T0353984

Taboo Genocide

Taboo Genocide

Holodomor 1933 & the Extermination of Ukraine

Before the *Holocaust*, there was the *Holodomor*

The Triad Trilogy: FDR, Stalin & Hitler:
A Strategy for War and Peace,
& the New World Order

The Never Before Told Story
of the Anglo-American Consortium
& the 1933 Terror-Famine in Soviet Ukraine

BOOK I of II Volumes

Kris Dietrich

ISBN: Softcover 978-1-4990-5609-9
eBook 978-1-4990-5608-2

Print information available on the last page.

Photo credits on Cover (left to right): Sir Winston Spencer Churchill (Public Domain), Teddy Roosevelt (Public Domain), Joseph Stalin (Public Domain), Holodomor victim (Public Domain), Skull and Bones, YALE (Public Domain), Hitler (source Hinterland by A. Nagorski), Rothschild Coat of Arms Five Arrows (image source <HYPERLINK "http://redicecreations.com" redicecreations.com>, US Presidents H. Hoover and FDR (Library of Congress, Public Domain), A-Bomb over Nagasaki (Public Domain), Photo of image of painting of Ukrainian woman by Dimitri (Kyiv)

Rev. date: 08/28/2015

For more information, links, up-to-date developments, and photos, please visit www.taboogenocide.com

To order additional copies of this book, contact:
Xlibris
1-888-795-4274
www.Xlibris.com
Orders@Xlibris.com
550204

CONTENTS

INTRODUCTION - *HOLODOMOR*: "DEATH BY FORCED HUNGER" 1933

This is a story of war and peace. It may have been the greatest crime of the century after the Bolshevik coup and Russian Revolution and the murder of the Russian Romanov Tsar Nicholas II, his wife Tsarina Alexandra and their five young children: four Grand Duchesses Olga, Anastasia, Tatiana, Marie and the Tsarevich, Alexis.

It is our story. And I want to share it with you now because it is *your* story too.

What am I to say to you? What?

The spirit of Tchekov, and Doestoevsky and Solzhenitsyn weigh heavy on this tale of more masterly tales preserved by great writers, so many who perished here; Mayakovsky, Mandelstam, Gorky, Bulgakov ... Yes! But Pasternak lived through it all. He survived! Stalin didn't kill him! He didn't "preserve" him to make him squirm.

Please read, and live! I am in a hurry. It is very cold outside and the fire is burning...

We all live and share it every day of our lives. It is embedded deep in our hearts and minds and in our cultures and history. In one way or another, this story is in us all.

And yet almost nobody knows about it. It was taboo. It was a story not to be told. Even in hushed whispers and lowered eyes an utterance of the truth was strictly forbidden, and maybe get you killed. Now reader, hold on, you have to surf a little so stay on the board...

What would you think if someone told you they knew rich people in a country investing in a foreign war killing millions of people mostly young and untrained men and at the last minute that country joined the great war to win it, all the while the rich people who occupied the government and owned the factories and businesses of national economy now make a killing in war profits to keep the industrial machine war going, then when they are good and ready lead a million poor souls shipping them far overseas where ten percent of them are killed, this over 100,000 of the young men are dead and many thousands more are wounded and maimed for life, and then these same rich men of big corporations and banks who sold the same people and their families paper called Liberty Bonds urging them with great national demonstrations and rallies and advertising with movie star celebrities and banking and business leaders walking hand in hand with government officials and newspapers creating a national war frenzy telling the people they must take a financial stake in the war and make a profit too, so the bankers float and syndicate billions of dollars in war loans and in the chaos of war and destruction these same men stage a coup to take down the largest and richest empire in the world in a strange and distant land, a great power speaking a foreign language among the greatest powers in the world and with the fastest accelerating modern economy yet a great nation of peasants and the bread-basket of Europe, – and these same men who sent the young men to die and urged their families to buy a stake in the war now destroy that foreign empire in their quest for global dominance in the future which they do so successfully killing the royal family of four young daughters and a little boy crown prince, backing a small group of cut-throat penniless wretched professional revolutionaries, bandits and thieves who slaughter a cultured ruling class aristocracy evolved over centuries and these same ideological bandits lead an illiterate rag-tag army promising peace, land and food; then these same people invest in a one-party dictatorship enslaving 160 million people under a system of slave labor and terror, starving millions at the point of bayonet and filling concentration labor camps and massive man-made famine killing some ten million of the best farmers in the land and turn the screws so tight until it is time to win another world war, and this time the same rich people stay out of the war but promise food and aid to the dictatorship bleeding itself to death for claiming victory for themselves, but it is really only a victory of its foreign masters who own the banks and corporations with their politicians that invest in the war factories and the slave dictatorship while their own country is wallowing for years in a terrible economic depression but now having come out of the second war again richer than ever in the entire history of the world, and in fact just so that the population of the foreign rich masters could prosper while these rich masters themselves control the world populations and resources when the dictatorship is used to sustain a world ideology keeping the entire world populations transfixed in a state of paralysis of terror and fear so that the rich masters get even more rich and their population enjoys mindless prosperity all the while the slave population of the dictatorship suffers a most terrible fate as it falls deeper and deeper into a bottomless pit of terror and fear and economic bankruptcy until three generations later their false state collapses. Essentially this is what really happened in the rise and fall of the Soviet Russia and the emergence of the American global empire. But who were these rich and powerful people and how did they do all these terrible things and get away with it and even become the envy of them all, these downtrodden and oppressed peoples of the world who marvel at them singing and dancing in the name of Democracy and their national pursuit of happiness and freedom?

In Soviet Russia to speak about it meant prison. Likely death. In America to mention it would leave people thinking the subject is too far-fetched to be taken seriously. It seemed too incredible to be believed and people didn't know what it meant or how to think about it. Both countries were highly brainwashed and suspicious while living in fear though the cultural climate was markedly different then and during the Cold War years leading a half century later to the fall of the Soviet Union in 1991.

To borrow a quote from England's fearless and unflappable Prime Minister Winston Churchill, a principal actor in this ethos of the World War Two, the 1933 Holodomor Terror-Famine in the Ukraine holds a special place in the heroic and tragic of wartime Russia, always that inscrutable "riddle, wrapped in a mystery, inside an enigma".

In fact, as the story unfolds it becomes evident that the Holodomor is a vital link compelling Hitler to launch his invasion plan *Barbarossa* to seize the fertile fields of wheat of the Ukraine (after the spring sowing in 1941) and compelled Roosevelt to make his fatal pact with Stalin beginning officially in 1933, already a one-man cult in the Communist Party hierarchy of the ramshackle rattletrap of Soviet Russia, a year after the 15th anniversary of the Revolution led by Lenin eternally asleep in the Kremlin.

One of the most strange aspects of US government relations towards the USSR prior to the outbreak of World War II is that neither Hoover, nor Stimson nor FDR in these years of the twenties and early thirties of US economic and technological trade collaboration with the Soviets and for the Holodomor years Stalin seldom and very rarely is ever the subject of State Department memoranda nor is Stalin cited in Stimson's personal diary as I was able to determine for this book during close to a decade of research. Thousands of skilled American workers and engineers lived in the Soviet Union at this time building the new Soviet Socialist dictatorship.

An evil silence pervaded throughout the USSR that shrouded Russian society in secrecy. In both countries of powerful myths and icons the Holodomor story seems to assume a dimension even more evil with time. That is, until now.

Having intercepted German wire transmissions and warned Stalin that Hitler's invasion is imminent, on the same day he struck June 22, 1941 Churchill in a national radio broadcast declares "A wonderful story is unfolding before our eyes. How it will end we are not allowed to know. But on both sides of the Atlantic we all feel, I repeat, all, that we are a part of it, that our future and that of many generations is at stake. We are sure that the character of human society will be shaped by the resolves we take and the deeds we do."

On the day of invasion Churchill tells the world, "This is no class war, but a war in which the whole British Empire and Commonwealth of Nations is engaged without distinction of race, creed or party … if Hitler imagines that his attack on Soviet Russia will cause the slightest division of aims or slackening of effort in the great Democracies who are resolved upon his doom, he is woefully mistaken. On the contrary, we shall be fortified and encouraged in our efforts to rescue mankind from his tyranny." Before the speech is delivered his personal secretary recalls how Churchill had once said that he had sought to "strangle in its cradle" Bolshevism, Churchill now quips, "If Hitler invaded Hell, I would make at least a favourable reference to the Devil in the House of Commons." ("Alliance with Russia", radio broadcast, June 22, 1941, *Never Give In!,* ed. Winston S. Churchill, NY: Hyperion, 2003)

With America still on the sidelines CBS newsman Edward R. Murrow on the same day of the invasion gave his radio broadcast with the opener that made him famous "This is London". In his low gruff voice Ed Murrow said, "As you know, the Prime Minister made a broadcast this evening. Never before has he been so violent in his denunciation of Hitler, whom he termed a bloodthirsty guttersnipe. Mr. Churchill made a solemn prophecy that there would be misery and famine without equal in history; India and China were next on the Nazi list. He said a thousand million more human beings were menaced. The Prime Minister brought all his oratorical power to the appeal for aid to the Soviet Union, which he has always hated– and still does. ... What he implied was that the Russians, after all, are human but the Germans aren't. Russia's danger, he said, is our danger." Then

Murrow adds a recent broadcast statement to America by Churchill, "'But time is short'. If Russia is beaten quickly and decisively, time will be much shorter." (*In Search of Light, The Broadcasts of Edward R. Murrow 1938-61*, Ed. with Intro. by Edward Bliss, Jr., NY: Knopf, 1967, 47-8)

Our story unfolded not long ago during the lives of our parents and their parents in a far away land of buttermilk and honey, happy robust maidens and strong men of the earth, pagan spirits and Christian saints. Fertile farmland enriched by centuries of toil, golden wheat fields in bloom and tall birch forests suddenly poured rivers of blood into the Dnieper River as it flows from the north down into the Black Sea.

We return to a hidden and murky past to find behind dark clouds, sealed vaults and hushed voices the story brought to light of the creation of the world we all inherited and live every day of our lives. As it emerged with new industrial technologies and a capacity for war more violent than ever before seen or imagined by the ordinary illiterate man, this world was heralded the "modern civilization" or "Brave New World' and took over the landscape with a bold new mythology and borders drawn by prominent generals, bankers and politicians of the era. Little did I know when in my senior year at prep school I was honored with the History Prize –, a classic encyclopedia of mythology, that it would guide me through the illusions and signs of the Cold War. More appropriate perhaps a book on rhetoric, but we already had Wilson's speeches for that; a few years at Yale under phenomenology professor Edward S. Casey recently at Stony Brook University Manhattan began to make sense of it all.

H. G. Wells along with many great writers both contemporary and past, including George Bernard Shaw, Aldous Huxley, George Orwell, and many others are witness and in some cases even enthusiastic participants as the fascist horror all fell into place during the years of peace and world war promising happiness, prosperity and freedom to the children and future generations after years of terrible cruelty and unspeakable crimes. Never mind. I know what I know and will tell you as it is for you to know the soul of truth in the story that has never been told before as we can know it in our time.

What did we learn?

War is a dirty business. War is good business. Genocide works. *Cui bono?* To understand it better just remember what the Romans said: "Who benefits?"

Only a few years ago far from Washington and on the opposite side of the world the former President of Ukraine Viktor Yushchenko declared November 21 a day of national mourning in honor of ten million victims of Terror-Famine of the Ukraine known as the *Holodomor* ("Death by Hunger" in Ukrainian pronounced with a "G" as in "*Golo*"). In fact, as terrible as it really was maybe the death toll was as high as 14.5 million as declared by former Soviet Premier Mikhail Sergeyevich Gorbachev. Impossible? Unthinkable? Or, perhaps the true death figure is "between three and six million". Or, as "claimed from six to eleven million lives, depending on how the estimates are made". (*Martin Malia, The Soviet Tragedy, A History of Socialism in Russia, 1917-1991, NY:*

Free Press-Macmillan, 1994, 1999; Orest Subtelny, Ukraine, A History, Univ. of Toronto Press, 1988, 1994, 415)

The exact number will probably not ever be known. Yet, the Washington-Moscow story of the Holodomor of the 1932-34 years has never been told. That too compounds the shocking truth of regenerated numbers if you think about it. Still, as we untangle the knot of censorship and historical disinformation we find the real story of Genocide in Ukraine embedded in the greater 1933-45 war period of extraordinary Machiavellian strategic political and financial intrigue resulting in the destruction of lives and property reaching epic proportions encompassing the two World Wars. Ukraine was the most ravaged survivor of a doomed planet calling out for help in their most dire time of need.

FREUD AND THE DEATH INSTINCT OF CIVILIZATION

The Nazi menace tears asunder the work and family of Sigmund Freud. Renowned Austrian psychoanalyst Freud near the end of his life during this time of Nazi persecution of Jews and non-Aryans considered incompatible with German civilization finally must face the mystery and horror of man's Fate as an exterminator of his own species with an unmitigated destiny doomed by an aggressive will to power and sustained by a lust for the most powerful weapons of destruction. The confrontation of Western man with "the others" does not leave him unaffected nor does he escape untouched by this clash of traditions. On the eve of the outbreak of the Second World War literally at the end of his rope Freud is persuaded by his daughter Anna to abandon his precious library and flee the Nazi takeover of Vienna. He is, he declares, "a godless Jew" who painfully must forsake any role as prophet. Ultimately, and no less ironic to our story, Freud is saved from the death camps by Roosevelt and his intermediaries and escapes from Europe in the darkness on a night train and ship across the Channel to safety in England where soon thereafter in exile he dies safe and free.

Freud seriously ponders what kind of Europe his seven grandchildren would inherit. During the rise of fascism he dreads the lapse of freedom. "But who can foresee the prospects and the outcome?" The question begs to be answered by us all.

We learn how Freud dreads the repressive and brutal tyrants and faces the challenging questions of responsibility of moral choice living under conditions of fascism. His seminal work *Civilization and Its Discontents* (1930), – reader, we are precisely in our own most relevant time here, – should be perceived as a final testament to his investigation of the human conflict between Eros and Death. Remember Freud is the leading psychoanalyst in the West, he invented the practice! – to investigate myths and symbols in the "alien" worlds of the unconscious to grasp the dynamism of man's destructive psyche "impelled by historical forces other than those which have shaped the history of Western world". (M. Eliade, *Myths Dreams, and Mysteries*, 10)

"My courage sinks to stand up before my fellow humans as a prophet," Freud declares, "and I bow before their reproach that I do not know how to bring them consolation – for that is fundamentally what they all demand, the wildest revolutionaries no less passionately than the most conformist pious believers." When Freud wrote this a maddening arms race and incessant drive of modern progress and technological innovation did not hold out much promise for the future. With less than a decade to live and with mankind now facing nearly insurmountable hurdles, he sighed, "Men have now gone so far in the mastery of natural forces that with their help they could easily exterminate one another to the last man. They know this, hence a large part of their current unrest, their unhappiness, their mood of anxiety." (Peter Gay, *Freud: A Life For Our Time*, NY: Norton, 1988, 551-2)

Freud harbored no illusions in the aspirations for the ideal New Proletarian Man (and Woman) construed by the Soviet Russia's supreme Dictator and the Communist Party, vanguard of the working class and the protagonist of history. "I can recognize its psychological presupposition as an untenable illusion." As he understood the predicament of civilized humanity when he argues that aggression "was not created by property", and could not be controlled by it. Aggression, unfortunately, is a peculiar pleasure and man is not inclined to reject it. "They do not feel comfortable without it,"

Freud declares. A compulsion he describes as "the narcissism of small differences" appears to spur men to find certain pleasure in persecuting and torturing others. In another comment he reflects, "all the massacres of Jews in the Middle Ages were not enough to make that age more peaceful and more secure for their Christian comrades." (P. Gay, *Freud,* 549)

THE STORY YOUR TEACHERS NEVER TOLD YOU

This is a story your teachers never told you in high school or college. Survivors of Ukraine dispersed living around the world and in their Motherland still whisper chilling memories to their children of the time when they were hungry, sick with bloated bellies, without bread and bodies everywhere. Most of what is taught in American schools about geopolitical history of the last few generations is either a ton of crap to hide the dirt or shrewdly deceptive and misguiding. Computer technology today will aid the avid reader find facts to help navigate an intelligible course through the rocky shoals of treacherous deception and deep uncharted waters. Under all that there are glimmers of the truth like the lotus flower worshiped because it rises above all the mud. From Buddha to Jesus on the cross and Shakespeare they would tell you the same in a proverb.

In Russia the Holodomor is for the most part ignored or forgotten; from Hollywood to New York City the Holodomor truth is overshadowed with an apparently incessant daily news stream of the Jewish Holocaust with no sign of it waning for the future.

And yet this predecessor of the Holocaust was even more horrific preceded the Holocaust by only a few years. There was never a Nuremberg Judgment to condemn it or exorcise the guilt of a Humanity betrayed by Holodomor Genocide perpetuated on an innocent population by Stalin and his world. It was our world, too, torn asunder in a clash of forces, good and evil deeds, and, as this book reveals, a world transfixed in collaboration with the West. It happens during the prewar years of "peace" during the rocking "Roaring Twenties" and the Great Depression. Your teachers most likely never knew about the evil bleak reality shadowed behind the dark clouds. They didn't want to know the truth until it was too late. It was and has always been taboo. The Consortium had arranged the agenda especially before Genocide ever became a crime in violation of "the laws of Humanity" in the aftermath of World War II in the Nuremberg Judgment trials. Since it was chartered in 1948, the United Nations, another instrument of Consortium work or order the world, has been primarily responsible for the selective processing to prosecute certain nefarious crimes against humanity.

It still *is* taboo, off the history map in the political lexicon. Rather, it *was* all taboo but that is now changing today with the transparency accelerated by the Internet and Wikileaks or Facebook and U-tube type organizations with video blogs and news sharing in an endlessly continuous streaming of data files.

Nor did your teachers tell you about the details of American engineers and technicians, thousands of American specialists sent to Russia in the 1928-1934 years of the Five-Year Plans to modernize the Soviet economy during the Hoover and Roosevelt administrations (1928-1945). With their complicit knowledge a small but incredibly wealthy and powerful group of Anglo-American political and industrial leaders secretly helped build the Communist state of terror under Stalin. This clique with a power center based in Washington and led by Roosevelt and his men then rapidly supplied Stalin with everything he needed to slow Hitler's race to Moscow across Ukraine and the Eastern Front to save Europe and the West from what Churchill called "the curse of Hitler" for "the survival of Christian civilization" from certain destruction and domination by the German Nazi military machine.

THE HORROR, THE SECRETS, THE TABOO

No pictures of Consortium communist horror appear in *Time* or *Life* created and owned by Henry Luce and his Skull and Bones chums from Yale. No photos of the GULAG (*Glavnoye Upravleniye Lagerey*), the vast administrative network of prisons and forced labor concentration camps headed by Yagoda of the OGPU secret police when its established in 1930 in every province stretching all across the Soviet Union. Only happy smiling faces of strong young peasants and workers in the fields and factories were shown in the country and abroad. The Soviet Russians knew but were silenced by the mortal fear of death embedded in their lives Soviet justice enforced by Stalin's executioners and a nation of paranoid informers so far remote from the comprehension of the West. And for the most part Soviet records are unreliable or unavailable, either lost, non-existent or kept totally secret. And, unfortunately, that practice of secret government is not alien to America with its millions of newly classified documents kept under lock and key every year and denying the people their right to know First Amendment Constitutional Rights.

The Soviet Union keeps their secrets. So does England and America. The business of the Consortium in the Soviet Union was considered by them to be their private business as it is today. The scions of American wealth and power with their links in London and Paris are at the center of this money and influence gang of world centralized banks, global corporate industry and government. It is a natural extension of colonial power by the masters that be– the Rothschilds, DuPonts, Mellons, Morgans, Harrimans, Rockefellers and their kind.

A taboos concealing the truth kept secret by unlawful power protecting falsehoods and corruption in democratic and totalitarian dictatorship lose their grip over public awareness; the internet has pushed societies forward beyond the condition of what the poet Yevgeny Yevtushenko in a reference in 1974 to dissident Soviet writer Aleksandr Isayevich Solzhenitsyn and the doomed poet Osip Mandelstam call living the lie of silence.

The taboo is exposed in controversy. In the past *Time-Life* publisher Henry Luce and various Consortium servants in the press trumpeted the wonders of Soviet "progress", perpetuating the American war mythology in the thirties of Soviet communism and American democracy while the secret truth remained concealed in classified government papers and various other scattered sources. This is the story about what really happened in a planned and systematic extermination by Stalin of millions of Ukrainians, men women and children during the peak of the 1933 Holodomor and the Consortium cover-up leading to World War II and the Soviet strategic alliance with the West between Roosevelt, Churchill and Stalin.

(*Note. One of the best known Russian Soviet poets in the 1950's and 1960's, Yevgeny Aleksandrovich Yevtushenko, born to a peasant family in Siberia in July 1931 was of mixed Russian, Ukrainian and Tartar heritage. His family is exiled after the 1881 assassination of Emperor Alexander II. His early poem *So mnoyu chto-to proiskhodt / Something is happening to me* becomes a very popular song; praised by Pasternak, Sandburg and Frost; his most famous poem, *Babi Yar*, denounced Soviet distortion of the Nazi massacre of the Jews in Kiev September 1941. Also a film director of prolific talent Yevtushenko is made an honorary member of the American Academy of Arts and Letters, in 1987, and two years later while backing Gorbachev's *perestroika* reforms he's elected as a representative for Kharkov in the Soviet Parliament. Yevtushenko is not without literary and social critics, rebuked as a false dissident and collaborator. Anatoly Kudryavitsky (*A Night in the Nabokov Hotel*) considers him more a "naughty child of the regime" than a leader of protest against the totalitarian regime. Yevtushenko even maligns Boris Pasternak's widow, Olga Ivinskaya imprisoned on bogus charges of foreign currency violations. And he sneers that "*Doctor Zhivago* is not worth publishing in the Soviet Union". Soon after her release from prison poet Irina Ratushinskaya dismisses Yevtushenko as an official poet; novelist Vasily Aksionov refuses any contact. This is a tumultuous moment in Ukraine's national history, and Dr. James Mace in Kiev makes headlines rekindling Soviet responsibility for the Holodomor Terror-Famine.

The consequences of the Holodomor are far reaching then and now. Don't kid yourself and believe otherwise. Dictatorships are potent rivals. Great superpowers make for even greater dictatorships. Dictatorships rule. Communist China and Putin's Russia are ominous adversaries for the United States in any future world conflict. Free-thinking democracies are burdensome with so many institutions difficult to manage and lengthy legislative and judicial processes. Of course Bush proved that the country could be easily pushed into line to support the Home Land Security Patriot Act and the Iraq War with its bogus allegations of weapons of mass destruction. American presidents know well that it requires special Executive War powers to fight foreign wars and a vote by Congress. Dictatorships don't require bi-partisan endorsements. There are even people living in the United States who believe passionately that America is no longer a healthy and pluralistic democracy, but instead a land spoiled by the seeds of industrial military dictatorship.

When people don't have enough to eat after a time they will starve and die. They lose the ability to live. That will always be a human tragedy. When those same people live in a land of fertile soil with abundant grain and wheat harvests and work hard every day tilling the rich soil that nurtures them and protects their families and then one day that food is taken away from the people who work on the land to plant cut and collect the harvest as they have done for centuries and many people die the tragedy is worse. The authorities with machine guns and bayonets come again and take away all the seed and villagers and leave villages barren and empty and the tragedy is worse than ever. Yet when millions die the tragedy is epic. Despite all reservations it did occur.

When the starvation is man-made and caused by political expediency it is a crime against Humanity. And when the murder of the people is a deliberate act of extermination by careful selection and the people are of a certain biological or national origin this criminal act against Humanity is called Genocide. (I prefer using the capital "G" when referring to this horror of all horrors known to man.) This was the reality of the Holodomor in Soviet Ukraine 1933. It is an epic story about the two most powerful nations to emerge in the East and the West in a world of shifting Empire and wealth gone amok with Fascism and greed. (We also might omit the use of the capital letter "F" but won't for other reasons than not to be redundant.)

What would you do if you discovered that your friend was a descendant of a Consortium family who not only knew about the famine in Soviet Russia and the Ukraine but was heavily invested in it? Does it raise serious questions of morality relevant to society today? Murder is committed in the name of a God or ideology or merely the act to serve a higher purpose. For America, this is a real dilemma that requires focus and context for a new generation of Ukrainians in search of national identity after its independence from Russia in 1991 as well as in terms of defining its relations with nations and peoples of the world. It isn't a small gesture for President Barak Obama to urge that America and Russia "reboot" relations.

But what does this mean really?

This book hopes to help you understand the dilemma of the paradox as is evident when democracy is used as a tool of fascism to control the free world and render people powerless and without a clear voice of resistance. Unfortunately, that trend still seems absolutely unchanged today magnified by an ever greater crescendo of the democracy debate rhetoric that obfuscates the real issues of who and which institutions and corporations control wealth and power and what they are doing with it.

In short, the Ukrainian Genocide of the Holodomor is a most remarkable story. In the natural course of events no one could possibly tell it completely long after the pain and suffering of death is gone with the dead. Yet truth has its own mysterious way of revealing secrets long lost and hidden from view. In a strange way the revelation may be a sort of recovery for both the victims and the survivors. To hear and see the truth that has eluded the general public for generations the writer has resorted to original sources and documented works to unearth buried lies.

The Holodomor remains an ever-present and frightening truth, and ever more so if people do nothing to neither acknowledge it nor ask questions about such an event ever occurring again in the future. Much research remains to be done to reveal more of the truth of what happened and find records of those millions of people lost with families and entire villages annihilated. As we see with resistance from Moscow so too within the operatives and institutions of the Consortium is this true.

Powerful financial, economic, political and social organizations inside and outside of government do not readily reveal their secrets. It is your responsibility, if you care about your freedom and your life, to seek the truth and do what you can to preserve it and make life worth living. To find a good map through life may help you find peace and happiness, and not get lost in a bad logic such as the logic that promoted and condoned a Terror-Famine with all the consequential suffering and killing of millions of lives by a logic secret and unbridled corporate greed, fascism and the betrayal of democratic ideals, government corruption, massive death and despair. In the Great Game of post-colonial Empire and ruthless capitalism Genocide was more than a by-product; it was both a strategic process of practical utility for an end result with still greater consequences for the Holocaust and the Second World War.

THE CURRENT DEBATE

The current debate surrounding issues of the Holodomor is in need of serious historical correction. The reality of Consortium intrigue with "the Kremlin"* illuminates the reasons why for so long the story of Stalin's terror against the peasants in the Ukraine did not even merit the status of a detail in American history books. Disgraced *New York Times* and Pulitzer Prize reporter Walter Duranty reduced the killing of millions of Ukrainians to no more significance than a mere "incident" of history. During the Stalinist era it was intended to be effaced from human memory. (*The Old Square *Staraya Ploshchad* in Moscow, site of the headquarters of the Central Committee of the CPSU and the center of Russian political authority.)

The 1932-33 Holodomor was deleted from official history but it could not be erased from the collective memory. "The first step in liquidation of a people is to erase its memory. Destroy its books, its culture, its history. Then have somebody write new books, manufacture a new culture, invent a new history. Before long the nation will begin to forget what it is and what it was," writes Czech author Milan Kundera about life under communist dictatorship in *The Book of Laughter and Forgetting.*

This is a history with a perspective where even the most backward, as in uneducated, and innocent individual of a forgotten country weighs in the balance with a significance also as potent as the terror and evil that crept out of the depths of a complex modern world, and which was an undeniable part of the collective history of the Ukraine, the Soviet Union, the United States. It was then, and remains today, a world order of nations, and a claim on the sake of Humanity whatever that meant or was appeared to be.

Likewise, any responsible review of the Holodomor must ask how Americans, for the most part considered widely as warm-hearted, generous, and loving people noted for their common sense as once observed the English-born American revolutionary patriot, Thomas Paine, were deprived of information which might otherwise have compelled them to pressure their leaders in Washington to aid the Ukraine and alter the course of history driving them with an industrial pace akin to madness over the edge to the death, horror and flames of yet another World War. Currently as we go to press the most recent leaks and revelations by former National Security Agency employee Edward Snowdon blanket the world media as he warns Americans and the world of the massive unprecedented deprivation and abuse of American privacy and civil rights by government spying and the alleged illegal and unauthorized misuse of technology. (Milan Kundera, *The Book of Laughter and Forgetting,* NY: HarperCollins, 1978)

But if war really is good and dirty business, and if Genocide really does "work", then how did it work?

Are the masses really just idiots and fodder for political men in power to do away with as they please like sheep sent to the slaughter? And in particular, how did the Holodomor play into the hands of the all-empowered Machiavellians? Moreover, the perpetrators of Genocide always deny it ever happened even when proven guilty by an international tribunal of justice in a court of law in the context of a Crime Against Humanity. And that too, given the scope of the mechanics of international preparations and calculations for war even in the advent of possible prevention, or provocation, raises further the complexity of the issues leading to war itself as genocidal by nature in the arrangements for power and dominance. Defenders of freedom are difficultly perceived as perpetrators of such outrageous immoral monstrosities.

An excellent historian and storyteller, foreign correspondent and editor of Britain's *Evening Standard* and *Daily Telegraph* Max Hastings writes in *Inferno* (Knopf 2011) that following of the 1939 German-Soviet Non-Aggression Pact Hitler was allowed to see Stalin's war preparations from manufacturing plants far deep inside Russia, even in Siberia. When a German military intelligence report arrived on his desk, Hitler tells his generals, "Now you see how far these people have already got. We must strike at once." The British World War II historian and author of some 20 books Max Hastings describes the genocidal strategy of Hitler's Wehrmacht killing machine: "The destruction of Bolshevism and the enslavement of the Soviet Union's vast population were core objectives of Nazism, flagged in Hitler's speeches and writings since the 1920's. Overlaid on them was the desire to appropriate Russia's enormous natural resources."

But Hitler is already too late. Hitler compounds one mistake after another on his mad path to war. He blindly misconstrues the White House engagement with Stalin, certainly one of his most fatal strategic blunders. For over three decades Stalin is duped by his own Bolshevik-Soviet ruse cast over the empire; the leader himself is duped by an elaborate communist propaganda megalopolis of Kremlin power and dogma that holds bourgeois capitalists in contempt for inflicting Armageddon against the proletarian masses.

In as much as Stalin believes that the Non-Aggression Pact will hold Hitler back from launching an attack, Hitler believes that the America President will let both England and Russia fall in his hand rather than risk the spread of international communism infect Europe and enslave the world. From the beginning, hindered by hatred and ambition, Hitler is doomed. Many of his countrymen know it. But already there are too many Nazis everywhere in Europe. The German invasion will tear open such a deep visceral wound only an unconditional and overwhelming Russian victory could heal and leave a leave a deep scar marked by the Iron Curtain and Berlin Wall.

Ukrainians played the primary role in the Red Army Soviet victory. On the website of Holodomor historian Andrew Gregorovich spotlights how the Ukrainian experience unlike the "Russian glory" and the Jewish Holocaust has passed virtually unrecognized by western and Russian war historians. He observed how no English language history is available to recall the sacrifice, pain, and terror of the suffering of the Ukrainian nation in the "Great Patriotic War" as Stalin preferred it to be known as it unified all the ethnic peoples in a tidal surge of humanity to save Mother Russia. Gregorovich is executive director of the Ukrainian Canadian Research and Documentation Center (UCRD), Toronto, founded in 1982. In 1984 the UCRD produced the award-winning film *Harvest of Despair* by director Slavko Nowytski.

Nor has there been an accounting of the priceless cultural treasures of architecture of Ukraine, world art and literature destroyed and looted.

In the "Patriotic War" Ukraine lost about ten million people or, one out of four of its sons and daughters. We can only wonder what beauty, genius, and talent was lost to the world as a result of the Nazi German and Soviet annihilation of the Ukrainian people in 1939-1945. About 4.5 million Ukrainians served in the Soviet army (2.5 million were decorated which might mean 2 million combatants perished) with another 1.3 million fighting in militia and partisan units against Germany. Hundreds of thousands served in the guerrilla partisan armies fighting both totalitarian powers, Nazi Germany and Red Soviet Russia. At least 350 Ukrainian generals and marshals served in the Red Army and were responsible for many of the victories at Stalingrad and Leningrad. Apparently, and unknown to most Ukrainians today, Berlin was captured principally by Ukrainian troops; many of the 102,000 killed were Ukrainians who died there and are buried in the Berlin cemetery. That's close to the number of the entire loss of Americans in the First World War.

Stalin even uses Ukrainian national patriotism in the war instituting the Order of Bohdan Khmelnytsky medal for the four Ukrainian Front Armies in 1943. They included prominent marshals – the majority of marshals of the USSR were said to be Ukrainians – and generals born in the Ukraine: Marshal Simon Tymoshenko, Marshal Rodion Malinovsky, Marshal Ivan Konev, Marshal Yakiv Fedorenko, Marshal Kiril Maoskalenko, Marshal Serhiy Rudenko, General Andrey Grechko, Marshal Peter Koshoviy, Marshal Petro Leliushenko, Marshal Kliment Voroshilov, Marshal Andrey Yeremenko, General Yakiv Cherevichenko, General Fyodor Kostenko, Col. General Micahael Kirponos, Col. General Andrey Kravchenko, Admiral Mykola Basisty, General Iosif Apanesenko, and Marshal Alexander Vasilevsky. (Figures sourced from Andrew Gregorovich website 1995)

The greatest hero of World War II is of Ukrainian origin, – the brilliant Marshal Georgi Zhukov who signed the German surrender after sacking Berlin. First he taught the Japanese a lesson in their worst military defeat during six months of an undeclared war in 1939; two years later it was the German's turn to do battle with this great military leader who dared to speak openly to Stalin. Too few Americans in our time know his name or have any idea of the role he played in defeating Nazi fascism and capturing victory and for the free world. Zhukov received the major credit for the Battle of the Dnieper and the capture of Berlin (which the Ukrainian Front Army of Ivan Konev nearly seized before him).

Born in Kaluga, Zhukov's original family name was Zhuk and his Ukrainian family was from Birky village in the Poltava region of Ukraine according to the information of Zhukov's relative Varvara Hryshko. On the verge of taking Berlin Zhukov promised Nikita Khrushchev, then Head of the Communist Party of Ukraine, that when he captured Hitler he would first ship him in a cage to Kiev so that Ukraine could see him before Moscow. However, Hitler's suicide left only the Fuehrer's charred body to be found by the Soviet Army. The search party into the Nazi command bunker in Berlin which found Hitler's remains was led by Ukrainian Lt. General Ivan Klimenko. (A. Gregorovich website, 1995, *Molod' Ukrainy* 14. X. 1994, 2)

Sixty-five percent of all Allied military deaths British historian Max Hastings writes in this long overdue book *Inferno* a testimony to the incredible sacrifice of the USSR to saving the free world from Hitler's *Wehrmacht* invasion thrust to Moscow through the Ukraine. It was here where the most remarkable battles of World War Two, or as the Soviets call it, "The Great Patriotic War", were fought, victories won and ground lost.

It was the war in Russia that defeated Hitler's Nazi schematic plan for world domination, not the D-Day Normandy Allied invasion or the Liberation of Paris as most Americans have been taught to believe. Compared to the war in Russia Western Europe was a sideshow. Military chiefs in London and Washington understood that well. If Russia fell, England would be doomed and would be forced to wait for isolationist America to help them regain their freedom.

In *Overlord,* Brutish war historian Max Hastings writes in 1983, debunking what he describes as "chauvinistic post-war platitudes" and "comfortable chauvinistic legends" and the "astonishing" twist of historical record that endures "40 years after the battle". That euphoria of the battle endures even today in America eager to find and remember its heroes as countless books hit the market commemorating D-Day, which may be all well and good yet do not forget, reader, as the Russian poet Yevgeny Yevtushenko reminds us in his introduction to the ground-breaking novel by Solzhenitsyn exposing the Soviet reality of the Gulag, *One Day in the Life of Ivan Denisovich,* that "Bertolt Brecht once observed that a country which needs heroes is an unfortunate one." Published in 1962 in *Novy Mir* under the Khrushchev regime, this short novel became an overnight sensation and bestseller in the Soviet Union; rehabilitated in 1956, Solzhenitsyn is then again banned by Khrushchev fearing that he had gone too far; the *Gulag Archipelago* is suppressed as "too dangerous"; arrested in 1974 by his successor Brezhnev the next day Solzhenitsyn is expelled to Frankfurt and literally dumped out of Soviet society tossed out of the country.

Max Hastings writes "The struggle for Normandy was the decisive western battle of the Second World War, the last moment at which the German army might conceivably have saved Hitler from catastrophe. The post-war generation grew up with the legend of the Allied campaign in 1944-45 as a triumphal progress across Europe, somewhere unrelated to the terrible but misty struggle that had taken place in the east. Today, we can recognize that the Russians made a decisive contribution to the western war by destroying the best of the German army, killing some two million men, before the first Allied soldier stepped ashore on 6 June 1944. It is the fact that the battle for Normandy took place against this background which makes the events of June and July so remarkable." (Max Hastings, *Overlord, D-Day, June 6, 1945*, NY: Simon & Schuster, 1984, 11; Yevgeny Yevtushenko, "Intro.", xi, A. I. Solzhenitsyn, *One Day in the Life of Ivan Denisovich*, NY: Signet Classics-Penguin, 1962, 2008 ed.)

British historian Hastings does not want us to misconstrue what was essential to the outcome of the war due to the fact that "90 percent of all Germans killed in combat met their fate" on the Eastern Front." Mostly all the territories of the Ukraine victimized by Stalin's Holodomor are revisited by Hitler's invasion and retreat, the principal battleground ravaged by both armies during four years of fierce engagement between the world's two most formidable belligerents. Hastings here makes a crucial observation: "Between 1941 and 1945, British and American sailors and airmen fought at sea and in the sky, but relatively small numbers of Western Allied ground troops engaged the Axis in North Africa, Italy, Asia and the Pacific. The Soviet Union suffered 65 percent of all Allied military deaths… the United States and Britain 2 percent each ... One Russian in four died, against one in twenty British Commonwealth combatants and one in thirty-four American servicemen. Some 3.66 percent of Marines died, compared with 2.5 percent of the

Army and 1.5 percent of the Navy." (Max Hastings, *Inferno, The World at War, 1939-1945,* NY: Knopf, 2011)

For his part, in 1933 when the American president instead extends the olive branch and continued financial and industrial support to Moscow and chooses to ignore and leave to their fate the millions of victims of the Holodomor Genocide, FDR proves himself able as any Machiavellian and as ruthless a warrior President on a path leading inevitably toward world war as his partner in the Kremlin, And yet, distinguished by a unique intellectual and cultural nature he appeared benignly apathetic to his principal adversaries the arch-villain sadist Stalin and the deranged Austrian militarist who resembles a garment salesman more than a Prussian militarist that he could never be. Imagine that! A political man of genteel education and culture in a wheel chair out-maneuvers them both!

Once victory is in view FDR's concession will be sealed in February 1945 at the Yalta talks in the Crimea. Ever since they both reached their apogee in 1933, it may have been FDR's most carefully guarded secret to allow Hitler to be led like a dog to believe that the American President would not raise a finger or even blink at the 1933 Ukrainian Genocide. For that matter, why would he be bothered by the German eradication of the communists deprived of their fertile wheat lands in south Russia. Hitler thought it would be perceived in the West as a stroke of brilliance to replace Ukrainian Slavs ruled by the barbarian Russian communist dictator with the cultured German Third Reich already deep in the pockets of the Anglo-American capitalists of the Consortium. Reader, turn to Neil Ascherson's *Black Sea* and his edifying account of barbarian lore: "Barbarians, by definition, are so-called; they do not consider themselves to be barbarous. ... When Blok ('Yes – we are Scythians. Yes– we are Asiatics, / With slanted and avid eyes... / For the last time come to your senses, old World! To the brotherly feast of work and peace, / For the last time to the bright brotherly feast/ The barbarian lyre calls.' sic) snatched up the 'barbarian' conceit for revolutionary Russia, it had already been well-worn in the service of imperial nationalism, above all in Germany. ... The Third Reich hardened this fashion into a full cultural dogma ...." (N. Ashcerson, *Black Sea,* 108-9)

THE WAR GAME: FROM HOLODOMOR TO HOLOCAUST

The genocidal impact of the Holodomor on Ukrainians and Russians was not lost on Hitler alone. In fact, with the entire Nazi fascist organization operating under a specific Aryan racist agenda extermination excelled at mass killing and slaughter of Slavs, Jews and non-Aryan races.

The Ukrainians were doomed long in advance. The Holodomor was just a beginning of the end for what was soon to tear apart their ancient and beloved country. The numbers are terrifying and may seem incredibly unbelievable even to historians and researchers. For most Americans who enjoy the benefits of peaceful isolation while living in a country that was never occupied or invaded apart from perhaps the experience of the American Revolution some 300 years ago, – and the Genocide inflicted on the native Americans –, the death toll defies the imagination unless otherwise experienced.

Reader, please bear in mind that the total military loss in World War II for the USSR alone was 8,668,400 which includes Ukraine, Byelorussia, Russia, Lithuania, Latvia, Estonia, Armenia, Georgia, Uzbekistan, Kazakhstan, Tadjikistan and its other republics, according to General M. Moiseyev, Chief of General Staff, USSR Armed forces. Compare the figures and think again about history and the strategy of leaders: Ukraine lost 19 per cent of its population, while Great Britain lost 0.7 percent and the USA lost 0.2 percent. (Andrew Gregorovich, "Population Loss by Country WWII, citing "*Voennoistoricheskiy zhurnal*", no. 3, March 1990 cited by Peter G. Tsouras, *The Great Patriotic War*, 240, A. Gregorovich, *Forum Ukrainian Review* No. 92, Spring 1995)

From May 1989 after Mikhail Gorbachev opened the first session of the Congress of People's Soviets, the Russian masses were beginning to speak openly about the mass-murder of the Holodomor that began with Lenin as the prelude of mass-killing under Stalin with the worst yet to come during the Second World War. George Orwell wrote, under the cloud of Katyn and the Nazi death camps, in 1944, "'Atrocities' had come to be looked on as synonymous with 'lies'." Before long the banned books of Solzhenitsyn become bestsellers available in bookshops and libraries. And this is the man who had to dodge GPU agents; then they called themselves NKVD, and after that KGB. And he had to dodge them all, sometimes finding them hiding in his attic, always tapping his phones, opening his mail, agents posing as helpful couriers to smuggle – no steal! – his manuscripts all when he is still considered "an enemy of the people" and all "active measures" were taken to persecute him inside his own country and to see that he was discredited abroad in the western press.

If the Holodomor numbers were incredible they only make the toll of the war even that more spectacularly unbelievable, obscene and unimaginable to a mind not yet gone mad or supra-rational in the sterile calculation of numbers and statistics. But these were not rational times and the accounting remained contentious and inconclusive. The powers imposed greater censorship as the killing went on. True figures were never reported to the outside world nor to the Russian people even to this day.

Struggle and persistence is usually rewarding. Like Dostoyevsky to be exiled and imprisoned and forced to write in secret can produce great work. "To plunge underground", writes Solzhenitsyn, "to make it your concern not to win the world's recognition, – Heaven forbid! – but on the contrary to shun it: this variant of the writer's lot is peculiarly our own, purely Russian, Russian and Soviet!" (Christopher Andrew and Vasili Mitrokhin, *The Sword and the Shield, The Mitrokhin Archive and the Secret History of the KGB*, NY: Basic Books – Perseus Books Grp, 1999, 31)

In his 1998 essay "Genocide in Ukraine 1933", senior Canadian documentalist was disturbed and puzzled by what he found in the undeniable causal proximity of the extermination campaigns between Stalin and Hitler and, in particular, targeting Ukrainians. Stalin became the teacher of Hitler. We can only speculate what might have happened if Stalin's secret Genocide by famine had been fully exposed to the world. Would Hitler's terrible secretive Holocaust of 6,000,000 Jews been possible?

"We also know", Andrew Gregorovich observes, "that Hitler in World War II adopted Stalin's famine weapon and starved millions of Soviet prisoners of war including many Ukrainians. Aided by his incisive scrutiny Andrew Gregorovich cites figures by Dr. Wolodynmry Kosyk (*The Third Reich and Ukraine*, 1993) as high as 2.5 million military and 4.5 million civilian deaths resulting in "a total loss of 7 million for Ukraine compared to a total German loss of 6.5 million". Losses by other countries in World War II include Poland, more than 5 million, Japan 2.36 million, Yugoslavia 1.7 million, France 600,000, Italy 500,000, Romania 500,000, Greece 450,000, Hungary 430,000, Great Britain 350,000, Czechoslovakia 340,000, Austria 374,000, USA 300,000, Holland 210,000, Belgium 88,000 and Canada 42,000. Byelorussia lost 2,198,000 civilians. The Russian SFSR, or Russia, he states "lost 1,781,000 civilians and about 3 to 4 million military or about 5 to 6 million total according to Kosyk." (George Orwell, *Tribune*, 31 March 1944, M. Hastings, "Victims", in *Inferno*, 499; A. Gregorovich, reprinted from *Forum Ukrainian Review* No. 92, Spring 1995; A. Gregorovich, address, "Genocide in Ukraine 1933, Town Hall, Hamilton, Ontario, Nov. 14, 1998)

That's not the worst of it. In many Ukrainian villages the eager Nazi exterminators ordered all the men, women and children into the local church, sealed it and burned them alive. Academician Yuri Kondufor, Director of the Institute of History, Ukrainian Academy of Sciences, in Kiev, revealed figures in 1984 of precise statistics of Ukrainian population losses in World War II. Kondufor calculated, according to Gregorovich, "that there was a total loss of 7.5 million (7,509,045) including the dead and those taken as slave laborers to Germany. The German occupation and World War II resulted in the extermination and death in Ukraine of 3,898,457 civilians and 1,366,588 military and prisoners-of-war for a total of 5,265,045." These figures loom over the shadow of the Holodomor victims to which they were all doomed. (A. Gregorovich, *Forum* No. 61, reprinted from *Forum Ukrainian Review,* No. 92, Spring 1995).

This is an essential history not to be overlooked in the story of the Holodomor and its aftermath. The number of villages in the Ukraine destroyed by Stalin and his squads of executioners during the Holodomor extermination was *surpassed* by Hitler and his Wehrmacht.

Canadian researcher of Ukrainian ancestry Andrew Gregorovich of the Toronto-based Ukrainian Canadian Research and Documentation Center (UCRD) writes, "In the space of about three years Ukraine suffered devastation from the scorched earth policy of two cruel totalitarian governments. He points to figures in Soviet Ukraine that "the retreating Germans "razed and burned over 28,000 villages and 714 cities and towns, leaving 10,000,000 people without shelter. More than 16,000 industrial enterprises, more than 200,000 industrial production sites, 27,910 collective and 872 state farms, 1,300 machine and tractor stations, and 32,930 general schools, vocational secondary schools and higher educational institutions of Ukraine had been destroyed. The direct damage to the Ukrainian national economy caused by the fascist (Nazi German) occupation came to 285,000,000,000 rubles ..."

Gregorovich found material losses for Ukraine amounted to "about $60,000,000,000 prewar dollars for Ukraine or *trillions* of dollars today". No wonder Premier Nikita Khrushchev rebuffed Averell Harriman over a paltry $11 billion Lend-Lease bill when the freedom of the western world was in hock to the Russians to a degree far greater. But by then the world had changed and the Soviet-Russian war debt would be renegotiated under new agreements for the postwar New World Order economy. In due course in Moscow during the Kennedy administration after arduous negotiations Khrushchev invites Harriman into the Kremlin for dinner to celebrate their agreement with Britain for a limited nuclear test ban treaty July 1963. As they walked past the Old Palace formerly Stalin's gloomy fortress and now a public park.

Schlesinger tells the story in *A Thousand Days*: "Harriman remarked that he saw few security men around. 'I don't like being surrounded by security men,' Khrushchev said. 'In Stalin's time we never knew whether they were protecting us or watching us'." Then Khrushchev turned towards the public crowd, and joked, "This is *Gospodin Garriman.* We've just signed a test-ban treaty. I'm going to take him to dinner. Do you think he's earned his dinner'." (A. Gregorovich, *Soviet Ukraine*, 155; Arthur M. Schlesinger, Jr., *A Thousand Days, John F. Kennedy in the White House*, Cambridge, MA.: Riverside Press-Houghton Mifflin, 908-9; italics added.)

Nikita Khrushchev wasn't the only one who thought he didn't have to pay back the Americans for Lend-Lease. With England shouldering the burden with Soviet Russia, and France already down and out, defeated and under Nazi occupation, "the British strenuously resisted" what they considered Roosevelt's gracious and friendly high-handedness. The fact that the Americans stayed out of the war while Britain had to fight Nazi fascism virtually alone, did not improve Anglo-American relations and certainly strained it within the Consortium's own ranks where the British exerted their individual means of persuasion.

Former Moscow AP correspondent Lynne Olson writes in her book, *Citizens of London*, (2010) of the pros and cons in the aid deal that preceded US entry into the war and official alliance as a disinterested Ally: "In the summer of 1941, the Roosevelt administration proposed that, as a payback for Lend-Lease, the British agree to end its imperial preference system. ... Although a staunch imperialist, Churchill did not much like the imperial preference system. But he and his cabinet were vehemently opposed to the idea of being coerced into agreeing to a postwar economic order that favored the United States. Indeed, they wondered, why was there any need for a Lend-Lease payback at all?" Indeed, with good reason, and, as Olson adds, "In February 1942, Churchill raised that point in an irate cable to Roosevelt that was never sent: 'It must be remembered that for a large part of 27 months we carried on the struggle single-handed... Had we failed, the full malice of the Axis Powers ... would have fallen upon the United States.' In a cable that *was* dispatched to the president, Churchill noted that the British cabinet had already decided the issue. It voted against swapping imperial preference for Lend-Lease, feeling that, if Britain did so, 'we should have accepted an intervention in the domestic affairs of the British Empire'." (Lynne Olson, *Citizens of London, The Americans Who Stood with Britain in its Darkest, Finest Hour*, Random House, 2010, 299-300)

War historian Max Hastings hasn't much to say about Lend-Lease given the delay of Americans to get into the war while England struggles and millions of Russians are left to fight Hitler's military machine alone on the continent. "American supplies made a critical contribution," Hasting writes, and he adds, It was often suggested in Washington and London that the Soviets were ungrateful. Stalin might have given the contemptuous response he once gave to Zinoviev, who made the same charge; 'Gratitude? Gratitude is a dog's disease!'" Hastings adds, "Churchill observed, with justice, that Britain entered the war in 1939 as a matter of principle, and fought alone for almost two years, while Russia was content to play vulture on the carcasses of Hitler's kills until Germany invaded the Soviet Union. It was impossible to dispute, however, that Stalin's people were overwhelmingly responsible for destroying Hitler's armies." (M. Hastings, *Armageddon*, NY: Knopf, 2004, 114)

Gregorovich goes on to declare in reference to Professor Kondufor as "there were also 2,244,000 Ukrainian citizens taken to Germany for slave labor in the German war industry. Most of these probably perished in Allied bombing raids. According to these statistics provided by Prof. Kondufor, Ukraine's total World War II loss was 7.5 million. To this should be added the loss of 250,159 in Carpatho-Ukraine and Crimea giving a total of 5,515,204 dead according to Kosyk or 7,759,204 total lost including Zakarpatia and Crimea. This includes about 600,000 Ukrainian Jews. Kondufor's statistics, perhaps the most accurate of all, probably cover the period from June 1941 rather than September 1939." (A. Gregorovich, *Forum Ukrainian Review,* No. 92, Spring 1995)

Gregorovich also noted a particular reference quoting from the *Encyclopedia of Ukraine*: "An estimated 6.8 million Ukrainians were killed. ... About 200,000 Ukrainian displaced persons (DPs) ended up in the emigration to the West; the vast majority were returned to Soviet rule through forced repatriation." He adds, "Bohdan Krawchenko states that, 'In the course of the conflict 6.8 million people were killed, of whom 600,000 were Jews and 1.4 million were military personnel who either perished at the front or died as prisoners of war (POWs)'." (Y. Boshyk, *Ukraine during World War II*, 15; *Encyclopedia of Ukraine,* Univ. of Toronto Press, v. 5, 727)

Toronto-based historian Orest Subtelny observes in his *Ukraine, A History* (1994), "Even a cursory listing of losses reflects the terrible impact that the Second World War had on Ukraine and its inhabitants. About 5.3 million, or *one of six inhabitants of Ukraine*, perished in the conflict. An additional 2.3 million had been shipped to Germany to perform forced labor." Millions of captured Soviet soldiers and the Ukrainian population died there in the factories and death camps. (Orest Subtelny, *Ukraine, A History,* Univ. of Toronto Press, 1994, 479. italics added)

The official Soviet encyclopedia (1978) statistics state: "During this war over 20 million Soviet people were killed including many peaceful citizens. On the territory of Ukraine along the Hitlerites destroyed over 5 million people and more than 2 million people were carried off into slavery to Germany." (*Ukrainska Radyanska Entsyklopedia*, Kyiv 1978, v. 2, 152 cited by A. Gregorovich)

For another perspective on the Soviet involvement in bringing about the end of Nazi Germany Gregorovich observes, "Even if we accept the conservative figure offered by Prof. Kondufor (during Soviet rule it should be mentioned), Ukraine's loss of about 7.5 million people is greater than the total military loss of the USA, Canada, British Commonwealth, France, Germany and Italy all put together. According to the *Encyclopedia Britannica* the total military losses of these countries in World War II was 4,305,214. The statistics are: USA 292,100; British Commonwealth 544,596 (including 39,139 Canadians); France 210,671 (+107,847 civilians); Germany 2,850,000, and Italy 300,000. In conclusion it seems reasonable to estimate that because of the German occupation and the Soviet repression from 1939 to 1945 during World War II, *that Ukraine lost about 10,000,000 citizens or one Ukrainian out of four."* (italics added)

The body count tells the story. "It is reasonably estimated that about *50 million people* perished because of World War II which means *20 per cent of all the victims were Ukrainians*; in this figure are about 600,000 Ukrainian Jews. In 1939, as Andrew Gregorovich observes, the Jewish population of Ukraine was 1.5 million (1,532,776) or 3% of the total population of Ukraine. When the War started on June 22, 1941 the Soviet Government first of all ordered the execution of all 19,000 Ukrainian political prisoners in western Ukraine (750,000 had already been killed or exiled to Siberia) and then the evacuation of 3.5 million key personnel to the east, to Russia. These evacuees included many Jews who were highly educated, and were scientists, skilled workers, Communist bureaucrats, and NKVD secret police. *The total evacuated was estimated to be about one-half to two-thirds of the total Jewish population of Ukraine*." Would any of this have been possible had world leaders vigorously objected to the Holodomor Genocide? (Italics added)

"As the German Army swept east across Ukraine it included German *Einsatzgruppen* with 500 to 1,000 men which were special mobile killing squads ordered to carry out "The Final Solution" of killing all Jews. Ukraine had been the major part of the Jewish Pale of Settlement in the Russian Empire and in the 19th century probably had the most Jews of any country in the world. Within a few days of capturing Ukrainian cities like Lutsk, Zhitomir and Berdichev in the summer of 1941 thousands of Jews were killed. Most of these executions were carried out by the *SS Standartfuehrer* Paul Blobel who was the officer of the *Sonderkommando 4A, Einsatzgruppe* C. Only German personnel, no Ukrainians, were members of the *Einsatzgruppe* C and D which were assigned to Ukraine." (Reitlinger 251 cited in A. Gregorovich online, "World War II in Ukraine: Jewish Holocaust in Ukraine", <www.infoukes.com/history/ww2/page-25.html>, Infoukes, Ontario, Canada)

From this historical perspective Ukrainian fatality figures for the two World Wars are astounding. In his essay "Ukraine's Population Losses in World War II: 7.5 million or 13,614,000?", Andrew Gregorovich makes it unmistakably clear that Ukraine lost more people in World War II than any other European country.

"At the beginning of the war," Gregorovich observes, "Ukraine's population was 41.9 million. Let us review some of the estimates of losses from largest to smallest. According to *A Short History of Ukraine* published by the Ukrainian Academy of Sciences in Kiev in 1986, as a result of the Second World War: 'The population (of Ukraine) contracted by 13,614,000.' This statistic is not explained. In 1977 Stephan G. Prociuk estimates in a detailed analysis that Ukraine's World War II loss of population was 11 million." (*Annals of the Ukrainian Academy of Arts and Sciences in the USSR,* NY, 1977, v. 13 no. 23-50)

He goes on to tell us that "The American journalist Edgar Snow, who visits Ukraine in 1943 during the war, and at the end of the war in 1945, reported in his book *The Pattern of Soviet Power* (1945) that according to a high Ukrainian official 'No fewer than 10,000,000 people had been lost to ... Ukraine since 1941.' This statistic excluded 'men and women mobilized in the armed forces'. Yet it was not till I went on a sobering journey into this twilight of war that I fully realized the price which 40,000,000 Ukrainians paid for Soviet—and Allied—victory. The whole titanic struggle, which some are apt to dismiss as 'the Russian glory', was *first of all a Ukrainian war. ...* I was told by a high Ukrainian official. That excluded men and women mobilized for the armed forces. A relatively small part of the Russian Soviet Republic itself was actually invaded, but the whole Ukraine, whose people were economically the most advanced and numerically the second largest in the Soviet Union, was devastated from the Carpathian frontier to the Donets and Don rivers, where Russia proper begins. No single European country suffered deeper wounds to its cities, its industry, its farmland and its humanity." (*A Short History of Ukraine*, Ukrainian Academy of Sciences, Kiev, 1986; Edgar Snow, *The Pattern of Soviet Power,* NY: Random House, 1945, 73; italics added)

The Russian counter-offensive to Berlin left behind a country of decimated ruins. Gregorovich tells us his former homeland's population had fallen "by 25 per cent – that is, by approximately 10.5 million people; 6.8 million had been killed or died of hunger or disease, and the remainder had been evacuated or deported to Soviet Asia as political prisoners or had ended up as slave laborers or emigrés in Hitler's German," states Ann Lencyk Pawliczko in *Ukraine and Ukrainians Throughout the World* (1994). Prof. Kubijovych, a geographer, says "the population of the *Reichskommisariat Ukraine* fell from 24,100,000 in 1939 to 16,900,000– a drop of 30 percent. The population of the larger cities dropped by 53 percent. ... We may assume that in 1943 the population of the Ukrainian SSR in the current boundaries was about 30 million, that is, 10.5 million less than in 1939." Trembitsky in *Ukraine: A Concise Encyclopedia* (1963) gives a total of war losses to Ukraine in 1941-45 of 8,545,000. (*Za Vilnu Ukrainu*, 24 serpnia, 1994 3; Ukrainian leader Volodymyr Shcherbitsky gives a "statistic" of 6,750,000 as Ukraine's World War II losses. (*Radyanska Ukraina*, 18 October, 1974); Ann Lencyk Pawliczko in *Ukraine and Ukrainians Throughout the World,* Univ. of

Toronto Press, 1994, 62; Trembitsky, *Ukraine: A Concise Encyclopedia*, Univ. of Toronto Press, 1963, v.1, 204)

Andrei Gogorovich states in his online essay “Koch vs Rosenberg”, that Nazi *Reichskommissar* Koch for the Ukraine “was ordered to provide 450,000 workers a year from Ukraine for German industry by “ruthless” means, according to Reitlinger. German documents said that the Ukrainian *Ostarbeiter* would be ‘*worked to death.*’ Although 40,000 Ukrainians a month were being sent to Germany as *Ostarbeiter* (slave laborers), Hitler’s young chief architect and armaments minister Albert Speer (1942-45) complained that his work force was dwindling. This would mean that more than 40,000 were dying *every month.* In one memorandum from Fritz Sauckel to Alfred Rosenberg there was a demand for one million men and women in four months at the rate of 10,000 a day and more than two-thirds were to come from Ukraine. In all the major Ukrainian cities the German army kidnapped young adults off the streets and shipped them to Germany as virtual slave laborers to work in the worst and most dangerous conditions. On the orders of the German administration Ukrainian cities were to be permanently depopulated by starvation and deportation. About three-quarters of the over 3,000,000 *Ostarbeiter* were Ukrainians. Prof. Kondufor’s statistic is that 2,244,000 Ukrainians were forced into slave labor in Germany during World War II. Another statistic cited by David Dallin (1961) put the total at 2,196,166 for Ukrainian *Ostarbeiter* slaves in Germany. Both of these statistics probably do not include the several hundreds of thousands of Galician Ukrainians, so a final total could be about 2.5 million.” (D. Dallin, 452, in A. Gregorovich; Ibid.)

“There were slightly more women than men *Ostarbeiter* employed in agriculture, mining, manufacturing armaments, metal production and railroads,” Gregorovich writes. “For example, on September 3, 1942 Hitler demanded that half a million Ukrainian women be brought to Germany to free German women from housekeeping. Hitler thought there was a Germanic strain in Ukraine because the Ostro-Goths and Visi-Goths had lived in southern Ukraine 1,800 years earlier and the ‘chaste peasant virtues of Ukrainian women’ appealed to him. In the end only about 15,000 girls were taken to Germany to work as domestics. The other two million Ukrainians worked mostly in the armaments factories including the V-2 rocket factory at Peenemunde.”

At the end of the war some 120,000 Ukrainians registered themselves as displaced persons (DPs). Most Ukrainians who survived the war in Germany were forcibly repatriated to the USSR because of the Yalta agreement. Repatriation almost always meant death or exile in Siberia. General Koch served eight years in Polish prisons, avoided Soviet imprisonment. Never tried for his war crimes that occurred in the Ukraine he lived a free man in Poland until 1986, apparently at peace, tolerated and granted a ripe old age dying at 90. Americans never knew him or his horrors. (D. Dallin, “The Soviet Union, From Lenin to Khrushchev”, Washington DC, US Government Printing Office, House Document No. 139, 1961, 452)

The Nazi Germans were no less exacting in their killing as they were in the documentation of Stalin’s crimes. Gregorovich recounts, for example, how

German experts excavated mass-killing by the Soviet NKVD secret police in Vinnytsia, a Ukrainian city 120 miles south-west of Kiev. In 1939 it had a population of about 100,000. On May 25, 1943 a German team of professors of forensic science and international experts started excavating three mass murder sites there of 1937 and 1938. The local population thought that about 20,000 people who had disappeared had probably been murdered there by the NKVD on orders from Moscow.

Once Germany invaded Stalin adopted extreme measures of internal counter-espionage and subversion of the Wehrmacht. Boris Levytsky writes, "The NKVD rendered inestimable service in the defense of the Soviet Union. Their fanaticism contributed decisively to raising the morale of the fighting forces. Still more valuable was their services to the armaments industry. ... The NKVD was unique in its display of toughness, iron discipline, and loyalty to the regime." Much of the responsibility of organization in the Caucasus fell to Beria and Kagonovich including State security services, intelligence, and espionage. The creation of Smersh, "the anti-espionage department of the People's Commissariat of Defense, with the title of 'Death to Spies', in Russian *Smerty Shpionam.* This gave Stalin all he needed .... On each staff there was a Smersh office which de factor watched all officers. ... The Smersh gradually became a weapon of offense," Levytsky writes. Soon it handles "more and more political tasks." It penetrates the partisans flushing out anti-communists and infiltrates the Gestapo. "At the end of 1942 the NKGB succeeded in activating the network of its secret agents in the areas occupied by Germany. Their task was trenchantly formulated by Stalin himself– 'to make life behind the enemy lines intolerable for them'. Their agents infiltrated all the activities of the Gestapo and other authorities." (B. Levytsky, "In the Front Line of the 'Patriotic War'", 156-75)

Procedures were systematically followed by the German investigators and carefully documented. Victims had their hands tied behind their backs and were shot in the back of the head. From May to October 1943 there were 9,432 corpses, including 169 women, found in three burial places. Of these 679 were identified from their documents and garments by relatives. The Soviet government had hidden the graves in a pear orchard and by building a Public Park on top of the mass graves with swings and playground equipment. (A. Gregorovich, "Vinnytsia", on the web)

Gregorovich reminds us that "most of the executions in Ukraine were carried out by shooting the victims (because all the death camps like Auschwitz were in Poland) (although) some people were killed by hanging and others in trucks by gas." The Ukrainian author Anatoly Kuznetsov writes: "On one occasion a gas-van arrived full of women. When the usual procedure was over and the shouting and banging had died down the door was opened. After the fumes had cleared, the van was seen to be packed full of naked girls. There were more than a hundred of them, pressed tightly together, sitting on each other's knees. They all had their hair done up in scarves, as women do when they take a bath. They had probably been told when they were put into the van that they were on their way to the baths. Many were found to have rings and watches, lipstick and other small things hidden in their headscarves. The drunken Germans hooted with laughter, explaining they were waitresses from the Kiev night-clubs .... When Davydov lifted them and laid them on the stack ... still warm, the breath would come out of their mouths with a faint noise, and he got the impression again that they were alive but had simply lost consciousness. They were all burnt on the fire in Babyn Yar." (Anatoly Kuznetsov, *Babi Yar*, NY: Penguin, 1982, 377-8; Kamenetsky; Zayas, 204, 240-4; A. Gregorovich, "Kiev Waitresses", online)

For ill-fated Ukraine more horrific tragedy would follow the Holodomor as it escalates into a larger more terrible world catastrophe and realignment of world power. "The great puzzle is: Did Hitler or Stalin during WW II kill the most Ukrainians?", Gregorovich asks hauntingly. Unfortunately, this is a most relevant question and no more absurd than the silence of the West to ignore it. And ever more so relevant today with Genocide currently inflicted on defenseless populations in various forms. His reply is no less creepy: "Hitler's crimes in Ukraine have been better documented and are better known. Stalin said that history is written by the winners. As a victor over Nazi Germany Stalin's USSR was able to hide its Genocide of Ukrainians. After the war Stalin conceded that 7 million Soviet citizens died but we know he concealed the real figures. Premier Nikita Khrushchev, in 1961, set the death toll in the USSR at 20 million and this seems to be an accurate accounting. More recently Moscow has set figures as high as 25 million; in Washington in 1990 Gorbachev declared 27 million dead but he may have included non-combat deaths as well. (F. Wilheilm Christians, *Paths to Russia, from War to Peace*, NY: Macmillan, 1990)

These latest figures are either sheer propaganda or estimates based on new information about Stalin's Genocide of Ukrainians and other Soviet citizens during the War. Both Hitler and Stalin saw the Ukrainian nation as an obstacle to their plans and goals. Hitler wanted Ukraine as German *Lebensraum* ("Living space") and Stalin feared that Ukrainian nationalism and an independent Ukraine would wreck the Soviet Russian Empire. Both were guilty of war crimes and Genocide in Ukraine on such a massive scale that they are virtually unequaled in history. We are not speaking here of thousands, or tens of thousands, or even hundreds of thousands of victims of mass murder. We are talking of millions of Ukrainians killed by both Hitler and Stalin." Within that space of argument we are led back to Stalin's mass-killing of the Holodomor Genocide.

Gregorovich then goes on to declare, "No documentary evidence exists of Hitler's order to eliminate all Jews in Europe but we know this is true. Likewise, we have no Hitler order to annihilate the Ukrainians. But we do have the evidence: 1) Millions of civilian victims perished which could not be 'accidental'; 2) Documentary evidence of the wholesale executions of Ukrainians; 3) The order to execute up to 100 innocent Ukrainians for one German soldier shot by the partisans (and 460,000 German soldiers were killed by partisans and guerillas); 4) The *Ostarbeiter* Ukrainian slaves were to be 'worked to death' in Germany; 5) Millions of prisoners of war were intentionally starved to death in concentration camps; 6) Ukrainian cities were starved to death according to plan; 7) Nazi leaders said that Ukraine as the *Lebensraum* of Nazi Germany would be colonized by

German population and some Ukrainians would be used as slave labor.'" And we find Stalin's written expressed dread of losing the Ukraine that would seriously weaken Russia and threaten Moscow's control and post-imperial communist dominance." (A. Gregorovich)

Hitler's Final Solution applied to the extermination of the Ukrainians as well as Jews; and the destruction of everything Ukrainian. It was Hitler who ultimately was in charge of the Nazi Empire. "Of the 650 major legislative orders issued during the war", Niall Ferguson observes, "all but 72 were decrees or orders issued in his name. It was Hitler who argued, shortly after the invasion of the Soviet Union, that 'In view of the vast sie of the conquered territories in the east, the forces available for establishing security in these areas will be sufficient only if, instead of punishing resistance by sentences in a court of law, the occupying forces spread such terror as to crush every will to resist among the population'. It was Hitler whose preferred method for pacifying occupied territory was 'shooting everyone who looked in any way suspicious'." (N. Ferguson, *Civilization*, 194)

"What about the other Ukrainians?" Gregorovich asks. "As late as 1943," he observed, writing, "Hitler refused status to Ukraine and when Ukrainians offered to form an army against the USSR it had to be named Galicia Division until the very last few minutes of the war in 1945 when it was renamed the Ukrainian National Army". Furthermore, Gregorovich reminds us, "Ukraine's disproportionate civilian losses compared to military also indicates a special Nazi German campaign. It would be naive to think that Adolf Hitler and the Nazi German government was not bent on destroying as many Ukrainian *Untermensch* as possible in view of the statements which prove it. For example, *Reichmarshal* Göering, who was second to Hitler in power said: 'This year between *twenty and thirty million* persons will die (in Ukraine) and Russia of hunger. Perhaps it is well that it should be so, for certain nations must be decimated'." (Hermann Göering, Nov. 24-7, 1941, A. Gregorovich, in D. Dallin, 123; italics added)

FDR: WHAT IS A US PRESIDENT TO DO?

From day one in his first administration as the nation's Commander-in-Chief FDR kept steady vigilance standing by on the bridge preparing for the inevitability of war and final American acceptance necessary to get in it. A full two years before Pearl Harbor and America's declaration of war on Japan and Germany, FDR wrote his ambassador in London, Joseph Kennedy on October 30, 1939, "We over here, in spite of the great strides towards national unity during the past six years, still have much to learn of the 'relativity' of world geography and the rapid annihilation of distance and purely local economics." Kennedy installs his eight children with him in the Embassy compound at the Court of St. James with its floral gardens and grand mansion that once belonged to banker JP. Morgan. But Kennedy is not very popular here for his pro-German views confident that Hitler would crush England. MI5 keeps him under close surveillance; his phones are tapped, associates are followed and secretly searched. When the bombs began to fall on London, "the American Embassy was, to Roosevelt's disgust, the first to flee from the capitol", writes Churchill's personal secretary Jock Colville. Kennedy prefers refuge in his large country home. Roosevelt promptly fires him. (John Colville, *The Fringes of Power*, 753)

Ever since the disillusionment of Wilson's promises during America's strategic role in WWI and its turn inward into euphoric isolationism shackled suddenly by the mind-numbing economic Depression, popular conditions convinced President Roosevelt that only an overt act of war against the United States would rally the people to fight. When Hitler was on the verge of invading Czechoslovakia, Ambassador Kennedy held a cozy press conference and exposed high ranking anti-Hilter coup plotters including General Ludwig Beck, Chief of the German General Staff and his deputy General Franz Halder. Kennedy's pro-Hitlerite defeatism persists up to 1941 when in his commencement address at Notre Dame his constant anti-British remarks were reported back to the White House, and particularly infuriated the Roosevelt team for having said, more or less in a paraphrased summary of his remarks that "Hitler was the greatest genius of the century. (His) diplomatic ability was superior to anything the British could hope to muster. ... Britain is hopelessly licked and there will be a negotiated peace within sixty days."

Seymour Hersh disclosed in *The Dark Side of Camelot* that British intelligence compiled a secret file on ambassador Joe Kennedy "known as the 'Kennediana' file, which would not be declassified until after the war. In those pages Sir Robert Vansitart, Undersecretary of the Foreign Office in early 1940: 'Mr. Kennedy is a very foul specimen of a double-crosser and defeatist. He thinks of nothing but his own pocket. I hope that this war will at least see the elimination of his type'." (M. Hastings, *Inferno*, "We over here ...", 180; re. Kennedy at Notre Dame, Joseph E. Persico, "A Secret Unshared", *Roosevelt's Secret War: FDR and World War II Espionage*, NY: Random House, 2001 337; S. M. Hersh, 65)

President Franklin Delano Roosevelt was a grandmaster at handling the American press. Driving hard against the isolationist currents resisting American intervention in the European war FDR artfully cultivates their support with the sharpest instincts of a political animal. He steadily held firm his course towards nothing less than unconditional surrender of the enemy. The man in the wheel chair is most unsuspectingly undetectable and formidable adversary. His closest advisers are often baffled by the secrecy of his intentions. In a style not unlike JFK a generation later, Roosevelt forbids newspapers to photograph his steel braces needed to overcome painful adversity and earns him the confidence of the nation, winning an unprecedented four presidential terms in the White House, and he lives to see American troops embarking to the Normandy coast on their way to Paris and Berlin. Knowing that America soon has atomic weapons, and with victory nearly in hand, FDR sits for a presidential painting in the White House, then feels a blaring pain in the back of his head, and dies a few months before Hitler commits suicide in his underground steel and concrete bunker.

Two years after American rearmament had begun with a $1.15 billion Naval Expansion Bill, passed in May 1938, and then a Cash-and-Carry Bill, passed in November, 1939 which also modified the Neutrality Act officially opening the door for weapons sales to France and England, in particular, Hitler invaded Norway in April 1940. Then, two months before France's capitulation, the President holds another carefully contrived and artfully controlled press conference. The press love Roosevelt and he has them eating of his hand.

When asked if America faced a greater threat of war he replied with deliberate circumspection that veiled his steady preparation to enter the conflict. Roosevelt declares, "You can put it this way: that the events of the past forty-eight hours will undoubtedly cause a great many more Americans to think about the potentialities of war." It was finally the fall of France that persuaded FDR to stay the course and win reelection to keep his hands on the helm as Commander-in-Chief for a third term. His close adviser at State, Adolf Berle Jr., – both are experienced veterans of the First World War–, recalls on May 15, "The question of whether Roosevelt would run is being settled somewhere on the banks of the Meuse River." In a special meeting with his chiefs of staff Roosevelt instructed preparations for war and expansion of the armed forces. This same year the White House rams through Congress the Selective Service Act imposing the draft and his $15 billion rearmament plan.

America is slow to get into the war. Not everyone agrees with FDR's foresight. Harvard's treasurer William Clafin advises Harvard's president, "Hitler's going to win. Let's be friends with him." Two years after the disgrace of Chamberlain isolationists in America still held sway on national public opinion against intervention in a foreign war; Kingman Brewster, Yale's controversial president signs an editorial manifesto published in the *Atlantic Monthly* September 1940 against armed intervention to save England from Nazi domination. Thirty years later students would teach Brewster and his friends a hard lesson about Consortium politics and support of murderous Right-wing fascist regimes supporting US Consortium politics in the State Department during the free love and rock & roll sixties and anti-Vietnam War protests as white middleclass students mixed with radical Black Panthers demanding an end to the war. The American youth had enough of the appeaseniks and Cold War hawks of the Kennan-Acheson-Rusk gang. The youth (and not those privileged sons too stoned and anesthetized in the drug culture of prep school nirvana) were fed up and had enough of the lies and deception of the older generation. Finally they had come of age to teach their fathers a lesson just how terribly wrong they had been for far too long waging their insanely Genocidal campaign about the national liberation struggle of Ho Chi Minh a pseudonym of Nguyen Sinh Cung), Gen. Vo Nguyen Giap and the Viet Minh (a youthful Giap, victor in 1954 at Dien Bien Phu studied Napoleonic strategy at the Ecole Coloniale in France) but only after over twenty years of armed struggle and over fifty thousand dead American soldiers and more than a million dead Vietnamese.

In a poll taken the day before FDR wins the presidential contest with 55 percent of the vote, *Fortune* found that only 16 percent favored sending US forces to join England's war for freedom. FDR understood well in advance of the nation that to defeat Nazi Germany, Hitler's enemies had to destroy his *Wehrmacht*.

In the events carefully calculated by FDR compelling Japan to launch a suicidal attack on America Undersecretary Berle remains throughout the war a key intelligence link between his Commander-in-Chief and the urbane Henry L. Stimson who received perhaps his worst brow-beating from the president over delayed 1941 Lend-Lease shipments to Russia, instead diverted to England. Weeks after the German invasion FDR harangued Stimson in a cabinet meeting August 1, 1941 that the Russians weren't receiving fast enough what they asked for including some 140 P-40 fighter planes packed in crates and sent to England instead.

"The Russians have been given the run-around," then Stimson insists. "I am sick and tired of hearing that they are going to get this and they are going to get that. Whatever we are going to give them, it has to be over there by the first of October, and the only answer I want to hear is that it is under way." As we enter the dark labyrinth of the war powers of these giant nation states it will become clear reader how the Stalin's man-made Genocide Terror-Famine of the Holodomor figures into the steely cold-hearted calculations of rapidly cascading events and the spiral into the Second World War in 1941.

In March of the decisive year 1942 Roosevelt tells his close friend and cabinet adviser Morganthau, "Nothing would be worse than to have the Russians collapse…I would rather lose New Zealand, Australia, or anything else than have the Russians collapse." The following year Russia took the offensive. (Beatrice B. Berle, and Travis B. Jacobs, *Navigating the Rapids, 1918-1971*, Harcourt Brace, 1973, 314, cited in M. Hastings, *Inferno,* 181-3; Robert B. Stinnett, *Day of Deceit: The Truth about FDR and Pearl Harbor,* NY: Simon & Schuster, The Free Press, 2000; Ted Morgan, *FDR: A Biography*, NY: Simon & Schuster, 1985, 593; Eric Larrabee, *Commander in Chief: Franklin Delano Roosevelt, His Lieutenants & Their War*, NY: HarperCollins, 1987, 629)

"The senior officers of the Wehrmacht", writes historian Max Hastings, "flattered themselves that they represented a cultured nation, yet they readily acquiesced in the barbarities designed into the Barbarossa plan. These included the starvation of at least 30 million Russians, in order that their food supplies might be diverted to Germany, originally a conception of Nazi agriculture chief Herbert Backe. At a meeting held on 2 May 1941 to discuss the occupation of the Soviet Union, the army's armament-planning secretariat recorded its commitment to a policy noteworthy even in the context of the Third Reich: 1. The war can only be continued, if the entire Wehrmacht is fed from Russia in the third year. 2. If we take what we need out of the country, there can be no doubt that many millions of people will die of starvation." The Hitlerian extermination plan also included total starvation and destruction of Petrograd to be replaced by a modern marvel of futuristic Germanic urbanism. (*Germany and the Second World War, Potsdam*, v. 4, Research Institute for Military History, Oxford Univ. Press, 341, in Max Hastings, *Inferno, The World at War, 1939-1945*, NY: Knopf, 2011, 138-9)

The peasants didn't know what hit them. It was as though a sudden natural disaster, a tsunami or earthquake had toppled and swept away the innocents. They didn't understand the monstrosity of the crime perpetuated against them in their utter weakness against the merciless crushing force of such a cruel fate. After all, they were only peasants, illiterate, uneducated tillers of the Earth. There were farmers. They knew what was in store for them, – government procurements by police agents stealing all their grain, and seed! The global picture of geopolitics was too high over their heads to comprehend. So it was easy for the Soviets and their state communist propaganda machine to blame the victims for their misfortune.

The peasants are the least to blame. But how could they even dream that the American leaders in the free world could be so utterly cynical and evil unless of course they were the corrupt bourgeois counter-revolutionary capitalists of the West. The name of President Hoover and the American Red Cross persisted as symbols of goodwill since the American intervention during the Russian famine immediately after the First World War. Was there no other way to build "the New Society" of the great new communist state? Did life in Soviet Ukraine have to be a fascist communist hell in a maze of absurd totalitarian nightmares? In 1929 in April when the Sixteenth Communist Party Conference adopted the first Five-Year Plan for the Development of the People's Economy, the peasants made up over eighty percent of the total population in the Soviet Union. "A hundred thousand tractors will turn the *muzhik*, the peasant, into a Communist," declared Lenin. *Newsweek* bureau chief in Moscow, Owen Mathews (of Ukrainian descent) writes that in that year there are only five tractors for the spring planting in the Ukraine. (Owen Mathews, *Stalin's Children: Three Generations of Love, War, and Survival*, NY: Walker, 2008, 25-6)

FDR cajoles that he is a farmer too, "a gentleman farmer" on his 1500 acre estate "Springwood", high overlooking the Hudson River; his friendly neighbor and close adviser Henry Morgenthau, Jr., is also an apple farmer. His father, President Wilson's politically appointed ambassador in Turkey in 1915 witnessed the Armenian Genocide and pleads with Ottoman government officials and his own State Department to intervene to cease the bloodshed of mass extermination but it was all in vain. Now his son enjoys trading secrets of good cultivation and prized fruits of their farm labor tilling the soil of the earth under the sun. FDR's Secretary of Agriculture and future vice-president, is also a farmer. Whereas for the gentlemen farmers this work is a hobby; and relief from the stress of Consortium business, politics and war, for Henry Wallace, FDR's vice-president during the Holodomor years, farming is a living passion that assumes a cosmic mystical delight. Wallace is fascinated by the life of plants, and what he calls plant "intelligence". None of these men ever lift a finger to save the Ukrainian population of peasants from Stalin's campaign of extermination by hunger and terror.

Fascism, pure and simple? Call a spade a spade. Is it not so that it was always meant to be the way it was? The America President Woodrow Wilson, a great expert on the Constitution and former President of Princeton University, saw it already infesting his government during the first year of his first term and fought valiantly but in vain for the ideals of democracy till his death in 1924, repudiated at home and abroad, isolated, and alone. In 1921 Lenin warns his band of Communist

Party Commissars of the Politburo which this year becomes the real center of power in the country, to adopt his pro-capitalist New Economic Program (NEP) with food distribution rather than a food tax as the incentive of food production by the peasants still burdened in their backwardness, that fatal curse gripping Russia for centuries. His days are long but his time is brief. Lenin will be dead too soon to see it implemented. Uncertain of a new beginning he warns others in his political testament to remove Stalin, and slowly wasted away poisoned, "incapacitated by his third stroke in March 1923", and, nearing his end he and his wife are kept virtually a prisoner of Stalin who he had fatally made General Secretary, head of the Secretariat of the communist bureaucracy in 1922 which allows him to stack the *nomenklatura* and emerge the incontestably the dominant master of the Party by 1929. For Mother Russia it was too late. (C. Andrew and V. Mitrokhin, *The Sword and the Shield,* 31)

The seeds of fascism had already multiplied their deep roots into the culture of western democracy and totalitarianism. When foreign bankers and businessmen construct and invest in fascist regimes, with their arms soaked in the blood of dictators which they nurture and protect, financially and politically, does that not make them fascists too? Or were the duped American people not unlike the forlorn Ukrainian peasants, victims of the same injustice perpetrated against the poor people of the world by fascists with their incestuous and invisible links between government and corporations which today undermines codes of ethics by global corporations to justify their investment in corrupt pariah regimes.

The author is a child of the Cold War, born in 1954, a year after Stalin's death. My father served 44 months in the Second World War mostly in Japanese-infested islands of the Pacific. A US Signal Corps officer he joined the US Army after Cornell and Wharton Business School. Nearly everyone alive today are creatures of that era, by-products of Cold War culture which makes this book more pertinent than ever. Both the US and the former USSR are still heavily engaged in "Cold War" mentality and burdened by gigantic military expenditures while civilian populations confront issues of declining health and welfare. Only near the end of his life did he tell war stories of his years in the Pacific while I wondered how the politics in the country sent him there and stole away his youth. My father was in San Francisco on his first leave home in August 1945 when two A-bombs dropped on Hiroshima and Nagasaki.

Hunger occurs in various regions of the world as it did in Russia and in America in the thirties. The United Nations' global food security program reported "more than one billion people - a sixth of the world's population - are undernourished, according to a BBC report mid-October 2009. World hunger remains widespread increasing daily despite modern techniques of cultivation and mechanization by billionaire dollar corporations trading millions of shares daily such as Caterpillar, International Harvester, John Deere and others with improved seeds and fertilizer. How governments choose to deal with world hunger recalls an amazing story of greed, indifference and deceit during the Holodomor thirties when the gold-plated billionaire Consortium corporate culture was rotten to the core. Leaders and personalities of power in the governing institutions, giant businesses and banks combined to perpetuate a system that at present creates enduring situations of famine in the world worsening daily.

For example, the UN's Food and Agriculture Organization (FAO) based in Rome said there are today "more hungry people than at any time since 1970" during the Biafra crisis. The world financial crisis had seriously aggravated the problem reducing foreign aid and investment in poorer countries and cut remittances from those working abroad. More hunger. More poverty. More government corruption. More propaganda and unaccountability. American government leaders argue that Russia must change its "mentality".

Americans must do the same. So must many journalists responsible for honesty and integrity in their jobs of reporting the news and informing the public if not for anything more than to protect the rights of free speech and the freedom of information. For example, the two *Wall Street Journal* writers of recently published "*Enough, Why the World's Poorest Starve in an Age of Plenty* (Perseus Books 2009). A heart-wrenching story or an artful cover-up? First look at its funding sources: The Rockefeller Foundation, the Chicago Council on Global Affairs. Oh my God! I thought. What is this? What is going on here? And there it is, smack from page one the reader is told of the "patriotic duty" of DuPont; then followed by FDR's Secretary of Agriculture Henry Wallace praised for trail blazing "from the beginning, the Green Revolution"; on the next page ultra-conservative Republican Consortium boss Herbert Hoover and often more aptly described as the mysterious wizard behind the curtain is introduced as the "wealthy mining engineer (who) organized private food-aid drives that fed millions of Europeans during World War I". Reader, as we go hand-in-hand through this dense forest before catching your breath – keep up! Be careful! Try not to stray off the path for its so easy to get confused and feel lost,– that is what they want!, – we are told how Rockefeller Foundation's president Raymond B. Fosdick is praised for its research to increase harvests with a team of agronomists led by Harvard and Cornell.

The Rockefeller team of Roger Thurow and Scott Kilman write, "Like Wallace, the professors were big believers in 'scientific farming." Bulls-eye! Here again with a traditionally correct twist smacks of elite propagandizing ingenuity aimed to protect the most powerful interests in America and around the world. Rockefeller-funded scientists lead the way to solving the world hunger problem! Amazing, yes? Perhaps. Ha! On closer scrutiny its apparent that these two authors for no odd reason fail to tell readers that from Berlin to Moscow, Rockefeller money led to famine across the whole of the Soviet Union, Genocide in the Ukraine, and the Second World War. Nice little war game this, eh?

Reader, remember this: It's all about money, power and influence, - using it, taking it, and never offending it. All necessary ingredients they combine together to create paradigms of political equation. Woe to these guys who lost their place in what they liked to call "Our Game" when the USSR comes tumbling down in 1991. Read John Le Carre's novel by the same title and only five years with the British secret service to become England's great spy raconteur on par with Graham Greene and Ian Fleming, also former FO operatives of the Consortium. The *WSJ* authors promoted their cause on *National Public Radio* (*NPR*), America's most listened to propaganda agency with "news" virtually manufactured and approved for domestic consumption by the US government. Just substitute "Propaganda" for the "Public" before the brainwashing begins. It never ends. Everyday, more of the same, more or less. That's the way it goes.

Rising and uncertain oil prices, chemical fertilizers, biofuels, soil depletion, climate change, and a host of problems leave it strikingly unclear how world leaders will find the political will to resolve famine in the future. When Rockefeller oil money made the world what it is today, it will take more than money alone to change it. A free mind with new positive and constructive ideas is a good start. Even with a global push to increase food production by 50% by 2029, – and another 100 *million* people deprived by the 2008 economic slide of adequate means to buy food,– the awareness is growing that the problem is even more severe.

Neil MacFarquhar, reporter for *The New York Times* listened intently for the record. A senior economist at the organization Kostas G. Stamoulis tells him, "'The way we manage the global agriculture and food security system doesn't work. There is this paradox of increasing global food production, even in developing countries, yet there is hunger.'" (Roger Thurow and Scott Kilman, *Enough, Why the World's Poorest Starve in an Age of Plenty,* Perseus Books, 2009; Neil MacFarquhar, "Experts Worry as Population and Hunger Grow", *The NYT,* Oct. 21, 2009)

Not so long ago in Russia during the lives of our parents and grandparents forced to survive under the terror of state communism, famine and Genocide happened in the Ukraine and other soviet territories. It was the result of orders of communist dictator Premier Joseph Stalin. Memories still haunt Ukrainian family survivors who were children when their mothers and fathers were killed or vanished. Some experts say perhaps at least ten million people were killed. One-quarter of the entire nation perished. Three million Ukrainian children perished in three months! They knew and the survivors and descendants remember how they suffered and died.

But at the time the world outside their villages and country was kept from knowing the reality because the leaders of the West including two Presidents of the United States refused to intervene to stop it. Instead President Roosevelt in his first year in the White House officially refuses to acknowledge it. And *in the same year 1933* FDR officially recognized Stalin's regime of socialist terror. The following year the Soviet Union is invited to join the League of Nations, in September 1934 to put a good face on the strategic alliance forged in betrayal and treachery of the ideal of freedom and the dignity of mankind, but the League "was still a taboo issue in American politics", notes historian Joseph P. Lash in "From Pacifist to Anti-Fascist" from his book *Eleanor and Franklin* (1971). (Joseph P. Lash, *Eleanor and Franklin*, Forward by Arthur M. Schlesinger, Jr., NY: W. W. Norton, 1971, 556)

While editing this book living on my fifty-year-old 35-foot teak sloop I came across a book in the Block Island Free Library, *The Siberians* by Farley Mowat. This prolific Canadian writer and naturalist, born in 1921 and before the war spent his boyhood exploring the vast wilderness of mountains and plains of his homeland in Saskatchewan in the northwest. A few years later Farley Mowat is commanding a rifle platoon in Operation Husky, the early Allied landings of Sicily; he and later does intelligence work on the surrender of Nazi troops in Holland and on Operation Manna of secret food drops saving thousands of Dutch lives.

One of the most honored and distinguished writers in Canada and recipient of countless awards, Farley is banned from entering the US during the Reagan administration, and later, again banned, in 1998 when invited to an ecology conference. Hostile to his politics, the US Justice Department discloses that Mowat is "on the watch list as a suspected war criminal". After a public uproar the ban is lifted, but only temporarily.

Author of some twenty books (*People of the Deer*, 1952; *The Regiment,* 1955; *Lost in the Barrens,* 1956; *Never Cry Wolf,* 1963; *The Boat Who Wouldn't Float,* 1969 ...), and noted for his gregarious passion for ethnic peoples and the Arctic tundra in the mid-Sixties was invited to tour Soviet Russia. In Moscow attending a ceremony at the Tchaikovsky Theater in honor of the Ukrainian nationalist poet Ivan Franko (1814-1861) Farley was amused to find speakers addressing their distinguished audience in their national Ukrainian language although the Russian-speaking Minister of Culture for the Ukrainian Socialist Republic is obliged to ask for a translation.

On his tour through the Siberia taiga Mowat learns to appreciate the burden of false notions carried in the baggage of propaganda and their subtle differences between East and West. "Our belief (it is almost a tenet of faith)," Mowat writes, "that the Russians are mindlessly manipulated by their propaganda agencies like a bunch of automata is one of our more glaring misconceptions. In my experience most Russians are so immunized to the propaganda downpour that it runs off them like water off a duck. Furthermore, most Russian internal propaganda is so unpalatable, and is prepared by such unimaginative dullards, that nobody but a born fool would pay much attention to it. There are undoubtedly born fools in Russia but most Russians do not fall into this category. The real nature of the situation is summed up in the words of a Soviet correspondent who spent five years in the United States and with whom I once had a discussion about the relative effectiveness of propaganda in our mutual countries. 'I have the greatest admiration for your propaganda,' he told me. 'Propaganda in the West is carried on by experts who have had the best training in the world– in the field of advertising– and have mastered the techniques with exceptional proficiency.'

"'On the other hand,' he added, somewhat wryly, 'we never had such a training ground because we had very little to advertise. Consequently, our propagandists are mostly old-fashioned and inept, and they try to make up by sheer volume of words for what they lack in ability. Yours are subtle and pervasive, ours are crude and obvious. This is one thing. Another is that we Russians are not, by nature, a gullible people. We are, and always have been, suspicious of what we cannot see for ourselves. You can call it the peasant mentality if you like. At any rate it is quite a different attitude from the rather charming naviété which makes many

North Americans incapable of doubting or assessing what they are told by their leaders and their communications media. I think the fundamental difference between our two worlds, with regard to propaganda, is quite simple. You tend to believe yours... and we tend do disbelieve ours'." (Farley Mowat, *The Siberians*, NY: Penguin, 1970, 83-4)

GENOCIDE IN THE 21ST CENTURY

Genocide is a unique phenomenon for modern man. It has a special power to kill. And power is habit-forming. Stalin made a habit of it and his regime thrived because of it. Stalin extended his success in the Ukraine by exterminating other nationalities, and then extending to other groups and sectors of his population even including his own political hierarchy of the communist political soviet system. Jews were spared the terrible anti-Semite persecution they suffered under the Tsar. Many of the leading Bolsheviks were Jews, as were the commissars of the dreaded secret police, the Chekha. Stalin resorted to similar methods casting to their fate more people fighting for their Motherland in the war against the fascist Hitler which took another twenty or more million. (The experts are out on the exact calculation.) German efficiency perfected the crude, rough and barren methods of the Russian "barbarians" with their genocidal death camps of the Jews. Hitler's fanatical fascists would not spare even his most brilliant Jewish bankers and industrialists. Stalin's terror becomes Hitler's obsession and Russian Jewish communism his worst nightmare setting the world aflame.

Secrecy and deception is the *modus operandi* for all Presidents and their diplomatic agents from the shameless George Bush family– father and son, to George Washington and back to Franklin Delano Roosevelt when the Russian Soviet dictator Joseph Stalin decimated the Ukrainians in the 1932-34 famine terror. For years the communist man-made famine swept through their fertile land of rich black soil. Why did they have to perish? The Ukrainians never really knew what hit them. Did they all have to die so that the great new Soviet society could live?

What dark forces were behind the plan for extermination of millions of hardworking men, women and children? And why were they never told the truth of the almighty international political intrigue that sent them to their doom. It happened then, and with ignorance of its real causes it might happen again. That haunts Viktor Yushchenko, swept into the presidency during the 2004 Orange Revolution, and fuels his crusade against reactionary indifference of the Russofied citizens of the Ukraine.

For Americans, it was printed on every dollar: put your faith in God, - not men. The first president of the United States graces every US dollar bill with the words "In God We Trust". George Washington himself said, "The necessity of procuring good Intelligence is apparent need not be further urged. All that remains for me to add is, that you keep the whole matter as secret as possible. For upon Secrecy, Success depends in most Enterprises of the kind, & for want of it, they are generally defeated, however well planned & promising a favourable issue."

Governments seldom reveal their best kept secrets. FDR wrote in code, thought in code and spoke in code. Few leaders and advisers understood the full meaning of many of his pensive meanderings. Many associates insisted on documents and instructions in writing, some of which he delivered, mostly not. Memoirs for the most part are largely entertaining anecdotal histories; classified documents are more useful in distinguishing fact from fiction and idle pursuits of memory. Governments protect their government men, especially these men in the Washington and London living in their tidy homes, offices and clubs, and did nothing to help. These men in trim government suits let millions of poor people who proudly and faithfully tilled the soil of the Earth die a wretched death by hunger and starvation under a state socialized system of Terror-Famine and oppression that they had put in place and paid for in dollars and debts and machines of modern technology. Then when it went haywire as they knew it would they did what they had to do to save themselves, closed their secret files, and went to dinner to enjoy another tasty meal with their friends and families. Men of honor would have vomited out their guts if they had witnessed the consequences of what they did and did not do. Instead, Stalin's henchmen buried and burned the bodies while the proud diplomats, bankers and lawyers and businessmen of the Anglo-American Consortium that emerged politically omnipotent and fabulously rich from the mud and blood of WWI covered up their tracks and promoted each others' career.

And so it happened in Soviet Russia in the early 1930s that a *holodomor*, "death by starvation" was inflicted on this nation of peasants. *Holo* means hunger in Ukrainian, *domor* means death. As many as ten million people were deliberately killed according to widely quoted figures of some Holodomor protagonists. Perhaps to the reader it it sounds so incredible that it couldn't be true. Impossible! You say. A Genocide of that magnitude in the thirties? Could it really be true?

The Powers-that-Be buried the history with skulls and bones of the dead. The perpetrators of the notorious crime showed no mercy and left barely a trace to remember the victims and blasphemy of the crime. Ten million victims perished. That's a conservative estimate of Stalin, and his spokesman for *The New York Times* William Duranty. The death toll may be much higher.

Ten million is an astonishing figure, too abstract to imagine as real, yet Americans today have almost no memory of understanding of the twenty odd million loss, civilians and soldiers, including Ukrainians, who perished in the Second World War less than a decade after the Holodomor while in the same conflict the Americans officially suffered *only* 416,837 killed.* The incredible disparity of losses among Allies claiming victory over Nazi Germany and Japan alone ought to raise eye-brows that something dark and secret is buried in those figures master-minded by the warmongers seeking empire, i.e. world domination. This same logic of machination is still spell-bound in a fragile balance of political, military and diplomatic intrigue between the superpowers. (*WWII death toll from the US Congressional Research Report, "American War and Military Operations Casualties", Feb. 26, 2010. The same report cites 10,725,345 Soviet dead and some 6 million captured. Russia today estimates are closer to 17 million military war dead, and twice that of civilian victims.)

Exposure of their role as perpetrators of the crime was too painful to confront or admit and so they remained shielded by their estates and headlines of a different nature. Their intention was to divert, mask, conceal. And they did so deftly, wielding economic and political power to control society and rendered the masses ignorant of the truth and impotent to resist. And for more than a half-century the perpetrators leveled layer upon level of diversion and concealment of the true historicity of their complicity cast in their crime.

Down to this day when few have dared to risk their academic careers exposing the traditional version of "History" as the trumped and tragic fake it really was. As I write this week *The New York Times* published a story on the declining numbers of contemporary diplomatic and political history courses offered at American universities teaching establishment history, culturally political correct interpretations which mostly have very little to do with the realities of the actual events. At the same time the Dean of Faculty at Johns Hopkins University maintained that "traditional diplomatic and economic history are still the specialties that are best suited to deal with American problem's today". However, one historian selected to put the priority of knowledge in context as we become more socially, culturally aware. "We'll widen our frame of reference, while not losing sight of the remarkable fact that a very small number of people still have the power to lead nations into war." ("Great Caesar's Ghost! Vanishing on Campus", *The NYT*, June 11, 2009)

In 2007, the Ukrainian delegation to the General Assembly raised the question of recognizing the Holodomor as an act of Genocide against the Ukrainian people. Putin's alarming resurgence of a Stalinist-inspired monolithic Russian dictatorship and Ukraine's president Viktor Yanukovich's regressive return power with a fiercely pro-Russian alignment are both decidedly against it. *The Day* newspaper published in Kiev observed "Russia's official representatives at the UN did everything possible to have the definition of the Holodomor as an act of Genocide excluded from the Joint Statement of 36 nations on the 70th anniversary of Ukrainian Holodomor." (*The Day*, Nov. 22, 2005)

The following year on October 23 the European Parliament adopted a resolution that recognized "the artificial famine of 1932-1933" of the Holodomor as a crime against Humanity. (EU Parliament Press Release, October 23, 2008). Earlier in May, on the occasion of a state visit by President Yushchenko to the Canadian Parliament where he was welcomed by Prime Minister Stephen Harper, the Holodomor was formally recognized as Genocide, and to establish a Ukrainian Famine and Genocide Memorial Day (Bill c-459).

PRESIDENT YUSHCHENKO AND THE UKRAINIAN PARLIAMENT

In November 2008, Russian President Dmitri Medvedev writes Ukraine President Yushchenko refusing to participate in Ukraine's 75th commemoration events of what he described officially as "the so-called Holodomor". Medvedev is Putin's pawn following in Putin's steps. When Putin won his contested 2012 presidential election, he immediately switched places with Medvedev stepping down to become Russia's new Prime Minister in Putin's new government.

Medvedev left no stone unturned in Putin's attack blaming Yushchenko even for exploiting the tragedy for personal political gain. President Medvedev wrote, "I am forced to point out that, in our opinion, the tragic events of the early 1930s in Ukraine are being used to achieve immediate short-term political goals. In this regard, the thesis on the 'centrally planned genocidal famine of Ukrainians' is being gravely manipulated. As a result, including thanks to your personal efforts, this interpretation has even received legislative support. In particular, I am referring to the law passed on 28 November 2006 by the *Verkhovnaya Rada* (Ukrainian parliament) that you signed, which states that "the famine of 1932-1933 in Ukraine was a genocide against the Ukrainian people".

The Russian president rejected the argument that Stalin deliberately sought to destroy Ukrainian nationalists and the Ukraine as a separate nation. "The famine," Medvedev declared," in the Soviet Union in 1932-1933 was not aimed at the destruction of any one nation. It was the result of a drought, forced collectivization and dekulakization (campaign of political repressions of the better-off peasants and their families) and affected the entire country, not only Ukraine. Millions of people in the middle and lower Volga regions, northern Caucasus, central Russia, southern Urals, western Siberia, Kazakhstan and Belarus died. We do not condone the repression carried out by the Stalinist regime against the entire Soviet people. But to say that it was aimed at the destruction of Ukrainians means going against the facts and trying to give a nationalist subtext to a common tragedy." And yet, only during this period earlier in the mid-eighties under the easing of restraints and Gorbachev's call for *glasnost* reforms, or openness in Communist Soviet society which of course in turn dealt a death blow to corrupt Marxist-Leninist dogma out of sync with a younger generation born long after Stalin's departure, and the opening up of mass graves, the digging up skulls and bones of murdered victims as the upsurge of Ukrainian nationalism shook even within Soviet army units based in Ukraine and running throughout the ranks of the Soviet army in which 17 per cent of its recruits came from Ukraine.

Formerly the *Financial Times* correspondent in Moscow before and after the Gorbachev era David Satter makes a very good point of this essential struggle to uncover the truth of the Holodomor with this compelling link between the surviving memory of the Holodomor and the final resurgence of Ukrainian nationalism which struck at the bloodline of the Soviet Red Army responsible for maintaining internal order and national defense. In *Age of Delirium, The Decline and Fall of the Soviet Union* (1996), Satter handily traces recent insurgent Ukrainian nationalism in this unfolding drama, and he writes, "The Russian soldiers feared they would be excluded from a Ukrainian army or forced to leave Ukraine. Almost all of them were skeptical of the Ukrainian nationalists and pointed out that the blue and yellow Ukrainian flag had been used by partisans who committed atrocities during the war. ... They spoke about the 1933 famine and Communist Party corruption and argued that the only future for Ukraine was an independent state ... an entire air-defense regiment refused to carry out the order to transfer its base to Semipalatinsk, where nuclear tests were conducted. The wives of the officers went on a hunger strike in the town's central square and officers asked Kravchuk* for political asylum." (David Satter, *Age of Delirium, The Decline and Fall of the Soviet Union*, NY: Knopf, 1996, 374-5; * Leonid Makarovych Kravchuk, the first President of post-Soviet Ukraine (1991-1994) was born in 1934 in the peasant village of Velykyi Zhytyn (*Żytyń Wielki*) in Poland which became part of Rivne Oblast in the Ukrainian Soviet Socialist Republic after the 1939 Soviet invasion.)

We know from Stalin's own hand, however, that by 1932 he feared "losing the Ukraine". Stalin regarded Ukrainian nationalism as an enemy to be crushed at all cost. As both Communist Party leader and Soviet Premier Stalin imposed a greater tyranny on the people of Ukraine no less terrible than under the Russian Czars and worse than suffered under Ivan IV in the 16th century.

Three hundred years after Ivan, the astute French diplomat Marquis de Custine in his 19th century classic travel account to Russia told of his journey to St. Petersburg and Moscow,— and exactly one hundred years before Hitler invaded Poland in 1939. His words ring true today as well they did when he first laid eyes on the East. "In Russia, the government dominates everything and gives life to nothing. In this vast Empire, the people, if they are not tranquil, are silent; death hovers over all heads and strikes them capriciously – this serves to create doubt of the supreme justice; there man has two coffins – the cradle and the tomb." (Marquis de Custine, *The Russian Journals of Marquis de Custine, Journey For Our Time*, Gateway Ed., 1987)

THE HOLODOMOR DEATH TOLL

How many Ukrainians died? The total count of victims from Stalin's repressions resulting from abortive soviet state agricultural policies is mind-boggling. Twenty million persons are said to have died of starvation in all the afflicted Soviet territories. In the Ukraine alone the number of victims of the famine of the 1932-33 period increased from 3.5 million to 7 million, with estimates surpassing even 10 million. Most Holodomor experts concur that the famine was most severe in the Ukraine, the North Caucasus Kuban, the middle and lower Volga, and in Kazakhstan. Furthermore, the Terror-Famine was most severe in the fertile grain-producing sectors where state collectivization reforms, propaganda violent suppression of the peasant population were most intensive.

A generation passed after the Holodomor before anyone reopened US State Department government files on the Holodomor. These official state records had been processed, and sequestered in remote places where they had been ignored and might have been entirely lost or forgotten until a US government agricultural specialist sought them out for his study published in 1964 entitled "The Great Famine in Ukraine 1932-34". An economist with the US Department of Agriculture, and formerly attached to the USAID, Dr. Dana Dalrymple used these "previously unopened records of the US Department of State for 1933" in an effort to get the causes and numbers straight and assemble an accurate picture of what happened in those years. (Dr. Dana Dalrymple, "The Great Famine in Ukraine 1932-34" originally published in *Soviet Studies,* Jan. 1964)

Extracting coherence from these records was no simple task. Dr. Dalrymple assembled and published various accounts of the Genocide. Dalrymple also recorded eye-witness stories. While the dying and the dead were to be found at first on the streets of the main cities, it is in the villages where famine killed most. There were many reasons to be frustrated. "At the outset," Dalrymple writes, "it is difficult to make a precise estimate of the number of deaths from the famine." Dalrymple received no assistance from Moscow albeit the inquiry occurred during the apex of Cold War hostilities of the Kennedy-Johnson era. At the time Dalrymple stated, "The Soviet government not only has refused official recognition of its existence, but has not published any figures that might be used to calculate mortality." He methodically combed through evidence in the absence of "crude birth or death rates during the famine period" none of which were disclosed by Soviet authorities. However, his findings indicated detailed knowledge of the Terror-Famine at the time among the diplomatic corps in Moscow.

Following publication of the Dalrymple findings, that same year the State Department accepts the death toll figure of 5 million Holdomor victims. The US government officially describes the Holodomor as "among the worst famines of all time". It was a no brainer but still a step in the right direction, albeit dicey. In 1948, in his book *Europe on the Move* published by Columbia University, an Ivy League establishment icon, writer Eugene Kulischer indicated that at the least 5 million deaths occurred as a result of Stalin's collectivization drive. Two years earlier, with the Cold War enveloping geopolitics, the New York firm Dutton published Nicholas Timasheff's *The Great Retreat* with an 8 million death count. (Eugene M. Kulischer, *Europe on the Move*, Columbia Univ. Press, NY, 1948, 96. Kulischer suggests the publication of annual mortality data ceased *before* the famine;Nicholas S. Timasheff, *The Great Retreat*, NY: Dutton, 1946)

But it was during the crisis it was commonly accepted by well-informed diplomats that the Holodomor was far worse than the terrible famine during the Lenin era with intervention by the Hoover American Relief Administration (ARA), and it was not unthinkable to estimate a total mortality at least be as high as eight million victims. For the record Dr. Dalrymple drew attention to the transcript of a conversation between the astute diplomat Felix Cole, US Chargé d'affaires in Riga, Latvia, and junior embassy officer John Lehrs with "a member of the staff of a foreign legation in Moscow." The famine, Dalrymple observes, "was frankly admitted on several occasions by officials of the Commissariat for Foreign Affairs to members of the Moscow diplomatic corps." (W. Horsley Gantt, "A Medical Review of Soviet Russia: Results of the First Five-Year Plan," *British Medical Journal*, July 4 and 18, 1936, 19 and 128, reprinted in his *Russian Medicine*, v. XX of *Clio Medica*, NY: Harper & Bros, 1937. Dalrymple benefited from conversations with Dr. Gantt (1892-1980) in Dec. 1963 and Oct. 1964, and from a letter dated March 6, 1964; Lorimer; Felix Cole to Sec. of State dispatch

No. 1633, Oct. 4, 1933, US State Department General Records, National Archives Record Group 59, SDDF 861.48/2450; Dr. D. Dalrymple, "The Great Famine in Ukraine 1932-34", *Soviet Studies* Jan. 1964; D. Dalrymple, Letter from Warren Eason, Department of Economics, Princeton Univ., March 27, 1963)

All things considered– excluding mortality by disease–, assessment of the official Holodomor death toll confronts a vast abyss where some five to ten million people perished. Ten million! Men, women, children. Civilians. Ordinary people. Families. Common hard-working field peasants of the Soviet bread-basket. We will never know how many perished. Published by *Neva* in the Soviet Union, in 1962, two years prior to Dalrymple's paper, Ivan Stadnyuk wrote in his realistic novel, *Lyudi ne angely* (*People Are Not Angels*), "The men died first, then the children, and finally the women," Stadnyuk wrote in the story of a young boy who proudly returns to his country village as an Soviet Air Cadet, dressed in shiny boots and red epaulets only to be denounced by jealous informers. His father commits suicide.

Soon it would be the Jews in Germany and Eastern Europe. The victims are defenseless Ukrainians and other Russians, many of them Christians whose religion worshiped pagan goddesses of fertility and rebirth and celebrated harvest holidays that followed the sun and moon and seasons. Their ancient and traditional beliefs fused with the Christian God and their saints. These were a holy people of the Earth, with a rich and deep spiritual past. Yet, in this ancient land the vestiges of that epic tragedy survived the onslaught. Nationalist Ukrainian traditions embedded in customs, language and memory merge with the modern complexity of contemporary Ukraine reflected in the symbols of mass media and market trends.

The human cry of the Holodomor strives to pierce the cacophony of capitalist globalization and be heard above the silence of despair.

There are very few books on the Ukrainian famine. Russia has never recognized the Holodomor. It ought to strike the reader odd that the Jews have thousands of books and daily media steaming televised and radio commentary to preserve the memory of their Nazi Holocaust but the Ukrainians are virtually ignored despite the higher death toll during the same period of foreign investment and Hitler's ascendancy with the National Socialist Party in Germany. There are many reasons to explain why that is that surface in the story of the Holodomor.

The initiative set down by Ukrainian President Viktor Yushchenko since his hard-fought election victory in 2005 witnessed for months on millions of screens around the world aimed to change that with the establishment of a national Holodomor research institution.

APRIL 23, 1986: US CONGRESSIONAL COMMISSION UKRAINE FAMINE 1932-33

In 1987 in New York, Dr. James Mace calls America's role in the Holodomor "perhaps the single most successful denial of genocide in history." Speaking openly about the Terror-Famine during a New York conference of his findings in a paper titled, "The United States and the Famine, Recognition and Denial of

Genocide and Mass Killing in the 20th Century". "The US government knew a great deal about the man-made famine of 1932-1933 in Ukraine," Mace declares, "and chose not to acknowledge what it knew or to respond in any meaningful way. Some members of the American press corps also knew a great deal which they chose not to report and, in some cases, actively denied in public what they confirmed in private. This constituted collaboration of the perpetrator's denial of genocide ..."

The story resurfaced in the year before when two important events occur in publishing details of the Holodomor Famine Terror: Harvard's Ukrainian Institute publishes Mace's book *Famine in the Soviet Ukraine 1931-33;* Oxford University publishes *Harvest of Sorrow* by Robert Conquest. When Harvard and Oxford converge with simultaneous publications of this magnitude something is up. A coincidence? Extraordinary timing, or rather, is something we don't see at work here. Then, in this same year, in Washington DC, US Congressional Commission on the Ukraine Famine, on April 23, 1986 records testimony by Dr. Mace and others. Just three days later in a quiet little village in Chernobyl north of Kiev on the Dniepr during a safety test the nuclear reactor explodes and melts releasing radiation at highly dangerous levels. Brave men die in a heroic and furious effort to contain it. All these events occur exactly five decades after the worst of Stalin's man-made Holodomor killing millions of men, women and children. My God! Poor Mother Ukraine! The problem of radiation leakage from the nuclear reactor is still unresolved three decades after the accident. No way to point at an foreign plot here! ("Investigation of the Ukrainian Famine 1932-33", *US Congressional Commission on the Ukraine Famine*, Second Interim Report, April 23, 1986, US Government Printing Office, Washington, DC, 1988)

Dr. Mace does not, however, expound upon another aspect of the tragedy, citing though without specific details contentious "issues dealing with grain production because of direct competition between American and Soviet wheat exports on the world market." At the time of the Depression thirties, there were economic strategic issues embraced by the capitalist Consortium and plans for the rapid industrialization of the Soviet socialist gulag state financed in part with desperately needed foreign exchange from Soviet exports of grain on the international grain market sold at depressed world grain prices, and confiscated from the Ukrainians who were for the most part either ruined and left destitute without resources, shot, and exterminated. (Dr. James E. Mace, "The United States and the Famine, Recognition Denial of Genocide and Mass Killing in the 20th Century", presented NYC, Nov. 13, 1987)

But that's not all. The next year, in 1988, the Holodomor Terror-Famine Genocide is officially recognized by the United States Government. Before the American Congress and again at the United Nations, Dr. James Mace of the Commission on the Ukraine Famine 1931-1932 drives his wedge deeper reopening living memories and old wounds of the Holodomor polemic when he presents a series of easy to follow facts that made it difficult to mount the least possible resistance or reject his conclusions and all this during the Gorbachev-Reagan thaw in Cold War tensions only a year before the destruction of the Berlin Wall.

SOVIET PREMIER GORBACHEV CONFESSES HIS SECRETS

Soviet Premier Mikhail Sergeyevich Gorbachev was born on March 2, 1931, in Privolnoe, a farming village in southern Russia of the North Caucasus. For generations his family worked the fields of his ancestors. Young Mikhail barely survived the Holodomor famine conditions of arson, riots and open rebellion against Soviet confiscation and extermination of the peasants. His grandfather Andrei Gorbachev is sent to a gulag charged with hiding forty pounds of grain for his family, a very serious offense. It's a miracle he isn't shot. His father Sergei is an operator of tractors and combines made from American factories with American technology.

Only much later apparently does Mikhail Gorbachev comprehend that Stalin's man-made famine had inflicted "an estimated 14.5 million deaths from hunger and famine." Soviet Premier Gorbachev is not unaffected by the repression of his own family members; he carries the family scars with him describing his grandfather as a "middle peasant" in the class of peasants who own a small amount of land they farmed.

Only long after the Khrushchev era and once he becomes General Secretary of the Party, Gorbachev speaks to "a commemorative session on the seventieth anniversary of the Bolshevik revolution, with a lingering sense of grievance at the 'injustice' and 'excesses' committed against the middle peasants in the thirties." According to an account of the event by writers Dusko Doder and Louise Branson in *Heretic in the Kremlin* (1990), Gorbachev declares that those peasants were the "staunch and dependable ally of the working class, an ally on a new basis." (Dusko Doder and Louise Branson, *Heretic in the Kremlin*, NY: Viking, 1990, 1-5)

PREMIER GORBACHEV RECALLS "...HALF THE FAMILY DIED OF HUNGER..."

In *Lenin's Tomb* (1993) describing the rapid breakdown of the Soviet Communist Party during the Gorbachev years the former Moscow correspondent David Remnick recalls the moment when the Soviet Premier let it slip that his own family had been destroyed by Stalin and collectivization! Reader this is an extraordinary moment in the life of the Soviet Union. The game is up! This an incredible event and naturally it does not pass unnoticed. Never before during his life and ascendancy within the *nomenklatura* of the privileged few enjoying "a life in which everything flows easily" would the smart legal-minded Gorbachev allow such an utterance to fall from his lips!

Four years *Washington Post* correspondent in Moscow, Jewish, Princeton, and fluent in Russian, Remnick writes, "Gorbachev's climb to power took place inside the Soviet Communist Party, an institution that valued aggressive obedience and secrecy. The initiator of glasnost revealed little of himself except through political performance... For all his support of glasnost, for all his talk of the need to fill in the 'blank spots' of history, Gorbachev kept to himself a central fact of his early life for more than five years coming to power. It was only in December 1990, when he was alienating the entire liberal intelligentsia, inlcuding Shevardnadze and Yakolev, by cooperating with the hard-liners in the Party, that Gorbachev revealed that both of his grandfathers had been repressed under Stalin. You had to be listening carefully to catch it. Late one night, Central Television broadcast a tape of one of Gorbachev's meetings with a large group of leading writers and journalists. Somehow, Gorbachev was trying to justify his swing to the right but at the same time to win back the respect of the intelligentsia. 'Look at my two grandfathers,' Gorbachev said. '*One was denounced for not fulfilling the sowing plan in 1933, a year when half the family died of hunger...*'." He truly wants to confess! To an American journalist of the *Washington Post*! "Why now?" David Remnick conjectures, "Why hadn't he said anything in 1988 when the battle for history had been raging?" When did it ever stop. Look at the reactionary power-crazed Tsar Putin deploying Cossacks to control the crowds at the 2014 Winter Olympics at Sochi. (italics added)

In 1990 Remnick hears another taboo of the Gorbachev family story again this time recounted by the Soviet boss himself: "'They took him away to Irkutsk to a timber-producing camp, and the rest of the family was broken, half-destroyed in that year. And the other grandfather – he was an organizer of collective farms, later a local administrator, a peasant of average means. He was in prison for fourteen months. They interrogated him and demanded that he admit what he'd never done. Thank God, he survived. But when he returned home, people considered his house a plague house, a house of an 'enemy of the people'. Relatives and dear ones were not able to visit, otherwise 'they' would have come after them, too'." (David Remnick, *Lenin's Tomb, The Last Days of the Soviet Empire*, NY: Random House, 1993, ed. 1994, 148-9)

Remnick made a radical career change. Or was it? He left both Russia, and his job at the *Washington Post* to assume in 1992 the honorable repose of the Edward R. Murrow Fellow of the Council of Foreign Relations (CFR), yet another beneficiary of the Rockefellers, granted a transitional sabbatical not quite the prize for the spy who came in from the cold, so to speak, before he joins *The New Yorker* magazine, Manhattan's slick icon of the publishing elite; by 1998 Remnick reemerges as its chief editor helping it reclaim status as a first-rate publication of liberal American intellectual culture. The former journalist is readily positioned to earn millions of dollars with all the perks and status of the rich and famous in America, and empowered with a national platform to write freely and often about Israel and the Holocaust towering above the largest Jewish community outside Jerusalem. Still summing up some editorial changes for this book while visiting the Caribbean in a televised report on the 2013 Boston Marathon killings. The networks of the media circus seem intent to walk their stars out of the stables from time to time and circulate among the current opinion makers of the culture's mass media on and off the air in "living time".

In April 1967, when he was 49 years old, Aleksandr Solzhenitsyn commented on "the crippling and cowardly secretiveness from which all our country's misfortunes come" to add, "a noose was draped around my neck two years ago, but not drawn tight, and I want to see what will happen next spring if I jerk my head slightly. Whether the noose will break or I shall be strangled cannot with any certainty be foreseen." Solzhenitsyn recalls in that incredible moment, nothing short of what seem the miraculous opening of the door toward freedom by the Twenty-second Congress."

Only a decade earlier in 1956, Solzhenitsyn continues, "there was no way of foreseeing the sudden fury, the reckless eloquence of the attack on Stalin which Khrushchev would decide upon for the Twenty-second! Nor, try as we might, could we, the uninitiated, ever explain it! But there it was –and not even a secret attack, as at the Twentieth Congress, but a public one! I could not remember when I had read anything as interesting as the speeches at the Twenty-Second Congress. In my little room in a decaying wooden house where one unlucky match might send all my manuscripts, years and years of work, up in smoke. I read and reread those speeches, and the walls of my secret world swayed like curtains in the theater, wavered, expanded and carried me queasily with them: had it arrived, then, the long-awaited moment of terrible joy, the moment when my head must break water?" But he had to wait for over three more decades to pass until the Soviet Union collapsed in 1991 after a failed army coup against Gorbachev's *glasnost* regime that smashed the myths of the inevitability of a world-wide Communist victory and of absolute power of the Marxist-Leninist grip on the people shaking their heads while lost in their crisis of broken faith. (A. I. Solzhenitsyn, *The Oak and the Calf: Sketches of Literary Life in the Soviet Union*, NY: Harper & Row, 1979, 14)

Then came Yeltsin. And still yet an even more incredible personal narrative of the Holodomor by the supreme Russian leader. Another child of the Holodomor, Gorbachev's protégé and the Party boss of Moscow, Boris Yeltsin presides over the dissolution of the USSR while his family and a handful of powerful oligarchs plunder state resources as it slips helplessly back into fractured anarchy and neo-Stalinist nationalism. Yeltsin, too, lied about his peasant kulak family past. Born in 1931 young Boris was raised in the farm village of his ancestors; Butka, in the Sverdlovsk Region of the Urals is where the Yeltsin clan sowed the fields, ploughed the wheat, and barely survives the Bolshevik takeover of Tsarist Russia.

Yeltsin recalled the family story when he nearly drowned at his own baptism: "The birthrate was quite high and baptisms took place once a month, so the day was rather hectic for the priest. The baptisms took place in the most primitive of fashions. There was a barrel, containing some kind of holy liquid, the child was completely immersed in it, then the squealing infant was pulled out, blessed, given a name and entered into the church register. As was the custom in villages, the parents then presented the priest with a glass of booze, vodka, moonshine ... Considering that my turn only came around in the second half of the day, the priest was by that time having trouble keeping his feet. I was passed to him, he lowered me into the barrel and forgot to take me out, instead starting to discuss and argue with the onlookers about something. My parents were some distance away, and didn't grasp the problem at first. When they did understand, my mother jumped up with a cry, caught me somewhere around the bottom and pulled me out. … My child-life was hard. There was no food. The harvests were abysmal.

Everyone was herded into a *kolkhoz* – it was a time of mass dispossession for the kulaks. Moreover, war-bands roamed the land – almost every day there were gunfights, murders, and thievery. We lived in poverty. A small house, a cow, there was a horse but it soon died so there was nothing to plow with ... In 1935, when even the cow died and it became completely unbearable, father decided to find work at a construction site, to save the family. This was the so-called period of industrialization. We hitched ourselves to the cart, threw our last few possessions onto it and headed towards the station, thirty-two kilometers away."

The Yeltsin family moved into a tiny wooden barracks, six sleeping on the floor. They bought a goat, for milk and warmth during the thirty degree below winters. It is true. A goat saved them all.

But that was an artful and socially acceptable rendering of the Yeltsin peasant family to cover the truth. The reality was much different, according to author Sol Shulman (*Kings of the Kremlin*). The Yeltsins are "a solid and well-to-do peasant clan...with deep roots in the Ural soil. The grandfather on the father's side was a well-known blacksmith and church elder." He was arrested and his farm confiscated under the "revolutionary morality" of the Soviet law in his case, "merciful". According to Internal Security Case # 56-44, grandfather Yeltsin was charged with having "a large village home, two mills – one water, one wind, he also owned a threshing-machine, an automated harvester, five horses, four cows, and twelve hectares of land. He also kept helpers, hired hands." The grandson recalls that his grandfather *kulak* "in the best peasant tradition 'took to the hills'" and dies four months later.

Yeltsin's father Nikolai is a talented handyman and fortunate to be allowed by a kind *kolkhoz* chairman to travel to the city to work. Otherwise the family faced starvation. In order to survive the family packs up and resettles at Berezniki, in the Urals, where his father finds work on a construction site. More hardship burdened the Yeltsins;, in April 1934 when Bill Bullitt prepares to arrive in Moscow to reopen the US embassy Boris Yeltsin's uncle Nokolai and four co-workers are arrested and charged with sabotage.

The actual cause of his arrest was an incident when Boris' 22-year old uncle dumped a canteen of foul soup and unleashed an outburst of anti-Soviet curses that sent his father and uncle to the labour camps for three years. Yeltsin recalls the nightmare that every family feared might befall them in *Notes of a President*: "'It is night. People walk into the wood barracks. Mother shouts, she is crying. I wake up and also start to cry. I'm not crying because they are taking father away. I am still little and don't understand what is going on. I can see that mother is crying, and how scared she is ... Father is taken away, mother rushes to me and embraces me. I calm down and go to sleep. Three years after father returned from the camps'." (Sol Shulman, *Kings of the Kremlin*, Brasseys/Chrysalis, 2002, 281)

Understand reader that straight through to Putin Russian leaders have never recognized the Holodomor. Nor does Putin who thinks of himself as a normal Stalinist. That is, he kills less but that won't convince the Chechins, or survivors of the current bloodbath in Syria.

As long as he stays within politically safe limits Dr. James Mace received timely US support from Washington to Kiev where he was a university professor. This is happening during the crackup just prior to the final collapse of the Soviet Union. Mace published a high-lighted list of his findings:

"1) There is no doubt that large numbers of inhabitants of the Ukrainian SSR and the North Caucasus Territory starved to death in a man-made famine in 1932-1933, caused by the seizure of the 1932 crop by Soviet authorities.
2) The victims of the Ukrainian Famine numbered in the millions.
3) Official Soviet allegations of "kulak sabotage," upon which all "difficulties" were blamed during the Famine, are false.
4) The Famine was not, as is often alleged, related to drought.
5) In 1931-1932, the official Soviet response to a drought-induced grain shortage outside Ukraine was to send aid to the areas affected and to make a series of concessions to the peasantry.
6) In mid-1932, following complaints by officials in the Ukrainian SSR that excessive grain procurements (seizures) had led to localized outbreaks of famine, Moscow reversed course and took an increasingly hard line toward the peasantry.
7) The inability of Soviet authorities in Ukraine to meet the grain procurements quota forced them to introduce increasingly severe measures to extract the maximum quantity of grain from the peasants.
8) In the Fall of 1932 Stalin used the resulting "procurements crisis" in Ukraine as an excuse to tighten his control in Ukraine and to intensify grain seizures further.
9) The Ukrainian Famine of 1932-1933 was caused by the maximum extraction of agricultural produce from the rural population.
10) Officials in charge of grain seizures also lived in fear of punishment.
11) Stalin knew that people were starving to death in Ukraine by late 1932.
12) In January 1933, Stalin used the "laxity" of the Ukrainian authorities in seizing grain to strengthen further his control over the Communist Party of Ukraine and mandated actions which worsened the situation and maximized the loss of life.
13) Postyshev had a dual mandate from Moscow: to intensify the grain seizures (and therefore the Famine) in Ukraine and to eliminate such modest national self-assertion as Ukrainians had hitherto been allowed by the USSR.
14) While famine also took place during the 1932-1933 agricultural year in the Volga Basin and the North Caucasus Territory as a whole, the invasiveness of Stalin's interventions of both the Fall of 1932 and January 1933 in Ukraine are paralleled only in the ethnically Ukrainian Kuban region of the North Caucasus.
15) Attempts were made to prevent the starving from traveling to areas where food was more available.

16) Joseph Stalin and those around him committed genocide against Ukrainians in 1932-1933.
17) The American government had ample and timely information about the Famine but failed to take any steps which might have ameliorated the situation. Instead, the Administration extended diplomatic recognition to the Soviet government in November 1933, immediately after the Famine.
18) During the Famine certain members of the American press corps cooperated with the Soviet government to deny the existence of the Ukrainian Famine." (Dr. James Mace)

Genocide is a political nightmare for governments. It is a sort of undeclared war against the innocent people of the world and in today's war-torn poverty-stricken media-assaulted environment the issue of Genocide risks the "fifteen-minute" claim to fame of media redundancy. In today's Internet culture, ironically, important news becomes old news almost instantly. Instead of dealing with simple and logical priority of political responsibility, the Genocide Debate is played out on a complacent and overwhelmed public much to the satisfaction of the perpetrators who remain at large, disguised or virtually unseen. These masters and princes yielding world power remain protected and untouchable behind tall walls and guarded gates isolated in their luxury, wealth and privilege. As a result too much time and energy is spent on this other debacle, this endless highly politicized debate over definitions: famine vs. Genocide; forced or man-made famine vs. natural or artificially induced mass-murder, et cetera. Academicians indulge in this sort of mental gymnastics debating numbers and definitions that obscure the fundamental issues.

Protagonists of this false debate defy human rights advocates and economists. These "experts" not only want a full belly, but immortality, – that cheap fame that comes from succumbing to peer pressure with their names engraved on institutes instead of gravestones. Clear lines of distinction are obscured; victims are confused with the aggressors. Think about it: numbers of victims quickly become abstract. A victim becomes a number. Solzhenitsyn has a wonderful description of woman prisoners in the Soviet gulags refusing to wear a number, – "the sign of the devil!" they screamed. Forced to withstand sub-freezing conditions nonetheless they preferred their light undergarments than wear the scarlet letter of evil. To be nothing! To be a mere statistic! To the women it is an intolerable human dignity. The Nazis learned from Stalin, and, after the invasion of June 1941 subjugated the Ukrainians as sub-humans to be treated worse than animals.

Stalin became supreme ruler of the Soviet state, always using cunning skill and diabolical intelligence to plan his strategic moves well in advance. It was easy to eliminate the Ukrainians *en masse*. For the Russian communists the Ukrainian nationals didn't even rate as a statistic. No IBM index card for them. Watson, the chairman of IBM, was more interested in organizing the Nazi empire used as well for cataloging Holocaust victims for which he was honored by Hitler, that is, before he sold his machines to Stalin. This at a time as many Consortium leaders voice their infatuation for the fascist movement. General Motors senior executive on his return from Germany, for example, William Knudsen, in a comment for the press, portrayed Hitler as "the miracle of Europe". A few peasants might be noticed. But a million! Never! No one would believe it. Would you? Where did they all go? To Mars? And so they denied it. All the leaders publicly denied the extermination while privately talking it over in low whispers between themselves behind closed doors, in classified dispatches and secret orders.

The West feared Stalin just as a decade earlier they had feared Lenin and Trotsky ubiquitously absent at Versailles. And the Cheka-OGPU-NKVD? (Under Putin the state secret police is renamed again, as FSB). Nor were these secret police executioners above the law of Soviet justice! They too must be made to pay for their crimes. There is always a crime to be found if not in the past, in the future. Their plots and schemes will undo them. Are not the executioners also victims for having expedited orders to the excess? Historians for the most part concur that seven to ten million people perished in Stalin's forced famine.

WHO WAS JOSEPH STALIN?

Who was Joseph Stalin? Apparently he was born in 1879 in Georgia of the North Caucasus (though a theory has it that his father was Ossetian and Stalin "Georgianized" his family name to Dzhugashvili). Chosen General Secretary of the Communist Party in 1922, his Bolshevik party name was "Koba". Soviet Defense Commissar Trotsky (Leon Bronstein/Lev Davidovich) was the same age as Stalin, more popular, a cosmopolitan intellectual, and inflammatory speaker and generally expected to succeed Lenin. When Lenin's health fails, Stalin isolates Lenin and most probably poisons him, in 1924, while he outmaneuvers Trotsky pushing him completely out of the Communist Party in 1927.

In the Soviet Union Party hierarchy this is a worse than death. But Trotsky is still too popular to kill without provoking serious suspicions. Comrade Stalin knew all too well if you don't use your teeth you get nothing. For Trotsky his time is soon up. Two years later Lenin's Commissar for War and founder of the Red Army, Leon Trotsky, having refused to admit "crimes against the Party", is accosted by an OGPU detachment that morning and ordered to leave his flat January 17, 1928. One of the officers recognized his former leader and added to the drama as he cracked and wept, "Shoot me, Comrade Trotsky, shoot me." They usher him by car to the Trans-Siberian Express taking him far from Moscow in Alma-Ata. (C. Andrew and V. Mitrokhin, 39, re. Leon Trotsky, *My Life,* Gloucester, Mass.: Peter Smith, 1970, 539; Issac Deutscher, *Trotsky*, Oxford Univ. Press, 1970, 692-4; Dimitri Volkogonov, *Trotsky, The Eternal Revolutionary*, London: HarperCollins, 1996, 305)

The sky is still too dark for Stalin. He regrets leaving Trotsky too much freedom out of his control but at least he's out of the way where he can't stir up trouble. It happened to the Tsar and it might happen to him, at any moment, a bullet in the back of the head; perhaps the honors of a firing squad he must have wondered. Or, a hunting accident on one of his few hunting trips. He is given a desk, writing materials and sends "about 550 telegrams and 800 'political letters', to his supporters while he is allowed during this time to receive a thousand letters and seven hundred telegrams. How many were confiscated, destroyed or sent to Stalin surely must have been much more he thought. The head of the OGPU and Stalin pour over the stream of correspondence for the slightest hint of conspiracy. "Stalin," writes Christopher Andrew, who never failed to overreact to opposition, cannot but have been unfavorably impressed by letters which regularly described him and his supporters as "degenerates'." (C. Andrew and V. Mitrokhin, 39)

A decade passes when Trotsky, still in Mexico is assassinated by a Soviet NKVD agent who slams an ice pick into his brain.

Was his death a tragedy?

"WHEN ONE DIES, IT IS A TRAGEDY. WHEN A MILLION DIE, IT IS A STATISTIC"

Stalin methods of mass purges seldom left any trace. This deserves some reflection. "When one dies, it is a tragedy. When a million die, it is a statistic", Stalin is reported to have said. The remark by Stalin to Churchill at the Teheran Conference late November 1943 may have been paraphrased in translation: "When one man dies it is a tragedy, when thousands die it's statistics", quoting David McCullough's, *Truman* (1991): "Churchill had been arguing that a premature opening of a second front in France would result in an unjustified loss of tens of thousands of Allied soldiers. Stalin responded that 'when one man dies it is a tragedy, when thousands die it's statistics'." Teheran proves to be an important conference, in particular for Churchill and Stalin to overcome their natural disposition of mutual suspicion and distrust, and their mood is more relaxed and occasionally they are able to talk together as "men and brothers". (A. I. Solzhenitsyn,"a full belly" quoted "Asphyxiation" in *The Oak and the Calf,* 247; Gerard Colby, *DuPont Dynasty,* 1974, 1984, 326; David McCullough, *Truman,* NY: Simon & Schuster, 1991; D. McCullough from *The Time of Stalin: Portrait of Tyranny* by Anton Antonov-Ovseyenko, 278. David McCullough (b.1933, Bones 1955; Alexandra Robbins, *Secrets of the Tomb: Skull and Bones, the Ivy League, and the Hidden Paths of Power*, Boston: Little Brown, 2002, 12)

CHURCHILL: "IF HITLER INVADED HELL ..."

By that time the war had been extremely problematic, costly in lives and resources, and highly unpredictable. When England had been alone in standing up to Hitler, and before *Barbarossa,*– the anticipated German invasion of Russia, – Prime Minister Churchill entertained a small dinner party at Chequers as was his custom. Among his guests were his Personal Secretary Jock Colville, Foreign Secretary Anthony Eden, and US ambassador John Winant. "Hitler was counting on enlisting capitalist and Right Wing sympathizers in this country and the U.S.A," Churchill said, and he added, when the attack comes, "We should go all out to help Russia." Churchill held that line all during the war, never trusting

Stalin, yet never does he belittle their sacrifice and extraordinary losses. Winant reaffirms Roosevelt's support for Churchill "welcoming Soviet Russia as an ally". With the dinner guests away Colville and Churchill talked about cuddling with Stalin, and Churchill remarks, "I have only one purpose, the destruction of Hitler, and my life is much simplified thereby. If Hitler invaded Hell I would make at least a favorable reference to the Devil in the House of Commons."

In a curious twist of fate, it was a Russian emigrant Jew who greatly advanced America's code-breaking effort. Churchill and Roosevelt, armed with Ultra and Magic, were essentially fighting a techno-savvy spy war with codes and ciphers and cryptanalysts while Stalin endlessly throws hordes of divisions after divisions ranking up millions in war dead to overwhelm rapidly depleting German forces in armaments, men and supplies. William Friedman coined the term "cryptanalysis". According to the inimitable British historian John Keegan, "Friedman was largely responsible for the most important of America's cryptanalytic successes, the breaking of Purple."

The Purple machine, the latest Japanese encryption device, has a similar effect as the German Enigma. F. W. Winterbotham, a senior Air Staff man in the British Secret Intelligence Service for ten years before the outbreak of war in 1939, was largely responsible with other 'backroom boys' of the Ultra code-breaking operations housed at Bletchley. Throughout the war the top secret ciphered and decoded transmissions were guarded with the utmost security that earns the attribution by Churchill as "my most secret source" in his campaign to win the war. The information includes high-level communication from Hitler and his commanders on their Enigma cipher machines. With the decoded intercepts the British know in advance German preparations for the 1940 Battle of Britain, for example, and the position of U-Boats and surface ships. Enigma intercepts are surreptitiously diffused to alert Stalin of Hitler's Russian war plan "Barbarossa" down to the day and hour of invasion while Churchill carefully guards the origin of his secret source. Stalin dismisses the warnings as Anglo disinformation not to be trusted or taken seriously. Donovan's OSS agents bought an Enigma from the Finn code experts "for a suite case full of cash".

Group Captain F. W. Winterbotham reveals in his popular book *The Ultra Secret* (1974) that the British War Office and the Air Ministry on Intelligence long in advance had trails of reports on Hitler's use of "the dive bomber in the armoured blitzkrieg.... General von Reichenau had explained to me ... how the blitzkrieg would work against Russia, way back in Berlin in 1935." (J. E. Persico, "Spies versus Ciphers" in *Roosevelt's Secret War*, 101; *Life's History of World War II*, NY: Time Inc., 1950, 66; John Keegan, *Intelligence in War*, Knopf, 2003, 193; F. W. Winterbotham, *The Ultra Secret*, Dell, 1974, ed, 1978, 55; re Soviet ciphers and decrypts, C. Andrew and V. Mitrokhin, *The Sword and the Shield,* 1999; David Kahn, *Seizing the Enigma, The Race to Break the Enigma U-Boat Codes 1939-1943*, NY: Barnes & Noble, 1991; P. K. O'Donnell, 268)

We know that certain political leaders of the western governments were not unintentionally blind to the Holodomor, nor were they ignorant of Hitler's preparations for the invasion of Russia. Friendly European consulates and embassies witnessed it. British ambassador Sir Esmond Ovey and his officers regularly send reports home to the Foreign Office where they were hushed up. The author was first amazed at the tepid response of US officials who apparently closed their eyes and looked away preferring not to see or hear cries for help from Stalin's terrified Ukrainians, who, as the State Department officially declared, were already forsaken as victims "powerless to take any steps which might have ameliorated the situation".

Cut them out. Let them go. "Reset", Obama declares. Start over. With what? The same program, the same mentality of a cynical debauched political leadership of the so-called democracies with their orchestrated media side-shows reset for mainstream consumer consumption? Some call it chaos and randomness; others see an alarming orderly consequential logic set in motion. In the end, whether duped or duked, its all the same result.

But wait! The American government did in fact have detailed knowledge of the Holodomor Genocide. It's not until the late 1980s that Dr. James Mace declares that in fact the State Department had been more than adequately informed about the famine and that it had for years kept detailed official memoranda monitoring famine conditions in the Ukraine. It was an initiation into the dark shadows of the Holodomor and US foreign policy where few dare venture. It is not called "Foggy Bottom" for nothing. There transparency is not good for business. In fact, its code of ethics is decidedly contrary to an overt code of moral ethics. The honorable Dr. James Mace, too, chose not to dig deeper. There were for him, in fact, to get as far as he did, "special considerations", special safe limits of Washington's politically correct agenda beyond which he does not dare transgress during his lifetime.

CONSPIRACY: THE EVIL HAND OF OFFICIAL GOVERNMENT SECRECY

Why be bothered by corpses! The dead don't tell lies. The Holodomor remains politically steeped in controversy. Jobs are at stake. Careers and lifetime security and social status may certainly be jeopardized by the vanity of crying Genocide to deafened ears. How many were killed because they knew too much, or lived to keep silent about exposing more details of what may have been known of American complicity with Stalin during the Holodomor years? And all that denigrating the memory of the dead to impoverish the morality of the living with the poison of their selfish contempt if not for anything but the sacred truth of it while for such crime-masters there is nothing sacred at all, where greed and profits hold sway over the ignorant masses under the heel of stoic educators of culture and religion. For that matter, why should Dr. Mace care if Roosevelt turned a blind eye to the Genocide and extend official recognition of the Soviet communist regime?

But that is exactly the nub of the problem. And that problem persists even today with stench and rot of a festering wound infecting those who dare to turning away and ignore it. There were political motives for leaving the Ukrainians to their fate. Engagement with Stalin! As his first major foreign policy decision of his new administration in November 1933 FDR legitimized a *de facto* policy (real but undeclared) of the US government at the time of American economic engagement with the Soviet communist dictatorship of gulags and slave labor.

Dr. Mace ventured into the labyrinth of original perpetrators of the crime estimated at a loss in human life "at the rate of 25,000 per day – or 1,000 per hour. Nearly a quarter of Ukraine's rural population – the backbone of the nation". And of those lost, perhaps as many as three million children. There is absolutely no excuse for avoiding the truth, and averting others from spreading seeds of illusion that bear more rotten fruit. It is an intellectual desecration of the worst sort. Reader beware.

A half-truth is also a half-lie. By not pursuing the leads, for fear of implicating the imperial Presidency posing as the defender of "the forgotten man", the idol-smashing high priest of American democratic capitalism, FDR was throughout the decade of his Presidency in bed with Stalin and cronies of the Consortium. Not a nice place to be, even for Dr. Mace suddenly within the maze of Consortium intrigue. Solzhenitsyn warned us of such persons who dared to know, even write, cutting away the truth, these so-called truth-seekers who undertake a journey only to suddenly stop and turn away. Have they "... taken fright? Gone soft with fame? And betrayed the dead?" he asks. (A. I. Solzhenitsyn, *The Oak and the Calf, Sketches of Literary Life in the Soviet Union*, Harper & Row, 1975, 1979 ed., 311)

Declassified government documents, mostly State Department files, provided many of the detailed dispatches and correspondences revealing knowledge and concern by US government officials of the Holodomor and the cover-up in Washington. Currently, the activities of secret government are a constant menace to a free and democratic society and undermine its basic foundation and principles. Co-authors dedicated to the preservation of civil liberties and free speech for an open, honest and transparent democratic government Jesse Ventura and Dick Russell write in their book, *63 Documents the Government Doesn't Want You To Read (*2011), citing the *Washington Post*, "there are now 854,000 American citizens with top secret clearances. The number of new secrets rose 75 percent between 1996 and 2009, and the number of documents using those secrets went from 5.6 million in 1996 to 54.6 million last year. There are an astounding 16 million documents being classified top secret by our government every year! Today, pretty much everything the government *does* is presumed secret. Isn't it time we asked ourselves whether this is really necessary for the conduct of foreign affairs or the internal operation of governments? Doesn't secrecy actually protect the favored classes and allow them to continue to help themselves at the expense of the rest of us? Isn't this a cancer growing on democracy?"

As for Julian Assange and Wikileaks, Vetura and Russell state unequivocally, "Julian Assange is a hero... Wikileaks is exposing our government officials for the frauds that they are. They also show us how governments work together to lie to their citizens when they are waging war .... If our State Department is asking diplomats to steal personal information from UN officials and human rights groups, in violation of international laws, then shouldn't the world know about it and demand corrective action? Maybe if they know they're potentially going to be exposed, the powers that hide behind a cloak of secrecy will think twice before they plot the next Big Lie." (Jesse Ventura and Dick Russell, *63 Documents the Government Doesn't Want You To Read*, NY: Skyhorse, 2011, 3-9; That number has increased to "more than a million", writes Steve Coll, "Comment: The President and the Press", *The New Yorker*, June 10, 2013)

THE DEAD TELL NO LIES

How much more he knew about the evil hand behind the Holodomor Dr. Mace did not say. It was his choice. He chose not to. But in every act, there lay the so-called non-act, that which is not done. It is what is undone, and left for others to do. In the case of the Holodomor, that which he didn't do, – and this is where lay the moral dilemma,– is left implied in what Dr. Mace does reveal.

The other side of good is evil. Dr. Mace did not deliver us from evil. Implicitly, however, Dr. Mace leaves it behind for another time, for others to sort out. That moral dilemma is omnipresent. It doesn't go away by willing it to disappear. It's there even when you don't see it. It's always there when Roosevelt turns his eyes away to ignore it completely. Nor does the Holodomor go away by not thinking openly about it or discussing it with notes among his closest advisers. Or when Putin says it's not so, or that Stalin was not at fault.

What we do know ever so carefully broached by Dr. Mace is that the record still hidden of evil deeds by Stalin and the Consortium then is clearly out front and right behind him pushing forward, and bankrolling his grandiose communist social and economic scheme were all politically linked as they were aware of events of the Holodomor during those years before and after in what amounted to "the worst Holocaust the world has ever known …", observes US Senator Charles Schumer from New York, FDR's home state in a memorial ceremony in November 2009. (Remarks by Senator Charles Schumer at the 2009 annual Memorial Service hosted each year by the Eastern Eparchy of the Ukrainian Orthodox Church in America with the Stamford Eparchy of the Ukrainian Catholic Church, in November. The senator's official website declared, "After graduating from Harvard College and Harvard Law School in 1974, Chuck returned home and ran for the New York State Assembly, becoming at 23, the youngest member of the State Legislature since Theodore Roosevelt…")

You would have to be a veritable idiot defying the logic of gravity not to expect that FDR and his liberal-leaning wife Eleanor Delano were not both alarmed by press reports and private conversations and documents that filtered through the State Department. Roosevelt played with consummate skill the leading actor in the center role, a grandmaster many steps ahead of his advisers, and who with a wave of the back side of his hand could nonchalantly dismiss the infiltration of Soviet spies and betrayal in his government as though he knew more about them than they knew themselves. High above the valley with the Hudson flowing from the mountain streams and forests to the wide ocean there at Hyde Park Roosevelt may have felt aloft on his Everest above the temptations of life and removed from its fears and where a Christian is compelled by an inner force and intuition to act and cannot resist the workings of History. As we are told in good counsel by the reflections of French philosopher and professor of the history of religion at the University of Chicago, Mircea Eliade, writing of our epoch, "evasion is forbidden to the Christian. And for him there is no other issue; since the Incarnation took place in History, since the Advent of Christ marks the last and the highest manifestation of the sacred in the world in *Myths, Dreams and Mysteries* (1957): the Christian can save himself (and mankind sic) only with the concrete, historical life, the life that was chosen and lived by Christ." (sect. "Powers and History" in "Power and Holiness" of Mircea Eliade, *Myths, Dreams and Mysteries*, Paris: Gallimard; NY: Harper & Row, 1957, 1960 ed., 154)

Politics follows different patterns in defiance of the laws of Nature. Why was news about the Holodomor taboo in free and democratic America? The consequences can be equally tragic and as we saw with the unfolding events of the thirties culminating in the Second World War and the Holocaust subsequent events were even more catastrophically horrific ultimately leading to not disease and pestilence this time but atomic annihilation giving birth to a new globalized world order of federated nations and increasingly powerful centralized banks and giant media organizations bent on Cold War mythology churning out constant propaganda. What were the reasons for the censorship and black-out by the editors at home?

At the same time in Soviet Russia a distant association to a Ukrainian was grounds for arrest and even execution.

It also seemed odd that neither the distinguished and highly honored American in Kiev Dr. Mace nor the ranks of apparently earnest researchers of the Holodomor pursued those most important questions of moral imperative inherent in public service and humanitarian aid which today act as cornerstones bridging freedom with the legal system of an open democratic society. Dr. Dalrymple draws some valuable lessons from his experience as a researcher into the Holodomor and the problem of Genocide in general as it was handled at the time. "American and English studies on the USSR," Dalrymple writes, "occasionally mention a famine in Ukraine. But that is the end of it, and in most cases, lack all details." The question of ethics is banished along with the problem. If the problem doesn't exist then there is no ethical question to discuss. Divert, change the subject, "reset" or reposition the debate. Move on. And that's what happened. We know that the American presidents Herbert Hoover and FDR did nothing to stop it. Instead, they exploited it to their advantage, secretly and in partnership with the Kremlin, and in particular, Joseph Stalin, arch-mass murderer in our time of the century and in likelihood in all of human history.

HOLODOMOR GENOCIDE FILES: CLASSIFIED OR DECLASSIFIED?

In spite of an international outcry and national protests in the streets and newspapers in the United States and abroad, the Holodomor Terror-Famine was neither officially recognized nor examined. Instead, and in spite of the continuing forced death of millions of Ukrainians and other Russians FDR granted his "brother" Stalin official diplomatic recognition in 1933. American businesses and banks continued to build the industrial infrastructure of the economy of the Soviet totalitarian monopoly.

How many of famine-related documents in US State Department archives remained classified, inaccessible, misplaced, lost or destroyed is not known. Over a span of decades hundreds of uncounted hours, endless weeks and months in the vaulted archives of Yale, Harvard and Princeton I can personally attest to that.

Since Dr. Mace went public, scholars and historians debate the maze of numbers in the tragic toll. "As with the Holocaust and the Armenian massacres," Mace declares, "the exact number of victims can only be estimated. But we know that the 1926 Soviet census counted 31.2 million Ukrainians and that the probably inflated census of 1939 counted only 28.1 million, an absolute decline of 3.1 million or 10 percent. Once probable population growth for the period is considered, the probable number of victims is in the range of 5 to 7 million, more probably closer to the higher end of this range than to the lower."

In New York, in November 2009, the Ukrainian Orthodox Church of the USA declared the figure of "ten million men, women and children lost in Josef Stalin's horrifying effort to destroy a people – a nation – long proud of their rich land, which was known as the "bread basket of Europe". And always when examining "official' facts and records in the Soviet Union under Stalin, in particular, even the numbers can be life-threatening, if not satisfactory to the always right Stalin, as with his first census in the thirties, discontent led to executions of the census takers until he got the numbers respecting the "perfection" of his bold new socialist society.

THE 1988 US CONGRESSIONAL COMMISSION

In a unique concurrence of political events a newly established United States Congress Commission on the Ukraine famine in 1988 examines the role of foreign journalists, among them the Americans Walter Duranty, Louis Fisher, William Chamberlin, Ralph Barnes and three Britons– Gareth Jones, Eugene Lyons, and Malcolm Muggeridge. They all witnessed and reported in varying measure with wide divergences and contradiction the Holodomor Terror-Famine. Some deliberately told the truth. Others intentionally suppressed it. But the truth was not forgotten and found its way out of the depths of despair and denial. A serious and dramatic correction in the compass of inquiry was needed before facing the truth.

Between the original revelations and more recent research by Dalrymple and Mace over a span of a half-century had passed before the compass needle of the official record began pointing in the right direction. They both concluded that in spite of the official blackout and denial by Americans and the Soviets newspapers had reported worsening famine conditions and soaring numbers of fatalities. It was all too evident that both the Hoover and Roosevelt administrations adopted a policy of denial. Their "out of sight out of mind" approach towards business investment in the USSR shadowed the Holodmor victims and relegated them to the back pages of tabloids in scattered articles and classified government documents long sealed away from public scrutiny. Meanwhile politicians and diplomats in the White House State" Department met with bankers of the Federal Reserve America dealt with their own problem of collecting the foreign reparations debts from Germany, England and France. Meanwhile during the years of the Great Depression of the thirties the Consortium gang pursued their corporate profits and investments banking in the struggling American economy and fascist regimes abroad.

During the mounting crisis of the 1932-1934 Holodomor years the risk of exposing at the heart of the matter the Federal Reserve system of centralized and partner banks with its inept currency manipulations strikes at the core of the integrity of America's democratic institutions. The risk was great of incriminating many of the country's highest ranked corporate leaders and model citizens of the Consortium, the baronesque wealth of the DuPonts, Mellons, Morgans, Harrimans, Rockefellers and their set, certain to be compromised by any investigation into America's economic arrangements with Mussolini, Hitler and Stalin. According to Gerard Colby in his extensive detailed inquiry *DuPont Dynasty* (1974) fierce anti-communist rhetoric of the conservative end of the political parties provokes a real threat of a military take-over of the US government in a scheme financed by Gerald MacGuire, "a lawyer in the Morgan brokerage office of Grayson M. Murphy and an official of the American Legion". (Gerard Colby, *DuPont Dynasty: Behind the Nylon Curtain,* Secaucus, New Jersey: Lyle Stuart, 1974, 1984 ed., 324-30)

BANKING, GENOCIDE & THE GREAT DEPRESSION

In view of the 2008 financial crash and world economic slowdown, the dysfunctional years of the Great Depression and Holodomor are brought up-to-date with an understanding that strikes home. Then, as well as today, it was obvious that the economy of the nation was in need of a major over-haul, something more than a correction or drop in the fed interest rate both in terms of the moral leadership of its political leaders and the way the country conducts business at home and abroad. In comparison with the Holodomor thirties, the global banking crisis and economic recession of the last few years since the Wall Street meltdown in 2008 uncovers alarming parallels with that same period of the Great Depression and political turmoil that something is fundamentally and structurally wrong with capitalism in America. Then, too, increasing numbers in the ranks of the hungry and unemployed begged for a correction.

The secret Geitner-Paulson deals between Treasury and the Bank of America killed the giant investment firms Lehman Brothers and Bear Stearns and lost trillions of dollars sunk in toxic overly- leveraged debt leaving the Obama administration and the US Congress facing a $14 trillion debt in scale with a $30 *trillion* financial meltdown. World Bank president Robert Zoellick in Washington warned against the unaccountable authority of the Fed's "independent and powerful technocrats" who far exceed the limits of Congress to hold it responsible and in check". Not everyone lost, – not by a long shot. In the debacle

JP Morgan-Chase and Goldman Sachs stack up over $3 billion profits. Soul-searching Goldman Sachs' chairman Lloyd C. Blankfein set aside $16.7 *billion* in bonus money averaging $700,000 for each of his 31,700 workers. Goldman Sachs is perceived as the prime culprit for the total loss of the major global stock exchanges that dropped just under $45 trillion "down from a peak of almost $62 trillion at the end of 2007, before the subprime meltdown wrecked the global economy", according a report by *Bloomberg*. Blankfein pockets another $34 million pay package from his firm from 2010-11.

The next day the world learns that J. P. Morgan bought out its investment bank partner Cazenove in London described as "a 190-year-old British brokerage that counts the Queen among its clients" with the aim to consolidate its activities in business in Europe, the Middle East and Africa for the $1.7 billion deal. At the same time England's Parliament and the City,– London's financial investment district,– is thrown into mayhem following the Bank of England's rescue deals that by the end of 2009 cost U.K. taxpayers about 850 billion pounds. And as the bankers count the billions that came and went elsewhere in America unemployment lines grow longer so that by the end of 2009 some 7.3 million workers lose their jobs within the last two years. In the wake of the meltdown by January 2010 a total of 10.5 million people were receiving unemployment benefits all the while Jamie Dimon laughs his way to the bank. (Julia Werdigier, "J. P. Morgan Buys Out a British Banking Partner", *Bloomberg*, Nov. 18, 2009; *The NYT*, Nov. 19, 2009; Caroline Binham, "Turner Plan on 'Socially Useless' Trades Make Bankers See Red", *Bloomberg*, Jan. 7, 2010; *Bloomberg*, Jan. 8, 2010)

On August 1, 2013, a jury decision in New York found Fabrice Torre, a 34 year old former Goldman Sachs vice-president Fabrice Torre guilty on seven counts of charges of insider trading and fraud in a failed mortgage deal that went terribly wrong in 2007 costing investors billions. Goldman had bartered with the SEC back in July 2010 and pay $550 million to bury the case over Abacus, and neither admit nor deny any wrongdoing while at the same time it concedes, according to Reuters, that "some of its marketing materials were misleading." Reuters added, "Wall Street crashed the global financial system and almost caused a second Great Depression," according to Dennis Kelleher, chief executive of financial regulation advocacy group Better Markets, and he declared, "the SEC failed to go after Wall Street's bonus-bloated executives who ran the banks that sold trillions of dollars of worthless securities," adding that the SEC merely needed Toure as an isolated lone "scapegoat" with an incriminating trail of emails in which "bragged" about the deal and imminent collapse of the markets to his girlfriend. The SEC had earlier, in November 2012, backed off from pursing civil charges against, a former director at GSC Capital Corp involving a $1.1 billion CDO crafted by JP Morgan Chase. To avoid the law suit both two banks settled out of court a nine-figure payment neither admitting or denying the charges. As I write the Jamie Dimon, chief of JP Morgan-Chase late September 2013 announced a deal with the US Justice Department for a $13 billion settlement to end the government's inquiry into its "questionable mortgage practices". And that doesn't include Dimon's $9.3 billion payoff to the lawyers. (Nate Raymond, "SEC wins as ex-Goldman executive Tourre found liable for fraud", *Reuters*, Aug. 2, 2013; Ben Protess, Jessica Silver-Greenberg, "JP Morgan Said to Be Near Deal on Mortgages", *The NYT*, Sept. 27, 2013)

Despite intervention by the world's central bankers pumping trillions into failed banks and credit institutions newspapers report daily stories by world economists and bankers predicting that the US and global economy is still close to the brink of a gigantic financial *tsuami.* In the wake of billion dollar bonus payouts to Wall Street investment banking investment firms (Goldman Sachs, JP Morgan-Chase, Morgan Stanley, Bank of America, Merrill Lynch), the Fed bail-out of the banks ensnares the Obama administration in a fury over the lack of accountability and transparency. Just where all the money went no one knows with any certainty leaving the people in a lurch and the economy in a steadily declining free-for-all tailspin.

In our time Americans appear to take a more critical look into the secrets of the Federal Reserve Bank operations and its taciturn chairman. In October 2009 *The New York Times* published an Op-ed. piece titled "Who's Looking at the Fed's Books?" by William A. Barnett, a former Fed staffer, and at present professor of macroeconomics at the University of Kansas and the editor of the journal *Macroeconomic Dynamics.* William Barnett wrote, "it should be clear that we depend on the Fed for high-quality financial data and that the Fed should be held to the highest standards of transparency. And yet we cannot be assured of either of these things unless the Fed is subjected to a thorough audit of its numbers. I know that without comprehensive audits to double-check Federal Reserve data, the risk exists of inadequate and sloppy accounting from the Fed." Oh, but nothing criminal, no arrests or prison terms for the elite. They are untouchable, so far. In the words of billionaire T. Boone Pickens referring to a high price of oil,– which speaks same for Consortium control of the Fed and economic uncertainty, the Texan grunted, "Get used to it. You're going to have to live with it." In other words, "eat it and shut up". Putin's Russian expressions are more vulgar and direct. ("World Bank Head Expects Dollar's Role to Diminish", *The NYT*, Sept. 29, 2009; "Return of Record Paydays", *The NYT*, Oct. 16, 2009; William A. Barnett, "Who's Looking at the Fed's Books?", *The NYT*, Oct. 22, 2009; "Oil Skyrockets Above $80 as the Dollar Sinks", *The NYT*, Oct. 22, 2009)

2008 MELTDOWN: BUBBLE TALK FROM WASHINGTON

Were the masses suddenly waking up? In November 2009 Connecticut Senator Christopher Dodd who chaired the Senate Banking Committee called for revamping the Federal Reserve Bank and strip it of its supervisory powers the Obama administration bailed out the financial system with the $700 billion of taxpayer money channeled through its Troubled Asset Relief Program. Two months later Dodd sheepishly told the press he would not seek re-election bloodied by the press implicating his responsibility for accepting preferential treatment in a loan by Country Financial, a fallen subprime lender subsequently salvaged by

Bank of America. Rumours abound over bailouts in the works TARP's capital-purchase program injected nearly $205 billion into more than 600 financial institutions.

Bloomberg News reported John Mack, chief executive officer at Morgan Stanley saying banking procedures had gone haywire and justified a Fed crackdown: "We cannot control ourselves," he told a panel discussion audience hosted by *Bloomberg News* and *Vanity Fair.* Mack added,. "You have to step in and control the Street." Meanwhile President Obama urgently seeks a way out of the storm's path by further relying on the Fed's staff of 220 Ph.D. economists to identify risks and run mathematical models to see the fallout to bank profits as global markets pop in another bubble. If they couldn't' predict this bubble, how will they predict the next?

The Consortium's mass media of talking heads constantly spin virtual simulations of the future to save the economic system that is melting down with trillions evaporated in thin air while a billion people of the world are programmed to starve to death in calculated doom as 6 million Americans barely survive on food stamps. In January 2010, *The New York Times* reports Morgan-Chase and other banks forcing foreclosures selling homes on the cheap from "roughly 15 million American homeowners who are underwater, meaning they owe the bank more than their home is worth". Of course these economists performed wonders not predicting the collapse of the banks causing a world financial meltdown worst than the Great Depression of 1929 era. (Craig Torres and Michael McKee, "Fed Makes Monitoring Capital Foremost Concern Amid Bubble Talk, *Bloomberg News*, Nov. 20, 2009; "US Loan Effort Is Seen as Adding to Housing Woes", *The NYT*, Jan. 1, 2010)

Its amazing to follow the financial events unfolding on Wall Street while watching the role and response of the White House in the ongoing spectacle of severe economic insecurity reminiscent of the thirties. Particularly exposed is the US Congress which having proved intimidated by the Bush-led "War on Terror" and failed wars in Iraq and Afghanistan and to see it transformed into a stage of the absurd where politicians scurry to capture voters mad about the government bailout of bankers who retain their jobs and bonuses while the peoples' life savings are wiped out, again. "The Federal Reserve, which has printed money in exchange for assets from the nation's banks, has long operated opaquely. It is virtually impossible to size up its balance sheet," reporter Andrew Ross Sorkin wrote November 23, 2009 in the *NY Times* during the national debate in Congress over attempts to impose legislative oversight on the Fed as the national debt staggers "in excess of $12 trillion".

While US central banker Fed chairman Bernanke and the Obama Goldman Sachs team are pushing Congress to give the Fed even more control over financial firms, *The New York Times* then runs with its story asking why is it possible that the Fed, with its touted stable of hundreds of Ph.D. "experts" failed to explain "how they missed the biggest bubble of our time." In his story on January 2010 reporter David Leonhardt writes that five years has passed since "Bernanke– then a Bush administration official– said a housing bubble was "a pretty unlikely possibility."

As late as May 2007, Bernanke argued that Fed officials "do not expect significant spillovers from the subprime market to the rest of the economy." But that's exactly what happened and the writing was on the wall for everyone to see it except that few did. The fact that Mr. Bernanke and other regulators still have not explained why they failed to recognize the last bubble is the weakest link in the Fed's push for more power. It raises the question: Why should Congress, or anyone else, have faith that future Fed officials will recognize the next bubble? (David Leonhardt, "If Fed Missed This Bubble, Will It See a New One?", *The NYT*, Jan. 6, 2010; Andrew Ross Sorkin, "Beware the Result of Outrage", *The NYT*, Nov. 23, 2009, B1)

And who is to regulate the regulators? This was the same problem that bedeviled America in the bankrupt thirties with the Consortium clique investing in the regimes of Hitler and Stalin. Americans were powerless to change the nation's destiny in the hands of the central bankers and their political heads. Furthermore, then as now, the Consortium corporate gang controlled the newspapers and radio, long before the advent of television or the Internet two generations later. Across the globe disgruntled politicians voice public opposition to the absence of transparency by centralized bankers forced to keep discounted interest rates low. In London, bankers in the City feel the mood swing like a razor-sharp pendulum over their tapered collars.

Captioned in a photo alongside Bank of England's Governor Mervyn King, a visiting professor at the London School of Economics John Kay is headlined saying, "You have a group of politically powerful oligarchs, whom other people hate, but who are entrenched there". John Kay adds, "It will require something of a political earthquake to reduce the bankers' sway." No wonder. Kay is speaking after an event hosted at the Royal Society for the encouragement of Arts, Manufactures and Commerce, known as the RSA when later in that day November 12 he delivers a lecture hosted by the Institute of Economic Affairs in London and chaired by Bank of England Deputy Governor Paul Tucker. When it comes down to the bottom line we live as we have always lived; the bankers decide the fate of nation states and populations. The bankers rule. Its something they like to remind us from time to time. Reader, never forget that. (Brian Swint, "Banker 'Oligarchs' Block Break-Up Moves, Kay says", *Bloomberg News*, Nov. 13, 2009)

GOLDMAN SACHS "DOING GOD'S WORK"

That followed another eye-popper when The *Sunday Times* (London) on November 8 ran its long story by John Arlidge on Goldman Sachs'and its obtuse chairman Blankfein ("I'm doing 'God's work'. Meet Mr. Goldman Sachs"). The "world's most powerful, and most secretive, investment bank" then announced the cancellation of the company's notoriously lavish Christmas bash, far too flashy next to headlines of rising double-digit unemployment.

Even at Goldman the average tenure for a partner is eight years. For the third quarter, Goldman announced a profit of $3.19 billion and said it has set aside nearly half of its revenue to reward its employees. After the real estate bubble popped, and in 2008 of this first year of major impact hitting the world stock market meltdown, Goldman paid out $4.8 *billion* in bonuses, awarding 953 employees at least $1 million each and 78 employees at least $4 million. "If there's anything worse than a secret Federal Reserve, it's Congress controlling it," said Sen. Jim DeMint, Republican of South Carolina, the Wall Street Journal reported the next day. "But I do think that there's a wide majority of Americans who want to know what the Federal Reserve is doing and to make sure that it's achieving its primary purpose, which is to protect the value of our dollar." (Brian Swint, "Banker 'Oligarchs' Block Break-Up Moves, Kay Says", *Bloomberg*, Nov. 13, 2009; John Arlidge, "I'm doing 'God's work'. Meet Mr Goldman Sachs", *Sunday Times*, London, Nov. 8, 2009; Sudeep Reddy, Damian Paletta, "House Attacks Fed, Treasury, Panel Votes for Tighter Political Rein on Central Bank; Some Call for Geitner to Quit", *WSJ*, Nov. 20, 2009)

Goldman Sachs people mix deep with Consortium government types. They always have. They always will. They personify the revolving door syndrome exploiting influence and secrecy of that hidden world of obscure and mighty finance pumping the politicians with a steady flow of campaign dollars in exchange for the right buttons pushed after elections. The expanded Goldman family today regulates the regulators through their maze of partner banks and investment houses. UK journalist John Arlidge wrote, "after selling their soul to Goldman doing good does not mean running an HIV clinic in Kinshasa, it means getting top jobs in treasuries, central banks and stock exchanges around the world.

The list of former Goldman executives who have held key posts in the US administration and vital global institutions in New York and Washington alone is mind-boggling. It includes: treasury Secretary under Bill Clinton (Robert Rubin); treasury Secretary under George Bush (Hank Paulson); current president and former chairman of the New York Fed (William Dudley and Stephen Friedman); chief of staff to Treasury Secretary Timothy Geitner (Mark Patterson); chief of staff under President Bush (Joshua Bolten); the economic adviser to Secretary of State, Hillary Clinton (Robert Hormats); chairman of the US Commodity Futures Trading Commission (Gary Gensler); under-Secretary of State for economic, business, and agricultural affairs under President Bush (Reuben Jeffery); past and current heads of the New York Stock Exchange (John Thain and Duncan Niederauer); ceo of the Securities and Exchange Commission's enforcement division (Adam Storch).

Moreover, Goldman's new top lobbyist in Washington, Michael Paese, used to work for Barney Frank, the congressman who chairs the House Financial Services Committee. To put this in perspective, imagine that Alistair Darling, the chancellor, and his key advisers, Mervyn King, Governor of the Bank of England, Xavier Rolet, the boss of the London Stock Exchange, and Hector Sants, head of the Financial Services Authority, all used to work at the same City firm before shifting to to government postions. Small wonder that another of Goldman's nicknames is "Government Sachs". Critics say having friends in high places gives the firm the vital edge. Key government officials, they argue, discuss policy – privately – with Goldman chiefs more than executives from other banks. Understand reader, government is not some mystical elaboration; its access to a huge public architecture of tremendous accounts of money feeding the private sector and leveraging power with a lot of bureaucratic red tape. (John Arlidge, "'I'm doing 'God's work'. Meet Mr Goldman Sachs", *Sunday Times*, London, Nov. 8, 2009)

BIG BANKS & THE "TOO BIG TO FAIL" LIE

In his new book, *Too Big to Fail*, Andrew Ross Sorkin reports one pivotal meeting. Blankfein's predecessor, Paulson had promised not to talk to Goldman when he moved from the bank to the US Treasury, but last June he happened to be in Moscow at the same time that Goldman's board of directors was having dinner there with Mikhail Gorbachev, the former Soviet Premier. Paulson got approval from treasury lawyers to meet his old chums, since it would be a "social event". Paulson proceeded to regale them with stories about his time in the treasury and his predictions for the global economy. Goldman's board questioned him about the possibility of another bank blowing up, like Bear Stearns. Recently released documents reveal that a few months later during the height of the crisis when Paulson was working on the bail-out of AIG, Blankfein's name appeared on his call sheet 24 times in six days. Big banks that held AIG insurance contracts, including Goldman, were paid off in full, rather than at the 60 cents on the dollar that AIG negotiators had been pressing for, prompting allegations of a "sweetheart deal" between Paulson and Blankfein." (John Arlidge, "'I'm doing 'God's work'. Meet Mr. Goldman Sachs", *Sunday Times, London,* Nov. 8, 2009)

The prince of Wall Street Jamie Dimon and his bank JP Morgan Chase is off the hook. David Reilly of *Bloomberg News* runs his story December 4 on the traders with at least $2 trillion on its balance sheet. Morgan, not Goldman holds the "No. 1 in the too-big-to-fail bank club" bailed out by the Fed's rescue squad with double Goldman's assets "and twice the notional (or face) value of over-the-counter derivatives contracts". Morgan's retail operations hold $868 billion in deposits which Reilly says are "20 times the amount Goldman."

Morgan gets a whitewash while Goldman shareholders and US taxpayers are shouting from the streets to conference rooms at Goldman's 16.7 billion. Goldman gets flack over "a back-door government bailout" by AIG (American International Group) while Morgan bankers sneak away with a little publicized "rescue" via Bear Stearns earlier that helped JP Morgan "the biggest player in global derivatives markets with about $80 trillion in contracts." Reilly added, "Bear was a big derivatives-markets player itself; it had contracts with a face value of $14.3 trillion as of March 30, 2007. The firm's failure would have threatened the $600 *trillion* derivatives market. JP Morgan had the most to lose if this happened. In light of that, its purchase of Bear doesn't look exactly altruistic. And JP Morgan didn't have to do all the heavy lifting itself. The Federal Reserve agreed to backstop losses on $29 billion of Bear's problem assets once JP Morgan had eaten $1 billion in red ink." (italics added.)

By September 30, 2009 the Fed reported those Morgan assets worth $26.14 billion with beleaguered US taxpayers "on the hook for more than $2 billion in

Bear losses" as Morgan declared a third quarter *profit* of $3.6 billion, and got away with it. As does the Consortium, so do the bankers take care of their own. Which is exactly the problem in America during the thirties when there was no one outside the system to signal the alarm to prevent the Holodomor, or even recognize it once it was too late to save a soul. It required a war to take America out of bankruptcy then and the Ukrainians were the first to be sacrificed to pay the price.

Once again symptoms of the same syndrome surfaced only now with blatant disregard for public scrutiny and under our own eyes, defying transparency and blogs with the impudence of elite conceit for the masses. America's cut-throat bankers showed their true colours like brazen peacocks when they took billions from their own posh Ivy League schools in the 2008 financial meltdown. Harvard's endowment tumbled a record 30 percent to $26 billion from its peak of $36.9 billion in June 2008, and its cash account lost $1.8 billion four years after its financial directors sealed agreements that locked in interest rates on $2.3 billion of bonds.

The deals were handled by James Dimon, chairman at JP Morgan Chase, a 1982 Harvard Business School alumnus, Larry Summers, president of Harvard, currently President Obama's chief economic adviser, and James Rothenberg, – Harvard to the core – Harvard undergrad, Harvard Business School and at the time of the swap strategy serves as Harvard's Treasurer on the Board of Harvard Corporation. Dimon called in cash collateral payments – ultimately totaling almost $1 billion – that Harvard agrees to pay if the value of the swaps fall.

None of the eight schools in the elite Ivy League of the New England escaped the speculative disaster; Yale, Columbia, Cornell all got badly burned when tumbling interest rates plunged to zero. Harvard's glorious endowment sheared 22 percent from July 2008 through October 2008. By 2012 Harvard had recovered some to report a $30.4 billion level, significantly above Yale, whose endowment staff had been hailed for pioneering heavy investment in derivative and alternative investments in particular the real estate debacle. Yale reports a meager endowment of $16 billion (September 2009), having equally suffered a 30 percent meltdown in a single year.

Harvard's bankers panicked, paying premium rates "to get out of the swaps at the worst possible time. According to *Bloomberg News* ("Harvard Swaps Are So Toxic Even Summers Won't Explain") Summers, Rubin and the Fed chairman Alan Greenspan had originally opposed regulation proposed in 1998 by the US Commodity Futures Trading Commission's to guard against potential pitfalls inherent in -the-counter derivatives including interest rate swap agreements. The risk is a gigantic bet that interest rates would rise and cost a $1 billion to dump them. At the time, Summers is Robert Rubin's deputy Secretary in Clinton's Treasury. Rubin (Harvard, Yale Law 1964) is the chairman at Goldman Sachs, apparently a brilliant inside financial player from a Jewish family raised in New York and Miami; apparently he lobbied for Summers to get the Harvard presidency. Rothenberg, former Harvard treasurer in 2004 chairs Capital Research & Management Co., the investment advisory unit of Capital Group (Los Angeles) that manages the second-largest stock and bond mutual funds in the country, incidentally called American Funds. Daniel Shore, Harvard's chief financial officer, minimized Harvard's gigantic loss describing it "less than ideal, but the surrounding context was less than ideal as well." (Michael McDonald, John Lauerman and Gillian Wee, "Harvard Swaps Are So Toxic Even Summers Won't Explain", *Bloomberg News*, Dec. 18, 2009)

Economics professor at Harvard's Business School and a highly respected writer to several generations of cultured Americans, John Kenneth Galbraith, a Kennedy insider and dove during the Vietnam War who had served on the US Strategic Bombing Survey along with George Ball and Walt Whitman Rostow, born in New York City to a Russian Jewish immigrant family (Yale, Oxford, Columbia, OSS) Kennedy and Johnson's National Secretary adviser (1961-69), and a thousand other "experts" set up in 1944 under Stimson, describes how clear and pertinent weighed the burden of economic misery on the two successive administrations on deck if not at the helm of Consortium investment in the USSR: "After the Great Crash came the Great Depression, which lasted, with varying severity, for ten years. In 1933, GNP (total production in the economy) was nearly a third less than in 1929. Not until 1937 did the physical volume of production recover to the levels of 1929, and then it promptly slipped back again. Until 1941 the dollar value of production remained below 1929. Between 1930 and 1940 only once, in 1937, did the average number unemployed during the year drop below eight million. In 1933 nearly thirteen million were out of work, or about one in every four in the labor force. In 1938 one person in five was still out of work."

Reader, be on guard – always – to spot the Consortium player. Even here when reading Galbraith who hobnobs with the Brahmin boys and Consortium power types. *The New York Times* featured its lead story on his son Peter W. Galbraith a "former American ambassador" pocketing hundreds of millions of dollars in a suspicious oil deal with a Norwegian company and the Kurds in northern Iran. (John K. Galbraith, *The Great Crash 1929,* Boston: Houghton Mifflin, 1954, 168; James Glanz and Walter Gibbs, "American adviser to Kurds Stands to Reap Oil Profits", *The NYT,* Nov. 11, 2009)

So let us return to the Holodomor with the perspective and clarity of knowledge gained from research into those past years and events systemic of the Terror-Famine and understood in view of the experience of our current failed banking and political institutions of the Consortium. Once again Wall Street and the banks are at the forefront of the debacle only it is the welfare of populations of the western nations that is sacrificed instead of millions of once robust and healthy Ukrainians deliberately persecuted and left starving, or shot en masse, arrested, and sent to certain death and long imprisonment, entirely uprooted and displaced from their homes, villages and country. Sad Ukraine! A more terrible perfect storm could not have been dreamed as though the most foul curse of the darkest nightmare had cast the evil spell upon their people.

The Consortium scheme for the Soviet Union was far more nefarious than some Russian fairytale of incantations from witches of Gogol or Mikhail Bulgakov. Launched in the first year of Hoover's Presidency, in the winter of 1929-30, with an all-out collectivization drive of Soviet agriculture, the first phase of the Plan (actually there were two Plans) was ceremoniously completed under extraordinary pressure from the Kremlin in 1932, just three months before his rude defeat to Roosevelt. Another Five-Year Plan is then launched again orchestrated by the Consortium and Stalin's die-hard members of the Soviet State Central Communist Party, and their imprisoned engineers and technocrats (virtually working under house arrest). Roosevelt's collusion with Stalin went far beyond the partisan politics of Washington's stage shows before the democratically-elected American Congress.

At the apex of power it is entirely a Consortium affair which has become the venue for which America's new President endorsed and continued support to the consolidated Soviet dictatorship of mass murder and enslavement of the Russian peoples. In the eclipse of the final pre-nuclear era this was all part of an enveloping global strategy of war and destruction leading the nations of the planet directly into the Second World War. For the barons and lords of the British realm mixing top tier Pilgrims with Consortium billionaires, scions of industry and finance, this would be their last gasp in the Great Game of Empire when war is the means to a greater end such as it did when England lost 60,000 men in a single day in the Battle of the Somme during the First World War and England's Empire was no less the "meat-grinder" it was during Stalin's Holodomor years and the attrition of its army ranks during the Second World War.

Compounding the violent campaign of collectivization of the Ukrainian farm peasants with forced procurements and confiscation of their seeds and grain, grain prices plummeted on the world grain markets depriving Moscow of desperately needed foreign exchange to finance the Soviet Plan of Industrialization vital to prepare national defense against the rising German Nazi forces on its western frontier and invasion by Japan in the East all of which necessitated massive stockpiling of grain to feed the Soviet army. In the Great Game of Empire these were the consequences of the Consortium investment for peacetime profits while the politicians, bankers and industrial leaders prepared for world war.

Messrs. Dr. Darlymple and Dr. Mace are among the first to note that during the late twenties and early thirties some two dozen Americans and Europeans including doctors, journalists and émigrés traveled in the Soviet Union and on the scene to observe the Holodomor. For the most part they are not newcomers on the scene and are accustomed to living conditions under the restraint of the Soviet authorities and constant surveillance by the secret police.

Both Darlymple and Mace report a wide divergence in the figures of the Holodomor death toll with estimates for the period ranging from 1 to 10 million and average 5.5 million. Ralph Barnes for the *New York Herald Tribune* estimates one million deaths; Walter Duranty (*NYT*) 2 million; Bill Chamberlin (*Christian Science Monitor, Foreign Affairs*) 4 to 7.5 million; Bernard Pares, Whiting Williams; Eugene Lyons (UPI) 5 million; Thomas Walker (Hearst), 6 million, Richard Sallet, 10 million. (James E. Mace, "The United States and the Famine", "Recognition and Denial of genocide and Mass Killing in the 20th Century', a paper presented in NYC, November 13, 1987; Dr. D. Dalrymple, "The Great Famine in Ukraine in 1932-1933', *Soviet Studies,* Jan. 1964; Petro

Dolyna, "Famine as Political Weapon"; Individual accounts of the famine and excerpts from several Russian-language newspapers, v. 2 of *The Black Deeds of the Kremlin; A White Book*, ed. by S. O. Pidhainy, DOBRUS, Detroit, 1955, 712. DOBRUS - Democratic Organization of Ukrainians Formerly Persecuted by the Soviet Regime ; R. W. Barnes, "Grain Shortage in the Ukraine Results From Admitted Failure of the Soviet Agricultural Plan," *NY Herald Tribune*, Jan. 15, 1933, pt. II; R. W. Barnes, "Million Feared Dead of Hunger in South Russia," *NY Herald Tribune*, Aug. 21, 1933, 7)

A full generation after the Holodomor and nearly a half century ago these death figures were corroborated by Dr. Dana Dalrymple, a specialist in the US Department of Agriculture. He found that the most authoritative reference to the cause of death Holodomor Terror-Famine had been made by Dr. W. Horsley Gantt of the Johns Hopkins Medical School. Dr. Gantt's observations of the famine had first appeared in the *British Medical Journal* and were known to the Moscow correspondents on the scene, including the hard-knuckle foreign correspondent for the *New York Herald Tribune* Ralph Barnes who reports famine deaths at one million.

Dr. W. Horsley Gantt is highly respected by both the Americans and Russians and earns the status of a "Hero of the Soviet Union" as head of Herbert Hoover's American Relief Administration's (ARA) medical section of the Leningrad Unit (1922-23), as well as for his work in Pavlov's famous laboratories (1925-1929). Dr. Gantt returned to the Soviet Union in 1933, ostensibly Dalrymple writes, "to continue his work with Pavlov". Yet, his name is curiously absent from State Department files of registered interviews in the National Archive microfilm collection for the period. Whatever happened to his records?

If famine didn't kill disease did. Typhus is the worst. Dr. Gantt focused on associated deficiency diseases and contagious epidemics. A hiatus of the epidemic finished them off. Deaths from typhus are classified as "Form No. 2". Starvation is complicated by disease making it virtually impossible to know which took more victims.(Dr. D. Dalrymple, 1932-1934 Great Famine: some further reference", published addendum to his article "The Great Famine in Ukraine 1932-34", originally published in *Soviet Studies,* Jan., 1964)

"Stalin's motto was 'machines instead of food'," remarks Dr. Gantt who travels freely through the famine regions off-limits to journalists. His mortality figures are the highest estimate at 10 million deaths; Soviet authorities privately tell Gantt that the mortality figure from starvation and disease is more realistically closer to *15 million*; Frederick L. Schuman, *Soviet Politics at Home and Abroad*, Knopf, 1946, cited by Dr. Dana Dalrymple; F. L. Schuman, *Russia Since 1917*, NY: Knopf, 1962; Homer Smith, *Black Man in Red Russia*, Chicago: Johnson Publishing, 1964)

Who cares about five or ten million peasants living peacefully in the grain-belt on the edge of Europe? The fascists certainly do, enough and in so far as they enslaved them with a tyranny more complete and ruthless than ever known under the Russian Czars. Simple, hardworking strong and resistant people, in the beautiful grain lands of Europe, where Ukraine is known as a country of song, where young girls sing in the fields barefoot, with wreaths of leaves in their hair, dancing gracefully in the wind, their words flowing melodiously like rivers to Christian angels. Here on Mother Earth all people were protected by the Mother Goddess *Berehynia* and surrounded by the *domovyk, polyovyk, lisovyk, vodyanyk* (home, field, forest and river spirits), *mavka* and *nyavka* (river maidens). These spirits and practices invoking them persist to this day. In Gogol's words, song in the Ukraine is the thread of life and sacred to "poetry, history and one's father's grave".

UKRAINE: EUROPE'S OLDEST CIVILIZATION?

Ukrainians are descendants of this Trypillian culture of Europe's first land-tilling population that has existed as far back as 2200 B.C. Ancient Trypillian culture dates to the 4th to 2nd millennia BC and is well-represented by mystical clay figurines of women, tributes to fertility and motherhood. Slavonic civilization is thought to have existed 2,000 years. Since the first century before Christ, when Iranian nomads including the Cimmerians, Scythians and Sarmatians inhabited the vast steppe lands of South-Ukraine and on the northern shores of the Black Sea, ancient Slavic city states were established by both Greek and Asia Minor's settlers.

Scythian travels and conquests are preserved in ancient chronicles. In *History of Greek and Persian Wars* Herodotus described the Scythian movement from their Asian lands settling on the steppes from the Don to the Danube. From there they ruled from the 7th to 3rd century BC before the Sarmatians established their own villages within Ukraine. Art and folkcraft of Kyiv Rus' of the 11th to 13th centuries was inherited by ancient Ukrainian goldsmiths. Archeological gold treasures found in Scythian burial mounds tell of funeral rites practiced by the Eastern Slavs with their supernatural belief of the existence of the other world and the immortality of the soul. Archeological findings "prove that the Trypillians were the first to invent the wheel (6,500 years ago), domesticated horses and cows (8,000 years ago), and cultivated 12 varieties of grain (including three kinds of wheat, barley, rye, and peas)."

"Trypillian ceramics are beautiful," writes Svitlana Bozhko from Kyiv. "Long before the Sumer and Chinese civilizations our forefathers decorated their earthenware with signs and symbols that would spread across Europe and the Orient, including yin and yang; *svarha*, the symbol of the sun; the cross, symbolizing the sun, fire, and eternal life; and an image of the Primeval Mother - the woman-protectress." Anyone who has visited or lived in the Ukraine or has had the fortune to know Ukrainians may have discovered that their homeland is endowed with strong spiritual powers, forces and myth transforming their vast plains and birch forests where young men tilled fields and seldom left their villages except to fight Tsarist wars during the last three hundred years of Russian dominance. The primordial image and power of "the Earth-Mother" is "an image we find everywhere in the world, in countless forms and varieties", writes Mircea Eliade. (Svitlana Bozhko, "Solving Ancient Mysteries", *The Day*, Kyiv, July 24, 2007; "Mother Earth and the Cosmic Hierogamies" in M. Eliade, *Myths, Dreams and Mysteries*, 155-89)

Ukrainian folk traditions date back thousands of years. Innumerable sources testify that the Ukraine is an ancient land of spooky fairy tales. For example, ask children in Russia and the Ukraine today about "Baba Yaga", the witch who lives in the woods in a hut made of chicken feet. Tribal beliefs were preserved in original ritual songs and dances. The *rushnyk* (embroideries) and *pysanka* (Easter eggs) known to every household are based on worshiping the forces of Nature. These and village games were dedicated to the tillers' seasons and calendar holidays, and the might of the heavens such as *Kolyada* (Christmas carols), *Vesna* (Spring) and *Kupalo* (St. John's Eve).

Kiev Rus' flourished in the 10th and 11th centuries. It was a time of heroic epics and ballads accompanied by *skomoroskhy* minstrels and the *husli.* Legend recalls how St. Andrew stood on a hill atop Kiev, which is the site of St. Andrews Church on Andrievsky near the Witches Hill overlooking the Dnieper River and proclaimed Christianity would flourish here before Prince Volodymyr the Great resolutely baptized Kiev Rus', in 988 AD. (*Forests of the Vampire, Slavic Myth,* Duncan Baird Publishers, 2003)

In present day Ukraine still retains the feeling and wonder of a mystical land as though the Mother Earth spirit refuses to be stained by patriarchal abuse. Here in Ukraine, don't ever foul the Mother Goddess. If offended she will destroy. Fate will not be kind to the man who dares to usurp the power of the female goddess spirit against her. Stalin is dead and widely demystified and Mother Ukraine is developing again, and growing stronger every day with the energy of youth and every new spring of hope and promise.

Visitors are always welcome to Ukraine to experience the power and beauty of the land, and see in the faces of the smiling women, and hear their laughter and feel it sparkle and shine. The cultural motif that Ukrainian men drink too much, having been toughened and cowed into unemployment and limited ambition may also be forced to adjust to new social attitudes as Ukraine develops into a "free market economy", but because of dominant capitalist forces such as Proctor & Gamble, Coca Cola, MacDonalds, Gillette, Pizza Hut that eagerly reach out to a younger and new Ukraine to suck up market share and the Ukrainian *hrvna* of the workers emerging out of the shadow economy of communist dictatorship. The author was on the ground in Kiev, Kharkov (Kharkiv) and other towns and cities during the momentous shift of the wintery political upheaval canvassing Target shopping malls and trendy MacDonald franchises to witness the western advertising blitz attempt to transform post-Soviet orthodox religious holiday into a commercial feast.

Agence France-Presse in Moscow on March 2, 2003 reported "up to 30 million people are estimated by Western historians to have died between 1918 and 1956 in Stalinist repression, civil war, famine and collectivization, although the true figure may never be known." How many people in all the republics of the USSR did Stalin order killed? "No one really knows, not even here," a Ukrainian in Kiev connected with the intelligence services told me.

Standard assessments indicate that the Soviet Union lost over 20 million people during the Second World War. Historian Nikolai Tolstoy makes a convincing case that the actual total is probably closer to 30 million, maybe even more – with about a third of these deaths attributable to Axis actions. Only after the Second World War did foreign offices begin to do a body count excluding World War II casualties. "The British guessed perhaps seven, eight millions", *BBC* reported, and adds, "Progressive liberal people in both Britain and America were reluctant to believe that he'd ever executed anybody except genuine, dangerous party plotters."

Whereas the U. S. State Department, besieged with paranoia about Communists under every bed and spies in every office, estimated a more conservative figure of twenty million. Finally, in 1991, released Russian archives (those the Soviets filtered) cited 27 million. Estimates vary but the general figure is somewhere between 40 and 50 million people estimated to have died or disappeared as a result of Stalin's inhuman policies of terror and repression. John Mosier, in *Deathride* (2010) cites 25 to 27 million Russian deaths by the war.

Poison is historically considered the customary method for assassination in the Kremlin. A few years after the Holodomor Lavrenti Pavlovich Beria, like Stalin a Georgian Bolshevik, is promoted Commissar of Soviet internal affairs in charge of the secret police and national security and later feared more than any man in the USSR. Stalin dies in 1953, most probably poisoned by his closest associate since 1938 and who he feared most, the wretched Beria who takes control of the NKVD in 1939. It is widely accepted that Stalin was poisoned by one of Beria's men. Ryumin, the secret police official who engineers the "doctors' case" that apparently murdered Stalin is quickly liquidated in 1953. After Stalin's sudden death,– most likely by Beria's men, Beria himself was quickly eliminated by the Molotov-Khrushchev gang.

In that same year, 1957, it's the veteran Bolshevik and Stalin's foreign minister Vyacheslav Molotov's turn, spared by Khrushchev in the so-called anti-Party coup. It is all part of the brief Soviet thaw against the Stalin's totalitarian dictatorship and the rehabilitation of those purged by the Great Dictator. In 1961, followed the next year by the sensational publication of Solzhenitsyn's gulag novel, *One Day in the Life of Ivan Denisovich.* Molotov loses his relatively minor job in Vienna as the Soviet rep to the International Atomic Energy Agency, then is finally ousted from the Party and retires to a *dom otdykhya*, a ministry rest home shared with junior and mid-level diplomats, in Chkalovskaya, a small village outside Moscow where he is observed by Arkady N. Shevchenko, who later becomes the highest ranking Soviet defector from the UN General Secretariat in Manhattan. In 1984, Molotov is rehabilitated under Brezhnev (a die-hard Stalinist who despises Sakharov) leading to his readmission to the Party, at 94. (Arkady N. Shevchenko, *Breaking With Moscow*, NY: Knopf, 1985, 111; Amy Knight, *Beria*, Princeton Univ. Press, 1995)

FEAR AND SILENCE – FDR AND THE SECRET PRESIDENCY

Whereas FDR might have imposed moral restraint on Stalin, the American president instead shows no moral outrage or indignation at his ceaseless butchery. To outsiders that may have appeared odd especially when the large American

Consortium interests were invested in the Soviet Union, and could have easily ascertained that much was wrong in Moscow and in its vast outer territories. But this generation of leaders has emerged from the colossal rubble of the devastation they had inflicted in the First World War with some hundred million casualties on all fronts and disease.

Part of the problem of dealing with the historicity of the Holodomor is academic. War-time death figures dwarf Holodomor numbers. Responsibility for as many as 23 million deaths is placed with Stalin and his NKVD* henchmen ...." But then the figures are complicated by the institutional conditions of living under a state of totalitarian terror. In his article *Stalin's War; Victims and Accomplices,* Charles Lutton declares, "The Stalinist policy to deceive the West is well-know to anyone who traveled to the Soviet Union as a tourist or journalist. Everything must be locked away – every image of the slave labour camp, torture chamber, execution squad, even pictures of the daily, dreary life of the people, the daily bread and soap queues, everything except the model farms dolled up for showing off to foreign visitors." (*NKVD, *Narodnyi Komissariat Vnutrennikh Del,* political police, 1934 successor to OGPU, *Obeydinennoe gosudarstvennoe politcheskoe upravelenie*)

In addition to killing a million or more returning Soviet soldiers, repatriated after WWII as promised in a secret understanding and official diplomatic relations between FDR and Stalin, the Soviet leader was given a free hand to continue his postwar genocidal schemes against the Russian populations. Lutton underscores the fact that "Stalin's forcible resettlement of over 1.5 million people, mostly Muslims, during and after World War II is viewed by many human rights experts in Russia as one of his most drastic genocidal acts. Volga Germans and seven nationalities of Crimea and the northern Caucasus were deported: the Crimean Tatars, Kalmyks, Chechens, Ingush, Balkars, Karachai, and Meskhetians. Other minorities evicted from the Black Sea coastal region included Bulgarians, Greeks, and Armenians."

Nikolai Tolstoy in *The Secret War* (1981) describes the fierce campaign Stalin waged against the Russian population - a struggle which often took priority over pressing military problems. For example, Stalin tied up much of the rail network in western Russia with slave trains of captives from the Baltic states instead of devoting all rolling stock to the reinforcement of the front-lines. At Lvov, six hours west of Kiev, where the Soviet 4th Army was fighting to prevent defeat, Stalin's concern was that the NKVD finish liquidating potential Ukrainian opponents of the regime rather than order the local security forces to join in the battle against advancing Axis units. While Stalin pleaded with the British to rush more aid and take further action, NKVD labor camp guards were doubled from 500,000 to one million heavily armed men. Solzhenitsyn writes how three million returning Soviet POWs were then imprisoned and liquidated by Soviet secret police for "treason of the Motherland", and to keep them from talking about a better life in Europe. (Charles Lutton, "*Stalin's War: Victims and Accomplices*", *Journal of Historical Review,* v. 5, no. 1, Institute for Historical Review, 2007, 84-94; Nikolai Tolstoy, *Stalin's Secret War*, NY: Holt, Rinehart & Winston, 1981)

THE STRANGE FINDINGS OF DR. JAMES MACE

Why the American professor in Kiev James Mace stopped short of examining the political implications of the grain market economics where it becomes particularly relevant is not clear and at first glance seems odd to say the least. This is where the world turned on the commodity markets. It is where the bankers, the US grain producers, price fluctuations on the international grain market, jobs and unemployment issues connected to the US depression, and general world monetary instability were having a seriously negative impact on the world markets from New York and London to Berlin and Moscow. It would have been crazy, so they thought in the White House, to gamble with the requirements of domestic politics and reach out to the Ukrainians.

Unfortunately, research by Dr. Mace and others did not pursue trails leading to the White House of questions of engagement and responsibility for the famine, in terms of their trade or financial obligations between American banks and businesses providing essential support to Stalin's systematic campaign of terror.

Nor does Mace consider the unlikelihood of any political fallout between Stalin and FDR prior to their future military alliance against Nazi fascism that was a major feature of his reelection campaign 1936. With the risk of exposing top-secret strategic links between the capitalists and their communist proxy on all fronts – political, economic, industrial and military, FDR and his gang were not inclined to publicly accuse Stalin and Soviet Communism of political inefficiency and gross neglect in its inability to feed its own people. President Roosevelt and the State Department knew how Stalin was using the food weapon to inflict terror and famine on his own people.

Nor did Mace explore in any significant way the reasons for governmental denial and policy of diversion waged by newspapers publishers and their editors and journalists in America and England to conceal the truth about Soviet Russia. Investments by the Bank of England, Rothschild and the American family of Federal Reserve banks combined to yield an awesome power linked to the Democratic administrations of Hoover and FDR. Few scholars and writers apart from pioneering works by Antony C. Sutton (1925-2002) and Eustace C. Mullins (1923-2010) have traced the money trail of Stalin-supported repression and Genocide leading straight back to FDR's White House, thereby setting a pattern of arrangements that had placed Bolsheviks in power since 1917 and all done in complicity with the American Red Cross intelligence mission under the direction of the Morgan Bank in New York, with agents on the ground in Moscow and St. Petersburg and Jewish bankers in Hamburg, Frankfurt, London and New York.

It is remarkable that during this era of consolidation of war and revolution the occurrence of world tragedies of epic proportions followed a particular logic and pattern. The Consortium is ever-present. The impact of its involvement was immediate and consequential. Far too little has been published about the Holodomor, with virtually nothing in the book stores and mass media. British spy Robert Conquest's *Harvest of Sorrow* (1986), and *The Great Terror* (1973) are on American university reading lists. Professor James E. Mace's lesser known work was dedicated to restore the memory of the Ukrainian Holodomor as an act of Genocide to be forever acknowledged by the world community.

BEHIND CLOSED DOORS – THE STATE DEPARTMENT KNEW

Only a few months in 2005 separated the deaths of two key individuals to the Holodomor story. Their disappearance is not insignificant: Holodomor specialist Dr. James Mace (1952-2004) and diplomat George Kennan (1904-2005), the American icon of "containment" of "the Cold War" and perhaps the State Department's first official mystifier of the Holodomor. The Consortium takes care of its own. That's how it works and maintains its power. Immediately after World War II Kennan co-authored the euphemism "Cold War". By then it was forgotten that George "X" Kennan deserved more than a little credit for his role in the State Department's Holodomor debacle as well as its internment deep in the classified secret government archives buried safely away from public scrutiny.

In this story no two people could be further unlike one another and yet were mingled with mutual sympathies and aversions. George Kennan was a crafty soft-spoken Department pundit and ought to be remembered as the man who betrayed the American people about the real nature of events spiraling out of control in the Soviet Union. There should be no doubt that in order to further his career in the diplomatic service for which he was amply rewarded Kennan choose to cover up the traces of the activities of Stalinist terror and the Consortium players with the intent not to expose their schemes which remained concealed in classified files behind the curtain of foreign policy and national defense kept secret removed from public scrutiny.

In this 800-page Kennan biography (2010) Yale American history professor John Lewis Gaddis presents a soft portrait of the American icon of the US State Department prone more as a primer for high school students while omitting to mention one word about the Holodomor or the state system of totalitarian soviet terror sustained by western technology. Ironically, the safe Yale-Gaddis treatment confirms Kennan's philosophy on Soviet life which sheds not the slightest honest reference to famine, terror or gulag slave labor concentration death camps, and nothing of the great Five-Year Plans nor a word on collectivization, or industrialization and western technology. Nor is there any hint of an extermination or Genocide or suggestion of a secret Roosevelt war strategy with the Stalin. Of course the book received the standard fanfare of establishment accolades. Incredible! Academic propagandizing is still an institutional prerequisite of Consortium gamesmanship and very much alive in Yale culture for the 21st century. Pity those undergraduates without the convictions to know more than what they are told are dare to. (John L. Gaddis, *George F. Kennan: An American Life*, NY: Penguin, 2011; Frank Costigliola, "Is This George Kennan?", *The New York Review of Books*, Dec. 8, 2011)

The Consortium takes care of its own. That's how it works so well. It would be foolhardy to look for whistle-blowers. You won't find any. More wise to quietly pursue your own research and link. As it were, while serving two masters, – Stalin and the Consortium, – Kennan deceived and betrayed the American people and deprived them of knowing the true nature and extent of Consortium investment in the Soviet gulag. George Kennan was a poor, sickly junior officer in the elite diplomatic Foreign Service who learned fast how to serve his masters; he survived department dismantling of the Russian section and remained close to America's first ambassador to the Soviet Union, William C. Bullitt, described by Washington columnist Marquis Childs as the "Iago of Iagos". Kennan climbed the career ladder under more heavy handlers, political shyster and Bullitt's successor in Moscow, Joe Davies, and the inimitable Ave" Harriman, arch don of State US Department hierarchy. (re. Iago, J. E. Persico, *Roosevelt's Secret War*, 256)

For a society that stands on freedom taboos are always more dangerous than the secrets they protect. Unfortunately, much valuable time crucial to advancing Holodomor research had been lost due to the fact that Dr. James Mace never went so far in his findings and disclosures as to substantiate western rationality justifying the famine in terms of the political and economic expedience critical to Anglo-American Consortium power. For Mace to push forward his Holodomor agenda he has to take carefully measured small steps, or risk facing oblivion, or worse. Moreover, Mace stays away the taboo of Jewish domination of the Bolshevik leadership and Cheka secret police. Nor did Mace turn his attention to examining the Bolshevik practice of Jews killing Ukrainians by the millions, a not so popular topic for Steven Spielberg or the American mass media when you consider for decades the American government gives over $1 billion each year in foreign aid to Israel and the extent of Jewish influence in Hollywood and the American press.

It was decidedly more advantageous for Mace at the moment to duck that problem in order to finally achieve public recognition of the existence of the Terror-Famine Genocide by the US Congress and do it even when the reactionary Ukrainian government remained under the control of the pro-Russian President Kuchma nearly two decades before the Orange Revolution that brought Yushchenko to power in 2005. Part of his legacy to historians is the lesson not to denigrate history by avoiding sometimes painful issues that lay behind the causes of the tragedy. It is s too superficial to say that under Stalin everyone was a victim and to leave it there. Whereas the Jewish Holocaust dominates the world press the story of the Holodomor Terror-Famine in Soviet Russia attracts only very rare interest in the West. Dr. Mace courageously recasts the Holodomor agenda forward for a new generation.

Meetings and encounters with distinguished world personalities of history and culture import significant meanings to the turn of events shaping our experience. Occasionally a writer or researcher may hit a dead end or suddenly veer away from the tirade of misinformation, deception and denial to take another course and see on the horizon details of the big picture. Like what happens when stepping out of the fantasy world and entering the real one. Or, sharpening your focus from a kaleidoscopic maze of bewilderment. Wake up reader. A slight twist in the telling can alter everything you once thought to be true, and in a certain context maybe it was. Even dead objects in museums invoke new lively interpretations.

Strange and momentous encounters can be life-changing, especially when you are young. When I shook hands with Aleksandr Solzhenitsyn at Harvard a bond was formed that made this book possible. Understand reader, this is the man who when Khrushchev in 1962 finally publishes *One Day In the Life of Ivan Denisovich*, it was as if the entire Soviet Union, and the rest of the world, suddenly, overnight woke up to the reality of the Gulag and the Soviet prison state. Before no one dare talk about it, at least not openly, and always weary of denunciation and arrest so people learned to keep their mouths shut and get on with living the best they could.

A few years after Yale, while talking with my dear friend Roger Baldwin (Harvard Law 1910), indefatigable founder in 1917 of the American Civil Liberties Union (ACLU), and there honored with a front row seat at Harvard's 1978 commencement, a man tapped my shoulder requesting that I step aside to make way to the podium. I had abruptly left a private lunch with three generations of Lodges, my friend and the latest Lodge to graduate Harvard, Henry Cabot Lodge III (who turned an eye to let me crash nights in the Fly Club), his father George, a charmingly quixotic and talented Harvard Business School professor, and the venerable ambassador himself, a State Department icon Henry Cabot Lodge II, Eisenhower's former ambassador to South Vietnam and the United Nations, and grandson of the mighty HCL of President Wilson's era, with Hughes and Root the Republican stalwart in the Senate and one of the architects of American foreign policy behind Taft and Teddy Roosevelt and credited with having built the State Department in the late 19th century. A slight tap on my back and I turn around and in a moment dwarfed by a mountainous presence towering overhead. Solzhenitsyn waits to take the stage. The Soviet Union's "Center", its international organization of intelligence officers and agents quickly arrange a secret viewing of the Solzhenitsyn speech for officials in Moscow.

A life can change forever in a moment. But *you* have to seize the moment and make it the right one for you. Action is everything. There under the immense sky stood the legendary Aleksandr Solzhenitsyn himself, in flesh either to teach the dons a lesson in Cold War politics or to give the sacred Harvard Yard his blessing! Not a statuesque archetype of resistance and perseverance but the man who shook the Kremlin and who decades before had emerged from the belly of Siberian concentration camps and the haunting Soviet era! Amazingly, he had come this far! The survivor of dead souls and forbidden secrets, of human memory itself here in the flesh, a living icon of the Holodomor years, surviving battles as an artillery ("sound ranging") battery commander with Soviet Red Army in the Great Patriotic War of WWII, ranked by his unit at the top for military actions and discipline; then eleven years in gulag that transform him into a dissident writer of conscience of the national experience.(Just before the war he graduated with honors and a degree in mathematics and physics from Rostov University, not likely either without confirmed loyalty to the regime.)

In 1973, Solzhenitsyn sent shock waves around the world sensation when his trilogy *The Gulag Archipelago* was published, in Paris, revealing in comic satire the absurd horrors of an entire generation under Stalin. The book is named for the network of prison camps that stretched across the USSR. Solzhenitsyn had survived! Of all places here he was at Harvard! But even Stalin didn't understand America's unique connection with the Great Butcher of the New Society of Russian communists.

The Associated Press announces September 10, 2009 that the Russian Education Ministry had authorized Solzhenitsyn's three volume magna opus, *The Gulag Archipelago* as required reading for Russian students. Only six years earlier Russia had banned a history text critical of Stalin. Three years after he is awarded the Nobel Prize for literature, *Gulag* is published, in 1973, leading to his expulsion the next year and exile to the United States where he lives with his family for two decades writing in the remote peace of the Vermont woods in the small town Cavendish. This was a time when both superpowers were soon to confront the most powerful challenges in their history, when President Ford and Soviet Premier Brezhnev negotiated the disarmament SALT agreements, in 1974.

Looming high over the heads of his highly privileged and educated audience Solzhenitsyn resembles the stoic hermit returned from the wilderness. But his message, perhaps garbled in translation falls on deaf ears. "How did the West decline from its triumphal march to its present sickness?", he asks rhetorically. It is clearly the wrong question at the wrong time. The gathering of young graduates and aging alumni would have been better served not by this harangue to a war-weary America still feeling its wounds after the dishonorable retreat from Saigon and the tragedy of the Vietnamese refugee "boat people" in flight and erupting Genocide in Cambodia under the American-backed Pol Pot regime in full terror.

Solzhenitsyn blames the sons for condoning the mistakes of their fathers. And whereas what he said rings of truth the clarity of his message instead would have been better served had he addressed the role of American corporate and financial backing of Stalin in creating the Gulag converting the entire Soviet Union into a concentration slave factory the leading Russian dissident "denounced those in the West whose silence and inertia had made them 'accomplices in the suffering imposed on those who lived under Communist rule'," declares Christopher Andrew. (C. Andrew and V. Mitrokhin, 321)

Solzhenitsyn had been too long in the Vermont woods living in exile estranged from his beloved Russia to fully grasp the diabolical nexus of US-Soviet relations. Embittered and dogmatic, feeling the outrage, and alienation from the Power Establishment, that he, too, embraced the "truth even while it eludes us, the illusion still lingers of knowing it", he said. Out of step with contemporary culture, he missed his mark and berates the young generation for all the wrong reasons, in particular, the excesses of the West and its unrestrained materialism. The nation is weary of Vietnam and losing the war. The same year of *The Gulag Archipelago* publication, headlines of the Vietnam War Paris Peace Talks and the agreement signed in January are superseded by the Watergate White House Presidential scandal will force Nixon's resignation in disgrace.

By 1978 the students have moved on. Neither they nor their alumni care much to hear the Soviet dissident's tirade, and Solzhenitsyn leaves them more confused after his talk then they already were before they took their seats. Only two years before Moscow becomes the world showcase hosting the Winter Olympics, and unsure of what he might better have said, Solzhenitsyn left Harvard confused and no wiser for it, but with an understanding put in his own words, "just as today the West does not understand Russia in communist captivity." It was a fine summer day in June in Harvard Yard filled with alumni and graduating students, and Solzhenitsyn missed his mark.

At the end of the next year militants of the Iranian Revolution would seize the American embassy in Teheran and hold it hostage for 444 days infuriated over Western support of deposed Shah Mohammad Reza Pahlavi and its replacement with an Islamic republic under Ayatollah Khomeini. America's geo-strategists in the White House, Solzhenitsyn argues, and only six months before the flight in exile of the Shah, needs a more demonstrative deployment of armed force around the world or risk being perceived as a paper tiger. It is a strange and uneasy encounter with this surviving icon of the Soviet gulag, with *perestroika* and *glasnost* just around the corner, amidst the affluent and comfortable Class of 1978 whose elders in the Consortium remain keen to keep their secrets. The students would have preferred instead a good laugh with Timothy Leary or the Dalai Lama instead of this throwback to Tolstoyian spiritualism. *The New York Times* dismissed Solzhenitsyn's "world view" as "far more dangerous than the easy-going spirit which he finds so exasperating"; the *Washington Post* pans his "gross misunderstanding of western society". (*The NYT*, and *WP,* in C. Andrew and V, Mitrokhin, 321, citing D. M. Thomas, Alexand*er Solzhenitsyn, A Century in His Life*, London: Abacus, 1999, 462)

But Solzhenitsyn's presence at Harvard was no doubt political and part of a greater drama being played out at a higher level. Nevertheless, he did take a swing at Kennan and disarmament advocates. "Very well known representatives of your society," Solzhenitsyn declares, "such as George Kennan, say: we cannot apply moral criteria to politics. Thus we mix good and evil, right and wrong and make space for the absolute triumph of absolute Evil in the world. On the contrary, only moral criteria can help the West against communism's well planned world strategy. There are no other criteria." And remember reader, at the time Communist Poland is seething with revolt soon to erupt in a national uprising that emerges on 31 August 1980 at the Gdańsk Shipyard led by Lech Wałęsa, a dissident electrician, organizer and devout Roman Catholic, and backed by the trade union "Solidarity" federation that within a year spurred a movement of ten million supporters. Three years later Walesa won the Nobel Peace Prize and in a decade is elected President of a liberated Poland that had shattered the shackles of Russian communism. In confronting the brute force of Soviet communism the problem for Solzhenitsyn seemed more acute than ever if America was to successfully deploy its inexhaustible moral force to bring about peaceful democratic change and prosperity to the world of developing nations.

Currently, *The New York Times* reported the dictator described as the butcher and mass murderer of hundreds of thousands of prisoners in the systematized criminal system called the Corrective Labor Camps and Colonies (*Gulag* in Russian) has at present been "voted by Russians as their third greatest historical figure, and lyrics praising him have been inscribed in the vestibule of a prominent Moscow subway". This is the world's celebrated Russian dissident writer and humanitarian whose funeral President Bush Jr. snubs preferring to watch barely-clad volley beach ball girls prancing in the sand at the Chinese Olympic Games. ("Russian Schools to Teach 'The Gulag Archipelago', *The NYT*, Sept. 10, 2009)

For this Soviet dissident to survive those Holodomor years of gulag, famine, purges and war while writing of *The Gulag Archipelago* is still another seemingly incredible superhuman feat and an act of indominable strength of mind. Weaker men collapsed mentally and physically, reduced to crumbs and went insane. Smuggling the mass of papers assembled into a manuscript sent abroad outwitted the constant surveillance of the NKVD and GR. Just that alone was a task of the near impossible and required Solzhenitsyn and his supporters to always be at least one step ahead of the soviet thugs locked on his every move.

Solzhenitsyn recalls the ordeal in *The Oak and the Calf* (1975): "My work was going to pieces. I was short of air, short of room to move. I couldn't even go near the windows, in case someone spotted a stranger. I had put myself in jail, except that the windows had no 'muzzles' and I was not on short rations. But oh, how reluctant I was to go to the Lubyanka! Those who *know* what it is like. ... On the whole, I was on a firm footing. I had been allowed to get away with a lot. But I would not get away with *Gulag!* If they caught it on the way out, before anyone knew about it, they would smother it and me with it." It is a "must- read" for anyone seeking to grasp the simplicity of understanding freedom within the context of US-Soviet *rapproachment* made complex by its estrangement especially once they had been seized by the *Gulag*.

During the sudden international uproar over the Sakharov affair and *Gulag's* secret appearance in the West, Solzhenitsyn observed, "Eastern tyranny found even stauncher supporters in Western businessmen: in other words, the most loyal supporters of the "dictatorship of the proletariat" were the capitalists. They tried to persuade the US Congress that *trade* was the very thing to reinforce the rights of man in the USSR!" Even Solzhenitsyn could not fathom the depth of Consortium double-play. (A. I. Solzhenitsyn, *The Oak and the Calf*, 358)

Just how incredible was the event of the 1917 Bolshevik coup for Russia would not be clear until a generation after when the dust had settled. Unending terror: arrest, incarceration, torture, disappearance, deportation and executions often without trial for over half a century converted beautiful Russia into a vast Soviet prison camp of slave labor. Strange that on summer day in 1979 at Harvard I had never seen so much security in America, secret service agents descending everywhere. I had been working that year in the UN Secretariat in New York with my everlasting friend and mentor Hans Janitschek (1934-08), former Secretary General of the Socialist International, Austrian journalist in the UN Department of Public Information (DPI). After his warning to the West carried by *Time* Solzhenitsyn conferred momentarily with several Russian Orthodox priests, then vanished in a black limo. I wonder who could tell you how many Soviet KGB agents were in Harvard Yard that day.

During the Russian Revolution the ACLU (American Civil Liberties Union) has been cloaking its Bolshevism under a banner of patriotism a done so ever since its very inception in1917. It was Baldwin so long ago who as a friend of John Reed in the turbulent days of war and revolution who passed on to Louise Bryant the letters Reed sent from Red October in Moscow and St. Petersburg; Baldwin advised Louis Lochner of the Communist People's Council in a letter back in August 1917 when he wrote, "Do steer away from making it (the People's Council) look like a Socialist enterprise. Too many people have already gotten the idea that it is nine-tenths a Socialist movement ...." This same ACLU icon later declares, "I am for socialism, disarmament, and, ultimately, for abolishing the state itself.... I seek the social ownership of property, the abolition of the propertied class, and the sole control of those who produce wealth. Communism is the goal." (See CFR and Trilateral Commission websites)

MASS MURDERER AND DICTATOR JOSEPH STALIN

In 1932, Stalin wrote the commission Party chief of a major grain-growing region in Ukraine, "Unless we immediately start to improve the situation in Ukraine, we might lose Ukraine." For Stalin, it was imperative that the Ukraine never again collapse into civil war or lose it to the Poles or Germany. During the fall and winter of 1932-33, the work of the Communist Party commissars resulted in more famine. Eyewitness reports of the famine and accounts from victims testify to the severity of famine and Soviet repression. From its listening post at Riga in the Balkans the State Department was well informed. It is extraordinary that instead of recognizing the problem of famine and open negotiations to alleviate it, FDR used Bill Bullitt to send Stalin hearty congratulations on the resounding success of Soviet communism and the Five-Year Plans when everything there is breaking apart at the seams. Roosevelt was more interested in indulging in his public relations image as a true comrade of the working class. With his roots and education deeply rooted under the towers of Groton, Harvard and Columbia nothing could have been more absurd. Why should FDR be seen helping Ukrainian peasants when American farmers were suffering from agricultural and economic depression at home?

Not once did FDR condemn the repression or oppose Stalin's totalitarian dictatorship that since the beginning had been financed and supported largely by banks and industrialists of the Anglo-American Consortium. When FDR and Stalin extended their hands in partnership, their deal was sealed by the blood and lives of millions of Ukrainians. Furthermore, the socialist economic policies of both FDR and Hitler also precluded any solution of the Ukrainian problem. These were clever and secret plans to consolidate federal and fascist takeover of their own governments. A decade earlier Herbert Hoover bailed out Lenin and the Bolsheviks during the first famine of 1920-21. Soon Hoover labels Roosevelt's National Recovery Administration (NRA) a "fascist" program.

Where Hoover failed, FDR, Hitler and Stalin succeeded. The FDR gang eventually got the war they prepared for plus the A-bomb which came to FDR like a cherry on a Cold War multi-layered cake to inaugurate the New World Order. Instead of returning to a hero's welcome, returning POWs found victory bittersweet, condemned for having survived when true communist fighters, more courageous and patriotic in fulfilling their proletarian duty, died a hero's death. Stalin was merciless, and he quickly applied the pressure of the prewar system filling the gulag prisons. Each day more names are added to he executioner's list. The American people, for their part, become indebted to that great American Dream of a higher standard of living with spiraling inflation and trillion dollar debt from defense expenditures sold to them by "representative" politicians in bed with the Consortium's corporate lobbyists in return for easy profits, all packed together with incentives, subsidies and constraints.

Ukraine's population – not unlike the American masses - never had a clue how they are trapped. The "Great Game" of geopolitics played over their swollen bodies and gaping mouths unable to catch their last dying breath. And who dare credit American capitalists for the success of the great Soviet socialist transformation! This was Stalin's turf. The foremost and, in fact, for quite a long time the only British Russian expert Bernard Pares (Harrow, Trinity College, Cambridge) had spent four years on the Russian front during the First World War recalled in his book *Day by Day With The Russian Army.* Under increasing pressure he takes pains in passing the buck to Stalin to credit the dictator for checkered progress under the Five-Year Plans of industrialization and collectivization. Only it is principally the American buck that pays for it with mostly American machinery, American engineers and American technical assistance. Subsidies and federally-insured loans paid for by US tax-payers also figure into the calculation of aid to the USSR.

Long after the Terror-Famine of the Ukrainian Genocide British Slavic scholar Pares writes, "The foreign capitalist was indispensable, as the heavy plant had to be obtained from abroad, but he was attracted by the possibilities of this practical program. The foreign technician was equally indispensable at the outset, and he too was attracted by the scope for his enterprise ...." (Bernard Pares, *A History of Russia*, Dorset, 524)

THE USSR AND THE ANGLO-AMERICAN CORPORATE CONSORTIUM

From the beginning the Soviet Union was a client state of the Anglo-American Consortium clique of central bankers and Wall Street industrialists from New York and London that had evolved from a peculiar Russian Tsarist historical condition easily adaptable to the absolute centralized power of socialist nationalism under Stalin. They had learned their craft of espionage from the British during the First World War. Many members of the British ruling class were members of the Pilgrims Society, the Consortium's inner sanctum of privilege and power in London which tapped Americans into their activities of Empire. Marxist-Leninism called the Bolshevik state terror organization the "Dictatorship of the Proletariat". The Russians were duped and suckered to believe that it was something wonderful and real, an ideal state without private property and where everything belonged to the State. Instead it was an infernal meat-grinder of incessant Bolshevik propaganda and Moscow's dreaded secret political police.

"The historical process is not necessarily social progress; very often it is regression," wrote professor Stanislav Kulchytsky, also deputy director of the Institute of Ukrainian History at the National Academy of Sciences in the national Ukrainian newspaper, *The Day*. Kulchytsky has written extensively on the famine Genocide and the Soviet Union. Of the Russian famine of 1920-21 agriculture specialist Dr. Dalyrmple writes in 1964: "There is a curious parallel here with the action of the Soviet authorities in 1921 when the government not only withheld news of famine conditions in Ukraine, but levied a food tax and continued to ship out grain. Fisher indicated that 'One cannot escape the feeling that fear or political expediency, or both, influenced the official policy in these regions'." (Stanislav Kulchytsky, *The Day*, No. 26, Sept. 6, 2005; "The Great Famine in Ukraine 1932-1934", *Soviet Studies*, 1/1964; Harold H. Fisher, *The Famine in Soviet Russia, 1919-1923*, Macmillan, 1927. H. H. Fisher, Hoover Institution director, professor Russian history, Stanford Univ.)

History is a set of vicious dynamos. Ten years after the Holodomor 1932-34, FDR, Stalin and Winston Churchill gather together at the Yalta Conference of WWII. There they divide the world amongst themselves. Tens of millions more people perished and millions more were forced into Soviet captivity before the end of the war. The victorious powers continued to conceal US-Soviet economic collaboration behind the veil of Cold War propaganda. Americans forget that the Russians were first in Berlin and that the Americans were the last to leave Vienna. The Cold War was all a Great Lie of the Consortium myth-makers, just another chapter in what has long been most cynically perpetuated long before Kipling called it "the Great Game". The "nukes" rendered it eternally life-threatening to the planet. During the Reagan eighties I was educated by their awesome group at the Washington-based Johns Hopkins University of Advanced International Studies, counting warheads and talking nuke scenarios with Consortium big-wigs Harold Brown, former Vietnam War Secretary of the Army and later US Defense Secretary, the dapper State Department don Paul Nitze *et cetera*... Nor do I wish to forget the extraordinary satisfaction of study and friendship shared with Middle East specialist and Palestinian Fouad Ajami at SAIS and Princeton.

From the beginning while American banks and corporations promoted trade with the Soviet government, the Soviet Union developed a system of extreme repression and terror that inflicted forced famines, purges, executions, and arrests in the Soviet Union. Under Stalin who welded the ruling Communist Party to his iron fist, forced-labor concentration camps in Siberia became the pillar of Soviet Communism by which he exerted absolute control over the lives and decisions of all the people in the Union of Socialist Soviet Republics. At least fifty million people died as a result of Stalin's inhuman policies of terror and repression while American engineers walked over the fields and cities of the torturers and their victims.

See the big picture. Researchers N. G. Okhotin and A. B. Roginsky publish *On the Scope of Political Repression in the USSR under Stalin's Rule: 1921–1953,* in Moscow in 2003 declare, "Then the number of the victims of Bolshevism will also encompass various categories of deportees, people who died in artificial famines, those killed in engineered armed conflicts, casualties in numerous wars waged in the name of communism, those children that were never born because their potential parents had been repressed or starved to death, and many others. In this case, the estimate of the total number of the regime's victims will approach 100 million persons (a number of the same order of magnitude as the country's population itself)." (N.G. Okhotin, A.B. Roginsky, *On the Scope of Political Repression in the USSR under Stalin's Rule: 1921-1953*, Memorial Society, Moscow, 2003; <www.osa.ceu.hu>)

The brunt of the man-made famine hit the defenseless Ukrainians during the worst years 1932-34. It came like a howling wind across the vast fertile plains of "Little Russia" – as Ukrainia was known for centuries. The ancient land of Kiev Rus', once so mighty peaceful and prosperous is unlike any other place in the world blessed by Mother Earth covered with a blanket of rich black soil that endowed its culture with traditions and customs enduring two thousand years. Many of them were not even arrested or given the chance to reach what Solzhenitsyn called that "breaking point" that strikes like lightning that scores a direct hit on you.

There were too many to send off to the far away unknown islands of Solovky the place of no return in that frozen gulag archipelago where 1,111 "counter-revolutionaries" were shot in the back of the head in November and December 1937 and hundreds others horribly tortured to death,– Ukrainian writers, scholars, workers and peasants. No, sending them away was would be unnecessary. Why pay the price? Just raid their houses of every trace of food, and throw terror into their hearts. Dig up the grain! Show us the hidden pits! Stalin's OGPU agents set the village peasants on them, they too like scared dogs terrorized by the secret police, threatened with arrest and exile for aiding the criminals against the social order. Entire households and villages were left with nothing to eat, not a grain, or a seed or a cow. The lazy kulaks will disappear and eliminated, secretly shot and burned. Good riddance! And they waved their hand in the air saying, "Who wants to remember them anyway! No one will miss them. Soon the world will forget. Russia has millions more of ignorant masses, wave after wave of the Russian horde resting on the edge of Europe poised to invade the civilized West. No one will want the burden of memory to inherit the moral responsibility of our crimes unless absolutely necessary."

Communication technologies then seem primitive compared to the 21st century age of mobile cell telephones, internet and 24-hour satellite TV. Then the telephone and telegraph became standards in the West. Newspapers abounded everywhere. Radio suddenly was the craze. Another standard was set by the propaganda machines of government censorship and news spin by the privately owned press industry and the Soviet Kremlin. In fact, there was famine every year from 1930 on leading to the Holodomor.

WHEN ARTHUR KOESTLER MOCKED STALIN AND THE PUSSY RIOT HITS PUTIN

With vigor and constant demonstration President Herbert Hoover and his Secretary of State Henry L. Stimson asserted no obstacles are to stand in the way of the Consortium to finance and aggressively implement Stalin's Five-Year Plans (FYPs) of collectivization and industrialization while he consolidated his regime of terror and brutality that would go down in history as the most systematically murderous regime ever in the world, as the former communist turned anti-Stalinist, and writer Arthur Koestler mocked in his novel *Darkness At Noon* (1941).

Koestler wrote that "history ran on rails according to an infallible plan and an infallible pointsman". While living abroad, mostly in exile in Paris, meeting to talk and drink together daily with Albert Camus and Jean-Paul Satre late into the night, in 1945, the year it was published in France, along with later that same year *Yogi and the Commissar* – both biographical fictions denouncing totalitarianism. Koestler with uncanny accuracy estimated that Stalinism took up to *a hundred million victims*. And in a near total news blackout! In that first postwar year in Paris Camus is finishing *The Plague* and asking questions about courage and the responsibility of the writer as the world's witness to speak out against the "infallible". (Arthur Koestler, *Darkness At Noon*, Macmillan, 1941)

While Washington only recently has recognized that Stalin committed Genocide in the Ukraine, the US Government, nevertheless, continues to seal its role with silence and perversely orchestrated distortions. Reader any sane person would have to wonder about that. Washington still carries on expecting Americans and the world to believe that its leaders acted with "the highest integrity" in its dealings with the Soviet Union during those white-washed and wretched Holodomor years.

Arthur Koestler witnessed the Holodomor. The young communist living during "the famine winter of 1932-33 in Kharkov, amid millions of starving Ukrainians," notes *The New York Times* in 2009, Koestler had been a member of the German Communist Party. He's one who got away and lived to tell after he turned against Stalin and became one of his most fierce anti-communist critics recruited by the British secret service. Allowed privileged access to territories and contacts with individuals aware of the famine Koestler personally observed the terror and remained affiliated with the Comintern. In the Spanish Civil War Koestler is accredited to a British paper, the *News Chronicle*, and is captured with the rebels in the fall of Málaga on February 9, 1937, jailed with condemned prisoners hundreds whom are executed weekly by Franco's fascists. At 32, he's a long way from "the cultured Jewish milieu of the Hapsburg twilight" and his origins in Budapest. "The consciousness of being confined acts like a slow poison, transforming the entire character," he wrote. "Now it is beginning gradually to dawn on me what the slave mentality really is." Through efforts initiated by his wife, Dorothee, an international outcry for his release, led by Hearst and British notables leads to Koestler being transferred to Seville and ultimately he is narrowly escapes a crueler fate saved in a prisoner exchange. He quits the Party, and remains a stoic anti-fascist anti-totalitarian and for nearly two decades devotes his writing to the political cause of freedom of the oppressed masses. Three years after his release Koestler publishes *Darkness At Noon* in 1941;in the year after the war with the Nazi occupiers crushed by Stalin and France liberated by the Allies, it sells over 400,000 copies, mostly in the United States, and later in France after the war. A literary sensation about the grim reality of a man condemned in Communist Russia the book never went out of print nor should it become any less popular under the arbitrary miscarriage of justice and post-KGB terror of the Putin regime. (Michael Scammell, *Arthur Koestler: The Literary and Political Odyssey of a Twentieth-Century Skeptic*, NY: Random House, 2009; Christopher Caldwell, "Man of Darkness", *The NYT*, Dec. 24, 2009)

Equipped with knowledge of the Holodomor, and an understanding of Solzhenitsyn, Stalin's legacy hits home with a force lacking in those early years of Cold War America. Rubashov is Koestler's anti-hero in the novel and not that different from Dostoevsky's Raskolnikov in *Crime And Punishment.* Issues of morality, ethics, and historical revolutionary necessity in the context of Genocide and mass murder under Stalin and the CP hound the aging Bolshevik leader Rubashov as he sits in a cell cleaning his pince-nez glasses on his sleeve during the Purge – in Russian *chistka*, or "cleansing"– in a socialist reality that denigrated the individual to the property of the State. His nightmare is our nightmare, his world, our world, his choices, our choices as he awaits sentencing and contemplates how the Bolshevik socialist revolution came to this, abandoning decency and individual vanity to follow a logic of usefulness of "historical necessity". The anti-hero (it could be Trotsky, Zinoviev, or any of the CC Party members, opens his conscience to the reader: "The whole thing was a pretty grotesque comedy, Rubashov thought; at bottom all this jugglery with 'revolutionary philosophy' was merely a means to consolidate the dictatorship, which, though so depressing a phenomenon, yet seemed to represent a historical necessity. So much the worse for him who took the comedy seriously, who only saw what happened on the stage, and not the machinery behind it." (Arthur Koestler, *Darkness At Noon*, 178)

Ukraine's Holodomor remains one of the worst crimes of man in his technological evolution in the 21st century. Koestler's Rubashov is taunted by his co-conspirator and interrogator Ivanov. In Stalin's revolutionary world the table turns interminably. Today's hero is tomorrow's "enemy of the state", the brilliant engineer who fails is shot as a "wrecker" or counterrevolutionary. They debate the essential questions which shook the Consortium's client regime of collective Soviet socialism under the dictatorship of "No. 1" and which concern us all at present decades after the Soviet Union has ceased to exist.

Koestler lived "the comedy", his euphemism for the staged performance of Party debates and submission to Stalin. Referring to the Holodomor in a parody of proletarian dictatorship and Stalin's purge trials and mass murder, Koestler's anti-hero in *Darkness At Noon* (1940), Rubashov tells us, "Yes," and he explains, "So consequent, that in the interests of a just distribution of land we deliberately let die of starvation about five million farmers and their families in one year.

So consequent were we in the liberation of human beings from the shackles of industrial exploitation that we sent about ten million people to do forced labour in the Arctic regions and the jungles of the East, under conditions similar to those of antique galley slaves. So consequent that, to settle a difference of opinion, we know only one argument; death, whether it is a matter of submarines, manure, or the Party line to be followed in Indo-China. Our engineers work with the constant knowledge that an effort in calculation may take them to prison or the scaffold; the higher officials in our administration ruin and destroy their subordinates, because they know that they will be held responsible for the slightest slip and be destroyed themselves; our poets settle discussions on questions of style by denunciations to the Secret Police, because the expressionists consider the naturalistic style counter-revolutionary, and *vice versa.*

"Acting consequentially in the interests of the coming generations, we have lived such terrible privations on the present one that its average length of life is shortened by a quarter. In order to defend the existence of the country, we have to take exceptional measures and make transition-stage laws, which are in every point contrary to the aims of the Revolution. The people's standard of life is lower than it was before the Revolution; the labour conditions are harder, the discipline is more inhuman, the piecework drudgery worse than in colonial countries with native coolies; we have lowered the age limit for capital punishment down to twelve years; our sexual laws are more narrow-minded than those of England, our leader-worship more Byzantine than that of the reactionary dictatorships.

"Our Press and our schools cultivate Chauvinism, militarism, dogmatism, conformism and ignorance. The arbitrary power of the Government is unlimited, and unexampled in history; freedom of the Press, of opinion and of movement are as thoroughly exterminated as though the proclamation of the Rights of Man had never been. We have built up the most gigantic police apparatus, with informers made a national institution, and with the most refined scientific system of physical and mental torture. We whip the groaning masses of the country towards a theoretical future happiness, which only we can see. For the energies of this generation are exhausted; they were spent in the Revolution; for this generation is bled white and there is nothing left of it but a moaning, numbed, apathetic lump of sacrificial flesh... Those are the consequences of our consequentialness." (Arthur Koestler, *Darkness At Noon,* Macmillan, 1940)

Diplomats, lawyers, politicians and businessmen of the Consortium invested in Stalin's regime of communist socialized terror using these words in similar fashion to justify their crime against the men, women and children of the Ukraine wiping out entire families and villages with hunger and famine. This was the Holodomor of the early thirties. These words – "the highest integrity" – lost their meaning, infecting the words with another meaning, for they still have meaning and are not empty of it for they are not meaningless of what they mean to express. Endowed with other meaning, the opposite and contrary, the words act with the power of demons, as evil as the lie wrapped, embedded in their words given what they are intended to do. Words have intentionality, a usefulness, and here in their use meant to deceive.

The New York Times castigates Russia as a black market economy and institutionalized corruption writing June 26, 2009: "Russia often passes abroad for a country where a corrupt judiciary and blackmail are staples of business life" as in the heinous assassination of journalists in particular investigative reporter and human rights activist Anna Politkovskaya, in 2006, and Paul Klebnikov, editor of Russian language version of *Forbes* shot dead in 2004. Both are murdered while investigating organized crime. This does not help Putin's Russia image abroad. Politkovskaya had recently written *Putin's Russia: Life in a Failing Democracy* published the previous year in the West. Born in 1958 in New York City where her Ukrainian parents served as diplomats Anna Politkovskaya returned to Russia to work for *Izvestiya*, official mouthpiece for the Soviet Central Committee.

In the forward to *A Russian Diary*, published posthumously (2007), Scott Simon writes, "Pravda, the other best-known daily (but in no sense a competitor) was the official voice of the Communist Party. *Pravda* means 'truth', *Izvestiya* means 'news', and the joke among Russians was, 'There is no news in Pravda and no truth in Izvestiya'." Three suspects said to have been FSB agents were acquitted in a trial; in 2011 the prosecution won the right for a new trial to bring her killer(s) to justice. (Anna Politkovskaya, *A Russian Diary: A Journalist's Final Account of Life, Corruption, and Death in Putin's Russia*, NY: Random House, 2007, viii)

Scott Simon adds, "It is dangerous to be a real journalist in Russia today. A conscientious Russian journalist, unlike reporters in North America or Western Europe, doesn't have to travel into war zones to risk his life. Danger comes to his or her doorstep, car, or apartment block. The Glasnost Defense Foundation, led by Alexey Simonov of the Moscow Helsinki Group, reports that during 2005 alone, six Russian journalists were murdered, sixty-three assaulted, forty-seven were arrested, and forty-two were prosecuted. The editorial offices of twelve publications or broadcasters were attacked. Twenty-three editorial offices were closed. Ten were evicted from their premises. Thirty-eight times, the government refused to let material be printed or distributed." The Helsinki Group, the leading human rights organization in Russia which since 20 years received major funding from UA AID via MHG, an NGO (Non-government organization), and a member of the International Helsinki Federation for Human Rights (IHF). That was cut in November 2012 by Putin when Russia ordered USAID to cease its activities in the country starting October 1, claiming that the agency allegedly "tried to influence the political process in the country through its financial grants." The State Department claims that during its 20 years of work in Russia the agency spent $2.7 billion on various programs with a third aimed at the development of democracy. Looking at the latest crackdown Putin has reason to be concerned. How much are they spending now? (A. Politkovskaya, *A Russian Diary*, xiii)

By 2009 at least 17 journalists have been assassinated in Russia since the election of Vladimir Putin as President of the Russian Federation in 2000, leaving his office as director of FSB, Russia's federal security bureau (ex-KGB). He succeeded a drunken and pathetically disgraced Boris Yeltsin deeply embroiled in corruption scandals. His first official act was to grant the Yeltsin family total amnesty from any judicial prosecution. Three years after the death of her close friend Politkovskaya, human rights activist Natalya Estemirova was found murdered on July 15, 2009, abducted and killed in Grozny and her body dumped on the roadside nearby in Ingushetia. Two highly courageous women journalists slain. After the murder of Gadzhimurat Kamalov in the Russian province of Dagestan in the Caucasus by six shots to his chest people are afraid to write anything against the corrupt economy and mafia thugs. Putin's crackdown on the freedom of the press intensified immediately after his reelection to the Presidency in 2012 where to urge political dissent against the regime is no mere joke but seriously life-threatening. Ask the Pussy Riot protesters ...

After a mock trial Russian anti-corruption opposition leader Alexii Navalny was sentenced to five years on trumped charges of theft, and cuffed by prison guards, the latest of Putin's targets to see their freedom disappear. That eliminates him from staging a threat to Putin's iron-fist hold on power in the future 2018 Presidential contest. "Opposition politician Boris Nemtsov, who attended the hearing, told Reuters that he was "shocked" by the ruling, and he added, "Putin has told the whole world he is a dictator who sends his political opponents to prison". The Reuters news agency quotes the imprisoned former oil billionaire and head of Yukos, Mikhail Khodorkovsky declaring, "'For Russia, there is nothing unusual about convicting political opponents on criminal charges'." Khodorkovsky compared the Navalny case to similar tactics of Stalinist "terror" in the 1930s. In Putin's xenophobic Russia the Ukrainian Holodomor is still just a fairytale of anti-Stalinist lies sponsored by the imperialist West. With thousands of Ukrainians protesting on the streets of Kiev denouncing President Yanokovich's kowtowing to Putin, the Russian dictator surprises the world with a general amnesty in December 2013 days before the long Christmas holidays and released the Pussy Riot women. In a separate arrangement Putin also freed Khodorkovsky who never admitted guilt and vowed not to return to politics but instead use his hidden fortune to help secure the release of Russia's fellow political prisoners. (Gabriela Baczynska, "Russia jails top opposition leader; Putin denounced as dictator", *Reuters*, July 18, 2013)

There is no Game, no war, no skillfully managed enterprise of terror without propaganda using words to deceive. *The NY Times* had their Duranty to lie and conceal the reality of Stalin's systematic campaign of mass-murder and rewarded him a Pulitzer and refuses to this day to take it back. Like he said, no omelets without breaking eggs, and once the egg is broken it is no more. So it is with the word; abuse it and lose it. Words lose their meaning, and men lose their values. The words and their men of the Consortium became empty shells.

Entrenched in the Kremlin Putin rules over 109 million cynical, terrified and disenfranchised voters. Commenting on the oppressive climate of a neo-Soviet system of loyal gangster oligarchs feeding on the postmortem ruins of a parliamentary democracy, in which the three branches of power in Russia, – the executive, the judiciary and the legislature – are welded in the fists of Putin, Politkovksaya once said quoting Molotov's grandson, "Ivan the Terrible and Stalin are more to the taste of the Russian people."

Whether Putin can survive to transform his state oligarchy into a pluralist economy of denationalized capitalist companies without taking "decades to collapse through creeping stagnation" and elections "rigged in the Soviet fashion", remains to be seen. As I write *Moscow Times* reports "The Kremlin has compiled a dossier on the 126 members of the Public Chamber that measures their degree of loyalty and whether they would be willing to act on Kremlin orders, *Novaya Gazeta* reported. If confirmed, the internal documents would back suspicions that the Public Chamber, an elected group of citizens that was formed in 2005 with a mandate to influence government policy is little more than window dressing of a civil society.

The document shows how the presidential administration rules its own court of civil society," *Novaya Gazeta* columnist Andrei Kolesnikov said in an introduction to a 42-page dossier published by the newspaper three days before. Meanwhile, human rights activists in Russia continue mounting pressure on the Putin regime and had hoped to shed more light on the 2009 prison death by beating of lawyer Sergei Magnitsky, 37, who worked for Hermitage Capital implicated in the disappearance of $230 million. Obliged to sign the Magnitsky Act passed by the US Congress in December 2012 which bars Russians suspected of complicity in his death and other human rights abusers from entering the United States and freezes assets their assets, Obama played down the case opting instead for more "permanent normal trade relations" and a pro-trade Department of Commerce pushing for a $20 billion share of the Russian market. In a decision prompting attacks of Stalinist tactics Putin's Russian court convicted Magnitsky guilty of tax evasion in Russia's first posthumous trial. The court also condemned his former client William Browder, a Briton who had spearheaded an international campaign to expose corruption and punish Russian officials he accused of killing Magnitsky. Hermitage Capitol immediately issued a statement declaring some $230 million had been stolen from the Russian state. ("Siberian Waterloo", *The NYT*, June 26, 2009; Anna Politkovskaya, *Putin's Russia: Life in a Failing Democracy published the previous year in the West, Metropolitan*, 2005; A. Politkovskaya, *A Russian Diary*, 11; Alexandr Bratersky, "Kremlin Has Secret Dossiers on Public Chambers Members", *Moscow Times,* 21 May 2012. See also Masha Gessen, *Putin: The Man Without a Face*, 2012; Gessen is interviewed Jan. 8, 2014 by NPR upon the release of her latest book on *Pussy Riot*; Maria Tsvetkova and Steve Gutterman, "Russia finds dead lawyer Magnitsky guilty in posthumous trial", *Reuters*, July 11, 2013)

STALIN TO PUTIN: OFFICIAL EXTERMINATION

Stalin and his cohorts from the West planned it more or less that way. Stalin succeeded in entrenching Russians into the darkness from which they are still afraid and hesitate to emerge. Ruling over a state of gangsters and fear over two hundred journalists have been killed in Russia, according to Simonov. "Unfortunately, in the heart of most Russians is an urge to not stand out, and it is particularly in evidence today," Politkovskaya observed. "We do not want to attract the evil eye of repressive institutions. We want to stay in the shadows."

Politkovskaya adds, "but keeping to the shadows lies much deeper in the heart of every Russian. After all that has happened here in the twentieth century alone, it is perhaps hardly surprising." (A. Politkovskaya, *A Russian Diary*, 321)

The extermination of the population in the Ukraine and in other regions of the USSR in the early thirties was a coldly calculated and ruthlessly executed program of Soviet-style socialization, a vicious form of state terrorism against its own citizens and holding the populations in captivity with the complicit engagement of foreign companies, especially a significant number of giant American corporations like General Electric, Ford, DuPont, General Motors and the Rockefeller oil and banking empire (Standard Oil/ Exxon/Mobil/Amoco/ Chevron/Chase et cetera). What could they people do to resist. When the peasants revolted they were crushed. The people, suspicious and fearful turned away.

"We are sometimes called a society of millions of slaves and a handful of masters, and told that is how it will be for centuries to come, a continuation of the self-owning system. We often speak about ourselves in that way too, but I never do. The courage of the Soviet dissidents brought forward the collapse of the Soviet system, and even today, when the mobs chant 'We love Putin!' there are individuals who continue to think for themselves and use what opportunities exist to express their view of what is happening in Russia, even when their attempts seem futile." (A. Politkovskaya, *A Russian Diary*, 293)

The Holodomor was shrouded in secrecy, denial and distortion. Officially it never happened. That view no longer holds. Change always confronts resistance. It remains inside Russia a zealously guarded secret as Putin stages new culture wars in search for identity and power in the Stalinist syndrome of post-Soviet society. Archived State Department documents reveal eye-witness accounts of famine in the Ukraine all meticulously recorded in American embassies and consulates before being transmitted to Washington and organized by the Department's Eastern Europe Affairs Division. Documents were buried away and many perhaps lost forever. At the same time Stalin's Sovietized Russians shot burned and buried Ukrainians official US government files were grounded in deep silence inside the Hoover-Roosevelt administrations with entangling roots of incalculable dire consequences for the health and integrity of future democracies. Startling testimonies, combined with facts and figures from all directions inside and outside the former Soviet Republic of the Ukraine, bear witness to the extent of the Famine Terror.

This was unmistakably a deliberate and planned Genocide against the Ukrainian people. And it spreads this deterioration of Democracy with a sickening gangrene on Humanity in general. Understand reader this is no accident. What to do? Get the poison out of the system or chuck the system. Is recovery a viable option? For the vibrant fresh scent of youth it most certainly is. But for the sordid stale putrid smell of rotten cynical businessmen and bankers and seasoned diplomats a reversal of their fortunes is not in their deck. For them the game is stacked in their favor. Look at the power of the central banks and their button-pushing politicians asking for more.

Fortunately in the West government documents and private archives are more accessible. With an increasing number of journalists assassinated inside Russia freedom of expression in 2009 appears not only dangerous but sometimes fatal. A few years ago Russians were tearing down statues of Stalin; at present criticism of the dictator will likely lead to a imprisonment. *The NYT* reports late 2009 the official push by Russia's enduring Communist Party celebrating Stalin's 130th birthday, part of Putin's never ending drive to brighten the image of Stalin with "an appeal for people not to bring up the more unseemly aspects of his record."

The evil of fascism always seeks to strengthen its hand in the struggle against the good. "Stalin is a polarizing figure in Russia, still popular for winning World War II and industrializing the Soviet Union while reviled for the purges that killed or displaced millions of people," the *NY Times* added, without citing the number of Stalinists parading at Red Square to lay flowers on his grave. "'We would like very much on this day for the discussion about any mistakes of the Stalin era to stop, so that people can reflect on the personality of Stalin as a creator, thinker and patriot,' said Ivan Melnikov, a senior party official". (Clifford J Levy, "Russia: A celebration of Stalin", *The NYT*, Dec. 22, 2009)

In Russia already by mid-year 2009 there were three journalists killed, and over 19 assaults on crime reporters investigating corruption at the to Not a low risk preoccupation here where western concerns of morality are considered a joke. Among the conservative oligarchs in the Kremlin, an extremely tight network of former KGB officers consolidating power after the Gorbachev *glasnost* era of the 1980s, have reversed any trend towards liberalization and access to these invaluable official archives. In Washington State Department documents pertinent to the famine terror were sequestered out of site, classified, and remained inaccessible to the public for nearly half a century despite the Freedom of Information Act. Who really knows what records been misplaced, or destroyed?

So why all the secrecy?

Would exposure have compromised America's foreign policy? Was it done to protect the Presidency and the State Department from public scrutiny, and subsequent embarrassment from public scrutiny over the lack of accountability? Would it have weakened the moral fiber of the image and example of American democracy exported around the world if government secrets had been exposed? The denial and secreting away of official recognition of the Famine Terror was in fact part of a carefully orchestrated political maneuvering within the ranks of Washington and Wall Street stretching to the capitals of world powers unbeknownst to the American public and the masses of the so-called free world.

In November 1933 Roosevelt invited Stalin's foreign envoy Maxim Litvinov (born Meir Henoch Mojszaewicz Wallach-Finkelstein 1876-51) to the White House. They shook hands and then signed their notorious "Gentleman's Agreement" granting official American recognition of Stalin's terrorist communist dictatorship. Did the American president cynically sacrifice America's extolled fundamentals principles of Humanity lost to his generation and quite possibly for generations to come? And why was their meeting– exposed as a farce mocking the entire free world– further jaded by the Consortium's strategic geopolitical agenda of the inevitable war with Hitler and Japan?

The official record does not bear kind witness that President Roosevelt suffered any sleep over Stalin's mass murder of untold millions of Ukrainians. Just another day at the office in a world gone mad, or just to make the people think while they hold their breath living in fear and ignorance and told to mind their own business. Champagne toasts, handshakes, back-slapping, this was a festive day in Washington and far away in Stalin's fortified labyrinth of the Tsarist Kremlin. No spilled tears here. An amazing campaign of disinformation and suppression in the western press of the reality of the Soviet death camps and slave labor system working in tandem with corporate America.

FDR did not leave much behind if any visible record of agonizing soul-searching over their tragic plight. No trace of compassion for the Ukrainians emerged from the White House. This fit with his complex and aloof style of playing White House politics with his advisors and closest insiders while preserving his all options.

The President's ally in Moscow was soon to be America's "Uncle Joe". Between Stalin and FDR not even God could save the Ukrainians from their fated destinies more than a decade before Yalta and Roosevelt's selling out of half of Europe to the Soviet Communist dictatorship intertwined with the plots and purse strings of the powerful Consortium that unleashed the terror that eventually divided Germany, but saved Paris and Western Europe from occupation by a Soviet Russian nuclear superpower. Of course for the innocent hardworking peasants in the fields, all this was far over their heads, and only a decade away on the path.

What they could not trust they knew to be true. Men, not God, betrayed the Ukrainians. Believers knew it was so. Even to this day skeptics, particularly post-Soviet apologists in the Kremlin and their friends found the scale of horrors of the Ukrainian Holodomor utterly unimaginable. FDR and the State Department ignored it, brushing it aside off the public record, branding it a virtual taboo. Even the Soviet Union could boldly disclaim preposterous lies by enemies of Russia's communist state for the socialist future of the New World Order. But these were no lies or mere excesses. Stalin systematically exterminated the indigenous population of the Ukraine, selecting not one group among many but instead all but the least resistant rural peasant and factory workers as well as engineers and the national intelligentsia. Putin's Russia – Putinism – maintains a policy of secrecy and denial that keeps state archives off-limits and this at a time when the Holodomor has already become a football in the culture wars of Russia's contemporary identity crisis with Washington.

In 2003, the Ukrainian Government conducted a special hearing about the famine and pledged to build a National Famine Memorial Complex. That year it drafted a resolution for the 58th Session of the General Assembly of the United Nations to "secure recognition of the famine in Ukraine as an act of political genocide against the Ukrainian people." It was a giant first step that had been the lifelong ambition of Holodomor historian Dr. James Mace who died in 2005. That year President George Bush awarded Robert Conquest a US Medal of Freedom, the nation's highest civil award, citing his book *The Great Terror*. Ukrainian President Viktor Yushchenko's own father was a victim of the purges sent to the Belomorkanal construction project. Not until the election victory of Yushchenko in 2004 rejecting more than a decade of Soviet dominance did Ukraine gain its first genuine independence. Yushchenko continues to manifest publicly his sincere respect to the millions of tragic famine victims killed by Stalin's totalitarian dictatorship however contested by the oppositionist Yanokovich pro-Russian camp.

This book is dedicated to the memory of the victims and to encourage efforts like those by President Viktor Yushchenko, himself a former head of Ukraine's central bank during the turbulent 1990s under Yeltsin and Kuchma. Nor did he forget them. And a special place of dedication is reserved to the living who still have their memory buried in their hearts bearing witness to those painful years. Friends and acquaintances in Kiev and around the world where Ukrainians have settled tell me about their *babushkas* and grandfathers who disappeared, and of survivors who remember how they barely lived while others were more or less fortunate.

Under Yushchenko stories and pictures of the 1932-34 Holodomor appeared more frequently on Ukrainian national television and in the press. The Ukrainian government recently began preserving recorded testimonies of survivors, scorched memories that never heal, bearers of history that has been etched on their hearts.

Oles Yanchuk's film *Holod-33*, produced in 1991, will probably never be surpassed for its terrifying dramatization of the 1930s famine. A *New York Times* review of the film stated, "The Soviet forces who carry out the savagery are portrayed as uniformly monstrous. They take sadistic pleasure in flaunting their grain, vodka and sausages in the faces of the hungry and think nothing of slaughtering hundreds of unarmed protesting farmers with machine guns. When Myron Katrannyk (Georgi Moroziuk), the head of the household, is suspected of hiding a sacred chalice, he is summoned to Communist party headquarters, suspended on a rack and beaten. After he and his wife, Odarka (Halyna Sulyma), refuse to talk, they are held prisoner and their children are left to fend for themselves. One of the perils they face is being kidnapped and eaten." (Stephen Holden, *The NYT*, Dec. 15, 1993)

Ukrainian journalist Oksana Shapova recounted a true story how the young girl Vera barely lived through the repressions only to then lose all her relatives in WWII and postwar misery. As Milan Kundera reminds us, "The struggle of man against power is the struggle of memory against forgetting." As Oksana Shapova tells us the Holodomor Genocide is "a history that is impossible not only to forget but which cannot be converted into a mere succession of historical facts, happenings, and dates. These people are reliving it every day of their lives. They wake up and fall asleep, looking back on the past with a fear that this might reoccur someday...Only God knows how much love and care it takes to ease their tormented hearts. Whoever considers himself human cannot help bowing to the memory of these people and do his best to alleviate their sufferings today and ensure that tomorrow will not create a hell on earth." During Yushchenko's presidency Holodomor stories surfaced weekly of remembered personal histories rebuilding Ukraine's collective identity and preserving respect to their lost but not forgotten ancestors. (Oksana Shapova, "Wounds that Time Cannot Heal", *The Day*, Kiev, March 28, 2006)

The Holodomor is a tragic human story etched in the memory and hearts of the survivors and in rare letters of grief, suffering, and hope. Hope for survival, love and Humanity and all the good things worth living for in the countryside of vast golden fields of wheat. Mythical pagan goddesses blended with Christian ritual over a higher law of this land of milk and honey. The Bolsheviks changed all that. Death came slowly day by day over the years taking new victims. Stalin converted a failed program of agricultural collectivization into a national campaign of communist terror and mass extermination of indigenous populations in the Soviet republics. His commissars and secret police seized grain and seed from the deeply religious peasants who kept God in their hearts and icons of the Mother of God and Jesus in their modest homes within view of photos of Marx and Lenin.

Death took away their last seed of hope. Millions died from hunger in Stalin's "secret" war against the peasants. It was an American secret shrouded in official silence. In the White House under Presidents Hoover and Roosevelt knowledge of the Holodomor was jealously guarded over by their Consortium men in the State Department and Commerce and Treasury Departments. Details rarely leaked into the press but were never officially released by the men in dark suits and stiff white colors. In 1939 in a radio broadcast Winston Churchill described Russia as "a riddle, wrapped in a mystery, inside an enigma". Exactly what she would do he said he didn't know. A former journalist in the Boer War, elected to parliament and Minister of Munitions in the war government under Prime Minister Lloyd George, Winston Churchill well understood how effectively government censorship gagged Britain's press in wartime. The British spymasters and empire-builders led the way teaching the Americans how to do it. When America finally entered the war, in 1917, President Wilson protected the Consortium's secrets by controlling America's journalists through the Committee of Public Information (CPI), the national propaganda agency backed by emergency laws of sedition targeting dissidents.

The government has one story, the "free" press another. They are seldom if ever the same. To understand the Holodomor, its causes and consequences are all part of the greater web with spiders everywhere spinning the saga. There are so many filters to obscure the truth mixed in a kaleidoscope of fictions that it may seem even too dangerous to open a door and step into a strange and multifaceted world turned upside down in revolution and Bolsheviki chaos of the revolutionary consciousness of the proletarian new society with its own collective language and consciousness and objects of the new age. That is, before the simple order of it all.

Welcome to Soviet-style Putinesque Russia. Vladimir Putin's reelection to a new six-year term in March 2012 calculated no higher than 53% is widely contested by thousands of Russian and international observers and denounced as "an insult delivered to civil society" declared Russia's League of Voters. Putin's national security force immediately began arresting opposition leaders for protesting against the election results. In Putin's modern day Russia we are again dealing with unseen forces, written and unwritten truths, a spinning world sometimes beyond reach where it may be difficult to maintain balance and a perspective in focus especially when watching *CNN* or *NBC*.

"About contemporary Russia: there is no proof of anything that happened", *Washington Post* columnist the gulag writer Anne Applebaum observes in her *NYT* book review of Gessen's *The Man Without a Face: The Unlikely Rise of Vladimir Putin* (2012). Even with the Old Bolsheviks gone Stalinist-style corruption and the lack of government transparency and accountability are the order of the day in Putin's Russia as the people grope for threads of the past to survive in an uncertain future and in a world of fallen but not forgotten heroes. (Fred Weir, 'An Insult': Russian election observers reject Putin's win", *The Christian Science Monitor*, March 7, 2012; Anne Applebaum, "Vladimir's Tale", *The New York Review of Books*, April 26, 2012)

THE COVER-UP TODAY

How do you put "a face on the faceless"?

Former British intelligence op Robert Conquest tried to do it in 1986 with his book *Harvest of Sorrow: Soviet Collectivization and the Terror-Famine*. Information is disinformation. That might seem like a contradiction in logic. It is not. It is no mere coincidence that the Conquest famine book was published the same year research findings were published by Holodomor historian and Kiev resident James Mace and the US Commission Investigation of the Ukrainian Famine, 1932-1933. Two years later Washington published the *US Congress Report on the Ukraine Famine* (1988). An interesting synchronicity was in play.

In fact, Mace and Conquest actually collaborated on their famine research. Both were Harvard research fellows and at the time both were funded by Harvard University's Ukrainian Research Institute.

Think about it. Immediately that should tell raise eyebrows. Follow the money. There are always strings attached. And they can be cut as easily as they are pulled. Don't bite the hand that feeds you. Leave it to the Harvard, Princeton and Yale cronies and that's what you get: the Harvard-Princeton-Yale take. Conformity has many versions of coercion with subtle but no less brutal methods of persuasion. It took me a long time to get that clear in my head; my Kent prep school roomie at Yale, a Varsity oarsman for three years – (the first up in the morning and the last to eat in the day, double training routines) –, refused the cap-and-gown parade; his father was Yale but with one credit to go, he bucked it. No diploma, freed of the Yale karma. Don't get me wrong here, reader. I love the place. Like when I found "the King" himself, Blues legend B. B. King standing in the vestibule to the Calhoun College dining room, apparently feeling out of place and a little lost, alone under the stain-tall glass windows, Gothic gargoyles and paneled walls. So I asked Mr. King if he wouldn't be inconvenienced to join me for lunch. The King and I. I still feel the chills when he recalled his childhood. Such rare honors are not that infrequent at Yale. Such grace and dignity tempered by timeless inspiring humility. God save the King!

But neither Conquest nor Mace could completely get away with ignoring, distorting or suppressing the truth. A rational person might think it would be very hard to kill some ten million people and get away with it. But these were not very rational times. And they did, then, and many scholars and politicians, businessmen and financiers with their hacks in media still intend to keep the truth buried today. Funny, he then went on to introduce garbage recycling on conveyor belts in the late seventies.

Conquest and Mace had to move quickly to get their propaganda version neatly embedded in historicity of the politically correct and indelible path of memory, if not only to reach beyond the landscape of bitter suffering and truth that surfaced a decade before, in 1973, when Solzhenitsyn made public his remarkable trilogy of *The Gulag Archipelago.* After all, the Russian writer and former Soviet army officer had lived and witnessed first-hand the Holodomor terrorism of those same years, when it was called the "Plague". It was incredible. How could it be! He wrote how so many were lost, without the odes and poets to recall the souls of these dead Ukrainians and fellow Soviet citizens of famished territories.

Solzhenitsyn recalls the vanquished lives before their last traces vanished completely from the collective memory. "Fifteen million souls. Fifteen million lives. They weren't educated people, of course. They couldn't play the violin. They didn't know who Meyerhold was, or how interesting it is to be a nuclear physicist ... about the silent, treacherous Plague which starved fifteen million of our peasants to death, choosing its victims carefully and destroying, the backbone and mainstay of the Russian stones mark the crossroads where they went in creaking carts to their doom. Our finest humanists, so sensitive to today's injustices, in those years only nodded approvingly: Quite right, too! Just what they deserve! It was all kept so dark, every stain so carefully scratched out, every whisper so swiftly choked, that whereas I now have to refuse kind offers of material on the camps – 'No more, my friends, I have masses of such stories, I don't know where to put them!' – nobody brings me a thing about the deported peasants. Who is the person that could tell us about them? Where is he? ... I cannot document even one chapter thoroughly. All the same, I shall make a beginning. Set my chapter down as a marker, like those first stones – to mark the place where the new Temple of Christ the Savior will someday be raised."

So, throwing up his hands in frustration, Solzhenitsyn asked, "Where did it all start?" Why not start with 1929 and its "murder lists, the confiscations, the deportations", and the gavel crashing down on the peasants with the official Party decree of February 1, 1930 for "complete confiscation of the property of the kulaks" and deportation from their village homes "to points beyond the boundaries of certain regions and provinces". (A. I. Solzhenitsyn, *The Gulag Archipelago,* v. 3, 350-2)

Solzhenitsyn had survived the Terror-Famine and the Purges, prison camps, the propaganda of The Plans and Stalinization of Russia transformed into one giant monopoly of foreign investment and development by the unseen hand of the Anglo-American Consortium. He lived through all that and assiduously kept a record in three published volumes describing the Soviet human experience under the political absurdity of centralized planning by the Soviet socialized state. That is a very good question: "Where did it all start?"

In the same year 1973 Solzhenitsyn's *Gulag Archipelago* saw the light of day, another truth-telling event of the Russian Soviet experience surfaced in the West, another set of three volumes precisely researched and clearly written that revealed details buried by the so-called Cold War, that euphemism for the next phase of American power by one of the same State Department bureaucracy's literary architects skilled in producing propaganda of the Holodomor, namely the virtuoso George Kennan in Moscow.

If you want a new perspective on history you owe it to yourself to discover Aleksandr Solzhenitsyn. Put his volumes alongside Tolstoy, Dostoevsky and Antony Sutton's *Western Technology and Soviet Economic Development 1917-1965,* monumental contribution published ironically by the conservative Hoover Institute at Stanford University from 1968 to 1973. With exhaustive detail and source referencing Sutton showed the extent of financial and industrial collaboration and technology transfer between Washington and Moscow behind Stalin's Five-Year Plans and the Terror-Famine totalitarian regime of the Holodomor. Capital and technology imported from the West; slave labor, police terror and propaganda, a home brew of Marxist-Leninist Bolshevism and totalitarian Stalinism cooked up from East.

"WILL THERE BE SOUP?"

Washington and Moscow. Hoover and Roosevelt and Stalin. Capitalism and Communism. Together these forces combined to secretly build the Soviet gulag state system implementing a Consortium strategy in a race with time to crush the rising pyramid of Hitler's Nazi fascism and emerge as unchallenged victors of the Second World War. Most uncanny bedfellows! The political observer Gareth Jones wrote in November 1932 nearing the peak of the Holodomor winter "In short it forecasts that in this the last winter of the Five-Year Plan the question will still be: "Will there be soup?"

By the mid-1930s economic conditions in America and Soviet Russia began to improve. Recognition of the Communist regime by the richest capitalized nation is a boost of enormous magnitude as were the huge industrial complexes installed under the supervision of Bolshevik commissars, Soviet and American engineers and their American companies all with household names: General Electric, with its headquarters in Schenectady, New York, Westinghouse, Detroit's Ford Motor Company, US Steel, DuPont, American Caterpillar and many more well-known and lesser known firms including the controlling investments by the Rockefellers, Morgans, Mellons, Harrimans and others. When pro-Stalin supporters cheered the great achievement of the military and industrial success of the USSR's first and second Five-Year Plans, it was never said that the technology came mostly from the West. To admit Stalin was a patsy of the capitalists was a counterrevolutionary attack on sacred Communist Party doctrine. Anyone in the Soviet Union who dared to make such a claim would regret it, and probably shot as an "enemy of the people". After all, didn't the Party provide the mass labor necessary to build and run the factories and industrial plants?

The Ukrainian Terror-Famine was man-made as was its concealment, two sides of the very same coin. Master-minded in the labyrinth of the ornate rooms of the ancient fortified Palace of Russian Czars, the Kremlin is as daunting and mysterious as the men who lived there, as it were, haunted by the ghosts of Ivan the Terrible and his successors who ruled the empire after pushing back the Moguls in the 13th century. Protected in this ancient fortress for over three decades Stalin ruled like a God controlling the fate of more than a hundred million people of diverse ethnicity living in nations that became republics of Moscow's central authority symbolized by the impregnable Kremlin. Those who caught a glimpse of the omnipotent ruler overlooking the glorious Red Army on May Day parade or for the anniversary of the Bolshevik Revolution of 1917. From here Stalin issued orders to implement his Terror-Famine campaign of the Holodomor against the Ukraine with blood-soaked hands of his accomplices in the Anglo-American Consortium's network of banks, law firms and corporations eager to use the slave labor of soviet terrorism for profit.

The Holodomor cover-up does not end there. It continues today with conferences and memorial ceremonies orchestrated by propagandists from Washington and academics invited the honorable universities where they are rewarded with lofty salaries and publishing deals unthinkable in the Ukraine. Oh! Don't offend the conference hosts at Harvard's Ukrainian Institute, or Princeton's George Kennan Center or at Yale's Slavic Studies. These good people relish the rituals living in America with healthy salaries and benefits, neat incentives for their career? But who is to blame them?

Even when President Barak Obama visits Russia in mid-July 2009 and vows to "reboot" relations with Russia, the disinformation keeps one foot in the past. At the same time in the United Nations General Assembly delegates gathered in July to debate what *The New York Times* described as "the concept known as 'the responsibility to protect'." Shortened to "R2P" in diplo-speak, the nations of the world have yet to understand "how the world body should intervene to stop genocide, war crimes, crimes against Humanity and ethnic cleansing". Delegates worry "that the more it is debated, the less consensus will emerge". ("When to Step in to Stop War Crimes Causes Fissures", *The NYT*, July 23, 2009)

REAL WORLD POLITICS OF GENOCIDE: FROM GULAG TO WORLD WAR

Genocide and politics are inseparable partners in organized crime against Humanity. Denial is always mixed with accusations and counter-accusations of responsibility. In the geo-political balance of power of the "Big Lie" of the Kiplingesque "Great Game" no one is innocent." Make no mistake about it.

Politics is proxy war played out in times of peace. The content of propaganda may shift with the focus but it comes from the same culture that thrives on war and destruction for which the masses always pay dearly with their lives, and some are fatally cut short.

Holodomor revisionist Robert Conquest was a British spy. A paid informer easily capable of betrayal (after all it was his job), Conquest, born in 1917, educated at Oxford, was a cagey writer eagerly serving the agenda of distraction and subterfuge rather than assume a personal risk exposing the role played by his masters in the British Foreign Office during the Holodomor years. Like others of his kind he was hired to keep the secrets, not expose them.

Even today London prefers the modest wonder boy Gareth Jones for breaking through the barrier of press censorship rather than having to deal with the tedious mendacity of the Foreign Office and Britain's complicity with the Kremlin, and this at a time when all the puppet strings lead back to the Empire's links with the Consortium culture. Quite a twist of Fate that cost Jones his life. For his part in the Holodomor controversy Conquest opted for a comfortable professional life as a paid civil servant of the British Foreign Office's disinformation and propaganda department (IRD). There during the Second World War he served his British masters until 1956 when he leaves the cloak of government to join the private publishing sector that he had so skillfully infiltrated as a former communist and British informer before the era of the "the supreme muzhik Nikita Khrushchev". Or Yeltsin in his resurrected Russia. (A. I. Solzhenitsyn, "the supreme muzhik Nikita Khrushchev", in *The Oak and the Calf: Sketches of Literary Life in the Soviet Union,* Harper & Row, 1979, 21)

As we examine later, the shadow of his past shatters the flimsy political motives and any claim to integrity of Conquest's anti-communist books. It is clear that Conquest like his predecessors was bent on protecting the puppet-masters both in London and Washington from public exposure for their hidden complicity and denial in the Ukrainian Holodomor for over a half-century. This is not an incidental or trite piece of rhetorical disorder. Moreover it's an intellectual corruption of the first order. But lets face it; his career and pension depended on that complicity and subterfuge. Instead of academic exile the intellectual is rewarded for his complicity in the crime of cover-up, deception and denial. And his sordid career lends itself to the masquerade of a darker wretchedness. Conquest is a tool of the spymasters.

The case of the young Welshman Gareth Jones as we shall see is also invariably tied with intractable knots and emboldened mystery. During Ukraine's newly resurgence and all too brief break from Moscow, the chapter of the Holodomor in world history enters a new revision of political football between Moscow and Washington, each with their own agenda to protect. In 2005 President George Bush the Younger actually awards Conquest the Presidential Medal of Freedom, America's highest acclaim for civilians exercising exemplary patriotism in their craft, yet slight compensation for a second-rate spy who never achieved the fame or notoriety shared by Smiley's people or the likes of contemporaries Somerset Maugham, Lawrence Durrell, Graham Greene or John Le Carre.

First Duranty then came Conquest. The Consortium always honor their own. It's a process for the continuity of legitimacy of power, lies and deceit. There is a long line of establishment academic writers lining up and waiting to pay their dues for just rewards. When monuments are erected in Washington for the victims of the Holodomor, what will these future historians write then?

In the early 1930s, Ukraine was ravaged by the wholesale slaughter and destruction of peasant village communities. No body count has ever been released by the Soviet Russian authorities. Bodies disappeared, buried in the fields burned or vanished in unmarked and mass graves along the route in all directions to forced labor concentration camps in the mines and forests deep inside the immense regions of the Soviet Union and never to be seen or heard from again. Party hierarchies in the Ukraine, and elsewhere were regularly purged of "wreckers", "saboteurs", "bloodsuckers", and "enemies of the people". Survivors would soon perish a few years later fighting the German Nazi invasion in World War Two. After the collapse of the Soviet Union in 1991 mass graves of executed prisoners began to appear in the press of shattered propaganda myths and smashed communist icons.

No family in the Ukraine was immune or unaffected. It is hard to put words on a political and humanitarian catastrophe of such unthinkable proportions. But that is just it, the problem is that it is not unthinkable and never was. Few were spared first Stalin's, then Hitler's machinations. "This was the nub of the plan," observed Solzhenitsyn, writing, "the peasant's seed must perish together, with the adults. Since Herod was no more, only the Vanguard Doctrine has shown us how to destroy utterly down to the very babes. Hitler was a mere disciple, but he had all the luck; his murder camps have made him famous, whereas no one has any interest in ours at all."(A. I. Solzhenitsyn, *The Gulag Archipelago,* v. 3, 359)

Serious establishment authors who refuse to recognize the vital role played principally by American corporations in the development of the modern Soviet state are simply not credible. "A regular flow of American machines and industrial equipment fueled soviet industrial development", wrote Kings College historian Richard Overy and British journalist Andrew Wheatcroft in their book *The Road to War* (1987). Unfortunately, they too failed to observe that the flow continued virtually uninterrupted until the era of the Holodomor in the Ukraine and famine elsewhere disrupting life throughout the Soviet Union and threatened to shake Stalin's tyranny and end his inhumane regime of terror, forced labor, and propaganda. Such misreading of the historical record is overtly suspicious of complicity with the secret agenda of the Consortium and its agents in academia and publishing. (Richard Overy and Andrew Wheatcroft, *The Road to War: The Origins of World War II*, 1987)

THE ASCENDANCY OF VIKTOR ANDRIIOVYCH YUSHCHENKO

The Terror-Famine was a personal tragedy suffered by all Ukraine. In 2004 the Holodomor became a symbol of national solidarity with the official backing of resident Viktor Andriiovych Yushchenko and his wife Katrina, a former American-born citizen from Chicago of Ukrainian descent. Another "must-read" on contemporary Ukraine is the work of Andrew Wilson, author of *Ukraine's Orange Revolution* (2005). At the time, Andrew Wilson was at the School of Slavonic and East European Studies (SSEES) of the University College in London, and since promoted to senior policy fellow at the European Council on Foreign Relations and honorary fellow of the Royal Institute of International Affairs.

Viktor Andriiovych Yushchenko was born in 1954. Both his father and mother were villager teachers; his father Andrei taught foreign languages and his mother Barbara, mathematics. Viktor Yushchenko's father who came from Sumy served in the Red Army was captured, but escaped from *seven* Nazi concentration camps (Auschwitz, Buchenwald, Dachau…). The elder Yushchenko died in 1992. In *Ukraine's Orange Revolution* British writer Andrew Wilson observes with keen perspicacity : "Many of those who returned to the Soviet Union were shot, and others shot before they could return, so young Viktor was doubly lucky to be born... Viktor Yushchenko is a country boy. He speaks with an accent that involves some *surzhyk*, a unique convergence of Russian and Ukrainian; his perilous hobby is bee-keeping. Yushchenko has heard terrible stories in his youth of the Great Famine 1932-33 caused by Stalin's collectivization and grain-requisitioning policies, when rural regions such as Sumy were ravaged by some of the highest death rates, estimated at between 15 to 20 percent of the local population – some four hundred souls in Yushchenko's immediate region." (Andrew Wilson, *Ukraine's Orange Revolution*, Yale Univ. Press, 2005)

The early personal history of Katherine Yushchenko-Chumachenko, Viktor Yushchenko's second wife, is also a tale that touches the miraculous. Originally came from the Ukrainian disapora, her parents separately survived the Holodomor only to be captured by the Nazis. They meet in Germany, where they are both *ostarbeiters* (slave laborers from Eastern Europe) and liberated after the war somehow find their way to Chicago. After studying economics at Georgetown University, Katherine earns her MBA at the University of Chicago (1986) before joining President Reagan's State Department. She moves to Kiev (1993) where she works with the international consulting firm KPMG, and marries Viktor (1998) when he is the "highly successful" head of the Ukrainian National Bank according to Wilson; that's a bold understatement given the country's dire status for double-book corruption, money-laundering economy, and ingenious tax scams. During the 2004 election campaign, the Yushchenkos suffer "vicious attacks", in particular, against his wife over alleged CIA connection, but not about money-laundering and corruption which hit too close to home President Kuchma and state institutions. All in all, during the election the press construct for the world a very clean image if not total white-wash of the ascendancy of Victor Yushchenko. And nothing is ever disclosed how the Americans swept in quickly depossessing the Ukraine of its nuclear arsenal after it broke away can reclaimed its national independence. That full story awaits to be told.

Yet in view of the disappearance of hundreds of millions of dollars and billions from the decommissioned nuclear arsenal of the former Soviet Russian empire hidden in the Ukraine, Wilson writes "the NBU (National Bank of Ukraine) was guilty of *extremely* creative accounting. The IMF stopped funding Ukraine, despite Yushchenko's apology. The NBU's inelegant defense is that they did what they had to do to survive in the conditions of the time". But why did the CIA, and the State Department's USAID wait so long to enter the fray after the US government swept clean the nuclear missiles buying them up en masse for peanuts soon after the collapse of the USSR in 1991. Inside the fury of oppositional politics I arrived in Kiev in late 2004 and was struck immediately by the absence of any national student democratic organization to lanch the new generation against the older corrupt master political class. (A.Wilson, *Ukraine's Orange Revolution*; <www. Faminegenocide.com>; italics added.)

Less than two years after the popular victory of the people's so-called "Orange Revolution" during which Yushchenko was severely poisoned and his face (that too had been publicly contested) - the love affair with hope for the future rid of corruption faded and died, badly scarred, with the quick return of the Yanukovich gang loyal to Moscow. In 2010 Ukraine headed to a showdown in the presidential contest. Yushchenko's five-year term came to an abrupt and climatic end. His popularity falls to new lows. Murders pass unsolved, jails remain empty of the perpetrators and the politicians openly clashed, sometimes violently on camera in parliament for all the world to see that capitalism in the Ukrainian still faces a very hard road ahead. Corruption is widespread and a thorn in the side of Euro-enthusiasts. And his contentious former Prime Minister Ulia Tymoshenko, heroine of the "Orange Revolution", courts death languishing for years isolated in hospital under guard while facing multiple long prison terms. After months of mass protest erupting in bloody violence in mid-February 2014 and over 75 anti-government protesters killed by Yanukovych troops and riot police, opposition leaders in Ukraine's Parliament reached an agreement for Tymoshenko's release and hold new elections.

In 2013, as I write, Ukrainians, after uninterrupted deprivation, scarcity of goods and government subsidy, suffer two-digit inflation and higher prices for food and clothing, gas and electricity. In October 2008, the Ukrainian national economy suffered a major hit during the global financial meltdown prompting an emergency $16 billion loan from the IMF. With its economy contracting 15 per cent and hit by the IMF's refusal of a $15 billion bailout by the end of the decade and unaided by lackluster reform efforts, Ukraine's debt problem grew steadily worse sending the hryvnia, Ukraine's currency sliding to a three year low. As of late 2012, Ukraine had achieved world status as basketcase default risk rated the six highest of 93 countries, according to a study published by *Bloomberg*, and reported in London's *Financial Times*. ("Ukraine Requests Fresh IMF Bailout", *Financial Times,* Nov. 30, 2012)

While it owes the owes the IMF $5.9 billion, and with its weak economy strained by a poor grain harvest, a domestic credit crunch, and reduced demand for steel exports, it's largest revenue resource, it seems unlikely the country will be able to roll over about $10 billion in external sovereign due in 2013.

Burdened by heavy feelings of betrayal, the Ukrainian population was besieged by an advertising blitz selling the Hollywood-manufactured American dream of market capitalism spear-headed by brand-name corporations led by MacDonalds, Coca-Cola, Gillette, Ford, Phillip Morris tobacco to name a few among the many international firms grabbing market share to the beat of kitsch pop music imports.

After the 2004 election Ukraine rushed to find a place in the new market economy. Inflation rose with the pace of rising real estate values. Ukrainian folk culture stepped in spiritually and artistically rich national traditions added an eerie incongruity to the modern tempo of life. In that climate of public enthusiasm for change and die-hard reactionary blowback to the Stalinist nightmare of stability balanced with that frightening knock on the door in the dark hours of night, President Yushchenko had to walk a political tightrope to combat Holodomor apologists and preserve the memory for a nation of survivors and for the world as its witness.

SOVIET RUSSIA UNDER STALIN: MADE BY "USA INC."

It staggers the mind to think of the combined global wealth of America's giant international corporations and the enormous power imposed over less privileged sovereign states. The 1932-34 famine years read like a Pandora Box taking us back to an era when easily identifiable American companies shared key roles in building up the war-based national economies of Nazi fascism in Germany rivaled by Stalin's Soviet communism.

General Motors, Ford, General Electric (GE), DuPont, IBM are only some of the big name brand companies who were active in that war trade that figured in the extermination of the millions of Ukrainians. DuPont maintained a secret exchange of confidential scientific findings with Nazi chemicals giant IG Farben until 1945; on January 1, 1926, DuPont men arrived at Hamburg, Germany for a secret meeting and signed a "gentleman's agreement" with agents from Germany's two huge explosive makers – Dynamit Aktien Gesellschaft (DAG), and Koln Rottweiler, soon both Farben companies. In the deal, both German companies received, according to Gerard Colby who did extensive research into the DuPont family empire holds "the first option of any new processes and products developed by the other. This included black powder, disruptive explosives, smokeless propellants for 'sporting' purposes, detonation, safety fuses, powder fuses, and 'generally all devices for initial detoxication or ignition'." Writer Gerard Colby observed that the deal opened the door for the German Nazi fascists providing them with access to "all patents and secret inventions covering commercial explosives".

The 1934 US Senate munitions hearings discover the DuPont ruse to mix commercial explosives with military explosives, and skirts the ban of any sort of German rearmament under the Treaty of Versailles. The DuPonts pleaded innocence but a letter found in DuPont files revealed "that IG Farben had an explosives capacity comparable to 'a large, rapidly mobilizable force, or a large number of guns, or a fleet". Writer Gerard Colby found that "Colonel Aiken

Simons, head of DuPont's military sales, wrote DuPont Vice President Casey and gave the State Department's Allen Dulles as the authority officially confirming the US policy of allowing German arms smuggling to 'swell' the reparation fund." Actually, acknowledged by the Senate Munitions Committee, "Dulles had made this policy clear at the pre-Geneva meetings of 1925."

Soon the DuPonts begin investing millions in Farben subsidiaries, which include, in 1929, an 80 percent stake in Adam Opel, AG, Germany's biggest auto manufacturer, and a sum increased to over $33 million by 1931 "giving GM a 100% investment. … A year later, DuPont's European sales agent, Colonel William Taylor, again reported to Wilmington of German rearmament, including the smuggling of American arms to Nazis by way of the Dutch rivers that flow into Germany. 'There is a certain amount of contraband among the river shippers,' he writes, 'mainly from America. Arms of all kinds. The principal arms coming from America are Thompson submachine guns and revolvers. The number is great." (G. Colby, 335-7)

Gerard Colby discloses further DuPont's confidence in the good business of arming Hitler's Nazis during this dark period of the Holodomor. Remember reader, the Holocaust is just around the corner. "Significantly," he reveals in 1974, "the only America firm licensed to manufacture and sell the Thompson submachine gun was Federal Laboratories, with which DuPont shared joint sales agencies. In January 1933 Taylor sent another excited report of Dutch gunrunning to Nazis in the Cologne area. Within a month, DuPont made its decision to take a direct plunge into the German munitions smuggling." (G. Colby, 335-7)

Again we can refer to Colby's exhaustive inquiry into the DuPont Nazi business: "On February 1, 1933, A. Felix DuPont, Sr., the suave, young-looking head of DuPont's foreign sales, along with Vice President K.K.V. Casey, secretly met with two Hitler agents, Jungo Giera and Count Westar Westarp was the more easily identifiable of the two; he was a representative of the German General Staff. Giera, however, kept his real identity to himself. Actually, he was Peter Brenner, a former German spy in the United States during World War I who had become a counterspy to avoid US prosecution. After the war Brenner continued sleuthing, selling his talents to at least thirteen different nations." When it became clear that Germany was going to produce the arms themselves the deal was dropped but not before paying off Giera $25,000 for his silence; the DuPonts would activate Giera later for sales to Japan. Colby wrote that DuPont, together with the British company Imperial Chemicals by 1934 "owned 20 percent of Hitler's largest munitions makers, DAG, part of the IG Farben combine." DuPont has other cartel agreements for German rearmament including its ownership of Remington Arms which include German sales of Remington cartridges to the US government. (G. Colby, 337)

Many people knew but seldom spoke of the fact that American companies were building up the world's most mighty industrial war machines in Berlin and Moscow. Sounds absurd? Read history. Internet will help debunk the lies still popular with high school History 101. Search the bibliographies, read the books with painstaking research of facts brought to light and made easily accessible to inform you intelligently on the business of war and the stakes involved. Dig deep under all the poof and puff.

At any moment in the 1930s the European powder keg could have exploded into another world war. And they knew it. FDR and the Consortium players all knew it too. Rockefeller was even invested in the Nazi death camps, though it is a fact today that might seem so banal that even the extensive network of Rockefeller-owned publishing companies won't lose any sleep over it. Michael Beschloss writes in *The Conquerors* (Simon & Schuster, 2002) the Senate investigations over American war preparedness and defense company links to the German cartels helped boost Harry Truman from the corner to top ranks of the Democratic Party and into the White House but with only a $10,000 budget there is little he could do before America entered the war after Pearl. Further Beschloss adds, "Deals between the German behemoth IG Farben and companies such as Standard Oil and Alcoa (Mellon sic) were charged with threatening dangerous wartime shortfalls in magnesium and synthetic rubber." (Michael Beschloss, *The Conquerors, Roosevelt, Truman and the Destruction of Hitler's Germany, 1941-1945*, NY: Simon & Schuster, 2002)

And Antony C. Sutton wrote some three decades earlier, "The US was desperate for such a formula. Standard Oil provided the Nazis with numerous other patents critical to their war effort, and owned a half-interest in the death camp at Auschwitz, together with their partner, IG Farben."

Fascism was widespread in the elite hallways of power American institutions. It was no secret. FDR and his Secretary of Agriculture and future Vice President Henry Wallace warned Americans about it. Many of the Consortium Nazi war factories were never bombed. Nazi death camps were overlooked as non-strategic targets. Roosevelt and his War Secretary Stimson argued that his business was killing Germans, not saving Jews.

By the early thirties Stalin already had his own peculiar Gulag system of forced labor death camps with vast wilderness of timber and mines and millions more prisoners to replace the millions dead from malnutrition, severe below freezing temperatures and physical exhaustion.

The Jews were next. Time was running out for them, too. Hitler made no secret of that. First, in Germany and the Baltics, then the Ukraine and Belorussia. It would not have surprised shareholders to know that the strategic capability to engage in the massive destruction of the Second World War would not have been possible without the collusion of American and international banks and corporations working in tandem for the socialist reconstruction of Europe and Russia after the Armageddon unleashed in the First World War. Anti-Semitism was not limited to the Nazis. (Daniel J. Goldhagen, *Hitler's Willing Executioners, Ordinary Germans and the Holocaust*, NY: Vintage-Random House, 1996)

THE CONSORTIUM BANKERS: AMERICA'S PRESTIGIOUS FAMILIES

Behind most of these huge American corporations of the Consortium reaping colossal fortunes are some of the richest and most prestigious families in America including the Rockefellers, Mellons, DuPonts and Harrimans. Their extensive families are likewise interconnected with their corporate network including National City, National Bank of Commerce and Morgan's Guaranty Trust all of whom made windfall war fortunes.

For example, JP Morgan and Co., under the direction of Henry Pomeroy Davison was purchasing agent for the Allied Powers, and personally involved on site with the central Bank of London and Paris the London-New York gold shipments vital to secure Allied loans to prolong the war against Germany. No small irony that once America was dragged into the war by the banking fiasco of apocalyptic proportions H. P. Davison (HPD) himself became Chairman of the American Red Cross. The 1934 public Senate hearings into the war trade confirmed that Morgan was the principal bank that maneuvered America into the war.

Harry Davison is JP Morgan's right-hand man until his last breath. He fell under the national spotlight only a few years before the outbreak of war when he sat alongside America's giant of finance and skillfully rebutted public scorn and scandal-mongerers at the highly publicized Senate Pujo Committee hearings during eight months between May 1912 and January 1913 over the Money Trust monopolies of millionaires (equivalent to today's billionaires), and the Congressional inquiry into the Panic of 1907 and the rescue of New York City from financial bankruptcy by Morgan's elaborate network "of overlapping directorships or interlocking directorates of the top banking houses and major financial institutions" of the United States. It all happened just prior to setting up the national Federal Reserve. It was at that very same time that the Fed system of a centralized national bank, which today controls America's money supply of deficits and debt was pushed on the newly elected US President Woodrow Wilson who reluctantly signs it into legislation in 1913 – landmark legislation of his first year in office.

The Senate Pujo Committee aimed to prove Wilson's contention of money and capital "the great monopoly in this country", and is headed by Samuel Untermeyer (1858-1940), a New York lawyer (Columbia Law School), and the prosperous son of a German Jewish veteran killed in the American Civil War fighting for the Confederate Army. On the stand Pierpont Morgan proved a most willing and cooperative witness "unfailing polite and frank when it came to giving testimony". Susie Pak observes, "Fundamentally, he acted like someone in charge, and he was not afraid to name names or be held accountable unlike many of the other witnesses." George Baker, 73, had a harder time of it, naturally unable "to remember everything". Jacob Schiff proved to be a stunning if not impeccable example of banking stewardship and disposed to exalting the "honor" and "moral responsibility" of the "gentlemen" bankers and attributing their success to individual freedom and character. "We do not make brains," he said. "Brains are created by a higher Power." And he admonished the Committee, declaring, "I would not limit, in any instance, individual freedom in anything, because I believe the law of nature governs that better than any law of man." In the shadows behind the scene Schiff is secretly funding the Bolshevik revolutionaries to overthrow the Russian autocracy and destroy an entire empire. The Morgan partners grew to detest the "beast" Untermeyer; Tom Lamont preferred to have him smeared as an "irresponsible muck-raker". Suzie Pak describes Untermeyer "by all accounts, a formidable prosecutor". (S. J. Pak, 26-31)

The Fed then bankrolled the First World War making some choice firms and people fantastically rich and positioned and just long enough for the Americans to get in and clean up while suffering a comparably minimal loss of American lives while forcing Germany to prolong the war until Wilson and the Allies could impose their postwar reconstruction plans for New World Order imposed on the vanquished by their glorious terms of unconditional surrender. Although "HPD" was not Yale and so never eligible to be "tapped" by Yale's ultra-secret society Skull & Bones, his son Henry Pomeroy Davison, Jr., ("Trubee"), and grandsons Endicott and Daniel ("Coty" & "Danny") continued the elite tradition of privileged leadership otherwise known as America's division of the classes as two more of its emboldened initiates. Trubee later becomes chief of personnel at the CIA; eventually the two grandsons serve distinguishedly a few years a few feet across the hall from Yale University President Kingman Brewster as the President of Yale Corporation, and president and chairman of London's posh banking firm Morgan Grenfell, senior partner of Morgan Guaranty in New York, before his crowning achievements as head of US Trust. The latter quixotic younger brother "Danny" Davison who this author was privileged to know, distinguished his exemplary career with a particular uncanny brilliance marked by a quick stringent, at times baffling wit, always elegant, and extremely secretive with an unobtrusive and casual demeanor evolved over a lifetime of smoothly mixing with eccentric aristocrats and royal cousins on the other side of the Atlantic. (Kathleen Burk, *Morgan, Grenfell 1838-1988: The Biography of a Merchant Bank*, NY: Oxford Univ. Press, 1989)

Danny Davison also married a distinguished woman, a refugee, but not an ordinary Russian refugee of the 1917 Russian Revolution, and there thousands of them, that is, the lucky ones who managed to escape the Bolsheviks and prosper in exile. Yes, this was a very special Russian, a Tsarist princess, Katusha, of the vastly rich Sheremetyev landowning aristocrats. Their name is since immortalized as Moscow's very own Sheremetyevo airport. Great stories of intrigue and fabulous wealth followed the pleasures and sorrows of the Count and Countess Sheremetyev and their life in their magnificent residence that vividly conjures up illustrious associations with the court of Catherine II when Uvarov once discharged from the Empress's bedroom is honored with the rank of regimental commander of the Grenadier Guards back "in Petersburg's dawning days, soon after a branch of that 'nameless little river', the Neva...", as Serena Vitale so graciously enlightens us in her book *Pushkin's Button.* When the Count died in 1835 the poet Pushkin (Alexander Sergeevich Pushkin), the most outrageously beloved bard of Czar Alexander and foe of his Ministry's official censors added to his notoriety– Russia's "greatest man of literature" and "the most famous poet it has ever had"– when he attempts to plunge into the fortune of the soon-to-be-deceased Dmitry Nikolaevich Sheremetev, only that the young Count stages a remarkable recovery after a near fatal illness and much ceremony, and returns to his domaine of "600,000 desyatins (about 1,627,000 acres and a couple of hundred thousand serfs". (Serena Vitale, *Pushkin's Button,* Transl. A. Goldstein and J. Rothschild, NY: Farrar, Straus and Giroux, 1995, 127-32. Pushkin dies in 1837 after a duel to defend his wife's honor; he survived for 36 hours, time enough to receive a pardon and blessing from the Tsar and assurances "that his wife and little children would be properly cared for. Witnesses are astounded when 50,000 people "of all classes" visited his funeral chamber.)

For his part, the older grandson of HPD, Endicott Peabody Davison, "Coty", married President Bill Taft's grand-niece, Jane Ingalls. No coincidence there; US President Taft's father was co-founder of Skull & Bones in 1832. (*Life* publishes for June 2012 a special issue, "The Hidden World of Secret Societies"; on the last page dedicated to Skull & Bones, with 1920 member page taken from the yearbook. The *Life* story has no story. It is just more disinformation revealing no secrets. We are not the secret society, they are. Fifteen names of men are listed under the S & B "322" logo. Three of the names I know very well: Henry Pomeroy Davison, Jr., David Sinton Ingalls and Henry Robinson Luce. Dave Ingalls was the flying ace in the First World War when he volunteered to fly with the British fighter pilots before America entered the war. He was the first ace in the US Navy. His friend Trubee helped create the Yale Unit, fighter pilots under the command of their own squadron before the US Army was in the air. Jane Ingalls married one of his three sons "Coty" Davison; their son David Ingalls Davison graduated Groton and Yale ('77), not a S&B member nonetheless is a lawyer and flying enthusiast, a staunch Democrat and the most modest and generous person who I have the pleasure of knowing since our youthful days together at Yale. Janie is still very active, recently celebrating her birthday at 87 in 2013, a lover of horses agile and fearless in the saddle, and one of the most kind, and fun-loving people you would ever wish to know. If you visited Wikipedia for Skull & Bones in July 2013, reader we find the S&B photo for the Yale Senior year and there standing in the back row of a group of men for their private group photo besides George Bush, next to the grandfather clock, a few inches from his right ear is Endicott Peabody Davison, son of Trubee. But reader be assured none of this seems to matter anymore, unless as we know from the revealing connections of the Consortium Holodomor story then these names printed on the Skull & Bones card are more than hieroglyphics. These people are real with loving families. You have to have a more than just a name. Or just a face as with the Wikipedia photo with no other name than George Herbert Walker Bush.

Remember what Graham Greene says in *The Comedians*: "War is Horror. Horror is real." Otherwise all you have is more of the same disinformation. The Davisons I know are all fine people with families who value traditions as well as their friends and their privacy. It is difficult even painful to imagine that the goodness of innocence is so easily corruptible (if it even exists at all) by the evil of politically ignorant and criminal events and no excuse for good intentions. In Paris my friend from SAIS told me, "History is what it is and that's what it." (He was head of the French head of the Gallop pollsters of public opinion). Yes, reader, the Holodomor as these men of Skull & Bones lived not so long ago. William

Faulkner wrote, "The past is never dead. It's not even past." Remember reader children never choose their parents and the wholeness of the spirit that lives in them and in all of us is greater than the sum of the parts. And the powers that be and the forces in play in that time of the Holodomor are still very much a part of the historicity of our lives and the future.

A year before the war JP Morgan sails away from his banking fortress megapolis never to return, to Europe, convokes the spirits of the ancient Pharaohs at the pyramids in Egypt (and collecting priceless artifact), kneels in prayer to his God with the Pope and, then still in Rome, quietly passed away in his sleep March 1913. H. P. Davison, assisted principally by Tom Lamont, takes the helm and single-handily transforms the Morgan financial colossus into an even greater empire to secure war loans and fill the Fed vaults with British gold. Once America was officially in the Great War (the Consortium gang had been trading in contraband munitions throughout the so-called neutrality years) Davison then stoically carried the banner freedom and democracy as chairman of the American Red Cross raising millions of dollars from American workers in Liberty Loan fund-raising drives. "HPD" did more than any other American to finance the First World War, and, it can well be argued, to facilitate the popular mobilization of the American masses to support it behind the lines and in the trenches.

In her chapter on the Morgan bank's syndication of war loans during the First World War Suzie Pak (*Gentleman Bankers*) marks December 1914 when "the House of Morgan became the buying agent for the British and French governments, essentially 'coordinating the vast and growing war purchases both countries were making in the United States'." In fact, the bank was busy straight away that late summer in England arranging the financing for the war with gold shipments from London to New York assuring the extension of armed conflict into total world war so that by 1915 Morgan through its syndicated banking network floated a $500 million Anglo-French loan "organized by Henry P. Davison and managed by Edward R. Stettinius, whom Thomas Lamont recruited" into their firm. By January 1, 1917, four months before America officially enters the war, with the Russian Czar doomed and Davison head of the American Red Cross war lobby, the Morgan war loans total over a billion in financial securities marketed by their partners and friends on Wall Street. This is how it was. Not for the wives and children to know. Dollar-a-year patriots, outstanding men of distinction with cigars and pipes in low voices behind closed doors protected from public scrutiny in their private dens and members only clubs and dining rooms. Exterminators and destroyers of the old world take their turn in the grab for empire. (Suzie J. Pak, *Gentlemen Bankers The World of JP Morgan*, Cambridge, MA: Harvard Univ. Press, 2013, 112)

Once the Romanov Russian Czar abdicated and was out of the way, president Wilson joined the Allies and Harry Davison on whispering terms with the Windsor Palace as well as the Bank of England micromanaged from his downtown Manhattan office on Wall Street the American Red Cross spy mission to St. Petersburg and Moscow diverting millions of dollars for the Bolshevik coup staged by Lenin, Trotsky and his revolutionary Bolshevik troubadours after Lenin's arrival at Finland station in a sealed train from Germany.

Writer Eustace Mullins in his book *Secrets of the Federal Reserve* (1983) astutely observed in Wilson's April 1917 war message "an incredible tribute to the Communists in Russia who were busy slaughtering the middle class in that unfortunate country." Wilson declares, "Assurance has been added to our hope for the future peace of the world by the wonderful and heartening things that have been happening in Russia. Here is a fit partner for a League of Honor." The war had dragged on too long. By the time the Americans arrived to fight a few months snatching up the pieces of falling empires like fruit falling from the tree, there remained a lot of mopping up to do.

After four years of war, by 1918 Europe is in ruins and on the brink of a widespread disease sweeping over borders and out of control. Russia has fallen into a state of utter disintegration. The Romanov monarchy is on the rocks; the center could not hold. After the sudden Armistice Wilson sends US troops to intervene in Russia's Civil War. America's brief exodus overseas leaves 108,000 dead US soldiers, with the League of Nations battered in disgraced Versailles negotiations and a scandal of secret treaties. Repudiated morally and politically the President falls seriously ill and retreats into seclusion at home with his wife in the capital. For the 1924 presidential contest and with Harding Republicans, burned and tarnished by highly publicized notoriety over the oil corruption deals of the Teapot Dome navy oil lease scandal, HPD is considered a GOP favorite for the Presidency but he collapses from a brain tumor and is gone. (E. Mullins, *Secrets of the Federal Reserve*, 1983, 85; G. Colby, *DuPont Dynasty*)

HARRIMAN AND MORGAN CREATE THE SOVIET RUSSIAN BANK

From the beginning, Morgan's role in the Russian-Ukrainian nightmare was huge. Averell Harriman and Morgan's Guaranty Trust together created the first Soviet international bank, Ruskombank. A vice president at the Morgan bank Guaranty Trust, Max May came from Chicago's First National Bank, in 1904, and was a director at Ruskombank. Max May became its first vice president in charge of its foreign operations. Max May was also an associate of the key Nazi powerbroker and Morgan banker Hjalmar Horace Greeley Schacht. During the apogee of the Holodomor in early 1933 Schacht emerges as the cornerstone of German rearmament and Hitler's rise to power. FDR liked to laugh retelling the story when Schacht comes to the White House weeping on the President's desk and begs FDR to save Germany; after Roosevelt dies that spring 1945 Harriman will warn President Truman that the Russian "barbarians" will have to be held back from sweeping over all of Europe.

This astounded author-engineer-historian Antony C. Sutton who wrote about but never really experienced firsthand the secretive Yale Bones culture. Sutton writes, "an American banker under guidance of a member of The Order had a key post in a Soviet bank!"

Averell Harriman is the closest link to Stalin and Churchill after Hitler invaded in 1941 the key negotiator handling the administration's Lend-Lease supply line to Great Britain and the Red Army. The significance of this unfolds in the US-Soviet politics of famine from the fall of the Imperial Czarist Empire and the return to Moscow of Lenin and Trotsky.

Other researchers and writers stayed in the loop becoming awed and inspired to pull back the curtains on these makers of mega profits and doom. In his article "Building Communism" in *American Opinion* (1975) Gary Allen writes, "After the Czar abdicated, Leon Trotsky was sent to Russia from New York on an American passport supplied by Woodrow Wilson. The interim Socialist boss in Moscow was A.F. Kerensky who spent the remainder of his days in New York. When he died he left behind sealed records to be opened after 1987 detailing the 'conspiratorial organizations modeled on freemasons lodges' which were responsible for the revolution. It is now clear that an arcane conspiracy, backed by finance capitalists in the United States, has been behind the Reds from the beginning." But 1987 came and went and nothing apparently was revealed. (Gary Allen, "Building Communism", *American Opinion*, Dec. 1975)

The Ukrainian Holodomor had all the trappings of the conspiratorial plot. Only it was much more than that. Murder by man-made famine, by deportations of the peasants in below freezing conditions to Arctic death camps, sent to work on giant industrial projects from Magnitogorsk, to the White Sea Canal, the Volga Canal was normal business under "dekulakisation". Solzhenitsyn described the chaos and devastation caused by eradication of the peasants already occurring in 1929, a scene repeated in all directions and once prosperous villages during the next five years.

Solzhenitsyn wrote, "Great streams of deported peasants poured through Archangel, and for a time the whole town became one big transit prison. ... This was how they lived in that plague-stricken winter. They could not wash. Their bodies were covered with festering sores. Spotted fever developed. People were dying. Strict orders were given to the people of Archangel not to help the special *resettlers* (as the deported peasants were now called)! Dying peasants roamed the town, but no one could take a single one of them into his home, feed him, or carry tea out to him: the militia seized local inhabitants who tried to do so and took away their passports. A starving man would stagger along the street, stumble, fall – and die. But even the dead could not be picked up (beside the militia, plainclothesmen went around on the lookout for acts of kindness). At the same time market gardeners and livestock breeders from areas near big towns were also being expelled, whole villages at a time (once again – what about the theory that they were supposed to arrest exploiters only?), and the residents of Archangel themselves dreaded deportation. They were afraid even to stop and look down at a dead body. (There was one lying near GPU headquarters, which no one would remove.) They were buried in *organized* fashion: by the sanitation department. Without coffins, of course, in common graves, next to the old city cemetery on Vologda Street – out in open country. No memorials were erected."

(A. I. Solzhenitsyn, "The Peasant Plague", *The Gulag Archipelago, 1918-1956, An Experiment in Literary Investigation*, v. 3, V-VII, 361-2)

In order to accomplish their goals, the Anglo-American Consortium (call it what you will, Order, Elite,– don't be confused, it's the same) mixed public policy with private business to profit themselves and corporate shareholders with vast holdings in the companies they controlled. Strategic calculations for short and long-term objectives were the business of the day, and the livelihood of generations of the elite. Their goal was always the same, relentlessly pursued in secrecy and fear to control the accumulation of unlimited power and enormous wealth. And by controlling the public debate from generation to generation – they still do— through a web of ownership of media conglomerates, private institutes, foundations and universities, the depth and magnitude of their penetration of power stretched throughout society virtually unchecked. This Consortium linked first by method and access to the centralized national banks of England and France, then used the Fed's system of select banks make and finance war, trade in armaments and supplies with belligerents, mobilize national armies, negotiate peace conditions, scheme and intrigue launching reconstruction plans for the conflicts that follow.

Make no mistake about it. There is a ruling class in America. It is mercilessly proud and arrogant when it needs to be but for the most part when seen in public members of the ruling class take special pleasure to appear at ease engendering a consensus of fusion between the national and local community. Of course, with the agenda is always set to serve their ends of continuity of power and control over the comfortable masses. They like to wear a happy smile while appearing unabashfully benign and innocuous, even folksy. The reality is different behind the mask. These same families of extraordinary and exponential wealth assumed the social status that only that kind of wealth can afford and for whom hundreds of thousands dollars are counted as nickels and dimes. They comprise the class that rules and governs, long thought to have been a thing of the past, superseded by the proliferation of fortunes and wealth, but actually meticulously maintained in career positions filtered and selected to advance their agenda decided by their fathers and their fathers, going back generations. In so doing the very rich and chosen few protected and extended their invaluable legacy of wealth, possessions and social reputations. And get away with murder by proxy.

While a relatively miniscule number of members of the capitalist Consortium blithely calculated and accumulated vast fortunes, the Consortium reduced Nazi Germany and the USSR to the status of slave-like client states, vassal proxies, and destroyed the lives of millions of people forever lost in an abyss of ignorance. Stalin reduced the Ukrainians to a statelessness torpor of animal existence. What did they reap in the deal? Nothing but misery, hardship, famine and death inflicted on them by Stalin, Hitler, and Mussolini, all favorite clients of the Anglo-American Consortium of the West. Diplomats and governments they represent ought to be made to pay for their crimes. But how? The Consortium controlled the national and international courts. Do you really believe today they do not? Take your blinders off! The American masses retreat further into passive indifference, bloated inertia unable to march on Washington after the Bush election coup or mount a serious movement of dissent against the give-away of trillions of unaccountable government dollars to the same the banks responsible for the financial meltdown in 2008-2009.

For the supporters of Stalin's social transformation of Bolshevik Russia into a totalitarian monopoly trading with the West the gain far outweighed the cost counted in dollars, not human lives US relations with Stalin was paved in American dollars and cheap Soviet slave labor without which the investment would not ever have been possible. In fact by 1928 the bankrupt Soviet economy starved of foreign exchange would take only Red gold and dollars to pay for Stalin's crash Five-Year Plan for national industrialization. During six years of the two Five-Year Plans (July 1929-January 1, 1934) the number of prisoners incarcerated in labor camps increased 23 fold. (Sistema ispravitel'no-trudovjkh lageri v SSR 1923-1960, 35)

By 1928 Stalin is ready to resume the social and economic revolution in Russia. A "Five-Year Plan" is announced to replace the NEP program for a state capitalist monopoly under Soviet communism. From the beginning Stalin's primary objective of each plant is to satisfy military requirements. Sutton writes, "It is ironic, from the Western viewpoint, that contracts viewed as serving the cause of world peace (Henry Ford, for example, elected to build the Gorki tractor plant to advance peace) should have been utilized immediately for military purposes." The masses desired peace more than anything so the Consortium let them believe they had it. Rockefeller's publicist Ivy Lee used this double standard adopted by all public relations employees of private corporations to legitimate and morally condone their business relations with autocratic monopolies.

THE AMERICANIZATION OF SOVIET INDUSTRY

This was the Americanization of Soviet Industry. Industrial death camps and wheat fields as far as the eye could see but who in America heard the screams of raped, killed and exiled victims of the Soviet state communist system built with American and western technology, credits and loans? Ukrainians were targeted by Stalin because of their strong Slavic national and cultural ethnicity, a serious break-away threat of national resistance. The peasants hated the communists! Young children, old men– few were spared. Death scarred the fertile land with the tides of repression during three decades of Soviet terror. The Consortium had taken the former Russian empire with all its vast and mostly untapped resources, impoverished by institutionalized fear and mistrust, ingrained with centuries of serfdom and the lack of freedom intrinsic to Czarist bureaucracy, and controlled its fate in an arrangement where almost anything was permitted as long as the spies were kept at home. In three decades Tsarist Russia was transformed into a world superpower, a feat not possible without capital, technology and management expertise from the western Consortium players.

At what cost to human life? At what cost to human posterity?

The figures boggle the mind. The Terror-Famine led to even more terrible repressions – and denial. Stalin raised a great hue and cry claiming the whole party was in danger, having been "penetrated" by Trotsky's spies and foreign agents. Mass arrests, deportations to forced labor camps, and executions included not only the suspects, but also their families, supporters, friends and acquaintances. Guilt by association was reason enough for long prison terms or death. Soviet writer and a former prisoner of the Gulag Alexander I. Solzhenitsyn (b.1918) estimated that some 40 million Soviet citizens lost their lives under Stalin's rule. The *minimum* estimate, including the war, stands at 53 million, including World War II, estimated *at least* at some 27 million lives. However, the exact total number of those killed during collectivization, in the purges up to Stalin's death in March 1953, and the Second World War is disputed and may never be known. (A. I. Solzhenitsyn, *The Gulag Archipelago, 1918-1956*)

Even in Ukraine the name of Rockefeller carries legendary awe and fascination of an impossible dream. While the country slides back into "mafia-type post-communism" and the average salary stagnates under $400 a month the ordinary Ukrainian cannot imagine the capital wealth and power of that much money possessed by a single man. Perhaps, except for Bill Gates who has an uphill battle to end computer piracy where any student for less than two dollars can obtain a complete Microsoft Windows pirate copy CD.

The Rockefeller-Khrushchev story may be more fact than fiction. In 1963, a bad harvest year, it became clear that the central government had not managed to accumulate the reserves of grain required to resist the event of natural calamity. Did the Consortium Rockefeller gang push Khrushchev out during his precipitous departure?

There were frequent bread shortages in many parts of the Soviet Union. After the Patriotic War, in 1947, once again, as in the Holodomor thirties, long lines formed as bread sales were rationed in the gulag state. The southern parts of the country suffered terrible famine, especially, areas such as the Northern Caucasus and southern Ukraine.

Under Khrushchev the Soviet central government began massive purchases of grain from abroad draining available gold reserves. More than 13 million tons of grain are bought. Khrushchev will soon be severely attacked for it; in Stalin's time the citizens would simply have been left to swell up and die of starvation. But now Rockefeller and the Consortium have new players and a modified agenda. Khrushchev's Politburo opts to exchange gold for bread distancing himself and his government further from the crimes of Stalin.

The Holodomor grates at the memory of its surviving son who had participated in the Terror-Famine Genocide. The Great Patriotic War ends, the Red Army saves Moscow and takes Berlin, and in less than a decade the immortal and invincible Stalin is dead as a door and eulogized into myth and madness. Ironically Khrushchev's last desperate attempt to find a way out of the agricultural impasse is connected with the drought and the bad harvest of 1963. His hopes for the extensive development of agriculture through the use of the new lands, particularly in Kazakhstan and Siberia fail. The entire agricultural system has to be transformed. But in order for this to work agriculture had to be intensive even for a country as large and diverse as the USSR. The example of the United States, where 3.5 percent of the population produces enough not only to feed the country but to export huge quantities of food is reason enough that other more efficient methods promise a better way. To some extent Khrushchev hoped to duplicate the American experience, if not surpass it, but his approach is too bombastic and his methods are mechanically unsound. The differences between the two superpowers both economically and socially are so great that the peasant Premier grossly miscalculates the hunger for freedom of its people terrorized and living in a state of stunted growth and deprivation and fear.

Apparently safe in his lofty perch on top of Lenin's mausoleum in the Kremlin's Red Square, Stalin,– and here reader allow this reflection in reference to the work of the brilliant religious historian and philosopher Mircea Eliade – "consoled himself for the terror of History"– by transforming into an untouchable modern Asiatic despot. Shortly after the outbreak of the Second World War, FDR is obliged to let multimillionaire industrialist W. Averell ("Ave") Harriman oversee American military aid to the Moscow front. After the Nazi invasion in June 1941, FDR appoints Harriman with Harry Hopkins to run America's wartime Lend-Lease emergency war provisions program to London and Moscow and subsequently appointed him ambassador to help Stalin cross his last and final bridge, his Rubicon. After repulsing the German invasion, while insisting for years the West launch a second front, Stalin continued to benefit from massive American wartime equipment one half of which was available for postwar reconstruction and the Cold War. (re. "terror of History", "Mythologies of Memory and Forgetting", M. Eliade, *Myth and Reality*, 137)

In fact, any serious accounting the great Barbarossa invasion of Soviet Russia by Hitler's generals at the outset is horrifyingly extraordinary and the worst ever battle casualties of any war ever in the recorded history of mankind, well over half-million Russian losses in less than three weeks of fighting. That's more than the Americans lost in the entire Second World War of 1941 to 1945. For example, Chris Bellamy writes, "The 'border' or 'frontier' battles lasted from 22 June to 9 July in the Baltic (North-West Front) and Belorussian (Western Front) areas, and until 6 July in western Ukraine and, later, Moldova (the South-Western Front and Southern Front's Eighteenth Army). The average daily losses were 23,207 in Belorussia, against Army Group Centre, and 16,106 in Western Ukraine, against Army Group South, with some also falling to Ukrainian nationalists." To the Russians it is called the Great Patriotic War.

"The losses were terrifying. An attacking force, with only a modest superiority in numbers of men, and inferior in numbers of tanks, guns and aircraft, had been able to drive the defending Russians back between 300 and 600 kilometers and inflict irrecoverable looses – killed, prisoners and missing, officially numbered at 589,537 in between fifteen and eighteen days. According to that arithmetic, losing more than 44,000 men a day, how much longer could the Soviet Union last". Bellamy observes that in the first three weeks of combat the Wehrmacht had lost 92,120 or some 3.6 percent of its total strength, killing "one to twelve or thirteen, overall, but only one to five in the air" suffering "only a fraction – between a sixth or a seventh – of the Red Army, air force and NKVD casualties". (C. Bellamy, 206)

The economic industrial growth of the U.S.S.R, according to G. Warren Nutter's book, *The Growth of Industrial Production in the Soviet Union* (1962) in fact greatly benefited from the stimulus of those Consortium Lend-Lease provisions supplying the Soviets with *one-third* of its prewar industrial output. Separately, writers Sutton and Nutter both traced the emergence of the USSR from the utter destruction and ruin by the War with a powerfully devastating factor concealed in the apparent and immediate advantage assured them by America's Lend-Lease "pipeline agreement" providing that Lend-Lease supplies continued *after* the war through 1947 at a time of extreme postwar deprivation and outrageous repressions by Stalin who denied the good Russian people the fruits of their hard sacrifice and victory over Nazi fascism.

Sutton in a similar light concludes, "There is no question that the Soviets ended World War II with greater industrial capacity than in 1940 – in spite of the war damage – and on a technical parity with the United States." Furthermore, capital flows from the occupied countries significantly contributed to rebuilding the postwar Soviet economy. Soviet forces stripped and transported whatever they could salvage in the reconstruction effort. Sutton found that 25 percent of the economy of the USSR was destroyed by the Germans. Still, Russian factories "were far better off in terms of both capacity and technology by 1946 than before the war when at that time its steel production compared with 70 percent of the Americans. Destroyed facilities were more than replaced by debt repayments and Lend-Lease, and more, importantly, replaced with equipment 10 to 15 years more advanced." Nor were these observations overlooked by the British and American war strategists. (A. C. Sutton, *Western Technology and Soviet Economic Development 1917 to 1930*, Hoover Institution Press, Stanford Univ., CA. 345-6. v. II, 1968; G. Warren Nutter, *The Growth of Industrial Production in the Soviet Union*, Princeton, 1962)

LEND-LEASE: FDR'S SECRET WEAPON AND LIFE-LINE TO RUSSIA

In fact, Lend-Lease fit nicely into FDR's war strategy consistent with peacetime collaboration with the Soviet Union since the late twenties and well into the thirties. Bellamy writes that rather than Great Britain and Russia becoming straight-out allies, (Churchill only ever refers to the USSR as "Russia"), they engage as "co-belligerents", they both shared one common enemy and aim "to do Germany all the harm we can". Some British officers were more explicit and the idea sleeping in the same bed with the Russian Bolsheviks was less than fanciful "for the Russians are a dirty lot of murdering thieves themselves and double-crossers of the deepest dye. It is good to see the two biggest cut-throats in Europe, Hitler and Stalin, going for each other." (Remark of Lt. General Henry Pownall, Vice-Chief of the Imperial General Staff, Chris Bellamy, *Absolute War: Soviet Russia in the Second World War,* Knopf, 2007, 409, citing Pownall Diary, in Joan Beaumont, *Comrades in Arms: British Aid to Russia, 1941-45*, London: Davis Poynter, 1980)

"The Russians remained anxious that the British might now make a separate peace with the Germans," Chris Bellamy writes in *Absolute* War (2007), "although they reckoned, quite rightly, that the constant British quest for intelligence was to evaluate the length of the breathing space available before Germany smashed Russia and turned back against Britain." Stalingrad was the great turning point in the war. After the long siege destroying the city and their surrender Germany could never win. However, in the early days of the war, July 12, 1941 with the odds against him Molotov signs a vague mutual agreement with the astute British lawyer and avowed Marxist ambassador Sir Strafford Cripps – not a treaty– for war. They both needed the Americans if they were going to survive; anything less than an unconditional surrender with Germany would be fatal to either London or Moscow.

Bellamy writes, "the Americans were in a quite different position. From a geographical point of view, they had more secure – longer – communications with the western Soviet Union through Alaska and Siberia and allied sea routes through the Arctic Circle, north of Norway, Sweden and Finland and down to Russia through the White Sea to Arkhangel'sk and Murmansk, as well as the northern route through Turkey and Iran." Even after the US declared war on Japan Stalin is careful not to provoke the Japanese and considered invaluable Lend-Lease convoy shipments to Vladivostok "undesirable." Instead, Allied convoy ships sailed through German submarine infested waters to reach northern Russia. Of twenty four ships that sailed April 8, 1942 from Iceland bound for Russia only seven arrived, one sank and sixteen turned back. (C. Bellamy, 410-9)

Bellamy's contemporary book on Russia's strategic importance on winning the war against Germany is so far the best I have seen on the Lend-Lease aid program. In July 1941 Roosevelt proposed a three-nation committee with Hopkins and Anastas Mikoyan. Bellamy writes in his chapter "Grand Alliance":"Just after Barbarossa, an opinion poll showed that 54 per cent of those questioned opposed sending munitions to Russia." FDR promises Stalin "aid to the hilt" and tells the Soviet rep in Washington Comrade Umanskii he can be relied on for his request of $1.8 billion worth of guns, airplanes, ammunition and even an entire war producing industrial plant.

The three-day Moscow Conference takes place September 29 concluding that Great Britain would supply Moscow monthly beginning with "500 tanks, 300 anti-tank guns, plus aluminum, tin, lead molybdenum, cobalt, copper and zinc, and other 'equipment'. The US would supply 1,250 tons of toluol (toluene) – used to make high-grade aviation fuel – per month, and 100 tons of phosphorous, while the UK would supply $150,000 worth of (industrial diamonds). In fact, only half a million dollars' worth of aid arrived in November and December – 1 per cent of the amount promised." (C. Bellamy, 420-1. For sources on Lend-Lease Bellamy refers to Robert Hugh Jones, *The Road to Russia: US Lend-Lease to the Soviet Union,* (Oklahoma, 1969). Bellamy cites as principal source material, "Wartime International Agreements: Soviet Supply Protocols," US Department of State, Publication 2759, European Series 22, Washington DC, 1948)

Russia might easily have fallen in 1942 had it not been for the American aid Furthermore, the Japanese, after impressed by Moscow's fierce defense, opt not to attack the Soviet Union and instead concentrate on the expansion in China, Southeast Asia and the Pacific, and so fall into FDR's trap for a first-strike against the Americans.

Queried by Molotov, in London in May, Churchill replied that the British Empire and the United States together would defeat Nazi Berlin. By that time the Russians had already lost "their entire prewar army in 1941 – millions of men and women, the equivalent of a small nuclear attack". On August 12, 1942 Churchill lands at Moscow Central Airport on Leningradskii Prospekt. Stalin doesn't understand English, and Englishmen less. Due to mechanical problems obliging his advisers Commanding General A. Wavell (postwar Viceroy of India sacked by Attlee in 1947), Sir Alan Brooke and Sir Alexander Cadogan to turn around back to Tehran, Churchill is left virtually on his own, as he prefers, and works out details with Harriman.

Lend-Lease proved to be a lifeline not only for the USSR but also for the West contributing a significant difference in the progress of the Soviet armies against Hitler's armies. As he had contained the importance of western aid in its industrial and military preparations for war, although it constituted about 15 per cent of the total equipment used by the USSR Stalin and Party leaders tried to play down the role of wartime Lend-Lease.

In particular, almost one-half million American trucks were delivered to the USSR to aid its war effort. The Ukrainian T-34 tanks with their wide tracks and the American-made Studebaker trucks transporting Katushya rocket launchers rallied the Red Army against the highly trained Wehrmacht Panzer forces. Gregorovich's findings agree with the account that the USA supplied the USSR with "6,430 planes, 3,734 tanks, 104 ships and boats, 210,000 vehicles, 3,000 anti-aircraft guns, 245,000 field telephones, gasoline, aluminum, copper, zinc, steel and five million tons of food. This was enough to feed an army of 12 million every day of the war. Britain supplied 5,800 planes, 4,292 tanks, and 12 minesweepers. Canada supplied 1,188 tanks, 842 armoured cars, nearly one million shells, and 208,000 tons of wheat and flour. The USSR depended on American trucks for its mobility since 427,000 out of 665,000 motor vehicles (trucks and jeeps) at the end of the war were of western origin." (A. Gregorovich, *Forum Ukrainian Review*, No. 92, Spring 1995. Scranton, PA; John Mosier's *Deathride* (2010) has a unique reassessment of Soviet military numbers and effectiveness against a superior mechanized Nazi Wehrmacht; Max Hasting, *Armageddon,* 2004)

In Hitler's petulant illusion for a quick victory by late November 1941, the Germans had planned to feed and fuel their war machine with resources plundered from the Ukraine. "The first German 'Military-geographical study of European Russia' was completed by 10 August 1940," Bellamy writes. "The main targets were Ukraine, which produced 90 per cent of the USSR's sugar beet, 60 per cent of its coal, 60 per cent of its iron and 20 percent of its wheat, plus Moscow, the capital, and Leningrad. ... the competing attractions for these objectives play havoc with the selection and maintenance of Hitler's aim." (C. Bellamy, 168)

US RECOGNITION & DOLLARS FOR STALIN

FDR's recognition of the Soviet Union was the ultimate death blow to the Ukrainians, their *coup de grace*. The two major flows of financial aid and technological assistance came from the West, but this book is not so much concerned with the wartime contribution as with the prewar input from 1930-34 and the influential strategic economic and political relationship that preceded. This occurred during the same time as the famine-terror and extermination of the Ukrainians. How it exactly fit into FDR's global war plans is disturbing as it effected every individual and group decision that was concerned with FDR's Russian policy. If it was not a *quid pro quo* sealed by official diplomatic ties in the recognition deal in November 1933 between FDR and Stalin, then how do we account for the benign and overt censorship by both leaders, and by the western press as well as by Stalin's communist-controlled propaganda media, the State Department– at the time and ever since– and eye-witness accounts of American professors from the most prestigious universities.

For the hundred millions of Russian citizens in the former Czarist Empire, the recognition deal stifles their hopes for freedom and doomed them to an oblivion masterminded by Stalin and paid for and bought by Roosevelt and the all-powerful men of the Consortium.

The 1933 Roosevelt-Stalin recognition deal is packed with intention and earth-shaking consequences. Official diplomatic recognition of the Soviet Union in the grip of Stalin's regime of tyranny is the most important foreign policy decision in the first year of FDR's first of four consecutive terms in office. Not only does it set the stage for cooperation and alliance during the inevitable war but it will influence the future of America for the generations to come leaving no American or Russian unaffected, and certainly no surviving Ukrainian. The crisis in Kiev of January 2014 is unequivocable testimony to that as the Ukraine problem turns violent putting to the test the grip of the Yanukovych-Putin coalition.

Furthermore, it begets the question of the responsibility of the Roosevelt administration and the Consortium cronies in the State Department for complicity in the Holodomor as well as an accessory of a totalitarian regime of mass murder? In view of the outcome of the war and American hegemony over nuclear power these questions may appear irrelevant, if not utterly distasteful to the Western observer.

But what is to be said for the problem when world leaders let people starve to death, cover up the facts and deceive the public well in advance of the crisis, and do nothing to stop it? Are the leaders guilty of complicity in the crime beyond their own national borders? And then, after a round of toasts, turn and shake hands with the murderer! Of course diplomats are all protected by diplomatic immunity. After all, such privilege is the cardinal law of civilization. Diplomats also protect the nation's secrets, and working hand in hand with the "free" press, they write their memoirs, invent history, and cook the culture fed to the masses in a ritual act of daily national consumption.

Few today contest the facts that prove America helped construct Nazi fascism and the Soviet totalitarian colossus. Of course interpretations and definitions are mixed deliberately with academic and political motives. One destroyed the other. Both exterminated populations. Holocaust literature occupies shelves in America's public libraries. Yet it is rare to find a single citation about the fate of the Ukrainians and the Holodomor in the American history textbook. Ukraine has finally wrenched its independence from the Soviet Union. It is hoped that a new awareness may forever throw back the veil of silence. And as the Soviet historians had to constantly revise their textbooks so too does this come to pass in America as the new revelations endure and replace old ones and truth takes another swing at persistently recurring mythologies.

Even Britain's reputable historian A. J. Taylor reconstructs history as the hapless result of inept and bungling diplomats. But diplomats are no more than the messengers and communicators of policy than the mailmen who deliver the mail write the letters. War is a deliberate, carefully planned policy of a particular international strategy. It may be wrong, prepared for and managed by incompetents, and destined to fail, but to characterize it simply as "a mistake" is to paint the sky black. It's a "mistake" only for the losers, in this case, Hitler's national fascists at war with Soviet Russia's communists. In the "winner takes all" scenario, mistakes belong to the enemy. But that's too easy a reduction and obscures vision.

This was true especially in the world of Soviet Russia where under Stalin's regime it was a crime against Mother Russia to escape alive from the Germans! Betrayers! Sons of Kulaks! Solzhenitsyn's worst nightmare. Heroic simple soldiers discharged from the Red Army in disgrace! Shot, or imprisoned in labor death camps and a fate for many worse than death. In that upside down world vision was obscured, totally. Of course historians are more discreet, and devious when they need to be.

A. J. Taylor writes, "She had still far to go: her population was still impoverished, her resources were hardly tapped. But Germany had not much time if she was to escape being overshadowed, and still less if she hoped to seize the Soviet Ukraine. Here again, it would have made sense for Hitler to plan a great war against Soviet Russia. But, though he often talked of such a war, he did not plan it. German armaments were not designed for such a war. … The Germans had to improvise furiously when they went to war against Soviet Russia in June 1941; and they failed to achieve a quick decisive victory there largely because they had altogether neglected to prepare transport for a war of this nature. In the end, it is hard to tell whether Hitler took the project of war against Soviet Russia seriously; or whether it was an attractive illusion with which he hoped to mesmerize Western statesmen. … The war of 1939, far from being premeditated, was a mistake, the result on both sides of diplomatic blunders." If you believe that establishment rubbish then you will believe just what the Consortium people want – more entertainment and ridiculous fantasy. Weird is cool for the Consortium hypsters. (A. J. Taylor, *The Origins of the Second World War*, NY: Atheneum, 1962)

MODERN UKRAINE: FROM REMEMBRANCE TO NATIONAL RESURGENCE

In daily news broadcasts from Kiev heard around the world thousands of people representing a new generation of Ukrainians occupied the streets in protest of the 2004 presidential election fraud. This author was there on the scene with international journalists and Canadian election observers. The Ukrainians were trying to come to terms with their recent history, with one foot stepped in the past, and the other in the present taking them to a future without much of a clue and less certain who or what is in control of their destiny.

Post-Soviet Ukraine is riddled with corruption. Official government deception prevailed under the banner of democracy and an uncertain market economy severely weakened by the 2008 global financial downturn. But in 2004, pro-West politicians seized center stage at Independence Square and surfed the waves of peaceful protest in the cold rain and snow and seduced a nation hungry for change with rock music and popular slogans of hope.

I joined a tour across the country, twenty cars of the Pora (громадянська партія ПОРА/ "Its time!") caravan of election observers from city to city meeting increasing numbers of men, women and children day and night who braved the freezing winter in solidarity, sharing stories of corruption by officials of the old regime. With a coordinated organization that impressed this outsider, young people squeezed into hundreds of improvised tents on Khreshchatyk Street, Kiev's Champs Elysées. A national outpouring of support maintains a permanent vigil at Independence Plaza in the center of the city. Days turned into weeks then months of occupation. Young women set up makeshift soup kitchens and served *borsch* and bread and coffee or tea in sub-freezing snow, and vodka and cognac flowed freely while couples snuggled in their sleeping bags to keep warm. An unmistakable upsurge of freedom enthused the spirit of liberation in the air as a new generation of Ukrainians seized the opportunity to reject their Russian masters that had drained Ukraine of ninety percent of their economy.

The tension over inaugurating a genuine revolutionary change in the course of daily life was exhilarating; at any moment a new announcement declared more support for the protest movement. A lively spirit of common fellowship exuded throughout the city. Truckloads of plain-clothed Russian soldiers were rumored to have clandestinely entered Kiev. All kinds of speculation circulated on the streets about their intentions. Were they agents-provocateurs? Was President Kushma implicated in the killing of journalist going to stay out of the fight or force a violent repression and bloodshed?

An outbreak of violence was expected at any moment. It was said most of the men in the protest were armed but few dared to show their weapons. A leader in the radio press station which sat like a nest on a steel scaffold blaring out rock music with intermittent news announcements stopped me on the stairway and raised his coat to reveal a pistol tucked under his belt. "The people are ready", he said.

But the real revolution was not to be. Students lacked leaders and the mass movement mentality forged from years of organized discipline. Where were the student leaders? There weren't any. This observer was amazed to find that there was no national underground student organization or movement in position ready to defy the government leaders steeped in corruption. It was all too easy from across the dividing lines for the veteran political leaders of the mainstream center to cross the bridge defended by the green youthful protagonists and snatch victory and call it their own.

In 2005 when new president Viktor Yushchenko took office, his face freshly scared from an attempt to kill him with poison, and named his prime minister the firebrand opposition leader Ulia Tymoshenko to form the new government. Dressed in expensive Paris fashions and with her blonde hair coiffed in the traditional style of a Ukrainian maiden, and praised for her defiant embrace of democratic values for a new Ukraine, Tymoshenko overnight became a world celebrity. In the spirit of legitimate and hard-fought victory she effusively thanked her supporters, occupied office and chose her ministers putting politics above consensus. Yushchenko fragile government was doomed.

The protesters disbanded for the Christmas holidays and returned to their village homes and warm apartments to get drunk. After the New Year hangover, political turmoil seized the parliament. Within a year the bright orange banners faded. Fist-fights broke out in parliament caught on national television. It became apparent that power had merely shifted the national debate for reform from the street to the corrupt political institutions of the old regime entrenched for decades.

A YOUNG GENERATION SCREWED: ROCK KILLS THE YOUTH REVOLUTION

The fight was bitter. Cronies of the old regime are desperate. What else could they do? Jobs are scarce and they have to eat too! In less than a year the protesters who had forced the politicians into the streets and disgraced in full view of the world found themselves screwed by the "Orange Revolution" of 2004. Or, by a "revolution" concocted in the media for the press by the West and its organizers inside Ukraine, a huge rock music spectacle televised abroad. In less than five years the old regime had retaken power. Change seems too slow, if at all.

The Old Guard had left only to come back stronger. Ulia Tymoshenko, darling of the Orange Revolution, was sentenced to seven years for a crooked deal over Russian natural gas and taxing her Ukrainians with higher prices, banned from public office for an additional three years, and levied a $190 million fine. In 2012 she went on a hunger strike protesting beatings by guards and a lack of medical care. After European countries boycotted a political reunion, in Kiev, German Chancellor Angela Merkel called Ukraine a "dictatorship" similar to Belarus. Accusations of alleged government corruption by President Yanukovich's clique including two sons who managed to become among the richest men in the country have stalled an IMF emergency loan of $16 billion and explains Yanukovich's warm invitation to election oversight by foreign observers.

Putin's re-election as President for another term and his tough stance towards "Little Russia" augers badly for Ukraine in decline and its economic independence severely tied to Russian oil and natural gas. With the "Orange Revolution" totally discredited and Putin flexing his muscles, support for the Holodomor suffered a new crisis of national identity. Amidst a steadily increasing percentage of capital and equity outflows leaving the country anti-Putin protesters promise to fight against a return to the corrupt old style of doing business.

As I write Tymoshenko suffers prolonged incarceration while Russia and Ukraine continue to flaunt international appeals for her release by the United States and the European Union. Ukraine's interior minister Yuriy Lutsenko and defense minister Valery Ivashenko were equally jailed on similar charges of abuse of office in a case supporters claim was politically motivated as Ukraine falls deeper into the grip of Russia's reactionary nationalist hardliners under Putin's control of the dreaded secret security forces (FSB), the former KGB. A report from the foreign affairs committee of the House of Commons in Great Britain released in October 2012 over the Khodorkovsky-Magnitsky affair in Putin's takeover of the Russian oil company, and, in particular, Sergei' Magnitsky's brutal death while in prison, declared that each year in Russia between 50 and 60 people die in pretrial detention facilities in Russia. At the same time the Russian Federal Penitentiary Service declared 107,800 deaths occurred in pre-trial detention in Russia.

LIFE AND DEATH IN "PUTANIA"

The consequences of denying truths that in turn betray the Spirit are never healthy. The megalomania of Putin's nationalist drive highlight his intention to control that too as witnessed by the attempt to imprison even the internal revolution of the Spirit and capture the emotions of the people. Putin appears content to removes all obstacles that threaten to stop him dragging Russia deeper into the darkness of a Stalinist-style state nationalism while plundering the national economy and country resources including Russia's 2% of world oil supply.

Corruption is a real, not virtual, condition a veritable state institution. Transparency International ranked this so-called "Putania" 143 in its 2011 survey of a total of 182 countries, tied with Belarus only slightly ahead of Ukraine (152) with Burma, North Korea and Somalia coming up last. It could hardly be worse. But then again, look what happened in 2013; the Nobel Peace laureate and indefatigable defender of the peoples' human rights against military oppression in Burma Aung San Suu Kyi made a triumphant return to power and takes a seat in Parliament where she can rekindle hope and stand up and lead her party against the Army's dictatorship and a chance to share in the world's prosperity.

So what does all this have to do with the Holodomor? Everything. As with the current political crisis, the Holodomor sadly falls into the abyss of politics and national identity. A life that follows knowledge and acceptance of truths instead of falsehood leads to understanding and compassion, and in this case that means a better chance for realizing positive change in a society that may prevent humanitarian tragedies in the future. Instead of facing courtrooms and confessing for their crimes, the corrupt cadre played musical chairs. His presidency may be easily forgotten but Viktor Yushchenko earned honors for remembering the Holodomor as a national day of mourning for the victims of Soviet persecution. However, contrary to overwhelming evidence, Yanukovich adopted the pro-Stalinist line of Putin and Russian hardliners to dismiss the Holodomor as a Genocide against Ukraine.

Archival film, photographs and documents resurface daily on national TV and challenge the memory and will of Ukrainians not to forget the tragedy that traumatized the country. In Kiev in the fall 2006 I watched as the news announced that 5,000 more documents have been found and declassified attesting to Stalin's absolute repression, and diverting food relief away from the stricken regions. What those documents do not reveal nor do those scarcely few books and conferences on the subject of the Terror-Famine is that those millions of Ukrainians who died in the worst Genocide of all time were sacrificed by the West as a political concession to Stalin. It's a fact. This was not simply the "cost" of doing business with Stalin. For God's sake if not for the Ukrainians – Oh, yes, these were godless heathens exterminating the Faithful! Only none of that weighs for the reactionaries.

During the Stalin era cost and price for the fascist capitalists no longer figures during the time of economic heyday and depression. There is another calculus at play. Soon the Nazis will go one step further to exterminate the Slavs as barbarians treated with less dignity than their vicious dogs. It was *quid pro quo.* Fascism for the fascists. It was that simple. And they were proud to say it. And all the while the devious Roosevelt and his gang of insiders rant about "freedom from fear", and transforming the country into an "arsenal for democracy".

THE GREAT GAME OF EMPIRE

The British writer Rudyard Kipling who Orwell called the "prophet of imperialism" inspired the politics of Empire-building into mainstream use as the "Great Game" in his novel *Kim* (1901) though the term may have first been used by an intelligence officer in the British East India Company. The ultimate goal is power and control. Stalin understood that in exercising expedient ruthless power against all his fellow Bolsheviks and eliminating them. FDR could afford to be more refined in his methods. Some people may think it cynical to have a partnership under this condition. Of course, Stalin and FDR left questions of evil and responsibility to the philosophers and priests. They, too, like the Columbia professor John Dewey (1859-1952), a pro-Communist academic philosopher and educator of "pragmatism", who for decades trained the elite in their universities to cultivate young minds endowed with social status, set the liberal mindset of a generation of Americans. Enthusiasts, like Dewey, could hardly have been entirely ignorant of the human costs of the Soviet "experiment," including hunger and bloodshed. Their engagement with Russia thus required a certain clinical detachment. Pro-communist liberals in academia set up the national debate of dissent within safe boundaries of the men in the Consortium who controlled public opinion.

Dissent in America is as harmless as children playing in a sandbox. Understand that these breeding grounds of language and philosophy constitute the very backbone of America's national "culture". In a telling remark, Dewey called the socialist state experiment "by all means the most interesting going on upon our globe– though I am quite frank to say that for selfish reasons I prefer seeing it tried out in Russia rather than in my own country." It's the Duranty pro-Stalin line in different words; in a different place, back home in an Ivy League university environment of the youth where the sons and daughters of the Consortium plan their careers. The Duranty-Dewey message is the same "you can't make an omelet without breaking eggs". But America's eggheads preferred to disregard the Russian costs while awaiting the universal benefits for the American Dream. For who else? Certainly not *them*. Not for the Ukrainians. Call it the "Birth of a Nation"; the Holodomor is the end of theirs.

As it were, while Stalinist apologists politicized universities and government circles from Chicago to Boston, Washington and Moscow may cite the noble fervor of revolutionary idealism striving to entrench the agenda of a "Cultural Revolution" necessary to build a new heroic society of communist socialism the dark reality of tyrannical absolutism in a few hard-pressed years shattered any illusionist dream that deviated from strict party conformity to the utility of party discipline under the Marxist-Leninist dictatorship enshrined in the Kremlin. Everything must serve the New Society of the Proletariat, the dictatorship, the people. Any deviation from the norm was stained as counter-revolutionary. The dissenter was a social deviant, a parasite, the "enemy of the people". Consortium plans for the reconstruction of soviet industry and agriculture under Stalin's iron fist would allow no blind spot there. Stalin's brand of totalitarianism was cast in fear and terror. From the beginning the peasants resisted with outrage and violence and they were smashed.

In the early thirties with support from the West Stalin emerges as FDR's most precious dictator to stop the German Nazis from taking all of Europe. But of course, the Soviet Russians might have defeated them first, and pushed them into the Atlantic Ocean before the Americans had time to launch their Operation Overlord, the Allied D-Day invasion in Normandy. There would have been no one to stop the Russians from taking vengeance on Napoleon and the French as any reader of *War and Peace* knows.

But long before the Normandy invasion there were the most serious national security issues of strategic importance for world order, and in particular European security and the future of a divided Germany, already decided by the American-Anglo Consortium. The Americans got their H-Bomb in the nick of time. Only a handful of insiders including General George C. Marshall, Henry L. Stimson and his Undersecretary Harvey Hollister Bundy could breath comfortably knowing Stalin could be restrained. The American-Anglo war planners had finally beaten Stalin then making his final assault to Berlin to claim the Russian victory. Stalin's forces raced through Eastern Europe and towards Japan in order to get there before the Americans. But the big bomb stopped the Red Army in its tracks and changed history for the next half century.

By the end of the Second World War, the strategy of fascist terror that swept away the Ukrainians in the early thirties gripped the entire world with the ultimate horror ever inflicted on mankind. The Atomic Bomb changed forever the nature of "The Game". America dropped not just one, but two A-Bombs, and after the massive fire-bomb air raids by American planes and crew that converted traditional wood homes of Tokyo into one giant fireball. That display of unmitigated destruction was also intended as a warning to Soviet Russia to stay out of Japan as well as Western Europe. But Stalin would soon have his A-Bomb too and the ensuing Cold War would deny its citizens freedom for decades to come. The Soviets successfully detonate their first A-Bomb on August 29, 1949 dubbed "Joe-1" by the Americans, a 22 kiloton blast at their Semipalatinsk test site in Kazakhstan. The nuclear arms race has begun. Three years later the Americans set off an even bigger blast, code name "Mike", a stunning success of ten megatons with a blast force of at least 700 Hiroshima bombs. A generation later when Kennedy faced down Khrushchev in October 1962 during the Cuban Missile Crisis "America's arsenal contained 3,000 nuclear warheads and nearly 300 missile launchers – far more than the Soviet Union's 250 warheads (including those in Cuba) and estimated 24 to 44 missile launchers", Seymour Hersh writes in *The Dark Side of Camelot* (1997).

One of my good friends from Yale is the grandson of one of the original few A-Bomb strategists, Harvey Bundy who as Stimson's right-hand man was part of the Manhattan Project secret management team for FDR's race to be first with the new super-weapon even though they calculated the Nazis had a two year head start. His son McGeorge Bundy miscalculated Soviet capacity and siding with the generals nearly pushed the world into nuclear oblivion but was overruled by the Kennedy brothers. Know your history reader; the historical record is a fact. In October 1962 Kennedy got the Soviet leader to agree to remove the missiles from Cuba and saved the world. A year later JFK is killed in a terrible conspiracy. For the Consortium the only thing sacred is money and power and their unrestricted right to have it.

The Americans were quick to exploit their victory in the East. The fire-bombing of a million Japanese civilians in 1945 had been planned with statistical analysis for General Curtis LeMay who commanded a bomber group and flew a lead plane by number-cruncher Robert S. McNamara, the future Secretary of Defense under Presidents JFK and Johnson and a chief architect in the early years of America's doomed war in Vietnam that killed millions of Vietnamese; then names of 57,939 American soldiers killed or missing in action are inscribed on two converging walls of black granite in the 1982 Vietnam War Memorial dedicated in Washington, DC, designed by Chinese-American student Maya Ying Li, a Yale graduate. In a press conference during his vice-presidential bid as a candidate in 1968 on the George Wallace ticket LeMay was unwilling to rule out the nuclear option in order to "win" the war in Vietnam. (Louis Menand, "Nuke of Hazard: Eric Schlosser's 'Command and Control'," *The New Yorker*, Sept. 30, 2013; Richard Rhodes, *The Making of the Atomic Bomb*, NY: Simon & Schuster, 1986, with an extensive bibliography)

After seven years at Defense, McNamara finally acted on his convictions backed by numbers that the war was a no-win catastrophe of epic proportions from the beginning; by 1968 after the Tet escalation he resigned. Johnson and the Consortium bosses grant him another thirteen years of virtually unlimited power as President of the World Bank. Meanwhile Harriman stays on the White House payroll in the shadows as Number One at State, a vital link to negotiations with Moscow. The younger McNamara wields power and influence that was the dream of princes. When he dies, in July 2009, *The NYT* published a photo of him smiling and sharing drinks with Joe Alsop, syndicated *Washington Post* columnist, CIA operative and confirmed hawk of the Vietnam War, who with his wife Susan Mary were formidable hosts tagged the "grand couple of Georgetown". Oddly, Alsop has been dead two decades, since 1989 but this ghost lives on. A more recent obit for CBS anchorman and icon Walter Cronkite revealed that he and McNamara, in fact, had served together on *The Washington Post's* board "a sinecure he was awarded after he had helped send some 50,000 Americans to pointless deaths." That sort of collusion irks Cronkite, a staunch anti-Vietnam critic who each day on the evening news with ritual vigor adjusts the rising body count of slain American soldiers while also on another tack he gives the *Post*'s Watergate reporting national coverage just days before President Nixon's reelection in 1972, then followed Nixon's downfall by public humiliation, near impeachment and resignation the following year.

THE CONSORTIUM ROAD - WAR PROFITS AT THE BANK

The Consortium war planners, however, never defeated the Russians or the Ukrainians who had survived the Second World War. That task was left to Stalin and his paranoid despotism. After their return from Germany and the West, renewed mass repressions and purges against the heroic Red Army denied the Russian people the fruit of their sacrifice and courage. There would be no cease-fire to Stalinist terror against the Soviet citizens. The fruit of victory was snatched away before they could taste it. Instead of returning as triumphant combatants, victory was exchanged for the virtues socialist sacrifice and "progress". (*The NYT*, "And That's Not the Way It Is", July 26, 2009)

During the first years of the Terror-Famine President Hoover's Secretary of State was Henry L. Stimson (1867-50). Stimson is the dean of the American diplomats. Yale, Class of 1888, Skull & Bones, with a mansion in Washington to rival the White House, an estate and stables on Long Island with all the right friends, the right clubs and the steady companionship of a wife at his side he adored. A crucial detail overlooked by most historians is the fact that the stoic Stimson becomes FDR's indispensable Secretary of War (1940-45); in fact it is Stimson who oversees the top-secret Manhattan Project to build an atomic bomb ordered by the President in June 1942 as liaison between Brigadier General Leslie Graves and FDR. Stimson was old school who had to do some fast catching up to read other gentlemen's mail from Japanese intercepts in the twenties over their Manchurian conquests to German and Soviet code-breakers before and during the WWII. Stimson would have been rudely surprised to know that the Soviets had intelligence reports from their spy network "Centre", that Roosevelt on June 20 had secretly conferred with Churchill during their meeting in Washington for an all-out joint effort on building the nuke. Soviet expert Christopher Andrew and Vasili Mitrokhin write in *The Sword and the Shield* (1999), "On October 6, following extensive consultation with Soviet scientists, the Centre submitted the first detailed report on Anglo-American plans to construct an atomic bomb to the Central Committee and the State Defense Committee, both chaired by Stalin." Before the year is out Stalin gave the order to beat the West and build the first Soviet atomic bomb. (C. Andrew and V. Mitrokhin, 114)

A full generation earlier and just a few years before the outbreak of the First World War Stimson had been the friend President William H. Taft and his Secretary of War. Few Americans today know that it was Stimson who returned to coordinate the nuclear destruction of Hiroshima and Nagasaki to end the Second World War. Taft too is Yale, Skull and Bones, Class of 1878, and son of Alphonso Taft, a co-founder in 1833 of that secret society. Overseas England was completing its anti-slavery campaigns to ban the slave trade and outlaw slavery itself throughout the British possessions with $100 million in compensation for the disenfranchised masters; all slaves were set free on August 1, 1834, three years before Victoria, barely eighteen, becomes Queen; three years later she marries cousin Albert who belonged to the same family of princes from which her mother came. For the rest of the century while Gladstone and Disraeli fought their parliamentary battles in the House of Commons under the reign of Queen Victoria, Taft, father of the future US president serves as the American Secretary of War in President Grant's notoriously corrupt administration, and later takes the post of Attorney General before his brief appointment as US Minister to Czarist Russia. Two major political operators of the Consortium who oversee America's emergence as an industrial and military superpower.

When in the early 1920s, the Federal Reserve Bank plays the decisive role in the re-entry of Russia into the international finance order, the law firm Winthrop and Stimson prove to be an effective main link between Russian and American bankers. Enter Bill Phillips. It is Stimson, and his assistant Phillips, who set up the secret path towards official relations with the USSR after the 1932 presidential election when US recognition of the Soviet Union comes as an anti-climax, the icing on the cake of US-Soviet relations with the American-Anglo Consortium of Morgan-Rockefeller-Harriman clan of businesses and banks, and in particular the National City Bank, predecessor to Citibank anxious to collect on its bad Russian loans.

Stimson is the Consortium's veteran standard-bearer in world diplomacy. All power in Washington ultimately passed through his office. It was the Stimson again in the summer of 1932 during the Geneva disarmament talks who first tips off Soviet foreign affairs Commissar Maxim Litvinov of Washington's readiness to revive recognition talks with the Soviet Union. Ten years later, with Stimson in position as America's Secretary of War, and only six months after the creation of the top-secret spy organization, the OSS (Office of Strategic Service) by FDR's personal spymaster, General William J. Donovon sends, in early July 1942, a cable from London to ambassador Phillips at his Back Bay home of Boston requesting that he run the OSS London office.

Bill Phillips is surprised and awed by the spy mission. And according to former OSS agent and author Elizabeth McIntosh in her book, *Sisterhoood of Spies The Women of the OSS* (1998) Phillips admits, "'I knew nothing about OSS except that it had been created by the President a few months earlier," he said of his appointment.

Bill Phillips writes in his book *Ventures in Diplomacy* (1953) that he moved cautiously, contacting Roosevelt for presidential approval. Roosevelt's response was immediate and couldn't have been more pleased. (Had FDR suggested Phillips as first choice?)

"Delighted with the idea!", exalted the President. Without exposing Phillips' unique and long intimate connections with the Brits, author McIntosh described his sudden thrill at getting back into the privileged shadows the empire game: "Intrigued by the prospect of an entirely new type of career, Phillips went to Washington where he met Donovan for the first time at breakfast at the general's Georgetown home. The new recruit was immediately charmed. 'He had an in depth knowledge of world affairs, coupled with an immense vitality and an unwavering conviction that OSS would play an important part of the war'." McIntosh keynoted the extensive experience of British sophistication in spy and intelligence activities accrued over the last four hundred years, though without a remark how the British artfully used propaganda and terror techniques while masterminding America's entry into the First World War.

At first the Americans work out of their embassy while their offices were set up at Grosvenor Street in the posh section of the city not far from Claridges. Again McIntosh: "Here Phillips was briefed on the relationship between OSS and British intelligence. He learned that the newly spawned American spies were considered upstarts by a service that dated back to the sixteenth century, when Queen Elizabeth I had established England's first far-reaching intelligence agency. Her ambassadors abroad were also secret agents, with a supporting attaché system; Jesuit priests spied on political activities within their own church; third countries such as Italy were used to mount subversive action against the queen's archenemy, Spain; disinformation campaigns were developed that kept the Spanish Armada from attacking England for at least a year. Phillips was up against a spy system that had been in place for four centuries. The British were not his only adversaries." (William A. Phillips, *Ventures in Diplomacy*, Boston: Beacon Hill, 1953; Elizabeth McIntosh, *Sisterhoood of Spies: The Women of the OSS*, Annapolis: Naval Institute Press, 1998, 84-5)

Despite Hoover's staunch opposition to recognition of the Soviet regime American history professor Katherine Siegel observes in her book *Loans and Legitimacy* (1996) that Secretary of State Stimson "saw the advantages of recognition for strategic and peace considerations after Japan's annexation of Manchuria in 1931". Unfortunately she stops short of exploring the unique and special advantages enjoyed by the Morgan Bank and other Consortium corporations "anxious to protect their large investments in Japan, Manchuria, Korea and Taiwan" and which lead directly to World War and the American plundering of the Japanese gold fortune in a deal saving the heads of Japanese war criminals and restoring the prewar corrupt Japanese economic power structure. (S. Seagrave and P. Seagrave, *The Yamato Dynasty*, 166; Katherine A.S. Siegel, *Loans and Legitimacy,* The Evolution of Soviet-American Relations, 1919-1933, Kentucky Univ. Press, 1996)

However, what's not clearly examined is the glaring inconsistency of Hoover's stance. Nor does Stimson push the recognition card with Hoover apparently blocked by the President's obstinately refusal to accept that "a nation of Japan's size could unsettle the futures of two countries as large as China and Russia", that recorded in his diary May 16, 1932, and only months before Bullitt surfaces with the Bols again in Moscow. His predecessor at State Frank Kellogg writes Stimson just days after FDR's victory confirming Stimson's position enhanced by the unique economic incentives of Soviet dictatorship.

In his last year in office, Hoover conceded to use his newly created Reconstruction Finance Corporation to extend a $4 million publicly financed credit to the Soviet dictatorship by which Amtorg, a Soviet state-run trading company in New York, would be able to finance cotton purchases but he was out of office by the time it was implemented." Amtorg has been around for eight years and trades aggressively for American dollars combining business with espionage work. (HLS Diary May 16, 1932, HLS Papers, reel 4, Library of Congress, cited by Andrew J. Williams, *Trading with the Bolsheviks 1920-1939*, Manchester Univ. Press, 1992, 167, 185, Frank Kellogg to H. L. Stimson, Nov. 18, 1932; the cotton deal cited in Jesse H. Jones to President June 24, 1933; J. H. Jones to H. Morgenthau, Jr., June 27,1933, Henry Morgenthau, Jr. Papers, box 243; K. Siegel, *Loans and Legitimacy*)

FDR AND THE 1932 CAMPAIGN TO THE PRESIDENCY

That is left to Yale man William C. Bullitt, FDR's choice for ambassador and mislabeled by FDR biographer Ted Morgan as FDR's "foreign policy adviser during the 1932 campaign". That he was most definitely not. (Roosevelt has quite a few in his pocket.) A true fellow countryman, but you'll never see Bullitt on a postage stamp. He was a bit of a prig, and a confirmed cad. Bullitt wrote the invitation letter to FDR on November 23, 1933 destined to be sent to Bolshevik Commissar Kalinin in Moscow "to promote trade between our two countries" and "the desirability of an effort to end the abnormal relations between the 125,000,000 people of the United States and the 160,000,000 people of Russia". FDR later put his signature on a slightly different version, in his letter to "Max" Litvinov who arrives in Washington to personally discuss terms with the President. FDR gives Stalin's emissary the full red carpet, and he bellows brightly, "The cooperation of our governments in the great work of preserving peace should be the cornerstone of an enduring friendship." (T. Morgan, *FDR*, 392)

As we will see in more precise detail millions of Ukrainians had already starved to death that year and millions more were dying though "the people of the United States" were never informed or allowed to know the truth about Roosevelt's Consortium deal backing Stalin. Bullitt was never one to be trusted, but only after he had ingratiated himself into the Roosevelt election campaign FDR put him in place for Moscow where he could make good use of him. After all, he was the President's favorite, a hand-picked man. President Truman's future Secretary of State, Dean Acheson, shared the halls of power during Bullitt's brief career at State detested Bullitt and spared no kind words for Bullitt's spineless moral character, summing up his contempt in his memoirs for his fellow "Yalie" with "a singularly ironic middle name".

Prior to the public announcement on normalization of diplomatic relations William Christian Bullitt, a descendant from a modestly endowed Philadelphia old-line family, a former editor of the *Yale Daily News*, and divorced only a few years from Louise Bryant, wife and lover of John Reed, the Harvard socialist radical who wrote the classic *Ten Days That Shook The World*, an eye-witness account of the Russian Revolution. Bullitt told his Soviet counterpart that "no normal relations between our peoples are possible until they shall have been settled in a manner which will satisfy the people of the United States".

Yet, after recognition of the Soviet Union, there was a ray of light that the Americans might return to end the horrific nightmare as had Herbert Hoover in the Harding years. Americans arrived there with food relief to reduce to reduce the famine during Lenin's regime of terror from 1919 to 1923 and consolidate Bolsheviks in power. No such luck this time. In previous years James Goodrich, a former Governor of Indiana, had been chosen, in 1921, by President Harding's Secretary of Commerce Herbert Hoover to make an initial survey of the Russian famine. (Dean Acheson, *Present At The Creation*, NY: W.W. Norton, 1969)

PRESIDENT HOOVER AND LENIN'S RUSSIAN FAMINE

Two years later Goodrich is officially pressing for "some sort of relations with Russia". Hoover balks and Goodrich quit over the State Department's secret non-recognition policy pushed by his Consortium peers. By 1932, not one prayer, not a single word (!) was uttered by Roosevelt or his advisers to hint at the systemic and forced starvation and Genocide of the Ukrainians. Saving the Ukraine from annihilation was never on the agenda. That much was tacitly understood as part of Roosevelt's done deal with the Soviets. It never went to Congress for a vote and consent of "the people of the United States". This time no one came to their aid.

The tragic personal story of the Holodomor was clouded in Stalin's cauldron of internal affairs linked irrevocably to a Soviet foreign policy of communist propaganda and subversion. Ten million peasants and intelligentsia in the Ukraine perished under Stalin's crash program of collectivization of farmland and the shift to modern military industrialization for war. FDR could not have not known that Soviet "progress" as it was understood in the state socialist ideology, was sustained by American financial and technical investment needed for Soviet

Russia's survival in the Second World War. By the early thirties plans for another world conflagration were well underway; even as early as the late twenties when Hitler's Nazi ascension to power was considered likely and world war loomed constantly imminent and inevitable.

The extermination and Genocide of peasants in Soviet Ukraine was a prelude to Hitler's mass extermination and Genocide of the Jews. This is crucial. The Holodomor and the Holocaust were stillborn twins of the same war, spawned and nurtured by financial and corporate manipulations of the Consortium. It was a cynical *quid pro quo*: if Stalin can exterminate the Ukrainians and get away with it, then Hitler's Nazis can kill the Jews and no one will stop him. That this story is not understood in these terms today is testament to the power, organization, wealth and intelligence of the Jews and the alliance of the United States to the new state of Israel created after the dust settled from the war.

Neither the State Department nor Presidents Hoover or FDR *overtly* saw it that way. In the unfolding New World Order events and decisions bore consequences of an inherent logical determination that cannot be easily dismissed. Responsibility can always be denied to suit expedience. It took a long time before Stalin was personally identified as the culprit behind the methods used in building the New Society that defined him for the cunning despot he was and the all-pervasive meaning of Stalinism. Exterminate all the brutes! Reads like a page out of the polish expatriate writer Joseph Conrad's eerie *Heart of Darkness*. (Poland once occupied most of western Ukraine.)

Furthermore, Hitler never in his worst dreams imagined that FDR would try to stop him. How Nazi intelligence failed him is another question. Nor did the Japanese at first seek war with the Americans; on the contrary, Japan in desperate need of natural resources to feed its expansion sought to avoid a direct clash. Nor did FDR ever try to stop Stalin or even launch any serious protest against his repression of internal elements within the USSR. On the contrary, FDR's diplomatic deal gave Stalin a green light to continue his campaign of state terrorism. It may even have encouraged him not to relent especially with the Americans in the bag. And much to the chagrin of the Jews, Hitler could easily get away with his *Mein Kampf* repression and still enjoy favorable headlines in the western press and investment by the Consortium.

"... FDR WAITED UNTIL THE ULTIMATE MOMENT TO ENTER THE WAR ..."

History does tell us that FDR waited until the ultimate moment to enter the war long after the persecution of Jews in Germany had started. By late 1941, Great Britain's empire was on its knees hardly able to fight back. France had conceded to Nazi occupation. Against overwhelming odds the Russians heroically fought to save Stalingrad sacrificed in order to save Moscow.

A. J. Taylor studied Hitler's follies. In the chapter titled "The War of Nerves" of his book, *The Origins of the Second World War*, Taylor pin-points one of Hitler's many fatal blunders writing, "The United States had greater economic resources than the three European Great Powers combined: and her lead increased with the years. It would have made sense if Hitler had planned to unite Europe against the 'American danger'. He did not do so. For some obscure reason – perhaps the willful ignorance of a land-bound Austrian – he never took the United States seriously, either in economics or politics. He supposed that, like the Western Powers, they were rooted by democracy; and Roosevelt's moral exhortations increased his contempt. It seemed inconceivable to him that these exhortations could ever be translated into material force; and he had no idea that he was bringing a formidable enemy down upon Germany when he declared war against the United States in December 1941."

From the White House FDR watches events unfold between two colossal fascist powers bearing down on each other, both armed and reconstructed essentially with American industry and finance. Taylor writes, "The economic advance of Soviet Russia, on the other hand, obsessed Hitler. It was indeed startling. During the ten years between 1929 and 1939, while the manufacturing production of Germany increased 27 percent, and that of Great Britain by 17 percent, Soviet Russia's increased by 400 percent; and the process was only beginning." Roosevelt could take comfort in thinking his bet against the Holodomor would some day pay off in huge dividends for his Consortium with rivers of Russian blood from Moscow to Berlin.

God velikogo pereloma. / Год великого перелома/ Year of Great Change. Stalin vowed, "There are no fortresses that Bolsheviks cannot storm" channeling the spirit of the civil war ethos towards for modernization. Taylor's assessment is consistent with history. A decade earlier, on November 7, 1929, *Pravda* quotes Stalin's declaration to push full throttle to increase the pace of industrialization to develop the Soviet Union that had become "a country of metal, a country of automobiles, a country of tractors". Ford, Deere, Caterpillar, International Harvester ... At that time Soviet authorities reported a 19.2 percent growth in industrial production under the first FY ... Between 1928 and 1932 the volume of retail trade increased 175 percent. The number of workers employed in industry more than doubled. By 1932, industrial output stood at 219 percent of its 1928 totals," Scott Palmer observes in his book *Dictatorship of the Air: Aviation Culture and the Fate of Modern Russia* (2006).

These are some of the striking figures that did not escape the attention of the American industrial giants during the Great Depression. The urgency was daunting, the challenges colossal. Nothing of the scale had ever been attempted before in the History of the Modern World. The whirlwind of change catapulted its citizens with a frenzy that left them spell-bound, enthusing the young and innocent with passions not shared by the older and more cynical generation of their parents. Palmer examined the consequence of technological transfer from the West with its inevitable and "unprecedented upheaval, inefficiency, and waste." And Palmer adds, "As forests were razed, rivers damned, and resources consumed for the cause of development, so too were ordinary men, women, and their children. In the villages, the onset of the FYP was accompanied by deportations and death." A. J. Taylor concludes that "By 1938, Soviet Russia was the second industrial Power in the world, ranking only after the United States." (Scott W. Palmer, *Dictatorship of the Air: Aviation Culture and the Fate of Modern Russia*, NY: Cambridge Univ. Press, 2006; Iosif Stalin, *Pravda*, 7 Nov. 1929; Peter Kenez, *A History of the Soviet Union from Beginning to End*, Cambridge Univ. Press, 1999, 91,196)

At the 1932 Geneva disarmament talks Soviet foreign affairs commissar Litvinov was calling for total disarmament. In reality, and Stalin knew it, Soviet Russia faced total war. In a few years the peasant Holodomor would be overshadowed by the technocrat's nuclear madness. The Consortium called it a deterrent even when only they had "The Bomb". Consequently the Big Business war hawks finally got what they had promised,– a totally industrially militarized New World Order scenario calling for new and more terrible advanced weaponry, superior to any adversary, short of nuclear annihilation. It's always just a figure of speech, rhetoric. "The War to End All Wars" this time is called "MAD",– Mutually Assured Destruction–, a curious jingoism defining the Cold War, the quick fix, the surest way to end everything, or the world as they knew it. Reconstruction would not be in your lifetime, if ever. In fact, the "nukes" nearly had their way during Kennedy's Cuban Missile Crisis in the very tense face-off with Khrushchev in the fall of 1962. As I write a brief report December 2013 on *NPR* radio recalls when in 1993 two years after the collapse of the old and bankrupt Soviet system Moscow sold 20,000 warheads to the Americans to disarm the weapons and turn over uranium needed to power nuclear plants in exchange for $17 billion; Americans called the Russian sell-off the deal of the century. Yeltsin and Putin got very rich while the rest of Russia and the Ukraine suffered extreme economic misery with little left to eat besides food Americans serve their pets.

HENRY STIMSON AND THE AMERICAN ELITE

In 1945 Secretary of War Stimson uses position to compel FDR's inexperienced successor President Truman to unleash atomic holocaust on the Japanese. Many thought Roosevelt had conceded too much to Stalin at Yalta. A few weeks later the President suddenly collapses dead. Before he's sworn the former VP Harry Truman had never seen FDR's map room nor known it existed and had never been consulted on military strategy. If Roosevelt had been poisoned no one is going to tell.

The Consortium's immediate policy goal is to stop cold the long-awaited advance of the barbaric Russian Slavs eastward and west, in addition to saving a million American lives in the planned invasion of Japan now shelved. Imagine that! This, after all, had been Hitler's plan! Now it is left to the Americans. One day it's the Nazi mission, next day it's the Americans who take charge. It is enough to confuse anyone until the A-Bomb. No wonder Stimson and General Marshall felt comfortable and could finally breathe a sigh of relief having the A-Bomb. Japanese civilians get toasted to teach the Russians a lesson. Was all that really necessary to preempt a Russian invasion and save their revenge brewing ever since their humiliating defeat in 1905 in eastern Siberia? Old hawks thought so. Or was it just luck?

Yet, it was one of the reasons the Consortium players took out the Czar when they did in the First World War easing President Wilson's official entry into battle, but not before the French had narrowly avoided losing Paris and all of their colonies. For it was then in August 1914 that the Allies shrewdly expended the Czar's army of peasants on the Eastern Front transforming a short-term tit-for-tat between feuding royals and mismanaged mobilization of armies into a four-year quagmire of unimaginable mechanized destruction. Tens of millions of soldiers and civilians were sacrificed in the carnage. More Russians then were killed then all the other countries combined. Another hundred million people may have perished by the influenza epidemic which ultimately stopped the war.

The Anglo-American Consortium's campaign of terror however is not to be put out of action. Far from it. The reader will remember that as the Consortium masters engage their End of the World scenarios for war and peace its plan remains unfulfilled promising new beginnings for the wonders of the future. It unleashes more terror destroying more worlds as it moves forward.

Not long after Stalin's man-made famine and extermination of the Ukrainians Josef Goebbels' Nazi propaganda inflames passions with revived tales of the ancient hordes of Russofied Mongols sweeping across Germany and sacking Europe. To fuel public consumption and assure their success, the Consortium men enacted a new historic drama on the world stage and declared noble and glorious aims to match their deeds if only to kindle fears of Russian expansionism, first militarily, and economically as well as ideologically, poisoning hearts and minds of the so-called "free world" with the best security their world order had to offer the governed.

By late 1947 the *quid pro quo* balance beam using their instruments of artful deception (individuals, institutions *et cetera)* bought and sold the Cold War mythology to the American people who were led to believe that once again Russian hoards of forever invading barbarians descending from the Ural steppes were preparing to invade the Western Hemisphere. As long as Henry Luce's *Life* and *Time* propaganda magazines said it was so, they believed it. Such control over the masses by an elite had never been so thoroughly organized and orchestrated.

Whatever you wish to call it, an apparatus, a process, a confidentially organized power of birds of the same feather who flock together across a scenery of their own production, the Consortium owns the stage hands, write the union laws, and pay their discounted production bills. As Hoover's Secretary of State, Stimson, a skillful lawyer, senior Bonesman in the secret society hierarchy of private clubs, hidden mansions and class protocol, an American imperialist through and through, a kinsman of Teddy Roosevelt with more tempered tastes, possessed in his own right firsthand knowledge of Consortium investment in German Nazism and Stalin's Five-Year Plans for national repression and development. Then later, while serving under Presidents Roosevelt and Truman, Stimson again proves to be without a doubt one of the most important decision-makers in US foreign policy dealing directly with presidential executive authority from his days with

President Taft and TR to working out an approach with Marshall and Truman in handling the A-Bomb. All the while Stimson appears relatively distant, quiet if not remote, even lame towards Stalin under Roosevelt's decided agenda of trade and cooperation and accept strategic losses in order to use Stalin against America's enemies. Remember reader, after Berlin the Russians were preparing to invade Japan had Roosevelt got there first. Later, it becomes "collateral damage" becomes the namesake for national security interests in Washington.

And it was Stimson on deck at the helm with Hoover during the first year of the Holodomor.

To a not insignificant degree it is not historically incorrect to think that the cool and implacable Henry Stimson lacked personal knowledge of the Russians or Ukrainian history. On the contrary, Stimson was the ultimate keeper of secrets, famous for his saying "Gentlemen don't read other gentlemen's mail." What irony! A good alibi to keep secrets from the American people and prepares America's entry into World War II. (Stimson was a pioneer advocate of crypto analysis intercepting Japanese wire transmissions in the 1920s and 1930s leading to prior knowledge of Pearl Harbor.)

Decision makers and leaders skirted responsibility with a hands-on and hands-off approach to the Kremlin. It's the preferred position in the client-dictator relationship. No guilt, no blood-stains on the clean starched white shirts and Panama suits of the sons of imperialism from Puerto Rico to the bloody massacres in the Philippines that turned that acquisition into a turkey shoot for the American soldier. Stimson was also a privileged member of the Pilgrims Society among other Masonic groups of the self-anointed elite and super-rich American capitalists of "Golden Nineties". We know from the memoirs of the chief architect of the North Atlantic Treaty (NATO) Secretary Dean Acheson that the tradition of extending Anglo-American relations required "the duty of every Secretary of State by addressing a gala of distinguished company gathered at a dinner of the London branch of the Society of Pilgrims ...."

THE SECRET SOCIETY OF THE ANGLO "PILGRIMS"

Stimson, Lodge, Hughes, Page, Wilson, House, Taft, Whitney, Vanderbilt, Root, Roosevelt, DuPont, Harriman, Morgan, Rockefeller .... These were all household names of an era, the best and the brightest who transformed America into a modern global power. But if Henry Stimson didn't grasp the tragedy of the peasant famine and terror of the 1932-33 Holodomor– which any geopolitical statesman must be compelled to understand, either by experience or conviction–, then his sense of tradition was fatally flawed. Unlikely, you might say, or absolutely out of the question?

Stimson and his class obscured the reality and rigged the debate. Even today, after the collusion of no less innocuous men like Robert Conquest and James Mace under the shadow of Harvard, the rivalry between Washington and Moscow threatens to push the debate deeper into the darkness of an unmitigated crime against the past and the memory of the victims. Victims remain victims. The dead die twice in the presence of the living who bear the burden of the eternal witness. (D. Acheson, *Present At The Creation*, 392)

Was the 1932-33 Holodomor of ten million victims an exception? Or was it part of an old tradition with a new face, a great plan with a new name that would soon be passed off and dismissed from public awareness in the blur of war fulfilled with a new promise of the nuclear age?

Experts often say, "look at the numbers; it's all in the numbers." The Second World War destroyed 40 percent of Ukraine's Russian wealth, and 30 percent of the entire wealth of the USSR. Conservative estimates of the death toll figure some 5.3 million killed, or one in six inhabitants. Around 2.3 million more people, including children, were shipped to Nazi labor camps. Few barely survived. Some 700 cities and towns and 28,000 villages were destroyed. Twenty-eight thousand collective farms were ruined and 16,000 industrial factories wasted. The USSR lost some 32,000 factories and 100,000 collective and state farms, and 52,000 miles of rails destroyed. Just as it had happened in the First World War when the West took out its ally the Czar, "Uncle Joe's" Russia was crippled in the Second. Betrayal is sweet. Should anyone really have to second-guess to wonder why Stalin never trusts the West?

Victory for the Ukrainians was bittersweet. There was more famine and repressions. Fields went unplowed, sowings were inadequate. Of course in 1946 the harvest failed again. When Khrushchev was asked about famine in the USSR, he talked about 1947, not 1933. State grain quotas described by Nikita as "really a system of extortion" forced farms to surrender their meager harvest below the yields of the two previous years.

"THEY SHOOT CANNIBALS, DON'T THEY?"

Acting under orders of Comrade Stalin, Khrushchev emerged as the Party boss of the Ukraine, chairman of the Council of People's Commissars and first Secretary of the Ukrainian Central Committee. "Then the cannibalism started," Khrushchev wrote. "I received a report that a human head and the soles of feet had been found under a little bridge near Vasilovo, a town outside of Kiev. Apparently the corpse had been eaten. A Party chief from Odessa told Khrushchev a case how people survived the winter. Hideous tales of strange murders reached the Kremlin. "The woman had the corpse of her own child on the table and she was cutting it up. She was chattering away while she worked, 'We've eaten *Manechka* ("*Little Maria*"). Now we'll salt down *Vanechka* ("Little Ivan"). This will keep us for some time'."

Ukraine Party boss Nikita Khrushchev sheepishly wrote, "There was nothing I could do." He was right. No one could raise their eyes and expose "the Great Butcher" if they wanted to save their own neck and their family. Half the returning veterans lived in rural areas, mostly bombed ruins and ravaged and scarred fields. At the May 9, 1945 Victory Parade in Red Square, Stalin stood perched safely above the totalitarian ritual of the cookie-cut parade of high-stepping boot clicking defenders of the Motherland.

Instead of praising human sacrifice and exalting heroes, Premier Stalin reduced Soviet men and women to nothing more than "the little screws and bolts" of his glorious Soviet state. Nearly a fifth of more than five and a half million Soviet citizens who returned to the Motherland in 1946 after years of imprisonment and forced labor in Nazi camps and factories are either executed or sentenced up to 25 years of hard labor. Some 1.8 million returning POWs are seized by the fanatic and most dreaded secret security agents of SMERSh (State Directorate of Counter-Intelligence), Stalin's new system of military police after 1943 and held in concentration camps, including conveniently refurbished Nazi death camps like the extermination camp at Sachsenhausen.

Concentration camp labor was essential to Stalin's Five-Year Plan started in 1946. "There was actually a branch of industry which was monopolized by the concentration camps; the expansion of forestry in Siberia and other areas beyond the Urals was exclusively reserved for forced labor.... It is impossible to state exactly the total number of concentration camp inmates. Expert estimates vary between eight and twenty million.... if we say about twelve million in and around 1950 that would make about 16 per cent of the adult population," Boris Levytsky writes in *The Uses of Terror.* (Boris Levytsky, *The Uses of Terror, The Soviet Secret Police 1917-1970*, 1972, 184)

Stalin continued his deportations and liquidations of Ukrainians, particularly insurgent nationalist partisans of Western Ukraine in yet another hopeless civil war against Stalin and the communists. Before it was suppressed in 1950, at least 300,000 people had been imprisoned and deported from western Ukraine by special troops and secret police, successors of the elite Special Forces OSMBON Motorized Infantry Brigade of the NKVD. Khrushchev later wrote that Stalin would have deported all the Ukrainians if only he had somewhere to put them.

Both Khrushchev and Lazar Kaganovich, one of Stalin's most ruthless and loyal servants, were intimately involved in the crimes of the Stalin era in the Ukraine and throughout the USSR. (John Mosier notes that among the thousands and millions of condemned Russians among them was Lazar Kaganovich's brother Mikhail Kaganovich, in charge of the aircraft factories while Lazar is an intimate member of the Party Central Committee often close to Stalin himself. Stalin accused the Russian Jew Mikhail the "designated head of Hitler's puppet government". It was absurd but, of course, true, Stalin insisting, "I have the testimonies". Stalin was always right. Anyone who thought different and was found out had no future. Criticism of Stalin after 1931 is considered anti-Soviet defeatism, "sabotage" and part of the capitalist and imperialist conspiracy to undermine Soviet socialism. There is no place for "enemies of the people" in the new proletarian culture. (John Mosier, *Deathride, Hitler vs. Stalin, The Eastern Front, 1941-1945*, NY: Simon & Schuster, 2010)

Historian Martin Malia makes this perfectly clear in his *The Soviety Tragedy,* although the fundamental logic of Stalin's one-dimensional culture emerging into an ideological dictatorship in which the revolution devours its own children somehow eludes the State Department Russian experts. "The same fate befell the discipline of history the following year, in 1931", Malia writes of Stalin's arrangements leading to his man-made Holodomor, and he adds, "This time the turn was announced in a letter of Stalin to the editors of the journal *Proletarian Revolution* and concerned Party history. The journal had printed an article analyzing certain mistakes of Lenin in dealing with the Second International. Stalin replied that Lenin had never made mistakes, thereby laying down the rule that there was a single correct view of Party history, of Lenin's role in it, and, by implication, of his– Stalin's position as Lenin's successor. The new orthodoxy came to be that Lenin and his Party had always been right; that Stalin had been Lenin's closest collaborator in building the Party and in leading the October Revolution; and that Stalin was now completing that Revolution by building socialism.... The next step in the taming of history was to combine Party and prerevolutionary Russian history.... By 1934, however, as the new order was nearing completion, such disparagement of the national past came to be viewed by the leadership as demoralizing to the citizens of the new state. This was so because the glory of Russia was to have created the world's first socialist society; that is, the Old Regime was to be viewed not as a Russian past, but as the past of a radical new entity, the Soviet Union.... In particular, the new history was to emphasize the creation of a centralized Russian state as a progressive development; Peter the Great and Ivan the Terrible, therefore, became heroes insofar as they had been mighty state-builders." (M. Malia, *The Soviet Tragedy*, 234-5)

In 1934, with famine ravaging the countryside and peasants still resisting the collectivization of their households and communities, Khrushchev was promoted to the Central Party. The next year he took over as first Secretary of the Moscow regional Party Committee under Kaganovich. Simon Serbag Montefiore in *Stalin, The Court of the Red Tsar* (2004) describes Stalin's Party henchman Lazar Kaganovich who first stamped "Stalinism" as the genre of the new generation. "The fact that neither Khrushchev nor his immediate circle were free of guilt" wrote the Soviet Marxist historian Roy A. Medvedev, "made them immensely vulnerable. Sowing the wind, would they have to reap the whirlwind?" Undoubtedly these sentiments were also felt in Washington while FDR secretly made preparations as well as priming public opinion to move America closer to war in Europe. (R. A. Medvedev, 165; Simon Serbag Montefiore, *Stalin, The Court of the Red Tsar*, NY: Knopf, 2004)

In spite of her refined research professor Catherine Merridale who taught history at the University of London overlooked the compelling theme paramount to the Russian soldier's plight to hold Moscow to the last man, woman and child, and prevent capture of the Soviet government from the invading Nazi troops which nearly happened in 1941.

"Just as seriously," Merridale writes in *Ivan's War* (2005) "the whole of Europe and even the United States, would have faced an unthinkable catastrophe. Stalingrad, Kursk, and Berlin were real victories, and not for Moscow only but for its allies, too. Their human cost paid was paid by Stalin's people, and whether they were willing soldiers or not, all but a small minority believed that they were on the right side in a true just war."

Author Merridale even goes so far as to blame "the Soviet people, who had acquiesced, however unwillingly, in the emergence of Stalinism, and who had also fought and suffered to defend it, would now permit the tyrant to remain." The Merridale account obviously intended to leave unwitting readers more dumb and blind than the Russian peasants themselves as to knowledge of the essential role played by western technology in building Stalin's communist industrial war machine. This is no mere unintentional oversight on such an important element in military issues by an establishment journalist writing about the war and completely ignores Sutton's exhaustive three volumes on western prewar investment and technological transfer to the USSR. More than embarrassing, was this oversight is intellectually flawed and just plain stupid? Worse, it was deliberate and she was paid for it.

Nor was Berlin spared Stalin's wrath and Russia's vengeance from the war inflicted on Humanity by the Consortium's instruments of war. A book review by Brian Ladd in *The New York Times* of Richard Bessel's *Germany 1945, The Ghosts of Berlin* (2009) declared that 4 million Russians poured into Germany in January 1945 killing more that month than "the total wartime losses of either the United States or Britain". Furthermore, it states, "The formidable *Wehrmacht* was hopelessly outnumbered and outgunned". Ladd writes that Bessel blames Hitler for Germany's fate, "Hitler, who chose to destroy his country rather than surrender and face death. For the German people – many bombed or chased out of their homes, all at the mercy of the occupying armies – this was the legacy of the Third Reich: not conquest and glory, nor genocide and guilt, but betrayal and ruin, rubble and grief." (Brian Ladd, *The NYT*, Aug. 16, 2009, 17; Richard Bessel, *Germany 1945, The Ghosts of Berlin*, HarperCollins, 2009)

Max Hastings in Armageddon (2004) reminds that the pace of killing quickened in the last year of the war: "Those who survived did so merely by accident, because the Nazi death machine faltered amid the disruptions and administrative inconveniences imposed by defeat.... Germany also presided over the killing of a host of people who were not Jewish. At least three million Russians and hundreds of thousands of other enemies of Hitler died in captivity. Two million Soviet prisoners, Poles, Gypsies and other 'anti-social elements' were killed at Auschwitz alone, in addition to two million Jews. Many victims we merely allowed to perish in the concentration camp system, rather than being deliberately gassed. Every Western allied prisoner who glimpsed a compound inhabited by Russians recognized how fortunate were his own circumstances in comparison. Germany's excuse was that the Soviet Union was not a signatory to the Geneva Convention, and thus that Stalin's soldiers could not expect its protection. Every day in every camp in which Russians were held, men (and women and children sic) died of disease, hunger or cruelty."

FDR and his generals took their sweet time before launching the D-Day Normandy invasion, and after two million of the best men of the Nazi Reich were dead and millions of Russians and others languished in Nazi labor concentration camps and death factories vital to the Third Reich's war effort. Hastings writes how they waited and suffered, "'They could have been quicker, said Nikolai

Maslennikov, for three years an inmate of concentration camps.' The Western allies only started to fight when the Germans were almost beaten. They were bloody slow. They were too late for too many." (M. Hastings, *Armageddon*, 382-3)

On the same theme of the horrors of brutality inflicted civilians, journalist Daniel Johnson writes in his article for the *Telegraph*, in London (2002) "Red Army troops raped even Russian women as they freed them from camps": "Perhaps 30 million inhabitants of the Soviet Union are now thought to have died during the war, including more than three million who were deliberately starved in German POW camps. The Germans, having shown no quarter, could expect none in return. Their casualties were also on a vast scale. In the Battle of Berlin alone more than a million German soldiers were killed or died later in captivity, plus at least 100,000 civilians. The Soviet Union lost more than 300,000 men. Against this horrific background, Stalin and his commanders condoned or even justified rape, not only against Germans but also their allies in Hungary, Romania and Croatia. When the Yugoslav Communist Milovan Djilas protested to Stalin, the dictator exploded: 'Can't he understand it if a soldier who has crossed thousands of kilometres through blood and fire and death has fun with a woman or takes some trifle?' And when German Communists warned him that the rapes were turning the population against them, Stalin fumed: 'I will not allow anyone to drag the reputation of the Red Army in the mud.'" When told of rough Russian army behavior, the American Commander of Allied Forces in Europe General Eisenhower thought best not to get involved in a spat with Stalin and his generals.

"The rapes had begun as soon as the Red Army entered East Prussia and Silesia in 1944. In many towns and villages every female, aged from 10 to 80, was raped. Nobel laureate Alexander Solzhenitsyn was a young officer and described the horror in his narrative poem *Prussian Nights:* 'The little daughter's on the mattress,/ Dead. How many have been on it/ A platoon, a company perhaps?' But Solzhenitsyn was rare," and Johnson adds, "most of his comrades regarded rape as legitimate. As the offensive struck deep into Germany, the orders of Marshal Zhukov, their commander, stated: 'Woe to the land of the murderers. We will get a terrible revenge for everything."

By the time the Red Army reached Berlin its reputation, reinforced by Nazi propaganda, had already terrified the population, many of whom fled. Though the hopeless struggle came to an end in May 1945, the ordeal of German women did not. How many German women were raped? One can only guess, but a high proportion of at least 15 million women who either lived in the Soviet Union zone or were expelled from the eastern provinces. The scale of rape is suggested by the fact that about two million women had illegal abortions every year between 1945 and 1948. (Daniel Johnson, "Red Army troops raped even Russian women as they freed them from camps", *Telegraph,* London, Jan. 24, 2002)

"...THEY RAPE THEM ON A COLLECTIVE BASIS..."

Military historian Antony Beevor, author of *The Fall of Berlin* (Penguin, 2002) wrote :"Red Army soldiers don't believe in 'individual liaisons' with

German women," wrote the playwright Zakhar Agranenko in his diary when serving as an officer of marine infantry in East Prussia. 'Nine, ten, twelve men at a time - they rape them on a collective basis.' The Soviet armies advancing into East Prussia in January 1945, in huge, long columns, were an extraordinary mixture of modern and medieval: tank troops in padded black helmets, Cossack cavalrymen on shaggy mounts with loot strapped to the saddle, lend-lease Studebakers and Dodges towing light field guns, and then a second echelon in horse-draw n carts. The variety of character among the soldiers was almost as great as that of their military equipment. There were freebooters who drank and raped quite shamelessly, and there were idealistic, austere communists and members of the intelligentsia appalled by such behavior." (Antony Beevor, *The Guardian*, May 1, 2002; A. Beevor, *The Fall of Berlin*, Penguin, 2002)

Beevor brings back the memory of our historical consciousness of what should never be forgotten or erased as one tragedy is consequential to another. Reader do we dare ask can it ever? How tragic would that be to compound horror upon horror, this bedrock of our happiness and protected lives? The Holodomor. Militarization. Nanking. Non-Aggression-Pacts. Invasion. The Holocaust. The rape of Berlin... "Calls to avenge the Motherland," Beevor wrote, "violated by the Wehrmacht's invasion, had given the idea that almost any cruelty would be allowed. Even many young women soldiers and medical staff in the Red Army did not appear to disapprove. 'Our soldiers' behavior towards Germans, particularly German women, is absolutely correct!' said a 21-year-old from Agranenko's reconnaissance detachment. A number seemed to find it amusing. Several German women recorded how Soviet servicewomen watched and laughed when they were raped. But some women were deeply shaken by what they witnessed in Germany. Natalya Gesse, a close friend of physicist Andrei Sakharov, had observed the Red Army in action in 1945 as a Soviet war correspondent. 'The Russian soldiers were raping every German female from eight to eighty," she recounted later. 'It was an army of rapists'."

"Famous wartime Soviet novelist Vasily Grossman, and a journalist attached to the invading Red Army, discovers soon after Berlin is sacked that rape victims are not just Germans. Polish women also suffered horribly. So did young Russian, Belorussian and Ukrainian women who had been sent back to Germany by the Wehrmacht for slave labour. 'Liberated Soviet girls quite often complain that our soldiers rape them,' he noted. "One girl said to me in tears: 'He was an old man, older than my father'.'The rape of Soviet women and girls seriously undermines Russian attempts to justify Red Army behavior on the grounds of revenge for German brutality in the Soviet Union. On March 29, 1945 the central committee of the Komsomol (the youth organization of the Soviet Union) informed Stalin's associate Malenkov of a report from the 1st Ukrainian Front. 'On the night of 24 February,' General Tsygankov recorded in the first of many examples, 'a group of 35 provisional lieutenants on a course and their battalion commander entered the women's dormitory in the village of Gutenberg and raped them.' In Berlin, many women were simply not prepared for the shock of Russian revenge, however much horror propaganda they had heard from Goebbels. Many reassured themselves that, although the danger must be great out in the countryside, mass rapes could hardly take place in the city in front of everybody. In Dahlem, Soviet officers visited Sister Kunigunde, the mother superior of Haus Dahlem, a maternity clinic and orphanage. The officers and their men behaved impeccably. In fact, the officers even warned Sister Kunigunde about the second-line troops following on behind. Their prediction proved entirely accurate. Nuns, young girls, old women, pregnant women and mothers who had just given birth were all raped without pity. Yet within a couple of days, a pattern emerged of soldiers flashing torches in the faces of women huddled in the bunkers to choose their victims. This process of selection, as opposed to the indiscriminate violence shown earlier, indicates a definite change. By this stage Soviet soldiers started to treat German women more as sexual spoils of war than as substitutes for the Wehrmacht on which to vent their rage." Remember reader, "war is horror". It may be hard to stomach when in a "civilized nation" a high standard of living is thrives on the war economy. (A. Beevor, "They raped every German female from eight to 80", *The Guardian*)

The whole world had changed and Stalin too. But how? After the Second World War, nearly half of the Soviet Union lay in ruins, tens of millions of its citizens dead. It cost some three and a half trillion rubles or roughly one third the entire wealth of the USSR. Unlike America, war did not bring prosperity to the families of the victorious Red Army. Instead the Soviet regime became even more dark and forbidden.

A new tidal wave of Soviet culture then besieged the communists trapped in mythology and austerity of the Cold War launched in September 1947. Soviet reconstruction was swift, and in no small measure the result of forced labor in the timber camps in the Caucasus and Siberian mines freshly restocked with Russian POWs returning from Nazi camps and ex-combatants. There life was less valuable than a ton of coal. Many of the camp authorities were vengeful former prisoners, kulaks exiled from the Ukraine in the thirties. "'As soon as your officers' backs are turned,' one of them hissed, 'we're going to kill you with hunger and hard labor. And you deserve it because in 1929-30 you were the ones who dekulakized us'."

Yes reader, you must, you really ought to read Solzhenitsyn when he writes of the glorious work in the timber camps, especially during the war years "(on war rations), the camp inmates called three weeks at logging *dry execution*." And they were the lucky ones, not yet thrown to the Front.

Almost before the last guns were silent Stalin tempered the people's exaltation for peace, calling it "progress" not victory. Once again, after the incredible victory of war, individualism and freedom are stamped out under the boot heel of Soviet state terrorism. "Stalin would set the official tone," Catherine Merridale observes in her account of the battle-worn experience of the Red Army soldier, man and woman, husbands and wives, parents and children of the USSR. "He was proud to take credit for the victory but reluctant to share it... By 1948, within three years of the peace, public remembrance of the war was all but banned," she writes. The USSR was thrust back to socialist empire-building and glorification of Stalinism." (William Taubman, *Khrushchev*, NY: Norton, 2003, 154, 200-1; Catherine Merridale, *Ivan's War*, NY: Metropolitan Books, 2006, 353)

To care for some 2.75 million surviving invalids, the dictator's solution was simple. Stalin in 1947 orders Soviet streets cleared of beggars and maimed veterans, many of them amputees, and crammed them onto trains for the north, like the Island Valaam, on the far side of Lake Ladoga where most of them died in dreary exile. Such was the terrible fate Stalin had in store for the Soviet soldier returning from Germany, infected, or infiltrated by exposure to the West, who fought in the Great Patriotic War to defeat the fascist Nazi military machine constructed and paid for in large measure by the elite Anglo-American Consortium of the Morgan-Rockefeller-Harriman crowd.

None of this much surprised or alarmed Henry Stimson (Bones 1888). He regrets FDR's deals with Stalin at Yalta and harbors little credence to free "elections" in Poland under Russian control. With Averell Harriman (Bones 1913) as America ambassador in the Kremlin, and assured America possesses the all-powerful A-Bomb Stimson records in his war diary, on May 1945: "I told him (John J. McCloy, CFR chairman, 1953-70 sic) that my own opinion was that the time now and the method now to deal with Russia was to keep our mouths shut and let our actions speak for words. The Russians will understand them better than anything else. It is a case where we have got to regain the lead and perhaps do it in a pretty rough and realistic way. They have rather taken it away from us because we have talked too much and have been too lavish with our benefices to them. I told him this was a place where we really held all the cards. I called it a royal straight flush and we mustn't be a fool about the way we play it. They can't get along without our help and industries and we have coming into action a weapon which will be unique. Now the thing is not to get into unnecessary quarrels by talking too much and not to indicate any weakness by talking too much; let our actions speak for themselves."

On the top secret atomic bomb mission under the codename "S-1" Stimson works closely with Harvey H. Bundy (Bones 1909, Harvard Law 1914) and Edward R. Stettinius Jr., the Morgan man and FDR's Lend-Lease administrator before filling in as Secretary of State,– two of "the very few men who know it". Stettinius is virtually unknown in America today but his vestige can be seen behind FDR at Yalta in the famous photos with Churchill and Stalin and their aides Harriman, Eden, and Molotov, respectively. It is Stettinius who takes over at State replacing Hull with Sumner Welles out of the picture publicly axed in a sleazy bit of scandal mongering by Bullitt's leaked rumors of homosexuality. His passage, however, is transitional and brief. Morgenthau, too, is bitter about losing out for the job and calls Stettinius little more than "a good clerk". Interior Secretary Harold I. Ickes, another jealous Roosevelt insider thinks Stettinius lacks intellectual depth. (Irwin F. Gellman, *Secret Affairs, Franklin Roosevelt, Cordell Hull, and Sumner Welles,* Johns Hopkins Univ. Press, 1995, 367)

Also in Stimson's key inner circle is Robert Abercrombie Lovett Jr. (Bones, 1918), a Harriman man brought up in the footsteps of his father, Secretary of War for Air and former head of Brown Brothers Harriman. Bob Lovett has skills later exemplified by Robert S. McNamara in the Vietnam War fiasco. McNamara, fresh out of Harvard Business School he excelled at statistical planning for the massive bombing raids in WWII killing hundreds of thousands of civilians in Europe and Japan. Afterward he goes from war business to the Ford Motor company quickly becoming a director then chairman, in 1960, before taking the top Defense Dept. job for JFK. Credited with having lost that war and for unleashing massive terror on the Vietnamese in a futile logic to win it, McNamara was rewarded with the plum of the presidency of the World Bank with all its princely money power, perks and privileges fit for a prince of lofty Consortium status.

From war to war, corporation to corporation, and generation to generation the Lovetts are a good example how the Consortium incarnates its power. Continuity flows with blood. Robert Lovett Sr. had been Edward Harriman's personal lawyer as well as executor of his will. As sworn Harriman men, the Lovetts benefit as sworn guardians, devout missionaries of capital of the colossal Harriman fortune. Together Consortium safe-keepers of world order envision "possible" UN control of nuclear weapons under the UN Charter drafted that spring. George Herbert "Bertie" Walker, grandfather of President George Walker Bush, joined Brown Brothers Harriman run by Bob Lovett Jr.. More on that later. During the Second World War, Lovett later became Secretary of Defense and later serves as an adviser to John F. Kennedy with the Bundy brothers, "Mac" and Bill. These were men the British historian Godfrey Hodgson liked to describe as having come "from a tradition of service and who possessed a certain confidence ..." So they did. The safe-keepers of the New World Order. (Godfrey Hodgson, *The Colonel, The Life and Wars of Henry Stimson 1867-1950*, NY: Knopf, 1990)

September 1933 Stimson's Assistant Secretary of State Bill Phillips is brought a step closer to the Holodomor in a most personal and direct way. Phillips is handed an urgent radiogram. Phillips is Stimson's right-hand man and second in rank at State he is a most trusted minister of foreign affairs. But this telegram has been sent from his son safely outside the USSR. Phillips is told that the current crisis is "one of the world's greatest famines". Did he need to hear it from his son? But the magnitude of the calamity falls on his desk with no more impact than an insignificant event of little importance and bearing no consequences for the US government however much relief Phillips harbors for his son.

Ask virtually any American today who was Phillips and they don't have a clue. Why is that? Yet Bill Phillips during the Holodomor years is one of the most influential, – and wealthy, – actors in the game of diplomacy at State. He is a consummate Consortium man. No one ought to have had a clearer understanding how the Russian observers in the Department had filed reports of famine on the Ukraine grain-belt for years. The radiogram is precise and clear and here his son tells his father, "The present famine is so directly due to (the Communists' policies) that they are trying in every possible way to deny and cover it up. This the people know... Seed grain is state property and any withholding it is stealing from the state and punishable with death. Children are given Soviet honors for revealing any concealment even by their parents."

HOLODOMOR TABOO: A GOVERNMENT CONSPIRACY?

Phillips remains calm and nonplussed. Surely there is no cause of alarm to ruffle the feathers of an arcane and highly astute diplomat. This is much more than just "old news" to be forgotten and passed over lightly or not at all. Stalin is an odd fellow, no doubt. So what is there to do? Phillips has lived through famines before. And so while perhaps no less startled by the obvious absence of either private or official reaction to the Holodomor Terror-Famine, the reader can be assured that it is extremely rare to find any trace whatsoever be it in private archived memoirs, declassified State Department memoranda, internal or official government dispatches that either Stimson, Phillips or other senior diplomats recognized the famine, absent as it was, from such official files and reports, as though to leave the impression that there might have been an Executive Order or some such confidential instruction from above not to comment in any way or fashion, nor even mention the famine in conversation or glib note to acknowledge the startling account described in the radiogram by his son.

What was going on? Was there a deliberate purge in place? Had the Holodomor taken on the force of a clear and implicit taboo with all the hallmarks of a government conspiracy to cover-up? Might it be that the protagonists in the Anglo-American Consortium are so much up to their necks in wicked and unsavory engagements with criminal and immoral elements that they have much to worry about should their role be exposed to the media entailing the risk of a general public inquiry? Was it too late to stop the cover-up? After all, what is there go be gained by exposure of Stalin's skullduggery?

Bill Phillips was born an insider with impeccable family history and personal connections. He is one of America's premier diplomats in Washington and London and at home in every capital of Europe, and elsewhere. His peers might say he holds the world in the palm of his hand. Certainly, ever since Versailles quite a few Americans feel they do. Yet few Americans today have any clue who he was, or that he even existed yet alone know the extent of his wealth and influence or the role he played in the Holodomor disinformation. His career path in the Foreign Service was paved with gold.

Formerly assistant to Wilson's Secretary of State, the Anglophile Robert Lansing during the First World War, Phillips is the State Department's point-man during that era's pivotal unfolding events – the Bolshevik coup in 1917, the Russian Civil War and then Herbert Hoover's famine relief imbroglio entrenching power with the recently installed Bolsheviks Lenin and Trotsky. It would behoove one not to suspect Phillips knows all too well the details of US monetary and economic support by the American International Corporation (AIC) based in New York to the murderous Bolsheviks and their communist doctrine. Such operations are as common and seamless to these men as the air they breathe. More on the banking operations of AIC will become clear later as our story unfolds.

Phillips wasn't inclined to speak openly about any of this. The stain would be too messy, a severe blemish on them all, right down to the reporters and observers in the field, to the journalists themselves, arch beacons of America's free press and its deeply embedded intelligence agents. Exposure would be too great, the whiplash too harmful to their entire multilayered structure of economic and political power in society and risk shaking the foundations of institutions from church to state. What on earth did Phillips do with the information?

WHO REALLY IS BILL PHILLIPS AT STATE ?

William A. Phillips seemed perfectly tailored for his role as career diplomat of the highest rank and certainly could have been Secretary of State but was like Harriman more powerful behind the curtain. His family came from good old New England stock descended from settlers with the Massachusetts Bay Colony when Boston Common was a meadow and every man had a cow, or two. That was a long time ago. Bill Phillips (1878-68) returned to the imperial fold when in late 1942 when word got out Phillips was handpicked by FDR to act as the American Viceroy to India then embroiled in its revolt for independence from centuries of British imperial domination, *Time* said of Phillips that he "has no State Department rival save Undersecretary Sumner Welles for tall, aristocratic elegance." Born in Beverly, Massachusetts, Phillips graduated Harvard College, then Harvard Law, 1903. Thereupon he was sent immediately to London where he was blended with the British ruling class and served as Secretary to Ambassador Joseph Hodges Choate. From there Bill Phillips was sent in 1908 to China, a timely arrival on the scene just a few years before the fall of the Qing dynasty.

Phillips stays in China until 1911, long after the Boxer Rebellion and the Siege of the Legations in Peking in 1900 – the foreign legations were never taken though the Chinese did fire away with their antiquated Mausers and Mannlichers – when the Manchu government declared war on the imperialist powers, and the final storming of the Imperial City by American General Chaffee and his Anglo counterpart. After the row Phillips returned to London.

Two years later William A. Phillips married Caroline Astor Drayton. Once upon a time her grandfather was the wealthiest man in America. Her grandmother, Caroline Astor of New York reigned over American society of the famous *"400" of the Gilded 1890s. Caroline Astor was the daughter Charlotte Augusta Astor, who in turn was the daughter of William Backhouse Astor II, famous for having spent some $20 million before he died, a royal fortune in those days; her uncle was John Jacob Astor IV, father of her first cousin Vincent Astor (1891-1959), born in the old William Astor mansion at Fifth Avenue and 34th Street on the site of the old Waldorf Astoria Hotel. His mother was the beautiful and spoiled grand princess of Philadelphia.*

In 1912, John Jacob Astor IV was the grandson of John Jacob Astor made the biggest fortune in America in furs and real estate. The younger was not so lucky; he went down on the Titanic. The New York Times estimates the Astor family wealth at around $100 million ($2.5 billion) with $41 ($1 billion) million in New York real estate. Legend recalls that as water fills the Titanic's grandiose staterooms Astor and put his pregnant young wife into a lifeboat a ship's officer said, "Only women allowed aboard, sir." J.J. Astor IV calmly lit a cigarette and tossed his wife his gloves. Another legend has it that after the ship hit the iceberg he quipped, "I asked for ice, but this is ridiculous." Col. Astor drowned, – in icy waters, but his pregnant eighteen year old bride Madeleine survived and months later gave birth to a son, John Jacob Astor IV.

The ill-fated Astor (Harvard '88) willed his huge fortune to young Vincent, estimated at a cool $200 million. His widow walks off with only a "pre-nup" $5 million, something to be expected in this crowd. He has prepped at Eton in England instead of St. Pauls School in Vermont and becomes a freshman at Harvard. Then, suddenly in 1912 he inherits $60 million in Manhattan real estate, including large hotels among them the old Waldorf later joined to the Astoria; the St. Regis, the Knickerbocker, and the Astor. He also owns the grand Astor House. Vincent builds his own house in 1927 at 130 East 80th Street designed (at present the Junior League). Astor continues investing and building in Manhattan including on East End Avenue, less pricey than Fifth Avenue and with apartments renting out at only $22,000 a year in 1931 it's all "perfectly adequate if you had an estate in Glen Cove, a big house in the Berkshires and a shooting plantation in South Carolina". ("Mrs. Astor's Starter Home", *The NYT*, July 26, 2009)

ASTOR & THE AMERICAN CULTURE OF BILLIONAIRES

That keeps him comfortably in billionaire status in rank with the Vanderbilts, Rockefellers, Whitneys, Morgans and others oligarchic clans on the elite Social Register. Jack London's brand of literary socialism was the rage. When Mayor Fiorello H. La Guardia took over New York, Astor transferred his ghetto holdings to the newly organized Municipal Housing Authority in exchange for a long-term low mortgage. America was faced with a choice, – reform social institutions or face revolution in the streets. Vincent Astor sold the family's New York City slum housing, built a large housing complex in the Bronx with a children's playground and another in Harlem. When *Forbes* compiled its first list of America's wealthiest Vincent Astor came in a poor 12th.

Cruel fate struck the Astors again this time at Vincent's wedding in 1913; he came down with the mumps which sterilized him. And although the Bush family is indelibly stamped on postwar America most people never heard of Vincent Astor or know that in 1948 he marries the divorced wife of James S. Bush, and her third husband. (James Bush is brother to Sen. Prescott S. Bush and uncle of George the First.) The Astor enclave nestles in at Ferncliff on 500 acres overlooking the forested green hills of the Hudson; his choice of Rhinebeck on a 3,000 acre stretch of private grounds in Rhinebeck, New York, and only a short crow's flight from "Springwood", the Roosevelt Hyde Park retreat situated near the Delano, Rockefeller and Vanderbilt family estates on the Hudson River more suited his commutes to New York on fast trains that stopped for his convenience. There the Astors join the famous Livingston and Armstrong families to whom they aspired in social status.

The New York Times does its best to ingratiate Astor wealth with fantasies for the masses and at every turn seize the chance to publish details of his opulence, particularly the choice of Ferncliff, such as headlines "Mansions on the Hudson: His Estate at Rhinecliffe" to take its place up the river from Manhattan in the realm of extraordinary wealth encased in such homes as the half-million dollar construction of the McKim Mead & White designed mansion of Ogden Mills. ("Mansions on the Hudson", *The NYT*, Sept. 6, 1897)

During the 1932 campaign, Astor backed FDR and for a time was a New Dealer until FDR's economy adviser the Columbia University professor Raymond Moley broke with the White House and teamed with Astor of all people to launch the *Today* magazine. Apparently Vincent had gone sour on New Dealism or was just teasing his cousin and baffling the masses at will playing the devil's advocate.) Together, in 1937, Harriman and Astor absorb *Today* into *News-week. Time* and *Newsweek* become culture beacons of American propaganda, *Time*, a Luce property serving its master's vision and friends, and its founder a Yalie after Harriman's own heart, a fellow Bonesman (1920) in tandem with Lovett and their clan. *Time* and *Newsweek*, Yale and Harvard. It's all fair play in the game of extended families and Consortium millionaires.

On April 9, 1934 *Time* puts Vincent Astor on its cover. But just try to get anything of the famine or American complicity with Stalin's state terrorism published in those rags! Fat chance! Take a walk today through the Yale University campus in New Haven, Connecticut. The Luce legacy at present penetrates American society from Yale's grand Henry R. Luce Hall, host to the Center for International and Area Studies, or visit the Luce Foundation Center at the Smithsonian American Art Museum in Washington DC, bold pavillons of splendor grand enough to rival the envy of even the ancient gods of Rome.

After priming in London Phillips sees first-hand how the empires of the Great Game have survived to dawn on modern times. The three years Phillips passes in China alone could fill a political thriller to sequel a Peter Fleming story on the fall of the Manchu dynasty by America and the Big Four Powers. The Empress Dowager dies in 1908; three years later a revolution topples the Manchu rulers and sets China on track towards modernization. Bill Phillips, 30, is dispatched there to direct State's Division of Far Eastern Affairs.

Its interesting to observe two decades later that Luce's *Time* writes periodically glowing praise of Phillips during the aftermath of the Holodomor in the Ukraine once the dust settles the stench of the dead. Shortly after Roosevelt appoints him Ambassador-at-Large, Bill Phillips again emerges from the shadows of Foggy Bottom in a December 1935 story occasioned by the US delegation to the Naval Limitation Conference in London led by Norman H. Davis, a friend of Hull from Tennessee who previously headed the US commission to the League of Nations debacle. Davis is a professional diplomat, served in Wilson's cabinet as Assistant Secretary of the Treasury during wartime, and later becomes president of the CFR from 1936 until he dies in 1944. He's a front man and has carries no weight at the disarmament conference that May in Geneva. Yet *Time* magazine features Davis on its cover while downplaying the fanfare as "a new Naval Conference which all oracles have doomed to fail". Unable to come to terms on tonnage and ratios for construction all the parties will violate their agreements by 1938 while the Consortium strives to increase its share of the booming arms business with the fascist regimes of Stalin, Hitler, Mussolini and the Japanese militarists behind the Imperial palace of Emperor Hirohito. ("Naval Conference: Doom's Double Barrels", *Time,* Dec. 16, 1935)

See how Luce as one well-placed insider here takes care of one of their own. With his tight personal links to corporate and government officials Henry Luce portrays "Billy" Phillips, not exactly one of FDR's "forgotten" men: "Undersecretary of State William Phillips was selected because of special circumstances... Everything that the late Henry James could have hoped for in a U.S. diplomat has been the property of 'Billy' Phillips from birth. His family arrived in New England in the person of the Rev. George Phillips in 1630, founded Phillips Andover and Phillips Exeter Academies. The first mayor of the city of Boston was his great-grandfather. Although Boston was founded in 1630, it was governed by town meeting until 1822. In that year it adopted a city charter, elected its first mayor John Phillips, one of whose sons was the famed abolitionist Wendell Phillips.

"The Phillips family fortune, made in shipping and real estate and preserved in the best New England tradition, stands behind him. His shapely head, long nose and aristocratically petulant mouth were born to him. He went to Harvard in the same class (1900) with, three other young men who grew up to be eminent U. S. diplomats by profession, William R. Castle Jr., Robert Woods Bliss, Peter Augustus Jay. Billy Phillips' career matched his endowments. After college a classmate and a fellow Porcellian* Bayard Cutting, elder brother of the late Senator from New Mexico, went to London as private Secretary to U. S. Ambassador Joseph H. Choate. Tiring of diplomacy, Cutting, in 1903, designates Phillips as his successor. Two years later William Woodville Rockhill, U. S. Minister to China, met the suave and elegant young Phillips in London, took him to Peking as second Secretary at the U. S. legation. Because China was so far away, Billy Phillips resigns, gave up his seniority, returns to Washington, and started over again at the bottom with an office boy's salary as an assistant to the Third Assistant Secretary of State. That was in 1907."

Odd rather, that Luce chooses to omit any mention of Phillips' early training in the law firm of his mentors Stimson and Root. The plot thickens as corporate and financial elites take over broadening their interlocking social base and control of government. The *Time* accolade runs on:

"Within two years he had won such esteem in the Department that he was sent to London as first Secretary of the Embassy, a doubly important post because Ambassador Whitelaw Reid was in very poor health. It was during that period that he married Caroline Astor Drayton. Mrs. Phillips is a descendant of the Draytons whose name means as much in the history of Charleston, South Carolina as her husband's does in Boston. In 1912 at the ripe age of 34, William Phillips retired to become regent of the college and Secretary of the Corporation of Harvard. Short-Sighted Hostess. In marrying Caroline, Mr. Phillips not only married more family and more money, but also more tact and more charm which was to stand him in good stead when his diplomatic career began again. Nowadays Mrs. Phillips is rated rather snobbish, but obstinate would be a better word for it. She refuses to wear glasses although she is so shortsighted that she cannot recognize her best friends across a room. As his hostess in Washington when Woodrow Wilson called him back to the State Department just before the War, as his hostess at The Hague when he was appointed Minister to The Netherlands (1920), in Brussels when he became Ambassador to Belgium (1924) and at Ottawa when he was appointed first U. S. Minister to Canada (1927), she played a notable part in her husband's career.

"The wealth of the Phillipses which has opened to him posts which were closed to other career diplomats has also been a drawback, for they have ever found difficulty in securing adequate living quarters. In Brussels they lived for some time in the two front rooms of a pension. When Secretary of State and Mrs. Hughes arrived to visit them they had to give up their own beds and find others at the back of the house. Later they rented the palatial Hôtel d'Assche which had been the home of King Albert and Queen Elisabeth before their elevation to the throne. There old Cardinal Mercier used to drop in to play with the five Phillips children and there the King & Queen called often. Crown Prince (now King sic) Leopold attended all their better parties, and the Socialist leader Emile Vandervelde went there to discuss with his friend Phillips the social problems of the underprivileged. Recall. After Brussels, Ottawa was a comedown in rank, accepted deliberately, when Calvin Coolidge offered it, so that the Phillips children could attend school in the U. S. In Canada Mr. & Mrs. Phillips never found a house large enough to suit them. After two years, therefore, Mr. Phillips, aged 51, resigned and retired once more to Beverly, Massachusetts. There he headed the Massachusetts drive of Herbert Hoover's private Committee on Unemployment until in 1933 Franklin Roosevelt, one of his old Wartime friends, called him back to be Undersecretary of State. Such is William Phillips' career, a career which never put him in a tight place, diplomatic or otherwise. But capable is the diplomat whose career is uncheckered. No one has ever alleged that the present Undersecretary of State is an eagle of intellect, but he has done many a job competently and quietly." ("Professionals to London", *Time*, Dec. 9, 1935; *Porcellian, or simply "the Porc", is Harvard's elite club, a knotch above the Fly. Other top Harvard clubs, A.D., Spee, Delphic and Owl. Yale has Fence, (Groton and St. Pauls), Delta Kappa Epsilon-DKE (Exeter and Andover), Zeta Psi and St. Anthony's; Skull and Bones (founded 1832) and Scroll and Key (founded 1842) the two top ranked, campus leaders, and "more polished men of the senior class"; Princeton reserves the Ivy and Bogue for its most prestigious members.)

Had the editors at *Time* wished to pursue a more objective journalism they would have referred to the Phillips mission ("a one man diplomatic corps") to Canada as a landmark in US foreign policy establishing a legation for the first time, in Ottawa, frequently standing side-by-side with the Canadian Prime Minister MacKenzie King, with a column of top State Department men as a gesture to loosen the King's empire grip there and recognize the autonomous statehood of Canada beyond the reach of its imperial masters in London.

Time is already telling more than it wanted Americans to know about this mystery man and the good company he kept of well-informed insiders well aware of repression, famine and forced labor in the Soviet Union. After all, these are Pilgrims and Consortium men working in key positions of national and international institutions with their hands on the levers of world corporate power, media and the dictators they control. So *Time* proffers a portrait of the Consortium players with harmless rhapsody to enamor its readers with whimsical prose of patriotic hype reminiscent of the "One Dollar-A-Year" businessmen faithfully performing their duties in Wilson's War Department during the First World War. Reader, do you wonder why did *Time* wait so long to bring this key insider Bill Phillips into the spotlight of American public opinion? Back to the Belgium baby-killing propaganda reinforcing that cultural mindset of a few years ago. Remember, reader! It's the big "Game". It helped win the war for America and its Allies against those beastly Germans! (John Hilliker, *Canada's Department of External Affairs*, 2001, 112)

Time went on adding this juicy tidbit: "Among them was the distribution of $1,000,000, willed by a Sharon, Pa. millionaire, Frank H. Buhl, to improve the lot of Belgian orphans. The fund was so well administered by an unpaid staff that it has only recently been exhausted, all the orphans having grown up. Today Mr. & Mrs. Phillips live in a commodious house on upper Massachusetts Ave., sharing a garden with their next-door neighbor, Hungary's Count Laszlo Szechenyi. There they dine the diplomats whom it is their job to dine, but otherwise do not entertain inordinately.

"Aloof and polished Bill Phillips has many friends but few close ones. In spite of a good sense of humor, he is so cautious and deliberate in his choice of words that he supplies his small world with few *bons mots*. Iron Man. Occasionally on a sunny afternoon passersby before Woodley*, formerly Stimson's 18-acre estate in heart of Washington, DC, might see in the distance a curious sight. On the lawn adorned by a large 18-century Federal house, the regal host Stimson, the well-born patrician Manhattan lawyer, Secretary of State Cordell Hull, the white-haired modest politician from Tennessee's hill country, and Undersecretary Phillips, the Boston blue blood, engaged in a threesome of croquet, elder gentlemen generally deep in a discussion of the most important of government affairs, and Phillips leaning on his mallet in graceful attention. (Woodley is now site of the Maret School.)

"On the political front William Phillips plays no apparent role. At least, that is, the strings are invisible. During his retirement in 1932 he did declare that as an Independent he favored Franklin Roosevelt for President, but that was all. His job at the State Department is not to put new irons into the international fire but to tend those already in, seeing to it that none gets too hot to handle. He is the professional manager of the Department, the top-notch careerist who knows how to deal deftly with the other careerists in the Foreign Service, the diplomatic pinch hitter who can always go to bat for Secretary Hull and never strike out. Wellington proclaimed that the battle of Waterloo was won on the playing field of Eton." (Churchill preferred Harrow.)

"So far as Undersecretary Phillips is concerned, the battles of diplomacy are won on the platform of Waterloo. For during the first, two years of his career, as private Secretary to Ambassador Choate, he spent much time waiting on the platforms of London's railway stations to greet U. S. diplomats passing through London on their way to & from their posts. There he learned patience, tact and the ability to absorb jars. This week when he steps off the boat train in Waterloo Station, what he learned there in other years will be called as never before into the service of his country." Ten years Phillips returns to London accepting Stimson's offer run the newly formed American super-spy war agency, the OSS, predecessor to the CIA.

In 1927, Henry Luce offers him *Time*'s glowing send-off to Canada. "Choose an ambassador for his wife" is a saying not applicable to William Phillips. He has himself charm enough for the most difficult social encounter. "He is the only man," said one traveler, "who could be popular in Europe with a cross-eyed termagant for a wife. It happens, however, that Mr. Phillips, having reached age 32, married some years ago a Manhattan girl (Caroline Astor Drayton) whose charm matched his, and whose beauty outshone his manners."

"Few would compliment John D. Rockefeller Jr. on his wealth. Thousands have blundered into complimenting the Phillipses on their charm. The important thing Mr. Phillips about Diplomat Phillips is that, regardless of personality, he is a good diplomat. It is widely conceded that there is no better equipped diplomat in the U. S. service. For 23 years he has been equipping himself. He began as private Secretary to Ambassador Choate at the Court of St. James's. He served in Peking. He accepted demotion in order to return to Washington, to work "with the office boys of the State Department underworld." He soon became chief of the Division of Far Eastern Affairs. President Taft, aware of his abilities, sent him back to London (where his career had begun) to the duties of Ambassador, Whitelaw Reid* being in ill health. President Wilson, aware, made him Assistant Secretary of State during the War, and later gave to him the post of Minister to the Netherlands. In 1924 he reached the top title, Ambassador, his assignment being to Belgium. He is to be demoted to a Minister. It is a demotion *cum laude*, President Coolidge evidently desiring that the first U. S. minister to Canada should be the most competent diplomat available."

Read again. Luce writes Bill Phillips joined "Hoover's private Committee on Unemployment until in 1933 Franklin Roosevelt, one of his old Wartime friends, called him back to be Undersecretary of State". Imagine that. Bill Phillips on the Hoover's Committee of Unemployment! Bill Phillips never had a job he didn't get by appointment. In the same breath Luce refers to FDR as "one of his old Wartime friends". Very chummy all that sort of thing, both members of the Fly or "Porc". But to come back as "Undersecretary" is putting him just a little down. With Stimson gone, Phillips runs State. It's his territory but he doesn't appear to know the Soviet Union and his only personal contact with conditions there apart from paper pushing is a letter about the famine crisis from his son at school there. But there is another little secret Luce omits to tell his largely middle-class readers who if they don't already know certainly don't *need* to be told.

His wife is an Astor!

Caroline Astor Drayton is the grand-daughter of the man richer than Midas. (Luce conveniently drops Astor from her name.). In London in 1910 assisting US

Ambassador Choate, Bill Phillips marries the Astor girl; in 1931, their cousins, Lady Nancy Langhorne Astor, from Virginia, and her husband enjoy a royal tour with British playwright George Bernard Shaw in Moscow under the protective security of the Kremlin's Chekists. Shaw has joined Lady Astor and other well-known appeasers not unfriendly to the fascism sweeping over the European continent and affected by many among the British aristocratic upper class. During the thirties this powerful and influential social group coined the name of "the Cliveden set" infamous for its occultist pro-Hitlerian sympathies shared at sumptuous weekends at their manor estate of the same name. Bill Phillips ought to have shared some interesting conversations with Lady Astor and Mr. Shaw ....

Long before the American people indulge a fascination bordering on cult worship for the Kennedy family celebrity it is the mystique of the Astors that captured their imagination. While FDR is a close relation to Vincent Astor, – distant cousins both living in America –, on the other side of the Consortium set we find that his uncle Waldorf Astor is an intimate friend and political patron of David Lloyd George, and who, himself, in fact served as his Parliament Secretary during the First World War.

Upon the death of his father he inherited a fortune including *The Observer*, bought by his father in 1911 from press baron Lord Northcliffe. He also occupies the chairmanship at the Royal Institute of International Affairs 1935 to 1949. Waldorf Astor, 2nd Viscount Astor (1879-1952) was born William Waldorf Astor, the builder of the 1939 America's most famous hotel, the Waldorf Astoria Hotel on Park Avenue in Manhattan where he was born, son of William Waldorf Astor (1848-1919) who moved with his family to England. When he was twelve he did as all proper sons of Lords and upper class boys, go to Eton and Oxford. His father, called Waldorf Astor, married the American divorcee Nancy Witcher Langhorne; for a wedding present his father gave him the family estate at Cliveden.

Britain's industrialists and press barons collude seamlessly with the government. The Astors prove to be a convenient link of Consortium homogeneity to Roosevelt and Lloyd George. Whereas Waldorf Astor owns the *Observer* newspaper, brother John Astor owns the *Times*, both of London, and both inherited from their father William Waldorf Astor (1848-1919). The *Times*' editor Geoffrey Dawson, elected Fellow of All Souls College, Oxford and one of Lord Milner's "kindergarten" young men when he served as private secretary to Colonial Secretary Joseph Chamberlain will soon invite scorn from their peers as another self-declared appeaser of Nazi Germany.

William Astor used his wealth lavishly to raid Europe of its art treasures many which he stole away to Clivedon including ancient Roman and Greek treasures some raided from the Villa Borghese in Rome. Italy wants them returned but will have to wait in line. The Sacrophagus with Theseus with scenes of King Minos, the Minotaur and Daedalus filled his bastion of wealth alongside his vast collection of sculptures and paintings scattered around his rooms and gardens. More were secreted away his newly acquired home Hever Castle of Kent where he retired in 1906 preferring this ancestral home of Ann Boleyn. In 1916 William

Astor was awarded a barony and the next year elevated to Viscount Astor. The next year Nancy Astor welcomed the King of England for dinner.

Clivedon is a center attracting the social elite of London and its friends from around the world. Nancy Langhorne Astor brightened up her family's manor with memorable parties transforming it into a Mecca of England's intellectual high-brow political culture. She counts Soviet apologist George Bernard Shaw as among her best of friends. American ex-patriot Henry James living in Paris is a frequent guest. So is Rudyard Kipling and Churchill. Arthur Balfour and Lord Curzon are often seen there. Charlie Chaplin occasionally drops in between films and openings whenever in London and passing through Europe. The banking Grenfells are regulars; actress Joyce Grenfell is Nancy Astor's niece married to Reggie Grenfell.

Nancy Langhorne Astor, daughter of Chiswell Dabney Langhorne, the railroad millionaire of the prominent Virginian family of Lynchberg, were once wealthy slave-owners big in tobacco until the American Civil War. Langhorne rebuilds the family fortune including "five Southern Belle daughters, ante-bellum survivors living out the Confederacy in late 19th-century America, ready to export his daughters across the Atlantic to marry into the English peerage in exchange for a smuge of their cultural heritage.

To these stately Virginians going to the grand hunting estates in England feels like coming home. Indeed, Nancy Astor's father-in-law left the United States definitely, declaring "America is not a fit place for a gentleman to live". In 1919, upon the death of his father which obliges him to forfeit his seat in Commons, came the title to enter the House of Lords. The younger Astor assumes the title 2nd Viscount Astor. His wife quickly occupied the vacancy and so became the first woman ever to sit in the House. (Philip Hoare, "Catastrophe strikes the Cliveden Set: war and revolution drove the Anglo-American plutocracy off the rails", *The Independent,* Dec. 12, 1998)

And, so, in view of the indelible linkage of America with Great Britain, a family bond that remains to this day, it is not insignificant that while FDR was more than a mere friend to Vincent Astor, either in America, or across the Atlantic on the other side of the Consortium set, we find that uncle Waldorf Astor, colored by a decidedly outspoken anti-Semitic persuasion, and intimately linked to the government of the Prime Minister Lloyd George, in fact, holds a seat in Parliament for Plymouth serving as his Parliament Secretary during the First World War; Astor, indeed, was also his Food Minister and took a position after the Armistice cabinet in a reorganized Health ministry. His son, David Astor, who in more recent times succumbed in 2001, at the overripe age of 89, presided over *The Observer*, which ranks as "Britain's oldest Sunday newspaper".

YALE, HARVARD, PRINCETON & THEIR SECRET SOCIETIES

And, so in December 1935, Henry Luce's magazine *Time* elaborated ever so nicely a few branches of the family tree so Americans could finally discover who really might be this man in charge with so much responsibility at the State

Department, two years after he's in position and nearly three years after the peak of the Holodomor. "Mr. Phillips is a Harvard man of wealth and deep Bostonian rootage. He had a classmate (1900) from St. Louis: Robert Woods Bliss, who also married a Manhattan girl of wealth and grace (Mildred Barnes). Mr. Bliss began to serve the U. S. in Porto Rico and has subsequently been skillful at Venice, Petrograd, Brussels, Buenos Aires, Paris, The Hague, Washington. Last week he reached the top title, the Secretary of State announcing his promotion from U. S. Minister to Sweden to become U. S. Ambassador to Argentina. In Buenos Aires, the Blisses will be responsible for the most expensive of all U. S. embassies. There is no doubt as to their financial, social or intellectual qualifications."

Time adds, "Another St. Louis-Harvard man is Frederick Augustine Sterling. He was a big ranchman and woolen manufacturer until he was 35, when he began his diplomatic career at Petrograd. Since then he has toasted monarchs and men at Peking, at Petrograd again, at Washington, Paris, Lima. He has been second in command of the U. S. embassy in London since 1923. In 1922 the Irish Free State was founded. Last week the Secretary of State announced his appointment as first U. S. Minister to that part of Ireland which is governed from Dublin. Many an Irish-American was vexed that he was not a Sullivan, O'Rourke, Kelley, Callahan, Collins, Gallagher or Shean. But loud were the praises for the administration for having made its appointments from 'career men,' not politicians.'" Or political payback for the appointees. That year Luce and *Time* lists Andrew Mellon (1855-37), father to Paul Mellon (1907-99), and his brother Richard as two of the America's four richest men alongside John D. Rockefeller and Henry Ford. When he died Rockefeller's net worth has been publicly estimated at $200 *billion*. (*Time*, December 1935)

This was Henry Luce's *Time Magazine* launched and initially financed with his Skull & Bones friends at Yale, one of whom is founder of Pan American Airlines, Juan Tripp and Trubee Davison, all having flown in the daring Yale Unit of WWI, America's first naval air force organized by Trubee and his brother and financed by their father, Morgan's own HPD. Neighbors were more fascinated than peeved by the stirring motors heard on take-offs and landings at his Long Island estate on Peacock Point. Many of them had planes of their own anyway, as flying is the fashion of the rich and young daring of the elite.

William C. Bullitt, for his part, when he's plucked by FDR to be America's first ambassador to the U.S.S.R, is decidedly on the odd-ball fringe of this batch of blue-bloods, even he did hail from Philadelphia. And *Time* won't elaborate on the relations between Phillips, Root, and Stimson and nor their inner circle of friends and clients at Morgan, an extended family that includes bright, privileged and very gifted set, the handsome elite. Thomas W. Lamont (1870-48), Harvard 1892 following his older brother Hammond '86; Tom entered the freshman class while J.P. "Jack" Morgan, Jr. was a senior. He becomes a Morgan partner in 1911 – and on the Board of Overseers at Harvard with Jack Morgan –, a mentor of several presidents and chairman of JP Morgan in 1943 His son Thomas Stilwell Lamont, (Harvard '21), becomes a vice-chairman of Morgan Guaranty Trust and Harvard Corporation fellow, and a stand out among others in this Harvard-Yale set. (In

1933 Tom W. Lamont, Sr. publishes an biographical tribute of chief Morgan banker HPD.)

Tom Lamont, son of a modest minister living in upstate New York, owes his distinguished career to the social links and status accrued in the educative formative years of early manhood; he'll send all three sons to Phillips Exeter and Harvard; Corliss Lamont, Exeter, Harvard '24, with Austin Lamont '27, became a socialist distancing himself from his father and the family fortune. I met Corliss in the late 1970s uptown in his very modest apartment in Manhattan while researching a book on his radical past. He was getting old and seemed bitter and irritated by some of my questions about his radical past so I left. (Thomas W. Lamont, *Henry P. Davison*, 1933)

EYE ON THE JAPANESE EMPIRE IN KOREA AND CHINA

In China, Bill Phillips works closely with Willard Straight. The pair play their parts as American traditionalists reaching out into the global empire with an eye on Russia. But remember, when they are born the country has existed for barely one hundred years and narrowly survived a bloody Civil War still fresh in the memory of their families.

Let's follow Straight into the center of his Consortium activities to have a better idea of finance, business, war, humanitarian relief, the press and other fields of operation under their control for the fulfillment of the people's destiny. He enjoys an amazingly illustrious but all too brief life, the envy of Midas (married into the Whitney family fortune) full of exotic adventure and excitement. Born an orphan in 1880 in New York, Straight studied architecture at Cornell (1901) where he's elected in his senior year to Sphinx. Upon graduation he's off to China with the Imperial Maritime Customs Service in Peking, clerking as secretary to Sir Robert Hart, the Service's Inspector General, and packed off to Korea in 1904 as personal Secretary to Edwin V. Morgan, US Consul General to the Kingdom of Korea. There Straight is able to get a good taste of Empire politics while looking on as the Japanese push the Chinese out of Korea, break down negotiations with the Russians over Manchuria and Korea, launch their surprise attack in Manchuria and cripple the Russian fleet at Port Arthur thus instigating a war with the Czar Nicholas lasting over a year before destroying Russia's Baltic Fleet in the Battle of Tsushima annexing Korea and south Manchuria. This severely alters the balance of power in the Far East and ends Czarist ambitions to teach "the monkeys" a lesson, as some officials in the Czarist court called the Japanese. (Louis Graves, "An American in Asia, V. Willard Straight as Consul General in Mukden", *Asia and the Americas*, v. 21, 1921)

In the clash and grab of nineteenth-century empire building, Japan sacked Korea, first with threat of force, then sending troops and outwitting the Russians who preferred to let Japan have a free hand "but all of Manchuria was to remain outside the sphere of Japanese interests. Furthermore, as professor Ki-Baik Lee observes in his history of Korea (Harvard 1988), Russia had also maintained that "the territory of Korea north of the thirty-ninth parallel be declared a neutral zone into which neither country would be permitted to introduce troops."

The Japanese are not amused. Russia's imperial adventure into Manchuria makes war with Japan a sure thing. When negotiations reach an impasse, the Japan launch its surprise attack at Port Arthur, and after warnings by their ambassador Kurino go unheeded; their emissary to negotiate, "the greatest of Japanese statesmen" Marquis Ito is snubbed when he visits St. Petersburg in February 1904. "Russia has been made by bayonets, not diplomacy," declares Vyacheslav Plehve, minister of the Interior. Having signed its Anglo-Japanese Alliance in 1902 aimed at containing the Russians, and especially weary of Russian designs in the Far East and the building of the Trans-Siberian railway, Tokyo could rely on assurances from London and Washington to support their expansionist thrust into Korea and China, in particular Manchuria.

Scholar Ki-Baik Lee in *A New History of Korea* (1988) helps to make clear what the American diplomats preferred to conceal, and which is overlooked by western historians in general, and he writes, "It no longer mattered what the Koreans wanted, for Japan's policy already was set.... The Treaty (of Portsmouth 1905 sic) first of all gave full authority over all aspects of Korea's relations with foreign countries to the Japanese Foreign Office. Secondly, it forbade the Korean government from entering into any further treaties or agreements of an international character 'except through the medium' of the Japanese government. Thirdly, it provided for the appointment of a Japanese resident-general to a position directly under the Korean emperor, to take charge of Korea's foreign relations. In sum, Japan had completely divested Korea of the sovereign power to maintain relations with foreign governments." (Robert K. Massie, *Nicholas and Alexandra*, NY: Baatam Doubleday Dell, 1967, 91-100)

In less than an hour, the Japanese fleet under Admiral Togo blasted the returning Russian battleships streaming through the Strait of Tsushima, sinking and destroying one Czarist ship after another, eight battleships in all, twelve cruisers and six destroyers. After the signing of peace in New Hampshire, the Russian minister Sergius Witte is invited by President Teddy Roosevelt to lunch at his Sagamore Hill family compound in Oyster Bay on the shores of Long Island not far from Manhattan. Witte is not impressed by the unpretentious American style of official hospitality and finds the food "for a European, almost indigestible. There was no tablecloth and ice water was served instead of wine ... Americans have no culinary taste and ... they can eat almost anything that comes their way." Roosevelt shares an equally dim view of his guest who he remembered as "a very selfish man, totally without ideals". Czar Nicholas is more impressed by his jubilant minister boasting of his brilliant negotiations and aboard his grand imperial yacht *Standart*, the Czar creates him a Count. Nicholas recalls, "He went quite stiff with emotion and then tried three times to kiss my hand!" (R. K. Massie, 97)

Reader, here again we encounter that beguiling and treacherous "iceberg" effect of pseudo history, or the myth-making and entertaining side of our Ivy League historians, in this case Massie of Yale. Why talk about the food on

Roosevelt's table when the real meat is missing from the story. A few minutes on the internet and you will see that the Roosevelt presence in the Japanese-Russian conflict is far more entertaining and revealed elsewhere. For example, consult the book on the secret voyage of the Roosevelt-Taft-Schiff ship to Japan and Asia, in *The Imperial Cruise*, by James Bradley (1910), and *Heroes and Friends, Behind the Scenes at the Treaty of Portsmouth*, by Michiko Nakanishi (2006). Light entertaining fiction passed off for significant historical context is one thing, serious treatment of what's really going on is another; it all takes place on the same stairway but you have to walk the steps. Its a long way up to the top.

All of this was quite clear and tacitly confirmed by Roosevelt, Taft, Root, Hughes and the America's foreign policy Consortium architects who stood by while Korea is converted into a police state under the control of imperial Japanese fascists as they take their turn dismembering Asia. Anyone not cooperating with the Japanese authorities was subject to prison, or worse. Nationalist newspapers were banned and the Korean language suppressed. By 1910 the Kingdom of Korea had become a subjugated colony of Japan exercising its hegemony through a Government-General, replacing the former Residency-General, and appointed by the Japanese militarists "generals or admirals on active duty, and all legislative, executive and judicial powers" which he possessed. Koreans became second-class citizens in their own country dominated by Japanese military police and thousands of Korean thugs "auxiliaries recruited from the dregs of Korean society". None of this history should have escaped the attention of our US President Taft, and his distinguished Secretary of State Henry Simpson. Quite the contrary, as their friend and fellow politician Teddy Roosevelt made the Russian Japanese experience all too clear. The Americans are merely bidding their time which will surely come and Stimson will live to see it and even be the man who decides with Truman to A-bomb "the little Japs" to end WWII in 1945 and then Herbert Hoover, the Groton Morgan man Joe Grew, Gen. MacArthur and their American cohorts go in for the real killing, taking the Japanese loot and gold estimated possibly as high as a trillion dollars worth, and secreted into slush fund bank accounts around the world.

For Americans today can tell you much if anything at all about this Korean-Japanese history. There is another side to the story of the great American liberation of Philippines from their Spanish priests. In exchange for western recognition of the annexation and plundering of Korea of virtually all its wealth and the subjugation of an entire ancient nation's population by the Japanese, US President Teddy Roosevelt received his *quid pro quo* recognition of the US military conquest and bloody annexation of the Philippines. In the conflagration of the First World War, Japan joined the Allies providing minerals and badly needed raw materials from increased mining operations in Korea. The American leaders know their day will come, so for now, let the "plucky little Japs" have their fun at The Game of conquest. Their day will come. And we all know what happens then. Winner takes all...

Ki-Baik observes, "Japan was interested not only in land but in all of Korea's natural resources. For further development of its capitalist economy Japan had to convert to the gold standard, and it relied on Korea for an assured supply of that precious material. Accordingly, Japan took gold from Korea by whatever predatory methods, and the availability of Korean gold played a decisive role in Japan's adoption of the gold standard. Following the annexation the Government-General surveyed Korea's mineral deposits and turned them over to the Japanese *zaibatsu* conglomerates for exploitation. The result was a dramatic increase in mining output. Such minerals as gold, silver, iron, lead, tungsten, and coal registered increases that were five-or six-fold in some cases or even several thousand times in others." (Ki-Baik Lee, "Japanese Aggression and the Struggle of the 'Righteous Armies', *A New History of Korea*, Harvard, 1988, 306-20)

So, while the Anglo-American Consortium during their war production in the First World War increases their war profits from violent Japanese oppression of the Koreans, and reducing the number of adversary empires with the elimination of the Austrian Hapsburgs and Russian Romanovs, they remain confident that when the opportune time came, the Japanese would be next to fall. But before that time was to come, the industrialists and bankers set it all up there for an easy killing. And that includes the Japanese and Korean financial institutions, and of course, the Korean rail lines, and national electric power services as well, in 1898, facilitated by "a company capitalized jointly by Korean and US interests".

Here is Ki-Baik of that: "Japanese financial institutions appeared in Korea just after the opening of the ports. By around 1900 a number of Japanese banks – the Daiichi Ginko most importantly but many others as well – had established branch or agency offices in Korea and had come to play the leading role in the country's financial activities. Early in 1905, when the Korea branch of the Daiichi Ginko was given authority to issue currency, it assume the role of a central bank for Korea, buying gold and silver bullion, making loans to the Government, collecting customs duties at the open ports, and otherwise undertaking a wide range of central banking functions. With the establishment of the Bank of Korea in 1909 these functions became its responsibility, but the manager of the Daiichi Ginko's general offices in Seoul was concurrently appointed to the governorship of the new bank...." In essence national banking in Korea was a Japanese affair. And the Morgan-Rockefeller-Rothschild bankers of the Consortium knew it very well and had no problem taking care of the burden of the massive Korean debt which accumulated in 1910 to some 45 million yen. (Ki-Baik Lee, sect. "Japanese Aggression and the Struggle of the 'Righteous Armies', 306-23)

Straight also plots his intrigue to advance the interests of banker Jacob Henry Schiff (1847-1920) flush with access to the Rothschild billions and responsible for at least $200 million in loans betting on the Russian defeat. Since 1897 Straight serves as junior rep for railroad tycoon E. H. Harriman involved at the time in Kuhn Loeb's reorganization of the Union Pacific railroad with Harriman, executive chairman of UP. Harriman keeps up an active correspondence with HPD *de facto* acting chairman of the all-powerful Morgan Bank on Wall Street. This is only a few years after President Teddy Roosevelt lent his support to the Japanese victory over the Russians in the Portsmouth Treaty signed in New Hampshire in exchange for Japanese endorsement of the American annexation of the Philippines and thereby enhancing a friendship that would endure for two decades until, in 1924, the US tightened its immigration laws barring Japanese immigration.

After the 1905 Russo-Japanese War, Straight briefly joins the Reuters news agency. A dash of diplomatic fun as Vice Consul and Secretary to the American minister to Seoul (Keijo) before catching some rays in Havana, and he's back in China, US Consul-General at Mukden, Manchuria in 1908 where he also serves as head of State's Division of Far Eastern Affairs. Here and now Straight renegotiates Morgan loans which facilitates Japanese repression of the Koreans and keeps the oligarchs dependent and in their control.

Living in China with his wife, Straight manages Consortium syndicate business of the Morgan partners developing railway lines in Manchuria including the Russo-Chinese Siberian. In northern China his progress is blocked by continuing hostilities between Russia and Japan. Among his official duties Straight works for Harriman interests in the Hukuang railways of the Chinese Eastern Railway negotiations. Always on the make, he has a love affair with Mary Harriman, but her father E. H. Harriman stops it cold. Announcing his engagement instead to Dorothy Whitney, they marry, in Geneva, in 1911. *The New York Times* describes him "on the rare road to fortune in his own right. This dashing giant, with his blue eyes and blonde hair and towering frame ... the poor missionary's son". Following the collapse of the Chinese Qing dynasty and the ascendancy of Sun Yat-sen as president of the new Chinese republic January 1912, the Straights sail away from the Orient and reclaim their lives in New York City's uptown millionaire social circuit. Meanwhile, the grand patriarch J. P. Morgan attends to his personal legacies including his magnificent private library as well as the New York Public Library, and leaves for Egypt, the ancient land of pharaohs and pyramids, and Europe where he indulges further in extraordinary acquisitions adding to his personal art collections, visits Rome for one final audience with the Pope, God's Holy messenger, and dies there, in 1913, just before Wilson signs the Federal Reserve Bank into law and a year before the clash of empires sparking the First World War.

Meanwhile, Harry Payne Whitney, brother of Dorothy and Payne Whitney, also sits on the board of directors of Morgan's Guaranty Trust during the Russian Revolution. He once owned *Metropolitan Magazine* that published the newly arrived brazen socialist John Reed during his rise to national fame with on-the-scene reporting of the Ludlow, Colorado mining massacre scandal by Rockefeller-financed thugs, and his reporting from Mexico on the trail with Pancho Villa in 1914, when Reed is fast eclipsing Jack London as the best writer in America, already one step ahead of F. Scott Fitzgerald and two leaps in front of Ernest Hemingway. Reed's connection to that capitalist Morgan property does not go unnoticed by his peers and exposes him to sharp rebuke by leftist radicals and fellow socialists, including his friend and Harvard classmate Walter Lippmann. (*The NYT*, July 30, 1911)

With his wife's huge Whitney fortune Straight bankrolls liberal public opinion in America. During the First World War, in 1915, Straight launches

The New Republic magazine, edited by Herbert Croly and Harvard's Walter Lippmann. The self-proclaimed champion of liberal causes Lippmann (of Jewish descent but few knew), just seven years after he graduates from Harvard, – along with Reed and T. S. Eliot among others of that distinguished class of 1910,– drafts Wilson's controversial Fourteen Points 1917 Peace Plan devised to smooth the America's official entry into the Great War for democracy, and, they proclaimed "to end all wars". (Reed and Lippmann become fiercely jealous rivals.) And the people believed that! But what else could they do in the time of war when minds go mad with irrational passions? Better to just tell the people what they want to hear and repeat it endlessly until they think not differently.

Straight leaves the Morgan bank to work for the American International Corporation (AIC). Once the Russian Czar abdicates clearing the way for Wilson, son a minister and defender of the faith, declares war on Kaiser Wilhelm which leaves Straight in his job in charge of the President's War Risk Insurance Bureau selling life insurance to 250,000 American soldiers overseas. It raises more than $1 billion for their war chest. Straight and Secretary of State Lansing negotiated American war loans from National City Bank.

Thus personally enriched by the combined Payne Whitney fortunes Straight deftly steers the liberal Left discreetly financing both *The Nation* magazine *and* the *New Republic.* But his stellar life suddenly ends tragically when shortly after the Armistice, in November 1918, Straight, 38, dies, in Paris, a casualty of the dreaded influenza epidemic decimating world populations by the tens of millions and prompting an abrupt abrogation of the war business and imposing a *cordon sanitaire* on Europe's Eastern Front with Russia. Straight's negotiations for Morgan with Japan's Imperial Emperor Hirohito, and his militarist family clans are maintained and strengthened in the twenties by Morgan men including Tom Lamont, Joe Grew and Jack Morgan, as well as Hoover and Stimson in the White House.

With Straight's passing, newspaper editor and Consortium conduit Herbert Croly, mutually close to muckraking journalist Lincoln Steffens and maverick Reed, writes Bill Bullitt, on July 23, 1918, lingering at the State Department, informing him that Tom Lamont who had once been a junior reporter has secretly acquired *The New York Evening Post.* The property had actually been offered to Davison, Morgan's chief banker and the man sent to England during the summer of 1914 to assure Allied gold shipments to the US in exchange for lucrative war industry supply orders that prolonged the war for years. He declines the *Post* deal. With America sending troops to Europe Harry Davison is appointed chairman of the American Red Cross.

Besides handling the Bank of England's gold shipments to the United States – he had been a principal founder of the Federal Reserve Bank in 1913, – H. P. Davison is an active "Dollar-A-Year" volunteer in the war effort through the War Department responsible for Liberty Loan campaigns raising millions of dollars from the American people whipped into a frenzy to get into the war with a promise of paid dividends as a good return on their noble sacrifice and contribution. It is hailed as "patriotism", this at a time war critics are shackled in jail cells under the country's emergency sedition and espionage laws rushed through Congress, along with contentious objectors to the imperial slaughter in Europe.

Overnight it became a crime risking arrest, indictment and prison to publish articles against the war. Soon *The Masses*, published on the Lower East Side of Manhattan by Max Eastman and his wife Crystal is suppressed inflaming America's nascent revolutionary left-wing socialists led by John Reed. On the opposite side of the political spectrum, Charlie Merrill, chief of the investment firm he co-founds, Merrill Lynch, based on the same Liberty Bond premise proving the reliability of the maxim that the masses could themselves share in the democratic fruits of the nation's newly enriched prosperity and soon become robust capitalist shareholders and own a piece of the great American corporate enterprise system of the expanding economy.

To run *The Post*, Tom Lamont forms an investor group bringing together Consortium bigwigs Ellery Sedgwick of the *Atlantic Monthly*, Henry Smith Pritchett, an ex-President of MIT and a trustee of the Carnegie Institute, and Theodore Vail principal owner of American Telegraph and Telephone Company (AT&T) and Western Union. Lamont asks Croly to list names "of any people who were in my opinion competent to make *The Post* a progressive and independent publication, and I suggested you as a person with whom he should at least talk over his plans". Herbert Croly, himself considered by many too "radical" at the *New Republic* to take over as chief editor at *The Post*, passes the offer to Bill Bullitt. Croly sends Bullitt a note to use the newspaper as an instrument, he declares, for building "an independent vigorous vehicle of American progressive thought", that is, of course, all within the structure and restraint of the politically correct. It would be yet another media tool to pacify the American masses, and of course owned and controlled by the Consortium, but that much goes without mention. With Straight's unexpected departure, Croly retires to write Straight's biography, published in 1924, with intriguing details long since forgotten and for the most part ignored, about the Morgan links to revolutionary China during the end of the Manchu Dynasty. Six years later Croly joins his Maker, but not without first regretting in a last fatalistic judgment, that his own life has been a public failure.

With Soviet Russia always very much on his mind, the young and brassy Bullitt has big plans. He graciously declines the top journalist position and instead crept closer to Col. House, his political godfather.

THE ENIGMATIC AND STRANGE MR. HOUSE

Bullitt began a life-long and intimate friendship with the "Colonel". House was a key Consortium insider, and former White House player in the Wilson administration during the rapidly unfolding events of Czarist Russian chaos in the Great War and Lenin's Bolshevik coup Bullitt had blundered terribly then and knows he ought to play a more sophisticated role inside the political machinations of the great Game that channeled the stories that editors censored under the Committee of Public Information (CPI) wartime censorship bureau shaping public opinion. Croly and Bullitt had been friends then. They stay in touch.

After Bullitt's failed million for House to Lenin in Moscow, and his return from Petrograd with journalists Lincoln Steffens and Arthur Ransome on August 1, 1919 Croly invites Bullitt to leave his home at 222 West Rittenhouse Square in Philadelphia's smart district for a summer jaunt in Maine and a little "camping in a huge house formerly occupied by the President, and as we have very few servants".

Croly adds, "I have never had a chance, yet of telling you how much I admire and sympathized with your action in openly protesting against the Treaty of Peace. If a dozen other people had the guts to follow your example the whole apple cart might have been upset. Nobody's record in the whole matter was anything like as good as yours."

The American political scene repositioned after the Versailles debacle. The Wall Street office of Cravath, Saine & Moore ranks high among Consortium law firms. Squashing any official US-Soviet trade deal in Paris House is assisted by a young lawyer Gordon Auchincloss (1886-43) who married his daughter, Janet House, in 1912. He's a heavy hitter with real clout, the Manhattan corporate lawyer the Anglophile Paul D. Cravath (1861-40) for Kuhn Loeb. House used his position to overstep Wilson's authority, out-flanks Baruch, Lansing and other advisors with privileged access and even advised the President to stay in Washington and not attend the Versailles Conference. Cravath is a Pilgrim and soon co-founder of the Council on Foreign Relations (CFR), and a Davison neighbor in Long Island's lush Locust Valley.

As we see during the Holodomor years as anyone in the Consortium Paul Cravath is an expert on Stalin, US-Soviet trade and US foreign policy. In 1917 when the Americans entered the war in Cravath was already in London and Paris attached to the US Treasury Department with the US Mission of the Inter-Allied Council on War Purchases and Finance for which he would be proudly honored with a chest full of medals, from France, Romania and Italy.

Lenin does not get the official diplomatic recognition and the financial aid he so urgently needs to counter the civil war raging between the Communist Reds and the Whites apparently backed by the Anglo-American interventionists.

In April 1919, in Paris Bullitt's plans for Lenin undergo a serious revision. House and the Auchincloss brothers draft a proposal "which would have been practically an offer to feed Soviet Russia, provided full control of its railways was placed in the hands of foreigners, etc., etc.". Of course that doesn't fly. It fails to capture Lenin's endorsement. Bullitt is furious, and the Americans think Bullitt had gone native, crossed over to Lenin and the Bolshevik side. "I blew up entirely", Bullitt wrote after his return to the West. He spends the next few years "in diplomatic exile" in the French sun on the Riviera.

Who are they? Bear with me reader as the genealogy does wind with the spiraling complexity of DNA into branches of the expansive family tree with cousins everywhere and leading straight into the White House and top levels of the State Department.

Lawyer Gordon Auchincloss has done very well for himself. He is a big player. Only ten years before the War he was a senior at Groton, then Yale (1908) and Harvard Law School (1911). Born in New York in 1886, the seventh of eight children of Edgar Stirling Auchincloss and Maria La Grange (Sloan) Auchincloss, Hugh is one of his brothers along with Charles, James, and Reginald. Waspy enough?

Gordon is only six when his father, a Manhattan merchant dies. The family survives with a comfortable inheritance of vast wealth from his mother who lives to 1930, a daughter of Samuel Sloan, president of the Delaware, Lackawanna & Western Railroad and the Hudson River Railroad. A year after Yale, Gordon meets Janet House in Europe during a summer vacation. They marry three years later. Their first child, Louise is born in 1914; the second, Edward House Jr., in 1929.

From Harvard Gordon joins the firm of Hawkins, Delafield & Longfellow in 1911; in April 1915, he's working in the Miller & Auchincloss firm with his cousin David Hunter Miller. (Col. House's wife Louise is a Hunter.) He assists his father-in-law House who introduces him to all the right people in Wilson's Democratic administration including Wilson's son-in-law, William Gibbs McAdoo, Thomas Watt Gregory, Vance McCormick, Frank L. Polk and other prominent men.

By 1916 Gordon takes an active part in Wilson's reelection campaign as assistant treasurer of the Democratic National Committee. After Wilson's victory Auchincloss enters at the top level at State, moves to Washington and assumes his responsibilities as personal secretary to Frank Polk, virtually taking over the office when Polk falls ill in April 1918 right when America enters the war. When Auchincloss travels to London and Paris in 1917 Gordon is by his side as secretary of the American War Mission and at the Inter-Allied Conference, and stays with House in Paris during Armistice negotiations and at Versailles, also mixed up with the organization of the League of Nations, and on Hoover's ARA work in Russia.

Gordon Auchincloss returns to the United States in August 1919. His Washington law firm expands with more partners and changes to Parker, Marshall, Miller & Auchincloss. Gordon is considered a rising star in the nation's capitol with a stunning Consortium client list of trustees and receiverships with his firm litigating major bankruptcies and reorganizations. Less than a decade out of Harvard Law School Gordon Auchincloss is the envy of lesser peers and sits on a stack of corporate boards, national and foreign. But his life won't be long and he dies in 1943.

Hugh Auchincloss is sometimes confused with his cousin, the younger Hugh Dudley Auchincloss, Jr. (1897-76), Groton, Yale (1920) Columbia Law (1924), and the son of Hugh D. Auchincloss, Sr. (1858-13), a merchant and financier. HDA, Jr. becomes a lawyer and stockbroker, and the father-in-law the future wife of JFK, Jacqueline ("Jackie") Kennedy. (Harvey Bundy's youngest daughter Katherine Lawrence Bundy married Hugh Auchincloss, Jr.)

Hugh was born on the family's Hammersmith Farm in Newport, and he's the nephew of Edgar Stirling Auchincloss and John Winthrop Auchincloss. So it follows that his father is the youngest brother of Edgar Stirling Auchincloss Sr., the father of Gordon and his brother Hugh, and also cousin of the politician James C. Auchincloss. All of them are part and parcel of the Consortium players. One big happy family. During both World Wars the younger Hugh Auchincloss joins in Naval intelligence and State, and he, too, is to be found working with Hoover's Commerce Department; still later, in 1927, we see him linking with the Morgan men and Dwight Whitney Morrow on aviation issues. Four years later, in 1931, upon a vast inheritance from his mother he resigns from government work to build his own Washington brokerage firm, Auchincloss, Parker & Redpath, and associated with Chase National Bank, Solvay, Sofina, and the Gross & Blackwell firm. And through a succession of marriages Hugh Auchincloss becomes father-in-law to both Gore Vidal and Jacqueline Bouvier, the future First Lady Mrs. John F. Kennedy. (Col. Edward House Papers Yale Univ. Archives; Gordon Auchincloss Papers, Yale Archives)

Investment banker Lewis L. Strauss (Kuhn, Loeb) who Bullitt succeeds as ambassador in Paris, late 1936, after his Holodomor years, also happens to be in Russia at this time and admitted that "he was one of four American delegates" conferring with the Germans at Brussels in March 1919 on the final Armistice, according to Eustace Mullins who doesn't tell us who were the other "delegates" or what exactly Strauss was doing in Russia.

On November 11, 1918, *The New York Times* headlines, "REDS GRIP ON GERMANY: Königsberg, Frankfurt-on-Main, Strassburg now controlled by Spartacist Soviets". Next day the newspaper states, "The revolution in Germany is today, to all intents and purposes, an accomplished fact." It also runs a banner headline "Splendor Reigns Again; Jewels Ablaze" assuring the "Dollar-A-Year" millionaires on President Wilson's War Industries Board that indeed the war was over and peace restored.

Life in Manhattan could return back to the unabashed prewar pomp and celebrity comforts the Consortium wives and their husbands enjoyed, having been assured by key Consortium financiers in AIC behind the Bols once Russia withdrew from the war. The occasion was a gala evening at the Metropolitan Opera, with Caruso and Homer signing *Samson and Delilah.* Also in attendance among the guests were the Otto Kahns with the French Consul General, the George F. Bakers and his sister Mrs. Goadby Loew, Cornelius Vanderbilt and his daughters, the Whitneys, the JP Morgans, the E.T. Stotesburys, the Fricks, and Mrs. Bernard Baruch. Her husband remains in Europe. What better reason to take the wives to the Opera.

Later, on October 1, 1919, Bullitt writes his friend Croly and sends him a reading list, commenting "economic theory is a thing I know nothing about. I have never even read a word of Marx or Henry George." A curious confession having boasted of intimate talks with Lenin. "Will you treat me as a child who craves a knowledge of Economics, History and Politics?" Bullitt adds. Remember, reader, Bullitt will soon be FDR's bellwether in Moscow face to face with Stalin.

That winter Bullitt rents Croly's summer house in Cornish, Vermont; on November 26, when President Wilson fell ill and remained sequestered with his wife and intimate assistant, Joseph Tumulty, Croly wrote, "I understand, by the way, that Wilson is really pretty bad. I heard on excellent authority yesterday that Col. House has not seen him since his return to this country and that Wilson himself does not know even that Colonel House is in this country. He does not know anything that Tumulty does not want him to know." During US military intervention against the Bols, Tumulty and Wall Street mogul "Bernie" Baruch are among the few visitors permitted to visit the infirm President. The falling out between House and Wilson is a most curious affair of suspicion and betrayal that ought to intrigue historians and non-specialists alike. It was not pretty nor was the world they left behind but that particular relationship it is not the focus of this book.

Godfrey Hodgson, another protector of closely guarded secrets and author of a clean Yale version of the House story (and published in part with funds from a foundation established at Yale), *Woodrow Wilson's Right Hand* (2007), however notes regarding House's dubious loyalty to the dying President: "House was nevertheless moved by Wilson's death. ... House intended to go to the funeral but was told by Bernard Baruch that he would not be admitted. So he gave up and went to Madison Square Garden, where the service was broadcast, but he arrived too late and had to stand outside in the rain." Reader, mark that from this point of view it is clear something very odd affected one of the most strange and powerful relationships that ever existed in the White House and that involved much more than "the collapse of their hopes for the league" with consequences affecting the peace and prosperity of the entire world. (Godfrey Hodgson, *Woodrow Wilson's Right Hand*, Yale Univ. Press, 2007, 263)

Moscow had been his baptism where he underwent his first experience with the Bolsheviks fighting for survival besieged by civil war and a foreign invasion. In her book, *Loans and Legitimacy* (1996), Katherine Siegel is unimpressed by Bullitt's early 1919 mission finding him to be more the postering flamboyant, a sort of decadent bohemian play-acting on the world stage. "All parties including House and Wilson," Siegel writes, "envisioned the trip as an 'exploratory' effort sounding out the Bols "rather than a serious negotiating session. Everyone, that is, except Bullitt."

Lenin and Bullitt meet on March 11. Trotsky resists Anglo-American terms that Soviets remain in control of their occupied areas, and the West would end the Allied intervention and blockade after agreement on an eight point plan set by Archibald ("Archie") Philip Kerr, another of Lord Milner and private Secretary to British Prime Minister David Lloyd George. More subterfuge during the secret undeclared war in eastern Europe and revolutionary Russia? Col. House hopes, according to Siegel's account, that by sending Bullitt to see Soviet Russia first hand, it might "cure him of his Bolshevism". While Steffens boasts about seeing the future "and it works", Bullitt rejoiced proclaiming "the red terror is over", convinced the best justification of that insight is that "prostitutes have disappeared from sight, the economic reasons for their career having ceased to exist". Perhaps he arrived too late or, too early. (K. Siegel, *Loans and Legitimacy,* 42)

"In the Ukraine," Lenin assures British journalist Arthur Ransome in early 1919 during Bullitt's mission, "you will certainly see our policy modified. Civil war, whatever happens, is likely to be more bitter in the Ukraine than elsewhere, because there the instinct of property has been further developed in the peasantry, and the minority and majority will be more equal."

Stalinist measures of 'dekulaksation" are still a decade off. But for primers in his book *Russia in 1919* Arthur Ransome describes the political chaos of the revolutionary era as the Bols seized power in Moscow, Petrograd and throughout Russia. Ukraine repeatedly fell in and out of the hands of Germany's Russian White Guards under the ruthless General Deniken aided by "the least civilized colonial troops of the Entente" along the Black Sea in the Crimea. The Republic had been proclaimed in Kharkov, but at that time Kiev was still in the hands of the Directorate Lenin urges Ransome to travel and see for himself "saying that I could go down to Kiev to watch the revolution there as I had watched it in Moscow".

Over a decade passes and in 1934 Stalin personally and emphatically insisting upon Bullitt tells Roosevelt's man the Soviet Union urgently needs heavy railway track and locomotives if it is to adequately counter the challenge of an inevitable war with the Japanese in the vast wilderness of Russia's Far Eastern frontier; it is the same refrain of 1919 when Bullitt heard the urgent appeal by Lenin and the Moscow Soviet embroiled in civil war in sore need of locomotives and tractors, and fuel, to move resources along the rails to feed the population dying of famine. What a tremendous opportunity for the Consortium masters! Ransome leaves Russia together with Steffens and Bullitt, journalists and spies each and every one playing out their unique roles in the Great Game. (Arthur Ransome, *Russia in 1919,* 229)

Bill Phillips over at State is already working for his third "C.C." in the White House. Phillips teams with the Department's Consortium lawyers Frank L. Polk who during the war worked closely with Sir William ("Willie") Wiseman of the British Secret Service. Polk heads the American Legation in the Versailles peace negotiations. In 1915 Polk was appointed Counselor to Secretary of State Robert Lansing, and was essentially second-in-command there. Wiseman is privy to direct and privileged contact with Col. House who considered their relationship most favorably and superseded the British ambassador Sir Cecil Spring Rice; William Franklin Sands in Washington and the American-Russian Industrial Syndicate in Manhattan to coordinate Consortium tactics of payments for the Bolshevik takeover of Russia's tottering imperial empire. Phillips, Lansing, Polk, Sands, Wiseman. They are some of the key figures at State for the Consortium with eyes turned toward Russia.

The American-Russian Industrial Syndicate was the predecessor to the American-Russian Chamber of Commerce (ARCC) at 261 Fifth Avenue in Manhattan with backing from brothers of the Jewish House of Guggenheim with a fortune assured by their flagship American Smelting and Refining and offices at 120 Broadway, New York City, associates of William Boyce Thompson of the New York Fed and the Red Cross spy mission sent to St. Petersburg to facilitate the Bolshevik coup Harry F. Sinclair, president of Sinclair Gulf, a Rockefeller operation, was also located at 120 Broadway. J. G. White and the American-Russian Industrial Syndicate share addresses at 43 Exchange Place. The plot thickens leading to the Holodomor in the near distant future.

The Guggenheims of New York made a fortune during WWI mostly in copper needed for cable and electricity. Their mines from Mexico to North America, Alaska down to Chile worked 24 hours a day for maximum output. Biographer John H.

Davis writes in his chapter "Harvest of War": "The estimate of the Guggenheim's net worth of from $200 to $300 million after World War I is based on the family's holdings in Utah Copper, Chile Copper, Kennecott Copper, and American Smelting and Refining in 1920... by the end of 1923 Guggenheim's holdings are worth close to $253 million (over $2 billion). (J. H. Davis, *The Guggenheims*, 554)

James G. White (b. 1861) of J. G. White Engineering, a big Consortium firm in the US-Soviet reconstruction under Stalin with offices in Washington, DC and London. White became an engineering contractor in New York in 1890 and a Pilgrim by 1903. A director in the American-Russian Industrial Syndicate, White prospers as a principal foreign contractor on the huge Soviet Svir hydroelectric dam built with soviet slave labor from Stalin's national system of communist gulag death camps. He became president of General Reinsurance Corp., director of various public utility corporations as well as a member of the Japan Society and Italy-America Society in Manhattan, both Pilgrims Society fronts still active today. (Keith Jeffrey, *The Secret History of MI6*, NY: Penguin Press, 2010, 113-4)

After Versailles, Bill Phillips who two decades later will head OSS operations in London, shifts his attention to the European theater and reconstruction as US minister to the Netherlands (1920-1922), then ambassador to Luxembourg and Belgium (1924-1927); in 1927, he became America's minister to Canada then still very much under the British crown where he stays before joining Stimson in Washington at State as his chief foreign affairs adviser for a few more years under FDR.

That's when *Time Magazine* brought him out from behind the curtain and pegged him as one of "Cordell Hull's croquet-playing cronies", a cute falsification to divert public attention from the real course of power. *Time* sets the stage for consumption of public opinion; this is what Luce does and he profits handily from it creating quite a reputation for himself and his small but fast-growing corporate empire. An innuendo of diversion the opposite was true. Phillips had neither the time, nor interest in Hull nor croquet. He's a top Consortium man, and later joins the diplomatic embassy network in Europe with Bullitt in Paris, Joe Kennedy in London, and Joe Davies in Moscow.

Keeping his hands in Europe's prewar politics, the suave and gracious puppeteer replaced Breckinridge Long to smooth relations with Mussolini in Rome after his Ethiopian adventure (Long had opposed oil embargo) and from where he can observe more closely his German friends in the Reich. The same day the Japanese bomb Pearl Harbor Phillips leaves Italy for Washington. He will soon be called to coordinate the State Department's handling of "Wild Bill" Donovan's newly authorized wartime spy agency, the Office of Strategic Services (OSS), precursor to the CIA.

For more on FDR's handling of top-secret intercepts of Japanese transmissions leading up to Pearl Harbor, and Phillips'conversation with Bill Donovan and Edward R. Murrow, CBS TV news correspondent, read Robert B. Stinnett's *Day of Deceit: The Truth about FDR and Pearl Harbo*r (2000). Stinnett's conclusions of FDR's cunning waiting game to get America into the war and overcome an isolationist American public includes research from over 200,000 documents and interviews many obtained under the Freedom of Information Act. His findings include over a hundred pages of detailed notes revealing volumes of intercepted coded and decrypted Japanese cables indicating conclusively that "Roosevelt knew of the impending attack by the Japanese" as "a systematic plan had been in place long before Pearl Harbor that would climax with the attack". (R. B. Stinnett, 258-9)

Almost to the day a year later, on December 21, 1942, *Time* writes, "At 64, Ambassador Phillips is "a patient, conservative diplomat who has never ruffled feathers nor interfered with history." Over pressure from Churchill over Phillip's meddling with the Indian independence movement of Mahatma Gandhi, Pandit Nehru and opposition leader J. P. Narayan, in 1943 FDR shifts Phillips over to Gen. Eisenhower's staff headquarters as special adviser; subsequently he oversees the brief *sejour* of Edward Stettinius when he becomes Secretary of State.

Unfortunately for the Ukrainians the spineless Hull shows more remarkably more passion for croquet at Woodley and free trade issues against protective tariffs than he did for the cunning statecraft skills of his peers who usurp his back woods style of authority. Hull likes to retire at Stimson's Woodley estate late evenings for mint julips and a good gentlemanly game on the finely trimmed lawn. It is his only recreation. There Hull and his wife escape from Washington's formal diplomatic dinners of the very rich, high and mighty. Hull plays the fool during the Terror-Famine years of the Holodomor while Stimson, Phillips and FDR run the show from the White House.

Acquired by Stimson in 1929 for $800,000 Woodley with its vast private grounds Hull is privileged to use it for his Washington residence. Woodley held a specially endowed place in American history. The land had once been the hunting grounds of the Nacotchtank Indians who in the seventeenth century lived on the far side of the Anacostia River. England's Lord Baltimore granted the land to Henry Darnell in 1668. This was the time when the young Russia Czar Peter built the Venice of the North, St. Petersburg out of a swamp exacting the labor from every corner of his realm including foreign guests.

If only the walls could speak! Woodley had served as the summer home to four presidents. President Grover Cleveland lived there with his family, as did Martin van Buren, eighth President of the United States voted out of office after the banking Panic of 1837. General George Patton rented it and galloped his polo ponies over its grand lawns. There Col. House negotiated America's secret war plans with the Germans in 1916; a career insider at the State Department Adolf A. Berle Jr. (1895-71) since the First World War moves in and occupies the estate with his family when the Stimsons are away and later rents it in 1939. Stimson owns the house until 1946, and finally shortly before his death donates it to his beloved Andover prep school. (David F. Schmitz, *Henry L. Stimson*, Delaware, 2001)

Edward R. Stettinius, Sr. is another key Consortium player adept at the business of war and reconstruction. A Morgan partner Stettinius Sr. is appointed in 1917 surveyor-general in the War Department to oversee *all* war-related purchases for the government. His liaison in Paris is H. Herman Harjes, the 39-year-old senior partner of the Morgan-Harjes Bank. There Harjes works hand in glove with US Ambassador Robert Bacon, likewise a Morgan man appointed by Republican President Taft in 1909.

With Consortium men of the position and rank in the network of Stettinius and Davison, Baruch and Schiff and so many others that here we are at the tip of the pyramid, America emerged from the First World War as a global empire and the world's largest arms manufacturer with an industrial capacity surpassing England and France combined. After his war work, Stettinius left Washington and works out of the London office where he continues channeling mass purchases in their Foreign Commerce Corp. created to finance world trade and rebuild Europe.

Stettinius Sr., as is common among insiders, likes to pass stock tips exchanging between partners and other players. Stettinius is also empowered with managing the personal stock accounts of Jack Morgan, son and heir of J.P Senior, along with Tom Lamont; in 1922, Stettinius warns H. P. Davison against buying a certain stock until a statement showing a debt "of about $58 million as indicated in the memo attached hereto ... shall have been published". That sort of insider confidentiality among partners is worth millions and pays Stettinius handsome career dividends. His son, E. Stettinius Jr. (1900-49) leaves the University of Virginia without a degree though gains access inside UV's secret Seven Society with its bizarre cult traditions. Frank Wisner (OSS- CIA) is another member.

In 1931 the younger Stettinius succeeds family friend John Lee Pratt as vice president of General Motors, created in 1908 by William C. Durant which under DuPont's direction and financial control becomes America's largest corporation. After a brief stint in 1933 on the advisory board of Roosevelt's NRA the next year he rejoins Pratt at US Steel; in 1939 Stettinius returns to government as FDR's head of Office of Production Management and chairman of the War Resources Board. Both Pratt and Stettinius are not indifferent to Stalin's industrialization and steel production capacity managed under conditions of prison slave labor. To think otherwise would be to logically and similarly deny the German people knowledge and responsibility of Hitler's Nazi campaign of extermination of Jews, Slavs and ethnic minorities.

By 1941, Stettinius is promoted to manage FDR's brainchild to aid Stalin and heads Lend-Lease operations alongside Harriman, officially becoming an undersecretary, in 1943; the next year Stettinius takes over as Secretary of State pushing aside an embittered and physically weakened Hull. That leaves Harriman to shadow FDR, Churchill and Stalin. Hull steps further in the background complaining of physical exhaustion. The stress of Consortium war work grievously hinders Stettinius, too, and cuts him down at his prime. Stettinius. Four years after the end of WWII, and just short of fifty Stettinius dies suddenly, and is buried in the family cemetery plot at Locust Valley, Long Island. (R. Chernow, *The House of Morgan*, 189, 306; D. Acheson, 88; G. Colby, *DuPont Dynasty,* 1974, 1984, ed.)

THE ODD COUPLE: ROOSEVELT AND HIS AMBASSADOR IN MOSCOW

Roosevelt and Bullitt share as strange as any relationship perhaps ever between an American president and his diplomatic rep in Moscow. It certainly would not bid well for the Ukrainians. A long-time supporter of Soviet recognition, Bullitt always felt personally indebted to FDR, wrote many of his campaign speeches and affectionately considered him a father substitute. Republicans who hate FDR never fully understood the President or how many American lives he actually saved through his support of Stalin *before* and during the war. It was easier to brand FDR a communist than begrudgingly credit any success – even if they did win the war.

Stalin's repression continued unabated in the Ukraine. Human life disappeared into numbers and statistics. After FDR agrees to official recognition of the USSR, Stalin continues sending hoards of OGPU secret police to exterminate Ukrainian and Russian peasants and cleansed the Communist Party, military and Soviet society of dissident opposition, Stalin played cat and mouse with Bullitt. So did FDR on top of his own game of brinksmanship with the dictator. But when Stalin toys with the lives of men and women he plays for keeps; Stalin's aim is always to show that only he decides their fate.

Hand-picked and sent to Moscow on the sole authority of the President, Bullitt is instructed not to intervene in any way with Stalin's campaign of terror. From the beginning FDR aims to placate Stalin. Long before Munich FDR is the grand appeaser and not unlike the supreme dictator plays a game of wait and see and let the sadistic tyrant construct his defensive fortress to counter the Nazi fascism. Bullitt in Moscow is assisted by small staff of Russian experts based in Riga, Latvia on the Russian border; for years since the US closed its embassy during the Bolshevik revolution Riga serves as a listening post. Throughout the 1930s the fear of another outbreak of war leaves the world leaders spellbound and fearing the worst. Bullitt ignores the Holodomor Genocide and quickly wearies of the dull Soviet life and proves to be entirely ineffectual apart from indulging his passion for real estate in procuring the building to house the new American embassy.

By 1937 FDR sweeps out the door virtually all the top Russian hands except for only a few. George Kennan and Chip Bohlen are spared. Both speak Russian. Bullitt's replacement is a political appointee Joe Davies, the corporate lawyer from Wisconsin who gained national notoriety defending Ford Motor Company shareholders in a highly publicized tax case winning millions against the US Treasury and pays tribute to FDR's ascendancy to the White House, adding to his fame by a recent marriage to the glamorous and talented cereal heiress Marjorie Merriweather Post. Reader, do you really think for one minute that the insider lawyer for the Ford Motor Co. would be ignorant about the US-Soviet truck-tank conversion war factory business? Hard to swallow? Think again. You don't have to drink endless toasts of vodka to get the picture. And how else would Stalin move so rapidly hundreds of thousands of prisoners to the gulag cattle-car trains? Thank you, Mr. Ford.

Although foreign policy falls constitutionally under the mandate of the President, FDR was in no way solely responsible for his policy towards Stalin and the Ukraine. So, who really controlled the dance with the devil? No two men were more strikingly incompatible and devious than FDR and Stalin who were as much separated as they were united by their differences. Who were the players who could? Where was the power behind the President in his Oval Office? As one of FDR's intermediaries with Stalin, the reader will see how the record shows that Bullitt was no more than a pawn on the chessboard of power politics, global alliances and secret treaties. The colossal destruction and political disaster of the First World War, led to Versailles which in turn directly led to the reconstruction and rearmament of Europe and Russia.

Reader, follow this closely. Stay on course. That war revealed for the 20th century how diplomats and generals born in the 19th century played out their roles in the war games of an arbitrary and virtually inhuman power eminent within the structure of an all-mighty Consortium of combinations of finance and industry that would affect generations well into the 21st century. Guardians of American history and culture intended it to be that way once they had deposited their fortunes *outside* government, and *in* private foundations, universities, mega corporations and banks while always holding onto the strings of government and public service. Their associates were embedded in useful positions wherever needed to extend their influence and master the power of their control.

Absolute tyranny destroys absolutely. Today freedom in the Ukraine creates new conditions for freedom to progress in the future. Ukraine struggles to realize its own destiny and to meet the challenge to measure up to the task to interpret this chapter in its Soviet history between the two world wars and understand how the western powers ruled over its fate. Therein lay the even more terrible and sinister story of the Ukrainian Terror-Famine.

Stalin could not have existed without the policies of elite industrialists and bankers inside the State Department, and administrations of Hoover and FDR, and the capital and technology provided by their political support in Washington. It is an indisputable fact that billions of dollars worth of American technology credits and loans, indeed some of the most advanced technology in the world, had not prevented what may very well be the single most devastating famine in world history.

That same investment in state-of-the-art industrial technology and technical support principally provided by the Americans sustained Stalin and the Russian communist leadership in the Kremlin as masters of a giant national military industrial production. Again the principal burden of war fell upon the Ukrainians. When Hitler broke the German-Soviet Non-Aggression Pact in June 1941, Stalin quickly reaffirmed his alliance with Roosevelt and the West to defeat Nazi Germany and liberate Europe from fascism.

It was both a blessing and a curse. Only six months after Hitler's Nazis invaded the Ukraine, June 22, 1941, the Soviet Red Army had lost at least *four and a half million* men. Hitler called the Battle of Kiev "the greatest battle in the history of the world". In only a few weeks the defense of Kiev left 700,000 dead or missing; on September 19 the Germans occupy Kiev. Nazi occupation lasts 778 days. Kiev's population in 1940 of 900,000 is leveled to only 186,000 by 1945. During four years of war Soviet officers are killed at a rate fourteen times that suffered by Russian Czarist troops in the First World War. Millions of civilians perished, survivors of Stalin's Terror-Famine which persisted into the years of the Purges used to build his absolute despotism in preparation for war against Hitler.

When Stalin ceased the Great Purge the Soviet Army trained in the thirties was literally destroyed; its numbers at least doubled during the war. Some thirty-nine million men were mobilized, including 800,000 women who share the hardships at the front. By April 1942, a new Soviet law frees the kulaks, early victims of the Terror-Famine desperately needed and most to perish in the defense of the Motherland. (C. Merridale, *Ivan's War*)

STALIN'S ECONOMIC PLANS & THE GREAT DEPRESSION

The year before America's 1929 Great Depression on Wall Street Stalin pushed through his plan of agricultural repressions in the Ukrainian countryside. Stalin's state socialist terrorism was praised by America's elite banking and corporate Consortium as a Brave New World controlled by international finance and trade. Stalin needed a positive image. Up until then the USSR had enjoyed several years of relative progress and freedom with an explosion in society and the arts. Then JD Rockefeller, Jr.'s personal assistant Ivy Lee reappears on the Moscow scene.

Ivy Lee is member of the elite Pilgrims and the Council of Foreign Relations (CFR), Princeton fund-raiser, and master spinner of Consortium PR.; dubbed "Poison Ivy Lee" by a union during the Ludlow affair and for many it stuck. In May 1927, Lee had travels to Soviet Russia as Rockefeller's agent to promote US-Soviet trade and raise capital selling Bolshevik bonds through the Morgan-Rockefeller banking syndicate. Lee publishes a pro-Soviet propaganda book to whitewash Soviet terror and hype Stalin's Five-Year Plans (*Piatiletka)* for agriculture and industry, actually a crash program for military conversion of peacetime trade. Lee is well paid to paint a pretty picture of the USSR as a favorable environment for US capital and trade.

Only a few top insiders and engineers are privy to the details The Plans many of whom were Morgan men and mostly all the same trained and experienced architects and managers of President Wilson's huge trade of the First World War. This is the same group which eagerly sold patriotic Liberty Bonds to the American people finance the European war while banking millions of dollars for their own private banks while publicly declaring that their jobs were voluntary service to the war effort. These "dollar-a-year" men – no salary – liked to appear to the public as self-sacrificing model citizens, volunteers for the great national cause. In reality they are experts at fraud and organized crime only there were no lawyers to prosecute them. They and many of their best friends are lawyers, protectors and beneficiaries.

Immediately after the 1917 October Bolshevik coup, Rockefeller's Standard Oil of New Jersey obtained 50% of Nobel's huge Caucasus oil fields in southern Russia, – but not the Rothschilds Baku wells. During the Russian Civil War operatives at Standard Oil and the Rothschilds make deals with both Whites and the Reds. In the midst of the great Russian famine the International Barnsdall Corporation owned by Morgan's Guaranty Trust (a Rothschild front) in 1921 reopens the Caucasian oil fields for Lenin providing desperately needed foreign exchange which helps launch his vision for rebuilding Russia, the New Economic Policy (NEP). "Socialism," Lenin declared, "is merely the next step forward from State capitalist monopoly. Or in other words, socialism is merely state capitalist monopoly which is made to serve the interests of the whole people and has to that extent ceased to be capitalist monopoly." More on Baku oil as we get deeper into the story. (V. Lenin, *Collected Works*)

By the early 1930s and dating back to his first administration FDR is determined to get America into a second world war. In fact, it was war business as usual; the agenda of the First World War was still uncompleted, when in 1918 the world influenza epidemic precipitated the sudden peace Armistice. As long as American bankers were free to fund the arms race, war once again seems inevitable.

Stalin had good reason to be primarily concerned with the dangers inherent in expansionist capitalism. When Lenin dies in 1924 Russia's industrial production was significantly less than fifteen percent of the 1913 prewar level. For the next four years the NEP aided largely from foreign concessions and partial development of private industry parallel to state planning helps close the gap. By 1925 Americans possess only eight of ninety "active" concessions; within four years forty new technical assistance contracts are held by American firms, more than any other foreign competitor. Katherine Siegel observes that during this period "over thirteen hundred engineers and technicians, mainly Americans and Germans" were operating inside Soviet Russia as "consultants". In fact, the number is significantly much higher, confirmed by sundry sources indicating that the real figure is closer to 3,000 skilled engineers and technicians needed by Stalin to transfer technology from the West. In that transitional period phasing out the NEP (1925-26), with Stalin preparing for the next onslaught against the freedom of the general population of peasants and workers, from a total of 482 applications only 110 resulted concessions turned operational. Harriman would say concessions under the Bols offered dim rewards as these accounted for only one half of one percent of production for 1926-27. On the French Mediterranean coast in Cannes, Churchill advised Harriman to save his money and get out of the Soviet Union. (K. Siegel, *Loans and Legitimacy*, quoting V. A. Shishkin, 111-28)

Fresh out of Yale and baptized during America's War Trade business during the heated pressures of the First World War, the future don of the State Department and postwar presidential candidate Averell Harriman found himself on the bridge running the American Ship and Commerce Corp. while taking over Harriman & Co.. He keeps the Harriman seat on the board at Morgan's Guaranty Trust.

From New York to London, Paris to Berlin and Moscow, "Ave" Harriman cuts a sleek figure racing across the globe from chic-to-chic, the great organizer of managerial men, corporations and chaos. He's generally portrayed as irresistibly "ebullient" with an effusive charming personality, quixotic even perhaps reflecting the multi-faceted dimensions of his portfolio, enigmatically, put by writer Kathleen Siegel, his "transportation, financial and administrative experience". Be that as it may, this billionaire capitalist in August 1921 virtually stole Derutra as a war bargain, the German shipping firm rendered defenseless by the German defeat. (P. Collier and D. Horowitz, "The Chemistry of Hate"; R. Chernow, *The Warburgs*, 267)

To facilitate his German pickings Harriman's business interests were helped by the leading Jewish investment banker Max Warburg dubbed "the Uncrowned King of Hamburg", a title that incurred the patronage and wrath of both Nazis and Jews –, and his extensive connections in the German financial and corporate elite of German cartels. The Germany economy continued to boom right up to 1938 to become the world's second largest economy. Times were good for the fascists eager for money and power. Consortium capitalists, Nazis and bankers alike. When Hitler betrays Stalin and orders his generals to launch the invasion into Russia German stocks peak.

Investor writer Barton Biggs looked at the Berlin CDAX Index "adjusted for inflation from 1930-1950", and Biggs concludes, "From the 1932 bottom until the 1937-1938 high, Germany was the best market in the world as the domestic economy enjoyed a strong recovery from the horrors of the 1920s. Unquestionably the strong leadership and charisma of Hitler were also important factors. Then from the late spring of 1938 until the end of 1939 German investors experience the same misgivings as the aristocracy and the Prussian generals about the risks of Hitler running with his aggressive actions in Europe.... Rumors of the coups and concentration camps were circulating. In late 1939, however, well ahead of the *Blitzkrieg* ("lightning strike") stock prices began to anticipate the overwhelming victories of 1940. By 1940 and throughout 1941 the German economy was booming from military production." (Barton Biggs, *Wealth, War and Wisdom,* Wiley, 2008, 120-9)

By the end of 1927 the NEP is a proven failure due principally to the unworkable policy of concessions and inadequate grain procurements needed to finance escalating costs of too rapid industrialization. Russian industrial output already attains prewar 1914. This year Standard Oil of New York builds an oil refinery in Russia; in 1928, Rockefeller's Chase Bank joins the banking syndicate selling Soviet Bonds to US investors, and, in so doing acts as a prime mover on the international front to fund Stalin's Soviet dictatorship. Western business interests accelerate their investment drive and push for more opportunities and profit. Westinghouse with its long special relationship in Russia has been operating a plant since 1920 exempt from Lenin's nationalization. Charles Coleman (b. 1865) also a Pilgrim member, associated with the Lehigh Valley Railroad (Vanderbilt and Rockefeller ownership) is a director of the American-Russian Chamber of Commerce (ARCC) since its founding in 1922, the same year as war-torn Russia had emerged from total chaos and economic ruin, disease and armed foreign intervention compelling Lenin to admit that communist system had failed and determined to save the "Proletarian Revolution" sought participation by western aid and state capitalism under his New Economic Program (NEP).

In 1924, Harriman negotiated a unique concession deal of manganese mines in Georgia ("Georgia Mining Corporation") to provide Soviet Russia with more foreign exchange to purchase western technology. Harriman and an older Yalie chum, Frederick Winthrop Allen, Yale, Bones 1900, establish the Georgian Manganese Company.

Maj. Alan Wardwell Yale, Bones 1904, of the Red Cross spy mission during the 1917 Bolshevik coup is also made a director and vice president in 1929 of the American-Russian Chamber of Commerce (ARCC). Reeve Schley is president, assisted by Wardwell, the son of Thomas Wardwell, Standard Oil treasurer and law partner in the prestigious Wall Street law firm, Stetson, Jennings & Russell. Stetson's son, Eugene Stetson Jr., is Yale, Bones 1934; Wardwell's son Edward Rogers Wardwell is "tapped" Bones in 1927 rewarding the father with another family distinction.

These are the sort of connections in the American power establishment that engender continuity and smoothly directs America's emergence as a global power in world affairs. Fathers and sons pull the strings, make the deals, elect fellow men to their ranks, instruct government leaders, and generally conduct business as usual. It's a neatly ordered world of clubs and boardrooms, yachts and exquisite suites, sumptuous black tie dinners in elaborate royal setting. And whenever affairs get a bit messy, they send in their men to set affairs back in order. (Charles C. Tansill, *America Goes to War,* 1938: C. C. Tansill, *Back Door to War: the Roosevelt Foreign Policy, 1933-1941*, Chicago: H. Regnery, 1952; A. C. Sutton, *Western Technology and Soviet Economic Development 1917 to 1930*; A. C. Sutton, *FDR*)

So, eager was the astute Yalie to push the Harriman family empire into Soviet business, that by 1924 and with the aid of Clifford Carver, the Harriman interests exploit their deal with Krassin and the Hamburg-Amerika line. (Author-scholar Katherine Siegel oddly omits to identify it as a Harriman property.) Derutra handled shipments including those for the Russian Red Cross and other trade including "shipped cotton, timber, scrap iron, asbestos, flax, furs" as well as "Hebrew National Kosher Sausage relief packages". By 1926 his Soviet Derutra line is doing "better than any of the line's offices in Europe". But irregularities in making a profit cause him to drop the line and turn it over to the Soviets while he pursues manganese ore mines at Chiaturi in Georgia invaluable in the production of steel and the source of half of the world's wartime supply, as well as an element in dyes, paints and glass.

In 1925 Harriman telegraphs his office "PRICE MANGANESE ASSURES LARGE PROFIT". Harriman's aim is to seize the "exceptional opportunity to control enormous basic industry with very limited capital and risk". By holding a major stake in the Soviet minerals monopoly Harriman intends to make a killing cornering the world manganese market. It promises to be yet the biggest soviet concession worth at least $120 million ($1.3 billion).

Harriman is ecstatic. He boasts to a colleague writing, "we have succeeded in obtaining control of one of the most valuable as well as one of the largest natural deposits of essential raw materials in the world". He signs the deal in June. By summer the next year he has paid nearly $3.5 million for excavation rights with a promise to invest $3 million in local mines and railways for which he advanced $1 million to the Soviet Gosbank.

The new Harriman Soviet venture is called the Georgia Manganese Company. Harriman proudly takes the chairman seat claiming it risks his company's "reputations as conservative businessmen". The enterprise quickly signs up orders for the high grade ore from Bethlehem Steel and other companies for over 110,000 tons of manganese millions of tons of peroxide.

One of Hoover's own ARA confidence men, Capt. T.T.C. Gregory endorses Harriman's scheme. Harriman anticipates Ford Motor Company to be a buyer with the largest orders. But production of ore by the German firm Rawack and Grunweld, already managing the Soviet firm Nikopol in the Ukraine with 40 percent of the Soviet market leaving Harriman with sixty percent is, nevertheless, able to surpass Harriman's domination of price of manganese on the international market.

By 1927, after only five years of production the Soviet-German firm produces nearly ten times the output of 1922, raising ore production from its mines to 615,000 tons triggering a crash in world prices. Stalin assigns Commissar Trotsky to pacify the Harriman people over their Georgian mine debacle.

Harriman still lacks his vital railway link to the Black Sea ports. He fails to persuade the State Department, or his friends at Treasury or Commerce, to persuade President Hoover to grant trade credits for Russia. Harriman urges a cutback in supply, reduces production to push up the world price. He backs down from demanding payments from the Soviet government owed for railway construction. With Nikopol's output reduced, the Harriman mine increases its output 25 percent to 20 million tons for a twenty year contract. After an impasse over foreign exchange and infuriated further when obliged to trade currency at the official Soviet bank rate instead of the black market, the Harriman firm pulls out taking out only "a small profit". (K. Siegel, *Loans and Legitimacy,* 1996; A. J. Williams, *Trading with the Bolsheviks*, 42-3. Mr. Williams, lecturer at the University of Kent, Canterbury, England; W. Averell Harriman Papers, Library of Congress, Washington DC, Box 698)

During the 1933 peak of the Holodomor famine, US Congressman Louis McFadden, himself a former banker, in the week of June 15, 1933 entered in the Congressional Record his instruction to the American public and their political reps in Washington: "Find out what business has been transacted for the State Bank of Soviet Russia by its correspondent, the Chase Bank of New York".

TO IMPEACH MELLON & THE FEDERAL RESERVE BANK

McFadden is inclined to spill it all and tell the American people what really was going on between the Consortium corporate instruments and the Communist Soviet totalitarian regime. That May 1933, as the last breath is crushed out the Ukraine, Congressman Louis McFadden introduced House Resolution No. 158, articles of impeachment for the Secretary of the Treasury Andrew Mellon, two assistant Secretaries of the Treasury, the entire Board of Governors of the Federal Reserve, and the officers and directors of its twelve regional banks. How little did they know what common thread links these events.

By then Mellon had already left the country to run the US embassy in London rendering mute McFadden's attack. America is more preoccupied with Roosevelt New Dealism and a way out of domestic hunger and unemployment. This isn't the first time either that McFadden has gone after the Fed. On June 10, 1932, McFadden, facing re-election, makes a bold 25-minute speech before Congress and accused the Federal Reserve of deliberately causing the Great Depression. *Wall Street bankers,* he charged, *funded the Bolshevik Revolution through the Federal Reserve banks and the European central banks with which it cooperated.* McFadden moves to impeach Hoover in 1932, and also introduced a resolution bringing conspiracy charges against the entire Board of Governors of the Federal Reserve. The impeachment resolution is crushed by an overwhelming vote of 361 to 8. And the blow is trumped by the mainstream media of the Consortium oligarchs as a big vote of confidence for their pawns in the Congress. With FDR in the White House evidently the nation is all too desperate to push forward. The press follows the piper.

Congressman McFadden is no small cheese. For over ten years, he is Chairman of the House Banking and Currency Committee. The Chase Soviet loans are part of America's financial and political engagement with Stalin and singled out at a most crucial time in the Ukrainian famine when it was still possible for the American government to pressure Stalin to lessen the bloodshed and forced death by starvation. "The Soviet government," McFadden declares, "has been given US Treasury funds by the Federal Reserve Banks acting through the Chase Bank and Morgan Guaranty Trust and other banks in New York City.... Open the books of Amtorg and Gostorg, the general office of the Soviet Trade Organization, and the State Bank of the USSR and you will be staggered to see how much American money has been taken from the US Treasury for the benefit of Russia." Then, suddenly, in 1936, during a visit to New York, Congressman McFadden, 60, collapsed dead under "mysterious circumstances". And like that he is gone. "Old stuff", harked the Republicans when he had raised his resolution to impeach Hoover and attacked Mellon. A mere drop in the ocean.

What in hell is happening?

Spring 1930. Amtorg as the trade representative of the Soviet government is taking a lot of heat from anticommunists in America screaming at Washington for using the trade offices for "subversive propaganda" by so-called faked documents issued from the office of New York Police Commissioner Whalen. Conservative businessmen not unlike Kelley, Kennan, Henderson and others in the State Department are alarmed at the casual ease with which Stalin's undercover Soviet intelligence acting as Amtorg commercial agents have access to the most advanced technical methods and technology available.

"From the late 1920s the Soviet intelligence services had operated in the United States as if our open society were a well-stocked hunting preserve," recalls veteran masterspy, OSS bureaucrat and CIA boss Richard Helms observed in his book *A Look Over My Shoulder* (2005). The naivété of Americans unconcerned by potential breaches of security astounded the highly trained Soviet officers. Defector Hedda Massing exclaims, "I could have walked into most of the government officers in Washington wearing a sandwich board saying 'Soviet spy on the prowl,' without attracting the least attention."

The American Russian Chamber of Commerce (ARCC) fights back, with a committee represented by Wardwell, vice-president, New York banker Samuel R. Bertron, chairman and Hugh Cooper, the famous hydroelectric dam engineer, director H. H. Dewey of GE. On May 27 they meet with US Commerce Secretary Tom Lamont. Cooper and GE are already deep into their Russian projects. A classic meeting with Consortium power-brokers on both sides of the table. Morgan man Tom Lamont raises no objections to hinder their plans.

STALIN'S REPRESSION OF THE PEASANTS

Back in the USSR the Kremlin ratchets up its repression of the peasants. Yuriy Shapoval of the National Academy of Sciences Ukraine, in 2009, with information sourced from secret files, publishes "Foreign Diplomats on the Holodomor in Ukraine" telling of the existence of an internal political Soviet memorandum specifically targeting the peasants of Ukraine "written in connection with the 'policy of liquidating the kulaks as a class'." Shapoval reveals this occurred "during the period from January 20 to February 12, 1930. The head of the GPU of the Ukrainian SSR Vsevolod Balytsky reports that a total of 12,000 people had taken part in 37 mass peasant protests in January; as of February 9, 1930, 11,865 people had been arrested, and peasants had carried out 40 terrorist acts in response to the policy of 'dekulakization.' Balytsky was even forced to head an 'operational headquarters' for the struggle against peasant protests and was in charge of crushing these protests in various regions of Ukraine."

On March 31, 1930 in GPU Order No. 74 of the Ukrainian SSR Balytsky reported GPU agents of the Ukrainian SSR "with the active participation of poor peasants and leading rural activists, completed an operation to expel kulaks from districts of all-out collectivization in Ukraine." (Yuriy Shapoval, "Foreign Diplomats on the Holodomor in Ukraine", *Holodomor Studies*, v. 1, Issue 1, 2009, citing Andrea Graziosi, "Collectivisation, révoltes paysannes et politiques gouvernementales à travers les rapports de GPU d'Ukraine de février-mars 1930," *Cahiers du monde russe 3*, 1994, 480-1)

After consultations between Allen Wardwell and Commerce Secretary Lamont, Amtorg is off the hook. Again its business as usual for Stalin and the Consortium syndicates. Amtorg chairman Peter Bogdanov, and Boris E. Skvirsky, Stalin's economic and political commissar in the USSR prior to FDR's normalization of diplomatic relations, are publicly exonerated while OGPU secret police thugs go unmolested running an underground spy organization in the US that drives FBI director J. Edgar Hoover mad with rage. Siegel's work also reveals that with America deep in economic depression, Amtorg and its Soviet affiliates in 1931 purchase hefty amounts of American industrial exports placing its orders in principal industries: "58.7 percent of all locomotive equipment, 59 percent of metalworking equipment, 65.6 percent of lathes, 73.8 percent of foundry equipment, and 97.4 percent of turbines. In 1930 and 1931, at least 60 percent of all

US orders for the Soviet Union originated in five states in the industrial Midwest." Ford, Caterpillar, International Harvester, John Deere, Bethlehem Steel, Baldwin Locomotive et cetera. (K. Siegel, *Loans and Legitimacy*, 133; correspondence Reeve Schley to T. Lamont, May 19, 1930; S. R. Bertron, Allen Wardwell, Hugh Cooper, Dewey on ARCC, June 14, 1930 to members of ARCC, in the Gumberg Papers. Fish Committee hearings, quoted by Hugh Cooper; Budish and Shipman, *Soviet Foreign Trade*; E. Filene, *Americans and the Soviet Experiment*; *NY Herald Tribune*, July 29, 1930; ARCC to Hoover, Mellon and Lamont, July 30, 1930 in the ARCCP, box 22; A. J. Williams, *Trading with the Bolsheviks*; Americans reaction to cutbacks see H. Cooper to A. Mellon, Nov. 27, 1930 in Alexander Gumberg Papers; Spencer Williams to H. Cooper, Oct. 8, 1931)

Scholar Katherine Siegel reveals some illuminating figures of US-Soviet credits and loans leading America straight into the hell of the Holodomor: "In 1932," Siegel informs, "total Soviet purchases in the United States plunged to a paltry $12.6 million, one-tenth of the previous year's tally. American economic nationalism was not entirely to blame, however, since the Soviet Union had its own reason for cutting back. The country was heavily in debt. By 1931, following the flurry of large purchases under the Five-Year Plan, Russia owed $500 million in credits, largely to Germany and Britain. These foreign purchases, along with a sluggish demand for Soviet raw materials and slow delivery of grain from the peasants who had been forcibly collectivized the year before, had contributed to $150 trade deficit, making continued large-scale purchases in Western countries difficult … between 1930 and 1932, Soviet orders abroad dropped by one-third. Yet certain maintained a strong share of the existing orders, facilitated by trade agreements. German sales to Russia in 1932 and 1933 amounted to 45 percent of the goods imported by the Soviet Union over those years, while the United States' comparable figure was only 5 percent." The disastrous 1931 harvest in the Ukraine provides scant relief. (K. Siegel, *Loans and Legitimacy,* 135)

Even the alleged arch anticommunist Hoover in 1932, in an effort to take some strain off the crashing American economy, extended a $4 million publicly financed credit to Amtorg towards cotton purchases in the US. Edward Filene, the department store retailer and socialistic political fundraiser favored it to advance "Soviet-American trade and international peace". *New York Times* Stalin watcher Walter Duranty said "there is a good deal of interest and a general feeling that recognition might help … where immediate business interests of groups or individuals are involved. For example, the General Electric and General Motors people are quite keen on finding a way if it can be done with proper dignity – I might almost say on finding a way anyway." Figures reported in the press range from $1 to $5 billion of extra business for America flaunted recognition as an impetus certain to get the American economy moving again. American Locomotive, Baldwin Locomotive, International Harvester …

The death toll varied from mouth to mouth, and month to month. 1933 is the worst year of the Holodomor. Villages are ravaged. Naum Jasny, in *The Socialized Agriculture of the USSR* (1949) writes, "The climax of starvation was not reached until the spring of 1933. The livestock herd also was then at its smallest, and total grain utilization was at the lowest point." This is consistent with the findings of Fedor Belov in *The History of a Soviet Collective Farm* (1955), writing, "The worst time came during May and June 1933." (Naum Jasny, *The Socialized Agriculture of the USSR*, Stanford Univ., 1949; Fedor Belov, *The History of a Soviet Collective Farm*, NY: Praeger, 1955)

Throughout the famine years Amtorg remains active. Promising handsome rewards it recruits eager American engineers, and contracts American firms desperate for orders to keep factories open and create jobs. Its political intelligence agents and secret police conduct industrial espionage on a sorely weakened American economy at grips to hold on. In 1930 Amtorg itself became the target of a Congressional "Investigation of Communist Propaganda". Another committee, a report, a little press, and the story quietly passes away with hardly a ripple. Later after the German invasion in June 1941 and with Harriman in Moscow the Roosevelt gang arranges to channel through Amtorg the government's Lend-Lease war provisions. (See 71st Congress, 3rd session, Report No. 22-90, Jan. 17, 1931, 48 ff.)

The same year of McFadden's Congressional review of Chase in Russia, *The NY Times* Moscow correspondent Walter Duranty, in June 1933, persists in writing lies to falsify and conceal the mass starvation overwhelming the Ukraine and other regions. The previous year Duranty had earned a Pulitzer, no mere compensation for his part in concealing the Terror-Famine and priming the pump for recognition of Stalin's communist dictatorship. A half century later, The New York Times Company report praised Duranty for his "dispassionate, interpretive reporting of the news from Russia"; in the 1932 the citation for his award praised his dispatches for their "scholarship, profundity" and "sound judgment and exceptional clarity" in that they were, states *The NY Times*, "excellent examples of the best type of foreign correspondence". Conquest added his two cents of propaganda, writing, "The praise which went to Duranty was clearly not due to a desire to know the truth, but to a desire of many to be told what they wished to hear. Duranty's own motives need no explaining." Wow! Of course they do. That's just the tip of the problem. Conquest wanted to shut the lid tight. A deft master of the metaphor, Conquest too excels at rhetorical ambiguity while serving to unseen masters. That citation by *The New York Times* might have just as well been written by Stalin or FDR himself. Odd, that there is not even a single reference to Roosevelt in the Conquest book, *Harvest of Sorrow*, a deliberate attempt to steer the Holodomor debate away from Roosevelt and Washington. (R. Conquest, *Harvest of Sorrow*, 320)

Why mislead the public to conceal a humanitarian catastrophe of such devilish magnitude? Obsessed over leaks and constantly suspicious of betrayal, Chekist agents tracked down the heels of diplomats suspicious of their every step and cracked down on journalists. No foreigners are above suspicion. Duranty meekly tried to explain to American readers that Stalin had the food crisis under control, that the Bolshevik leaders only needed to "swing all the forces in their command into an effort to overcome peasant apathy, individualism, dislike of novel collective methods and the previous mismanagement of collective farms."

Foreign correspondents are banned from touring the countryside. That includes Stalin's puppet Duranty.

Anecdotal glimpses into the origin and family control of this cornerstone of 21st century American journalism proffered by co-authors Susan E. Tifft and Alex S. Jones in their book *The Trust, The Private and Powerful Family Behind The New York Times* (1993), provides a glimpse into the role played by "Colonel" Arthur Ochs, who as a Jewish immigrant in the mid-19th century boldly finagled up the ladder of power on his way into the opulent world of America's oligarchy to buy a quarter-century later the bankrupt paper backed by a syndicate of industrialists and bankers. This was no haphazard accident.

Here is a glimpse of the tale recalled by Tifft and Jones: "The list of investors in The New York Times Publishing Company, as the syndicate was called, read like a who's who of America's business plutocracy: among its roughly sixty-two members were James J. Hill, who ran the Great Northern and Northern Pacific Railroad, and banking luminaries JP Morgan, Jacob Schiff, and August Belmont. ... In 1896 with the *Times* rumored to be weeks away from extinction, a populist gale from the South and West began to blow through the Democratic Party, making it critical to members of the party's conservative wing that *The New York Times* be kept afloat to represent their advocacy of sound money. Of this group, no one was more concerned about the fate of the dollar than the Equitable Life Assurance Society, the largest insurer in the world and one of the most powerful 'combines of capital' in the country with diverse holdings in banks, trust companies, real estate, railroads, and syndicates. Equitable had $50,000 invested in New York Times Publishing Company stock, and several of its directors, including Belmont, Hill, Marcellus Hartley, and Jacob Schiff, either owned *Times* shares themselves or controlled shares through others." (Susan E. Tifft and Alex S. Jones, *The Trust, The Private and Powerful Family Behind The New York Times*, NY: Little Brown, 1993)

But these authors omit an essential aspect to the tale, – the Rothschild connection –, and impart only casual reference to the pivotal role played by George Foster Peabody, who just happens to be Treasurer Democratic National Party (1904-05), a director on the board of the New York Federal Reserve Bank (1914-21) and a proprietor of Warm Springs, in Georgia relished by his friend FDR. Further, Peabody is "business partner" to Spencer Trask (1844-09, Princeton 1866) and a very well-endowed investor in Thomas Edison's light-bulb invention, as well as General Electric Princeton and Edison Electric Light. It is left to Spencer Task and his friends to guide Ochs in the Morgan-Rothschild scheme setting up the revived entity of The New York Times Company. Tifft and Jones write, "With $1 million in stock and $500,000 in bonds secured by a mortgage on everything the *Times* owned, from broken-down chairs to its name" and a royal five percent interest on the bonds. Ochs meets with JP Morgan at 23 Wall Street and accepts the titian's "$25,000 in old *Times* stock in just fifteen minutes."

Schiff turned over his shares as a "personal endorsement" of Ochs and the new enterprise. A generation later, a Rothschild secures for Arthur Ochs Sulzberger, the *Times*' heir and publisher their spacious five-story townhouse at 5 East Eightieth Street off Fifth Avenue and around the corner from the Metropolitan Museum of Art. Post territory. Prime New York real estate. In 1929 Arthur Sulzberger briefly visits the Soviet Union to see Stalin's great experiment to create the new man of the machine age, and finds the communist "experiment" entirely rude to his tastes and is personally offended but what he experiences there and finds to be true about the place.

But reader, let's not get too far ahead in this story too fast or get too entangled in so many loose ends and trapped in knots. We're in Yo-Yo land here; we can play "Walk the Dog", but everything is attached and on a string. That's just what the Consortium would like to see happen!

We are on a long journey here. Sometimes we take a few steps at a time, and even a few steps back again before a sudden leap. Remember to be patient on the way and see how these knots untie themselves as the story unfolds. There are so many strings in this tale so don't get caught and tied up! (A. S. Jones and S. E. Tifft, *The Trust*, 31-7; Naomi W. Cohen, *Jacob H. Schiff: A Study in American Jewish Leadership*, Hanover: Brandeis Univ. Press, 1999)

During the stormy Holodomor years the doomed Ukrainians are forced to sell all their possessions for a crust of bread. The weak fell exhausted and died on the streets of Kiev and Kharkov, many tortured, abandoned to starvation, dehumanized, – (how much dignity remains after total humiliation?) executed or exiled from their homes to Siberian gulags and forced labor camps, bullied by Stalin's secret police Organs. A debate ignited in America in 1933 when it was still possible to save lives and reduce the suffering described by the brave young journalist from Wales.

Duranty too is caught in the net. He's shunned by Stalin as well as Moscow's foreign press pool ever since both Malcolm Muggeridge and Gareth Jones in late March 1933 circumvent the official Soviet ban on famine stories. Exposed Stalin withdrew into the shadows again.

The young Welshman Jones walked among the villages in Ukraine and talked in Russian to the poor starving peasants who pleaded with him for food from well-prepared sack, and begged that he not forget their tale suffering. Jones returns to Germany and Russia almost every year since 1920, until his death in 1935, killed by a Soviet double agent in Manchuria to silence the man who exposed Stalin's "man-made" Holodomor to the world. An anonymous letter dated September 1935 written in London to the "Rt. Hon. D. Lloyd George. Re the matter of Gareth Jones" confirmed his death "that the poor man was treacherously betrayed by his colleague the German. They were both in possession of valuable information which was too vital for more than one to have, one had to be got rid of ..." Spies, double-agents, informers, secret police, journalist lies, diplomatic cover … this is the dark and secret world of profits, war and intrigue behind the Holodomor. (For letter to D. Lloyd George see Gareth Jones website)

For two years Gareth Jones told that story in local and major papers of the world press. His 1933 articles are the first to expose the famine and the scandal that erupts in a campaign of diversion by foreign media, men such as Duranty who reporting for *The New York Times* joined the Stalinists and their friends blaming the peasants' "degeneration and apathy" aggravated by scarcity "already widespread and serious" and poor prospects for the new harvest.

"ONE LIFE, ONE KOPECK"

On June 23 Duranty wrote his friend and fellow Pulitzer journalist "Knick" (H. R. Knickerbocker) in Berlin to encourage he drop the famine story calling news stories of the Holodomor in the Ukraine "mostly bunk as I told you, except maybe in Kazakhstan and the Alti, where they wouldn't let you go. If you did want a visa, I think you'll get it alright, but the FO in particular is rather crockety about reporters travelling these days." To this present day *The New York Times* routinely dismisses calls for the revocation of Duranty's 1932 Pulitzer Prize for his role in the Holodomor disinformation campaign.

Stuck in Moscow and isolated by Stalin and his paranoid contacts in the Party, Duranty called the Bolsheviks "fanatics (who) do not care about the costs in blood or money." It was more convenient for Duranty to throw the peasant burden which he called "not strictly a Soviet phenomenon". He writes, "It is cruel ... but the Union of Soviet Socialist Republics is near to cruel Asia, and the proverb 'One Life, One Kopeck' was a century-old expression of human values in Czarist Russia." Duranty would admit only that "life here is hard and menaced by malnutrition and diseases ... it once again underlined the ultimate goal justifying these sacrifices: the leadership's 'fanatic fervor' for industrialization." In a few years Muggeridge joins with other writers like Graham Green and Stephen Spender feathering "his young nest" at the wartime Ministry of Information set up in Bloomsbury in the University College buildings on Gower Street with its doors open to all kinds of demiurgical manipulations, dilettanti and dubious charlatans during the war concocting British propaganda. Now he concludes in his apologia for sadism that Duranty ranks as "the greatest liar of any journalist I have ever met." (Norman Sherry, *The Life of Graham Greene*, Vol. II, NY: Viking, 1995, 35)

STALIN AND THE MOSCOW FOREIGN PRESS CORPS

Among the other foreign correspondents then in Moscow were William Stoneman for the *Chicago Daily News*, William Henry Chamberlin for the *Christian Science Monitor*, Eugene Lyons among a half-dozen others. By August 21, 1933, Ralph W. Barnes covering the Holodomor for *The New York Herald Tribune* is telling his readers that the press ban is one reason they're not getting news about the "unfavorable" conditions in the USSR. The Soviet authorities promptly impose a travel ban all movements of the foreign correspondents outside Moscow. Later in the year when Stalin sends the Politburo's delegation led by Soviet Foreign Commissar Litvinov to meet with FDR in Washington the issue of the freedom of the press or manipulation by the Kremlin is never broached and kept off the table. (Dispatch Jan. 29, 1933; W. Duranty, "Russia's Peasant: The Hub of a Vast Drama", "Duranty Reports Russia", *The NYT*, Feb. 2, 1933, Feb. 27, 1933; W. Duranty to The New York Times Co., June 17, 1933 and Edwin

James to Arthur Sulzberger, June 17, 1933, both on reel 33, Edwin James Papers; W. Duranty to H. R. Knickerbocker, June 27, 1933, H. R. Knickerbocker Papers, Columbia Univ. Library)

The younger Welshman Gareth Jones must have seemed like a fish out of water in the Ivy Lee Associates offices. Bright, dynamic and well-connected in the Great Britain's elite Foreign Office, as it was his talent Jones adapted his socialist fervor and wrote splendid newspaper stories of the 1931 American on a wide range of topics from economic depression, unemployment and the Presidential race for the White House. His style was sharp, direct, and clear and always captured a focus on the human dimension in his writing that he pursued with the dedication of a craftsman, loose and fluid without pretensions. Truth was in the nature of his art. There is a distinctly profound and personal aspect, as he wrote with a intelligence that preserved the unadulterated nature of subject of inquiry. He found his muse in the Ukraine.

In reporting the famine Gareth Jones celebrates life on the edge of the abyss and destroyed by the masters who trained him and schooled him and published his articles. It was the force that rivaled this Humanity that killed him and the millions Ukrainians he had tried to save from terror and oblivion. His disappearance had never been forgotten by his family. His niece Dr. Margaret Siriol Colley recalls, "Both his sisters, Miss Gwyneth Vaughan Jones and Mrs. Eirian Lewis lived to be a hundred years old and before their deaths, they recounted the story of the traumatic event to his great-great nephew and nieces. So, the family saga has been carried down through the family verbally. This, we have in common with those Ukrainians who lost loved ones in their own personal tragedies and we have deepest sympathy for them in this respect." That much cannot be said for the war planners who collaborated knowingly and profited from their death and destruction.

The predicament of Jones is also a puzzle for the philosopher-historian aware of the danger of falling into a twilight zone of flashing mirrors. In establishing how things were we must be careful not to be convinced by false and lesser imaginings of how things might have been. Somehow the plain unadulterated truth eludes Jones and his trackers. But it eludes most people on the European scene including FDR's earnest American ambassador in Berlin. Or did it? Is truth no more than a concept? Is truth in the sense of establishing the meaning of what happens just another dialectical twist of the tongue? Are you laughing! This no mere folly of the intellect here. It is a very real problem in unraveling the story of plots and intrigues, declarations and guesswork. This is the stuff of history and decides the fate of men and nations! Or is truth as the philosophers, scientists and men and women of religion lead us on to believe an animation in the mind of something more profound, impermanent, absolute and fundamental to the spiritual meaning of life and human existence. And as I write this I can see Stalin twisting his mustache and with that squint in his eye so many times marked by visitors. And there it is again, that eerie grin on his face!

The Bolsheviks mock religion; they have to construct *Soviet hominicus.* Marxists-Leninists consider religion "the opium of the masses". *Das Capital* is their new Bible. But the Ukraine and elsewhere throughout Old Russia, women still sing prayers and sonnets of pagan spirits and saints with power of the natural order of their world bringing posterity or ruin, protectors of the soul.

Bullitt was more cynical morally in step with the FDR gang. For his part although Jones was very well-educated yet perhaps too young and naive to be able to absorb the magnitude of the problem that was overwhelming his career and the world. In spite of his sensitive and pacifist temperament, Jones never attacked the problem of exposing the complicated forces set in motion and converging directly upon the Ukrainians in the Holodomor until it was far too late for them. And he was cut down before he could do more to warn the world of the war nobody wanted but didn't stop from happening anyway. Yet as a foreign policy wiz and razor-sharp investigative journalist Jones ought to have known better to comprehend the nature of events unfolding all around him. Particularly his fate depended on it.

THE STRANGE CASE OF MR. JONES

Jones might have done far better to open the Ivy Lee files and see for himself how Lee's Consortium clients were investing in Nazi Germany and the communist Russia. Vacuum Oil and General Electric were active in Germany during the rise of Hitler and Stalin. For example, in 1935, the Rockefeller-controlled Socony Vacuum announced that it had bought oil from Russia since 1927, the year Stalin announced the first of his Five-Year Plans for Industry and Agriculture at the Fifteenth Party Congress in Moscow in December followed by the next Congress in April.

In 1935 FDR's ambassador in Berlin William Edward Dodd records in his diary: "January 23. Thursday. Our Commercial Attaché brought Dr. Engelbrecht, chairman of the Vacuum Oil Company in Hamburg, to see me. Engelbrecht repeated what he had said a year ago: 'The Standard Oil Company of New York, the parent company of the Vacuum, has spent 10,000,000 marks in Germany trying to find oil resources and building a great refinery near the Hamburg harbor.' Engelbrecht is still boring wells and finding a good deal of crude oil in the Hanover region, but he had no hope of great deposits. He hopes Dr. Schacht will subsidize his company as he does some German companies that have found no crude oil. The Vacuum spends all its earnings here, employs 1,000 men and never sends any of its money home. I could give him no encouragement." Ambassador Dodd and Dr. Schacht will see each other often and he becomes the American ambassador's friendly and helpful guide into the novelties of Nazi Germany.

A troubling fact is that after the war, reps of this pro-Nazi American Rockefeller company and others were given jobs inside the Control Commission to remove the Nazis." Imagine that! Nazis appointed to de-Nazify the Nazis. The Nazis needn't worry. Their companies took good care of them. Stalin's commercial and finance commissars were also dealing directly with the office of Hitler's economic czar in the Third Reich. Farben and Standard Oil shared an understanding on petroleum and refined gasoline; Farben agrees not to compete with Standard in oil. Their cartel agreement would turn out to be essential to the Nazi war effort even after they secure the Soviet Baku oil fields when Stalin and the Soviet high command (Stavka) was still confused on the strategy of the German generals; by the end of the Second World War Nazi Germany is producing nearly seventy-five percent of all its fuel synthetically. By the late thirties Farben is producing the poisonous Sarin gas for Hitler's lethal weapons arsenal. Why did Allied bombers spare these industrial sites from strategic bombing runs? At the end of the war some thirty of its refineries were still operating with only minor damage.

In *Armageddon* Hastings writes, "To continue the war, Hitler was overwhelmingly dependent upon the production of synthetic fuel. The Germans found it incomprehensible that, until May 1944, no systematic attempt had been made by the Allied air force to strike their oil plants." But that changed when the American Eight Air Force joined by Fifteenth Air Force from Italy thundering overhead blackening the daylight sky with their formations and bombs crippling German supplies from 927,000 tons to 472,000 tons in June. The Luftwaffe supply of fuel dropped more than a third to 50,000 tons, in June and only 10,000 tons in August when its minimal requirement is 30,000 tons a month, and this when it has already lost 31,000 air crew from January to June. (William E. Dodd, *Woodrow Wilson and His Work*, NY: Doubleday Page, 1920; W. E. Dodd, Ray S. Baker, *The Public Papers of Woodrow Wilson*; W. E. Dodd *Ambassador Dodd's Diary, 1933-1938*, NY: Harcourt Brace, 1941; G. Colby, *DuPont Dynasty,* 1974, 1984 ed.; M. Hastings, *Armageddon,* 301-2)

HITLER, MORGAN & THE INIMITABLE DR. SCHACHT

Dr. Schacht met frequently, many times per month, with the American ambassador, a renowned author, Southern gentleman and history professor from the University of Chicago. Dodd considers the German economics minister and president of the German Central Bank "a financial wizard" credited for having made Germany the only major industrial economy to rapidly emerge from the undertow of the Great Depression.

The financial wizard turned historical writer Barton Biggs was fascinated by the Schacht connection with the bigwigs in the Consortium. His instinctive intentions were animated with good reason in search for answers secreted in the hidden agenda. In *Wealth, War and Wisdom,* Biggs writes, "He had supervised the construction of the autobahn and overseen the public works programs of the Nazi era that had stimulated the economy." FDR biographer Ted Morgan leaves us a few anecdotes on FDR, Dodd and Schacht and he too merely scratches the surface of reflections. During their conversation in the White House June 16, 1933 over lunch, "FDR told Dodd that his first glimpse of the Nazi regime had been via the overbearing Dr. Hjalmar Schacht, who had as head of the German Reichsbank threatened to stop paying debts owed to American creditors. FDR had told Hull to receive Schacht but to pretend to be deeply engaged in looking for papers, leaving him standing awkwardly for a few minutes. Then Hull would discover a note from FDR indicating serious opposition to any defaults, hand it to him, and watch his face turn color. Another way to humiliate him was to say that he could not receive him because he had to receive the Japanese ambassador." FDR thrills in his penchant for whimsical gamesmanship keeping lesser players off-balance and in the dark. (T. Morgan, *FDR*, 395)

Dodd, however, is fascinated with Herr Dr. Schacht and his timeless role now at stake with the Nazi leadership. Contemporary author Biggs observes, "With advice from John Maynard Keynes, he had cured the hyperinflation of the 1920s. In 1935, he was at one time president of the Reichsbank, Minister of Economics, and Hitler's economic czar. Schacht was an economist, but he had no economic religion. Basically he played each situation by ear and intuition." His brilliance and capacity for survival astounded his peers, whether dining with the German Jewish elite trading insider stock tips or forever casually smoking cigars under Hitler's nose which few dared to do. "Schacht was able to print money and cleverly manipulate the currency," Biggs writes, and he adds, "He implemented measures to enforce savings and devised new methods of government finance."

It all worked. From 1932 to 1936, unemployment was reduced from 6 million to less than 1 million. Industrial production rose 102% from 1932 to 1937. Wages were essentially frozen, strikes were *verboten*, tourism was promoted, and margins and profits boomed ... By 1938, the German economy was, if not booming, at least healthier than that of any other major industrial country. After the United States, it was the second largest economy in the world. By the early fall of 1941, with German armies thundering across Soviet Russia and vast riches pouring into Germany from the occupied countries, German stocks soared, and in *real* terms, German equities finally surpassed the highs of 1910." German stocks continued to reach new highs in the months prior to Hitler's monumental Operation Barbarossa. In fact, the German market held until the imminent crushing defeat of their troops at Moscow. (B. Biggs, 225)

In January 1936 upon Schacht's return from Basle conference of the International Bank of Settlements, Dodd sits opposite Hitler's favorite Nazi Jew at his desk in the palatial office of the Reichsbank. Schacht is fascinated by the Nye Senate Committee investigation into renewed allegations of Morgan bankers pirating billions while financing the First World War. Dodd writes in his diary, "Schacht wanted to know if I thought Wilson had entered the World War for financial and trade advantage. I replied in the negative, giving Wilson's statement to me August 5, 1916, about his attitude which was to intervene in case it became clear that the Berlin military dictators were about to dominate all Europe. Schacht avoided a reply, except to say that he did not believe Wilson was pulled into the war by the New York bankers."

These were busy days for James Foster Dulles in Berlin. The future Secretary of State ruminated over Dodd's pessimism and constant battering by Nazi military propaganda. Dulles, in particular, is frustrated over "difficulties in financial matters here" and his sister's passion for the Nazi. "My sister lives here," Dulles confides to Dodd. "She is an enthusiastic Hitlerite, and anxious to show me the movie *Unser Wehrmacht* (*Our Defense Power*), proof she said of the German desire for peace. I sat through the show, but the war planes, big guns, pictures of violent attacks upon cities and the enthusiastic attitudes of Hitler, Göering and Goebbels, as they stood looking at the devastating work, took from my mind all thought of peace as an object of the show." Dulles tells Dodd "such a display in the United States would be hissed off the screen".

Dulles also recalled for Dodd some reminiscences of his own unique experience working under President Wilson and Secretary of State Lansing who he said was "indignant at the charges of the Senate Committee (under Senator Nye sic) that Wilson entered the World War to make money for the United States." A gross understatement.

Wilson was never good at banking which is why his son-in-law as well as the bank gang were able to use him so easily and he proves to be a most convenient front. Wilson was an ideal if not perfect shield for the pro-war bankers as the noble patrician face shadowing the evil of the worst sort that financed the war killing tens of millions of young men and civilians. Dodd's book on Woodrow Wilson was published in 1920. Dodd learns from Dulles that his uncle, Lansing himself, "recognized the bankers' role and attitude during 1915-16"; however, he stops there and denies "the President had any contacts with the Morgans". He didn't have to! Wilson never liked or trusted the bankers. Instead, Lansing is in place to handle the bankers. Such distinctions are part of the Consortium checkerboard.

The most frightening aspect of this American nation is that deadly toxic tentacles with vast reach grip America's culture and daily inject its venom into the veins of society where spreads unchecked and where it may be least detected. Take for example the Dulles factor. It is downright scary. Few Americans today recall that the recently deceased Avery "Cardinal" Dulles (1918-08) was a professor of Religion and Society with some eighty honorary degrees! Avery Dulles turned out to be the first American ever to be named a cardinal who was not a bishop, touched by God with the formal blessing of the Pope – just a few years before they both died, a sure ticket through the Gates of Heaven. And the Pope renamed Dulles in his image. No less incredible to be true.

Just follow the Rothschild-Morgan money into the impregnable bank vaults of the Vatican. They can do it, and they did. Avery's father was John Foster Dulles. After the war this Cold War maniac serves in the Eisenhower cabinet as Secretary of State and offered two nuclear bombs to the French in their doomed colonial war against Ho Chi Minh and General Giap. The French decline. Young Avery had been an agnostic at Harvard ('40), is assigned to US Navy intelligence before he joins the Jesus in the Society of Jesus, in 1946, while his father and uncle are busy setting up their brave new world. By the time he is ordained a priest at the Fordham University Church in 1956 *The New York Times* gives the Dulles boy their blessing with a lead front page story. The Holodomor never rated that kind of space.

This is America and in America that's how it's done. This defines to the core America; it is "the American way". Anything less is considered unpatriotic and un-American. It's just not apple pie. Rather, its not *kosher*. (Fredrik Logevall, *John Foster Dulles, Embers of War, The Fall of an Empire and the Making of America's Vietnam*, NY: Random House, 2012)

The Consortium takes care of their own first and foremost, and take all they dare get away with then bless the souls of the masses for stupid and blind obedience. Of course, the Consortium propaganda is intentionally fabricated to distract and pacify the masses to render dissent impotent and harmless. The Consortium wants to control the whole game. Before she lost her head the Austrian Queen of France Marie Antoinette ridiculed the starving French masses with the retort, "Let them eat cake (*"Qu'ils mangent de la brioche."*) Enough to drive any man or woman insane.

In America, the Hollywood factory pours out an instant and endless stream of celluloid and celebrity madness to constipate mass consumption. Meanwhile Congress increases appropriations for crowd control and Home Land security. Whereas Stalinist methods of propaganda and suppression may have seemed obtuse and crude, the subtleties and nuances of persuasion in the American Dream Factory have a dual purpose; increase consumption, and perpetuate the corrupt structure of the *status quo.* The Consortium reigns by fear and terror, too, and it is content and satisfied all of us not privy to the elite status befuddled and docile idiots.

A slight digression will go a long way to better understanding the stakes at play by certain political forces around the White House and Wall Street that played into Stalin's hands and facilitated his Genocide in the Ukraine. That John Foster Dulles should travel to Berlin to feel out Dodd at this time was no coincidence. Loose tongues make graves.

Let's not be too careless with understatement here. The British lost over 900,000 men in the First World War whereas the Russians lost *at least ten million*, and the Americans some 10 percent of the British toll while stripping England and France of all its gold bullion. Why is that relevant to the Holodomor? The historical record shows how that proved to be irrelevant after the war when poor Woodrow was pickled by the ranks of the Consortium peacemakers, most of whom are financiers, Wall Street industrialists and bigwig corporate lawyers. In both wars for the Americans and British it's the same Anglo-American gang running the show and taking home the gold while the masses, workers and peasants, get slaughtered *en masse.*

THE DULLES BOYS

From the beginning the Dulles boys are groomed princes of the first rank in the Consortium. First in his class at Princeton and considered by many to have the finest legal mind in the America, James Foster Dulles held a much higher rank in the Order than ambassador Dodd. Discreet and loyal to his clan Dulles fit the Consortium mold and straight out of university into America's top firm Cromwell & Sullivan. The genteel southerner was disposed to agree with Dulles but Dodd displayed a natural contempt for all the Consortium men in bed with Hitler. "I am inclined to the belief," that night Dodd wrote in diary "that Lansing was not altogether free from strong banking influences." History 101! Written "for the record" by the Rockefeller-funded Chicago University history professor! Surely this is an understatement bordering on hyperbole.

Dodd has good reason more than ever to fear that FDR and his docile Secretary of State Cordell Hull, a backwoods laddie born in a small cabin of most modern circumstances, has fallen under the same pressures just as Wilson had been up to his neck with the money men and their contraband arms dealers! Before the guns of August 1914 the Consortium bankers had taken over the White House and virtually ran the government.

As Wilson's wartime Secretary of State Robert Lansing is a Wall Street Consortium operative given to carefully polished Anglophile tendencies to exact perfect King's English still so keen to the ears of listeners of NPR broadcasts and feel more at ease in the presence of the Pilgrim set and ceremonies with the King and Queen. Lansing is Dulles' uncle; his father-in-law was John W. Foster, Secretary of State in President Harrison's administration (1889-1893); John W. Foster is grandfather to John Foster Dulles and Allen Dulles, both Pilgrims, and both descendents from distinguished colonial ancestors. A graduate of Amherst (1886), he married Eleanor Foster, the daughter of John W.. Poor Harrison is dead in office serving only 29 days. Lansing was a trustee of the Carnegie Endowment for International Peace, a powerful tool of the Consortium. Lansing founded the American Society for International Law in 1906, an organization with highly questionable views about United States sovereignty; in 1921, with lessons learned from his sophisticated British imperialist mentors, Lansing authored *Notes on Sovereignty.* (W. E. Dodd, *Ambassador Dodd's Diary,* 1941, 304; Charles Savoie, *World Money Power III*, 2005)

By 1933 western arms merchants intensified sales to Hitler's regime. The State Department facilitates the deals with a wink and a nod. "With Hitler's triumph," Gerard Colby observes, "German munitions companies were flooded with war orders as rearmament began full blast, and any new DuPont chemical discoveries, under its cartel agreements, became immediately available to the Nazi war machine. One DuPont discovery that was particularly priceless was neoprene – synthetic rubber. Under the patent agreement, this 1931 discovery was open to IG Farben's inspection and subsequent use. Not surprisingly, in 1933, IG Farben also 'discovered' neoprene, and was free to set up manufacturing plants like DuPont's Deepwater Point plant."

After 1933, William Shirer reports in *The Rise and Fall of the Third Reich,* "the Nazi government gave IG Farben the go-ahead with orders to raise its synthetic oil production to 300,000 tons a year by 1937. By that time the company had also discovered how to make synthetic rubber from coal and other products of which Germany had a sufficiency, and the first of four plants was set up at Schkopau for large-scale production of buna, as the artificial rubber became known. By the beginning of 1934, plans were approved by the Working Committee of the Reich Defense Council for the mobilization of some 240,000 plants for war orders. By the end of the year rearmament, in all its phases, had become so massive it was obvious that it could no longer be concealed from the suspicious and uneasy powers of Versailles." (G. Colby, 340; W. Shirer, *The Rise and Fall of the Third Reich*, 389)

But the American ambassador is left out of the Consortium loop by the Dulles brothers. Dodd describes what happened next. "These men were hardly out of the building before the lawyer came in again to report his difficulties. I could not do anything. I asked him, however: Why did the Standard Oil Company of New York send $1,000,000 over here in December, 1933, to aid the Germans in making gasoline from soft coal for war emergencies? Why do the International Harvester people continue to manufacture in Germany when their company gets nothing out of the country and when it has failed to collect its war losses? He saw my point and agreed that it looked foolish and that it only means greater losses if another war breaks loose." Germany still had not paid its reparations debt from the First World War which was basically written off by new bank loans and deals. If Dodd has to ask, Dulles is not inclined to tell.

It is not left to Dulles to reveal secrets of Consortium business affairs and strategy. Dodd or Bullitt might just have well asked about the business arrangements of International Harvester or Caterpillar or Ford Motor Co. with the Bolsheviks where wheat reapers and tractors under collectivization promises to transform farming in the Ukraine displacing millions of peasants no longer needed to harvest their traditional crops when one machine could do the work of hundreds of workers and livestock. Stalin wants these peasants in the factories and in the mines and on the great industrial construction projects of his Plans. But they don't ask, at least not to leave an easy trace for historians. Nothing went well according to plan. So there were new plans, constantly.

The logic of Consortium investment in the Nazis seriously troubles Dodd. He didn't understand and feels redundant, passed over, and played for a fool. Among the few papers not destroyed by Col. House and stored behind locked iron gates in Yale University Archives is a letter from Dodd written October 29, 1936, two years before House dies with his secrets. Dodd asks why American corporations were building weapons for Hitler even when they couldn't get their profits out of Germany because of the exchange controls. (W. E. Dodd, *Ambassador Dodd's Diary,* 303; W. E. Dodd to Col. House, Col. Edward House Papers, Sterling Memorial Library Archives, Yale Univ.)

FORD, HARVESTER & RUSSIAN COLLECTIVIZATION

Let's return to International Harvester. Katherine Siegel in *Loans and Legitimacy* writes, "the Soviet Union 'used the (Harvester) arrangement in many countries as a lever to obtain similar or more advantageous arrangements', quoting Fayette Allport a rep for the Bureau of Foreign and Domestic Commerce (Brussels)."

The Russian communist market promised to be a boom for American companies. Of course it was a Consortium Harvester deal mutually advantageous to both communists and capitalists alike. Good for Stalin, and good for the western banks. That's why they do the business. Siegel notes, "Harvester machines were, as always, highly desired in Russia, and the company's terms were actually better than those of its chief rival, Ford Motor Company. The Dearborn firm offered no credit until late 1925 yet still managed to get the lion's share of the Soviet tractor market through that year owing to the efforts of Armand Hammer's export agency and the passion for all Ford products and methods, which were thought to be the wave of the future." Hammer (1898-90) cut another curious figure of the era. The Barnes & Noble website describes him in an overview of the book by widely-read and praised investigative writer Jay Edward Epstein, *Armand Hammer: The Darker Side* (2011): "Dr. Hammer was a man skilled in bribing world leaders and collecting old masters and young mistresses." According to the Armand Hammer Collections website Hammer, born in New York to Russian immigrant parents, returned to revolutionary Russia and negotiated with the Bolsheviks to trade American grain for Russian goods. It was then he saw an easy fortune to be captured in Russia's vast art collections so, with his brother, a Princetonian specializing in art, they establish the Hammer Galleries in uptown Manhattan.

At the time Ford had forty percent of the American auto market, the other fifty percent gone to Chrysler and General Motors. By 1925 at least 10 percent of all tractors manufactured by the Ford Motor Co. were bought by the Soviet Union. Obviously Ford's animosity towards Jewish Soviet commissars or NKVD thugs did not deter his capitalist incentive to push for more profits. Through Amtorg the Soviets order a $1.5 million Harvester contract late 1924, half credit, half payment. The company confirmed payment "was made promptly at maturity". International, according to Siegel's account quoting Allport, "was 'the first of any importance to extend credit to the Russian Government'." That prompts Ford to jump in the game offering 25 percent credit late 1925.

The Harvester agent in Moscow George Sandomirsky writes, "The Commissar of Foreign Trade had been dealing with the Ford and trying to get Ford tractors on a credit basis, with the hope that, if they offered Ford an order for 10,000 tractors, they might expect to receive them with a fifty percent (credit) from 6-9 months'." Excusing the Consortium for consorting with the devil-worshipping communists, Siegel writes the Soviet Union "used the (Harvester) arrangements ... as a lever" to get their easy credit deals. Harvester still felt burned by Bolshevik nationalization. Consequently, Harvester lowers its risk and "did not permit the outstanding amount at any given moment to exceed $4 million and always received a bank guarantee for its credit from the Soviet banks in London." Foreign companies line up to fill in the gap; firms from Canada, Sweden, Germany and Czechoslovakia offered even better terms than the Americans; the Swedes, for example, proposed two year credit "with no cash down". (K. Siegel, *Loans and Legitimacy,* 101; David A. Mayers, *The Ambassadors and America's Soviet Policy,* Oxford Univ. Press, 1995)

Harvester sees a prize market ready to be snatched. According to Siegel, "Sandomirsky believed that Harvester could still get a share of the Soviet tractor business, estimated at $7.5 million ($85 million sic) or about eighteen thousand tractors for 1925-1926, if only the 'percent of cash payments were reduced'." The Soviets play various capitalist firms one off the other. Harvester, Deering and the

Fordson tractors compete with German factories with their trading partner as Deutsche Works and Krupp this year hold a combined $10 million order. Harvester in 1925 proves more flexible and grants terms $2.5 million credit over eighteen months. Ford holds out. The Soviets fail to gain better credit terms. (K. Siegel, *Loans and Legitimacy,* 102; D. A. Mayers, *The Ambassadors and America's Soviet Policy*; A. C. Sutton, *Western Technology and Soviet Economic Development 1917 to 1965, Hoover Institute, Stanford, 1968*)

Farming machines fill the bulk of American orders to the soviets between 1925 and 1929 worth a total of around fifty million rubles. That includes "twenty thousand tractors, mainly the Fordsons, but also lesser quantities of International (Harvester sic), Harris, Keyes, and Advance Rumely models", concurs professor Siegel. The Soviet market is an attractive fruit to put in their basket representing a quarter of the entire US export of tractors during the same period. For the Bolsheviks the new machinery is vital to their economic and political survival. Throughout the Russian and Ukrainian countryside American manufactured tractors appear synonymous with the bold new force of the communist revolution. "The tractor is to the Russian Communist something more than a machine; in his heart of hearts he regards it as in some way a mystical symbol of the new faith," observes L. E. Hubbard, author of *Economics of Soviet Agriculture* (1939). American engineers find all that out for themselves and so knew it was true. If only they grasped the full measure of that inexhaustible power of mystical imagination that animates the mystery of the vast steppes and wilderness of Russia and over the hills in far away Ukraine.

To think that the Americans would not take notice of the wretched famine devastating their export paradise is not only inconsistent with American business ethos, as we understand it today, it violates everything that defines the ethos of the profit-driven American manufacturer. Once their market dried up in the Holodomor wasteland, emptied of peasants, tractors rusting in the rains and lacking spare parts, fields and harvests devastated, the American capitalists are obliged to phase down their investment, in part, harassed by Stalin's Great Purge that begins 1937 through the next year creeping precipitously towards his defensive 1939 Friendship Pact with Hitler.

In addition to an increase of trade in oil and essential raw materials needed for German's war plans the Pact called for a special prisoner exchange. Dissident nuclear physicist Andrei Sakharov, the "father" of the Soviet H-Bomb and longtime critic of the regime commented on "the puzzling alliance with Hitler", observing that "it wasn't until later that we found out about the secret clauses in the Soviet-German pact and the swap of prisoners between the Gestapo and the NKVD." Nazi Germany exploited their fortuitous inspection of Russian industrial facilities and resources; Stalin permits twice the quantity of grain imports from the Ukraine after the signing of a new trade agreement January 10, 1941 while promising the Nazis an unlimited supply of foodstuffs necessary for Germany to pursue its military strategy.

Stalin does even more to avert German aggression. Richard Evans in his exemplary book *The Third Reich at War* (2009) recounts how "Stalin hurriedly launched a futile policy of trying to appease the Germans by stepping up Soviet deliveries of Asian rubber and other supplies under the trade agreement signed in January 1941."

As an adept Marxist-Leninist, Stalin remains convinced that Hitler's regime is a tool of German monopoly capitalism, so therefore if he made available everything German business wants, there ought to be no logical reason to invade, at least not for the present allowing more time to prepare defenses. Already, under trade provisions agreed under the Nazi-Soviet Pact early the previous year, the Soviet Union was supplying nearly three-quarters of Germany's requirement of phosphates, over two-thirds of its imported asbestos, only a little less of its chrome ore, over half its manganese, over a third of its imported nickel, and, even more critically, more than a third of its imported oil." Stalin dismissed numerous warnings from Soviet agents abroad "and even from members of the German embassy in Moscow", convinced all such reports were "disinformation". (Richard J. Evans, *The Third Reich at War*, Penguin, 2009, 165; A. Sakharov, 36; see M. Hastings)

Village after village Ukrainians appear as ghosts of the Holdomor years. Throughout the Russian countryside what the civilian population is forced to endure would fill endless volumes of wretched and unspeakable horror and hardship leaving deep scars. The people changed, their mentalities are profoundly affected, personalities twisted if not utterly and completely destroyed. Ukraine would never be the same and the mentality of an entire nation went through a rude culture shock from which it would never fully recover. *Washington Post* foreign correspondent David Remnick during his four years in Moscow observed the gravity of the profound change suffered and engrained in the mentality of several generations of Ukrainians and Russians in his fine book *Lenin's Tomb*, published in 1994 a few years after the fall of Gorbachev. How can a society ever become "normal" when the people have been severely changed forever and are not? Time cannot be reversed nor experience effaced but perhaps some of the damage can be healed by restored memory, awareness and understanding which is part of the aim of this book.

Just imagine! How would you feel after days, weeks, years and generations of shock therapy? And people in America wonder why some Russians, or Ukrainians "are not like us". To be fair, how would Americans ever know if the true history had been underplayed, ignored, or worse, deliberately falsified? It would seem, perhaps tragic, if the people were not free. Otherwise, it risks being morally depraved and criminally heartless and if not altogether spiritually corrupt.

Max Hastings cites salient passages from the artillery field officer Nikolai Belov of the Red Army. Its a poignant story though only his diary written for posterity survived the war and is finally published more than a half century later in 1997.

Major General Nikolai Nikanorovich Belov (1896-41) preserved an image of what he saw and experienced. Born in Kharkov, Nikolai is wounded during a few weeks after the German invasion and insists on staying with his men to fight instead of escaping by aircraft. Belov is killed within the week. He had served in the Czar's Army, joins the Reds after the October Revolution, and fights in the Russian Civil War. Then came Stalin and the Holodomor, more terror and the Great Purges. Belov writes, "A family of refugees stands in front of me now. They are so thin and gaunt, one can see through them. It is especially hard to look at the little ones – three of them, one a baby, the others a little older. There is no milk. These people have suffered as much as us, the soldiers, or even worse. Bombs, shells and mines no longer scare them." Multiply that by the millions and you might begin to better understand the experience of Russia and the Ukraine. The horror of horrors.

"Even those Russians," Hastings explains, "who did not suffer siege or bombardment spent the war laboring in conditions of extreme privation: they received 500 calories a day less nourishment than their British or German counterparts, a thousand fewer than Americans. Some 2 million perished of hunger in territories under Soviet control, while a further 13 million died under bombardment or in German-occupied regions; prisoners in the gulag's labour camps occupied the lowest place in the hierarchy of priority for rations, and one in four of them died in each of the war years. Russians suffered widespread scurvy as a consequence of vitamin deficiency, together with other conditions associated with hunger and overwork." (M. Hastings, *Inferno*, 316-7, 328-9; N.F. Belov, *Front Diary of N. F. Belov, 1941-44,* Vologda, 1997)

Cambridge professor Richard Evans observed, "None of the generals raised any open objections to Hitler's orders ... Only a very few, such as Field Marshal Fedor von Bock or Lieutenant-Colonel Henning von Tresckow, quietly instructed their officers to ignore the order to kill commissars and civilians as incompatible with international law or dangerous to discipline, or both. The vast majority of the generals transmitted the orders further down the line. ... The normal rules were set aside. Officers were not just officers but also leaders in a racial struggle against 'Jewish Bolshevism'. ... In the light of the orders it had received, the German army had no interest in keeping hundreds of thousands of prisoners of war alive... Tens of thousands were taken to concentration camps in Germany and killed there by firing squads. During the first weeks, many ordinary troops were also shot immediately on capture as well." (R. J. Evans, 176-86)

Hastings writes of rugged Russian resistance against the merciless total war. Yet, for reasons that are not made clear to the reader this venerable British historian consistently overlooks the place taken by the lessons of the Holodomor on the Ukraine and Russia's striking capacity to defend their homeland after decades of Bolshevik indoctrination and severe repression. There is an alarming tendency of most establishment historians of the same Ivy League and "Oxbridge" academic vintage to pass over the consequences of the Holodomor and its implications for the war from virtually every aspect whereas it otherwise would prove to be rich with instructive material of the unfolding tragedy suddenly thrust upon the Ukrainians.

Years of unforgiving silence and denial was the response to Stalin's repression through collectivization conceived and necessitated to rebuild Russia's capacity for its national defense. All the belligerents knew about it. While it is disturbing that the taboo of Genocide has been for decades summarily ignored, there should be no little consternation or wonder that historians today continue to have difficulty in scrutinizing the Holodomor, in particular, its consequences and implications their historical dissertations, for example, when they write of the German atrocities in southern Ukraine and Crimea. After the war the Holodomor was dismissed and ignored eclipsed by the war followed by more repression, imprisonment, famine and a desperate struggle to survive that continued unabated until Stalin's death in 1953.

Nothing can compete with the Holocaust for outrageous crimes against Humanity; nothing except the Holodomor which surpasses not it not in kind but in numbers of victims and complicity with the West.

Yet, the Holocaust, – and not the Holodomor, established the moral agenda for the historical interpretation and review of the Second World War. This is a major mistake that began ever since the first pictures of the Nazi concentration camps appeared in the western press. Nor should one ever overlook the unspeakable extermination campaigns of the Japanese militarists in China and elsewhere in Southeast Asia and the Pacific basin.

Hastings also endeavors to treat this difficult and contentious point which to him remains self-evident. Reader, lets not fool ourselves here. Hastings writes, "Most of Germany's generals, in the dark recesses of their souls, knew that they had made their nation and its entire army – it was a myth that only the SS committed atrocities – complicit in crimes against humanity, *and especially Russian humanity*, such as their enemies would never forgive, *even before the Holocaust began.* They saw nothing to lose by fighting on, except more millions of lives; it deserves emphasis that a large majority of the war's victims perished from 1942 onwards. Only victories might induce the Allies to make terms."

Certainly Hitler's visionary madness asserted in his outraged refusal not to retreat from Stalingrad in the 1942-43 campaign was exacerbated in defeat by a superior enemy but the blame for that madness of the Reich's extermination of the Russians and Slavs is not his burden to be shared alone. A reading of the more recent inquiry into the German national Nazi psychosis underlined in the book by Daniel Jonah Boldhagen, *Hitler's Willing Executioners: Ordinary Germans and the Holocaust* (1996) along with William Shirer's classic *Inside the Rise and Fall of the Third Reich* (1959) will lead to a strikingly better understanding of all this. (M. Hastings, *Inferno*, 295-6; italics added)

Historian Max Hastings makes another essential remark of the logic of the Second World War (or as it is better known in Russia, "The Great Patriotic War") and its cost in human lives, writing, "To defeat Nazi Germany, it was indispensable for its enemies to destroy the *Wehrmacht*. It was the Western Allies' extreme good fortune that the Russians, and not themselves, paid almost the entire 'butcher's bill' for doing this, accepting *95 percent of the military casualties of the three major powers of the Grand Alliance*." General Zhukov's great regret after storming Hitler's Berlin bunker is to find him dead by his own gun; he is unable to put Hitler in a cage for all of the Ukraine to see, on the route to Stalin in Moscow. (italics added)

Hastings then comments on the belated Second Front expected but not forthcoming from FDR and Churchill until 1944 by which time the *Wehrmacht* had already been crushed by the Soviet Red Army: "In 1940-41, the British Empire defied Hitler alone. Thereafter, the United States made a dominant material contribution to Germany's defeat, by supplying aid to Russia and Britain which assumed massive proportions from 1943 onwards, and by creating great air and naval armadas. The Anglo-American bomber offensive made an increasingly heavy impact on Germany. The Western Allied armies, however, by deferring a major landing on the Continent until 1944, restricted themselves to a marginal role. The Russians eventually killed more than 4.5 million German soldiers, while American and British ground and air forces accounted for only about 500,000. These figures emphasize the disparity between respective battlefield contributions."

Hitler's pursuit of a war of "annihilation" unleashed extraordinary civilian losses, totaling in the millions all the while Stalin is urging FDR to launch a Second Front in the west. The Allies are not ready, and when they do they confront on the Normandy coast a significantly weaker *Wehrmacht* "following a year of attrition on the Eastern Front". Nice word, "attrition", very neat, like "ethnic-cleansing"; in other words, butchery, extermination, "mass-murder". Genocide.

Hastings' research reveals the burden carried by the Russians on the Ukrainian fronts. The experience of a single embattled captain says it all, and Hastings writes, "Roosevelt and Churchill were able to exercise the luxury of choice denied to the Red Army, which continuously confronted Hitler's armies. Capt. Pavel Kovalenko was among many Russians embittered by the Western Allies supposed pusillanimity, which conveniently ignored the Soviet Union's ignominious role between 1939 and June 1941. Kovalenko wrote from the front on 26 March 1943: 'Winston Churchill made a speech on the radio, (saying): 'I can imagine that some time in the next year or possibly the one after, we shall be able to accomplish the defeat of Hitler' What can one expect from these bastards of 'allies'? Cheats, scoundrels. They want to join the fighting when the outcome is decided."

Not one to ever cringe from challenge to lead an intelligent offensive, just prior to the Normandy D-Day landing, Churchill's stake in the "terrible business" of war was tempered with deliberate caution, as when haunted by memories of the First World War; he tells Roosevelt's adjunct, and Stimson's Assistant Secretary of War John J. McCloy, "If you think I'm dragging my feet, it is not because I am afraid of casualties, it is because I am afraid of what those casualties will be. No one can accuse me of a lack of zeal. I cannot endure the loss of another British generation."

Instead, the Russians have to face not one generation but three. Fortunately for the Churchill and his friends as the British RAF proved in August 1940 Germany no longer had superiority of the air. (This time around RAF pilots came not from the decimated ranks of the aristocrats but low middle-class instead.) Their factories short on materials could not match output in either Russia, England or America. A similar sentiment was voiced by Churchill, when in June 1920, in his cabinet position as Secretary of State for War in Lloyd George's government and with Trotsky's Red Army was about to overcome Warsaw, he restrained his Prime Minister from declaring war on Lenin and the Bols. Churchill declared in the press that the British had sacrificed enough: "They are thoroughly tired of war. They have learned during five bitter years too much of its iron slavery, its squalor, its mocking disappointments, its ever-dwelling sense of loss."

An examination by Hasting of the clumsy and inept handling of the Allied invasion on Germany's southern flank in 1943 is more telling of the astonishment of the German commanders whose gallant troops were overwhelmed by sheer numbers. Hastings: "Fifty thousand Germans had held half a million Allied soldiers at bay for five weeks. ... Again and again Allied forces failed – as they would again fail in northwest Europe – to translate captures of ground into destruction of enemy forces. The Sicilian campaign represented the only significant summer 1943 land operation against the Germans by the United States and Britain, engaging eight Allied divisions and costing 6,000 dead. During the same season, 4 million men were locked in combat around Kursk and Orel, where *half a million Russians perished.* Some German civilians, desperate for an end of the war, lamented the sluggishness of Western Allied progress." (italics added)

Given the snail pace of the Allied military response, the Russians had good reason to gripe. After decades of research and more than twenty books to his name, Hastings concludes, "repeated Anglo-American failures to destroy Hitler's armies, despite successes in displacing them from occupied territories, meant that the Red Army remained until 1945, as it had been since 1941, the main engine of Nazism's destruction." Hastings carefully substantiates overwhelming Russian engagement with the enemy faced with the delay of England and the Americans. He concludes, for example, "While the Russians had been fighting continuously for three years, less than a dozen formations of the US Army had fought the Germans ... statistically, in May 1944, less than half of Churchill's army had fired a shot in anger ..." (M. Hastings, *Inferno*, 427-38; Martin Gilbert, *In Search of Churchill,* Wiley & Sons, 1994, 101-5)

War historian Richard Evans from Cambridge observed that "By 1942, he (Hitler) thought, the USA might well have entered the war on the Allied side. Defeating the Soviets would put Germany in a strong position to deal with the Americans. It would encourage Japan to come into the war against America by eliminating a major threat to Japan's west. And it would isolate the British still further and perhaps finally force them to the negotiating table."

Hitler was convinced that once Russia was irreparably crushed England most certainly would be next to fall. Ensuing events proved his judgment fatally flawed. Soviet industrialization and Stalin's Purges had left the USSR unprepared and virtually leaderless to effectively withstand the *Wehrmacht* assault. The Ukraine was decimated, Stalingrad nothing but rubble and by the summer of 1942, there were literally no more Jews to kill in areas under Nazi control. (R. J. Evans, 161-2; M. Hastings, *Inferno*, 505)

Then, too, the population in the Ukraine suffered further scarcity of grain when the 1939 Nazi Friendship Pact sent prices sky-rocketing forcing horrendous shortages of grain and other precious foodstuffs. A vivid experience of that deprivation is recalled in the engaging memoir *Nina's Journey*. This is a lively autobiographical narrative of Nina Markovna (1989), in her youth a sprite ballet dancer living in a small ancient coastal town on the Sea of Azov: "The bread supply was especially affected. Ships loaded with grain were departing from Odessa regularly for Germany. Trains loaded to bursting with more precious grain hurried toward German borders. Feodosia's granaries began to empty. Crimea, which had served ancient Greece as a breadbasket, became exhausted under the heavy demands of our Nazi allies to be fed, and fed well." (Nina Markovna, *Nina's Journey*, Washington DC, Regnery Gateway, 1989)

THEN CAME ELECTRICITY & THE AMERICAN TRACTOR

Before Stalin forced collectivization on the peasants the Americans were producing metal and electrical equipment ("grinding machines, high-speed precision lathes, and mining, boring, and quarrying implements") increasing output of American firms such as Cincinnati Milling, American Tool, Pratt and Whitney, Brown and Sharpe and others totally some 25 million roubles. The Soviet oil industry alone bought some 15 million roubles of state of the art American technology and mining equipment. Soviet commissars and their foreign guests, high-level Party goons drive in Harley Davidsons, Buicks, Fords and Dodges worth three and a half million roubles.

Without overtly describing the Soviet Plans as Consortium blueprints for the totalitarian's regime tyranny over the people Siegel confirms Sutton conclusion that soviet dependence on modern American manufacturing and "foreign technical assistance" was so great "that International Harvester claimed in 1930 that the Soviets were trying to get 150 American engineers and other technical workers at Harvester and GE to leave their jobs and work in Russian plants by offering raises of 50 to 100 percent". In fact, it was just business as usual in post-revolutionary Russia. (K. Siegel, 104)

In a short essay titled "The American Tractor Comes to Soviet Architecture: The Transfer of a Technology" (1964), its quite clear that the State Department agricultural expert Dana G. Dalyrmple understood there had been a cover-up ever since Lenin and the Bolshevik Revolution. "In 1924 there were only 1,000 tractors in operation, by 1934 the number had increased to over 200,000," Dr. Dalrymple observed. A transformation literally overnight of a Russian or Ukrainian village of thatched huts with wood fires resembling the Middle Ages into the era of machinery and modern innovation. "This technology, however,", Dalrymple adds, "did not spring from the Russian soil; *it came almost entirely from the United States*." (italics added)

Peasant girls marveled at the "miracle". Hardened elders who with their ancestors for centuries had tilled the land in harmony with their animals and the sounds of nature cringed at the mechanical metallic giant with fire in its nose. But it was neither a miracle nor a monster. Ironically, it is the Ford Motor Company that is transforming the Soviet Revolution "made in the USA". Stalin knew it was so. Yet when the Soviet pre-revolutionary Czarist educated engineers tried to customize communist Russia Soviet-style it proves to literally impossible. Generations of engineering innovation, automated production, worker company loyalty and Henry Ford's personal keenness at tinkering condensed in a few slogans and idiotic textbooks can hardly deliver the same result. They were doomed.

Advanced technology is power and whoever has the power controlled the technology and the culture it transforms. It wasn't easy to be Stalinist, but what was the alternative for the lonely gray wolf in the Kremlin? They had him and he knew it. But as long as he had millions of Russians to sacrifice, the people would pay the price of modernization with their lives.

In 1934, Abby Aldrich Rockefeller gave the Museum of Modern Art in New York a painting by Charles Sheeler of Ford's River Rouge Plant "the human-built world has become an American landscape", writes Thomas Parke in "Technology and Culture" from his book titled *Human-Built World: How to Think about Technology and Culture* (2004). This was the "Year of Our Ford". Evidently his publisher, – Rockefeller's own University of Chicago – wants us to know this and have it firmly fossilized in our brains. It's hard to imagine a more depressing industrial image of the "American landscape" blotching the Ukraine, unless we look at it duplicated as it was by the Soviets with slave labor.

On its fifth anniversary in 1896, Rockefeller pontificates in a speech at the University which he has already endowed with $10 million, "The good Lord gave me the money and how could I withhold it from Chicago!" In 1905 he repeats that conviction to a journalist in *Woman Home Companion*, "God gave me my money." Its an apt translation voiced by JP Morgan who decries, "I owe the public nothing!" By 1913, J. D. Rockefeller Sr. had given a colossal $23 million to the University of Chicago, and rose in two decades to $35 million. And that year JP Morgan sees the sun set for the last time, dead in the shadow of Vatican in Rome. (Thomas Parke Hughes, *Human-Built World: How to Think about Technology and Culture*, Univ. of Chicago Press, 2004; Dana G. Dalrymple, "The American Tractor Comes to Soviet Architecture: The Transfer of a Technology", *Technology and Culture*, Johns Hopkins Univ. Press, v. 5, No. 2, Spring 1964, 191-214; *Who's Who in America*, v. VII 1912-1913, ed. Albert N. Marquis, Chicago; Jules Abels, *The Rockefeller Billions, The Story of the World's Most Stupendous Fortune*, NY: Macmillan, 1965, 279; Walter Lord, in "Big Stick, Big Business" from *The Good Years, from 1900 to the First World War*, NY: Harper & Row, 1960)

BILL DODD: FDR'S MAN IN BERLIN

Who was William E. Dodd? The most unlikely choice for a man to confront Hitler, Roosevelt wanted his own man in Berlin and he chose Dodd.

The son of one of the founders of the Federal Reserve Bank "Jimmy" Warburg proposed Harriman for the job. Dodd's literary editor, the left-center fellow historian of American history Charles A. Beard writes that Dodd who came from a long lineage of landowners and clergy represents "the best in the American democratic tradition ... old English stock, born in Clayton, North Carolina, in 1869, a graduate of the Virginia Polytechnic Institute, the holder of doctor's degree from the University of Leipzig, won in 1900 by three years of hard work, crowned by a dissertation on Thomas Jefferson's return ot politics in 1796 ("Jefferson's *Ruckkehr zur Politik*"). A history professor at the University of Chicago since 1908, a Baptist with a "dry ironical humor typically his". Dodd joined the faculty in 1908, two years after the premature death of its first president, William Rainey Harper, himself a precocious poor boy born in a log cabin in Ohio; before he turns twenty he completes graduate studies at Yale, and specialized in Hebrew and biblical studies. He has lived nearly half of his professional life in Chicago on Rockefeller turf since the university is founded in 1890.

Professor Dodd keeps a small 400-acre farm family farm near the Blue Ridge Mountains in Virginia back country. "Democracy has never really been tried," was one of his favorite quips. Dodd is a Wilson scholar, and in Berlin had good reason to be particularly interested in John Foster Dulles' experience in Wilson's White House. In 1920 his book *Woodrow Wilson and His Work* told a certain story followed by dedicated editing for *The Public Papers of Woodrow Wilson* (1924), which he published in collaboration with Wilsonian loyalist, the journalist Ray Stannard Baker who writes the definitive collection of 15 volumes on Wilson–yes, 15!, (all that to bury the truth?), earning a Pulitzer in 1940. But his Rubicon is "The Old South" in four volumes.

Ambassador Dodd's Diary 1933-1938 carries an introductory biography by standout contemporary economic historian and free thinker, former Columbia professor Charles A. Beard (1874-1948). Beard first achieved national recognition in 1913 with *An Economic Interpretation of the Constitution of the United States.* Four years later he resigns in protest against the university trustees in 1917 and their support of the world war over there in Europe. Beard establishes the alternative New School in downtown Greenwich Village. A best-selling and influential historian he publishes *The Rise of American Civilization* in 1927. When Dodd gets the call for the Berlin job Beard sits at the top of his profession holding the presidency of the American Historical Association. He breaks with FDR's New Dealism and as a non-interventionalist, opposes US entry into the war and writes two more controversial books, *American Foreign Policy in the Making, 1932-1940,* and *President Roosevelt and the Coming of the War, 1941*, published the year he dies in 1948.

Dodd spoke German well but did he fail to anticipate the organized carnage of world war and Genocide? By the time the book on Dodd appears in 1941 Hitler leads Germany's revenge, Russia is burning and Dodd is gone from the scene but he's belatedly praised for his "loyalty to the humanistic traditions of American democracy", and Beard observes, Dodd exercised an "esteem for the finest features of old Germany and the affectionate warmth he felt for her people". That too might not have gone over too well. Beard, and America, remain isolationist, but that changes in a few months with the bombing of Pear Harbor.

Beard writes Dodd "saw more clearly than most of his colleagues, American and foreign, in the diplomatic corps, the hard drift of things toward the tragedy of the coming years. … He divined the frightful crash bound to come from the policy of appeasement, intrigue, and vacillation, and he fought relentlessly, as far as he was able, to stop it. That Russia was to play a decisive role in Western affairs, Mr. Dodd understood from the beginning of his mission." (Charles A. Beard in W. E. Dodd, *Ambassador Dodd's Diary*, xv)

Dodd arrives with family in Berlin mid-July and stay at the sumptuous Hotel Esplanade on the Bellevuestrasse where all the stars like to be seen. (Garbo and Chaplin had stayed there.) In advance of his arrival his Embassy affairs are prepared by the urbane and talented career diplomat and US Consul General in Germany, George S. Messersmith. He's assisted by Raymond Geist. They soon settle in at the sumptuous embassy at the end of the street off *Tiergarten*, Berlin's Central Park, formerly a royal hunting preserve converted into a 600-acre oasis with riding paths and walks stretching from Brandenburg Gate to Charlottenburg with its famous zoo that the Russians later destroy leaving the wild animals, cats and lions free to roam after Hitler is dead.

Dodd has a lot of catching up to do to keep pace with Hitler's marching Reich, and soon make the rounds presenting his ravishing naughty daughter Margaret at the diplomatic parties given by his hosts Goebbels, Göring and their Nazi gang. At first Dodd appears pretty much out of step with the whole new Nazi Party reality of postwar Berlin. Unlike the other millionaire ambassadors in the American diplomatic corps Dodd prefers to appear frugal, a wise attitude if dependent on the miserly State Department salary of $17,500, which under the circumstances, even in Berlin's dog days of Depression is extremely modest by old continent standards when sumptuous galas and dinner parties are naturally to be expected from the richest nation in the world for the princely aristocrats and their friends. Berliners make him appear a sort of odd ball in the diplomat set of top hats and long shiny black limousines; Dodd feels more at home driving his old Chevy which he shipped to Berlin from his farm in Jeffersonian Virginia named "Stoneleigh" for the rocks spread about the property under abundant apple trees that formed a perfect setting for his tales of history and southern hospitality recounted in his four-volumes titled *The Rise and Fall of the Old South.* His ancestors included two veterans of the Civil War at Appomattox present at the surrender of their Confederate General Robert E. Lee.

In their first days there Dodd gets briefings from Sigrid Schultz, the *Chicago Tribune's* foreign correspondent and learns of the KZ concentration camps, *Konzentrationslagger*, the pride of the Hitler's henchman, the former chicken farmer more easily mistaken for resembling a country school teacher, Heinrich Himmler.

Nearly a year has passed since that unforgettable call Thursday, June 8, 1933. Dodd is in his university office. Dodd picks up the receiver.

"This is Franklin Roosevelt. I want to know if you will render the government a distinct service. I want you to go to Germany as Ambassador." Dodd asks for time to think about it. Roosevelt said he could have two hours and praised his work "as a liberal and a scholar and his experience at the German University."

"Why me?" Dodd asks.

Roosevelt tells the professor, "I want an American liberal in Germany as a standing example". The embassy has been without an ambassador since March when Frederick Sackett packed his bags.

No one in FDR's cabinet opposes the appointment. The President is concerned about the Consortium's favorite Nazi banker Hjalmar Schacht's threat to default in August over reparation loans at 6-7 percent on $1 billion owed American creditors. Schacht's visit to Washington had not gone well, kept waiting by Hull before being handed the personal note from Roosevelt urging him to cooperate. Many years later, on April 12 1945, the night before he died, Roosevelt is visited by a strange memory during a small dinner party at Warms Springs, with Morgenthau, a Russian painter of the president's portrait and some favorite guests. He has a vision of Schacht coming to see him as he did "three or four times saying that the Germans were going broke and they never did!" (J. E. Persico, *Roosevelt's Secret War*, 433)

Before leaving the country for Berlin Dodd meets with the President and is briefed on Germany's anti-Semitism and the violent Nazi treatment of Jews. FDR tells Dodd it is "not a governmental affair" and not to make it one. FDR added, "We can do nothing except for American citizens who happen to be made victims. We must protect them, and whatever we can do to moderate the general persecution by unofficial and personal influence ought to be done." Nothing is found of a similar tone or instruction to Bullitt to urge lessening the repression of the Ukrainians. FDR instructs Dodd "to make arrangements on certain items and thus increase German exports so as to aid them in their debt repayments."

FDR tells Dodd, "If European states refused to make tariff concessions, we shall make special arrangements with Canada and Latin America and develop a mutual trade policy which will give us markets for our surplus products." Dodd warns against a US policy "that would soon lead us into a new feudalism which would tend to make peasants and day laborers of farmers, and proletarians of all unorganized city workers." Both agree that only a cutback in the escalation of arms trade would bring peace. Dodd meets Ray Moley attached to the State Department, and finds him unsympathetic to the Jews and ignorant of economic affairs, trade or tariffs.

Dodd is no more impressed by Undersecretary Bill Phillips who also strikes the good American as decidedly a Back-Bay Boston Brahmin elitist. In one comment he described a businessman as "my little Jewish friend from Boston". In the interview Dodd is alarmed at Phillips unabashed anti-Semitism, as when he casually remarks about his recent trip to Atlantic City, and tells him, "The whole place is infested with Jews. In fact, the whole beach scene on Saturday afternoon and Sunday was an extraordinary sight – very little sand to be seen, the whole beach covered by slightly clothed Jews and Jewesses." Phillips just finds that absolutely astounding! Not a word about Hitler but plenty to say about too many half-naked Jews on the beaches of Atlantic City. Ray Monk writes of the tribulations of Robert Oppenheimer, the son of German Jewish immigrants and a student in the twenties at Harvard under the presidency of Abbot Lawrence Lowell where Jews in the student body "had risen sharply from 10 to 20 percent", higher than at Yale (7 percent) and Princeton (3 percent). Monk writes, that despite significant gifts from Schiff, Felix Warburg "and other eminent Jews from New York City ... among both staff and students there was growing talk about the 'Jewish problem'. Harvard, it was said, was going the same way as Columbia ... where, by 1920, 40 percent of the students were Jewish. For Lowell, vice president of the Immigration Restriction League and a firm believer in the superiority of both the Christian religion and the 'Anglo-Saxon race', this was an intolerable prospect ... in order to pursue his vision of Harvard as an institution for the education of the 'Anglo-Saxon' elite." (re. anti-Semitism at Harvard in the twenties under President Abbot Lawrence Lowell, in "Harvard", from Ray Monk, *Robert Oppenheimer, A Life Inside the Center*, NY: Doubleday, 2012, 53-86)

Erik Larson in his bestselling book *In the Garden of Beasts* (2011) focused on Dodd's Nazified Berlin observes that "Phillips hated Jews", and as corroboration he cites research by Richard Breitman and Alan M. Kraut published in their book *American Refugee Policy and European Jewry, 1933-1945* (1987). Senior Undersecretary William J. Carr in charge of the consular service is inclined to call Jews "kikes", and harbors no compassion for Russian and Polish immigrants, brazenly writing, "They are filthy, Un-American and often dangerous in their habits." During a trip to Detroit, Carr observes the city covered with "dust, smoke, dirt, Jews."

Bill Carr, too, is disgusted every day during his trip to Atlantic City February 1934 by the sight of Jews and comments in his diary an endless slew of negative slurs. "In all our day's journey along the Boardwalk we saw but few Gentiles," the high-level State Department official writes. "Jews everywhere, and of the commonest kind." At the Claridges for dinner again he is annoyed to be out in public with Jews commenting that "few presented a good appearance". Carr and his wife dined the next night at the Marlborough-Blenheim hotel, and Carr notes with a great sigh of relief and satisfaction, "I like it. How different from the Jewish atmosphere of the Claridge." (Erik Larson, *In the Garden of Beasts*, NY: Crown, 2011, 30-1; I. F. Gellman, 37; Richard Breitman and Alan M. Kraut, *American Refugee Policy and European Jewry, 1933-1945*, Indiana Univ. Press, 1987, 32-6)

In New York Dodd meets bankers at the Century Club, and at their offices, National City Bank. He is surprised to learn about $1.2 billion of German loans and securities held by National City and Chase. The bank's vice president Floyd Blair complains that American investors had been deceived into making loans to German corporations and paid back in "cheap marks" forcing American bondholders to sell at 30 cents to the dollar. Bankers fear the negative impact on US banks in the United States. Dodd writes in his diary, "The National City Bank and the Chase National Bank hold more than a hundred millions of German bonds! If they could be sure of 4 percent interest, instead of the original 7 per cent, they would be satisfied." Its odd, rather that in Erik Larson's entertaining account of the Dodd embassy scene *In the Garden of Beasts* he omits any reference to the Standard Oil business, and he cites only $1 million of National City-Chase German bonds acceptable at a negotiated 30 cents to the dollar payback, or default.

In New York for consultations Dodd also meets with Felix Warburg of the Warburg banking family who happens to be married to Frieda, the daughter of Jacob Schiff. Jews are being killed "all the time", said Warburg, and many forced to suicide, their property confiscated. And this despite Hitler's assurance to Schacht that Jewish bankers and financiers would not be persecuted. Warburg tells him of the recent suicide in Frankfurt of two relatives, Moritz and Kathie Oppenheim. He also meets with Judge Irving Lehman of the New York Court of Appeals and the brother of the NY Governor, along with Rabbi Stephen S. Wise and Max Kohler, biographer of the Seligman family of New York of the prestigious merchant banking house J. & W. Seligman. The Jewish leaders urge Dodd to press the Nazis regime to put an end to their persecution of Jews. And who are these Seligmans?

BEFORE MORGAN THERE ARE THE ROTHSCHILDS ...

To answer that read for a start Eustace Mullins here. As we will see the Rothschild-Peabody connection becomes a primodial connection to the American culture of the nation's banking elite from Morgan to the Groton School and Roosevelt. Mullins writes, "Birmingham notes in *Our Crowd*: 'In the autumn of 1874, Baron de Rothschild summoned Isaac Seligman to his office – some $55 million of US Bonds were to be offered by three houses, the House of Seligman, the House of Morgan, and the House of Rothschild.' This was the first time that the Seligmans had been asked to participate in an issue with the Rothschilds. They were more than grateful, and thus another ally of the Rothschilds began to operate in America. A notable advantage o JP Morgan's work for the House of Rothschild was the carefully cultivated belief that Morgan, if not openly 'anti-Semitic', avoided participating in operations with Jewish banking firms, and that his firm would not hire anyone of Jewish background. It was the same deception which Nathan Mayer Rothschild had hired Morgan's predecessor, George Peabody, to perform in London. It was a traditional belief on Wall Street that if you wished to deal with a 'gentiles only' firm, you went to JP Morgan; if you wanted a Jewish firm, there were a number of houses available, but the most influential, by far, was Kuhn, Loeb Company. In either case, the customer was never made aware that he was dealing with an American representative of the House of Rothschild." (E. Mullins, *The History Project*; Stephen Birmingham, *Our Crowd – The Great Jewish Families of New York*)

My God!, if only we knew where to begin with the power of the Rothschilds who with all their diversified investments, relations and managers are reputed to own half the world. They seem to be everywhere. "For more than a century, a widespread belief has been deliberately fostered in the United States that the Rothschilds were of little significance in the American financial scene. With this cover, the tremendous financial power of the Jewish Rothschild banking family have been able to manipulate political and financial developments in the United States to their own advantage. Morgan's father, Junius S. Morgan, had been a London partner of George Peabody & Company, renamed the Junius S. Morgan

Company, a Rothschild front agent. As "an unidentified agent for Lord Nathan Rothschild as early as 1835", Mullins observes, "George Peabody had established his business in England through his connection with Brown Brothers", – later named Brown Bros. Harriman.

In 1837 the Rothschilds let their American representative W. L. & M. S. Joseph go bankrupt in the Crash while they throw their cash reserves behind a newcomer, August Belmont, and their secret rep, George Peabody of London.

Again Mullins refers to Birmingham's *Our Crowd*: "In the Panic of 1837, Belmont was able to perform a service which he would repeat in subsequent panics, thanks to the hugeness of the Rothschild reservoir of capital, to start out in America operating his own Federal Reserve System." That same year the firm August Belmont & Company opened in New York with Belmont "to be a manager of the Rothschild interests" and immediately earns the reputation of one of the leading houses. (S. Birmingham, *Our Crowd*)

After 1837, August Belmont (Schönberg) was publicly advertised in the financial press as the American representative of the Rothschilds. When Belmont participated in a financial operation, everyone knew that the Rothschilds were involved. When Belmont took no part, and the transaction was handled by JP Morgan & Co., and/or by Kuhn, Loeb Co., everyone "knew" (that is, "assumed") that the Rothschilds were not involved.

Although there is no statue of George Peabody in the Wall Street area, there is one in London, just opposite the Bank of England. George Peabody became "the favorite American" of Queen Victoria, no stranger in the glorious Rothschild mansions, Empress of India who ruled over 300 million subjects yet never visited her empire there, or virtually anywhere for in all of her sixty-three years, she ventured no further than Berlin to the east, or San Sebastian of northern Spain. His old lunchbox occupies a prominent place in the London office of Morgan Stanley to this day.

In 1860, while all the time representing Rothschild banking interests, August Belmont rises to the pinnacle of the Democratic Party and chairs the Democratic National Convention for the party's second convention, in Baltimore, after pandemonium over the slavery issue bashes the first attempt in Charleston, South Carolina.

By 1861, George Peabody has become the largest trader of American securities in the world. To put pressure on the Lincoln government, he began dumping them and drives prices down. It's the old Waterloo trick again masterminded by the boys from Jew Street when in 1815 Nathan crashed the London market using carrier pigeons (there was no telegraph cable) and pocketed a fortune. Junius Morgan, in league with Morris Ketchum, drains the American gold supply shipping it to England. He drives the price up from $126 ounce to $171 ounce, reaping a handsome profit, and squeezes the Lincoln government all the time while trading with the South. It's only one of an array of financial intrigues engineered by the Rothschilds. Impoverished aristocrats are lining up for loans to sustain their high empire standard of living and keep up appearances of their debaunched and cultured elite dominant class.

George Peabody had neither son nor heir; he partners in 1854 with Junius S. Morgan, father of John Pierpont Morgan, who before his death in 1913 became known as "the most powerful banker in the world", which suits the House of Rothschild secretly taking their commissions. George Peabody, 74, died in 1869 and is honored with a rare and highly publicized funeral ceremony and even accorded temporary burial in Westminster Abbey approved by his friend the Queen where in the centre aisle of the nave near the west door his name is written in stone commemorating "the temporary burial of George Peabody, American merchant and philanthropist".

Yale considers him "the first great modern philanthropist and one of the best known world figures of the 19th century", according to the Peabody Museum of Natural History website; his successful floatation of a loan that saved Baltimore is not forgotten: "After 5 business trips to Europe, in 1837 he decided to settle in London, where he established the banking house of George Peabody and Company, specializing in foreign exchange and American securities." No mention of Rothschild.

Educated with the elite at Trinity College, Cambridge, Reverend Endicott Peabody works briefly in his grandfather's prestigious Lee Higginson firm in Boston that had made fortunes for its Boston Brahmin partners in the China opium trade. Harvard Divinity School, a spell taming beasts, brutes and whores during the Gold Rush in the Wild West of Tomestone, Arizona, administering the Christian faith, Rev. Peabody returns to Massachusetts and creates the Groton School. His father Samuel Peabody, and JP Morgan Sr. are directors on Groton's first board of the elite boys preparatory school in the proximity of Harvard in 1884. (Jim Sterba, *Frankie's Place,* Grove/Atlantic, 2004, 153)

If the public had been paying closer attention to read between the lines they would have known more from a slight reference in *The NY Times* on October 26, 1907 of a curious connection Morgan and the New York Panic of 1907: "In conversation with *The New York Times* correspondent, Lord (Nathaniel) Rothschild paid a high tribute to JP Morgan for his efforts in the present financial juncture in New York. 'He is worthy of his reputation as a great financier and a man of wonders. His latest action fills one with admiration and respect for him.'" It was indeed very rare if ever that a Rothschild praised any banker who was not immediate Rothschild family.

More light casts darker shadows on the Peabody-Morgan connection and how it links with the Groton School for boys (and girls) with their obscure Anglo-American bridge to the London-based Rothschild banking empire. In Jim Sterba's idyllic *Frankie's Place* (2004) he writes, "George Peabody (1795-69) moved to London in 1837. In 1851 Peabody moved into railroad securities and partnered with Julius Morgan to form Peabody, Morgan & Company. His $8 million given to charity through the Peabody Trust for cheap housing in London 'for the deserving poor' established him as the pioneer in philanthropy before Morgan, Rockefeller and the ruling American elite. ... Next to the Royal Exchange a statue unveiled months before he died eternally stands in the City of London."

George Peabody had no children. Endicott Peabody is the son of Samuel Peabody who was himself a descendant of Joseph Peabody and John Endicott who first came to America in the early part of the 17th century. John Endicott (1601-64), being a Puritan landed at Naumkeag in 1628. He becomes the first Governor of Massachusetts Bay Colony, fought the Pequot Indian war, tortured and executed Quakers and other religious dissenters and kept the peace for King Charles of England for whose graces he so gallantly serves in this new land of native savages and formidable natural beauty and resource. One of their favorite torture techniques was pounding a burning iron nail through women's tongues until they recanted their non-Puritan religious beliefs. The unrepentant dissidents who resist persecution and torture are disgracefully hanged. Joseph Peabody (1757-44) became a revolutionary privateer who survives capture and prospers in the opium trade.

So, two generations after Peabody's passing, Dodd went to see Rothschild's taciturn Colonel House at his Beverly Farms home outside Boston. House insists to be kept in the loop. As President Wilson's chief political adviser during the First World War it's Col. House himself who had overseen British intelligence operations with Sir William Wiseman, tenth baronet of Ulster and head of British intelligence in the US, and made him feel quite at ease inside the JP Morgan bank and its Wall Street investment firms handling syndicated British loans. For his arduous discretion Wiseman is rewarded in 1929 by Kuhn, Loeb & Co. and made a general partner of the country's second greatest private banking house.

Dodd finds Edward House, 75, "mentally very alert". They talk for two hours over breakfast. Dodd learns that it was Nicholas Murray Butler known for his supremacist views held in common with his friend Elihu Root who had recommended Dodd for Berlin. Butler is President of the American sect of the Pilgrims Society serving as its president (1928-46) at the same time he's president of The American Academy of Arts and Letters and president of Columbia University for forty-three years until 1945. Further, he is on the board of the Carnegie Foundation for International Peace, and in 1931 shares the Nobel Peace Prize with pioneer social reformer Jane Addams and clearly on the opposite end of the political spectrum than his corporate Consortium gang. But little does Dodd know about the Pilgrims who plucked him for the Berlin post. Newton Baker, a lawyer, and formerly Wilson's Secretary of War, had already declined the job which House assures Dodd is "the most difficult post in Europe".

House urges Dodd to do his best "to ameliorate Jewish sufferings." But he should just go so far, says House, who adds, "They are clearly wrong and even terrible; but the Jews should not be allowed to dominate economic or intellectual life in Berlin as they have done for a long time."

In New York Dodd gets more warnings about the Jews when he visits the imposing Manhattan apartment of banker Charles R. Crane (1858–39) and benefactor of the University of Chicago where he endowed Harper's son in a chair of the Russian history department. Dodd is greeted and ushered into the Park Avenue home decorated with "a marvelous display of Russian and Asiatic works of art" accumulated by Crane on missions abroad during Wilson's war years. In addition to his interest in China Crane retains his passion for Middle Eastern oil.

Crane indeed is about to become fabulously rich opening up Saudi Arabian oil concessions which Roosevelt will consummate on his return from the 1945 Yalta conference inviting King Ibn Saud aboard the *USS Quincy*. Among his holdings and estates include a former palace in Prague refurbished as a US government building. Dodd quickly learns that this senior Consortium member is overtly hostile to the Bolsheviks, Jews and at the same time "enthusiastic about the Hitler regime in Germany". (Harry St. J. B. Philby, *Sa'udi Arabia*, NY: Praeger, 1955)

Crane feels no compulsion to hide his contempt for the Jews, whether they live in New York, Russia or in the Middle East. "Jews are anathema to him," Dodd writes, "and he hopes to see them put in their place." A passionate spokesman for the Arab states, opposed to Rothschild's Zionists pushing for an independent Jewish Palestine, Crane is credited with obtaining the first American concession, in 1931, for oil in Saudi Arabia. President Taft asked for Crane's resignation as his newly appointed ambassador to China in 1909 after hearing Crane respond to his election victory saying, "Well, now that Taft is President, I suppose that Jake Schiff and his Jew crowd will have a great deal to say in our national affairs." (David Philipson, *My Life as an American Jew: An Autobiography*, 1941, 32-3; Frank W. Brecher, "Charles R. Crane's Crusade for the Arabs, 1919-39," *Middle Eastern Studies*, XXIV, Jan., 1988; 46-7; Elliott A Green, "The Curious Careers of Two Advocates of Arab Nationalism," *Crossroads*, 33,1992; F. W. Brecher, *Reluctant Ally: United States Foreign Policy toward the Jews from Wilson to Roosevelt*, NY: Greenwood Press, 1991)

"The Jews, after winning the war, galloping along at a swift pace, getting Russia, England and Palestine," praising his appointment Crane writes professor Dodd, "being caught in the act of trying to seize Germany, too, and meeting their first real rebuff have gone plumb crazy and are deluging the world – particularly easy America – with anti-German propaganda – I strongly advise you to resist every social invitation." Dodd writes in his diary, "His advice to me was, of course, 'Let Hitler have his way'." (E. Larson, 38-9; W. E. Dodd, *Ambassador Dodd's Diary;* R. Chernow, *The Warburgs: The Twentieth-Century Odyssey of a Remarkable Jewish Family,* NY: Random House, 1993)

And so at the time of the Soviet Terror-Famine extremely powerful American financial and industrial interests maneuvered behind Stalin's communist Soviet monopoly, many with decidedly harsh contempt for the Jews and little interest in illiterate peasants anywhere. These same financial and corporate interests were indispensable in building Hitler's fascist war machine. Their German cartels produced the bulk of key German war materials used in World War II. Their Versailles Treaty was a ticking time bomb set to the watches of the victors of the First World War.

GLOBAL WAR: ROCKEFELLER STANDARD OIL FOR STALIN AND HITLER

Rockefeller's Standard Oil's contributions to the Nazi war effort were critical to Hitler's success. There were a ton of secret industrial patent deals paramount to the Nazi war plan. For example, without the gasoline additive tetra-ethyl supplied by Standard Oil, according to a 1943 IG Farben special report 'the war effort would have been impossible'." Examine the US military intelligence files for the Nazi period and you find the Consortium's US-owned companies Ford, DuPont, General Motors, Standard Oil, General Electric and others generously accommodating their fascist Nazi and Soviet communist partners even to the detriment of the American government. This did not escape the ambassador's suspicions. When Standard Oil provided Hitler with a patent for synthetic rubber the Consortium kept transactions secret even to the US military. After all, the State Department works performs admirably working to further their interests, not the other way around.

Why was Standard Oil such a formidable empire of capital and influence?

For over a generation and ever since Ohio's state legislature honored its anti-trust laws in 1892 forcing Standard Oil of Ohio to split off from the rest of the company which leading to a breakup of the giant monopolistic trust, JD Rockefeller builds the biggest oil fortune in the world all the time consolidating his oil monopoly. When it got too big, and its repression of the working class too vicious, and publicly embarrassing in the heat of the violent class struggle in New Jersey in 1899, clever lawyers applied their craft to modified its incorporation statutes. Apparently it was all that was necessary to effectively allow JDR's lawyers to recreate the trust as a single holding company, Standard Oil.

At its peak Standard holds a 90% share of the market for kerosene products. Turning sixty and richer than Midas in 1896 Rockefeller stepped back from actively directing Standard Oil while retaining the presidency until 1911 when he is finally brought up against the Supreme Court of the United States during the Taft administration.

Under attack for protecting billionaire monopolists holding American industry by the neck controlling prices and rates throughout the country Teddy Roosevelt, with his eye on the upcoming presidential election on the Progressive ticket, splitting the Republican Party by stealing victory out of the mouth of Eugene Debs and his Socialist Party, and a team of Consortium lawyers from Wall Street and Washington dismantled Standard Oil's sixty-four percent of the market. The giant oil combine is divided into at least 35 new companies: Continental Oil (Conoco), Standard of Indiana (Amoco), Standard of California (Chevron), Standard of New Jersey (Exxon), Standard of New York (Mobil), Standard of Ohio (Sohio). Rockefeller seldom ever sold shares. He held stock in all the new oil companies. At the time he died in 1937 his net worth has been estimated as high as $200 billion.

ALARMING REVELATIONS BY ANTONY SUTTON OF STANFORD UNIVERSITY

A research Fellow at Stanford University's Hoover Institution during the Nixon years (1968-1973), Antony C. Sutton had been an economics professor at California State University in Los Angeles. Born in London, in 1925, and having earned a D.Sc. degree from the University of Southampton, England, with training as an engineer, Sutton went on to study at a variety of universities in London, Gottingen and California. Not unlike Robert Conquest, Sutton, too is a Brit who with a passion for America. They both settled in California. Had they ever met it would have most interesting to be present while they discuss the Anglo-American economic links with Stalin.

"After 16 books and 25 years in basic research I thought I'd heard it all," Sutton declared, "the world was a confused mess, probably beyond understanding and certainly beyond salvation – and there was little I could do about it." In 1968 the Hoover Institution at Berkeley published the first of three volumes of *Western Technology and Soviet Economic Development*." They probably wished they hadn't. No light-weight this guy Sutton. But it was too late. The cat was out of the bag.

"I detailed how the West had built the Soviet Union', Sutton explains. "However, the work generated a seemingly insoluble puzzle - why have we done this? Why did we build the Soviet Union, while we also transferred technology to Hitler's Germany? Why does Washington want to conceal these facts? Why have we boosted Soviet military power? And simultaneously boosted our own?"

Somehow before the resourcefulness of the Internet Sutton had the clarity of mind to see with uncanny precision albeit his engineering training eased with the common sense approach of a unadulterated child having grown up out of the reach of American propaganda that enabled him to penetrate the data and grasp the meaning of facts directly under his nose.

Most Americans in his day were "dumbed" and "spoon-fed" conveniently placed Cold War propaganda and other nonsensical misinformation. So they missed it or for whatever reason lacked the time and energy to go down that long hard trail that is the scholar's dubious fortune. Tending towards the absurd or ridiculous instead of hard-nose facts Americans in this pre-Internet era were left by and by senseless about realities in the Soviet Union. Consequently the Holodomor Terror-Famine of the thirties made no sense at all. Americans, deprived of mindfulness were driven senseless. Another victory for the Consortium hacks and their masters! Its daunting to wonder how two populations of the two superpowers could be so incredibly ignorant about themselves and each other. But this is exactly the Consortium's intention. And they succeed until Solzhenitsyn and Sutton return us to that era of Holodomor gulags and mass murder and Genocide against the peasants in the Ukraine and South Russia.

In 1973 Sutton completed what he thought would have been his magnum opus on the surreptitious investment of US banks and corporations in the USSR. But one thing led to another. One day Sutton received in the mail an anonymous heavy 8 inch thick package of papers revealing names of Yale's secret society Skull & Bones during the last 150 years since its founding in 1832 by a Yale graduate who made a fortune in the China Opium trade. Almost every day for four years at Yale in the 1970s this author walked between the freshman Old Campus on one side of "the Fence" past the Skull & Bones "Tomb" building on the other not having a clue about its ominous secrets within. That always felt creepy. And my best friend's father was Skull & Bones with Bush & Co. It was never something to talk about. It took an outsider to blow those tomb doors wide open.

The awesome impenetrable-looking "Tomb" sits serene and uninviting to outsiders, a discreet and awesome gray stone building resembling a death house or mausoleum. Initiations take place on Maine's Deer Island in the St. Lawrence River owned by the Russell Trust Association. Some Bonesmen say the place at present looks like "a dump". Members sojourn for regular reunions to "the Tomb" a few steps from the freshman Old Campus. Initiation rites are always weird and may be strenuous. A tapped initiate may be "immersed naked in mud, and in a coffin" and recount sexual tales of their private life. Truly bizarre but they did get off on it. (Webster Griffin Tarpley and Anton Chaitkin, *The Unauthorized Biography of George Bush*)

The package struck like a lightning bolt. Once he had names, combined with facts of exhaustive research, he started connecting the dots of corporate power and America's elite society as it evolved out of the cocoon of the Harvard-Princeton-Yale "good 'ole boys" clique.

Sutton wrote, "The Order has only initiated about 2500 members in its history in the United States. Each year 15 new members are initiated, no more, no less. On the other hand, between 800,000 and 1 million persons receive college degrees each year from an institute of higher learning, including about 30,000 doctorates. When you follow the chain of influence below, hold in mind that out of 30-40 million degree holders, a few hundred men (never women) or in this case *less than a dozen men*, are presumed to be the only ones fit to occupy top posts in government. No one else is even seriously considered. We are asked to believe that only a few hundred members of The Order are capable of guiding the United States." (italics added)

"GOD, COUNTRY, AND YALE"

Sutton was as perplexed as many Yale students and even alumni are about the bizarre aura of Yale's mystique. So he grabbed the bulldog by the horns. "So obvious," he writes, "in fact, that in 1892 a young Harvard philosophy instructor, George Santayana, went to Yale to investigate this 'disturbing legend' of Yale power. Santayana quoted a Harvard alumnus who aimed to send his son to Yale – because in real life 'all the Harvard men are working for Yale men.' But no one has previously asked an obvious question - Why? What is this 'Yale power'?" Santayana is remembered more having said – and he is quoted by William Shirer as a lead to his book *The Rise and Fall of the Third Reich* (1959), – "Those who do not remember the past are condemned to relive it."

Ever since the Russian Revolution in 1917 American banks and large corporate businesses financed and sustained the Soviet socialist experiment and its dreaded secret police state. But to understand how this happened and how it all came about the reader must first understand that long before America's entry into the First World War (1914-18), the US President Woodrow Wilson and his closest adviser, the enigmatic Colonel Edward Mandell House – whose life-size portrait hangs over the entrance to the prestigious reading room of the Yale University Archives housed in the imposing Gothic cathedralesque Sterling Memorial Library – were deeply involved with British intelligence, international bankers, in a war of Empire. When the Russia and the Czar fell, they were there to pick up the pieces and put it all back together again.

Wall Street bankers and investment firms controlled America's money supply. Together in 1913 they establish the Federal Reserve banking system. Political adviser House, central banker Paul Warburg, Rockefeller, Rhodes Island Senator Aldrich, Morgan banker Davison and others guided President Wilson after much reluctance and apprehension on his part to officially usher into the American political establishment a centralized national bank, the element essential to finance the First World War that would reshape the world order for generations to follow.

A prerequisite to their plan was the destruction of Czarist power that would let fall into their hands the vast oil and mineral resources of the Imperial Russian Empire. The Anglo-American Consortium that emerged victorious in a carefully calculated but precipitously terminated First World War then set out immediately to consolidate their winnings over the Russian monopoly by facilitating consolidation of the Lenin-Trotsky Bolshevik stranglehold over the Russian masses duped to become servile citizens under the newly created socialist Russian federated republic later named the USSR. One of their first actions under the triad control of Lenin, Trotsky and Stalin of the new Soviet regime was to create Russia's new state centralized national bank. Trotsky, – Lev Davidovich Bronstein –, was, in fact, a Ukrainian-Russian born 1879 in southern Ukraine in the village Yanovka, near Kherson.

This tightly-knit group of individuals in America's invisible government was distinguished by its peculiar identity as a secretive and elite power group linking lawyers and bankers from generations of the elite Harvard-Princeton-Yale Ivy League set of the Eastern Establishment where the elite of eight New England colleges educate men to occupy positions in the institutions to govern the world controlled by the higher echelon of the Consortium. Day after day these players assure that The Game never ends. This inner sanctum was composed primarily of the self-proclaimed American elite from institutions like Yale's Skull & Bones secret society or Anglophile members of the Pilgrims Society that correspondingly worked in tandem with other interlocking organizations influencing national and foreign policy decisions of the White House.

With members mainly living in Philadelphia, New York and Boston this firmly entrenched and extremely wealthy network reached out hand-in-glove to Washington, London, Paris and Berlin. Members of these corporate and financial groups managed and financed Trotsky and Lenin's Bolshevik underground revolutionary network, installing and sustaining the Bolsheviks in Leningrad to consolidate the largest national socialist monopoly in the world.

The new Bolshevik dictatorship consolidated under Lenin from 1917-18 was to play a major role in their plan for European reconstruction. The sacrifice of more than fifty millions of men, women and children of the consolidated Russian empire in the new Soviet state was just part of the price and somebody had to pay for it so they paid for it with their lives.

A nation overthrown and torn apart by revolution and civil war emerged under the absolute control of Stalin, parallel with Hitler's fascist Germany. Both fascist regimes were willing partners of the Consortium's business interests hell-bent and ready to profit from an unlimited supply of cheap labor and enslaved oppressed masses stripped of individual identity and private property while the Old Imperialists and Empire builders and capitalists vociferously seek and grab the riches of impoverished empires. The Czarist fortune accumulated over centuries of costly conquest and tributes make the bankers drunk with envy. Who got the Czarist gold? They did, naturally. Whatever do you think! Few Americans ever knew it, much less even think or speak of it. Oh no, reader, mark my words. These cultivated, highly educated or crafty men and cut-throat escapadiers are not idiots! Seek and thee shall find, and they did.

Periodically the awesome financial reach and power of the Rothschilds would blip the radar screen of the nation's press, and even today as well as during the earlier era, for example, when Hearst's *Chicago Evening American* commented, Dec. 3, 1923, after the Russian debacle and shortly before Lenin's death at the hands of Stalin: "The Rothschilds can start or prevent wars. Their word could make or break empires."

Researcher historian Eustace Mullins in *The World Order*, cites William Randolph Hearst in a specific reference, writing that in their "quest for wealth, the Rothschilds did not overlook either the small farmer or the stockpiling and wholesaling of grain. They developed a 'farm loan' system which has been the curse of the farmers for more than a century. R.F. Pettigrew noted in the *British Guardian*, "This system of banking (causing the ultimate ruin of all those who cultivate the soil) was the invention of Lord Overstone, with the assistance of the Rothschilds, bankers of Europe."

As they had no interest in Napoleon's longevity (reportedly poisoned in exile by a Rothschild) the Russian Romanov's were on the Rothschild black list. "One of their greatest triumphs was the successful outcome of the Rothschilds' protracted war against the Russian Imperial Family," Mullins observes. "The family name of the Romanovs was derived from Roma Nova, New Rome. It embodied the ancient prophecy that Moscow was to become 'the New Rome.' The family originated with Prince Prus, brother of Emperor August of Rome, who founded Prussia. In 1614, Michael became the first Romanov Czar. After the fall of Napoleon, the Rothschilds turned all their hatred against the Romanovs. In 1825, they poisoned Alexander I; in 1855, they poisoned Nicholas I. Other assassinations followed, culminating on the night of Nov. 6, 1917, when a dozen Red Guards drove a truck up to the Imperial Bank Building in Moscow. They loaded the Imperial jewel collection and $700 million gold, loot totalling more than $1 billion. (Multiply that by at least twenty times for current equivalent exchange value. sic) The new regime also confiscated the 150 million acres in Russia personally owned by the Czar." Its hard to believe. A dozen guards? And all the while millions of men on the front already dead, or soon to die blown to bits in another insane battle charge to take another yard of blood-soaked mud.(Eustace Mullins, *The World Order*)

And what about all that gold the Czar had stashed around the world inflaming the envy of the bankers? Where did the banknotes go, the cash?

Lets stay with Mullins for a sell as he writes (though few trembling academics dare defy their pristine masters!) in *The History Project*: "Of equal importance were the enormous cash reserves which the Czar had invested abroad in European and American banks. The *New York Times* stated that the Czar had $5 million in Guaranty Trust, and $1 million in the National City Bank; other authorities stated it was $5 million in each bank. Between 1905 and 1910 the Czar had sent more than $900 million to be deposited in six leading New York banks: Chase, National City, Guaranty Trust, JP Morgan, Hanover and Manufacturers Trust. These were the principal banks controlled by the House of Rothschild through their American agents: JP Morgan and Kuhn, Loeb, Co.. These were also the six New York banks which bought the controlling stock in the Federal Reserve Bank of New York in 1914. They have held control of the stock ever since. The Czar also had $115 million in four English banks. He had $35 million in the Bank of England, $25 million in Barings, $25 million in Barclays, and $30 million in Lloyd's Bank. In Paris, the Czar had $100 million in Banque de France, and $80 million in the Rothschild Bank of Paris. In Berlin, he had $132 million in the Mendelsoln Bank, which had long been bankers to Russia. None of these sums has ever been disbursed; at compound interest since 1916, they amount to more than $50 billion. Two claimants later appeared, a son, Alexis, and a daughter, Anastasia. Despite a great deal of proof substantiating their claims, Peter Kurth notes in 'Anastasia' that: 'Lord Mountbatten put up the money for court battles against Anastasia. Although he was Empress Alexandra's nephew, he was the guiding force behind Anastasia's opposition.' The Battenbergs, or Mountbattens, were also related to the Rothschild family. They did not wish to see the Czar's fortune reclaimed and removed from the Rothschild banks. Kurth also notes: 'In a 1959 series on the history of the great British banks, for example, the *Observer* of London remarked of Baring Brothers, "The Romanovs were among their most distinguished clients. It is affirmed that Barings still holds a deposit of more than forty million pounds that was left them by the Romanovs." Anthony Sampson, editor in chief, said no protests were made. This story is generally considered to be true."

YALE CONNECTION: THE ORDER OF SKULL & BONES

Before the proliferation throughout the American society of the giant fortunes of great wealth, the Order of Skull & Bones possessed a veritable spell-binding hold over the political and economic destiny of the American democracy. Ever since the most recent prominence of the Bush father and son's presidencies, Yale's Skull & Bones has attracted sporadic notoriety in the press. President Bush's vice-president Dick Cheney left Yale in the 1960s without graduating, unusual behavior given the high number of the Cheney's in The Order (at least eleven since its inception in 1833!) topped only by the Walker family line.

The way it used to work each year, Skull and Bones members taps 15 third year students to replace them in the senior group the following year. Graduating members are given a sizable cash bonus to help them get started in life. Older graduate members, the so-called "Patriarchs," give special backing in business, politics, espionage and legal careers to graduate Bonesmen who exhibit talent or usefulness. But there's been a ton of publicity in the last couple of decades and "the Tomb" even conducts tours to special groups. It's part of the new ethics code of "transparency". The Rothschilds do the same thing in the time as I write this. In this Internet Age of over-exposure and ubiquity, as far as Rothschild and the Consortium cares, the more you see, the less you really know. And anyway, in the end, so what? Apathy can go a long way. With overexposure and people inundated and bombarded more than ever with technogadgets, who cares? Even monkeys push buttons all day long just to be satiated. They make good pets.

During the of that Consortium generation of the Holodomor era Prescott Bush walked that path paved with gold and reaped the benefits of his close association with the arch-deacons Roland and Averell Harriman ever since Yale at Brown Brothers Harriman which long maintained close ties to the secret society. Bonesmen take care of each other. Theres a lot here that goes with the territory. If you lose your job, which would probably never happen, they give you you a ton of money, a job, a life-line career. When I was at Yale I heard it was a $100,000 a year; today a million doesn't mean much so it's more like a few. Like when Prescott Bush at Brown Brothers Harriman lost his small Wall Street fortune in the 1929 stock crash, "Ave" Harriman gave it back to him.

American history in the 20th century fell under the stealthy hand of secret society men recruited into Skull & Bones at Yale College. And although the society was secret, the men risked public exposure of their secret which they for the most part guarded as though not only their lives but the success of the entire Order depended on it.

Were they working for a secret agenda? It certainly appears so.

Bonesmen were prominent members of England's Pilgrims Society and other organizations that shaped foreign policy and domestic policy. Their decisions and policies were pivotal in the First World War. The fall of Czarist Russia was not an accident of revolution. It was a carefully planned and executed operation of strategic and precise calculation in what appeared to the world, and on the streets as a terrible and incomprehensible chaos. The bankers did what they had to do to keep Lenin and Trotsky in power.

Then came Stalin who masterfully wormed his way eliminating all opposition of the Old Bolsheviks in the Communist Party hierarchy and set into motion his Five-Year Plans for agriculture and industry. His Terror-Famine swept across the countryside in the Ukraine and ten million peasants perished in their villages, in exile. And another class of initates took their vows to the Order of Skull & Bones while others graduated to follow in the footsteps of their elders investing in Hitler and Stalin preparations for the Second World War.

Anglophile American families shared a peculiar affinity in this arcane inner sanctum of bonded brotherhood. Gilded Age billionaires Harrimans, Whitneys,

Vanderbilts and many others regaled inside isolated chambers immune from the outside world and reaffirmed their steadfast loyalty. It was a core nucleus within the Consortium's sundry private clubs. Here "God, Country and Yale" mixed the vows of initiates blending fortunes and firms with the families that ruled America. Here Harriman might mix with the Tafts, Lords and Bundys, or with the Walkers and Bushes, the Sloans and the Cheneys, and with the Coffins and Brewsters, or even the Ishams, Coits, Gilmans or Davisons and Pratts. The cream of the American Establishment elite in young nation's political economy are adept at rhetoric assisted by their friends in publishing and the press and seamlessly spinning tales woven into the fabric of a culture of deception. Is it any wonder that Roosevelt himself was called "The Great Communicator"? Don't kid yourself. Together these men expanded their wealth and influence through the financial and military power centers of the world.

First there was Stimson, then there was Harriman. A seamless flow of Skull & Bones influence reigned through the State Department in 20th century America. In was an incredible time to live in the Consortium era when the Morgans, Rockefellers, Vanderbilts, Harrimans and others in their social mileu lived from mansion to mansion with hundreds of servants to make them feel comfortable and take care of their personal needs. That luxury was mostly phased out in the thirties and then the coming of age of America's "Lost Generation" between the wars.

The politically aggressive Morgan Guaranty Trust Company is run almost entirely by Skull and Bones initiates. It was a financial vehicle of these families in the early 1900s. Guaranty Trust's support for the Bolshevik and Nazi coups overlapped the more intense endeavors in these fields by the Harriman brothers, George Walker, and Prescott Bush and other Consortium operatives in offices located only a few blocks away, and in Berlin. From 1913 onward Skull and Bones was dominated by the inner circle of friends and associates of Averell Harriman; his firm Brown Brothers and Harriman is stacked with S & B initiates.

Adviser to presidents Herbert Hoover and Franklin D. Roosevelt during the Holodomor era of the early thirties, Stimson earned the inimitable status as the foremost legal stalwart guiding America's extension of power around the globe. He had served as President Taft's Secretary of War (1911-13). During the 1932-33 Holodomor, Bonesman Stimson (Class of 1888) returns to the White House cabinet as President Hoover's confident and Secretary of State (1929-33).

Very few Americans today know that after five years as FDR's Secretary of War (1940-45), and during FDR's long illness in 1945 Stimson as chairman of the top-secret Interim Committee in charge of the Manhattan Atomic Bomb project convinced President Truman, the former senator and son of a tailor selling hats in a haberdashery, to drop the atomic bomb on the Japanese. (Truman needed little coaxing though Stimson succeeds in sparing Kyoto and is deeply troubled by incendiary bombing raids on Tokyo that year.) This decision involved much more than mere pragmatic military considerations; it was a Consortium decision executed by the President.

Consortium power has long deep roots in Yale's Skull & Bones. Stimson was third-generation Bones. During the 19th century American railroad boom

Chauncey M. Depew (Bones 1856) had been general counsel for the Vanderbilt railroads and guided the Harriman family into high society of the Guilded Age while remaining one of the few intimate family friends of JP Morgan. Frederick E. Weyerhaeuser (Bones 1896), acquired huge tracts of American forest in the northwest, and was a follower of the Roosevelt-Pinchot environmentalism of that era. The Weyerhaeusers intrigued with diamond mining scion and arch supreme racist Cecil Rhodes of the British Empire. Fellow Bonesman Gifford Pinchot (1889) concocts a scheme accepted by the aristocrats' "conservation" movement as President Theodore Roosevelt's chief forester "substituting federal land-control in place of Abraham Lincoln's free-land-to-families farm creation program". Pinchot's British Empire activism surfaced at the International Eugenics Congress in 1912. In America he extended his views as a member of the American Academy of Political and Social Science and the elite Cosmos Club, Washington, DC, two well established Consortium front organizations.

Secrecy is the code, loyalty the law. A former teacher of a young George Herbert Walker Bush, whose father Prescott Bush was the first Bush family Bonesman publicly admitted that his father took sweet pleasure stabbing his priceless Skull and Bones pin into his skin to keep it in place when bathing. Throughout their lives members continue to unburden themselves of psycho-sexual thoughts to their bonded Bones Brothers "even if they are no longer sitting in a coffin" as in the case of US President George Bush Sr. for whom these ties are reported to have morbid ontological relevance. Imagine that! Beyond the psychological mindfuck associated with free masonic mummery there are esoteric primal almost culturally Darwinian reasons for Bush's strong carnal affections to identify with this bizarre behavioral political cult. (Webster Griffin Tarpley and Anton Chaitkin, *The Unauthorized Biography of George Bush*)

Skull and Bones – originally known as the Russell Trust Association – was first established among Yale College 1833 graduates not long after the days of burning witches in Salem, Massachusetts. Its founder is William Huntington Russell of Middletown, Connecticut. The Russell family is a clever accumulator of incalculable wealth derived from what today would be described as "the largest US criminal organization of the era". Russell & Co. was an opium syndicate in the "China trade". Their contemporaries today might likely resemble the Bush-Cheney Consortium gang trafficking Middle Eastern oil and dope in Afghanistan.

Russell had good reason to create a secret society to deflect deep suspicions prevalent in America at the time against freemasonry and secret organizations in the government of the United States Anti-masonic writings of ex-President John Quincy Adams aroused national revulsion that America's democracy had been penetrated by elite sects politically sworn to serve powerful international secret societies instead of the people. The Russells already mix state politics within Connecticut's Anglophile power hierarchy with the blood of proud families running in each other's veins with names like Pierpont, Edwards, Burr, Griswold, Day, Alsop, Hubbard … (actually far too many to mention here but any check of alumni magazines and school rosters of the prestigious institutions and the picture appears more clear.)

William Lloyd Garrison (1805-79), who settled in New England, and the father of Wendell Philips Garrison (Harvard 1861), a co-founder and literary editor for forty years of the *Nation* who in that earlier year, in December 1833 joined other anti-colonial abolitionists, men and women uniting their full possession of instinct, empathy and rational will against Empire representing ten states to the American Anti-Slavery Society (AAS), precursor to the NCAAP, founded by his grandson son Oswald Garrison Villard Jr., in 1910, and served as its treasurer when he publishes *John Brown 1800-1859: A Biography Fifty Years After. In the tumult of the First World War as America secretly exploits its contraband war trade Villard, an active pacifist writes Germany Embattled* (1915) and champions civil liberties well aware of the direction the President Wilson's government is taking under embattered imperialist democracy and manipulations by House, his closest adviser, and head of British intelligence in the United States Wiseman; Villard's opposition to the US military, political and economic engagement in the imperialist War of clashing empires is not shared, however, by everyone in the Villard family; his nephew Henry S. Villard, a teenager, sails over to join an ambulance unit on the embattled European front, and when wounded befriends the correspondent 2nd. Lt. Ernest Hemingway in July 1918 in the trenches also wounded and recovering in their hospital in Milan and after the war embraces Harvard where shares his passions on the staff of the Crimson and from there on seems to have enjoyed a wonderfully full life of diplomatic and literary adventures that would have amazed and alarmed his most famous ancestors.

Building an empire is never a simple affair but Yale and Skull & Bones knew how to make it seem like it was and the tradition transcends generations. From the beginning the Bonesmen share resources and shape the American politics. That is all part of their agenda. Alphonso Taft, father of the future US President, was Russell's classmate and Bonesman co-founder. As US Attorney General (1876-77) Alphonso Taft helped seal the deal of the Electoral Commission and fix the deadlocked 1876 presidential election over withdraw of US troops from the South. The shady bargain gives Rutherford B. Hayes the American Presidency (1877-81) with William M. Evarts subsequently the US Secretary of State in office until 1881. Taft is assisted by Yale classmate Morris R. Waite (Bones 1837), a US Supreme Court Chief Justice (1874-88) whose decisions after the Civil War annul many newly gained rights of African-Americans; Waite is by his fellow cohorts Taft and Evarts, another Bonesman (1837), and Wall Street lawyer for British and southern slave-owners. In the scheme of artful planning to take over Washington and dominate the nation's government of most powerful elected offices and institutions, with the power to appoint their selected candidates as they saw fit, and place them every in national institutions and embassies around the world, they arrange for Alphonso's son, William H. Taft (Bones, 1878) to became US President (1909-13); President Taft's son, Robert Alphonso Taft (Bones, 1910) will join "the Club" becoming a US Senator after the Second World War. Within the Consortium hierarchy power and social prominence in the corporate interests of the families ruling the affairs of the nation is always secured and projected from generation to generation.

Settled along its coast and inland amongst the hills, ponds and forests Connecticut was historically a refuge to marauding fortune seekers from the 19th century to the 20th century including opium drug traffickers and bootleggers, respectively. By the 1830s, the Russells had bought out the Perkins syndicate and made Connecticut the primary center of the US opium racket. Massachusetts families (Coolidge, Sturgis, Forbes, and Delano) joined the Connecticut Alsop brothers (Joseph IV, Joe, Stewart, John) from Middletown and New York Lows, all well-to-do smuggler-millionaires in league with the Russell brothers and their British partners.

Many great American fortunes were made in the lucrative China opium trade.

The Delano captain of Roosevelt fame braved the high seas and foreign shores to capture his loot. FDR joked about it often and even kept a clipper ship near his desk in the White House as a reminder how Uncle Delano made a million in drugs, then lost it in the American stock market only to returned to China to make another million which he did. So great was the American Dream riveted in the history of Skull & Bones that the story of opium and empire veered into a sharp struggle for political advantage over the young Republic.

It was Sam Russell, second cousin to William, who established the Russell and Company in 1823 in order to acquire opium from Turkey and smuggle it into China where it was strictly banned under the monopoly and guns of the British Royal Navy and this not long after the War of 1812 and Wellington's victory at Waterloo in 1815. So it was that Napoleon ended his rule as the French Emperor.

British ships ransacked the Chinese coasts demanding huge ransoms, stealing territory by signed treaties, and compelling strict obedience to British might. The predominant American gang in this romp over weaker nations had been the syndicate created by Thomas H. Perkins of Newburyport, Massachusetts, a colony of renegade "blue bloods", suddenly the newly hailed Brahmins hailing of good pedigree breeding from Boston's north shore. Squeezed out of the despicable but lucrative African slave trade by US law and slave revolts in the Caribbean, ambitious leaders of the Massachusetts clans of Cabot Lowell, Higginson, Forbes, Cushing, and Sturgis families keen on keeping their loot all married with the Perkins opium syndicate from where they originally gained fortune and fame while inspiring the envy of their social prestige fixed with money and a lot of it under the protection of the British pound and flag. (Kris Milligen, *Boodle Boys: The Order of Skull & Bones*)

Sam and Bill Russell – (or if you prefer Sammuel and William Huntington Russell) – were quiet, shrewd builders who loathed publicity while amassing their capital. An intimate colleague of opium dealer Sam Russell wrote: "While he lived no friend of his would venture to mention his name in print. While in China, he lived for about twenty-five years almost as a hermit, hardly known outside of his factory (the Canton warehouse compound) except by the chosen few who enjoyed his intimacy, and by his good friend, Hoqua (Chinese security director for the East India Company), but studying commerce in its broadest sense, as well as its minutest details. Returning home with well-earned wealth he lived hospitably in the midst of his family, and a small circle of intimates. Scorning words and pretensions from the bottom of his heart, he was the truest and staunchest of friends; hating notoriety, he could always be absolutely counted on for every good work which did not involve publicity."

According to the Forbes House Museum, – (formerly known as the Museum of the American China Trade but "China Trade" is a synonym for the opium connection),– "Captain (Robert Bennet Forbes sic), born in Jamaica Plain, Massachusetts, in 1804, was introduced into the China Trade at age 12 by his uncle Thomas Handasyd Perkins (1764-54), who, along with his brothers James (1761-22) and Samuel (1767-47), established the Boston-based Perkins & Company in 1803, later becoming the Russell & Company." (Forbes House Museum website)

In 1832-33, under the Russell pirate flag Skull and Bones was launched. Among early initiates to the order were Henry Rootes Jackson (Bones 1839), one of the leaders of the 1861 Georgia Secession Convention and post-Civil War president of the Georgia Historical Society; John Perkins, Jr. (Bones 1840), chairman of the 1861 Louisiana Secession Convention; and William T. Sullivan Barry (Bones 1841), a national leader of the secessionist wing of the Democratic Party during the 1850s, and chairman of the 1861 Mississippi Secession Convention. The Russells' Skull and Bones Society was the most important of their domestic projects "which did not involve publicity."... Yale was the northern college favored by southern slave-owning would-be aristocrats. Among Yale's southern students are the future US Vice-President John C. Calhoun, later ardent as the defender of slavery in South Carolina against nationalism, and Judah Benjamin, the Confederacy's Secretary of State. For posterity Yale unabashedly crowned on its twelve undergraduate residential dorms named after Calhoun. I rowed a triumphant eight for Calhoun and they gave me a medal. Hats off!

The Skull and Bones influence in building the image and character of a national American ethos and elitist culture through countless educational institutions and business entities would be incomplete and not what it was without Daniel Coit Gilman (1831-06) and Bonesman Yale Class of 1852. Gilman is one of the co-incorporators of "The Order" in the transformation of the Russell Trust in 1856 under the name "Russell Trust Association."

"The Order", in fact, was the euphemism under which Skull & Bones was known among the members. By special act of the state legislature in 1943, its trustees are exempted from the normal requirement of filing corporate reports with the Connecticut Secretary of state. Gilman was born July 8, 1831 in Norwich, Connecticut near New London in a family linked to Yale College. Originally, the Gilmans came to the United States from Norfolk, England in 1638. On his mother's side, the Coit family came from Wales to Salem Massachusetts before 1638.

Few Americans today realize the extent of influence Gilman plays in the culture set-up scene as president of the University of California (1872) Gilman is the key activist in the revolution of education in his early 1870s.

After Yale, Gilman was also the founding president of Johns Hopkins University (1875) that becomes a center for the racialist eugenics movement. Among his twelve points in his 1876 inaugural address as the first president of The Johns Hopkins University, Gilman declares, "Remote utility is quite as worthy to be thought of as immediate advantage... The best scholars will almost invariably be those who make special attainments on the foundation of a broad and liberal culture. ... The object of the university is to develop character–to make men. ... strengthen judgment, and invigorate the intellectual and moral forces. It should prepare for the service of society a class of students who will be wise, thoughtful, progressive guides in whatever department of work or thought they may be engaged." Irving Fisher (Bones 1888) became Yale's racialist high priest of the economics faculty (1896-46), and a famous purveyor of British Empire propaganda for free trade and the reduction of the non-white population. Fisher was founding president of the American Eugenics Society under the financial largesse of Ave Harriman's mother.

America's privileged sons were largely all educated with the same sophistry from New England's preparatory schools to universities private and public as they were created with the wealth accumulated by generations of capitalists rising higher with each new bottomed layer of illiterate immigrant workers and an expanding American class of enlightened leaders. The leadership culture was imbued in their training. They permitted no crossing over. The values of their education and fathers had to be obeyed and respected with cardinal loyalty. This formation of character led to career advancement and social security and with it came unswerving loyalty to the group and its elders. Family was clan and the clan made the class. Young men with molded passions were tapped or appointed to occupy positions of power and influence this select and very conservative elite. And in all the wars of their fathers many brave young sons give their lives to perpetuate the culture of their class and the monopoly of its power for future generations.

Uncle Henry Coit Kingsley (Bones 1834) was a classmate of relation to Daniel Coit Gilman, George Gilman, Spencer, and Treasurer of Yale from 1862 to 1886. James L. Kingsley was Gilman's uncle and a Professor at Yale. William M. Kingsley, a cousin, was editor of the influential journal *New Englander*. Daniel Coit Gilman entered Yale in 1848. The prominent Coit family deserves mention. The Coits descended from Rev. Joseph Coit (1673-50), Harvard 1697, Yale, 1702. On the Coit side of the family, Joshua Coit was a member of The Order in 1853 as well as William Coit in 1887. Gilman's brother-in law was the Reverend Joseph Parrish Thompson (Yale 1838).

St. Pauls School in New Hampshire traces its conception to Herny Augustus Coit, brother of Joseph H. Coit (Bones 1853), and further back to Levi Coit, a prosperous merchant and stockbroker who emigrated to New York.

His eldest son joined the financier Rothschild's man August Belmont (Schönberg) in business. Levi Coit married a Mayflower Howland. One of his later descendants is merchant banker and financier, Robert Coit (Bones 1850) treasurer and president of New London & Northern Railroad, president of New London Savings Bank, and president of Union Bank, Connecticut's oldest banking institution and one of the oldest in the country. A Republican state politician he was elected mayor of New London (1879-82).

In 1852, Gilman studied for a few months at Harvard College, living in the home of Prof. Arnold Guyot, a Swiss national educated in Berlin. With his classmate, Andrew D. White (Bones 1853), Gilman sails to Europe as diplomats attached to the American legation at St. Petersburg, Russia where together they dream of revolution and the iberation of the peasants and making a grab for the vastly rich Czarist Russian empire tottering with civil discontent and outbursts of rebellion. (In a few years the peasants are liberated by their own Czar.)

Daniel Coit Gilman spends the winter of 1855 in Germany before returning to Yale where he stays for nearly two decades. His friend Andrew D. White goes on to become the founding president of Cornell University as well as a diplomatic cohort of the Venetian, Russian and British oligarchies. Gilman's first task at Yale, in 1856, is to incorporate the Skull & Bones secret society as a legal entity under the name of The Russell Trust. In doing so Gilman becomes Bones treasurer under co-founder and now president, William H. Russell. As a student in German for a year, Russell had received permission to form a chapter of the German secret society. And reader we know that Russell and Alphonso Taft, the father of the future US President Taft, had originally set up *their* chapter in 1832.

After he launches University of California, followed three years later by Johns Hopkins University in Baltimore, Gilman is hit by a shock when the Baltimore & Ohio Railroad suspended dividends on the common stock, which formed the bulk of the endowment. Gilman remained in Baltimore until the 1890s. It is interesting to note that the B&O was largely financed initially by Barings Bank, which issued 6% bonds worth £1 million before 1880. The B&O also sold 2 million pounds of its securities through Morgan's London office and almost that many more at a reduced price a few years later–still before 1880. Most of the B&O creditors, therefore, were British, and they demanded that the interest on the bonds be guaranteed by Barings and Morgan. (W. G. Tarpley and A. Chaitkin, in "The Tomb", from *The Unauthorized Biography of George Bush*)

The American power establishment inside the Anglo-American Consortium at the time emerges after a closer look. Harry Payne of the Whitney-Payne-Vanderbilt family holds one of the richest fortunes in America. He's a nephew of Harry B. Payne (1810-96) whose daughter Flora Payne married W. C. Whitney. Both Payne and Whitney were close friends at Yale in the Class of 1863 when it was a small college in New Haven, Connecticut. And both were tapped into Skull & Bones.

The senior H. B. Payne made a fortune as a railroad lawyer before using his money to buy his way into politics and the Democrat Party, first in Congress and then the Senate in 1884 with funds from Standard Oil. Originally from Ohio, he was thought to have descended from Thomas Paine, the English radical of American revolutionary fame. Payne was a co-founder of the Cleveland and Columbus railroad, oversaw Electoral Commission legislation, and was a director of twenty or more corporations. His son Oliver H. Payne, went to the British-modeled Andover Phillips Academy and Yale (Bones 1863).

Oliver H. Payne fought in the Civil War earning the rank of Brigadier General in the "scorch and burn" destruction of Atlanta campaign with Union General

Sherman. Subsequently he made such a great fortune in Cleveland oil refineries that by 1870 it rivaled Rockefeller's Standard Oil. But not for long. In 1872 he's one of twelve original partners with Rockefeller holding 180 shares in the American Cooperative Refining Company; Rockefeller also holds 180 shares, with H. M. Flagler. Deemed the "aristocrat" with a hauteur "akin to God", Col. Oliver H. Payne, – the only college man in the Standard hierarchy –, sells his refining firm Clark Payne and Co. to Standard Oil paid off in stock worth $400,000, and sings on as an company executive becoming treasurer thereby substantially consolidating status and prestige. The company more than doubles its capitalization to $2.5 million in 1872; Rockefeller manages to gain half of Standard and quickly absorbs the refineries of Cleveland producing a quarter of the country's refined oil or close to 11,000 barrels a day. With a near monopoly and advantages from railroads and rail rebates in his pocket Rockefeller forces out his competition obliged to sell or wait to be "crushed". In 1875, Standard Oil is again recapitalized to $3.5 million; among the new shareholders is William H. Vanderbilt, the railroad baron.

In 1876, Rockefeller said, "The coal-oil business belongs to us. We have sufficient money laid aside to wipe out any concern that starts in this business." In America Payne's wealth is exceeded only by J. D. Rockefeller, the Charles Pratt estate and the Harkness family. In order to peddle influence and better secure government favors, Payne buys his son a seat in Washington and is alleged to have paid the way for his son's friend, and future son-in-law, W. C. Whitney's appointment as Navy Secretary under US President Cleveland. (J. Abels, *The Rockefeller Billions*, 110)

FROM SKULL & BONES TO A GOVERNMENT BOUGHT BY BIG OIL DOLLARS

During this era of money barons and muckrakers chronicled by journalist Ida Tarbell in *History of the Standard Oil Company* (1904) Americans were given a look into the workings of Big Oil that bought the United States Senate and fueled the coming of Pax Americana. It's a lesson that sadly may not be lost on Putin with all that Russian oil money awash in the Russian parliament.

Young Oliver becomes a key stockholder in American Tobacco Company and US Steel but prefers to reign as Commodore of the New York Yacht Club mixing with fellow members among them JP Morgan and Cornelius Vanderbilt on their super yachts, mystifying floating palaces and the envy of European royalty. Before buying immortality at Yale with a $1 million donation (he also gave $500,000 to Cornell), Oliver Payne lives and travels in luxury between his Fifth Avenue apartment and his hunting estates.

Another heir worth billions, Cornelius Vanderbilt IV, great-grandson of Cornelius, had the most unfortunate fate of "accident" to be born a Vanderbilt, on the wrong side of the family, son of capricious and mentally unsound parents made all the more worse by their peculiar union; born 1898, he's the progeny of Grace and Cornelius Vanderbilt who entertained "at least ten thousand guests each year at 640 Fifth Avenue, at Beaulieu, and aboard the *North Star*". The same inimitable woman TR once observed "sees herself in a kind of perpetual fairy tale". Fate was barely more kind to Winston Churchill who was hit by a car leaving their mansion in December 1931 having been warned by Grace "about mixing drinks". Great God's teeth! Churchill survived, and so did the free world. (*Vanderbilt,* 310)

Harry Payne left most of his estate (there were no income taxes) to his favorite nephews Payne Whitney (Bones1898) and Harry Payne Bingham, related to his friend Egert Bryon Bingham (Bones 1863), and Charles Tiffany Bingham (Bones 1928). Oliver Hazard Payne's brother-in-law William Collins Whitney (1841-04) married Flora Payne, and made his own personal fortune; after she died. Further down the family tree, W. C. Whitney married Gertrude Vanderbilt; she mothers three children: Flora Payne Whitney (1897), Cornelius Vanderbilt Whitney, and Barbara Whitney. Her son Payne Whitney married Helen Jay, daughter of Teddy Roosevelt's Secretary of State John Jay and outstanding member of the Pilgrims Society. In another odd coincidence of my adolescence was a friendship with Flora Whitney, a direct descendant and found a very old vintage bottle of wine from the old days. We opened it and it tasted no better than vinegar.

Harvard Law, Massachusetts Puritan stock, son of a Brigadier General and descended from John Whitney who came to America in 1635. William C. Whitney (Yale S & B 1863) was a big financier and promoter of the Naval Shipyards and America's Great White Fleet that sailed around the world. His *Report of the Secretary of the Navy* in 1885 warned "the United States had no vessel of war which could have kept the seas for one week as against any other first-rate naval power". He is also a director of the Guaranty Trust since its reorganization in 1892. Harry Payne Whitney (Bones 1894), took over from 1899 to 1930; and Cornelius Vanderbilt Whitney (Bones 1922) is a director from 1926 to 1940 during the Stalinist Holodomor war years.

By 1902 W. C. Whitney retires from Metropolitan Street Railway Company. His fortune boasts ten palatial residences. Whitney's New York mansion on Fifth and 68th is an Italian Renaissance showcase designed by the famous architectural firm of McKim Mead & White. In the style fitting of an English country Lord, Whitney retires to his Lexington stables in Kentucky; his horse *Volodyovski* wins the 1901 English Derby, a crowning social achievement when thoroughbred racing is literally the sport of Kings. He dies the following year. His son Harry Payne Whitney (Bones 1894) is a combination of two giant fortunes, a Consortium dream. H. Whitney keeps up his father's fortune and traditions, and towers over horse racing with the highest earnings in the 1920s where he is often spotted mixing with the Harrimans and Belmonts.

During the era of the Great Depression and Soviet famine-terror, C.V. Whitney win over $1 million dollars horse racing in those Holodomor years. That fatal summer 1933 at the peak of the Holodomor Americans are distracted watching the sport of kings; Whitney's *Seabiscuit* thunders his way into Horse Racing's Hall of Fame. Oh, how nice to be a billionaire in times of Depression and Famine. In Russia, they eat horses, don't they?

In 1904, Harry Payne Whitney inherits $24 million from his father and in 1917 approximately another $12 million from his uncle, Col. Oliver Payne. The Whitney legacy endures. (The Whitney Museum of Modern Art in Manhattan is public testimony to it inspite of its high ticket price of admission.) At present the Whitney fortune is more or less intact. In 1997, keeping up with tradition, the New *York Times* ran a piece on Marylou Whitney, widow of Cornelius Vanderbilt Whitney relating how in 1981 for Christmas she added a "copy" of an 1810 chapel for the 135-acre Cady Hill Farm in Saratoga Springs, New York. As the "Queen of Saratoga" Marylou fancies riding to her annual horse racing ball "in carriages shaped like pumpkins or towed by horses disguised as unicorns". Mrs. Whitney also gave lavish parties at the farm in Lexington. She was known to dance in the mud at a Grateful Dead concert and ride the Steamin' Demon roller coaster at the Great Escape Fun Park. She is a dedicated outdoors woman, who in recent years has developed an affection for the Iditarod, a famously grueling Alaska dog sled race. When away from Cady Hill, when weary of the Manhattan set entertained at Fifth Avenue; she and "Sonny" would fly out to their 550-acre farm in Lexington, Kentucky "where they bred the stakes winners that carried the Eton blue and brown colors of the C. V. Whitney Racing Stable; in Palm Beach, in Spain, "and on their 52,000-acre estate in the Adirondacks…". Be assured, the Consortium is alive and well. ("Marylou Whitney: Life at the Gallop", January 10, 1997, *The NYT*)

The Whitney family invested big in the American Tobacco Company. Whitney's brother-in-law, Oliver H. Payne funded Cornell University's medical school; Thomas F. Ryan, a director at American Tobacco is William C. Whitney's partner. Sutton notes that Pierre Jay's (Bones 1892) "only claim to fame in 1913 was to run a private school and be an obscure vice president of Manhattan Bank yet he became first Chairman of the New York Federal Reserve Bank".

The Whitney family of extended relations sends eight of its sons to Yale to become Bonesmen. By his second marriage to the divorced wife of Cornelius Vanderbilt Whitney, W. Averell Harriman seamlessly merged with the vast Whitney Standard Oil fortune,– (it seems all a bit like walking through rooms of the same big house, doesn't it though?), – and becomes stepfather to her son Harry Payne Whitney II. Wherever he ventured Harriman was encircled by fellow Pilgrims Society members and CFR bureaucrats in and out of the State Department. In 1941 after implementing critical American war aid under FDR's Lend-Lease arrangements, first to Churchill, then to Stalin he becomes ambassador to Russia.

Averell Harriman had no equal in the Consortium during the Holodomor years and rise of Stalin's totalitarian communist dictatorship. In fact few Americans today realize that Harriman remains a pivotal player in between the three most powerful leaders during the war and America's most senior powerbroker for the next half-century.

The Payne-Whitneys became some of Wall Street's most powerful financiers through the Guaranty and Knickerbocker Trust Companies linking their railroad, oil and mining fortunes to investments of the Harrimans, Walkers and Bushes to the Nazi and Bolshevik-Soviet regimes.

Thomas Fortune Ryan from Virginia is thought to be one of the richest men on the planet with a fortune in 1905 estimated at $50 million. Ryan had organised American Tobacco with William C. Whitney who called him a "most adroit, suave, and noiseless man"; Whitney predicts that Ryan might some day have "all the money in the world." Ryan is part of the Chase National Bank syndicate of New York together with Paul Warburg, William Rockefeller, George F. Baker, Moses Taylor Pyne, Percy Pyne, JP Morgan, H. P. Davison and a host of others who partly own and control by the New York Federal Bank. Ryan also holds 5100 shares of National Bank of Commerce stock in 1914. His son John Barry Ryan of National City Bank (Citibank) marries Otto Kahn's daughter; Kahn is a partner of Warburg and has access to Schiff at Kuhn, Loeb & Co. Otto Kahn had married the daughter of Khun, Loeb partner Abraham Wolffe. Jacob Schiff had also become a partner after his marriage to Therese Loeb. (Personal relations between Schiff and Kahn, however, are stiff and impersonal stemming from "their substantial differences in style and inclination".) Further on, Ryan's granddaughter Virginia Fortune Ryan marries M. M. Warburg, chairman of J. Henry Schroeder. (S. J. Pak, 117)

Follow the money. The Consortium family links go on and on …

The Schiffs, Loebs, Lehmans, and Warburgs all intermarry mixing bloodlines and fortunes. There are exceptions but rarely in the earlier first generations do the American WASPS (White Anglo-Saxon Protestant) cross bloodlines with the Jewish money elite. For example, as Jacob Schiff married Theresa Loeb, Nina Loeb married Paul Warburg (1868-32), and so on. Mortimor Schiff's son, John (1904-87), grandson of Jacob Schiff, joins Khun, Loeb & Co. in 1929 and marries Edith Baker, grand-daughter of George F. Baker of First National. "Their's was the first significant link between the social circles of Khun, Loeb and the Morgans, a direct tie between George F. Baker and Jacob Schiff's families," aptly observed by Suzie Pak, in *Gentlemen Bankers*. (S. J. Pak, 128-9. Pak explores in greater detail family and business relations between the Jewish and Gentilles. Assistant history professor at Harvard, Pak writes, "In the 1920s, a Jews began to marry with Gentiles and with greater frequency, they stopped referring to themselves as a 'race' as had once been the norm. In the late nineteenth century, Jews did not classify themselves, for example, on their birth certificate or immigration forms as anything but white. For Jacob Schiff or Felix Warburg, who were naturalized Americans, whiteness was a necessary identity to gain American citizenship. But like Jacob Schiff, Jews in the late nineteenth century did not see this classification as contrary to calling themselves a Jewish race. This was not necessarily the case twenty years later.")

These personal family relations with capital in the Consortium played a significant deciding hand investing in the state socialist economy of Soviet Russia and Stalin's terror dictatorship before and during the Holodomor as well as its influence in the White House, the State Department and the political economy of the country. Naturally endowed with so much power it the Consortium has no difficulty in setting the agenda of national debate and controlling the "free press" which it owns across the board from coast to coast. (Ron Chernow, *The House of*

Morgan, An American Banking Dynasty and the Rise of Modern Finance, Grove Press, 2001, 545)

As we recall the Belmonts descended from August Belmont worked with the Rothschilds. Eustace Mullins and Antony Sutton trace how at the turn of the 19th century American capitalists such as JP Morgan, Andrew Carnegie, Edward H. Harriman are actually operatives working on their behalf of not only enriching themselves but more importantly filling the coffers of the Jewish House of Rothschild which became Europe's wealthiest banking establishment for the past two hundred years with tentacles wrapped around all the empires, the predecessors to the current global financial strata.

August Belmont began his education as a child, in 1822, in Frankfurt, in the charge of his grandmother Gertrude whose husband Hajum Hanau was connected to the Rothschild banking family already embedded in the empires whose expansion and fortunes depended Rothschild brothers established in London, Paris, Vienna, and Naples. Prince Metternich once described the Rothschilds as Europe's richest family and made the five Rothschild brothers barons with the obligatory family coat of arms.

In his chapter on the Rothschilds in *The World Order* (1985) Eustace Mullins writes, "After 1837, August Belmont (Schönberg) was publicly advertised in the financial press as the American representative of the Rothschilds. When Belmont participated in a financial operation, everyone knew that the Rothschilds were involved. When Belmont took no part, and the transaction was handled by JP Morgan & Co., and or by Kuhn, Loeb Co., everyone 'knew' that the Rothschilds were not involved."

August Belmont, in fact, was Prince Metternich's Secretary four years; by 1857, Belmont is sending the younger Rothschilds small gifts – dozens of bottles of first-class Madeira for Alphonse, thousands of Havana cigars for Gustav. When Lincoln was assassinated, rumors spread that Belmont had been a member of the plot to liquidate the triad of Lincoln, Secretary of State Seward and General Stanton. Evidently the information leaked "through a servant in Belmont's employ" linking General McClellan, August Belmont, Fernando Wood, Charles H. Haswell (inventer of the first steam launch) and Jeremiah Larocque and "all together at a supper at Belmont's house with J. Wilkes Booth".

Cross a Rothschild and you pay the consequences as we see here in one of the countless interesting anecdotes of the Rothschild-Belmont business, there is the instance when Belmont is flatly turned down. Mullins writes, "In the years since his arrival Belmont had been so successful at channeling Rothschild funds into the United States Treasury in return for government securities that he was rewarded, in 1844, by being appointed United States Consul General to Austria, a move designed not only to provide Mr. Belmont with prestige but also to place him close to the Vienna House of Rothschild where he could be of further usefulness. Things, of course, did not always go smoothly. When the State of Pennsylvania defaulted on thirty five million worth of State bonds held by British investors, including the Rothschilds, Belmont, in Paris trying to place another US Federal Government loan, was icily told by Baron de Rothschild, "Tell them you have seen the man who is at the head of the finances of Europe, and that he has told you that they cannot borrow a dollar. Not a dollar'." August Belmont was also closely linked to the financial machinations of the Hayes-Cleveland administrations and the 1878 Silver Bill legislation passed by Congress… (*Our Crowd*, 73, cited by E. Mullins; David Black, *The King of Fifth Avenue: The Fortunes of August Belmont*, Dial Press, 1981, 266; E. Mullins, "The Rothschilds", from *The World Order*)

During the war the Bolshevik organization was disorganized. Lenin. Trotsky and Stalin were all living in separate exile. Antony C. Sutton observes in *Wall Street and the Bolshevik Revolution* that most of those who took part in the 1917 Russian Revolution came from New York. Sutton writes, "In 1905, while Russia was engaged in the Russo-Japanese War, the Communists tried to get the farmers to revolt against the Czar, but they refused. After this aborted attempt, the Czar deposited $400,000,000 in the Chase Bank, National City Bank, Guaranty Trust Bank, the Hanover Trust Bank, and Manufacturers Trust Bank, and $80,000,000 in the Rothschild Bank in Paris, because he knew who was behind the growing revolutionary movement, and hoped to end it. The Rothschilds, through Milner, planned the Russian Revolution, and along with Schiff (who gave $20 million), Sir George Buchanan, the Warburgs, the Rockefellers, the partners of JP Morgan (who gave at least $1 million), Olaf Aschberg (of the Nye Bank of Stockholm, Sweden), the Rhine Westphalian Syndicate, a financier named Jovotovsky (whose daughter later marries Leon Trotsky), William Boyce Thompson (a director of Chase National Bank who contributed $1 million), and Albert H. Wiggin (President of Chase National Bank of NY), helped finance it."

There is also a blue-blood-Belmont connection that eludes most people's attention but it is not insignificant for an understanding of America's Consortium elite as it evolved and encompassed FDR and his generation in the thirties and Stalin's Terror-Famine against the Ukrainians and FDR's war plans for a postwar European reconstruction. It has to do with the preparatory St. Pauls School, a prestigious blue-blood affair with heavy endowment from the Morgan banking fortune during the late 19th and early 20th century era. (E. Digby Baltzell, *The Protestant Establishment Aristocracy & Caste in America*, NY: Random House, 1964)

St. Pauls rivals Groton and Phillips Academy (Andover and Exeter). Its first Rector, Henry A. Coit, is a grandson of Levi Coit who married Lydia Howland of a Mayflower family when it all began in America. Levi Coit is a rich merchant and stockbroker who emigrated to the US. His eldest son joins August Belmont in business.

Henry Augustus Coit of Columbia and Princeton Theological School is a Presbyterian who converts to become an Episcopalian Deacon ordained by the influential Bishop Griswold of the vastly rich New England Griswolds. Phillips Academy (Andover) continues to rank as one of the nation's most prestigious and privileged independent schools; in 2002 it topped the list with the largest fund-raising campaign in independent school history with $208.9 million. ("At $208.9 million, Andover concludes largest fund-raising campaign in independent school history," Philips Academy News website, July 24, 2002)

Few WASPS in those anti-Semitic days of exclusive banking and social demarcations would appreciate knowing the intriguing details of how the Rothschild-Belmont-Coit connection consequently maintained St. Pauls School as the breeding ground for the sons of the American elite modeled on Eton and Harrow in England. Rector Henry A. Coit, for instance, is brother to Joseph H. Coit, Bones 1853.

The accumulated wealth from America's industrial revolution of railroads, trade and oil reinforced these kinds of family relations in a social hierarchy of tight political control over most of the resources of the nation under the capitalists and their monopoly system of producing wealth and wielding political control to protect it. Once these monopoly capitalists took control of the banking system and centralized it with their centralized Federal Reserve Banking system and government, this Consortium elite managed their resources for their war for democracy and determined the political settlements that led to the October Bolshevik coup and Lenin's consolidation of Bolshevik socialist monopoly. Stalin's Terror-Famine came in time and followed the same logic. Political and economic systems are abstract combinations of very real individuals and their social relations that determine them.

These empire-builders were interested in much more than Czarist gold. Russia was a fabulous rich bastion of precious minerals and metals. The vast interconnected capitalist networks of the Harriman and Rockefeller family fortunes moved quickly to strike at the vast ancient empire out of step with modern automation and companies like General Electric and Ford.

Oil and mining concessions were first to go. In return, Lenin traded with the capitalists to build his so-called "Dictatorship of the Proletariat", a ruse for state monopoly control elaborated in his NEP program before he fell ill from assassination attacks and withered away poisoned by Stalin. Imagine their excitement colored in thick cigar smoke and rich cognac as they eyed maps spanning one sixth of the world's global surface teeming with hundreds of millions of illiterate, hungry socialist workers driven like cogs in a wheel amid the devastation of colossal poverty and war by an incomprehensible foreign ideology to build the great modern state for the future of international communism and freedom of the world's working class against the tyrants of global imperialism? A collective capitalists' dream! A haven for capitalist-communist propaganda, albeit advertising for the masses. There was no lack of Soviet propaganda cameras to champion Soviet success portrayed by beautiful Ukrainian maidens dressed in traditional embroidered garments dancing in village festivals or on parade embracing with wheat stalks. Meanwhile NKVD police "shock brigades" raided villages, ransacked farms, confiscated stashes of sacks of grain buried under the fields, homes or hidden elsewhere, and arrested villagers and shot resisters.

Who would have thought that the Ukrainian Holodomor tragedy of Russia's defenseless peasants would expose the international Jewish banking Consortium alliance with the America's Wall Street WASP establishment, together with the FED and the Bank of England, the Nazi Reich and the tyrant in the Kremlin? But it does. Only a handful of Americans knew that the Washington-New York elite clique was actually led by the Jewish Rothschild banking agents in London and Wall Street, with family links instrumental in drafting the original US governmental legislation that created their own private monopoly in the Federal Reserve banking system.

Their history remains obscure even today while many of their names are so familiar they risk nothing were their obscure past exposed from their deeds and the consequences inflicted on an even more treacherous and indifferent world of oppressors, men and women duped and enamoured by their smug complicity in conspiracy. The vanguard of this front were the associates Otto Kahn, Jacob Schiff, Otto Kuhn of Kuhn Loeb & Co., Paul Warburg, Lehman Brothers to name only a few, respecting the untouchable Rockefellers and Harrimans, icons of the American wealth and their new empire for the 21st century. They were all familiar with the peculiar blend of intrigue and conspiracy of Leningrad and Moscow under Bolshevik Marxist-Leninist tyranny.

It was all a brilliant scheme played out in utter secret on the world stage. There is nothing mysterious about conspiracy which means only that strategic planning goals and tactics are kept in secret which is the practice of every company in the competitive market economy. The same Consortium of bankers and industrialists and their friends owned and controlled the nation's major news and information syndicates from *The New York Times* to AP and UPI wire services.

Other Morgan bankers, including Tom Lamont, the brilliant son of a Methodist minister who had worked his way through Harvard and still had time to become freshman editor of the *Crimson*, and Harry Payne, Yale's great benefactor. Lamont controls the *New York Evening Post*, and Payne holds the *Metropolitan World*. The 1933 anonymously published book, *Mirrors on Wall Street*, tells this of Lamont, born 1870: "Lamont of Morgan and Company has become its envoy extraordinary, its glorified propagandist, part of a money-making machine. He has never recovered from his earlier impressions of the elder Mr. Morgan. No peasant ever bowed more humbly before the Roman pontiff than Lamont bowed before Mr. Morgan. His word was dogma. And now after twenty years, he genuflects before the old gentlemen's chair and thanks God that he was chosen to live in his beatified shadow. ... The partners of Morgan and Company are chosen as carefully as are the members of the College of Cardinals, if for different reasons. There is no club quite so select. Members are invited to join; they are not recruited from the ranks. With three notable exceptions, no employee of the firm has ever sat at the table unless the blood of a member ran in his veins. It is an unusual role—typically Morganesque. Candidates for admission must be approved by Mr. Lamont before Mr. Morgan signs their partnership". (R. Chernow, *The House of Morgan,* 99-101)

As we see with the set up of the USRS, the Morgan business is very relevant to how Washington conducts foreign policy. Morgan operatives exercise their influence impacting on all the principal participants of the world wars touching every capital and every major industry. Lamont, for instance, chooses Russell Leffingwell, who is an undersecretary at Treasury under McAdoo in charge of floating the Liberty Loans. Leffingwell, (b. 1878, is Bones '99), comes from a New York City family, Columbia Law School ('02), editor of the *Columbia Law Review*, and practices corporate law at Cravath, Henderson, Leffingwell & de Gersdorff until World War I at which time he learns a lot about handling foreign bank loans and is so good at it he takes charge of international finance when the Allied loans are negotiated, a trade he pursues during the Harding administration; Leffingwell is still only in his early thirties; at 27, when he too joins Wilson's administration an undersecretary at Treasury; in the Harding administration he handles loans and debts as Agent General of Reparations (1924-30) having succeeded Owen Young. Then he joins the Morgan bank as a young partner and stays there until he retires as chairman of the bank in 1950. ("Died, Russell Cornell Leffingwell, 82, former board chairman of J. P. Morgan & Co. of cancer; in Manhattan", *Time Magazine*, Oct. 17, 1960. *Time* writes Leffingwell "joined Morgan in 1923 floating loans for the postwar recovery of Europe's economy".; R. Chernow, *The House of Morgan*)

For his assistant Leffingwell takes with him to Washington a personable, yet unknown recent graduate of Harvard Law School, Seymour Parker Gilbert (1892-38), and formerly Editor of the *Harvard Law Review* (1913-15), joins the War Department, rises in postwar Versailles- Treasury negotiations and officially joins the Morgan firm in 1931 and shows little interest of the need to restructure the national economy. "The remedy," he declares, "is for people to stop watching the ticker, listening to the radio, drinking bootleg gin, and dancing to jazz ... and return to the old economics and prosperity based on saving and working." Gilbert is in a position to know more than anyone else about the workings of that division of the Treasury. Leffingwell retires taking his knowledge to "The Corner". Gilbert succeeded him at Treasury. Gilbert's son, S. Parker Gilbert Jr. becomes head of Morgan Stanley to capitalize on the deregulation of the Reagan Eighties. (Peter Bernstein, *The Wedding of The Waters*, NY: Norton, 2005, 23)

Russell Leffingwell is also an active member of the CFR, its director and president (1944-46); from 1946 to 1953 he serves as the CFR's first chairman. A Pilgrims Society member he makes chairman of the excom of J. P. Morgan & Company until he dies of a heart attack, in 1938. In *Who's Who* (1961) Leffingwell's listing includes his membership in the Royal Economic Society, an organization similar to its counterpart at Vanderbilt University, opposed to silver and gold as money and considers "fronts for fiat money creators". Barton Biggs cites Leffingwell who bemoans, "The Allies cannot subjugate the Germans. There are too many of the devils and they are too competent." And was right, but leaves the Russians out of the count. (A. C. Sutton, *Mirrors on Wall Street*; Charles Savoie, *World Money Order III* on the net; B. Biggs, *Wealth, War and Wisdom*; "S. Parker Gilbert is Dead Here at 45", *The NYT*, Feb. 24, 1938; The private papers of Seymour Gilbert were destroyed by his widow; some papers were found in files of Cravath, Henderon & de Gersdorff for the period 1915-18. His alma mater Rutgers University may have papers.)

Men of the corporate Consortium culture share a unique sameness, different in kind yet are all respectable pillars of society, protected by foundations and trusts of personal wealth, and philanthropies constructing the character of the culture they envision, carefully plan out and control where money can buy anything and it usually does. From dictators to American presidents and Soviet Premiers, no one is immune or can afford to be indifferent except the deaf, dumb and blind. Lenin considered the masses little more than "deaf-mutes".

Part of the chimera played out on a global scale, in Moscow and Washington, was the role of the intelligence "law and order" agencies from the FBI to the CIA which simultaneous maintained the illusions of a domestic subversive threat financed and controlled from Moscow. It was a hoax involving the gamet of society from academics to senior public officials, lawyers, bankers, newsmen, and your local town minister. In the center of this web of deception, was America's most prestigious bank, JP Morgan, later Morgan Guaranty, then JP Morgan-Chase, a holy marriage if ever there was one as they have been together from their earliest days.

Before the Bolshevik Revolution in Russia, American socialists liked to depict the Wall Street banking industrialists with particular humor. A cartoon by Robert Minor who worked with Reed and Eastman at *The Masses,* here appearing in a 1911 edition in the *St. Louis Dispatch* depicting Karl Marx, that loving father of world socialism, being blessed by astute followers - JP Morgan, Morgan partner George W. Perkins, a smug John D. Rockefeller Sr., John D. Ryan of National City Bank (Citibank), and "TR", Teddy Roosevelt – characteristically shining his famous teeth all of them draped by Red flags with a Wall Street crowd hailing Marx as a friend of the New York financial district. Strange perhaps? Not really. Perkins is expert in Trust creation and the brains behind the giant International Harvester monopoly a decade earlier.

America lived under the looming shadow of the Rothschild fortune. Americans never really understood the ramifications of the very important detail that the great Morgan banking fortune was directly linked to the Rothschilds of nineteenth-century Europe. What does it matter to those who live blindly in the present when legacies of the past are lost in illusions of the future?

The American Dream, for example, is one such illusion. Democracy in America is another. But the masses of consumers are cultured with dope of such illusions from Hollywood to constant bombardments of the daily media swarming on the Internet competing for attention with porn and the latest Grammy pop singer.

John Pierpont Morgan (1837-13) was the dominant American financier before the First World War. JP Morgan dies in 1913 in Rome with over 50,000 miles of railroads in the United States under his control. Morgan and Carnegie had contrived millions with US Steel along with sundry other corporate combinations and rivalries. In the United States, John Pierpont Morgan, Jr. succeeded his father as head of the colossal Morgan banking empire. Rothschild, through his operatives at Kuhn, Loeb Co is the largest holder of railroads in America during the First World War.

Stalin's first request to FDR's ambassador, in 1934, is for 80,000 miles of used steel rails, not a problem for the Consortium. Before the First World War became the Second, the same Morgan Wall Street family of extended partners and network of friends, built colossal fortunes of capital, centralized and empowered the American national banking system into a private banking monopoly of the

Federal Reserve under their direct political control. This was an intimate family affair. They invested millions and billions of dollars, private and public, and trusted only their family connections and loyal servants employed in corporations, universities and public government. In America, public service is a very private business. They have the power to make and finance wars, small proxy wars and world wars. Their interest is to control the Game, absolutely, at least as best they can, one way or another, exerting the ultimate power. (A. C. Sutton re. Kuhn Loeb)

These same architects of American corporate finance aided and sustained the Bolshevik Revolution of 1917 and sustained Stalin's totalitarian repression personified in his Five-Year Plans of Industrialization and Collectivization. For FDR and his army of government federalists and corporate socialists during his administrations throughout the thirties, the cost in human lives did not figure in their balance sheet of profits and losses. At the very same time that Stalin issued orders extending the forced famine that killed millions of Ukrainian peasants in a campaign of ethnic extermination, FDR secretly prepared official diplomatic relations with the United States. Put it all into perspective. That the Hoover and Roosevelt administrations could blithely ignore Stalinist brutality should not surprise Americans familiar with their own country's brief and barbaric early history. Only a hundred years before the American Civil War war to free the slaves, Benjamin Franklin wrote about the massacre on December 14, 1763 in cold blood of defenseless and harmless Indians, peaceful women and children in their shelters hacked to death and scalped, the deeds of white men at Conestogoe Manor by "some of Frontier Townships". That's in Pennsylvania.

From the earliest days of settlement and throughout the westward expansion, American history is marked by the extermination, enslavement and betrayal of millions of native Indians of North America by the "civilized" superior White Race dominating non-Christian tribal peoples without that peculiar Anglo-Saxon worship of private property. For the "primitive" indigenous native only Mother Earth and their spiritual world were sacred. In comparison, the Ukrainian Genocide has to stand as one of the most shameful episodes in American history on the same scale in the balance with the lawless massacres during the Philippine pacification of 1900 and a million dead Filipinos and the subjugation of indigenous populations everywhere to satisfy the greed and lust for power and wealth in total disregard of respect for the civility of different peoples and human life. Although the democratic government of United States was still less than two centuries old, the cunning and spurious hypocrisy of Americans had long been established by their representative leaders by an arrogance known throughout the world as no less dangerous than the Nazi fascists and murderous Bolsheviks empowered by the elite Anglo-American Consortium.

For contemporary Ukrainian the Terror-Famine of the 1930s remains a vivid and haunting memory. The Jews never forget their Holocaust and they won't let the world forget it either nor should they. The Jewish Genocide was short and brutal. However information about the forced starvation and executions in the Soviet Union was kept out of the foreign press, and not pursued by its editors or Consortium publishers. These papers were controlled by the same corporate establishment that was doing business with Stalin. This corporate monopolistic elite appeared dignified and elegant whenever they did appear publicly emerging from their secluded rural estates and luxurious city apartments to flaunt their *richesse* and their *grandeur* at philanthropic galas.

These families of America's ruling class were trained and groomed in the best schools of America and granted entitlements to the most exclusive private clubs of "High Society". They worked and vacationed together, married cousins in mansions with hundreds of servants and traded business deals like they traded their sons and daughters. Consortium money and power stayed in the family. With succeeding generations naturally their power expanded and multiplied. Today there should be no mistake in minimalizing their predominance. It was their special kind of "democratic" plutocracy, or mafia. Whatever word you wish to use, its only a different name for the same thing, the tightly knit Consortium with heads all of the same monster.

From big commodity trusts to the money trusts of the Federal Reserve Banking system assuring billions gained on the ruins the war, the wasps of the Morgan-Rockefeller-Harriman networked with their Jewish families of Warburgs, Schiffs, Kuhns, Lehmans and Rothschilds. Together they pooled their multiples of billions of dollars of the nation's wealth to create a New World Order under their direct control. The world was their sandbox. Their descendant heirs in the Consortium hierarchy remained on the interlocking boards that control the international banks today. These bankers in no small measure financed the Bolshevik Revolution exercising control of the vast resources of the Soviet Union. They were so greedy to collect the spoils left behind by the Russian Empire destroyed by war that they nonchalantly killed for it. In fact for many it was all a little sad but amusing at the same time.

The Allied Powers who "won" the First World War had not treated very nicely their former ally, Czarist Russia. Poor Nicholas! So quickly had they forgotten 300,000 Russian soldiers of the Czarist army lost each month during the first ten months of war, forcing Germany to fight on two fronts. French diplomacy and the Russian army saved Paris from an immediate and humiliating defeat. The Germans never wanted a long war. Few expected it. But the French Anglo-American bankers had far different plans for the future world order of the 20th century. Consequently, by the time America and the Allies forced Germany into unconditional surrender, Russia lost another four million men before the Armistice was declared on November 11, 1918. America lost less than 60,000 combat soldiers. America won the war! That in only eight months of engagement! Churchill watched as the British lost over 55,000 men in a single day at the Somme.

The Versailles Peace Treaty excludes the Soviet delegates. Russia lost territory it had already paid for in blood. The Bolshevik Revolution and their call for a world communist revolution against the war capitalist democracies hangs like a dark cloud over every conversation at Versailles. It spooked Hoover. Soviet Foreign Commissar Georgii V. Chicherin (1872-36) flatly rejects war retributions attached to prospective Western credits. The West demanded the payment of

Czarist debts. Muddied by accusations of war guilt, the Consortium delegates of diplomats and bankers seek the restoration of foreign property nationalized by the Bolsheviks, and the securing of Western credits and loans held by key Soviet assets under Western control.

One way or the other, Wall Street always gets its people in the White House no matter how bad the news at home or abroad. For example, when President Hoover loses favor, the Wall Street crowd tapped FDR who is waiting behind the curtain and already owes them a ton of money. During his inauguration in the spring 1933, Stalin's forced Terror-Famine ravaged the Ukraine in full force sucking all the life of the once flourishing countryside. But with thousands of banks crashing all around him Russia is the last thing on Roosevelt's mind.

By spring 1933 workers in factories throughout the stricken territories are laid off, desert the plants looking for food, returning to impoverished villages and defying travel restrictions in order to forage in the more populated towns and cities. Even for the privileged class in the cities there is little food just enough to get by. Wandering peasants who had left their farms find little if any relief. A resident of the Caucasus summed up their plight in mid-summer : "The individual peasants are in special danger, since they are completely abandoned to their wretched lot, whereas the members of the collective farms are given some state assistance, though it be at best quite insufficient." European social activist Ewald Ammende points out, "In this way, the individual peasants were completely eliminated; either they entered the collective farms in so far as they were allowed to, or they died of starvation." (Ewald Ammende, *Human Life in Russia*, George Allen and Unwin, London, 1936, 61-2, 179; Malcolm Muggeridge, "Russia Revealed," *The Morning Post* (London), June 5, 1933, 9; W. H. Chamberlin, *Foreign Affairs*, April 1934; Pierre Berland, July 1933; M. Muggeridge, "A Citizen of Soviet Russia, "Famine in Northern Caucasus" (letter), *Manchester Guardian*, Aug. 28, 1933, 16.; see also Pearson and Paarlberg, 4; Eugene M. Kulischer, *Europe on the Move*, Columbia Univ. Press, 1948, 98, 103; Clarence Manning, *Ukrainian Under the Soviets*, NY: Bookman Associates, 1953, 99-100)

Albeit from Moscow to Berlin, London and New York, the famine is widely reported in the world press mixed with deliberate ambiguity and sheer nonsense. FDR does nothing to stop it. Nowhere in the private papers of Bill Bullitt kept under lock and key in the vaults of Yale's Archives is there a single trace to acknowledge between the newly-elected President, a Democrat, and his loyal Undersecretary of State nor even the slightest concern or remark about the Ukrainian famine. Not a request for information, nor any suggestion to prepare a public response to the human tragedy. Nothing. Millions of people have already died. Millions more are dying and will soon be dead if nothing is done to help them.

The exigency of domestic politics in his first year in the White House required that FDR ignore it. His political advisors and spin doctors had to wonder how would it look if Roosevelt was seen running to the aid of the Soviet communists while Americans go hungry throughout America and particularly in the hard-hit western farm-belt, with families in the cities across America facing yet another day without enough food for their children. About the Ukrainians, it's too simple and false to say the new President just does not appear to know nor show decisive determination what to do or that he made a mistake in his policy of denial and deception. Roosevelt never does understand the Russians, or Stalin. FDR does not see beyond his own nose when looking down his long cigarette holder. Nor does he have too. Moscow is just too far away to matter.

"THE YALE SPIRIT"

Not much more than a century ago, in the era of the grandfathers of the current postwar baby-boomers, – and that includes the generation of Presidents Bush Jr., Clinton and Obama, George Santayana went to Yale to investigate this a strange phenomena he described as the 'disturbing legend' of Yale power. Santayana quoted a Harvard alumnus who intended to send his son to Yale - because in real life 'all the Harvard men are working for Yale men.' But no one has previously asked an obvious question - Why? What is this 'Yale power'?"

The Yale College motto is "For God, Country, and Yale". It's on the university banner hanging in most every dorm room. That it is the whole of it found in the heart and soul of the men, women and the place.

World history may have taken a different course had the Ukrainians' prayers for life and peace not been silenced, their letters unanswered. America's great men who played no small part in the Russian-Soviet trade, and who endowed the finest universities, – Harvard-Princeton-Yale, – where their sons (women were not yet allowed in these sacred grounds until 1970) dined regally at lily white cotton draped tables in huge darkly paneled banquet halls feasting and carrying on in those jolly postwar years (many of them dead too in distant islands of the Pacific Ocean, and in Europe), served by white-gloved Afro-American servants all in true imperial style. For these young men too had to learn how to use the means of power with which to master society and make things work for private industry as well as providing for "the public good".

When this author first arrived at Yale, he recalls the amiable greeting by Yale President Kingman Brewster (1963-77), a lawyer and a former partner of the Root, Stimson and Winthrop firm. His sermon in Woolsey Hall around the corner from his office on Wall Street bellowed into the heads of freshmen awed by the Yale mission suddenly bestowed upon them in the spirit of public service. It was a very impressive seance in an archaic hall with worn wooden pews that hosted generations of predecessors, and the names of all those killed in the service of God & Country immortalized in marble and stone. A Groton boy of one of America's most distinguished old families and a Pilgrims Society member Kingman Brewster also enjoyed the rites of the Court of St. James living in the gold-plated ambassadorial embassy. Few in the great hall knew that Kingman had snubbed Skull & Bones before his senior year in 1941. (Geoffrey Kabaservice, *The Guardians*, NY: Henry Holt and Company, 2005)

In an annual ritual at Yale, Harvard and Princeton, as well as at the other Ivy League colleges, freshmen are indoctrinated with a good dose of traditional "Yale spirit", an intoxicating euphemism to enamor the privileged sons (and later daughters) to government and public service as though their destinies depend on conditions prescribed by elders and ancestors. Their names are eternally chiseled in stone on Yale's Gothic walls under haunting gargoyles that lord over their dominion casting spells as though to beckon greater private tax-deductible endowments from generation to generation to instill new life into the spirit of the place.

Whoever owns the bank owns the industries, as well as the private and public universities in America, those pristine institutions for education and higher learning determined to own history, keepers of the secrets holding the keys to the tomb of dark designs leading to even darker crimes for their sons to commit once they too take those keys in hand. These great men of the elite hold in their hands the tools that make history seem as they wish it to appear in the mass media. Of course with private endowments by less well-heeled patrons and modest variations in the pattern with succeeding generations to a degree, or two.

Instead of peace they pursued profits, scorching the earth with war and destruction. They really believed they could lock the truth away with bloodlines that crossed families that married like mafia and royalty and protect their careers and investments with the same fierce devotion, culture and mentality. And as their image expanded into the mainstream, their power and identity has become inversely more secret and inaccessible carefully guarded identities, protected lives in shielded communities and six-figure salaries with a platinum health plan.

It used to be called the "Old Boy" network in the pre-Internet era of the Information Age with innovative tech aps transforming communication channels.. The Presidents of the United States and top advisers destined to occupy key positions in government, politics, Big Business and investment banking and the armed services were for their part, in the land of opportunity, given their channeled positions, like an inheritance or royal succession. The emphasis was on duty, continuity and respecting traditions and preserving the system that kept it all together and made it worthy of obedience and sustained by a loyalty reenforced by the discipline of unquestioned values.

Robots in the linear mechanical world. That's not true anymore, not in the virtual reality of the digital world. That world is long since gone. Societies have changed. Different structures of evolved or radically different hierarchies reorient methods and procedures so that even the objects of reality are perceived not as they used to be, or maybe they are completely new as the old is transformed into a sterile and sleek new world beckoning description to define new values and meaning. In such a world patterns of estrangement leave fathers and mothers out of touch and their children out of reach searching for new roads to travel. In such a world battles are fought with drones not divisions, computer chips, surgical precision and extraordinary sophisticated data links managed by armchair warriors who never face a combat mission or know courage under fire. There are no medals for such executants, not even a Purple Heart. (Mark Bowden, "The Killing Machines, How to Think about Drones", *The Atlantic*, Sept. 2013)

Same families, same schools, same secret societies, same clubs, same company networks under one government in one world. A monopoly of Consortium power. They all know the rules, and they all play together. Most of them are members of the Council of Foreign Relations (CFR) that has a lot less prestige today than when there were fewer organizations and members with big money in the past. The CFR still remains a significant gateway to the network of higher echelons of power up the pearly steps to paradise.

Most of the American Presidents came from the secret society Skull & Bones at Yale or corresponding clubs at Harvard and Princeton. Since power emanates from the top down in the American Democracy regardless of what the Consortium controlled news tells you, it's no wonder that at present "the Yale Spirit" of the Harvard-Princeton-Yale syndrome still conjures up a plethora of feelings and attitudes engrained as it is in the national ethos. One man of the past who was determined that "the Yale Spirit" be engraved in stone as an indelible motto of status, influence and power was Yale's prewar historian Anson Phelps Stokes (1874-58, Bones) compiled the basic principles of the Yale creed in his book published months before the outbreak of the First World War.

Titled *Memorials of Eminent Yale Men* in 1914 Stokes publishes a limited edition of only 150 copies only destined for Bonesmen just to remind them who they are, where they come from and what it takes to hold the golden future in their princely hands. If America is to have a chosen elite of favored sons then these men and their attributes and endowments are central to the core. His son, Anson Phelps Stokes, Jr., graduates in the same class (1927) with George Herbert Walker Jr. and Edward Rogers Wardwell. The elder Stokes, born in London, a merchant banker, industrialist and philanthropist, dies, in 1913, age 75; first thought to have amassed a personal fortune of $25 million, or about $580,723,906 in today's dollar; in reality it was a few million less, $17.5 million. (Anson Phelps Stokes, *Memorials of Eminent Yale Men,* Yale Univ. Press, May 1914)

ANSON PHELPS STOKES: "CHARACTERISTICS OF MOST EMINENT YALE MEN"

Here is an extract from chapter eleven titled, "Common Characteristics of Most Eminent Yale Men":

"Let it be said at the outset that it is impossible to find any group of characteristics common to all Yale men of distinction. Yet every historical university has a personality, and leaves its impress upon its students. This is specially marked in the undergraduate course where students are in residence together for several successive years, enjoying a common life, and handing down the college traditions from one generation to another. It is true of families living in an ancestral home, of clearly differentiated communities, as well as of religious and social organizations, so it is natural that it should hold good of a university which shares many of the characteristics of such institutions, in addition to being primary a place of intellectual training. Its atmosphere is one of the most important educational assets, but this is nothing else than the associations and ideals handed down by officers and students living in the same place, with kindred purposes, through the course of the years. These bring up the past, influencing youth unconsciously by the ideals of those who have gone before. Many a man in a cathedral of the Old World has been enveloped by a feeling that the prayers of thousands of men and women have consecrated the place during several centuries. This is a help to worship, just as the living in a community where strong men have wrought unconsciously stimulates young men to imitate their example. Ivy-grown walls, ancient customs, and long-existing organizations, all have their effect in transmitting what earlier generations have achieved."

"This is one of the most precious gifts of an ancient university. Anyone who has lived as a student at Oxford knows the reality of the power, the spell of the place, with its traditions of classical culture, idealism, and conservatives. So it is at Harvard, where the atmosphere has been for generations one of independence, individualism, criticism, liberalism, and culture, forming well-defined traditions and ideals. These differ considerably from those at Yale, but only prejudice could deny that their contributions to American education are of vital importance. Both the spirit of Harvard and the spirit of Yale have their advantages and limitations. Each of them makes some impress on every student's point of view, occasionally by reaction, but generally by direct influence.

"What then is the Yale ideal which has been generally reproduced by our most representative graduates? The main definite factors of undergraduate influence – scholarship, religion, inspiring teachers and association with men … we are concerned with the atmosphere of the place which has had its effect on the general attitude of mind of eminent graduates. The Yale ideal, historically considered, has four main elements, which deserve separate consideration. It is a combination of them, corresponding in a rough unscientific way to certain attributes of personality, or perhaps better, to four activities of the individual. Socially it expresses itself in democracy, spiritually in faith, intellectually in conservatism, and morally in constructive activity."

"…democracy has played a prominent part as one side of the college ideal. It has been a factor in the services rendered by the University, in the two great American crises – the Revolution and the Civil War, *and it has been characteristic of almost all eminent Yalensians*. Of the seventy-nine names chosen for biographies by as objective tests as possible, most have been *genuine and whole-souled exponents of democracy*. Not one has been a snob, and only two (Samuel Seabury and William Smith were both loyalists) showed a lack of sympathy with republican institutions."

FAITH

"The typical graduate has the believing attitude of mind. He has faith in God, in his country, in his University, in his fellow men. A Yale atheist, or a Yale cynic, or a Yale pessimist, is rarely found."

"Faith is the essence of the spirit of the place. Its earliest and most characteristic manifestation is in the sphere of religion. The first words of the original charter, obtained in 1701, put this in the foreground, where it has ever remained: 'Whereas several well disposed, and Publick spirited Persons of their Sincere Regard to & Zeal for upholding & Propagating of the Christian Religion …' et cetera. The successors of these 'Publick spirited Persons' – the life members of the Yale Corporation – have always included a majority of ministers of the Gospel, Corporation meetings have always opened with prayer, the corporate Communion service has been held regularly at the College, which has the most influential and next to oldest undenominational University department of Divinity in America. ... the Yale brotherhood has been the first among American universities to found a support a Christian college in the mission field. These are merely representative facts. They are thoroughly reflected in the spiritual attitude of our graduates. ... There is not a professed atheist among them...The faith characteristic of Yale as indicated above is broader than the scope of religion, and affects a man's whole outlook on life. It is just as essential ion making a man a good patriot, or an educational leader in a democracy, as it is in developing a prophetic preacher. *It involves the implication that there are better days ahead for Humanity, and that they are worth working for.* The roots of this faith which makes a man cheer heartily and work enthusiastically 'For God, For Country and for Yale', find their religious beginnings in old New England, but these were broadened and chastened by the humanitarianism which followed the Revolution. ... They have been growing as the University has become more and more a national institution. It is hard for a man today in the college atmosphere, with its inherited traditions of religion and democracy, reinforced by the never rending stream of manly lads from Christian homes 'working their way through', not to have faith in God and man." (italics added)

CONSERVATISM

"It is undoubtedly true, whether a trait to be admired or not, that the intellectual note of Yale is conservatism rather than radicalism. There is not and never has been anything hidebound or reactionary in the University's attitude, but its educational policy has been marked by caution, by an unwillingness to make extreme and untried experiments in methods of instruction."

YALE AND THE RULING CLASS

"If these unusually mobile conditions of American life, and the need of evolving a higher civilization from the old, are granted, nothing is more necessary than that there should be some viable and potent national institutions emphasizing historical continuity. The absence of a ruling house and of a recognized aristocracy, and the short terms of elective office, make all this more necessary. No sooner have a President and a Cabinet secured a position of dignified influence than they are superseded." (A. P. Stokes, 383)

WAR, EDUCATION AND THE NATIONAL ETHOS

Chapter "Historical Universities in a Democracy", "Lack of Bonds with the Past in America"

"This is the more noticeable as there is not great center in which the past is summed up for the nation – as Athens does it for Greece, or Rome for Italy. We have no compulsory military service with the practically identical education for the youth of all sections which goes with it. We are thankful for the youth of all sections which goes with it. We are thankful for this, but there can be no doubt that such training as seem in Prussia is highly influential in handing down national traditions. A couple of years of military duty, with the details of life and much of the framework of thought directed from the central government, makes it relatively easy to transmit the country's ideals from generation to generation. The American public school system does not entirely take its place, as its connections are mainly local. It is a vital part of the life of the community, but at most its traditions are only state-wide. In spite of annual meetings of teachers, and of a potentially powerful but poorly supported Bureau of Education in Washington, there is no national *esprit de corps* among our public schools such as there is in the arm of France or of Italy." (A. P. Stokes, 383)

"More powerful than journalism is English literature. Yet it hardly satisfies our desideratum. ... No writer of our own soil has as yet expressed the genius of our people in a way to compare with Plato or Aristotle for Greece, Cicero for Rome, Goethe for Germany. We must believe that the greatest names in distinctively American literature are yet to appear. (A. P. Stokes, v. II, 384)

"A written constitution in a measure meets the need and yet only in a measure. It is not sufficiently living to be able to reflect the Zeitgeist at the same time that it reminds us of the past. But we should be thankful for it and for the Supreme Court, its interpreter, as these alone are ion any large degree reliable forces of political continuity in America. They are the bulwarks of the federal government. To them we must continue to look if we would make sure that we do not ruthlessly break with our history. Liberty and law are equally necessary in a democracy, and these ancient cornerstones of our political system help support both. If respect for them were eliminated, the future would bring change but not progress. ... We have no historic cathedrals, no St. Paul's or Westminster Abbey for centuries identified with the heroes of the nation...'

"The experience of other countries would indicate that probably only a few of them (universities) can be truly representative of the higher life of the whole nation. In England, Oxford and Cambridge stand by themselves. They have had an effect upon the thought and ideals of Great Britain, over a long period that is far deeper than that of any other modern institution of learning upon its own country. In France there are several excellent universities, but that of Paris alone broadly represents the nation. In Germany the habit of students migrating from one center to another as so to sit at the feet of more great masters than can be collected in a single place, has brought about a somewhat different situation. Yet the University of Berlin, at the capital of the empire, and with the unusually rich associations of a century's identification with great scholars, is the most representative institution. (A. P. Stokes, 386; *Not so. Women were poorly represented if at all. For example, we may recall Edith Hamilton (1867-63), the top woman classicist in her day, author *The Greek Way* (1930) and *The Roman Way* (1932), born in Dresden (great-aunt to my roommate at Yale) and her sister at turn-of-the-century Berlin, and the first woman member of Harvard's faculty some forty years later.)

"There is a widespread feeling in America that a great university can be created anywhere in a year by adequate gifts of money. … As a matter of fact, a collegiate foundation can only have its deepest effect after its character and ideals meet the threefold test which can be successfully applied in England to Oxford and Cambridge – influence on the nation's history, breadth of constituency, and established standing in the public mine. … a state university is fitted by its constitution to serve its own commonwealth rather than the whole nation. Deriving its main support from taxation and legislative grants, rather than from endowments, and having to satisfy the taxpayer, it is apt to err in overemphasizing the value of immediate utility in education, just as its older rivals tend to underestimate it. There is no danger that the spirit of the enthusiastic supporter of the old classical course who thanked God that he had learned nothing practical in college, will ever dominate a state institution. ... Most of these universities established in new communities in the latter half of the nineteenth century, with the help of the Morrill Land Grant to encourage 'Agriculture and the Mechanic Arts', must almost inevitably strike a different note from Harvard, founded in the seventeenth century for 'the education of youth. … In knowledge and godliness', or from Yale, which received its charter half a century later for the purpose of fitting men for 'Publick Employment both in Church and Civil State'." (A. P. Stokes, Vol. II, 388)

"We are therefore driven back in our search to historic and endowed universities such as Harvard, Yale, Princeton, and Columbia. Harvard fairly maintains the position of leadership among our schools of learning that is naturally hers by right of age, while the first two universities are the only American institutions in any field which have been for over two centuries factors of national influence. They alone remain as conspicuous, visible symbols of that first century of New England Puritanism to which we are indebted for laying deep the foundations of religion and of democracy. They are enduring monuments of that respect for education which has meant so much to all our commonwealths. Each institution has its strong individuality and hands down loyally its own interpretation, modified in the course of years, of the great purposes for which these shores were settled. Each stands prominently before the American people as a definite entity which reflects and helps to mold public opinion. They both carry, in organization and life, and in the careers of their graduates, the marks of every struggle through which the people of the country have passed. In their atmosphere every student should feel conscious of the great currents of history, and should lean the lesson that the most lasting changes are those built upon experience. They have an advantage over their Constitutional neighbors and over many of the state universities. … So it is that residential universities and colleges, like those of New England, of New Jersey, and of Virginia, and especially those separated from the changing and complex life of great cities, are best adapted to transmit to the future a body of worthy ideals." (A. P. Stokes, 388)

"We can hardly overestimate the service rendered by our old collegiate foundations as links with the life of earlier generations. Harvard would not be Harvard but for her identification with the Adamses and the Lowells (and the Lodges, sic) and with many leading American men off letters of the nineteenth century. Princeton would not be Princeton without the rich associations with Revolutionary struggles and the great names of President Madison. Columbia is justly proud of John Jay and of Alexander Hamilton; and Williams of President Garfield. At Yale it is the line of theologians beginning with Jonathan Edwards, and of scientists from Benjamin Silliman on, and the figures of Nathan Hale and of Chancellor Kent, that make the spirit of the place what it is." (the spy that got caught with intelligence on him and could only muster up a patriotic oath, naturally preserved by the mindful and law-abiding royal British servants). … President Witherspoon at Princeton and President Stiles at Yale were leaders of public opinion at the time of the Revolution, and well represented the spirit of the graduates and students." (A. P. Stokes, 389-90)

Another Yaleman was Eleazar Wheelock, founder and first President of Dartmouth College. Stokes wrote, "Born in 1711 in Windham, Connecticut, Eleazar Wheelock was a farmer "of respectable New England stock", received a legacy from his grandfather, at Yale in the era of Reverend Elisha Williams, along with Aaron Burr (a Berkeley scholar at Yale, Class of 1735, elected second President of Princeton when he was only 32 years old and considered to have had a major impact on the future of the institution, and married the daughter of Jonathan Edwards, his son not a Yale man was Vice President of the US), John Sergeant, Philip Livingston and David Wooster, Peter V. B. Livingston (Class 1731, one of the original Trustees of Princeton), among other prominent Yalesians, taking morning prayer at six o'clock from spring to summer and otherwise at sunrise. College rules required students to speak in Latin "in their Chambers and when they are together". Theodore Dwight Woolsey (1801-89) of the Yale Class 1820 became President of Yale; his mother was a sister of the first President. Dwight (Yale BA 1769), making him a great-grandson of Jonathan Edwards (Yale BA 1720). (A. Stokes, Vol. II 207, "Eleazer Wheelock, Class of 1733")

"All undergraduates except who shall Read English into Greek, shall Read some part of ye old testament out of Hebrew into Greek In ye morning and shall turn some part of ye new testament out of ye English or Latin into ye Greek att evening att ye time of Recitation before they being to Recite ye original tongues." (A. P. Stokes, Vol. II, 206)

Wheelock's role was a curious one setting a pattern for good Yale tradition. Stokes: "After graduation, Wheelock entered the Congregational ministry in Lebanon Ct., Columbia Ct., founded the Moor's Indian Charity School "with the purpose of training Indians as missionaries to their own people". With his friend Harvard graduate Rev Whitaker, and the Indian Ocean, the latter two went to England to seek funds from the King and the Earl of Dartmouth, and obtained 12,000 pounds. Through Governor Wentworth, granted the charter for Dartmouth College, in 1770. Indian boys walked from Lebanon, Ct. to Hanover, New Hampshire, - 100 miles- for the auspicious beginnings of the college. Actually the royal charter established Eleazer Wheelock, "the founder of said College", as its first President, and empowered him with the right to name his successor, and that was to be his son, Rev John Wheelock, (Yale 1771) left New Haven to join his father in New Hampshire. (A. P. Stokes, Vol. I, 210)

And here is Stokes on the guiding ethos inculcated into young minds of the Ivy League: "The fact is that American collegiate history is full of romance and of thrillingly interesting occurrences of which more should be made. The founding of Dartmouth College in the wilderness by Eleazar Wheelock for the purpose of education Indian youth."

YALE & THE STRANGE ROLE OF DANIEL COIT GILMAN ('52 SKULL & BONES)

Member of Russell Sage Foundation Daniel Coit Gilman was Yale Class 1852. Gilman's career is especially revealing and extremely rich with importance to the founding of the Consortium ethos and the spirit of Yale. He became the first President of Johns Hopkins University. Born in modest conditions in Norwich, Connecticut, Daniel Coit Gilman son of a merchant, lead member of the Linonian Society, which according to his classmate Andrew D White was "then in all its glory – the oldest and probably the best debating society in the United States". Gilman was editor of *Yale Literary Magazine*, and in his senior year becomes chairman of the Board of Editors. It is perhaps the oldest of American college magazines. In his essay, one of many, titled 'The Claims of Yale College to the Regard of its Students', he wrote "What makes the jurist tired and weary with his public life, return to the Academic shades, and stroll around to find the faces of those who one knew him and the places he once knew? What makes the Reveries of a Bachelor turn back to college as 'the noon of his life?' What makes the poet linger here for inspiration and find it in these college haunts?

"Behold the undergraduates, moreover, possessed of an *esprit du corps* which makes them all desire to aid, befriend and counsel one another, to preserve memorials of college life, and when the day of parting comes, to part with real fraternal feelings. Tell me, both graduates and undergraduates, is it not true that the simple words 'Yale College' are always enough to draw your immediate attention? ...Are not your sympathies more easily awakened for one in public life, whose name may be found on the triennial? And do you not lament a death more keenly, because the life was past at Yale, and the number of your brothers therefore has been lessened?"

"Yes, I am sure you all will bear witness, that Yale College is which your sentinel gives instant heed. Men who have been educated here, may seal their hearts against the stranger's approach – they may firmly lock with 'permutation fastenings' each entrance to their feelings, but if you wish to know what arrangements of the letters of the key will fling back the bolts and open wide the door, you will see it in the four which form that suggestive and potent word of *Yale*!" (A. P. Stokes, 267)

Among Gilman's numerous accomplishments he edits de Tocqueville's *Democracy in America*, and *Life of James Dwight Dana*, considered by Stokes to be "of special interest to Yale men", and "an ideal citizen" "active in the establishment and management of local philanthropies, was a member of the school board, and was on the commission to draft a new city charter...one of a Yale majority of three on President Cleveland's Venezuelan Commission, is a trustee of the Slater and Peabody funds for education in the South, and of the Russell Sage Foundation, and was one of the incorporators of the General Education Board...served as President of the American Oriental Society, of the American Bible Society, and the National Civil Service Reform League." Gilman leaves Johns Hopkins to take over as President of the Carnegie Foundation in order, he proclaims, to assume leadership in "the advancement of teaching" in America.

"YALE, THE MOTHER OF COLLEGES"

"The University's main contribution to education has been the impress it has made upon the minds an character of its graduates. Our United States would be a very different place were it not for the leaven of that measure of wisdom and of culture which historic universities have been trying to supply or over two centuries. ... No other American school o higher learning has, through a long history, contributed more regularly to the production of able men of high purpose who have founded and conducted the colleges scattered throughout the land. This zeal for education is part of Yale's inheritance from her founders, to whom preaching and teaching, the church and the school, were merely two sides of the same shield." William L Kingsley's much referred to study, *Yale College* (1879), includes a chapter tit-led "Yale, the Mother of Colleges". (A.P. Stokes, V. II, Chap III: "Educational Leaders, The University's Contribution to Education")

Stokes writes, in 1914, "Of its justification there can be no doubt, and cited "one hundred and fifty-seven graduates who have been college presidents". Johns Hopkins, Cornell, King's (Columbia) College, Dartmouth, Williams, Hamilton, University of Georgia, Kenyon, Tulane, University of Chicago etc. Yalesians ventured coast to coast with expansion and nation-building across the frontiers founders of state as well as privately endowed institutions including Ohio University "the oldest college in the Northwest Territory", and the University of Minnesota. Again Stokes leaves no doubt of the importance of Yale in the heart and soul, - and backbone of the United States as it framed the laws and instilled values dear to it and calls it "the Yale inheritance, and to some extent the Yale type, as it has gone through the country". Stokes writes, "The direct influence of our alumni in this way, especially in the development of the Western states, has been very large. It is exceeded by no other contribution which the University has made to national life, and has not been equaled in the same field." That distinct educational or missionary was not limited to within the country's borders, and quickly evolved into an internationalism of a very peculiar nature to shape the stability and conduct of foreign nations, ergo an instrument of *de facto* foreign policy.

Anson Phelps Stokes quotes "a Western university President" at Yale's Bicentennial "Most of the Yale men who have engaged in the work of education have had on them, all their lives, the stamp of Yale College, and have cherished the Yale ideas and have followed the Yale methods. A similar experience might also be made of the University's influence on educational institutions in foreign lands. Its most striking manifestation is in the Yale Mission College in Changsha, China, where graduates are attempting to adjust Yale ideals to the needs of an Oriental people." The Yale-China Mission is flourishing today through the Yale's Luce Center. (A. P. Stokes, 188, 191)

Stokes, at the end of his work puts the utmost emphasis on tradition and the earliest ties and deepest roots of the American past which he considers virtually inseparable from Yale "the priceless heritage of participation I the building of the nation." It remained in the twentieth century the indelible link to prestige and privilege, if not a moral responsibility to leadership and necessary to sustain it. "Let us not forget that association with the makers of history is, in terms of the spirit, an asset of first importance." Yale, Princeton and Harvard remained primary links with the vestiges essential to their "sacred associations of the past – the type of thing to which men of feeling are so sensitive when they enter an ancient church where good people have worshiped for centuries" as well as "a determination to meet the needs of the present and of the future". (A. P. Stokes, V II, "Historic Universities in a Democracy", 393)

It was left to Stokes to characterize the crowning persona of the consummate Yale man even when challenged by Darwinian forces asserting constant pressures to adapt and evolve through war and peace.. In his concluding remarks to his two volume quintessential history of the rank and distinction of Yale incarnating the highest values of national identity Stokes concludes, ominously, writing in the same year of the Great War: "Our most venerable universities were centers of ardent patriotism and of progress at the time of the Revolution and of the Civil War. They sent out men by the hundreds to fight the battles of liberty. This fact bound them with bands of steel to the nation's heart. They must continue to be actively on the side of progress in solving the many social, political, and industrial problems of today, or else forfeit their claim to represent the American people. Their contact with enthusiastic youth from all sections, combined with their firm sense of dependence upon the past, should make them well-balanced leaders in meeting the country's needs. The link between Harvard (1638), Yale (1701), Princeton (1746), the University of Pennsylvania (1751) and Columbia (1754 – the same year Samuel Davies returned from England funds to build Nassau Hall) – the only existing universities* firmly established with wide influence before the Revolution – and the most important chapters in our history, will be broken by any institution which, in the struggles for freedom upon us, throws its strength to the side of reaction. Universities may be liberal, as in Russia, or conservative, as in England, and yet continue forces for good. But the moment they become reactionary they will forfeit that respect of the people which is necessary for any successful institution in a democracy." (*Note by Stokes: "William and Mary (1693) and Washington and Lee (1749) are Virginia colleges rather than national universities. Dartmouth and Rutgers were founded only just prior to the Revolution (1770). Brown was established in 1765.")

In addition to over a hundred ships obtained by the Navy Department for their engagement in the 1898 Spanish-American War, the Consortium offered up their private yachts to shore up the national defense, such as "Colonel" Astor's *Nourmahal* and Hearst's *Buccaneer*, as well as four large liners used as troop transports – the *St. Paul, St. Louis, New York* and *Paris* were leased at $500 a day, large ships at 15,000 tons aptly armed with eight 5" guns and engines that could drive them at 22 knots. The latter two were renamed for the occasion, *Harvard* and *Yale*, respectively and were sadly missed at annual Yale crew races in New London that summer.

Then, on the eve of the world blowing itself up, it was Stokes final grand stroke of mastery and his most propitious rendering of American history about to seize its glory as the greatest power of the 20th century. It was Stokes' last grand "hurrah" sending the sons of the American elite of the Consortium's Ivy League to fight the war of their fathers. "It is the privilege and duty," Stokes reminded his elite "of that small group of universities whose history and constituency entitle them to be considered factors of national influence to lead the country today in interpreting its best aspirations. In this way they will be true to their past by passing on the best American traditions to the future without any break in historic continuity. *DIU FLOREAT ALMA MATER YALENSIS*."

AMERICAN EMPIRE IN "THE GREAT GAME"

The really big "Game" operates continuously seeking new players and dedicated members to keep the secrets. Many of them appear frequently in the news and on TV. Occasionally you read about in their work and family profiles. They never tell their secrets. As far as they are concerned its not for you to know how they operate inside governments, banks and international corporations. For nearly a century, in America, they owned the Game. Their educational research laboratories and espionage agencies invent ways to control how ought to people think. They fix the dialogue and frame the debate for public consumption. They control the newspapers, the ink, the press, the giant paper companies, television and radio stations. Today they want to control the Internet.

They are an organized mafia amongst themselves, shrewd, devious and artful in their cunning, diabolical in their designs, and calculations. People are reduced to the level of a statistic, a number. In their eyes, if you are not one of them, then you are only a number to be used and dispensed with at their will. Stalin understood that to the world the death on a single man might be murder, but a million was only a statistic. How could the world ever deal with a million slaughtered individuals. It was preposterous! This is what happened to the Ukrainians under the new Soviet government, financed and strengthened by the international bankers of Wall Street and their business alliances in Germany who supported Hitler. Both the Stalin communist and Hitler Nazi fascist regimes were in bed with the Americans. FDR saw, calculated and planned for war while he worried about a fascist takeover of the US government by the Consortium. So, by 1932 FDR claiming his election victory would prevent it wins the Presidency. Ostensibly America abhors fascists at home.

The American banking and industrial establishment that backed Wilson's election in 1912, pushed through the Federal Reserve banking legislation in 1913, made fortunes in WWI and were in position again in the thirties to prepare for the next war. They all expected it. War was in the air, an in their bank accounts. FDR's campaign speeches in 1936 constantly spoke against isolationism and advance of fascism in Europe. For them war was much more than a logical inevitability. It was a necessity. In the same sense the Ukrainians were doomed. They had to go. The Second World War was no accident. War like the Terror-Famine was man-made. The Consortium war planners in London, Washington and New York arranged for it, controlling events as best they could and to leave nothing to chance. Bankers do not like too much risk. Industrial corporations desire stability. For them, war is a business of massive governmental spending, public appropriations, costly infrastructure, massive production, huge profit margins and public relations twisted into news for general interest stories composed for mass consumption and Wall Street. The human factor is diminished as a necessary but insignificant liability. Human lives don't figure. Dead bodies don't sell. Public debates are always a Consortium controlled entertainment for show.

Global corporate collaboration with the Nazis went far beyond the usual routine of transacting business. Anglo-American corporations sold secrets vital to national security yet none of these Americans were put on trial at Nuremberg with their Nazi colleagues. IG Farben's Berlin N.W. 7 office is the key Nazi overseas spy center under Farben director Max Ilgner, nephew of IG Farben president Hermann Schmitz. Ilgner and Hermann Schmitz share the board table with American IG Farben fellow directors Henry Ford of Ford Motor Company, Charles E. Mitchell and of the New York Federal Reserve Bank and Paul Warburg of the Bank of Manhattan. Warburg is a key architect of the Federal Reserve Act signed by President Wilson on December 1913 and a key insider in Wilson's war trade. DuPont is deep into Farben too.

"The Warburgs were on the board of IG Farben in the US and Germany," Sutton wrote of the American-Nazi business connection. He added, "In 1938 the Warburgs were being ejected by the Nazis from Germany". It had happened with Hitler, and repeated throughout history, most recently when Saddam Hussein went haywire in Iraq. Sometimes America's monsters go out of control. Add Hitler for his part, and Stalin to the list. (Antony C. Sutton, *Wall Street and the Rise of Hitler*, Seal Beach: '76 Press, 1976)

The German industrial cartels are the backbone of Hitler's Nazi war machine. They were aided through financial manipulations of the Dawes-Young Plans in the twenties at the same time Dulles, Cravath and other Consortium lawyers secretly went through neat loopholes into backdoor German rearmament deals. By 1933 US ambassador Dodd directs them sometimes begrudgingly through the revolving door of embassy protocol straight into Hitler's central bank.

The timing of FDR's recognition of the USSR was odd. Further, negotiations between Bullitt and the Soviet rep Maxim Litvinov were bogged down over a hotly contested debt owed National City. Compared to American Consortium investment in the Nazi Republic, which confused the Soviet spy network, Bullitt's Russian mission seems comic bordering on the absurd, a most curious side-show that monopolized time, energy and became the butt of many sardonic jokes by FDR himself. It can better be understood as a deliberate ruse by FDR intended to test Stalin, and shadow Washington's overall war strategy in Europe, Russia and the Far East. The Consortium banks and investors were spending billions on reconstruction and infrastructure. Why stumble over a few million, most of it inflated back interest? Write it off and move on! But the bankers wanted their money. Or did they? For what it looks like Roosevelt played the bankers too.

The Russians would soon pay big time in blood. Tens of millions of dead Russians. Rivers of blood pouring down the Dnieper into the Crimea and the Black Sea. Stalin too played his own cat and mouse game with Bullitt all the while the extermination of Ukraine's population took its toll day by day – from illiterate peasants to nationalist intellectuals. It provoked not a single official protest from the White House.

This was a double-edged tragedy. These industrial cartels delivered the Nazis to power in 1933 at the very time of an acute period of the Ukraine Genocide. US-owned companies like IG Farben, GE, Standard Oil of New Jersey (Exxon) and Ford, for example, knew about the Holodomor from German consulates in Kiev and Kharkov. The officers of Germany's Foreign Service were precise and methodical. Germany's economic growth prospered with Soviet orders. These same cartels empowered and financed Hitler with funds directly transferred from Farben and GE to Chancellor Hitler through the Consortium's own Nazi banker Hjalmar Schacht who we know is a Morgan breed.

The famine is common knowledge to the Morgan bankers as well as to other facilitators in the Consortium. Its an unpleasant business, rather but German reports of the famine are detailed and accurate. The German specialist on Russian agriculture, Otto Auhagen, writing in the well-informed *Berlin Osteuropa* August 1932, described the situation in rural districts of the Ukraine... as *'famine in the full sense of the word'*. This is sent from the Riga office in Latvia to State in Washington. Dr. Auhagen leaves the German embassy in Moscow where he had been agricultural expert, and now directs the Osteuropa Institut in Breslau. The gravity of the famine is common knowledge to diplomats in London and Washington. Many of these reports in their original form most probably disappeared in the destruction of the War. (italics added)

More famine reports came from Dr. Otto Schiller, German agricultural attaché and Auhagaen's trusted colleague. Schiller is one of the best-informed foreigners in Moscow. His 1932 field reports described in detail the dire conditions overtaking the Soviet countryside during a long tour with a modestly exacting and little known Canadian wheat expert Andrew Cairns working for the Commonwealth. Some of his findings appeared in a German article published February 1933. The British FO had already transmitted Cairns' reports via their ambassador in Moscow Sir Esmond Ovey. Wishing not to offend Germany and avoid a scandalous investigation with ripples in the world press the Soviets merely dismiss the reports by Schiller and Auhagen as "impudent and undisguised espionage".

More reports arrive from the Italian consulates. The Italians also keep reports and could easily inform the West. "As early as 1928 officials of the Italian Consulate, who were analyzing the situation of the peasants and the government's policies toward them, say that famine is to be expected, and that the communists' own actions "are building up the counter-revolution." (Otto Auhagen, "Wirtschaftslage der Sowjetunion im Sommer 1932", *Osteuropa* 7, Aug. 1932; "As early as 1928", cited by Yuriy Shapoval, "Foreign Diplomats on the Holodomor in Ukraine", *Holodomor Studies*, 2009)

Two months after relaying his information about the existence of famine to the US Embassy in Moscow, Harvard's Russian studies professor Bruce C. Hopper actually catches up with the young Welshman Gareth Jones. It was propitious that these two young men should meet. Both were Russian experts with knowledge of the catastrophic famine conditions in the Ukraine. Hopper is an American, Jones a Brit. Hopper earned his Ph.D at Harvard in 1930. Both are at the start of their careers with access to Pilgrims and other insiders of the trans-Atlantic Consortium. Both have communicated their concern. Their timely encounter should not have been uneventful. Together they could very well have exploded Stalin's Genocide of the Ukraine wide open. Jones too had the easy choice to work for his Consortium masters and take the long safe road or court high risk and an untimely end, often the price of holding on to uncompromised moral ideals and passionate beliefs instilled in the rebel cry of youth. If they had acted differently, would history have been any different?

Military agent, political spy, Ivy League academic whatever the role Bruce Hopper is always the Consortium player. From the start he becomes Harvard's proud and respectable authority on Russian Soviet affairs and associate professor (1937-60) teaching the elite including the Kennedy sons Joseph, John and Edward. Hopper was thesis adviser for JFK. Author of a well-known book *Why England Slept*, Hopper screens and filters young men for government work and was on the payroll of the US Air Force, and a frequent guest lecturer on Soviet and Cold War politics at military institutions. It has been said that Bruce Hopper was the first OSS man.

Fate promised contrary destinies. Hopper will live a long career as an illustrious academic don tucked away safely at Cambridge inside Harvard even when doing intelligence gathering in Soviet Russia during the Holodomor for State; in June 1942 he is sent for the OSS to set up operations in Sweden. Gareth Jones has the selfless courage to tell the truth and will soon die for it. They cross paths in September. Jones informs his two handlers – Lloyd George in London, Rockefeller publicist Ivy Lee in NY: "I had a long talk with Bruce Hopper ...".

The reader will remember that Jones is a foreign policy assistant to Lloyd George, former British Prime Minister during the First World War and the Bolshevik takeover in the Russian Revolution. Lloyd George has been instrumental with Lord

Milner, Lord Robert Cecil, the trustees of the Rhodes Trust and the Rothschild-Morgan bankers backing Lenin, Trotsky and the Bolshevik coup d'état. Lord Milner and Lord Robert Cecil were both associates to the House of Rothschild banking family and Great Britain's royal family. What Lloyd George didn't tell his young protégé would kill him. When you are that close to the fire its easy to get burned. (See E. Mullins, *The World Order;* J. E. Persico, *Inside the Reich*)

The Rothschild wealth yields unsurpassed power and influence to this day. The money trusts are set up to last lifetimes and grow from generation to generation. Take a look at the uproar a few years back, in London, over bribes to the Tory Party. The public sometimes, albeit rarely, may catch a glimpse of the invisible Rothschild hand, as in a six-column London scandal story bounced in *The New York Times* late October 2008. As it happened, Nathaniel Rothschild described only as "the co-founder of the successful hedge fund Atticus Capital" was in the public eye over private remarks spread in the press involving an alleged secret donation between Oleg Deripaska, the Russian aluminum scion and reportedly "the richest man in Russia" and Britain's conservative Tory party's George Osborne. They had met at Davos, in Switzerland for the annual World Economic Forum, a genuine Consortium affair where they quietly conducted business in isolation of the island of Corfu aboard Oleg's $150 million 238-foot yacht. Even that big it comes with only a half-dozen bedroom suites. (Sarah Lyall, "A Case of Loose Lips in an Elite Social Scene Leads to Trouble for British Tories", *The NYT,* A6, Oct. 23, 2008)

There was a time when a Rothschild could speak openly of the common man being "cannon fodder" while planning a world of excavated natural resources balanced with the finest pleasures to indulge the elite. For Stalin the formula was simple and consistent with the bankers' bottom line. Reduce man to a mechanical existence extracting the maximum produce and capital with the minimum cost. The peasants supplied an inexhaustible resource of cheap slave labor. Illiterate but far from ignorant about nature and oppression, the soviet labor in the Ukraine pool of tens of millions of Slavs knew very well what to expect from the Bolsheviks enriched by their impoverishment they proudly called Soviet "justice". The more grain confiscated the better for the State. Less mouths to feed, more grain to sell on world markets. More capital to pay for technology imported from the West. Both World Wars proved the bankers maxim true. Peasants made extremely good "cannon fodder". Hitler and Stalin refined the Rothschild maxim to economize the cost of extermination with a single bullet in the back of the neck, mass starvation, mass burials with victims still alive, poison gas and crematoriums.

How many people know that the Bank of England is controlled in part by the Rothschild and Schroeder financial interests linked to the consolidated Rockefeller and Morgan firms as they evolved from merger and acquisition to this day. For example, Rockefeller and Chase-Morgan firms have long been linked to the New York Fed, Standard Oil, the Meyer family to Allied Chemical, and Morgan's Equitable Life. That combination at present continues to exert controls directly and indirectly on many of America's common household firms like Chrysler, GM, Firestone, R. H. Macy, Northwest Airlines, AT&T, American Express, Hewlett

Packard, Exxon, Wachovia, General Electric, Scott Paper, R.J. Reynolds, US Steel, Sperry Rand, an so on. The US Fed banks of Boston and New York tie up neatly with the Schroeder–Rockefeller-Morgan-Carnegie interests.

That includes a huge list of corporations which include Mellon National, New England Telephone, Equitable Life, Twentieth Century Fox just to name a few. Andrew Mellon, for example, had to resign from fifty directorships when he was publicly appointed Treasury Secretary. William Hoffman's unauthorized biography of Mellon, *Paul Mellon—Portrait of an Oil Baron* (1974) observed how a Congressional investigation of Mellon Bank revealed incredible wealth and influence interlocking directorships with four major chemical companies, twelve steel companies, along with Westinghouse Electric and General Electric, two conglomerates with significant investments in Nazi Germany and communist Russia. The same pattern is repeated with the Rockefeller brothers, sons of JDR Jr.: JDR III, Nelson Aldrich, Laurence Spelman, Winthrop, and David.

Today the Mellon empire is financially thriving, as is its celebrity with Yale's endowment posterity. Today Mellon is a Yale icon and a favorite advertiser in chic reborn *The New Yorker* magazine targeting well-heeled left-wing intellectuals and trust fund baby-boomers descended from the Cold War. Admission is free to the Mellon Museum, adjacent to Vanderbilt Hall and Skull & Bones, and that's very rare in America, indeed. With billions surpassing into trillions, the Mellons can well afford it. (William Hoffman, *Paul Mellon—Portrait of an Oil Baron,* 1974)

Upon returning to London from Soviet Ukraine, Gareth Jones writes Ivy Lee. Apparently Jones is not unaware of the extent of Lee's Rockefeller connections and uneasy about his zeal in promoting Soviet socialism. Westerners returning from summer travel carried with them horrid tales of widespread starvation. Bruce Hopper was more cautious. Hopper knew Moscow's foreign correspondents and how they parlayed their careers and journalism. But even Hooper could not remain silent, and in the dead of summer 1932 he sent word to his friend Bob Kelley at State that "there is definite famine in Ukraine."

As long as Bruce Hopper keeps tight-lipped about Consortium politics it pays off for him if not for that alone as Harvard rewards him making him director of its Russian Studies department. Hopper makes it his career. Why should he trade off an outstanding academic distinction as a para-government spokesman and intelligence operative. Hopper is frequently asked to teach at US military education centers.

No man probably did more than anyone to keep silence over the Holodomor than Hooper's friend from Harvard, Robert Francis Kelley (1894-76), the State's top man on the Soviets. As part of his functions during the phase of US recognition of the USSR, Bob Kelley prepares a "Daily Report for Eastern Europe" for the Secretary of State and the President. A former junior military intelligence officer during the First World War, Kelley stays in the US Army. After the Armistice Kelley is sent to the Baltic countries and became a keen Russian observer based in Riga on Latvia's eastern border with Russian frontier. In 1922, he returns to Washington and joins the State Department's Eastern European Affairs Division handling matters pertaining to Russia including Siberia, Estonia, Finland, City of

Danzig, Latvia, Lithuania, and Poland. With George Kennan and Loy Henderson he remains until FDR shuts it down in 1937 under pressure from the White House.

In 1926 Kelley takes over as head of the Far Eastern Division after the promotions of Evan Young and William R. Castle who remains a key Stimson's aide since 1918 when he heads the Division of Eastern European Affairs. As far as promotion in the Consortium it doesn't much matter that Kelley is Harvard. Even with all the points earned from his participation in the Holodomor hush-up Kelley comes from the wrong side of the Charles River, born in Somerville across from Cambridge, – Massachusetts, not England.

An obedient Foreign Service careerist, Kelley at least is assured the perks and security of the loyal insiders role as the State Department's key point-man in the Terror-Famine. Hopper writes Kelley. Kelley writes Phillips. Phillips informs Stimson. Stimson chats with President Hoover. Although Kelley thought he deserved the top Russian job at State, it's not going to happen. Kelley Harvard, Bullitt Yale. Different colours but the same beast.

It's not insignificant that both Kelley and Bullitt came of age with their generation during the First World War. Both share experience with the early Bolsheviks. Bullitt has what Kelley lacks, – money, social connections, and flair but most people at State find Bullitt outrageous. Between him and Stimson there is certainly no love lost. Stimson considers Bullitt lacking in character, eccentric and too unpredictable to be trusted with secrets of national security. Bill Bullitt has both wit and charm; Kelley neither. And, to be sure, Bullitt has performed special intelligence work for Col. House.

Bullitt marries Louise Bryant, adding fury to farce, on December 5, 1923 three years after her close friend and lover John Reed died of typhus in Russia. The marriage is doomed. So was Reed. Lenin, too. Within weeks Lenin loses his mistress Inessa Armand, a beautiful sexually liberated French woman he had met in Paris in 1910. Ten years later Lenin sends Inessa to the Caucasus to restore her health but she dies there of cholera. When Lenin receives an urgent telegram and is gravely shocked and devastated by the loss of his lover. It was a rude blow, but then compounded with the death of his favorite American comrade who sat near him on the Politburo. Afterward Lenin's own health rapidly deteriorates. This is a time when people are dropping dead like flies from typhus, influenza and starvation and before Hoover's ARA mission arrives to stop it from infecting all of Europe.

The Bullitt-Bryant marriage is a disastrous union that destroys her. If anyone had the wisdom to know how she had been taken by a living death she did haunted by memories of the man she loved and lost too soon.

From the beginning the marriage is doomed. Bullitt claimed to be the father. She had love in her heart only for Jack. Reed was a radical socialist and poet who shared writing classes with T. S. Eliot, both Harvard Class of 1910, and overnight became one of the best writers and foreign correspondents in America, heir apparent to Jack London who he eclipsed in his reporting on the Mexican revolution even though he published in the Morgan-owned press. Soon after he met Bryant in Greenwich Village and they became lovers. Blacklisted by Teddy Roosevelt and the Consortium-owned press for his outspoken opposition to the war (and having boasted of firing a gun from the German trenches towards the French lines) late summer 1917 Reed is on the government's black list, censored and gagged by Wilson's draconian Sedition Act; no newspaper will touch him so he travels to Russia and there on scene and witnesses the Bolshevik coup while dashing about with diplomats and spies of the American colony. He very quickly befriended Lenin and Trotsky and crossed over to the Bolshevik side. His story is a world scoop, *Ten Days That Shook the World. The New York Times* rated it among the top ten best books of the 20th century. Stalin, however, was never too keen about the book that barely mentions his name. It has been suggested that Reed may have been a double-agent, too, – so many people had suspicious associations in this hectic period, – but in decades of biographical research that speculation remains unsubstantiated. Overshadowed by Lenin and Trotsky, his book is suppressed under Stalin who even had the book rewritten to increase his own prestige.

He spent his time handling spies and other emigrants while processing reports to Washington on Russia and Bolshevism. As a Department analyst Kelley was as familiar as anyone in Washington of the details of Bolshevik terror under their leaders Lenin and Trotsky, and now Stalin. (Virginia Gardner. *Friend and Lover: The Life of Louise Bryant,* NY: Horizon Press, 1982)

From the beginning Kelley and his team fill their files with reports with traces of the millions of Ukrainians killed. Reader beware of that there can be no doubt. The burden of proof that it was otherwise is theirs alone. It is their job to know. This is what they do. It is why they are there, to watch and observe, and inform their superiors in Washington. Along with George Kennan from Princeton (1925), Bob Kelley worked with Chip Bohlen (1904-1974), an insider from the prestigious St. Pauls School and Harvard and best friends with Kennan. Both Kennan and "Chip" Bohlen will one day serve as ambassadors in Moscow, Kennan only briefly. Although Bohlen became Harriman's number two at the embassy in Moscow during the war, and translated for Roosevelt with Stalin and Churchill at Yalta, he never met his boss Stimson. Kelley eventually was pushed off the Russian desk by Hopkins and FDR's wife. Bohlen moved fast up the ranks becoming a White House aide at State the same year, 1945, when Kelley left but remained in government; in 1951, Kelley helps launch "Amcomlib", a Cold War propaganda agenda for Radio Liberty. He loved the work so much he stays sixteen years handling various emigré groups and moderating broadcasts disseminated in the USSR. Much of Kelley's collection over the years of Russian Soviet newspapers, periodicals and documents were saved from destruction by Bohlen who arranged their transfer to the Library of Congress. He must have been eating his heart out to see to see Kennan and Harriman take all the Consortium laurels. Like a good soldier he did his duty. (Charles E. Bohlen, *Witness to History 1929-1969*, NY: W.W. Norton, 1973)

BUT WHAT DID HE EVER KNOW OF "ARTICLE 58"?

Solzhenitsyn writes of the communist code of repression symbolized in real terror in "the heavy hand of Article 58": "Paradoxically enough, every act of the all-penetrating, eternally wakeful 'Organs', over a span of many years, was based solely on 'one' article of the 140 articles of the nongeneral division of the Criminal Code of 1926. One can find more epithets in praise of this article than Turgenev once assembled to praise the Russian language, or Nekrasov to praise Mother Russia: great, powerful, abundant, highly ramified, multiform, wide sweeping 58, which summoned up the world not so much through the exact terms of its sections as in their extended dialectical interpretation. Who among us has not experienced its all-encompassing embrace? In all truth, there is no step, thought, action, or lack of action under the heavens which could not be punished by the heavy hand of Article 58. ... All are simply criminals." (A. I. Solzhenitsyn, *The Gulag Archipelago*, 60)

Check out the Russian section again. Robert Kelley is stationed in Riga in the spring 1920. Warsaw and Poland are ravaged by violent civil war and invasion by Trotsky's Red Army. Kelley is the newly appointed assistant chief of State's Easter European Affairs Division under Evan Young. In 1924, Evan Young writes an essay titled "The Attitude of the United States Government towards the Soviet Régime" published in *The Annals of the American Academy of Political and Social Science*; in the same publication that year appears Kelley's essay "Political Organization of the Soviet Power".

The path is clear for the shuffle. Evan Young replaces Bill Castle, in 1925, to take over the Division. That year too President Coolidge gives Young a restful break in the Caribbean sun as ambassador to the Dominican Republic, replacing William E. Russell, a former Massachusetts governor sent off for one year to the land of monks and colorful water markets in exotic Bangkok and the golden court of the King of Siam surrounded by sublime Apsara dancers. (Russell has replaced ambassador Edward E. Brodie there for three years, an unusually long mission.) A few months later Kelley takes over as Division chief. Evan Young, a senior member of the Consular service is the new commissioner to the Baltic States and serves under key Consortium operative Christian Herter. He too has experience in Riga based there during Hoover's ARA famine relief mission (1921-23) and helps stabilize Lenin's Bolshevik regime over the Russians and the Ukraine. After Harvard and a trip to Europe in the Foreign Service along with Walter Lippmann and John Foster Dulles attached to the American delegation at Versailles Herter joins Hoover as his assistant in European food relief work and at the Commerce Department. Hoover then advises the six-foot-five Boston Brahmin to try politics; in 1930 Herter represents his Boston district in Congress. After the war he follows Henry Cabot Lodge and the Eastern Republicans to Paris, urges Eisenhower to run for President, vacates his seat to unsuccessfully join the race for Governor of Massachusetts, joins Dulles at State as "the number two-man in a one-man department", and when he resigns becomes the 53rd Secretary of State. When Herter went before the secret session of the Senate Foreign Relations Committee investigating the Gary Powers-piloted U-2 Richard Helms of the CIA altered his testimony; "If that's not perjury, then I don't know the meaning of the word," Herter remarks.

During the 1920s postwar boom in America when Consortium corporations become the backbone of the Soviet economy, Kennan, Loy Henderson, Kelley and western observers at State know about Stalin's system of prisons. All except for FDR who succumbs to polio paralysis in 1921 and never does regain the use of his legs. (Nobody, not voters nor adversaries and very few insiders will ever see how Roosevelt had to be carried by two men lifting a leg on each side to move the President to his automobile. He conceals that weakness too, and masters publicity shots with virtuoso skill.)

For suffering Russia these years of civil war, terrible famine, international armed intervention by America and the Allies culminate in 1924 with Lenin's death at the hands of Stalin. On top of the rubble heap high in the ancient Kremlin fortress of the great autocratic Czars Stalin oversaw a vast system of extreme repression and terror that inflicted forced famines, arbitrary arrests, purges and executions. Thousands of workers waited hours in 30-degree below zero cold weather in the snow to pay their respect to Lenin. Churchill too later regarded Lenin's death as a great national tragedy, writing "He alone could have found the way back to the causeway ... The Russian people were left floundering in the bog. Their worst misfortune was his birth … their next worse, his death."

STALIN – "MAN OF STEEL"

Stalin, the pseudonym means "Man of Steel". That should have been a warning to everybody. His real name was Josef Djugushvili. Stalin was a Georgian not a Russian. He always spoke Russian with a heavy Georgian accent. Stalin was unlike Lenin and Trotsky in almost every way except in perhaps Lenin's personal frugality. Of course, once they were installed as rulers of the former Russian empire, neither needed money. Stalin proved very resourceful for the Bolshevik intellectuals. He honored his name every day of his life.

This was Welsh journalist Gareth Jones' take on Stalin: "The secret of Stalin's power has been a matter of recent comment. It is amazing how he put out Trotsky, a man of equal, but of a more fiery and self-assertive nature. Stalin has maintained his position and advanced his strength by a special technique – achieving by seeming to put aside. He cloaks himself with the authority of the Party when it makes declarations. Yet at the same time, those are always his opinions and coincide with his will.

Christian Science Monitor reporter William H. Chamberlin, fluent in Russian and author of a dozen books including *Collectivism, A False Utopia* (1937), spends twelve years in the USSR, and taught at Harvard. He liked to tell an amusing example of his technique. "It seems that a foreign journalist put in an application to see Stalin when they were both at the same summer resort. The answer came back, 'Stalin never gives interviews unless the Party commands him to do so.' Thus does the 'man of steel' identify himself with Party discipline and play upon the Communist rule that is opposed to any kind of self-assertive flamboyant leadership."

Stalin came from a poor family. Marxist historian Roy Medvedev describes his humble beginnings in *Stalin and Stalinism* (1979): "Even as a child he was obstinate, striving for superiority, and determined to achieve fame. He was utterly contemptuous of his schoolmates when they were beaten, yet intensely afraid of being beaten himself; frequent blows at the hands of his father, whom he resembled, left the young Stalin resentful and vindictive. From an early age he loved to read, and as an adolescent was particularly impressed by a novel by the Georgian romantic, Alexander Kazbeg, titled *The Patricide*. The events of this novel take place in the 1840s and revolve around Shamil's struggle against autocracy. But the real hero is Koba, a fearless, indomitable fighter, who provided the young Djugashvili with the image of his own ideal. He began to call himself 'Koba', forcing his friends to call him by this name as well. Not an intellectual, he was profoundly affected by his early education."

Taught to become a Georgian Priest, Djugashvili shirks it off after five years of instruction at the church school in Gori and three more at the Tiflis Theological Seminary. His early years shape his personality and character that turn him into a ruthless trickster and absolutely corrupting usurper. He actually revels with insatiable delight over his power to deceive and inspire terror in other men and women, encouraging him, to be sure, – and this is no new discovery –, in later years to reap devastation as well as exalting adulation from millions of followers who worship and fear him reducing their admiration to a sort of primordial idol worship. Stalin becomes their proletarian savior, their new Czar, their contemporary Godhead.

Medvedev writes, "Life at the seminary was dominated by obscurantism, hypocrisy, and mutual denunciation; in that atmosphere students learned to be cunning and resourceful as well as dogmatic and intolerant ... Stalin never forgot the years he spent at the Tiflis seminary." Stalin became active in Social Democratic Party in 1908 robbing banks and forcing "expropriations". (Roy Medvedev, *On Stalin and Stalinism*, Oxford Univ. Press, 1979)

Early on Stalin learns fast how to survive and make the exploit the real advantages of bureaucracy by placing his supporters in choice positions throughout the Party hierarchy. This is common to any power entrenched hierarchy. The Consortium uses the same device. As early as 1912 he is part of the Central Committee. Stalin seizes control of the Purge committees. Initially Stalin supports Bukharin and the NEP, but as Lenin's influence waned Stalin mounts intrigues to subvert Trotsky. He simply out-maneuvers him.

In 1924, the year Lenin dies Stalin published the pamphlet, "Socialism in One Country". It is perceived as an attack on Trotsky who believes in the need for world revolution if socialist communism were ever to succeed. Whereas Trotsky does not oppose the concept of building Socialism in one country, Stalin departs from the former Bolshevik doctrine that world revolution is necessary for the Russian revolution to survive, stating that Socialism could be built in one country but could not be complete until revolution erupts all over the world.

By 1925, Kamenev and Zinoviev realized that Stalin is a mortal enemy out to get absolute power. Their alliance with Trotsky comes too late. Stalin dominates the party apparat although the chairmanship of the Politburo is occupied by Zinoviev (1922-24), succeeded by Kamenev (1924-25). However, they are helpless in the face of the Stalin-packed Party Congress and Supreme Soviet, as well as his control of the radio and the press.

In order to stay in the Party they backtrack, deviate with another tactic in reverse; they decide to admit they were in the wrong. His game of playing opponents off against one another is obvious in the Party debate on industrialization (1924-27) which turns out to be the last openly public policy debate in the Communist Party until Gorbachev's 1988 CP conference.

Since there was agreement by all leaders on the need to industrialize the USSR (in 1924, Russia is renamed the Soviet Union, or the Union of Soviet Socialist Republics), the debate focuses on how fast and by what means to proceed. There are two opposing sides: the "Right" led by Bukharin and supported by Stalin, argues for the continued development of agriculture within the NEP framework leaving private, family farms to produce within traditional communes (*mirs*). They argue that surplus production should be exported to obtain capital for investment in industry; the "Left", led by Trotsky and supported by the economist Yevgeny A. Preobrazhensky (1886-37), himself soon exiled with the Trotsky Leftists along with Leonty Rakovsky and G. L. Pyatakov, one of Lenin's closest collaborators and both liquidated in the 1937 trial purges denounced for the famine "irregularities", scapegoats neatly disposed of for wanting to "bleed" the peasants by collectivizing the farms to control production and prices. The net difference between the higher prices from state shops in the towns and the state prices for food produce paid to the collective farms failed to provide sufficient capital to pay for industrialization. Trotsky proposes a 10% annual growth rate in industrial production; Stalin supports the "Right" and openly ridicules Trotsky's proposal as "unrealistic."

In 1928 Stalin pushes ahead with his Plans for Collectivization and Industrialization. Finally its time for Trotsky to go; Stalin deports the creator of the Red Army to Alma Ata, Kazakhstan, in January and, later that year, expels him from the Soviet Union. For the next decade Trotsky remains Stalin's eternal Enemy No. 1. The "Red Lion" continues to oppose Stalin from abroad until he's murdered in 1940 by a Stalin agent in Mexico. Only after Gorbachev comes to power do Russians find the grand maestro of the Bolshevik Revolution mentioned in Soviet texts. (R. Medvedev, 1)

AMERICA'S HOLODOMOR STATE DEPARTMENT & THE FED

Forced-labor camps in Siberia became the pillar of that system as one of the principal techniques by which Stalin exerted absolute control over Russia and the Republics. The State Department's Loy Henderson provides one of the few portraits of his boss Bob Kelley, the man most responsible for reading and processing sensitive information before, during, and after the Holodmor Genocide streaming into Washington destined for Stimson and the White House all packed with eye-witness details about Stalin's carefully orchestrated famine and system of State Terror.

Henderson recalls how his friend at State Bob Kelley, at 31, "was at the time the youngest assistant chief of a political division .... I found that an exception had been made partly because Young, under whom Kelley had worked in Riga, had insisted that the latter be his first assistant, and partly because during the year that Kelley had served in the division he had displayed both marked ability and stamina."

Bullitt on the other hand acts at times more like a royal sycophant and an upper-class odd-ball dashing from palace to palace which is fine among the insiders where animated eccentricities are common and so not entirely out of place and even adds a colourful diversion to the all too-often sedate diplomatic set punctuated with a fair share of Anglophiles leftover from the last century. FDR keeps a jar of affectionate nicknames for Bullitt. Stimson prefers other company and keeps his distance. Kelley, however, is and will always be an outsider, an anti-communist, low-level civil servant tool working for the Consortium. In this way Kelley not unlike professor Dodd, the discreet aged scholar-historian whose unemotional objectivity inspires the trust of the President until his diplomatic shortcomings become a problem with Hitler and his Nazi chums in Berlin.

Anyone wishing to enter the reading room of Yale University Archives must first pass through a cherished gateway under the life-size oil portrait of Colonel Edward M. House peering down from his eternal resting place. What makes the eerie feeling of his cryptic stare even more bizarre is that he never studied at Yale nor was he ever a military man per se.

Texas power-broker and close adviser of President Woodrow Wilson, in 1912, House published *Phillip Dru: Administrator*, a sort of quixotic attempt at literary self-indulgence. He used it to promote, he writes, "socialism as dreamed of by Karl Marx". So one might have thought House a closet Marxist.

The next year President Wilson in his first months in the White House and just two days before the Christmas break rammed the Federal Reserve Act through Congress creating America's new central banking system. It was neither federal nor a reserve. It had originally been planned at a secret meeting in 1910 on Jekyl Island a 6000-acre enclave isolated off the Georgia coast. There a group of bankers and politicians assembled including Col. House, Morgan's Henry Pomeroy Davison and Frank A. Vanderlip of National City.

Very few know that Jekyl Island had been taken over in 1886 by J. D. Rockefeller and a few of his special friends as a winter retreat far from peering eyes of the annoying press and public. With their extraordinary wealth, the Consortium kingpins – JDR, Astor, Gould, Morgan, Pulitzer, Vanderbilt, Harriman *et cetera* -, all built huge mansions. Jekyl is their very own private island club, – one among the many dozens – but this one had the richest combined membership estimated at *one-sixth* of the world's wealth. Jekyl is a Consortium haven. Secluded in their private mansions of this tiny island retreat off the coast of Georgia the bankers scheme how their central bank would control peacetime economies and manage the financial exchanges necessary to make world war profitable for their banks and industries. The bankers' Federal Reserve Act transferred the power to create money from the American government to a group of bankers who then financed the First World War for the Bank of England and the Bank of France. Whoever said that the Fed was a government-controlled bank got confused in the nuance.

In his first year of office President Woodrow Wilson in 1913 has strong doubts about a relatively small group of men controlling the national currency. Its power remains undiminished, its secrets and inner workings guarded and as little understood by the public today as it was then. Not much has changed since except the millions became billions then trillions.

During his jaunt in Moscow, Bill Bullitt did little more than house-keeping and bill collecting for National City. To FDR he boasts how he had charmed Stalin to find a building for the new US Embassy and Consulate no less impressive than Jefferson's Monticello and entertains the diplomatic and Kremlin Communist Party hierarchy. Often bored and "homesick", Bullitt takes ample opportunity to skirt about Europe and frequently meets with Dodd in Berlin. Alarmed over American industrial and financial backing of Nazi fascism, Ambassador William Dodd has no warm feelings for the Morgan-Rockefeller-Harriman Consortium and their years of collaboration with Hitler's industrial fascists. In fact Dodd loathes them with a natural suspicion and instinct worthy of his best nature. Dodd keeps a detailed diary and sends frequent reports to Hull.

WHO WAS CORDELL HULL?
WHAT TO DO WITH SUMNER WELLES?

Few Americans today have even the slightest notion. Nor should they. Fate is not kind to Hull. As FDR's Secretary of State in 1933 he served his master until a bitter retirement November 1944. The next year before his unceremonious exit by the rear Hull is rewarded with the Nobel Peace Prize for his lackey devotion to the Consortium agenda – and for staying out of Roosevelt's hair.

The man who presided over the foreign policy of the United States survived unstained by the famine-terror years. Quiet and soft-spoken, Hull was a former US Army captain in the American Spanish War when over a million Philippine natives were killed, many of them tortured – a little known "item" of history not taught in American high schools. Hull served as a federal judge and congressman in Tennessee from 1907-21. He, too, has a role in the national scheme of America's powerful banking establishment behind the new Federal Reserve Banking system. On the powerful Ways and Means Committee Hull favors low tariffs and claimed authorship of the Federal Income Tax bill as well as the federal State income tax laws of 1913, and Inheritance Tax bill three years later in 1916.

Hull was never a specialist in foreign policy and he impressed his British counterparts no less.

At the wartime Quebec Conference wrangling with British foreign minister Antony Eden, Sir Alexander Cadogan called Hull "a dreadful old man", effuse and incomprehensible "and rather pig-headed, but quite a nice old thing, I dare say." (T. Morgan, 687)

Undersecretary Dean Acheson had been at State when Hull was Secretary, and writes sparsely of him in his memoirs. A veteran of long sometimes painfully enduring years playing FDR's paper Secretary Hull had told his close friend Breck Long faithfully by the Secretary's side since his return from a trip abroad to Europe that he'd resign after the 1944 November election. Long wrote in his diary, "It was a somber conversation. ... He was tired of intrigue ... tired of being by-passed ... tired of being relied upon in public and ignored in private ... tired of fighting battles which were not appreciated ... tired of making speeches and holding press interviews—tired of talking and tired of service. ... The end of a long career is at hand – ending not in satisfaction, as it should, but in bitterness." (D. Acheson, 86.)

Cordell Hull is not "in" with the Consortium bankers. Hull was tall and proud with a dignified humility that might have otherwise have passed off as obsequious obedience to Roosevelt's infectious personality and the awesome power of the Executive. His is a Southerly nature formed in his youth. Born on October 2, 1871, young Hull was raised in a rented log cabin with only two-windows on the front, in Brydstown, Overton (Pickett) County on the foothills of the Cumberland Mountains in Tennessee recalling the style of Abe Lincoln and Dick Nixon.

The most distinguished thing about his family past is perhaps that his father as a Confederate soldier in the American Civil War had his nose shot off by a Yankee. Hull was one of five sons taught how to read and write by their mother Elizabeth. Seven people in that house no bigger than a shoe-box. The kids were trained in Bible school at the local Baptist church. Hull's own father, in fact, was a a farmer and logger, but that didn't bring him any closer to the wheat fields or timber camps in Russia. Nothing would. His father moved to Carthage and went into business for himself setting up a general store with a post office. There he and the family prospered.

"Cord" Hull didn't have to farm or cut wood anymore, and graduated from Cumberland Law School after only ten months in 1891 and passed the exams admitted to Tennessee bar before his 21st birthday. He joins the Army as a captain ind the 1898 Spanish-American war. Five years later Hull is appointed a circuit judge, sharpens his political skills and joins the Democratic Party elected to the state legislature at 22. Since most native folks in Tennessee were farmers so Hull focused on taxes, tariff issues, agricultural imports and exports.

All that should have made Hull sensitive to his fellow farmers in the Ukraine. Yes? Not a chance. From 1903-07 Hull serves as a local judge; later he was elected to the House where he served 22 years in eleven terms (1907-21 and 1923-31). As a US Congressman Hull supported the standard democratic reforms of Wilson's administration: lower tariffs, child labor legislation, the eight hour day, but was on the wrong side of history voting against woman's suffrage and the 19th amendment. Hull's voting record was also decidedly anti-immigration. He favored a congressional act for a graduated income tax and in 1906 for the passage by Congress of the income tax 16th amendment. Methodical, legalistic, and cautious Hull was the antithesis of Roosevelt's effusive and extrovert nature.

Hull's maternal ancestors were good hard-working eighteenth century Tennessee folk. His mother was a humanitarian with a reputation for doing more than her share to care for her less fortunate brothers and sisters. If she could relieve the suffering and poverty of her community, she would do just that and they loved her for it. Tennessee liked Cord Hull. He seemed like a good man, an honest man. Hull understood the needs of poor people. He understood farmers and people who worked off the land and he would help them with their problems. People put their faith and trust in Hull. So why didn't Hull help the Ukrainians? How do such men live with their conscience?

Hull marries a woman from Staunton, Virginia, Frances Witz, the daughter of Issac Witz, a banker descended from a family of Austrian bankers and Confederate Army soldier. Her mother was a regular at the local Episcopal Church raised in "a socially prominent family with strong Presbyterian and Episcopalian attachments". She graduated from the Augusta Female Seminary, and moved to Washington. Her mother's first husband disappeared somewhere in East Asia; they waited until he was legally declared dead and marry on Thanksgiving Day November 24, 1917.

The Hulls have no children. They are an inseparable couple with unshakable religious convictions seen frequently attending Washington's St. Margaret Episcopal Church on Connecticut Avenue. After President Wilson's death in 1924 she remains a close friend of his widow. Together the Hulls live modestly in a seven-room apartment at the Carlton Hotel within walking distance to the White House. It is where they prefer to pass their quiet evenings at home rather than attend official dinners and formal receptions.

Money never impresses Hull very much. He knows his place and the power of wealth that drives men and fuels the empire. Standing next to Averell Harriman, a baronial landowner of vast estates employing small enclaves as servants, with miles upon miles of riding trails around valleys and lakes all his own, as a poor country boy Hull must have always felt the odd-ball, a politician useful to the big money men. By hard work and strict living Hull's father had lifted himself out of poverty rising from the status of a industrious small farmer to owner of a country store and speculator in real estate. When he dies in 1923, young Hull, a Tennessee congressman, made his father proud and leaves his son $200,000 of property including some land in Florida. By 1924 Hull owns six farms, a landowner in his own fashion.

When Wilson and the Democrats lose in 1920, Hull lost his seat in Congress. He stays on as Democratic Party chairman charged with rebuilding the party organization. Years later he advises Albert Gore Sr. then a junior state senator to run for the US Congress in 1938. Hull was also close to John W. Davis, the Party's nominee for President in 1924, another Morgan link towards FDR then closely allied to Al Smith. In 1927 Hull even considered his own possible role as lawyer and a trustee of the Rockefeller Foundation; he backs Al Smith in 1928 and is himself considered for nomination. "Hull for President" committees sprung up in southern states including Tennessee in anticipation of Smith losing. But a southern Democrat is too unlikely and Smith wins on first ballot. FDR favors Hull as VP with Smith, but it doesn't fly. During the Depression Hull won his Senate race in 1930. It was only in February 1932 when FDR looked strong in the presidential campaign race that Hull backed out and joined the Roosevelt lobby in the Senate as a possible running mate. John Davis will later replace Bullitt in Moscow.

So why does FDR choose a Tennessee Democrat with no experience in foreign affairs to head the State Department? Obviously FDR wants to be a hands-on President and call the shots from afar behind the curtain.

With Hull out in front, standing lean and six feet tall with dark eyes and white hair, Hull projected a proper cosmetic cover to the Ivy League clique. He looked and played the part expected of him. FDR brings Bill Phillips back to State as Stimson's virtual successor leaving Hull the work of the consummate bureaucrat leaving the Consortium press to spin the perspective and make the public think Hull is in charge. The appearance was completely different than the reality. Anyway, foreign policy is the constitutional prerogative of the executive branch with the nation's C.C. in charge.

Stimson would approve of Hull's training in law even though he's not an Andover-Yale man. Bill Phillips, too, learns to work the veteran congressman's natural restraint which makes it easier to find compromise and consensus in Congress. Phillips, Welles and others in the Consortium maintained the reality of American power abroad, and in particular, where it concerned the Ukraine and Soviet Russia while Hull shuffles the bureaucratic papers at home.

It was a tumultuous turnover of political power. Party considerations also prompted Roosevelt to add a loyal and steadfast regular from the South to his New Deal coalition. Well-known in Washington Hull had served in both houses of Congress and promoted Roosevelt's successful presidential bid culminating in the victorious return of the Democrats to the White House after more than a decade of Republican control of Washington.

Hiram Johnson, Republican senator from California tells Roosevelt in January that the new Secretary of State should be distanced from Wall Street. The Consortium gang had stacked Wilson's administration and ran that Democratic President's war cabinet and it looks bad especially during the Depression and Nye's Senate Committee investigation into war profits from the First World War if Roosevelt were to do the same. With peace more distant and war looming over European borders Americans have good reason to be sensitive about Wall Street and the failure of Hoover's disarmament talks in Geneva.

FDR assures Johnson he found someone with just the right "American outlook" who fit the mold. Hull was a favorite of FDR political adviser Louis Howe "because he reflected the domestic concerns for most American voters". Hull's selection surprised Johnson and caught Washington off-guard. Carter Glass, Virginia Democratic Senator, thought Hull was a terrible choice, unable to talk clearly or make much intelligible sense of complicated issues when the country needed clear decisions. But Senator Johnson understood Hull was harmless and would cause FDR little trouble or embarrassment and would keep quiet with the press. Hull was little more than "a pleasant, kindly disposed individual," observed Johnson, "utterly colorless, wholly without position in the body at all.

... To describe Hull as a tower of strength in the Senate, whose removal seriously affects the Senate, has been the subject of a good deal of laughter and joking the last couple of weeks. He is a nice man, and ... may develop into a great man. He has not thus far in his sixty years displayed any elements which would lead one to believe in this development."

The economy was fragile and the future uncertain. FDR sent Raymond Moley to sound Hull out for the job of Secretary of State. Hull knew it was all politics, a payback for the Southern vote, building support in Congress where the President would need it most. Hull promptly accepted the offer.

Hull kept his own comfortable circle of close advisers: Cecil "Joe", a fellow Tennessee man, and soft-spoken adviser on European affairs; his old pal George Milton, a newspaper man from home; James ("Jimmy") Clement Dunn – "Hull's closest adviser on European affairs" comes from a wealthy New Jersey family and married Mary Armour of Chicago's meat-packing fortune advanced under Hoover to be head of protocol and has family at St ate but depends on Hull for his career. In the tariff debates at the 1933 London Economic Conference Dunn played his cards right siding with his boss in the split with Moley and eventually becomes head of Western European Affairs. After Phillips resigned as Acting Secretary to replace "Breck" Long in Rome (1936) in the Welles State Department shuffle (1937), Dunn's power in Hull's office increased, a concession due more to his loyalty than brains. (T. Morgan, *FDR*, 439)

Hull is an easy target, and sometimes has to deflect heat meant for the President. Like when the *American Bulletin* in its August issue brands Hull the "Slave of Morgan and Jews". It declares, Hull "an example of American 'Statesmanship' of today. Men who are elected or appointed to an office of trust to represent the interests of the American people – the puppets of money magnates, betraying that office to satisfy the greed of money changers". Hull knows he's under the spotlight but feels in the slight a cheap personal slur and it shakes his feelings but there was truth in it and he knew it. For all the wrong they did poor Hull has to bear mean-spirited political attacks of the powerful publisher W. R. Hearst against the Consortium bankers. Hull side-steps the slander by those he says who "choose to equivocate, refusing to act boldly". FDR orders, Hull defers.

Of course Hull knows that the President ignores his advice and privately mocks him with ribald mimicry. "Far more insulting was the president's habit," the historian Irwin Gellman writes in his book *Secret Affairs* (1995), "without directly mentioning the Secretary, of condemning the State Department in public for its antiquated procedures and thus indirectly attacking the Secretary's competence. These actions deeply offended Hull. He could never fully trust a president who could publicly embarrass him and for no apparent reason. Above all else, the Secretary dreaded this kind of insult." FDR knew it, taking inane pleasure exploiting his subordinates, playing one off the other while mastering control over men and government. (I. Gellman, 99-100)

It was a curious thing. Foreign policy is the executive domain of the President. FDR replaced Secretary Stimson with someone who he could control who would be compliant to the whims of the chief executive. The Democratic Senator from

Tennessee had virtually no background in international affairs. And FDR was an ambitious President determined to make his name known forever on the world stage of history. Hull would act as FDR's figurehead, allowing FDR to run the show and reap the success. The most important foreign policy gesture of Roosevelt's first year in office was normalization of diplomatic relations with Russia and recognition of Stalin's Soviet terror regime and a complete turning away from the Genocide killing millions in the Ukraine, Upper Volga and the Caucasus. War threatened on the horizon in Manchuria and the Far East. While Hull sat in the head office of the State Department and into the Second World War the next generation of Americans don't even know his name, who he was or what he what his real role was for FDR's administration.

Hull's three predecessors had all been together in the clique of wealthy influential Republicans – Charles E. Hughes, Frank B. Kellogg, Henry L. Stimson. The Ivy League Skull & Bones faction entrenched more than ever continues to flourish. But times were fast changing and the Consortium needed more cover and less exposure than in the previous era now under close congressional scrutiny into the Wilson-Morgan banking imbroglio of warmongering and profits from the First World War and the *modus operandi* of America's investment in war mixed with the global investments of America's most opulent millionaires. With a Groton-Harvard elitist as President, the image of the Great Communicator wouldn't look the same if Stimson stayed in the spotlight. That was the old look. And it wouldn't appear right to have one foot in the past and one in the present going ahead to make a new future. No, that wouldn't do now would it? America had matured since the Taft-Stimson days prior to that war. On meeting Hull briefly before he left his bastion Stimson described Hull with an unflattering impression: "a tall gentlemanly man, with a pleasant Southern quiet manner, rather slow... On the whole I got a rather discouraging impression of his vitality and vigor".

The choice of Hull to head the Department sent the upper hierarchy into a spin. Why would FDR put in a man whose domestic concerns of solely an economic aspect would dictate foreign policy decisions of great political importance for the security of the country and the world? With the depressed economy Hull would push the Democratic line for a liberal free market and lower trade barriers. Undersecretary Bill Castle, sufficiently rich with a huge family fortune in Hawaii, writes Hugh Wilson February 1933: "Although he (Hull) knows nothing about foreign affairs, he is a tremendously fine man and has never believed in the spoils system". Harvard law professor, a brilliant Jew and Roosevelt insider Felix Frankfurter curries proximity to the Secretary. (re. W. Castle in I. Gellman, 21; W. Castle to Hugh Wilson, Hugh Wilson Papers, Hoover Institute, Stanford Univ.)

No matter how cunning and distasteful FDR's choice of a successor, Stimson, however, saw the pieces fall in place reassured that he would not lose his influence at State from his Woodley seclusion on the park. Bill Phillips is back in place, as uneasy as Stimson about Hull's appointment and decidedly less enthusiastic. Stimson calls the choice "lamentable" but has to live with losing Hoover. FDR intends to run his own foreign policy show keeping Stimson at arms reach but in the loop. Eight years later, when the Japanese attack Pearl Harbor, the first call

FDR makes is to Stimson then having lunch at Woodley. J. Pierrepont Moffat, Division head of Western European Affairs, perceives FDR's plan to be "his own Secretary of State in the best TR and Wilson tradition". Moffat stays eleven years with FDR and watches how the President always keeps his cards down relying on few advisers. When it came to foreign policy, FDR didn't feel obliged to be overly assertive, and it's not clear even if he had anything to assert in the wake of crushing economic domestic turmoil.

Stimson's concern shifted to alarm the next day when he learned that Roosevelt told Hull "that he intended to be his own Secretary of State, and Hull had knuckled down to it." Hull grouped had his own followers known as the "croquet clique". Hull liked to play croquet and played often during the week at Woodley, Stimson's estate near Rock Creek Park in the northwestern part of Washington in arms reach to the President. (Pratt-Hull, *Memoirs*; HLS Diary, Feb. 25, 26, 1933, Oct.18, 1933 v. 26; I. Gellman, 91-2)

FDR was a specialist in the art of diversion to conceal intrigue leaving him more options for difficult choices which lay down the road. The timely decision to put Hull in place was part of more general considerations to further Consortium strategy for America's positioning in the preparation of the future inevitable war in Europe now at risk with and the problems of Stalin's dictatorship all the more reason to by-pass any obstructionism within the State Department. Stimson had changed the script with Litvinov in Geneva. Now FDR himself would finish acting out the play. After getting his own house at home in order with New Deal reconstruction FDR took steps to deflate any antagonism against the Stalin and the Soviet regime from within Department ranks. Hull was the perfect bureaucrat, bland and unassuming without airs of social prominence. A perfect bore.

James Farley, chairman of the Democratic National Committee, FDR's campaign manager and choice for Postmaster General describes Hull as "very determined in his opinions", which may well be true, if and when he had them, and although he would never show it he could be at times "a bit domineering". Hull went along playing with the team and even would go out of his way to get "along well with other men". Hull would not make problems. Hull "never gets excited", Farley said. Hull would survive FDR's first term, dry and colorless, in the shadows without casting one. FDR's man to the core, he would never get the vice-presidency. The Consortium would never allow it.

This is the man that FDR put into the highest ranking position in the federal government. FDR, owner of the ship, had his captain on the bridge leaving him free to choose the course and enjoy the passage. He knew that Woodrow Wilson, and not his Secretary of State Robert Lansing made the headlines and occupied center stage. FDR intended to do the same asserting his influence in foreign affairs in much of the same manner he perceived his role the leader of the American people at home appearing to incarnate their will into his own and project it aboard albeit with little or no force at all.

A Tennessee Democrat "who had virtually no qualifications in international affairs" Hull would keep the job eleven and a half years until he was replaced on December 1, 1944 by a key Consortium player, Edward R. Stettinius Jr..

Irregardless of his modest past and uneventful career as a Senator, history cannot absolve Secretary Hull of direct complicity for his role he played to ignore and shirk responsibility of his office towards the plight of millions of Ukrainians especially at a time when Americans are still actively contributing to major agricultural and industrial projects essential to the Plans of the Consortium's support for Stalin's dictatorship of terror, forced labor and mass murder.

Dr. Stanley K. Hornbeck (1883-1966) is another key player in the US-Russian-China-Japan imbroglio. Mostly overlooked by historians Hornbeck, a Rhodes Oxford scholar (1907) enjoys his part played in Hull's "croquet clique". By the late twenties Undersecretary Hornbeck is very much on the scene and considered by the Consortium bosses as a serious highly educated, experienced career State Department man who knows just how to flatter his boss, avoid enmities, and totally loyal to the sworn mandates of the State Department mission he serves. More importantly, he enjoys Stimson's complete confidence in his expertise as they apparently try to balance the Japanese and Chinese tinderbox in Manchurian while making a mess of it and all of which will come back to bite them in the ass. Still, what they least desire now is to have a world war explode in the region. But it is still too early for that.

The presence of Hornbeck at State is a curious addition to the table. As an utterly immune technocrat he shows no compassion nor any intention whatsoever to help the Ukrainians, and this in spite of postwar experience as an intelligence gatherer for the US Army in President Wilson's exploratory mission to Armenia and the Anatolia region. Rather, Stanley evolves under his mentors into a rabid anti-communist up 'til the mid-Sixties when long since retired, he supports US armed intervention in Vietnam. A loser and for the most part forgotten among those many discarded historical figures who had considered their role so vital to the freedom and American prosperity. How is it that such personalities who appear to genuinely believe in the suppression of tyrants bent on the subjugation of nations do nothing to help the oppressed masses?

The son of a Methodist minister, he spends his childhood in the West, in Colorado, far from where he was born in born in Franklin, Massachusetts, and takes his diploma at the University of Denver (1903); four years later he studies with the sons of empire at Oxford before returning to assume a teaching post in political science at the University of Wisconsin where he picks up his Ph.D. on commercial tariff problems. Then Hornbeck is global-trotting again, this time abroad for five years as an instructor in various Chinese government institutions (Hangchow, Mukden) during the fall of the Manchu Dynasty and the Dowager Empress. Bill Phillips is also there, so is Willard Straight along with the Morgan syndicate banking crowd. Here the seeds are planted for his illustrious but brief career at State.

Back from China at Wisconsin U. the young professor Hornbeck publishes his first of eight books, *Contemporary Politics in the Far East* and it puts him on the map, a small island no doubt in a very big sea. But Dr. Hornbeck is now recognized as an "expert" now on the Far East and the Lodge, Root, Hughes and Taft masters of the senior generation need good young men to what is to come. In fact, the nation will need a plethora of able bureaucratic minded middle- managers to serve the technocracy of America's grab for empire.

Hornbeck, however, warns of Japanese expansion and future war in China threatening US interests there. The next year Hornbeck turns his back on an academic career and enters government in Washington first on Wilson's newly formed Tariff Commission, and when the America enters the war he joins the US Army's Ordnance Department where he soon captures the attention of Col. House. Hornbeck joins the 23 other members of the "Inquiry" group organized by House and dispatched to the Paris Peace Conference to solve postwar problems, in particular questions of occupation in the Far East (Tientsin, Shantung ...). (See Stanley K. Hornbeck Papers, Hoover Institution Archives, Stanford. His career history still awaits a keen biographer.)

Soon after joining the Army, Hornbeck received an invitation to join President Woodrow Wilson's Inquiry – a team of experts organized to devise postwar solutions to the world's problems, where he supervised research on Far Eastern issues. In November 1918, Hornbeck was one of the 23 members of the Inquiry chosen to accompany the American delegation to the Paris Peace Conference. In Paris in 1919, his position changed from a "general assistant" to the American delegation to the technical expert on the Far Eastern Division of the American Commission to Negotiate Peace. In the latter capacity, he represented the US on the commission studying the disposition of Tientsin and opposed (however unsuccessfully) Japanese retention of the Chinese province of Shantung. Hornbeck's mission in Paris ended on August 15, 1919. (Stanley K. Hornbeck biography, Register of the Stanley K. Hornbeck Papers, Op. cit.; Justus D. Doenecke, "Hornbeck, Stanley Kuhl," Op. cit.; Hu Shizhang, *Stanley K. Hornbeck and the Open Door Policy, 1919-1937*, Westport, CT: Greenwood Press, 1995, 45-6, 51-2; Noriko Kawamura, *Turbulence in the Pacific: Japanese-US Relations During World War I*, Praeger, 2000, 136)

Hornbeck is given an early introduction to the horrors of Armenian Genocide, and he learns the ropes how the Consortium Crowd manages to deny moral responsibility. Able to see firsthand how America intends to extend its global mission in the postwar land grab, after his first mission ends August 15, 1919 Hornbeck is promoted Captain in Wilson's American Military Mission to Armenia, a 50-member group under Maj. Gen. James G. Harbord (Commission to the Near East) dispatched from Paris on instructions from Secretary of State Lansing "to investigate and report on the political, military, geographic, administrative, economic, and such other considerations involved in possible American interests and responsibilities in the region." It would appear that their goal is to see what role if any America should play with respect to Armenia and the Asia Minor Trans-Caucasus territories (Anatolia).

In fact, there are two US government missions set up to explore the Middle East and report back to Congress on postwar problems. The other group, specifically civilian, also concerned with Wilson's League of Nations Mandate System, is headed by theologian and Oberlin college president Henry Churchill King and Democratic Party power boss Charles R. Crane (known as the King-Crane

Commission) officially called the 1919 Inter-Allied Commission on Mandates in Turkey begins work in June 1919, concerned with the disposition of non-Turkish areas within the former Ottoman Empire, and produces its report on 28 August 1919. The report is not published until 1922. By then Wilson's health failed, the country turns inward, isolationist, weary of foreign commitments, and a new Republican administration has taken control of the White House spirited by a Republican majority in Congress. Arriving in Istanbul (Constantinople) to confer with the Ottoman government. The delegation proceeded by train to Adana, Aleppo, and Mardin then by motor car through Diyarbakir, Harput, Malatya, Sivas, Erzincan, Erzurum, Kars, Etchmiadzin, Erivan, and on to Tiflis. Part of their group breaks off at Sivas to study conditions at Marsovan, Samsun, and along the Black Sea coast reaching as far as Trebizond. In Eastern Anatolia the Harbord report observes the local inhabitants are predominantly Turks stating "the temptation to reprisals for past wrongs" would make it extremely difficult to maintain peace in the region." The King-Crane group toured areas of Palestine, Syria, Lebanon, and Anatolia. In both cases, the missions are basically abortive exercises in the politics of diplomacy as both Great Britain and France have spurned Wilson's League, concluded their business at Versailles with their secret treaties still intact. Notwithstanding, the awkwardness of British translators, and the evident profound distaste for either British or French overseers as colonial powers, the American commissions was successful in conducting the first-ever public survey of Arab popular opinion to determine their readiness for self-determination. (James G. Harbord, *Report of the American Military Mission to Armenia,* US Government Printing Office, 1920)

To insure the growth of independent self-sufficient states, the King report recommends American occupation of the region instead of imperial domination by the British or French. But it won't fly in the US Senate, in 1918 under a Republicans majority in the Senate. The proposed Palestine mandate collapsed under provision drafted in the Treaty of Sevres. War Prime Minister Lloyd George comments that "the friendship of France is worth ten Syrias." In the secret treaties France seizes Syria while Britain snatched Mesopotania (Iraq) and Palestine. The report isn't made public until 1922 and then only after the US Senate and House passes a joint resolution favoring the establishment of a Jewish National Home in Palestine along the lines of the Balfour Declaration.

By this time public opinion is too divided to do anything about the Arab appeal for an American mandate with a democratically elected constituent assembly. Its particularly interesting to note currently given the Syria crisis and Assad's genocidal assault on the country's population that at the time of the Commission the delegates termed the territory it was investigating "Syria" covering the Arab territories of the defunct Ottoman Syria, or what would today encompass Syria, Lebanon, Israel, Jordan and the Palestinian territories. It further concludes, in 1922, that the Middle East is not ready for independence and urged Mandates be established to further the process of transition to self-determination. The King-Crane report is also noteworthy in regard to commitment towards the creation of a Jewish state in the Middle East. "Not only you as president but the American people as a whole should realize that if the American government decided to support the establishment of a Jewish state in Palestine, they are committing the American people to the use of force in that area, since only by force can a Jewish state in Palestine be established or maintained." For his part, Crane opposes the establishment of a Jewish state, while remaining an outspoken advocate of the independence of the Arab states, alarmed widespread anti-Zionist hostility in Palestine and Syria, and unwilling to underestimate the holy nature of the land for both Christians and Moslems nor should the Jews be given preference when their population attributes to only 10% of the peoples of Palestine. *Hornbeck's commission favors the creation of an Armenian state and dismisses Turkish claims to respect Armenian rights in the future.*

Hornbeck returns to the Tariff Commission, but Wilson's new minister to China Charles Crane in March 1920 taps him to as his private secretary on his extensive travels through China's interior. Hornbeck quickly becomes Crane's confidant and adviser, but Harding's Republican victory obliges them to pack their bags. No problem for Crane. With no time to lose, Flush with war profits while the empires are bankrupt, and now the world's banker, a creditor to debtors, America is anxious to capitalize on its heightened status in world affairs recalled to Washington. His work finished with King officially ends July 2, 1921. By then he and Hornbeck are already on the Manchurian railway to Siberia arriving there late June at Chita, then the capital of a short-lived "buffer" Far Eastern Republic commonly known in Russia as DVR, by the abbreviation of its Russian name. There Hornbeck assists Crane in meetings with the DVR minister of foreign affairs Ignaty Yurin (pseudonym of Polish-born revolutionary Ignatii Leonovich Dzevaltovsky/ Ignacy Gintowt-Dziewałtowski in the DVR). Crane gives assurances that America will take steps to end the Japanese occupation of part of the Maritime Region and Siberia.

On July 2 permission arrives from Moscow granting Crane the rights of passage; Crane leaves Chita traveling in his private railway coach "as a private citizen" en route to Prague across revolutionary Russia. US Army Captain Hornbeck meanwhile stays on in Chita where he met Boris Skvirsky acting as assistant foreign minister of the DVR. They plan to meet again in the US. Hornbeck makes his way to Vladivostok and sails to Japan, checks in at the US Embassy in Tokyo. and receives his instructions from State to proceed to Washington, DC for his new assignment as a delegate at the forthcoming Washington Conference on Limitation of Armaments (November 12, 1921 to February 6, 1922.).

America and Japan are now the two biggest war powers and future rivals. At State Hornbeck joins a small group in the Office of Economic Advisers attached as a "specialist" to its Far Eastern Division. He then resumes talks with his Soviet counterpart Skvirsky officially an "observer" at the conference as part of the DVR "trade delegation" since the breaking off of diplomatic relations between the US and Russia since the Bolshevik coup; in December 1922 Skvirsky becomes the Kremlin's top unofficial agent in the USA. The issue of non-recognition of the Soviet government is a hotly contested political issue. Commercial relations between the Consortium and the Kremlin are strictly "off the record" away from the press, and kept secret by Bill Sands and others at State.

Hornbeck finds it opportune to join the Harvard faculty, in 1924, where he lectures on the Far East. The following summer he helps create the Institute of Pacific Relations in Honolulu, a Rockefeller funded project initiated in a letter to JDR, Jr. by Ray Lyman Wilbur, Stanford University president and Hoover's Secretary of the Interior. Hornbeck remains active on trade and tariff legislation attending the Special Conference on Tariff Autonomy in Peking. Meanwhile, – according to Russian diplomatic records –, Hornbeck continues to maintain dialogue with Skvirsky. In January 1928, Hornbeck resigns from Harvard to accept his appointment as Chief of the Division of Far Eastern Affairs. After graduating Princeton in 1929, during his round-the-world honeymoon cruise the next year JDR, Jr. stops over in Kyoto to attend the IPR conference where he enjoys the hospitality of Japanese leaders behind the Manchuria conquest no less eager for his generous patronage. (re. Institute of Pacific Relations, P. Collier and D. Horowitz, ft. 676)

From 1928 to 1937, Hornbeck heads the Division of Far Eastern Affairs. Soon, he becomes known as the department's leading foe of Japanese expansion in the Far East. With the Japanese taking over Manchuria and establishing the puppet state of Manchukuo from September 1931 onward Hornbeck criticized moral persuasion as diplomatic instrument and advocates such remedies as a Western boycott of Japanese goods, and embargo on private loans to Japan – along with a defensive alliance in the Pacific and keeping the US naval superiority in the region.

At the same time nearing spring in 1932 Hornbeck continues back-door contact with Skvirsky in Washington and through other channels to send certain "signals" to the Soviet leadership. For instance, on March 7 and March 21 Hornbeck has lengthy discussions with New York TASS Bureau head K. Duranty. They discuss "a possibility of the Japanese attack against Siberia. Hornbeck insists that Moscow should "pay greater attention to the position taken by the USA in 1921 regarding the Japanese intervention in Siberia". Hornbeck conveys Stimson's deep regret that "the Soviet government had not taken any steps to contain the Japanese in Manchuko." He estimates "at the moment the Japanese attack would be favorable for Moscow," since "it would be better to settle these problems (the Japanese claims in Siberia) now, while Japan faces a difficult situation in Shanghai," while concluding with a rhetorical question: "Why would the United States take any steps to prevent the Japanese intervention into Siberia when Moscow is doing nothing to defend its interests in Manchuko?" The Japanese got more than they expected in battle losses from the furious battles with the Soviet Red Army and suffered some 50,000 killed, a major blow to Japanese prestige that did not go unnoticed by Tokyo.

However, during the fatal Holodomor summer of 1933 Hornbeck strongly opposes US intervention in East Asia and recommends American passivity concerning Japanese encroachments in China convinced that Sino-Japanese confrontation will eventually devastate both China and Japan exhausted by the conflict. In the general carnage the Chinese will lose some twenty million dead soldiers and citizens in WWII, and some 100 million displaced with shattered and uprooted lives.

At the same time Hornbeck is engaged in frequent and secret conversations with Skvirsky. Constant on their agenda is "confrontation between Japan and the USSR". Hornbeck assures the deputy soviet commissar that in the worst case scenario "the sympathies of America would definitely be on the side of the USSR, however, America would not join either of the sides." Fast forward to February 1936. On the eve of Skvirsky's departure from America Hornbeck tells the Russian to assure his government of Roosevelt intentions along with the British to support Stalin in the Far East.

Since September 1937, and clearly at odds with ambassador Grew's work on behalf of the Morgan financial interests bankrolling Tokyo's militarist expansion, Hornbeck continues advocating the need to put pressure on Japan, recommending such measures vital to protecting American interests in the Far East, not ruling out, for example, the sending of US heavy cruisers. At the Nine Power Treaty Conference in Brussels in November 1937 Hornbeck stresses the importance of providing Japan guarantees for access to raw materials and markets essential for her growth and development but ultimately with the aim to maintain peace. Sterling and Peggy Seagrave in *The Yamato Dynasty* describes the constant intrigues and plots around the Japanese Emperor Hirohito during their period of the start of the Chinese War lasting eight years after a provocation in July by the Kwantung Army sparking retaliation by the Japanese. FDR's call for sanctions and an economic "quarantine" against the Japanese "epidemic" but it dies without support in Congress and is crushed by "the powerful Wall Street pro-Japan lobby." The Seagraves write further, "Morgan Bank and a number of other major American corporations were anxious to protect their large investments in Japan, Manchuria, Korea and Taiwan." The Japanese immediately lay siege to Shanghai and prepare their full scale bloody offensive on Nanking. "Contrary to the impression created by postwar propaganda, dozens of imperial family members, including Hirohito's brothers, uncles and first cousins, served on active duty at the front in Manchuria, China, Southeast Asia and the Pacific Islands," the Seagraves observe. (S. Seagrave and P. Seagrave, *The Yamato Dynasty,* 162-96)

Hull's close friend and aide is "Judge" R. Walton Moore, the former Congressmen and a senior judge from Virginia. Both are from the south with parallel careers in law and politics. Moore had served in Congress with Hull. The very rich and devious Welles who jealously covets the job at State and never cared much for the old "Judge" whom he pushes aside as he ignores Bullitt. For his part Moore is uneasy and suspicious by the power which Sumner Welles is able to yield over Hull "whose judgment the President does not trust". Wallace McClure is another Hull economic adviser who stays on to help resolve serious trade issues aggravated by the worsening global economy that hits economies in individual nations like falling dominoes. Another longtime friend from Tennessee, McClure and Hull had worked together in Congress on reciprocal trade agreements for lower bilateral trade barriers as preferable to imposing across the board restrictive tariffs used by Wilson Democrats under the Underwood tariff. However, congressional die-hards adhere to the Wilsonian approach until the Roosevelt's election. Both Hornbeck and McClure agree that discrimination against US goods should be monitored, and stress negotiation against retaliation. To counter payment imbalances and increased protectionism against US exports during the debt crisis years of the twenties and early thirties three successive Republican administrations of US Presidents – Harding, Coolidge, and Hoover –, rely on private capital flows to augment payments imbalances of impoverished economies like Germany created by war debts and reparations damaged further by skyrocketing unemployment all of which proves overwhelmingly inadequate to stem inflation and stabilize the economy.

Ernest Hemingway remembers just really how bad it was in Germany when he was there in September 1922, and from Kehl he observes during these immediate postwar years how terribly the German mark had lost all its value. That year the exchange rate plummets from 162 marks to the US dollar to 7000. In a year it fell off the cliff to 4200 *billion* marks for a dollar. One fine day Hemingway looks on as pandemonium breaks out in a pastry shop with tempers rising because while the Germans starve the French are free to walk the bridge crossing the border to buy only all they could eat. Well, who won the war anyway? "The miracle of exchange," Hemingway writes, "makes a swinish spectacle where the youth of the town of Strasbourg crowd into the German pastry shop to eat themselves sick and gorge on fluffy, cream-filled slices of German cake at 5 marks the slice. The contents of a pastry shop are swept clear in half an hour ... The proprietor and his helper were surly and didn't seem particularly happy when all the cakes were sold. The mark was falling faster than they could bake." Unfortunately for Hemingway readers "the Old Man" and the sea this time is off Cuba in the summer of 1934, and apparently never happier then far away from the shoreline out of view on his boat *Pilar* catching 450-pound Marlin. (John Carey, *Eyewitness to History*, essay by Ernest Hemingway, "German Inflation, 19 Sept. 1922", Cambridge, MA.: Harvard Univ. Press, 1988, 497-501)

Congress reinforced its commitment to protectionism passing the Smoot-Hawley Act in 1930 raising tension between traditional trading partners particularly Britain and Canada hurt by getting shut out of the American market instead of gaining preferential trade status. Their governments retaliate to protect themselves politically reinforcing the effects of global depression. Nor is the US economy immune from injurious effects of its own protective trade measures in an increasingly complex global system where trade no longer can be treated as an independent domestic policy issue. After the debacle of the First World War which cripples Europe rendering governments and nations hostage to the international bankers, Wall Street syndicated bonds and loans of their credit markets and with the British Empire dethroned and virtually stripped naked from its pre-1914 rank no less helped when London in 1925 returns to the gold standard, London requires greater intervention by the American Federal Reserve to sustain its own political superiority in the Consortium if it is to remain on the forefront of world power *main en main* with the Americans. Smoot-Hawley Act raised the bar demonstrating the costs of protectionism are too high and need more innovative solutions in trade policy in which trade instruments such as unconditional MFN treatment might be used to lower trade barriers and increase the flow of goods and capital across borders. (I. Gellman, 143; D. Acheson, 11)

All that and more preoccupies Hull during the Holodomor years 1933-34. Preoccupied with the liberalization of trade as the stimulus for America's economic recovery, Hull lobbies for passage of the 1934 Reciprocal Trade Agreements Act (RTTA) to serve as the motor of a multilateral regime of commercial cooperation based on sound economic principles and institutions. FDR is able to wield the hand of Congress to cede to executive power to set and manage the trade agenda in exchange for promises to compensate producers disadvantaged by unprofitable trade. Trade barriers are lowered, reciprocal practices engaged, Congress placated, and unconditional MFN status established to maximize bilateral treaties. But none of this would improve the welfare of the Ukrainians left to suffer under the Consortium's Soviet monopoly. FDR takes the helm while dark clouds shadow Consortium-CFR engineered foreign policy constructive engagement with Stalin's terror gulag regime as thousands of engineers do their work for the big corporations, General Electric, Vickers, Westinghouse, Ford, DuPont, Caterpillar, Deering...

Hull's conservative southern temperament naturally estranged him FDR's more garrulous persuasion. He lacking his confidence or subsequently lacked access to the White House. Whereas Stimson had an "Open Door Policy" of access to Hoover, Hull was always an outsider and kept in the dark. During the 1935 Congressional budget review, for example, Hull was obliged to go before the House Appropriations Committee with "no grasp of the facts and figures" and unable to make a statement. Hull signed a letter of protest, on a reduced budget, but refused to deliver it to the President. Hull feared offending his boss and having to give up his to FDR's friend Sumner Welles. Wilbur Carr, a Hull adviser recalled, "Hull seems amazingly diffident, lacking in courage or lacking in close relationship to President. Other cabinet officers demand things of the President. Why not he?"

That summer Hull thought of resigning. His wife worried his health might break down "with many problems which increasingly come up." If there was ever to be anyone at State to stand up and help Ukraine against FDR and Stalin it would never be Cordell Hull. (I. Gellman, 101)

From his first days as Secretary, Hull saw how FDR intended to spin the world on the tip of his own finger. That was made unmistakably clear on the occasion when FDR met the French ambassador Laboulaye he invited former Premier Edouard Herriot to the White House and completely forgot Hull and State protocol. Not to matter, the French have their share of problems. After French President Paul Doumer is assassinated by a Russian émigré, the anti-communist government of Tardieu fell; French radicals and socialists increased their representation in the French Chamber of Deputies under the leadership of Herriot's new government in June. Then, Herriot set out to improve Franco-Soviet relations and, in November signs the Franco-Soviet nonaggression pact after having resumed trade talks in September "stalled on the issue of credit or guarantees for Soviet purchases in France". (French-Soviet trade, 1928-1939; Michael Jabara Carley, "Five Kopecks for Five Kopecks"; *Cahiers du Monde russe et sovietique,* XXXIII (I) janvier-mars 1992, 38)

Hull prefers to live alone with his wife and send Phillips or any one of the other undersecretaries to diplomatic receptions and state functions. Hull's memoirs are deceptive and unreliable, for example, writing how in his first term FDR was so swamped by New Deal legislative battles with Congress "that he left me in full charge of foreign affairs ...." The opposite is more likely true though Moley and Harry F. Payer leave in their first year, replaced by a friends of Hull including Judge Moore, a family friend of Bullitt, and Francis B. Sayre, President Wilson's son-in-law, a lawyer and Harvard professor who assists drafting reciprocal trade agreements.

It seems everyone at State is out of the loop on Russia during that pitiful summer in the Ukraine when Stalin's shock brigades deprived the peasants of all their grain. The conservative and inexperienced Hull is awed more than impressed by the flimsy and aloof Welles. But Welles, too, has nothing to do with the problems of Eastern Europe or Russia. From May to December, Welles is obsessed by junta politics in Cuba.

By 1935 Hull thought he's cut off direct access to FDR overstepped by more ambitious underlings and shadowy political appointees. He issues an order to respect the correct protocol of his office but it has little effect. From the beginning Bill Phillips is top man on his team and tight with Stimson. Extraordinarily rich, brilliant and endowed with a finest of New England heritage, Phillips is Harvard through and through. Phillips is flanked by George Messersmith, Adolf Berle Jr., Hugh R. Wilson, Henry F Grady, G. Howland Shaw, and Dean G. Acheson who ten years later replaces Joseph Grew for the top slot at State.

Welles and FDR grew up together at Groton and Harvard. It was intimate world known only to the select few, a world that groomed young boys to occupy positions of prestige, privilege and leadership Stimson, Yale, and the veteran patriarch of Skull & Bones, Taft's former Secretary of War two decades before. Ultimate strategy of foreign was decided by these three men. Welles had a haughty inaccessible personality, impetuous, even unpredictable and untimely after a few drinks. He would be at the center of more than one sexual indiscretions that would have cost anyone else his job. FDR kept him in place until Bullitt later exposed Welles throughout the State Department in a bid for his displace. FDR already had the FBI investigation documents on Welles and was not about to crucify his schoolboy chum from Groton and famous in the social circuit from Washington to New York. In those days it mattered not just a little. It made a big difference in who you knew and what people thought about you. It set the tone. Whether you're St. Pauls, Phillips Exeter, Andover, Groton or schools of lesser prominence like Kent, Loomis, Hotchkiss, Choate, Lawrenceville ... however these prep schools rank for the chosen golden boys of the American aristocracy share lectures and assemblies, and are teammates promised an inside track from the cradle to the grave if they play the game. But for Welles the damage is done and his career takes a dive.

Stimson, Welles, Berle, Moffat, Carr, Moore, Sayre, Phillips, Bundy, Acheson … are among the top tier selected or appointed to the foreign policy hierarchy in the twenties and thirties amused more than impressed by Bullitt's reappearance and sudden rise to power. Few if any know him well, if at all. Except for Judge Moore they remain suspicious of his temerity, and none more than Welles.

Benjamin Sumner Welles is heir to a wealthy family of the old establishment. He had many rivals and no few rivals. As a child Welles entered an America that was vastly different from the one he would come to know as an adult. In the year of his birth, the European empires elevated their legations in Washington to the status of embassies, a move confirming America's emerging big power status. The most recent census had declared the American frontier closed. The quest for new overseas markets and colonies accelerated, and the United States was on the verge of becoming a great industrialized world power.

Welles could trace his lineage to the initial settlement of the American colonies. Born on October 10, 1892, the same year as Bullitt, Hopper, and Henderson – this was their generation – in New York City and raised in Islip on Long Island. To escape a legal battle when he lost all his property over his puritan faith, Thomas Welles emigrated from England to the New World in 1635, appointed by the King of England Governor and first Treasurer of the colony of Connecticut. He settled in Hartford. Gideon Welles had been chosen by Lincoln as a New Englander in his cabinet where he reorganized the Navy at the outbreak of the Civil War when it was lost to the South.

Welles' great uncle, Charles Sumner (1811-74), graduated Harvard in 1830 and became a famous Republican abolitionist Senator from Massachusetts. An early visit to Washington persuaded him to leave in moral outrage; he returned to Boston to practice law and teach at Harvard Law School. Charles Sumner traveled widely abroad, fluent in French, German and Italian, and visited England in 1838. Among his Harvard neighbors were his friends Henry Wadsworth Longfellow and Ralph Waldo Emerson. Sumner believed that environment had "an important, if not controlling influence" in shaping individuals and that by creating a society where "knowledge, virtue and religion" took precedence "the most forlorn shall grow into forms of unimagined strength and beauty".

Moral law, then, was as important for governments as it was for individuals, and laws which inhibited a man's ability to grow – like slavery or segregation – were acts of evil. Charles Sumner married the daughter of a Massachusetts Congressman in 1866, but divorced in 1873 after her fling with a German aristocrat. After the Civil War Sumner chaired the Senate Foreign Relations Committee; his speech in April 1867 swayed the vote in favor of the treaty protecting commercial interests of New England whalers and traders eager for access to North Pacific waters. Charles Sumner had been a close adviser to Lincoln who called him "my idea of a Bishop", spoke out relentlessly for emancipation in the case of Dred Scott, and proved himself as a confirmed abolitionist against the southern seizure of the federal government. In 1865, Sumner declared, "Judicial baseness reached its lowest point on that occasion. You have not forgotten that terrible decision where a most unrighteous judgment was sustained by a falsification of history. Of course, the Constitution of the United States and every principle of Liberty was falsified, but historical truth was falsified again…"

Charles Sumner acquired the reputation as "the South's most hated foe and the Negro's bravest friend". An enemy of the 1850 Fugitive Slave Act he was nearly killed in 1856 on the Senate floor in a severe fight with Preston Brooks from South Carolina. He left with severe head trauma, recovered and returned three years later to champion the Union cause in the Civil War, but broke with Grant over corruption in the Republican Party. Grant became a bitter opponent of Sumner in 1870 when Grant needed his support in a plan to annex Santo Domingo. Charles Sumner was also involved in an abortive scheme to grab the whole of Canada in a dispute over its Civil War trade with the Confederacy at the expense of human life and for "that other damage, immense and infinite, caused by the prolongation of the war." A Geneva arbitrations court rejected his claims against Great Britain. Welles' ancestor's persistence not to compromise with corruption did not harm his popularity as a champion in the struggle against slavery. Emancipation empowered him.

The younger Welles might have been cut from the same family cloth but lacked his character. Throughout his career Sumner would benefit from his close relationship with other established New York families of the Social Register, in particular the Oyster Bay branch of the very much extended Roosevelt clan. Their association went back many years. Welles was "family". Sumner's mother and FDR's mother-in-law were close friends, and he and Eleanor shared a godmother. In 1905, the twelve-year-old Sumner attended Franklin and Eleanor's wedding where he carried the bride's train as she walked down the aisle on the arm of her uncle Teddy, the President, and into the arms of husband. Reverend Endicott Peabody of Groton officiated. On another occasion FDR invited Rev. Peabody to the White House to entertain for an anniversary party for his tight family of cherished Grotonians.

The Roosevelt connection was also important symbolically. Many of Welles' contemporaries would be challenged by the example of Teddy's commitment to public service. Whereas many members of the American privileged class thought public life beneath them, Theodore Roosevelt sought to make it seem respectable, even noble. Charities also gave the rich something to do placing them in the spotlight on the front page of society to raise the general standard of living and help their fellow man and less fortunate. Welles was a sickly child, dominated by his mother throughout his early years. Contemporaries would later joke that the fastidious Sumner wore white gloves as a child at play. Nonetheless, his upbringing within the cloistered and privileged world of the New York elite reinforced his feelings of superiority over others and contributed to an uncanny inability to relate well with those from different backgrounds. The Welles family made regular trips to Europe, where young Sumner formed early opinions and impressions about many of the countries that proved useful in his diplomatic career. Following in the footsteps of Roosevelt, Welles went to Groton at a time when the student body includes classmates Ave Harriman, Dean Acheson, and Eleanor Roosevelt's brother, Hall, a Welles roommate.

Groton served to structure the American establishment as Eton or Harrow did the English. The school was conspicuously inbred; more than half the student body would be the sons of alumni. Both Welles and Franklin Roosevelt send their sons there. Like Roosevelt before him, Welles fell under the spell of headmaster Endicott Peabody, a stern New Englander educated in England at Cheltenham and Trinity College, Cambridge who charmed his boys with real stories he lived out in the American frontier of the Wild West. Peabody modeled Groton after Cheltenham, arranging the students in British-style "forms" rather than American "grades" and favoring British spellings over American. Students enforced their hierarchies by strict hazing rituals and various other torments of which the headmaster approved, believing they contributed to the development of "manly Christian character".

In *Secret Affairs* Irwin Gellman writes of the civil servants and Foreign Service men at the State Department. And although Gellman observed that FDR "continued to harbor suspicions about the motives of the white Anglo-Saxon males who made up the tightly knit foreign service fraternity", that seems ludicrous in light of the tradition of hazing and initiations of young boys at Groton before, during and after FDR's years there as a pubescent student on the verge of manhood. That the men "hailed from the East and had grown up with wealth, attended Ivy League Schools, and entered the government to take their place as enlightened leaders in the service of their country" did not in any way contradict the traditions that FDR had inherited and fostered by the practice of his ways.

Inept at sports and unpopular with his classmates, Welles' sarcastic wit and weird personality left off the playing field. Apart from his classmates brothers and cousins Welles fell short of Peabody's ideal of fraternity. Yet Groton nonetheless seems to have left its burnished seal on the lad as it always does on the rich and spoiled. Peabody told successive generations of Grotonians that public service was a high and noble calling, and many graduates would later acknowledge the school's profound influence on their careers. Franklin Roosevelt called Peabody the "biggest influence on my life." Welles once told Peabody, "If I ever achieve anything in this world, even amount to anything, and I mean to, it will be due very greatly to you."

Upon Peabody's advice, Welles went off to Harvard in 1910, the same year some of America's best writers and political observers including T. S. Eliot, John Reed and Walter Lippmann had graduated late spring. Welles was also following in the path of FDR, Class of 1904. By his own admission his Harvard years were not happy ones. Welles spent much of his time drinking heavily and living with whores in choice brothels and acquired a reputation of a rich degenerate. Welles was unpopular, played no sports, and was undesired by the clubs. Even the *Crimson* rejected him. Welles was an irreducible effete snob. He left little impression, if any, and if his classmates remembered him at all, it was for his finely tailored Brooks Brothers suits, stickpin, stiff collar, and distance. In 1913, he contemplated dropping out of college, and traveled abroad but returned to join the Class of 1914. That year the Crimson team dumped Princeton Tigers in a 20-0 rout, captained by their All-American star running back and hockey legend Hobey Baker. It was their last great hurrah before the outbreak of war in Europe in August.

Welles drifts to the Foreign Service enlisting a helping hand from fellow Harvard grad Bill Phillips who had married Welles's cousin in 1910, Caroline Astor Drayton. By then Phillips already holds a senior position at State. FDR also intervenes to get him in. "I am delighted to learn that you are going to take the diplomatic examinations this Spring," Roosevelt writes, "and am gladly sending you a line to go with your application." Welles had asked FDR, then assistant Secretary of the Navy, to recommend him to Secretary of State William Jennings Bryan. "I have known", Roosevelt wrote Bryan of Welles, "since he was a small boy and have seen him go through school and college and I should be most glad to see him successful in entering the Diplomatic Corps." Welles receives the highest score on the diplomatic examinations. America was on the march to war under Wilson's policy of armed neutrality. American factories boomed with war orders and Federal Reserve banks stacked Allied gold for payments on goods shipped from London, Paris and Moscow. Welles learned hands-on how to play the Great Game of Empire. "We had been thrilled to the depths of our emotional and intellectual being," he wrote years later, "by the vision that Woodrow Wilson had held out to us a world order founded on justice and on democracy."

The same year he enters the Foreign Service Welles marries Esther Slater, the sister of a Harvard classmate and hunting chum. Her family possessed a sprawling textile empire in Webster, Massachusetts. Rev. Peabody of Groton blessed them all in the best Groton tradition. The Governor attends. Three thousand townspeople cheer their benefactor. A first son Benjamin is born in 1916, followed by Arnold two years later. Welles soon distinguished himself in postings from Tokyo where he observes Japanese treatment of German internees; a posting to Buenos Aires finds him out-maneuvering rival British merchants in the Argentine market.

Welles' meteoric rise at State is confirmed when he returns to Washington, in 1920, and just shy of his twenty-ninth birthday is appointed the youngest division chief yet with senior rank on Latin American affairs. There he helps draft the Wilson Plan for the withdrawal of American troops from the Dominican Republic as part of America's "Good Neighbor Policy" over client dictatorships. Personally, however, his wealth and curt demeanor didn't enamour him to the Foreign Service career men. It was hard to read Welles. It was observed by insiders that "many influential leaders had grown to detest him, viewing him as pompous, self-righteous, and moralistic and a rigid ego-maniac. He had a low, controlled voice, which he cultivated to heighten the impression of pomposity. He seldom laughed, and when he did he seemed to want to apologize for disturbing his normally solemn demeanor. Welles appeared to enjoy the idea that the troubles of the world somehow rested on his shoulders alone. ... His willingness to go directly to the highest possible authority and his unwillingness to solicit the opinions of his peers further alienated them. Just as Welles himself saw nothing in shades of gray, those who knew him either liked or disliked him, with no middle ground." (George W.

Baer-Loy Henderson, "The Effect of the Depression on the International Situation January 1931 – March 1933', *A Question of Truth: The Origins of US-Soviet Diplomatic Relations, The Memoirs of Loy W. Henderson,* ed., Hoover Institution Press, Stanford Univ., 1986, 68, 206-7)

In pursuit of career, influence and more power to advance his fledging career, Welles cultivated a close relationship with President Harding's Secretary of State, the Republican leader Charles Evans Hughes. Hughes taps him for his personal envoy for Latin America but Welles will be forced to resign over a breakdown in his marriage and of sexual promiscuity with other women and as well as men especially black porters on the private rail cars. In one liaison Welles used his wife's money to buy $100,000 worth of jewelry for a mistress. He precipitously left the State Department in March 1922. He tried his hand at making money but failed. Then Hughes sends him as US Commissioner to the Dominican Republic where he assumed other portfolios including an appointment as President Coolidge's personal negotiator in the Honduran civil war with favorable press by the Consortium gang.

Welles again went too far with his sex scandals when he attended the 1924 Democratic convention (which nominated Coolidge's opponent) accompanied by the prominent heiress Mathilde Townsend Gerry, wife of Rhodes Island Senator Peter Gerry and close friend of Coolidge. Welles is forced to resign, and after the convention sails for Paris with Mathilde leaving their lawyers to settle the divorce settlements. By late 1925, Coolidge's Secretary of State, Frank Kellogg nearly appointed Welles as an Undersecretary for Latin America or ambassador to one of America's Banana Republics but the Prohibitionist President kills it. "So long as I am President, that young man will never even be a minister," Coolidge tells the press. When Welles and Mathilde marry in 1925 in a "quiet ceremony", *The New York Times* runs the story on its front page. Welles and Mathilde spend most of their time at Oxon Hill Manor, a 49-room "country cottage" in the heart of Maryland hunt country some twenty miles outside Washington DC. Oxon Hill retains its reputation as a regular drinking hole fêting foreign dignitaries and diplomats, entertaining the President, and hosting informal gatherings of Consortium men and their families. Roosevelt, too, prefers Oxon Hill when he wants a quick escape from the White House to sip mint juleps with casual and intimate company on the veranda overlooking the Potomac.

As a former Senator's wife Mathilde is a conspicuous Washington presence. Her grandfather had made a fortune in Pennsylvania Railroad that put them in the league with the Vanderbilts and Astors of American aristocrats. Welles and his wife are comfortably at ease playing the grand host and hostess of the nation's capitol; her mother had been one of the social queens of Washington society during Mrs. Astor's "Guilded Nineties". And Welles and Mathilde move their staff of fifteen servants into the colossal Townsend Mansion on Massachusetts Avenue, a replica of Marie Antoinette's *Petit Trianon.*

For three years while he keeps his hand in Latin American and Caribbean affairs, Welles flirted with joining a Wall Street investment bank. He authors a book, *Naboth's Vineyard: The Dominican Republic, 1844-1924 (*1928). "No nation can live unto itself alone," he wrote. "If the United States, therefore, is to maintain itself as one of the greatest forces in the world of the future ... the time is at hand when it must reach the conviction that in the Western Hemisphere lies its strength and its support." Just a few miles south of Cuba another dictator takes over in 1930, Rafael Trujillo the Dominican Republic who joined the US marines during the occupation in 1916 and in nine years is promoted Commander-in-Chief. He rules the country with an iron fist for 31 years from 1930 until his assassination in 1961 by the CIA; the country is still haunted by his genocidal killing of 50,000 Haitians while he, on a not too infrequent manner, deflowers kidnapped young school girls. Still on his discretionary sabbatical Welles remains active at home joining the CFR and the Woodrow Wilson Foundation.

Although now morally estranged from the conservative puritanical wing of Republican Party, Welles identified with Roosevelt's ascendancy serving as a foreign policy expert for the Democrats sending FDR regular briefs on Latin America. During the 1928 presidential contest against Hoover, Welles collaborates with Roosevelt and frequently gives speeches on foreign policy for the Democratic nominee Al Smith. Welles even ghost-writes an article for Roosevelt in *Foreign Affairs*, helping to mold the image of FDR as a multilateralist and disarmament advocate while sketching a portrait of his friend as a truly converted non-interventionist, and at the same time parlays a sharp attack on the Coolidge's use of marines in Nicaragua despite FDR's support for Wilson having done the same in Haiti. Welles later easily exploited his presence in Central and South America to eclipse Hull's trips there. The skillful tactician also keeps up close ties to Eleanor Roosevelt with frequent letters and visits to Springwood, her Hyde Park estate in the rolling hills.

Once a Grotonian always a Grotonian. Welles and Roosevelt together ride the political express. They survived their ritualistic boyhood initiations and remain bonded friends for life. When FDR became New York's governor in 1928 Welles joined his shadow cabinet at Hyde Park and at the governor's mansion in Albany. As foreign affairs adviser they prepared political attacks on the Hoover-Stimson handling of foreign policy. This was heavy stuff, taking on the stalwart Stimson on military and foreign policy. It was only a logical step for Welles at the 1932 Democratic National Convention in Chicago to draft the party's platform on Latin America with some help from his friend the Washington journalist Drew Pearson in his popular national column.

Money follows ambition. All through the fall until victory Welles uses his fortune and influence to advise FDR directing the presidential campaign. Nationally syndicated columnist Drew Pearson in the *Baltimore Post* on September 28, 1932 speculates that Welles, although barely half the age of Stimson might succeed the patriarch. Instead FDR keeps him on Latin America affairs in one of many appointments that undercut Hull and embeds the Consortium network more firmly in place for the future. (FDR to Welles, March 9, 1932, President's Personal File (PPF) 2961, FDRL; S. Welles to Roosevelt, Dec. 19, 1932, PPF 2961, FDRL Roosevelt to S. Welles, Feb. 1, 1933, PPF 2961, FDRL; Eleanor Roosevelt to Sumner Welles, Dec. 7, 1932, box 148, Sumner Welles papers; Eleanor Roosevelt to Mathilde Welles, Feb. 17, 1933, box 149, folder 2, S. Welles papers, FDR; For an account of Hull's inability to control US foreign policy, see Julius Pratt, *The Ordeal of Cordell Hull, Review of Politics*, Jan. 1966, 76-98)

A generation later Dean Acheson recalled in his memoirs (1963) that the State Department was a "house divided against itself". FDR liked it that way and he played with Hull and Welles as he did his other advisers while surrounding himself with loyalists. "Suspicious by nature," speaking of Hull Acheson recalled, "he brooded over what he thought were slights and grievances, which more forthright handling might have set straight. His brooding led, in accordance with Tennessee-mountain tradition, to feuds. His hatreds were implacable – not hot hatreds, but long cold ones. In no hurry to 'get' his enemy, 'get' him he usually did." (D. Acheson, 9-11)

These three men sat high in the Consortium surrounded by advisers and specialists, junior secretaries and assistants eager to carry out their slightest whims. They made up FDR's top tier of his foreign policy team. When he ran for President, FDR made only a few general statements about the world. The Depression, joblessness and the economy were the issues that decided the Presidential election. Not Stalin, Hitler or war preparations. Foreign policy and the affairs of Germany and Europe, Russia and Japan made occasional headlines but they hardly could make the world seem much less distant than the vast barren plains that covered the dust bowl of the Midwest. Hull was cast as a well-respected and elderly politician, but oddly without any experience in foreign affairs. The longest tenure of any Secretary of State ever, Hull was remarkably ill at ease in his post, and so insecure, he often writes "READ AND DESTROY" on sensitive correspondence while keeping carbons for his file. Hull had no training in foreign affairs. In a world of Episcopalians he obsessed over his wife's Jewish ancestry. At one time Hull had been considered a Presidential contender. With rotting teeth, false wooden dentures, and diabetic, he is diagnosed tubercular *before* he joined Roosevelt's cabinet. (Pratt-Hull, Preface, ix)

Sumner Welles was a character of a decidedly different and distinct nature who had more in common with Roosevelt than many of his peers. His role in Soviet affairs is significant by his having none except to target Bullitt's outing from State sent once again into diplomatic exile. But this would come about years after Bullitt plays out his hand in the masquerade. Welles is intellectually aloof and pompous with enough wit and wealth with credentials to match to permit an eccentricity privy to the England's genteel upper class. Both covet the top job at State.

To say that Hull and Welles were worlds apart would be ridiculous understatement. Welles managed to leap over his rivals and rise from undersecretary to acting Secretary of State within a decade, a virtually impossible feat given his pariah social status as three times married, divorced, coloured by a scandalous reputation as "homosexual, unions with black railroad porters, shoeshine boys, and taxicab drivers". At times they never seem to share the same universe. Bullitt is a jealous and devious rival. No wonder Roosevelt chose Hull to steady the rocky ship of State with nuances of balance.

Welles acquired a perversely personal interest in Cuba and Latin affairs; his alleged homosexuality arouses suspicions and dark rumours about his sexual preference for men of Latino and African origin. He drinks heavily and indulges his passion to his personal detriment and the satisfaction of his enemies ready to exploit his careless promiscuity. It could easily compromise national security as well. By the mid-thirties the Soviets are widening their espionage activities which the famous "Cambridge Five"* as well as moles in the State Department, in Treasury and with access to the President's inner circle. Roosevelt's close friend, and candidate for the top job at State Sumner Welles could very well be a target of the INO, the OGPU's foreign intelligence directorate. (* "The Five": Kim Philby, Guy Burgess, Donald Maclean, John Cairncross, Antony Blunt. It was precisely during this period of the Holodomor years 1932-1934 when Philby, who graduates from Cambridge in June 1933 and his friends began to organize their underground network as Soviet agents against international fascism; Maclean and Burgess are recruited in 1934, Cairncross in 1937.)

STALIN SENDS HIS NKVD AGENTS TO PENETRATE, SPY AND STEAL

I defer and recommend to the reader the findings of Christopher Andrew with Vasili Mitrokhin, writing in *The Sword and the Shield* (1999) not only as to origins and activities of the INO during the time of our Holodomor crisis, (regrettably there is a big gap covering the Holodomor itself which has no mention the Andrew book which seems odd), but also, NKVD penetration of the US government during the Roosevelt years. They write, "The NKVD succeeded none the less in penetrating the most sensitive sections of the Roosevelt administration. ... There was thus a breathtaking gulf between the intelligence supplied to Stalin on the United States and that available to Roosevelt on the Soviet Union. Whereas the Centre had penetrated every major branch of Roosevelt's administration, OSS – like SIS – had not a single agent in Moscow." And in a footnote to his chapter "Grand Alliance", Andrew tells more, writing of Soviet spying in the US "as a base from which to collect intelligence on Germany and Japan"; and in reference to the Venona decrypts that in the nineties surfaced "overwhelmingly" incriminating Alger Hiss as a spy, he writes: "The VENONA decrypts of NKVD wartime telegrams from the United States include the codenames of approximately 200 agents (about half of whom remain unidentified). Since these telegrams represent only a fraction of the wartime communications between the Center and its American residences, the total NKVD network must have been substantially larger.... Mitrokhin gives the occupations of only thirty-six others, of whom twenty-two were journalists. Many of the agents were immigrants and refugees." In another footnote, Andrew adds, "Soviet agents at OSS headquarters were probably well into the double figures. Communists (not all of them agents) have been identified in the Russian, Spanish, Balkan, Hungarian and Latin American sections of OSS's R&A division, and its operational German, Japanese, Korean, Italian, Spanish, Hungarian and Indonesian divisions." Front the start, the OSS is seriously compromised by an American NKVD spy and recruited by Donovan as his personal assistant. Writer O'Donnell observes, "The most prominent Soviet agent was Duncan Lee, who had worked for Donovan's law firm before the war.... and through this sensitive position Lee was privy to some of the organization's most important secrets." More on this later. (C. Andrew with V. Mitrokhin, 110-1, ft.1, 29, 40. One of the greatest secrets of WWI and postwar period Venona recognized "as the codebraker's Rosetta stone", remained classified until 1996 and consists of "nearly 3,000 decrypted Soviet secret messages sent between 1940 and 1948" and provided American intelligence "an unparalleled glimpse into how the NKVD ... operated ... and "clues on new ways to crack other Russian codes", writes Patrick K. O'Donnell in *Operatives, Spies and Saboteurs, The Unknown Story of Men and Women of WWII's OSS*, NY: Free Press-Simon & Schuster, 2004, 269-70, 310)

Established by Lenin in 1922 under its first chief was Mikhail Abramovich Trilisser, "a Russian Jew who had become a professional revolutionary in 1901 at the age of eighteen." His world was the underground of Czarist secret police, spies, cut-throat agents, criminals and Bolsheviks for who he hunted down informers and other "counter-revolutionaries" inside the Bolshevik organization and among Ukrainian nationalists and the defeated White Armies. Lenin warned his comrades, "A beaten Army learns much." That includes the Czarist White Guards exiled mainly in Warsaw, Paris, and Berlin. This included the Ukrainian nationalist General Yurko Tutyunnik suspected of conspiring with Ukrainian leader Simon Petlyura (1879-1942), and members of his government-in-exile. In 1923, Tutyunnik is betrayed, and captured upon crossing the frontier. Imprisoned for six years he is executed by Stalin in 1929. Stalin's assassins eventually catch up with Petlyura in Paris. (C. Andrew and V. Mitrokhin, 33)

Welles is advised by Lawrence Duggan and Berle. He uses Drew Pearson to promote views whenever it suits him. During the Cuban mix-up Welles became ambassador but keeps the post only but a few months, succeeded by the Old School and innocuous diplomat Jefferson Caffery as Undersecretary for Latin American affairs. With Bullitt away in Moscow and Paris, FDR and Welles propagated American "good neighbor" policy in Latin America. During the Holodomor years Welles worked closely with Laurence Duggan (Phillips Exeter, Harvard), promoted three times in 1935 as chief of the Latin American division leaving the way open for Welles to take the top job at State. (Pratt-Hull, xi)

By the late thirties Lawrence Duggan who later becomes chief of the Latin American division is is targeted for recruitment by the NKVD intelligence operations in Washington under code names "19", later FRANK; described by soviet agents as "a very soft guy"... "cultural and reserved", he is first approached in 1934. By 1936 Duggan is turning over documents transmitted to Moscow including diplomatic dispatches from American embassies in Europe on the Spanish Civil War and a Bullitt cable from Moscow proposing reforms at State in the advent of the next world war. Even though his cover was blown by the defection of an NKVD operations chief for Europe (shortly thereafter kidnapped from a restaurant in Lausanne, Switzerland, shot and dumped on the road), Duggan continues supplying his NKVD handler documents including "confidential discussions of peace prospects undertaken on Roosevelt's and Secretary of State Cordell Hull's behalf in Europe by an American diplomat". His motive is candour, not cash. But then Duggan complains that his trusted good friends are disappearing in Moscow's Great Purge; "... all this seems to him 'a remote, incomprehensible nightmare... he cannot understand it, he is embarrassed, he cannot sleep." Moscow persists to convert Duggan into a loyal spy, instructing his handler: "All puzzling questions from (Duggan) must receive exhaustive answers from you. Leave nothing unclear and not satisfied.... We cannot lose him for any reason". (For breaches of security in FDR's administrations including activities of Alger Hiss, Whittaker Chambers, Harry Dexter White and Comintern agents of the NKVD and GRU, as well as Martha Dodd, daughter of FDR's ambassador in Berlin and her alarming career as a Soviet agent see C. Andrew and V. Mitrokhin, Chapter 7, "The Grand Alliance"; Allen Weinstein and Alexander Vassiliev, Chapter 1, "Communist Romantics, I: The Reluctant Laurence Duggan", *The Haunted Wood, Soviet Espionage in America – The Stalin Era*, NY: Random House, 1999; its two principal sources are File 36857, v. 1, 11-13, KGB Archives, Moscow; Paul Sudoplatov and Anatoli Sudoplatov, *Special Tasks: The Memoirs of an Unwanted Witness – A Soviet Spymaster*, NY: Little Brown, 1995, 3-21)

"Roosevelt, even though he knew that his health was failing, never explained his major foreign policy objectives to Vice-President Harry Truman or anyone else", Irwin Gellman wrote describing FDR's visceral disgust of Hitler: "Roosevelt grew to loathe German militarism. .... The American chief executive ultimately came to despise everything the Nazis represented, especially their renewed efforts at rearmament and the brutality that they unleashed upon their opponents. Almost from the very start of the New Deal, Roosevelt spoke out forcefully against the German government's persecution of its Jewish population. The president drew attention to this emerging reign of terror in its infancy because it offended the sense of decency and fair play that had been preached to him and those of his social class since his days at Groton." Hard to believe that Peabody of Groton ever spoke out against the slaughter of the people of the Philippines? ... He deplored the brutality of Hitler heaped upon a vulnerable minority, nothing more." Clearly there is a double standard at play here if true, ergo, reader, we are well in our right mind to ponder why Gellman choose to ignore the Soviet crisis in the Ukraine at the very moment FDR in secret but blatant denial of the reports goes deep cover on the famine doing nothing to help the Ukrainians? But so does all the Establishment historians and writers. *Quoi de neuf*? (What's new?) (I. Gellman, 16-7)

But Gellman prefers more confusion to obscure FDR's real and genuine intentions as he deals out decisions of foreign policy on the Consortium path to war. It's the sort of bunk that renders history superfluous and assured grants and scholarships to Oxford or any of the other top universities in the country. "Indeed, the president never followed a consistent set of principles in his conduct of international affairs," Irwin Gellman writes, and he adds, "He had not carefully studied the subject in school, nor had he developed a scholarly interest in it in subsequent years. His views had been nurtured since childhood."

FDR's direction of policy according to Irwin's take on it proceeds as though the Consortium and foreign investment in the fascist regimes never happened at all. Not a word from Gellman about Stalin's American engineers, Ford, Caterpillar and Harvester machines or the famine. For FDR, Gellman surmised, US foreign policy meant "collective security" and "unqualified support" to a Wilsonian post-Versailles brand of internationalism through the League of Nations which virtually collapsed with the Japanese walking out of Geneva in 1932, and Nazi Germany in 1934. "To win the presidency twelve years later," Gellman wrote, "he was forced to repudiate his earlier position endorsing US entrance into the League of Nations, but he never totally abandoned the concept of global cooperation. As president, he cautiously advocated it as a means of bringing about a more peaceful world, but whenever opponents challenged him on this emotional issue, he retreated. He vividly remembered the humiliation of losing the 1920 election and had no intention of repeating the experience." (I. Gellman, 16-8)

On foreign policy FDR was a disaster. "Diplomatic affairs were another matter," Gellman observes. "Roosevelt came to the presidency with a frame of reference for deciding foreign policy issues that few before him had possessed. Always an elitist, he truly believed that he could resolve any problem by himself. Although his self-assurance helped him in making many decisions, it also brought to the fore his inherent weaknesses. He was not a team player and he greatly exaggerated the extent of his knowledge; he was secretive, and sometimes insensitive and inconsiderate. He set out to play a dominant role without fully trusting the Foreign Service, and he acted unilaterally to illustrate his distrust. He had his own private agenda, which he seldom shared with anyone." That manner of doing business frustrates Stimson to no end, and though he praises FDR as the greatest war president the country ever had he finds relief in his successor Harry Truman who did away with the endless anecdotal chit-chat. Regarding relief in Russia Ukraine they never do, and focus instead on the economic revival of America abandoning the Ukrainians to their fate.

Through the Holodomor years FDR navigated his own traditional "good neighbor" foreign policy. For example, during his press conference March 20, 1935 when asked about Hitler's vamping up German rearmament, FDR answers, playing the fool to outwit Hitler and resurgent Nazi militarism: "I think we can only properly maintain the general principles of the good neighbor and hope that the American principle will be extended to Europe and will become more and more effectual and contribute to the peaceful solution of problems and, incidentally with it, as a very necessary component part, the reduction of armaments".

Gellman rightly finds that Roosevelt's projected persona "established himself as an activist president, and his promoters waxed ecstatic about the quality of his leadership in the Oval Office." Here Gellman interjects, "They, of course, gave him too much credit, but he seemed successful enough to perpetuate the myth of his omnipotence." For generations then and after this myth served the sycophants and the interests of the Consortium who then forever strive at their best to keep Roosevelt within bounds, never an easy task at that! Stimson winced. Hull grimaced. Welles squeaked. Bullitt squeals. Only a few months advising the

President Foley and Warburg resign. His steadfast political mentor and campaign manager Farley describe him "absolutely sure of himself – uncanny in his wisdom and judgment of things generally." Farley considers FDR acutely prescient, shrewd, competent to lead the country out of the Depression.

What about peace or war? FDR is praised for "good humor and ever-increasing aplomb". His detractors think different. Stimson and his undersecretary Bill Castle and others distrust Roosevelt's unpredictability and find it hard to read the man behind the mask and feigned grin. (I. Gellman, 87-91)

With Soviet socialism eclipsing into unbridled Stalinist terror, and the Ukraine crushed by the Holodomor, the ambassador scholar Dodd feels stuck in the heart of Europe, his soul darkened as he wades deeper in the darkening world of fascism funded and fueled with US corporate investment. Dodd agonizes over the prospect of war and peace in Europe. He feels uncomfortably lost and dangerously adrift in currents marching steadily to the breaking point. "Much as I believe in peace as our best policy," the ambassador writes the President October 19, 1936, "I cannot avoid the fears which Wilson emphasized more than once in conversations with me, August 15, 1915 and later: the breakdown of democracy in all Europe will be a disaster to the people. But what can you do? At the present moment more than a hundred American corporations have subsidiaries here or cooperative understandings.

The DuPonts have three allies in Germany that are aiding in the armament business. Their chief ally is the IG Farben Company, a part of the Government which gives 200,000 marks a year to one propaganda organization operating on American opinion. Standard Oil Company (New York sub-company) sent $2,000,000 here in December 1933 and has made $500,000 a year helping Germans make Ersatz gas for war purposes; but Standard Oil cannot take any of its earnings out of the country except in goods. They do little of this, report their earnings at home, but do not explain the facts. The International Harvester Company president told me their business here rose 33% a year (arms manufacture, I believe), but they could take nothing out." Dodd refers to Fowler McCormick, elected chairman and president at Harvester succeeding Alexander Legge; Harvester is the world's leader manufacturer of technologically superior heavy trucks easy for war conversion and the latest farm machinery needed for Nazi occupation of the Ukraine. The ambassador tells Roosevelt, "Even our airplane people have secret arrangement with Krupps. General Motor Company and Ford do enormous business here through their subsidiaries and take no profits out. I mention these facts because they complicate things and add to war dangers." (G. Colby, *DuPont Dynasty*, 1974).

INTERNATIONAL HARVESTER, MORGAN & THE ROCKEFELLERS

International Harvester is the model of American corporate enterprise and remains a top *Fortune* 100 corporation competing with Deere until its undoing in the late 1970s. An industrial giant it competes globally since it was started by

Cyrus Hall McCormick (1809-1884) and continues to be run by his son Cyrus H. McCormick Jr. who dies in 1936. Theirs is the reaping machine that revolutionized agriculture on par with the revolutionary invention of Eli Whitney's cotton gin for textiles in 1793 separating cotton seeds from cotton fiber. Unlike Russia the great stretches of flat, stoneless plains of America's future farm-belt lacks the millions of peasants needed to do the harvesting. Once the South had their cotton-picking slaves to build their economy and ill-gotten fortunes. McCormick found the substitute for hand labor in the mechanical reaper.

McCormick patented a modified version his original McCormick Reaper in 1834 near the time when Skull & Bones incorporates at Yale. (The McCormicks prefer the bucolic cow pastures of Princeton.) By 1847, he was turning out reapers from his Chicago factory while buying up rival patent rights and seizing the monopoly in production. A half-century later, in 1902, the McCormick company merged with four other leading agricultural machinery manufacturers to form International Harvester Company and began manufacturing tractors using an International stationary engine mounted on a chassis. A pulley wheel on the engine engaged the pulley on the chassis, producing a friction drive to the tractor. By 1909 technical innovation and marketing made Harvester the fourth-largest corporation in America and world leader in farm equipment technology and trucks. International Harvester promised to produce machinery to feed the world. (Scott Supply Co. website)

The road to monopoly is paved with blood and guts, and big money. The Deerings and McCormicks earned their battle scars in their greed for profits and market share. In these robber baron days of Wall Street sharks and cartel manipulators they're in over their heads and they knew it. Then the really big money kept the fighting families from cutting each others throats and missing the big picture. A hardworking ace in the insurance business caught the attention of the bankers. A Morgan partner George W. Perkins spells it out to them and his skilled maneuvering brought to principals to the table to merge the five largest harvester companies in America.

Perkins pulls off a deal to form International Harvester (IH) in 1902. The two largest of the group are McCormick Harvesting Machine Company and Deering Harvester, founded by William Deering (no connection with John Deere). From 1902 to 1912 Perkins and his partners at Morgan devise new schemes to exploit the giant global monopoly of the McCormick –Deering families.

Eventually, the McCormicks take control of the company's management. IH retained the old brand names while continuing to sell equipment under "McCormick," "Deering," "Champion", "Milwaukee" and other brands well into the early. Around 1923 the company dropped all of the separate brand names for the American market and began marketing farm equipment under the "McCormick-Deering" line. Abroad they keep the old brand names. Wherever the "Deering" brand name is dominant, such as Europe, International Harvester keeps it. (Lee Grady, researcher, Wisconsin Historical Library)

"Throughout ensuing negotiations," Barbara Marsh observes in her book, *A Corporate Tragedy: The Agony of International Harvester*, "he maneuvered to assure the Morgan firm controlling power in the new company.". But when the McCormicks resent Perkins' insistence for control, the banker agrees to the their concerns while keeping his stake of control in a voting trust lasting ten years and holding all the corporate stock. George Perkins, Cyrus McCormick, and Charles Deering serve as trustees.

"To oversee this empire," Marsh writes, "Perkins selected eighteen directors, ten of whom represented the five original companies. He quickly cemented Morgan's clout by installing himself and another Morgan representative as directors and also tapped two Morgan-connected directors of US Steel for board duty. He put himself in charge of the board's powerful finance committee, made Charles Deering chairman of the executive committee and Cyrus McCormick president of the company, and doled out vice-presidencies to principals from the other merging firms." (Barbara Marsh, *A Corporate Tragedy: The Agony of International Harvester*, NY: Doubleday, 1985, 40-1)

In the Guilded Age of extraordinary monopoly wealth and power it was only natural that the emerging ruling class in America, accustomed and jealous of their splendid isolation, protected and secure, combine socially as well as economically and politically. Individuals of wealthy families merged in parallel with their corporate holdings as the wealthy purveyors of the industrial revolution seized control over industry and government and reigned over the affairs of men.

Power in America quickly became a family thing and never more in evidence than in the McCormick-Morgan-Rockefeller consolidations. Heir to his father's International Harvester fortune, Harold Fowler McCormick, graduates from Princeton in 1895 and after a brief summer courtship marries Edith Rockefeller, one of the three daughters of John D. Rockefeller, Sr. and sister to JDR, Jr., or "Junior", as is his true family namesake. After the marriage JDR, Sr. holds some $30 million of Harvester securities ($750 million at present value).

Harold F. McCormick is named the third Trustee alongside John D. Rockefeller Jr. and Frederick T. Gates, JDR's close adviser, a Baptist minister and financial wizard to oversee the Rockefeller Foundation established in 1910 with $100 million initial funding which includes $50 million stake held in Standard Oil shares; by 1919 he had given the Foundation another $82.8 million for a total in the first ten years of close to $2 billion in current dollars. This is the time when the US government dissolved his Standard Oil monopoly in contentious Congressional proceedings. Actually, it was a windfall for the oil tycoon. His retains all his holdings now scattered into 33 independent subsidiary companies. When Carnegie passed by the Pocantico estate he found Rockefeller "tall and spare and smiling, beaming". Standard Oil stock had doubled. Wall Street had good reason to echo his prayer, "Oh Merciful Providence, give us another dissolution!"

Ron Chernow writes, "Those who had seen the Standard Oil dissolution as condign punishment for Rockefeller were in for a sad surprise. It proved to be the luckiest stroke of his career. Precisely because he lost the antitrust suit, Rockefeller was converted from a mere millionaire, with an estimated net worth of $300 million in 1911, into something just short of history's first billionaire. In December 1911, he was finally able to jettison the presidency of Standard Oil, but he continued to hold on to his immense holdings. As the owner of about one quarter of the shares of the old trust, Rockefeller now got a one-quarter share of the new Standard Oil of New Jersey, plus one quarter of the thirty-three independent subsidiary companies created by the decision.... Standard Oil of New Jersey remained the world's largest oil company, second only to US Steel in size among American enterprises and retaining 43 percent of the value of the old trust. Five of the newly divested companies stood among the country's two hundred largest industrial firms. Since all the companies had identical owners, it was hard to foresee vigorous competition. As Roosevelt (Teddy sic) complained, 'All the companies are still under the same control, or at least working in such close alliance that the effect is precisely the same.' ... the trustbusters helped to preserve Rockefeller's legacy for posterity and unquestionably made him the world's richest man." (R. Chernow, *Titan*, 556-9)

The next year JDR, Jr.'s father-in-law Senator Nelson Aldrich drafts a bill creating a federal charter to make the trust the largest philanthropic foundation ever; chartered in 1913 the foundation declares its purpose "to promote the well-being of mankind throughout the world." This is the same year the Aldrich-Warburg plan for the Federal Reserve Bank Act is put on President Wilson's desk and signed into law preparing the way to finance and prolong world war.

Harold' son H. Fowler McCormick (Groton, Princeton) worked his way up from the shop floor before earning the right to join the Harvester board which he does by 1936, and, as chairman replacing his older brother; Fowler McCormick, a favorite of JDR, Sr., also becomes a trustee of the University of Chicago, Rockefeller's crown jewel. In years of research I have found nothing to indicate that either the Rockefellers or their foundations, nor the International Harvester Company manifest any consideration or interest toward the causes or consequences of the Holodomor Terror-Famine. As regards the victims, the Rockefellers did nothing to intervene or even acknowledge that they exist. Jules Abels in *The Rockefeller Billions* (1965) states the Foundation in 1963 reported equity of $658 million held in stocks and "no less than $351,092,000 is invested in Standard Oil of New Jersey". In 1935 the Foundation gave close to $30 million in appropriations around the world. In the Consortium world of philanthropy beware of free gifts. Remember reader, in the world of givers and takers, there is no free lunch; philanthrophy is a double-edged tax deduction. Everything has a price. (J. Abels, 340)

Edith returns to Chicago hoping for reconciliation but her husband has other plans. He's hired Paul Cravath who had already brought from Europe a damaging witness. He sues, she signs, and before the papers are litigated, JDR sends his son-in-law a $1000 check for Christmas while his Edith falls deeper into debt after squandering $14 million from her father. Before the ink is dry in 1922 Harold McCormick marries the Russian-born Ganna Walska; both spouses seem to go haywire from then on. He spent thousands of dollars on singing lessons for her, all in vain. The primadonna became the model for Orsen Welles' classic film *Citizen Kane* rated on of Hollywood's all time best films. McCormick became just another number in a string of six marriages and countless lovers. After extensive effort including major surgery involving animal gland transplants to restore potency it all ends and he divorces Ganna in 1931.

As the second son of Harold and Edith Rockefeller, Harold Fowler McCormick, Jr. (1898-73), – "Fowler", as he was known, – is brought up in the Chicago family mansion on Lake Shore Drive. His older brother, baptized John Rockefeller McCormick after their grandfather, dies in childhood of scarlet fever in 1901. The grand hostess was entertaining when given news of her son's death. Edith kept up appearances with lavish grace not daring to interrupt the party. The shock is too great. She has already lost her nine-month old daughter. Instant freefall. Afterward Edith Rockefeller McCormick plunges into profound depression.

In one moment the richest woman in the world is suddenly doomed. Tragedy comes to both rich and poor alike and no one can escape their fate.

The rich indulge their fantasies, chase any whim, build whatever they wish, more grand and more sumptuous or taller than anyone dare dream, and they usually do. The "Villa Turicum" mansion is constructed in the hope it might help ease the pain of Edith's loss and distract her from her loss. But vanity is only a temporary cure for sorrow and it does not relieve her suffering or make her happy. A virtual fortress the immense villa towers over extravagant gardens and terraces encased with fountains and pavilions to highlight the beauty and pleasures of country life. Modeled after the "Villa d 'Este" ("settlement on water") in Tivoli, she chooses the name used by the Helvetian Celtic town of Zurich, Switzerland. To design the vast estate Harold McCormick contracts Charles Adams Platt at a cost of $5 million. A hidden elevator shaft and tunnel leads to surrounding structures to serve those not wishing to step outside its walls. Edith Rockefeller McCormick emerges once again as Chicago's most prominent hostess with grand entertainments and generous patronage of the Arts giving away Rockefeller money to the Chicago Opera and the Art Institute of Chicago, her principal pet charities.

But the ruse fails. Her life is shattered and she becomes in time unhinged. In fact she never recovers. The next year, 1913, she travels to Zurich for treatment under the care of Carl Jung. She is accompanied by Fowler, his sister Muriel, and an entourage of family servants and tutors in tow. By 1915 the entire McCormick family are undergoing Jungian psychoanalysis. She remains abroad for eight years and a devoted patron of Jung's practice. The Rockefeller family is perplexed that the old man JDR, Sr. harbors an "impenetrable" special affection for the young Fowler McCormick, "the only son of his renegade daughter" which did not go unnoticed by his other grandchildren. The grandparents look after them on their huge country retreat Pocantico in Westchester County on the Hudson both during school vacations before the First World War. "They knew that they were not his favorites .... Yet he liked them well enough and saw far more of them than any of his other grandchildren," Collier and Horowitz observed. Then Fowler is off to Groton, and Princeton. (P. Collier and D. Horowitz, 184-5)

During her absence her prized "Villa Turicum" is strangely silent except for the constant care of a full maintenance crew and staff, its gardens immaculately manicured. Edith never returned and there are no more grand soirees. Unable to manager her financial affairs, her estate dwindles to 1.5 million dollars with twice that in outstanding debts forcing her even to sell her precious jewels to the Cartier house for cash. Finally her tightfisted father JD Rockefeller, Sr. and "Junior", who in 1921 takes over the bulk of the $500 million fortune transferred over four years, – "about the same amount his father had already given away" –, cuts her off without a cent more. Ten years after her divorce, she dies, in 1932. A public auction of her personal property brought depression prices, $25,000 for $3 million worth of art and furnishings.

Abandoned and neglected the doomed estate fell into ruins. For her it was the End of the World. If there was Paradise, JDR most definitely every day at the appointed hour prays for it on the other side of the family. With all that Rockefeller money streaming into Berlin and Moscow through dozens of corporations and subsidiaries the Rockefellers show no concern for the Stalin's victims, and what they do few might have expected. Mircea Eliade (1907-86), formerly a University of Chicago department chairman and professor of religious history writes in of the vital collective and mythic practitioner of the Elect: "They react against the terror of History with an energy that only the extremity of despair can arouse." Yes, in fact, they do nothing. (M. Eliade, *Myth and Reality*, 68)

Through its ownership of mass media the capitalist ruling class is relentlessly clever in tweaking the nervous adulation with a life filled with pleasurable dreams that will never be experienced in reality. *Time* magazine's Henry Luce masters the art of nourishing the hunger for what's common in a democracy. Luce and his editors are well aware, even cynically excited by the fact that the rising mass of workers in America went starving without their tidbits of information fed to them daily, weekly and monthly in supplements with clockwork regularity of rationed medicine. Mass marketing and advertising experts empowered by students of modern psychology understand that the population gets fixated and mesmerized by doped information. They feed on it like kids at the circus.

Given enough over time the cultured masses would be ripened, fattened, softened and stuffed with the dope marketed and dished out by the corporate owners intent on the response that increased their corporate profits and took their excess in shares traded on Wall Street which in turn they leveraged as a barometer of the national economy they regulate with quarterly and annual earnings reports. And all of it convenient controlled with the Federal Reserve system of centralized banking and its friends at the center of the wheel. For Yale Bonesman Henry Luce his print and photo magazines, - *Time, Life, Fortune,* were all profitable tools of empire to seduce and control. Once Roosevelt was assured by the Consortium that the publishers, editors and journalists were solidly behind the Presidency, he reached out with radio, exploiting the technology to enter the homes and minds of Americans and capture their imagination to accept his secret war agenda with hope for recovery. (W. A. Swanberg, *Luce and His Empire*, NY: Charles Scribner's Sons, 1972)

And so it was that *Life* magazine on September 5, 1938 unfolds an array of photos of James A Stillman still active director of National City Bank arriving in New York for the marriage of Guy Fowler McCormick and "Fifi", - Anne Urquhart Potter Stillman, Stillman's former wife. Luce's editor's had called the

Stillman divorce "the most spectacular divorce case of the decade", and forced his resignation as bank president. Her mother had married Percy A. Rockefeller in 1901 when she was barely 16. The day of her divorce in 1931 she married Fowler McCormick, a grandson of JD Rockefeller. *Life* celebrates the affair with lusty enchantment for the gossip-hungry masses marveling in the private sensations of the ruling class. Upon graduating from Princeton in 1924 young Fowler "shocked his family by declaring his intention to marry Fifi, the mother of his college roommate once she divorced her husband, his roommate's father". Fifi is twenty years older than the young Fowler, and mother of four Stillman children. Psychologist Carl Jung, conjurer of the collective unconscious, was summoned from his home in Zurich to help Fifi "find herself" but at first was unable to make the long journey to the United States, and instead opted to send his assistant Peter Baynes, himself then distraught with his own marital crisis. Two years later the Stillmans divorce. The scandalous lovers married five years later. In June 1924, *The NY Times* announce the engagement of Anne Stillman to Morgan banker HPD, Jr. Davison Jr. becomes a partner five years later. They divorce in 1946.

Eventually Jung took a steamer to New York and met dockside by Fowler and his close friend George Potter. They install Jung at the University Club on Fifth Avenue, bastion of Consortium chieftains. On Christmas Eve the trio leave New York by train for Chicago where Jung stays as Porter's guest. Porter has also divorced and remarried. Jung then traveled westward through the Grand Canyon to Taos and the tiny commune of Mabel Dodge deep into Taos Pueblo Indian culture. Dodge is the former flame of John Reed and D. H. Lawrence and now apparently completely satisfied with her new lover Tony Luhan.

The Indian festivities included a spiritual ceremony of the "Buffalo Dance". Jung encounters the Hopi elder Mountain Lake who listens to the Zurich psychologist speak of "the mythology of the sun". Mountain Lake reveals to the wise white man tribal secrets "divulging various Hopi myths about the sun, the moon, and the state of the world". In *Protocols,* Jung recorded elements of pagan folklore in the Indian culture, writing, "The sun is their father and they help him rise. The sun wasn't made by God. It is the God." And they talked about Americans. Mountain Lake tells Jung, "What is wrong with the Americans. They are crazy, they think with their head, and not with their heart."

With his mother gone the "Villa Turicum" mansion now neglected and quiet fell to ruins. During the war years Fowler and his wife Anne settled in the West buying up vast parcels of land to create the 160-acre McCormick Ranch later purchased in part by the Cheney family. At the time of Anne's death in 1969 their ranch had grown to some seven square miles on 4,236 acres with 640 acres irrigated for livestock and wildlife and used in part for raising Arabian horses and Angus cattle. Eventually Fowler McCormick donates 100 acres of his sacred Arizona Hopi Indian countryside outside Scottsdale on condition that it be used as a public park for the laboring masses to enjoy and admire.

The McCormicks leave a legacy more familiar to visitors of Scottsdale than the stories of the famous and fabulously wealthy women Edith and Fifi. Their son later donated the family's railroad calling it "Paradise & Pacific Railroad" better known as the McCormick-Stillman Railroad Park equipped with three vintage steam engines, three diesel engines, a 1907 Baldwin locomotive, box cars, gondola cars and even a Pullman, one of six cars built in 1928 at a cost of $205,000 and used by Presidents Hoover Roosevelt, Truman and Eisenhower during their campaign rallies to the White House. The family created an Indian Arts and Crafts center near Shea Blvd with 7 *hogans* built from materials transported from the Hopi Reservation. After 1969, the remainder of the ranch was sold for 12 million dollars to the Kaiser Aetna insurance corporation to settle estate taxes. (Deirdre Blair, *Jung*, NY: Little Brown, 2004, 331-6)

A few years before Fowler McCormick discusses confidential Harvester affairs with the US Ambassador in Berlin, the naked truth of how quickly economic prosperity had spilled into the giddiness of a booming stock market bubble could be traced back to the false victory of a patriotic war and blood-soaked war profits enriching a handful of liars and crooks in Wall Street and Washington. Now in Berlin a Rockefeller grandson is staring the in the face while back home few Americans have a clue or even cared to know the real nature of Herbert Hoover or how he had emerged out of the death and ruins of the First World War as Bernie Baruch's Food Administrator in the War Industries Board. At that time President Wilson was lecturing the nation about the great and noble ideals of American democracy and Hoover was making secret deals to prolong the world war and make millions for the Consortium. Some "killing", eh?

In 1929 International Harvester stock trades near its peak of $142 a share. Following a series of furious mergers and acquisitions during the Harvester had regained its preeminence in the industry with domestic farm equipment sales of $150 million, tripling its closest competitor Deere & Co., of Moline, Illinois. *Fortune* calls the company "the greatest single agricultural enterprise in the world". As with Ford, windfall business from the First World War brought a boom to Harvester's truck production. Orders skyrocketed from 6,000 in 1910 to 227,000 in 1918 while worldwide truck sales remained modest. Under Legge's presidency the company focused on new production of its "Model S" speed trucks allowing farmers to whisk their ton-and-a half crop load faster to market. Since 1922 it began its Fort Wayne, Indiana plant Harvester has become the "Heavy Truck Capital in the World" Its ten-ton haulers and a massive Hall Scott four-cylinder engine beat out the competition throughout North America. By 1937, Harvester will have grown from its origins producing farm equipment to producing half-ton pickup trucks cutting into the profits of Ford and GM. None of this is known to the peasants in the fields of the Ukraine whose lives are radically transformed by Harvester and Ford machines on which their fate hinged. Are you kidding me? Their world, their families, everything they used to know is spinning away in the nightmare before their eyes, Cheka thugs digging up hidden grain stocks, villages condemned and abandoned to the dead and quarantined, families shattered, freight cars rolling to the gulag work camps…

HARVESTER, LEGGE AND THE WHEAT MARKETS

The stock bubble wipes out most of Harvester's shareholders slashing the stock to $10.37 in 1932. Prices of farm commodities wheat, corn, oats and barley which barely recovered from the depressed levels of the early 1920s plummet to new lows. After a brief rally in 1930 money for investment abroad decreased sharply. Countries cut back orders. Imports fall. Foreign leaders shuffle in a panic to shore up the value of their plunging currencies. By 1933 all major currencies will have quit the gold standard, except the French. Commodity prices continue to drop yet to reach bottom. Farmland values slump. Farmers hike production raking up surpluses which force prices into a downward spiral with the result that the total postwar net income made only small gains in ten years from $6.2 billion to $9.6 billion since the 1919 high.

The farmers clamored for price supports on their agricultural produce. In an effort to stabilize markets and deal with economic disaster in America's farm-belt. Baruch brings in Alexander Legge from International Harvester as one of Hoover's hirelings to stabilize wheat prices. During the war Legge had been food and raw material director under Baruch, and chief of service of the armies of the anti-German coalition; a decade later as the economy spirals into the Great Depression Hoover plucked him again from Harvester to head his Federal Farm Board. (B. Marsh, 56-7)

Legge leaves his $100,000 industry job. The government's new farm boss is paid a $12,000-stipend to manage a $500 million relief program. He must confront a bear market unwilling to take on U. S. farm surpluses. Foreign countries impose trade tariffs. President Hoover was famous for resisting government regulation of free markets. Canada and the Soviet Union are accused of dumping. A virtual war descends on the international wheat market with the world's poor drowning in a surplus of wheat production. Instead of relief, they starve to death.

Overnight Legge becomes one of most controversial personalities in the country. Legge's face is featured on the cover of *Time*. He's accused of bailing out corporations with government loans intended to off-set seasonal commodity price swings through the sale, purchase and storage of crops and at the same time tells wheat farmers to cut production. The farmers want the federal government to buy surplus stocks pushing the wheat price back to 60 cents a bushel. In the next three years the farmer's income will drop 70 per cent. "Wheat prices," *Time* wrote, "refused to rise when the Board tried to bull the market by direct buying." Hoover runs up against resistance by free market advocates who "flayed the Board for its 'socialistic program' of government-in-business." The President extends Legge's term to six years "long enough to make or break the current farm experiment and Mr. Hoover's maximum expectancy for White House residence." Hoover imagines he can buck the tide of Depression and impoverished voters facing unemployment, breadlines, and angry at seeing their savings wiped out by shrewd Wall Street speculators.

Legge is a Consortium player. A former cowboy rancher chosen by the McCormick Rockefellers to run Harvester he's a first-generation American whose parents sailed from Scotland to Wisconsin in 1857. After his family moved to Nebraska, he worked on his father's cattle farm and for a time in Wyoming before a lung condition obliges him to take an office job in 1891 as a collector at McCormick Harvesting Machine Co.. There a fortuitous encounter with Harold Fowler McCormick, then learning the family business on the ground floor in Nebraska, persuades McCormick when he relocated to headquarters in Chicago to bring along Legge to oversee worldwide claims.

Already in the Consortium world of big business Legge is fast on the way up. When the First World Way breaks out Legge catches the attention of Baruch in Washington who hires him as his vice chairman in the War Industries Board in charge of its Requirements Division; on the Allied Purchasing Commission Alexander Legge excelled at applying his corporate skills of the war business where he earned the approval of the Hoover government men under the American food czar, ARA famine relief in Communist Russia under Lenin and Trotsky. To crown his war-oriented activities Legge is honored with a Distinguished Service Medal and selected to join the US government's economic section negotiating the Treaty of Versailles. After the war in 1919, Harold McCormick took over as president of the International Harvester; three years later he resigned and succeeded by Legge. McCormick remained chairman. The next year Legge wins a key anti-trust suit and prevents the break-up of the giant company. That was ten years ago. ("Husbandry Legge & Job", *Time*, June 23, 1930)

Having been recalled back to Washington under President Hoover Legge is instructed to manage the surplus of American wheat production for the international market. From Grandfield, Oklahoma earlier that month federal officers moved the first carload of the year's harvest "all the way from farm to final buyer through cooperative marketing agencies," *Time* wrote quoting the Farmers National Grain Corporation. But the international grain market is in a slide as the prices of commodities tumble.

Indebted Farmers are nervous, their earnings slashed. Legge is unable to keep prices from falling. "The July figure in Chicago slumped to $1 per bu. – 7¢ below last year's mark", *Time* wrote. "Traders in the pit spoke of a 'panicky feeling'. Growers out in the country wondered when, if ever, the Farm Board would get them better prices. Meanwhile the National Grain Corp. braced itself to handle 300 million bushels of wheat (about one-third of the crop total) through its elevators and co-operative agencies." American farmers needing foreign buyers of the surplus are hit by rising tariff barriers. Worldwide economic depression continued to reduce US exports and imports declined. Now the social gains of the 1920s are wiped out. Between 1929 and 1932 national income in the United States falls by 38 per cent, the same level as the drop of the prices of manufactured goods; food prices drop by 48 per cent, and the prices for raw materials fall by 56 per cent.

Time tells only a part of the story: "Looming over the whole wheat market was an economic situation more potent than the Farm Board as a price-fixer. The visible world supply of wheat in May was 470 million bu., of which almost half (225,000,000 bu.) was held in the U. S. The Farm Board had advocated this holdover-from-1929 policy which now hung like an incubus over 1930 prices. The U. S. Department of Agriculture last week estimated the 1930 winter wheat crop at 532 million bu.—46 million bu. below last year's harvest of the same grain. But even this apparent cut did not materially aid prices." On the other side of the world, in Odessa foreign officials such diplomats of the Turkish Consulate carefully noted that the Kremlin is continuing to load and ship wheat "forcing its working class and the entire population to starve." (Yuriy Shapoval, "Foreign Diplomats on the Holodomor in Ukraine", "*Holodomor Studies,* 2009, citing HDA SBU, Kyiv fond 13, file 418, v. 1, pt. 3, fol. 632)

Everyday Americans opened their newspapers to find new lows as stocks continue to fall. Hoover's farm program is a failure; by 1932 the Farm Board agency is disbanded. In the same period Harvester's stock price mirrored the plunge in falling domestic sales down to $59 million, a 78 per cent drop. In 1932, for the first time since its creation with Rockefeller thirty years earlier, the company suffered a loss, of 7.6 million, and nearly $2 million lost in 1933. It will take another world war to bring it back to its 1929 high of $37 million in company earnings. Unemployment in the industrial countries hovers around 30 million workers and farmers who have lost their means of support. "In 1932, (the worst year for industrial countries)," J.M Roberts, in his *History of the World* (1976) observed, "the index of industrial production for the United States and Germany was in each case just above half of what it had been in 1929. ... There was to be no world recovery before another great war." (J. M. Roberts, *The History of the World*, Penguin-Knopf, 1976, 1995 ed., 880)

The book *Collectivism, A False Utopia* by Consortium journalist Bill Chamberlin is published in 1937 attributing "of the hunger in the towns and the famine in the country districts" in Russia (he doesn't cite Ukraine) as 'the accompaniment of Russia's rapid industrialization after 1929". Without describing mass murder or the systematic use of terror under Soviet dictatorship Chamberlin assures American farmers that "Russians, by and large, are eating less and worse than before the Revolution" and that life is better in the US. Misconceptions arise from false reports in the USSR. He writes, "America's troubles started from every newspaper and magazine headline, while Russia's were carefully concealed by an all-embracing censorship. There was plenty of publicity for the debt-ridden farmers of the Middle West, not a word for the starving peasants of southern and southeastern Russia (the Ukraine sic). The sufferings of the American unemployed were mirrored in hundreds of books and thousands of articles. One could search files of the Soviet press in vain for a single description of the sufferings of Russia's compulsorily employed exiles in timber camps and new construction enterprises, housed in foul barracks and dugouts, often under arctic conditions, receiving 'as pay' barely enough food to make it physically possible for them to perform their allotted tasks." The 1935 grain harvest "was well above those of 1931 and 1932, which were an immediate prelude to famine" while the "the per capita grain yield of 1913 was not quite attained". Chamberlin calls the 1935 harvest crop "the best harvest since the Revolution" at 91.6 million metric tons compared with 76 million metric tons in 1913, for a population of 171 million in 1935 compared to 138 million 1913. He quotes government figures from *Izvestia* showing livestock levels decimated, comparing 1916 and 1935: horses 35.1 million/ 15.9 million;

large horned cattle 58.9 million/ 49.2 million; sheep and goats 115.2 million/61 million; pigs 20.3 million to 22.5 million. But these ""official" estimates are still ludicrously high and meaningless. (William H. Chamberlin, *Collectivism, A False Utopia*, NY: Macmillan, 1937, 75, 88)

In these depression years that see America's industrial production cut in half and a quarter of its workers lost their jobs tens of thousands of Harvester's proud employees were cut from the company. As Stalin increases repression in the Ukraine and South Russia and Caucasus while collectivization of Soviet agriculture decimates villages and destroys lives of millions of peasants Legge returned to Harvester and not long after died of a heart attack. (Wheat Exports and Net Exports: Measured in 1000 bushels. Flour is converted into wheat at a ratio of 1 barrel of flour equals 4.7 bushels 1909-17 and 1921-39; US Treasury, *Annual Reports on Commerce and Navigation*, various years; "The Grain Trade of the United States," *Monthly Summary for Commerce and Finance*, Jan. 1900, 56th Cong, 1st Sess., Doc No. 15, pt. 7, 2022; linked to USDA, *Agricultural Statistics*: 1940, 9-10. Figures and sources cited by Joseph H. Davis, Vanguard Group, Christopher Hanes, NY State Univ., Paul W. Rhode, North Carolina Univ., "Harvests and Business Cycles in Nineteenth-Century America", June 2004; B. Marsh, 58)

HOOVER & ROTHSCHILD: AMERICAN FOOD CZAR OF BOLSHEVIK RUSSIA

The American most responsible during this period for complicity in American transfer of trade and technology to the Soviet Union in the incipient time of the Holodomor Terror-Famine was former Commerce Secretary and US President Herbert Hoover, Commander-in-Chief, and CEO of USA Inc. Eustace Mullins exposed dark secrets about this enigmatic stalwart of the Republican Party who looms over Consortium power in the White House for more than a decade since the October Russian Revolution, Bolshevik coup, the rise and fall of Lenin, and the consolidation of Soviet power under Stalin's proletarian dictatorship of the CP.

Mullins wrote, in *The World Order,* "As a mining stock promoter in London, Hoover had been barred from dealing on the London Stock Exchange, and his associate, who apparently took the rap, went to prison for several years. The incident brought Hoover to the favorable attention of the Rothschilds, who made him a director of their firm, Rio Tinto." Rio Tinto is the giant metal combine. Its chairman until 1925 was none other than Lord Milner, the founder of the Round Tables transformed into the Royal Institute for International Affairs, England's predecessor to the Council on Foreign Relations in the United States. Today Rio Tinto founded in 1873 is a world leader in finding, mining and processing the earth's mineral resources with headquarters in London. In 2012 it ranked as the fourth largest mining company in the world with a market capitalization of $134 billion, down from $147 in 2007. In the 1880s under the control of the Rothschilds is was the world's leading producer of copper. Soon his major rival will be Daniel Guggenheim.

From there Mullins traces the intrigue of Hoover's food deals during the First World War prolonging the carnage killing young men and civilians in so-called heroic exploits of courage while the future American President and his gang rake in colossal profits. Mullins tells an intriguing tale:

"In 1916, the promoters of World War I were dismayed when Germany insisted she could not continue in the war, because of shortages of food and money. The Czar's physician, Gleb Botkin, revealed in 1931 that the Kaiser's chief military adviser, and chief of his armies on the Russian border, Grand Duke of Hesse-Darmstadt, risked his life on a secret mission to Russia to Czarskoe Selo, the Imperial Palace, where he asked his sister, Empress Alexandra, to let him talk to the Czar about making a separate peace with Germany. The Empress, fearful of criticism, refused to receive him, and after spending the night at the palace, he was escorted back to the German lines. To keep Germany in the war, Paul Warburg, head of the Federal Reserve System, hastily arranged for credits to be routed to his brother, Max Warburg, through Stockholm to M. M. Warburg Co. in Hamburg. Food presented a more difficult problem. It was finally decided to ship it directly to Belgium as 'relief for the starving Belgians'. The supplies could then be shipped over Rothschild railway lines into Germany. As director for this 'relief' operation the Rothschilds choose Herbert Hoover. His partner in the Belgian Relief Commission was Emilie Francqui, chosen by Baron Lambert, head of the Belgian Rothschild family. The plan was so successful that it kept World War I going for an additional two years, allowing the US to get into the 'war to end wars'.

John Hamill, author of *The Strange Career of Herbert Hoover* states that Emile Francqui, director of Société Génerale, a Jesuit bank, opened an office in his bank as the National Relief and Food Committee, with a letter of authorization from the German Gov. Gen. von der Goltz. Francqui then went to London with this letter, accompanied by Baron Lambert, and Hugh S. Gibson, Secretary of the American Legation in Brussels." In 1952 ambassador Hugh Gibson is appointed Director of the Provisional Intergovernmental Committee on the Movement of Migrants from Europe. During the war he writes two books, *The Problems of Lasting Peace*, (1942) with co-author Herbert Hoover, and *The Road to Foreign Policy*, (1944). (John Hamill, *The Strange Career of Herbert Hoover*, NY: William Faro, 1931)

The US, AMERICAN CORPORATIONS AND NAZI WAR PREPARATIONS

American assistance steadily bolstered German economic reconstruction with giant firms doing a brisk business eventually underpinning Hitler's Reich economy from 1933 onwards into his rearmament years reinvesting their profits in German industries. For example, the two largest manufacturers of tanks were Opel, a wholly owned subsidiary of General Motors and the Ford's German subsidiary, Ford A.G. Morgan holds important stock portfolios in General Motors. In 1914, Pierre DuPont moved into the automobile industry buying General

Motors shares; the next year he held a seat on the board on his way to taking over the company as chairman after a $25 million purchase of GM stock and DuPont became GM's president. Soon GM became the number one automobile company in the world. Dodd was referring to Consortium Nazi deals such as the GM-Opel tax-exempt contract in 1936 with the Nazis enabling General Motors to expand its production under condition it reinvests profits in German industry production. All these plants and factories had war conversion capacity. Other leading American companies in the service of the Reich's economy included Ford, IBM, Alcoa (Mellon) and Dow Chemical (Mellon), Vacuum Oil (Rockefeller), Caterpillar-Deering (McCormick)

Uneasy about Japanese incursions on his eastern border Stalin welcomed official US diplomatic recognition and so-called "normalization" of relations. He has nothing to lose. Before extending the olive branch FDR waits until Stalin claimed victory in his war of Genocidal extermination of the Ukrainian peasants. Franklin Roosevelt would never mention the Holodomor. Like his predecessor it is strictly taboo. The Consortium' press organs controlled the debate and kept it off the front page. Luce, rabidly anti-communist, chides Ivy Lee and warns US businessmen not to be led into a trap, writing, "Prayers must be numerous and fervent indeed to stop Stalin, 'The Man of Steel', but he can be stopped the moment Business unites with the Church in an economic boycott of the Soviet Union. For Stalin's whole program is based on importing Ford tractors and U.S. technicians, exporting grain and raw materials."

In his cover story June 1930 showing an evil faced Stalin around whom conspirators plot, and titled "Stalin & Friends" *Time* tells its readers, "His business friends include Ford, International Harvester, General Electric, Radio Corp., DuPont, Standard Oil, Ivy Lee." Already in 1929 Stalin and US corporations had benefited from $108 million dollars of business under the Plans. His trip to Russia in May 1932 leaves him disgruntled and it seems at every turn he openly loathes the Russia and the Russians with their "atrocious body odor". On the train from Siberia to Moscow he observed, "It is not merely a pungent sort of barnyard odor. It is a decayed odor. It is everywhere the same. The nearest one could come to a definition was: the odor of rotten eggs in a damp cellar." Was it the smelter furnaces of the Magnitogorsk coke and chemical plant? Or, perhaps the incineration of peasants and workers? (W. A. Swanberg, *Luce and his Empire*, 100)

The American Consortium found in Germany a more advanced industrial client and more attractive investment than the USSR while building up military industrial economies in both fascist states. Stalin knew Germany was not yet prepared to begin hostilities. Such mania and madness of political and economic rivalry seduced the grab for power since the First World War. Versailles had set the tone and debate for war and rearmament. Rapid reconstruction remains the mantra and the Consortium led the way for the inevitable showdown between Nazi Germany and Communist Russia. A US-Soviet alliance had long been in the cards they both knew well. As our story unfolds we will see how Stalin smashes insurgent Ukrainian nationalism and exterminated its population by deportations and to slave labor camps and by starving them to death as prelude to war with

Germany. And although many Ukrainians who survived Stalin's repressions either joined or fought the Germans including nationalist partisans fighting for independence from Moscow's hegemony, in the end, the Ukrainians got smashed worst of all by all the Great Patriotic War. That's the real tragedy of the Ukraine. They never had much of a chance to defend themselves.

Ambassador Dodd in Berlin was more concerned by the financial and technical activities of Rockefeller's Vacuum Oil Company in building up military gasoline facilities for Hitler than shown by Bullitt's passivity over Vaccum Oil dealings with Stalin. Again, we have Sutton to thank for his research into the Wall Street-Nazi connection. Sutton wrote, "Standard Oil of New Jersey not only aided Hitler's war machine, but had knowledge of this assistance. Emil Helfferich, the board chairman of a Standard of New Jersey subsidiary, was a member of the Keppler Circle before Hitler came to power; he continued to give financial contributions to Himmler's Circle as late as 1944." The rise of Hitler paralleled contributions by Rockefeller's Vacuum Oil and General Electric. Dodd was overwhelmed by the monetary and technical contribution of Rockefeller's Vacuum Oil Co. behind Nazi gasoline facilities. Dodd tries repeatedly to warn Roosevelt. FDR, however, doesn't seem too interested in Dodd's litany of warnings and suspicions apart from encouraging him to carry on the best he can.

Alas Poor Dodd. How could he have known that Roosevelt started his legal career on the payroll of Standard Oil as a client of his firm. Rockefeller and Rothschild money is everywhere. It is just a fact of life never to change for a long, long while. Dodd may have naively hoped FDR would intervene. But Roosevelt himself is backed by these same oil interests. Walter Teagle, chairman of Standard Oil of New Jersey, for example, backs Roosevelt's New Dealism and sits on the board of FDR's Warm Springs Foundation. These are his friends and business partners. And though many of the Roosevelts on the other side of the family living in Oyster Bay on Long Island Sound consider Franklin a traitor, why should that matter to him when he has the whole world eating out of his hand, or starving. You can hear him now, with his head cocked backwards over the edge of his chair, laughing all the way to the bank. Laughing until at Yalta when the sly Russian wolf eats him alive while he devours half of Europe. Stalin survives, so tell me reader, who has the last laugh?

Unfortunately for Dodd he lacks the inside track that Bullitt cultivated with FDR. It frustrated him immensely. Paul Warburg's son, James Paul Warburg, vice-chairman of Bank of Manhattan, is Bullitt's personal friend evidenced by their amiable correspondence in September 1933. "Bill" and "Jimmie" were pals, a welcomed guest at Warburg's sumptuous town house at 34 East 74th Street in Manhattan, near Fifth Avenue and Central Park. His father, Paul Warburg, architect of America's Fed died, in 1932.

When FDR takes office in 1933 he appoints James Warburg Director of the Budget. Warburg sails to the London banking summit that summer but promptly resigned over FDR's voodoo economics. During WWII, Warburg set up the US Office of War Information, the government's official propaganda agency. In his 1950 testimony before the Senate Foreign Relations Committee, James Warburg said, "we shall have a world government, whether or not we like it. The question is only whether world government will be achieved by consent or by conquest." The Warburgs with vast holdings in Europe eventually became part of the elite New York Social Register set of millionaire society men, some of whom were part of the inner core of Pilgrims and their outer ring of CFR members who they control and use to execute their internationalist ambitions.

THE PILGRIMS SOCIETY

Once a King's man, always a King's man. These are all the King's men. God bless the Queen, their royal patroness. When writer Charles Savoie was researching the British crown-driven elite core of Anglo-Consortium men in the Pilgrims Society, he obtained a very rare to be seen 1969 Pilgrims Society membership list. It was leaked. Savoie learns how a particular set of these so-called "Pilgrims" are forever "locked in a struggle between the forces of 'created' money issued by central banks, and a movement to return to the use of true money – gold and silver. ... Baron Beresford, Admiral Charles William de la Poer Beresford (1846-1919)", –and a navy man since the age of 13, – "was a founder of The Pilgrims and close personal friend of King Edward VII who bombarded Alexandria, Egypt, and who, in 1882, authored *The Break-up of China* (1899). His brother, who attended a prep school appropriately located in Stabbington, England, was Military Attaché at the British Embassy in Saint Petersburg, Russia, 1898-1903. The financial powers whose base originated in North America joined the British Empire plan before the founding of the Society. Members of The Pilgrims have been active since the very beginning, first in bringing the Bolsheviks to power in Russia, in the formation of the USSR, in its industrial development and its break-up, and in the transition of China first to Communist rule, now mutating into a semi-capitalistic state." (Charles Savoie's reference to "the 2002 Pilgrim Book" in *World Money Power III*, 2005)

Pilgrims Society member Charles Hitchcock Sherrill (born 1867), a trustee of New York University was ambassador to Turkey from 1932 to 1933 and was so perfectly placed to monitor the Holodomor and tell about it but he never did nor would he ever. Sherrill claimed literary fame instead for having written a book based on his experience with foreign leaders titled *Prime Ministers and Presidents* (1922). It echoes the tone of sentiments echoed by followers of Cecil Rhodes who said of his Pilgrims Society "patent", "I am on the lookout for those who will do the governing of the nations in the years that are to come." In such a world as this is it any wonder why no one cared about the poor Slavs!

The Royal Institute on International Affairs (RIIA) was the brainchild of Cecil Rhodes founded as a means to "expand British hegemony globally and to regain Britain's control of the United States." America follows the path of the Crown, more or less. As the American spin-off of the British Royal Institute on International Affairs (RIIA), Rockefeller created the Council on Foreign Relations (CFR) in 1921.

The mandate of the CFR provides a national forum to influence US foreign policy. It was also a primary mover behind the United Nations. As it were, the CFR receives major funding for its activities from the private collective of Consortium of banks conveniently called the Federal Reserve Bank. Since the Fed collects all income tax money from US Treasury deposits and most of the interest on the US national debt, it wields astronomical financial power and influence.

When the Fed chairman sneezes, watch out!

Imagine why the Fed banks like debt so much…A fine system to tie up the hard-working masses into a knot of debts! Just lower interest rates and sweep them away in the flood, seizing property and assets overnight !

Today their program is coined "globalization". Research by Charles Savoie suggests that this anachronistic Pilgrims Society membership included the major heavy powerbrokers and representatives of key foundations and institutes hungry for longevity and more power. Their ranks did not overlook Andrew Carnegie who "was openly loyal to the King of England, one of the patrons of The Pilgrims", as indeed was his friend and fellow Scotsman President Woodrow Wilson.

Their design was a politically managed world government and centrally controlled economic monopolies rendering sovereign nation States powerless to defy their combined international financial and corporate power. The Royal Institute of International Relations and the CFR were under their influence as well as later versions acting through fronts that include virtually all important organizations: the Trilateral Commission, Council of the Americas, Asia Society, Japan Society, Committee for Economic Development National Corporation for Housing Partnerships, Atlantic Institute for International Affairs, Woodrow Wilson International Center for Scholars, International Executive Service Corps, California Institute of Technology, Stanford Research Council, Bilderberg *et cetera*.

Senior-ranking Pilgrims sit on steering committees and head major banks and corporations. David Rockefeller founded the Bilderberg group in 1954; it was no mere coincidence that Pilgrim member David Rockefeller, chairman of the CFR and son of its founder, took special pride in his Moscow address for Chase Manhattan Bank at 1 Karl Marx Square. It seemed like the perfect place from where to open up new channels to export Soviet resources and oversee trade for the Soviet communist masses. Even before Sutton published his findings on US-Soviet trade, Emanuel Josephson's *Rockefeller Internationalist* appeared in 1952 with a chapter on the Rockefeller family's connections inside the U.S.S.R….

Reader be patient. This Holodomor, Stalin, the Russification of the Ukraine, Genocide, World War Two and its consequences were so befuddling to the world as it had been for centuries that to understand it requires a rather good long look up close. Oh, and lets not forget that little creature the A-Bomb and its nuclear offspring proliferating out of control. So, kindly bear in mind the same Consortium interests backing Hitler and Stalin are also backing Roosevelt in one way or another.

Fascism was in fashion, a trend that comes and goes never without leaving a stench. (And whose to say its out of fashion now!) This is the way it was.

And one has got to ask how could it be any other way. The powerbrokers and junior members of these earlier organizations were groomed with initiations, pomp and ceremony with a protocol dedicated to their privilege, where public service was to mean how best to use government to pursue their private agenda agreeing to keep most of their experience and knowledge to themselves. American investors mixed with the boot-stepping Nazis saluting Hitler and persecuting Jews. That clearly frustrated the naïve ambassador who felt utterly powerless there whereas Bullitt was cynical and obsequious to the rich and powerful he envied and tried to emulate. And reader we know Walter Teagle of Standard Oil of New Jersey is a major contributor to FDR and his NRA economic domestic policy. It's one of many instances where the Consortium company was simultaneously consolidating Bolshevik Russia, the Nazi industrial war machine, and the NRA legislation of Roosevelt's New Deal. (Sources include Mullins, Savoie, Sutton, among the many.)

In the politics of famine, the role of influential US companies inside the Consortium elite raises profound questions that had been surreptitiously avoided and circumvented. Almost all of the German directors of German General Electric were financial supporters of Hitler and associated not only with AEG (German General Electric) but with other companies financing Hitler. AEG was sold to a Franco-Belgian holding company and evaded the conditions of the Young Plan. US Consortium investment in Nazi Germany did not escape the attention of the Chief of the Economic Warfare Division of the US Department of Justice who observed "The AEG of Germany was largely controlled by the American company, General Electric." These are facts that American establishment historians don't teach and feel uncomfortable putting into context with Roosevelt's foreign policy. But that did not deter Antony Sutton from lifting the veil.

Why was the famine allowed to proceed unabated for so long and worsen year after year? For this writer, and former investigative journalist, this was the first question that came to mind. Why were the facts known to American and British Moscow-based western journalists covered up? Why did the State Department and FDR in the White House assume an official policy of silence and inaction while maintaining business as usual with Stalin? Why did Washington and London back Stalin and his Five-Year Plans for industry and agriculture transforming the communist regime into a slave state run by bureaucrats and secret police? When the crimes of the Bolsheviks filled intelligence files with an endless stream of official internal documents why did the western leaders stand-by and do nothing to stop Stalin's extermination of the Ukrainians and other ethnic peoples of the USSR and millions of Russians through systematically organized mass murder, terror, depopulation?

The experience of the Great War of 1914-18 served a lesson how the masses were slaughtered while the international bankers and corporate industrialists of the Consortium ruled over empire and legislated their politics of war profit and greed. In the decade after the war they survived and held the power among themselves and sons all the while proclaiming themselves to be champions of freedom and democracy at any cost necessary in human life and human values.

These self-serving men created, bought or financed the institutions of society controlling even freedom of thought. They defined how things ought to be and prepared every day for the spoon-fed, hard-working and playful masses. The Consortium motto for the masses might just have well been "You work with your hands, we work with your minds."

"YOU WORK WITH YOU HANDS, WE WORK WITH YOUR MINDS"

The Consortium seemed to own virtually everything. They owned and fabricated their own culture as well as the mainstream. Their lawyers drafted legislation and stacked the courts with state and federal judges up through the Supreme Court. Law and order was their eminent domain. The Consortium set the tone and standard of right and wrong. They could even justify war and mass murder and ethnic cleansing in the national interests. Their politicians controlled Washington and implemented policy decisions handed down to them from above. So it was no mere coincidence that when the famine struck worst in the Ukraine at the same time the General Electric corporation risked public scandal as a prominent supplier of funds for the puny ex-corporal from the trenches in 1918. For his meteoric rise to power as German Chancellor in 1933 those funds were funneled through its GE's subsidiary AEG and Osram, an electric light bulb manufacturer. A blip on the radar that passed unnoticed by the public in the form of a bank transfer slip dated March 2, 1933 from AEG to Delbruck Schickler & Co. in Berlin requests that 60,000 Reichsmark be deposited "for Hitler's use" in the Nationale Treuhand (National Trusteeship) account. This at a time when FDR has his hand on the Bible and swearing under oath to protect liberty so precious to the American Constitution giving new meaning to his status as leader of the most powerful democracy in the free world then in the grip of moral, economic and political bankruptcy. IG Farben was the most important of the domestic financial backers of Hitler and in 1933 IG Farben contributed 30 percent of the Hitler National Trusteeship (or takeover) fund.

William L. Shirer, eye-witness of the ascendancy of the Reich, American foreign correspondent in Berlin and author of the several authoritative books of the Hitler era – *Berlin Diary* (1941), *The Rise and Fall of Adolf Hitler* (1961), *The Collapse of the Third Republic* (1969) ..., – and zeroed in on the Farben-Krupp connection to the Reich's military industrial success. The Krupps represent one of the most prominent dynastic families in Germany. Dating back four centuries they became famous for their steel production, ammunition and armaments. The family business, known as Friedrich Krupp AG Hoesch-Krupp, in Essen, is the largest company in Europe at the beginning of the 20th century. In 1999 it merges with Thyssen AG to form the industrial conglomerate ThyssenKrupp AG.

William Shirer (1904-93), writes for the Col. McCormick's *Chicago Tribune*, and will be the first reporter hired by Edward Murrow for his CBS radio team set up in London in 1937. Shirer writes, "A visitor to the Ruhr and Rhineland industrial areas in those days might have been struck by the intense activity of the armament works, especially those of Krupp, chief German gun makers for three quarters of a century, and I. G. Farben, the great chemical trust. Although Krupp had been forbidden by the Allies to continue in the armament business after 1919, the company had not really been idle. As Krupp would boast in 1942, when the German armies occupied most of Europe, 'the basic principle of armament and turret design for tanks had already been worked out in 1926. ... Of the guns being used in 1939-1941, the most important ones were already complete in 1933."

Having discovered how to make synthetic rubber from coal and overcome the handicap of the lack of an essential war materials that still had to be imported until 1933, "the Nazi government gives IG Farben the go-ahead with orders to raise its synthetic oil production to 300,000 tons a year by 1937. ... By the beginning of 1934, plans were approved by the Working Committee of Reich Defense Council for the mobilization of some 240,000 plants for war orders. By the end of that year, rearmament, in all its phases, had become so massive it was obvious that it could not longer be concealed from the suspicious and uneasy powers of Versailles." (William L. Shirer, *The Rise and Fall of the Third Reich*, 1959, 282)

IG Farben controls American subsidiary. Moreover, several directors of AEG (German GE) are also on the IG Farben parent company board. Hermann Bucher, chairman of AEG sit on the IG Farben board along with AEG directors Julius Flechtheim and Walter von Rath. On March 2, 1933, for example, another transfer slip was sent from AEG to the Delbrück, Schickler Bank in Berlin, instructed payment of 60,000 RM to the *Nationale Treuhand* fund used to elect Hitler in March 1933, and administered by Rudolph Hess and Hjalmar Schacht. We will explore more of the Rockefeller–IG Farben (Interssen Gemeinschaft Farben) connection later. (Nuremberg Military Tribunal, document No. 391-5)

The German industrialists and bankers wrote the then acting Reich President Field Marshall von Hindenburg to appoint Hitler as Chancellor. *The Brown Book of Nazi and War Criminals* (1965) recalled what happened next: "After the big monopolies had brought Hitler to power, even more funds were made available to the nazi party and its organizations. Under the name 'Adolf Hitler Donation of the German Economy' the capitalist enterprises, on the initiative of the big trusts – especially Krupp, IG Farben, Flick and Thyssen, etc., – made available to the nazi party from 1933 to 1945 over 60 million RM a year. In 1934, Dresdner Bank alone paid over 120,000 RM to the nazi party. ... Besides the payments to the Hitler Donation Fund, the armament monopolies made large financial contributions to the SS and other organs of the nazi terror apparatus. Friedrich Flick was among the most ardent of the donors and supporters of the Nazi party. Along with steady payments to the so-called "Circle of Friends" of Himmler – annually over 100,000 RM – Flick paid large sums to the 'Adolf Hitler Donation Fund' and to all local organizations of the Nazi party. The Steel Works in Riesa, which belonged to his trust, for example, transferred over 34,000 RM to the local SA and SS units from 24 February 1933 to the end of 1934."

William L. Shirer in his book *The Rise and Fall of the Third Reich* (1960) observes how the Nazi industrialists first stood back then supported Hitler such as Krupp von Bohlen und Halbach, "king of the munitions makers", becoming "a super Nazi". "How much the bankers and businessmen actually contributed to the Nazi Party in those last three years before January 1933 has never been established. ... Thyssen estimates it at two millions a year ; he says he himself personally gave one million marks...One of the most enthusiastic of them at this time – as he was one of the most bitterly disillusioned of them afterward – was Dr. Schacht, who in 1930 resigns his presidency of the Reichsbank in protest to the Young Plan, meets with Göering in that year and Hitler, in 1931, and for the next two years devoted all of his considerable abilities to bringing the Nazi power center closer to his central bank and industrialist friends and ever closer to the great goal of the new Chancellor. By 1932 this economic wizard, whose responsibility for the coming of the Third Reich and for its early successes proved to be immeasurably great, was writing Hitler "you can always count of me as your loyal supporter".

With the Nazis in power Schacht becomes Hitler's Economics czar with full control over German industry "empowered ... to integrate independent enterprises into the cartel system and bring them under cartel control," ascertains Norman Rich (Yale) working for the State Department at Nuremberg. The extraordinary Herr Schacht! The Consortium's own Nazi monopolist is empowered by the Nazi decree February 27, 1934 that leaves no illusion who controls the cartels. The law authorizes Schacht to form and control business associations "and eventually to ensure state control over all associations and their members", according to Rich who becomes professor emeritus of American history at Brown. As long as Schacht remains at the top of the German economy the Consortium is in position to exert control of Hitler's war machine.

While Roosevelt is sailing on the Astor yacht *Nourmahal, and nearly assassinated in Miami by a lone crazed immigrant, in Berlin* Schacht organizes a secret meeting February 20 at Göering's Reichstag President's Palace. "Göering and Hitler," Shirer writes, "laid down the line to a couple of dozen of Germany's leading magnates, including Krupp von Vohlen, who had become an enthusiastic Nazi overnight, Bosch and Schnitzler of IG Farben, and Voegler, heard of the United States Steel Works." Hitler promised to impose authority and economic stability by force. Hitler declares, "All the worldly goods we possess we owe to the struggle of the chosen. ... We must not forget that all the benefits of culture must be introduced more or less with an iron fist." Krupp and Thyssen applaud Hitler's plans for repression. Shirer adds, "Dr. Schacht then passed the hat. 'I collected three million marks,' he recalled at Nuremberg." It was to be paid immediately apparently for Hitler's electoral campaign but in reality it's slush money for Hitler's "other weapons"; two days later Goering orders 40,000 SS and SA soldiers into the Prussian police force, the cornerstone in the Nazi terror program. As our story unfolds we will see a lot more of Hitler's favorite Jewish Nazi banker and friend of the West Dr. Schacht. (*Brown Book of Nazi and War Criminals,* 1965, 1968; W. L. Shirer, *The Rise and Fall of the Third Reich*, 145, 190; R. Payne, *The Life and Death of Adolf Hitler*, 253)

But reader, we must not get too far ahead of the famine story in the Ukraine, that rich territory which Hitler covets so madly even when he wishes to destroy the Slavic culture of the Russians which he loathes with demonic madness. As we explore more of the Consortium's buildup of Germany's war monopolies we also realize that many top GE managers join America's wartime Office of Strategic Services, the OSS. More recently, in November 2007, IG Farben surfaced again in a paid advertisement published in *The New York Times* with a scathing attack on Bush's Iraq War by French President Nicholas Sarkozy and the pharmaceutical industry on the occasion of his visit to the White House and Congress. A real *faux pas*!

What happened to IG Farben after the US Justice Department confiscated it at the beginning of the war? Seymour Hersh in *The Dark Side of Camelot* (1997) in a footnote explains how JFK passed it over in a pay-off to Stanislaus Radziwill, an exiled Polish prince, brother-in-law to the First Lady, Jackie Bouvier Kennedy and "vote-getter for the Kennedy-Johnson ticket". Hersh writes, "The family's vehicle for rewarding Radziwill turned out to be the General Aniline & Film Corporation, an American chemical company once owned by Germany's IG Farben. After the war it mysteriously passed into a Swiss holding company, Interhandel."

The Swiss want it; negotiations followed in the fifties with former GE president Charles E. Wilson as the Swiss intermediary. People in the Eisenhower administration called the Swiss ploy a front for the original Nazi owners. The day JFK was nominated for the Presidency his brother Bobby got involved; Wilson was replaced by Radizwill. A deal went down whereby the company stock was put on the market and sold on Wall Street in 1963 for $207 million, a handsome reward for everyone involved and one that Joe Kennedy Sr., FDR's former SEC chairman, would have been proud to tell his friends if he could but is paralyzed and unable to speak. (Seymour M. Hersh, *The Dark Side of Camelot*, NY: Little Brown, 1997, ftn. 235-6)

There are alarming implications raised over these same corporate forces plying within Roosevelt's New Deal emergency program to alleviate the economic depression that swept across America in those critical years 1932 and 1933. Could this have been a reason for their dulled insensitivity to the crushing of the peasants the Ukraine? Americans watched in shock as their savings vanished overnight. Thousands of banks closed. Thousands teetered on the brink.

Few Americans knew that when Rockefeller's Ivy Lee was peddling communist propaganda to push Soviet bonds on Wall Street in Baruch early in 1928 outlined FDR's future New Deal socialism for a speech in Boston. Sutton found a disturbing parallel between the rise of Germany's national socialists bearing "a remarkable resemblance" to the Swope Plan for a "New Deal" in America engineered by Gerard Swope, board chairman of GE and International GE, and traces an economic convergence in philosophy straight back to Walter Rathenau of Germany. Swope is another of the top Consortium insiders of the FDR administration. His counterpart in Germany is Rathenau (1867-22) himself a director of the German subsidiary founded by his father Emil Rathenau (1838-15), *Allgemeine Elektrizitätsgesellschaft* (AEG), in 1899, and in the early part of the 20th century on the board of at least one hundred corporations. In fact, the Rathenau Plan is a masterful blueprint for Roosevelt's New Deal customized by Swope. Sutton's conclusion here is irreversible, and he writes, "We have the extraordinary coincidence that the authors of New Deal-like plans in the USSR and Germany were also prime backers of their implementers: Hitler in Germany and Roosevelt in the USSR".

Enter Stalin. These Consortium men all share in common the control of an internationally linked combination of national central banks, huge cartels and monopolies of industrial resources, and highly organized and disciplined labor. Keep reading as we pass through this labyrinth! You will see how first the Ukrainians were caught in the squeeze, along with the Jews and even the Old Bolshevik revolutionaries themselves when "The Game" spins out of control and Hitler starts attacking all of Europe in his mad pursuit for world domination of the master race.

Or, as we see with these wars and depressions did these men really ever have their affairs in control in their dark evil and creepy world? In the world of force and resistance, power must always use its power to have any. The Consortium must remain in control however discreet and seemingly innocuous. This maxim is obvious but overlooked only by the powerless. People are always attracted to ministers and their power. Political power, military power, corporate power, sexual power. Power attracts like an aphrodisiac. GE power stations ran virtually the entire Soviet electrical power industry. Without GE the Soviet regime would be without power. What would the smart Bolsheviks do then? Certainly many people wondered was Stalin, the Communist Party of the USSR, and for that matter, the entire Soviet Union now dependent on GE and the Consortium for their survival?

With news of the Holdomor Terror-Famine now reaching a peak across the vast plains and cities of the Ukraine, South Russia and the Caucasus, and featured widely in the international press of the world's capitals, in Washington on June 16, 1933 the National Industry Recovery Act becomes the law of the land. FDR appoints a tough pug-nosed Brig. General Hugh Johnson to run the National Recovery Administration (NRA) assisted by Swope now free to spread his ideas through the US Chamber of Commerce. Swope, of course, is also a high-ranking member of the CFR linking the domestic agenda with the Consortium's plan for the new world order. With broad powers to regulate wages, prices, and working conditions, it was, as Herbert Hoover stamped in his memoirs "... pure fascism... merely a remaking of Mussolini's 'corporate state'...." In a few years the US Supreme Court will strike it down ruling the NRA unconstitutional. In the land of liberty where the spirit of human freedom strikes a nerve, some dogs just won't fly. (Herbert Hoover, *The Memoirs of Herbert Hoover: The Great Depression, 1929-1941*, NY: Macmillan, 1952)

EUSTACE MULLINS REVEALS "SECRETS OF THE FEDERAL RESERVE"

Revelations from extensive by Antony C. Sutton and Eustace Mullins combined with readings of historians and writers in and out of the Establishment mold help to identify the convergent roles of Gerard Swope. Here in the nexus of the culture of American power the economics of Big Business and the politics of totalitarian fascism rising on the gamet of social and political fronts in America and abroad pivot with key figures of the American network of the Consortium. We find Morgan-Rockefeller-Harriman nexus at its center.

As repressive conditions of collectivization and industrialization in 1932 severely increase the plight of the peasants and the Holodomor shows more signs of breaking out into a most terrible human catastrophe, GE are heavily invested in both Soviet state communist terrorism and Nazi fascism. At the same time American directors of Germany's GE operations are prominently connected with the US financial and political elite: chairman of International GE, president of GE, director of National City Bank (and other companies), director of AEG and Osram in Germany… As author of FDR's New Deal and member of numerous Roosevelt organizations, Swope also heads GE's board and serves as deputy chairman of the New York Federal Reserve.

Through the JP Morgan bank Swope's influence showS the preparation of the Young Plan which supersedeS the Dawes Plan in 1929. It was Charles Dawes who arranged, in 1924, an $800 million loan package to consolidate steel and chemical corporations into giant German cartels including 'the Farben'. Georgetown professor Carroll Quigley describes the Dawes Plan "largely a JP Morgan production".

"In brief," Sutton underscores, "we have hard evidence of unquestioned authenticity to show that German General Electric contributed substantial sums to Hitler's political fund." Eighty percent of AEG was owned by International General Electric with four American directors on the board making them "the greatest single influence in AEG actions and policies". But that's not all. Through their connections with other German firms like IG Farben and Accumulatoren Fabrik, nearly all other AEG directors were contributors to Hitler's political fund! In less than a decade, this Nazi regime with its publicly declared extermination program will invade the Ukraine to liquidate what had barely survived years of Stalin's Terror-Famine. (Antony C. Sutton, *Wall Street and the Rise of Hitler*, Seal Beach: '76 Press, 1976)

TO THE VICTOR GOES THE SPOILS

In order to comprehend the influence of the Consortium relationship during the famine, fast-forward a few years and see what happened at the postwar trial of Nazi war criminals at Nuremberg. The court of the victors did as much as to exonerate and conceal the American pro-Nazi role as it did to condemn the leaders of the German fascists. Nazi industry for electrical equipment was controlled by a few corporations linked within an international cartel by stock ownership to two major US corporations, General Electric and the International Telephone & Telegraph Corporation (IT&T). Only German directors of AEG were tried in 1945. Not DuPont. Not Standard Oil. The Military Tribunal in Nuremberg 1945-46 set a precedent for US corporations investing in the dictatorships of foreign countries protecting them from prosecution for crimes against Humanity. More than a half century will have to pass before private companies were obliged, by internal shareholder pressure brought on by persistent social activism, to adopt principles for ethical development as an integral part of their business plan, in particular against their use of forced labor to increase profits and shareholder equity.

Germany served as a convenient third party for American corporations doing business with Stalin's huge communist monopolies. The Soviet chemical industry, for example, contracted with DuPont and Nitrogen Engineering for synthetic nitrogen, ammonia and nitric acid technology, to Westvaco for chlorine and to H. Gibbs to supplement IG Farben in the Aniline Dye Trust. If there were reports on the Ukraine filed for the President in the Holodomor year of 1933 Roosevelt ignored them. FDR had his own top advisers including John Raskob of DuPont; Walter Teagle of Standard Oil and Edward Filene. Together they composed the triumvirate pushing Roosevelt's NRA. The latest industrial equipment used in producing ammonia is also shipped to the USSR by DuPont and Nitrogen Engineering. FDR's State Department authorized this "peaceful trade" conveniently ignoring that one of the by-products producing ammonia is nitric acid essential to making explosives. Developed by German chemists to overcome the American blockade in Chilean nitrates, and a chemical company before it was merged with other chemical companies to form the cartel, IG Farben produced the killer chlorine gas used in World War I. (US Congressional Record, Oct. 3, 1975, E5215-E5216; (A. C. Sutton, *Wall Street and the Rise of Hitler*)

During the Depression years with GE and DuPont stock selling for cents on the dollar the Nazi-Soviet business promised rewards not forthcoming in the chaotic American economy. Documents corroborated to Sutton that "General Electric worked out a cartel agreement with Krupp to pool the patents of both parties and to give General Electric a monopoly control of tungsten carbide in the United States". This is only one of a daunting number of incriminating cases of direct collusion, indicative of the general operating strategy of Consortium activities in which GE figured prominently. Sutton writes, "General Electric – with the cooperation of another Hitler supporter, Krupp – jointly obtained for G.E. a monopoly in the US for tungsten carbide."

By 1939 Germany's electrical industry was closely affiliated with two US firms: International GE and IT&T. The Nazi German electrical industry was never a prime target for bombing in World War II. AEG and IT&T plants were rarely and minimally damaged by air raids. The electrical equipment plants bombed as targets were not those affiliated with US firms. GE retains a monopoly on tungsten carbide at around $450 a pound – almost ten times more than the 1928 price and unavailable in the US. As a result, German production of electrical war equipment rises steadily throughout World War II, peaking as late as 1944. According to the US Strategic Bombing Survey reports, "In the opinion of Speer's assistants and plant officials," Sutton writes, "the war effort in Germany was never hindered in any important manner by any shortage of electrical equipment." In Germany, as in the Soviet Union, peacetime industrial factory production was designed for rapid conversion to war work. This was common knowledge to the Consortium principals active in their financing and development. (A. C. Sutton, *Wall Street and the Rise of Hitler*)

Surely ambassador Dodd *en route* to Berlin must have known before his meeting Crane in New York that for decades Westinghouse activities in Russia were organized by industrialist Charles R. Crane, a Washington lobbyist, and senior member of the cherished Pilgrims Society. This former chairman of the finance committee of the Democratic Party between 1890 and 1930 made made no fewer than twenty-three visits to Russia. It was Elihu Root, a long-time Standard Oil lawyer and Taft's Secretary of State who later taps Crane to join the famous Root Mission to Russia in 1917 after the fall of Tsar Nicolas months prior to the Bolshevik coup that topples Kerensky's Provisional Government. Then Wilson's bankers bankrolled Lenin's terror and blood purge in the former empire of the Romanovs.

Elihu Root, Charlie Crane, Henry Simpson head the State Department's genteel club. As the Consortium's personal emissary, Root was given one hundred million dollars from Wilson's Special Emergency War Fund to prop up Bolshevik regime. Interviewed by journalist Lincoln Steffens and Bill Bullitt late winter 1919 after they arrived in Petrograd and Moscow in an attempt to negotiate a peaceful end to the American, French and British expeditionary intervention, Lenin spoke of the imperialist war that killed millions, and now reeked famine, a fierce Russian Civil War with unspeakable atrocities committed by both Reds and Whites, the Allied blockade compelling mass starvation and the use of terror just to survive another day as the ruins of war in Europe burned and crumbled and the amputees and wounded soldiers returned to a world as unrecognizable as themselves.

In his biography of Lincoln Steffens (1974) Pulitzer prize writer Justin Kaplan observes Lenin's defense of the Russian terror and killings by the Bolshevik state secret police, the newly-formed ranks of the Cheka:

"'Do you mean to tell me," Lenin demanded, 'that those men who have just generalized the slaughter of seventeen millions of men in a purposeless war are concerned over a few thousands that have been killed in a revolution which has a conscious aim: to get out of the necessity of war – and armed peace? Then he became resigned. 'But never mind, do not deny the Terror. Don't minimize any of the evils of a revolution. They occur. They must be counted upon. If we have to have a revolution, we have to pay the price of it'." (Justin Kaplan. *A Biography of Lincoln Steffens*, NY: Simon & Schuster, 1974, 247-8, with a dedication to Joseph Barnes)

Harrison E. Salisbury had occasion to know both Stalin and Khrushchev. His beat was Moscow during the war years, first in 1944 as head of the UP bureau, then joined *The New York Times* as bureau chief in 1949 for five years and remains in Russia five years more. In 1955 his *Russia Re-Viewed* wins him a Pulitzer. Other works include his superb account of the heroic battle of Stalingrad, the city completely destroyed by both armies in one of the greatest siege battles in the war and perhaps ever in world history. Two decades passed while compiling unforgettable memories and facts in gripping detail of the heroic battle for survival before publishing his vivid and thrilling account based on extensive Russian sources of the extraordinary defense of Leningrad (1969) and the horrible loss of a million Russians.

Yet, while amassing his account of the glory and gore of Russian courage and sacrifice Salisbury ignores any responsibility or role played by a Consortium power stratagem in the military rearmament and economic reconstruction of the Soviet State. That in itself is enough to leave a doubt as if to suggest while affirming the credit it deserves nonetheless to admit that "Uncle Joe" and his Red Army do a darn good job destroying the Nazi war machine. A commendable feat, indeed, and not without a price of some 25 million dead Russians, - and this all published during the détente years of the Cold War thaw.

So, while dismissing Marxist Bolshevism from Lenin to Khrushchev as a complete fiasco nor do we find any reference to activity to overthrow Czarist Russia by Jewish, banking and empire machination as though this incredible human catastrophe came about out of the blue sort of dropping out of the sky in the aftermath of diplomatic and political blunder. If only the Leningraders like the Ukrainians a few years earlier really knew what hit them in the logic of war before and behind Hitler's ruthless attempt to destroy the city and starve the population into non-existence as they fought for the survival of Mother Russia against world domination or a thousand year Reich. Salisbury is pure establishment historicity. Hitler's plan for total annihilation and extermination of the Russian peoples was not so idiotic; easier to exterminate then convert. Just try it. The Russians prefer their own good Russian butter to all the spam, chocolate and chewing gum shipped from America.

A proven stalwart iconoclast and insatiable veteran investigative reporter for Sulzburger's *NY Times*, Salisbury instead, implies that it was obviously clear for any pea-brain to see that from the beginning nothing the leaders of the Russian Communist Revolution could do would set things right. Later came his turn-about and anti-war coverage of the Vietnam War, a genuine turn-of-heart and audacious act of courage, – or bravado. Or is it really a behind-the-scene Consortium ploy toward inevitable withdrawal of US commitment once the chips were down and the White House was confronted with hostile public opinion and anti-war riots breaking out in cities and college campuses all across America?

From the start their course was doomed. Lenin had decided, as this he told Steffens, that "in the long run of history it will have been better for us to have tried our Marx to a finish than to have made a mixed success." By January 1924 Lenin is a dead man, isolated, crushed and poisoned by Stalin. His wife, the inimitable Nadezhda Konstantinovna Krupskaya arrested under the Tsar and married young Vladimir Ilyich also under arrest in Siberian exile, in Ufa, is intimidated, threatened with Siberian exile, or worse. She even insists that upon Vladimir's death there should be no grand-standing state funeral with all the pomp and circumstance that he detests, no cultist appropriating his legacy, and certainly no eternal embalment in a mausoleum with millions of awed mourners mesmerized that harsh Moscow winter.

But Stalin gets his way.

The socialist communist monolith drifted in Party debates over Lenin's NEP shift dependent on engagement with the western capitalists in order to pull Russia out of the rubble of war, disease and general devastation. Stalin emerges from the ruin more empowered and treacherous than his rivals. Many would carry precious impressions when even then the Ukraine and the USSR was wrecked by famine and saved intact by Hoover's ARA emergency food mission feeding millions of survivors and firming up the ruthless Bolsheviks in the Kremlin for whom he showed only contempt and suspicion.

Upon his quick return from Bolshevik Russia Lincoln Steffens met with Hoover over lunch on April 7, 1919 pushing for a humanitarian relief program combined with an economic trade package "to take the blooming philanthropy out of the thing and make it a simple proposition to stops fighting on both sides and begin to trade." Hoover is more inclined to treat the Russians as little more than a helpless and starving calamity of war. Hoover asks Stevens, "Can those Communists make a go of their food system?"(J. Kaplan, 247-52)

"Lenin," Harrison Salisbury would have us believe, "never did get around to defining Communism except for one speech in which he said it was 'electrification – plus Soviet power', which made it sound something like the Tennessee Valley Authority." Yes! Salisbury was close to defining the Consortium truth behind Leninism. In fact, had Salisbury written "Westinghouse – plus Soviet power", or mentioned Col. Hugh Cooper, the American dam engineer in the USSR, perhaps he would have risked revealing the predominant Soviet dependence on American science and technology and risk exposing the history of Westinghouse, General Electric and the role played by the American Pilgrims inside the CFR behind US foreign policy. Imagine the controversy arising from all the ills of the Soviet Union and the myth of the Cold War hype meant more to contain American fear and paranoia! Better to have a Cold War, an arms race, and threat of nuclear war with the Reds marching to Main Street! If Harrison had been more objective then perhaps the whole house of cards might have fallen long before it was time to follow Russia's interim provisional government president Kerensky to America after he was rushed out of Moscow in a US Embassy car.

Although the American correspondent fell under the shadow of Stalin's Holodomor he showed more generosity towards Lenin's earlier challenge, the ever-important predicament of agriculture and recurring famine in Russia. "The biggest problems," Harrison Salisbury writes, "in the Soviet economy almost from the start have centered on agriculture. … Karl Marx was a city man. His interests lay in the factory system and the urban proletariat. He paid little attention to the European peasant and farming problems. … Lenin at the time of his death left farming in the Russia almost entirely in the hands of individual peasants. The state operated a few large grain and cattle farms (most of them estates that had been expropriated). There was a handful of cooperative, or 'collective', farms. That was all. Stalin decided to change all this. He had three objectives. First, he wished to break the political will power of rural Russia, which could by simply reducing sown crops or by withholding food from the market, bring enormous pressure to bear on the Government. Second, he wanted to extract from the peasants every possible kopek of profit from their production – profit to be utilized in financing industrialization; Third, he though he could increase farm output by combining the individual peasant plots into larger, better-managed units. Stalin won his drive to collectivize Soviet agriculture. In a space of less than three years more than 95 % of Russian farm lands were incorporated in farm collectives or state farms which were directly operated by the Government."

Of some 29 books two which cover the war, veritable textbooks on the Soviet history of Russia during the war years, in particular *Stalingrad,* and, *The 900 Days – The Siege of Leningrad*, the latter which at the time of this writing is now in its 85th edition. Yet Salisbury, to be sure, offers only a slightly different account than his older *NY Times* colleague Walter Duranty.

At first the apparent subtlety of distinction boggles the mind yet both place the burden of guilt for the Holodomor on peasant resistance. Salisbury, a tall, lanky self-described "flat-toned Midwesterner", passes the worst Genocide in human history with a terse rebuff, writing, "…the price was colossal. Millions of kulaks, or rich peasants, were uprooted and shipped to Siberia. Civil war broke out in some regions. Peasants retaliated against the Kremlin by slaughtering their cattle, burning the harvests, concealing crops from the grain collectors. The toll in lives reached into the millions and many regions were struck by famine." It reads like incredulous Duranty verbatim. Had he read Sutton's ground-breaking work on technology transfers? Reader, we know that we'd better wonder. And when you think about it as with Duranty's pro-Stalin bias this superb reporter slams another slap in the face of Ukrainian revolt and independence. Establishment reporting at its best, in bed with the Bullitt breed of diplomats, and yes, deserving of another Polk or Pulitzer. A veritable establishment journalist icon of professional integrity, a mover and shaker, of the Kennan-Conquest set, Shirer is *The NY Times* man who knows how to play "the Game". Reader, beware. The Consortium plays for keeps…

In his book, *Without Fear or Favor: The New York Times and Its Times* (1981), after Duranty dies on October 4, 1957 Harrison Salisbury returns to the famine correspondents controversy writing, "He had long since run through all his funds and in a pathetic letter to Arthur Hays Sulzberger, in August appealed for a pension Sulzberger sent him his personal check for $2,500 on September 5, 1957." All fed by the same paymaster, so what difference does it make, Mr. Salisbury? (H. Salisbury, *Russia,* 52; *The New York Times* Archives 495; Harrison Salisbury, *Without Fear or Favor: The New York Times and Its Times*, NY: Ballentine Books, 1981)

While he is mostly remembered for his Russian books and staunch defiance of Stalinist censorship, among his innumerable hallmarks was the coverage of the JFK assassination by his *NYT* desk, and later his controversial visit to North Vietnam in 1966 where Salisbury suddenly emerges as the first mainstream American journalist to question President Johnson's massive aerial bombing campaign. Again, he narrowly misses out for another Pulitzer by the jury still decidedly pro-war. Salisbury dies in 1993, at 84.

From the beginning, periodically and long before Stalin officially launched the Five-Year Plan for collectivization of agriculture the peasants revolted against Bolshevik repression. In his study "Foreign Diplomats on the Holodomor in Ukraine" (2009) Yuriy Shyapoval notes how "representatives of foreign missions recorded revolt by the peasants although foreign correspondents suppressed it in their reports choosing not to offend soviet authorities and risk losing a return visa and the perks and rewards of their profession. According to the opinion shared by an Italian diplomat, raised in July 1930, and this before 1928, "it was possible to consider that the Government will be able to overcome the crisis, but today, in connection with the latest failed collectivization measures that have sparked powerful resistance on the part of the population, it is evident that the Soviet government will not be able to cope with the tasks that it is facing." (Yuriy Shapoval, "Foreign Diplomats on the Holodomor in Ukraine", *Holodomor Studies*, 2009. Shapoval cites as sources : Andrea Graziosi, ed., "Lettres de Char'kov'. La famine en Ukraine et dans le Caucase du Nord à travers les rapports des diplomates italiens, 1932-34," Cahiers du monde russe et soviétique, 1-2, 1989; Andrea Graziosi, ed., Lettere da Kharkov. La carestia in Ucraina e nel Caucaso del Nord nei rapporti dei diplomatici italiani, 1932-33, Torino : Einaudi, 1991; Marco Carynnyk, Lubomyr Luciuk and Bohdan Kordan, eds., *The Foreign Office and the Famine: British Documents on Ukraine and the Great Famine of 1932-33*, Kingston, ON, Limestone Press, 1988; Dymitri Zlepko, ed., *Der ukrainische Hunger-Holocaust*, Sonnenbühl: Verlag Helmut Wild, 1988; "Ukraina. Holod 1932-33 rokiv : za povidomlenniamy brytanskykh dyplomativ," Vsesvit 11,1989: 153-62; Upokorennia holodom. Zbirnyk dokumentiv, Kyiv: Instytut ukrainskoi arkheohrafii, 1993, 47-101; Wsevolod Isajiw, Famine-Genocide in Ukraine, 1932-33: Western Archives, Testimonies and New Research, Toronto: Ukrainian Canadian Research and Documentation Centre, 2003; Lysty z Kharkova. Holod v Ukraini ta na Pivnichnomu Kavkazi v povidomlenniakh italiiskykh dyplomativ, 1932-33 roky, Kharkiv: Folio, 2007 ; Andrii Kudriachenko, "Holodomor v Ukraini 1932-33 rokiv ta ioho suspilno-politychni naslidky za otsinkamy dokumentiv politychnoho arkhivu MZS Nimechchyny," in Holodomor v Ukraini: Odeska oblast. 1921-23, 1932-33, 1946-47. Doslidzhennia, spohady, dokumenty, Odesa: Astroprynt, 2007, 20-7)

"THE GAME": DECEIT, DENIAL & DECEPTION

It all came back to haunt poor Ukraine. How magical it was to see an electric light for the first time ever! First there was Light! They called it "a miracle". But they did not know the truth of it. To the extent of blurring the origin of Lenin's famous dictim that "socialism is electrification" so too did Salisbury do a smooth job glossing it over.

Why?

A Consortium deal.

General Electric was among the main "shareholders" in the joint-stock company created with Electroexploatsia, the second largest Soviet trust founded in June 1924 specifically to provide Soviet electrical systems and promote the use of electricity in the Ukraine and other rural areas. Lenin praised electricity as illumination by the October Revolution and proof of the victory of the proletariat. It was GE.

The huge Soviet trust was responsible to build new district electrical stations and provided state and collective farms with electric generators and motors. GE's Swedish subsidiary, ASEA, held shares purchased at 250,000 rubles paid in cash. Other shareholders included the Soviet People's Commissariat for Agriculture, Gosstrakh, Gossprit and Sakharotrust. ASEA's role was to organize and provide the equipment. That made GE a prime mover behind the draconian state collectivization program and methods. Just as Marxist-Leninism is inseparable from Stalinism and the harness of the cult of personality that binds Russia to this day under Putin there's no yellow brick road paved with good intentions.

Under the eyes of the US government and with its participation in German rearmament monopolies Hitler secretly started to prepare for a new war immediately after they had lost the first. Step by step the plans unfold, passing through the hands of such people as Harriman, the Morgan bankers, the Rockefellers and their loyal servants like Prescott Bush across the board from the deeply embedded Dulles brothers of Sullivan & Cromwell to countless other American law firms and international investment houses.

Gustav Krupp von Bohlen und Halbach declared in January 1944 that the success of the German military economy had been due largely to their early preparation. "Only due to this work of the German enterprises which was shrouded in silence", Herr Krupp in a speech declared, "…was it possible immediately after 1933 to find speedy solutions to the new tasks of rearming".

In the end Hitler benefits by living a little longer, instead of ending up a lifeless victim at the hands of the Rockefeller-funded SS. On top of that he either got nothing, or a promise from the Rockefellers' – owners of Chase-Manhattan and Standard Oil and Mobil, and partners with IG Farben at Auschwitz, and their fellow Nazis supporters in America – the record suggests not implausibly albeit outrageous as it may seem – (is it any more incredible than the Holodomor that preceded it by a few years and served as a precedent ?),– that in return for his Holocaust, they would use their influence over the US government and the military to prevent an invasion of Europe *for nearly two and one-half years.*

And they did just that. Of course the evidence for that "promise" is circumstantial. If it exists in any secret protocols, pacts or treaties, it hasn't yet been found. How else do you explain Hitler's suddenly insane diversion of resources, the reversal of his ten-year old policy of deporting Jews, and the two and half year delay by FDR before invading Europe? Actually the deportations continued to the very end of the war. (Charles Higham, *Trading With the Enemy,* NY: Delacorte Press, 1983, 20-2; A. C. Sutton, *Wall Street and the Rise of Hitler,* Seal Beach: '76 Press, 1976. Chase and Manhattan merge in 1956.)

Hitler could not have waged world war as long as he did without the help of the West. Standard Oil's contributions to the Nazi war effort were absolutely vital to the success of Hitler war plans. After Roosevelt's death, these monopolists took control of the State Department. A good look at military intelligence files for the period ought to be revealing. Hitler received enormous, indispensable, and really unbelievable support from the most powerful elements in the country including many top American corporations as Ford Motor Co., DuPont, GM, and, of course, GE.

General Electric's Japanese business in the thirties ought equally to be of interest in following the web of links and connections inside the Japanese nexus. GE director Clark Minor sits on the board of Japan Electric Bond. Rockefellers' Standard Oil provides Hitler's war machine with a patent for synthetic rubber, while keeping that dirty secret out of sight of the US military – even after Pearl Harbor! The US is desperate for such a formula.

Nor do leaders outside thte Consortium, including FDR's American ambassador, know that Standard Oil is providing the Nazi Reich with numerous other patents critical to their war effort, and owned a half-interest in the death camp at Auschwitz with their partner, IG Farben. A 1943 IG Farben special report pointed out that without the gasoline additive tetraethyl supplied by Standard Oil, "the war effort would have been impossible." (C. Higham, 216; A. C. Sutton, *Wall Street and the Rise of Hitler*)

Soon after the war it was disclosed that from 1933 until the end in 1945 the giant IG Farben made significant payments to Hitler's war chest. Armament companies interconnected with Germany's central government and linked to Germany's most powerful trusts provided funds and expertise to advance Hitler's national socialist fascist agenda for world domination. This is no trivial joke. Nor is it incidental. It is real and it happened. Carl Krauch, for example, emerges as Czar of Hitler's chemical industry and weapons program as chairman of the supervisory board of IG Farbenindustrie AG, Carl Krauch. Krauch also happens to be director of the "Reich Office for Economic Development" as well as the "general agent for special questions of chemical productions".

After the invasion of the Ukraine in June 1941, Farben directors hold key and highly sensitive posts from armaments to banking and the Foreign Office as well as government and party offices attached to military commanders and Reich commissioners in the occupied territories of the Ukraine and elsewhere.

From the start Ukraine figures as a target of Nazi expansionism. After the eclipse of the Holodomor, by early 1935 when FDR's hand-picked ambassador frequently shuttles between Berlin to Moscow, Stalin has already begun to intensify his campaign for mass terrorism removing any hint of threat to his absolute power, glee with success after the successful liquidation of Ukrainian resistance and Roosevelt's recognition of his regime and concentrates of eliminating the last of his recalcitrant Bols and tens of thousands of top military officers. None of this escaped the attention of Nazi intelligence. Furthermore, IG Farben creates the *Vermittlungsstelle W*, its Military Liaison Office empowered to calculate the economic details of war and mobilization with the Military Economy Office of the High Command of the *Wehrmacht*. From the Ukraine the Germans sought grain, coal, ore and Caucasian oil concentrating German military settlements in the Kuban and Caucasus territories. Once again death reared its ugly head towards the peasant villages as the German fascists particularly in the giant armament monopolies systematically prepared to plunder the Soviet Union.

Thus, only a few days after Hitler launches the Nazi invasion of the Ukraine on June 22, 1941 – a date engraved in the memory of all Ukrainians – IG Farben agents methodically list all the Soviet plants it aims to takeover. The Prussianized Germans are a very disciplined and organized race, systematic in executing orders much like one expects from wooden soldiers or robots and not wishing to leave anything to chance or accident. It is ingrained in them, and in their body motion, and in the way they think and organize their logic and thought processes. Marx mastered the Hegelian dialectical materialism but the Russians always had a problem with its application, or, even making sense of it, and lost sight of reality in the abstraction mixed with peculiar jaded Russian humour, the result of centuries of Russian custom.

Five years of perestroika and glasnost shattered the myth and icons of the Marxist-Leninist dogma revealing the corruption of an empty faith inconsistent with reality that promised only more misery and failed to deliver the goods. Angry Russians fed up with abuse and hardship cried out denouncing their managers who betrayed them, managers of a failed economy who stole and sold the goods for a song.

We can refer to David Satter who observed events before and after the end of the Soviet Union. In his book *Age of Delirium* (1996, 2001), Satter writes, "The rate of economic growth fell sharply and, in 1990, production started to decline. In a system of fixed prices, suppressed inflation led to the collapse of the consumer market. In the summer of 1989, of 211 food products, it was possible to buy freely only 23". Americans and the West should understand that Russians in their very nature are survivors and evolved from cultural experiences Americans find hard to comprehend. They endure and keep a stern firm face on hardship. Still the recent Soviet collapse was not as bad as in former days after the Germans blew up the Petrograd food warehouse in 1941. Again Russia's indomitable *babushkas* cried of inevitable famine. Here the voice of the women of Mother Russia are always at the heart of the matter. (D. Satter, *Age of Delirium*, 79)

Gorbachev's attempt at reform of the state economy contradicted private initiative. State controls clashed with market dynamism and entrepreneurs demanding democratization for a free market. The result was social chaos and economic anarchy. What would the "Lenin of today" with his NEP think of all this mess? In 1991 when the house finally came tumbling down on top of them. Politburo members were jeered. Party leaders faced a defiant stronger opposition. Some people have to learn the hard way, if they learn anything at all. In the Ukraine, the Chernobyl nuclear explosion and meltdown on April 26, 1986 is the fatal blow occurring just three days after the US Congressional Committee hearing on the Holodomor. Famine Genocide and nuclear meltdown. Ukraine is hit with a double whammy! Both are man-made tragedies of epic proportions; both occur in the Ukraine under the responsibility of the power in the Kremlin. This time although the Kremlin tries it is unable to coverup the magnitude of the disaster as the leaked radiation that fills the skies blowing west over Europe threatens the entire the world. Nuclear contaminants know no closed borders. Poor Ukraine! Another colossal tragedy. Another burden to carry. Once they could see from their windows high above the Dniepr Russian Ukrainian blood that poured into the Dniepr; now when they drink the water they cannot even what is killing them. Before they prayed and asked why; now no one knows when the end will come or how. To the hapless Ukrainians old memories of unseen terror long since past are not forgotten. And some hardened Stalinists shook their fists. "Its the Americans, the capitalist! They are to fault for this new terror! The bloody damn American nuclear technology! But we made the Hydrogen bomb with American technology. And bigger!"

It may even be attempted to interpret a connection in the coincidence of the conference in Washington to the explosion in Chernobyl and even perhaps evoke a historico-cultural correspondence in this ancient world where women were dominant in the "matrilocal and matriarchal society" even with the lapse of time. But reader let me defer to historico-religious philsopher Mircea Eliade, author of *Myths, Dreams and Mysteries*: "We should speak of *tendencies* rather than historical *realities*." (M. Eliade, *Myths, Dreams and Mysteries*, 176)

More golden tears of fearless love and suffering. No one can deny that the Tartar-Russian Slavic Ukrainians are survivors. Brave firefighters volunteer and work furiously to cover the reactor proud of their "duty" to save the nation. Many are decorated, and dozens die. Thousands of children suffer thyroid cancers and will for the years to come. Estimates vary widely as high as 200,000 people risk contamination but no one can say for sure how many will suffer and die. How many children will be born tomorrow with deformities from bizarre mutations in the gene pool of mothers and fathers as a result of the radiation no one can say but it is probable that the scenario corresponds in a great measure to the realities.

And again the Holodomor story is swept off the front page, not by Hitler's fascism and persecution of the Jews but a possible nuclear Holocaust any day now. Within five years the population of a new younger generation fed up with the lies and corruption of the ruling Communist Party hiding behind a false and failed ideology. As the country sinks deeper into economic stagnation the Soviet Union ceases to exist.

A new younger post-Stalinist generation had to suffer what their parents and grandparents went through during the Holodomor years. Party officials lied in a massive cover-up and the list of fatalities never ceased to rise under glasnost. The Ukrainian parliament asserted Ukraine's right sovereignty, to control its own resources and the right to establish Ukrainian citizenship organize its own national army.

When a deadly silence once hung over the villages where only old women whispered in hushed voices now they spoke out openly for their dead ancestors and destroyed villages. David Satter tells the story of the family of Olexandra Ovdijuk and their family lost in the Poltava region of Targan subsisting on grain stalks, bark, dirt, roots, anything not to starve. Satter writes, "At first, the villagers thought there had been some terrible mistake, but as the days passed, they started to realize they were the objects of a diabolical plot. First, medical and government representatives stopped coming, then roadblocks are set up along the highways to keep the peasants from leaving. Military guards surround the railroad stations, even the most insignificant. The villagers saw, to their horror, that the authorities had decided to imprison them in the countryside and that there was no food.... People dug up acorns and ate mice, rats, sparrows, ants, and earthworms. They ate tree bark, blades of grass, and autumn leaves. First the children died, then the old people. As the famine deepened, one student after another in Ovdijuk's school stopped coming to class. One day, shortly before the school was closed, the teacher asked Ovdijuk and two other children to find out why Timosh Babenko had not come to class. When the children went to Babenko's home, they learned that his mother, driven mad by hunger, had chopped him up with an ax. By late February, the sounds of normal life in the village had given way to an impenetrable silence...."

Ukrainian historian, Volodymyr Manyak invited Ovjijuki to Kiev to speak at a symposium on the Holodomor in Targan. Manyak said, "What happened in 1933 exceeded all the dark dreams of all the hangmen of the world. The perpetrators had high positions in the Communist system and turned their punishing sword on their own people. In the earth lie 9 million of our people. A similar act of bestiality does not exist in history... There is no analog to such a crime of a government toward its own people. The famine was directed against Ukraine and specifically against the village. The village was the guardian of the national spirit and the national language and customs." All around the country the national anthem could be heard as the people sang "Ukraine Has Not Yet Died." (D. Satter, "Ukraine", *Age of Delirium*, 351-79)

American shareholders benefited by the slaughter of Ukraine. Profits from German investments are reinvested in German operations. In fact there were restrictions to prevent taking profits outside of the country. Profits *had* to be reinvested in the Nazi regime. GE's German subsidiary was 80 percent owned by its mother American company. Similarly, the Farben established a special company for Soviet spoils, the AEF Ostlandwerk GmbH.

The Germans not only scorched and conquered the vast fields, they soon supplanted their employment of slave labor with Ukrainian Jews and war prisoners. Those who lived were fed food unfit for animals. As early as February 1942 the German Minister of Labor wrote a memorandum, "The present difficulties with regard to the employment of labour would not have arisen if one had decided in good time to make extensive use of Russian prisoners of war; 3.9 million Russians were available. There are now only 1.1 million left." Russian and Polish children were dragged off to Nazi armament factories and systematically put to work. The Hescho Trust, linked to the Deutsche Bank, employed children eight years old. Splendid German efficiency! (1.1 million figure cited in *Brown Book of Nazi and War Criminals,* 1965, 1968, 26)

Concentration camps were converted into cheap labor factories for the monopolies. They followed Stalin's re-education camp propaganda, for example, like at Dachau and Auschwitz, where they were called "labor reform camps" in "agreement with the Gestapo...to stop breaches of works discipline" .... The "systematic extermination of children, women and old people began in Treblinka, Belzec and Auschwitz. The most powerful monopolies immediately participated in this criminal business. They invented and practiced the method – Extermination through Work'. In the immediate vicinity of the extermination camps they built huge factories. Here the Jews were driven to work, without pay, given the worst food possible and had to live under completely inadequate sanitary conditions. The Auschwitz concentration camp commandant Rudolf Hoss, in his affidavit (Nt, IG Farben Trial, NI 034) named the monopolies – IG Farben, Siemens, and Halske, Krupp, Daimler-Benz and Henschel among others – which exploited concentration camp prisoners in the most inhuman way and on a large scale."

Workers were exploited to physical exhaustion, terminated, and replaced by a new work force. The monopoly tycoons at IG Farben even made a death profit supplying its Zyklon B poison gas. These companies continued to invest their war profits after the war. Some of the companies developed through American subsidiaries. For example, the IG Farben successor company, Farbenfabriken Bayer AG founded an American subsidiary in 1951, in Kansas City, Missouri, the Chemagro Corporation, to supply "the US Army with poison gases" developed by Bayer AG thus evading then the obligations of international law under the Geneva Convention banning German production of warfare agents and transferring operations to the US.

What happened to Stalin after massacring the Ukrainians? FDR rewarded him with the Lend-Lease give-away under the "Grand Alliance". Add to that at least twenty million dead Russians and Easts Europeans, Yalta, Poland and the freedom of half of Europe sacrificed topped off with a Cold War to further throw a totalitarian propaganda wall financed by American citizens on one side and on the other Soviet citizens who remained mutually isolated and in the dark about the traffic of business between the two monolithic world powers.

Wearied by Roosevelt's delay in mounting a second front in Europe Stalin's close aide and wartime foreign minister, Molotov pleads with Churchill, in 1942, and later tells him, "Well, if you can't help us with a second front, help us with arms, help us with aircraft. If they had opened the second front in 1942 or 1943 or 1944 it would have gone very hard for them, but it would have helped us immensely...."

To expect help from "the American people" in defense of soviet socialism?

It was too risky a gamble for the Consortium, and not necessarily as long as Germany bled red with Russian blood. The Bolsheviks would have been idiots to believe it anyway. A friend in Kiev, whose father was a doctor on the front (and his mother a spy in Austria) recalled to me in his underground office over coffee, nuts and cognac, with a touch of gratitude mixed with ridicule, how America sent canned meat and powdered eggs instead of soldiers.

Entire books can be written on Yalta and what transpired between FDR, Churchill and Stalin. A good primer is Jon Meacham's *Franklin and Winston, An Intimate Portrait of an Epic Friendship* (2003). Establishment history, with interesting personal anecdotes of heavy drinking, late night visits in the Kremlin,

Hyde Park and the White House, with sodden adventures over Russian banquets in Ukraine's Crimea that defied self-determination. It's definitely a good read.

"Ave" Harriman is there, too, with his charming wife Kathleen. Churchill's air chief writes Churchill's daughter of the meeting Feburary 8, 1945 at Livadia Palace at Yalta in the Crimea. "FDR was very wet indeed and just blathered. U.J. ("Uncle Joe" Stalin, sic) in marvelous form & so was big W, but as usual he ran away from the interpreter & was untranslatable ... Honestly, FDR spoke more tripe to the minute than I have ever heard before, sentimental twaddle without a spark of real wit." Future ambassador to the Soviet Union (1953-57) Chip Bohlen is there. He finds Roosevelt "ill...but he was effective." Harriman observes, "The fact that we tried and failed left the main responsibility for the Cold War with Stalin, where it belongs."

For FDR's motivation towards the US author Jon Meacham cites trade and confirmation of the *status quo*. During the bouts of heavy drinking on the last night February 10, 1945 in the heavily bugged Vorontsov villa Churchill declares of Stalin, "... The fire of war has burnt up the misunderstandings of the past. We feel we have a friend whom we can trust, and I hope he will continue to feel the same about us. I pray he may live to see his beloved Russia not only glorious in war, but also happy in peace." Churchill keeps on singing "a few lines from his favorite song 'Keep right on to the end of the road'. Stalin looked extremely puzzled..." (Jon Meacham, *Franklin and Winston, An Intimate Portrait of an Epic Friendship,* Random House, 2003, 319-20)

During the Yalta conference negotiations FDR only allows nations to become vassal states of the Soviet Union. FDR actually gave Poland to the Communists. That shocks Churchill. Had Roosevelt forgotten that it had been the Nazi violation of Polish sovereignty which at the start brought Britain and France into the war to stop Hitler? Roosevelt then agrees to "repatriate" those Eastern Europeans who had fought against the Soviets condemning them all. Photos of the Big Three show Stalin, smug and very confidently at ease in his chair and with good reason, having been fully informed by his spies in Washington and London before the summit of negotiating positions of both FDR and Churchill.

The reader might be well advised to consult Julius Epstein's book *Operation Keelhaul*, and visit the Museum of Communism. Russians, in German uniforms, turned against Stalin fighting alongside German troops on the Eastern front to defeat the communist Russians, Cossacks, and Ukrainians fighting with Poles for a liberated Poland, fighting with or against Poles. The Soviets allegedly sent one million Poles to death camps in Siberia. Similar fates greeted the residents of Estonia, Latvia and Lithuania, all part of FDR's postwar settlement to appease.

FDR was off-balanced to do it, and dying. Actually, he didn't have to. But he did it ostensibly using the favorite argument that it was necessary in order to save American lives, and it follows logically to let the Russians take the full weight of the Nazi war machine in defense of the Eastern front. FDR was like that. Like Duranty said, "They are only Russians."

At Yalta did FDR speak for America's best interests?

It is hard to say. Apparently Roosevelt at this time in his life, it may be argued, was an insanely deranged man. Bullitt should have known it. Bullitt had labored arduously with Austrian psychoanalyst Sigmund Freud over Wilson's self-torment and disturbed psyche, and, in fact with Freud co-authored a book about the former American leader who waged the phony war for Humanity and democracy and then pontificated with missionary zeal a bit too much to a nation weary of war and foreign engagements and died alone and forgotten in his Washington home, cripple and paralyzed, like Lenin in 1924. Wilson and Lenin. Two burned-out old men, once great leaders on the world stage but overnight by-gone and pathetic creatures who perish the same year, bed-ridden after their debacle and the world stage.

In Paris some twenty years ago I learned of the poisoning of Lenin by Stalin from a family relation of the Gorbachev's Foreign Minister Eduard Shevardnadze, but you will have a hard time proving it with forensic tests now that Putin has decided to stay with Lenin in the Kremlin. Stalin controlled access to Lenin, and quarreled bitterly with his Jewish wife, Krupskaya. The dying Lenin in his famous "testament" saved by his wife warned senior Bolshevik leaders of the "inordinate power" Stalin had amassed as General Secretary, who owed everything to Lenin since his return from arctic exile in 1917, that Stalin can be dangerously "too rude" in the most vulgar way that only a Russian can best appreciate and should be removed from his post though kept among the leaders.

Most of the survivors of the Holodomor a few years later perished in the most destructive war in world history. Perhaps the scale of that war's destruction was so massive that it makes a Genocide relatively insignificant in comparison. Perhaps that was also in cynical mind of House, Baruch, Roosevelt, FDR and dozen the war planners with vast experience in calculating numbers and statistics and profits from the previous Great War. They did have vast experience, and they did profit handsomely. So a few million more bodies here or there, as long as there are not too many Americans – a few thousand perhaps but please not millions.

Leave it to Stalin, right?

That is the logic in Washington. And that's what happened. Add those POWs from Poland, to the Kresy-Siberian list, and one might dare to diminish the peasant count from the 1932-34 Terror-Famine Genocide. That eastern Polish Kresy-Siberian list adds another 1.7 million Polish citizens – look at the map, Poland borders western Ukraine, and they share a long rivaly for territory and tradition – people of shared and different faiths and ethnicities (Ukrainian, Polish, Catholic, Orthodox, Belorussian, Jew …). These people were deported from eastern Poland of Kresy region in 1940 to 1942 by Stalin to labor concentration camps in Siberia, Kazakhstan and elsewhere in Soviet Russia. Over a hundred thousand more were taken through Persia in 1942, families and soldiers in Anders Army. The war that FDR and Stalin planned, independently, and uprooted and destroyed millions of people who hadn't already starved to death under Stalin, or were excuted by his NKVD secret service terror squads. (<www.aforgottenodyssey.com/memorial/>)

Following Hopkin's visit to Moscow to confer with Stalin in the fall the next year Molotov arrives in Washington and signs the Lend-Lease agreement.

Molotov walks in Stalin's shadow loyal to the end. In the White House and elsewhere he has many occasions to observe FDR in action. "Like all good capitalists Roosevelt believed in dollars. Not that he believed in nothing else, but he considered America to be so rich, and we so poor and worn out, that we would surely come begging. 'Then we'll kick their ass, but for now we have to help them keep going.' That's where he miscalculated. They weren't Marxists, and we were. They woke up only when half of Europe had passed from them....A poor country with no industry, no bread – they will come begging. They will have nowhere else to go'."

Molotov stays overnight as FDR's personal guest. In a message for the Soviet leader Roosevelt assures Molotov that Churchill during "intimate dinners" in Teheran and Yalta, confided, "I get up in the morning and pray that Stalin is alive and well. Only Stalin can save the peace!"... His cheeks were wet with tears. Not without reason did England lose a little more than 200,000 people while we had more than twenty million victims. That's why they needed us. That man hated us and tried to use us. But we used him, too." Molotov was right. It was Winston Churchill, First Lord of the Admiralty during the First World War, and the aristocratic descendant of the Duke of Marlborough, who had in former days not long ago flamboyantly urged war against Lenin to strangle Bolshevism in its cradle. (Vyacheslav Molotov, *Molotov Remember: Inside Kremlin Politics*, Chicago, Ivan R. Dee, 1993)

OVER FIFTY MILLION DEAD RUSSIANS IN "THE GREAT PATRIOTIC WAR"

After the famine years of the 1930s, more millions of Ukrainians and Russians perish in Stalin's Terror Purges under the watchful eyes of the Consortium. This too shortly before Hitler's invasion of Poland sending a clear warning to the Ukraine of imminent invasion. Over *fifty million* men, women and children in the Union of Soviet Socialist Republics died from the famine, terror and two world wars. Nearly three of every four Soviet soldiers in Stalin's Red Army are from peasant families. When Hitler unleashed the Nazi guns and divisions within a week the *Werhmacht* penetrate 200 miles deep into Soviet territory, one third the distance to Moscow. Within ten days Minsk falls. By the end of summer 1941, most of the Ukraine, the Baltic and Belorussia are all in Nazi hands; by August 21 the railway line between Moscow and Leningrad is cut; Panzer divisions slice across Ukraine's wheat fields now lost in their race towards Moscow and push east towards Stalingrad and Caucasus oilfields. German fascist invaders destroyed entire villages that had not been laid waste by Stalin, burning alive men women and children, torturing and hanging partisans and innocent hostage civilians.

After fierce fighting the Germans occupy Kiev on 26 September 1941. Leningrad is cut off from its lines of supply. Hitler expects to capture the city and enter Moscow before winter. Hitler's rape of the Ukraine exceeded everything imaginable in the painful days of Stalin's extermination with a drunken spirit for more killing. A German commander of a Panzer Tank Division south of the

Leningrad Front sends in a report: "The number of Soviet military deaths was even greater than the number of prisoners we took...Each night the villages went on burning, coloring the low clouds with a blood-red light." By October the mechanized Nazi advance had trapped nearly half of the population of almost 90 million people. The Red Army had lost over 3 million men. Stalin was said to have fled Moscow. Factories were shut down. Directors, managers and Party commissars panicked and ran. NKVD squads would descend to shoot the cowardly defeatists! Stalin tolerated no deserters. His fearsome OSMBON, Motorized Infantry Brigade of the NKVD Special Forces were ordered not to let Moscow surrender. Buildings were mined for the final Battle of Moscow which resumed in mid-November. Red Army soldiers and citizens fought back German tanks for the victory preserved in every Soviet child's heart. Hitler's decision to turn north towards Moscow extending his reach too far deep across the endlessly vast plains and away from the precious oil fields in the Caucausus along with his declaration of war against the United States was a telltale sign to Generals and troops alike that the icy doom of December in Russia sealed the fate of Germany.

Issues surrounding the Holodomor raise disturbing and relevant questions pertaining to the structure and orientation of contemporary life. With increasing governmental intervention in society, distinctions between capitalism, socialism and communism have become obscure. What is the difference between capitalism and socialism? Since the collapse and breakup of the former USSR, distinctions appear seamlessly academic bridging the gap between democratic societies and states with centralized planning for budgets and public services for example, for housing, education, medical care and health insurance. As in the Ukraine and other former Socialist Republics those state entitlements once provided to every Soviet citizen have virtually all but disappeared replaced by global capitalism the "free" market. The dollar sign replaced the hammer and sickle. Expensive designer jeans are the vogue. At Macy's department store in New York today white Christmas shopping bags are ablaze with the communist red star. The Second World War divided the world into two East-West blocs and nurtured the Cold War. Capitalism was still perceived by socialists and communists as the exploitation of man by man, while socialism remained the exact opposite. So, what really became of socialism?

A Russian proverb emerged: "Socialism is the longest and rockiest road from capitalism back to capitalism."

After Mikail Gorbachev's botched liberalisation and Boris Yeltsin's indulgence, the Russsian government under Vladimir Putin's iron heel refuses to acknowledge the Famine-Genocide of the early and mid-thirties. Premier Nikita Khrushchev own rise to power was linked to repression in the Ukraine. Khrushchev continued the assault on Ukrainian culture with thousands of secret exiles and deportations sent to prisoner labor camps where abuses of rape, deprivation and endless brutalities were routine. In December 1963, seven years after his denunciation of Stalin and his "cult of personality", Khrushchev acknowledged for the first time that starvation in the Ukraine had existed under Stalin and Molotov. (Vyacheslav Mikihailovich Molotov was ousted by

Khrushchev in 1957; he survives three more decades outlasting all the gout-ridden old men of the Politburo and dies of old age in 1986.)

That same year Khrushchev allows Solzhenitsyn's novel *A Day in the Life of Ivan Denisovich* to speak openly to Soviet citizens about the hard reality of Stalin's death camps and their assault on human freedom. Perhaps a million survivors of the camps returned. "The novel the effect of a political bomb," Yevgeny Yevtushenko recalls. "It took millions of stunned readers – Soviet and foreign – behind the barbed wire, dissecting for them the horrible life of daily self-genocide."

Reader you will recall that Khrushchev had been a active participant in the crimes of the Holodomor, and although in 1956 at the 20th Party Congress he denounces Stalin as a murderer he fails to admonish his own role only to crush the Hungarian revolt this year, prolong the system of the gulag and builds the Berlin Wall! "Khrushchev's tragic flaw was that he was both a Stalinist and an anti-Stalinist," explains Yevtushenko. "There were many reasons for this. On the one hand, he came from a poor family of serfs that had sufferend under the yoke of the czars. They also suffered under Stalin, a new czar, whom Khrushchev served simultaneously as courtier and serf. Yet Khrushchev hated Stalin for the mockery to which he subjected him. (Once Stalin placed a piece of cake on Khrushchev's chair when he rose to toast the great leader.) Khrushchev also hated Stalin for making him handle the executions of other high-ranking serfs in various Soviet republics, thereby making Khrushchev a collaborator in his bloody crimes. And he hated Stalin because he knew he could be arrested any night, branded an 'enemy of the people'. On the other hand, Khrushchev would occasionally try to rationalize Stalin's actions and maintain that Stalin despite his cruelty, was a great man. Khrushchev, after all, needed to justify his own existence and protect his life.... Khrushchev continued to vacillate between fits of Stalinism and anti-Stalinism. To support the latter position, he needed a book documenting Stalin's crimes. In other words, if Solzhenitsyn had not existed, Khrushchev would have had to invent him" (Yevgeny Yevtushenko, Introduction, xiii, A. I. Solzhenitsyn, *One Day in the Life of Ivan Denisovich*, NY: Penguin, 2008)

Reader, when the American journalist Edward Crankshaw tells you that he has "read almost every word of Khrushchev's that has been published since the late 1920s" and that he has met him various times "face to face", and he tells you in his introduction to *Khrushchev Remembers* (1970) where he returns to the years of the Holodomor, that "there's no mistaking the authentic tone" of Khrushchev's memoirs, you'd better believe its true listen up. The Stalinist thug from a family of peasants who becomes the viceroy of the Ukraine in 1938, escaped his purges and survived the war and Stalin himself emerged from behind the curtain, years after he had been dismissed from the Politburo "older now, tired, diminished by sickness, his vitality no longer what it was", but his stories retained an authenticity "all the more self-revealing because of that." In his short essay Ed Crankshaw captured the man captured in a nutshell.

It was his extraordinary Secret Speech at the Twentieth Party Congress denouncing Stalin in 1956. Premier Khrushchev virtually smashed the illusions of the Grand Dictator and his communist mafia one-party organization of dictatorship. Unfortunately at the time events and circumstances prolonged the system for another generation until it crumbled to pieces. (Apparently it served the Consortium's interests to propagate the Cold War mythology and prop it up as long as possible, while the hawks died one by ne or faded into luxurious retirement, or, in fact, until the youth themselves tore down the Berlin Wall and overthrew Gorbachev and the putchists.)

"Khrushchev", writes Crankshaw, "had inherited the system from Stalin and made it his own. He could conceive of no other. But in old age, there are flashes here and there which suggest that he has had second thoughts about a number of things. In this connection perhaps the most interesting feature is the short section on the collectivization of agriculture in which he states astonishingly but with perfect accuracy that 'the Stalin branch of collectivization brought us nothing but misery'". And reader you know enough to appreciate Crankshaw's following comment, as he writes, "He is speaking of that fearful, man-made catastrophe which cause the deaths of millions, virtually halved the agricultural production of the Soviet Union...". (Nikita Khrushchev, *Khrushchev Remembers*, Boston: Little Brown, Intro. Edward Crankshaw, Transl. Strobe Talbott, 1970, vi-xix)

During that brief thaw in the late fifties Khrushchev, half-liberal, half-Stalinist, shifts again, losing his nerve. The country froze up again. And Khrushchev was out in the cold. The Party censor soon reimposed the ban. Putin still refuses to open its secret archives on the Holodomor or the Cheka-GPU-NKVD files of the Soviet secret police.

Crankshaw's description of Khrushchev from the point of view of a western journalist is as good as you'll find anywhere. He writes, "Of course, he remained a prisoner of his past until the end". Since Khrushchev was both witness and participant in the Holodomor we find an excellent specimen of how Stalin and his henchmen play out their disastrous and corrupt destruction of the former Czarist Empire and, in particular, exterminated the Ukrainians under the watchful eyes of the West. Crankshaw writes, "In some ways he transcended the system which made him and which he helped to make. But he could never escape it entirely, and in the end it destroyed him. His achievement was extraordinary all the same. And the qualities which he began to exhibit toward the end of his career were not suddenly added to him; they must have been latent all the time, when, to all appearance, as a determinedly ambitious Party professional, sycophantic toward his master, bullying toward his subordinates, maneuvering around his rivals with deep peasant cunning, he was simly a thug among thugs, visibly distinguished from the others only by a certain liveliness of imagination, a warmth of feeling, a sturdy self-reliance, and at times the recklessness of a born gambler. Paradoxically, in one so committed to the Stalinist bandwagon, he had about him, I should think from the earliest days, a certain quality of apartness." So what, the bastard liked to plant potatoes and show off how great a peasant he was and showing off "unquestioning acceptance of some of the vilest of the vile". The butcher needs sharp knives but the wise man needs no knives at all. Better men suffered and died while he played farmer planting potatoes before returning to the his Kremlin fortress bemused in his delusion as the most powerful man (or clown)in the world. (N. Khrushchev, "Intro.", Edward Crankshaw, *Khrushchev Remembers*, xii-xiii)

Solzhenitsyn has much to tell about the methods and practices of the Cheka (abbreviation of *Vecheka*). From the early days of the Russian Revolution in 1917 Lenin and the Bolshevik leaders used them as their secret police to arrest counterrevolutionaries and terrorize the people into submission to communist principles of state tyranny on the pretense of the superiority of the Marxist-Leninist "Dictatorship of the Proletariat". Of course, only good communists comprised the "Proletariat".

Here is Solzhenitsyn, who lived the eternal terror of the Cheka and Lubyanka, Moscow headquarters of the secret police: "Most of Stalin's victims were convicted on the basis of article 58 of the Soviet Criminal Code of 1926. This catch-all article had 14 sections: Section 1 stated that any action directed toward the weakening of state power was considered "counter-revolutionary." This could be interpreted to mean a prisoner's refusal to work. In 1934, new subsections la, lb, lc, and ld, were added dealing with 'treason to the motherland'. (Changed to 'treason *of* the Motherland'). Thus, all and any actions directed against the military might of the USSR carried the penalty of ten years of prison (la) or death (lb), though the latter was most common. This meant that Soviet soldiers who were taken prisoner during the war, were given 10 year sentences for 'betraying the motherland.' Some Russians who emigrated abroad after the revolution or civil war, and had the misfortune of being swept up in the Red Army's advance into Eastern and Central Europe, were handed over by the allies and were also convicted on the basis of this article. So were Poles who had fought in the Polish underground army against the Germans in the territories annexed by the USSR in 1939 and then occupied by the Germans, e.g. the Vilnius region in Lithuania and the L'viv region in western Ukraine. Soviet law treated them as Soviet citizens who had committed treason against the USSR. (Those who resisted arrest or/and incorporation in the Red Army received either death sentences or were condemned to many years in labor camps).

"The section on 'treason' was broadened by article 19 of the criminal code, which allowed 'intent' to suffice for conviction. Indeed, the criminal code stated that it drew no distinction between intention and the crime itself, and that this showed the superiority of Soviet over 'bourgeois' legislation. Of course, the NKVD, forced the accused to confess that he or she 'intended' to betray the USSR. Section 2 of the criminal code stated that armed rebellion, seizure of power in the capital or in the provinces, especially with the intention of severing a part of the USSR by force, was treason. This was read to mean that all Polish resistance fighters against the Germans who were active in former eastern Poland, as well as Baltic, Ukrainian or Transcaucasian patriots, were guilty of treason and received automatic sentences of 10 or even 25 years of prison. Section 10 dealt with propaganda and agitation for the overthrow or weakening of Soviet power, or the preparation and/or circulation of literary material with the same intent. This section could even apply to private conversations reported by informers, or to private letters opened by the censors."

Solzhenitsyn was once arrested and convicted for joking about Stalin in a letter to a friend. Another time he was arrested because he had a friend who knew a Ukrainian so that made him an "enemy of the people". For that he gets a "tenner" in the gulag.

Sunday, March 4, 1934. For ambassador Dodd a day of reflection worried over division in France between pacifists holding the same French attitude "since 1920" at odds with "official" French militarists eager to seize the Rhineland in a preventive attack against Germany this spring. His diary is full of hopes and fears. "Today is the anniversary of President Roosevelt's first day in office... It was a decisive moment in history, like the beginning of the American Revolution in 1774." Dodd privately asserts the era is testing how the spirit of individualism will adjust to the increased pressures of government and federal controls over "individual independence, equality and initiative". He adds "...Roosevelt sees this in spite of the fact that his training at Groton and Harvard was faulty, even viscous, and the wealth of his family burdensome". The ambassador compares the irony of FDR's task to "Jefferson's effort to abolish slavery" while a southern slave owner. (W. E. Dodd, *Ambassador Dodd's Diary*)

History is never too kind to accidents or coincidences that burden its course with chance and deviations and compel constant corrections and adjustments. It should be remembered that eight years prior to the Nazi conquest of Poland, and only eight months in the White House, Franklin D. Roosevelt, on November 16, 1933, officially recognized the Soviet Union. Stalin's prestige rose immediately. Not long ago Roosevelt had been assistant-Secretary of the Navy and watched in the wings as Woodrow Wilson waited, lied and deliberately prepared the American entry into the First World War. Consortium men attached to Wilson's war administration earned billions of dollars and nearly snatched victory at Versailles. Less than 60,000 American soldiers were killed in combat. Many more were wounded. Disease killed more American soldiers than fell in combat. The lesson was hard learned especially with bodies piling up in city morgues back home making it even more tough for Charlie Chaplin, Mary Pickford, Douglas Fairbanks and other movie stars to sell Liberty Bonds. Two decades later Roosevelt knew well in advance of the German invasion of the Ukraine that the deaths of millions of Soviets incurred in Nazi defeats would save Americans from spilling their own blood. In strategic calculations between Hitler and the Morgan-Rockefeller-Harriman Consortium, Stalin lost. In the early hours of that fateful morning on June 22, 1941, the fascist Nazi armies blasted away at the Soviet Union and overwhelmed the main forces of the Red Army, taking Kiev, Odessa and much of the Ukraine. Many of the peasant survivors of Stalin's Terror-Famine now perished or fled from the invaders.

THE BANK FOR INTERNATIONAL SETTLEMENTS (BIS)

A professor of Bill Clinton at Georgetown University was Dr. Carroll Quigley. In his course on international relations he Quigley focused on investment bankers and the enormous control exercised by central government banks. In *Tragedy and Hope* (1966) the professor brought attention to the apex of this Consortium pyramid of international finance before and during the Second World War, in particular, and naming the Bank for International Settlements (BIS) based in Geneva with banking agents from the United States and throughout Europe. The BIS Nazi rep in Berlin is Hitler's own financial wizard and Reichsbank president, the inimitable Dr. Hjalmar Schacht.

Presently, this world strategic bank includes as board members Mr. Bernake, chairman of the United States Federal Reserve Board, and the head of the NY Fed, with over twenty years at Goldman Sachs. Former OSS career spook during the Vietnam era and Watergate then ambassador to Iran in Teheran for the fall of the Shah, the former CIA boss Richard Helms is proud to recall his maternal grandfather Gates W. McGarrah was appointed the bank's first president when it was first created to manage the Versailles debt payments from Germany. During the Holodmor years the young Helms picked up UP reporters job in Berlin and by a quirk of chance, or fate, was invited to lunch with Hitler on the occasion of a Nazi Party Day (*Parteitag*) in 1936. In their open Mercedes Helms sat alongside Alfred Rosenberg. Helms is impressed by Hitler's fascination at a fleet of Luftwaffe bombers blackening the sky overhead as they streaked past Nuremberg "and that the Fuehrer had then pointed east, toward the Ukraine." Helms recalled, "I managed to hear and make a note of the most dramatic bit of Hitler's hyperbole. In effect, he mused tht if Germany had the riches of the Ukraine, the country would be 'swimming in plenty'. (Richard Helms, *A Look Over My Shoulder:* NY: Random House, 2003, 15-25)

From 1933 to1945, two BIS directors include Nazi Walter Funk and Emil Puhl, convicted war criminals at the Nuremberg trials. Also among the select BIS board directors sit Herman Schmitz, IG Farben director and Baron von Schroeder, owner of the J. H. Stein Bank that holds the Gestapo deposits. It is alleged that the BIS bankers conspired hand-in-hand with Gestapo agents looting assets wherever they could find them.

The BIS was an intriguing arrangement. "There does exist and has existed for a generation," Quigley wrote, "an international ... network which operates, to some extent, in the way the radical right believes the Communists act. In fact, this network, which we may identify as the Round Table Groups, has no aversion to cooperating with the Communists, or any other groups and frequently does so. I know of the operations of this network because I have studied it for twenty years and was permitted for two years, in the early 1960s, to examine its papers and secret records. I have no aversion to it or to most of its aims and have, for much of my life, been close to it and to many of its instruments. I have objected, both in the past and recently, to a few of its policies... but in general my chief difference of opinion is that it wishes to remain unknown, and I believe its role in history is significant enough to be known."

Their objective, Prof. Quigley remarks, is "nothing less than to create a world system of financial control in private hands able to dominate the political system of each country and the economy of the world as a whole... controlled in a feudalist fashion by the central banks of the world acting in concert, by secret agreements arrived at in frequent private meetings and conferences." (Carroll Quigley, *Tragedy and Hope: A History of the World in Our Time*, G. S. G. & Assoc. 1966, 1975)

"One of Professor Quigley's most shocking revelations," declares California radio talk show host Dr. Monteith in his address titled "None Dare Call It Genocide", in 2004, "was the fact that the American Communist Party was partly financed by J. Morgan and Company.... J. Morgan and his associates financed the Republican Party, the Democratic Party, conservative groups, liberal organizations, communist groups and anti-communist organizations. Thus we should not be surprised to learn that someone purchased Professor Quigley's publisher and destroyed the plates to the first half of his book so it couldn't be reprinted." In his July 16, 1992 acceptance speech at the Democratic Convention Presidential nominee Clinton cited Dr. Quigley in a very rare and surprising honorable mention. That year Clinton defeated establishment icon and incumbent President George Bush Sr.. (Dr. Stanley K. Monteith, "None Dare Call It Genocide", M.D. Radio Liberty Conference, 2004)

The Versailles Peace Treaty and subsequent plans for the economic reconstruction of postwar Europe permitted the architects of the First World War to impose entirely new conditions on European politics. A new era required a new plan of violence, rearmament and industrial growth while feeding the masses before they are ready for the next battlefields. Lenin and Stalin both understood the far-reaching power of international investment banking Establishment.

Trotsky and lesser known Bolsheviks transferred funds to support the Bolshevik Soviet government long before 1917. In this regard Charles Savoie observed, "The main purveyors of funds for the revolution, however, were neither the crackpot Russian millionaires nor the armed bandits of Lenin. The real money came from certain British and American circles which for a long time past had lent their support to the Russian revolutionary cause." In his autobiography *My Life*, Trotsky tells of "a large loan granted in 1907 by a financier belonging to the British Liberal Party. This loan was to be repaid at some future date after the overthrow of the Czarist regime ... the obligation was scrupulously met by the revolution." Although no name is mentioned he was obviously in the circle of the Rothschilds, Schiffs and Morgans "among the British to support the Russian revolution with large financial donations."

All share one thing in common – monopoly. Whereas it was in the interests of these bankers and lawyers to advance the political careers of loyal operatives to consolidate their financial scheme for the Anglo-American Consortium, their link to German reconstruction of Hitler's national socialism and the social transformation of the USSR, under Stalin's state communism has been least understood. A.F. Kerensky head of the Russian Provisional Government deposed by Lenin and the Bolsheviks in 1917 spent much of his latter life in New York. Kerensky's secret papers were kept sealed until 1987 revealing the plots of "conspiratorial organizations modeled on freemasons lodges" responsible for the Bolshevik Revolution.

A creature of his class and wealth, son of a railroad lawyer, cousin to Teddy Roosevelt, born into elite and privilege, with all the benefits of American culture entitled him, FDR talked freedom and democracy to at least twelve million unemployed American workers and farmers. Yet there is no record that the President ever dared to take the high ground with Soviet Communist Party leader Joseph Stalin to curb his crimes and put him in his place. On the contrary, FDR chose not too. With the Soviet monopoly eager to do business with the Consortium brokers FDR preferred not to antagonize their favorite and most powerful client dictator. How do you castigate a dictator when he's one of your own?

Once installed in power, as supreme commander in chief of the nation, FDR immediately embarked on a road of profitable industrial and military strategy of cooperation paved in American dollars and Russian lives, – particularly Ukrainians, all sacrificed by Stalin and ignored by Roosevelt. President Hoover helped the Bols in the post WWI Russian famine years of 1919-23. But that was also a dodgy affair and too close to the secret American armed intervention in Russia's Civil War.

The Ukrainians never had a prayer in Washington as far as FDR and the State Department were concerned. Not ten million. Stalin ruled as supreme dictator and Roosevelt was his partner in crime. Only they were never charged with one. Welcome to the Consortium. During his decade in government, and as Commerce Secretary for eight years in two different administrations, and then serving as President from 1929 to 1933, Herbert Hoover remained aloof and indifferent to suffering in Russia. His business associates in the Consortium rush to invest huge sums in Stalin's consolidated dictatorship within the economic framework of the Soviet Party's Five-Year Plan.

For the professor of Russian and Slavic history Sheila Fitzpatrick, author of *Stalin's Peasants* (1994) chose to view the catastrophe of repression, terror and famine imposed on the countryside as stemming from the bungling errors of a confusing social experiment, rather than the result of any systematic orchestration of western political intrigue or Stalinist usurpation of centralized power. Fitzpatrick followed in the footsteps of her predecessors, Harvard's Hopper and Harper, also from University of Chicago's Russian department. Rich in rhetoric but poor in deeds Bolshevik methods did seem completely absurd to the Russian peasant mentality considered by the Leninist-Marxists as backward, inert and ignorant. However, they were anything but benign, naturally suspicious of the urbanites and more cunning in order to survive impossible procurement quotas depriving them of seed, grain and livestock without which they were doomed.

Fitzpatrick is compelled, nevertheless with painstakingly subtle naivété, to concede the breakneck force of industrialization imposed on the backs of these tillers of the land. "The frenetic collectivization", Fitzpatrick writes, "and mass expropriation of kulaks that burst forth in the winter of 1929-30 were the climax of two and a half years of rising political and social tension…and preparation of the First Five Year Plan that was to launch the Soviet Union into a new era of rapid, centrally planned industrial growth." You won't find in her work how American and foreign investment, in 1929, helped unleash special terror brigades sent to ravage whole villages in the Ukrainians, arresting kulaks, expropriating property of the "class enemies of the people", seizing grain procurements, barricading villages for days in unheated barns, and isolating resistance. (Sheila Fitzpatrick, *Stalin's Peasants, Resistance and Survival in the Russian Village After Collectivization*, Oxford Univ. Press, 1994, 37-9)

In retrospect, any scenario by FDR would have been better. With the spectre of the Japanese threat in Siberia and the Far East, and Hitler pulling out of the League of Nations in October, FDR had Stalin over a barrel, so, in 1933, he recognized the Kremlin communists with official diplomatic relations for the first time and kept hostile anti-communist critics at the door. FDR's slap-dash strategy was simple. It was the American democratic way passed down from President Wilson and the Consortium men in his war administration to FDR in the rearmament years of thirties. Make money and save American lives. Then heavily tax Americans and make them pay for the war managed and controlled by the Consortium elite and their all too willing newcomers inside the American government. Get the picture?

The convergence of corporations by consolidations and mergers follows the same logic. FDR, Stalin and Hitler used government regulation and terror to achieve national welfare states with control of their national military and police agencies. They all were masters at national propaganda and advertising, skilled in the art of habit-forming rhetoric and culture building techniques in media and communication. Rhetoric was actually a 19th century major in English and American elite universities. These Consortium instruments all shared the same mentors from Ivy Lee, Walter Lippmann, Edward Bernays and others. Sounds incredible? Sometimes the truth is hard to digest. People love a good gangster action movie or thriller. It distracts and absorbs superficially, skimming along on the surface of life, promoting more violence and criminality. When you don't like what you see, just zap it away. Therein lies real harm. The sense of awe and danger and powerlessness in the real world is suddenly overwhelming and inconceivable except in an oversimplified movie scenario or virtual video game or horror movie. Think about it. Politics today is fashioned to fit the news, "cut to fit" made for TV like a pair of sexy close fitting designer jeans. Truth is packaged for the 15 seconds of fame a phrase punned by advertising-trained pop artist Andy Warhol, incidentally of Ukrainian descent and craftily clever to package image and ink in a name brand canvas traded for millions of dollars. Society functions this way and in the end, no one is immune. Those inoculated by it inevitably suffer with a numbing insensitivity to pursuits of the intellect and quick and cheap pleasures. So the mind turns away, killing motivation and ambition and the desire to read and seek answers. It is a serious problem today in so-called free and open societies and repeated throughout the world governed by organized power over the political economy of countries everywhere. With global technology and mass communications the speed of change accelerates inversely to our response to cope with the problems people face every day. Wired in? Or wired out? In the Information Age, even history, – life as it was and the lessons to be learned in the inexorable process of memory and interpretation –, seem more precious and rare.

For *The Washington Post* journalist David Remnick reporting on the last years of the Soviet Union under *perestroika* and *glasnost* and the downfall of Gorbachev in the failed military coup and emergence of Yeltsin atop a Soviet tank protected by citizens hungry for freedom and an end to domination by the Party apparatchiks. In his book *Lenin's Tomb* (1993) he describes the daunting, incongruity leaving citizens dazed and at times terrified in the rarefied atmosphere of Russia facing a "new and vulgar image of what Leninists once called the 'shining future'", of western capitalism confronting vestiges of Stalinist dictatorship, where now in Moscow the occupant of the luxurious apartment of the former head of the state secret police gazes over the crimson arc of MacDonalds in the era of Russian mafia capitalism instead of the hammer and sickle.

Remnick writes, "When once the Russian landscape was littered with one kind of propaganda –'We are Marching toward Leninism!' etc. – television, radio and the newspapers are now filled with a propaganda of a different sort; advertising for unaffordable luxuries, fantastic commercials geared toward lives that hardly exist. One minute you are *Homo Sovieticus* surrounded by the aggressive blandness of communism, the next minute you are watching a Slavic vixen sucking on a maraschino cherry and telling you which casino to visit. There is something profoundly irritating (and American) about ads for investment funds or 'premium' cat food in a country where the vast majority live in poverty. A year or two of exposure to American-style commercials has produced what decades of Communist propaganda could not; genuine indignation on the part of honest people against the excesses of capitalism. But the intelligentsia is bewildered by it all and incapable of providing moral guidance. 'They struggle for a new life and it turned out that this life deceived them'." A Russian intellectual and dinner guest at a swank foreign restaurant tells the American "everyone wants it. This is *all* they think about. They don't think about novels or plays or poetry. If it is true that everything in America is about dollars, it is even more true now in Russia. This is a hungry country and it wants to be fed.'" (D. Remnick, 540-1)

Are citizens of democracies really motivated to think about the forces controlling their lives? This isn't a rap song, yet. Maybe then more people would get the message. Only its goes deeper. To want to know requires first a moral discipline to think and act with a deliberate motivation to live without fear and to live a truthful life. The choice is not to live a life of quiet desperation or complicity or carefree indifference which is equally mindless. Have people really been overcome by inertia and distraction, made meek and timid by superior forces operating in government that rule over their lives? Have they lost their individuality to instruments of power that dominate society, strip them to blind obedience while instilling fear and hatred?

Few dare or even have the mental reflexes to challenge the public debate set and staged in incessant news broadcasts that unfold enveloping their brain with reprocessed entertainment intended not to stimulate or provoke social unrest but to simulate with variations of a common theme because the script has already been written like a commercial of endless repetition. When even critical thinking is redundant, irrelevant and unresponsive freedom assumes the profile of a nuisance.

Mindful citizens in a "free" society then feel disempowered and incapable of altering prevailing structures of geopolitics or the international monetary policy of centralized banks. A Ph.D. in economics from the best university isn't going to be of much use.. Like the politicians and the anchor news people, read the prompter. News becomes a steady spew of information spin thick like molasses and thin like tin foil. Chew it and spit it back out. Today people are restricted by increasing government laws and regulations. Bankers rule the world with the luxury of organized crime in league with government Consortium players lining their pockets with all the pretense of the selfless public servant. Hah! Modern Ukraine is a glaring proof of the Holodomor nightmare inherited by Washington and Moscow now playing out their roles for the masters of "The Game".

In the thirties eye-witness foreign correspondents gave the Ukraine Terror-Famine a good spin. And they kept spinning it for years. Its not apparent that the American public ever saw in their minds the horror of bloated bodies and defenseless starving people begging for a piece of bread on their knees in the dusty streets of the harvest season, or in the snow of the harsh Russian winter without the strength to cry out? Their fate was left hanging in the air without knowing why.

JONES & MUGGERIDGE BREAK THE BARRIER OF LIES

Gareth Jones and Malcolm Muggeridge broke open the famine lies. Yet these two men, too, were captive of their culture. Muggeridge inherited a large estate, won a seat in Parliament and retired to the comfortable life of an English country squire. Gareth Jones, the son of "Major Jones", a mere ten-year-old lad when the British sacrificed an entire generation of their own finest ruling class officers at the Somme and Verdun, was educated in postwar England and on the path for a brilliant career in the Foreign Office. Destiny struck him down. Jones was murdered before his thirtieth birthday in remote region of far eastern Manchuria in a possible attempt to reenter the Soviet Union undetected by Soviet police. Stalin and his NKVD agents were his probable assassins. The British Foreign Office let it pass without any official inquiry preferring it be perceived that he had dropped off the map with no official consequence.

Had the two intrepid British reporters Jones or Muggeridge followed the money of Anglo-American investment they would have told a decidedly different story of capitalism and communism and the Marxist class struggle between the rich an the poor as it was perceived at that time, in reality as well as fiction. Many people find it hard to believe that the Bolshevik revolutionary movement was penetrated and funded in part by the Rothschild-Morgan banking syndicate from New York City. Historians and readers who specialize in the opaque world of intelligence and government intrigue find that all quite plausible and even cliché. The extent of their concentrated wealth controlled by a relatively small number of individuals boggles the imagination. So does the 1932-34 famine only the Ukrainian peasants didn't know much beyond their village or what was at stake in the arena of global politics during the fragile peace between the two world wars.

Gareth Jones lives with the spirit of Tolstoy's Olenin of the memorable story *The Cossacks* (1852), "that capacity to be entirely transformed into an aspiration or idea – the capacity to wish and to do – to throw oneself headlong into a bottomless abyss without knowing why or wherefore." He takes breaks from the quiet country life in Wales to tour the Ukrainian villages once abundant with the joy of living but when he returned in the late twenties he found them isolated and barren reporting; in 1930 Jones found "great suffering" and "many deaths" from "starvation". By 1930 Jones was enough aware of Stalin's repressive politics inside the Kremlin Party hierarchy from the top down to the countryside where Stalin unleashed a war against the peasants forcing them into collective state farms and confiscated their individual property. Stalin crushed the peasant resistance and smashed insurgent Ukrainian nationalism so that by 1941 when the Nazi's invaded and razed the Ukraine they did so with methodological precision of the Wehrmacht intelligence analysts who had systematically prepared their extermination plan.

Stalin had given Hitler a good lesson just how easy it was to exterminate a race. And he had done it during peacetime. In a few short weeks of war the German army captured 2.5 million soldiers of the Red Army. Lenin, Stalin and Hitler well knew that without the Ukraine all of Russia would collapse. It nearly did that year. Peasants who had survived the 1932-34 Holodomor now fought to save the Motherland and "the Great Butcher" pushed on by the *politruks*, Party commissars and other hacks dispatched to draft the soldiers with propaganda and keep the girls and vodka for themselves.

The wholesale suffering and slaughter of peasants, starved, excuted, tortured and imprisoned in slave labor camps was of such a colossal magnitude that those who recorded and recalled the tragedy dared not minimize or forget the individual loss suffered by the victims. The Ukrainians received no compensation. Worse, the survivors were repaid a few years later with more communist repression and the Nazi invasion.

As we trace the pattern of crimes in the unfolding tale of geopolitics and war Stalin was not the sole culprit. The tragedy of the Ukrainian famine is revealed in the web of intrigue of the bankers and their support for Stalin and communism. This author's research into the late 19th and early 20th century era of muckraking investigative journalism that pried into the private fortunes of the American gilded billionaires permits an enriched appreciation of Antony Sutton's unfettered rejection of obscurism when he put the pieces of the puzzle together revealing a very different picture of American history than taught in the nation's elite secondary preparatory schools. For good reason too, for most of their "in the box" professors at these public government funded schools as well as privately endowed prep schools, Sutton and other historians are taboo. The result is startling apparent, and reveals a very obvious, and seamless pattern of unfolding deception and arcane logic. It is a logic of destruction and war for profits, or as Wall Street speculator and Democratic powerbroker Bernard Baruch liked to joke, a logic "taking the profits out of war" and straight to their private bank accounts.

History is always a complex blend of fact and fiction. Sometimes looking for it is like diving to find a sunken ship lost under oceans of sand and rust. You may run out of time and oxygen before finding what remains. Sometimes its staring you right in the face. History remembered and recalled rests with the storyteller and writer. By the time events occur, it's a done deal. Better to move on, go forward. If you want to change the past, try first understanding the present. The present and future are born in the past and evolve out of the past. The real challenge of the future is not to repeat the mistakes of the past. Open your eyes, read, learn. Move you mind, instead of watching images flash and za Its all an illusion made to look and seem more or less real. The reality of life really is much more than it was. It must be so. Only you can make it so by determined inquiry and persistent questioning and reflection. That's why this book is for you. The Russian philosopher Nicolai Berdyaev (1874-1948), born in Kiev, friend of the revolutionary poets and writers, spared and exiled by Lenin in 1922, said a creative life is by necessity always a beginning and an end.

The history of US-Soviet relations in regards to Ukraine is not a pretty picture under Presidents Hoover and FDR. Both are political sharks and tools of the most powerfully rich people in America. Hoover has an important stake in Belgium copper mines in the Congo. FDR too is fascinated by the Delano fortune of his wife with millions made in the 19th century China opium trade, and an ever-present Mother. Nothing they do helped the twenty million Ukrainians and fellow Russians starved and killed by the famine and its epidemics during the Holodomor years.

Tens of thousands dead each day at the height of the famine, or a thousand people dead per hour. Dying from hunger, deprived of their bread and livestock. Hunger torments terribly. Abandoned in isolated villages. Cut off from the world. Walking kilometers day and night in the frost through fields and in forests where wolves prowled. Living for one more day of hope and gnawing hunger, from village to village, house to house where there may still be people who can trade for grain. So many are reduced to barbarism. If only to find some birch bark and grind it into gruel! If only not to have to worry about food anymore! Hunger is something terrible you cannot get used to. The head starts spinning, surroundings blur. Colored lights swirl before your eyes. The hours drag, the body weakens as strength goes away. American corporations ignored the civilians as though they did not even exist.

Hunger. Reader, have you tasted in your soul when your gut is crying out the pain of it because your soul may be all that there is left that can utter a sound. And there is no one better than Solzhenitsyn to help you understand the harm and pity of it or perhaps the women of Mother Russia know it better than he but lack his words. He lived it, in the camps, learned about it from the Ukrainians and in the Red Army when he fought for the Fatherland.

In *The Gulag Archipelago* Solzhenitsyn tells us how it was in the Russian mind and body and soul. Here is only a glimpse but I pray it is enough to find more to nourish the life that binds us all to those camps, and villages, towns and cities where the men, women and children were dying on "the wings of hunger" across the Ukraine of the Holodomor. Take a good hard look. Bet your life they did. Regrettably in every way, the men in the Department did not., "Philosophers, psychologists, medical men, and writers," writes Solzhenitsyn, "could have observed in our camps, as nowhere else, in detail and on a large scale the special process of the narrowing of the intellectual and spiritual horizons of a human being, the reduction of the human being to an animal and the process of dying alive. But the psychologists who got into our camps were for the most part not up to observing; they themselves had fallen into that very same stream that was dissolving the personality into feces and ash...You in your medical sections and your storerooms, you never knew hunger there, orthodox loyalist gentlemen!"

"It has been known for centuries that Hunger...rules the world! (And all your Progressive Doctrine is, incidentally, built against the well-fed.) Hunger rules every hungry human being, unless he has himself consciously decided to die. Hunger, which forces an honest person to reach out and steal ('When the belly rumbles, conscience flees'). Hunger, which compels the most unselfish person to look with envy into someone else's bowl, and to try painfully to estimate what weight of ration his neighbor is receiving. Hunger, which darkens the brain and refuses to allow it to be distracted by anything else at all, or to think about anything else at all, or to speak about anything else at all except food, food, and food. Hunger, from which it is impossible to escape even in dreams – dreams are about food, and insomnia is over food. And soon – just insomnia. Hunger, after which one cannot even eat up; the man has by then turned into a one-way pipe and everything emerges from him in exactly the same state in which it was swallowed." (A. I. Solzhenitsyn, *The Gulag Archipelago*, v. III-IV, 208-9)

A young man in the thirties Solzhenitsyn personally experienced the grain crisis and Stalinist repressions of "the Organs", administration security apparatchiks of the secret police and Communist Party *nomenklatura*. He lived the Soviet system, a soldier who was imprisoned because he knew someone who had known someone on the Ukrainian Front during WWII! If only American writers had used their writing skills to describe the repressive Soviet system when it was in full stride as he did while living its perpetual state of terror, arrests, and imprisonment not to forget the distant journeys to nowhere. He survived intact, a forceful and formidable opponent of Stalin and the Soviet propaganda machine.

The Russians and Ukrainians will have to wait a good long. It took two decades after Stalin's death before *The Gulag Archipelago* is finally published abroad, in 1973, in the United Sates (three years after they give him the Nobel prize!) and like its author stands as an incomparable testament of the methods and psychology of the Stalin's socialist police state inflicted on the Russian people. The secret police didn't need a reason to arrest somebody. If they didn't execute orders it was their head that would be next. They had general orders, and quotas to fill the prisons and camps of the Gulag state.

These secret police, Chekists, OGPU, NKVD agents, precursors to the KGB-FSB of Putin's era. Here let us see how Solzhenitsyn describes these dregs of the earth, the "Bluecaps": "The bluecaps understood the workings of the meat grinder and loved it. ... 'Just give us a person – and we'll create the 'case' !" The Model

Kh AZ-241 meat grinder was a Soviet innovation. The American journalists didn't fully comprehend the Soviet methods that evolved out of that dark mysterious Russian culture they otherwise found it convenient to generalize for the abuses of power without understanding its nature or feeling the blow.

Solzhenitsyn: "What prompted them all to slip into harness and pursue so zealously not truth but 'totals' of the processed and condemned? Because it was 'most comfortable' for them not to be different from the others. And because these totals meant an easy life, supplementary pay, awards and decorations, promotions in rank, and the expansion and prosperity of the 'Organs' themselves. If they ran up high totals, they could loaf when they felt like it, or do poor work or go ouot and enjoy themselves at night. And that is just what they did. Low totals led to their being kicked out, to the loss of their feedbag. For Stalin could never be convinced that in any district, or city, or military unit, he might suddenly cease to have enemies. That was why they felt no mercy, but instead, an explosion of resentment and rage toward those maliciously stubborn prisoners who opposed long fitted into the totals, who would not capitulate to sleeplessness or the punishment cell or hunger. By refusing to confess they menaced the interrogator's personal standing. It was as though they wanted to bring 'him' down. In such circumstances all measures were justified! If its to be war, then war it will be! We'll ram the tube down your throat – swallow the salt water! Excluded by the nature of their work and by deliberate choice from the higher sphere of human existence, the servitors of the Blue Institution lived in their lower sphere with all the greater intensity and avidity. And there they were possessed and directed by the two strongest instincts of the lower sphere, other than hunger and sex: greed for 'power' and greed for 'gain'.

Particularly for power. In recent decades it has turned out to be more important than money. Power is a poison well known for thousands of years. If only no one were ever to acquire material power over others! But to the human being who has faith in some force that holds dominion over all of us, and who is therefore conscious of his own limitations, power is not necessarily fatal. For those, however, who are unaware of any higher sphere, it is a deadly poison. For them there is no antidote." (A. I. Solzhenitsyn, *The Gulag Archipelago,* Chpt. 4, 1973)

The symbiotic relationship between communism and capitalism went undetected to mainstream America. Instead the American populace were doped on government propaganda and diverted by fabricated news that stereotyped the Soviets as inhumane communist heathens bent on destroying the God-given America way of life. Reagan perpetuated the myth with his rhetoric about the Soviet "Evil Empire", and claimed an astounding military victory when their proxy Syria in 1982 lost eighty-one Syrian piloted MiGs shot down by Israel's F-15 and F-16 fighters. And to top it off on March 23, 1983, Reagan announced in a televised message his Strategic Defense Initiative declaring a sort of space shield defense against any Soviet ICBM threat. Reagan's Star Wars challenge to Soviet defense planners literally meant gulag or total breakdown and bankruptcy of the USSR. It was a bluff by a master joker in the White House but who was to know better than the President of the United States?

Historically, denigrating the Slavic Russians of the East was a prerequisite for the Europeans before invading their territory. The Poles, Swedes, Germans and French fought for centuries to occupy the Ukraine. Three years later Sakharov, then still in exile in Gorky, was released followed by hundreds of other political prisoners. And for the first time the USSR publicly admitted in a lecture to a youth newspaper in Kishinev, a small town on the river Byk in Bessarabia in the time of Pushkin over a century ago that had changed hands often with Russian Czars and the Ottoman Empire, that "we are lagging behind", not catching up about to "bury" the West. Yet still in psychiatric hospitals and labour camps like Perm 35 hardened criminals mixed with politicos and members of the intelligentsia, – teachers, doctors and lawyers, resembling images from the Nazi concentration camps languished helplessly in barbaric conditions starving in the Communist Gulag under the supervision of the KGB and fed rations so poor they preferred to eat grass or maggots. Human rights? Civil liberties? Since its founding in 1978 Helsinki Watch activists tried to inform the world but who was listening? Soviet authorities tended to dismiss appeals from the West as more evidence of the mass psychosis of a weak and decadent West.

After decades of Cold War hysteria, America lived its own unique perversions dehumanizing Soviet citizens as something less than real people. Americans at home in their own country, of course, are most comfortable in their own hometown and back yard. Most people are. While Americans are habituated to their isolationism, they are used to 'the melting pot". They are suspicious of strangers who don't conform or fit the mold. Ethnic groups form ethnic communities. Americans who lived estranged from Russians found them, like myself, a world apart. In the Soviet Union, sameness and uniformity were the norm. Individual differences were measured by adoption of the same socialist standards. American diversity appealed to their instinct for freedom but threatened their Marxist-Leninist vision of bourgeois contradictions and the alleged American threat against the greater Soviet socialist future. The Cold War separated two very different nations speaking different languages now united by a tenuous nuclear bond in one very dangerous world.

THE CULTURE OF AMERICAN MYTHOLOGY – SOLZHENITSYN GOES WEST

The mythology was awesome. It worked like magic! Illusions do that. The spinners made it even look real in films and on television. It's so easy to brainwash the masses with TV. Every advertiser and newsperson knows that. Former heads of the CIA still talk about it a historical necessity, an absolute physical fact of life instead of an artificial concept they fabricated. At least until the Americans – and Harriman too – rejected the Vietnam War with massive demonstrations and sometimes violent draft-card buring protests with Vietnam veterans throwing their medals over the White House fence. Strange that the messager of Truth of

US corporate investment in Ronald Reagan's "Evil Empire" was a Soviet citizen and former prisoner of Stalin's gulags.

Overnight the preposterous became ordinary news. America was investing in the enemy, and the enemy was the American. When I visited the Ukraine for the first time and fell spellbound by Russians and these Ukrainians in former Soviet empire, I never felt that I was the enemy, or that the woman I loved was my enemy. That's something the Americans never liked to accept. "Make love, not war." During the Vietnam War, remember Nixon shaking his head, pleading for forgiveness when he said "I am not a crook!"

On June 30, 1975, Aleksandr I. Solzhenitsyn, the recipient of the 1973 Nobel Prize for Literature, gives an address with ground-breaking revelations that most certainly shook his audience gathered in the Washington Hilton located minutes away from the White House of the existence of a mysterious alliance, "at first glance a strange one, a surprising one - but if you think about it, one which is well grounded and easy to understand. This is the alliance between our Communist leaders and your Capitalists."

The alliance, he said, was not new. Great capitalists of the United States helped Lenin "in the first years of the Revolution," and that since then "we observe continuous and steady support by the businessmen of the West of the Soviet Communist leaders." Solzhenitsyn tells his incredulous listeners that the Soviet economy is so clumsy and awkward that it will never overcome its own difficulties by itself. That's an understatement known to anyone who has lived a short while in any of the former Soviet republics. Solzhenitsyn makes the allegation that the enslaved Russian masses could have thrown off Communism several times had not Western assistance been poured into the USSR to prevent the collapse of the Communist leadership before its collapse in 1991.

Solzhenitsyn tells his audience that "the major construction projects in the initial five-year plan were built exclusively with American technology and materials". Those massive projects were built in the 1920s with forced labor and American engineers. Welshman Gareth Jones had interviewed some of those engineers during his trip to the Soviet factories, in 1931, when the huge canals hydroelectric dam projects were built by hundreds of thousands of forced laborers. (US Congressional Record, 8, July, 1975, 11951-11956)

In August 1975, William F Buckley's *National Review*, the incorrigible Red-baiting flagship of American conservatism, triumphed the eventual demise of Soviet Communism in its story "The Strangled Cry of Solzhenitsyn". "WFB" was well-connected to the Consortium gang - Yale, Skull & Bones, married rich, an accomplished yachtsman who loved to drink, sing merrily and play the harpsichord for his friends in his Stamford home by the sea. (I was there in his home in Stamford by the sea on Shippan Point at a graduation party for his son, the distinguished writer Christopher Buckley.)

According to Solzhenitsyn, Stalin recognized that two-thirds of required resources came from the West. He wrote, "If today the Soviet Union has powerful military and police forces ... used to crush our movement for freedom in the Soviet Union ... we have Western capital to thank for this also." Americans had little if any idea how real was the movement for freedom behind the Iron Curtain. Marxism, he said, was viewed with contempt and ridiculed by the people outside the Communist Party *nomenklatura*, or elite of rank and privileges. "In the Soviet Union today,' he said, "Marxism has fallen so low it's simply an object of contempt. No serious person in our-country today, even students in schools, can talk about Marxism without smiling." Yet, at Yale and Harvard, historical materialism theory of Marxian dialectical thinking was still taught with intellectual prestige well into the mid-1970s.

(Note. See excerpt from "The Strangled Cry of Solzhenitsyn," *National Review*, August 29, 1975, Editor's Note: William F. Buckley Jr. 929-938: "But the proud skyscrapers stand on, point to the sky, and say: it will never happen here. This will never come to us, It is not possible here. We are slaves, but we are striving for freedom. You, however, were born free. If so, then why do you help our slave owners? And these two crises, the political crisis of today's world and the oncoming spiritual crisis, are occurring at the same time. Has the Berlin Wall convinced anyone? No again. It's being ignored. It's there, but it doesn't affect us. We'll never have a wall like that.... For communists to have a dialogue with Christianity! In the Soviet Union this dialogue was a simple matter; they used machine guns and revolvers. In the meantime, you've been outplayed in West Berlin, you've been skillfully outplayed in Portugal. In the Near East you've been outplayed. One shouldn't have such a low opinion of one's opponent. The tanks rumble through Budapest. It is nothing. The tanks roar into Czechoslovakia. It is nothing. No one else could have been forgiven, but Communism can be excused. And the person who signs these treaties with you now—these very men and no others – at the same time give orders for persons to be confined in mental hospitals and prisons. Take the SALT talks alone: in these negotiations your opponent is continually deceiving you. Either he is test radar in a way which is forbidden by the agreement; or he is violating the limitations on the dimensions of missiles.

So two years after Watergate, the departure of the disgraced Republican President Nixon and defeat of US Armed Forces in Vietnam, Solzhenitsyn continues on his mission traveling from Washington to New York speaking in his native Russian tongue and relates the same story of the Cold War hoax thrust on the duped American tax-payer that underwrites the Soviet socialist monopoly that imprisons, tortures and kills the Soviet people. A sweet story to shock the true believer of the Great American Dream. He emphasizes that the "whole existence of our slave owners from beginning to end, has depended on Western economic assistance." This is not light-headed stuff nor what Americans are prepared to understand after ten years fighting "slant-eyed Commie Reds" in Southeast Asian jungle with 58,000 dead US soldiers over 150,000 wounded and more than a million Vietcong personnel and North Vietnamese army fatalities, families and personal lives devastated and villages destroyed along with the entire country bombarded, mined and contaminated for generations to come. It was a place where Americans had no business being there in the first place. Unfortunately, at that time too many students on US college campuses are too numbed, dazed and stoned to comprehend the complications involved here, and turn off, prefer euphoric hallucinogens to feel cool, and willing or unable to feel genuine compassion care anymore. This was the age of the cool and alienated anti-Establishment and anti-System generation a decade before the Yuppies took over in the Reagan-Bush era.

Still, Solzhenitsyn drives home his point depicting the reality of the Soviet condition. "We are slaves there from birth. We are born slaves. I'm not young anymore, and I myself was born a slave; this is even more true for those who are younger. We are slaves, but we are striving for freedom. You, however, were born free. If so, then why do you help our slave owners? In my last address I only requested one thing and I make the same request now: When they bury us in the ground alive ... please do not send them shovels. Please do not send them the most modern earth-moving equipment."

Before retreating with his wife to live eighteen years in exile in Cavendish, a small town in the remote forests of Vermont, not unlike a Siberian gulag wilderness, Solzhenitsyn explained that the Russian people also were misinformed about the role of America inside the Soviet Union. Instead, the big picture was clouded by proxy rivalries between the espionage agencies. Civil populations and low-level bureaucracies were poisoned with never-ending lies. Senior leaders knew better.

For Solzhenitsyn that world of living memory was divided into two camps, East and West. American presidents were their nemesis. "Our country is taking your assistance but in the schools they are teaching and in newspapers they are writing and in the lectures they are saying, `Look at the Western world, it's beginning to rot. Look at the economy of the Western world, it's coming to an end. The great predictions of Marx, Engels, and Lenin are coming true. Capitalism is breathing its last. It's already dead. It has demonstrated once and for all the triumph of Communism'."

Americans wondered how the Solzhenitsyn revelations could possibly be true? How could it be that any Americans armed and financed their enemy in the Cold War? "Is the West," he declared, inquisitively, "particularly the United States, responsible for building and sustaining the Communist enemy?" Whoever would dare to believe a Russian communist? Article III, Section 3, of the United States Constitution defines treason as "giving aid and comfort to the enemy." What Americans didn't understand was that outside the Communist Party, not all Russians were communists! Three years later Solzhenitsyn took the same message to Harvard's Commencement ceremony as guest speaker. Today, each side still blames the other. For many the memory is still a vivid reality and nightmare. In 1994, Solzhenitsyn returned to Russia. "I knew I would come home to die in Russia", he swore. (D. Remnick, 542)

Forty years after Stalin's Terror-Famine, Solzhenitsyn ignited a debate underpinning the logic and intent of the America's alleged Cold War crusade against Soviet Russia. No one asked to know the reasons why the American Council of Foreign Relations, from the Yale's Buckleys to the Harvard's Lodges chose Solzhenitsyn then and there to ease the way to ending the Cold War hysteria. The war in Vietnam launched by President Johnson after the fictitious provocation of the Gulf of Tonkin in August 1964 leading to the US escalation of the Tet Offensive in February and the secret bombing of Cambodia and Laos intensified during the summer of 1972 unleashed new terrors and Genocide in Cambodia killing over two million people by the Khmer Rouge forces led by Pol Pot (born Sarlot Sar) and triggering the exodus of the fragile US-backed Lon Nol coalition government in 1975.

Take a trip today up Route 13 from Vietnam into southern Laos driving east on Route 9 and see for yourself as Stan Sesser did past poor villages that survived the bombing that left craters thirty feet in diameter. The Americans never did manage to shut down the Ho Chi Minh Trail but they did shut down information about the CIA's secret 9-year war that began a year after Kennedy's assassination and recalled in *The Ravens*, by British journalist Christopher Robbins.

Stan Sesser writes in *The Lands of Charm and Cruelty,* "The war was fought largely with bombs – an unprecedented rain of bombs. By 1973, when the bombing stopped, the United States had dropped 2,093,100 tons of bombs on Laos; the tonnage was a third higher than that of the American bombs that devastated Nazi Germany in the Second World War, and three times the tonnage dropped during the Korean War. The total number of sorties during that period was 580, 944 – an average of 177 a day, or one planeload of bombs every eight minutes around the clock for nine years. The cost of the bombing was $7.2 billion, or more than $2 million a day." The bombing was a total military failure; in 1975 the Pathet Lao forces took the capital Vietiane and abolished the monarchy. What the American's failed to kill by bombs they poisoned with toxic chemicals like Agent Orange. "The use of defoliants remained a secret far longer than the bombing itself. Only in 1982 did the United States Air Force confirm charges by antiwar groups that it had dumped two hundred thousand gallons of herbicides on Laos in 1965 and 1966," Stan Sesser writes. (Stan Sesser, "Laos, the Forgotten Country", *The Lands of Charm and Cruelty,* NY: Knopf, 1993, 69-124)

Reader I implore you to remember this period well. Ambassador Thomas Enders (Yale) became Nixon's ambassador in Cambodia targeting villages for destruction; I knew his two daughters, both undergraduates at Yale and visited Claire Enders in the new Yale student hospital, a spirited bright young woman in pain. We all seemed so powerless to stop the killing. There were so many secrets and so much pain in our lives.

The slain Senator Bobby Kennedy was right; the nation needed urgently a complete "cleansing" to be free of the poison infecting its soul. His voice articulated what so many felt; his voice spoke for the youth and the future. And he was killed with the others, JFK, Edgars, King, Malcolm X, Bobby... What did America get next? The hawkish Republicans: Nixon, Reagan, the Bush father and son, ...

US Congressman John M. Ashbrook on March 6, 1974 declares, "... US technical trade with the Soviet Union and other East European countries has `gained significant momentum' since the May, 1972 Moscow summit conference and will undoubtedly continue to increase at a gradual rate. The American share of Soviet imports of plants and equipment from the West is now running about

20 percent of the total. It is ironic that while American businessmen are trading hundreds of millions of dollars for plants and equipment to the Soviet Union, the Administration is asking for an increased defense budget to meet the Soviet military threat-a threat which, in part, is being built with American technology."

Then, in 1974, while President Carter and Premier Brezhnev hash out yet another Salt disarmament agreement further bankrupting the Soviet Union, the shameless Congressman Steve Symms goes public with what the Consortium never wanted Americans to know. Symms declares, "Few Americans fully appreciate the extent to which their tax dollars are being used to finance their own destruction. The dealings of the Export-Import Bank are a good example. US 'loans' to the Soviet Union through the bank now total over 760 million dollars to finance projects like constructing the world's largest truck plant on the Kama River. Only two weeks ago an additional $67.5 million of your money was provided for this project, along with a 20 million dollar loan for a Russian acetic acid plant. Another $180 million is now being earmarked for a chemical complex in the USSR and $49.5 million for a gas exploration project in Eastern Siberia."

Symms argued that the basic problem is that the USSR is arming the very enemy whose intentions as the governments and press would have everyone believe were understood to destroy western capitalist democracies. So, he goes on to say, clearly US foreign policy is fundamentally screwed up by the system and the US government's relations with world, as well as all the hammered-out notions of freedom, democracy and collective security so far interpreted by their America's elected and appointed government officials. In other words, he is asking, what ever happened to the American Dream? Is America living a dream, or dreaming a nightmare with nothing real but illusions spinning in their heads. (US Congressional Record, March 6, 1974, E1176)

"... US tax dollars are not only propping up a ruthless dictatorship," declares Symms, "but they are helping to arm our enemy to the teeth. While America is bust building factories and other valuable strategic facilities on Russian soil, the Kremlin is diverting proportionally more of its own resources toward sophisticated offensive weaponry. It makes one wonder whose side the Export-Import Bank officials are really on. Modern-day liberals often refer to these kinds of suicidal give-aways as `meaningful cooperation in the spirit of detente.' It used to be called treason."

The former Chairman of the House Committee on Internal Security – abolished months later, – was next to speak out. Congressman Richard H. Ichord was the top ranking member of the House Armed Services Committee. He offered little relief or reason for the "hate the Russian" mind-set of the Cold War era which made no sense when Americans were divested of their taxes so that private corporations could reap profits building up the "enemy". "We are especially alarmed," Ichord declared, "by the report that the Bank (Export-Import Bank) is on the verge of granting $49 million in credit to the Soviet Union for exploration of Eastern Siberian gas fields. We believe that American financing of Soviet gas exploration at this particular time in history, especially at an interest rate of 6% (which is in effect to be subsidized by the American taxpayer), smacks not only of poor business judgment but suggests a disregard for our national security. Every nation's defense capacity is directly related to its energy resources. The real question is why do we spend some $80 billion a year to maintain such a large military establishment? ... This has enabled the Soviet Union to engage in the largest peacetime military buildup in the history of man. We cannot afford to adopt any trade or credit policies that will allow the Soviets to further expand their military machine."

In a French documentary produced in 2003 of CIA operations during the Cold War with interviews of top cabinet and CIA officials including Bush's current director William Gates, a former CIA official was quoted saying that the US government's clandestine operations in Afghanistan broke the USSR and it only cost the US taxpayer 3 billion dollars, "a bargain", he said. In the entire documentary there was no reference to US investment or profits gained each year while the US financed and maintained the military might of the Soviet "enemy". (American Security Council, *Washington Report*, Feb. 1974).

Enter US Senator Richard Schweiker. The Senator makes headlines which he might have regretted later. Acting bewildered, and very misinformed for a national leader, Schweiker quotes Soviet trade concessions in a "$6.1 billion gas exploration project in Western Siberia and a $49.5 million oil exploration project in the Yakutsk area of Eastern Siberia" as being against US national interest. The *Los Angeles Times* reports Schweiker contended that "lending American capital at low (6%) interest for such projects when there is an energy crisis in the United States" didn't make sense. So why was the Export-Import Bank charging 6% interest when the prime rate was 10%? The Russian exchange issue is greater when one realizes "when Congress is depreciating the dollar at 5% per year, you have to charge 10% to make even five. If a buyer borrows dollars at 6% for Five-Years, and in that period the dollar has depreciated 25%, the buyer has only paid 1% per year for his loan." Who pays the interest subsidy? The bank? The Soviet Union? When the buyer defaults the US government sucks up the loss thereby increasing the national debt. (*Los Angeles Times*, March 9, 1974, Part 3; US Congressional Record, Feb. 19, 1974, E 694).

Forty years after Bullitt's long summer memo to FDR, the Russian bear is blamed for everything wrong in American food shops from higher prices to sour milk. Could America, in 1974, asked Illinois Congressman Philip Crane, ignore that the rise in the cost of bread to the American consumer is a direct result of the recent Russian wheat deal estimated at approximately $290 million or pay the extra cost to the beef industry for feed grains from increased beef prices. "What happened in the wheat deal, of course," Crane declares, "was that the United States sold the Soviet Union and Communist China wheat at a low, subsidized price, with the difference being made up by American taxpayers. As a result, the Soviet Union was saved from famine, and was saved from having to reform its system of forced collectivization..." Just think of his voracity! Four decades after the Ukrainian forced famine of Stalin's genocidal collectivization, financed and equipped by American banks, tractors and industrial plants, neither America nor the Soviet Union has yet recognized the 1932-34 famine.

The Republican Congressman from Chicago raves on unaware what he was up against and finding his way no better than a man chasing shadows in the dark. "The kind of trade the Soviets want, and which we have been willing to participate in, is not trade for consumer goods, such as refrigerators, radios, television sets, and automobiles. They want heavy-industry help, such as machine tools, ball bearings, and precision calibrators. These have military potential, and will hardly improve the living standards of the Russian people.... so that the people are kept poor slaves. To provide the Soviet Union with the sophisticated technology it needs to surpass us, while not demanding any concessions in return, and subsidizing the transaction in addition, is a one-sided policy designed solely to our own detriment." So why hadn't anyone told the junior Congressman how things worked in US-Soviet relations since the beginning? (US Congressional Record, July 10, 1973, H5896).

On July 10, 1973 Representative Earl F. Landgrebe, a Republican die-hard supporter of Richard Nixon during this crucial year of the Watergate break-investigation (Landgrebe makes headlines with his remark, "Don't confuse me with the facts."), – jumps on the wagon flabbergasted. "We are playing into the hands of the Communist rulers," he said, "when we come to their rescue with food and other products of this great free nation, when their whole problem is the fact that the people are trying to lift the Communist domination and pressure from their shoulders by refusing to produce. I would say that America is walking right into this situation and actually prolonging the control of the good people of Russia, and the Russian people are good people. But, as I say, they are under slavery by their Communist rulers. And when we make these deals with the Communist rulers we are perpetuating the slavery of the Russian people." The Indiana businessman is only telling half the story denied the voters. These congressmen had to know better, right? How can men of power be that dumb or were they paid to just act that way performing public theatrics?

There's the rub. In America it was, and still is politically incorrect, a subject not pursued by editors and publishers as well as the people's democratic representatives to speak about US trade with the communist regimes in Moscow, or Peking. For over ten years the US government had waged a criminal war killing millions of people to defeat "the Reds" in a Vietnamese civil war for national liberation until they were defeated not by Soviet weapons, but American weapons captured by the North Vietnamese themselves. Are they all referring to trade items that threaten American homeland security? Ten years later the CIA is secretly providing weapons to warlords in Afghanistan, creating the uncontrollable Taliban, then crediting themselves for "defeating the Soviet Union". The Congressional Record of February 7, 1974, revealed even more strategically vital and lethal trade to the Soviet Union facilitated through the US Export-Import Bank. It was not new. As early as 1934 Bullitt called upon the Export-Import Bank to provide loans and credits to the USSR. (US Congressional Record, July 10, 1973, H5894)

As the hearings continued to unfold the astonishing of US-Soviet trade newly elected Congressman Steve Symms on October 16, 1973 asks for more specifics on Consortium investment in the Soviet Union. Symms will last twenty years in

Washington serving four terrms in Congress and two terms in the Senate. The Republican from Idaho, a specialist in agriculture, speaking for the public record, declares, "So far in 1973, credits and credit guarantees from the US Export-Import Bank in the amount of $202.6 million have been made available to the Soviet Union. The credits carried an interest rate of 6 percent, and grace periods, before repayment begins, of up to 10 years. These transactions supplement the $750 million line of credit for grain purchases made available in 1972 by the Commodity Credit Corporation. In addition to these actual credits, major transactions involving the Soviets and American firms that have been announced this year envision US Export-Import Bank credits of approximately $3 billion."

Republican Congressman Symms makes more headlines when he reveals that his government extended loans worth nearly one billion dollars to the Kremlin *when America was still fighting the Soviet Union in Vietnam*! Senior Senator Henry Jackson said to his colleagues in the Senate, "Reliable reports have reached the West that Secretary Leonid Brezhnev has told Eastern European Communist leaders that improved relations with the West are, in fact, a tactic to permit the Soviet bloc to establish its superiority in the next 12 to 15 years. Tactical flexibility is, of course, a prime component of Leninist political doctrine. Will we find that, in 15 years, the Soviet Union has established a position of superiority which will allow it to disregard detente altogether?" The Senators shake their heads in disbelief, and fear. Is the cat out of the bag?

Sen. Jackson was wrong. By that time the fabric of political double think of Soviet society and propaganda and its perverse Party hierarchy weakened further by its failed invasion of Afghanistan is unraveling. But Solzhenitsyn is even more bitter, and he has nothing to lose defying the Morgan-Rockefeller-Harriman Consortium clique and their Kennan-Nitzocrats anchored in Washington and think-tanks across the country who now welcome him with open arms into their "free world" of coups and assassinations that has clandestinely built and maintained the Communist slave world from day one.

Premier Leonid Brezhnev was born in 1906 in Kamenskoye (later known as Dneprodzerzhinsk), an area where the 25,000 residents centered around the giant metallurgical factory. He began his working life in 1921 in a dairy of his city of Kursk, two decades later there on the plains the greatest tank battle ever in world history, where the waves of Russians pushed back the German Panzer tanks reversing the fortunes of war. When the Russians realized the Panzers lacked machine guns they blew up these modern dinosaurs with hand grenades and "Molotov cocktails". Major General Brezhev will survive the war and live to celebrate victory over the Germans and the disgrace of Stalin but not the end of the Stalinists.

After graduating from the Dniprodzerzhynsk Metallurgical Technicum, young Brezhnev excels as a metallurgical engineer in the iron and steel industry, in Ukraine. In 1923 he joins Komsomol; in 1929 becomes an active member of the Communist Party.

In 1931 a young Brezhnev leaves the Urals and is back in the Ukraine in his home town; four years later he serves as political commissar of a tank company.

He escapes the bullets of the Great Purge and afterward meets Khrushchev who had succeeded Kaganovich as First Secretary of the Ukrainian Politburo in 1938. When Deputy Party leader Brezhnev replaced Khrushchev in a bloodless coup in 1964, a joke circulated, "Stalin, Khrushchev and Brezhnev are sitting in the sleeper of a train called 'Communism', a train which seems utterly unable to move. 'Execute everyone!' Stalin orders. The executions are carried out, but the train refuses to budge. Stalin dies. 'Rehabilitate everyone!' Khrushchev orders. Everyone is rehabilitated, but the train still refuses to move. Khrushchev is deposed. 'Close the blinds on the all the windows, and act as if we are moving!' orders Brezhnev." (Freemen Report, February 15, 1974, 1; US Congressional Record, Sept. 20, 1973, S17053; S. Shulman, 205)

At the time of the Solzhenitsyn reception in the US, several low-ranking Congressmen rally to cut-off trade to the US-backed Soviet Gulag. Of course it never happens. For fifteen seconds people begin to think and ask who was to blame? Congressman Symms chides the Soviet state-run economy, not the American free market system, "History has proven that the Soviet Union's planned industry feeds on the industrial freedom of the West. It would long ago have died a natural death, had it not been for the repeated injections of lifeblood that are still being pumped into it today." Will Americans ever wake up? Any high school kid in America if left to think straight could understand the problem better than the Harvard Business School of Ethics.

How many Americans ever remember US Congressman Dr. Larry McDonald. "He was the most principled man in Congress", Ron Paul tells the *Philadelphia Inquirer* after McDonald disappears aboard the doomed KAL 007 along with with 268 fellow passengers and crew. It was shot down August 31, 1983 by Soviet interceptors. Reagan is the US President and KGB chief Uri Andropov is Soviet Premier. US Secretary of State George Shultz announces the South Korean airliner took 12 minutes to disappear off radar screens. It happens to be the same flight that Richard Nixon was suddenly ordered to get off in Nome, Alaska. It is later learned that the KGB Major General A. I. Romanenko, Commander of the Sakhalin and Kuril Islands frontier guard in charge of a Soviet delegation handling the incident disappeared; it is officially classified as a suicide.

In June 2012 Sen. Scott Brown of Massachusetts signed on to a petition urging US President Obama to open an investigation into the doomed flight where McDonald and 60 other Americans went missing in circumstances that have never been resolved. At the time of this writing early November no news has come of any change from the White House. (Bert Schlossberg, *The Untold Story of KAL 007 and Its Survivors,* 2001)

On March 10, 1975 the far right conservative Democrat from Georgia speaks out to Congress opposing US credit and trade transfers. Referring to the report of the Committee on Appropriations Congressman McDonald declares, "the United States has provided $1,033,400,000 in foreign aid and assistance to the Soviet Union from 1946 through 1974. Presumably this was done under authority other than the Foreign Assistance Act, which prohibits such aid. When you also consider the so-called lend-lease program - so- called because as things turned out it was neither lend nor lease but outright charity to the tune of $11 to $12 billion – and the passing over our post-World War II occupational currency production capability, – the true figure of aid to the heartland of totalitarian communism would be somewhere between $30 to $40 billion. Most Americans are staggered upon learning that the USSR has been the No. 1 beneficiary of US aid in this century .... All of this certainly destroys the accepted view that the United States has an anti-communist foreign policy."

McDonald doesn't stop there. Again for the official Congressional record McDonald quotes from a review of Antony C. Sutton's book *National Suicide*: "It was primarily US technology that kept the Bolsheviks on their feet after their 1917 coup d'état, that maintained them through the Depression, and that has kept them alive to this date .... The major areas of technical assistance to the Soviet Union, which have been directly or indirectly used in military applications are: (1) weapons, including explosives, ammunition and guns; (2) tanks, trucks and armored cars; (3) ships; (4) airplanes; (5) space technology; (6) missiles; and (7) computers. In the area of weapons, aid was forthcoming from the United States even before the Bolsheviks had consolidated their hold on Russia after the coup." How had the history textbooks missed that? (House Report 94-53, H.R. 4592, March 10, 1975; US Congressional Record, Oct. 16, 1973, Freeman Report, 15 Feb. 1974; US Congressional Record, Oct. 3, 1975, E5215)

After the 2005 presidential election many of these same corporations buy out Ukrainian dairy and grain firms seizing shelf-space and advertising on Ukrainian television to sell everything from expensive American and European brand-name products from chips to chocolates when the people have barely enough to feed themselves and their children and buy decent clothes. News of the Terror-Famine was common knowledge in Moscow, but taboo in the American press. Yet American energy conglomerates used slave labor heralded as great strides in federated socialism while Stalin's Soviet state savagely and not without perversely cynical Russian humor humiliated a kind and loving people in a campaign to exterminate them. Even a John Bircher like McDonald who opposes federal busing to integrate southern schools apparently is taken for a ride with no return.

Thus it was obvious to any observer that successive regimes of the former Soviet Union and the United States combined a campaign of suppression of the truth of a concealed US-Soviet collaboration in keeping with such a low profile in the western press as to suppose deliberate suppression of the truth. Such collusion entailed further complicity in the denial of the Terror-Famine. Slave labor provides a steady workforce for the factories and fields and soldiers to fill the ranks. America invested in the Soviet Union for business and war profit.

Long after the end of the Vietnam War, and in spite of the volumes by Sutton and Solzhenitsyn's message to the West the American people continued to act as though they were uninformed about US cooperation with the Soviet Union during the Cold War years. That wall of silence still stands tall long after Stalin's death in 1953. Less than ten years later, in 1961 Khrushchev erects the Berlin Wall. That stands for nearly thirty years, a symbol of the ultimate epitome of the charade of East-West relations masking Consortium complicity behind the Kremlin.

Consortium diplomats and war-makers in the West have a party lasting another generation. Short of nuclear war this was a brilliant and lethal card in "The Game" to raise Cold War tensions and keep the Consortium in business. Both mass populations in the East and the West, in the Ukraine and the other Republic vassal states of the USSR, and the Americans were kept in control and uninformed of the reality that held them hostage to Washington and the Kremlin, and the even more ridiculous irony of the entrapment was their own paralysis by nuclear parity and the apparently unstoppable nuclear arms race. Political dissidents were sent to prison and psychiatric institutions.

The gulag system worked both in the East and the West, different in style and degree. Of course the Soviet henchmen perfected Party discipline coherent with Party doctrine. The effect was the same : incarceration and containment of social deviation. The Consortium had its prisoners on both sides of the Berlin Wall. Before he left office, President Dwight Eisenhower warned America and the world about the ominous and voracious appetite of "the industrial military complex". The growth of the American defense industry saved the country from gnawing and stagnant depression and restored the American Dream, allowed for expansion of the economy building neat suburbs of a blooming white middle class. The same men of the two world wars knew well that war is very profitable for their corporate business. Business had never been so good as during the years of the Cold War. The Berlin Wall and the Vietnam War guaranteed that the good years would continue for a good many more years and that made the good'ole boys of the Consortium very rich and feeling smug with goodness about themselves and each other.

The gulags and psychiatric institutions remained full of political prisoners, violently beaten and abused, drugged into dementia so that the weaker prisoners shattered. Many died. These conditions continued right up through the 1980s and the final collapse of Gorbachev's *perestroika* reforms. The purge mania ended with Stalin departure but censorship and repression of freedoms for behavior contrary to Party doctrine remain in place ready to smash any revolt against the state authorities. Putin's repressions of civil liberties and ease with which he brushes aside the Holodomor issues with the back of his hand, emerging from Kremlin and the shadows of Stalin and snickering in public crude Russian jokes are more of the same measures indicative of post-Stalinist hardline reactionaries. He wields the tremendous power of a Czar mocking liberal reforms of the West content to stay in power and not slide back into political chaos and the social and economic anarchy of the 1990s, or let Russia fall into rebellion of the sort that marked the failed coups of 1991 and 1993.

Russians and Ukrainians still don't get it. Nor do Americans. And the rift between the two superpowers continues to widen in particular exasperated by Israel and its tight grip on the American press and academic institutions riveting the country with incessant Holocaust propaganda. There is a good reason for it too. The New York metropolitan area is home to the largest Jewish population in the world outside Israel. A 2001 census report shows the total world Jewish population of 13.3 million Jews live primarily in three regions: the United States (46 per cent,

6.5 million), Israel (37 per cent, 4.95 million) and in Europe and Russia (12 per cent, 1.6 million). More Jews live in Los Angeles (621,000/*490,000) and Miami and southeast Florida (514,000/*535,000) than in Jerusalem (570,000/497,000**). Within the metropolitan areas of New York City, Los Angeles, and Miami lives nearly one quarter of the world's Jews, according to a 2008 census report. Moscow and Kiev count 200,000 and 110,000 Jewish population, respectively, and 100,000* in St. Petersburg. (**The Jewish Population of the World*, American-Israeli Cooperative Enterprise, World Jewish Congress, Lerner Publications 1998; ** The figure of 497,000 Jews living in Jerusalem in 2011 reported by Wikipedia November 2012. As of May 24, 2006, Jerusalem's population is 724,000 – about 10% of the total population of Israel, of which 65.0% are Jews, according to the Israel Central Bureau of Statistics.)

Disinformation and ideological confusion fall into a bad pattern in favor of special interests and still in effect to the advantage of global corporations investing in dictatorships for oil, natural gas and other strategic resources. Kill a million islanders in the Philippines in 1900 and call it "liberation" of colonial subjects during the Taft-Stimson- Roosevelt era ("Uncle Teddy"), – or slaughter a million retreating Iraqi soldiers as President George Herbert Walker Bush did in the 1991 Gulf War and feel good about trashing America's bad-boy dictator Saddam Hussein while preparing for the next nice little war for George Bush, Jr. . Historians are already describing the Bush wars as the most outrageously inept blunders in the American foreign policy. There is an ever-growing literature on the Bushes and their wars; your reading list should include the best-selling Pulitzer book, *Takeover, The Return of the Imperial Presidency and the Subversion of American Democracy*, a concise review of the alarming evolution of presidential executive power by Charlie Savage (Harvard, Yale Law School 2007), a Pulitzer writer for the *Boston Globe*; *Fiasco, The American Military Adventure in Iraq*, (2006) by Thomas E. Ricks, *Washington Post's* senior Pentagon correspondent; *Family of Secrets – The Bush Dynasty, America's Invisible Government,* and the *Hidden History of the Last Fifty Years*, by Russ Baker, well-known writer and former contributing editor to the Columbia Journalism Review; John Dean's *Worse Than Watergate – The Secret Presidency of George W. Bush* (2004). That's just a handful in a sea of volumes currently within reach. Actually, the Bush era was a boom for publishing books on the dangers of government secrecy and a White House that considers the Executive Office of the President above the law of the land.

Too few books, however, examine the evolution of elite Consortium power in America. All the more reason to pick up the Russ Baker book on the Bush factor, in particular its close look at the origins of their so-called 'dynastic" sway over the American electorate, with the seeds of what Baker calls "the story that lay behind the political rise of the entire Bush clan", and, in particular, those same foundations established by the earlier generations of Sam and Prescott Bush, the former US Senator and their links to the Yale Skull & Bones Taft-Stimson-Harriman crowd. Baker's concluding chapter of that era highlights the core background of the forces at work underlying this book on the "man-made"

Terror-Famine Genocide in the Ukraine and US government support of Stalin's Communist Party dictatorship in concert with the war-making Consortium and its tools in the US State Department. Read the Russ Baker book and others like it. *Takeover* is a particularly astute and highly readable review of the misuse of presidential authority by the Bush-Cheney team and their manipulation of the Republican-led Congress. Many Americans are still incredibly clueless how that resulted in a "truly historic expansion of the president's power to impose martial law" using the Military Commissions Act "to virtually eliminate the possibility that the Supreme Court could ever again act as a check on a president's power in the war or terrorism". Or anything else. This is a must read book of alarming implications on the end of civil liberties and the freedom of information by the secret government of the United States.

The peasants were "only Russians", declares *The New York Times'* Stalinist hack and Pultizer journalist Walter Duranty in 1932. African-Americans and descendants of former slaves were denigrated by racists in elite corporate America ready and willing to supersede the British Empire in its imperial habits from the Philippines to the Banana Republics. The picture is not pretty. Most Americans don't seem to care as long as it's not their funeral and left "free" to believe in their pursuit of American dream and maintain a general picture of the ideal Christian American standard of living and way of life. Is this religious fanaticism, or what? Bill Bullitt wrote of responses to the communist Revolution by Main Line Philadelphia society and the political Right in England including the Lord Northcliffe press baron who disavowed his mission to Lenin, and in his novel *It's Not Done* (1926) Bullitt wrote, "They've all become atheists, and I'm for blockading them and starving them and killing them till they return to their senses and become Christians again." (J. Kaplan, 265)

Only a few very determined people, mostly men in strategically-oriented top positions in industry, finance and government are able to control the world order. A hundred years ago in America, a small group of men, perhaps a few hundred, or less, from prestigious schools and secret societies, wealthy and intermarried families, working in government, private industry, within federal and international banks, and educational and religious institutions, all linked and interconnected, were able to control the legislative, judicial executive offices of the government of the United States, manage the national and international press with strategic alliances and friends in high places, set the domestic and foreign policy within a framework of war, national defense, control the national currency, pursue a logic of destruction, and mold the future and mind-set of the nation.

It may sound improbable but it was true. To the civilized humanist it might have seemed odd that the Consortium thought it justifiable they use the Bolsheviks to takeover the Russian Czarist Empire as their own private monopoly and in doing business with the communist Soviet dictators omit to utter a word for the millions of people they killed. Of course, they covered it up the best they could. And no one stopped them. Not then, not now. This kind of horror cast upon the civilized world is almost as frightening as the horror and terror inflicted on the victims. A slow immoral death can be less virtuous and more painful than a bullet in the back of the head, a common practice of the soviet butchers with less blood spilled. A brilliant economy of bullet and blood. Whatever one may be induced to call it, ideological rape, mental castration, it still remains an abomination of morality dragging exalted values and national identity in the gutter.

During the Holodomor years of the early thirties each country had its own elite organizations of ownership and control to sustain the Soviet socialist regime. The Consortium of big international banks of Wall Street in New York, on "the Street" in London, around "La Bourse" in Paris and in the German marketplace of Berlin, Munich and Frankfurt shared a common goal with the highly capitalized American corporations and trained American engineers, as well as British linked and controlled in the hands of a most secret and powerful elite, most of them working through embassies, banks and reputable firms in Berlin.

If you take the high figure, Ukraine lost at least ten million men, women and children in the Holodomor years. The price for Americans would be bitter but they paid for it when America after World War II bought the Cold War in a brilliant arrangement with all the cunning of the devil with the innocence of a virgin. The men and their group who made the Cold War were the same architects of the previous two world wars. Bernard Baruch, his close friend Wall Street friend, Eugene Meyer, Paul Warburg, Rockefeller, Harriman, Stimson, McCloy and their groups of friends making billions of dollars in the WWI, profiting handsomely in wealth and social prestige, sometimes at the cost of the lives of their sons, a very small number indeed compared to the tens of millions of innocent civilians who died because war was more profitable than peace. They live in lofty estates, manors and plantations. They live like barons and princes in isolated and protected seclusion. They send their favorite sons to Harvard, Princeton and Yale, and enshrine their perpetuity with the names of fallen heroes engraved in stone. At Yale's Woolsey Hall and on the imposing edifice of the Commons dining hall their names echo the immemorial battles of WWI in France casting shadows over their descendants and heirs but revealing nothing of the pointless stupid waste of human life. Gazing up at their names engraved in stone gives the impression that it has fallen from the Gods from above is not far from mind. The Consortium and its survivors repeated the same mistakes in the next war but it would be the Russians this time who would lose millions upon millions of soldiers and civilians and this time insist on their rewards.

Son of poor Jewish immigrants Bernard Baruch made his early fortune on Wall Street in the 1890s market boom. Baruch was very rich with his reputation of success (he is known as the "Lone Wolf of Wall Street") he had no trouble penetrating the ranks of the eastern establishment of America's ruling class of landed gentry and industrialists. He was intimate with Wilson who vacationed at his southern estate on thousands of acres of secluded coastline and marshlands. Not long after making a killing on Wall Street Baruch purchases his "Hobcaw Barony", a winter residence that over the years grows to some 17,500 acres 71 square kilometers on the coast of South Carolina. There he welcomed presidents Wilson and Roosevelt in need of a peaceful and isolated natural retreat away from

Washington. On a visit there Sir Winston Churchill is bumped by a taxi, fortunately it was a light-headed fender bender and the minister is not seriously injured.

It is not difficult to see the America experience reflected in Ukraine. How could it not be so? When they wrote their exhaustive histories, Antony Sutton and Carroll Quigley knew it would be hard for most Americans to understand that what they wrote was true. It's there to see but as with things in life an effort is required to look beyond the surface of illusions. Most people are not willing to make that effort. Most don't even see what's at the end of their nose. Sometimes you have to go away, far away, to see where you came from, and to see where you are. Like with a mirror held up to the past, its possible to discern the names and machinations of individuals and processes that affected the Ukraine by holding up their historical landscape to reflect the panorama of America's past. Sometimes to be or not to be requires a lot of thinking before actions make the picture comes into focus and what is beyond the spin and behind the curtain reveals itself. What hasn't been shredded burned and destroyed is still here to see in one form or another. Call it illumination, revelation, or truth.

Persistence also necessarily entails vigilance before it can deliver a practical reward. The Consortium gate-keepers are not relenting either tenaciously holding on to anachronistic tenets of cronyism as stewards of the politically correct intent on keeping their voters in step. Hah! They will be the first to flee to their hideaway retreats when the people wake up, turn off their TVs, fling the DVDs out the window and take to the open streets! Its all there to be seen and studied unfolding before your eyes daily. To have a perspective, and a fresh view and renewed strength to go on. For a sea change. Clean air even if you reader dares to breathe a breath of protest. Untie those knots of ill-will and deception. Shed the falseness! Clear skies and a broad long view, peace and quiet. And the stillness that comes from somewhere. No one can say for sure what will happen next. It doesn't matter really, as long as you keep your bearings and don't lose your balance. Change will happen anyway inside and around you. And also because you are aware that your ideas change and evolve along with your faith that you can make change happen. And you want change to happen that evolves and transforms and enriches your life and your world. And you want to be on the side of change at that point in your life when you are not afraid anymore. This book is meant to help you on your path of understanding and awareness of these nefarious forces messing up your own natural healthy energies.

If you have the good fortune to meet Ukrainians undoubtedly the encounter will leave an impression that Ukrainians for the most part are modest, courageous and simple loving people with basic instincts. Certainly it is an understatement to say that Ukrainians are a testimony of human endurance. To survive is everything. It is their first and foremost preoccupation and perhaps they are animated an instinct of flesh and blood that is foreign to Americans in their experience of remote and splendid isolation. Educated Ukrainians are articulate, intelligent, and well-read. Look at them today and as Bulgakov made clear in his literature hailed as some of the best verse in Russia you will discover something mysteriously beautiful about them. You must do that to know what is behind that mystery.

There are secret spirits and forces that belong only to Mother Ukraine. Respect for the eternal Mother is a sacred ancient Ukrainian and Russian custom. In the Ukraine, the *babushkas* rule over the spirit of the land.

Lenin was a Russian intellectual. He passes only a year or so in the Russian countryside on a family estate in the Volga. Stalin was from a village in Georgia, in the Caucasus but lived his whole adult life in the city. Trotsky was a cosmopolitan Jew. No one in Kiev today speaks about Nikita Khrushchev or his humble peasant origins.

As though transfixed forever in a Gogol paradox Ukraine persists, both a land enriched with wondrous joy and tales of epic survival, a tragic land heavy with the spirit of dead souls wandering through a cultural quagmire of death and destruction. It is a land that remains at the same time a very positive and a very negative place. Perhaps the dark dead souls have been reborn in lower realms than human life. Cockroaches! It has been said by lamas that Hitler was reborn a dog in Holland.

Many secrets will forever remain inaccessible as to how the manipulations of international bankers and American businessmen with their international partners joined together in a common union for power and control of the world's governments and resources. But the obvious remains here at the tip of your nose. You just have to see it, and touch it, and understand.

What made Sutton's findings so unique compared to Establishment historians was that his identification of the problem differed significantly. Much of that history, he wrote, has been for nearly a century "brushed under the rug of history because they do not fit the accepted conceptual spectrum of political left and political right." Soon a river of new black tanks would pour into the Ukraine and Russia emblazoned with swastikas and soldiers standing at attention in neat uniforms invading as conquerors killing millions at the front. More terror and so much blood. Poor Russia. When would peace ever come? The years of war and famine never seemed to end. Nazi Germany like a giant steamroller pressed down on Russia as onto a piece of iron squeezed flat where nothing remains. All of the original shape destroyed by the invading German fascists.

MORE CONSORTIUM PLAYERS – THE NAZI BROWN BOOK OF WAR CRIMINALS

Hitlerians were more efficient than Stalin. Whose fault is it that sons are killed and mothers weep? Based on State archives of the German Democratic Republic, the *Brown Book of Nazi and War Criminals* made international headlines when it was first published in July 1965, two decades after the defeat of the Nazi system which had been "guilty of the death of 55 million people". In the preface to the 1968 second edition, it stated, "Already once before, in 1933, German anti-fascists – with active international support, published a *Brown Book* at a time when many people in Germany and abroad did not yet perceive the dangers arising from Hitler's seizure of power. In Paris, they published that famous *Brown Book* which revealed the first crimes of Hitlerites." This when Stalin was killing millions of defenseless Ukrainians by starvation and forced exile to slave labor camps so many dying on the way without food or clothing. (*Brown Book of Nazi and War Criminals,* 1965. A second edition was published 1968)

While the *Brown Book* did not explore international banking and investment in the Nazi regime, its research on early Nazi investment and Nazi aggression in the Soviet Union portrayed a grim picture when superimposed on the tragedy of Stalin's Terror-Famine. Ukraine suffered the worst atrocities of the 1941 Nazi invasion. Many of those who survived the famine were horribly tortured and killed in the first ten weeks of war by special Nazi SS death squads with black and white banners of skull and bones with the single objective to exterminate the people.

The *Brown Book* traced the careers of the German war monopolists. "Only a few of the armament industrialists were convicted by the American military court and given mild sentences. They did not even have to serve their time in jail thanks to the intervention of the Bonn government. Today (1968 sic) those chiefly responsible for the Nazi war crimes, the IG Farben directors, Flick, Krupp and other armament industrialists, are among the most powerful people in West Germany ... No important decision is made by the West German government without their consent." It's too naive and not serious to think that neither the State Department or Military Intelligence lacked information on Hitler's funding; on the contrary, failure to do so would have constituted a severe breach of competence and professional incompetence. Ambassador Dodd mingled with a steady stream of American lawyers and bankers passing through his Berlin Embassy. He dined and entertained the Nazis of different temperaments and knew their minds weary over Jewish persecution and German militarism.

In fact, after the war, virtually not a single of Hitler's economic war planners in the industrial monopolies and banks were imprisoned for any long term. Those who became "defendants" at Nuremberg emerged as senior officials in the "reconstructed" Federal Republic of Germany. Many of the senior economic war planners joined American corporations, for instance, Dr. Hans Heyne, AEG general manager on the supervisory board and leader of the main committee for aircraft armament and war production, member of the industrial council of development of aircraft equipment for the Luftwaffe. Among the many companies he joined after the war (AEG, Seimens, Telefunken, Deutsche Bank …), was General Electric, one of the world's largest atomic weapons producers. AEG (German General Electric) had, in 1965, a 55% stake in the joint company, among their activities, making plutonium. Another IG Farben representative, Siegfriend Balke, replaces Deutsche Bank board member H. C. Paulsen, one of Hitler's economic chiefs in the armaments industry, who steps down as chairman of the Aluminiumindustrie Singen AG.

Further, the *Brown Book* also listed hundreds of war criminals, former SS, SD and Gestapo murderers and Nazi leaders who later penetrated the state apparatus of West Germany. They included butchers like Dr. Otto Dippelhofer, a major in the SS police who had "massacred thousands of Slavs and Jews in Eastern Europe"; Reinhard Dullien, member of the NSDAP since 1933, head of the main department III in the general commissariat in Volhynia and Podolia of the Reich commissioner for the Ukraine; Gunther Hermann, SS operation commando leader in the Soviet Union, head of SS Gestapo; Hartmann Lauterbacher, SS, involved in mass shootings of Soviet POWs at the Seelhorst cemetery; Gerhard Oehl, SA officer in the gendarmerie in Simferopol of the Crimea I southern Ukraine ... Their number is too many to list, their Gestapo crimes obscured by oblivion. Many found refuge as police in West Germany.

Journalist and Soviet Commissar Vasily Grossman is a brave and brilliant Jewish writer from Ukraine. His mother was executed by the Nazis in the Berdychiv massacres and he would have been too. Commissars are first on the Nazi death list. On the highway leading to Berlin from Moscow to enter the defeated capital of fascism, he rode with the Red Army in a Willys jeep with the first Soviet troops. There he found Germans eager to obey their conquerors and noted the absence of partisan resistance. He took his readers into the office of the Soviet Colonel General Nicolai Berzarin, of the Fifth Shock Army, the most popular commander under Zhukov, and toured the city bombed by the Americans and English. Grossman himself narrowly escaped Stalin's anti-Semitism. Stalin dies in 1953 before he could give him the taste of the Gulag. However Grossman's writings too closely parallel Nazism with Stalinism. The "supreme muzhik Nikita Khrushchev persecutes him, confiscating the manuscript of his last and most famous novel *Life and Fate*, actually the sequel to his previous novel *For the Right Cause*. Smuggled out of Russia on microfilm it is reportedly transcribed by the highly esteemed member of Soviet Academy of Sciences Andrei Dmitrievich Sakharov and published in Switzerland.

Appearing a year after his death Andrei Sakharov's *Memoirs (*1990) is an irreplaceable document of his Russian experience living under Stalin and the Communist Party power regime. His family were talented and educated intelligentsia descended from various regions of Russia. Andrei was a baby of the Revolution, born in Moscow in 1921 he lived in a communal apartment in a leaky old house across shared with four Sakharov families. One of his ancestors was Nikolai Yakushkin, a direct descendant of the Decembrist Revolt of in 1825, the radical Ivan Yakushkin seeking liberation of the serfs and a constitutional monarchy and as with all the other literate radicals of the movement knew Pushkin's poems and "Ode to Freedom" by heart: "Fallen slaves, take heart like men, / Listen to these words and rise." His grandfather had been a prominent lawyer, instructor at the Second Moscow State University and a outspoken opponent to capital punishment. The Sakharovs enjoyed a cultured society of skilled and learned professionals in the arts and sciences. That all changed with war and revolution. They shared Russia's tragedy of starvation. His grandfather died of typhus, in Kislovodsk, in the Caucasus cut off from central Russia by civil war. His parents were stranded in the south on the Black Sea. Another grandfather died of typhus in Kharkov. Other family members starved and died of disease. (Elaine Feinstein, *Pushkin, A Biography*, New Jersey: Ecco Press, 1998, 44)

Andrei Sakharov recalls, "I heard this tragic story in my infancy; it was one of my earliest memories...I vaguely recall their telling me about a night they spent in an enormous barn crowded with Red Army soldiers delirious from typhoid fever, about the machine-gunning of Kalmyk families, men, women, and children, trying to escape from famine, and about starving people frozen to death on the steppe."

Andrei Sakharov narrowly survived those years only to confront the thirties. These were the traumatic days of the Russian famine when Hoover intervened with Congressional funds and American aid dispersed by the ARC. The family settled back in their house in Moscow on Granatny Lane for the next two decades across the street on a stately mansion nationalized by the Bolsheviks converted to the Bureau of Weights and Measures of the All-Union Institute of Standards hung a banner displayed "every November 7 and May 1: 'The Comintern Is the Gravedigger of Capitalism".

The future Nobel Peace Prize laureate, father of the hydrogen bomb, "Hero of the Soviet Union" and its leading Soviet dissident recalled, "I began to hear the words 'arrest' and 'search' more and more often. Hardly a single family remained untouched, and ours was no exception." Uncle Ivan lost two sons in the civil war; eventually this dexterious natural engineer, friend of Bukharin and Valerian Osinsky, both later Bolsheviks, excelled at finance, ran afoul of authorities over when he loaned a friend his passport, enlisted Yagoda to intervene, when he was already deputy head of the OGPU, but went to prison for two years. After his release, after some time arrested again, sent away, arrested a third time and dies in a Krasnoyarsk prison hospital during the war of malnutrition. And there was the story of his Aunt Valya, and her second husband: "a man named Belgardt, had been an officer, first in the Czar's forces and then in Admiral Kolchak's army; in the mid-1930s, like most former White Guard officers, he was arrested and shot. Mother's elder brother, Vladimir, was arrested and died in a camp. Also in the mid-1930s, my cousin Evgeny, was sent to a labor camp, where he drowned while rafting timber down a river. His son Yura had spent a summer with us at the dacha, and we'd all become very fond of him. In the winter of 1938, Yura contracted meningitis and died in the hospital. In 1937, Uncle Knostantin, another of Mother's brothers, was arrested, along with his younger sister Tusya and Tusya's husband, Gennady Sarkisov ... Konstantin had worked at a military plant – and in those days, having family links both to foreigners and to military technology was more than sufficient grounds for arrest. Konstantin was an amateur photographer and also a highly skilled radio amateur. As early as 1930, he'd built a homemade television set with a mechanical scanning device, using a Nipkow disc – an absolute miracle for that time. He died during the course of the investigation ... Was our family's chronicle of tragedies exceptional? Every family I know suffered casualties, and many lost more members than ours did." (Andrei Sakharov, *Memoirs*, Knopf, 1990, 4-36)

Declared a "nonperson" Vasily Grossman died in 1964. During his days in May 1945 in Berlin Grossman observed the charred remains of Josef Goebbels who had poisoned his six children and shot his wife; he walked through Hitler's bunker, examining papers and desk. Grossman wrote "A day in Berzarin's office. The creation of the World. Germans, Germans, Germans – Burgenmeisters, directors of Berlin's electricity supply, Berlin water, sewerage, trams, gas, factory owners, (and other) characters. They obtain new positions in this office. Vice-directors become directors, chiefs of regional enterprises become chiefs on a national scale. Shuffling of feet, greetings, whispers. ... Oh, how weak human nature is! All these big officials brought up by Hitler, successful and sleek, how quickly and passionately they have forsaken and cursed their regime, their leaders, their Party." On May 2, 1945, he wrote in his diary, "In smoke among gthe ruins, in flames, amid hundreds of corpses in the streets. Corpses squashed by tanks, squeezed out like tubes. Almost all of them are clutching grenades and sub-machine guns in their hands.... Most of the dead men are dressed in brown shirts. They were Party activists who defended the approaches to the Reichstag and the Reichschancellery." (Vasily Grossman, *A Writer At War*, 2005, 338)

It should now be clearer to you reader that from the beginning Stalin and his Communist Party *nomenklatura* were assured of the support within the inner presidential sanctum of both Presidents Hoover and FDR. You want more details? Okay, you get them here. Stay with it because this is the story of the century. In fact, ever since the 1917 collapse of autocratic Czarist Russia, the prerequisite to America's entry into First World War preparing for shipment of Bolsheviks to stage the October Revolution, all subsequent American administrations and their influential friends in finance and industry supported Lenin's Marxist Bolsheviks and the Communist Party, vanguard of the working class proletarian dictatorship. Their support continues to sustain Stalin's two Five-Year Plans for industrial workers and agriculture, the mainstay programs for political stability and economic growth of the US backed by the mind-numbing ideology of dialectical reasoning. Stalin is given a free-hand at repression and extermination. US government-backed loans, insured by the Federal Reserve central banks, private national banks and US business investment endorse and further encourage Stalin's repressions. Sabre-rattling pacts of Berlin, Rome and Tokyo further push Stalin towards the West which he suspects plotting intrigue against him and add to his mental derangement and seclusion inside the walls of the Kremlin where he is protected by hundreds of special secret police, soldiers and bodyguards.

Reader, do you *get* it now?

In exchange for their share of destroying but not irrevocably shattering the former Russian empire, the powerful ruling elite of imperialist foreign powers maintained a devious business relationship inside the governments of England and America. The Communist leaders Lenin, Trotsky and Stalin each desperate in their time of need for capital, foreign exchange, technology and industry including agriculture had no where else to turn.

Their logic was incontrovertible: to keep the lid on the disintegration threat, from Lenin to Stalin, whoever wanted to create a collective (communist, socialist, whatever) – it was all monopolist society in a country populated primarily of peasants. Neither FDR, the Consortium or Stalin were not prepared to could not stop half-way. These extraordinarily rich and powerful men who back the nation's politicians looking and talking respectably in the spectacle of the nation's public arena, and who financed and advised America's two political parties and their democratically elected Presidents remained enigmatic like their strategies of control. They planned it that way. That much is true today.

America in the First World War was governed and controlled by a socially tightly-knit, enormously wealthy business and financial elite. A serious study of Wilson's war years, the Versailles Treaty and postwar reconstruction is indispensable. It inevitably leads to a better understanding of the Terror-Famine and the betrayal and extermination of the oppressed and defenseless Ukrainian population. Consortium operatives like banker Paul Warburg, Wall Street speculator Bernard Baruch, Col. House, – one of its most enigmatic characters who for over a century has escaped serious scrutiny, – and a very tight clique quickly saw in the war a golden opportunity to capture the national economy.

Baruch's design of Wilson's War Industries Board for the First World War was similar in concept to cooperative trade associations favored by Wall Street to control market competition. His scheme was easy to put in place: committees of industry, big and small, with reps in Washington. Baruch biographer William White wrote that Baruch, a major campaign contributor to both Wilson and Roosevelt was startled when told by House that Wilson refused to sign the bill which had secretly been written by Warburg.

The Federal Reserve Bank was originally proposed to be "controlled by Congress" with the majority of the directors were to be chosen, "directly or indirectly" by the banks of the association. This infuriated President Wilson who refused to participate in the scheme. Jefferson, Andrew Jackson, and Wilson feared the over-reaching hands of the bankers in a democratic nation dedicated to free markets, determined to defend human rights and the liberty of sovereign nations and uncomfortable with imperialist empires. Not much more than a century has passed since American founding father Benjamin Franklin observed, "There are two passions which have a powerful influence on human affairs: love of power and love of money.... When they are united they produce the most frightful outcomes."

THE GREAT AMERICAN JEWS: THE SCHIFFS, THE WARBURGS, THE KAHNS ...

The Federal Reserve banking system is the largest generator of debt in the world. Warburg and Baruch persuaded the President to arrange details to create the national centralized bank by the "administrative processes". It was a refined Warburg plan whereby Federal Board Governors would be appointed by the President of the United States. In reality the Board would be controlled by a Federal advisory Council meeting with the Governor; and it would be the directors of the twelve Federal Reserve Banks who choose the Council members. Their identity was not to be revealed to the public. Only then Wilson agreed to let the bankers have their way. He signed the Federal Reserve Act on December 23, 1913 and regretted it soon after.

The Schiffs, the Warburgs, the Kahns, the Rockefellers, Harrimans and Morgans all put their faith in House. George Sylvester Viereck, the prolific author of *The Strangest Friendship in History, Woodrow Wilson and Col. House* (1932) writes, "When the Federal Reserve legislation at last assumed definite shape, House was the intermediary between the White House and the financiers…. Col. House looks upon the reform of the monetary system as the crowning internal achievement of the Wilson Administration." It's not unlikely that House's father had been a Rothschild agent in Texas. The following day Schiff wrote House, "My dear Col. House. I want to say a word to you for the silent, but no doubt effective work you have done in the interest of currency legislation…" In a carefully planned campaign, two professors at Harvard and the Rockefeller endowed University of Chicago were responsible for propaganda to promote the new federal banking system with a five million dollar slush fund of the "National Citizen's League". (Col. Edward Mandell House, *The Intimate Papers of Col. House*, ed. by Charles Seymour, Houghton Mifflin, 1926-28, v. 1, 157; George Sylvester Viereck, *The Strangest Friendship in History, Woodrow Wilson and Col. House,* NY: Liveright, 1932. Hodgson notes it was published in 1933 after an estranged collaboration with House when Viereck bought the rights to House's memoirs. G. Hodgson, *Woodrow Wilson's Right Hand*, 265)

Head of Kuhn, Loeb & Co. in Manhattan Jacob Schiff had come from Germany, born 1847 in Frankfurt to a prominent rabbinical family emigrating in 1865; ten years later he marries Theresa Loeb, daughter of Solomon Loeb, head of Kuhn, Loeb, and is soon head of the firm linking up with the Belmont and Morgan. Schiff's wealth extended to an array of Judaic philanthropies as well as Pax Americana organisatons from the Red Cross to the Boy Scouts. In the 1904-1905 Russo-Japanese war, Schiff contributed at least $200 million in loans to ensure a Japanese victory and provoked the failed 1905 Russian revolution. Japanese Emperor Meiji awarded Schiff the Order of the Rising Sun. No foreigner had ever before been so honored.

On the eve of the First World War Lord Rothschild sent a telegram to the German Kaiser Wilhelm II: "This banker, with all that amount of Jewish money behind him, could have embarrassed us as much as Schiff of New York embarrassed Russia." On the Street it was a poorly kept secret that Kuhn, Loeb was a principal agent for the Rothschilds financial empire. *The New York Times* wrote a pertinent reference to Kuhn, Loeb and Company in Schiff's obituary, "During the world War certain of its members were in constant contact with the Government in an advisory capacity. It shared in the conferences which were held regarding the organization and formation of the Federal Reserve System." In 1785 the Schiffs and Rothschilds families shared a five-story house in Germany known as "The Green Shield".

Writer Eustace Mullins adds, "The 1920 Schiff obituary revealed for the first time that Jacob Schiff, like the Warburgs, also had two brothers in Germany during World War I, Philip and Ludwig Schiff, of Frankfurt-on-Main, who also were active as bankers to the German Government! This was not a circumstance to be taken lightly, as on neither side of the Atlantic were the said bankers obscure individuals who had no influence in the conduct of the war. On the contrary, the Kuhn, Loeb partners held the highest governmental posts in the United States during World War I, while in Germany, Max and Fritz Warburg, and Philip and Ludwig Schiff, moved in the highest councils of government. According to Warburg, 'The Kaiser thumbed the table violently and shouted, "Must you always be right?" but then listened carefully to Max's view on financial matters.' Ten years after Jacob passed away, Mortimer Schiff prefaced a book about his father's life recalling his anti-Russian and anti-Czarist dealings." (Cyrus H. Adler, *Jacob Schiff, His Life and Letters*, 1929, London: Rothschild to Wilhelm II; Emil Ludwig, *June 1914; The NYT*, Sept. 26, 1920; Max Warburg, *Memoirs of Max Warburg*, Berlin, 1936, in E. Mullins, *Secrets of the Federal Reserve*)

The Rothschild extended family of preeminent Jewish bankers ranks them supreme in world finance. Mullins observes, "On July 27, 1844, (Giuseppe) Mazzini said, "Rothschild could be King of France if he so desired." The Jewish Encyclopedia noted (1909 edition): "In the year 1848 the Paris house (of Rothschild) was reckoned to be worth 600,000,000 francs as against 352,000,000 francs held by all the other Paris bankers." In "Jews and Modern Capitalism", Prof. Werner Sombart wrote: "The principal loan floaters of the world, the Rothschilds, were later the first railway kings. The period of 1820 onwards became the 'Age of the Rothschilds' so that at the middle of the century it was a common dictum: There is only one power in Europe and that is Rothschild." Hearst's *Chicago Evening American* comments on December 3, 1923: "The Rothschilds can start or prevent wars. Their word could make or break empires." Reeves notes, "The fall of Napoleon was the rise of Rothschild." Napoleon was later slowly poisoned to death with arsenic by a Rothschild agent. They had no need of another "return from exile". (E. Mullins, *The World Order*)

That that same year just prior to the passage of the Federal Reserve Act President Wilson's *The New Freedom* was published. A curious piece of rhetoric by the Princetonian who studied rhetoric in preparation for his thesis on constitutional law. It reads like propaganda it is. However it carries a strange warning that rings true. "Since I entered politics," Wilson wrote, "I have chiefly had men's views confided to me privately. Some of the biggest men in the US, in the field of commerce and manufacturing, are afraid of somebody, are afraid of something. They know that there is a power somewhere so organized, so subtle, so watchful, so interlocked, so complete, so pervasive, that they had better not speak above their breath when they speak in condemnation of it."

With Col. House and the bankers raising their glasses to toast profits and victory in war, President Wilson descended further into doubt and despair, suffering a crisis of faith not to be expected by the son of a prominent southern Presbyterian minister and the maternal grandson of a Scottish preacher. He lost control of the government to some of the same bankers he had done battle with at Princeton when he made national headlines as president of the university up against the Trustees, powerful alumni and the elite club system. In 1916, he wrote a treatise titled *National Economy and the Banking System*, and, he declared, "Our system of credit is concentrated (in the Federal Reserve System sic). The growth of the nation, therefore, and all our activities, are in the hands of a few men." (Sen. Doc. No. 3, No. 223, 76th Congress, 1st session, 1939)

Antony Sutton traced the Paul Warburg family members in their role as influential bankers and insiders of the American banking establishment and particularly their involvement with the Russian Revolution or Bolshevik uprising led by Lenin and Trotsky. People and details seem to fall into place that curiously, and it might appear to some observers most strangely indicate that after staging the Lenin-Trotsky coup in the Petrograd Soviet in 1917, the Consortium people within President Wilson's administration maintain key links of engagement. Intriguing with these centralized bankers was the enigmatic Colonel Edward M. House (1858-38) and the younger William Wiseman (1885-62). Wiseman works behind the scene pushing the progaganda of noble British war aims against German infanticidal maniacs and rapists of the Prussian militarists while he and his agents secretly disrupt German trade and camouflage the illegal munitions commerce between England and America. A familiar face to Wall Street's Consoritum bankers, in particular Kuhn, Loeb, the main investment firm with Morgan in the munitions trade and behind the Bolshevik coup

COL. HOUSE, THE ROTHSCHILDS & THE FED CONNECTION

Very little is known about the secretive and influential Col. House who served as a buffer and conduit to Wilson's two terms in the White House and liaison with the State Department, Wall Street and the imperialists of the British Empire. "Mr. House is my second personality," Wilson confided. "He is my independent self. His thoughts and mine are one." Sutton is one of the very few historians to penetrate the enigma of House's background and found him to be "the son of a Rothschild agent in Texas, and succeeded as a master at playing politics there electing five consecutive governors before joining Wilson's 1912 Presidential Election bid. It was House (and Baruch) who compelled Wilson to sign the Federal Reserve Act in close cooperation with head banker Paul Warburg and lobbied Congress for rapid passage. That set the common course to control the American government for world war and revolution to be managed by the bankers and their interlocking network of corporate directorates. Then Wiseman and House collaborated closely to maneuver Wilson into the Great War." (G. Hodgson, *Woodrow Wilson's Right Hand,* 2009. This book obscures more than it reveals using a wide brush with alarming inaccuracy.)

Wilson was a political captive if ever there was one of the bankers of Standard Oil of New Jersey where he was Governor before making his step towards the White House. His daughter marries William Gibbs McAdoo, Wilson's Treasury Secretary throughout the war years stepping down in 1919 while remaining "ex officio" of the Fed. Neither can withstand the powerful men of Wall Street. After the war Wilson's daughter drifted off to India and remote ashrams for meditation and perhaps karmic reincarnation away from the finance men and Washington society. Hegelian philosophers, Marxists and socialists enjoy the synthesis of contradictions and would find little irony that Wilson was destroyed by the men of war pontificating principles of peace that eluded him.

WHO GOT THE SHARES IN THE FEDERAL RESERVE BANK

To have a better idea how the Fed system was set up for and by the bankers take a look. The nation's third large purchase of Federal Reserve Bank of New York stock in 1914 was the National Bank of Commerce which issued 250,000 shares; JP Morgan, through his controlling interest in Equitable Life held 24,700 shares and Mutual Life which held 17,294 shares of National Bank of Commerce also held another 10,000 shares of National Bank of Commerce through JP Morgan and Co., which held 7,800 shares; JP Morgan, Jr., held 1,100 shares, equal in number to those given to Morgan's top partner H. P. Davison; Paul Warburg, a Governor of the Federal Reserve Board of Governors stood out with 3,000 shares of National Bank of Commerce; Warburg's partner Jacob Schiff also held 1,000 shares of National Bank of Commerce controlled by the Morgan bank which actually was a subsidiary of Junius S. Morgan Company and the N.M. Rothschild Company, both of London. I once asked a descendant and confidential friend, of one of the original shareholder families, "What happened to all these shares?" No answer. Silence. Play dumb and people *will* think you are really stupid, or just as empty as silence itself. Reader, wake up! Ask questions and find the answers.

In regard to the Consortium play of the Great Game the Schiff Jewish legacy is outstanding. As scion of prestigious banking firm Kuhn, Loeb & Company Jacob Schiff was an avowed enemy of Czarist Russia. For years Schiff financed anti-Czarist revolutionary activities to overthrow Czar Nicholas and the Romanov monarchy.

During WWI when the Czarist regime tumbles early spring 1917 Schiff publicly takes credit for having financed the revolutionary movement with $12 million *before* the outbreak of war. Paul Warburg became a partner at Kuhn, Loeb when he was hired from his firm Warburg & Warburg in Hamburg, Germany at a half-million dollars. With war on the horizon, imagine how was it possible that a recent immigrant from Germany was able to assemble the pillars of the American banking establishment at Jekyll Island in 1910 as co-founders of the Federal Reserve national banking system.

This was when in the dark of night on a deserted railway platform in Hoboken, New Jersey these most powerful men came together in secret for a mission that would revolutionize international finance. Their cover if caught by journalists was they were off on a Thanksgiving duck hunting vacation. Warburg is joined by HPD and Frank A. Vanderlip of National City Bank, Senator Nelson W. Aldrich of Rhodes Island, A. Piatt Andrew, Wilson's Assistant Secretary of the Treasury and Special Assistant of the National Monetary Commission, and Charles D. Norton, president First National Bank, another Morgan bank. When war breaks out Piatt becomes the chief organizer of the American Field Service sending collegiate volunteers to the Front to do their patriotic duty for the Anglo-American war profiteers. Also on the Hoboken train platform there to send them off to Jekyll Island is Benjamin Strong; a Morgan man, president of the Bankers Trust, Strong will later become the first governor of the New York Federal Reserve Bank until his death in 1928. (Nathaniel W. Stephenson, Chapter 14, "Jekyll Island", *Nelson W. Aldrich, A Leader in American Politics*, NY: Scribners, 1930)

JACOB SCHIFF AND THE BOLSHEVIK REVOLUTION

There is a preponderance of circumstantial evidence purporting Schiff's involvement in the fall of the Romanov Czars. A telegram from Jacob Schiff expressing support was publicly read on 23 March 1917 at a Bolshevik rally in Carnegie Hall in New York, and reprinted the next morning by *The New York Times*. Schiff later dismissed allegations as sensational press, but his grandson John thirty years later on 3 February 1949 in the *New York Journal American* conceded $20 million in funds went to the Bolshevik revolutionaries.

Sutton wrote, "There will appear influential persons at all levels of society, even very high ones, who will help the Stalinist formal Communism when it becomes, if not real, then at least objective Communism. Communism in Moscow, Capitalism in New York." Thesis and anti-thesis is the classic Hegelian Marxist dialectic method." Cheka-GPU interrogators often gave prisoners copies of Marx, Engles and Hegel for revolutionary re-education. Moscow is subjective Communism, but (objective State) Capitalism. New York: Capitalism subjective, but Communism objective. A personal synthesis, truth: the Financial International, the Capitalist-Communist one – 'They.' Schiff, the New York banker was listed with these words of praise: 'Mr. Schiff financed the enemies (Bolshevik) of autocratic Russia. It is not incredible that Schiff and his friends donated $20 million to Leon Trotsky and 'a band of 243 cut-throat Jews from New York's Lower East Side'." In 1928 in the Yaroslavl Central Prison, the Communist Nadezhda Surovtseva, as with other "long-termers" received harsh treatment. "However, the Secret Political Department of the GPU permitted her to have complete sets of Marx and Engles, Lenin and Hegel in her cell." (A. C. Sutton; E. Mullins, *Secrets of the Federal Reserve*; A. I. Solzhenitsyn, *The Gulag Archipelago*, 477)

Again from Sutton's findings we learn "A copy of *To Moscow* published in Rostov and dated September 23rd, 1919 told of the part allegedly played by Jacob Schiff in the 1917 revolution. Evidently, if not a forgery, – the French were experts at diplomatic intrigue, a document was given to the Americans in Washington originating from the French High Commissioner there. It read, 'In February 1916, it was learnt that a revolution was being fomented in Russia and that the following persons and business concerns were engaged in this destructive enterprise: 1) Jacob Schiff; 2) Kuhn, Loeb & Company (directors): Jacob Schiff, Felix Warburg, Otto Kahn, Mortimer Schiff, Jerome H. Hanauer*; 3) Guggenheim.'" And it was then in March 1917, Jacob Schiff publicly sent his telegram to the rally of Bolsheviks celebrating the collapse of the Russian Romanov autocracy declaring that it largely thanks to his financial support that the revolution in Russia is advancing.

Only after abdication by the Czar in spring 1917, in fact, does US President Wilson officially declare America in the war. Subsequently the Morgan men prepared a secret government's spy mission sent that summer to Petrograd, first the Root mission, then Davison's Amercan Red Cross spies and *agents provacateurs* arrived on the scene and went to work.

Following the Bolshevik takeover of the Constitutional Assembly *Washington Post* reported February 2, 1918 that Morgan interests also supported the Communist revolutionary cause in Russia with at least $1 million from the private account of Republican mining industrialist William Boyce Thompson of the New York Fed (1914-19). When he died in 1930 Thompson's mining empire ranks the world's third largest behind DeBeers (Rothschild) and Oppenheimer. 1930 was a bad year for the Guggenheim mining fortune; J. P. Morgan asked them to contribute a quarter of billion dollars into a pool fund to help Wall Street bounce back but it drops further and their holdings suffer heavy paper losses; their world nitrate monopoly also is threatened when in the previous year a German chemist makes a breakthrough to cheaply produce synthetic nitrate. And in 1930 Daniel Guggenheim dies, only 74. During the First World War Herbert Hoover's top assistant in the US Food Administration with its close link to the Schroeder banking operations is managed by Lewis Lichtenstein Strauss soon after a Kuhn Loeb partner; Lewis L. Strauss marries Alice Hanauer, daughter of Kuhn Loeb partner Jerome Hanauer who started at Khun, Loeb & Co. as an office boy in 1891 at sixteen rising to partner twenty years later. (Gary Allen, *None Dare Call It Conspiracy,* 1972; S. Pak, 278-9)

Why would capitalists financially back radical communists? Antony Sutton explained schematically how the Consortium operators made simple work and a lot of money using Marxist-Hegelian logic to do just that. Not many Americans have the patience to read *Das Kapital* by Karl Marx. After nearly a century of socialist rhetoric contemporary Russians and Ukrainians have for the most part evolved as excellent dialecticians in both theory and practice. If you're good at dialectics, argument with them can drive you insanely mad with frustration or fill you with stitches of laughter from absurd reasoning to comic relief. Reader, be brave and practice some dialectics! The top cadre of Bolsheviks, mostly intelligent Jews, were experts at arcane and often exasperating dialectical argument. They easily outwit, frustrate and wear down exasperated western bankers during loans and credits negotiations. Ambassador Bullitt repeatedly breaks down sickened and exhausted over endlessly futile meetings with Litvinov talking "Bolsheviki" getting no closer to a resolution of the Soviet debt owed National City.

If as incontrovertible evidence indicates that Schiff was foremost instrumental in bringing Stalin and the Bolsheviks to power, it is then most interesting to know his connections to the big power money of the Consortium. Jacob Schiff (1847-20) is considered to have been the Rothschild's agent to gain control of US railroads.

Schiff was born in the Rothschild House in Frankfurt, Germany, and then emigrated to the United States where he marries the daughter of Solomon Loeb, founder of Kuhn, Loeb. Subsequently Schiff became senior partner with extensive business with Morgan. In *Secrets of the Federal Reserve,* Eustace Mullins observes, "Congressional testimony showed that in the firm of Kuhn Loeb Company, Felix Warburg was supporting Taft, Paul Warburg and Jacob

Schiff were supporting Wilson, and Otto Kahn was supporting Roosevelt. The result was that a Democratic Congress and a Democratic President were elected in 1912 to get the central bank legislation passed." How ever it goes down, the Rothschild-Morgan gang gets their man in the White House. These people are all well known to Rockefeller's press agent Ivy Lee who begins as publicity man for the Democratic Party. (E. Mullins, *Secrets of the Federal Reserve,* Chapter 3, 1952)

JEWISH CONSORTIUM LINKS

Jewish financial links tie in very tightly within the American industrial corporate and political culture of the Consortium of the Morgan-Rockefeller-Harriman links. Jacob Schiff and his Kuhn, Loeb, for example, partners handled investments building the great Harriman's railroad fortune. Harriman's widow held 5000 shares in National Bank of Commerce, stockholder in the New York Fed bank at the time in 1910 of the Pujo Senate hearings on the Money Trust in America when Senator Robert L. Owen publicly identified Kuhn Loeb as the representative of the Rothschild bankers in the United States. The American masses were due for another history lesson. In 1912, Schiff was exposed by *Truth* magazine writer George Conroy as "the financial minister" to Rockefeller's Standard Oil and the dominant financial power behind American railroad expansion. "Mr. Schiff is head of the great private banking house of Kuhn, Loeb & Co., which represents the Rothschild interests on this side of the Atlantic. He has been described as a financial strategist and has been for years the financial minister of the great impersonal power known as Standard Oil. He was hand-in-glove with the Harrimans, the Goulds and the Rockefellers in all their railroad enterprises and has become the dominant power in the railroad and financial world of America." (George R. Conroy, *Truth,* Dec.16, 1912 and cited by E. Mullins, *The History Project;* S. J. Pak, *Gentlemen Bankers*)

Although he failed to overcome Brahmin opposition and get Louis Brandeis on his cabinet, President Wilson succeeds in appointing him, the first Jew ever to sit on the US Supreme Court. (Schiff is among those who oppose Brandeis as not one of them, in particular for opposing their railroad cartel.) Brandeis also happens to be a Kuhn Loeb lawyer. That's not all. Mullins relates how *The New York Times* "has been practically acquired by Kuhn, Loeb and Schiff" as revealed in a letter from British Ambassador in Washington during the war years Cecil Spring-Rice to Sir Valentine Chirol written on November 13, 1914 after the stalemate early in the First World War when the credit is sorely needed to prolong the conflict. Sir Spring-Rice described Warburg as Rothschild's agent behind the Kaiser. "'He practically controls the financial policy of the Administration … it was exactly like negotiating with Germany'." As they saw it the Rothschilds were happy to hedge their investment and take their percentage of profit from the empire builders and politicians financing their armament schemes to blow up the world and killing millions of people, remap borders and seize resources. Let them find crazy ruthless and sadistic dictators and other mad men to do the dirty tricks and fuel the passions of the empire builders and arms manufacturers making wars destroying the world just as long as the finance men and their institutions increase their capital ensuring their capability to finance the next war. (*Letters and Friendships of Sir Cecil Spring-Rice*, Houghton Mifflin, 219-20)

In the fall 2009 a *Bloomberg* business news story announces that the Rothschilds are launching a half-billion euro hedge fund ($711 million) through their family banks in London and Paris. The ghost of Mayer Amshel returns, dynasty founder who "started out buying and selling old coins in a Frankfurt Jewish ghetto in the late 1700s". *Bloomberg* informs us that "In the early 1800s, he sent his five sons to establish bases in London, Paris, Naples and Vienna, in addition to Frankfurt." The man running the show is David de Rothschild who persuades the newly elected socialist French President Francois Mitterand to return the bank his socialist government nationalized in the eighties ... A younger Rothschild leaves Bank of America to join the family business when they aren't watching their racehorses, racing yachts, and sampling grapes.

FOR OVER TWO CENTURIES THE ROTHSCHILDS FINANCE THE WORLD

For over two centuries the Rothschild family has played the crucial role in international finance. Frederick Morton writes in his amusing anecdotal book titled simply *The Rothschilds* (1961) nominated for a National Book Award: "For the last one hundred and fifty years the history of the House of Rothschild has been to an amazing extent the backstage history of Western Europe." They reaped huge profits because of their success in making loans to countries, not individuals. (Frederick Morton, *The Rothschilds,* NY: Atheneum, 1961)

In reference to William Guy Carr's *Pawns in the Game* (1958), Eustace Mullins recalls that since the family Rothschild patriarch ("Red Shield") embarked on a world banking empire that financed the story of the ages of the rise and fall of nations and kings. In *The World Order (*1985), Mullins observed, "As he prospered, Mayer Amschel placed a large red shield over his door of the house in the Judengasse, which he shared with the Schiff family. He took the name 'Rothschild' from his sign." His real name was Mayer Amschel Bauer and he assembled 12 wealthy men in his goldsmith shop in Frankfurt in 1773 and revealed his plan of twenty five points how to finance and control by force of the power of capital world revolution "to win ultimate control of the wealth, natural resources, and manpower of the entire world." They would emerge as masters of the wealth of aristocrats and kings, direct their wars and control their debt and fate. Point 14 reads "Panic and financial depressions would ultimately result in World Government, a new order of one world government." (E. Mullins in *Secrets of the Federal Reserve,* citing Ignatius Balla, *The Romance of the Rothschilds,* Everleigh Nash, London, 1913; William Guy Carr, *Pawns in the Gam*e, 1958; E. Mullins and Ezra Pound, *The World Order*)

Here is Mullins from *The World Order* (1985): "In 1812, when he died, he left one *billion* franks to his five sons. The eldest, Anselm, was placed in charge of the

Frankfort bank. He had no children, and the bank was later closed. The second son, Salomon, was sent to Vienna, where he soon took over the banking monopoly formerly shared among five Jewish families, Arnstein, Eskeles, Geymüller, Stein and Sina. The third son, Nathan, founded the London branch, after he had profited in some Manchester dealings in textiles and dyestuffs which caused him to be widely feared and hated. Karl, the fourth son, went to Naples, where he became head of the occult group, the Alta Vendita. The youngest son, James, founded the French branch of the House of Rothschild in Paris. Thus strategically located, the five sons began their lucrative operations in government finance. Today, their holdings are concentrated in the Five Arrows Fund of Curacao, and the Five Arrows Corp. Toronto, Canada. The name is taken from the Rothschild sign of an eagle with five arrows clutched in its talons, signifying the five sons. The first precept of success in making government loans lies in "creating a demand", that is, by taking part in the creation of financial panics, depressions, famines, wars and revolutions.

The overwhelming success of the Rothschilds lay in their willingness to do what had to be done. "For the last one hundred and fifty years," Frederick Morton explains, "the history of the House of Rothschild has been to an amazing degree the backstage history of Western Europe .... Because of their success in making loans not to individuals but to nations, they reaped huge profits .... Someone once said that the wealth of Rothschild consists of the bankruptcy of nations."

The Rothschilds did enormously well amassing fantastic wealth shorting nations forced into bankruptcy. E.C. Knuth writes, in *The Empire of the City*, (1948): "The fact that the House of Rothschild made its money in the great crashes of history and the great wars of history, the very periods when others lost their money, is beyond question." (E, Mullins, *The World Order* citing E.C. Knuth, *Empire of the City: A Basic History of International Power Politics,* 1948)

"Rothschild's war profits from the Napoleonic Wars," Richard Lewinsohn elucidates in *The Profits of War* (1937), "financed their later stock speculations. Under Metternich, Austria after long hesitation, finally agreed to accept financial direction from the House of Rothschild."

Mullins notes that "*The New York Times*, April 1, 1915 reported that in 1914, Baron Nathan Mayer de Rothschild went to court to suppress Ignatius Balla's book on the grounds that the Waterloo story about his grandfather was untrue and libelous. The court ruled that the story was true, dismissed Rothschild's suit, and ordered him to pay all costs. *The New York Times* noted in this story that 'The total Rothschild wealth has been estimated at $2 billion.' A previous story in *The New York Times* on May 27, 1905 noted that Baron Alphonse de Rothschild, head of the French house of Rothschild, possessed $60 million in American securities in his fortune, although the Rothschilds reputedly were not active in the American field. This explains why their agent, JP Morgan, had only $19 million in securities in his estate when he died in 1913, and securities handled by Morgan were actually owned by his employer, Rothschild.' After Waterloo and other successful speculations, Baron Nathan Mayer) Rothschild exclaimed, "I care not what puppet is placed upon the throne of England to rule the Empire on which the sun never sets. The man that controls Britain's money supply controls the British Empire, and I control the British money supply." (E. Mullins, *The Secrets of the Federal Reserve,* Chapter 5, First Amendment Books)

Eustace Mullins compiled much of his findings in *The World Order* on the ever-expanding empire of Rothschild's global investments. Mullins wrote, "In the early 19th century, the Rothschilds began to consolidate their profits from government loans into various business ventures, which have done very well. Fortuitous trading on the London Stock Exchange after Waterloo gave Nathaniel Mayer Rothschild a sizeable portion of the 'consols' (bonds) which formed the bulk of the deposits of the Bank of England. Joseph Wechsberg notes in *The Merchant Bankers*: 'There is the Sun Alliance life insurance company, most aristocratic of all insurance companies, founded by Nathan Rothschild in 1824; Brinco, the British Newfoundland Corp., founded by the British and French Rothschilds in 1952; the Anglo-American Corp., Bowater, Rio Tinto and others.

"Not only does the bank rate of the Bank of England affect the interest rates in other nations; the price of gold also plays a crucial role in the monetary affairs of nations, even if they are no longer on the gold standard. The dominant role played by the House of Rothschild in the Bank of England is augmented by another peculiar duty of the firm, the daily 'fixing' of the world price of gold. The *News Chronicle* of December 12, 1938, describes this ritual: 'The story of the gold-fixing has often been told. How every weekday at 11 a.m. the representatives of five firms of bullion brokers and one firm of refiners meet at the office of Messrs. Rothschild (except on Saturday) and there fix the sterling price of gold. There is, however, a great deal of activity which lies behind his final act – this centralization of the demand for, and the supply of gold in one office and the fixing of the price of gold on that basis. A price of gold is first suggested, probably by the representative of Messrs. Rothschild, who also acts for the Bank of England and the Exchange Equalization Account.

"The banking houses privileged to meet with the Rothschilds to set the world price of gold are known as 'the Club of Five'. In 1958, they were: N. M. Rothschild, Samuel Montagu, Moccata and Goldsmid, Sharps Pixley, and Johnson Matthey. In 1961, the London Accepting Houses operating by approval of the Governor of the Bank of England were: Barings, Brown Shipley, Arbuthnot Latham, Wm. Brandt's & Sons, Erlangers, Antony Gibbs & Co., Guinness Mahon Hawkins, S. Japhet, Kleinwort & Sons, Lazard Bros, Samuel Montagu, Morgan Grenfell, N.M. Rothschild, M. Samuel, J. Henry Schroeder, S.G. Warburg. *These chosen firms rule the financial establishment in 'the City' of London.* (italics added)

"In 1961, the leading business groups in England were listed by Wm. M. Clarke as: Morgan Grenfell Ltd. (Lord Bicester) the Peabody JP Morgan firm, Jardine Matheson, Rothschild-Samuel-Oppenheimer (group), comprising Rio Tinto, British South Africa Co., Shell Petroleum, Brinco (British Newfoundland Corp.), Lazard Brothers, Shell, English Electric, Canadian Eagle Oil, Lloyd's Bank, Barclay's Bank, Peninsular & Orient Lines, Cunard, Midland Group – Eagle Star – Higginson (Cavendish-Bentinck), Prudential (Assurance Co.), Imperial Chemical Industries, Bowater, Courtauld's Unilever. Although this list shows the Rothschild group as only one of fourteen, in fact they hold large positions or influence in the other groups of this list.

FROM WATERLOO TO THE PRESENT: THE ROTHSCHILD HOLDINGS

"In 1982, the principal directorships held by the London Rothschilds were: Lord (Jacob) Rothschild – N.M. Rothschild & Sons, Arcan N.V. Curacao, chairman Rothschild's Continuation, and Rothschild Inc. USA., Edmund Leopold de Rothschild – N.M. Rothschild & Sons, Alfred Dunhill Ltd., Rothschild Continuation, Rothschild Trust, Rothman's International, chmn Tokyo Pacific Holdings N. V., Baron Eric Rothschild – N.M. Rothschild & Sons, Evelyn de Rothschild – chmn N.M. Rothschild & Sons, DeBeers Consolidated Mines Ltd. South Africa, Eagle Star Insurance Co., chmn The Economist Newspaper Ltd., IBM UK Ltd., La Banque Privee S.A., Manufacturers Hanover Ltd., Rothschild Continuation Ltd., chamn United Race Courses Ltd, Leopold de Rothschild – N.M. Rothschild & Sons, Alliance Assurance Co., Bank of England, The London Assurance, Rothschild Continuation Ltd., Rothschild Continuation Holdings AG Switzerland, Sun Alliance and London Assurance Co., Sun Insurance Office Ltd."

Much has changed since Mullins first published *The World Order: A Study in the Hegemony of Parasitism,* a decade before the Internet but the fundamentals have expanded over generations and centuries. Mullins wrote, "The British firms comprising the major basis of the Rothschild fortune are: Sun Alliance Assurance, Eagle Star, DeBeers, and Rio Tinto. Eagle Star's directors include: Duncan Mackinnon, of (S.G.) Hambro Investment Trust, Earl Cadogan, whose mother was a Hambro, Sir Robert Clark, chairman Hill Samuel Co., Marquess Linlithgow (Charles Hope) whose mother was a Milner – he married Judith Baring, Evelyn de Rothschild, Sir Ian Stewart of Brown Shipley Co., who has been parliamentary private Secretary to the Chancellor of the Exchequer since 1979. DeBeers directors include: Harry F. Oppenheimer, Sir Philip Oppenheimer, A. E. Oppenheimer, N. F. Oppenheimer, Baron Evelyn de Rothschild, Sidney Spiro. Spiro is also a director of Rio Tinto, Hambros Bank, Barclays Bank, and Canadian Imperial Bank of Commerce. DeBeers interlocks with Anglo-American Corp. of South Africa, of which Harry F. Oppenheimer is chairman, and Anglo-American Gold Investment Co. of which Julian O. Thompson is chairman, and Harry F. Oppenheimer director. DeBeers interlocks with Hambros Bank, whose chairman is Jocelyn Hambro; directors are R. N. Hambro, C. E. Hambro, Hon. H. W. Astor (Hambros Bank went through quite a dissolution in 1980s and 1990s sic); Sir Ian Morrow, chairman UKO Int. and The Laird Group, International Harvester, Rolls Royce, and the Brush Group; J. M. Clay, director of the Bank of England; Mark Weinberg, and Sidney Spiro. Sir Charles Jocelyn Hambro (1897-63) was quite a rising star in his day on a constant ascendance since Eton where he was captain of the cricket team, in 1914, and immediately went to the Royal Military Academy Sandhurst, Ensign in the Coldstream Guards and action on the Western Front awarded an MC for conspicuous bravery in action; he and his wife lived with Harry Morgan while training at Guaranty Trust, and working at the family bank J. C. Hambro & Sons; at 30, in 1928 Charles is elected a director of the Bank of England and from 1930 to 1932 works closely with Montague C. Norman in the bank's exchange control division, and declines to succeed him in 1937. During the war he joined the Special Operations Executive for sabotage and smuggling in Scandinavia, joined activities with Danish resistance and heavy water sabotage in Norway, but clashes with Donovan of OSS and resigned his post as head of SOE, in 1943.

"Rio Tinto's chairman is Sir Anthony Tuke; he is also chairman Barclay's Bank, and member (of the) Trilateral Commission. Directors are Lord Shackleton, Lord Privy Seal, chairman RTZ Dev. Corp.; Lord Charteris of Amisfield, grandson of Earl of Wemys, married to daughter of Viscount Margesson, private Secretary to Queen Elizabeth, director of Claridge's Hotel, and Connaught Hotel; Sir David Orr, chairman Unilever; and Sidney Spiro, Hambros Bank. (Ernest Shackleton was commander of the National Antarctic Expedition of 1909, on the disaster-ridden trans-Antarctic expedition. After the Armistice, Shackleton was off to Murmansk as Director of Equipment and Transport Mobile Forces in the north Russia campaign, and died aboard ship off South Georgia, commanding the British Oceanographical and Sub-Antarctic Expedition in 1922. His son Edward Shackelton (1911-94) was also an explorer, member of parliament and a life peer in the House of Lords."

All highly placed in Empire-building, all very influential. Mullins went on: "The principal Rothschild firm is Sun Alliance Assurance, which Nathan Mayer Rothschild founded in 1824, with Sir Alex Baring, Samuel Gurney, and Sir Moses Montefiore, with an initial capital of five million pounds. The chairman of Sun Alliance is Lord Aldington (Toby Low) who is also chairman Westland Aircraft, director of Citibank, Citicorp, and GE Ltd; Lord Aberconway, de Chairman; H.V.A. Lambert, chairman Barclay's Bank; Earl of Crawford Robert A. Lindsay; Ronald Charles Lindsay, son of the 26th Earl of Crawford (1877-45, PC, CVO, GCB, KCMG, ambassador to Turkey 1925, Germany 1926, the USA 1930-39), whose mother was a Cavendish – he is also chairman National Westminister Bank, former private Secretary to the Secretary of Treasury. Minister of State for Defense, Minister of State for Foreign and Commercial Affairs; Lord Astor, whose mother was the daughter of Earl of Minto – he is the former chairman of *The* (*London*) *Times*; Sir Charles Ball, of Kleinwort Benson, also director of Chubb & Sons., Barclay's Bank, Cadbury Schweppes; Sir Alan Dalton, director Natl. Westminster Bank; Duke of Devonshire – his mother was a Cecil, one of England's three ruling families since the Middle Ages; Sir Derek Holden-Brown, chairman Allied Breweries, director Hiram Walker; J.N.C. James, trustee Grosvenor Estates, which owns large sections of London; Henry Keswick, chairman Matheson & Co.; Lord Kindersley, exec. director of Lazard Bros., director of Marconi, English Electric, British Match, Swedish Match; Sir Peter Matthews, chairman Vickers;J. M. Ricchie, chairman British Enkalon, director of Vickers, Bowater Ltd.; Evelyn de Rothschild, chairman N. M. Rothschild & Sons".

"The Rothschilds have had a large position in Vickers for many years. Chairman is Sir Peter Matthews (1922-06 sic), also director Lloyd's Bank and Sun Alliance. Directors are T. Neville; Baron Braybrooke; Earl of Warwick (the Salisburys, one of three ruling families in England); Sir Alastair Frame, chief exec. Rio Tinto Zinc, director of Plessey & Co. UK, and the Atomic Energy Authority. The chairman of Vickers in 1956 was Edward Knollys, son of the Private Secretary to King Edward VII forty years, and George V for 5 years." (E. Mullins, *The World Order: A Study in the Hegemony of Parasitism;* also referred to on the web as *The History Project*)

Author Mathew Josephson in *The Robber Barons* (1934) observes that the British Imperial Viceroy to India Lord Mountbatten, uncle to Prince Charles, is related through the Cassels to the Meyer Rothschilds of Frankfurt. Reader, now what does that tell you? In fact, Mountbatten marries "the richest woman in England", the granddaughter and sole heir to the banking fortune of Sir Ernest Joseph Cassels (1852-21). Cassels' daughter Amalia Mary Maud Cassel marries Wilfred Ashley, later 1st Baron Mount Temple, himself a grandson of the 7th Earl of Shaftesbury.

The English royal House of Windsor has a direct and very significant family relationship to the Rothschilds. With the constant deluge of baby photos of the never-ending courtships and marriages and lifestyle media blurps about the British royals, we lose focus of the real story. For example, Ashley's friend the Crown Prince Albert Edward attended the marriage eighteen days prior to his Coronation in January 1901; when Queen Victoria's son, Edward, becomes King Edward VII, he neatly re-establishes the Rothschild ties. Lord and Lady Mountbatten have two daughters: Lady Patricia Mountbatten, Countess Mountbatten of Burma (b.1924), sometime Lady-in-Waiting to the Queen, and Lady Pamela Carmen Louise (Hicks), (b.1929), who accompanies them to India in 1947 and sometime is also Lady-in-Waiting to the Queen. And through their father Wilfred Ashley they are also first cousins to Prince Philip, Duke of Edinburgh, born in 1921 is currently the oldest living great-great grandchild of Queen Victoria, as well as her oldest living descendant over whom so much fuss was made in the great empire-building days.

Digest Quigley, reader, about American establishment power. Fit the pieces neatly together and you begin to get the bigger picture of how things actually work in America and the realm of power. Don't expect to read about that in the American press or while your brainwaves are warped listening to NPR (National Propaganda Radio) which aims most of the time aims to pacify, console and confuse Americans with fantasy and entertainment and a steady dose of either Jewish or pro-Israel plugs. (Frederick Morton, *The Rothschilds*, NY: Fawcett,1961, 36; E. Mullins, *Secrets of the Federal Reserve*; Richard Lewinsohn, *The Profits of War,* E. Dutton, 1937; E.C. Knuth, *Empire of the City: A Basic History of International Power Politics*, 1948; Henry Clews, *Twenty-eight Years in Wall Street,* J. S. Ogilvie Publishing, 1901; Ignatius Balla, *The Romance of the Rothschilds*, London: Everleigh Nash, 1913; Mathew Josephson, *The Robber*

Barons, Harcourt Brace, 1934, 1995; Dr. J. Landowsky, *Red Symphony*, London: Plain Speaker. Landowsky is a doctor at the Purge trials 1937)

"AVE" HARRIMAN: FROM ROOSEVELT TO KENNEDY, THE DON AT STATE

Before the war Kuhn Loeb had shares along with the Kaiser in Germany's prestigious Hamburg-Amerika shipping line, and negotiated a flag transfer with Paul Warburg, recently sent from Hamburg who arrives in the US as a naturalized citizen to handle Germany's war business deals with Washington. In the grab for spoils after the war the Harriman-Walker firm takes over Hamburg-Amerika, a most convenient acquisition as that firm's first crucial global thrust to dominate German shipping and having been seized by the US government in an arrangement never disclosed publicly. The Hamburg-Amerika's commercial steamships which before the war had been the pride of the world shipping industry overnight become Harriman property.

Harriman, Vanderbilt, Phillips. These were a few of the key WASP capitalists of the young generation joining the ranks of the Consortium's elite rich and famous. Railroad baron Harriman would become America's most privileged contact to the devious wolf Commissar Stalin. He now controls the world's largest private shipping line. Fabulously rich, young, and handsome, just ten years out of Yale, in 1923 Harriman became co-owner of the Hamburg-Amerika Line with the Russians. Eventually, the Hamburg-Amerika Line would regain its vessels but at a steep price. Harriman reserved "the right to participate in 50 percent of all business" from Hamburg. For the next twenty years US Naval documents gave evidence that the Harriman firm had "complete control of all activities of the Hamburg line in the United States". The Hamburg-Amerika takeover created an effective means for shipping essential goods to Nazi Germany as well as effecting strategic economic influence over its economic development. In the deal, the Hamburg-Amerika line invested 50 percent of the capital and in return took 50 percent of the profits.

In bringing the Holodomor story up to date with Consortium control of government and the national agenda, reader we need to look closer at the Harriman-Bush Nazi business connection. In 1913 Prescott Bush enters Yale University in New Haven, Connecticut. A native of Columbus, Ohio, Prescott has spent the five years at St. George's Episcopal prep school on Newport's bucolic coast surrounded by huge estates and yachts of the Gilded Age. Prescott Bush's first college year was also the freshman year with E. Roland ("Bunny") Harriman. Older brother William Averell Harriman had graduated earlier that year. In the spring of 1916, Bush and Bunny were both initiates tapped in Skull & Bones. (Webster G. Tarpley & Anton Chaitkin, *George Bush: The Unauthorized Biography*)

Meanwhile, the two Skull & Bones patriarchs Averell Harriman (Yale 1913) and Percy Avery Rockefeller (Yale 1900), son of William Rockefeller, paid special attention to Prescott Bush's Class of 1917. The Harrimans were the unequivocal stars of this new Anglo-American elite. Averell's father, stock broker E.H. Harriman, gains control of the Union Pacific Railroad in 1898 with credit arranged by William Rockefeller, Percy's father, and by Kuhn Loeb & Co.'s British-affiliated bankers, Otto Kahn, Jacob Schiff and Felix Warburg. Rothschild controlled funds continue to flow in and out of the economic system in America, in particular through their Rockefeller and Morgan business and family connections. William Rockefeller, treasurer of Standard Oil and brother of Standard founder John D. Rockefeller, owns National City Bank (later Citibank) together with Texas-based James Stillman. In return for their backing, E.H. Harriman deposits vast receipts from his railroad lines in City. When he issued tens of millions of dollars of watered" (fraudulent) railroad stock, Harriman uses the firm Kuhn Loeb to sell most of his shares. Interesting to see a *New York Times* reporting E.H. Harriman "master of the greatest railword power" in the world, February 26, 1907 and in glaringly bold headlines, "HARRIMAN ON HIS FINANCING Admits $24,000,000 Profits from the Chicago and Alton Reorganization". By 1902 the Rockefeller fortune surpassed $200,000,000 ($3.2 billion in 1992 dollars) and is multiplying rapidly, with personal expenses less than a half-million on $58 million earned for that year. (Webster G. Tarpley & Anton Chaitkin, *George Bush: The Unauthorized Biography;* Bernice Kert, *Abby Aldrich Rockefeller*, NY: Random House, 1993, 99)

The First World War was a great boost for Prescott Bush's father, Samuel Bush (1863-1948). He entered into the bottom tier of the Eastern Establishment. But he was in, and as war loomed in 1914, National City Bank began reorganizing the US arms industry. When Percy A. Rockefeller (1878–34) took direct control of the Remington Arms company, he appoints his own man, Sam Pryor chief executive. The U.S entered World War I in 1917. In the spring of 1918 Sam Bush became head of the Ordnance, Small Arms and Ammunition Section of the War Industries Board responsible for government contracts with Remington and other weapons companies. An unusual appointment, indeed, but these were unusual times and the Consortium had to get their men in place in the expanding war bureaucracy. Prescott's father apparently had no previous background in munitions. In fact, Sam Bush had been president of the Buckeye Steel Castings Co. in Columbus, Ohio, makers of railcar parts! His whole career was railroads– supplying equipment to the Wall Street owners. Samuel Prescott Bush later became a close friend and adviser to President Hoover. His son Prescott Sheldon Bush (1895-1972) was born Columbus, Ohio. He marries Dorothy Walker, daughter of the successful St. Louis stockbroker who was born in Kennebunkport, Maine, the family compound of the future Bush enclave actually called Walker's Point of York Country. In 1992, while her son governed the country from the White House she dies at the Bush home in Greenwich, Connecticut. She had lived long enough to know of the collapse of the Soviet Union the previous year.

Back to Baruch. As chairman Bernard Baruch ran Wilson's War Industries Board in the conflict that finished the Russian Romanovs. Always a keen Wall Street speculator with close personal and business ties to the railroad men including E. H. Harriman, Baruch's investment firm had dealt with all sorts of Harriman stock deals. The Harriman fortune, in fact, is widely divested in mining, railroads, shipping and banking. As director of the Facilities Division of the War Industries Board Bush reported directly to Baruch, and to Clarence Douglas Dillon (1882-79) who Baruch hires as his assistant. Dillon is another successful and rich Wall Street investment banker. A Texan like Col. House and National City's James A. Stillman, Dillon was born in San Antonio, the son of Samuel Dillon and Bertha Lapowitz. (His paternal grandfather Samuel Lapowski was a poor Jewish immigrant from Poland, and settled in Texas after the Civil War. Clarence changes the family name to Dillon with a nice short and waspy sound to it.) Young Dillon becomes good Harvard stock, Class of 1905, known to be cold and aloof, seldom speaks, is a genius at poker with excellent timing. His friends call him "baron". He'll amass a fortune on Wall Street to become one of the country's richest men listed by *Fortune* in 1961 of somewhere between $100-$200 million. Four years out of Harvard his wife gives birth to a son, in Geneva, Switzerland, who one day a generation after Mellon will become Kennedy's Treasury Secretary in 1961, and resigns in 1965.

Through his Harvard friend Bill Phillips now comfortably married to an Astor and installed high up at State, Dillon is introduced in 1912 to William A. Read, founder of the Wall Street bond traders William A. Read and Co.. Dillon joins Read's Chicago office the next year; two years later he's in New York and does so well that when Read dies C. Douglas Dillon takes control with a majority interest. He joins Baruch war business in Washington; the grandson of a penniless Jewish immigrant from Poland earns his reputation as the "Czar of American Industry".

After the war, in 1920, the William A. Read firm's name was changed to Dillon, Read. In 1925 he buys Dodge Motors for $146 million in cash; three years later Dillon pulls off the Chrysler buyout of Dodge for $236 million; by 1929 he has his name on Harvard's real estate having restored Field House when it burned down. By 1930 he pulls away from the market to retire. In 1935 Dillon bought the Chateau Haut-Brion vineyard in the French Bordeaux region for $250,000 and today his granddaughter Joan Douglas Dillon, Princess of Luxembourg (widow of Prince Charles of Luxembourg) is honorary president; when she became the Duchess of Mouchy having married the duke Philippe de Noailles, Joan lost the rank of HRH and Luxembourg titles ceasing to be a member of *that* royal family due to her third marriage.

C. Douglas Dillon, who as a brilliant boy who read by the age of four, is educated in special schools (Pine Lodge School at Lakehurst, New Jersey, classmates with three Rockefellers - Nelson, Laurance, and John III, – then off to Groton, graduating and Harvard (1931). Afterward, he joins his father's firm and after distinguished service in the war with the Navy becomes the firm's chairman (1946), doubling the value of its investments in six years. During the Cold War fifties he takes another hiatus from Wall Street, backs Eisenhower's campaign to the White House, is appointed Undersecretary of State for economic and agricultural affairs, and ambassador to France (1953-75) and in 1959, is promoted Assistant secretary of State. During the Kennedy years, although a Republican

Dillon serves on his cabinet ExComm during the Cuban Missile Crisis. In New York's social scene the Dillons assume prominence as longtime trustee and chairman of the New York Metropolitan Museum (1970-77), and chairman of the Rockefeller Foundation (1972-75). Dillon had been president of the Harvard Board of Overseers, chairman of the Brookings Institution, and vice chairman of the CFR. In 1989 alongside George Kennan he is awarded the Medal of Freedom. Put it together, lord and master with his noble public servant. In bestowing the honor President George Bush lauds Dillon "for service to three presidents and for commitment to his fellow man. By fostering European economic and military unity, he furthered the cause of democracy. Through his leadership on economic issues, he helped make possible the material advance of a generation." That's quite an extraordinary history and acknowledgment by the President.

Meanwhile, the Soviet security organs remain fully operational repressing Ukrainians and Russians throughout the USSR. Kennedy School of Government Dean Graham T. Allison recalls Dillon had been "one of Harvard's most distinguished graduates of the 20th century"; *The Harvard Crimson* honors him "as one of a handful of top White House advisors deciding the fate of the world". Fortunately the "nukes" lost and the world is saved. Dillon was also a trade expert, and that includes the knowledge at the highest level of undisclosed business with the Kremlin. (*The NYT*, Jan. 12, 2003. *The Harvard Crimson*, June 5, 2003)

Clarence Dillon is director of American Foreign Securities Corporation, which he had set up in 1915 to finance the French Government's purchases of munitions in the United States.(In 1914 he began making a fortune with phenol and the Schlesingers of Milwaukee, an essential ingredient in explosives.) (Robert C. Perez and Edward F. Willett, *Clarence Dillon, A Wall Street Enigma*, 1995)

Dillon's right hand man at Dillon Read is James V. Forrestal (1892-1949), a Princetonian (1915) voted by his classmates "most likely to succeed". Wall Street's wonder boy sells bonds making partner in only seven years, and in 1926 becomes company vice president; by 1938 Forrestal replaces Dillon as president. During the war Forrestal accepts FDR's call to take over as Secretary of the Navy (upon the death of Frank Knox), and in 1947, Secretary of Defense. But suddenly his world falls apart and Forrestal dies under mysterious circumstances at a Federal hospital.

In his meteoric rise to power James Forrestal learned how to maneuver the Dillon Read banking business financing Adolph Hitler. "America's business dealings with the Nazis were hushed up by Forrestal's vice president who was in charge of postwar investigations into Nazi finances," write investigative journalist and lawyer John Luftus, and Mark Arronsn write in their book, *The Secret War Against the Jews, How Western Espionage Betrayed The Jewish People* (1994). "Forrestal was not himself a Nazi, nor even a Nazi supporter. He was an extremely strange mixture who supported President Roosevelt's New Deal banking reforms but was not himself a New Dealer...like several other Dulles allies, he was a corporate spy within the president's own ranks. While he didn't respect, let alone like, FDR, nevertheless, in mid-1940 he became one of the president's special administrative assistants." (John Luftus and Mark Arrons *The Secret War Against the Jews, How Western Espionage Betrayed The Jewish People,* St. Martin's Griffin, 1994, 156-61)

Forrestal helps set arrangements for Rockefeller oil to be shipped to the Nazis. But that's not all. "He even raised huge sums," Luftus and Arrons observe, "for the company (Caltex) and then joined the board of IG Farben-controlled General Aniline and Film Corporation, one of Allen Dulles key Nazi clients. While still Undersecretary of the Navy in 1941, and just before the United States joined the war, Forrestal gave immunity to Standard Oil of New Jersey ships supplying the Nazis with much-needed oil. He was also the banker for Caltex when it bought millions of dollars' worth of Saudi Arabian oil and the man who pulled the strings to procure King Ibn Saud's secret bribes from President Roosevelt. In fact, Forrestal's company, Dillon, Read, had helped finance Hitler in 1934. One of Forrestal's close business associates was an American Nazi collaborator named Alexander Kreuter, who obtained favorable treatment for Western financial interests from the Nazis. Kreuter later served as a Dulles contact in the secret peace negotiations with Germany."

After the war Forrestal is embroiled in the Israel-Arab conflict over oil and the future of Palestine with former Moscow hand Loy Henderson, then head of the Near and Middle Eastern Affairs desk and State Department Undersecretary Bob Lovett. Two years later Jim Forrestal is found found with a bed sheet tied around his neck after plunging to his death from his room in Bethesda Naval Hospital outside Washington where he was suffering from extreme psychosis and paranoia that Jews and Communists were out to get him. Few people knew that he had been linked to a secret government program to bring Ukrainian assassins of a group called *Nachtigall* (Nightingale) "who had worked for the Nazis exterminating Jews and Red Army supporters, to work clandestinely within the Soviet Union assassinating communists. Forrestal's private papers at Princeton's Mudd Library list a veritable *Who's Who* of Consortium players. (E. C. Mullins, *Secrets of the Federal Reserve,* Kasper and Horton, 1952; David Martin, *Who Killed James Forrestal*, 2004, on the web)

BERNIE BARUCH WAR TRADE: THE WAR INDUSTRIES BOARD (WIB)

Take a close look at the Baruch War Industries Board (WIB). Of particular importance to the functioning of the American government and the White House during the Holodomor years, and in particular, in view of "the dictatorial power exercised by Baruch during the war years", the WIB served as a training school for Consortium management in peace and war. Again Mullins put it clearly in focus when he writes that "From WIB and the American Commission to Negotiate the Peace came the Brookings Institution, which set national priorities for fifty years, NRA and the entire Roosevelt administration, and World War II.

The WIB is a wasp nest of Consortium men. Working with Baruch at the WIB is his asst. chairman, Clarence Dillion of Dillon, Read; Robert S. Brookings, chairman of the Price-Fixing Committee of War Industries Board, later founder of the Brookings Institution; Felix Frankfurter, chairman of the War Policies Labor Board and Harvard wiz; Herbert Hoover and T. F. Whitmarsh of the US Food Administration; H.B. Swope, journalist and publicity hack for Baruch; Harrison Williams; Albert Ritchie, later Govenor of Maryland; Gen. Goethals; and Rear Adm. F. F. Fletcher. General Goethals is replaced by Gen. Pierce, who is then replaced by Gen. Hugh Johnson, later Baruch's longtime right-hand man; Johnson stays on Baruch's payroll for two months after becoming chief of FDR's National Recovery Administration (NRA) during the New Deal. President Woodrow Wilson was known to have boasted of his close friend Baruch at the WIB, "Let the manufacturer see the club behind your door." Baruch tells investigators of the Graham Committee, "We fixed prices with the aid of potential Federal compulsion."

Mullins : "Left out in the Baruch-Wilson mutual esteem society was William Jennings Bryan, longtime head of the Democratic Party. Bryan not only opposed our entry into World War I – he dared to criticize the family which had organized the war, the Rothschilds. Because he dared to mention the Rothschilds, Bryan was promptly denounced as 'anti-Semitic'. He responded, 'Our opponents have sometimes tried to make it appear that we were attacking a race when we denounced the financial policy of the Rothschilds. But we are as much opposed to the financial policy of JP Morgan as we are to the financial policy of the Rothschilds.'" (E. Mullins, *The History Project)*

Along with Rockefeller, the Harriman railroad and mining interests are always high on the agenda in Russia, first under the Czar, then the Bols. We see it remains the top priority for Joseph Stalin at the inaugural reception with Bullitt to celebrate renewed good relations between Washington and Moscow.. In the confluence of Consortium power, the Harriman connection is also instrumental in the emergence of another American political dynasty of corporate America power wielded in the White House from the First World War an up to the last two decades. In the postwar grab for bits and pieces of the broken empires, in November 1919, Bert Walker of the Bush lineage organized the W. A. Harriman & Co. private bank. Walker became the bank's president and chief executive; Averell ("Ave") Harriman was chairman and controlling co-owner with his brother Edward Roland Noel ("Bunny") Harriman. Bunny's friend at Yale and Bones was Prescott Bush and the father of George Herbert Walker Bush; Prescott married Walker's daughter. Among the wedding guests are Henry Isham, and Isabelle Stillman Rockefeller, and Percy Avery Rockefeller,(Yale Bones 1900) and a key player, for he is the son of William Rockefeller, and a director and a founding financial backer.

Heyward Isham.(1926-2009) graduated Yale (1947), Columbia University Russian Institute, State Department 1950, assigned to Berlin embassy, chief consular section and political office US embassy, Moscow 1955-57, worked with Henry Kissinger on the failed US peace accord with North Vietnam signed in 1973. Called a "peace" with honor" it was neither; instead it was designed to give Nixon a political way out to ditch the unpopular war before North Vietnam would break the cease-fire two years later and take back South Vietnam abandoned by the Americans long after the French learned their lesson having warned the Americans to do the same and stay out. Instead America gets two Kennedy's assassinate and a war that only the military and Consortium weapons business interests were so hungry to get and sustain the Cold War ideology. A former ambassador to Haiti, Heyward Isham played his hand in negotiating the lost war, then gets a neat ambassador posting to Porte au Prince to hold hands with the Duvalier dictator in Haiti before taking retirement rewriting the memoirs of friend and former Soviet foreign affairs commissar Andrei A. Gromyko (1957-1985) and their tale of the Consortium's Cold War for Doubleday; one of Isham's two sons, – both Groton and Yale, – heads the Washington news bureau for CBS; his younger brother married Alla von Ausberg from Europe, daughter and heiress of her mother's fortune salvaged from the Claus von Bulow family court scandal splashed across national newspapers in the eighties. Alla walked away with $50 million. David Remnick recalled in *The Washington Post*, how Gromyko said of an earlier leadership shakeup, upon his retirement by Gorbachev, after 50 years of loyal service, "You know how it is around here. It's a bit like the Bermuda Triangle. Every now and then one of us disappears'." David Remnick, *The Washington Post*, July 4, 1989)

It is Percy Rockefeller who, in 1932, caused the Kreuger swindle in a huge public investment scandal with some $200 million in losses ending in Kreuger's reported suicide. A Pilgrims Society member, Percy A. Rockefeller had directorships in over 50 corporations, including Guaranty Trust. Immediately after attending Yale he marries Isabel Goodrich Stillman, daughter of First National City Bank president James Jewett Stillman. Other founding directors of W. A. Harriman & Co. include Guaranty Trust directors Eugene G. Grace, William C. Potter and Eugene W. Stetson; President Ave Harriman and his brother Bunny Harriman (S & B 1913 & 1917), Frederick B. Adams and Percy A. Rockefeller (both S & B 1900), Harold Stanley (S & B 1908) and Joseph R. Swan (S & B 1902); also Wilbur F. Holt, Secretary and Treasurer; Elton Hoyt 2d; Henry Lockhart Jr.; Samuel F. Pryor; R. H. M. Robinson; J. D. Sawyer, Vice President; Joseph E. Uihlein; and G.H. Walker, "President. W. J. Sturgis is Vice President", (*The NYT*, Dec. 29, 1920, 23; F. Lundberg, *America's 60 Families,* 1937, ed. 1947; A. C. Sutton, *Wall Street and the Bolshevik Revolution*)

FROM YALE TO NAZI BERLIN AND THE KREMLIN

Averell Harriman begins his association with the German steel baron Fritz Thyssen in 1925. Three years out of Yale Averell Harriman (Yale, Bones 1913) became a director of the Guaranty Trust until 1941 when he became ambassador to Moscow. During the Holodomor thirties, the Harrimans maintain financial interest in the Union Banking Corp. controlled by the Dutch Bank voor Handel en Scheepvaart N.V., a front for Hitler's financier, Fritz Thyssen. During the Second World War UBC's assets are seized by the US government under the Trading With The Enemy Act and Executive Order No. 9095.

Fritz Thyssen and various members of the Harriman & Co. and its successor, Brown Brothers Harriman are directors of Thyssen's Union Banking Corporation which held German Nazi accounts with Guaranty Trust, Chase National Bank, and National City Bank Furthermore, the Harriman-Walker firm gained a tight hold on its management, with the not-so-subtle backing of postwar occupation of Germany by American and British troops.

Another Walker associate is one of the notorious death merchants. Chairman of Remington Arms' excom Sam Pryor is helped by Harriman arrangements in W.A. Harriman & Co. and works closely with Walker on the board of Harriman's front organization, the American Ship and Commerce Company. Stay in the saddle reader. There is much more to this underworld of riches and intrigue buried under the ashes and dust for far too long! We will return to this little matter.. But lets first see how the Bush gang gets in bed with Adolph.

Inside the Yale Bones brotherhood investment clique of the Consortium in Nazi Germany we finds the Walker-Bush-Harriman connection in bed with Hitler and Walker's associate David Francis, the bumbling American ambassador in St, Petersburg, a political appointee by Col. House and Robert Lansing in Wilson's administration during the 1917 Bolshevik coup with lethal consequences for the Ukrainian independence and the peasants in the coming years of more famine and coercive Bolshevik grain procurements. One famine follows another with a decade of respite until the Holodomor comes sweeping down from Moscow in the early thirties strategically crucial to Stalin's takeover of the Marxist-Leninist regime and leading up to the war and aftermath when, in 1941, after the German invasion Harriman leaves London to join Stalin and White House envoy Harry Hopkins to manage FDR's Lend-Lease war supply scheme in order to bolster the Red Army defense of Moscow and buy time for American manufacturing and readiness before FDR goes to Congress to officially enter the war against Japan and Germany. ("Thyssen Has $3,000,000 Cash in New York Vaults", *New York Herald Tribune*, July 31, 1941)

In 1926, concerned over soaring rail and port costs, Harriman meets with Stalin and Trotsky relegated chairman of the Concessions Committee. For four hours the Soviets negotiate with "the American capitalist from Yale". Trotsky, the ubiquitous and cosmopolitan internationalist who for a while had lived in Greenwich Village of lower Manhattan, confides to Litvinov at the Foreign Ministry that he suspects more treachery from Stalin. "Its already being said that I'm on Averell Harriman's payroll"!

Its on this trip that Harriman toured museums in Leningrad able to see the *bezprizornye*, – starved orphans who had escaped civil war and the Bolshevik facade for foreign consumption.

Harriman took advantage of his status and asked for a private rail car. For four days on his passage to Tiflis he traveled in Czarist comfort under gilt scroll work and wood inlay. Harriman enjoys wine from the Grand Duke Nicholas' cellars – a 1906 Bordeaux and 1860s Rhine wine – and the best caviar ever to be found. "By the time we emerged from the cellar we knew no pain," Harriman remarks. Nothing is too good for this Consortium emissary!

But the trip soon sours. Harriman returns home with only slight reduction in Soviet royalties and obligations to finance port railway reconstruction. A full half-century later, he told students at Lehigh University, "I became convinced that the Bolshevik Revolution was in fact a reactionary revolution and that it was not 'the wave of the future'." However, on leaving the Soviet Union, he sent a letter to the Yale Class Yearbook of a decidedly different hue, insisting that change in the Soviet Union must "come as a development of ideas from within the Communist Party".

Harriman praises Stalin as a man with whom he could do business, who is "not a dictator in any sense of the word, as has been expressed, but he is a political boss in the sense of Charles Murphy of Tammany Hall." Where are the notes of the Trotsky-Harriman 1926 talks? They might prove most revealing since Trotsky had extensive experience as an agent of the international bankers... Researchers might start with Trotsky Papers Collection at Harvard's Houghton Library, neatly arranged near the John Reed Collection ...

The next year, at the December Party Congress, Stalin reveals his ambitious plans to increase national production by 15 percent. To succeed it requires more than an intensive propaganda campaign to inspire the masses, already hard-pressed and suffering food shortages.

"Trotsky was able," Sutton writes, "to generate support among international capitalists, who, incidentally, were also supporters of Mussolini and Hitler." This was true also of the famous personalities like Rockefeller's publicist Ivy Lee and senior partner at Morgan Thomas W. Lamont. Sutton's extensive research tracked Trotsky's link to "international banking" through Kiev, capital of the Ukraine. "On the other hand," Sutton added, "the only known direct link between Trotsky and international banking is through his cousin Abram Givatovzo, who was a private banker in Kiev before the Russian Revolution and in Stockholm after the revolution. While Givatovzo professed anti-bolshevism, he was in fact acting in behalf of the Soviets in 1918 in currency transactions."

On his 1926 trip, Harriman meets with the bankers in Milan before his interview in Rome with the fascist dictator in the Dulce's ornate Italian renaissance palace. The little gangster refuses to sell Harriman the palace and Harriman refused to sell Italian bonds unless Mussolini stops meddling with the lira. That year Lamont arranges a $100 million loan to Mussolini.

When he was Coolidge's Treasury Secretary Andrew Mellon who had much more money than Harriman admired the "strong man" Benito Mussolini in 1924 Mellon admires the economic stability of dictatorship introduced into "the Italian government and not by bargaining" ; two years later and already a self-confessed fan of the vain Italian fascist Mellon remarks "Mussolini is making a new nation out of Italy. He is one of the world's most vigorous personalities. Many of his measures are unique indeed, but they are effective." (William Hoffman, *Mellon, Portrait of an Oil Baron*, Follett, 1974, 130; Charlies Savoie, *World Money Order III*)

Still, Consortium banks has problems with the State Department. When attempting unsecure financing, for example, in 1925 the Harriman & Co. sought to extend a $35 million credit to industrial firms in Germany for export to Russia. Harriman wanted a three hundred million mark credit to Russia for purchases of German-manufactured heavy and light equipment; he had already secured German government support from the central Reichsbank. At the State Department Leland Harrison opposes the deal stipulating that "the employment of American credit for the purpose of making an advance to the Soviet regime" violated American policy of no loans to Moscow. That didn't deter Chase National from pushing a syndicated loan deal to finance to sell Soviet railway bonds for the Soviet State Bank at 9 percent return to investors. That too was blocked by State Department. US ambassador in Berlin Jacob Gould Schurman told the German ambassador in Russa, Dr. H. von Dirksen, to wait until questions were resolved in the Young Plan before it could give a green light to financing a German loan to finance Soviet trade. (K. Siegel, *Loans and Legitimacy, Loans and Legitimacy*, 103)

Then there was the Industrial Credit Corporation set up under Soviet auspices in 1927 to facilitate deal-making with clients not wishing to go through Amtorg. Sherman boasted he used his own capital in a $3 million fund and had been unable to convince banks to buy its acceptance notes. The funds would be used to "assume the risk of postponed payments" thereby reassuring contract holders. More transparent credit arrangements were forthcoming. Siegel writes, "The trend toward greater accessibility in credit enabled the import-export trade to increase from 1923 to 1930 by more than 2300 percent, from $6 million to nearly $140 million. The great bulk of this was American exports, and most of this was American exports, and most of the increase took place after the Five-Year Plan had replaced the New Economic Policy in 1928." It was a tall order for heavy industry representing "a significant share of several sectors of the American economy, including drilling and refining equipment, agricultural implements, construction and mining machinery, and electrical and metalworking apparatus." (K. Siegel, *Loans and Legitimacy*, 104)

But during this early era of Bolshevism Harriman called for an end to US trade sanctions against Stalin in exchange for concessions. In 1926 Harriman and a German export group offered $42 million in long-term credits to the Soviet Union. Some people in the State Department wanted to know what was going on. Harriman met with Ambassador Jacob Gould Schurman and told him the deal was good for everybody allowing the Germans to export to the Russians and prevent Germany from dumping in the US. The deal collapsed. Before the war, Russia was known to have the greatest reserves of high-grade alloy minerals for steel. Harriman offered to rebuild an essential Russian port and restore steel production to prewar capacity for a cool $25 million. In the deal, the Soviets agreed to a $4 per ton payback on manganese. To settle Czarist claims after nationalization by the Bols confiscated the mines Harriman agreed to pay to pay its previous owners an additional dollar per ton. But that deal soured too when the market price of manganese plunged when new mining deposits were found in Africa. Meanwhile, the Soviets expanded production in the Donetz mining regions of western Ukraine. When Bullitt returned to Moscow manganese was high Bullitt's trade agenda.

In 1926 Prescott Bush, a future US Senator, leaves US Rubber to join fellow Yale Bonesmen in the Harriman investment bank. W. A. Harriman Company is owned by the two Harriman brothers, Averell ("Ave"), and Roland ("Bunny"), also both Yale and Bones. That same year, while "Ave" is in London playing polo with the Prince of Wales, Bush's future father-in-law, "Bertie" Walker buys Harriman a few race horses with stables thrown in for $225,000 (over $2 million), a gift price from the Belmonts. Walker is comfortably at peace living in an English country setting of Greenwich, Connecticut where he plays golf at the exclusive Round Hill Club with Bert, who also happens to be president of the USGA (US Golf Association), and commuting by motor yacht from his mansion on Stanwich Road to the fortress on Wall Street.

The Bush family is well on its way to over two decades of Bush Presidencies as they lay the stones along the path much of it backed with British, French and then the Russian, of the WWI era, and enhanced with Soviet gold. When he dies in 1972 at age 77, Sen. Prescott Bush enjoyed homes in Long Island, New York, and Greenwich, as well as the family compound in Maine and a 10,000 acre plantation in South Carolina. Oh, yes, let's not forget their island retreat off the coast of Florida. It is Harriman who first introduces Prescott Bush to William Paley, in 1932, before Paley became a major powerbroker and OSS man. And Paley puts Sen. Prescott Bush on his board at CBS (Columbia Broadcasting System), another Brown Brothers Harriman client. You see there is an insidious revolving ferris wheel verisimilitude involved in these paths of power. Ever since the notorious CIA days of the Kennedy assassination period right through the Iraq-Afghanistan fiasco boggles the American public mind may at times be too overwhelmed and conveniently distracted by post 9-11 trauma and the movie-celebrity propaganda culture to comprehend the full magnitude of an integrated network of connections and in particular the scope of the Bush family legacy. Historian William Manchester had an inside track on the Kennedys and the shock to Harriman when his friend the President is killed. He terminates lunch in the State Department dining room and over protests from aides including William H. Sullivan, he insists on conducting business as usual. "No", he replied, "the world must go on".... Even on the day of the assassination the spirit of JDR, Sr. stalks in the White House; first on Harriman's agenda is a meeting with a group from Standard Oil of New Jersey. The Rockefeller Foundation stocks are valued no less than $658 million with over $351 million held in Standard. When Jackie Kennedy is widowed and in a state of shock and trying to keep sane still living with her children in the White House she receives a call from Mrs. Averell Harriman offering the use of her home on N Street in Georgetown. (William Manchester, *The Death of a President,* NY: Harper & Row, 1967, 367,642; J. Abel, 340; Edward Klein, *Just Jackie*, NY: Ballentine Books, 1998)

By 1926, and with four years very profitable years in Berlin, W. A. Harriman and Co. trade and underwrite corporate foreign stocks and bonds. Knight Woolley, Yale 1917 Bones, godfather to the first Bush president, is general manager of the new Harriman Brothers bank located at 39 Broadway. Woolley had been Bullitt's friend back during the days of the Yale Dramat. In 1927 Bert Walker still manages his St. Louis firm buying stocks on margin. Woolley and Harriman prefer a cash only business or, as they say, "NOCD" – "Not Our Class, Dear".

In 1930, after the crash, Harriman tasks Prescott with examining all the Harriman company holdings. Brown Brothers does not escape by the crash unscathed and is forced to close both its Paris and Warsaw offices and trim their budge in Berlin. Poor Prescott is wiped out owing the firm a paper loss of in the hundreds of thousands of dollars. For these guys that's a small fortune when you don't have it. His pals appeal to the Harrimans with their cool $70 million of family inheritance ($777 million in 2004 terms). With the international economy in a slump and the European banking crisis rocking Nazified Germany, Harriman investments in Berlin plunge. That spring 1931 Germany's inflationary spiral render reichmarks worthless. The government issues a *Stillhalte*, freezing all foreign-exchange assets and putting a stop to debt payments to foreigners. BBH takes a $10 million hit.

Its just a bump in the road. Harriman personally covers their losses and bails out Bush and Woolley. This secret fraternity is bound together forever. But Bonesmen do that sort of thing. In addition, "The Tomb" keeps a handy slush fund for just these kinds of contingencies. After all, they mustn't be allowed to show vulnerability or weakness, or show a drop in standards even in such uncertain times. Harriman dips into his pocket and gives Bush and partners thirty-two thousand dollar salaries, the equivalent to $400,000 today. That should solidify their discretion and integrity for generations. It's only money anyway, right? The Harriman brothers survive the market crash handsomely and continue their lavish lifestyle.

Baruch got himself and his friends out early, telling Percy Rockefeller and other close friends to sell off and get out of the frenzy and buying on margin. On Wall Street as far back as 1896 when the Dow first opened up the secret world of insider trading Baruch has few peers in the market and never failed to attract the attention of the older set of Morgan, Whitney, Harriman and their generation of billionaires on the Street. But we're a generation later, in "Barney" Baruch's gay days with Roosevelt in Georgia savouring the healing waters of the Warms Springs resort which FDR buys hoping to cure his polio paralysis.

Additional reports of conversations between US diplomats and those who had traveled to the US tell of the alarming decimation of various sectors in the Ukraine and the North Caucasus. All of the reports are of a serious nature sent from American academics, businessmen, and engineers. Two letters, addressed in English, and sent in 1931 to the "Department at the City at Washington, the District of Columbia" arrive in Washington originally postmarked from Zhashkiv in the Cherkassy region five hours south of Kiev on the banks of the Dnieper River. Bob Kelley at State describes the first letter as "apparently written from Russia, with regard to alleged conditions in Russia." From the second letter Kelley again notes with a marked preference for evasive nuance the "alleged conditions… in the Ukraine".

The State Department under Presidents Hoover and Roosevelt keeps a very low profile about the famine. Their careers hang in the balance and depend on a modicum of precise discretion that determines their future in and out of the Foreign Service. If they did as they were advised they and their families will be assured a comfortable and prestigious life with all the perks of success. There's no lack of candidates applying to the Foreign Service. No one is indispensable here. To be sure they all have their orders at Foggy Bottom where secrets are no less persuasive then in Lubyanka although methods of career termination significantly differ from the caprice of a totalitarian Kremlin. So they do nothing in the way of leading to any action that might antagonize a higher authority or ameliorate the suffering of the Ukrainians and expose US investment and trade transfers sustaining Stalin's secret economy and ubiquitous police state. There are moles, double agents of the Fifth Column. The Soviet Union has is quickly evolving into a complex and colossal prison but this is kept secret from the public eye and suppressed by the western press owned by millionaires and corporations there to serve their shareholders. As millions of men, women and children are dying, and an entire culture lay waste from the rich lands of the Ukraine, Bullitt, Litvinov and other US and Soviet diplomats and financiers gladly shake hands in secret meetings to advance official diplomatic relations to be announced in October 1933.

Again Siegel's findings aptly provide a succinct description of the economic linkage between Stalin and the West labeled in contemporary rhetoric as "constructive engagement" with a military regime. She writes, "During the First Five-Year Plan, Soviet-American trade reached a peak, although the high sales were short-lived. From 1927 to 1930, spurred by the industrialization imperatives of the plan, US exports to Russia increased from $65 million to $114 million. In 1931 sales dropped to $104 million, but the Soviet government's orders still made it America's seventh largest customer. Soviet purchases of American manufactured goods in 1931 were 22 percent higher than those in 1929, a significant increase when compared to the more than 50 percent drop in overall American exports during this very depressed period. While $104 million amounted to only 14 percent of American GNP in 1931, it still represented 4.3 percent of American exports that year. *Russia had become the largest foreign customer of American industrial machinery*." (K. Siegel, *Loans and Legitimacy*, 133; italics added)

Siegel also notes the American Locomotive Sales "five-year financing arrangement with Moscow" followed by a five-year credit of an even greater amount by International General Electric". After a year of negotiating with the Soviets, and the State Department, GE proposes a $25 million credit for Soviet purchases of heavy electrical equipment. In the deal GE requests only a quarter payment up front and the balance paid in five years. GE's president Clark R Minor publicly declares the offer was good to GE shareholders since it required a "higher rate of interest charged" thereby resolving all outstanding nationalization claims of the company against Moscow ($1.75 million). But this runs counter to State Department policy insisting the Soviets honor claims before doing new business. *Tass* sees the deal as a victory for Moscow, writing "General Electric considers new business importanter (sic) than pre-Revolutionary claims." However State Department Undersecretary Castle found room to wiggle and calls it "merely a financial credit not involving Russian securities in the American market", and he concedes, "it was not a thing that we would disapprove formally."

The State Department steps aside to let the deal pass without a hitch. In fact, the corporate lawyers and their colleagues at State work together to facilitate the business. That year, 1928, Amtorg's Saul Bron declares, "About fifty first-class firms, each of which is a leader in its particular sphere, have offered considerably improved conditions for short-term credits." With long-term credits on the table, and enthusiastic for more Consortium funds pouring into the Soviet Plans, Bron rejoices, saying "all of this gives reason for a certain optimism in estimating the immediate prospect of development of the business relations between the USSR and the United States." Still right on course; in 1929, Amtorg reports that over 200 firms had signed contracts for one-year credit or more. (K. Siegel, *Loans and Legitimacy,* 103-4)

Meanwhile, the corporate men blue-bloods live a charmed social life with a calender full with elaborate parties and outings all in line with the good life deserving of Yale men. Bush and Woolley share a rail parlor car to New Haven for another reunion joined by fellow Harriman employees at Brown Brothers, their classmate and Bonesman James Sedgewick Ellery (1917), Robert Abercrombie Lovett, Jr. (Yale, Bones 1918) who had been a member of the Yale Aviation Unit with the Davison brothers and funded by their father Morgan banker's HPD during the First World War. Bob Lovett also at Brown Brothers has married the daughter of still another Brown partner. This Harriman set is one very tight "family". The Consortium insiders live like the princes they are, guarantees the best of everything in America and abroad. Having come of age in the First World War managed by their fathers and peers, and only a little more than ten years after Yale, they agree to link up the two Harriman firms with the Harrimans brothers tossing in another $10 million as partners. "Averell Harriman, his brother Roland Harriman, and members E. S. James and Knight Woolley, through the Union Bank (in which they held a major interest) are all "prime financial backers of Hitler". (See A. C. Sutton, *The Order*; E. Mullins)

The merger of W. A. Harriman & Company with Brown Brothers is no mince affair. The creation of Brown Brothers Harriman is carried by *The New York Times* in their story December 12, 1930. "This was an older financial house whose partners were also members of The Order," Sutton is one of the early writers to highlight the ominous presence of the strange and mysterious Skull & Bones secret society in the firm's far-ranging investments. He writes, "Alexander Brown was founded 1800 in New York and Philadelphia. By the 1970s the relatively unknown private international banking firm of Brown Brothers, Harriman, with assets of about one-half billion dollars, had taken in so many of 'the Brotherhood' that out of 26 individual partners, no fewer than 9 were members of The Order." Time-Life owner Henry Luce (Yale Bones 1920) assures that Harriman millions remain dazzling front page news to mesmerize readers still troubled by the failure of American banks. (Kitty Kelly, *The Family: The Real Story of the Bush Dynasty,* Doubleday, 2004, 39; A. C. Sutton, *The Order*)

That same year Stalin's favorite capitalist makes another merger consolidating his affair with the richest women in the world. Marie Norton Whitney had left her husband Cornelius Vanderbilt Whitney to marry the dashing Yalie, bringing their two young children along, Harry Payne Whitney and Nancy Marie Whitney. The market crash doesn't hamper the Harrimans' lifestyle which carries on with dramatic masquerade balls, lavish parties and countless social outings of High Society once the glittering domain of Lady Astor who at the turn of the century had reigned over New York's most prestigious 400 families. A few would survived the crash joined by the nouveau-riche of Wall Street commodity and industrial barons managed to preserve that prewar era here described by Walter Lord, author of *A Night to Remember* of the sinking of the *Titanic* in April 1912, and recalled in his book *The Good Years* (1960): "For this was the era of massive entertainment. Night after night the rich and fashionable vied with one another in achieving the spectacular. Two weeks after Mrs. Astor's ball, James Stillman installed an artificial waterfalls in his dining room for a dinner dance. On another occasion Rudolf Guggenheimer stocked the Waldorf's Myrtle Room with nightingales borrowed from the zoo. The Cornelius Vanderbilts imported the first act from the Broadway musical *The Wild Rose*, complete with cast and scenery, for an 'at-home' during one of Newport's famous tennis weeks. In the competitive whirl, some hosts simply turned to the bizarre. Cornelius K. G. Billings marked the completion of his $200,000 stable by giving a Horseback Dinner at Sherry's. Livery stable nags were brought by freight elevator to the grand ballroom. The honored guests mounted them and dined in the saddle from precariously balanced trays. The dinner was served by waiters disguised as grooms, while grooms (perhaps disguised as waiters) hovered in the rear to clean up any mess. At Newport, society was invited to a formal dinner to meet a new arrival, Prince del Drago of Corsica. The 'prince' turned out to be a monkey in full evening dress – the joint inspiration of Mrs. Stuyvesant Fish and her personal jester, Harry Lehr. The dinner went on, and as the money sipped his champagne, all agreed it was one of Mrs. Fish's cleverest ideas yet." (W. Lord, The Good Years, 1960, 104-19)

This fall, *Time* paints a primrose portrait of the hectic life of a millionaire's wife collecting a fortune of French modern art worth millions for their sundry estates of town houses, lavish apartments and secluded country homes on thousands of acres. Imagine the contrast of this garden setting of a Manhattan gallery opening with scenes of Stalinist terror police confiscating the tiny land plots given to peasants by the Bolsheviks after the First World War. Picture in contrast to the pomp and glamour the spot executions and arrests of villagers imprisoned and exiled to distant slave labor camps and huge industrial work projects managed by American and foreign engineer experts.

Their friend *Time*'s Henry Luce's told only one side of the story, writing, "In a welter of gardenias and orchids, amid the sheen of many emeralds, in an atmosphere fragrant with excellent things to drink, a new art gallery blossomed last week on Manhattan's artiest street, East 57th, with an opening exhibition that snapped one more spat-button of respectability on the artistic insurgents of 1918: Derain, Picasso, Van Gogh, Gauguin, Matisse. Grizzle-chinned Henri Matisse was present in person to confer a Parisian benediction. Owner and patron of the gallery was the beauteous Marie Norton Whitney Harriman, onetime daughter-in-law of Sculptress Gertrude Vanderbilt Whitney, present wife of Banker-Sportsman William Averell Harriman. The Marie Harriman Gallery will probably never feel that fear of financial disaster which hangs like a permanent black pall over most of its glittering neighbors." Poor Mrs. Harriman. How she fretted over her paintings and publicity. Time writes, "At the opening last week Mrs. Harriman gravely explained to reporters that she had been collecting French moderns for years, that her house had become so crowded that she must either stop buying pictures or rent more rooms to hang them. Hence the Marie Harriman Gallery. Art critics, dodging nervously among socialites, were impressed. Of the 29 canvases on view, not one was unimportant. Present were such frequently reproduced works as Picasso's mustachioed *Harlequin*, a good Tahiti Gauguin, Renoir's *Claude as a Clown in Red*, Cezanne's *Man with a Pipe*, eight irreproachable Derains." (*Time*, Oct. 13, 1930, W. A. Swanberg, *Whitney Father, Whitney Heiress: Two Generations of One of America's Richest Families*, NY: Scribners, 1980. Swanberg also the biographer of Pulitzer, Hearst and authored other books. In the Whitney book there are two rare photos of Bill Phillips, many photos of the Harrimans but oddly none of Averell Harriman. Also Swanberg writes a section on the Whitney-Morgan 1900 China investment scheme managed by Willard Straight for HPD.)

Future governor of New York and a Presidential contender, Averell Harriman is the main Wall Street investor of German Nazi Reich. But that won't become an issue when in August 1945 he stands tall with Stalin, and Generals Eisenhower and Zhukov of the Red Army atop Lenin's Tomb as victors while 10,000 Russian athletes parade in triumph. The friendship forged immediately between Eisenhower and Zhukov when they first met in Germany grew with each encounter and so unnerved Stalin that he banished the most decorated man in the history of the Soviet Union to the Black Sea where he sojourned until recalled by Khrushchev who appointed him Minister of Defense and rescues him from a coup plot only to be dispatched again into early retirement.

Solzhenitsyn's short story "Times of Crisis" traced the fall from grace and Khrushchev's jealousy of Zhukov's popularity and the general's chronic problem of the slippery dialectics of truth when truth like love or anything is just a concept: void of permanent meaning. "The problem was that the truth itself somehow steadily and irreversibly altered with the passage of time: the truth was one thing, under Khrushchev it was another; and there were many things that it was still premature to mention." There is some irony here; Zhukov was legendary without the legend and that's probably not a bad thing. Remember what she said, Marlene Dietrich, who soared into fame starring in Josepf von Sternberg's *Blonde Venus* (1932); when the Austrian film actor and director Maximilian Schell asks the actress what is the truth about her she answers, "The truth about me ... is that everything you read about me is untrue." (Michael Scammell, "The Master Returns – or Does He?", *New York Review of Books*, December 8, 2011, 57)

Among the long cast of characters of the Roosevelt reign in the White House and for nearly a half century of Cold-War politics, Averell Harriman is the quintessential personna of consummate elegance and discretion. The establishment calls that "integrity". He stands with and above all others in the Consortium. These guys make history and pay others to write it as they see it and want it to appear sanitized for the public eye by the nation's "free press". The same man who heads FDR's Lend-Lease wartime aid program to London and Moscow leads the whole Consortium bandwagon of American capitalists from the Rockefellers, DuPonts, Ford and every other major corporation that passed under the eyes of alerted friends in Washington and Berlin, and much to the astonishing bewilderment of US ambassador Dodd. Six days after Pearl Harbor, by order of FDR, Harriman Nazi's holdings are quietly but officially seized. (They are returned after the war.)

Bert Walker takes over operations at his bank, the UBC; Prescott Bush, a director, had one share of UBC. That bank was dissolved in 1951. (For all its name-dropping of Washington insiders, including the Bohlens, Nitzes, McNamaras and Bundys, to cite only a few, and particularly in view of the fact that her husband Phil Graham was an early member of the Lend-Lease operations even before America officially entered the war, Katherine Graham omits Harriman from her vivid autobiography, *Personal History.*

In return for an investment fee, the Harriman partners built up the business by doing for their friends and wives what they were doing for the Harrimans brothers in their private investment bank. They had no trouble finding clients. Bush became a director of many of them including Dresser Industries oil company and US Guaranty Insurance Co.

In 1931 Harriman became chairman of the Illinois Central Railroad Co.; in 1932, he's takes over the board at Union Pacific; in the year of the Holodomor 1933 Harriman teams up with his buddy Vincent Astor and together they acquire *Today* magazine to play with. Nothing inflammatory ever printed about the Holodomor there. In 1937 their *Newsweek* absorbs *Today*, yet another example how the Consortium super-rich controlled the American press and set the mind-think for the nation's culture and the limits of popular debate.

Through it all George Herbert "Bert" Walker stayed on as president of W. A. Harriman and Co. Walker despised Roosevelt especially after the passage of the Wheeler-Truman Act signed into law by FDR in 1940 that reorganized the railroads and placed them under the authority of the Interstate Commerce Commission. Truman had knocked Walker's firm for taking huge profits while bankrupting railroads. "We worship money instead of honor", Senator Truman declared in a speech citing the creed of Walker's law firm and Harriman's investment bankers which "load great transportation companies with debt in order to sell securities to savings banks and insurance companies so they can make a commission".

Bush downplays the importance of Harriman who is not involved in the day to day business. He later said "the fact that Averell was (there) didn't help us a damn bit at Brown Brothers Harriman. In fact, it was a little bit of a hurdle you had to take from time to time. Some big corporate client would say, 'What the hell is your partner doing down there with this red bunch of Communists and socialists? …

he was a good Ambassador to Russia ... He was at the very highest levels there with the Roosevelt administration."

After Hitler invades Poland and starts exterminating Jews, BBH tried to find cover behind a Swiss bank and conceal their business with the board of Nazi directors in their Silesian –American mining holdings since 1926. Three times FDR rejects their efforts to bypass the government ban on Nazi contracts. (K. Kelly, 57)

Walker's Union Banking Corporation (UBC) has been doing business with Germany since 1924 as a front for Fritz Thyssen, Germany's steel magnate. Thyssen holds an empire of coal mines and banks. Fritz knows Ave from earlier days and asks him to join a new New York bank. Instead, his brother "Bunny" Harriman and some of his partners join Thyssen's board, actually a subsidiary of his Dutch bank in Rotterdam but operated by BBH at 39 Broadway. UBC, the property of "Hitler's Angel" would be a dark cloud over the Bushes forever although at the time it is considered politically correct to carry on business with the Aryan-crazed Nazi fascists by Consortium standards. "No questions were raised about the ethics of continuing to accept fees from the man whose memoir was titled *I Paid Hitler*." writes author Kitty Kelly. (K. Kelly, 60)

But they did much more than merely take in fees; Bush, Lovett, Woolley and others shrewdly invested in the industrial war preparations of Nazi Germany and the planned Nazi assault on Europe, England and the world while at the same time minutely preparing cost-effective guidelines for extermination and enslavement of men, women and children in concentration camps and slave labor factories. "As German troops swept across Europe," Kelly writes, "absorbing Austria, bludgeoning Czechoslovakia, raping Poland, swallowing Denmark, Norway and Sweden, grabbing Luxembourg and Belgium, invading France and bombarding the British Isles, no one at Brown Brothers Harriman stepped forward to decry their continuing business ties with Germany. The remunerative relationship between Fritz Thyssen and Brown Brothers continued for sixteen years." (K. Kelly, 60)

Finally, in May 1940, after the Nazi invasion of Holland, FDR froze all Dutch assets in the United States including those held by UBC. No matter. Harriman was appointed FDR's emissary to London to expedite Lend-Lease aid to Churchill while his firm held $3 million of UBC's Nazi cash in New York vaults before taking over the Moscow Embassy with the junior Russian aide Kennan, Thompson and the Lend-Lease mission under General Bradley joined by Consortium insiders Tom Watson Jr. founder of IBM and others like Allen Wardwell of the 1917 Red Cross Bolshevik spy mission. That's in 1941.

With England under siege Harriman writes Bullitt from the London Embassy at 1 Grosvenor Square unhappy with Roosevelt's foot-dragging. "It is impossible for me to understand the ostrich-like attitude of America. Either we have an interest in the outcome of this war, or we have not. If we have not, why are we supplying England with the tools? If we have, why do we not realize that the situation could not be tougher and every day we delay direct participation – at least use of our Navy and Air Force—we are taking an extreme risk that either the war will be lost or the difficulty of winning it multiplied, in arithmetic if not geometric progression, for each week we delay". They might control him but FDR was still their "President". FDR liked to fool everyone. It amused him to no end. Even if he was their man he was still the President! Peter Clark, professor of British History at Cambridge, wrote in *The Last Thousand Days of the British Empire* of British stupefaction at surviving a war against the Nazis, or, after the war when the Americans retired their Lend-Lease life-line. "They subscribed hopefully to the common deal for the postwar world but had no idea how to survive the transition to it. Within weeks, therefore, Churchill was to ask Roosevelt personally what on earth would happen to the British economy when Lend-Lease had to stop." (Peter Clark, *The Last Thousand Days of the British Empire,* Bloomsbury, 2008, 33)

In *Secrets of the Federal Reserve*, Eustace Mullins immerses the reader in the murky details of the consolidation of Consortium power inside the Federal Reserve central bank. "After our entry into World War I," Mullins writes, "Woodrow Wilson turned the government of the United States over to a triumvirate of his campaign backers, Paul Warburg, Bernard Baruch and Eugene Meyer." Baruch runs the America's War Industries Board "with life and death powers over every factory in the United States". Wall Street's Eugene Meyer worked in the WIB and the War Savings Committee before taking over as chairman of the War Finance Corporation, in 1919. Warburg takes control of the nation's banking system.. All three men are highly successful Jews.

Meyer is the son of a long line of distinguished Jewish families from France; "that numbered many rabbis and civic leaders", writes his daughter, *Washington Post* owner Katherine Graham. She particularly cherished her family's link to Napoleon when Jacob Meyer, her great-great grandfather was awarded the Legion of Honour and had been "a member of the Sanhedrin, the college of Jewish notables called by Napoleon I in connection with recognizing the rights of Jews as citizens." Passing through Paris *en route* to America his father had the good fortune to be recommended by Alexander Freres (Lazard Freres), who set him up in San Francisco, around 1860, and the following year joined Lazard Freres in Los Angeles, then a small ramshackle town "made up of only three or four thousand inhabitants, mostly foreigners", he recalled.

Eugene Meyer arrives on the scene at a most propitious moment before the oil and movie boom. In her autobiography (1998), *Personal History,* Katherine Graham observes, "There were four brick houses – the rest were adobe with roofs that cracked. There were no paved streets or sewers. The water for both drinking and irrigation came from ditches. My grandfather stated in Los Angeles for the next twenty-two years." On the eve of the First World War Baruch persuades Meyer to move to leave Wall Street and move to Washington to run the War Finance Corp. "in charge of the loan program which financed the war". Warburg holds onto the reins of the Federal Reserve and national banking system. In fact, Eugene Meyer heads the Federal Reserve Board during the Holodomor years until 1933, and although Roosevelt asks him to stay he resigns. Both Eugene Meyer and his outspoken wife were decidedly staunch Republicans. Graham recalls, "In his eyes, Roosevelt's sins were many, but a few stood out; his experimentation with the dollar, his disregard for the gold standard, and his general lack of sophistication about economic and financial policies." (Katherine Graham, *Personal History*, NY: Random House, 1998, 4, 29, 57. Her autobiography describes with candor intimacies of her illustriously privileged life as the divine millionairess and publisher-owner of the *Washington Post* for a half-century and is no less remarkable for the fact of having no mention of the Warburgs, Stalin or Russia though it mentions her close friend Harriman in the Astor sale of *Newsweek* magazine in 1961. Tantalizing story-telling by a master Washington insider and international socialite. As I write her former editor Ben Bradlee in August 2013 is honored by Obama with the Medal of Freedom and joins that rare breed of some 500 fellow culture laureates.)

January 1932 Congress commissions Hoover's RFC (Reconstruction Finance Corp) with Eugene Meyer chairman. It will eventually disburse $10 billion in debt and capital to US corporations, with 40 percent of RFC capital going to bail out faltering financial institutions. (William D. Cohan, *The Last Tycoons, The Secret History of Lazard Freres & Co.,* NY: Doubleday, 2007)

Eustace Mullins helps us sort this out, and he writes, "Knowing, that the overwhelming sentiment of the American people during 1915 and 1916 had been anti-British and pro-German, our British allies viewed with some trepidation the prominence of Paul Warburg and Kuhn, Loeb Company in the prosecution of the war. They were uneasy about his high position in the Administration because his brother, Max Warburg, was at that time serving as head of the German Secret Service." (The Warburgs assist Morgan and his Wall Street bankers put together their abortive 1900 China loans.)

"On December 12, 1918, the United States Naval Secret Service Report on Mr. Warburg was as follows: 'WARBURG, PAUL: New York City. German, naturalized citizen, 1911, was decorated by the Kaiser in 1912, was vice chairman of the Federal Reserve Board. *Handled large sums furnished by Germany for Lenin and Trotsky.* Has a brother who is leader of the espionage system of Germany.' Strangely enough, this report, which must have been compiled much earlier, while we were at war with Germany, is not dated until December 12, 1918. After the Armistice had been signed. Also, it does not contain the information that Paul Warburg resigned from the Federal Reserve Board in May, 1918, which indicates that it was compiled before May 1918, when Paul Warburg would theoretically have been open to a charge of treason because of his brother's control of Germany's Secret Service. Paul Warburg's other brother Felix in New York was a director of the Prussian Life Insurance Company of Berlin." Mullins adds the comment that Warburg "presumably would not have liked to see too many of his policyholders killed in the war". (E. Mullins, Chapter 8, *Secrets of the Federal Reserve*; italics added)

Remember Ezra Pound? Creative genius and contemporary of James Joyce and Harvard's poet laureate T.S. Eliot. Mullins research, in fact, was triggered in part based on findings by Pound in spite of Pound's imprisonment for thirteen and a half years held captive inside an American medical institution. Their seminal work was published over a half century ago, in 1952, titled *The Federal Reserve Conspiracy*. More recent editions make it readily available though the book at time had been banned and ordered burned in Germany by the Bavarian Supreme Court with approval by the US High Commissioner to Germany, James B. Conant who incidentally had assumed the presidency of Harvard University in 1933, the year of the Holodomor. Who would have thought that the President of Harvard would have endorsed book burning?

As it were, for the first time Mullins and Pound exposed "the original stockholders of the Federal Reserve Banks" and traced back to "the parent companies the London Connection". Mullins tried unsuccessfully to secure Pound's freedom while he languishes in a federal sanatorium in Washington DC. The US government, Mullins observed, "has never owned a single share of stock in any Federal Reserve Bank; *all of its stock is owned by "private corporations"*. (When I queried a very close friend whose ancestor figured among the founding shareholders, I never received a reply. Silence. The taboo covering the truth about the Fed casts a large cloud over reality.; italics added)

In the Consortium hierarchy, another key Harriman man who figures unfolding the Machiavellian economic and military strategy of FDR's foreign policy that invests in the Stalin's Soviet gulag state terrorism that sacrifices the Ukrainians and prepared the way giving the world the Holodomor nightmare, – and cover-up, Nazi concentration camps, endless campaigns of mass genocides, and the world as we know it today, is Robert S. Lovett Sr.. Lovett too is Yale, Bones, a member of the Yale Flight Unit in the First World War, and a life-long Harriman crony. As President of Union Pacific Railroad, Lovett Sr. faithfully served as chief counsel to Edward H. Harriman overseeing his railroad empire, and executor of his will. During WWI Bob Lovett is appointed by Wilson and Baruch to manage national production and purchase "priorities". Quite simply this entitles Lovett to exercise enormous emergency war powers and reap personal advantage.

"Our firm", Baruch recalled, "did large business for Mr. Harriman .... In 1906 Harriman had (us) place heavy bets on the stealthy lawyer Charles Evans Hughes in his race for Governor of New York against William Randolph Hearst. After several hundred thousand dollars had been wagered, (our firm) stopped. Hearing of this, Harriman called, 'Didn't I tell you to bet?' he demanded. 'Now go on.'"

Roosevelt confided to the Harriman man lawyer Bob Lovett that his views on the elder Harriman were based on what JP Morgan had told him. Holodomor detractor and a Consortium hack in the US Embassy under Bullitt during the Famine-Terror Genoide, George Kennan's father was a E. H. Harriman protégé. Teddy Roosevelt considered the elder Harriman "an Enemy of the United States and free nations everywhere." Pretty strong stuff from the old Rough Rider from San Juan Hill fame who shot from the hip. Kennan does a lot of covering up for the Consortium which early on recognizes his talent for prose writing two anthologies on Wilson's armed insurrection and undeclared war during the Bolshevik Civil War and later an authorized Harriman biography. (Bernard M. Baruch, *My Own Story,* NY: Henry Holt, 1957, 138-9)

In *Wall Street and the Rise of Hitler* (1976) Antony Sutton reveals convincing evidence that the American financiers not only provided the money and materiel to

Hitler but planned to use him in order to launch World War II. Reader the primary lesson of the First World War stay in focus that the Consortium thrives on war. Its men – and women – are in place to pull the levers and bring in the cash tightening their grip on resources, property, and the weak and meek. Sutton traced the international bankers role in the financing of the Bolshevik revolution documented in his book *Wall Street and the Bolshevik Revolution* (1981) Sutton's volumes of *Western 1917-1965* (1973) leave no room for doubt that all the technology, the know-how, much of the raw material and most of the capital necessary to build the industrial and military machine with which the threatened the free world came from the United States. Before the First World War Czarist Russia was had one of the fastest economic growth rates in the world. Profits from war manufacturing industries made America for the first time a creditor nation with England and France in tatters with dangling empires imploding in discontent and national liberation struggles. Sutton diligently followed a trail of alarming facts to conclude that the military industrial machine of the Soviet Socialist Republics threatening the West was stamped "Made in the U.S.A.". (A. C. Sutton, *Western Technology and Soviet Economic Development 1917-1965*; Sutton, *Wall Street and the Rise of Hitler*, Seal Beach, CA: '76 Press, 1976; A. C. Sutton, *Wall Street and the Bolshevik Revolution,* NY: Arlington House, 1981)

During the First World War FDR lived the life of a lordly prince of imperial empire in the glittering world of millionaires, mansions and monopoly. In fact, FDR always lived with a silver spoon. In the war he was appointed Assistant Secretary of the Navy where he displayed a predilection for the covert in his duties as Director of the Office of Naval Intelligence in association with England's Admiral Blinker Hall. No application necessary. The Groton-Harvard elite are never in need. During the war he could do as he pleased and vacationed on America's battleships and cruisers and he did so as President. At the same time in London his Anglo-counterpart Winston Churchill was First Lord of the Admiralty. Churchill is of a distinctly more noble lineage being a direct descendant of the Duke of Marlborough with all the trimmings of the stately English manor. For his part, the renegade bank thief Joseph Stalin is a bandit turned revolutionary scoundrel without a life roaming about the Georgian Caucasian mountains. Early on this cunning wolf abandons the priesthood, pursues crime, is caught by Czarist police and exiled to Siberia.

The Triumvirate shares the same goal in common – Empire. Eventually, after some heavy Allied bombing of Germany raised the stakes as Russian troops poured into Eastern Europe in the race towards Berlin, this threesome would tee off again at Yalta on the Black Sea in Crimea of southern Ukraine and carve up the world between Stalinist communism in the East, and Anglo-Democratic capitalism in the West.

This time not long before the end of a war the stage was again set in advance for the next half century of a New World Order launching the stalemate between two nuclear superpowers which is soon called "Cold War". War by spy games and proxies, – Vietnam, North Korea, Congo, that kind of side-show war instead of blowing up Moscow and Washington or New York London and Paris. Certainly a preferable scenario, at least for the Consortium. In the equation the Holodomor never figured even as a statistic.

Stalin was left alone with his self-styled oriental state terrorism against the heroic yet forsaken battle-weary citizens of the USSR made even remote to the western mindset by the pernicious propaganda of a world apparently divided against itself. After the battles in Russia and the Ukraine countryside pushed the Germans pack to Berlin, and the guns silent after most destructive war in the world's history, the voices of the millions of famine victims of the Ukraine were long forgotten. In fact, Yalta was a business-as-usual deal for the Morgan-Rockerfeller-Harriman set only now much more certain of their organization plans for reconstruction of postwar Europe with Soviet Russia on the rebound and attrition wearing down the Nazi forces led by competent generals and a leader cracking under the strain who wouldn't heed their advice. Instead of Wilson's League of Nations, the same Wall Street gang has set their sights on a world government community as member in the Rockefeller-funded United Nations. The Anglo-American (and French) capitalists occupied seats in the UN Security Council with Communists from the USSR Soviet Union and Maoist China. "Communism is simply a front for something deeper", wrote Ralph Epperson, another author out of the box. "Communism is not the revolt of the poor, but the secret conspiracy of the rich. The international conspiracy arises not in Moscow but in New York." (Ralph Epperson, *The Hidden Hand*, St. Petersburg, 1996, 103)

THE INCREDIBLE REVELATIONS OF BOLSHEVIK RAKOVSKY

Another curious tale of money funneled to the Bolshevik revolutionaries by Consortium bankers, Morgan and Jewish financiers in London and New York comes to light just after the Holodomor years. The mysterious Bolshevik Rakovsky (Chaim Rakeover), a Bulgarian Trotskite revolutionary leader, recounts information shocking to Stalin's investigators during the tyrant's Great Purge show trials. Rakovsky relates how Bolsheviks and the Soviet Comintern had worked hand in hand with international bankers who not unlike their Marxist brothers – many who were Jewish –, sought to destroy all national borders and establish a one world dictatorship, not the proletarian kind but a federated financial oligarchy. It's the kind of power tripping that today irritates Putin as he lashes out against the despicable "cockroach" Russian billionaire industrialists who threaten his absolute power. Rakovsky reveals both sides work in tandem sharing mutual convenience. Likewise, agents of the Consortium and Jewish banking empire are financing Hitler's rearmament of Nazi Germany. Rakovsky served as soviet ambassador to France until he is replaced January 1928 by V.S. Dovgalevsky who Bullitt meets in the Kremlin upon his return to Russia late 1933…

Rakovsky recalls that prewar Czarist Russia and its reactionary monarchy presented a certain obstacle to their plans, on the one hand, yet provides a golden testing ground in social politics. In that early Bolshevik era Trotsky enjoys the confidence of the masters of the "interest spiderweb" – the Schiffs, Warburgs and other international financiers who place at his disposal mouth-watering sums. Even the pro-American transitional puppet prime minister Kerensky, according to Rakovsky, was one of the bankers' agents who yielded power to his "higher-ups" when they beckon as we learn in this account by J. Landowsky in *Red Symphony*:

"From the start 'Red Leon' became practically the complete master of Russia and the Bolshevik Party. Any attempts on the part of anyone else to occupy that role were decisively cut short. When Lenin began to exhibit excessive independence and make claims to real power it was Trotsky who organizes through the vicious Cheka police the Left Social-Revolutionary putsch, and then that fatal summer the Fanny Kaplan assassination attempt, as a result of which Vladimir Ilyich was once again put in his place. But the main achievement of the 'permanent revolution' was Trotsky's formation of the Red Army. As soon as he took charge of the War Commissariat and the Revolutionary War Soviet, uniforms and ammunition appeared as if by the stroke of magic. Only then did the Reds began to prevail over the Whites. The secret depositions of the former Paris ambassador confirmed that this breakthrough was the result not only of financing on the part of Lev Davidovich's international friends, but also the activities of agents of those very same friends within the ranks of the Whites. Other details are also worthy of attention: for example the fleeting reference in the text of *The Red Symphony* to 'your acquaintance Navachin', a garbled translation from Spanish of Dmitry Navashin – with whom Rakovsky was acquainted – the director of the Franco-Soviet Bank, safekeeper of Trotsky's funds and a leading Mason. Navachin was killed in 1935 outside Paris in mysterious circumstances. His wife told *Paris-Soir,* "They killed my husband, because he knew too much. He was the victim of powerful, worldwide occult forces." (J. Landowsky, *Red Symphony*, London: *The Plain Speaker*)

At his trial witnessed by the American ambassador Rakovsky tells Stalin what FDR already knows to be true. "The financial internationalists," Rakovsky said, "will make sure that the Allies declares war only on Hitler and not the USSR. On the contrary, the USSR ought to be helped. The USSR will not enter the war if it is not attacked. But USSR rulers can arrange that they will be attacked. The aggression against America can be invented. The Capitalistic States will destroy each other if one brings about a clash of their two wings: the fascist and the bourgeois."

In 1928 the American publisher Penguin releases Trotsky's defense of his leadership of the Bolshevik Revolution in *My Life, An Attempt at an Autobiography.* In the book of Rakovsky proffers a glowing tribute to a scarcely understood Bolshevik. It was by no means a casual or incidental reference.

"Christian G. Rakovsky is," Trotsky writes, "internationally, one of the best known figures in the European Socialist movement. A Bulgarian by birth, he is a Roumanian subject by dint of the Balkan map, a French physician by education, a Russian by connections, by sympathies and literary work. He speaks all the Balkan and four European languages; he has at various times played an active part in the inner workings of four Socialist parties - the Bulgarian, Russian, French and Romanian – to become eventually one of the leaders of the Soviet Federation, a founder of the Communist Intemational, President of the Ukrainian Soviet of People's Commissaries, and the diplomatic Soviet representative in England and France – only to share finally the fate of all the 'left' opposition. Rakovsky's personal traits, his broad international outlook, his profound nobility of character, have made him particularly odious to Stalin, who personifies the exact opposite."

Stalin despises Trotsky for all his skill and fame. That tribute should have alone been sufficient to seal Rakovsky's fate. But it was true! Stalin was no ideologue. He was Georgian with the instincts of a wolf with the refinement of a back-alley gypsy bandit. Was Trotsky sending a public message to Stalin anticipating the Purges still Five-Years distant? Why expose a secret double-agent? Rakovsky tells Stalin's Purge Tribunal, with the Great Dictator gasping in laughter behind chamber walls: "There is only one aim, one single aim: the triumph of Communism. It is not Moscow which will impose its will on the democratic States, but New York, not the 'Comintern,' but the 'Capintern' on Wall Street."

Rakovsky went on and none of this eclipsed the attentive hungry ears of the US State Department: "Who other than he could have been able to impose on Europe such an obvious and absolute contradiction? What force can lead it towards complete suicide? Only one force is able to do this: money. Money is power and the sole power." But of course! How improbable for it not to be true. The contradictions of the bourgoise capitalist! War! Capital! Suicide! And the capitalists needed their "Uncle Joe"! Compared to the Kirov-Zinoviev-Bukharin plot of petty Commissars shot after the 1936 show trials and Krylenko's interrogation of the old expert engineer Fedotov in the famous "wrecking" trial of 1930 Stalin has every reason to believe that this was something indeed that made sense.

While in prison, Rakovsky is interviewed by Stalin's foreign agent, Gavril (Gabriel) G. Kusmin. Rakovsky reveals an astounding plan for provoking World War II which not only intrigues Stalin, he accepts it, too. He bought it! Furthermore, Rakovsky says that Wall Street engineered "the stock market crash on October 24, 1929", describing it as "more important for even the revolution than the October Revolution. It was called a real revolution". It created the Great Depression and allows FDR to enact his NRA government-regulated welfare reforms, or socialism American-style.

"The four years of the government of Hoover", Rakovsky declares, "are years of revolutionary progress: twelve and fifteen million on strike. In February, 1933, there takes place the last stroke of the crisis with the closing of the banks. It is difficult to do more than Capital did in order to break the 'classical American', who was still on his industrial bases, and in the economic respect, enslaved by Wall Street. ... the four years of the rule of Hoover were used for the preparation of the seizure of power in the United States and the USSR; there, by means of a financial revolution, and here, with the help of war and the defeat which was to follow. ...You can understand that the execution of the plan on such a scale requires a special man, who can direct the executive power in the United States, who has been predetermined to be the organizing and deciding force."

These revelations might seem extraordinary but these are extraordinary times when the unbelievable and incredible are not only possible in the logic of endless Bolshevik absurdities, but capitalist advancements in technology from the radio and television, to electricity, turbine engines, tractors and the long-distance aeroplane were no less extraordinary to the barefoot illiterate Czarist peasant or Oklahoma farm boy nor were they far from the context of economic and political realities emerging in Europe, the USSR, England and America. So why shouldn't Rakovsky's disclosures be true. According to French intelligence sources, Leon Trotsky (Lev Davidovich) had penetrated the inner family circle of the Jewish banking world. Trotsky's ties to the world financial elite were well-known long before the publication of *The Red Symphony*. In 1919, the French government received from its informer in Washington, a detailed report where "Red Leon's" New York banking sponsors were listed, identified as document "1618-6 No. 912".

For some strange reason Stalin lets Rakovsky escape the executioner for a time and he is sent sent instead to the Gulag, sentenced to twenty years hard labor in Oryol Prison. Three years later when the Nazi invasion in June 1941 Rakovsky along with over 150 other "political" are shot on emergency orders from Stalin to the NKVD. In Russia it is known as the political prison Medvedev Forest massacre. Those shot include Olga Kameneva and Maria Spiridonova. Rakovsky's second wife, Alexandrina Alexandrescu is arrested, and held in Nutyrka prison where she suffers a series of heart attacks. His adoptive daughter, Elena Codreanu-Racovski, is expelled from her secretarial post at the Mossoviet Theater and deported to Siberia. She survives as did her memoirs *The Length and Breadth of the Century* with recollections of her father. Christian Rakovksy is rehabilitated by Gorbachev in 1988.

The Consortium – cartel, group network, private set, social club, corporate clique, family clan, political conspiracy– whatever name you wish to attach is redundant – of bankers and statesmen in New York and London put their money on Franklin D. Roosevelt in the US and on Hitler in Germany and on Stalin in the USSR. They already had Stalin securely in place in the Soviet Union, although "Red Leon" Trotsky was really their man ever since his marriage to the daughter of banker Abram Zhivotovsky thus conveniently establishing his connection with the financiers. These are the same people who have arranged for Lenin to be shot by Fanny Kaplan, member of the Social Revolutionary party in a Cheka-organized putsch in the summer of 1918. The organizer of the Red Army Leon Trotsky is that close to the top of the Consortium coup plotters.

THE WARBURGS, BAKERS, MORGANS, SCHIFFS, KUHN LOEB, SCHROEDER & CO.

And it is Trotsky, not Lenin, who brings us back to the fascinating connections of the Warburg family. (Lenin returns on the German-financed sealed train.) Remember reader, just five years have passed since Paul Warburg as co-founder of the financial system of the US Federal Reserve Bank established a centralized a network of affiliated Fed banks in America to finance the War and postwar reconstruction, including mopping up the dangling republics of the Russian Empire. It just so happens that Felix Warburg is one of the principal financial backers of the Bolshevik Russian Revolution. In the firm of Kuhn Loeb, Felix Warburg supported Taft.

Mullins and Sutton concur: "As one of the main financiers of the Russian Revolution Felix Warburg compromised himself to such a degree by his connections with the Bolsheviks that it was decided to remove him from the US Federal Reserve Board, in order to 'cover the traces' of American bankers' ties" to wretched yet well-organized and ruthless professional revolutionaries of the Russian Revolution whose names were added to the long list of anti-government intellectuals and great men since the days of Nicholas I. Remember reader, bloody revolutions are not won by nice guys with big hearts.

Over the course of two centuries the Rothschild dynasty perpetuated itself exclusively through close-relative marriages. An interesting and highly significant example of the Schiff relation to the Federal Reserve power system and how it relates to FDR is found in the Baker-Schiff link. In 1934, with Holodmor famine victims still pleading for food and dropping dead in starkly barren villages, towns and cities, Jacob Schiff's grandson, John Mortimer Schiff, marries Edith Brevort Baker, daughter of J George Baker Jr., and grand-daughter of the old scion himself Baker, Sr. theirs is a sumptuous banquet affair with most expensive trimmings that would arouse even the Astors. Baker's father is the president-founder of First National Bank. Coined "the Sphinx of Wall Street", George the Elder holds director seats on more than 40 companies; John M. Schiff also is privy to a nice handful of corporate directorships, Getty Oil, Uniroyal, Kennecott Copper, Westinghouse, CIT Financial, A & P to name only a few. When he assumes the board chairmanship at National City, in 1909, he possesses 20,000 shares worth $20 million ($500 million in 2011). When George Baker, Sr. dies, in 1931, he sits atop a cool $100 million National City bank fortune with engraved in the national consciousness his famous remark fit for a gravestone, "It's none of the public's business what I do!" (Expletives deleted.)

This is the same bank that sets Bill Bullitt, FDR's hack envoy to Moscow, spiraling in ceaseless diversionary talks with Stalin's men, even before his eventual appointment as ambassador. In other words, Bullitt's debt negotiations are mere subterfuge to shadow the Consortium operations.

Three years after his death *Time* magazine in its March 26, 1934 edition hails Baker as "the richest, most powerful and most taciturn commercial banker in U. S. history"; a decade earlier and years before the 1929 market crash, *Time* reported his wealth "twice as rich as the original JP Morgan", and the owner of "half a dozen railroads, several banks, scores of industrial concerns", and served on at least 22 corporate boards. (George F. Baker Private Papers, Harvard Business School)

At this time of Holodomor and the Bullitt bank negotiations with Moscow, because of all the Morgan men on the board First National is known by the Wall Street crowd as "the Morgan Bank". Three decades have passed since in 1914 it is the *second* largest purchaser of shares of the Federal Reserve Bank of New York.

Between the two of them Baker and his son hold 25% of their bank's total stock. Moreover, the Baker family multiplies their wealth extensively compounded by distinguishing marital arrangements; George F. Baker Sr.'s daughter Evelyn is married to Howard Bligh St. George, of the Baronet St. George family of London; her sister Florence married a Loew. Brother, George F. Baker, Jr., a year after the war wins a seat to the US Congress, and retains his seat for nearly two decades. The St. Georges settled in the United States; their daughter Katherine St. George, a Republican, also served in Congress. Katherine St. George's mother Catherine Delano Collier, is the younger sister of Sara Delano Roosevelt, mother of President Franklin Delano Roosevelt, and his first cousin. (Her daughter marries into the Duke tobacco family fortune.) Cousins and more cousins expand the Consortium universe and tighten control of the extended family resources.

More marriages and mergers consolidate the tight inner circle of power of the Consortium. The Jacob Schiff family is another huge Consortium legacy. John M. Schiff becomes honorary chairman of the merged Lehman Brothers Kuhn Loeb Company. The Morgan bank – and we can thank Mullins for his excellent research here –, is "really a subsidiary of Junius S. Morgan Company of London and the N. M. Rothschild Company, also of London, and Wall Street's Kuhn, Loeb Company, also widely considered as "a principal agent of the Rothschilds". Financier Thomas Fortune Ryan holds 5,100 shares of National Bank of Commerce; his son marries Otto Kahn's daughter; Ryan's grand-daughter, Virginia Fortune Ryan, marries Lord Airlie, destined to become the head of J. Henry Schroeder Banking Corp with headquarters in New York and London.

Prize winning historian and biographer Mathew Josephson writes in *The Robber Barons* (1934) of the Morgan acquisition taking direct control of National Bank of Commerce, adding to its part ownership of First National Bank run by Baker. Morgan already dominates the insurance business (New York Life, Equitable Life, Mutual Life) giving him a billion dollars in assets with fifty million dollars to invest each year. Meanwhile, the politicking former judge from Independence Missouri who left the family farm to join "the Club" of the US Senate as it was known, Harry S. Truman lambasts the four giant insurance companies for controlling some 60 percent of all the asssets of the insurance business in America. Morgan then easily linked his banks to others (Hanover, Liberty, Chase). "Does it surprise you why Mrs. St. George, a first cousin of FDR and New Dealer, said, 'Democracy is a failure'." (M. Josephson, *The Robber Barons,* Mariner Books, 1934, 1962; E. Mullins, *Secrets of the Federal Reserve,* 65; re. Truman on insurance companies, D. McCullough, *Truman*, 233)

Each and every Consortium family branched into very important roles and positions of dominance tightening the Consortium's grip on developments in America. Third generation Pilgrim member and Pilgrims Treasurer John Mortimer Schiff, in 1973, also marries into the George F. Baker family fortune (First National Bank of New York, General Electric, US Steel, General Motors, US Trust, Mutual Life Insurance ...) estimated at a half billion dollars in 1924 dollars ($20 billion). Warburg marries the daughter of Solomon Loeb of Kuhn Loeb Company. Otto Kahn is a partner of Warburg and Schiff in Kuhn, Loeb Company;

his daughter marries into the firm. Later, a Ryan grand-daughter married M. M. Warburg, chairman of J. Henry Schroeder, one of Hitler's favorite banking houses of the Consortium. Baker, Warburg, Schiff, Kuhn, Kahn, Rothschild, Ryan, Morgan, Lehman, Schroeder ... and on down the yellow brick road of the real world into the Oz culture of America.

These are the American architects of "globalism" who from their public schools, "Oxbridge" students, palatial mansions, grouse hunting estates, private clubs and cozy austere board rooms backed the Jewish intellectuals masterminding the Bolshevik coup of the October Revolution giving the world Stalin and the Holodomor. The international organization, – (cartel, group network, set, club, clique, clan – whatever name you wish to attach is merely redundant), – of bankers and statesmen in New York and London put their money on Franklin D. Roosevelt in the US, and Hitler in Germany. They already have Stalin entrenched in power and securely in place in the Kremlin, although "Red Leon" Trotsky was really their first choice ever since his marriage to the Zhivotovsky woman. Sutton concludes Felix Warburg is one of the principal financial backers of the Bolshevik Russian Revolution. In the arrangement Paul Warburg and Jacob Schiff support Woodrow Wilson; Otto Kahn supports Theodore Roosevelt. From the outset of his career in politics, Woodrow Wilson is also politically captive of Standard Oil of New Jersey, where he leaves Princeton to become Governor of the state, and beholden to the financiers if ever anyone could be.

During the 1920s Paul Warburg resigned from the Federal Reserve Board over public revelations of his brother Max in German wartime Intelligence. That didn't limit his power. Paul Warburg became the most powerful trade acceptance banker in the world. A Reserve Bank Governor for a year in the 1914-18 world war, Paul Warburg personally managed Board policies by meeting as President of the Federal advisory Council as well as President of the American Acceptance Council. From the time it was organized in 1920 until his death in 1932, Warburg remained Chairman of the Board of the International Acceptance Bank of New York (AIB). This was the largest acceptance bank in the world. Brother Felix M. Warburg, a Kuhn, Loeb partner, was director of the International Acceptance Bank. Paul Warburg's son, James Paul Warburg, was Vice-President. In addition, Paul Warburg was controlled important acceptance banks in this country with director seats at Westinghouse Acceptance Bank, for example, organized in the United States immediately after World War One when the headquarters of the international acceptance market was moved from London to New York. At any time in the late and early thirties, AIB certainly had the financial means to intervene in Moscow to persuade Stalin to alleviate conditions in the Ukraine but it lacked the political will to do it. (A. C. Sutton, Chapter 10, *Wall Street and the Rise of Hitler*)

By fall 1930 editors at *The New York Times* show a strange sudden interest in Hitler publishing several articles including "Hitler, Driving Force in Germany's Fascism" on September 21. In 1929 *The New York Times* had run only a single brief on Adolf Hitler. By 1931 it runs scores of Nazi Hitler stories including three "Portraits".

Sutton writes, "James Warburg's Sworn Affidavit New York City, James Warburg July 15, 1949 1. Concerning the wholly false and malicious allegations made by Rene Sonderegger of Zurich, Switzerland, et al., asset forth in the foregoing part of this statement, I, James Paul Warburg, of Greenwich, Connecticut, U.S.A., depose as follows: 5. I did not go to Germany at the request of the President of the Guaranty Trust Company in 1929, or at any other time." Sutton adds, "Note that Warburg, by his own statement, told his banking associates that Hitler would come to power. This claim was made in 1930 – and the Warburgs continued as directors with IG Farben and other pro-Nazi firms. Warburg did go to Germany in 1929 and 1930 for the International Acceptance Bank, Inc. "I did go to Germany on business for my own bank, The International Acceptance Bank Inc., of New York, in both 1929 and 1930. On neither of these occasions did I have anything to do with investigating the possible prevention of a Communist revolution in Germany by the promotion of a Nazi counter- revolution. As a matter of recorded fact, my opinion at the time was that there was relatively little danger of a Communist revolution in Germany and a considerable danger of a Nazi seizure of power, I am in a position to prove that, on my return from Germany after the Reichstag elections of 1930, I warned my associates that Hitler would very likely come to power in Germany and that the result would be either a Nazi-dominated Europe or a second world war – perhaps both. This can be corroborated as well as the fact that, as a consequence of my warning, my bank proceeded to reduce its German commitments as rapidly as possible." (A. C. Sutton, Chapter 10, *Wall Street and the Rise of Hitler*)

"Warburg did go to Germany in 1929 and 1930 for the International Acceptance Bank, Inc. 6. I did go to Germany on business for my own bank, the International Acceptance Bank Inc., of New York, in both 1929 and 1930. On neither of these occasions did I have anything to do with investigating the possible prevention of a Communist revolution in Germany by the promotion of a Nazi counter- revolution. As a matter of recorded fact, my opinion at the time was that there was relatively little danger of a Communist revolution in Germany and a considerable danger of a Nazi seizure of power, I am in a position to prove that, on my return from Germany after the Reichstag elections of 1930, I warned my associates that Hitler would very likely come to power in Germany and that the result would be either a Nazi- dominated Europe or a second world war - perhaps both. This can be corroborated as well as the fact that, as a consequence of my warning, my bank proceeded to reduce its German commitments as rapidly as possible." (A. C. Sutton, Chapter Ten, *Wall Street and the Rise of Hitler;* Ron Chernow, *The Warburgs*, NY: Random House, 1993)

"Note that Warburg, by his own statement, told his banking associates that Hitler would come to power. This claim was made in 1930 – and the Warburgs continued as directors with IG Farben and other pro-Nazi firms. 7. I had no discussions anywhere, at any time, with Hitler, with any Nazi officials, or with anyone else about providing funds for the Nazi Party. Specifically, I had no dealing of this sort with Mendelssohn & Co., or the Rotterdamsche Bankvereiniging or the Banca Italiana (Banca d'Italia sic).

There is no evidence to contradict this statement. So far as can be traced Warburgs were not connected with these banking firms except that the Italian correspondent of Warburg's Bank of Manhattan was 'Banca Commerciale Italiana' - Banca Italiana." (A. C. Sutton, Chapter Ten, *Wall Street and the Rise of Hitler*, 145)

"In February 1933 (see pages 191 and 192 of *Spanischer Sommer*) when I am alleged to have brought Hitler the last installment of American funds and to have been received by Göering and Goebbels as well as by Hitler himself, I can prove that I was not in Germany at all. I never set foot in Germany after the Nazis had come to power in January 1933. In January and February I was in New York and Washington, working both with my bank and with President-elect Roosevelt on the then-acute banking crisis. After Mr. Roosevelt's inauguration, on March 3, 1933, I was working with him continuously helping to prepare the agenda for the World Economic Conference, to which I was sent as Financial adviser in early June. This is a matter of public record. There is no evidence to contradict these statements. 'Sidney Warburg' provides no supporting evidence for his claims." (A. C. Sutton, *Wall Street and FDR*, NY: Arlington House, 1975; A. C. Sutton, Chapter Ten, *Wall Street and the Rise of Hitler*)

For years French intelligence sources place Trotsky inside the inner family circle of the Rothschild banking world linked to the international Jewish financiers backing the Revolution. For over two hundred years the Rothschild dynasty secured its future with marital predestination and holy contracts. This was a closed tightly-knit clan with marriages between the Dreyfuses, Lazards, Schiffs and Warburgs arranged among themselves. It was closed to outsiders without the necessary credentials.

Philosopher and eminent world authority and author on totalitarism, Hannah Arendt, who emigrated to the US, in 1941, unlike her friend and first cousin the brilliant but doomed Walter Benjamin who died of suicide unable to escaped from the Nazi Gestapo in France. She wrote, "Jewish banking capital became international, united through intersecting marriages, and turned into a real international caste ... What could be a more convincing illustration of the fantastic conception of a worldwide Jewish government than the Rothschild family, uniting citizens of five different governments the separate conflicts of which didn't affect the interests of their respective state banks even for a moment!"

Two highly readable contributions by Hannah Arendt *The Origins of Totalitarianism* (1951) and *The Human Condition* (1958) trace the roots of Stalinist Communism and Nazism. In her reporting for *The New Yorker* of the Eichmann trial summed up in her book *Eichmann in Jerusalem: A Report on the Banality of Evil* (1963), – and that close to twenty years after the Nuremberg Judgment –, Arendt coined the phrase "the banality of evil". She raised the question of whether evil is radical or a common and simple form of mere idiocy, a tendency of ordinary people to obey orders and conform to mass opinion without thinking, or exercising that critical evaluation that there are consequences to their action or inaction.

The prison memoirs of Reichsminister Albert Speer, Hitler's favorite Nazi architect sentenced October 1, 1946 by the eight judges of the Nuremberg

International Military Tribunal to twenty years for war crimes and crimes against humanity, spent most of his years consumed in reflection pondering the absurdity of their predicament under Hitler and descent of the German Nazi leaders into the obscenity and human debaseness neck deep in moral decrepitude. It was during the early months of his indictment and incarceration, in November 1946, in "the silence of the sanitorium" of his solitary prison cell, and the day after the son of the ailing scion of the Krupp works, a shy and surrogate son Alfred Krupp must suffer the Allies charges at Nuremberg.

Speer goes on: "Once again I am obsessed by the thought of Hitler's two faces, and that for so long a time I did not see the second behind the first. It was only toward the end, during the last months, that I suddenly became aware of the duality; and significantly my insight was connected with an aesthetic observation: I suddenly discovered how ugly, how repellent and ill proportioned Hitler's face was. How could I have overlooked that for so many years? Mysterious! Perhaps I saw the man himself too little and was intoxicated by the tremendous assignments, the plans, the cheers, the work. Only today have I recalled that on our tours of the country, when we were met with so much cheering, we again and again drove under screamers repeating the anti-semitic slogans of the very man with whom I had sat at an idyllic picnic listening to songs and accordion playing by his household steward, Kannenberg. I would never have believed this man capable of such a cruel rage for extermination. Sometimes I ask myself: Didn't I even notice those slogans, 'Jews undesirable here', or 'Jews enter this locality at their own risk'? Or did I simply overlook them as I overlooked Hitler's other face, which represented the reality I had banished from my world of illusion? ... Every day I learn anew how inhuman we really were. Now I do not mean the barbarism off persecution and extermination. Rather, the absolute dominion of utilitarian ends, such as I pursued as minister of armaments, is nothing but a form of inhumanity."

Albert Speer like others denied knowledge of the Final Solution. Yet, as the son of Nuremberg prosecutor, the US Senator Christopher Dodd writes in his book on his father's experience, *Letters from Nuremberg* (2007), Speer "ruled over a slave labor program that included the importation of five million workers to Germany." Speer wrote in his diary December 9, 1946, "At the trial I testified that I had no knowledge of the killings of the Jews. Justice Jackson and the Russian prosecutors did not even challenge this statement in cross-examination. Did they think I would lie anyhow? ... Even when we spoke of our own dead, we used the term 'casualties', and in general we were great at inventing euphemisms."

Speer managed to escape the hangman's rope. After the day court session US lawyer Thomas J. Dodd is furious that Speer slipped off the hook so easily due to the lack of cross-examing skills of US Supreme Court Justice Robert Jackson, and Dodd angrily writes his wife, "We finished von Papen and Speer and this morning we started von Neurath … I did not cross-examine Speer – but I wish I had done so. I urged the Justice to do it. I felt he needed it as Speer was the last one for whom the US had primary responsibility… Speer was ripe for plucking – but it didn't work out. Of course he will not escape – we have far too much on him. But we could have destroyed him – as he really deserved."

Again the central problem," Speer wrote from prison just over two months after his sentencing. "Everything comes down to this: Hitler always hated the Jews, he made no secret of that at any time. By 1939 at the latest I might have foreseen their fate; after 1942 I ought to have been certain of it. In the months before the outbreak of the Second World War, which surely did not come at a convenient moment for him, his tirades increased. World Jewry was insisting on war, he obstinately repeated; and later he said that the Jews alone had instigated this war and were to blame for it. ... If I had listened more closely, observed more careful, it would surely have dawned on me then that he was making such remarks in order to justify his own mass killings. ... He was capable of tossing off quite calmly, between the soup and the vegetable course, 'I want to annihilate the Jews of Europe. The war is the decisive confrontation between National Socialism and world Jewry. One or the other will bite the dust, and it certainly won't be us. It's lucky that as an Austrian I know the Jews so well. If we lose, they will destroy us. Why should I have pity on them?" (A. Speer, 25)

During the trial indictments, arguments and summaries are heard from the four victorious powers Thomas Dodd voiced his doubts about the Russians in whole Nuremberg process his wife, July 28, 1946, "It seems perfectly clear to me from observing them that even the Russian judges and Russian prosecutors are under control of these secret police officers. As I was listening to the arguments of Jackson and Shawcross, I was thinking of the Russians and it was ever in my mind that all of the crimes which the Nazis have committed have been committed by the Russians, and from what I hear – may still be committed by the Russians. The Russian participation in this prosecution is the Achilles heel of the great trial. Some day we may have to explain it. Thomas Dodd and his family lived in the same small New England town as do I as write, in Old Lyme, Connecticut; Senator Christopher J. Dodd still lives a few miles up the river somewhere in the woods. (Christopher J. Dodd, *Letters from Nuremberg, My Father's Narrative of a Quest for Justice,* NY: Crown, 2007, 41-2, 329-30; Speer, 20-4)

"Communism is simply a front for something deeper", wrote the American Ralph Epperson, in *The Hidden Hand.* "Communism is not the revolt of the poor, but the secret conspiracy of the rich. The international conspiracy arises not in Moscow but in New York." A similar assertion appears in his book *Where England is Going* (1927) published in Great Britain. After stating that the Comintern (Communist International) is a conservative organization comparable to the stock exchange in New York, Epperson asks, "Who's driving England toward revolution? Not Moscow, but New York".

During the 1937 Purge Trials Rakovsky singing for his life recounts stunning facts to Stalin's NKVD investigators. A veteran Bolshevik, Rakovsky had left his wealthy family in Roumania and by 1919 becoming a member of the Central Committee of the Russian Communist Party and a chairman of the Council of People's Commissars of the Ukraine. Rakovsky is an important link between the Bolsheviks and the Comintern's work hand in hand with the international bankers to establish a worldwide dictatorship under a financial oligarchy. By the mid-1930s, however, both Rakovsky and the Comintern are powerless as

Stalin had long renounced permanent world revolution as Soviet doctrine. The proletarian revolution is in effect the means of achieving government monopoly controlled by a socialist bureaucratic elite. (Ralph Epperson, *The Hidden Hand*, St. Petersburg, 1996, 103)

1930 CRACKDOWN OUT OF CONTROL

By January 5, 1930 in a decision by the Soviet Central Committee, the Communist Party decides to launch a major thrust against all the peasants. Author Owen Mathews describes in his book *Stalin's Children* (2008) this period as "a winter of virtual warfare—virtual because one side was unarmed." It is Stalin's first massive assault on the countryside far exceeding the attacks on the richer kulak families. In the 1930 wave of terror half of Ukraine's farms are collectivized by force. Propaganda and political indoctrination is intensified. The Party decision called for complete collectivization of the important agricultural zones by fall; elsewhere no later than after the next year's harvest, as Conquest writes in *The Terror*, "everything got out of hand, and in a few weeks the Party had been carried to the brink of disaster.

Between January and March 1930, the number of peasant holdings brought into the collective farms increased from 4 million to 14 million. Over half the total peasant households had been collectivized in five months. And in the countryside the peasants fought back with 'the sawed –off shotgun, the ax, the dagger, the knife'. At the same time, they destroyed their livestock rather than let it fall into the hands of the State." According to a report by the Secret-Political department of the OGPU of October 1931, in the first nine months of 1931 alone, in the USSR as a whole there had been more than 6,000 acts of 'kulak terror'. (*Sovetskaya derevnya glazami*, v. 3, book 1, 774-87, in M. Ellman, "The Role of Leadership Perceptions and of Intent in the Soviet Famine of 1931-1934", 2005; R. Conquest, *The Terror*, 18-9; O. Mathews*, Stalin's Children, 2008*)

The Holodomor is a personal story for Owen Mathews. His grandfather was Boris Biblikov, an official Party man at the new Kharkov Tractor Factory (KhTZ) completed by July 15 1931 in astounding record time in fifteen months. "By 25 August 1931 the first trial tractors were coming off the assembly line. …Twenty thousand people assembled in the giant machine hall for the official opeining. … A biplane flew over the site, scattering leaflets with a poem entitled 'Hail to the Giant of the Five Year Plan'. The foreign journalist with the yellow boots was there too, 'just as sloppy, but less confident.' Vavara, the peasant girl whom he had scoffed at, had been to the factory school and was now a qualified steel presse. Grigori Ivanovich Petrovksy, head of the All-Ukrainian Central Committee of the People's Economy, cut the ceremonial ribbon, walked inside the hall and rode out on a bright red tractor covered in carnations and driven by champion woman worker, Marusya Bugayeva, as the factory bank played the 'Internationale' …. Dozens of tractors followed. Poems are sung, slogans chanted. People cried, others screamed 'It's a miracle!' But behind the universal jubilation, further catastrophe was unfolding in the countryside. The KhTZ's tractors came too late to make an impact on the 1931 harvest, which, after the ravages of collectivization, was disastrous. The projected 'grain factories' were producing little more than half of what the same countryside had yielded five years before. The peasant's only way to protest against the loss of their land and homes was to slaughter their animals and eat as much of their food supplies as they could before the commissars came. Eyewitnesses from the Red Cross reported seeing peasants 'drunk on food', their eyes stupefied by their mad, self-destructive gluttony, and the knowledge of its consequences."

The Kremlin sells grain abroad. Mathews observes, "the state demanded grain not only to feed the cities but also to export for hard currency in order to buy foreign machinery for projects like the KhTZ. Soviet engineers were sent to the United States and Germany to buy steam hammers, sheet steel rolling machines and presses with trunkloads of Soviet gold, all earned from selling grain at Depression prices. The KhTZ's American steam hammer ("one of only two in the whole country" sic), which Biblikov was later accused of sabotaging, cost 40,000 rubles in gold, the equivalent of nearly a thousand tons of wheat, enough to feed a million people for three days."

For the month of October 1931 "the Soviet Government requisitioned 7.7 million tons of a meager total harvest of 18 million tons. Most went to feed the cities, strongholds of Soviet power, though two million tons was exported to the West. The result was one of the greatest famines of the century." Harvest figures for the period published on the Ukrainian Canadian Congress in Toronto (2008) reveals harvest figures: 18.3 millions of tons of grain (1931); 14.6 tons of grain (1932); 22.3 millions of tons of grain (1933). It adds, "The Soviet regime dumped 1.7 millions of tons of grain on the Western markets at the height of the Holodomor". The same Toronto report recalled, "In late 1932 – precisely when the famine struck – the Central Statistical Bureau in Moscow ceased to publish demographic data. On Stalin's orders, those who conducted the 1937 census, which revealed a sharp decrease in the Ukrainian population as a result of the Holodomor, were shot, while the census results were suppressed." (O. Mathews, 37; Ukrainian Canadian Congress website, <holdomorsurvivors.ca>, Holodomor Suvivor Documentation Project 2008, Toronto, Canada)

In fact, when Stalin imposes full repressive measures on the peasants in the USSR in early 1930 Rakovksy is one of the older Bolsheviks among the leading Trotskyists to see "the real results of collectivization" and critically challenge Stalin's scheme. Rakovsky writes in "Bolshevik' no 7":

"Behind the fiction of collective farmer-proprietors, behind the fiction of elected managers, a system of compulsion is being erected that goes far beyond anything that already exists in the state farms. The fact of the matter is that collective farmers will not be working for themselves. And the only thing that will grow, blossom and flourish will be the new collective farm bureaucracy, bureaucracy of every kind, the creation of a bureaucratic nightmare. ... Collective farms, with all strata of the peasantry united under one roof (with the exception of the obvious kulaks), will find themselves bound at every turn by the iron chains of the bureaucratic apparatus. The collective farmers will suffer privation in everything, but extensive compensation will be provided for this in the form of officials and protectors, open and secret. Once again this confirms the fact that bureaucratic socialism perpetually breeds new bureaucrats. The socialist society, therefore, which official scribblers assure us is already close at hand, can never be anything else but a kingdom of bureaucrats."

In advance by two years Rakovsky predicts the next step of Stalin's brutality and a throwback to Tsarist repression by the insistence on passports "to suppress their flight to towns and cities and reports from the terror-stricken death fields." None of that eludes the British Embassy which sends dispatch January 23, 1933 stating "there is small chance that Soviet agricultural production will respond favourably to the multiplication of elaborate paper ordinances such as these, any more than it does to open terror". (R. Conquest, *Harvest of Sorrow*, 171, citing Public Record Office Handbooks no. 13, *The Records of the Foreign Office, 1782-1939*, London, 1969; R. A. Medvedev, 78)

"During the Revolution I saw things that I would not want even my enemies to see," Bukharin writes before he is shot in the 1938 Purges. Party opposition to repressive collectivization in support of peasant resistance collapsed under the overpowering control of Stalin. Bukharin and the right-wing faction were too weak. Stalin won the contest for Party leadership. The famine split the rift between Stalin and the hardened Bolshevik old guard; Bukharin and others too were horrified at suffering inflicted by the Terror-Famine. "During the Revolution, Bukharin declared in the same statement, "I saw things that I would not want even my enemies to see," Bukharin writes before he was shot in the 1938 Purges. "Yet 1919 cannot be compared to what happened between 1930 and 1932. In 1919 we were fighting for our lives ... but in the later period we were conducting *a mass annihilation of completely defenseless men together with their wives and children.*" By late 1932 Stalin's assault on the peasants remaining in the villages leads to inevitable famine in the Ukraine, the North Caucasus and the Lower Volga. A Soviet publication in 1988 stated "this famine was organized by Stalin quite consciously and according to plan." (R. Conquest, *Harvest of Sorrow*, 20; O. Mathews, 39; italics added)

THE WASHINGTON CFR MEN PLAY "THE GAME"

Ever since its founding in 1921 by President Wilson's closest adviser "Colonel" Edward House, the CFR has dominated State Department thinking. Journalists are literally sworn to silence, for a paycheck and career opportunities that guarantee their family security. I graduated from Yale with many blue bloods of the Establishment, worked in New York in a special office attached to the Secretary-General at the United Nations Secretariat, spent some time in the Far East, for two years attended to the Washington's prestigious renamed Paul Nitze School of Advanced Studies in International Affairs (SAIS) before chucking that to take a humble sub-editorial post in the Paris-based *International Herald Tribune* (ownership shared by *The New York Times*, *Washington Post*, and the French). My university circle of friends and acquaintances included the Lodges, Brewsters, and Davisons, Bundys, Walkers, Cheneys and Ishams, Bohlens, Buckleys and Bunkers ... and so many others among that isolated gated community of the Yale crowd and defined how elite it all can be in that reality divorced from the real world of the oppressed and impoverished struggling humanity in need of food and water in order to live another day.

It was a special race. One giant yacht against another, a yacht with no name, and its owner skipper a mystery. We sailed after the Admirals Cup and the Fastnet from Cowes to Valletta for a sea race in the Sirocco winds of Sicily back to Malta. Our crew learned the challenger was Rothschild himself, aboard *Benbow,* an black eighty-foot maxi-racer; aboard *War Baby*, skippered by Warren Brown of Bermuda who had bought the ex-America's Cup boat converted to ocean racing from CNN-founder Ted Turner and racing legend. (Brown owned several racing boats from Turner, including the famous *Tenacious*). Reader what concerns us here is to understand that these people live in a very private world, indeed. Sometimes we are granted access and glimpses into their lifestyle, tidbits of amused pleasures of their everyday comforts.

The Baron and Brown. He came and went with the wind in the dark. No one on our racing boat ever saw our opponent in the flesh. In the tradition of Sopwith and Vanderbilt of the J-Boat era of the Holodomor thirties, two boats, two men in the private world of millionaires and manipulations on terraces overlooking the sea, in private gardens or behind thick doors that enclose secrets are tightly sealed by their keepers, and nothing left behind, not even a case of wine for their competition, our crew!

Educate yourself to "The Game". The CFR people own it. Forget television and mass media with their trickle-down entertainments. Don't be fooled. Or let yourself be reduced to 'deaf mute' status that Lenin and Stalin applied to the ignorant and manipulated Russian hordes of their Bolshevik Revolution, paid for and financed by international centrist bankers.

The CFRs, the Bilderbergers, Trilaterals of the world chain of international bankers and lawyers inside the IMF, the World Bank, the Export-Import Bank and sundry key institutions all share a common mission. Pushing forward, in June, 1991 the CFR co-sponsors an assembly titled "Rethinking America's Security: Beyond Cold War to New World Order", assembling 65 prestigious members of government, labor, academia, the media, military, and the professions from nine countries. Before long several of the conference participants joined some 100 other world leaders for another closed door meeting of the David Rockefeller's private *tete a tete*, the Bilderberg Society in Baden Baden, Germany.

The 1991 Bilderbergers' (European-based globalists) opening speaker is Chase bank chairman David Rockefeller himself endowed with untold billions. He tells his privileged and grateful disciples, "We are grateful to *The Washington Post The New York Times*, *Time*, and other publications whose directors have attended our meetings, and respected their promises of discretion for almost 40 years. It would have been impossible for us to develop our plan for the world if we had been subject to the bright lights of publicity during these years. But, the world is more sophisticated and prepared to march towards a world government. The supranational sovereignty of an intellectual elite and world bankers is surely preferable to the national auto-determination practiced in past centuries." Rockefeller donated $100 million to Harvard in 2007, part of $900 million dispersed in philanthropy. The Bilderbergers also exert considerable clout in determining the foreign policies of their respective governments. At that meeting David Rockefeller personally thanks the ranks of his fellow Consortium propaganda pundits. World centralized banking is programmed to run economies and keep The Game globalized and in Consortium control. Look at the present day financial crisis of 2008. It's the same old story with every new crisis. The classic French proverb uttered by the Rothschilds, Warburgs and Morgans in Paris and around the world is more appropriate than ever: *Plus ca change, c'est la meme chose.*

The principal leader for the Holodomor cover-up in the US media was *The New York Times*, followed by magazines *Time*, *Life*, and *Fortune*, all owned and personally promoted by their creator Henry Luce. I considered it a privilege to work with the editors and an honor to leave the *International Herald Tribune.* Installed in Paris with a new-born son I passed through there in those youthful days as a subaltern editor in finance and quickly got by as a junior writer with full page published byline but left after refusing to bow down to those masters of deceit after an internal row of jealousy with the Old Guard hacks who dine themselves royally in Parisian elegance while indulging in the banter and buffoonery of complicitly corrupt lives, delighting in rewarding themselves and fellow members with inane prize-giving and self-congratulatory celebrations. These men either love or cringe in the pomp and circumstance. *La noblesse oblige.* For the most part genuinely talented and sincere, above all else they are obliged to keep up their pretense as trustworthy citizens and honorable good men and women. Too many of these fake journalists are largely, by hook and crook, and cleverness, institutional liars clever at editing out the truth lest it embarrass their owners, and give away some of the secrets of "The Game".

Though I did get only a glimpse of the legendary *Washington Post* publisher herself Martha Graham, and one-third owner of the *IHT* when she visited our building in Neuilly, I remember the excitement when the otherwise staid editorial floor came to life in the August doldrums of a Parisian summer 1985 as the wires reported that Sakharov's wife, Elena Bonner, would be allowed to travel outside the country for medical treatment and that the Politburo had ended Sakharov's exile.

Gorbachev tells him, "You can return to Moscow together. You have an apartment there. Go back to your patriotic work!" "Gorbachev later acknowledged that," Christopher Andrew observes, "of all the deputies elected to the congress, Sakharov was 'unquestionably the most outstanding personality'." Before the end of the year and after a harsh snub by Gorbachev ignoring "tens of thousands" of signed telegrams calling for an end to the dictatorial one-party communist system, Sakrahov dies of a heart attack. The KGB's "Public Enemy Number One" and Nobel Prize winner is dead. That month I left "the *Trib*" with a high recommendation letter in my pocket from the chief editor Walter Wells, and with six months of French unemployment checks embarked on a journey into the digital revolution overtaking modern civilization and published into the next decade an international computer animation image magazine, *Tech Images*. It was one hell of a ride in the early days of the late eighties with Siggraph and the makers of the new wave of the digital age of the Internet that transformed the old economy into a new cyber world once a compressed digital animated data file could be pushed through the wires. (C. Andrew and V. Mitrokhin, 321-2, 333; late summer 2013 Amazon founder Jeff. B. Bezos with over $61 billion in sales bought *The Washington Post* for $250 million.)

That being said it's worthy to note the *Herald Tribune* ever since its origin in 1835 when it was first founded as a penny paper by James Gordon Bennett, is also the establishment paper where Joe Alsop (Groton, Harvard, OSS, CIA, Vietnam hawk, friend of Kennan and Harriman...) first got his start in New York as an reporter $18 a week city reporter. He stays three decades until it falls under its new owner-publisher-billionaire "Jock" Whitney it flounders; Alsop jumps to *The Washington Post*, in 1961. But in 1932 the *Herald Tribune* can still boast a half-million readers in a fat Sunday edition and 300,000 daily, and turns a profit even during the Depression with a circulation 70 percent of the city leader, *The New York Times.* With its offices in the big *Herald Tribune* building on West Fortieth Street, the paper that year adds Walter Lippmann to its syndicated columns, and carries an extensive network of foreign offices mainly from London, Paris, Berlin and Moscow. Unfortunately, events in Russia are too remote to concern Alsop; by 1932 with Stalin firmly in control of the Party and issuing orders to prepare for the Holodomor Terror Genocide directed at the grain belt of the Ukrainians. But Alsop observes none of that and leaves no account of the on-going American engagement there. (R. W. Merry, 44)

To be anyone of importance in this world you have to be an institutional player in "The Game", with weekly invitations which keep you in the welcoming line of the black tie balls and dinners of the privileged, institutes and conferences and rub shoulders with the Consortium types served by waiters in white gloves and black dinner jackets there to satisfy your every need. To this day, the media corporations represented in the CFR, and the more recent Trilateral Commission : *CBS, NBC, ABC, PBS, CNN, Washington Post, New York Times Co., Wall Street Journal, Newsweek, US News and World Report, Time, Associated Press* and *Reuters* (both of which local papers rely upon). Journalists profit from the social relations in their professional and private life. They like that. It doesn't matter too much to them if they are used as tools for semaphoric domination and control. Many senior TV news media celebrities are CFR and TV personalities, the old and new guard: Dan Rather, Mike Wallace, Walker Cronkite, Tom Brokaw, David Brinkley, John Chancellor, Barbara Walters, Diane Sawyer, Robin McNeil, Jim Lehrer, Daniel Schorr. David Brinkley (CFR), speaking to a meeting of the American TV/Radio Broadcasters Association, said this of the American people: "All they know about public policy is what we tell them." Their list of prominent "talking heads" in that era of the Holodomor is very long. Little has changed today. See for yourself today; go to some CFR functions and pinch the guest list.

The Holodomor tragedy is a world tragedy. It occurred in Ukraine but it was known to the powerful politicians throughout Europe, England and Washington. They chose to ignore it for political expediency, economic profits and global geopolitical strategy. These world leaders had altogether another plan to put into place. Equally devious they put a nice face on the demonic cataclysmic horror. Some insiders understood, marginals like Bill Bullitt, FDR's sidekick as America's first ambassador to Stalin stepped out of line, and duped one way and another are eventually overtaken by events and swept aside out of the rank and file. The ground may feel solid but when walking on thin ice even the most cynical and dispassionate observers are left behind in the wake by the monstrosity perpetuated on the world. No more medals and promotions for the unfaithful who no longer serve the cause of the masters.

Before official diplomatic relations confirmed the status quo, Stalin, by 1933, is firmly entrenched in power with the finance and technology of the Consortium from the victorious postwar nations and planning to liquidate the last of his rival Old Bolsheviks along with their families and friends. Stalin is the master Machiavellian; he hold on absolute power leaves space for no rival. Eventually when it suits his strategic interests during the war FDR likens Stalin as "his brother" much to the bewilderment of the Russian. Stalin never had a brother. Nor does he have friends. Those close to him in rank and position always fear him; Stalin only has victims and he prefers it that way. For her part FDR's wife, Eleanor, is a Delano, and surrounds herself with the liberal reform movement and communist sympathizers of the American Left. And when she is attacked in the press during FDR's 1936 campaign for supporting the American Labor Party, she wrote a woman judge that "I, too, must admit that the American Labor Party tempts me!" FDR easily wins a second term with a one-sided victory. The Consortium sees to it that Soviet dependency on US technology is contained and never becomes a serious issue to break the unity of their strategy. (J. P. Lash, *Eleanor and Franklin*, 449)

When the cry of Humanity is silenced, the outcry of the world is buried under their propaganda and plans of deception for the next war and world federation in the postwar settlement that collapsed after WWI. The second time around, these same architects for the New World Order, have aged, are more experienced They planned and executed the Consortium Big Business agenda with renewed vigor and determination culminating in the Stimson-Bundy-Acheson-Forrestal-Marshall-Harriman generation of the Cold War architects, and the secret "S-1" atomic bomb detonated in 1945. Some age well, mellowed like a fine wine, stout veterans of a righteous cause to the very end, and enjoy ripened years in sweet retirement; others turn sour, bitter, hardened with sealed lips and a weak vacuous look of veiled amnesia in their stare.

Since November 1933, after the more resistant peasants and workers had already been silenced and severely disciplined by the Party, FDR proudly reached out to congratulate the Great Dictator. At the time an alarming number of Consortium leaders openly envied Stalin's masterful hand over the population as an example to follow in America. That is a real concern to many observers across the political spectrum. Next year Stalin's emissaries are welcomed into the League of Nations, predecessor to the United Nations "club of dictators", as a UN diplomat and longtime friend preferred to call it.

Victims of the Holodomor warned the world of the treachery of Stalin. When newspapers were controlled by members of the Council of Foreign Relations, – or by Luce and other rabid anti-communists, – the lack of denunciation of western investment in Stalin's régime was consistent with the Consortium drive for technological mechanization of modern progress. Both the State Department and the media in America were partners in the perfidious denial. A few journalists and brave editors and publishers tried to get out news of gulag repressions, terror and the peasant famine. But they were quickly overcome by the majority of newspapers controlled by the powerful Morgan and Rockefeller interests, and marginalized. Their outrage perished with the cries of the victims in Ukraine.

The story of the Ukrainians sacrificed to the powerful financial interests in America who rule over the world economy through their American and global network of governmental, political, economic and social organizations and corporations, had long term consequences for succeeding generations. Today, in Ukraine and Russia, Franklin Delano Roosevelt has the reputation of "a great man". That is what the people of Ukraine think even today. Little do they know about him or the powerful financial forces operating in his administration and influencing his mind. These forces are still operating today, unchecked and more rich and powerful than ever.

Contemporary Ukraine is engulfed in a morass of post-Soviet corruption and gangsterism of billionaire politicians creating a new generation of elite mafia parliamentarian. Impoverished and raped of resources, this nation of beautiful and strong children and young adults risks to be engulfed by a calamity of misfortune leaving it ranked among the worlds poorest countries. And there was a joke circulating in Kiev where I lived for four years that the Ukrainian Parliament is "Kiev Knesset", renamed in honor of the legislative branch of the Israeli government, that passes all laws, elects the President and Prime Minister, appoints the cabinet. It is a fact of life that the Jews have returned to Kiev to take over the businesses from the less organized Russian Ukrainians. Go see for yourself and ask any well-informed Russian or Ukrainian and you may be surprised at what you hear. Nor would it be naïve to think that with Yushchenko gone there may be a movement inside the government and parliament to shadow the Holodomor as a day for national reckoning. It would be a sad day for Ukraine and the world if issues of the Holodomor were twisted by attacks of anti-semitism.

At present day the financial crisis that began to drastically unravel in October 2009 and in many ways was not dissimilar from the stock market in 1929 could happen any time for much the same reason with the multitrillion dollar American debt and the billion dollar interest subsequently accumulating each day added to the debt burden. The same organization and market forces that existed then, still exist today although more elaborate and sophisticated in their methods and mathematical models for creative accounting and the creation of money by these international bankers who have bankrupted America and threaten the world economy and world order. The American Federal Reserve Bank is at the heart of the system, a sort of center of the wheel around which all the organizations and personalities revolve. No one is immune from it today. All American taxpayers are dependent upon it and send their money to the government with checks endorsed by a Federal Reserve Bank. That money – and the gold – goes to the creditors of the US Treasury in payments of debt obligations. The money goes to international bankers. In the Federal Reserve Bank of New York alone, some *nine thousand tons of gold* worth on a given market day between 60 to 70 billion dollars is stored in its vaults in over a hundred compartments eighteen feet deep.

Little did the people comprehend how in 1932 Consortium men in the federal government control the network of Federal Reserve network of privately held banks and has done so ever since its creation in 1913. Consider the following excerpts from the *Washington Post Weekly* (May 4, 1992): "The IMF, the World Bank, and the major industrial nations have decided to take a risk with Russia and former Soviet Republics .... Russian Deputy Prime Minister Yegor Gaidar ... last week swept through Washington, reassuring business leaders, as well as finance ministers and central bankers from the Group of Seven major industrial nations."

The US taxpayer underwrites about 20% of the IMF and World Bank funding, but the aforementioned G-7 central bankers are also shareholders in America's Federal Reserve Bank. The *Washington Post* added, "In an effort to get the banking system under control," *The Washington Post* story continued, "Gerald Corrigan, the President of the New York Federal Reserve Bank (CFR and Trilateral Commission member sic), has been visiting Moscow regularly since September (1991) to advise the Central bank and commercial banks. An acquaintance of former Fed Chairman Paul A. Volcker (CFR and Trilateral Commission member, sic.), says Volcker is close to an agreement that would make him consultant to Russian President Boris Yeltzin."

A brief look at recent history sharpens the focus on the century's post-colonial slide into the "New World Order" of the Consortium's shaping of the world community as they intend it should be. During that tumultuous year of the Vietnam War mid-summer, on July 26, 1968, Republican candidate for the White House Nelson Rockefeller brazenly pledged support of the New World Order and carried in an Associated Press report. Rockefeller told the AP reporter that "as President, he would work toward international creation of a New World Order." Four years later during his visit to China in 1972 President Nixon raised his glass in a toast to veteran Communist leader Premier Chou En-lai (Zhou Enlai), a former CFR member and President of the People's Republic of China. Nixon put forward "the hope that each of us has to build a New World Order." The next year the Trilateral Commission is founded by David Rockefeller who taps Zbigniew Brzezinski, – soon President Carter's National Security adviser, – as the Commission's first director and thirty years later a chief architect in America's Middle East global strategy "to fight terror". Carter is also joins the Trilateral founding members.

In April, 1974, *Foreign Affairs* published the article "The Hard Road to World Order" written by a former Undersecretary of State, Trilateralist and CFR member

Richard Gardner. He wrote "the 'house of world order' will have to be built from the bottom up rather than from the top down... but an end run around national sovereignty, eroding it piece by piece, will accomplish much more than the old-fashioned frontal assault." Two decades pass before *Foreign Affairs* publishes an opening article by CFR Senior Fellow Michael Clough titled "Say Good-Bye To the 'Wise Men'", stating the "Wise Men" (e.g. Paul Nitze, Dean Acheson, George Kennan, John McCloy) have "assiduously guarded it i.e. American foreign policy for the past 50 years .... They ascended to power during World War II .... This was as it should be. National security and the national interest, they argued must transcend the special interests and passions of the people who make up America ....How was this small band of Atlantic-minded internationalists able to triumph.... Eastern internationalists were able to shape and staff the burgeoning foreign policy institutions .... As long as the Cold War endured and nuclear Armageddon seemed only a missile away, the public was willing to tolerate such an undemocratic foreign policy making system."

These are the same government insiders with their friends who kept the lid on top of the secrets of their support of Stalin and the Communist Party dictatorship. You understand, reader, that dictators are good for business. For the Consortium, there is nothing better than direct, secret, noncompetitive access to monopoly resources. To hell with the free world they say if you read their lips. Save all that rhetoric for the liberal bleeding hearts promoting freedom and democracy for the masses. True believers inside the Consortium understand their priorities and serve to protect with undivided loyalty. Wars are not won by idealists and dead heroes; they are won by courageous killers and ruthlessly doing their duty. (*Foreign Affairs*, "Say Good-Bye To the 'Wise Men", Jan./Feb., 1994)

"The Cold War should no longer be the kind of obsessive concern that it is," declares George Ball, former Undersecretary of State and senior CFR member. In his interview with *The New York Times* in January, 1988, Ball comments, "Neither side is going to attack the other deliberately. If we could internationalize by using the U.N. in conjunction with the Soviet Union, because we now no longer have to fear, in most cases, a Soviet veto, then we could begin to transform the shape of the world and might get the U. N. back to doing something useful... Sooner or later we are going to have to face restructuring our institutions so that they are not confined merely to the nation-states. Start first on a regional and ultimately you could move to a world basis."

Addressing a UN forum on December 7, 1988, Soviet President Mikhail Gorbachev called for mutual consensus saying, "World progress is only possible through a search for universal human consensus as we move forward to a New World Order". Six months later on May 12, 1989, President Bush choose a college student assembly in his home state Texas to declare that America is ready to welcome the Soviet Union back into 'the world order." With the end of the Soviet Union in sight Boris Yeltsin is elected President of the Russian Federation June 12, 1991 with 57.3% of the vote and a 74% national turnout, according to reports.

The scholar-journalist Neal Ascherson was there and provides an appropriate account ing in *Black Sea* (1999) when Yeltsin joined hundreds of demonstrators in front of the White House of the Russian parliament to silence the deafening roar of tanks sent by the army coup plotters. "They went on until the bows of the tans which had gone over to Boris Yeltsin touched the bowes of the lead tank still loyal to the army command. Then the demonstrators sprang on board and raised the Russian tricolour and yelled at the crew inside to surrender. In that night, between 20 August and 21 August 1991, the coup failed. Most of the foreign journalists wrote afterwards that it had been bound to fail; its preparation had been feeble, its organization slovenly and chaotic, its leaders drunk and irresolute.

"But I was there too, and I do not think so. In most of the provinces and republics of the Soviet Union, the leadership submitted or rallied to the plotters. The people, appalled but resigned, for the most part did nothing; if the usurpers had held on for another few days, the coup against Gorbachev might have consolidated. Only the determination of a few thousand people in Moscow and Leningrad, challenging the will o the plot leaders to slaughter them, broke their nerve."

And in the frontline there was a force even greater than all that of the coup plotters combined, more powerful than their weapons and will to conspire against the essence of the spirit throughout Russia and touching every heart and mind. I too saw this profound outpouring of human force and dignity constantly present day after day wherever you turned, on every street and market place, in every bus and tram and train later in 2004 during the Orange Revolution convulsion against Yanokovich and the old guard of reactionary pro-Russian Ukrainians in Kiev and Kharkov in Donetz and along the Crimean coastal towns. Never double cross your Mother! For all his crimes Stalin never betrayed his Mother; he even rebuilt her house in the Kremlin so she could be near to him making it into a shrine for all of Russia to see his humble proletarian past.

Ascherson knows this to be true. And reader, right at this moment as I write, protesters with rocks and sticks and shovels are killed in the streets of Kiev demonstrating against the corruption of the pro-Putin Yanokovich government mid-January 2014. Here Ascherson writes of the downfall of the USSR in 1991: "The front line of the Moscow resistance was a chain of women holding hands. They made a cordon across the far end of the Kalinin Bridge, looking up the dark boulevard along which the tanks would come. Every few minutes, somewhere in the distance, tank engineers who were both young and old, stood an anxious support group of husbands, lovers and brothers with flasks of tea, transistor radios and cigarettes. When I asked the women why they stood there, and why they were not afraid, they answered: 'Because we are mothers.' .... On the third morning, the sun came out and the plotters went away." (Neal Ascherson, *The Black Sea*, NY: Hill and Wang-Farrar, Straus and Giroux, 1995, 40-3)

On August 24 Gorbachev ceases to be General Secretary of the Communist Party of the Soviet Union. In Madrid, on October 30, two months after the failed military coup, Gorbachev used the forum of the Middle East Peace Talks to declare, "We are beginning to see practical support. And this is a very significant sign of the movement towards a new era, a new age... We see both in our country and elsewhere ... ghosts of the old thinking. ... When we rid ourselves of their presence, we will be better able to move toward a New World Order... relying on the relevant mechanisms of the United Nations." A week later, on November 6, Yeltsin issued a decree banning all Communist Party activities on Russian soil and the country rapidly disintegrates into social chaos and economic anarchy; Gorbachev resigned on 25 December and the Soviet Union was formally dissolved the following day; two days after Gorbachev vacates his office. With Putin at his side Yeltsin on 27 December assumes the leadership of the Russian Federation and remains in office until 1999. He has only eight years to live.

Alas, Gorbachev's world tumbled as the Soviet economy falls apart.. He calls it quits, rescued by the West where he puts his savings in a foundation for peace and disarmament. Next to go are Russia's vast resources in the great sell-off managed by Putin and his handful of clever and vicious oligarchs and the ruthlessly organized KGB gang. The Red Army is owed nearly a half-billion dollars in back pay so they start selling off their military bases to international arms dealers – tanks, airplanes, anything they can get their hands on. In the scramble for weapons the US works frantically to buy up all of Ukraine's nuclear arsenal, the worlds third largest. That story has never been told.

Believe what you will, but first filter the facts from fiction. Then quickly move on. Stalin reminds us that truth is protected by a battalion of lies. If you want to be a true believer, find the truth in the lie. Or be the idiot that the rulers and manipulators want you to be. Ask questions, find answers and stay on track, focused on events passing by before they fade from view. That's why historians and researchers always have to look backwards and return to events when they first occurred, looking for sources, records, traces of the past before its lost, forgotten or destroyed, then reconstruct until the pieces fit in the right places and then its clear again for all to see.

You don't have to be a clever dialectician turning concepts inside out and stripping them of any inherent meaning to find the truth in an argument, or behind the curtain or in the missing piece, that elusive Rosetta stone of understanding. Be careful of the diversions and false paths and dead-ends. Prepare yourself for some shocking revelations, and remember that for the most part, what you learned in high school you can toss away on the garbage heap of false history, rhetoric and propaganda, a fairy tale of incongruous dates, names, places, paths that lead nowhere, and ghosts.

Essentially even in this faster dynamic new digital world the same system operates in place. It is the system that financed the world wars, choose and supports dictators, and their corrupt politicians to expedite their business interests and bankroll managers. Of course, digital technology has a way of jolting tradition and spinning public school old dons on their heads morphing one clone into another. Everything moves faster and secrets become less easy to hide. Yet these same forces of individuals and organizations invested in Stalin and built the Soviet economy. It is a well documented fact. You can read scores of books on the subject. Now we can see how the terrible human tragedy of Ukraine, "Little Russia", was one of the first victims of that devious and cynical extension of centralized financial and corporate power, controlled by a few individuals in banks and political organizations in the United States, with their friends in England and abroad, in preparations to set up the New World Order of communism, containment capitalists, and the illusory Cold War. As I write the world media broadcasts from Kiev December 2013 as several hundreds of thousands of anti-government protestors in Kiev denounce Ukraine's further shift away from the European Union under Yanokovich and his lackluster capitulation to Putin's hardball economic pressure. In the continuing showdown Ukraine's PM denounces the opposition leaders forcing a shutdown of government bureaucracies and attempting to stage a "coup" against his government, charges that are quickly dismissed by western ambassadors as a normal process of popular participation in a democracy. Young people are digging up the old cobble streets to use as projectiles against the heavily-armored police reminiscent of the student uproar in Paris 1968.

FROM ATOMIC WAR TO COLD WAR

Versailles was bad but Yalta and Potsdam proved altogether disastrous for the free world and very nearly might have ended in nuclear Armageddon. The Cold War, like Stalin's Plan for Industrialization, was an incredibly good business deal for American industry. It was a natural logical by-product of World War Two, and a very good deal for its planners, with some exceptions, like the "Mr. X", – George Kennan–, the Russian "expert" and propagandist for the Cold War embedded in the Truman-Nitze generation of cold warriors. I met Paul Nitze (Harvard 1927, Dillon, Read & Co.) at SAIS in Washington, of Johns Hopkins University. Little did I know back in the early eighties there sitting alongside the affable and elegant man, that he and with his wife's Pratt-Standard oil fortune and baronial country estate, was in fact a charismatic Georgetown prince of the era. Paul Nitze along with Christian Herter were co-founders of the school while he performed war work as chief of the Metals and Minerals Branch of the Board of Economic Warfare on his way to becoming director of Foreign Procurement and Development in WWII.

Condemned for war crimes Nazi *Reichsministser* Albert Speer, in 1951, who always felt he shared much in common with Hitler's aesthetics, recalls meeting Nitze, "while I was in Flensburg". Nitze, for his part in the play, "interrogated me extensively about armaments and aerial bombing", and he "wrote expressing sympathy for my situation in Spandau." In prison Speer records his satisfaction from having been comforted by Nitze's interest: "in the midst of this world of underlings, of guards and directors, a man of my own background and position is speaking to me; a former enemy, moreover, who in this way testifies to his respect. Friendly as many of the guards are, I really enjoy not being 'Number 5' for once." Oh, sure! Great job the Germans did with their V-rockets killing hundreds and destined to flatten London.

Hitler's release of terror against England in the bombing of the London Blitz inspired retaliation led by the head of Bomber Command in February 1943, Sir Arthur Harris, or better known by his staff as "Butch", as in "the Butcher" and his plan to shorten the war and save Allied lives, bombing civilian targets day and night with "the right kinds of bombs". His logic to win with a new air war was simple: "It has been decided that the primary objective of your operations should now be focused on the morale of the enemy civil population in particular, of the industrial workers". On May 20 he exercised his first assault with hundreds of two-engine bombers dropping 14 hundred tons of mostly incendiary bombs on the ancient city of Cologne. At the Casablanca Conference in January 1943 Roosevelt and Churchill officially approved the directive by the British Chiefs of Staff calling for mass fire-bombing of civilian urban centers: "the progressive destruction and dislocation of the enemy's war industrial and economic system, and the undermining of his morale to a point where his capacity for armed resistance is fatally weakened".

Late May 1943 Bomber Command ordered the "total destruction" of Hamburg by "at least 10,000 bombs". Operation Gomorrah begun on the night of July 24, with Hamburg less damaged than Cologne with 1,500 killed by some 1,000 incendiary bombs; three days later close to 800 bombers, mostly Lancasters with Halifaxes and Stirlings flew across the channel dropped another 1,200 bombs. By midnight July 28 Pathfinders dropped yellow flares and bombs to keep Hamburg in flames. A flight officer observed that night was "the daddy of them all". Author Ricard Rhodes describes the event in *The Making of the Bomb* (1987): "The burning of Hamburg that night was remarkable in that I saw not many fires but one.... I saw no flames, no outlines of buildings, only brighter fires which flared like yellow torches against a background of bright red. Above the city was a misty red haze. I looked down, fascinated by aghast, satisfied but horrified." The one-hour bombing raid created a *Feuerstrum* (firestorm). Fire-fighters were helpless against engulfing the hurricane death winds, their hoses "no more than throwing a drop of water o n to a hot stone". Human beings melted, screaming as their hands and knees stuck in burning asphalt. Rhodes writes, "The firestorm completely burned out some eight square miles of the city, an area about half as large as Manhattan. The bodies of the dead cooked in pools of their own melted fat in sealed shelters like kilns or shriveled to small blackened bundles that littered the streets." (Richard Rhodes, *The Making of the Atomic Bomb*, NY: Simon & Schuster, 1986, 469-76)

Just two years before Hiroshima and Nagasaki, Bomber Command returned home leaving behind 45,000 dead, mostly civilians, old men, women and children. Mass-murder and extermination were bookends to the technological potential of total war. Churchill saw that clearly during the Dunkirk evacuation in 1940 and the advent of the Battle of Britain when he wrote his Minister of Aircraft Production: "... when I look round to see how we can win the war I see that there is only one sure path ... and that is absolutely devastating, exterminating attack by very heavy bombers from this country upon the Nazi homeland. We must be able to overwhelm them by this means, without which I do not see a way through."

Rhodes describes how this logical path of destruction and extermination combined with enhanced "death technologies" in a race against time to win and end the war. He writes, "The other way the belligerents could escale was to enlarge the range of permissible victims their death technologies might destroy. Civilians had the misfortune to be the only victims left available. Better hardware and software began to make them also accessible in increasing numbers. No great philosophical effort was required to discover acceptable rationales. War begot psychic numbing in combatants and civilians alike; psychic numbing prepared the way for increased escalation. Extend war by attrition to include civilians behind the lines and war becomes total. With improving technology so could death-making be. The bombing of Hamburg marked a significant step in the evolution of death technology itself, massed bombers deliberately churning conflagration. It was still too much a matter of luck, an elusive combination of weather and organization and hardware. It was still also expensive in crews and matérial. It was not yet perfect, as no technology can ever be, and therefore seemed to await perfection." (R. Rhodes, 469-75)

No comment from Speer about the Allied saturation bombing of Hamburg, an industrial target, in April 1945. Devastated by Operation Gomorrah the former elegant and thriving metropolis Hamburg was entirely incinerated with more than 80,000 casualties and some 42,600 civilians and a total of 118,000 people killed, nearly 300,000 houses destroyed, and three thousand ships sunk in the harbor. All of Hamburg's beauty and splendor acquired over centuries lay under 43 million cubic meters of ruin. In 1977 I delivered a German Admirals Cup racing yacht from Cowes to Hamburg and was stunned by its barren and starkly modern urban sterility. (R. Chernow, *The Warburgs*, 532)

Nor was Dresden spared. In February 1945 2000 planes annihilated 90 per cent of the city center, killing from 20,000 to 200,000 people depending on the estimates notwithstanding discrepancies in the numbers. (Speer declared Nazi war production in general was little affected by the massive Allied bombing and quickly recovered.) In one day and night 35,000 people were killed and though Dresden is a rail center "the city's railway links, pretext for the Allied bombardment, were relatively unscathed ... the city possessed no special significance," writes Max Hastings in *Armageddon.* But it was the British command, principally Sir Arthur Harris and Churchill who personally instructs him just prior to the Yalta conference to use massive air force against Germany's cities, with no regard to civilian casualties, as did the RAF squadron briefers "to show the Russians when they arrive what Bomber Command can do". Of course there were high airmen "casualties" on the Allied side; airmen are more likely to die than survive the war. RAF's Bomber Command lost 56,000 personnel "almost double the fatal casualties suffered by the American bomber men in Europe", Hastings observed. The Allies launch thousands of bombers darkening the skies Europe and Germany. In March another massive USAAF raid destroyed the famous Vienna Opera House burying 160,000 costumes and sets for 120 shows; the last performance was Wagner's *Gotterdammerung.* (M. Hastings, *Armageddon*, 335-7)

Paul Nitze (1907-04) was then an undersecretary in charge of Policy Planning Staff having left a successful career on Wall Street during the Depression years to follow his former boss Jim Forrestal, FDR's new appointee in charge of procurement and production for the Navy. The war for Nitze promises to be a winning ticket and his new career taks off; in 1944 he serves as vice chairman of the United States Strategic Bombing Survey leading to the decision to use nuclear bombs on Hiroshima and Nagasaki. Two decades later Nitze is sitting at the long table in Kennedy White House, part of his ExCom team during the fall 1962 Cuban Missile Crisis with full operative understanding of nuclear protocol procedures with Air Force commander General Curtis LeMay and Admiral Anderson; the hawkish Nitze is appointed Undersecretary of Defense during the Vietnam War, remaines active on CIA affairs, and in the Reagan era oversees SALT (Strategic Arms Limitations Talks) negotiations with the Soviets from 1969 to 1973.

As we know Pilgrims can afford to be very generous. Married to a Pratt (Rockefeller) oil heiress, Nitze gave a cool ten million dollars and persuading the Johns Hopkins University to rename its graduate program the Paul H. Nitze School of Advanced International Studies. That's how it works in America. I sat in a seminar with him for a while; it was strange to see this Cold War icon so relaxed talking about catastrophic military adventures but then again, he was one of the victors enjoying semi-retirement with a younger generation and no leader wishes to be redundant. They abhor it. Mandating history and buying institutional immortality for the perpetuity of the culture stamped yearly on new diplomas for young generations to hang on their walls every year. This is one way America's greatest values of virtue are sustained by evolving tradition and carved in stone. In America, money has its big rewards, whether you are an arms trafficker with your name on American University's library, or a Cold War hawk. (I skipped graduation having fallen in love with a talented astute beautiful French girl in Paris who two years later gave birth to our son. I never went back. *C'est la vie.*)

If only Russia was less suspicious about the benefits of philanthropy but it is already starting to take off. Russian philanthropy is still in its infancy. In 2010 Medvedev and Putin made both appearances at various charitable events and met with representatives of NGOs and foundations." "Philanthropy is going public. After years of mistrust and existence on the margins of society, philanthropy is finally coming out of shadows", declares Maria Chertok, in December 2011, director of CAF Russia and a board member of the Russian Donors Forum. With funds destined mostly to universities or various cultural institutions, "more than 40 endowments were created in the last 2-3 years", she said. (A. Speer, 172; Maria Chertok, "Trends in Institutional Philanthropy in Russia," <Philanthropynews. alliancemagazine. org>, Dec. 15, 2011)

Big Business and philanthropy are common bedfellows in the capitalist market economy. Philanthropy created and sustains democratic institutions and sustains private universities strengthening education and building lasting reputations. It's like that everywhere in the Ivy League whether at Columbia, Harvard Princeton or Yale. Kennan had to settle for a Princetonian Institute to promulgate his reputation as America's distinguished Russian expert and diplomat; he gave the name, not the money. Averell Harriman must be laughing ever since. (There is an institute in his name too, naturally.) Harriman occupied the US Embassy in Moscow to oversee operations there during the war. Kennan of lower rank will get his chance too, serving briefly as ambassador in Moscow, a token plum assignment, yet he knew he would never be an insider either in Moscow or Washington. There are only a few places for foreign policy decision-makers at the top of the Consortium.

Big names in Big Business and Big Politics like Big Partners. Just like Big Money likes Big Money. In order to take out Germany and Japan FDR needs Stalin and a Big War. Just like Stalin needed FDR. Each prepares for what they consider to be the inevitable world war and whether it be called a class struggle of capitalist imperialists or a grab for world hegemony and control of resources doesn't figure at the top. The Cold War was an even bigger business arrangement that would overwhelm both Stalin and two generations of American presidents.

How far ahead did the planners of the Cold War set it in motion? Once communism established its borders and could no longer function as an international movement, with Trotsky pushed out, and Stalin's renunciation of world communism, Stalin was already isolated, alone and contained with Hitler and the Japanese imperialists in the Eastern frontier breathing down his neck.

For the war planners, the Ukrainian problem was secondary and a major potential embarrassment. Cynicism prevailed after the First World War, the communist revolution and civil war. Those who survived the hardship and loss struggled to get on and rebuild. People were lost in the numbers. Even Death became abstract, incomprehensible. So what if a few people die...they were only Russians, right? What did it matter anyway when there were so many, and so many perished in WWI, twenty *million*, a figure too extraordinary for the American public to ever contemplate. So why tell them? For the most part Americans know what the corporate war makers wanted them to know. How could Americans even possibly conceive that Russian fatalities from World War II would amount to some twenty-eight million dead men, women and children? Americans have a hard enough time getting their numbers straight on their annual income tax forms or balancing food prices. Let the Americans play until its time to scare the hell out of them.

Strategies of cohesion and restraint have become a standard government public relations ploy to gain the loyalty of national voters before elections and wars. Its an old political trick later employed so voters would accept the democratically approved massive expenditures and consequent fatal casualties such as laid out in the master plan for the Cold War -NSC-68 which had been finalized only two months before the outbreak of the Korean War in which the Sino-Soviet rivalry played no small part. Cold War planners knew what they were doing. The military costs for the Cold War were high but substantially less than the cost to the impoverished world. This scenario is still operational in the post-Cold War of Bush's "War on Terrorism".

Negotiations in the of the First World War settlements didn't remove the chances for another outbreak of war. On the contrary, once the weakened powers were reconstituted, a second world war was clearly intended to finish what was left incomplete from the preceding one. Negotiations were incomplete and unsatisfactory. Versailles was a disaster. Borders needed to be redrawn. All Cold Warriors knew that. They only disagreed on how "The Game" was actually bought and paid for by American business deals with Stalin and the Soviets, and not to alarm too much the American public caught in the propaganda and war by proxy (Korea, East Asia, Africa, Central and South America).

Stalin always knew how dispensable peasants were to Russia's defense during wartime. It was always their duty and historical fate, to toil like farm animals, drink festively, praise the Motherland – Mother Earth –, during times of peace, and leave the land to defend it as they had done for centuries filling the ranks of the Czar's armies. In 1939, Stalin's comments to a small group of Comintern and Politburo members on September 7, where he spoke of maneuvering between the Anglo–French coalition and the Germans. "We see nothing wrong', Stalin said, 'in their having a good hard fight and weakening each other". Weeks later Stalin said: 'We preferred agreements with the so-called democratic countries and therefore conducted negotiations. But the English and French wanted us for farmhands … and at no cost!".

During World War II Stalin often repeated the same line to foreigners. Is it any wonder Stalin sent peasants to battle not with guns or ammunition but with orders to take weapons from dead Germans. He used the NKVD secret police organized in 1943 as SMERSh, military agents of counter-intelligence to shoot deserters and spies.

In Vasily Grossman's (1905-64) long suppressed memoir, *A Writer at War*, and finally published posthumously, in 2005, the former commissar observes, "Any soldier who failed to denounce and to shoot down comrades who attempted to desert was treated as an accomplice." As a war reporter Grossman covered the front with the Red Army and witnessed the battles of Moscow, Stalingrad, Kursk and Berlin. In the Ukraine and Poland he featured reports on Nazi ethnic cleansing there and, in 1943, he collected some of the first eye-witness Holocaust accounts of the Treblinka and Majdanek extermination camps. Conquest acknowledged that Grossman also denounced Stalin's extermination of the Ukrainians, as the inevitable result, he said, of collectivization and political repression of the peasants.

Vasily Grossman writes, "The decree about grain procurement required that the peasants of the Ukraine, the Don and the Kuban be put to death by starvation, put to death along with their little children." Before the war Grossman, too, narrowly escapes Stalin's Purges. (He had been nominated for the Stalin Prize but cut from the list personally by Stalin as too close to the Mencheviks.) His wife is arrested but released in 1938. He lost his mother living in Berdychiv when the Nazis invaded and exterminated tens of thousands of Jews there. Eventually, after the war, Grossman repeatedly clashes with Soviet officials and his manuscript of *Life and Fate* condemned in 1959. Grossman writes Khrushchev: "What is the point of me being physically free when the book I dedicated my life to is arrested. … I am not renouncing it.... I am requesting freedom for my book." (R. Conquest, *Harvest of Sorrow*)

After the war, Stalin executes and imprisons returning Soviet POWs, their crime having surrendered instead of fighting to the death to defend the Motherland. NKVD executions and death squads target deserters and stem a massive Russian retreat and collapse of military discipline, mass desertions and severe reprisals of soldiers and the civilian population suspected of aiding or giving comfort to the enemy. Commissar Beria's NKVD units produce at least 600,000 hardened liquidators.

"In the course of the war," British historian Max Hastings observes, "168,000 citizens were formally sentenced to death and executed for alleged cowardice or desertions; many more were shot out of hand, without a pretense of due process." A total of around 300,000 Russian soldiers are believed to have been killed by their own commanders – more than the entire toll of British troops who perished at enemy hands in the course of the war." Hastings adds, "Suicide units were composed of Soviet soldiers who escaped captivity and were captured by the NKVD; on average one unit for each Soviet army; others were sent to the camps and industrial plants in Siberia." (Geoffrey Roberts, *Stalin, the Pact with Nazi Germany, and the Origins of Postwar Soviet Diplomatic Historiography*, 94-5; V. Grossman, *A Writer at War,* 2005, 71; M. Hastings, *Inferno*, 148-9; Geoffrey Roberts, *Stalin's Wars: From World War to Cold War, 1939-1953*, Yale Univ. Press, 2006)

The players and interests were virtually the same planners for the Second World War. The war history could easily be interpreted as the greatest American business success story. Ideology and talk about democracy and freedom served a vision of splendid idealism to win the hearts and minds of simple people and the masses, with the aim to control them and make them subservient and obedient workers, and consumers, to pay taxes, in order that the powerful interests could realize colossal profits so that the leaders continue to play "The Game".

Well over two decades before the Internet revolutionized access and the flow of digitalized information instantaneously at your finger tips to assist scholars in their inquiry, Antony Sutton put his finger on facts laying dormant and covered up in countless State Department documents, many declassified and on microfilm. His findings indicate that it was the Kuhn Loeb firm which principally benefited as a primary partner that financed Stalin's two Five-Year Plans for the agricultural and industrial development of the Soviet Union in the late twenties and early thirties.

Sutton's work in our time remains largely ignored by the establishment mainstream press controlled by Consortium interests. Sutton's findings were and still are mind-boggling. In light of the continued suppression of the truth and given the evident and remarkable myopia of scholars or intentional neglect of the data, reader ask why Sutton is rarely cited in the source credits of these published scholars and writers as though his work never existed. The classic three volumes were in fact published by Stanford University (and the Hoover Institute!) in the 1970s. So, it can hardly be merely bad scholarship by this herd of establishment historians who depend on Consortium financed institutions for their lives. You see reader, disinformation and the continued denial and ignorance or dismissal of the data falls within the parameters of Consortium logic to maintain the taboo and divert attention to Consortium historiography. Sutton's conclusion comes after years of research focused on American investment and compiled his study of US-Soviet economic and trade transfers *Western Technology and Soviet Economic Development 1917-1960.*

Their avarice in the First World War was superseded with riches beyond the dreams of Kings - while destroying many of them – and earning themselves specially appointed seats in the American war government, all of whom were perfectly positioned in the militarized American society sent marching off to combat while they grab the spoils of the destabilized Russian Empire and literally overnight enslaved the Russian masses under "revolutionary" decrees building the "New Society" issued by their Bolshevik Politburo Central Committee.

Lenin, Trotsky and Stalin promised a "brilliant" future to mold the Soviet communist society. Instead, the people, Russian as well as American industrial workers and peasants were betrayed by their leaders. When the American people finally wake up and understand how they too have been deliberately lied to and cheated by the political power of their federal government and the politicians bending like reeds to special interest groups and lobbies of the Consortium, perhaps they will at least understand and appreciate the sacrifice of the Ukrainians and why they were liquidated without as much as a mummer or any official government outcry in Washington or London.

THE HOLODOMOR – A CLASSIFIED GOVERNMENT SECRET

The US State Department abhors controversy and handles it badly. Before the outbreak of famine it shadows the information and for decades after classify documents to keep them sealed off from the public.

There had to be good reasons for why such secrecy about the Holodomor is imposed by the US government. Much of the story of the Holodomor still remains either classified or destroyed. For a half-century the US government always maintained an official profile that it never existed in such severity, and certainly not in the context of the Consortium's logic of war and reconstruction for the new world of huge military defense appropriations and populations transfixed by fear of atomic Armageddon of the Cold War era. For the most part, official references to the famine are hard to find, and very few, out-of-date, and when they appear at all often appearing in secondary sources, memoirs, and books published long after the actual Terror-Famine repression. In fact, it was not a subject to be openly discussed. FDR's cleansing of the Russian section after Bullitt's tenure as ambassador suggests that the President wanted to turn the page on that sordid past and move on towards a closer relationship with his future partner in war against Nazi Germany. He would have to wait until Hitler's Wehrmacht invades the Soviet Union in June 1941. But even that wouldn't be enough for isolationist America to wake up and fight. So he waited until the Japanese hit Pearl Harbor with the Germans ill-equipped for winter and under heavy snow in full retreat from their siege of Moscow. One thing Americans don't appreciate is a kick in their butt or a slap in the face. So with *millions* of dead Russians and three thousand dead Americans at Pearl, America went to war to save its former allies England and France.

It becomes more clear why the State Department bureaucracy did not list or officially monitor for public disclosure US investment in the USSR. It was too political, but on what level? That brazen cloak of deception stood out like a sore thumb. Yet, for the engineer-historian Sutton, such collaboration raised too many unanswered questions vital to national security and inconsistent with America's entire Cold War status. Or was the Cold War a chimera masquerading a darker secret reality of collusion between the capitalists and the communists?.

"Such lack of ordered information", Sutton writes, "would go far to account for many of the remarkably inaccurate statements made to Congress by officials of the State Department and its consultants in the 1950s and 1960s - statements which sometimes so far removed from fact they might have been drawn from the pages of Alice in Wonderland rather than the testimony of senior US Executive Department personnel and prominent academicians. In brief, a possibility exists that there has been no real and pervasive knowledge of these technical transfers – even at the most 'informed' levels of Western governments. Further, it has to be hypothesized that the training of Western government officials is woefully deficient in the area of technology and development of economic systems, and that researchers have been either unable to visualize the possibility of Soviet technical dependence or unwilling, by reason of the bureaucratic aversion to 'rocking the boat,' to put forward research proposals to examine that possibility. This does not however explain why some of the outside consultants who were hired by all Western governments in such profusion, have not systematically explored the possibility. If it is argued, on the contrary, that Western Governments are aware of Soviet technical dependency, then how does one explain the national security problem?" (A. C. Sutton, *Western Technology and Soviet Economic Development,* 418)

Ineffective and weak, against a formidable adversary like Stalin, Bullitt was a complete fiasco in Moscow. The elite left him to flounder in his own delusion with no influence on the wolves in the Kremlin. Once the spectre of war recedes, in 1934, with the eclipse of the worst months of the Holodomor, Stalin turns his attention towards liquidation of the old remaining Bolsheviks. He plays with Bullitt and negotiations with the ambassador and soviet commissars sounds more like small violins weeping. Stalin is aloof, and their encounters are few and far between.

By October 1936, FDR packed Bullitt away from Moscow once Paris opens and there Bullitt finds the bliss he seeks enjoying the quaint bourgeois comforts near the Champs Elysées across from the Eiffel Tower and the gardens of the Louvre. There, at ease in his large apartment and chateau all he must do is entertain and await Hitler's *blitzkrieg.* France lacks an adequate air defense and has no will to fight another world war. Meanwhile, FDR dismantles the entire State Department's expert Russian section except for a few key insiders.

In Moscow Bullitt was still remembered for his secret mission in 1919 promoting recognition of Lenin's murderous Bolshevik regime and earning a public reputation as Washington's own Bolshevik. As ambassador he still curried favor from two aging power-brokers Col. House and Bernie Baruch. These two senior presidential advisers represented at least three decades of American ascendancy to global dominance and were still inside the loop backing FDR rise to the summit. To the Lenin-Marxists in the Kremlin, however, they were portrayed by the Communist Party as imperialists in the working class struggle of labor and capital and bound to perish along with the peasants of the backward Russian empire.

Ukraine, the ancient homeland of the Eastern Slavs. It is a beautiful land richly endowed with iron ore, coal, precious raw metals and some of the best black soil in the world making it the traditional breadbasket of Russia and Europe. Yet its grain lands were some of the worst hit by the "man-made" famine. Stalin forbid any food to be brought in to break popular resistance of the Ukrainian peasants. Meanwhile, badly in need of foreign exchange to pay for his bankrupt economy, Stalin ordered grain shipped and sold abroad on world markets.

Every bit of grain – and seed – was taken from the peasants not on collective farms. Stalin and his notorious secret police – the NKVD, until 1934 called the Cheka – starved them to death. Homes were regularly raided day and night. People were shot for "stealing" grain which they produced and needed to survive. Brainwashed children were publicly praised as heroes of the new Soviet socialist society for turning in their parents. Of those not killed off by famine, some 4 million Ukrainians were deported to labor camps in Siberia or to provide slave labor on mega-projects, for example, the building of the White Sea Canal, praised as a great bold example of Soviet success supervised by American engineers and technical advisers. It was an economic and humanitarian disaster.

Thousands of Ukrainian artists, writers and intellectuals vanished, the most brilliant and bold among them. Known as death camps or concentration camps a network of labor camps awaited the peasant spared from the executioner sentenced under Article 58 or by the "Special Board". Prisoners suffered extreme conditions where forced labor was extracted and classified under the Corrective Labor Codex in existence since 1918. Brutality of deprivation and sadism varied only in degree.

Conditions at prison camps on the northern White Sea were particularly severe. At the island Solovetski Monastery between 1929 and 1934 the average lifespan "did not exceed one or two years". The slave labor camps remained one of Stalin's best kept propaganda secrets. Instead of targets of virulent condemnation, from East to West they were praised as exemplary examples of revolutionary re-eduction under Soviet socialism. Criminals were mixed with "politicals"; non-criminal women were especially helpless in the mixed camps, frequently raped by camp guards, or mass-raped by "urkas", the name for criminals who lived by their own code. Women are forced to sell themselves for a crust of bread, or protection from camp authorities who anyhow will not relent to break them down if they resist.

Conquest writes in *The Great Terror*: "A typical story from the Baltic White Sea Canal camps is of a young woman who refused to give in to an official, who thereupon assigned her to a team of ordinary criminals who the same night blindfolded her, raped her, and pulled out several gold teeth. … There was no one to whom she could complain, for the camp chief himself was known to have raped several prisoners." Young village peasant girls, sixteen or seventeen were frequently seen in the camps, serving five years for stealing potatoes. My friend in Kiev told of his step-father who was a gulag director of a northern camp. "Not all criminals were ruthless to the politicals," he said. He liked my nickname for him, "Caponavich", saying it's a fitting description of contemporary Kiev with its lawless gangster culture. "It's only theory," my friend "Caponavich" said, "that said the criminals were inhumane. If you had education, the criminals would even look up to you *like a saint*." His voice rises slightly as though uttering their cry of hope. (R. Conquest, *The Great Terror*, 315)

Vira, a young girl born in 1920 in a village near Odessa on the Black Sea, comes alive again in a true story, "Wounds that time cannot heal / Ukrayina Incognita" published in the Ukrainian newspaper *The Day*. "Vira clearly remembers the events of the 1930s to this very day", wrote journalist Oksana Shapova. "Collectivisation was completed in the countryside by 1932. No wages were paid on the collective farm. Every villager had to complete 120 workdays in one working season. If someone failed to meet the target, she had to provide an explanation. At year's end, after the harvest was gathered, the greater part of it was consigned to the state, and a certain percentage of the remainder was divided into the number of days worked and then distributed among the peasants in the form of grain, peas, etc." (Oksana Shapova, "Wounds that time cannot heal, Ukrayina Incognita", *The Day*, March 26, 2006)

No one could silence the pain and wrenching heartache that successive American governments allowed to transpire without an official denunciation of Soviet terror that would certainly offend their client Stalin and disrupt the Realpolitik. How many tens or hundreds of thousands of young girls like Vira suffered unspeakable degradation and perished without a trace so that American companies could build Soviet tanks, Soviet aircraft, Soviet battleships, pump Soviet oil paid for by Soviet gold and the sweat of millions of strong and heroic people forced to work at the point of bayonets and machine guns and never lose their capacity for love of the Motherland and hope for survival?

Once the horrors of the First World War were suppressed, the Holodomor apocalypse might have been hard pill for shareholders to swallow. Political dynamite to spark a revolution of the masses in the United States infected with Soviet communist propaganda! Hardly, both shareholders and pro-Stalin liberals were already poisoned by greed or propaganda. The shame of it all! All Hell could break loose and turn on the elite clique in America that brought on the 1929 Wall Street crash and banking crisis. But that wasn't to be. What might the American Consortium authorities do? Declare a state of emergency in America because of dead Ukrainians in Russia? Not likely.

Contradictions of reality may appear more fantastic than the truth and become the stuff of true believers perverting their minds and actions with illusion, a chimera, the charade so that in the end the believer doesn't have a real clue of the true nature of the political reality. Instead, everything is defined and seen through a filter of false ideology, masterfully orchestrated by the magician illusion makers, in this case, the Communist Party ideologues in the Soviet Union, and the Consortium politicians and pundits in the national media. American propaganda is masterful and not less wicked than Stalin's Bolshevik machine. See who controlled the presses! In fact, the PR specialists in corporate advertising and message-making in American media, initially students of the British Ministry of Information and the Wilson's Committee of Public Information (CPI) during the Great War, trained the Bolsheviks on the art of mind-control and manipulation of the masses! It's a fact. The Marxist-Leninists owned the media. There were almost never any leaks. In America the news blackout of the Holodomor was a total success.

At Kharkov, the former capital of Soviet Ukraine, American engineers and managers knew of people dying on the city streets and the sudden absence of workers taken by the secret police but they remained silent about the horror and the crime. What could they do to help? Whatever could they do to stop this human catastrophe of which they too were part. Everyone knew. Russian observers and other State Department bureaucrats and journalists of the Moscow foreign press corps, acting no better than professional whores bought and paid for by the Consortium gang of influential newspapers like *The New York Times*, *Chicago Daily News*, *London Times*, UPI and AP wire services all of whom reported blamed the Ukrainians themselves for creating the conditions that destroyed them. Wined and dined by the Soviets, they blamed the victim for the crime. Promised land and freedom by the Bolshevik Revolution they lost everything they lost everything, condemned to death or prison for even owning a cow! Or a chicken! Capitalist pig stealing State property.

Of course the peasants hated the communists who made their life unbearable for everything they did. But oppressors never blame themselves. Why blame Comrade Stalin? Why scare off investors knocking at the door holding contracts and blueprints to build the glorious future of mega-factories, and who promised more shipments of western technology already pouring across Europe into southern Ukraine. So keen on victory of the socialist future, few in the power center cared to spoil the monopolists' dream with the agony of a humanitarian nightmare. Their logic was simple and not surprising: let the peasants starve and take the profits from war. In the general scheme, to the power elite it doesn't matter if ten or ten million peasants die. To paraphrase *New York Times* correspondent Walter Duranty, "No one is counting." Nor is Duranty, yet.

"In 1932," Vira recalled, "when it came time to distribute the earnings, it turned out that absolutely everything had been requisitioned. As people gradually found out, they began to contemplate using the previous year's reserves for the next year. At this very time the government decreed that all 'surplus' grain and other foodstuffs be consigned to the state because 'the country's working class was starving'... They would take away everything, no matter how many children there were in the family, or what age they were."

"Vira's peers, as well as younger and older children, stayed out of school. Instead, they would go to the harvested fields early in the morning to look for some thing edible. It was a great joy to find a mouse hole with a handful of grain inside. Whoever found such a hole would be over-joyed, while the other children looked on with envy. A wonderful find was an ear of corn or a frozen carrot... This lasted until the heavy snowfalls arrived. When the ground was covered with snow, the famine intensified. People ate everything they could get their hands on. There was not a single fowl, pig, or cow left in the village – even the dogs and cats began to be eaten. People were bloating and starving to death. Word spread that a mother had eaten her own child in a neighboring village and that human corpses were also eaten ... People died every day. They would fall dead right on the street, in the fields and houses; they were no longer buried or mourned. Pits were dug and several corpses were thrown inside one of them."

ODD COUPLE: THE SOVIET GULAG & THE AMERICAN DREAM

During the 1932-34 Terror-Famine, how many Americans would have dared to imagine that the communist Soviet Empire was a direct by-product of the American Dream? Reader, pause and think about it. Truth is a peculiar paradox. War is absurd, a sick rational for economic world order to benefit a few billionaires and their entourage. Give brainwashed people an illusion of freedom and security and they will march to any order. To the Consortium masters President Wilson and the Great War proved that all the lies of propaganda spin held a sacred truth. Only it's a Big Lie.

The masses neither in America nor in the Soviet Union were permitted to know what was happening behind their national economies. Anyone who dared to voice anti-Bolshevik theory or objections to the Party line were eliminated, deported to camps or killed; in America, Main Street lives in perpetual fear of the truth and is skilled in methods to contain it. The Consortium insiders knew the USSR to be the fruit of capital combined with Stalin's Five-Year Plans for agriculture and industry, which was for all practical purposes in reality a massively infused national industrial preparation for war driven by propaganda fed to both Soviet and American citizens with convoluted ideological dialectics spewing out Marxist-Leninist slogans and spurious catchy ideas tailored to consumption for everyone to swallow in both the USSR and the United States. And they did making the world dark and sick with the dead. In the fields and dusty streets of the Ukraine, but not on the finely manicured lawns of the rich Long Island estates or across the Sound where the Wall Streeters piloted their yachts to stately stone sanctuaries in Greenwich, Connecticut.

The aims of extermination of the Ukrainians were political. Once the wedge for gain and spoils was driven into the heart of Ukraine how could it not be so? Vira's dream was hardly the same American Dream portrayed in *The Saturday Evening Post*, *Life Magazine*, *Colliers* and other journals contrived by a few dozen giant American companies with familiar names like Ford, General Electric, Westinghouse, Standard Oil, International Harvester and so on. They were led by shrewd investors and banks under the relatively new centralized banking system of the Federal Reserve signed into law by President Wilson in 1913, the first year of his administration.. Her dream was survival.

In Depression America anyone interested in knowing the truth of American political ambitions for world power might have immediately suspected the nature of Stalin's terror-repression. Had they pieced together the news of Congressional hearings by United States Senator Gerald Nye's 1934 government investigations into the financial machinations and profits of the banks and "Dollar-A-Year" patriots and called death merchants running Wilson's war cabinet that managed the national economy with the thoroughness of a military dictatorship.

The portrayal of poetically-inspired rhetoric to honor the dead is a tired-out war theme. War is ugly and painful. FDR knew and lamented in a 1936 reelection campaign speech, "I hate war." But it didn't stop him or his clique from making it and taking the profits to their banks. Historians would never regard FDR as a humanitarian. FDR was a juggling trickster prone to long-winded anecdotal story-telling whereas Wilson acted no better than a pontificating liar. Whereas FDR fails to intercede to condemn or even acknowledge Stalin's war against the peasants, Wilson sharpened his own peculiar skills of rhetoric in 1880 as a student at Princeton. It was then a very English thing to do in Ivy League academia. FDR came out of the same private school system; both indulged in public oratory. Wilson's father was a God-fearing minister of the Christian church. Groton's Reverend Peabody too held sacred rituals and sermons that indoctrinated the sons of the elite to steer the nation from sin and educate the public to be good social citizens and follow their enlightened leaders. It is George Peabody who conducts the bible-swearing ceremonies to initiate Roosevelt's terms in the Oval Office.

CONGRESSMAN MCFADDEN DENOUNCES TREASON BY THE FED

In Washington DC, in 1932, Pennsylvania Republican Congressman Louis T. McFadden's statements about the Federal Reserve Banking System may have killed him. The entire investment scheme of the Morgan-Rockefeller-Harriman Consortium behind Stalin and the Five-Year plans of industrial and agricultural collectivization would most probably have been put at great risk from press exposure controlled by the same interests he publicly denounced. Intellectuals and academics on the Left would have had a field day attacking the insiders and war planners. As Chairman of the House Banking and Currency Committee Congressman McFadden declared America's centralized banking system was under the control of the men who also controlled the political economy of the nation - the banks, the politicians, the corporations, the newspapers. All of it. The whole circus. McFadden exposes numerous cases of currency and stock manipulations in the New York stock market crash leading to world depression, crushing foreign economies and foreign markets. Since the beginning of the slide in September 1929 to the end in July 1932, the Dow Jones Industrial Average fell off 89.2 percent. (William D. Cohan, *Lazard Freres*, 2007, 28)

On January 13, 1932, McFadden, serving nearly two decades in the House, had introduced a resolution indicting the Federal Reserve Board of Governors for "Criminal Conspiracy": "Whereas I charge them, jointly and severally, with the crime of having *treasonably* conspired and acted against the peace and security of the United States and having *treasonably* conspired to destroy constitutional government in the United States. Resolved, that the Committee on the Judiciary is authorized and directed as a whole or by subcommittee to investigate the official conduct of the Federal Reserve Board and agents to determine whether, in the opinion of the said committee, they have been guilty of any high crime or misdemeanour which in the contemplation of the Constitution requires the interposition of the Constitutional powers of the House." Congressman McFadden called the predatory international bankers a "dark crew of financial pirates who would cut a man's throat to get a dollar out of his pocket." (italics added)

On June 10, 1932, McFadden addressed the House of Representatives: "Some people think the Federal Reserve banks are United States Government institutions. They are not government institutions. They are private credit monopolies which prey upon the people of the United States for the benefit of themselves and their foreign customers." Today that may no longer sound very threatening, to a nation habituated to debt, and powerless to change the status quo or reduce their easy credit-debt obligations except by seeking more credit to pay spiraling debts. McFadden adds, "The Federal Reserve banks are the agents of the foreign central banks." That should have been enough to awaken most Americans out of their stupor. But they are infatuated with credit and debt making them virtually senseless to overcome the syndrome or recognize the role of the FED and the government controlling their lives.

McFadden quotes Henry Ford, another big investor in Soviet Russia, warning Americans, "The one aim of these financiers is world control by the creation of inextinguishable debts. The truth is the Federal Reserve Board has usurped the Government of the United States by the arrogant credit monopoly which operates the Federal Reserve Board and the Federal Reserve Banks." Ford also invested in Nazi Germany.

A smear campaign branded him insane. McFadden is publicly smeared and loses his seat in the next Congressional elections as money poured into his home district of Canton, Pennsylvania to defeat him. No action was taken on McFadden's resolution. So McFadden fought back and entered a motion on December 13, 1932 to impeach President Herbert Hoover. Only five Congressmen stood up to support it. The impeachment resolution was defeated by a vote of 361 to 8. Whoever dared to defy the power of the Consortium had no future in American political system. The Republican majority leader of the House uttered "Louis T. McFadden is now politically dead." He is removed from committees.

And yet to the very end in this year of the Holodomor McFadden persists to attack the Consortium banking nexus of the Fed. On May 23, 1933, he introduces House Resolution No. 158, Articles of Impeachment against the Secretary of the Treasury, two Assistant Secretaries of the Treasury, the Federal Reserve Board of Governors, and officers and directors of the twelve Federal Reserve Banks for their guilt and collusion in causing the Great Depression.

Congressman McFadden: "I charge them with having unlawfully taken over 80 billion dollars from the United States Government in the year 1928, the said unlawful taking consisting of the unlawful recreation of claims against the United States Treasury to the extent of over 80 billion dollars in the year 1928, and in each year subsequent, and by having robbed the United States Government and the people of the United States by their theft and sale of the gold reserve of the United States." The Resolution never reaches the floor. Critics including columnist Drew Pearson's *Merry-Go-Round* label him "crazy", anti-Semitic and widely quoted as pro-Hitler.

HOLODOMOR, SOVIET RECOGNITION AND THE 1932 BANK CRISIS

Shaken by the tumult of the banking crisis in 1932 the American people elected Franklin D. Roosevelt 35th President of the United States. That same year Paul Warburg died. For many skeptics FDR's election and Warburg's death meant freeing the people of America from the evil domination of Wall Street's investment banks. An era had passed so they said. That was far from the truth. On April 14, Mellon in haste vacates his office at Treasury for the plumb post as US ambassador to Great Britain at the Court of St. James. Personally welcomed by the Prince of Wales, Mellon settled into the luxurious compound, formerly JP Morgan's residence, and quickly became the favorite of Lords, Dukes and Earls. His son Paul Mellon and wife Bunny were frequent quests of His Royal Highness Prince Philip the Duke of Edinburgh and Queen Elizabeth who hosted in 1960 a reception in his honor at Buckingham Palace for promoting "Anglo-American understanding" (re. Anglo-American alliance) The Prince was a Pilgrim, of course. Among his sundry banking interests Mellon's son-in-law James Bruce, and a director of Federal Home Loan Bank of New York.

Author of over thirty books, William Hoffman's biography of Paul Mellon (1900-91) refers to the Mellon lion share of the $38 billion in US war profits from World War I. Mellon is the US Treasury Secretary during the decade of the twenties serving two presidents in a Republican White House, Coolidge and Hoover. After a dip in the market prompting Wall Street to close in 1914, it opened when European gold and orders flooded into America ending the American recession. Markets flourished. Wall Street boomed. Mellon's Alcoa, for example, sole producer of aluminium in America took in 72 million pounds in orders from Great Britain in the first two years. In "Financial Consequences of the War", an long and obscure academic paper by Francis Delaise published in the *Revue des Vivants* (Paris) in May 1933, – at the height of the Holodomor in the Ukraine and curiously at the same time of the World Economic Conference in London, revealed how as a result of the Great War, the United States had accumulated two thirds of the entire gold stock in the world. Timing is more than the mere coincidence of apparently dissimilar events which bear a causality of interconnectiveness bringing together what is more common than shared by their differences. These two events, the extermination of the Ukrainians in the Holodomor and the First World War both bear witness to the Consortium men of Versailles shoulder to shoulder on both sides o the balance holding gold in one hand and in the other the mass murder of the population of the Ukraine and in regions of their client state Soviet Russia elsewhere devastated by systematic starvation of Stalinist repression between the two world wars. (Pilgrim book, 2002, 45, re. 1960 reception; W. Hoffman, *Mellon*, 37; A. Shlaes, 113).

The Consortium bankers and businessmen reaped undreamed of profits, rewards and medals while young boys and men, and civilians were blasted to death in the faraway war. Take a look here in figures assembled by Lawrence Turner comparing wartime and prewar profits: gunpowder from DuPont: 1910-14 yearly average $6,000,000/ 1914-18 yearly average $58,000,000; Bethlehem Steel: 1910-14 yearly average $6,000,000/ 1914-18 yearly average $49,000,000; United States Steel: 1909-14 yearly average $105,000,000/1914-18 yearly average $240,000,000; Anaconda Copper: 1910-14 yearly average $10,000,000/ 1914-18 yearly average $34,000,000; Utah Copper: 1910-14 yearly average $5,000,000/ 1914-18 yearly average of $21,000,000; Central Leather Company: 1911-14 yearly average $1,167,000/ 1916 $15,000,000, increase of 1,100 per cent; General Chemical Company: 1911-14 yearly average $800,000/ War $12,000,000, increase 400 per cent; International Nickel Company: yearly average $4,000,000 to $73,000,000 yearly an increase of more than 1,700 per cent; American Sugar Refining Company averaged $2,000,000 a year for the three years before the war. American Sugar Refining Company recorded a profit of $6,000,000 in 1916. The 65th Congress tabulated corporate earnings and government revenues of profits during the war of 122 meat packers, 153 cotton manufacturers, 299 garment makers, 49 steel plants, and 340 coal producers. Turner observed, "Profits under 25 per cent were exceptional. For instance the coal companies made between 100 per cent and 7,856 per cent on their capital stock during the war. The Chicago packers doubled and tripled their earnings. The shoe people sold Uncle Sam 35,000,000 pairs of hobnailed service shoes. There were 4,000,000 soldiers. Eight pairs, and more, to a soldier. My regiment during the war had only one pair to a soldier." (US Sen. Doc. No. 259).

Leading those families who figure prominently over others who reaped exorbitant profits during the First World War are "the Rockefellers, who were very eager for the United States to enter World War I (and who) made far more than $200,000,000 from that conflict." Malcolm Pratt Aldrich was head of the Commonwealth Fund, another British Empire front, founded by Standard Oil billionaire Edward S. Harkness (b.1870), a member of London's Pilgrims Society. In 1924 the Harkness family fortune was estimated at $800 million. According to Ferdinand Lundberg (1902-95) in his book *The Rich and the Super Rich* (1969): "The Standard Oil branch of the Harkness family was found to be among the twenty largest stockholders in no fewer than 24 of the 200 largest companies, apparently a record." In the thirties the Harkness family left its name permanently built in stone at Yale University. One of its outstanding landmarks there is Harkness Tower centrally located, a few steps from Skull & Bones; a huge clock encased overhead with chimes keeps time for thousands of students and shadows the Old Campus, scene of Yale's graduation commencement ceremonies. Eternal vigilance. (F. Lundberg, *America's 60 Families,* 1947, 26; F. Lundberg, *The Rich and the Super Rich,* NY: Bantam, 1969, 189)

The Mellon fortune spread like fertilizer on the bedrock of American culture. Philanthropy is the art of giving your money away in order to have more and that freedom too is taken away by government taxes and nasty bureaucrats. An apparent contradiction perhaps, but not really. When they weren't giving paintings away for the masses, – the National Gallery and its art collection in Washington DC is a gift from Andrew Mellon –, they catered to the elite, for example, the Yale Art Gallery from Paul Mellon. The money of these billionaires is everywhere, but they shun publicity. It's a tax exemption while they evade public exposure at how their fabulous wealth nurtures the American political economy which they control through their elaborate combinations. Mellon ranks with Rockefeller among the richest Americans. Income-tax figures for 1923 released the next year show JDR, Jr. paid the highest at $7,435,169; his father liable only for $124,000, amounting not much more than pennies on billions. The Fords, Henry and Edsel were next, with $2,467,000 and $1,984,000, respectively. (J. Abels, 312)

Mellon also provides a prestigious headquarters for influential associates and functionaries including General Matthew Ridgeway, Allied Supreme Commander in Europe (1951-53), Truman's Army Chief of Staff until 1955 is also a Pilgrims Society member. He leaves government to chair the Mellon Institute (1955-60). In 1967 the Mellon and Carnegie institutes merged into Carnegie-Mellon University. When *Fortune* prepared its first list of the wealthiest Americans, in 1957, four of the richest eight people in the United States were Mellons (Paul, his sister Ailsa Mellon Bruce, and two cousins) with a combined fortune well over 2 billion dollars. A serene Mellon estate on the Connecticut River is located minutes away from my writing desk.

During the height of Stalin's Purge Trials in Moscow across on the other side of the world US Senator Gerald Nye's Investigation Committee hearings that began in 1934 rolling over the ruins of the economic wasteland as a result of delocation in the aftermath of the Great War (1914-18). Until their abrupt termination three years later the Senate hearings finally starts looking into corporate government accounts worth billions of dollars that poured into America's industrial war chest. Baruch is serene throughout the whole proceedings. "All wars are economic in their origin," he candidly tells the government's investigators. The Nye hearings get a boost with the Book-of-the-Month Club's bestselling book *Merchants of Death* by two bright scholars with degrees from H. C. Engelbrecht (University of Chicago, Columbia, Harvard) and former editor of *World Tomorrow,* and F. C. Hanighen, foreign correspondent for *The New York Times* and *New York Evening Post.* Morgan's war business as the enterprise and objective of their syndicated loan campaigns is specifically held responsible with their "corporation clients and banks which dominate the American arms industry". (S. J. Pak, 208)

Even with the Nye Senate inquiry into the Morgan-Rockefeller-Harriman clan running the US war industry as though it was their own private investment club, FDR, a former War Department man himself, knew the Senator was right on the money but went too far into Wilson's suspect dealings with Consortium war trafficking. After 200 witnesses and 93 hearings the senator's funds are cut and his vigilante circus shuts down. It was too much and had gone on too long. Nothing must interfere with the Consortium strategy for world war. Its time for "the Lost Generation" of the Hemingway twenties to start forgetting and get on with business as usual and doing things the traditional old way not because the doing is good but because its the way things are done before and as far as the old men with their old habits and old education think is the way of the future. Reader, are their heads screwed on backwards, or is yours?

Days before FDR's Inauguration the Congress was getting down to business hard on the Consortium banking system. The US Senate Pecora Hearings in 1933 on National City Co., and Morgan's lead investment house and strongest collaborator is and top syndicate partner is having its worst day ever as its private activity is under national exposure by the political investigation. In the years between 1895 and 1934, Suzie Pak concludes, National City held a total "over $1.6 billion with 391 participants for 110 unique clients (that) "was only surpassed by First National Bank of New York, which had a total of $2.7 billion and 709 participants. (First National has 189 unique clients.)" Then Jack Morgan is the first person called before the Nye Committee to testify on the practices of the private banking Consortium he leads and for which he is a national symbol of the progress and success of American capitalism. (S. J. Pak, 204)

National City Bank chairman Charles E. Mitchell is forced to resign. In the national press scandal Mitchell narrowly escapes prison for income tax invasion and pays a fine instead. He is personally assailed for unethical securities transactions.

Feeding on the public vigilante frenzy in his inaugural speech with Bible in hand Roosevelt attacks the bankers for casting sin and shame and misery on the American people. "Practices of the unscrupulous money-changers stand indicted in the court of public opinion, rejected by the hearts and minds of men.... Faced by failure of credit they have proposed only the lending of more money. Stripped of the lure of profit by which to induce our people to follow their false leadership, they have resorted to exhortations, pleading tearfully for restored confidence. They know only the rules of a generation of self-seekers. They have no vision, and when there is no vision the people perish. The money changers have fled their high seats in the temple of our civilization. We may now restore that temple to the ancient truths." (S. J. Pak, 205)

The approach of old men applying traditional answers to new problems is futile and counterproductive. Not only that it is also archaic and entirely wrong, or as Aldous Huxley put it clearly in *Brave New World* during this period, "hopelessly unsound", and like their educators who suffer in the "debaunched kinesthetic sense", being as they are, out of touch with the natural order and spirit of the universe in which they live and must nurture in order to survive and advance civilization to discover new understandings of the natural world and human existence. So when Roosevelt makes his bellicose and vague pronouncement reader, this may be hyperbole and out of step but its not. Huxley stressed the value of heeding the wisdom in the "educational methods" of the Australian F.

M. Alexander recognized by the predominant educator in America John Dewey of the day who contributed prefaces to three of his books, but lacked Alexander's particular disposition essential to knowledge. It is of concern here reader that from the start the logic of the "inveterate 'end-gainers'." and namely, the entire slew of our educated and ambitious Consortium opportunists and their friends as well as clients, is doomed. The tragedy is to be found there in the fact that it exists in all its wicked forms, and everything that contributes to it is there to be exposed to the public, its ultimate victim. That is why it is forbidden, kept secreted away, in prison cells and graves and in an endless trail of documents filed and locked in the dark. Huxley reminds us, from the start, noble ends never justify rotten means; it just won't work. At least not when the goal is health, peace and prosperity for more than the chosen few of self-proclaimed leaders and rulers of nations.

"We are anxious", Huxley writes, "to achieve some particular end that we never pay attention to the pyscho-physical means whereby that end is to be gained. So far as we are concerned, any old means is good enough. But the nature of the universe is such that ends can never justify means. On the contrary, the means always determine the end. Thus the end proposed by the Allies in the First World War was 'to make the world safe for democracy.' But the means employed was unrestricted violence, and unrestricted violence is incapable of producing world-wide democracy. Unrestricted violence produces such things as fear, hatred and social chaos. Chaos is followed by dictatorship and dictatorship combined with general fear and hatred leads once more to unrestricted violence. This is an extreme case; but the principle it illustrates is universally valid." (Aldous Huxley, 'The Education of an Amphibian", *Tomorrow, and Tomorrow, and Tomorrow, and other essays*, NY: Harper & Brothers, 1952, ed. 1956, 15. Huxley refers to four books by F. M. Alexander all still in print: *Man's Supreme Inheritance, Constructive Conscious Control, The Use of the Self, The Universal Constant of Living*)

In the end FDR denounces Senator Nye's Committee as an irresponsible and an irritating public nuisance. Intent on deceiving Americans once again, and secure in his second term, FDR turns his statecraft towards carefully preparing the nation for more of the same– psychological propaganda for the masses and profits for a few insiders at a cost of destruction and death for millions of people in foreign lands.

On the other side of town, however. a professor of American history at Georgetown University Charles Tansill (1890-64) is racing to complete his book on the war trade, *America Goes To War*, finally published in 1938 after the rape of Czechoslovakia and Finland and only a year before the outbreak of war when Hitler butchers Poland. Tansill argues that US involvement in the First World War could have been avoided but was unnecessarily complicated over American trade and neutrality and other legal technicalities. Charles Tansill observes that as early as 1915 FDR had anticipated a major clash with Imperial Japan. Had a generation needed to pass before America is yet to learn from its own history? Rather than finding new solutions to old problems it appears the old order with their thinking unchanged even by a world war is reset to the same course toward world destruction for the dismantling and rearrangement of empire. Huxley sets his eye on the debacle when he writes, "The degree of wrongness may be great or small; but since all bad habits tend to become worse with time, it is in the highest degree desirable that they should be corrected at the earliest opportunity." (Charles C. Tansill, *America Goes To War*, Boston: Little, Brown, 1938; Charles C. Tansill, *Back Door To War: The Roosevelt Foreign Policy, 1933–1941*, Chicago: H. Regnery, 1952; A. Huxley, "The Education of an Amphibian", 13)

The ultimate tragedy is the American people still suffering an economic depression subserviently lower their heads diverting their eyes while preserving their faith in their constitutional right to happiness incarnate in the promise of the American Dream. Unfortunately, they confuse that pursuit with the moral integrity of their leaders and willy-nilly esteem both to be righteous and pure only this time in the face of crumbling empires the unfolding story is not just about Christians killing Christians.

FDR's fireside radio take over the rites of ritual of the warrior chief with "chat" about "Freedom" and "Democracy", – those inimitable Americanized catch-words on the tongue of every newly Americanized true-believer.

At the same time Ukrainians were stripped of their freedom, starved, and executed by Stalin's NKVD henchmen often led by Jews seeking revenge for centuries of Russian pograms. The Bolshevik leadership was comprised mostly of educated Jews. When Stalin later turned against the Jews in the 1952-53 "Doctors Plot", his motivation, as Robert Conquest suggests in *The Great Terror*, was more "a matter of policy rather than dogma". Whereas in the Soviet Union anti-Semitism is a capitol crime against the working class and the Party, Hitler raved about the Jewish communist threat. Hitler passionately hated Jews and Slavs and wanted to exterminate them both. Stalin's Jewish commissars killed Ukrainians. Hitler killed Jews, Ukrainians and Russians. Stalin murdered while effectively terrorizing the mass group of those left untouched – Ukrainians, Germans, Russians and Jews. Stalin targeted the Ukrainian population, selectively, listing individuals, sections, villages and regions and as a mass ground. The ultimate modern despot! FDR's "Uncle Joe" may be smiling, rarely, but behind the mask lurked ghoulish treachery to surpass the brutality of Genghis Khan, Ivan the Terrible or Tamerlane combined, enjoying a renaissance of popularity under Russian President Vladimir Putin.

"HE'S A SON OF A BITCH, BUT HE'S *OUR* SON OF A BITCH"

Remember what FDR said about dictators. The capitalist monopolists of collective world order sometimes like to moan how hard it is sometimes to find a really good dictator. Two decades after Wilson first sent thousands of marines, to Nicaragua, ostensibly for democracy handled by the United Fruit Company, FDR declared about the dictator there, "He's a SOB (son of a bitch), but he's *our* SOB". That logic conveniently serves as the excuse for training death squads to kill national liberation leaders striving for non-aligned independence and as we see with ambassadors Guggenheim and Welles its their dilemma in Cuba. And they argued likewise such logic affords a legal license for rape and murder, auxiliary dividends of a repressive investment Wilson nor FDR may have claimed a moral or humanitarian right of neutrality when preparing for war but they were under no moral compulsion not to lie about it. Such claims were meant only in rhetoric for mass consumption and political expedience in a popular democracy where voters entrust the politicians with power make the laws and legislate authority in the name of the people. The same logic pervaded arguments of the Cold War. If you weren't a capitalist, then you had to have been a communist, an enemy of popular democracy in the republic. To justify his invasion of Iraq, lies about weapons of mass destruction, empowered by the so-called "War on Terrorism", President Bush, in 2006, played the same game with his line "If you are not with us, then you are against us."

During the First World War, many of the journalists and advertising men who worked in Wilson's propaganda department of the CPI (Committee of Public Information) propagated President Wilson's rhetoric to sell the war and Liberty Bonds to the American people and raised 20 billion dollars to pay for it. When it came time ten years later, in 1927, for the industrialists and bankers to boost Soviet reconstruction under Stalin, the same experienced war gang applied their tricks of fund-raising to sell Bolshevik bonds. This same Consortium gang knew how little truth was needed to sway the masses into obedience and submission. Give them a dream and put them to see Let them think that they are free and rich and they will be happy and content and work like slaves to embrace the illusion.

Few people outside government circles have sufficient understanding to know that the "Fed" was established by House, Aldrich, Warburg, McAdoo and others behind the Wilson administration in the prewar years, and signed into law in 1913, essentially as a Consortium instrument to legitimate the national banking system under their private control. It was a slam-dunk carefully drafted orchestration signed into law after it had been pushed down President Wilson's throat by a handful of bankers and industrialists who then used it to finance their profiteering in the First World War clash of Empire. This Consortium of famous names and "Dollar-A-Year" millionaire patriots, then stack the Peace Commissions with their agents and lawyers, diplomats and spies, and subsequently pocket billions of dollars in profits and credits to flood postwar reconstruction of Europe with blood-stained dollars while ransacking Europe and Russia of its treasures. The Carpetbaggers did it after the American Civil War and now the Consortium gang would do it again but this time on a global scale. Build, destroy and build again, locally and globally, nation-building on an international scale. What did it really matter for the common people to understand the nuts and bolts of the insidious links between commerce, finance and government as long as women get the latest sewing and washing machines and the men can drive the latest flashy model automobile, with all the other iconic techno-emblems of "progress" that spread the dream of success so precious to the heart of the bourgeois consumer-capitalist thinking in the box behind the white picket fence and stone walls.

Hoover's Secretary of the Treasury Andrew Mellon was one of America's richest men. Mellon's own take was at least $200 million of the combined at $38 billion dollar pretax profits of the American industrial elite in the First World War. That this dwarfs the combined wealth of the richest American families by a few billion was revealed in 1910 during Teddy Roosevelt's Trust investigations before the war and only a year before the US government's anti-Trust lawyers ordered the breakup of Rockefeller's Standard Oil Company. DuPont was another. Morgan. Harriman. Rockefeller. Icons of American industry, finance and global power. Meanwhile, wages fell during the war years, and American workers were more impoverished living under runaway inflation than they were before the war. (W. Hoffman, *Biography of Paul Mellon,* 1974; G. Colby, *DuPont Dynasty*, 1974)

Nearly fifty years after the 1932-34 Holodomor when Professor Mace pursued the horror story of the Ukrainian Genocide at the same time the British undercover agent Robert Conquest turned out to be one of the first writers in the West to unearth the story in his book *Harvest of Sorrow.*

The following year, on November 13, 1987, James Mace presents his paper in New York, "The United States and the Famine: Recognition and Denial of Genocide and Mass Killing in the 20th Century, The Man-made Famine". Mace declares, "given the absence of internationally recognized human rights norms and an administration committed to closer ties with the Soviets, was seen as an internal Soviet affair, viewed with skepticism, or simply not mentioned. Politicians and opinion makers either turned a blind eye toward Stalin's famine out of expediency or saw sympathy for the Soviet Union as a litmus test of one's commitment to a more just society in this country. The tragedy is that the reality of mass starvation and collective victimization became politicized such that the question of fact concerning whether there was a famine was subordinated to the question of one's political values." Contemporary standards of human rights violations for rape, torture, murder and other crimes against Humanity never figured in the mind-set of perpetrators and witnesses of the man-made famine Genocide of the Holodomor. (R. Conquest, *Harvest of Sorrow,* 1986)

Food is a political weapon. Famine is politics, Soviet politics, American politics. Link it an you get Soviet-American politics. FDR granted official recognition. Stalin was ready, always waiting patiently for the opportune moment to snatch his prey. Stalin had long been America's client. Recognition and normalization of relations was both a *quid pro quo* and *de facto fait accompli* of Realpolitik. How crazy of Hitler to attack Stalin. Hitler made two fatal mistakes: he was a poor student of American history, and he underestimated the warrior spirit behind Russian nationalism when he provoked the fury of the Russian bear.

Before he died in 2005, Mace stopped short of disclosing the sinister pattern of economic subsidy and political manipulation behind the Terror-Famine or its role in Stalin's defense strategy of war preparedness in the advent of an outbreak of war in Europe. Bullitt's Moscow private memoranda to FDR frequently highlight the inevitability of war with Germany. Internal papers at the State Department also clearly show a reluctance to document the fact that the Communist Party's First Five-Year Plan for Soviet industry was under construction by American companies necessary for the Soviet modernization of Stalin's armed forces.

DR. MACE & THE 1987 REPORT ON THE "COLLABORATION" OF US OFFICIALS

Dr James E. Mace wrote in his 1987 paper on "collaboration" of US government officials with Soviet authorities to mask the famine: "There can also be no doubt that both the State Department and the White House had access to plentiful and timely intelligence concerning the famine of 1932-33 in Ukraine and made a conscious decision not only to do nothing about it, but to never acknowledge it publicly. For political reasons largely related to FDR's determination to establish and maintain good relations with the USSR, the US government participated, albeit indirectly, in what is perhaps the single most successful denial of genocide in history."

In this the Americans were not alone. The British record, for example, has also been partially told and was, if anything, worse. Mace writes in his 1987 paper, "The US government was made aware of conditions in the USSR by its embassies and legations throughout Europe, which sent extensive reports based on interviews with American workers and visitors to the USSR, Soviet officials, the foreign press, Soviet citizens and foreign nationals, all of whom understood the gross inefficiency of the Soviet system, the mediocrity of local Soviet management and increasing hostility of the peasants long before diplomatic relations were established with the USSR. State Department officials were aware of thousands of Soviet citizens fleeing to Poland and Rumania and of soldiers and civilian brigades being sent into Ukraine to assist with the harvest. Washington even received letters from hungry Ukrainian peasants, asking for assistance. (Dr. James E. Mace, "The United States and the Famine, "Recognition and Denial of Genocide and Mass Killing in the 20th Century: Collaboration in the suppression of the Ukrainian famine", paper presented in New York, November 13, 1987, *The Ukrainian Weekly*, January 17, 1988, No. 3, v. LVI)

Mace perceived the US government response four-fold:

1. "The official response to all queries regarding the horrors of life in the Soviet Union was to refer to them as 'alleged conditions'."
2. "The term 'famine' was used in diplomatic dispatches as early as November 1932."
3. "Inundated by queries and information regarding the famine, the State Department sought and received confirmation from Athens and from Riga, the premier US listening post for Soviet affairs, a month before FDR recognized the Soviet government."
4. "There can be little doubt that American journalists collaborated with the Soviets in covering up the famine."

State Department files prove, however, that long before recognition of the USSR by FDR, the White House had the information of Stalin's man-made famine sent by the US observation post at Riga in Latvia under the Division of Eastern European Affairs at Washington. Mace's conclusions bear this out. "As early as 1931," professor Mace writes, "the excessive seizure of agricultural produce had led to localized outbreaks of famine in Ukraine. An early indication of the hardships wrought by the Soviet state, the number of refugees fleeing to Poland and Rumania, was duly reported to the State Department." Stimson's gentlemen bureaucracy calmly went about its business over lunch and dinner parties all the while it had exhaustive records of famine even before 1931! And Stalinist terror methods are constantly creeping up in State Department Russian files. Official silence and taboo took care of that problem with women and a good Russian cognac!

William Christian Bullitt (1896-70) had access to that information long before he embraced and kissed Stalin for FDR. We have no record that it ever mattered to "Billy" Bullitt that Stalin exterminated the Ukrainians. Nor is there a trace of a record that he ever lost any sleep over it or lift a finger to help them. Instead, Bullitt is sent on a mission to badger and tease Stalin's finance commissars to pay back the money he owned to his friends at National City Bank.

For years Bullitt negotiated bank loans for the State Department while keeping an ear to political turmoil in London and Paris. For the Moscow job, Bullitt also relied on his confidential relationships from two key corporately-owned journalists, none other than Walter Duranty and Louis Fischer, of *The New York Times*, and *The Nation*, respectively. FDR, not unlike Hoover, collaborated with Stalin in suppressing the truth. Using both Duranty and Fischer, news was censored by Soviet agents and passed directly to the western press. FDR, too, relied on both Duranty and Fischer for an inside track to Stalin. Certainly there was a famine black-out but not entirely. Not everybody played by the rules. The younger Gareth Jones had ideas of his own. But the price was high. Stalin eliminates his opponents. And Jones pays the heaviest price going out alone where he dare whereas Duranty and Fischer interact closely with each other and with members of Moscow's Central Committee, spoke Russian, lived with Russian women in large apartments, and survived.

Louis Fischer knows how to play the Consortium propaganda game. In fact he's a grandmaster player and ends up with Princeton taking his private papers to add to their collections of prestigious Americans; reader, keep an eye on Fischer and figure that one out. Born in Philadelphia he's the son of a Jewish fish peddler, but not in the same neighborhood as Bullitt. An old Bolshevik hand in Soviet Russia, Fischer first made a name for himself valuable as an American Jew journalist writing for the *New York Evening Post* about the 1921-22 famine where he encounters Duranty. He describes Hoover's massive humanitarian famine relief efforts disbursing $20 million in Congressional funds "one of the greatest deeds of charity that history records". That same Hoover mission is seriously questioned as a fake intervention in a deliberately arranged Genocide a decade before the Holodomor! Fischer reported, "No government rests securely when its population starves. The ARA (American Relief Administration) has thus very directly aided the present regime through its presence in Russia."

In 1923 Fischer begins writing for *The Nation.* George Kennan in Riga, Latvia for the State Department confirms Hoover's support of the Bolsheviks, writing "the Soviet government was, thus, importantly aided, not just in its economic undertakings, but in its political prestige and capacity for survival, by ARA's benevolent intervention. This political aid was desperately needed." Kennan described Hoover's food distribution as "benevolent" intervention. More points for Mr. Kennan as the Department's quintessential establishment historian. In fact, Kennan made no attempt to conceal that he always dreamed with his natural penchant for fiction what his life might have been had he pursued a literary career instead of doing quasi-official hack work covering up for the Consortium. (B. M. Weissman, 201; George Kennan, *Russia and the West under Lenin and Stalin*, Signet, 1962, 180)

Before Antony Sutton published his research on US-Soviet trade little was known of the story how Jacob Schiff, president of Khun, Loeb & Co. with Morgan bankers and National City financed the Bolsheviks while using a specially deployed American Red Cross spy mission as a front to funnel millions of dollars. Kennan's two-volume history of that collaboration (he was a junior officer in the US embassy in Moscow during the coup days) was an elaborate fabrication to divert the trail of the active role of the Consortium and its links to Lenin and Trotsky. That the same Consortium of highly placed US government officials in various departments and Wall Street collaborated through Amtorg, the Soviet liaison agency in New York to engineer postwar Russian reconstruction of Lenin's New Economic Policy (NEP) in 1924 as well as Stalin's Five-Year development plans for agriculture and industry from 1928-35 is little known and even less understood in the context of its implications for power and freedom and the distortion of these ideological concepts in contemporary American culture. While Kennan's legacy remains enshrined at Princeton'a School of International Affairs, we will give the reader enough fodder that exposes Kennan as the Consortium's tool and the principal mystifier at State of the Holodomor.

Famine relief aide served Bolshevik interests whereas for the reconstruction capitalists the ARA relief program presented itself as an opportunity to sharpen Lenin's break from "war communism" while opening the door to western technology and trade. Sutton concluded "there was a complete collapse under War Communism. This collapse had little to do with the Civil War. It was created at the very beginning of the period of War Communism by dispersion of skills, absurd decrees, and the removal of disciplinary market forces. ... More than $45 million was raised through public and private means, and 700,000 metric tons of food were distributed in Russia" under Hoover's ARA, wrote David Mayers in his portrait of US-Russian relations. Of course, Hoover is depicted as the arch-anticommunist who would never allow business to be conducted between US companies and an unrecognized terrorist government. ".... Hoover, vehemently anti-communist, produced no obvious results but won the suspicion – and later vilification – of the Soviet leadership." (A. C. Sutton, *Western Technology and Soviet Economic Development,* v. 1, 313; D. A. Mayers, 96)

That view is shared by Benjamin M. Weissman in *Herbert Hoover and Famine Relief to Soviet Russia: 1921 – 1923,* writing that "the legalization of free trade in farm produce – the most important reform of the NEP – had little meaning in a country paralyzed by famine… It was only after the fight against the famine was won that the incentives provided by the NEP began to take effect. The economy recovered. Soviet rule survived." With the New Economic Policy (1921-28) conceived with the Americans for rapid postwar reconstruction, Lenin and the Bolsheviks imposed a standardized tax to replace grain requisitioning from the peasants. It permitted limited private enterprise for small business and retail sectors. Centralized Soviet trusts controlled heavy industry, foreign trade and banking. Stalin's First Five-Year Plan adopted in 1928 launched in parallel with an intensive internal and foreign propaganda campaign to severely re-impose and tighten severe measures of centralized state planning over the economy to speed industrialization through absorption of western technology and trade transfers paid for mostly by oil managed by Rockefeller's Standard Oil, gold mined by forced labor, and Ukrainian grain depriving the peasants of their land through forced collectivization. (B. M. Weissman, 201; Alec Nove, *An Economic History of the US*, London, 1972; Silvana Malle, *The Economic Organization of War Communism, 1918-1921*, Cambridge, 1985; Alan M. Ball, *Russia's Last Capitalists: The Nepmen, 1921-1929*, Berkeley, 1987; Zara Witkin, *An American Engineer in Stalin's Russia: The Memoirs of Zara Witkin 1932–1934*, Univ. of CA.,1991; Dane Starbuck, *The Goodriches, An American Family*, Indianapolis: Liberty Fund, 2001,174)

It cannot be overstated that in the context of FDR and the Holodomor, Hoover's famine relief mission was extremely significant and a major power-play in the politics of famine and diplomacy of the era between the Hoover, President Harding, the Consortium and Lenin's Reds. It was a major event in the relations between America and the emerging Soviet state, covered in both Soviet and western press. Hundreds of Americans were hired by the ARA to help the Russians disperse over $20 million in food relief approved by Congress to be dispersed within three months and paid for with $10 million (20 million gold rubles). Both William Chamberlin and Duranty were among the foreign correspondents who wrote about this earlier famine and Hoover's ARA intervention.

Why then did these same experienced journalists deliberately tone down the Holodomor concealing catastrophe in the Ukraine and elsewhere a decade later?

Both enjoyed the privileges and perks of the Moscow foreign correspondent elite as long as they enhanced Stalin's prestige in the West. Duranty and Fischer vowed to keep Stalin's secrets. In exchange for special favors each had their own agenda and carefully guarded their access to Stalin and sources in the Central Committee. Bullitt warned his friends in the Senate and State Department to beware of Fischer's Bolshevik duplicity. Both journalists overtly lied in their stories about the Terror-Famine. After Gareth Jones publicly exposed and discredited Duranty, UPI wire correspondent Eugene Lyons published his book, in 1937, recounting how Duranty and Moscow's entire foreign press corps deliberately lied to conceal the truth about the famine. Lyons' apartment had been a favorite gathering place for Moscow society and sharing stories. (Eugene Lyons, *Herbert Hoover: A Biography*, Doubleday Page, 1964)

Before human rights became a pillar of the United Nations, knowledge of the 1932-34 Ukrainian Terror-Famine tragedy was sufficiently widespread to defy any political agenda or national strategy to justify or excuse the wholesale death of millions. "This is ever the case," Mace observed, "when human issues are viewed through the prism of one's commitment to the Right or the Left. If there is one lesson to be learned from this tragedy, it must reside in the universality of human rights and human suffering. If the quest for a 'greater good' or the struggle against some 'greater evil' is seen to require a double standard of blindness toward the injustice and evil perpetrated by those who claim to be on our side of the political spectrum, the victims will always be ignored."

Although he had spent decades in research Mace did not dare explain what he meant by "a double standard of blindness". What "double standard"? Did Mace not know about the State Department declassified files? And who exactly was Mace referring to when he wrote, "those who claim to be on our side of the political spectrum"? Mace found he was swimming in dangerous and murky waters and maybe in a little too deep over his head.

It becomes clear that Mace did not walk the bridge connecting Stalin's Terror-Famine and Hitlerian Nazi fascism that systematically exterminated Ukrainians and Jews, respectively, a bridge financed and constructed by the Morgan-Rockefeller-Harriman Anglo-American Consortium. Yet the evidence is so unmistakeably obvious that when you follow the big money and the industrial deals behind the political agenda it is simply not plausible to imagine that the victims weren't "ignored". They were systematically, deliberately and officially exterminated. This is complicity in the crime. It is certainly not "blindness".

That's just Mace coping with the heinous nature of Big Business. But Mace knew he was on thin ice if he wanted to get any recognition at all for the Holodomor by Washington or Kiev then still struggling under the heel of Moscow. The American professor in the Ukraine surely knew there was more to the story that had to be told if his findings were to have coherence especially a half-century after the fact. But why take a walk in a field of mines and risk something blowing up in your face. But Mace is in a minefield stepping over dead bodies tattooed "Made in the USA". It can get messy. Neat arrangements with academic order prove too weak when built on a foundation of lies. There are still too many missing pieces in the structure of a convincing argument to make it stand up to the truth. Academics intent on a career must be careful where and when they tread.

Viktor Yushchenko's coalition government was ripped apart by charges of corruption whether under the pro-Russian Prime Minister Viktor Yanokovich, himself a former President, or by his own Prime Minister Ulia Tymoshenko, herself mixed up in Russian gas deals. Today, in the independent Republic of Ukraine there is a heated debate with post-Soviet Russia over the Genocide of the Holodomor spilling over into Europe to the United States and into the United Nations. In the war of words Russia wants to change the vocabulary and dismiss entirely the issue of Genocide.

Once the Ukrainian Parliament declared independence for Ukraine, on August 24, 1991, Ukrainian leaders officially began to recognize the Soviet Genocide.

We find in the official volume "Ukraine, 5 Years of Independence", published in 1996 with official endorsements by Ukraine's national leaders, including President L. Kuchma, Yushchenko, then president of the National Bank of Ukraine, Yuri Yekhanurov, Chairman of the State Property Fund, both appointed by Kuchma, and Olexandre Moroz, Speaker of the Rada Parliament, and others, endorsement of this historical observation:

"The history of Ukraine in the 20th century has been particularly brutal. In an attempt to break Ukrainian and their resistance to collectivization, Stalin instigated a deliberate genocide, the Great Famine of 1932-33, which took 5 to 7 million lives in 15 months. During World War II, Ukraine was the principal battleground between the Soviet and German armies. The so-called 'Russian Front' in fact was in mostly the Ukraine not to minimize the northern losses in Belorussia. Of all the republics on the territory of the Soviet Union, Ukraine suffered the highest number of civilian deaths and the most extensive physical destruction. Every decade from the 1920s through the 1950s saw a progressive annihilation of the Ukrainian intelligentsia, through deportation and assassination. In the 1940s and 1950s millions of Ukrainians were permanently deported to labour camps in Siberia. In an attempt to create a 'Soviet man', the hegemony of Russian language and culture prevailed, and indigenous Ukrainian Catholic and Orthodox Churches were subsumed under the Russian Orthodox Church; the Ukrainian language was relegated to the status of a 'Russian' dialect." (*Ukraine, 5 Years of Independence*, Arc-Ukraine Publishers, Kiev, 1996)

At the time of 1932-34 Terror-Famine, two Democratic Party leaders sat in the White House. Herbert Hoover and Franklin Delano Roosevelt. Americans were under the sway of the Federal Reserve system, economic turmoil and the Great Depression. A not too startling revelation of political realities in Washington was made by FDR's vice president Henry Wallace during the 1936 re-election campaign. In 1932 reactionaries in America conspired to launch a military fascist coup Wallace declared in his confirmation speech. Indeed this was a bad time America the greatest and most powerful democracy in the world. FDR's election in November 1932 was claimed to have been the decisive factor in setting the course that America would take for the decade. It was then that month the State Department received reports from its officers in Berlin and Paris of an outbreak of serious famine in the Soviet Russia. American financiers and businessmen were eagerly investing in Stalin, Hitler and Mussolini. Meanwhile, the Ukrainians endured Communist Party tyranny, mass repression and extermination. So, when the famine peaked under FDR's watch, and Bullitt traded words with his Soviet counterparts in Washington to open diplomatic relations with Stalin. For the first time in the brief new history US-Soviet Russian history, it appeared that the US might gain an unprecedented privileged access to Soviet society and the dark secrets of the Kremlin. The reality was different.

Much different. But the White House opts for engagement with Moscow making the two great nations appear not so utterly incompatible and sharing more in common than their differences. A propaganda film manufactured by ambassador Joe Davies, *Mission To Moscow* stressed that fantasy to a level of the absurd. Russian observers and Soviet experts in America knew it was ridiculous; the Russians found it likewise amusing and incomprehensible. FDR and the Consortium were playing a very dangerous game. If the linkage failed, the house of cards would fly in all directions. The threat of an outbreak of war was ever-present. A spark in the powder-keg was too great a risk. FDR knew one mustn't stretch the tightrope too tight and there was enough elasticity to make it bounce without making the actors fall in the trickery act of balancing the whole show.

Agriculture Secretary and his future Vice-President Henry Wallace was a very clever choice t for handling the farm problem from the White House. After the debacle of Hoover the president elect was instantly overwhelming popular, embracing hopes and fears of working America judging from the 450,000 letters that poured into the White House during that dreary first week after his inauguration. Before he took the sacred oath of office he already appeared to have nearly the entire nation eating out of his hand. After his dealing with the banks and his first fireside chat, even the fierce anti-Roosevelt newspaper scion Randolph Hearst writes, "I guess at your next election we will make it unanimous."

Hearst is cited in a recently published book written by a *New York Times* editor attempting to make Obama parallels to the Roosevelt years. Unfortunately, Adam Cohen's book *Nothing to Fear* (2009) dishes out more boiled-over hogwash and is no pot-boiler. Roosevelt had no interest and never does balance the budget though what he did manage to do in creating the largest budget deficit in the country's history dwarfs compared to Obama's lame promotion of Federal Reserve Bank chairman Bernard Bernake for a second term as the head of the Federal Reserve while he's borrowing mind-blowing unprecedented amounts for spending programs. (Obama finally dumps Bernake late 2013 replaced by a woman, another first for his legacy.) Bloomberg reports late December, that the marketable debt of Obama's government tripled three-fold "to a record $7.17 trillion in November from $5.80 trillion at the end of last year."

The Consortium loves them both, with two wars in Afghanistan and the US government "bankrupt" with the money presses rolling 24/7. On its cover *Time* hails Bernake Man-of-the-Year 2009 blazened across supermarkets in America that would have the ghosts of Henry Luce and his Yale Skull & Bones group of investors dancing in their bones. But this much is true when Cohen writes, "Factory workers, farmers, and bankers all had their champions. The pragmatic Roosevelt listened to all of them, looking for ideas that would work. Many of the initiatives adopted during the Hundred Days were thought up by Roosevelt's closest advisers, but others came from members of Congress.... He took into account what the public wanted, what Congress would pass, and what was acceptable to his electoral coalition – from farm leaders, to union bosses, to Wall Street financiers. Sam Rayburn, the Texas Democrat who later became House speaker, said Roosevelt was 'the best jury to listen that I ever saw.' ... The idea of Roosevelt imposing a program to restore the nation to health could not be more wrong according to those who were there. 'Franklin Delano Roosevelt did not invent the New Deal; he does not own it', wrote John Franklin Carter, one of the era's leading journalists. 'He is its master of ceremonies, not the manager of the theater; its chief croupier, not the owner of the casino'." And so the critics declare FDR is not another Moses from the mountain top, or was he? (Adam Cohen, *Nothing to Fear, FDR's Inner Circle and the Hundred Days that Created Modern America,* NY: Penguin-Thorndike Press, 2009, 18)

William Faulkner said, "The past is never dead. It's not even past." Yet while the current economic crisis is week after week called the worst the country has seen since the Great Depression of the 1930s, comparisons are lame. First of all, the 2008-9 crisis is the worst financial debacle ever in the nation's history. But that's where the comparison stops. Journalists don't venture to understand enough of the dynamics at play during the crisis inherent in the current culture to see the big money at work in the market manipulations, shorts and insider trading that brought on the 1929 crash with Baruch, Dillon, the Whitneys and Harrimans, Rockefellers and others in the gang getting away with billions in capital gains as they swept away the small investors and other rising meager fortune-seekers pumping up the market artificially and then who dropped like suckers at the casino. The market collapse of 2008-9 was also for the Consortium a classic grab once the market tanked and shares plunged squeezing out the small-time player. Only this time it would be too obnoxiously blatant to print another Rothschild magazine cover, so they use their front-man lackey from Princeton Bernake instead.

When Franklin Delano Roosevelt took his oath of office in March 1933 as 10,000 banks tumble like dominoes in a tidal wave of panic and money-runs after the longest slide since the 1929 stock market bubble burst. The nation's fragile faith thin like their paper money harbored by frenzy, greed and sky-rocketing gains and promises dropped like a Rockefeller dime spinning to the ground with fantasies that would not come back to life until Hollywood's glamour movies with starring Ginger Rogers and Fred Astaire brought the glamour of riches of the Consortium back into their living rooms. More dreams. More fantasies and then there would be the Wizard behind the screen and Dorothy under the rainbow of Oz.

FDR played the role well with folksy Will Rogers by his side, the patrician appearing in step with America's favorite spokesman for the common man. Whatever might be said about Roosevelt it will never be said that he was no brilliant game player, striking the pose, playing the role, having his fun in his own peculiar way while bringing a quarter, or even a third of humbled unemployed American workers to his bosom. His speech writers have a field day. There would be Gershwin and Cole Porter to write spanking upbeat songs of Americana in the beat. And when there were fights over scraps of food from the beginning, speaking to millions with his resounding voice of the nation's Commander-in-Chief Roosevelt in his first fire-side chat used the economic depression to marshal the country on the road to recovery and war. Prosperity would have to wait once colossal orders of the war industry converted to postwar reconstruction with paralysis of fear instilled in the fake Cold War trembling in the embrace of the American Dream before making a run for the underground nuke shelter. While millions of Russians slogged in proletarian fever imprisoned in soviet gulag labor camps at the point of Bolshevik bayonets barely surviving on unhealthy rations, FDR told Americans "First of all, let me assert my firm belief that the only thing we have to fear is fear itself—nameless, unreasoning, unjustified terror, which paralyzes needed efforts to convert retreat into advance." Six years later German and Soviet troops stormed into Poland and Finland taking the Balkans precipitating world war."

Amazingly straight away Roosevelt didn't run for cover with the bankers; instead, he publicly shames them to run for cover and holds them at arm's length. And why not when their banks were crashing to the ground one after another on the streets across America. In the same breath, Roosevelt declares, "Yes, the money-changers have fled from their high seats in the temple of our civilization. We may now restore that temple to the ancient truths. ... This nation is asking for action, and action now. There must be a strict supervision of all banking and credits and investments. There must be an end to speculation with other people's money. And there must be provision for an adequate but sound currency."

Writer Adam Cohen, – as did America's New Left journalist Amy Goodman, – called Henry Wallace "an amazing man, a scientist, a farm journalist." Absolutely fantastic when the greatest farmers in the world, those peasants of the Ukraine whose ancestors had made Czarist Russia the world's largest grain producer, are most meticulously exterminated with typical fascist bureaucratic order.

Adam Cohen went on to say on the website of National Public Radio, guardian of liberal opinion in America (with daily reinforcement from the BBC): "And he came to Washington saying he was going to save the Farm Belt, or he would just go back home to Iowa. And the Farm Belt had actually been in depression much longer than the rest of the country. They had a terrible 1920s. So he comes to Washington, and he goes to FDR in the first week and says, "We need an agriculture plan." And FDR says, "Go talk to the farmers. See what they want." Wallace quickly holds a meeting of all the farm leaders. They agree to this subsidy program, which was critical then to saving the farms. And within a month or two, we had this incredibly revolutionary agriculture program that did save the farmers, save the Farm Belt. Another amazing fellow." Oh, how splendid, how wonderful, absolutely amazing, hogwash. And Amy Goodman and her "Democracy Now" website bought it too, a result not atypical in America. When the left turns news into a popularity contest it gets mainstreamed to center adding more muck to the rake.

Let's take a closer look at the food expert in Roosevelt's cabinet during the Holodomor. Henry Wallace came from a very different world than FDR, Harriman and the other Consortium men of his White House years. At six, Henry was taken on what he called "botanizing expeditions" with a brilliant black man and famous inventer and chemist George Washington Carver, a son of slaves born during the Civil War. At the time he was a little known thirty year old teaching assistant at Iowa State where he was able to escape the hatred and racism that still condoned lynching "negroes" for amusement. Two years later Carver is invited by Booker T. Washington to head the Agriculture Department at Tuskegee Institute, in Alabama, where he stays for nearly a half century. Henry Wallace Sr. had actually been one of his teachers at Iowa State. In 1916 Carver had been honored by England's Royal Society of Arts, a rarity at the time even for a white American. However, Carver's promotion of peanuts brings him more fame; during the war Carver and his close friend Henry Ford collaborated to produce synthetic rubber.

His was an odd but appropriate appointment as Agriculture Secretary succeeding his Republican father in the same office under Harding; the younger Wallace thought the bitter disagreements with Harding's Commerce Secretary Herbert Hoover took a serious toll on his health. Wallace, born in 1888, served until September 1940, when he resigned to accept the nomination for Vice President; elected in November 1940 with Roosevelt. In May 1943 Wallace landed in Siberia during his trip to the Far East. Authors White and Maze, in their book on Wallace (1995) described just how far the naïve and ignorant politician played into the hands of his Soviet hosts during his twenty-five day tour of "eighteen different centers, mainly inspecting mines, munitions factories, farms, and so on, and trying in his speeches, as he wrote, to bring about 'world security on the basis of broader understanding'." Harriman sent a dispatch to FDR that Wallace had even given a speech, in Tashkent, in Russian'."

"In 1944 FDR sent him on a disastrous trip to East Asia," establishment historian Arthur Schlesinger wrote in 2000. Wallace left on a personal mission to find and he added, "In the Soviet Union, the Russians fooled him by turning the slave labor camp at Magadan into a Potemkin village and in China, the columnist Joseph and Stewart Alsop*, a British infantry officer who in 1944 marries his eighteen-year-old sweetheart, and on D-Day parachutes behind enemy lines (like Schlesinger both Alsops were wartime OSS intelligenc sic) persuaded him to cable the president recommending that Gen. Joseph W. Stilwell be recalled. Wallace was really too naive for a hard world. Though he remained the favorite of labor and the liberals, a war-weary FDR dumped him as his running mate in 1944 in favor of Harry S Truman."

Joe Alsop was Harvard, Class of '32; like his father and grandfather Stewart Alsop went to Yale where he is "highly popular" in the Class of 1936 but leaves without a diploma; among his classmates include Whitelaw Reid of the *Herald Tribune,* Brendan Gill, John Hersey, and Walt Rostow. Alsop biographer Robert Merry writes of the collegiate atmosphere at Yale in the thirties before the war, "If Harvard taught young men to wear the robes of power with dignity and gentility, Yale's mission was to teach the art of accumulating power – in finance, politics, business, and society generally. As Yale graduate and professor Henry Seidel Canby put it, '(Yale) educated specifically for the harsh competition of capitalism, for the successful ... pursuit of the individual o power for himself, for class superiority, and for a success measured by the secure possession of the fruits of prosperity.' Canby noted that for Yale undergraduates, the competition for social awards was fiercer even than the competition for academic marks – fiercer, in fact, than anything known in the business world. And the social awards went to those who rose to the top in campus activities. At Harvard when the time came to judge potential initiates into the Porcellian and other exclusive clubs, it mattered more who you were, meaning who your parents were and your grandparents. But at Yale more emphasis was placed on campus accomplishments. As that fictional Dick Stover put it, one had to do something to be someone ... the underlying philosophy along Grove Street wasn't much different than that of those elite academies. But the tough competitive spirit at Yale was leavened by a strong belief in fair play and an idealistic approach to religion and patriotism. In rising to the top, the aim was to remain worthy not only of the ascent but of the social position that was the final prize." (Robert W. Merry, *Taking on the World, Joseph and Stewart Alsop, Guardians of the American Century*, NY: Viking Penguin, 1996, 39)

During the wartime Soviet trip "Wallace was sent on a wild goose chase by a Russian émigré shyster on a quest for drought-resistant grass". He yearned to compare what he called "the individuality of corn plants (to) the personality of animals or human beings". Wallace had talked about what he described as the holy significance of seeds in a public speech, "The Strength and Quietness of Grass". Perhaps he would have experienced a different vision had he dared to venture into the fields outside Kiev in 1933.

Wallace's own book of the trip, *Soviet Asia Mission*, gave "with few qualifications, a very complimentary, not to say, idealized, account of the tremendous developments taking place in Siberia, and of the apparently unanimously patriotic and optimistic spirit of the masses of 'volunteers' who had flocked there to realize the region's great potential." Wallace said nothing of the Holodomor; on the contrary his record of the trip stood as a proof that it never happened as he was prevented from learning the truth from the imprisoned Ukrainians and kulaks that inhibited the regions he visited under constant control and surveillance of the NKVD. Wallace wrote, "Komsomolsk was founded in 1932 by Komsomols, members of the Communist Youth Organization, to settle the wilderness. The first settlers were enthusiastic young men, who were soon joined by equally high-spirited young women from all over the Soviet Union." The town had become a major center of heavy industry."

A more recent look at Wallace appeared in *Henry A. Wallace: His Search for a New World Order* (1995), by Graham White and John Maze who observed, "Wallace knew something of the coercive nature of Stalin's resettlement schemes, but though he was not entirely blinkered (noting, for instance, that 'the young city of Komsomolsk looked disheveled and run down, and the people seemed overworked'), he seemed prepared at this moment to accept the official version of the town's beginnings. Of a visit to an anti-aircraft factory at Kranoyarsk, he wrote: 'The spirit at this plant was splendid ... The war-bond drive had been well organized, for (the captain in charge) said that purchases by employees averaged 12 per cent of their earnings. Often, patriotic individuals turn in all their savings, saying to the government, "Use it to buy a warplane or a tank'." (Graham White and John Maze, *Henry A. Wallace: His Search for a New World Order*, Univ. of North Carolina, 1995)

"On his travels through Siberia, Wallace wrote, his party was 'accompanied by 'old soldiers' with blue tops on their caps. Everybody treated them with great respect. They are members of the NKVD, which means the People's Commissariat of Internal Affairs. I became very fond of their leader, Major

Mikhail Cheremisenov'. But as Cheremisenov, Wallace also relates, 'was a "major of the Soviet secret service," it is little wonder his men were treated 'with great respect'. At Balkhash, Wallace was told again of the willing nature of the migrants. 'Founded by volunteers', the city's remarkable mayor (a woman) told us, "They came from Kiev, from Kharkov, from Moscow and Leningrad – 180 people 15 years ago. Now we have 70,000'."

White and Maze note the American vice-president's inclination during the war effort to deny the truth of Soviet terror. "Perhaps Wallace was finding it hard to choke all this down", and they added Wallace remained confused "that even though Americans might think the human cost of forced collectivization too great, that policy had produced the agricultural surplus necessary to create these new industrial towns. Yet it is hard to understand the naviété of comments such as the following, 'The Kolyma gold miners are big, husky young men, who came out to the Far East from European Russia. I spoke with some of them. They were keen about winning the war. "We wrote to Stalin asking to be sent to the front", their spokesman said, "but Stalin replied that we were needed more right here." Stalin had made gold mining a preferred war industry, we learned, and had frozen the men in it'." This account continued, "Subsequent 'defector' testimony has shown that the workers of Kolyma were not volunteers but prisoners, part of a vast system of forced labor on which Russian industry depended. They had hoped that Wallace's visit might improve their conditions, but instead saw him deceived by bogus displays of relative comfort and prosperity. Watch towers had been taken down by the authorities, starving prisoners removed, office workers disguised as farmhands, and stores temporarily stocked with goods. Such revelations, however, came to light much later ..."

Neither authors White and Maze, nor Wallace, make any reference to the Stalinist famine terror of the 1933 Holodomor. But at this point in the war, that pales compared to the consequences for the Ukraine and Russia: the war destroyed 40 percent of Ukraine's Russian wealth, and 30 percent of the entire wealth of the USSR. At least ten to twenty million are victims, with over two million people, including young children were shipped to Nazi labor camps with few survivors; hundreds of Soviet towns and cities ruined, 28,000 villages crushed and burned; nearly 30,000 collective farms and 16,000 industrial factories are destroyed. Understandably, when the Soviet Union suffered the destruction of 100,000 of its collective and state farms, it was not the time for Wallace to knock FDR's most important ally on the verge of pushing back the Nazi invaders on their way to smash Berlin. (Graham White and John Maze, *Henry A. Wallace*)

Writer Benson Bobrick in *East of the Sun* (1992), also cites an anecdotal reference to the 1944 Wallace visit to Magadan in Siberia with Prof. Owen Lattimore of the Office of War Information, the government's propaganda agency. Bobrick, too, finds it bizarre how Wallace apparently remained so dumb and blind to the human catastrophe of the workers he encountered at the Kolyma gold mines, describing "big husky young men" as "pioneers of the machine age, builders of cities". That much was true. These displaced people are robust and tough. They have to be in order to survive.

Instead of a description of the genuine brutal reality of contemporary soviet politics, Lattimore prefers a comparative regression to America's early settlement days of the Hudson Bay Company. Lattimore is suckered by local greenhouses producing "tomatoes, cucumbers, and even melons were grown to make sure that the hardy miners got enough vitamins". Conquest notes the Wallace-Lattimore camps were stocked with "fake girl swineherds, who were in fact NKVD office staff'." The American mystifiers playe along with Soviet propaganda. When asked about forced labor prison camps, Soviet Deputy Prime Minister Anastas Mikoyan told the UN investigators "there were no labor camps in Russia and the prisoners there were so well provided for that English and American workers had every reason to envy them". (Benson Bobrick, *East of the Sun: The Epic Conquest and Tragic History of Siberia*, Poseidon Books, 1992, 445; Karlo Stajner, *Seven Thousand Days in Siberia*, NY, 1988, 238; R. Conquest, *The Great Terror*, 239)

Reader, if you think that Kolyma might be a delightful travel destination read the saga of the American Alex Dolgun and think again. Dolgun, 22, had a routine job at the American embassy, on his way to meet a friend for lunch, is seized by the secret police, and within seconds his fate is in the hands of the KGB, and smuggled into prison where he was incessantly interrogated, tortured, and beaten before receiving a 25-year sentence at hard labor. Dolgun serves time in five camps, a self-described regular "Robinson Crusoe in hell" as he recounts how he lived with "political", hooligans, wretched animals and common thugs. Prisoners mutilated themselves in morbid fear to avoid transfer to Kolyma in Siberia: "One shaved dust from an indelible pencil with his *moika,* put the dust in his eye, and deliberately blinded himself. The eye ulcerated and had to be removed. And they still sent him to Kolyma. Another nailed his scrotum to the bunk and yelled, 'Kill me, you bastards!' Take me away, kill me!' They simply pulled out the nail with a claw hammer, poured iodine on it, and put him on the train." (Alexander Dolgun and Patrick Qatson, *Alexander Dolgun's Story, An American in the Gulag*, NY: Knopf, 1975)

In 1944 Wallace is denied renomination by his party and accepts the Commerce Secretary post serving one year. An Episcopalian like the Rockefellers and other true believers of their faith he went back to farming in South Salem, New York, and dies with his tomato patch, in 1965 in Danbury, Connecticut, not far from my childhood hometown. (Arthur Schlesinger, "Who was Henry Wallace, The Story of a Perplexing and Incredibly Naive Public Servant", *Los Angeles Times*, March 12, 2000; A. Cohen, Chapter 4, see ft. 18, *Nothing to Fear*)

The Soviets have their farmland reforms while the Americans try a different method. During his first weeks in office Roosevelt socializes the US government with massive federal programs. Writer Adam Cohen (*Nothing to Fear*) put it this way: "FDR comes in and says we need essentially to create a social welfare state. So that's why we get things like the Federal Emergency Relief Act, $500 million for a welfare program. We get the Agricultural Adjustment Act, the first time the government really intervenes in the agriculture markets in that way. We get the National Industrial Recovery Act, which had some ham-handed attempts to get government and business to work together, but it had that $3.3

billion in public works, money which then became the WPA and other famous public works programs. These fifteen bills were all passed incredibly quickly by a Congress that was willing to give FDR virtually anything he wan ted, because the country was in such dire straits. … And that's going to be the debate. It was the debate during FDR's time, too. The progressives wanted billions more, and the conservatives said there's no money at all. We're going to get that again. The Senate, McConnell, people like that are going to say there's not enough money. … FDR – Obama really needs to push for high levels of funding. The more that we can inject into the economy, the more jobs, the better we'll be right now." (A. Cohen, *Nothing to Fear)*

Today America is a good example of how the oppositional political opinion takes on Roosevelt's New Dealism. "FDR created," Adam Cohen observed, "in addition to the welfare state … the New Deal coalition. And the New Deal coalition incorporated lots of different groups that all voted Democratic, got the Republicans out, and FDR felt they were his constituency and he needed to keep them happy. So, that included union leaders who were very important, and that's why we got the right to organize. It was in the National Industrial Recovery Act, because the union leaders demanded that. Farmers were very important and had been fairly Republican. To keep them voting Democratic, FDR gives them, you know, a big relief program. Urban workers, the heart of the Democratic electorate, FDR gives them things like the first welfare program. And yes, when the union people spoke out, they got more things, they pushed back. So he was very responsive to pressure of this kind, and he wanted to keep everyone in the coalition happy." That is his theme song of the Democratic Party. *Happy Days Are Here Again.* Let the children play, keep them happy, that's all it takes, then they will be ready to march to a foreign war made by a Consortium gang some of whom they can see and touch but never really know and all the time they are willing to die and kill for it. Don't worry, be happy … (A. Cohen, *Nothing to Fear)*

It may strike readers as odd, but from Moscow to Washington, the Presidents of both Russia and America identify with Roosevelt, or at least in so far as they said it publicly and there is good reasoning for that. For Obama, the proximity is self-evident. BBC reporter Lucy Ash observed, "Mr. Putin says his role model is neither Peter (the Great sic) nor any of Russia's past leaders, but America's longest-serving president. He has often compared his mission in history with that of Franklin Roosevelt's in the 1930s. Just like FDR, the Russian president believes he has rescued his country from a Great Depression – in Russia's case, the chaos of the Yeltsin era in the 1990s – and laid the foundations for a new era of prosperity. Given the triad of nations, an appearance of tension fueled by increased armament expenditures may be just the perfect ruse to balance China's astral ascendancy into the 21st century realignment of the superpowers.

With Vladimir Putin drifting consolidating his dictatorial powers, it should not be difficult to understand his alignment with the American president, Stalin's partner in crime. The BBC compares Putin's drift toward dictatorship to FDR's hold on the Americans. Putin's unwillingness to yield power is reminiscent of FDR's unprecedented political longevity. Here reader you see we touch on another problem linked to our Holodomor story. Casting himself also as a national "savoir", it may appear that Putin aspires to a similar rank in Russian history; America's historically proximate and secret economic and political alliance with the tragic history of the Soviet Union from the start makes the parallel seem all the more problematical if no less logical and politically consistent with the past. And why not? One may wonder if Putin's new image makers are not in fact Consortium handlers. Ukraine in revolt again in January 2014 prompts criticism in Kiev among the protest movement that Obama cuddles too much favor from Putin's dictatorship instead of showing tepid support towards opposition leaders of the democracy movement while billions watch daily. (Lucy Ash, "How Putin is inspired by history", *BBC News,* online, Feb. 25, 2008)

A generation after the Holodomor and a decade after Stalin's death, the Hoover Institution published more than sixteen volumes of Stalin's collected works. That too should have seemed very strange since the dictator had been poisoned and discredited by his successor Khrushchev. Stalin, a pseudonym meaning "Man of Steel" (his real name was Iosif Vissarionovich) masterfully eliminated any threat to his complete and total authority as Party leader and Soviet dictator. Millions of people were arrested, imprisoned and killed as traitors to the Communist Party merely because under the Soviet criminal code they could be suspected of potentially acting against the regime and so, to serve the needs of the State of which they all are a small and expedient part, they were of course, guilty by confession.

At the same time the modern day incarnation of Soviet power, ex-KGB-FSB officer Putin enjoys maintaining Stalin's iron fist over Russia's millions of post-Soviet citizens and their children of the new era. The BBC reported his former prime minister turned "implacable opponent" Mikhail Kasyanov saying, "'He was, and is, an old KGB officer who leads, or tries to evaluate all events and future from that angle: how to control society, how not to allow people to directly participate because that brings risks," says Mr. Kasyanov of his former boss." Putin cultivates Stalin's as the country's "most successful leader". ("KGB old boys tightening grip on Russia, *BBC News*, Feb. 22, 2008)

Under Putin's reign the Terror-Famine remains a forbidden state secret buried under the chorus of sad Russian songs that evoke days of the Czars. The NKVD Soviet archive remains off-limits, out of reach of truth-seekers. The Holodomor is still too sensitive an international issue, political dynamite in the hands of detractors determined to exploit in in Cold War tensions between the pro-western democracies and communist voters. Informers and NKVD political police were everywhere to root out any dissent or negative observations of centralized state communism. The vast Soviet Union was a regime of mass terror with spies and informers literally everywhere. Yet, in a society that boasts about liberty and prides itself on freedom, the historical record reveals that the West maintained a pernicious veil of silence and complicity that deliberately shrouded and obscured the tragedy and one of the greatest humanitarian debacles of the 20th century. In fact, the actors in the Executive Office and State Department not only had access to information but possess detailed knowledge of mass starvation and

Stalin's campaign of extermination of the Ukrainians. Hoover and Roosevelt knew about it. Both Presidents choose not to intervene to lessen the human suffering deliberately caused by their strategic business client Stalin.

Once again, the policy of business as usual defines US-Soviet affairs unbeknownst to the American public kept in the dark by the privately-owned newspapers like *The New York Times*, *New York Herald Tribune*, and Associated Press and UPI wire services. In 1942, the general manager and executive boss of AP, Kent Cooper, spoke of this international news monopoly in his autobiography *Barriers Down*: "… the news of the world was it's own private property to be withheld, to be discolored to it's own purposes, or to be sold to whom and to where they directed." With the control of the money came the control of the news media. Kent Cooper declared, "International bankers under the House of Rothschild acquired an interest in the three leading European agencies." Thus the Rothschilds bought control of Reuters International News Agency, based in London, Havas of France, and Wolf in Germany, which controlled the dissemination of all news in Europe."

Mullins is more explicit citing a *Life* magazine story dated November 13, 1944: "Because of the secret planning needed to launch a major war, control of the communications media was essential". Cooper tells *Life*'s readers that "Before and during the First World War, the great German news agency Wolff was owned by the European banking house of Rothschild, which had its central headquarters in Berlin. A leading member of the firm was also Kaiser Wilhelm's personal banker (Max Warburg). What actually happened in Imperial Germany was that the Kaiser used Wolff to bind and excite his people to such a degree that they were eager for World War I. Twenty years later under Hitler the pattern was repeated and enormously magnified by DNB, Wolff's successors." It was no less an extraordinary revelation eclipsed unfortunately by the intensity and scope of the war effort. (E. Mullins, *Secrets of the Federal Reserve;* Kent Cooper, *Barriers Down, The Story of the News Agency Epoch*, Farrar & Rinehart, 1942, 21; Ben J. Bagdikian, *The Media Monopoly*, ETC, 1983)

After the Rothschilds seized control over the Bank of England early on in the nineteenth century a controlling interest, in fact, was also purchased in the Jewish-controlled Reuters newspaper based in London. Oh!, no one told you? With controlling interests in Wolff and Havas newspapers, the Rothschild House holds an international news monopoly.

WHO MAKES THE NEWS?

Do you still wonder who makes then news? The members of the Consortium surely know. Should it surprise the reader that the world news sources and services are well wired into the Council on Foreign Relations (CFR) and direct in part their affairs, including personnel as well as the editorial agenda. Of course its not something news organizations care to talk about. Skeptics should do more research.

At one time these CFR-ridden news organizations included Reuters, AP, UPI, *Wall Street Journal*, *Boston Globe*, *The New York Times*, *Los Angeles Times* and *Washington Post*, ABC, NBC, CBS, and RCA. Most national and international news is channeled from these sources. The CFR is deeply embedded in the leading energy corporations, the military and the US Government. As the CFR organization manages the news that molds public opinion about how to think and debate issues of world affairs, its members occupy key positions to influence democratic governments. Editors and journalists, writers and publishers are often members of the CFR, the CIA and other government organizations. A list of names would be too long to cite here. It's amazing when you realize who is on the list. Google it. How all this evolves with the transparency of the Internet Age explosion with its exponential proliferation of websites, blogheads, and social media from Facebook to Twitter and whatever is next is yet to be determined as countries weigh in to control it and users struggle to survive the deluge of electronic gimmickry and still make sense of their lives.

The historical record surrounding the Holodomor shows clearly that leadership from Moscow to Washington severely lacked moral discipline. An investigation into the story reveals that in their delusion and attachment to false ideologies and power, of a whole gang of elite leaders in power before the First World War acting like lower beings who have fallen into the lower depths of existence all the while proclaiming great deeds and self-less sacrifice for Humanity. From Stalin to FDR, the historical record shows how both leaders lacked any ethical restraint while secretly inflicting death and misery on helpless and innocent victims. Their actions led to the suffering and deaths of millions during war and peacetime. All that sets a very bad precedent for integrity in politics!

Circumstances could have been different indeed and prevented the endemic from suffering their logic of pathos. Communications are still primitive compared to the 21st century. Radio is all the craze. FDR and Bullitt often communicate by letters which take weeks to arrive. When he first lands in Moscow, Bullitt has no safe means to send cables; he is obliged to use the Berlin diplomatic pouch. And this when he is convinced Germany has all the American telegraph codes! Even in the former primitive media conditions of life without satellites when, as Edward Snowden disclosed, the NSA secretly listens to billions of private phone conversations daily terror could not be entirely concealed; his subsequent disclosures released to selected journalists for publication mid-January 2014 blanket alleging industrial spying targeting Germany's Siemens is particularly intriguing...

Terror and war are methods of greed for profit. In the thirties, their methods evolve logically and intrinsically link to a demented pursuit for control in the New World Order of emerging nations of declining empires. Despite signals of worsening starvation sent mostly by American-Ukrainians and eye-witnesses, alarming reports of the famine terror did nevertheless reach President Roosevelt and flooded Congress and the State Department. Both groups – concerned Americans and the Sovietized Ukrainians – were neglected and dismissed, abandoned as it were, sacrificed within the political framework of a scheme unfolding beyond their reach or understanding.

The emerging economic world order knew no mercy and was accustomed only to war and destruction on a massive and global scale. With both systems strategically linked for their destruction and survival and both propelled by parallel tendencies for centralized monopoly, within a few short years, the Sovietized republic of Ukraine, as well as other countries in the Soviet orbit were hanging in the balance of the capitalist governments for a second imperialist war.

For three hundred years Kremlin tyrants of the Muscovite nation subjugated the Ukrainians. Fields of village peasants between the towns and cities were all part of a vast and mixed population of indigenous Slavs, Indo-Europeans, Mongolians, Tatars, Cossacks and many other peoples whose ancestors could be traced back thousands of years to the steppe-roving Scythians described by the 5th century Greek historian Herodotus as particularly fierce. In the 1st century the Bosphoron kingdom gave way to the Roman Empire. There are still ruins of classic Greece throughout the southern Crimean coast along the Black Sea across from Turkey. The Slavic Kiev Rus' kingdom ruled a vast territory in the 11th century and embraced Christianity but not before Vladimir, a born pagan, had massacred ruthlessly his enemies and challengers to his authority while accumulating a numerous wives and hundreds of concubines from subdued tribes.

For Vladimir the path is heaven is not through Rome. He casts in his lot with Byzantium. After he is baptized and converted to Christianity Vladimir seals his political alliance with Constantinople and Emperor Basil II of Byzantium by marriage to his sister Princess Anna, in 989. The marriage ceremony was consecrated in Kherson and the city given as *veno,* the bridegroom gift for the emperor before Vladimir and his bride Anna arrive in Kiev surrounded by their flowing procession of ecclestiastics from the Crimea whose mission it is to convert the Russians and destroy the pagan idols. To mark his acceptance of the new faith Vladimir's first act was to have a huge statue of Perun, the Slavic thunder god, dragged down to the water and cast in the Dnieper where he orders his people baptised. Throughout the kingdom old pagan sancutaries are destroyed and replaced by new churches. The most remarkable built is the Kievan Church of the Dormition of the Holy Virgin completed in 996, the first of its kind in Russia inspiring the Hilarion to declare Vladimir of saintly status who has made the Church in Russia "a wonder to all surrounding lands".

By the end of the century Vladimir's expanded his territories with a population of five million and second to its rival the Holy Roman Empire with its center in Germany. He makes each of his twelve sons a prince ruling in an important city of his kingdom. Fratracide strife followed between the step-brothers and Vladimir's goal of stability fails until his son Yaroslav reclaims the throne of Kiev and turns his energies to the edification of the capitol which includes, in 1051, the appointment of the first Russian-born metropolitan, Hilarion, sovereign head of the Church in all of Russia.

A political strategy of royal alliances elevates the Slavic kingdom to new status. No longer are the Slavs and Russians to be perceived as uncultivated barbarians; that is an honor taken by the Ottoman Turks.

Yaroslav is also the first of Kiev to practice royal marriage to forge foreign alliances and strengthen the kingdom; he marries a Swedish princess; the King of Poland marries his sister; the kings of Norway, Hungary and France marry his daughters; four sons marry German princes. Another son marries a daughter of the Byzantium emperor's royal families. The literate and talented Princess Anna is wed to the French King Henry I to secure an alliance against the German emperor is able to sign her name while the King is capable of scratching out an "X". Kiev emerges a beautiful city under Yaroslav's reign and a center of political power in Russia.

Kiev Rus' falls under the Mongol invasion in the 13th century. Genghis Khan (Temuchin/ Temujin), – or if you prefer Chingis, – is an abandoned orphan saved by his brothers rose to head of his Mongol clan, in 1206; by 1215 he and his generals capture Peking, the capitol of the Chinese Empire before raiding west and south filling his army ranks as he went until he leads hundreds of thousands of warriors; by 1221 the Mongols destroy the defiant Shah Muhammad Ali, emperor of Khwarizm, Transoxiana, and Khurasan, a region covering Indus River basin in north India stretching across modern Iran to the Persian Gulf and sweep through the region to capture southern Russia, central Asia and most of Europe.

His reconnaissance troops of 20,000 horsemen on a two-year mission prepare the campaigns of Chingis' grandson Batu in 1237 and 1239) devastate a superior army of Georgian troops in southern and northern Rus' and opens the Russian steppes allowing them to sweep through to Eastern Europe into Galicia-Volhynia and round north to the Balkans. Russian medieval history scholar Charles J. Halperin in *Russia and the Golden Horde* (1987) tells us what happened next to stop the Mongol invasion westward: "The advance through Eastern Europe halted only when news of the death of the Great Khan, Ugedei, overtook the nomad armies. To attend the *quriltai*, the council to elect his successor, the Mongol leaders turned back .... The Mongols were never defeated in open battle. Because of their great mobility armies from the steppe, even if outnumbered, could generally defeat the armies of sedentary civilizations; so it was with the Mongol armies in Eastern and Central Europe in the 1240s, for they were more than a match for every army sent against them."

Afterwards, the Mongol generals swerve with thundering speed into northwest Persia when they decimate a 10,000 strong army of King George IV of Armenia; they drive their ranks with terrifying winds of deafening thunder north shaking the earth wherever they pass, and defeat in succession the Georgians, the Kipchak Turks from the Volga steppes; then next to succumb are the Bulgars of upper Volga. By 1223 it is Ukraine's turn to fall and the Crimea, too, is doomed to the Mongol onslaught where they withstood numerical superiority. After their conquest when their slaughter is complete in the east of northern China, and Korea, the Hordes defeat the Song rulers of southern China and sweep across northern Persia, through northern Iraq, Armenia, and Azerbaijan. In 1236 the great Khan's sons and grandsons sent their hordes north and west towards eastern Europe led by Batu and the tactical genius of Subedei, driving the horde north and west defeating the Bulgars from the middle Volga and the fierce Cumans from the steppes south.

They turn north invading Christian Russia in a ferocious winter campaign sweeping Rostov, Moscow and Vladimir with blazing speed. In 1240 Kiev fell and is destroyed. The next year the Mongols swallow Moravia, then Silesia, and turn south to take Hungary. Perhaps they might have gone all the way to Paris and witness the great Catholic cathedrals including Notre-Dame, completed in 1230 but their destiny chose another fate. (Charles J. Halperin, *Russia and the Golden Horde*, Bloomington: Indiana Univ. Press, 1987, 47)

The far-reaching expanse of conquered territories and empires dwarfed the legions of Rome. For the next twenty years the Mongols are the horror of horrors, annihilating armies and cities everywhere until out of the darkness in the north the Russians find their savior, the great Alexander, the prince of Novgorod and son of Yaroslav II, and in 1241 the victor over the Swedes. Henceforth he is known as Grand Prince Alexander Nevsky. When he dies at 43 in 1263, the modicum of peace he exerted over the Russian lands comes to an end and slips into Russia's dark ages. "The sun of Russia has set", announced the metropolitan of the Orthodox Church.

On his heels came the Turko-Mongol warrior Tamerlane ("Timur the Lame") who in the 14th century sends his hoards to conquer Asia and the Caucasus. Led by a vassal of Tamerlane – the new khan of the Golden Horde, Tokhtamych – and with his forces rebuilt for attacks Moscow in 1382, after Grand Prince Dimitri and the Russians are betrayed by a spineless vermin who throws open the gates, the Mogols sack and brutally burn and rape Moscow subjugating the entire region that lay at their mercy. The yoke of Mongol occupation weighs heavily upon Russia until 1480 when Khan Akmad of the Golden Horde abandons his assault on Moscow defended by Czar Ivan III the Great and withdraws from the Ugra River. In 1500 the Mongol reign is eventually crushed with a coup killing Khan Akmad by the Crimean Horde reinforced by Christian Russians from the north ending over two centuries of terror and repression. (N. V. Riasanovsky, *A History of Russia*; James P. Duffy and Vincent L. Ricci, *Czars, Russia's Rulers for over One Thousand Years*, Facts On File, Inc. 1995)

Nor are the Ukrainians sudden newcomers on the American scene. In North America, in fact the largest ethnic Ukrainian communities establish their new homes in the Chicago region and the mid-western farm belt. Ukrainians settled in three principal waves of refugee emigration – at the turn of the last century, between and after the two world wars. Today they number over a million, with at least another half million Ukrainians living in Canada.

In contemporary Ukraine, the consequences of "Russianfication" still blur many of their former differences. A Ukrainian friend in Kiev whose father was a communist Party member told me, "Ukrainians are more Russian than Ukrainian, and Russians are more Ukrainian than Russians." That might explain in part Putin's grasp on Ukraine. My girlfriend has lived all her life in Kiev with her Russians parents having moved to Kazakhstan, a former Soviet republic. Her eyes are Mongolian, she speaks the national Ukrainian language fluently with the poetry of song and better than most Ukrainians, and looks more like Brigitte Bardot with slanted eyes. She too jokingly doubts she has any Ukrainian ancestors. It is common knowledge in Kiev that having been raised as citizens of the greater USSR, Ukrainians generally speak better Russian than Ukrainian. Ukrainian nationalists work to see that change.

In the spring of 1933 the White House knows just how terribly Kazakhstan is suffering. A report dated March 1 sent to State is records the account by eye-witness Dr. Hoover to his friend Frederic Sackett appointed ambassador to Germany in 1930 under Stimson and one of his trusted advisers. Sackett is no stranger to Soviet terror politics and famine. Much later Dana Dalrymlpe, State's agriculture specialist, observes how Kazakhstan lost virtually all its livestock. Nomadic tribes like the Kirgiz or the Kazakhi raised cattle. Kazakhstan's nomadic tribes were forced into collective farms and died there. Under collectivization, with their livestock wiped out, the tribe suffered severe human mortality "perhaps higher than other areas" but because of its isolation little is known about the course of the famine. This phenomena is now being repeated by the Chinese government in Peking against the Mongolian Tibetans in the steppes deprived and deplaced from their ancestoral steppes.

Likewise, scattered reports identify famine stricken regions in White Russia, Central Asia and elsewhere in the USSR. "But even excluding these areas," Dr. Dalrymple concludes his report published in 1964, "along with Kazakhstan, the area and population in the grip of starvation exceeded the famine of 1921." (Dr. D. Dalrymple, "The Great Famine in Ukraine 1932-34", *Soviet Studies,* Jan. 1964; Alexander Markoff, "Famine in Russia", NY: Committee for the Relief of Famine, 1934, in D. Dallin, 167)

To this day few Americans know that the famine ever existed so naturally reader why would one ever suspect the role of American leaders and corporations in suppressing news about it. That would be unfair, now wouldn't it? But it's not unthinkable, And in fact, journalists themselves were remarkably pathetic in reporting the famine but efficient in suppressing the truth. Nor have Americans ever been fully told of the US foreign policy and activities of presidents Hoover and Roosevelt with Stalin's regime. The fact is they do nothing to stop it and instead connive publicly not to acknowledge either the famine or its victims killed in the Soviet "meat grinder" by the American client "Uncle Joe", – the epitome of Roosevelt's curious blend of jaded patrician cynicism.

The American public certainly did not know, for example, that the same man at State in charge of stonewalling letters appealing for government aid or assistance to the Ukrainians was a former US Army intelligence officer when Lenin prevailed all supreme in 1920. The same man is involved in the top secret transfer of Bolshevik gold shipped to San Francisco facilitated by Robert Dollar for deposit by Morgan bankers in the New York Federal Bank and worth at the equivalent gold rate nearly approximately $500 million today. Gold was then valued at $20 an ounce.

Anthony Sutton looked closely into the American International Corporation (AIC) and its extensive links in the nexus of Consortium power. Robert Dollar was one of the AIC directors. A few small pieces of the activity of AIC reveal a story astonishing to the innocent and unaware but not difficult to understand in the general scheme of political and corporate relations of the Anglo-American elite as it evolved. Crises tend to stir things up, shake up the murky bottom and both obscure and reveal the pieces falling into place once the waters clear. The darkness conceals and reveals. Follow the money. Today with electronic trading and hidden numbered bank accounts it is nearly impossible to trace the billions of secret illegally gained funds are transferred in nanoseconds from bank to bank, account to account, company front to company front. In the past there was more transparency. So the actors had to protect their secrets themselves. There were fewer banks, fewer actors. The Consortium was a very tight closely-knit arrangement. You either belonged, or you didn't. Only those who knew did. Of course that's changed slightly today where managers of suspicious offshore accounts refer to their anonymous clients known to them only by numbers. No names, number only please.

THE AMERICAN INTERNATIONAL CORPORATION – THE AIC

It sounds like the next step to God. To those insiders it felt like it, or the next best thing. Sutton researched it and his findings are an illumination into the power that played a key role in setting up the debacle that inflicted the Holodomor. Bestial greed, obsession with power, dehumanizing indifference, arrogant elitism... They had it all that and more of the evil that dwells in the utter baseness of war and crimes against Humanity. It may be said, too, that these powerful bankers actually relish Genocide. They actually embrace it, condone it, profit and exploit it. Look at the numbers in the First World War where impotent old "gentlemen" gallantly sacrifice an entire generation of their most educated and cultivated sons of aristocrats and the illiterate working class in battles with thousands and tens of thousands of fatalities in a day. The British Empire's own bard Kipling would lose his son; Teddy Roosevelt weaped when his youngest and most dear, a pilot lost over Belgium.

Genocide is part of "the Game", part of equation of Empire, power and the Consortium tasted the blood and they too suffered the sacrifice of war. It was then. And it still is today. To be sure, you may be a shareholder. In this global community no one is immune nor entirely innocent or independent of its nefarious tentacles. Reader, the recent NSA spying disclosures by Edward Snowden should make you think hard. Your government is most certainly invested with much at stake especially with the international financial system of centralized banks leaving the taxpayer neither innocent, immune or exempt. So much has changed since the feudal days of labor and wars to sustain the masters in their castles and fortresses. In the post-industrial age of technology wars for democracy are waged when taxes suffice dispensing with the need of Liberty Bonds. How quaint digital satellite age of nukes and drones. And all the rhetoric of diplomacy and media disinformation will change too. But lets go back and see what happened first when greater men willed their destiny and the weak and defenseless perished to their fate. Reed, Hemingway and the Lost Generation knew it had all been for nothing, a terrible ruse inflicted on the masses by the imperialists in Paris and London and Dollar-a-Year men in Washington and New York.

In November 1915, the AIC is formed when huge field guns were blasting and men dying daily by the thousands in the First World War, largely with munitions manufactured and shipped – illegally as contraband – from America. AIC's members included JP Morgan, the Rockefellers, National City, Joe Grace of W. R. Grace & Co., Otto Kahn, Kuhn, Loeb & Co.... We already saw that Willard Straight, a Morgan banker married to the Whitney fortune, with close ties to the Harriman family left Morgan to become VP of the AIC with its worldwide offices in all the right places, including Petrograd.

In 1917, the AIC took a big stake in the newly formed Grace Russian Company, a joint venture between W. R. Grace & Co. and the San Galli Trading Company of Petrograd. Take a walk down Manhattan, reader, and look up at the Grace skyscraper's curved glass and mirror facade glimmering in the sun, one of the most stylish modern architectural monuments built for the heirs to the shipping family's fortune when Peter Grace ran the company in the 1970s. Old money endures. AIC also invests in United Fruit Co. and spread its money to pay off revolutionary groups and stage political coups in Central and South America. The American International Shipbuilding Corp is a wholly owned entity of AIC. During the war it makes millions of dollars worth of contracts to build warships through the Emergency Fleet Corp..

"Another company operated by AIC," Sutton writes, "was G. Amsinck & Co., Inc. of New York; control of the company was acquired in November 1917. Amsinck was the source of financing for German espionage in the United States. In November 1917 the American International Corporation formed and wholly owned the Symington Forge Corporation, a major government contractor for shell forgings. Consequently, American International Corporation had significant interest in war contracts within the United States and overseas. It had, in a word, a vested interest in the continuance of World War I."

Acting on behalf of the Soviets the AIC director and San Francisco shipping magnate Robert Dollar attempted to import Czarist gold rubles into US in 1920, in contravention of US regulations. Other directors included Pierre S. DuPont, Philip A. S. Franklin and J. Grace (both directors of National City) alongside R. F. Herrick, director of New York Life Insurance. With them in the center of it all is Otto H. Kahn (1867-34), former president of the American Bankers Association, a trustee of the Carnegie Foundation. Otto H. Kahn runs Kuhn, Loeb (1916-31), and is a long standing client of the Stimson's law firm Harris, Winthrop linking up other prestigious clients in the financial world. Not to be left out is Percy Rockefeller married to the daughter of James A. Stillman of National City Bank. Stillman is president of AIC (1916-23). A. H. Wiggin, director of the NY Fed is also an AIC director, along with T. N. Vail, president of National City Bank of Troy, New York, and National City Bank president Frank Vanderlip in Manhattan.

The National City Bank has no fewer than ten directors on the board of AIC. It is the central element of the elite Consortium banking empire. At that time Stillman and Vanderlip are a most formidable force smoothly combining the Rockefeller-Morgan capital resources, partners and strategic interests. The DuPonts and Kuhn, Loeb each have one director, Stone & Webster have three on the board. At least four AIC directors – Saunders, Stone, Wiggin, and James T. Woodward (Hanover National) – are also directors on the NY Fed. Director of the NY Fed representing the nine-member board William Boyce Thompson paid millions to back Lenin, Trotsky and the Bolsheviks in the 1917 October Revolution coup. Having become its youngest president, in 1911, by the time America enters the First World War, Al Wiggin (1868-51) reigns as chairman at Chase National Bank transformed into an impregnable Rockefeller monolith. And like his cohorts Wiggin sits on some 50 boards of Consortium interests; in 1930 with America more deeply entrenched in the Soviet build-up under Stalin's regimentation of the Old Bolshevik regime Wiggin steps down at Chase succeeded by Winthrop W. Aldrich.

It should be clear in your mind that the unseen hands of the Consortium gang cast their dark shadows over the Holodomor. Again we can defer in good measure to Sutton's extensive findings corroborated by numerous other sources. It turns out that the AIC was a major player in determining how the Russian Revolution played out leading to Bolshevik Party coup that brought Lenin, Trotsky and Stalin to their height of revolutionary power taking over the Czarist Russian Empire. To do it the AIC used private and Federal Reserve central bank funds to finance key intelligence operations in parallel with the State Department sponsored activities.

In the Game no embassy is neutral. At the same time while advising and using the US Government channels through a network of elite Anglo-American Consortium bankers, lawyers, and businessmen, many whom were secret society members of the Skull & Bones of the Yale set, and the broader net of the upscale British Pilgrims Society, including President Wilson, and his extremely legalistic Secretary of State Robert Lansing.

AIC is fully engaged in Allied policy decisions on behalf of Lenin's newly installed Soviet regime. The best reading on this period is John Reed*'s Ten Days That Shook The World.* For three months in 1917 Petrograd and Moscow was in total chaos. The October Bolshevik coup rendered all of Czarist Russia into a war frenzy. In the turmoil, on January 16, 1918, William F. Sands, the AIC executive Secretary working in his New York office at 120 Wall Street, sent Lansing a long policy memorandum on Russia assuring him that the AIC had "various branches of American activity at work now in Russia ...". (Sands also intervenes at the highest levels to help left-wing radical journalist John Reed recover his notes and papers confiscated by government officials upon his return in early 1918 to the United States.) Fighting a civil war and threats of foreign intervention, the Bolsheviks negotiated with Germany for immediate withdrawal from the war; during that same spring 1918 Sands reprimands Secretary Lansing for obstructing

US recognition of Trotsky. "Whatever ground may have been lost should be regained now," Sands writes to Lansing, "even at the cost of a slight personal triumph for Trotsky." It should not be forgotten that it was President Wilson who personally intervened to free Trotsky from detention by Canadian and British authorities aboard a ship off Halifax en route to Petrograd in 1917 and secured him a US passport!

In a not so remarkable assessment by Eustace Mullins in *World Order 1984* as any amateur investigator can readily see once the arrangements are reassembled, it's funds from Rockerfeller's Standard Oil acting more like an investment firm which bankrolls Stalin's elimination of Trotsky. And this happens *after* Trotsky is appointed to head concessions negotiations, with Harriman, for example, which ultimately collapse but the damage is done and Trotsky is tainted for neo-capitalism, a definite violation of Marxist dogma even under Lenin's NEP. But to arrive at that juncture in the puzzle historians, scholars and investigative writers first have to come up with the pieces before the picture reappears in focus.

"The Rockefellers," Mullins observes, "figured in many pro-Soviet deals during the 1920s. Because of the struggle for power which developed between Stalin and Trotsky, the Rockefellers intervened in October, 1926, and backed Stalin, ousting Trotsky. Years later, they would again intervene when the Kremlin was racked by disagreements; David Rockefeller summarily fired Khrushchev."

Take a good look at Dan Morgan's excellent book *Merchants of Grain* (Viking, 1979) on the Soviet grain deals from the Kennedy years and on through the Nixon Presidency. It did not go unnoticed by Rockefeller and the Consortium that Khrushchev began importing grain from the US in 1960 to remedy shortcomings in the Soviet agrarian production. Here we should note that while both the US and the USSR had about the same amount of arable land, i.e., 11% of the total area, the US yields were, and remain high, while Soviet yields were much lower.

The instructions from AIC's William Sands were essentially predetermined for the government to implement as official policy. By then Czarist Russia is finished. It has ceased to exist. The takeover of Moscow and the Kremlin is assured by the coup under Bolshevik leadership. Trotsky commands the Red Army, first making peace with the Germans at Brest-Litvovsk, then dealing with a civil war raging across Russia but particularly hard fought on its European borders while the Americans launch their spring and summer offensives to finish off the last German offensive with the least loss of American combatants before the Armistice in November 1918.

Sands idyllically compares the Russian situation to "our own revolution", and he writes, "I have every reason to believe that the Administration plans for Russia will receive all possible support from Congress, and the hearty endorsement of public opinion in the United States." Since the Consortium men control the press and Congress the expectations of this former adviser to save the King of Korea from Japanese conquest and remarkable observer and participant of the unfolding drama are assured to bear fruit

By this time the Pilgrims Society members in London have already settled back in their deep leather chairs in their sundry clubs and estates confident that their men sitting in the British war cabinet under Lloyd George and Lord Milner have picked the winning ride of Lenin and Trotsky to finish ahead of the pack. As one of the directors of the NY Federal Reserve Bank William Sands feels confident that the million dollars sent to William Boyce Thompson in Petrograd destined for the Bolsheviks promises to be a terrific prize of the war if not the best deal of the century. Not since the Americans bagged the Philippines after the provocation sinking *Maine* off Cuba has an ever greater empire on a scale of boundless treasure and natural resource once the dream of kings and warlords been taken so easily, and at a cost so small, a few million dollars, and twenty million Russian lives.

MANCHURIA & THE CONSORTIUM'S ADVENTURE IN THE FAR EAST

The Consortium is ecstatic with greed and joy. Taking the Russian Empire is their steal of century. And it will allow them to set up the next few dominoes in the Great Game while they let the Japanese rape and loot Korea, Manchuria and the rest of China in their imperial conquest of Southeast Asia which will be there for the taking when the same Consortium gang ransacks Japan after dropping two atomic bombs in August 1945 forcing the Emperor's surrender to end the Second World War while they broker postwar deals sparing Japanese war criminals in exchange for hundreds of billions of dollars of gold and treasure secreted away to Consortium banks. This might seem like a mouthful, and it was. But this is how empires are made. In bits and pieces and some times a big war, and a coup from time to time. To bag Russia in a coup was a brilliant stroke of genius but it took the Great War to do it and that was no mince affair. It bankrupted both England and France and left the Americas masters of the Twentieth century. Reader, do you get it? Do you really think these educated fellows from Harvard and Yale and Princeton across the ocean and around this relatively small and overpopulated world to Oxford and Cambridge were really going to leave all that great Russian real estate with all its gold and valuable mineral resources to the sordid insane Bolsheviks? Really, you got to be kidding if you do. Wake up! Of course, the Consortium wants you to believe in their oversimplified staged establishment conventional textbook story. Sorry, but that's just a silly fairytale for children without pedigree.

William Franklin Sands (1874-46) is a most exceptional player in our story, a lawyer (Georgetown Law 1896), diplomat, author (*Our Jungle Diplomacy*, 1944), and law professor. Sutton observes Sands to be "a man with truly uncommon connections and influence" in Washington. A grandson of Benjamin Franklin, his early life was a tale of adventure and empire. Sands was one of the first graduates of the State Department diplomacy school, appointed second secretary of legation at Tokyo just prior to joining the US legation at Seoul as first secretary (1897-99). When two senior US officials Clarence Greathouse and Gen. Charles Legendre die within months of each other in 1899 Sands finds himself in the position of confidential adviser to Emperor Gojong of the Joseon Dynasty that has reigned for five centuries from 1392 to 1897 but whose future is very much at risk. In fact, this is the most important time in Korean history. (William Franklin Sands, *At the Court of Korea*, London: Century, Intro. Christopher Hitchens, ed., 1987)

In 1863 Gojong became King but the crown prince is still too young to rule. Three years later the Americans arrived and blasted the blissful Korean kingdom's isolation into the Twentieth century just around the corner. His father, Regent Heungseon Daewongun rules for him until Gojong reached adulthood. During the mid-1860s the Regent for Catholics and western missionaries is the much-detested instrument of the persecution, a Korean state policy that lead directly to the French campaign against Korea for decades to come. First it was Commodore Mathew C. Perry's flagship the war steamer *Mississippi* in 1853 sailing from Panama to Singapore and crossing the shifting shoals and dangerous reefs of the South China Sea to Macao, over the channel to Hong Kong, twelve years after it was seized by the British, for the voyage to Japan to secure ports for the American steamer trade which he said, in 1938, will be "a necessary arm of our naval strength to enable the country to sustain with ... dignity its maritime rights." (Peter Booth Wiley, *Yankees in the Land of the Gods, Commodore Perry and the Opening of Japan*, NY: Viking, 1990, 54)

When its Korea's turn, in July 1866, the *SS General Sherman* sails into Korean waters and attempt to explore upriver entering the Emperor's sacred capital Pyongyang. Only that the Koreans had not invited this rude and unexpected visit. Unfamiliar with the waters the ship ran aground outside Pyongyang. The crew on the General Sherman attempted to trade with the locals. Korean officials refused all trade offers although they provided the crew with the supply of foods. It seems the gun-toting Americans, uninvited and rude, and unaccustomed to the place, loud and obnoxiously unfamiliar with the local language and customs of an ancient kingdom organized with refined social protocol, made a mess of everything. The American crew imprisoned the Korean officials to force a trade negotiation. When that tactic failed to impress their reluctant hosts, the Americans showed them what Americans do best. The blasted away with their cannons killing curious civilian spectators who came to see the strange looking aliens in their strange looking ship. The result is seven dead Koreans and 5 wounded. Not too bright these Americans lost far from home in a hostile country which they ignite in resistance. The Koreans open fire on the ship. After four day battle, the *USS General Sherman* is a burning inferno. The Koreans take no prisoners hacking the crew to pieces. There are no survivors. Such is America's first display of "gunboat diplomacy".

Four years later more American gunships arrive in what the Koreans call the *Shinmiyangyo*, or Korean Expedition, in 1871, the first military action of America in Korea, near the island of Ganghwa. Again, the Americans lack the diplomatic initiative, and a battle ensues in June with ships blasting away and some 650 Americans armed with superior rolling block Remington rifles and 12 pound howitzers capture several forts, killing more than 200 Korean troops armed only with matchlock muskets and vintage weapons with a loss of only three American dead. Korea refuses to negotiate with these marauding demons until 1882. On board one of the five American warships is Rear Admiral John Rodgers and the US ambassador to China, Frederick F. Low. The Koreans forces known as "Tiger Hunters" are led by General Eo Jae-veon. Several Americans later received the Medal of Honor for their part in the battle. After a few weeks the US ships sailed to China. Subsequent efforts at a less threatening approach of diplomacy by the US fails to induce the Koreans who refuse to negotiate. The regent Daewon-gun instead entrenches deeper into a policy of isolation and issues a national proclamation against appeasing foreigners.

In 1873, King Gojong announced his assumption of royal rule. With the subsequent retirement of Heungseon Daewongun, the future Queen Min (later called Empress Myeongseong) gained complete control over her court, placing her family in high court positions. Not until 1876 after the Meiji Restoration in Tokyo when the Japanese acquire western military technology do Japanese ships again enter Ganghwado and threaten Seoul and force the hand of Joseon to sign the Treaty of Ganghwa do the Koreans enter into a trade treaty with their Asian neighbor opening three ports to trade and granting the Japanese extraterritoriality.. In the spring of 1882, America and Korea sign a 14-Article treaty which grants Korea a most favored trading status with the US. Three years later the British Navy arrive; they occupy Port Hamilton and that same year, 1885, they capture the King of Burma in their empire campaign of Asiatic colonization. It remains in place until the Japanese destroy Korea's sovereignty in its 1910 annexation.

Under the watchful eyes of the foreign powers including the United States, and, in particular England and Russia, the Japanese are eager for a successful military adventure abroad, having grown weak at home with thousands of samurai downgraded in status and in need of re-legitimization before they become utterly redundant. Japanese Home Minister Prince Yamagata transforms society into a police state obedient to his own forces drafted from powerful shogun families and the underworld of crime and corruption. Yamagata yearns to increase the sovereignty of Japan by suppressing another. In rivalry with the Chinese for power and influence in Korea, the Japanese sink a Chinese troop ship and push Chinese forces out of the country and seize southern Manchuria, then take Formosa in their negotiation for peace. Fearful of Czarist expansion along the Trans-Siberian railroad the Japanese sign with the British, in 1902, their naval treaty which guarantees British support should Japan go to war with more than one foreign adversary.

Embolden in their aggression by the Anglo-alliance the Japanese intensify their repression of the Koreans and balk in negotiations with Moscow instead launching a surprise attack in Manchuria, in 1904 against the Czarist fleet at Port Arthur in a war that endures for over a year. The Japanese are mauled by the Russians taking 60,000 casualties but then sink the Russian fleet and emerge victorious at Roosevelt's peace conference held in the US. With the backing of the Americans and their secret deal to let the Roosevelt and Taft have their way in the Philippines, the Japanese eagerly swallow Korea entirely by its complete annexation in 1910 while secretly murdering tens of thousands of Koreans on the pretext of fighting terrorism. Four decades later another Roosevelt will do all he can to deceive and defeat the Empire of the Rising Sun.

Just prior to the outbreak of war in 1904 Sands is obliged to leave in 1904; the Japanese find him too pro-Korean and no longer desirable to stay in the country. Bill Sands is replaced by Durham White Stevens, a very different kind of man. Stevens (1851-08) is a tragic figure long forgotten in America. In Korea he is a doomed man. Suspected of betraying the Korean people and employed by Japan's Foreign Ministry he is killed as an imperialist agent for Japanese occupation by Korean-American assassins. Durham White Stevens becomes "the first victim of Korean terrorism". A lawyer and graduate from Oberlin in Ohio he joined State in 1873. Grant appoints him to the US legation under nationally famous lawyer John Bingham involved with the trial of the Lincoln assassination. Stevens resigns from the State Department and in 1884 began to use his legal skills defending Japanese interests abroad in treaty negotiations, for example, with Mexico, and in Washington, as well as in Korea earning medals from the Emperor enhancing his reputation and wealth. During the First Sino-Japanese war he published an article in the *North American Review*, defending Japanese imperial ambitions and denouncing the "dry rot of Chinese conservatism" that hindered Korea's development. More medals, this time a Second Class of the Order of the Sacred Treasures. Stevens is hired to go with the Japanese mission to twice to Hawaii (1901, 1902) More decorations and rewards including Second Class of the Order of the Rising Sun; in October 1904, for the fourth time Stevens is decorated with the Grand Cross of the Sacred Treasure. Apparently while still employed by the Japanese government, in November 1904, Stevens is appointed adviser to the Korean Foreign Office. It's virtually a death sentence. Stevens is attacked in San Francisco, and buried in Washington DC. One of his pallbearers is the lawyer Elihu Root. The Korean assassins are considered heroes and patriots in their home country. (The William Franklin Sands story remains fertile and unexplored territory waiting for biographers and scholars. William Franklin Sands Papers, Philadelphia Archdiocesan Historical Research Center, Wynnewood, PA; W. F. Sands, *At the Court of Korea*, 1987)

As he had done in Korea Bill Sands moves seamlessly through the shadows and chambers of power. He acquires the reputation of the quiet fixer, a behind-the-scene trouble-shooter surprisingly cool and at ease in hot spots. Sands shows up in Panama during the revolt against Columbia over Teddy Roosevelt's seizure of the canal zone and reaches an understanding with radicals. Then there is his jaunt to Mexico, and Ecuador mixed up in the Alfaro-Estrada revolution while appearing to settle a projected construction of the Guayaquil waterworks as a countermeasure against the spread of yellow fever and bubonic plague. For the Taft-Stimson White House Bill Sands heads the US Embassy in Guatemala (1909). From 1898 to 1920, Guatemala is ruled by the dictator Manuel Estrada Cabrera whose access to the presidency is facilitated loyalty of a few generals and generous concessions to United Fruit Company when Minor Cooper Keith made his fortune there, and in Costa Rica and Panama, investing in railroads and bananas. It's during his long presidency that the United Fruit Company becomes a major force in Guatemala with a reputation of unrestrained violence of the workers including islanders shipped in from the Caribbean Basin.

Sands is one of the least known characters in the unfolding saga of how the Anglo-American Consortium took Russia. During the Great War he consults with Basil Miles on what to do with a million German prisoners of war, and some half-million displaced civilians. As is not uncommon in Washington, Sands enjoys a career that flows like sweet liquor between State and Wall Street. He knows all the right people and has little trouble when called negotiates an Ecuadorian loan for James Speyer's New York bank specializing in railroads in Central America and the Philippines, or to represent the Central Aguirre Sugar Company in Puerto Rico. During the years 1915 and 1916 he's back in London to represent the George McFadden company of Philadelphia for the solution of the British naval seizures of non-contraband cotton.

His long diplomatic career, however, will not be trumpeted by Henry Luce in *Time,* or Vincent Astor's *Newsweek,* or any other Consortium mouthpiece for middle-class America. Sands escapes having his privacy traded for the notoriety he deserves. During the war in 1916 Sands travels to Czarist Russia on an intelligence mission with Basil Miles undercover of the Red Cross. The stories Sands could tell of his elegant negotiations and adventurous encounters to please Le Carre's Smiley or Graham Greene's man in Havana. Many of his early letters tell of events that have escaped the peering eyes of scholars covering a range of adventures from the Boxer Rebellion to the Russo-Japanese war, and the political intrigues in Central America as well as the building of the Panama Canal. (See William Franklin Sands Papers)

Upon returning to New York Sands takes over the helm at at AIC. Miles, Sands and Bill Phillips are all AIC insiders and move funds from America to the Bolsheviks as well as maintaining a convenient governmental intelligence division for dealing with Russia.

Make no mistake about it. AIC and its Consortium advisers are calling the shots. Historian Sutton makes that clear, writing, "In early 1918 Sands became the known and intended recipient of certain Russian 'secret treaties'. If the State Department files are to be believed, it appears that Sands also acted as courier, and, that he had some prior access to official documents – prior, that is, to US government officials. On January 14, 1918, just two days before Sands wrote his memo on policy towards the Bolsheviks, Secretary Lansing caused the following cable to be sent in Green Cipher to the American legation in Stockholm: 'Important official papers for Sands to bring here were left at Legation. Have you forwarded them? Lansing. 'The reply of January 16 from (Ambassador Ira sic) Morris in Stockholm reads: 'Your 460 January 14, 5 pm. Said documents forwarded Department in pouch number 34 on December 28th.' To these documents is attached another memo, signed 'BM' (Basil Miles, an associate of Sands): 'Mr. Phillips. They failed to give Sands 1st installment of secret treaties wh. (which) he brought from Petrograd to Stockholm'."

Pulling back the curtain projecting the Consortium façade of history, Sutton found the clay that packed it together. Evidently, late 1917, the AIC executive secretary traveled from Petrograd to Stockholm on his secret mission. A few months later, on July 1, 1918, Sands wrote to Treasury Secretary McAdoo suggesting a commission for "economic assistance to Russia."

Sands urges that since it would be difficult for a government commission to "provide the machinery" for any such assistance, "it seems, therefore, necessary to call in the financial, commercial and manufacturing interest of the United States to provide such machinery under the control of the Chief Commissioner or whatever official is selected by the President for this purpose."

Sands is in position to arrange for the financial and economic exploitation of postwar Russia to be handled by a network of Consortium members pivoting around the AIC's offices near Wall Street at 120 Broadway, a well-known address with their men inside the New York Fed and Washington. These links include principally Guaranty Trust, the Guggenheims, General Electric, and other key corporations. As it were, Rockefeller's Sinclair Oil of New Jersey is linked with the enormous mining interests of Meyer Guggenheim and his seven sons, in particular, Daniel Guggenheim (1856-30) "to obtain concessions in Russia". Rockefeller and Rothschild both focus their interests on Russia's vast oil reserves at Baku and in the Caucasus which remain central to dealing with the Bolshevik leadership of the Soviet Communist Party.

Sad but true and war not famine is Bullitt's priority. This time the Americans cannot come to the rescue of Russia's peasants, not like with Hoover's ARA in 1919 during the Lenin regime. The Consortium will do nothing to help these people doomed under Stalin's totalitarian meat grinder. Millions starve. Stalin kills them. Then when the Nazis come millions more die.

But millions more came, and came again. Stalin orders wave after human wave of tanks and soldiers against Hitler's well-trained and heavily equipped Nazi divisions. Poorly prepared young "Volunteer" Soviet units are mowed down by Nazi gunners and Panzers. More keep coming, overwhelming the German soldiers, holding down the German advance into the Ukraine towards Moscow, and giving Stalin's generals more time to prepare defensive counterattacks. Could Stalin's totalitarian USSR hold out against a German invasion?

In his analysis of preparations for war Bullitt continues to display the logic of his ideas. The Soviet Union has virtually impregnable defenses he tells President Roosevelt, however, they will only be marginally effective abroad. Bad roads, railways, vast spaces and natural barriers all give Russia "an extraordinarily favorable position for defense, at the same time they make it extraordinarily difficult for the Red Army to operate effectively beyond its borders." The French (Laval, Leger, and the French ambassador in Moscow) "estimated at zero the value of the Red Army as a fighting force beyond the borders of the Soviet Union. … Various Japanese have expressed the same opinion to me. The same Frenchmen believe that the Soviet air force, in spite of the inferior quality of its machines, might have a minor value in a European conflict."

Catherine Merridale (*Ivan's War*) gives a fine account of what happened when the Germans invaded the Ukraine in the Sunday morning June 22, 1941. Luftwaffe aircraft take off from their airstrips at three o'clock on a Sunday morning, bombing and strafing Soviet airfields. By noon Stalin has lost 1,200 planes; within a week 2000 Soviet planes have been destroyed. Göering toured the front three weeks later ecstatic with amazement and for good reason. He learns in a western district, for example, 528 planes lay destroyed on the ground by German guns. With methodical precision and ease his Luftwaffe also hits strategic targets besides aircraft including fuel dumps, and anti-aircraft guns.

Fearing yet the worst is yet to come future president of Czechoslovakia Eduard Benes tells Bullitt that "the Soviets might use Czechoslovakia as a base to attack Germany but it required a dangerous path over Roumania's northern tip, so that "the new airplane line from Moscow to Prague had to be routed by way of Odessa, and Cluj in Transylvania – a very long way around." Unless the Soviets quickly received FDR's emergency Lend-Lease provisions military experts in both London and Washington estimate Russian resistance would crumble in *one to three months.* (C. Merridale, *Ivan's War*, 84-7)

Once the Holodomor has long since passed Bullitt writes FDR that any Franco-German alliance in Stalin's mind means losing the Ukraine to save France. And Stalin knows the French will do nothing to save the Ukraine. He understands how Paris had been spared from massive destruction or occupation in the First World War when the French caused the German command with little to spare was forced to transfer divisions from the West to the Eastern Front to stem the advance of Czarist armies. I remember stories told by my French aunt living in the Parisian family flat on rue Jacob in the Latin Quarter as she recalled childhood memories taking refuge underground in the coal cellar in the Great War (1914-18) when the infamous railway German "Paris gun" with its 120 km long-range shot 210 pound (94 kg) lobbed shells into the city. Reader, its self-evident that vivid memories of the First World War are still fresh in the minds of these veteran professionals of war.

"The present policy of the Soviet Union", Bullitt went on, "not only with regard to its European neighbors but also all other European states is very similar to the traditional British policy of the balance of power. The Soviet Union fears nothing so much as a general reconciliation of European hatreds, especially a reconciliation between Germany and France: (a) The Soviet Union fears that reconciliation in Europe may be based upon permission to Germany to obtain the economic outlets which she needs by acquisition of the Ukraine. (b) War in Europe is regarded as inevitable and ultimately desirable from the Communist point of view.

"The Soviet Government fears war in Europe at the present time because the Soviet Union is unprepared and it is feared that war this year or next in Europe would grow into world war with simultaneous attacks on the Soviet Union by Germany, Poland and Japan. But it is the conviction of the leaders of the Soviet Union that if war in Europe can be postponed until the Red Army is prepared and the railroads of the Soviet Union rebuilt, the Soviet Union will be able to intervene successfully in such a war, and will be able to protect and consolidate any communist government which may be set upon as a result of war and ensuing revolution in any European state. To keep Europe divided and to postpone the war which will certainly come if Europe remains divided, is the substance of Russian policy in Europe." Although Bullitt would reverse his opinion as the world watched in awe when Hitler attacked in June 1941, he is essentially accurate in his assessment that Stalin never trusted the English any more than he trusted the French. Churchill needed him. Narrowly defeated at Stalingrad, and Leningrad relentlessly bombed and starved to near extinction, and before Moscow successfully repelled the Germans in sight of the city's towers, Russia's future looked less dismally bleak. But that was before Churchill and Stalin became steadfast drinking chums, slicing up the world between empires. (re. "War in Europe…", W. Brownell and R. N. Billings, *So Close to Greatness*, 183)

In this same memorandum Bullitt transmits an obvious but nonetheless salient factor in the US-Soviet equation, and plays the card that would turn the trick. "It is, of course," he writes, "the heartiest hope of the Soviet Government that the United States will become involved in a war with Japan." He goes on, "If such a war should occur it would be the policy of the Soviet Union to remain outside the conflict and to gain whatever wealth might be acquired by supplying the United States with war materials via the west and supplying Japan with war materials in the east. *To think of the Soviet Union as a possible ally of the United States in case of war with Japan is to allow the wish to be farther to the thought.*" (italics added)

Here Bullitt is seriously mistaken. This is a moment reader for a brief review of how these beginnings in the twentieth century take a different direction. The Japanese attack Pearl Harbor six months after the Germans invade the Ukraine. Battling a two-front war the US and the USSR opt for the only strategy possible in order to survive total war. Bullitt here theorizes that the Soviets will wait for Japan to be crushed in order "to acquire Manchuria and Sovietize China" and until a communist government can then be established in Japan. The Japanese seizure of Manchuria in 1931 coming in the wake after decades of consolidated gains in the China territories over the past forty years is protected by a British treaty alliance and weak America complacency symbolized by Stimson's weak diplomatic posturing in vain and Hoover's lack of resolve combined with Consortium duplicity and Morgan investment incentives. Nor does the League of Nations show any serious intent back with resolve that it has power to impede their imperial conquest of China and Southeast Asia.

With Nazi Germany crushed and in ruins, the Russians in Berlin, and Hitler dead, in fact only two days after the Americans on August 6 1945 drop an atomic bomb code-name "Little Boy" with a uranium-235 warhead on Hiroshima killing at least one hundred thousand people, – mostly civilians, – the Russians declare war on Japan and launch a massive successful *blitzkrieg* overwhelming the Japanese in Manchuria. A few hours later in the morning on August 9, 1945, America drops a second atomic bomb, "Fat Man", armed with a plutonium 239 warhead on Nagasaki, a military industrial port, killing 40,000 people. In the chaos of rapid events the Japanese are caught completely by surprise when the Soviets declared war an hour before midnight on 8 August 1945, invading just after midnight on 9 August on three fronts simultaneously penetrating deeper into

Manchukuo and capture the former Chinese Emperor on an airstrip attempting to flee to Japan. By August 14, the Japanese Emperor Hirohito agrees to surrender preempting a Soviet invasion of Japan thus thwarting the worst fears of the Japanese civilian population.

Consortium insiders buried the famine story with the dead. They hold the essential positions in US government and news organizations. Influence is something to buy and they buy it all in the name of protecting their special interests. Monopoly is something the Consortium is very good at preserving as well as their control of necessary and valuable resources. Col. House works close with the British agent Wiseman advised Wilson during the First World War to suppress and gag any news organizations that oppose relations with the Bolsheviks.

Stalin has the Rockefeller-backed Council of Foreign Relations (CFR) on his side. By this time the capitalists have created a real problem. Stalin is free to virtually do anything he wants and get away with it. He can even takeover Europe when the time is right f he wants to go completely Bolshevik and fan the flames of communist world revolution taking his Red Army all the way through France to Paris and the Atlantic coastline. The Russians never forget that Napoleon burned Moscow...

In a war with Germany the American generals know that America will have to fight hard to prevent a total Soviet victory and Sovietization of Europe. After what the Germans did to the Ukrainians, the *Werhmacht* stood little chance against the full fury and unrelenting massive force of the Soviet Union. Hitler never learned the lesson of the full force of Stalin's use of terror against the Ukrainians until it was too. The Russians toppled Berlin. Only then did Hitler take the cyanide with a *coup de grace* bullet in the head.

"Not all the witnesses died", Solzhenitsyn writes. Nobel laureate and Soviet dissident Aleksandr Solzhenitsyn survived those famine years. Akin to a miracle Solzhenitsyn is also a survivor of the Second World War in the Red Army and survived Stalin's Gulag. After long exile in Vermont, he dies in his native homeland in the summer of 2008. Do not forget Stalin's crimes, he warns. "Deception. This, too, can be practiced thanks to total secrecy," Solzhenitsyn reminds us. Deception in any society, free or totalitarian, is a symptom of manipulation and a total public disconnect with events and processes endangering any community of shared responsibility and values. Solzhenitsyn was strong and robust, able to mentally and physically resist and not be broken. He was never defeated nor did he destroy himself like Hemingway.

During the Harvard commencement where he is guest speaker I am determined to meet this Russian soothsayer who came to bridge two disparate worlds. While approaching the stage, he stands behind me as he approaches the stage along the front row. Make no mistake as I turned to looked over my shoulder he appears a towering presence overhead and for an instant I felt he could crush me like an ant. Looking at him in those fleeting moments I saw Solzhenitsyn alone silhouetted like a mighty pillar standing alone with the force to hold the sky aloft. Everything suddenly seemed still, silent, more real. After his speech backstage

I gripped his hand as we met in a strange moment feeling the seconds pass into eternity. Again it was a same intense moment without equivalent in reality.

The Solzhenitsyn Harvard address is highly publicized. Three decades earlier Secretary of State George Marshall uses the same Harvard commencement platform, in 1947, to launch the $17 billion postwar Marshall Plan for the recovery of Europe.

"At no time have governments been moralists", Solzhenitsyn reminds us. How carefully FDR and his men guarded their secrets and employed ghostwriters skilled at crafting subtle fictions. "Sometimes we try to lie but our tongue will not allow us to," Solzhenitsyn wrote, and added prophetically, "And soon no one will call Stalin's government anything but a government of insanity and treason." Today a frightening trend is taking form under the regime of Putin and his thousands of former KGB officers who took over Russia from Yeltsin's widely reported indulgences. Stalinists are suddenly becoming the fashion. In 1963, Premier N.S. Khrushchev authorizes the publication of his book in the Soviet Union, *A Day in the Life of Ivan Denisovich* detailing the horror of the prison camps and the absurd logic of life as it truly was lived under communism under Stalin. Seven years later Solzhenitsyn is again target of the Kremlin and expulsed from the Soviet Writers Union, a sentence for a writer worse then death, silenced, banned and unable to publish or earn a living. After he is declared a Nobel Laureate winning the prize for literature Solzhenitsyn is banned from the Soviet Union, in 1974. For the next 20 years he lives a life of exile in Vermont until his return to Russia in 1994. (A. I. Solzhenitsyn, *A Day in the Life of Ivan Denisovich,* NY: Praeger, 1963; A. I. Solzhenitsyn, *The Gulag Archipelago 1918-1956*)

Since Red October and the consequent Civil War consolidating Bolshevik control of the communist revolution Lenin and the Bolsheviks fear losing the Ukraine and desperately need the support of the peasants to survive before they can inflict the Dictatorship of the Proletariat and ultimate rule by the CP. Stalin too fears Ukrainian nationalism and an independent Ukraine. Both fret over the destruction of the Soviet Union from foreign powers, including Germany, Japan, and the Anglo-American Entente. That is to say, Stalinism is not a sudden or isolated development. There are a multitude of reasons to point to the famine tragedy as not only man-made and provoked by Stalin's obsession with Ukraine, and his maniacal obsession in internal politics with absolute power, but also stems from a traditional Russian fear of encroachment and attack by the imperialist foreign nations.

Indeed, the entire Bolshevik crash program for economic recovery and development after the First World War proceeds in anticipation of an inevitable Second World War that would be far more terrible and costly than that which preceded it. With the world locked in motion on the brink of war and escalating armament, it's too simple to blame either a sick, paranoid and totalitarian tyrant or backward Russia with its Czarist oppression of peasants for the "man-made" famine. It's also naïve, and gives rise to a false reading of history.

The royal stewards of empire and elected leaders of developed nations were embarked on a technological arms race and wars of mass destruction. Survival depends on more than guesswork. War industries are given priority. Stalin resorts to mass slave labor imposed under the rule of socialist dictatorship of the so-called proletariat, – the workers and peasants, citizens of the Revolution. Russian reconstruction under the Bolshevik leadership is in the general scheme for reshaping the future of Europe, and this scheme is endorsed by all the leaders of the West who stood by passively and as their diplomats and engineers watch over the slaughter. Embassies filed their classified interviews and reports to their senior government officials. As America's client dictator and "our SOB" firmly in place, to use FDR's vernacular, and with soviet state terror a by-product of Anglo-American Consortium investment, why only blame Stalin for unrealistic quotas in factory production or colossal battlefield casualties? Behind his big desk in the Oval Office FDR's manicured hands were dripping with the blood of treachery and death on a scale never seen before in human history. The First World War is just a prelude, a prerequisite for the Second, moving Humanity from Total War to MAD, or "Mutually Assured Destruction", a suitably apt acronym for the Atomic Age and title of the most popular comics in the sixties and my favorite competing with *Boy's Life* and *Playboy.*

Stalin blamed the dancing, lazy, smiling illiterate peasants. Hitler blamed Stalin. The French and English blamed Hitler and Stalin. The French blamed the English (again). The English blamed everybody. Americans of course kept their head down, made a lot of money for themselves hiding behind England from across the sea and blamed Europe. America always blames Europe. America never blames itself. No nation does. Find a scapegoat. Or find something better for the "feel good" domestic consumption catharsis.

In the actual course of events the Realpolitik of US-Soviet relations is much a part of the Soviet Ukraine Holodomor. Call it the interactive dynamics of international relations, or call it patricide. It *is* patricide. It is and always will be too easy to simply blame Stalin. Hitler understands the dynamics evident in *Mein Kamf* to concentrate all the blame on one target, the evil enemy, in his case, the Jews. America never takes responsibility for its errors. As a superpower it doesn't have too. Governed by bankers, diplomats, and lawyers, *that* will never happen. These professionals never admit error. Bankers and lawyers never blame themselves. And of course, diplomats are paid not to reveal their secrets.

In the Kremlin there was no man more alone than Stalin. Nor more adroitly paranoid and afraid of losing his kingdom. His is a logic of the beast. Not far from his borders another world leader was born, in 1935. His Kingdom is Tibet. The 14th reincarnated God-King of Tibet lost his vast and ancient kingdom that had endured even long before the 5th Dalai Lama ruled and built the Potala Palace in Lhasa also becomes a victim of the nuclear arms race and general destablization in China and flees the Communist invaders in 1959 crossing the Himalayas to refuge in India. His Holiness the Dalai Lama does not need to know all the details of the complexity of the problem to understand its simple nature. (Thomas Laird, *Into Tibet, The CIA's First Atomic Spy and His Secret Expedition it to Lhasa*, NY: Grove Press, 2012)

Years ago when I would sit privately with him on several occasions and call him a friend, his awareness opened new paths of perception and understanding. The Chinese communists killed over a million Tibetans. "This blaming", His Holiness the Dalai Lama tells us, "will reinforce self-centered attitudes, like attachment and hatred. Through association with such deluded attitudes, we become attached to our belongings and beset by mistrust or even paranoia." This we see strikingly clear in the US-Soviet syndrome of alliance with Lenin and Stalin and their ascension to absolute despotism.

His Holiness the Dali Lama, who prefers to refer to himself as "a simple monk", observed, "The Chinese communists abandoned religion for the sake of what they saw as liberation. They call each other comrade and in the past made great sacrifices in the struggle for the liberation of their country. But after gaining power, they created political rivalries and often fight against each other. One tries to take advantage of the other, and eventually one destroys the other. Although socialism has the noble aim of working for the common welfare of the masses, the means for achieving that end have antagonized the community, and the attitude of the people has become confrontational. In this form Communism has become so destructive that all the energy of the government is directed toward repression rather than of liberation." During a meeting in early 1980 after mid-night in Benares His Holiness told me firmly, "The Tibetans will never be happy living under the Chinese by force." Thirty years have passed and still there is no accord between China and the Tibetans. Stalin's assault on the peasant population in the Ukraine and their resilient nationalism bears this wisdom out.

The paradigm of spiritual enlightenment personified in the Dalai Lama carries much wisdom to point us in the other direction of compassion rather than lead astray pursuing a logic of destruction through starvation and war. The enlightened Dalai Lama writes, "In contrast to the Communists many great practitioners have traveled the Buddhist path and led their lives on the basis of love and compassion. With such motives your basic intention would be to work for the benefit of sentient beings, for whose sake you are trying to cultivate positive states of mind. Even if the damage done by the Chinese Communists in Tibet and China had been matched by an equally extensive positive program, I doubt that they would have been able to contribute much to the betterment of society because they lack the motivation of great compassion. When we look at Karl Marx's own life and the actual origin of Marxism, we find that Karl Marx underwent great sufferings during his lifetime and advocated constant struggle to topple the bourgeois class. His outlook was based on confrontation. Because of that primary motive, the entire movement of Communism has failed. If the primary motive had been based on compassion and altruism, then things would have been very different." (His Holiness, the Dalai Lama of Tibet, *The Way to Freedom*, The Library of Tibet, Harper Collins, 1995)

I was a child of the Cold War. Stalin died March 5, 1953. I was born in New York City the following year. My entire family was a product of the Cold War, cousins, uncles, – two generation, those who fought and those who survived. My father served 44 months in the intelligence work in the US Army Signal Corps in the South Pacific islands. My memory as a child standing inside the family's tiny underground nuclear shelter remain a vivid image from early days growing up in the racist "sundown town" of Darien, Connecticut infamously portrayed in the Academy Award-winning film Gentleman's Agreement (1947) starring Gregory Peck and Dorothy McGuire which exposed its discriminatory real estate practices against Blacks and Jews, and when the only dark skin allowed in public were bronzed Wasps at the beach and country clubs.

There one summer I and a friend from Yale, a grandson of Harvey Bundy painted the towering steeple of the Protestant church on the Boston Post Road and where my father was a Deacon, treasurer and friend to its well-known minister, as well as his banker on occasion when some lost soul needed Christian charity. Leaving that insulated, privileged and unreal world I never returned and bare no regret.

Although I didn't know it at the time my future was Yale. There I passed through corridors of power and entered different worlds where I lived with the sons of the Consortium who had served in the Second World War of their fathers and drank punch with President Kingman Brewster who taught us young freshmen to be good public servants "of the highest integrity". Fortunately, I learned there are worlds beyond the reach of Yale and you should follow your own path to find and know them.

For nearly forty-five years after the war public attention in America was focused on the Cold War mythology of a death-struggle between capitalism and communism. Now the divisions are between terrorism and the free world impaired by a global financial debacle, and a very dubious juxtaposition of words and ideas by the spinners. It was a carefully deliberate diversion instilled in the young and old with enough potency to sting the mind and raise the soul. The Consortium powers that rule over the American people and the world are determined to protect their investments in the future of their sons and daughters with trusts of accumulated capital managed by the same banks that gave us several wars and peace to inspire the American Dream. The intent of these planners of military strategy and economic postwar reconstruction required a convenient manipulation of political forces inside governments using their monopolistic power to acquire and control world markets and assure profitable access to valuable resources.

Money and markets make miracles happen. Stalin knew this to be true. We all live in this post-Cold War world. The Holodomor which sacrificed peasants to let Stalin and American capital have its way was one step up the stairway to the paradise of prosperity for Americans who no longer need to struggle in order to survive. The US-Soviet deal signed in November 1933 led to straight to Yalta. It also led straight to Berlin. When the Big Three, – Churchill, Roosevelt, Stalin –, met in Teheran in 1943, the race to Berlin had already begun. The Americans were yet to have launched their Normandy invasion cross the English Channel to the beaches of northern France; as long as the Russians remained bogged down getting slaughtered pushing the Germans back out of the Ukraine, the Americans still had time to precision bomb and occupy Western Europe to minimize Allied casualties.

Inevitably it is the interest in monopoly motivated by greed that protects and maintains Consortium power with all the privileges and trimmings reserved to the top tier of the ruling hierarchy. Contrary to popular belief, under the Consortium system public service was a very private business. It still is. With the appearance of democratic popular participation, largely window-dressing to pacify the population, the Consortium rules behind closed doors. Don't fool yourself. The Consortium is very hostile to sharing power that might in any way threaten its agenda, present and future. Public service ensures its survival. Longevity in the families is their only option. Seeds are carefully planted and sowed.

FDR's economic policy at home administered through the National Reconstruction Administration parallels and shapes his political relations with the Kremlin. There may have been occasional corrections of the compass but Consortium policy remains as fixed as the stars in the sky. From his first days in the White House FDR holds true to course with occasional corrections to political and economic events which he executes with triumphant flare. No successor or predecessor ever exhibits or is capable of reproducing his artistry in command. Kennedy tried but he had his own loyal entourage to assist and protect the sanctity of the White House. And history being what it was he had Roosevelt's ghosts to guide him whereas Roosevelt had Stimson and Marshall but in the end dwelt in his own iconoclastic enigma. Military arrangements do not alter their direction or logic and change only insofar as they intensify the design of their true nature and intention. All the President's men are essentially the same advisors and operators in axis of power and control in the Consortium passed down from the Wilson era of the First World War and they remain close to their Commander-in-Chief responsible for the Second Big One.

Antony Sutton published the bulk of his Soviet-American research in the seventies. He called "corporate socialism", namely FDR's federation of financial and business forces inside government. After the 1912 US presidential election, the merger of capitalists with the federal legislation they administered left the American Socialist Party in their tracks; by 1916, its leader Eugene Debs was in prison. The Socialist Party in the US was a dead fish.

In 1916, Wilson was reelected on an arbitrary campaign pledge not to enter the war in Europe. The capitalists, however, by then had already taken over the government and were in control of Wilson's war cabinet. Since the beginning Morgan bankers financed the war and were determined to dominate any postwar settlement. The industrial gains of the First World War, along with the lessons learned for consolidating the power of the wealthy elite within a trained and technologically-equipped nation would be multiplied many times in a more efficiently managed and more violent war and a new generation of young men to fight it. Implementation of Soviet Five-Year Plans stayed the course. The Terror-Famine of Ukraine would be reduced to a mere footnote in world history buried under more terror and Genocide by Hitler and Stalin including Soviet in 1943-44 deportation and extermination of the peoples of the North Caucasus. Who would blame their saviors then? (R. Conquest, *The Nation Killers*, Macmillan, 1970;

New International Review, 1981, v.3, No.2; A. C. Sutton, *Western Technology and Soviet Economic Development*)

By the early thirties, the Russian people were breaking under the repressive Five-Year Plans of collective agriculture and industrialization mixed with famine, deaths and gulags. Communist leaders planned to save the Party by removing Stalin and blaming the Soviet economic fiasco on him alone. Stalin needed a way out.

Stalin's Soviet negotiator Maxim Litvinov sailed to the United States and secretly arrived in Washington to work out the language with Bullitt and FDR. Litvinov assured Roosevelt that American Communists would no longer seek to overthrow the United States government! FDR played into Stalin's hands. At this critical moment the United States chose to recognize the *status quo* and formalizes relations with the USSR. Stalin's prestige rose once Communist legitimacy was recognized by the world's greatest capitalist nation. The financial credit of the Communists skyrockets overnight. Communist idolatry soars to new heights heralding the Great Promise of the Proletarian New Man. With the Consortium's endorsement Stalin emerges the new God-head of Soviet Russia.

The intrepid Welsh reporter Gareth Jones knows all this to be true but had to see it for himself and reports back to British war prime minister David Lloyd George.. Harvard academic and war veteran Bruce Hopper from Harvard knows it, too. US Department insider Bullitt knows it from secret memoranda destined for FDR and Secretary Hull. They are all acting with strong links to the powerful Consortium players. And they all use their knowledge differently with uncanny convergence to the same end. But that's not the concern for the Ukrainians for they are doomed.

Long after Stalin had abandoned talking "Bolsheviki", spurred by mercurial impulse Bullitt is frightened that the Commie Reds are going to ferment world revolution against the capitalist West. Nothing was further from the truth. Bullitt has a direct link to FDR, and he's certainly not going to sound the alarm on world war out of step with the White House.

Roosevelt's "New Deal" for America included a secret trade alliance with Stalin and Soviet communism. It was one of the greatest mysteries of modern times. Nothing was ironic about the simultaneous bail-out of the two apparently diametrically opposed societies. The package was centered on the basic outlook shared by Wall Street and the system of centralized banks of the Federal Reserve. In the 1970s, Sutton and Solzhenitsyn found themselves to be common bedfellows. Was this timely coincidence so strange and sudden? They came into the public arena in the United States in the same period grasping how the world strategists combined forces to set up the *quid pro quo* paradigm prior to the Cold War. This by-product of the Second World War was already inscribed in the strategic alliances put in place from day one of the First World War and the international banking arrangements moving into place for the takeover of the Czarist Russian Empire via the Bolshevik coup in 1917.

Maxime Litvinov, the veteran Bolshevik diplomat who in London helped establish relations between Britain's Foreign Office and Lenin, in 1918, was one of the very few Bolshevik commissars who escaped Stalin's terror which eliminated most of his fellow diplomats and friends. Molotov later replaces Litvinov also survived, but not his wife, nor Kaganovich's brother. In 1933 Litvinov facetiously asked German diplomats impatient over communist propaganda their take on "the literary works of Hitler (*Mein Kampf*)?" "That was ten years ago," came his disingenuous reply. Inside the Narkomindel (Soviet Foreign Office) 'talking Bolshevik', circuitously tedious Marxist dialectics with fundamental reasoning based on the absolute invincibility of the proletarian working class, was rarely heard.

In contrast to what he might say in a speech at a party meeting, in his private communications Litvinov did not "speak Bolshevik". He once quipped to a foreign diplomat that of course he could use that "language" if the diplomat so desired. When he was led the Comintern in 1923, Litvinov wrote a letter wet with sarcasm to fellow commissar Zinoviev to call off his agents in Germany damaging relations with the Weimar. Two years later Litvinov and Chicherin sign a rare joint letter to the Politburo asking for the recall of the Soviet envoy in Paris. A. G. Shlyapnikov, the left oppositionist thought to be talking too much Bolsheviki and straining diplomatic relations recently renewed with France. Litvinov had succeeded Chicherin as commissar for foreign affairs during the 1920s. Litvinov even speaks openly with foreign diplomats about his disdain for the Comintern, castigating them as a group of idiot chatterboxes, scribblers and rabble-rousing radicals who ought to be invited *to leave* the Soviet Union. By that time, the Comintern had become an obstacle to better relations with the West, so that by the end of the 1920s Stalin brought it more or less under his control.

In 1959 Soviet Premier Nikita Khrushchev ridiculed America and the West after the Berlin Wall and U-2 spy plane crises and brandished his shoe in the General Assembly of the United Nations frequently threatening to "bury" the US. It was a ridiculous demonstration of Russian peasant bravado even though if you scratch this Russian you will find a Ukrainian. (Or vice verse.) He screamed out that he had caught the Americans red-handed! That he had captured the American pilot "alive and kicking". Americans were cheats, Khrushchev shouted to the world. Imagine that. And the world listened while he seized center stage. But it was mostly a show for to save his own skin.

At the same time he admonishes Harriman and Nixon proud to show the Soviet peasant neatly arranged maquettes of American housing each equipped with modern appliances. And all equipped with washing machines! It was typical Khrushchev showmanship showing his peasant origins for which he was famous and often resented. During the previous two decades Khrushchev had been Stalin's loyal henchman for the suppression of the Ukraine. A few years before, during a Geneva summit with President Eisenhower, the Soviet Premier was introduced to Nelson Rockefeller. "So this is Mr. Rockefeller," he said, as he playfully jabs Rockefeller in the gut. Rockefeller "took this as a joke and did the same thing to me," Khrushchev recalls.

Before the 1961 summit with Premier Khrushchev, and shortly after the failure of the Bay of Pigs Cuban fiasco and the October 1962 missile crisis,

President John F. Kennedy worried about Khrushchev's reputation for toughness. Averell Harriman tells him not to worry. "'Don't let him rattle you, he'll try to rattle you and frighten you, but don't pay any attention to that ... His style will be to attack and then see if he can get away with it. Laugh about it, don't get into a fight ... Have some fun'." Nelson's brother, David Rockefeller, often identified with his bank Chase Manhattan, is photographed in the Kremlin with Premier Aleksei Kosygin in a story by Gary Allen, "Building Communism" in *American Opinion*, December 1975, and he adds, "They look like old pals during an informal photo session." (W. Taubman, *Khrushchev,* 351, 494)

In the Crimea on a brief vacation two years later at this favorite dacha on the Black Sea, Nikita Khrushchev was suddenly ousted by his own Party leaders. A similar jolt happened to Gorbachev. But it was no joke when ten years later during Khrushchev's visit to the US Solzhenitsyn pleaded to Americans not to bury Soviet citizens with their American-produced tractors and shovels. Harriman was surprised his Russian friend had survived since his rise to power in the Holodomor thirties. Great power always attracts its share of rumors; it has been said he may have been removed by David Rockefeller in a dispute over insufficient Soviet state fertilizer purchases and the disastrous harvest of 1963 forcing Khrushchev to import over 10 million tons.

Ten years after Kennedy's assassination and confronted by the reality of US-Soviet trade, Sutton ridicules the deceit and hypocrisy of the Cold War ethos permeating American mediA. C. Sutton persisted. "The citizen who pays the piper is not calling the tune," he told an interviewer in 1998. "He doesn't even know the name of the tune." Twenty-five years earlier, in his 1973 Congressional testimony about US-Soviet trade, Sutton related a conversation between Stalin and Harriman at the end of World War II. Harriman reported back to the State Department, "Stalin paid tribute to the assistance rendered by the United States to Soviet industry before and during the War. Stalin said "that about in two-thirds of all the large industrial enterprises in the Soviet Union has been built with the United States help or technical assistance." Other researchers had explored the connection between Kennedy's sudden assassination and threats that Kennedy had made to restore the gold standard and undermine the Federal Reserve's monopoly over the American currency. Indications were clear to that, Sutton declared, that Germany's shipment of Lenin, Zinoviev and other Bolsheviks in 1917 in their sealed train into Russia is ample proof that from the beginning "the survival of the Soviet Union has been in the hands of Western governments." Concealment and secrecy were at the heart of the mystery. American involvement in the Soviet economy was so pervasive and to an extent so great and inverse to the openness in the public sphere so the people did not know. (Sutton testimony August 15, 1972 before Subcommittee VII of the Platform Committee, National Security Subcommittee, Miami Beach Republican convention.)

Wall Street loves a state monopoly. For decades, a particularly small inner circle on Wall Street had their eye on removing the Czar and taking over business in Petrograd from the reactionary and incompetent Czarist regime. Formerly St. Petersburg, the city was renamed Leningrad, and then renamed again St.

Petersburg after the breakup of the USSR. A monopoly is an ideal trading partner. Dictators need support and are easier to deal with then parliaments and elected representatives. The Communist Party, the Red Army, and the centralized Soviet Republics all wrapped up in one single authority of political Commissars of the CCCP with a General Secretary sitting on top of it all. And in an impregnable capitol fortress in Moscow, the Kremlin. Ideal!

British historian and a self-confessed Russophile Prof. Bernard Pares declares, "The Communist Party, which was throughout the real ruler of Russia, retained a complete monopoly of political power; it also retained an equally complete and inviolable monopoly on the Press; lastly, it maintained a monopoly of foreign trade, which could only flow through the channels of the Soviet Government." With safeguards assured for secrecy, bankers and industrialists were able to calculate without fear of exposure deals with the most hardened terrorists and criminal wits then known in recent history.

Ukraine's peasants were an economic and political problem to dispose of quickly and without public scandal like with Hitler's liquidation of the Jews with ovens and gas. FDR with his NRA program for social welfare under the reins of Big Business, and Stalin's evolution of the Communist Party into a despotic socialist monopoly both amply show that in order to preserve their ideal of social collectivity, – corporate and communist, – they measured progress counting dollars, not human lives. A perfect crime leaves no trace. We have a long historical record that leads us down many paths to the same conclusion. Is it any wonder in the summer of 1959 Soviet Premier Nikita Khrushchev jousted with Harriman when the American capitalist complained the Soviet $11 billion dollar Lend-Lease "debt" was never paid, a significant debt some critics argued was owed to the US Treasury and paid for out of the pockets of US tax-payers. The Soviets estimated the Germans owed them at least $10 billion.

For a half century Harriman prevails in Washington as one of the most influential of the Consortium men to oversee American foreign policy. The Soviet premier refused Harriman a mere $300 million to pay off the bankers. Selling Alaska was one mistake in kind that Premier Khrushchev isn't going to repeat. Remnants of Czarist outposts and abandoned forts still recall Russian settlements from across the Bering Strait and along the Pacific Northwest and down the coast into California. Their settlements included Fort Ross, around 1820 when 25 Russian explorers and fur trappers set up their outpost for a Russian-American enterprise.

Khrushchev knows American bankers can well afford to write off the wartime Lend-Lease debt like they did Germany's First World War reparations. Actually Schacht resigned his post in protest; Hitler tore up the onerous Versailles mandate. He tells Harriman that the Americans ought to be happy and content having already made enough profits in two world wars. (In fact after the war American banks possess 75 percent of the world's known gold reserves.) Khrushchev argues that due to exceptional circumstances, the United States capitalist system was favored by both World Wars in which it made money. Harriman tried to deny it. He said the US had given at least $11 billion dollars to the USSR and had made no profits.

Khrushchev expressed his appreciation for the aid but insisted that both wars were hugely profitable for the American businessman. The Soviets misconstrued the impetus of American war production as profit-making. Khrushchev told Harriman to balance his profits with 20 million dead Red Army soldiers. To say nothing of the material damage to homes and industry, towns, villages, and entire cities destroyed. Russian rivers ran red. He reminded the capitalist that compared to one and a quarter million Americans killed in the Second World War Harriman could keep his debt. President Kennedy, a battle-scarred Navy veteran, was more understanding and publicly acknowledged Soviet losses as the equivalent to laying waste all of the United States west of Chicago. How is America to pay for all the Russian blood spilled to stop Hitler before he subjugates the entire free world?

Those friendly talks prior to the Premier's visit to the United States recall similar talks that transpired in 1933-34 over an $86 million dollar debt-claim by Bullitt for the National City Bank – now Citibank – rejected by Litvinov. Follow the money to the bank and see how debts are played with politics. Trotsky, and his band of Bolshevik double-agents did just that working out deals with the "Bolshevik bankers from America". FDR was Stalin's best banking connection. Franklin Delano Roosevelt was in the bankers' pockets up to his neck. Roosevelt's uncle Frederic Delano (1863-53), an engineer by training (Harvard), railroad work in the Philippines, and a railroad executive, was also vice-chairman of the New York Federal Reserve Bank during the Great War (1914-16), succeeded by its co-founder Paul Warburg. International banking, as the Rothschilds, Warburgs and Schiffs have shown, is always better as a very tight family affair.

HARRIMAN, WALKER, BUSH & THE SOVIET'S RUSKOMBANK

Research by Eustace Mullins led him to conclude that the Bushes were "lackeys of the Harriman family at Union Pacific, and the Harrimans were lackeys of the Rothschilds who put up the money for Union Pacific". Follow the money and all that makes common sense. Wherever there is money and dependency there are strings and obligations that tie people and business activity together. Incorporated in 1862 the Union Pacific rapidly expanded to become the largest railroad network in the United States. William Averell Harriman of The Pilgrims Society, marries and merges his fortune with Standard Oil money. George Herbert Walker, who is the first President Bush's grandfather is head of Brown Brothers Harriman which handles all the Harriman investments. The Harrimans and Bushes are both Yale Bonesmen.

US State Department dean Henry Cabot Lodge and Harriman officially welcomes and guides Nikita Khrushchev during his 1959 trip to the United Nations Secretariat headquarters in Manhattan, Rockefeller turf when he bought in the previous decade several blocks on the East River. Harriman, Bohlen and Kennan stay on as Russian advisers in the Kennedy administration to deal with Khrushchev and his successor.

During that trip the Soviet Premier is also entertained by Harriman in his private townhouse at East 81st Street. Present also are J. D. Rockefeller III, and John J. McCloy, CFR head and the "unofficial chairman of the eastern establishment". McCloy is a "die in the wool" Rockefeller man. A former Cravath, Swaine lawyer he became a partner at Milbank Tweed where he handled the Rockefeller account; in 1953 he joins Chase replacing Winthrop Rockefeller who leaves to head the US Embassy in London. Two years pass before McCloy makes Chase the largest bank in the country after merging with the Manhattan Bank. McCloy declares, "The thrust towards global government can be well-documented but at the end of the twentieth century it does not look like a traditional conspiracy in the usual sense of a secret cabal of evil men meeting clandestinely behind closed doors. Rather, it is a 'networking' of like-minded individuals in high places to achieve a common goal, as described in Marilyn Ferguson's 1980 insider classic, *The Aquarian Conspiracy*." (E. Mullins, *The World Order*; James Dyer Interview, "A recent visit with Eustace Mullins, 2003; W. Taubman, *Khrushchev,* 428)

Unsuccessful in his bid for the Presidency, Harriman retires as the patrician stalwart of the Democratic Party. A good look at this kingpin to Stalin will bring the reader closer to the keys of the treasure chest. From London to Paris, Washington and New York, no one was more influential, rich or elegant than W. Averell Harriman. Few Americans knew more than Harriman as to how long and how much Western financial aid and trade has supported Stalin's communist dictatorship of socialist terror since Lenin's Bolshevik coup that seized power in the Petrograd Soviet in 1917.

Harriman companies had built railroads across Russia for the Czar and his ministers helping to transform the Romanov Empire through the practice and rewards of capitalism of the 19th century industrial revolution overtaking the West. The Rockefeller-Morgan-Harriman Consortium network had extensive dealings with Kremlin monopolists. The "people's socialist government" of the Soviet Union was governed not by transparent democratic procedure but by a centralized party hierarchy of the Central Committee based in Moscow – the CCC. Recalling his railroad experience in the prewar Czarist era, Harriman used his Hamburg American Company as early as 1921 to began talks with the Soviet Party leadership and established a jointly owned shipping firm, the Deutsch-Russiche Transport Company whereby the Kremlin owned half, reports *The New York Times*. Harriman then used his Berlin bank office of W. A. H. & Co. to buy discounted Russian notes guaranteed by his Soviet partner. This business was transacted only a few months after Trotsky's Red Army in March 1920 chased the General Deniken's White forces and the mass exodus of hundreds of thousands of refugees driven madly to the sea off Novorossisk and to the all too few British battleships of the Mediterranean Fleet sent up from Constantinople for the evacuation. Bolshevik artillery field guns fired on the Emperor of India and other ships so tightly packed with Cossack troops and the refugee mass on decks that 13.5 inch guns were unable to open fire over the heads of the refugees. A smaller White Russian warship blasted the Reds, setting fire to the railway station and storage tanks of Standard Oil Company and filled the sky with black smoke as the harbor town burned. Among them is the Cossack *Ataman* (chieftain) Piotr Nikolayevich Krasnov who fled with the broken remnants of the White armies and Don Cossacks; in Berlin Krasnov wrote a four volume history of the end translated into many languages. When the Germans invaded in 1941 he returned to lead Cossacks and survived with his nomadic troops, surrendering to the British in Austria in 1945; repatriated to Russia most of the Cossacks were shot or packed off to labor camps in the Far East and the Arctic. Krasnov was sentenced as an "enemy of the People", denied a firing squad and hanged in Moscow on August 26, 1946. (N. Ascherson, *Black Sea*; Piotr N. Krasnov, *Two Headed-Eagle to Red Flag*, 4 vols., London, 1923)

With an eye on vast reserves of Russian oil from the Siberian wilderness to Lake Baikal and Baku, Harriman and Morgan's Guaranty Trust created the first Soviet international bank, Ruskombank. They used British capital restricted by the Soviet foreign-trade monopoly. By this time Harriman is already in bed with Morgan's Nazi side of the family's Consortium banking affairs. Long before linking up with the Hitler, the Wehrmacht banker Hjalmar Schacht served as a member of the Workers and Soldiers Council (a Soviet) of Zehlendoff which he left in 1918 to join the Nationalbank fur Deutschland (DONAT); his co-director on the board at DONAT was Emil Wittenberg, a director in Ruskombank alongside Morgan's Max May, a vice president at Morgan's Guaranty Trust in New York. The brilliant Max May became a director in charge of Ruskombank's foreign department. These men were directly responsible for the first attempts to import Soviet gold into the United States. Between 1918 to 1922, Lenin transferred 600 million roubles in gold to Kuhn, Loeb according to former the Czarist ambassador in Washington Bakhmetiev. Whatever happened to 600 million gold roubles is a question few can answer.

CONSORTIUM BANKERS AND THE BOLSHEVIKS

The Consortium bankers who had backed the Bols moved quickly once the Russian gold started to fill their vaults. In 1920, Guaranty Trust renewed its interest in Soviet Russia confirmed in a letter January 21, 1920, written by Henry C. Emery of the banks' Foreign Department to the State Department's Consortium ace DeWitt C. Poole. Morgan Guaranty was soon in business again acting as the *de facto* financial agent for Lenin in the United States without official recognition by the US government of the Soviet regime. Two years later, the future US President, Secretary of Commerce, Herbert Hoover (1924-28) forwarded inside information to the State Department about a deal by Guaranty to do business with the "New State Bank at Moscow". Hoover wrote that the Morgan Guaranty plan "would not be objectionable if a stipulation were made that all monies coming into their possession should be used for the purchase of civilian commodities in the United States". He endorses the plan with the same philosophy operating behind the Consortium's early support and organization of the Bolsheviks, writing, "It might be advantageous to have these transactions organized in such a manner that we know what the movement is instead of disintegrated operations now current." It's a fact that one of the first official acts of Lenin was to nationalize Russia's banks as a centralized state monopoly under the Bolshevik control.

Neither Hoover nor Morgan are ever really genuinely interested in free market dynamics. Their game was monopoly. Hoover and the Morgan men wanted the Bolshevik trade for themselves. There was no hesitation on the part of the Consortium and their banks to use US State Department facilities for negotiations with the Soviets. No one dared make too strong a protest. State Department officials conducted business as usual passing it through official cables. Much to his consternation, Harding's Secretary of State (1921-25) and Consortium kingpin Charles E. Hughes feared the scheme was a disguised plan for *de facto* recognition of the Soviets.

Morgan's Guaranty Trust Co. and the Bolsheviks always enjoyed a smooth working relationship. Sutton uncovered a long established link between Bolshevik banker Olof Aschberg and Guaranty Trust Co. in New York "before, during, and after the Russian Revolution". Aschberg was Morgan's agent in Russia during Czarist days. It was Aschberg who negotiated Russian loans in the United States for the Great War. And it is Aschberg who acted as the go-between for Morgan with the Bolshevik revolutionaries. Aschberg then joined Max May as head of Ruskombank.

Olof Aschberg ran the Berlin branch of the Bank's deals for Russian concessions. Huge lumber sales to Germany did not go through the Trusts; the large German Mologa concession, for example, was financed on credit by Ruskombank and Deruwa, the German-Russian Merchandise Exchange Society. US diplomat Frederick W. B. Coleman, based in Riga, a businessman and lawyer appointed in 1922 as ambassador to the three Baltic States until October 1932, described the Mologa concession in his report sent May 19, 1927 showing "concrete manifestations of a Soviet-German rapprochement", and he remarked, "the reluctance of the international money market to make investments in the Soviet Union". However, the concession fails owing to "to irregular and rising costs, and unprofitable credit arrangements with the Soviets." (A. C Sutton 157; SDDF 316-135-615; Willi Münzenberg wrote his memoirs in 3 volumes titled, *En vandrande jude från Glasbruksgatan*, *Återkomsten*, and *Gästboken;* Margaret Buber-Neumann, *Under Two Dictators: Prisoner of Stalin and Hitler;* Sean McMeekin, *The Red Millionaire: A Political Biography of Willi Münzenberg, Moscow's Secret Propaganda Tsar in the West*, Yale Univ. Press, 2003)

Max May was the most enigmatic. German by both birth and education, born in 1861, as a trader in Darmstadt and Karlesruhe he became an expert in foreign exchange before emigrating to the US in 1883. Like Paul Warburg he became a naturalized American citizen, and, in 1888, and worked at Union, Atlas and First National Banks of Chicago until 1904, when he joined Guaranty Trust Co.. Before long he is head of its profitable foreign exchange office. During the First World War, Max May manages foreign exchange operations in tandem with the American Federal Reserve Bank; in 1918 he sets up the Foreign Trade Banking Corporation, America's first discount house which closed the year before he assumes his post at Ruskombank.

Until his retirement in 1925 May makes frequent trips to Moscow. When he dies, May 1931, *The New York Times* publishes an obit with the simple header "Max May Dies at 69; Formerly a Banker". It's amazing understatement with just the right reserve one expects of a banker.

The American-Russian syndicate was created in 1918 to obtain concessions was backed by the White, Guggenheim, and Sinclair mining and oil interests. Interlocking directorships controlled by these three financiers included Thomas W. Lamont (Guaranty Trust) and William Boyce Thompson (New York Federal Reserve Bank). The syndicate intended to immediately cash in on its role backing the Bols in the revolutionary chaos. Further, the Morgan firm Guaranty Trust plowed funds in 1919 into the Soviet Bureau run by the shadowy Alex Gumberg, his brother and other left-wing socialists in New York associated and not particularly liked by with John Reed.

Diplomatic circles observed how quickly the Swedish banker Olof Aschberg changed hats. Known as the "Soviet banker" who passed funds to Lenin and Trotsky in 1917, in the tumult of revolution and civil war it was Morgan money, provided by Aschberg to Trotsky that helped consolidate the first ranks of the Soviet Red Army. That might be hard to believe but memory is short and who remembers the debacle in 1991 when Gorbachev ran out of funds and failed to pay his corps of generals? For two decades Aschberg (Olaf Ashberg) of Stockholm's Nya Banken channeled money to the Bols. London's *Evening Standard* once reported a visit by Ashberg to Switzerland "for secret meetings with Swiss government officials and banking executives." (*Evening Standard,* 6 September 1948, source Mark Weber file)

Aschberg and the Consortium work in tandum. Sutton investigated further into the Aschberg connection. He found that Aschberg opened his bank Nya Banken in Stockholm in 1912; by 1916, in New York circles Aschberg is already known as the "Bolshevik banker" to the German press (*Bankier der Weltrevolutio*n). Nya Banken's codirectors include prominent members of Swedish cooperatives and Swedish socialists including G. W. Dahl, K. G. Rosling, and C. Gerhard Magnusson. That summer Aschberg is also representing Pierre Bark, former finance minister for the Czar. *The New York Times* reports a $50 million loan for Russia signed in June and arranged by Aschberg and Stillman's National City, at 7 1/2 percent interest per annum with a 150-million-ruble credit for the City syndicate in Russia. Stillman's bankers then sells the loan at 6 1/2 percent certificates in the US market for $50 million ($1.25 billion in 2007). (A. C. Sutton; *The NYT,* Aug. 4, 1916)

By 1918, Nya Banken shows up on on the Allied blacklist for trading with Germany, so the bank changes its name to Svensk Ekonomiebolaget. Its London agent is the British Bank of North Commerce chaired by Earl Grey, a close associate of Cecil Rhodes. Others associates include the Bolshevik Leonid Krassin, the Russian revolutionary, engineer and millionaire, formerly the Russian manager of Siemens-Schukert in Petrograd and Bolshevik Commissar of Foreign Trade (1920-24), Carl Furstenberg (1850-33), one of the most prominent German bankers of the nineteenth century, and Max May.

Aschberg passes large sums from the Germans to Russian revolutionaries to accelerate the fall of the Russian Empire. Before the Russian Revolution, the autocratic Czarist regime is generally regarded by the American press as a backward economic monolith and reactionary pariah of anti-Semitic oppression and a threat to civilization. Its the return of the old myth of Russian Mongolian barbarians. Aschberg tells American businessmen in New York to look towards Russia for big profits. "The opening for American capital and American initiative," he said, "with the awakening brought by the war, will be country-wide when the struggle is over. There are now many Americans in Petrograd, representatives of business firms, keeping in touch with the situation, and as soon as the change comes a huge American trade with Russia should spring up." After the revolution added to his fortune, the Jewish financier Aschberg turned philanthropist donated a priceless collection of Russian icons to the Swedish national museum, and privately lived in splendorous comfort owning several private estates including several elegant chateau outside Paris now French government property. Stalin, in 1934, and badly in need of cash, sold Aschberg the famous amber-coloured diamond from the Russian Crown Jewels collection that today ranks 27th on the list of yellow diamonds over 100 carat weight. That's a small drop in the ocean of $400 billion transferred from the Czarist vaults and safe-houses to Consortium banks in New York.

There was a time when the question came to mind of how to write this book. To tell the story with the real names and real faces, private lives and rare public appearances of men in a world of power when Internet was still three generations in the future and letters and newspapers took weeks to deliver overseas. Technology transformed industry and changed the geopolitics of war. Over ten million people disappeared, starved to death in the Terror-Famine but who remembers their faces. (Conquest estimated at least twenty million lost their lives in Stalin's terror gulags, depopulated kulaks and famine.) They were overcome by politics, war and experiments in progress. Perhaps it was something utterly different, something utterly more terrible that destroyed the Ukrainians with barely a trace, not even half-revealed human wrecks of bare bones. What can be more terrible than the tortured pain of death itself?

Ignorance and deceit are poor excuses for complicity. Is it any wonder why Stalin was never publicly exposed for the worst crime of the modern society? At every turn FDR nudged his top advisers – in particular veteran Bonesman Stimson and his Harvard dauphin Bill Phillips – to reconcile good relations with Stalin, supporting economic relations for bilateral trade which lead directly to a sustained war effort of US aid. Stimson and Phillips are the State Department's top men, both lawyers in a city of the nation's most powerful corporate lawyers serving the rich and privileged of the upper class while blue-collar workers in America slaved their lives away for subsistence wages in underground mines, sweatshop mills and urban factories. That's the way America works. While the rich constructed a patrimonial culture in America based on philanthropy to protect their estates and streamlined the public debate with university donations, think-tanks and its own media organizations, huge sums of industry and banking capital built institutions that ordered the national mind-set. The rich taught people how to think, act, and participate in society. Survival is always the priority of natural selection for both rich and poor. Capital, if you had it, provided a freedom of restraint, and luxury, and dreams for the middle-class. Capital offered time to think, and reflect on conditions to improve life and the lot of the fellow man, right?

When the Second World War fell upon the survivors it added more millions of Soviet fatalities and virtually obliterated the earlier victims from living memory as the armed powers once again blew themselves to bits. The Consortium found in FDR a charismatic politician to pry America out of joblessness and economic collapse never before seen in America since the "Great Awakening". Coming as it did a decade after the debacle of Wilson's plan for America in global empire, mainstream America turned inward during the "Roaring Twenties" while Consortium Big Business went to work making billions in reconstructing a new world order out of the rubble. FDR turned a problem into a solution.

The Great Depression provided conditions to modernize America's social and industrial infrastructure. The Consortium needed to wage another world war packed with the same explosive fury that obliterated all sense of moral responsibility for the actions that built the Soviet centralized state. It was justified along with Stalin's repression by terror that had become a necessary evil not only for sad and tragic Russia forced under absolute Bolshevik totalitarian monopoly but FDR too was inseparably and intrinsically linked by virtue of the Consortium's economic ties to the Bolsheviki, a devil sprouting two heads. FDR didn't' need the war to bring together the alliance. It happened all the same with his shuffling ambassadors, shifting diplomatic alliances, and covertly allowing the process to gradually unfold. Is it any wonder why the Consortium players encouraged crucial business investments and financial credit arrangements to sustain Stalin's barbaric regime, with methods well-known to Russians as "the meat grinder". Riga and the State Department knew it. Churchill and FDR knew it. Only a naive imbecile would think it otherwise. Or a blamelessly ignorant outsider.

For the most part they were the same. America was a nation of outsiders. The Consortium ruled. Its elaborate insider networks stretched the globe operating in the major capitals principally through banks and corporations with long tentacles penetrating throughout society and entrenched in academia and the outlets of national media, the bedrock of national culture telling the people how it is, or how should be and fill their minds with other trivial mindlessness.

In place of the memory of the Ukrainian victims of Genocide another image is sketched on the collective imprint of history, that of FDR sitting alongside Churchill and Stalin, at Yalta, in the Russian peninsula of the Crimea on the Black Sea. They would laugh and drink together about how three men were fated to survive two world wars and three decades of turmoil and empowered to carve up the world. And there not far away the spirits of millions of Holodomor dead lay buried and dispersed without a trace in the black soil and since obliterated with bombs and shrapnel of the war. In the forgotten land of Mother Ukraine, the breadbasket of Europe struggled again in death by hunger and war. With the end of the war in sight FDR would not live to witness the end of the war and all its ceremony.

Truman dropped the atomic bombs, and sat with Churchill and Stalin at Potsdam, conspicuously uncomfortable sitting next to the visibly worn and gray but confident dictator. History is rotten with ironies but nothing is more ironic than truth itself. Let the Truth now encompass as much as it can embrace. Its there somewhere among all the deliberate lies, diversions and rhetoric inside and outside government. After Wilson's war, America got used to the Second and ever since has been besieged by a tightly-linked and interconnected Consortium penetrating the economic fabric of the nation and mastering the global economy. Whether in the US or the USSR, criticism was controlled, tolerated more or less, and deviations effectively dealt with to disarm and destroy any real threat to the political and economic control of the Consortium. During the tragedy of the Ukrainian Genocide, Stalin's mass extermination of millions of men, women and children was carefully planned and orchestrated with knowledge by the Consortium with Presidents Hoover and Roosevelt's consistent public performance to deceive Americans and the world. Let the Truth be a vigil for the dead.

I seriously considered deleting some names of real persons, but why do that? For what reason? To protect the innocent? Among the benefactors there are none. They were criminals, organized mafia, outstanding leaders of society. And extraordinary sums of secreted wealth that vanish from sight. But this is no fiction. The strange fact is that some people I had known, now seem more like ghosts of a past that's not my own anymore, appearing as chimeras stepping in and out of tales of a bygone era belonging to a time shared but not lived. It was never completely my own experience as though the film were pulled through the back of a camera and the pictures got blurred in the making of what was supposed to appear real instead of only approximations of the past. How do you get face to face with the past? How do you look the monster in the eye and not get destroyed? A black and white photo in a history book. A hand-written note with a signature. It seems so vague and unreal. Even a little scarey too when you think how life slips through your fingers and the past recedes further away when it ought to be clearer in focus, magnified for a close-up when all perspective is lost.

As the aging and existential writer Norman Mailer declared in an *Esquire* interview, January 2007 prior to his novel about Hitler (*Castle in the Forest*). It suggests what people have been telling me all along. Writing is living your own experience in words and trying to make sense of it which is an insane improbability. Why should a world that doesn't make sense be a motivation to make sense of it? Perhaps its worth remembering the message when David Byrne of rock group Talking Heads sings, "Stop Making Sense". In all the documents, notes, conversations, incidents, transactions, contests and escapades, the motivations in the end are prompted by psychological torment, inner drives of greed and power, wanton and relentless ambition. Freedom carries a very high price which is why some people are willing to die for it.

In the story about Stalin, Hitler and Roosevelt, - and the omnipresent Churchill – even today the disappearance of over ten million men, women and children of the Ukraine is tossed about by extremists between reality and fiction long after the bodies were burned or buried or eaten by survivors and worms and insects while these leaders drank dozen of toasts to victory, war and peace. Mailer's demons were part of Hitler's vision for the future, a nightmarish reality with surreal names like "Werewolf" and "Typhoon". "Barbarossa" was the code-name for the invasion of Russia in June 1941. When that fails Hitler launched "Typhoon" to take Moscow.

Both Hitler and Stalin were determined to leave it a smoldering ruins like Stalingrad with orders to fight to the last man in hand to hand combat. Blow-back would have been more apt a code-name. The Russians mounted their fierce defense and forced the Germans to retreat in the harshest of winters smashing forever the myth of the invincible Nazis and recalling Napoleon's defeat in 1812. Barbarossa and Typhoon cost the Germans more than the loss of a quarter of their army of 3.2 million men on the Eastern Front. When they failed to beat the Russians in their surprise invasion, Hitler's wisest Generals knew they would lose the war. Odd that FDR's own Chief of Staff General George Marshall thought the Russians wouldn't last the summer. Hitler still had not taken the Caucasian oil fields south of Rostov-on-the-Don. Three months after the German invasion in 1941, Harriman met Stalin and Churchill at their Moscow conference late September.

The Consortium opened the Lend-Lease pipeline to bolster Stalin's defense until the Red Army could mount a counter-offensive and smash the Nazi invaders back to Berlin. After the invasion FDR put his Lend-Lease plan into operation. In addition to the German military inspection of Russian industrial facilities, Stalin permitted shipping to Germany of twice the quantity of grain exports from the Ukraine after the signing of a new trade agreement January 10, 1941 while promising the Nazis an unlimited supply of foodstuffs necessary for Germany to pursue its military strategy. In fact Stalin did even more to appease German aggression. "Stalin hurriedly launched a futile policy," historian Richard Evans observed, "of trying to appease the Germans by stepping up Soviet deliveries of Asian rubber and other supplies under the trade agreement signed in January 1941.

By the November and with winter coming down upon them over the steppes the Germans grind to a halt. During "Typhoon" Hitler's the assault on Moscow when the Wehrmacht arrived 25 km from the city and the temperature fell to 40 degrees Fahrenheit below freezing the German advance literally froze, tanks and vehicles abandoned. The Soviet T-34 tank with its compressed-air starter works in freezing conditions whereas the German tanks were transformed into coffins of dead metal. Then Japan attacked and America was finally at war, first with Japan, and then Hitler declared war on America in a desperate and failed attempt to prevent supplies across the Pacific from reaching Russia. Chelyabinsk, better known to some as Tankograd in the Urals, manufactured the new T-34. By 1942 the Soviets are already out-producing the Germans. In this period Russia delivered 21,700 aircraft to Germany's 14,700, for example, and the American aid started to arrive. In the last year of the war Russia's factories are close to 30,000 tanks and 40,000 aircraft. (M. Hastings, *Armageddon*, 114)

Max Hastings, in *Inferno*, explores the war package, writing: "Of the Red Army's 665,000 vehicles in 1945, 427,000 were American-built, including 51,000 jeeps. The United States provided half the Red Army's boots – loss of livestock made leather scarce – almost 2,000 railway locomotives, 15,000 aircraft, 247,000 telephones and nearly 4 million tyres. 'Our army suddenly found itself on wheels – and what wheels!' said Anastas Mikoyan with a generosity uncharacteristic of Stalin's ministers. 'When we started to receive American canned beef, fat, powdered eggs and other foodstuffs, this was worth a lot of extra calories.' Mikoyan believed that Lend-Lease supplies shortened the war by a year to eighteen months." (R. J. Evans, 165; M. Hastings, *Inferno*, 315)

History reads like a novel because it's the stuff of fiction. But it's not fiction. The fabricators teach it that way. Neither the writer nor the reader ever possess the whole story living it as it happened, thinking about events as they were in the plans and decisions, joy and pain, suffering and death of the days and actualities sliced and sandwiched together in headlines and battlefronts, close-door meetings and communiqués, classified documents and memoranda, diaries and notes, banquet dinners and hideaway retreats.

Epistemologically and heuristically that is impossible. It is also highly unnatural. The German and Bolshevik dialecticians knew this. Oxbridgians knew it and taught the art of rhetoric at American universities in the latter part of the nineteenth century along with the classics whereas American students learned the lessons of higher education at places like Heidelberg. Yes we are always in the dialectical clutches of historical falsifiers, occultists and soothsayers. Yet, that's all we have to deal with, all that is ever left behind, in the ruins and monuments, and histories that invoke what happened in the fictional idea of it all. Its more real that way All for nothing more than a very small and momentary glimpse. Stop the shreader! We hear the public call. Read Wikileaks. Free Julian Assange. Listen to Edward Snowden! Not a spy but self-confessed patriotic American in 1013 he revealed a ton of secrets of the years of current surveillance activity facilitated by the US government satellite and computer technology, including the monitoring of private cell phones of foreign leaders.

For over a half-century now the American NSA has been spying domestically on its citizens but they have to be knocked to their senses to imagine it is true, just imagining while a few more stories in the press, books and news media struggle to deal with it while the government issues more denials and holds its breath until the next outrageous public disclosure. The US federal government insists *he* broke the law and must return from exile to face "justice". Meanwhile President Obama says he needs to catch up to find out what his spying agencies are actually doing. Obviously Snowden makes it clear Obama ought to read *his* files first. Its an old story with a new twist. What kind of government exists in a democracy where secret spy agencies are spying on everybody including 35 heads of state and no one knows, even the President, what is going on or who is in control.

In its 100-year anniversary October issue *Vanity Fair* included a story on Julian Assange, "The Man Who Came To Dinner", by Sarah Allison who interviews Assange already more than a year living in asylum in tight quarters inside the Equador embassy in London's Knightsbridge district.

A little book that few people have read in over fifty years, *Why Don't We Learn From History,* was written by B. H. Liddle Hart, in 1943, an Oxford don not very popular with Churchill and the war cabinet. It's highly recommendable reading especially for historians. He declares, "Writing history is a very tough job – and one off the most exhausting ... (and) also the most exasperating of pursuits. Just as you have unraveled a knotting string of evidence, it coils up in a fresh tangle." In the search for historical truth, Sir Little Hart (the Queen knighted him in 1966 in spite of his opposition to the D-Day invasion) equated the endeavor to the most lofty "working out of God's purpose". His jewels of insight include essays titled "History and Truth", "War and Peace", "The Importance of Making Promises", How the Germs Work", "The Illusions of Victory", "The Problem of Disarmament", and other themes relevant to our story of how to understand and explain the Holodomor, and recommended reading for the not so feint at heart.

Charles Beard, the former Columbia University professor in his 1927 book, *The Rise of American Civilization,* tells us "The history of a civilization, if intelligently conceived, may be an instrument of civilization." What Beard had in mind was akin to the inquiry tht finds that "the history of a civilization may symbolize a certain coming to maturity in that civilization itself." And if we are to find the rub, he adds, "When the dust of the earth becomes conscious of the dust, a transformation began to take place in the face of the earth." The key is not to get lost in the metaphors but to see clearly under all that dust.

The story of the Ukrainians in the big world struggle for a New World Order challenges that notion of history. History is more than a mere glimpse in a moment of time and struggle. During this research I came across the photo of a beautiful woman, a Russian partisan led by three Germans to her execution. Her expression is haunting, reserved, full of grief and resolve. On her face is the expression of stoic and solemn resistance. She does not wear a look of pitiful resignation of her imminent death. She knows she had forsaken her own life long before her capture. Who is this woman. A partisan? A spy? A Slav? Russian? Ukrainian? We do not know her name or her village. An inner strength moves and protects her from the aggressors, these three men who violated the sanctity of her ancient Motherland which fed and nurtured her now soaked in blood. Behind her a German soldier laughs with the grin of a grotesque animal. Two other German captors look aside, history's villains, shamed with faces of evil. It is all captured in a furtive moment by the anonymous photographer. There is no neutrality possible here. It is too late for any lie. The photograph tells the real horror of the truth of the story that reads like an open book, expressions of Humanity, innocence and guilt written on their faces in the light for all to see. Moscow prepares its urgent defense where 500,000 men and women dig 185 miles of trench fortifications, felled trees and lay barbed-wire and Harriman and Molotov lay plans for American Lend-Lease provisions shipped from American factories. In London, the English parliament debated if

Churchill had given enough aid to defend Communist Russia. For this writer the bullet fired to end her life is the shot heard around the world. Do you hear it? Do you dare silence that stinging ring that echoes in your ear? Can you see it?

To see the photograph is to feel by some strange mysterious power drawn in and compelled to witness this scene with the eye of the photographer into the heart of the confined sacred moment of that horrible war. Can you imagine that some people in their psycho-perverted minds dared to even call this war "the good war?" How glorious it is to die a hero, how wanton to be dead. What good is that? Would they trade places with the dead?

The act compels a respect to understand, to know the woman, to be there. Perhaps that is what is most compelling. The photograph is a testimony of the life-death struggle. Death is only ever just a few steps away, and engulfs her nation. War and evil are terrifying, horrific. The Slavic woman is completely void of any trace of vanity. Spirit animates her now, not ideology or dogma, transcends barriers, concepts, names. The outsider is now caught, captured, as it were, in that moment that reveals more than it conceals. There is no place to hide. Neutrality is not permitted here. After years of extermination and famine we live in a world of total war only to have more of the same because cowards failed to act and condemn their leaders for their treachery and intrigue. The same force of the Spirit that dwells within her against the evil she fought and took her life and the lives of millions fighting back armed fascists who invaded their homes and lives. The Nazis will destroy her but they cannot defeat her or deny her Russia's vengeance.

Too much information overwhelms and confounds the reader. Information is superfluous. The reader is mislead and left alone, bewildered and estranged. Too much information can strangle the reader with loose-ends tied in knots. A reader should know where the history leads. That's very much part of the problem of reading history and building a knowledge base of understanding what happened and how and why it happened and to find the motivations and reasons behind decisions and policies that invariably lead to where we are today with new strategies and standards. Hitler had a plan. Stalin had a plan. Roosevelt and the Consortium had a plan. Their plans all clashed and converged during the turbulent thirties of the Terror-Famine prewar years of Depression. The stakes were raised, something had to give. FDR, Churchill and Stalin each waited their turn. Hitler struck the first blow. A fatal and inevitable mistake. Stalin had feared Hitler and found the betrayal incredible. It took him days to recover his senses and organize a national defense. He had been outmaneuvered! It shook him to his bones. History made it so. Truth always makes history inevitable and necessary. That is why politicians, so-called leaders, are forever determined to conceal it lest they and their plans be exposed.

Adolf Berle, Jr. (1895-71) is another gem of a Consortium player later in his career a confirmed Rockefeller man in the Kennedy fiasco when his National Security Council leads hims to the Bay of Pigs invasion of Cuba to overthrow Fidel Castro. A brilliant student he entered Harvard at 14, and was the youngest graduate of Harvard Law School before starting his government career in intelligence with the US Army during the First World War prior to joining the

American delegation at the Versailles Peace Conference outside Paris. Berle knew the turning point of WWI came long before Germany's defeat. Before joining Roosevelt's "Brain Trust' advisory clique Berle taught corporate law at Columbia Law School, and in 1932 co-authored with the economist Gardiner Means, *The Modern Corporation and Private Property*, a much-quoted reference to corporate governance.

Berle and Means showed that the means of production in the US economy were highly concentrated in the largest 200 corporations and that within these corporations managers controlled firms despite shareholders' formal ownership. Berle theorizes that the facts of economic concentration intend that the effects of competitive-price theory are in effect mythical. While some advocate trust-busting, breaking up the concentrations of firms into smaller entities in order to restore competitive forces, Berle contends that that would be economically inefficient. Instead, he argues for government regulation and became identified with the school of business statesmanship, which advocates that corporate leadership accept (and theorized that they had to a great extent already accepted) that they must fulfill responsibilities toward society in addition to their traditional responsibilities toward shareholders. In the end corporate law will reflect this new reality. Writing in *The Modern Corporation*, Berle and Means stipulate, "The law of corporations, accordingly, might well be considered as a potential constitutional law for the new economic state, while business practice is increasingly assuming the aspect of economic statesmanship." Rockefeller and Morgan could not have said it any better than their Consortium boys of America's capitalist architecture. (Adolph Berle Jr. and Gardiner Means, *The Modern Corporation and Private Property*, NY: Macmillan, 1932, 313)

Two decades later, in 1961, Berle is again on the front line occasionally advising President Kennedy on American initiatives towards Fidel Castro's communist Cuba on the eve of the botched Bay of Pigs invasion. Then, after two years, Berle publishes another work, *The American Economic Republic*, clearly defining the two fundamental ideas of economic theory: the relation of property to power, and the allocation of power. "Property is active and productive," Berle writes, "but is so because it is organized and administered, not because it is 'owned'. It sets up passive, exchangeable wealth, thanks to surrender by the wealth holder of owner's power, and to state-fostered mechanism giving liquidity to this wealth." And he concludes, "After a lifetime of privileged access and government service, the location of decision- making in the economic world has shifted. Ownership ceases to play much decision-making in from two thirds to three fourths of the American economic republic. Instead, that power lies in corporations managements, in administrators of savings-gathering institutions and pensions crust, in the offices of the larger commercial banks, in government agencies, and in an inchoate emerging group which may be called the 'scientific community'." (Adolph A. Berle, Jr., *The American Economic Republic*, NY: Harcourt Brace, 1963, 75)

In the late thirties Berle has access to confidential Reich communications of the upcoming Nazi invasion of Russia picked up from radio traffic passing between Berlin and Tokyo and cracked in April 1941. In the first intercept carried Göering's details to Hiroshi Oshimna, the Japanese ambassador in Berlin including the number and types of planes and divisions to be deployed. Roosevelt's top secret communications intercept program was code-named MAGIC. As early as December 1940 it is one of the sources that keeps Berle and a few others in the top drawer with Phillips, Stimson and FDR on Nazi intentions and strategic military operations. All with the exception of Hull are senior members of this tight inner circle of the Consortium. Hull was an *executant,* not a policy maker and he knew very well and much to his regret and seething aversion what was expected of him. It's not unlikely that Hull was not even aware of these intercepts.

The Japanese used a German machine, the Enigma, with Red and Purple Codes. When the Germans realized the Americans were intercepting messages, they informed the Japanese. Incredibly, the Japanese did not change their codes. Appointed US Ambassador to Soviet Russia in 1941, Laurence A. Steinhardt, on June 12, reports to the State Department that German divisions are positioning *en masse* along the Soviet border.

The German invasion began June 22, 1941. A message intercepted by the MAGIC team in July told the Americans that the Germans were bogged down in Russia, and now incapable of invading England because of "losses of tanks, airplanes, and materials", and that replacements would be "difficult". US Minister in Sweden since 1933, Lawrence Steinhardt had replaced ambassador Joseph E. Davies in Moscow, in August 1939, and finishes his mission there November 1941 to takeover the embassy in Turkey. A fellow Jew, Steinhardt helped many Hungarian Jews escape from Bergen Belsen concentration camp and prominent intellectuals flee Europe finding refuge in Turkey. In 1945 Truman appoints Steinhardt ambassador to Czechoslovakia, and to Canada (1948) where he died in a plane crash near Ontario two years later *en route* to Washington. (T. Morgan, *FDR*, 590-1)

By May 1942, "Wild Bill" Donovan of the OSS assisted by the War Department's Information/Propaganda minister Jimmy Warburg is already talking in terms of the need for a complete military German defeat. Unconditional surrender, again. Donovan declared, and deemed it "essential before we can begin to talk about a peace offensive on the part of the United Nations". Still uncertain is the future of the Soviet Union, the subject of a secret report commissioned by the JPWCC ("Measures in the Event of Russian Collapse in 1942, June 1 1942"). It is prepared by professor James Baxter III (1893-75), a Williams College graduate with degrees from Harvard and the founder of the research and intelligence division (R&A) of the OSS, and a president of Williams; after 1942, the group is led by Harvard Professor William L. Langer and stacked with Ivy Leaguers. Baxter's job at the Central Information Division (CID) is to recruit researchers, analysts, and scholars. Donovan, a Republican, had failed in his bid against Lehman for Governor of New York. FDR liked him and he liked FDR. On November 7, 1941, $12.9 million of appropriated funds passed over to Donovan's CID activities four weeks before FDR declared war after the Japanese attacked Pearl Harbor.

Warburg also worked with waspy Archibald MacLeish (Yale Bones), America's poet-laureate and a former head librarian of Congress and the Office of Facts and Figures. MacLeish excelled passionately in war work at the new Office of War Information (CWI) playing out his role as America's poet laureate and one of its principal propagandists "to tell the American people the truth about the war". MacLeish had been the first director in 1937 of Harvard's Nieman Fund as a recipient of America's most prestigious award in journalism. Ambassador Dodd's chair at Chicago University, in fact, was later endowed in part by MacLeish. Reader, now fancy that! Institutions have an uncanny tendency to germinate and reproduce from generation to generation, from war to war and from father to son forming a mesh deeply embedded in society. All together they define and contain the culture. Author of the 1935 anti-fascist play *Panic*, "Archi" MacLeish saw in himself America's cultural poet laureate war hero called by fate to celebrate the pain of defeat, the joy of victory. The Consortium always uses its wealth and influence to perpetuate its power over the masses. And what greater pundit of propaganda to serve this mission that the nation's own great poet. America's Civil War had its Whitman, the Great War had its Seeger. D-Day has its MacLeish.

The CWI was remarkably similar to the CPI (Committee of Public Information) that had been concocted by George Creel as President Wilson's government's news organization that propagandized and lied about WWI beguiling popular support for the war effort. Now, a generation later, in June 13, 1942, FDR officially created the Office of War Information "that Archie had proposed five months before".

With FDR exhausted by three terms in the White House, the banking crisis, Depression and massive unemployment, the rise of fascism then four years of world war and soon to die of a massive brain hemorrhage, MacLeish and others at State lent their hand to writing parts of the United Nations charter. Meanwhile Stimson and Marshal have one eye on keeping a handle on Stalin's occupation of Poland, Hungary and Eastern Europe and the other on the success of the Manhattan Project delivering the nuclear weapons, ending the war in a way that will forever change the world as they knew it once they hold in their hands the capacity to destroy the world and exterminate everyone. Stimson becomes obsessed with the fate of a humanity caught in the technological death grip of total war that has led to a total disregard for human life. In his last meeting with Roosevelt In their last meeting Stimson worried that in a few years the Russians would also have nuclear capability tries in vain to deal with the questions of sharing atomic secrets with the Russians already breaking his agreements but FDR died and nothing came of it. (See Richard Rhodes, Part 3, "Life and Death", *The Making of the Atomic Bomb*, 1987)

Also at the San Francisco conference creation of the UN with the delegates arriving in April 1945 to formulate the UN charter is a young lawyer from Illinois, Adlai Stevenson, the future Democratic nominee for President. In the fall of 1962 President John F. Kennedy sends ambassador Stevenson to the UN Secretariat in New York for his famous presentation to the world exposing the Soviet missile installation sites in Cuba. On June 28, 1945, President Truman endorsed world government in a speech: "It will be just as easy for nations to get along in a republic of the world as it is for us to get along in a republic of the United States." Four months later, on October 24, 1945 the United Nations Charter becomes effective, with Alger Hiss, an adviser to FDR at Yalta, now its general secretary in San Francisco, and not long after indicted as a Soviet spy although he protests his innocence. (In that affair Nixon fueled his presidential ambitions; secret papers pertinent to the case remain classified.) That same day Democratic Senator Glen Taylor of Idaho introduces Senate Resolution 183 to go on record as favoring the creation of a world republic including an international police force to fight terror. One of the first missions of MacLeish's new office is to organize London's overseas information radio broadcasting with close friend Jamie Warburg; they and their wives often vacation together. After the war, MacLeish rents Warburg's sumptuous uptown Manhattan apartment near the corner of Madison and Seventieth Street.

Two decades earlier, the gallant Scotsman learns that a close friend had burned in his fighter cockpit. Yale's one time poet laureate who played football there, who wrestled and fished with Hemingway and haunted the halls of both sides of the fascist social elite, right-wing conservatives as well as communists and liberals, was never sure of his place among them. E. E. Cummings described him as "a dangerous man on the wrong side." Archie MacLeish always carried the burden of the memory of his younger brother, Kenny, a junior pilot killed in WWI with the Lafayette Esquadrille. MacLeish writes, "The Young Dead Soldiers" while sitting in his director's office at the Library of Congress. "The young dead soldiers do not speak…They say: We leave you our deaths. Give them their meaning./ We were young, they say. We have died. Remember us." There is nothing better than a good war to consolidate close relations and partnership between friends and nations. (Scott Donaldson, *Archibald MacLeish, An American Life,* Houghton Mifflin, 1992, 361-74)

PAUL WARBURG AND HIS FAVORITE BANKERS

Whenever Wall Street called they changed the discount rate and performed open market operations with Government securities. Behind them was the figure of Paul Warburg, who exercised a continuous and dominant influence as President of the Federal Advisory Council, on which he had such men of common interests with himself as Winthrop Aldrich and JP Morgan.

Paul Warburg was never too occupied with his duties of organizing the big international trusts to supervise the nation's financial structures. His influence from 1902, when he arrived in this country as a Jewish immigrant from Germany, until 1932, the year of his death, was dependent on his European alliance with the banking cartel. During the Holodomor Paul Warburg's son, James Paul Warburg, continues to exercise such influence, if indeed only nominal, as Roosevelt's appointee, in 1933, as Director of the Budget. For the war he's on the scene setting up the Office of War Information. The Warburg-MacLeish friendship quaintly illustrates just how deeply embedded and widespread was the hierarchy of the ruling establishment in America and ever since has remained virtually unknown and unrecognized except to the insiders themselves, those primly chosen and appointed and self-anointed princes who know better than the general public of the pragmatic value of the so-called democratic interests that their government controlled only so long as they see fit to have it that way. For all practical purposes, they not only were the governed, they were, the government too. So here we have a situation where the ruling class reign over the governed. This can never be a healthy situation for a fragile democracy where these same citizens pride themselves and their kind as standing above the rule of law.

Reichsmarschall Göering's Luftwaffe's 1940 bombing of London, witnessed on the ground and transmitted in the chilly broadcasts by the American Edward Murrow, ignited a flame in MacLeish determined to sell the war to an isolationist-minded American. Ninety-five per cent of Americans polled in a 1936 Gallup survey said FDR should stay out of any future European wars; by January, 1941, with England on its knees and Churchill's baritone booming revenge 68% were willing to risk going to war. Murrow's broadcasts had much to do with that. "Democracy in Action is a cause for which the stones themselves will fight," Churchill thundered in November 1940 inside Boston's famed Revolutionary Faneuil Hall. Murrow not only reported on the war, he was in it, accompanying flyers into combat flying forty missions in two wars including bombers over Germany.

To reverse the tide of public opinion against the war, MacLeish and Jamie Warburg play out their roles "with British propaganda and information leaders, with an eye to ensuring that the same story was told on both sides…by helping the American people to decide what they were fighting for, what kind of world they wanted to live in after the war was over." Soon enough he's targeted for outlandish individualism and forced to resign, lamenting his saga to fellow Bonesmen and *Time* publisher Henry Luce: "I never expected to see you … act as a typhoid Mary..." The *Times-Herald* put him in his place with a Kiplingesque epithet "Oh, West is West and East is East, And so is Archibald MacLeish." He returns to the Library of Congress, nesting in his new abode outside Washington in the former childhood home of Robert E. Lee purchased by his wife's inheritance while working with the ARC; he once dares to advise General Patton, bound for North Africa, how "to make his troops more comfortable". (Roll 6 MF, 1642, Entry 190, RG 226, NA. On background estimation of the USSR by the OSS, see Betty Abrahamsen Dessants, "Ambivalent Allies 1941-45", *Intelligence and National Security*, 11/ 1996, 722-53; S. Donaldson, *MacLeish*, 36)

IBM in Soviet Russia and Nazi Germany is also dark knight in the Holodomor story. Thomas J. Watson president of International Business Machines Inc. was a prominent member of the board of directors American-Russian Chamber of Commerce (ARCC). Watson and IBM are a good example of 20th century Consortium politics. In *IBM and the Holocaust,* Edwin Black wrote, "For their part, the Russians in their zone were already utilizing the experienced staff and IBM machinery of the Reich Statistical Office in Berlin." Whether adorned in jackboots and swastikas, or Brooks Brothers suits and ties, accountability was demanded – after the war. Indeed the world understood that corporate collusion was the keystone to Hitler's terror. Businessmen who cooperated with Hitler were considered to be war criminals or 'accessories to war crimes', and that included Consortium members but they were never prosecuted. IBM machines were recovered from the concentration camps "and reabsorbed into the IBM asset list. They would be deployed another day, another way, for another client. No answers or explanations would be provided. Questions about Hitler's Holleriths were never even raised." (Edwin Black, *IBM and the Holocaust*, NY: Crown, 2001, 420-4)

The Soviets were interested also naturally interested in IBM's automated modern technology that performed computing marvels in German and the West. Sutton revealed IBM among the Soviet concessions. "Calculating machines, typewriters, sewing machines, clocks and watches, razor blades, drawing instruments, and similar items were all subject to agreements." By 1927 the Soviets bought several models of calculating machines including the IBM Hollerith, Burroughs, Monroe and Marchant. They would dismantle and copy the design. For marine and aviation, Soviet engineers copied Sperry Gyroscope, the US manufacturer from Cornell. (A. C. Sutton, 181)

Tom J. Watson of IBM was a proud member of board of directors American-Russian Chamber of Commerce. Watson, too, whose technology was essentially the processing machine of Hitler's Jewish Holocaust and Stalin's socialized terror, became a longtime director of the Guaranty Trust. Watson was actually a "Wasson", son of a tough Scottish lumberman raised in the Finger Lakes of Painted Post of New York State and set out determined to do more than farm or run horse teams pulling barges. Instead young Watson made money taking his cut on commissions from building and loan association stocks which he sold in saloons. Fast deals, easy money.

Neither a Brahmin nor Bones, Watson just loved to sell and was good at it. He got his big start selling American sewing machines. At 21, in 1895 when Baruch and his crowd were combining fortunes on Wall Street, Watson joined National Cash Register Co. (NCR) becoming its most persuasive and manipulating salesman eating up sales and driving out competition. In 1914 he joined CTR (Computing-Tabulating-Recording Company) of New York in 1914; after the war Watson ran CTR and took over the seized German assets of the company rendered virtually worthless by runaway postwar hyperinflation and the all-mighty dollar that destroyed Germany's currency.

By the mid-thirties, IBM was making huge profits. Watson used his same sales skills setting up IBM business with the Third Reich. IBM's German subsidiary enjoyed a seamless operation with the Third Reich's industries and government. In June, 1937, the year he received a medal from Hitler, the Merit Cross of the German Eagle (with Star) "honoring foreign nationals who have made themselves deserving of the German Reich", he wrote his son, and he added, "It was a white cross framed in gold and decorated with swastikas." Of all men it's Hjalmar Schacht as Germany Reich's economic minister who draped the Nazi medal around Watson's neck ...

Tom Watson recalls how he owed much of his start after the First World War to the shrewd Schacht. "From the day I returned to Germany after the War, to find my Company's affairs in the best safekeeping by your Alien Property Custodian, well-administered and conscientiously managed, from the highly satisfactory experience gained in my association with German industry after the War while building up my Company in Germany, all have felt a deep personal concern over Germany's fate and a growing attachment to the many Germans with whom I gained contact at home and abroad. This attitude has caused me to give public utterance to my impressions and convictions in favor of Germany at a time when public opinion in my country and elsewhere was predominantly unfavorable."

Watson writes Schacht that the world must extend "a sympathetic understanding to the German people and their aims under the leadership of Adolf Hitler". In 1940 Watson is obliged to return the medal to Hitler with a note writing he had accepted it "in recognition of my efforts for world peace and world trade". Despite his trouble to convince the Holocaust victims of his sincerity it doesn't fly. Still, IBM becomes the wonder mainframe company for three postwar decades. (E. Black, *IBM and the Holocaust*, 43)

Schacht claimed to have underestimated Hitler's megalomania. Eventually his game of balancing Jewish resources with Nazi militarization at the cost of civilian spending collapsed in a violent confrontation with Hitler at Berchtesgaden late 1938 that became legend. For one year more Hitler keeps Schacht in the Reichsbank but then he loses his role as finance minister to his number two Göering.

The Consortium finds another use for Schacht in Anglo-American war plans. Christof Mauch writing in *The Shadow War Against Hitler* (2003) describes how Bill Donovan felt convinced that Germany needs an internal revolt, and "someone of the old regime, such as Hjalmar Schacht, the former president of the Reichsbank, could get together secretly with the Governor of the Bank of England, Montagu Norman, against Hitler." Leave it to "Wild Bill" to think this one up! Schacht then figures as the impetus for the creation of his OSS for the "struggle against Hitler without weapons" with an intensive propaganda war effort against Nazi Germany. Among Donovan's many recruits are Holodomor journalist Edgar Ansel Mowrer (1892-1977), and Edmund Taylor who wrote *Strategy of Terror* describing the need for "rumor campaigns, radio operations, and the deployment of secret agents". (Christof Mauch, *The Shadow War Against Hitler*, Columbia Univ. Press, 2003)

THE MORGAN MAN & HITLER'S BANKER – H. HORACE GREELEY SCHACHT

Schacht was swept up in the tide of corporate fascism with the rest of them. He helped ease the Nazis into power part realization of his dream to revive the grandeur of German authoritarianism. Schacht was so important to the Consortium in fact the editors at *The New York Times* ran in their Sunday magazine September 1, 1935 the feature "Schacht Challenges the Nazi Hotheads" to familiarize readers. Certainly he was one of the most curious individuals in the Consortium-Nazi-Soviet maze of connections of the Holodomor Ukraine puzzle.

His full name was Hjalmar Horace Greeley Schacht. Born in 1877 to German-Danish parents who had lived in the United States young Schacht had lived in Brooklyn where he acquired his odd middle name. Schacht studies philosophy and earned a Ph.D. in economics. That he becomes Hitler's most trusted central banker and financial genie can be traced in part to the results of the Reichstag elections November 6, 1932 when the KPD (Communist Party of Germany) polled three times the votes of Hitler's National Socialist Party with only two million votes.

"I am in no doubt," Schacht writes Hitler, "that the present development can have but one end, and that is that you become Reich Chancellor. It seems that our efforts to get signatures for this from the country's economic circles have not been quite in vain ..." He had already resigned publicly from the Reichsbank in an ostensible and open split with the Consortium bankers of the Young Plan.

Schacht is the sphinx of sphinxes inside a labyrinth of high-risk intrigue. His father was William Schacht, a Morgan man. Ah! Interesting, and it becomes much more so. An American citizen William Schacht had worked thirty years for Morgan's upstanding firm Equitable Life inside Germany and owned a stately home in Berlin known as "Equitable Villa". Antony C. Sutton caught the connection between Schacht ties to Morgan and the Russian Revolution which he describes in *Wall Street and the Bolshevik Revolution.*

Sutton realized that the elder Schacht himself was actually a Morgan operative in the Berlin office of Equitable Trust Company of New York in the early twentieth century by then controlled by Rockefeller after his son JDR Jr. persuaded him to buy a major stake after Equitable Life Assurance Society is forced to sell once the 1911 reform legislation became law. Big money always attracts big money. Henceforth Equitable expands rapidly accumulating $254 million in deposits as the country's eighth largest bank and "an important part of the family's increasingly complex financial planning"; by 1929 it had absorbed fourteen smaller banks and attracts more funds overseas as it opens foreign offices. When the bank's president Chellis Austin suddenly dies in December JD Rockefeller, Jr. persuades his brother-in-law Winthrop Aldrich to run the bank.

So, as it were, Hjalmar was born in Germany rather, – not in New York, – by the coincidence of his mother's illness which prompted their return to Germany. And just to make it a little more interesting, the fact is Hjalmar's brother William Schacht is an American-born citizen.

Sutton delves more closely into the origins of the mysterious Dr. Schacht, and he writes, "To record his American origins, Hjalmar's middle names were designated 'Horace Greeley' after the well-know Democrat politician. Hjalmar spoke fluent English; the postwar interrogation of Schacht in 'Project Dustbin' was conducted in both German and English. The point to be made is that the Schacht family had its origins in New York, worked for the prominent Wall Street financial house of Equitable Trust (which was controlled by the Morgan firm), and throughout his life Hjalmar retained these Wall Street connections."

A. Voegler of the German steel cartel Stahlwerke Vereinigte was another the 1928 German delegates under the Dawes Plan was A. Voegler. Both Voegler and Schacht play important roles in the rise of Hitler's German economy and subsequent rearmament. Both Voegler and Schacht representing Germany negotiated with the Consortium's Morgan bankers, like the Warburgs, Paul and Max for the US, as they had done in earlier years, working with legations of the Dawes and Young Commissions with the result that many directors in the huge German economic trusts contributing to the rise of Hitler enjoy close links with the principal New York investment firms and Consortium banks restructuring world financial order.

American assistance to Nazi war efforts extended into other areas with giant firms doing business bolstering Hitler's Reich economy reinvesting their profits in German industries. The two largest manufacturers of tanks, for example, were Opel, a wholly owned subsidiary of General Motors, and Ford's German subsidiary. Sutton concludes GM was "controlled" by Morgan money. In 1936, Opel contracts a granted tax-exempt status with the Nazis enabling General Motors to expand its plant operations under condition it reinvests profits in German industry production. These plants have primary war material conversion capacity. To honor his service to the Reich's economy (and the Reich's war preparations) Henry Ford like Tom Watson of IBM is decorated by the Nazis.

Other companies such as Mellon's Alcoa and Dow Chemical arrange numerous transfers of domestic US technology into Hitler's war machine. Smaller companies like Bendix Aviation supplied Siemens & Halske A. G. with data on automatic pilots and aircraft instruments. GM was an important shareholder in Bendix Aviation. At the same time the Luftwaffe streaks across Europe and nearly bombs Britain to defeat. "Bendix Aviation supplied complete technical data to Robert Bosch for aircraft and diesel engine starters and received royalty payments in return," Sutton observed.

Both Bullitt and Lee are well informed on WWI debts and reparations, negotiating and writing press publicity, respectively. During Bullitt's handling of debt repayment negotiations with Commissar Litvinov and other Soviet communist authorities during the period of US companies and banks in the Consortium backing the Five-Year Plans for the reconstruction of the USSR were also significantly connected to building the Nazi economy. Thus, long before the Soviet-Nazi Non-Aggression Pact of 1939 the Americans and Soviets had their unofficial partnership of alliance for military preparations without the diplomatic obligations entailed in an accord of mutual defense. Sutton observes, "General Motors, Ford, General Electric, DuPont and the handful of US companies intimately involved with the development of Nazi Germany were– except for the Ford Motor Company– controlled by the Wall Street elite– the JP Morgan firm, the Rockefeller Chase Bank and to a lesser extent the Warburg Manhattan bank." (Henry H. Schloss, *The Bank for International Settlements*, Amsterdam: North Holland Publishing, 1958; John Hargrave, *Montagu Norman*, NY: Greystone Press, 108; G. Colby, *DuPont Dynasty,* 1974, 1984 ed.)

Particularly prominent in backing Ivy Lee's pro-Soviet lobby was the Rockefeller-controlled Socony Vacuum Oil which besides actively assisting in the creation of Bolshevik Russia is a significant contributor to the military build-up of Nazi Germany. It is also a well-known company with a popular print advertising campaign directed at the average consumer. These are not the most auspicious references when standing behind Roosevelt's New Deal seeking to appeal to "the Forgotten Man" out of luck and looking for a job in America. Lee's pro-Soviet lobby was not a conspicuous "Hands off Russia" public movement of left-wing communist freedom -fighters left over from the Bolshevik era (1919-21). Lee's clique was the top-end sophisticated Wall Street group represented by men such as George Whale of Socony Vacuum Oil and Charles A. Coffin, chairman of General Electric and M. A. Oudin, GE foreign manager shoulder to shoulder with the so-called "Wall Street Bolshevik" William Boyce Thompson of the New York Federal Reserve, Daniel Willard of the Baltimore & Ohio Railroad, and various prominent socialists.

Ivy Lee and Associates do public relations for Socony Vacuum Oil (1935-44) which also happens to be Standard Oil's producer of Mobil gasoline and products essential for making synthetic gasoline and explosives necessary for war. Production was consequently in the hands of two giant German cartels created by Wall Street loans under the brilliant and doomed Dawes Plan.

Seldom if ever in the Allied war press is it written that the British and French trench soldiers bled for oil. Many historians overlook the grab for oil as a real primary cause for the First World War. The German Kaiser Wilhelm was determined to have his railroad to Bagdad and seize Near Eastern oil then in the control of the British. The British needed it so badly for its Imperial Naval Empire that it agreed to let down the barriers to Standard Oil in order to push Wilson and the Americans into the "War to Save Democracy," a neat little trick of propaganda gimmickry, – and the nationalist patriotic masses bought it.

And yet it takes nearly a century for Americans to substitute oil for democracy and compete with the antiquated and crumbling British Empire for world dominance. In the postwar grab for territory under the Versailles Peace Treaty, Standard Oil wastes no time snatching concessions in Rumania, Bulgaria, Ethiopia, Sumatra, Persia, Kamchatka, Turkey and Saudi Arabia. In the Empire horse-trading the Rockefeller partners also obtain their share of oil monopolies including rich fields in Iraq to which the French Government was a partner, as well as in Czecho-Slovakia and in China.

After World War I the British seized the valuable Russian oil fields in Baku from the Turks and Germans, who had hitherto taken possession. After their withdrawal the British briefly supported the White Denikin Army in his mad pursuit of Bolsheviks, territory, fame and glory. In 1920 Standard Oil of New Jersey purchases the Baku oil holdings of Nobel Oil Company.

For eight years the Rockefeller Standard Oil group diplomatically plot against Royal Dutch and Shell for the Baku oil prize. When the Rockefeller-Standard Oil group came out the winner, Stalin is ready to conclude talks for recognition of the Soviet Government by the United States. Churchill chewed his cigar and winced while England gradually loses more of stake in empire to the Americans.

Lee's relations with the fascist regimes of Hitler and Stalin become more clear when examined in the light of the Mussolini-Rockefeller oil connection during the Holodomor famine years. For example, in 1933 there was organized, the African

Exploration and Development Company affiliated with Socony Vacuum Oil for exploration of the Ethiopian oil fields. Standard Oil moves closer to Mussolini intent on developing other sources of oil in the Mediterranean. With the French colonial masters in Algeria and the British deep in the Iraq-Iran basin, a subsidiary, the Anglo-American Oil Company obtains, in 1933, an exclusive concession in the northern half of the Harrar Province in Ethiopia. Evidently under British pressure, Sir Francis Rickett, the Rockefeller-Standard Oil negotiator made no headway with Haile Selassie. He turns to Rome and offered Mussolini a deal on Abyssinian oil. In return for the invasion of Abyssinia he offers Mussolini a Rockefeller a promise for no sanctions by the Rockefeller-controlled League of Nations through its executive undersecretary Raymond B. Fosdick, a Rockefeller Associate.

Peter Collier and David Horowitz in *The Rockefellers* (1976) elucidates Fosdick's entry into Washington politics as a Wilsonian Democrat, first in the Bureau of Social Hygiene, then transformed with Rockefeller "backing" ergo, dollars, "the Institute of Government Research, which shortly was transformed into the influential Brookings Institution". Rockefeller's Fosdick "worked to close every red light district in the United States and thus make soldiers 'fit to fight' when war came in 1917. Following tha war, President Wilson appointed Fosdick, an under secretary-general of the League of Nations; after the United States failed join the League, he became a moving force in the creation o the Foreign Policy Association and an organizer of the Council of Foreign Relations. It was Fosdick who got Rockefeller involved and interested in the question of realignment of global power that would begin to take place in the decade after World War I". (P. Collier and D. Horowitz, 142)

Consequently, Mussolini could count on Rockefeller oil from the Roumanian fields in exchange for a 30 year monopoly of the Italian oil market. Even during the war, Socony Vacuum built two refineries for the little fascist in Naples. In December 1935, Haile Selassie quickly signed for peace after a flash war lasting only two months giving up to Italy his oil-rich Fafan Valley and the lands west. The Rockefeller interests eventually get complete control of Ethiopian reserves in 1947 with the Standard Oil's Indiana subsidiary Sinclair Oil picking up the concession.

Looking at the broad array business research presented in Sutton's three volumes of the Wall Street-Nazi -Soviet trade, the same names reappear: Owen Young, Gerard Swope, Hjalmar Schacht, Bernie Baruch, Jack Morgan, Paul and Jamie Warburg, and so on; the same international banks: JP Morgan, Guaranty Trust, First National City, Chase Bank; and always the same location in New York: usually 120 Broadway. Peter Myers arrives at the same conclusions. Sutton writes: "This group of international bankers backed the Bolshevik Revolution and subsequently profited from the establishment of a Soviet Russia. This group backed Roosevelt and profited from New Deal socialism. This group also backed Hitler and certainly profited from German armament in the 1930s. When Big Business should have been running its business operations at Ford Motor, Standard Oil of New Jersey, and so on, we find it actively and deeply involved in political intrigue, revolutions and war. The version of history presented here is that the financial elite knowingly and with premeditation assisted the Bolshevik Revolution of 1917 in concert with German bankers."

By 1929, after profiting from hyper-inflationary bankruptcy which by 1923 had rendered German marks worthless and shifting the burden of German reparations to American investors Wall Street waves its magic wand only to find investors drowning in the 1929 financial doomsday.

TOM WATSON AND IBM INVEST BIG IN HITLER AND NAZI GERMAN FASCISM

To the victor goes the spoils. The Consortium fortune-seekers strip Germany naked. In *IBM and the Holocaust* author Edwin Black writes that Watson in 1933 possesses "an extraordinary investment in Germany". With the German currency virtually worthless in the early, Watson acquires the Hollerith equipment invented by Herman Hollerith, a German who "invented IBM". A precocious fifteen year old teenager Hollerith had moved to Manhattan earning an engineering degree with perfect grades from the Columbia School of Mines. He came across his idea of punch cards from seeing a train conductor use a similar albeit more primitive method, and designs the IBM punch card with standardized holes for different traits or characteristics (gender, nationality, age, occupation…). Millions of cards with standardized information could be stacked and rapidly sorted by finely calibrated machines. It is one of the great wonders of the industrial world. By 1884 the IBM punch card is prototyped; six years later Hollerith wins the 1890 US Census Bureau contest and promptly manufactures his first machines. Next, he took his machines to Europe and Russia selling them to Czar Nicholas II, eager to import Hollerith technology to make the first ever census of an estimated 120 million Russians.

Hollerith incorporates his wonder company in Georgetown, Washington DC as the Tabulating Machine Company, later to be known as International Business Machines (IBM). In 1911 Hollerith sells the company to Tom Watson's boss who creates CTR.

With the First World War grinding to an end and the empires exhausted or destroyed the German economy spiraled downward uncontrolled creating a devastating instability in the currency. German marks were as worthless as Czarist paper. Everything in Germany is up for grabs if you have dollars in your pocket. Watson went after and grabbed the German Hollerith license for a king's ransom, with poor Hollerith in wretched debt of 450 billion marks. In his excellent book *The Making of the Atomic Bomb* (1986) Richard Rhodes observed the ruined economy: "In the summer of 1922 the rate of exchange in Germany sank to 400 marks to the dollar. It fell to 7,000 at the beginning of January 1923, the truly terrible year. One hundred sixty thousand in July. One million in August. And 4.2 *trillion* marks to the dollar on November 23, 1923, when adjustment finally began. Banks advertised for bookkeepers good with zeroes and paid out cash withdrawals by weight. During the unusually cold winter German citizens burned the paper for heat; reichmarks were cheaper to burn than coal. Antique stores filled to the ceiling with the pawned treasures of the bankrupt middle class. A theater seat sold for an egg. Only those with hard currency – mostly foreigners – thrived at a time when it was possible to cross Germany by first-class railroad carriage for pennies, but they also earned the enmity of starving Germans. 'No, one did not feel guilty, 'the visiting Englishman crows, 'one felt it was perfectly normal, a gift from the gods'." (R. Rhodes, 18)

Whereas four years of total war and attrition had exhausted German manpower and resources, finally deprivation and disease broke the mighty Prussian Germanic will to fight and with communism threatening revolution at home the politicians and ministers knew the folly had gone on too long. The Allies failed to defeat Germany militarily so they destroyed the German and Austrian-Hungarian empires economically and financially. What could he do this young German inventor but throw up his hands and sell! It's the War! Champagne and riches for Watson! The American businessman strikes and takes 90 percent of the company for a song. IBM is born in 1924. He unleashes his IBM reps throughout Europe peddling the Hollerith machine technology and the punch card business.

1933 WHEN HITLER COMES TO POWER IN BERLIN

Where after in 1933 Hitler comes to power and the Nazi leadership immediately enacts its persecution e*n masse* of the Jews subordinate to the Master Race destined to rule Germany, Europe and the world under Nazi national socialism. The vitriolic scheme for extermination clearly described in *Mein Kamp* will, in fact, be implemented using IBM punch cards. Automation now cost thousands of Germans their jobs. Worse, Jewish businesses are violently suppressed. Jews dragged from homes, thrown out windows, beaten and humiliated, kidnapped and tortured with absolute German efficiency. Jews are stripped of their civil rights and dignity. Mr. Watson's profits soar. The new world of IBM calculating machines has begun.

By March 1933 the Holodomor Terror-Famine of extermination in the Ukraine breaks out in larger bold headlines in articles by Malcolm Muggeridge spread across London. Gareth Jones descends on Berlin and holds a press conference in Berlin. That horror is not contained by borders although the Soviet soldiers are there with guns with orders to shoot to kill those who flee; in Dachau, only ten kilometers from Munich sees its Jewish community converted into a slave labor concentration camp established on March 10,1933. It becomes the model prison for all the SS-organized camps and the first and most important camp of the Nazi medical experiments. Of the doctors there seven would be sentenced to death at Nuremberg. Merchant Jews from Essen and Muenster streamed through its barbed wire gates. London and Washington knew very well what was unfolding before their eyes when in Frankfurt Nazi Storm Troopers paraded and screamed "Kill the Jews". A London newspaper even publishes a map of Berlin Nazi torture houses.

In New York City, on March 27, 20,000 demonstrators protested at a mass rally held at Madison Square Garden and broadcast on radio worldwide followed by boycotts and more protests movement. In April, 60,000 more Jews are imprisoned and 10,000 more flee across the border to find refuge abroad. Signs posted everywhere shout "Jews Not Wanted Here". By May 10, one hundred thousand protesters assembled, businessmen step by step walking arm in arm with union workers, Jews and Christians alike in the mass march that blocked midtown Manhattan. Banners urge a boycott and end to business with Hitler. After this extraordinary mass demonstration no one could say they didn't know of the Nazi repression weaving its fascist roots infecting and poisoning life as it had once been before the red menace and economic hardship in the war between capitalism and communism. Concentration camps made news and the West saw it coming long before Nazified Germany turned on the gas.

In Europe as Jews as a race are harassed and persecuted, further to the East national Ukrainians are starved, shot, their homes and entire villages denuded and stripped of seeds and foodstuffs if indeed any are left to be found. Raids by crack soviet commando brigades served the attentive Hitlerites with a good lesson in techniques of Soviet-styled extermination and just how easy it is to get away with it, even in peacetime. History might have been radically altered had the Jews also protested against Stalin's systematic denigration of the Ukrainians. They too are expedited with the exacting efficiency of the Consortium's IBM machines. Eight years later, in addition to their resounding declarations for mass murdering Slavic Ukrainians, the Reich Nazis proceeded with its systematic extermination of Jews in dozens of towns and villages throughout the Ukraine, including Kiev where Jews accounted for more than one-quarter of the city's population. Today Jews number over 100,000, roughly five per cent of the city's population in 2001.

Estimates vary on the number of Ukrainian Jews killed by the Nazis. For example, it has been estimated that as many as 100,000 Ukrainian Jews were slaughtered at Babi Yar in 1941. *The New York Times* reported on October 6, 2007 "nearly 34,000 Jews in the Babi Yar ravine in Kiev" were murdered over 48 hours beginning September 29 and filled with some 100,000 bodies in ensuing months. Andrew Gregorovich writes, "Blobel commanded the killing of the Ukrainian Jews of Kiev at Babyn Yar (Babi Yar) on September 29-30, 1941. Blobel's unit killed 33,771 Jews in less than two days which was not equaled in Auschwitz or any other death camp." On its 50th Anniversary, in 1991, the Government of Ukraine commemorated Babyn Yar. Two monuments for the victims of Babyn Yar have also been erected. *SS-Standartenführer* (Colonel) Paul Blobel, a decorated veteran of the First World War, commanded *Sonderkommando 4a* of Ensatzgruppe C active in Ukraine, was condemned at Nuremberg and executed by hanging at Landsberg Prison in Bavaria on June 8, 1951. Unrepentant to the end his last words were "I die in the faith of my people. May the German people be aware of its enemies" (A. Gregorovich on the web.)

Kharkov remains the capital of Ukraine until 1934 when it was transferred to Kiev. Since their persecution under the Czar the Jewish population had increased over the centuries substantially and by 1939 surpassed 130,000. It had been estimated as many as 21,685 Jews were killed in the German invasion and occupation. French catholic priest Patrick Desbois and his team has raised previous estimates to "the murder of the 1.5 million Jews of Ukraine, shot dead and buried throughout the country". In Kharkov, on December 14, the *Stadtkommandant* ordered the Jewish population to be herded in a hut settlement in the vicinity of the Kharkov Tractor Factory. In two days, 20,000 Jews assembled there. Again *Sonderkommando* 4a, commanded by Blobel started shooting the first of them in December, and continued the slaughter throughout January in a gas van. German ingenuity refined their ordered efficiency. A modified truck with crammed 50 people drove around the city slowly gassed the people with carbon monoxide emitted and channeled into an airtight compartment. Furthermore, the German Army spread famine by confiscating food; by January 1942 one-third 300.000 remaining inhabitants in the cities were starving and many too weak to survive the winter. (Karel Margry, "Kharkov, After the Battle", Feb. 2001, Issue 112, 3-45; Ukrainian Historical Document, <www.history.org.ua/ JournALL/ journal/1999/6/8.pdf>)

Systematic extermination requires a systematic counter-force of resistance to stop it. People are not machines nor do they function like them even when processed by IBM. Popular mass protest movements could not compete against the mechanistic repression by the Consortium and their technologically-empowered totalitarian partners. Systematic extermination had given a new meaning to corporate socialism. Reader, it is with a pain of comic regret and consternation that I tell you a personal anecdote when I grew up in the suburbs of Manhattan commuters living Fairfield County in Connecticut. My father intended that I go to Andover but instead took summer courses and enrolled in The King School in Stamford; the son of the chairman of IBM, Frank Carey was a fellow student and friend. My mother worshiped her IBM stock, and would never sell, always delighted when it split. The past of IBM eclipsed the tranquility of the place with manicured lawns, country, swim and tennis clubs where life passed euphoric, decadent and rich and where middle-class values of honesty and integrity were snuffed out in the real estate boom of the Yuppidom Eighties and the causal relaxed quietly snob scene was replaced with the secluded gated communities and heavily policed neighborhoods with invisible private security companies. IBM was *the* company of the fifties and sixties. Until Bill Gates created Microsoft IBM was ubiquitous and even Tom Watson who lived in Greenwich across the town line was a very close friend with fellow yachtsman Warren Brown, a Bermuda legend in racing, – they sailed together to the South Pole – and with who I raced thousands of miles. I can tell you reader even now my hands are on an IBM; this notebook under my fingertips, is a vintage IBM ThinkPad.. (Edwin Black, *IBM and the Holocaust*, NY: Crown Publishers, 2001; *The Encyclopedia of Jewish Life Before and During the Holocaust*, Ed. Shmuel Spector, Forward by Elie Wiesel, NY Univ. Press, 2001. v. II, 618; *The NYT*, Oct. 6, 2007

"IBM did not import German merchandise, it merely exported American technology", wrote author Edwin Black. He added, "The name IBM did not even appear on any of thousands of index cards in the address files of leading New York boycott organizations. Moreover the power of punch cards as an automation tool had not yet been commonly identified. So the risk that highly visible trading might provoke economic retaliation seemed low…". Just when Watson was expanding his German operations in the Nazi regime, FDR became a big client and personal friend of IBM. The company more than doubled its size supplying machines that automated the administration's business of Roosevelts' National Recovery Act of 1933. The rapid expansion of government over the nation was an IBM windfall. The government needed to process all kinds of information about the nation's businesses and IBM's capacity to identify them. This was progress! (E. Black, *IBM*, 46)

"Nazi Germany offered Watson the opportunity to cater to government control, supervision, surveillance, and regimentation on a plane never before known in human history. The fact that Hitler planned to extend his Reich to other nations only magnified the prospective profits. In business terms, that was account growth. The technology was almost exclusively IBM's to purvey because the firm controlled about 90 percent of the world market in punch cards and sorters. As for the moral dilemma, it simply did not exist for IBM. Supplying the Nazis with the technology they needed was not even debated. The company whose first overseas census was undertaken for Czar Nicholas II, the company… saw Adolf Hitler as a valuable trading ally." (E. Black, *IBM*, 46-7)

Black writes, "In Hitler's Germany, the statistical and census community, overrun with doctrinaire Nazis, publicly boasted about the new demographic breakthroughs their equipment would achieve. Everything about the statistical tasks IBM would be undertaking for Germany was bound up in racial politics, Aryan domination, and Jewish identification and persecution... At the vanguard of Hitler's intellectual shock troops were the statisticians. Naturally, statistical offices and census departments were Dehomag's number one clients. In their journals, Nazi statistical experts boasted of what they expected their evolving science to deliver. All of their high expectations depended on the continuing innovation of IBM punch cards and tabulator technology…. to identify, sort, and quantify the population to separate Jews from Aryans…

"By necessity, that collaboration was intense, indispensable, and continuous. Indeed, the IBM method was to first anticipate the needs of government agencies and only then design proprietary data solutions, train official staff, and even implement the programs as sub-contractor when called upon. IBM machines were useless in crates. Tabulators and punch cards were not delivered ready to use like typewriters, adding machines, or even machine guns. Each Hollerith system had to be custom-designed by Dehomag engineers. Systems to inventory spare aircraft parts for the Luftwaffe, track railroad schedules for the Reichbahn, and register Jews within the population for the Reich Statistical Office were each designed by Dehomag engineers to be completely different from each other. Of course the holes could not be punched just anywhere. Each card had to be custom-designed with data fields and columns precisely designated for the card readers. Reich employees and to be trained to use the cards ... IBM New York reacted enthusiastically to the prospects of Nazism. While other fearful or reviled American businessmen were curtailing or canceling their dealings with Germany, Watson embarked upon a historic expansion…Just weeks after Hitler came to power, IBM NY invested more than 7 million Reichmarks – in excess of a million dollars – to dramatically expand the German subsidiary's ability to manufacture machines" (E. Black, *IBM*, 47-50)

This is heady stuff. IBM became a munitions manufacturer in the American war effort as well as producing Enigma machines used by both Allies and Germany. "It was an irony of the war that IBM equipment was used to encode and decode for both sides of the conflict." (Black, *IBM*, 344)

Black's book IBM reaped hube profits in the Consortium game of war and destruction. "War had always been good to IBM. In America war income was without equal. Within ninety days of Pearl Harbor, Watson was able to inform the media tht IBM had secured more than $150 million in munitions and other defense contracts. Total wartime sales and rentals tripled from approximately $46 million annually in 1940 to approximately $140 million annually by 1945." IBM machines used for the draft processing millions of men and women. At home IBM machines were used to tabulate the race specs of Japanese citizens and registered in the 1940 census. (E. Black, *IBM,* 345)

Naturally, Watson was able to parlay his role as country's chief industrial peace patriot as well as its chief industrial war patriot pledging "the loyal cooperation of every businessman in the United States". Profits for the company but at what cost to consumers and ordinary people? Black concluded, "For the Allies, IBM assistance came at a crucial point. But for the Jews of Europe it was too late. Hitler's Holleriths had been deployed against them for almost a decade and continued accelerating Nazi growth without abatement. Millions of Jews would now suffer the consequences of being identified and processed by IBM technologies." The machines would get you! No place to hide!

Writer Black describes how the Nazi's staged a conference January 20, 1942 – six months after the Barbarossa invasion of the Ukraine – in a sumptuous Berlin villa filled with Reich statisticians and Hollerith experts assembled to "outline the Final Solution of the Jewish problem in Europe. In this elegant civilized setting they scheme the murder of millions of Jews. Those present in the secret meeting of the senior Nazi leadership included Reinhard Heydrich, head of Security Police, Gestapo Chief Heinrich Muller, and "experts" in racial census and statistics including Adolf Eichmann. The demographic regions of Europe and Eastern territories were broken down for a total of 11 million Jews including the British Isles, and 5 million Russians. The experts had experience since the mid-thirties and were required to sign an oath of secrecy days before the conference. Himmler hand-picked statistical expert Richard Korherr prepares a report for Hitler submitted March 23, 1943 which includes eastern Russia's 1,449,692 Jews, all targets for extermination. Once again IBM's high-speed Hollerith punch-card machines would be used only this time the Jews would not be sent away from their offices or congregated into ghettos. Germany was now ready for mass shooting pits, gas chambers, crematoria, and an ambitious Hollerith-driven program known as 'extermination by labor' where Jews were systematically worked to death and disposed of like spent matches. For the Jews of Europe, it is their final encounter with this wonderful new technology of German automation. Nearly every Nazi concentration camp operate a Hollerith Department known as the Hollerith Abteilung. In some camps, such as Dachau and Storkow, as many as two dozen IBM sorters, tabulators, and printers were installed." Punch cards, statistics, specs and sorters. "Without IBM's machinery, continuing upkeep and service, as well as the supply of punch cards, Hitler's camps could have never managed the numbers they did. (E. Black, *IBM*, 350)

These IBM machines process all the production activities of extermination from the slave factories and farms to the gas chambers and crematoria. Black writes, "The *Arbeitseinsatz* housed the Hollerith equipment. In most camps, the *Arbeitseinsatz* tabulated not only work assignments, but also the camp hospital index and the general death and inmate statistics for the Political Section." (E. Black, *IBM*, 350)

In the chapter "The Spoils of Genocide", Black informs us that "No one will ever know exactly how many IBM machines clattered in which ghetto zone, train depot, or concentration camp. Nor will anyone prove exactly what IBM officials in Europe of New York understood about their location or use. Machines were often moved – with or without IBM's knowledge – from the officially listed commercial or government client to a deadly Nazi installation in another country, and then eventually transferred back again. … All that mattered was that the money would be waiting – once the smoke cleared." Although apparently obstructed by General Ruling 11 of the US Government (Trading with the Enemy Act), IBM circumvents US government restrictions by operating through neutral country subsidiaries. "Official American demands that business be curtailed were often ignored…The Reich could afford the best. And it purchased the best with the assets it stole." (E. Black, *IBM*, 375)

The staunch capitalist Tom Watson Sr. does a lot more than casually back FDR's bold overture to Stalin. They correspond regularly sending back and forth comments and suggestions. Watson liked to keep the letters in his pocket and often shows them off to impress his associates and occasionally drops in at the White House and at Hyde Park. Too busy making millions of dollars and building his global company Watson turns down FDR's offer of Commerce Secretary and even rebuffs the President when offered the London embassy; Joe Kennedy gets that job leaving Watson to serve "unofficially" as FDR's ombudsman in New York and wherever he goes peddling his machines. FDR uses him to entertain special guests like the crown prince of Sweden. "All Father had to do was press a button. He had a whole department that did nothing but set up company directors and other functions. They'd produce a guest list, and between one hundred and two hundred people would be splendidly entertained at the Union Club, all at IBM's expenses."

Even Cardinal Spellman "would be on hand to give the blessing". FDR liked to say, "I handle 'em in Washington, and Tom handles 'em in New York." Watson, his son recalls, "was very flattered by that". By 1936 with the country still suffering from the Depression, Watson is making more money than comedian-actor Will Rogers and holds America's top salary. - $365,000, and nicknamed the "Thousand-Dollar-A-Day-Man", or $3.5 million today. (Thomas J. Watson Jr. and Peter Petre, *Father, Son & Co.: My Life at IBM and Beyond,* NY: Bantam, 1990)

With Europe tottering on the brink of war, in 1935 Watson transferred the company's European headquarters to Geneva from Paris. New York, however, still made all the decisions. Werner Lier was IBM's top manager for Europe and based in Geneva until Germany surrendered. Lier oversaw nearly every transaction in every country during the war. "His function," Black writes, "was simply to monitor the business and keep the records. "The European Headquarters in Geneva," Lier explains, "are, in a way, a representative of the World Headquarters in New York, whose job it is to manage and control European affairs. ... In short, the functions of the Geneva Office are purely administrative." And Lier emphasized, "When the local offices (in different countries) require machines or material from our factories in the United States, they pass the order to the Geneva Office which, in turn, transmits it to the New York headquarters for handling and supplying the machines direct to the local office. Switzerland was the commercial nexus of World War II. It's famous financial secrecy laws, neutrality and willingness to trade with enemies made Switzerland the Third Reich's preferred repository for pilfered assets and a switchboard for Nazi-era commercial intrigue." (Edwin Black, "Then They Came for the Gypsies: The Legacy of Death's Calculator")

At the height of Stalin's Terror Watson' son passed through Russia, in 1939, en route to Siberia, Manchuria, Tokyo and Peking. On the trip Tom Jr. was guided by Gene Schwerdt, his Dutchman who runs operations there. Watson pleads to Ambassador Davies in a personal letter for Stalin on behalf of IBM to exempt the American company from Soviet government interference and to recognize IBM's business support of the Soviet socialist system all confirmed by younger Watson in his autobiography, "We did substantial business with the Soviets, who relied on IBM machines to manage vast quantities of statistics for their Five-Year Plans." Foreigners had become unpopular and many deported, arrested, exiled or shot.

Ambassador Davies intercedes and requests Soviet authorities allow IBM's Moscow rep "Mr. Shervdt" to be be allowed to stay unmolested. In his letter to Litvinov on August 10 1937 the USSR ambassador stresses America's "the "long-continued business relationship" with the Soviets and emphasized how the Soviet communist system benefited from IBM machines for "bookkeeping and accounting facilities". Davies urges Stalin that Shervdt be given the best operating advantage, and reminds the Kremlin master: "As a matter of fact, many branches of the soviet government are now using these machines which represent a very substantial capital investment". Davies even goes so far as to describe Watson's social consciousness and energy that he devotes to a large measure "to matters of public rather of private interest". And, of course, there is the pragmatic utility to use Watson as a leader in "liberal sections of American business". He remains a "close friend of our great President".

Thus, during the height of Stalin's Purges compounded by years of Terror-Famine in the Ukraine and throughout the vast Soviet socialist republics, the US ambassador, married to one of the richest women in the world, lies through his teeth to please "Uncle Joe". Davies remains perhaps the administration's most zealous supporter of Stalin, and throughout the war effort urges further Lend-Lease aid to Moscow turning the tide of war from imminent defeat to victory not only for Russians but in such a way that Churchill and FDR would also emerge victorious in the new world order. IBM's Tom Watson, the American ambassador now declares to Stalin, "is distinctly the type of man who would be sympathetic in connection with the humanitarian and impulses and enterprises upon which the Soviet Union is engaged".

Davies finds his rewards. In return for his usefulness during his brief two-year stay in the USSR, Stalin opens the sealed doors to hidden Czarist treasures allowing Davies and his wife to stealth away hundreds of millions of dollars worth of Russian art from Czarist vaults and smuggled aboard their magnificent yacht *Sea Cloud*: 89 Russian paintings including *Red Army in the Don Basin* (1930) by Pavel Petrovich Sokolov-Skalya, *Collective Farm in Georgia* (1934) by S. Anikin, *The Cable Factory* by Nikolai Alexandrovich Ionin, *The Colliery Terminus* (1930) by Finageev. Their stash includes twenty-three precious icons dating to the 16th century which he later donates to the University of Wisconsin-Madison in exchange for a multimillion tax break and feature as part of the permanent collection of the Chazen Museum of Art. Quite a brilliant and profitable coup! They must have had a good laugh toasting Stalin's crafty slight of hand for the US ambassador to avoid a heavy US government tax burden depriving American taxpayers while his alma mater scores a major donation in the art world. Another sweet deal in the game consortium billionaires are so good at won on the backs of the American workers afraid of the IRS government agents. Soviet socialist art for the American masses! (See Joseph E. Davies' pro-Soviet book and feature film, 1943, both titled *Mission to Moscow*).

"Be careful here", he tells Tom Jr.. No fool Schwerdt for his part warns the naïve American heir. "They'll try to set you up with a woman. They also mike your room, so don't say anything." Watson is told by the IBM rep that Stalin's Terror was in full swing. "Stalin established his power through executions right from the beginning," he recalled in his autobiography and then, – Schwerdt put it in sales terms – he steadily increased his quota until the shooting had become as common in Russia as traffic tickets in the USA." It was a serious briefing to knock sense into the young man to astutely watch his step. "I sat for two hours, hearing about propaganda, spies, the black markets, the terrible housing shortage, and the bureaucracy that paralyzed everything. By the time I left I was shocked."

His cards always kept close to his chest Tom Watson proudly cherishes his collection of White House letters including one from Hull, who his son considered as "a friend of Dad's". Watson finds Moscow's embassy staff, including Kennan, all down on the Russians. Kennan, he recalls in a letter to his father, was then "a thin, intense, dark-haired fellow, only thirty-three, and completely down on the Russian communist dictatorship, "and told me that he had come to Russia thinking that Communism was the world's ultimate solution and had slowly reached the view that it was 'an utter failure as it was being practiced'."

Watson Sr. assures his son that "the masses" are better off under the Stalin's socialist dictatorship than in the autocratic era of the Czar. "I am sure that you will find conditions in Russia much improved for the masses, as compared with prewar times. Furthermore, you must keep in mind that every country is in a position to figure out what is best for its own people. It is not our duty to either criticize or advise them in these matters." Watson is sent on a guided tour by NKVD agents posing as Intourist officials. Their itinerary includes the customary Potemkin collective outside Moscow. "It looked more or less like an ordinary US farm, but what did impress me was the way they cared for the children in clean, bright nurseries." When young Watson offers the kids money a guide rebuffs the gesture, saying "They don't want money. They have plenty." Watson sneaked it to a boy anyway who "leaped at it". During his visit Watson is joined by Peter Weil, nephew of a New York investment banker. (T. Watson, Jr., *Father, Son & Co.*, 57-8)

Tom Watson Jr. was first generation Ivy League, graduating from Brown University in Rhodes Island. He liked to recall how in the early thirties his father was head of New York's prestigious Merchants Association "socializing with people like John D. Rockefeller Jr. and Henry Luce". Watson Sr. kept a autographed photo of Charles Schwab "the great steel man" on their grand piano next to a photo of Mussolini. Dad's other "most influential friend" was FDR, he swore. Odd that later Republicans who loved their IBM stock and detested Roosevelt could never figure out correctly the nature of this odd couple but of course it boiled down to money and prestige and social status he sought in vain. Watson contributed significantly to FDR's political campaign buying access to the White House. His first visit was in that fatal summer of 1933. Ukraine and the Terror-Famine is far from Roosevelt's daily business fighting national and congressional opposition to his NRA mandated wage and price controls. Watson recommended easing up on government regulation. It hurt business. Infuriated, Roosevelt told the IBM boss, "Look here, Tom. You go back and tell your banker and businessman friends that I don't have time to worry about their future. I am trying to save this great nation. I think I am going to be successful. If I am successful, I'll save them along with everyone else." A consummate opportunist and brilliant politician FDR was brilliant at playing people off one another in order to get the best result whether for his personal or national interest. Often it would be hard to say which came first. Harriman observed how FDR style in managing his entourage as he did his cabinet. "He always enjoyed other people's discomfort. I think it is fair to say that it never bothered him very much when other people were unhappy." (Richard M. Kethum, *The Borrowed Years 1938-1941*, NY: Random House, 1989, 400)

Tom Watson Jr. was selected as a second pilot flying a B-24 bomber for General Bradley's Lend-Lease mission to Moscow and was there working in the fall of 1942 on Makhavaya Street across from the Kremlin "with the German armies less than thirty miles away". Young Tom liked to model himself after his friend Llewellyn Thompson who he had met in the US Embassy in 1942; Thompson who spoke fluent Russian would serve as US ambassador in Moscow under three American presidents – Eisenhower, Kennedy and Johnson. "Most of the embassy had been sent to the town of Kuybyshev five hundred miles to the rear." Kuybyshev, north of the Caspian Sea, 420 miles east of Moscow, was the temporary seat of the Stalin's Government with its top officials, diplomats and specialists but not Stalin who stayed in a small villa a good distance from the Kremlin and worked out of a nearby subway station Kirovskaya with the Stavka high command.

Henderson's account continues: "but Tommy … had been assigned to keep an eye on our Moscow facilities." With food scarce Watson flew Thompson to Teheran "to pick up provisions for the staff" loading some two tons of food supplies. Consortium tradition is keeper of the faith and so the very elite sons like their fathers become Pilgrims; In part to appease Harriman President Carter acknowledged the Watson-Soviet legacy naming Tom Watson Jr. ambassador in Moscow on the occasion of the 1979 Soviet invasion of Afghanistan.. Other Consortium players on IBM's corporate board included Secretary of Defense Harold Brown and Secretary of State Cyrus Vance, the inimitable lawyer from Yale. (G. W. Baer - L. Henderson, 424-5)

DESPERATE YEARS IN DEPRESSION AMERICA

In 1932 a cub city reporter for the *New York Journal* and a self-described "eye-witness" James D. Horan covered many of the big events of the era portrayed in *Desperate Years.* What does he say about the Ukrainian famine? He calls it as "a drastic food shortage", and he writes, "Premier Stalin promised the people of the Soviet Union that the second five-year plan would triple the amount of foodstuffs". Horan recalls the Wall Street crash and Hoover's promise that "poverty in the United States would be abolished for all time". With market fever of Wall Street 1929 and industrial development at its peak, automobiles sell for $10,000 and a comfortable Park Avenue apartment could be taken for "a trifling $45,000". James Horan observes, "The market was booming; there were hundreds of thousands, perhaps millions of new stockholders, including clerks, housewives, and truck drivers, and almost every one of them was making profits – on paper. Very few were taking their profits; most of the stock-buying was on margin. But no one worried, certainly not the small investors who had taken most of their savings out of the bank or mortgaged all they owned for cash to play the market. Taxi drivers paid as much attention to the stock quotations from Wall Street as to the score in the afternoon ball game." But when the stock craze turned ugly into a greedy frenzy of unchecked speculation the fall was a bitter lesson for city shop girl and the small Main Street American investor as well as the big banks in London, Paris and Berlin. September 1929 spelled disaster as the market plunged from the all-time high. A flood-tide of orders to sell swamped brokers as a total of 12,894,650 shares hit the board in a single day of trades and everybody, buyers and sellers lose.

James Horan recalls the scene when the Consortium bankers played the country's investors for fools. "Huge crowds watched the arrival that afternoon of the titans of Wall Street and the House of Morgan. There were the country's top five bankers: Charles E. Mitchell, chairman of the board of the National City Bank; Albert H. Wiggin, chairman of the board of the Chase National Bank; William Potter, chairman of the board of the Guaranty Trust Company; Seward

Prosser, chairman of the board of the Bankers Trust Company; and Thomas W. Lamont, senior partner of JP Morgan & Co. For a brief few days it seemed as if these giants of finance shoulder to shoulder, have averted disaster. After the meeting Lamont issued a statement to calm investors and stem the panic meltdown: 'There has been a little distress selling on the stock market. … There are no houses in difficulty and reports from brokers indicate that margins are being maintained satisfactorily". He said the nation's top bankers felt "many of the quotations on the Stock Market Exchange do not fairly represent the situation".

Stimson's good friend is Morgan banker Tom W. Lamont was for the most part considered as "directing intelligence" behind both the Dawes and Young Plans. And it is his son, Thomas Stilwell Lamont who we find in Japan arranging Morgan's Japanese loans, and after the war returns to the American corporate world as a leading Consortium industrialist, vice chairman and director Phelps-Dodge Corporation (1955-58), a copper mining fortune under chairman and Pilgrims Society member Louis S. Cates (1930-47). Its stock quadrupled during the same period. Lamont is also attached to International Minerals & Chemicals and Texas Gulf Sulphur. Later he became an overseer of Harvard as well as president of the Phillips Exeter Academy (1946-56), one of America's most elite prep schools on the level with Groton, St. Pauls School and Phillips Andover. (source Sutton)

Five days later, Black Tuesday, October 29. Wall Street hit the skids. Panic descended upon the city and the nation. The stock bubble burst. In one day sixteen million shares are dumped, virtually worthless. Losses figure up to five hundred billion dollars. Even then Hoover's Secretary of Commerce, Robert Lamont scoffs at doomsayers. Prosperity, he declares, "for the long run" is sure to come but few have a clue what he is talking about as they watched their financial security vaporize before their eyes into debts, joblessness and empty food cabinets. Lamont doesn't explain nor would he reveal how the manipulators of the Fed banks wiped out the savings of the *nouveau riche* and middle class buying stocks at bottom of the barrel prices, and sweeping away the nations' accumulated paper capital into their portfolios. (J. Horan, *Desperate Years,* 128)

By spring 1930 millions of American workers were jobless. Blue-collar and white. Factories were shut down. Massive layoffs leave 14.5 million unemployed men and women walking the streets. Earnings are slashed by layoffs and schedule reductions on the 59 cent hourly wage. Millionaires still wearing their three-piece business suits are reduced to selling apples trucked in from their country homes. By the end the year if he was lucky enough to keep his job an industrial worker on average took a 20% cut on an annual wage of $1500. Some people in Manhattan still have cash to buy winter coats "trimmed with Manchurian wolf" selling at $38.50 and karakul coats for $88. The price of a loaf of bread held at seven cents. The Young Communist League exploited the crisis with mass demonstrations against capitalism and calls to "Defend the Soviet Union" and the "7-Hour Day".

That March 1930 in the middle of the economic crisis former President and Supreme Court Justice William Howard Taft keeled over dead in his home in Washington DC. The obese 300-pound patriarch of Skull and Bones (1878) co-founded by his father Alphonso Taft in 1833 had served in more public offices than most any other American in the nation's history – thirteen in forty nine years – appointed, not elected to twelve posts since he started out as an assistant prosecutor in Ohio in 1881 a half-century before. His last post was US Chief Justice serving with with his longtime friend and former Secretary of State Elihu Root. His friend and Hoover's Secretary of State Henry Stimson joins the ten thousand mourners who shuffle by his coffin under the Capitol dome before a soldier's burial at Arlington Cemetery. In London the King of England proclaims Taft "a man of peace". The tides shift. A giant of the Old Guard of the Consortium had passed away. The hour-glass had turned. Who will be next?

The victorious New York Governor FDR is caught in a rare photo showing his leg braces under his formal black-tie seated next to New York's Lieutenant Governor Herbert Lehman, former chairman of the Democratic Party's Finance Committee (1928); Lehman became governor in 1933, serving until 1942. The son of a Jewish immigrant Meyer Lehman, he was one of three founders of the powerful Lehman Brothers investment firm. Herbert Lehman became partner in 1908 with cousin Philip and brother Arthur. Until the election of Eliot Spitzer, Herbert Lehman had held the distinction of having been not only the first but also the only Jewish governor of the State of New York. Later "in one of the most inflammatory campaigns in New York history" Lehman becomes the first Jewish senator in the nation defeating the Consortium prince John Foster Dulles. Out of a job Dulles seeks help from Dean Rusk, president of the Rockefeller Foundation in 1952, and chief of State's Far Eastern Affairs and soon to become Secretary of State; Rusk recommends Dulles to his boss Secretary of State Dean Acheson. Rusk later brings David Rockefeller and Henry Kissinger to the cabinet level. During the war Kissinger, 21, a Staff-Sergeant of the US Counter-Intelligence Corps, rounds up Nazi officials and Gestapo agents and recalls with nostalgia "this was the one period of my life when I felt completely American". Dulles is in Japan as part of the government's treaty negotiations with Emperor Hirohito and General McCarthy. Dulles, a trustee of the Rockefeller Foundation since 1935, becoming board chairman since 1950, then picks JD Rockefeller III to join him as his aide.

Following their mission Dulles is appointed chairman of the board of directors of the Japan Society in New York, and its president is JDR, III. Authors Collier and Horowitz write, "over the next two decades he was to entertain every Japanese Prime Minister and member of the royal family visiting the United States. Raising that part of the society's yearly budget that he didn't contribute to himself, he became a familiar face not only to the Japanese business leaders and statesmen who began streaming to the United States, but also to musicians, Kabuki troupes, and No players as well. He could often be found at Japan House, his tall figure draped in a kimono, hosting a tea for visiting dignitaries. He was so completely identified with the cause of bettered US-Japanese relations that when producer Josh Logan received the completed script of *Sayonara*, he sent it to Rockefeller for comments before starting to film." (P. Collier and D. Horowitz, *The Rockefellers*, 282-6; re Kissinger, M. Hastings, *Armageddon*, 359)

During World War II Lehman runs the Foreign Relief and Rehabilitation Operations for the State Department, a training ground for when he would become Director-General of the same such office in the postwar United Nations settlement. Barnard College has a building named after him. As is the tradition of rewards promising eternal remembrance, more illusions and cultural landmarks of posterity followed. His alma mater Williams College gave him a dorm, and Columbia University reserved a government professorship crowning his name in academia. Lehman's landslide victory for the New York Governorship gives Roosevelt the momentum he needs to reach the presidency. The Lehman Brothers investment bank is wiped out in the 2008 meltdown.

"Whatever you do Jim, is all right with me," the candidate told his campaign manager James A. Farley, a powerfully tall man and member of his first cabinet. As Hoover set up the RFC (Reconstruction Finance Corporation), Roosevelt set up his emergency unemployment committee in March 1930, later in August 1931 legislation was passed creating the Emergency Relief Administration, headed by Harry Hopkins. That provides $20 million to help New Yorkers get through the exceptionally severe 1931-32 winter.

America is at an all-time low. US farm prices slide precipitously. Factory production, retail trade follow stocks and bonds in the downward spiral. Cities nationwide are crisscrossed with long lines of the unemployed, starving and homeless. The ranks of the jobless might surpass 15 million. In the cities, men sell neckties, even pins and needles, roast chestnuts on the street, and just about anything to get by while in the farm belt fields are patrolled by armed guards with shotguns to keep foreclosure agents at bay. Midwinter the bank crisis flares up in headlines and clerks work feverishly trying to keep up with withdrawals. Banks sway trembling as though the ground underneath is about to give way.

CONSORTIUM MEN IN THE WALL STREET MARKET CRASH BOOM FIRE SALE

Not everyone lost in the stock took a dive. Far from it. Many Consortium insiders do well, cashing out ahead of the deluge. Some do very well indeed and reap huge profits in the killing. Reeve Schley (1881-60), for example, president of the American-Russian Chamber of Commerce in 1929, and Allen Wardwell, vp, both directors and members of the ARCC excom, both survive with family fortunes well intact. The younger Wardwell is a Standard Oil man. William T. Wardwell (1827-11) born in Bristol, Rhodes Island moved to Michigan when he was nine. Four years later, he joins his uncle, Samuel W. Hawes in the booming new oil business in Buffalo, New York. Wardwell gets in the oil bucks for himself; in 1875 when his business is bought out by Standard Oil he becomes treasurer of the Devoe Manufacturing Company, a subsidiary of the Standard. In 1898, under questioning by the Attorney General, John D. Rockefeller Sr. releases the names of Standard Oil Trust holders who redeemed their certificates. They include William T. Wardwell, Oliver H. Payne, and Charles Pratt. Wardwell ran unsuccessfully for Mayor of New York (1886) on the Democrats' Prohibition ticket, then Governor (1900). He dabbles in philanthropy as president and chief financial backer of the Red Cross Hospital. During WWI, his son Allen Wardwell served as a Major in the American Red Cross spy mission to Russia under H. P. Davison of Morgan, William Boyce Thompson, mining tycoon, investor and a director of the New York Fed, and Raymond Robbins all of them helping to prop up Lenin's revolutionary Bolshevik government during the Russian civil war.

Secret British War Cabinet papers record how Thompson arrives in London after the Bolshevik takeover and persuades Britain to shift policy away from Kerensky and support Trotsky and the Bols. Thompson is a key insider of the Consortium's Russian business seeking huge rich mining and other concessions. In Petrograd, in 1917, Thomson personally transfers to the Bolsheviks a million dollars from his own bank account. Soon after, in London, Thompson meets with war Prime Minister David Lloyd George to help coordinate their plans for postwar Russia. Donald McCormick's *The Mask of Merlin* (1964) found Lloyd George, the former munitions minister during the Great War "too deeply in the mesh of international armaments intrigues to be a free agent" and ensnarled with Sir Basil Zaharoff, the international arms dealer. In the early thirties we find that both Lloyd George and Rockefeller's Ivy Lee share a very unique personal connection on the eve of the Holodomor onslaught linked as they are through their young personal assistant Gareth Jones, journalist and specialist at the British Foreign Office. (Donald McCormick, *The Mask of Merlin, A Critical Biography of David Lloyd George,* Holt, Rinehart and Winston, 1970)

In 1919, Allen Wardwell is in New York alongside Rockefeller publicist Ivy L. Lee and Morgan's Guaranty Trust-Central Trust directors and trustees in the "charity" to raise money for the United Hospital Fund, a veritable Skull & Bones reunion campaign. Oliver G. Jennings, Lee, and Wardwell are all members of the campaign committee to raise millions for the United Hospital Fund in 1919. Other fund raisers included Guaranty Trust and Central Trust directors and trustees.

More traditional links to Old England families read like a "Who's Who" in the magazines of the "High Society" of Consortium culture, which works promoting a sort of made-to-order propaganda to allure the masses into the American Dream spirit of millionaire capitalism with rag to riches stories to spur economic development for middle-class tax funded government programs all of which keep the millionaires safe and secure from "the commie" Reds. Cornelius Bliss, Adrian Iselin Jr., JP Morgan, Percy R. Pyne II of National City and Princeton fame (an intimate friend and benefactor of All-American and WWI flyer Hobey Baker), George E. Roosevelt, James Speyer, and Albert H. Wiggin, and the wives of Speyer and Oliver Harriman; also Mrs. C. B. Alexander; M. N. Buckner (Bones 1895); Mrs. Benjamin Brewster (Bones 1882); W. V. Griffin,; Ogden L. Mills; William F. Morgan; Mrs. Henry L. Stimson (Bones 1888), Frank S. Witherbee (Bones 1874), Otto T. Bannard (Bones 1876). Philanthropic capitalism works wonders to preserve the spirit of freedom and individuality protecting private property, building national institutions, and preserving cultural traditions in America while it encourages a spirit to give wealth away or risk having it taken away by government taxes.

William Wardwell's second wife, Helen Rogers, a niece of Francis Lynde Stetson, senior partner of the prestigious law firm Stetson, Jennings & Russell representing Guaranty Trust; Wardwell was an executor of Stetson's estate willed to Williams College, a key lawyer in Stetson's New York City's Corp. Counsel under William C. Whitney, and personal friend and lawyer for JP Morgan Sr. and Jr.. From 1847-51, Stetson's father had been a US Congressman and a county judge in upstate Albany; Stetson is proud of his New England heritage, descendants of Robert Stetson, who settled in 1634, in Scituate, Massachusetts. (*The NYT*, April 15, 1930; "Standard Oil's Secrets", *The NYT*, Oct. 13, 1898; "Wm. T. Wardwell Dies Suddenly", *The NYT*, Jan. 4, 1911; "Under Red Terror", *The NYT*, Dec., 26, 1918; *The NYT*, Oct.25, 1919)

Allen Wardwell (1873-53) maintained his father's close ties with the Rockefellers and the Morgan men of Guaranty Trust. Legally trained, he partnered at Stetson, Jennings and Russell which became Davis, Polk, and Wardwell, the founding nexus flush with the Rockefeller Foundation of the Council of Foreign Relations (CFR). Partner Henry C. Alexander of JP Morgan Co. was vice chairman. Frank Polk served as Undersecretary of the US State Department under Lansing in Wilson's war cabinet. Polk remains an obscure and greatly underestimated Consortium insider who served on the excom of Davis Polk Wardwell Gardiner & Reed, counsel of Guaranty Trust. He also handles Davis' presidential bid in 1924. John W. Davis and Lansing Reed hold board seats at Guaranty Trust; his good friend Lansing Reed (Yale, Bones 1904) is a director at Guaranty Trust from 1924 to 1933.

Davis, Polk & Wardwell are always legal agents of Morgan and Rockefeller interests. The original firm name founded in 1921 was Davis, Polk, Wardwell, Gardiner & Reed then changed to Davis, Polk, Wardwell, Sunderland & Kiendl. Wardwell liked to keep up with public health work, for example, directing the Active Campaign Committee of the American Society for the Control of Cancer; in 1926 JD Rockefeller, Jr. sends a cool unconditional $100,000 gift to its congress meeting at Lake Mohonk. All three original partners of the firm died within a year following one after the other to the grave.

And to paint the faces into the picture for a better view of the close links of mutural interests we find Stetson, for instance, friendly associates of Thomas F. Ryan, W.C. Whitney's buddy in American Tobacco, both directors of the State Trust Company. After he bought control of Equitable Life Tom Ryan appointed the US President Grover Cleveland as one of the trustees of his stock in the company; Stetson and Ryan are both directors of the State Trust Company. Wilson Shannon Bissell (Bones 1869) was another of President Cleveland's early friends whom he appointed Postmaster General. Bissell (Richard Bissell of the OSS-CIA, Yale-MIT economics professor is the proud father of the U-2 spy plane dubbed "Bissell's bird", fiasco in 1960 when it crashs over Sverdlovsk in the Urals) is chums with the Yale Skull & Bones gang which includes US State Department don and FDR's senior adviser on foreign policy Henry Albert Stimson (1865), Edmund Coffin (1866) of GE, Henry Thompson Sloane (1866), Wilder Bennett Harding (1867), Horatio Seymour (1867), Peter Rawson Taft (Yale 1867), Chauncey Bunce

Brewster (1868), John Beach Isham (1869) and many others and their sons... Harry Payne Whitney (Bones 1894), H. W. Sage (1895) and A.G.C. Sage (1896) are also on the Bones play committee with Allen Wardwell for their dramatic farce antics. Other Sage family Bonesmen included Henry Manning Sage (1890), Dean Sage (1897). His son Edward R. Wardwell recharges the family Yale spirit tapped for Bones in the Class 1927. ("Interesting Yale Doings", *The NYT*, May 13, 1895; "Other Wedding Plans", *The NYT*, April 15, 1930)

Wardwell was "commissioner" of the Red Cross spy mission to Russia (1917-18) that secures Lenin's Bols in power; twenty years later, Wardwell is again alongside Harriman's Lend-Lease mission to Moscow as chairman of the Red Cross delegation to Stalin's Russia in 1941; the next year he ran the Russian War Relief Inc..

Lawyer Allen Wardwell is among the original founders in 1921 of the Rockefeller funded Consortium CFR men along with his partners John W. Davis and Frank L. Polk. Wardwell and Polk are all old Russian hands. Davis (American Telephone & Telegraph) had been ambassador in London during postwar reconstruction negotiations from 1918 to 1921. Davis and Polk were both Pilgrims Society members, and probably Wardwell, too. For two decades Polk remains a CFR director (1921-43) with Davis (1921-55). Allen Wardwell meanwhile performs his duties as president of the Association of the Bar of the City of New York (1927-29) followed by Davis (1931-32). In gratitude for all his Russian work the Consortium gives Wardwell, in 1943, a seat on the Bank of New York board. ("Wardwell to Head Russian Aid Drive", *The NYT*, May 24, 1942.)

Wardwell's CFR co-founder was Reeve Schley. Grant Barney Schley (1845-17) was a wiz at numbers, handsome with thick red hair, and often mistaken for Teddy Roosevelt. His brother, Evander, buys thousands of acres of farmland in New York and East New Jersey counties. Grant and Evander came from humble circumstances, a farm family in Chapinville, New York. Grant made his fortune and reputation as a tobacco banker; his brother William T. Schley (1840-12) used his legal skills to represent the New York Central Railroad. Its Grant's nephew, Reeve Schley Jr. who graduates from Yale (1903) and is a Fellow of Yale Corporation, in 1942, seven years after George Schley.

For twelve years Reeve Schley practices law with Simpson, Thacher & Bartlett until he resigns to become vp of Rockefeller's Chase National Bank; he had been on the board (1920-33), and so is intimately familiar with Chase's Russian loans that preoccupy FDR's ambassador Bill Bullitt. Reeve Schley is also Eastern treasurer of the Republican National Committee (1918-20) and, as more importantly concerns our story in 1929 serves as president of the American-Russian Chamber of Commerce (ARCC) during US investment in the Soviet Five-Year Plans under Stalin.

Which brings us closer to another Consortium FDR insider who made out splendidly in the crash. Floyd Bostwick Odlum, an associate of Reeve Schley Sr., and, by 1933, is one of the 10 richest men in the world. Odlum is chairman of the Howe Sound Company. He had a full hand of directorships including General Dynamics Corp., the Atlas Corp. (Atlas Utilities & Investors Company), the

United States Guarantee Co., the Chihuahua Mining Co., the Potosi Mining Co.... Odlum creates Atlas as an investment trust with $40,000 polled together into an investment fund in 1924. He, too, cashes out of most equities before the market collapse, solling half of Atlas, and with some eleven million dollars cash buys stocks at record lows diversifying into nearly every industry.

While on the other side of the world poor Ukrainians and Russians in the Volga region of the Caucasus are in the worst of the Holodomor tsunami of Genocide, *The New York Times*, on April 23, 1933, reported Atlas Corp owned $100,000,000 in aggregating assets and became one of the biggest investment trusts in the world making Odlum a billionaire many times over and his friends like Schley very rich patrons of Stalin and Roosevelt. Odlum was also a shareholder in RCA, General Dynamics, Greyhound Bus Lines, Northeast Airlines (nearly 90%), the Bonwit Teller department stores, Convair Aviation, United Fruit Company, and Madison Square Garden. In 1933, Atlas Corporation purchases Paramount Pictures at "basement" prices. Odlum is also chairman of RKO Studios; he sells RKO to Howard Hughes. Odlum also is a big player in Barnsdall. (More on Barnsdall later.) Oldum marries Jacqueline Cochran who became the fastest racing air pilot in the country and close friend of Amelie Earhart and her publisher husband George Putnam; Amelie makes world headlines as the first woman to fly solo across the Atlantic, in 1932. On May 9, 2004, the History News television network in America described Odlum: "A powerful financial wizard and industrialist, personally convinced Ike (Eisenhower) to seek the office." (*The NYT*, April 23, 1933; the Floyd Bostwick Odlum Collection are housed at the Eisenhower Library.)

Reeve Schley Sr. began working as a clerk at Wells, Butterfield & Co. in Syracuse, and got his big break when the firm was combined into Adams Express Company and he was sent to the money order department in New York. By 1874, Reeve Schley met George F. Baker (1840-31), the financier, director at American Express and co-founder and President of the First National Bank of New York. Baker is the American Croesus who gave millions to Harvard to create the Harvard Business School. In 1955 the First National Bank combines with the National City (Astor- Stillman-Rockefeller) and emerges as First National City Bank, or Citicorp.

Lets follow the money down the yellow brick road and see where it takes us. George Baker hires Reeve Schley to clerk at First National. Grant Schley soon married Baker's sister Elizabeth. After six years at the bank, he resigns in 1885, and becomes a partner with John G. Moore to start his own brokerage business, Groesbeck & Schley. Schley prospers in the boom years with railroad, mining and steel companies and takes directorships on the boards at American Smelting and Refining Co., Chihuahua Mining Co. (president), Coal Creek Mining and Manufacturing Co., president of the Coresus Gold Mining Co., Electric Storage Battery Co. (president), El Potosi (president), Elliott-Fisher Co., Northern Pacific Railway, Pittsburgh Coal Co., the Republic Iron and Steel Co., the American Smelting and Refining Co.. Schley money pours into developing Far Hills, New Jersey. In 1971, AT&T buys four hundred acres of Schley property for their corporate headquarters.

Grant Schley's estate "Fro Heim" in Somerset along the Lamington River, began in 1882, amassing forty farms on 5,000 acres with 1,500 under cultivation and requires 36 servants. In 1906 Grant Schley had built a large estate, Brook Cottage in the lush equestrian grounds of the landed gentry at Somerset Hills as a wedding gift to his daughter Evelyn; thirteen years later she died from the war's Spanish Influenza; their son Kenneth (Yale 1902) also worked on Wall Street, a prominent broker of Moore & Schley, and sits on numerous boards. In October 1941 during WWII he entertains the English royals, the Duke and Duchess of Windsor at his Somerset home built with terra-cotta bricks and shingles given by his friend JD Rockefeller. (Kenneth Jr. becomes a distinguished pilot during the Second World War; his sister Anne Caroline is also a licensed pilot.)

Follow Schley's family line and it takes the ARCC straight into the heart of the Consortium plutocracy in America. Grant B. Schley worked closely with Standard Oil treasurer Oliver Hazard Payne (1839-17), Yale, business partner of JD Rockefeller who with James B. Duke buys out Duke's competitors to create the American Tobacco Trust and US Steel with Carnegie. Both are directors of the Manhattan Trust Company and directors of Chase National Bank (later the Rockefellers' Chase-Manhattan, at present day JP Morgan-Chase. Payne's brother-in-law is William Collins Whitney (1841-04) married to his sister Flora Payne; when she dies widower Whitney marries Gertrude Vanderbilt. Her daughter will marry Averell Harriman; another son Payne Whitney marries Helen Jay, daughter of Teddy Roosevelt's Secretary of State John Jay (1885-89): Yale, Bones, Harvard Law, Puritan stock, son of a Brigadier General and descended from John Whitney who came to America in 1635.

The son of Harry Payne Whitney, Cornelius Vanderbilt Whitney, marries Marie Norton. After her divorce, Marie Norton Whitney marries W. Averell Harriman, his first wife. Sometimes it seemed that these men trade women the way they trade shares in their friend's companies, for profit and accumulated interest. The club prefers to treat all its fellow members fairly. (*The NYT*, Jan. 21, 1901 WF8; "Annual Bank Elections", *The NYT*, Jan. 13, 1904)

In 1893, George F. Baker replaced Fiske; by 1914, Baker is the third largest stockholder in the National Bank of Commerce after the Equitable Life and the Mutual Life; the largest stockholder in the Chase National, the First National; and the second largest in the Liberty National, after E.C. Converse. George F. Baker Jr. is the fifth largest stockholder in the First National.

Elected a Trustee of the Mutual Insurance Company in 1879, Baker closed the circle working with Henry H. Rogers, of the Charles Pratt oil firm, ringleader of the Mutual Insurance takeover who when he dies in 1909 had a fortune so large that surpasses JP Morgan and William Rockefeller. Two decades later Baker is elected a director of the First National Bank of Chicago, in 1903, along with James H. Hyde, Vice President of the Equitable Life Assurance Society, who, a year out of Harvard, inherits the company worth $400 million in assets when his father dies in 1899, leaving him a $100,000 annual salary while the fortune is held in trust until he turns thirty. H. H. Porter, Jr., is another director who succeeds his father on the board.

Max May of the Soviet Rumskobank came to Guaranty Trust in 1904 from Chicago's First National. Norman B. Ream and Clarence M. Woolley were directors of the First National and National Safe Deposit Company along with Baker in 1910.

Only four years before he died in 1960 Reeve Schley was elected chairman of the Underwood Corporation and remained chairman and director of the Somerville Trust Company. Reeve Schley's daughter, Eleanor Prentice Schley, married Webster B. Todd; they were the parents of New Jersey Governor Christine Todd Whitman, and the great-grandniece of Grant Schley. ("Miss Schley Bride of Webster B. Todd", *The NYT*, Oct. 11, 1933)

At the top end of the Consortium, and by the turn of the 19th century, William Collins Whitney (Yale, Bones) possesses one of the largest fortunes ever in America. C. Sutton listed some his vast estates: ". . . a city residence in New York, a Venetian palace and 5,000 acres in Wheatley Hills, near Jamaica, Long Island; a Sheepshead Bay house, with a private track covering 300 acres; a mansion at Berkshire Hills, Massachusetts, with 700 acres of land; October Mountain house, with a large tract of land; Stony Ford Farm, New York, used as an auxiliary to his Kentucky Stock Farm; an Adirondack game preserve of 16,000 acres; a lodge at Blue Mountain Lake with a fine golf course, a Blue Grass farm of 3,000 acres in Kentucky; and an estate at Aiken, South Carolina, comprising a mansion, race course, and 2,000 acres of hunting land." And that may not be all. In fact, the October Mountain spread by 1902 is a great game preserve of 10,000 acres situated four miles from Lenox, Massachusetts. *The New York Times* reports his newest acquisition, a bird "farm" with "several hundred of the beautiful English pheasants sometimes called Japanese green heads" enclosed on two acres surrounded by lynx, "wild cats", moose shipped in from Manitoba Canada in British Columbia, Montana black-tailed deer, more than two dozen buffaloes from the Rockies…

The Wardwell and Schley branches of the Consortium tree remain close family friends and move in the same social and professional circles with their fellow Yale Bonesmen. Close among them are George Schley Stillman (1935) with classmates, Charles Seymour, Jr. whose Bonesman father edited Col. House's private papers, in 1926, as a sort of sacred Trust. (House had deposited his papers at Yale, in 1923, and encouraged others to do the same, including son-in-law Gordon Auchincloss and Sir William Wiseman. (All archives scholars and researchers at Yale must pass by a creepy oil portrait of House that might just as well preside over a cabal of vampires.) Reader there are many who figure prominently with names that remain currently familiar: John Sargent Pillsbury Jr., Lyman B. Spitzer, Jr., Eugene William Stetson, Jr., (1934), Henry John Heinz II, (1931), Edward Rogers Wardwell (1927), Anson Phelps Stokes, Jr. (1927), George Herbert Walker, Jr. (1927), Charles Tiffany Bingham, (1928), John Rockefeller Prentice (1928), Henry Riddle Merrill (1929), James A. Stillman (1937) …

John Rockefeller Prentice is John D. Rockefeller's grandson; when cousin John Sterling Rockefeller, grandson of William Rockefeller and son of William Rockefeller (Yale 1892) joins the Paul Mellon group in Scroll & Key, *The New*

York Times commemorates his ascendancy as an event deserving of national headlines: "Senator's Son Gets Final Tap at Yale". The Rockefeller-Prentice family through mergers and business became the pillars behind the Milbank, Tweed firm and the Sterling Memorial Library at Yale, one of the largest ever constructed in the world famous for its towering Gothic architecture and design and located in the heart of the Yale campus. (*The NYT*, May 20, 1927)

Get the picture? It should be more clear now. America's top-tier family business and banking connections run on and on with a discernible logic to the pattern. Here we trace the links to the Wardwell-Schley connections leading into the ARCC's promotion of investment in Stalin's Soviet regime taking us into the nexus of Morgan Guaranty and politically influential corporations of the Consortium that extended their fortunes from the end of the 19th century into the 20th and 21st centuries. This is not insignificant nor should it be underestimated when it combines with the former Russian Empire's extraordinary natural and human resources, – a subjugated population of cheap slave labor of tens of millions of illiterate peasants under an unyielding totalitarian dictatorship. With the monopolistic wealth of America's Consortium capitalists combining to weld a strategic partnership during the Depression years embedded in the consolidated fortress of Stalin's machine of mass Terror American foreign policy decisions of the White House with its slew of advisers positioned in corporations, investment houses, law firms and government offices are ready for world war. Bring it on!

For example, by virtue of his marriage to Helen Rogers, the niece of Stetson, Allen Wardwell mixes his blood with a second generation tier of the banking Bakers, Ryans, Whitneys and Rockefellers. Thomas Fortune Ryan, the tobacco and transport scion was also a Schley business partner. Ryan's grandson eventually marries one of George F. Baker's grandchildren.

Baker's son Alan Ryan, marries Janet Newbold, a publishing heiress; she divorces him and for her third husband chose James S. Bush, brother of Prescott, father of George Herbert Walker Bush, the President. To show further how family relations keep the money and power in the family, George F. Baker's son, George F. Jr. marries Breevort Kane; their son George F. Baker III marries into the Drexel-Munn family, descendants of the Drexel banking house, a family derivative of JP Morgan's original Drexel-Morgan firm.

The Drexels for their part also tie up with the Dukes and Biddles, descendants of Nick Biddle, founder of the Second Bank of the United States, predecessor of the Federal Reserve. Further, George F. Baker's daughter, Flo, marries the son of a woman who was the grandson of one of the original bankers of Brown Brothers, precursor to Brown Brothers Harriman. To top that, Thomas Suffern Tailer then leaves Flo, and remarries a Sturgis of the Russell Trust (Skull & Bones) clan of the great by-gone China opium days when the British with a few Americans on the scene (Forbes, Russell, Delano, Perkins, etc.) started the Opium Wars after the Chinese dumped their precious opium product into the sea at Canton.

Baker's daughter Edith marries John Schiff, the son of New York's favorite Jew, Jacob Schiff, the power icon behind Kuhn-Loeb. John Schiff's great aunts Nina and Frieda are both married into the Warburg family; Nina marrires Paul

Warburg of the Federal Reserve. Frieda marries Felix; their grand-daughter marries Franklin D. Roosevelt, Jr.! And be sure to visit the Forbes collection at the George Peabody Museum, in Peabody, Massachusetts.

Follow the lineage of the great American families down the yellow brick road of Ozland. Where the money flows the power goes. Consortium establishment power, whether Wasp or Jew, continues to breed offspring in honor of the legacy of their ancestors; at present day a grandson of John Schiff and Edith Baker marries the daughter of former Vice President Al Gore. In this federated world where borders come crashing down and money flows through invisible channels so too are the old barriers rendered redundant and obsolete casting an eerie opaque shadow the strange geo-political architecture of foreign relations deciding war and peace.

Lets look closer at the Rockefeller- Wardwell-Rogers fortune. Henry H. Rogers migrated to the Pennsylvania oilfields in the early 1860s. There he meets Charles M. Pratt and joins him in Brooklyn in 1866. During the Standard oil wars in the next two decades, as happened with William Wardwell's company, Pratt interests were absorbed by Rockefeller's giant Standard Oil, in 1874. Rockefeller's mergers made fortunes and marriages.

As Chairman of the Manufacturing Committee at Standard Oil Henry H. Rogers organizes its pipeline system. He is also president of the Petroleum Refiners and Dealers of New York City and superintendant of the Charles L. Pratt plant. Rogers marries Abby Palmer Gifford of an old New England line. Rogers is a member of gas company syndicates along with William Rockefeller, with Moore & Schley as their brokers. William Rockefeller of the United Metals Selling Company takes over the interests of the Lewisohn Brothers to control by 1900 at least seventy percent of the America's copper production. For Standard Oil in Denmark, Rogers persuades the Danish Government to sell the Danish West Indian Islands, St. Johns, St. Croix, and St. Thomas, to the United States, pocketing a ten percent commission, and tells his Danish counterpart that he "controlled the votes of twenty-six United States Senators, who were at all times ready and willing to obey any order given them by the Standard Oil Company".

Henry Rogers is also a director of the Chicago, Milwaukee & St. Paul Railroad along with William Rockefeller and a director of Harriman's Union Pacific. Rogers and Rockefeller are also directors of the Amalgamated Copper Co. financed by an interest-free $39 million public loan from National City Bank to buy Amalgamated stock which they are forced to sell at a loss when copper plunged, and collect a neat $36 million in the deal. These were the tumultuous days of the railroad combinations making America's great industrial fortunes of the Consortium bankers, lawyers and investment houses. Kuhn-Loeb and Morgan joined to back James J. Hill buying up Northern Pacific Railroad in the 1890s; they then backed E. H. Harriman and the Rockefellers in 1901 over control of Northern Pacific. (Thomas Lawson, "Frenzied Finance", *The NYT*, August 20, 1904; "Standard Oil Plot Foreshadowed War", *The NYT*, May 1, 1900)

Consortium leaders with Tom Watson of IBM stack the board of the American-Russian Chamber of Commerce (ARCC) but it has its share of prominent insiders less visible to the American people. They include Samuel R. Bertron (1865-38), a New York banker and a ARCC chairman, Yale and Bones (1885) and a Pilgrims Society man; Charles Coleman with Lehigh Valley Railroad of the Vanderbilt and Rockefeller clans on the ARCC board since it was founded in 1922. Bertron was a senior vp at Guaranty Trust and board member of more than a dozen companies (Atlantic Safe Deposit, National Surety, United Gas & Electric, Electric Bond & Share, Wire Wheel Corp. of America, New York Indemnity, San Juan Sugar and International Equities Corp.…).

Bertron & Storrs conducts their investment banking through offices in Philadelphia and Manhattan. During the First World War Sam Bertron works closely with Robert Bacon and Harjes in Paris for the Relief Clearing House for France. These men also collaboratie with Senator McAdoo, President Wilson's son-in-law, on the Excess Profit Tax Board before McAdoo becomes Treasury Secretary. Bertron is one of the few tapped for the 1917 Root diplomatic mission to Russia during the political chaos that summer before the Bolshevik coup Root was a protégé of Taft whom he served as Secretary of War, then Teddy Roosevelt's Secretary of State, and Henry Stimson's mentor at his firm. Root's daughter married the grandson of President Ulysses Grant. For his work Root is honored with the 1912 Nobel Peace Prize and outlives most of his peers until passing away in 1937.

Wilson had sent Bertron on the Root-Crane mission to Russia along with John R. Mott (YMCA), Cyrus McCormick (International Harvester, Chicago), US Navy Rear Admiral Gennon, and journalist Charles E. Russell; Russell's graphic muckraking reports of the meat-packing health and labor conditions in Chicago's stockyards had been a source of inspiration for Upton Sinclair's best-selling expose *The Jungle* (1906) describing Chicago slums and diseased working conditions in the Armour family meatpacking plants echoed in Teddy Roosevelt's public attacks against these "malefactors of great wealth". Not yet fourteen, in 1897 he graduated from City College of New York and briefly studied at Columbia.. Lewis went on to win the 1930 Nobel Prize for Literature, the first American writer to win the award.

As more thousands of Ukrainians mortally succumb to the Holodomor Terror-Famine another key Consortium player in the loop with interest in Stalin's future makes a foray on the scene in Japan and Manchuria. Paul D. Cravath is an iconic figure among Wall Street's most prestigious law firms (Davis, Polk and Wardwell) located at 15 Broad Street in lower Manhattan in the Wall Street district. He later forms *Cravath, de Gersdorif, Swaine & Wood.* Born in the first year of the American Civil War, Cravath sits with the upper class Pilgrims Society set, a member since 1903.

Along with Davis and Wardwell of the Council of Foreign Relations (CFR) Cravath, too, is a director of the organization he jointly creates in 1921. He remains a lifetime director until his death in 1941. During the First World War Cravath's legal team represents the US Treasury at the Inter-Allied War Conference on War Purchases and Finance in London and Paris. These "Dollar-a-Year" volunteer Consortium millionaires earned their medals as they honored one another in the conflict that dooms over 100,000 Americans – and some 20 million Russians, including the Romanovs as they set up the chessboard for the decadees to come.

For all his "heroism" Cravath also receives a DSM (Distinguished Service Medal). The Allies cover his chest with numerous other postwar medals. Ever since 1888 Cravath's future is linked to the fortunes of law partner, Republican boss Charles Evans Hughes who in 1930 replaces former President Taft, now deceased, to become Chief Justice of the US Supreme Court. Ferdinand Lundberg's *America's 60 Families* (1947) writes, "In every detail of his life Hughes was joined with the Wall Street freebooters."

Fresh out of Columbia Law School, Hughes joins Cravath at Carter, Hughes & Cravath; the firm name was later changed to Hughes, Hubbard & Reed. Cravath keeps a mansion in Locust Valley, Long Island, not far from Harry Davison's baronial compound at Peacock Point on Long Island Sound, and the home of Stettinius, FDR's war boss of Lend-Lease. Cravath, Swaine & Moore remains an international powerhouse handling legal affairs of many illustrious personalities of our American saga including Madame Chiang Kai-shek. wife of the late client of the Consortium's corrupt warlord of the Nationalists waging war and extermination of Mao's millions of organized and dedicated communists fighting for freedom from poverty, hunger and disease. (Later Madame Chiang is a Cravath neighbor at Peacock Point renown in the community for her visits to the local hairdresser accompanied by a small army of bodyguards.

HOOVER, STIMSON, MORGAN & THE JAPANESE IMPERIAL CONNECTION

During the fatal winter of 1933-34 when Stalin continues murdering Ukrainians, Paul Cravath and his friend Alfred R. Whitney share a cruise through the Panama Canal before stepping aboard their luxurious private ship *Stella Polaris* cruising to the South Pacific islands on their way to checking up on the rumblings in Manchuria, China and Japan.

Cravath regrets having just missed his friend in passing international French banker Jean Monnet here for several months for the League of Nations. Monnet left for Hong Kong "while I had to be in Shanghai", Paul Cravath observes in a privately published book of his trip but he doesn't reveal the nature of his business in Asia on the verge of breaking out into another world war and a region where the Soviet underground reseau "The Center" keeps a close watch on influential figures as well as shadowing its own agents and sending reports back to Lubyanka in Moscow.

On his Far Eastern tour Cravath confers with America's favorite Asian heroin drug lord Chiang Kai-shek on the verge of losing his hold on Nanking in Manchuria after FDR drops the gold standard and the US Treasury stocked up on silver draining Chinese silver reserves and killing the Nanking bonds used to finance Chiang's anti-communist activities. Cravath seems to be more impressed that Gen. Chiang has been educated in Japan. His fact-finding mission in Japan heightens his alarm of rising tensions but he finds comfort from nubile bare-breasted Tahitian girls made famous in Gauguin paintings and he prefers them over even younger geishas presented to him in Tokyo when he makes the diplomatic rounds with the key link in the Consortium chain in Japan, Ambassador Joseph C. Grew, a Morgan man of paramount and intimate importance. When the Japanese in the fall of 1931 invaded Manchuria and set up the puppet state of Manchukuo, Chiang's third attempt with 300,000 troops and close to three dozen American Vought Corsair fighter-bombers approved by Hoover and Stimson fail to annihilate Mao's Red Army and stop his Long March to the west. (Dean King, *Unbound,* NY: Little Brown, 2010; Agnes Smedley, *China's Red Army Marches*, NY: Vanguard Press, 1934; Harrison E. Salisbury, *The Long March; The Untold Story*, NY: Harper & Row, 1985)

Both Groton and Harvard (1902) where they collaborate on the *Crimson,* Franklin and Joe share much more than collegiate affairs; Grew too is descended from Boston Brahmins who financed America's opium China traders tightly linked to the Russells, Forbes, Perrys and Delanoes. On a trip to Japan after graduating Harvard he met Alice Perry, the beautiful great-grand niece of Commodore Perry who sailed American naval ships into Tokyo Bay, in 1853, a defining moment obliging the Japanese to open commercial trade agreements with the United States. Grew returns to the US, and enters the Foreign Service. His first colonial experience was a posting in Egypt and honeymooned on the Nile, then after first passing through Mexico and Russia he and his wife arrive in Berlin in 1908, where he witnessed the outbreak of the First World War, and quickly turns away from embracing the German cause, and joins Hoover's food distribution operations in Germany before returning to the United States when Wilson entered America into the war.

Grew does his bit selling Liberty Bonds in the bankers' war effort selling the war to patriotic Americans who know nothing of the political and financial manipulations of the Consortium masters. Less than a year after the Manchurian Incident, in 1928, a little ploy of delayed action triggered of the assassination of the Manchurian warlord Chang Tso-lin when the Japs blew up his train blamed on Chinese troops prompting the Japanese three years later in "the Manchurian Incident of 1931" to provoke the seizure and occupation of the entire 440,000 square miles of Manchuria. Herbert Hoover and Joseph Grew combined their personal support of the Japanese expansion and takeover of Manchuria. (On the extraordinary secret manipulations by Herbert Hoover and Joseph Grew, in S. Seagrave and P. Seagrave, *The Yamato Dynasty*; Waldo H. Heinrichs Jr., *American Ambassador: Joseph C. Grew*; Herbert Hoover biographer George H. Nash, four vols.; Joseph Grew, *Turbulent Era*, NY: Houghton Mifflin, 1952)

According to the Seagraves' published findings in *The Yamato Dynasty* (1999) Herbert Hoover mortally feared Stalin and held the Russian communist factor entirely alien to the values of the civilized world so endearingly precious in West "culture". That is not credible. The Hoover story we know reader is far more complex. As a well-informed pragmatic and able politician Hoover knows better. However, during his trip through Europe in early 1938, on March 8 when he arrives from Prague to meet Gen. Göering and the Fuhrer now reaching his summit and months away from unleashing world war.

Hoover assures Hitler how impressed he is with "the splendid new highways, the new housing, and the general prosperity in the German towns and villages". It's the typical compliment praising the efficiency of trains running on time. Hoover's effusive and profound "admiration" is fundamental. He tells Hitler how wonderfully impressive he finds this upbeat "very hopeful, live atmosphere everywhere in Germany". For his part Hitler does his bit to use Hoover to build a bridge from America to the Nazi agenda that has "created a new security and stability of conditions, and in particular, security for the private capitalist" and likewise argues his government had satisfied had resolved Germany's economic problems "without Labor having to exercise pressure". The Fuhrer rages sufficiently against communists, Jews and Democracy to convince Hoover that he's probably more insane than eccentric. The Seagrave portrait of Hoover is an interesting one that merits repeating here, especially in light of their extensive investigations published in numerous notable books. (John Lucas, "Herbert Hoover Meets Adolf Hitler", *The American Scholar*, 1993)

"Like most conservatives," the Seagraves write, 'Hoover was more alarmed by Stalin and t he communist menace than by Hitler and the Nazis. In his eyes, there was nothing to choose between Nazi Germany and communist Russia. If pressed to choose, he would not have chosen Russia." Hoover was a mining engineer with early experience in China and personally acquainted with many Japanese leaders. "He had been visited at his California home by Prince Konoe and pro Nazi Foreign Minister Matsuoka, who both shared Hoover's fear of Russia and his contempt for Wilsonian pacificsm." (S. Seagrave and P. Seagrave, *The Yamato Dynasty*, 207. F. Konoe, three times Japan's prime minister (1937 to 1939) and at head of government during Rape of Nanking Massacre that began in December 1937, and Pearl Harbor attack four years later; Konoe remains on the US war criminal list, and commits suicide 1945)

Although headed in the right direction the Seagraves downplay the full extent of the shadowy government hand of Stimson and the full extent of Consortium power behind the grab for gold and influence in the East, a relatively odd turn of mind when they do in fact reveal very extensive holdings of Morgan, General Electric and Westinghouse in the Japanese Imperial economy. They do an excellent service in elaborating the role of Ambassador Joe Grew in Tokyo, – a figure practically completely overlooked by establishment historians, – and later undersecretary in Washington alongside Stimson and Hull becomes more clear in view of family links that tie together the Morgan fortune with the Nippon empire.

The Seagraves do excellent research which makes their exaggeration of Hull's importance all the more uncanny but then its not difficult to understand when little and almost next to no research has been published on these Consortium State Department connections with the American super rich turn-of-the-century family elites."

"On the Allied side," Sterling and Peggy Seagrave write, "the quasi-Christian network was a cat's cradle of powerful connections. One of its leaders was

US Undersecretary of State Joseph Grew... had longstanding ties to General Fellers* and to former president Hoover. Grew's wife, Alice Perry Grew, was a relation of Commodore Mathew Perry, father of the navy clan and leader of the ships that opened Japan to American trade. As a child, Alice attended school in Tokyo, became fluent in Japanese and was intimate friends with aristocratic Japanese girls, one of whom grew up to become Hirohito's mother. So Alice and Joseph Grew had unique access to aristocratic circles in Japan." Cousin Jane Norton Grew marries Jack Morgan, son of J. Pierpont Morgan, Sr. . In Japan the Morgan banking empire is known as 'the Morgan *zaibatsu.* From some of the findings highlighted by the Seagraves we can have a better understanding how Stimson's soft-step manipulation of America's foreign policy to accommodate the imperial Manchurian aggression and feigned neutrality is a springboard to Morgan investment. The Seagraves write, "Morgan made huge loans to Japan in the 1920s and 1930s and helped many big American corporations like General Electric to make investments there, So Grew, part of the extended Morgan family, also enjoyed a very cozy reception in the Japanese financial world. While he served as US ambassador to Japan in the 1930s, Grew associated with Japanese men and women who were reassuringly like the Boston Brahmins of his own childhood. With so many Quakers and Christians among them, Grew felt he was dealing with the Asian equivalent of New England Puritans." (Sterling and Peggy Seagrave, *The Yamato Dynasty: The Secret History of Japan's Imperial Family*, NY: Broadway Books, 1999, 11-2. * Gen. Bonner Fellers is attached to the OSS to assist Grew and Gen. MacArthur on the postwar longevity of Hirohito and the corrupt royal and warlord clans.)

Alice Perry Grew and her husband the Consortium's diplomat of choice to deal with the Japanese emperor and the shogun oligarchs set sail for Tokyo arriving there mid-summer 1932, a full century since his ancestors underwrote the Russell & Company opium traffickers and a half-century since Morgan established his bank for the Meiji Restoration once the British had polished off their "significant role in the Meiji coup" and lost no time in recognizing in 1868 the Restoration government and newly enthroned emperor overthrowing the shogun. (See "Out of the Cage", in Seagrave and P. Seagrave, *The Yamato Dynasty*, for an excellent description of British royal cultivation of the Japanese, who Lloyd George called a "steadfast ally" during the First World War, and the Anglo-Japanese Alliance (1902-21) intended to safeguard British interests in North Asia, 100-15)

Ambassador Grew proudly shows off his new Embassy. Cravath is overwhelmed with praise, describing it in his diary "palatial". Cravath writes, the Tokyo complex is "the finest American Embassy I have ever seen ... four buildings in a beautiful location on a hill in the suburbs, and comprises the Chancery, two dormitories for the staff, and a magnificent house for the Ambassador". It always pleases empire builders to see what money can do.

The previous embassy building had been destroyed in the 1923 Kanto earthquake followed by a horrific 36-foot tall tsunami drowning thousands living in wooden homes now a massive rubble of Tokyo set aflame when fires broke out toasting thousands more along the banks. That scene was terrific on a scale surpassing the devastation that ripped apart San Francisco decades earlier. "As the fires spread, the city of Tokyo became a single blaze. More than the earthquake itself, the fire wreaked havoc, incinerating many square miles of congested housing, while refugees fled in panic before walls of flame, converging on the banks of the Sumida River. The flames followed, igniting wooden bridges, roasting alive tens of thousands of people huddled along the river banks. Thousands fled into the waters of Tokyo Bay, where they were engulfed in new flames as 100,000 tons of fuel gushed from burst tanks at Yokosuka naval base. Firestorms raged through the night. By Sunday morning more than 300,000 buildings had vanished and two-thirds of the city was reduced to smoldering ashes. Aftershocks continued. On Monday morning, dazed survivors began sifting the debris for the remains of relatives. Over 140,000 people were lost from an urban population of 1.5 million. Property damage came to 2 percent of Japan's total national wealth. Two million people were homeless." Protected by a wide moat, the imperial palace survived intact. It was said that the Emperor Hirohito remained unshaken. (S. Seagrave and P. Seagrave, *The Yamato Dynasty*, 117)

Agriculture was not unaffected. Many farms were suffered damage. Warehouses were destroyed, collapsed and burned in the inferno. Americans donated canned beans, and much more.

For the Consortium bankers the Japanese disaster proves to be a golden opportunity. Flush with cash from the First World War, the banks cash in quite handily extending massive loans to their Asian partners. Not only do they save a the virtually bankrupt economy but the bankers now afford a capital investment base and modernization program that will escalate their military adventurism consolidated with privileged personal relationships to ensure their violent excursions into China, Manchuria from Shanghai to Nanking and along the southern Mongolian border with Russia.

Without connecting the lines the writing duo Sterling and Peggy Seagrave who over forty years researched the Japanese and Chinese dynasties from their centuries old past through the Second World War era to the present day, are well-qualified and astute in their findings about the financial web of the Consortium's partnerships with the opaque Imperial Japanese hierarchy. It was a very privileged access into the aristocratic elite palaces of shoguns and princes and seemed to mimic the aristocratic "structural corruption" of Boston society of New England blue-bloods and Wall Street. "America provided more than beans.

The Seagraves take it from there, writing, "Jack Morgan sponsored a $150 million loan package for earthquake reconstruction (an enormous sum in those days) and, in doing so, bought himself a piece of Japan's future. The House of Morgan had become involved in Japan nearly half a century earlier during the Meiji Restoration, when the bank was first established by Jack's father. ... Morgan could easily handle giant loans. The United States had come out of World War I with a lot of excess capital generated by wartime business. Morgan Banks in particular profited when it became the major purchasing agent for the British Army and Navy and for the French government. During the war, Morgan handled $3 billion in commercial transactions, netting $30 million in fees. Then there was a $500 million Anglo-French loan for which Morgan demanded a steep 6 percent interest, while generously waiving all other fees. Before the war was over, Morgan had arranged over $1.5 billion in credits. With this leverage, and the decline of Britain's dominance of international fiance, the House of Morgan became the world's most influential bank, 'America's premier foreign lender', and the sage of Wall Street. This tremendous economic clout had the result of moving the House of Morgan into the political arena of foreign policy, making the firm virtually an extension of the US government. As the bank became a global player, it turned its attention to Asia ...". Harry Davison and the Morgan men chose their latest Harvard gelding, Thomas Lamont, the youngest partner who joined the bank in 1911, and sent him to East Asia to scope out prospects. Dismayed by the confusing turmoil of China, Lamont saw a fortune to be made in Japan and set the stage for the political and military upheaval caused by the Japanese scourge throughout East Asia and all the way to Pearl Harbor and Hirohito's fateful indecision that promoted the nuclear destruction of Hiroshima and Nagasaki and little sympathy from the Americans who saved Japan from suffering a Russian invasion that was sure to come, otherwise.

Morgan's first significant offering with the $150 million Japanese loan in 1924 stepped over the ranking postion in Japan enjoyed for decades by Khun, Loeb and Jacob Schiff, I must now reader defer to Suzie Pak when she understands so well this banking connections with the Japanese militarist expansion in Korea and Manchuria. It is a wicked affair if there ever was inflicted on the Korean people. Bill Franklin Sands tried to stop it and the Japanese knew him and what he was trying to do and they respected him but they could not talk about it. It was forbidden and they would turn away with a hush. Of this they could not speak. Suzie Pak writes, of "the ways in which private banking at the Morgan firm were changing in the postwar period. Their relationship with Japan, in particular, demonstrates how the conditions under which the Morgans pursued their work were affected by America's rise to world power and the rise of state power. ... As the leading international bankers of the world's leading power and with Japan as their client, the Morgans could not afford to ignore "how much the conditions of their business had changed as national and international circumstances shifted the balance of power."

In her chapter "Unseating Khun, Loeb", Suzie Pak tells the story what happens when Morgan with the State Department takes over in Japan: "As an international bank, the Morgan firm's client base had always been diverse, but before the First World War, the scope of its business with Japan was limited by the strong and proprietary relationship that Kuhn, Loeb & Co. had as Japan's American banker. In 1904 alone, Kuhn, Loeb & Co.'s sales for the Japanese government amounted to 11,000,000 (pounds sterling) or approximately, $53,460,000. In total, Kuhn, Loeb & Co. made five loans for Japan during the Russo-Japanese War, of which 'the American share of the five loans combined amounted to over $196 million, a sum that was said to set a record for large-scale volume financing before World War I.'" And reader I assure you in here this will surprise even you! She reveals, "Jacob Shiff had such close ties with Baron Kaorekiyo Takahashi (1854-36), vice-governor of the Bank of Japan and later the Japanese minister of finance and premier, that Takahashi's fifteen-year-old daughter, Wakiko, lived with Schiff and his wife in New York for three years (1906-09). Takahashi met Schiff at a dinner in London in 1904 after he had been sent abroad as Japan's financial commissioner. He spent the better part of three years in Europe and the United States in order to raise money for the Japanese war effort. His life-long friendship

with Schiff started as a union of common interests against Russia. Takahashi had initially hoped to enlist Pierpont Morgan to Japan's cause, but he found Morgan to be unfriendly and rude. Pierpont's apparent disregard for and disinterest in Japan's business leaves open the field for his rival. While in New York in 1905, Takahashi told his associate Kentaro Kaneko, the brother-in-law of Takuma Dan, a financier and representative of the Mitsui industrial conglomerate, "Khun, Loeb is strong enough to prevent any mischief that might come from Morgan.' In 1906, after the Russo-Japanese War, Schiff was invited by the Japanese government to visit Japan, where h met central financial and political leaders, including the Japanese emperor, who 'presented (him) with the Order of the Rising Sun'. It was at the conclusion of that trip that Wakiko accompanied Schiff, whom she later referred to as 'Uncle', and his wife, Therese, to New York to live and study in the United States. After she returned to Japan, Wakiko stayed in touch with the Schiffs and she eventually moved to London with her husband, Toshikata Okubo, a member of the Yokohama Specie Bank and the son of Toshimichi Okubo, a Japanese statesman, who was one of the founders of modern Japan." This is top level insider control and very profitable.

"As long as Kuhn, Loeb & Co. retained their proprietary right as Japan's bank, JP Morgan & Co. could not poach Kuhn, Loeb's client without violating their informal code of conduct. Kuhn, Loeb & Co.'s break with Japan over its alliance with Russia and Jacob Schiff's death in 1920 offered the Morgans the opportunity to begin anew with Japan, now the dominant power in East Asia. By the early 1920s, the Morgans made critical steps towards replacing Kuhn, Loeb & Co. as Japan's leading foreign bank. ... The Morgans were able to leverage not only their position as the Allies banker, they were able to leverage their social status as Anglo-American elite bankers in order to supplant Kuhn, Loeb's proprietary rights." The assassination of Takahashi by right-wing nationalist extremists, followed by further militarist conquest and the rape of Nanking leads Roosevelt to denounce "the epidemic of world lawlessness" and Morgan. In her exhaustive accounting of the Morgan bank in Japan (though she ignores Morgan investments in Russia), Suzie J. Pak writes, "Having supported Japan in its imperial endeavors for more than two decades, the Morgans were forced to disavow their titles." (S. J. Pak, 162-3, 189-90)

Lamont and the Morgans in the 1927 co-managed a $20,640,000 loan to the City of Tokyo with their partners Kuhn, Loeb, National City Bank, First National Bank, Yokohama Specie Bank; the same bank syndicate in 1930 extend a $71 million loan to the Imperial Japanese Government (for debt refunding) and American share $50 million. Lamont sends a clear message to the Japanese that they should tell Kuhn, Loeb "that they had chosen the Morgans to take on the loan in order to secure 'co-operation throughout the entire American investment public. The implication, of course, was that Kuhn, Loeb & Co. could not. On all of the Japanese syndicates, which included loans to the cities of Yokohama and Tokyo, Kuhn, Loeb & Co. remained a co-manager, listed before the National City Bank and First National Bank, but always second to JP Morgan & Co.... During this period the Morgans continued to lend money to Japan ... and a guaranteed loan in 1931 to the Taiwan Electric Company. Morgan had also organized $25 million bank credit to the Yokohama Specie Bank for currency stabilization as Japan prepared to return to the gold standard in 1930. In 1932, JP Morgan & Co. advanced $127 million to the Yokohama Specie Bank for a short-term loan. That loan was made in November 1931 after the September invasion of China." Between 1924 and 1931, JP Morgan & Co. 'floated bond issues totaling $263 million for Japanese borrowers ... the largest amount for any country outside Europe." (S. J. Pak, 187, ft.328)

The minister's son is now perceived as Morgan's investment agent and Japan's stand-out PR financial representative in the United States backing Japanese rape and murder along with conquest and plunder in China and risking a major war with Russia. It was self-evident and need no further justification to see as Lamont and the Morgans with encouragement from ambassador Grew, and with no end in sight, believed their relationship to Japan important enough, as author Suzie Pak confirms in *Gentlemen Bankers* (2013) "that Lamont continued his campaign of persuasion of key officials and persons in the United States into the 1930s, producing propaganda in support of Japanese colonial militarism. His main concession was that he avoided doing so publicly." In 1931 he readily prepares publicity documents and acts as a Japanese lobbyist to assure his client gets the desired reception in the American press. For the two years with Roosevelt in the White House relations between America and Japan deteriorate with the Morgans in the middle. Lamont tries to lay low but he is spotlighted and he and the bank remain, Harvard's Susie Pak concludes, "a publicity problem".

Harvard's Lamont and Morgan partners are fueling Japan's war engines while American manufacturers are building their fighter and bomber airplanes, as well as those of Chiang's nationalist exterminators of Mao's desperate and small communist people's army. To be sure, America has a lot of irons in the fire. Late June the *China Weekly Review* published an article "Morgan & Company and the Japanese 'Hands-Off' Doctrine" and Martin Egan of Morgan sends a Lamont letter with the story to Ambassador Hiroshi Saito (1887-1939) asking for his opinion. It appears that the Japanese militarists are getting away with murder and protected behind the shield of "the New York banking house of Morgan and Company ... the silent partners in Japan's 'hands-off' declaration." Lamont personally is targeted in the article and singled out for having told the Japanese press that he supports the Japanese presence in China but furthermore declared "that any future investments in China *must rest on the necessary condition that the Nanking Government will honor all its existing loans"*. Pak confirms, "Lamont had in fact made these arguments repeatedly through the IBC." Lamont has come a long way since the First World War President Wilson had appointed him as chairman of the excomm of the China Famine Relief Fund alongside the social reformer and outspoken leader of civil rights for women, Jane Addams. In 1928, the Women's International League opposed Morgan's loans to Japan "in connection with the Manchurian railway" sent a strong protest letter to Lamont. (S. J. Pak, 185)

All heads turned towards Lamont as the unlucky scapegoat to go down with the ship if it came to that. But the Consortium is loyal and the members take care of their own society and club men. Particularly when the loans are syndicated and the partners spread out. The Rockefellers felt compelled to distance the Foundation from the stain of suspicion on its reputation. Aware privately of having acknowledged to the Bank of Japan after the shocking reports from Nanking that "the whole civilized world is aghast at these bombings by the Japanese military of innocent lives", Lamont defended himself in 1937 in a letter to Abby Rockefeller, grand-daughter of JDR, Sr., against "that fantastic tale" that the Morgan bank, in fact, is financing the Japanese government and its military war lords behind the taciturn emperor with a life-long obsession for Disney's Mickey Mouse cartoon character. "I hardly have to tell you there is not the slightest foundation for it. We have not loaned a dollar to the Japanese Government for years." His son and member of the bank, Tom S. Lamont replied to a similar query from a Presbyterian missionary associated with the Chinese Medical Board of the Rockefeller Foundation, "... we are of course a purely private firm. We are lending no money to any phase of Japanese activity, nor have we done so for some years past." (S. J. Pak, 187-91, 164; original italics)

Four years before the Lamont-Rockefeller letter, Tom Lamont, in June 1934, prepares an internal memorandum for his partners "JP Morgan & Co. and Their Relation to the Public". He wrote, "We are a private firm of merchants ... . And as private merchants there is no theoretical reason why we should have public relations." But, of course, these are definitions of structure, not utility. Lamont immediately elaborates, "... practically we have such relations, and they are inevitable and proper because of the nature and importance of the firm's transactions". In other words, their private business is irrevocably and undeniably linked to the public destiny of governments and their interests, domestic and foreign. Then Lamont provides a partial list of high government positions occupied by Morgan partners including Secretary of State (Robert Bacon), Assistant Secretary of the Treasury (Russell Cornell Leffingwell (1878-60), S. Parker Gilbert, "H.P.D's work in the American Red Cross during the war", Jack Morgan on the 1922 Bankers' Committee (Reparations) etc..

Suzie Pak has a peculiar take on the Lamont Morgan stream-lining company performance with the intrusive somewhat annoying often venomous rapport between Morgan's private financial business and the people's perception of these architects of finance in and out of government and the bank's role in extending and articulating government foreign policy. Her study is Japan and China to the exclusion of Russia except for the Manchurian factor and increasing excursions by the Morgan-backed Japanese imperial forces along the south and east of the Russian border. If Lamont insists on JP Morgan & Co. as "a purely private firm" the lines of demarcation are never black or white but definitely opaque and blurred in the shadows of gray and Lamont makes that perfectly clear listing former senior cabinet and State Department posts in public government held by socially intimate, wealthy, and elite partners of the "purely private firm". The convergence of private financial might with national government authority comes to a peak in the Roosevelt administration much to their regret during the banking crisis of 1933 and the 1934 Nye Senate investigations into the armament business of the bank's financial underwriting of the First World War. Suzie Pak writes in *Gentlemen Bankers*, "The Morgans embrace of an identity of the private banker as a public servant was a significant shift from its nineteenth-century past. Ironically, it was also made possible by the American nationalism to which the firm was now resigned and even embraced. In other words, by the postwar period, the Morgans realized that concessions to national discourse did not fundamentally challenge the separate spheres model that was so important to the traditions and practices of gentlemen banking. To the contrary, accepting the nationalism of their time, particularly given America's changing position in the world, was actually essential if the Morgans wanted to protect the private nature of their work and associations." (S. Pak, 215)

In their brilliant book recently published on the power elite of Imperial Japan, *The Yamato Dynasty* (1999) tracing its "uneasy history from Emperor Meiji in 1852 to the present day", the Seagraves present a picture of Consortium Wall Street investment inside the mysterious and secret channels of the royal palace and its ruling families, and, in particular, the role of Thomas Lamont for Morgan. There are only two minor references to Secretary of State Stimson's and the State Department "strong ties to the Morgan Bank", and a bizarre overestimation of the role of US Secretary of State Hull covering for Roosevelt unfortunately inaccurate and misleading but this dimension within the nexus of Anglo-American corporate intrigue is not their prime focus. When editing for publication I came across the Seagraves research and its most illuminating on the imperial connections and the elitist method of Morgan banking in Tokyo before and after the war.

The Seagraves in *The Yamato Dynasty:* "There are many linkages between conservative US business and the Japan Crowd... The Japan Crowd influenced Washington at the highest levels. Secretary of Commerce W. Averell Harriman was a principal in the investment firm of Brown Brothers Harriman, and was part-owner of the magazine *Newsweek*. Secretary of Defense James Forrestal was a key figure at the investment bank of Dillon, Reed, headed by future Treasure Secretary C. Douglas Dillon (and) one of a group of investment banks, called the Club of Seventeen, which handled 70 percent of Wall Street underwriting. Former Secretary of War Henry L. Stimson had ties to Morgan and Dillon Reed through his law firm. In their thinking about Japan, all were influenced by Lamont, Hoover and Grew." (Sterling and Peggy Seagrave, *The Yamato Dynasty: The Secret History of Japan's Imperial Family*, NY: Random House-Broadway Books, 1999. See H. L. Stimson, 146, ft., 230, "Unclean Hands")

Grew gives Cravath the last word on Japanese militarism. "The Japanese", Cravath reiterated, "are certainly pursuing with great vigor the policy of achieving the greatest possible economic independence of the rest of the world. They seem to think that their greatest gain from acquiring control of Manchuria will be the increased supply of raw materials which now have to be imported from other countries." Cravath knows the Japanese are preparing for war, but when? "I should say the chief financial danger that confronts Japan is that she will have a war with Russia before she completes her policy of achieving the maximum of independence, Cravath observed, and he added, "In view of her present unpopularity throughout the world and the prevailing impression as to her financial unsoundness, she would, in case of war, soon have difficulty in financing the imports of the production of the sinews of war. The fortuitous combination of circumstances which enabled her to place loans abroad to finance her last war with Russia are not likely to occur again. It was rumored that Japan has already accumulated a large amount of the imports which would be needed in case of war." From Seattle Cravath boarded a twelve-passenger Boeing for a hair-raising cross-country home flight back to New York to resume his work at Cravath, Henderson, Leffingwell, & de Gersdorff (1920). (F. Lundberg, *America's 60 Families*, 129, Citadel Press, 1947; Paul D. Cravath, *Letters Home From the South Sea Islands, China and Japan,* Privately Printed, 1934; S. J. Pak, 215)

Days away from the FDR's presidential inauguration on March 2, 1933 at least 12 states had already closed their banks. "FDR sat down in front of a microphone for the first of his famous fireside chats and said, "I want to talk for a few minutes with the people of the United States about banking".

Mellon wants to close the banks to prevent full-fledged run on the nations' cash savings. He urges the governors in New York and Illinois to shut their doors. The nation's credit system is crumbling before everybody's eyes threatened collapse of the national economy. Everyone held their breath, uncertain about their future. How were they to even think about the dead in Communist Russia and the Ukraine. On March 3 the Fed's board reports in the last week a quarter billion dollars in gold has been moved out of its vaults. At any hour New York banks threatened to close their doors to depositors precipitating a national panic and run on the banks. The nation's economy is precipitously falling off the cliff of greed, cheap money and wanton speculation.

Hoover urges the President-Elect to make a joint statement declaring a national emergency. FDR declines, preferring to distance himself from Hoover and his politics while choosing to act in his own good time, not when America is going bust. The next day, Saturday March 4 nearly all the country's banks and factories close. City and state workers are sacked and payrolls left unpaid. Never before had the nation seen such economic despair and needed more faith in their leaders.

With Ukrainians starving and on their knees praying to the heavens and Stalin for relief, FDR sat in his wheel chair for the presidential inauguration under a cold gray sky. "First of all," he said, "let me assert my firm belief that the only thing we have to fear is fear itself – nameless, unreasoning, unjustified terror which paralyzes need efforts to convert retreat into advance. That same weekend Bill Bullitt writes a letter to FDR playing on the galloping psychology of the president fused with his own. "Washington and Jefferson and Henry spoke through you at that minute and in your address you struck so firmly the old note of (sic) 1776 that every man who cares about the essential spirit of this country felt deeply glad. May God be with you ..."

Whose side was God on? Bullitt's task, he reminds the President, is to keep "working out the problems of the Economic Conference, debts etc." FDR plans an Economic Conference in Washington that spring over war debts, the reparations, and stabilization of the dollar to the pound. Bullitt assures FDR "France would make the December 15th payment at once." Bullitt writes nothing about Russia while the monetary experts plan for a big meeting in London. On March 9 the new US Congress pushes through legislation to give FDR special presidential powers over national banking and the dollar. The next day FDR signs the banking act into law.

Meanwhile, in the scramble for gold and dollars, the government leaders battle for mens' minds. FDR is helped by his long-time associate Louis McHenry Howe. During the pre-convention frenzy over teetering unemployment levels, FDR's campaign team concocted the 1932 slogan "The Forgotten Man". On the other side of the world the Soviet propaganda machines around the clock produce slogans and posters trumpeting their industrial advance praising the young communist hero of the "New Society" at the time when the Russians and Ukrainians are pushed deeper into hardship and misery under the sickle and the hammer and the gulag, and as the weight of their burden increases daily from pressures by the Consortium capitalists in ARCC and the CFR and the bankers always clamoring about Russian money owed Chase. The year 1932 was the first terrible year of the great Holodomor and the official end of the first Five Year Plan now reduced to four by Stalin's "extraordinary measures".

That year American veterans of the First World War marched on Washington towards the White House demanding their bonus promised by the government. An army of 700 mounted policemen clashed with protesters. It looked like a Czarist revolution might erupt in the streets of Washington.

Gerard Colby in *DuPont Dynasty* (1974) describes this Hoover's military repression of the demonstrators: "Hoover's image had already suffered a crushing blow by the Depression. Industrial production was down 50 percent, according to the Federal Reserve Board; iron and steel, 85 percent; lumber, 77 percent; cement, 65 percent. Factory payrolls had been slashed 65 percent, employment 44 percent. Over 13 million workers were jobless and over 4,000 banks had failed. But the *coup de grace* to Hoover's career was delivered in June 1932, by his own hand. A 'bonus army' of thousands of tired, unemployed veterans and their families arrived that month in Washington demanding a federal bonus promised them by law, but not payable until the 1940's. They had traveled thousands of miles in battered jalopies, trucks, and wagons; many had even walked. And when Hoover wouldn't even receive them, they pitched tents, erected shacks, and slept in the capitol's parks to petition Congress. As soon as Congress adjourned after refusing to grant the marchers any relief, Hoover made a show of force.

"On July 28 a police attempt to evict some of the squatters resulted in the killing of two veterans. Hoover then called in the Army. Army Chief of Staff General Douglas MacArthur, who described the marchers as 'a mob ... animated by the essence of revolution', delayed the use of troops only long enough to have his swagger stick and medal-covered uniform arrive from a nearby fort. Aided by Colonel Dwight D. Eisenhower and Major George Patton, MacArthur ordered tanks, four troops of cavalry with drawn sabers, and a column of steel-helmeted infantry with fixed bayonets to enter downtown Washington and advance on the unarmed veterans. From Pennsylvania Avenue, MacArthur's proud army marched across the Anacostia Bridge, thousands of veterans and their wives and children fleeing before them, and advanced on their shanty village, lobbying tear gas bombs and setting its shacks and tents afire. An infant died from the tear gas, an 11 year-old boy was blinded for life, and many veterans were wounded. MacArthur, responding to a reporter's claim of having seen a cavalryman use his saber to slash off a veteran's ear, explained, somewhat amused, that that was quite impossible. "You don't slash with a saber,'" he told the press, "you lunge", and striking the correct pose for photographers, he demonstrated the proper thrust ... The next day the press was informed that 'the President was pleased'." (G. Colby, *DuPont Dynasty*, 1974, 1984 ed., 324)

In 1924 Congress had passed a bill providing for "adjusted compensation" or a bonus to WWI veterans. Hoover's Treasury Secretary Mellon sought to block payments "for twenty years". Congressman Wright Patman inflamed the public outrage. "Filthy rich" Patman declares, "didn't lack fo' anything on earth, and there he was, attemptin' to keep needy veterans who fought and bled fo' their country from gettin' what was already theirs." During the protest, Washington Police Chief Pelham G. Glassford, a retired brigadier general is hit in the head. An appeal for calm is met with a quick reply, "Hell, a lot of us were killed in France."

Mellon's Gulf oil corporation in 1929 is worth some $761 million in assets alone, according to Patman. In 1930 Patman introduced a bill to oblige Mellon to pay off the veteran bonus certificates but an American Legion convention in Boston failed to endorse his measure. "The invisible hand of Mellonism was present" Patman roared to reporters "misleading, and false statements were circulated that the Legion should not take action on my proposals ..." They called it "a strictly partisan matter" accusing Patman of a hate-campaign against Mellon particularly targeting his suspicious reorganization of his aluminium company. In January 1932 Patman had moved to impeach Mellon for "high crimes and misdemeanors". Hersh wrote, "One swollen rumor, which alleged a two-hundred-million dollar Koppers contract to oversee the erection of villages of coking ovens in the Soviet Union by convict laborers, broke down on investigation to a $383,000 sale of engineering plans and the transitory reassignment of seventeen unemployed technicians." (Burton Hersh, *The Mellon Family*, William Morrow, 1978, 246)

Congressman Patman describes Mellon's bank paying 200 percent dividends during the dark days of the Depression. In 1928 private police equipped with machine guns patrolled Mellon-owned mines. Patman declared the Mellon fortune represented "twice as much money as the average amount of money that has been in circulation during the past three years. It is equal to two-thirds of all the gold in the entire world. It is equal to one-half the value of all the property in the United States in the year 1860."

As head of the Debt Funding Commission, and anti-cancellation protagonist, Mellon issues a statement to the Ways and Means Committee in Congress, on January 4, 1926. "Europe is our largest customer," Mellon declared. "Unless the finances of Europe can be restored, her currency placed on a sound basis, and her people able to earn and to spend, this country will not be able to dispose of its surplus products of food, materials and goods." And then he adds: "The entire foreign debt is not worth as much to the American people in dollars and cents as a prosperous Europe as a customer."

To be sure, reader, the secret hand of the Consortium wasn't above reproach. This is an art of strategic balance by one of its top men in America. Nor is it not without its pride and injury as happens in all councils and courts of intrigue and rivalry. In a direct attack on Stimson, the *New Republic* magazine said it was regrettable that "an American Secretary of State had used his high office to persuade the National City Bank of New York to grant an unsound bank credit to the government of Columbia as a means of obtaining one of the world's largest oil concessions for a company controlled by the interests of Mr. Mellon, our Secretary of the Treasury."

The assault came from the Democratic left-wing on the political spectrum. The Senate Finance Committee investigation exposed some delicate connections that linked Allen Dulles, a former Undersecretary of State during the Versailles Treaty negotiations in Paris to Morgan which he represented in the Barco scandal over its Columbian oil concession. It turns out that Herbert Stabler, the former head the Department's Latin American division works for Mellon's Gulf Oil and that Mellon's former top aide, Garrard Winston (Yale 1904) is family with Frederick S. Winston (Yale 1877) and his brother a National City lawyer and Chicago politician, Dudley Winston (1886 Bones) who died in 1898 under mysterious circumstances on a train to NY's Grand Central Station. Their father was Gen. F. H. Winston, is the former US minister to Persia in 1885. Garrard B. Winston (1882-55), in fact serves Mellon as an undersecretary at Treasury (1923-27) before leaving to become a partner in Shearman & Sterling, a leading Wall Street law firm whose partners were members of the super-elite Pilgrims Society of London. Winston wore other hats too, including his appointment as Secretary of the banking front of the American Debt Funding Commission, membership at the prestigious Manhattan Links Club and treasurer for the Roosevelt Hospital.

Representative Patman has another lance to throw at the opaque Consortium squeeze on America's fragile political economy. "The man who freely stole millions from government during wartime was now running the US government Treasury," Patman tells the American people. With increasing joblessness and voters anger rising daily Congress is listening. Its Andrew Mellon, Patman declares who is "more responsible for the country's poor economic condition than any other person." Andrew Mellon ought to be impeached, Patman tells

Congress. His research team found enough scandals to hang any small town crook. But Mellon was no cheap gangster. The Consortium mafia links to thugs and gangsters leave them nonetheless virtually untouchable. Their methods are the sort that would make the post-Soviet Union thugs look like amateurs after the collapse of Gorbachev's regime in 1991 and the total breakup of the USSR when they stripped state assets. Mellon tells his trusted valet to start packing and prepare the servants …

Between March 1930 and March 1931 unemployment in the United States doubled to eight million disenfranchised workers between March 1930 and March 1931. In his book *The Mellon Family* (1978) historian Burton Hersh describes the scene left by Mellon and other Consortium industrialists in Pennsylvania: "Destitution everywhere was nauseating. Pittsburgh even – one place where a man with a back on him and sense to tip his cap could always find something. Families survived in culverts, where cars went by children squirmed out from underneath upturned dinghies or the Citizens secreted themselves in the weeds around dumps until the refuse was unloaded and the trucks rolled out and they might freely claw open the steaming piles with boughs and sticks. Hoovervilles. Unemployment in Pennsylvania approached a third, worst around the soft-coal areas. … relief was negligible, the women wandered barefoot, starving children were normally too lethargic to whimper. 'This is a hell if there is a hell anywhere,' (Gifford) Pinchot quoted one miner. 'No work, starving, afraid of being shot, it is a shame for a man to tell such bad truth'."

Against such a backdrops of domestic poverty and hopelessness in the streets of America its not hard to imagine how difficult it may have been for Americans to turn their heads and care enough to relieve the problems of suffering Ukrainians in the Soviet Union when the Consortium crushed their own workers in factories and coal mines in Pittsburgh and across the country. (B. Hersh, *The Mellon Family*, 1978, 292, 306)

The Mellons fortune (Andrew and Richard) is one of the four largest fortunes in existence, alongside the Rothschilds and Rockefellers. Eustace Mullins figured the Windsors (British Royals) as a close fourth. With the national economy unraveling and rising unemployment the shifting public mood turned on Mellon's fortune. The Congressman held up the Treasury Secretary as "more responsible for the country's poor economic condition than any other person." In 1957, when *Fortune* prepared its first list of the wealthiest Americans, the four Mellon cousins (Richard, Sarah, Paul and Ailsa) ranked amongst the richest eight people in the United States, with fortunes conservatively estimated at 400 to 700 million dollars each, with significant tax arrangements to provide generous philanthropies for the public good.

Congressman Patman exposes Mellon's pirating of the War Department that had paid Mellon's Koppers Company $18,582,428.44 in First World War profits when Koppers could not even prove it had produced a single dollar of goods. Yet somehow President Wilson's government had granted contracts for Koppers to purchase for $600,000 buildings and machinery that had cost the American taxpayer $2,987,200; and for materials Koppers paid $300,000 that were valued at $5,558,000. This latter deal was made despite the fact that a different company had bid $700,000 "the technical project" founding the Magnitogorsk coke and chemical plant "with elements of the McKee project".

John Scott (1912–76) is the pseudonym of the son of the well-known and radical political economist and prolific writer Scott Nearing (1883-83) indicted in 1918 under the Espionage Act in New York during the First World War. While in Russia Scott marries Mariya Ivanovna Kikareva. He returns to the US and writes *Behind the Urals: An American Worker in Russia's City of Steel* (1941). During the war he joined the OSS. (W. Hoffman, *Mellon,* 54; John Scott, 154; B. Hersh, *The Mellon Family,* 247; re. Wright Patman hearings on A.W. Mellon; C. Savoie, *World Money Order III*)

Scott Nearing was hounded by government and justice officials during the war years and finally prosecuted in the US for his writing *The Great Madness: A Victory for the American Plutocracy;* he is charged with "obstruction to the recruiting and enlistment service of the United States." Nearing spends two months in the Soviet Union, in 1925, observing social conditions which served the basis of his book *Education in Soviet Russia* published the following year. After two years of contentious membership Nearing is formally expelled from the Communist Party in the US. (Scott Nearing wrote the author shortly before his death vividly recalling his friendship with John Reed.)

In 1930, "John Scott" lands a job at that Magnitogorsk plant in most difficult conditions for two years squeezing benzol out of coke gas using mostly imported equipment in the benzol department equipped with four stills producing sixty tons a day. McKee had one of the largest contracts for the construction of seven blast furnaces, steel mills and an entire town at Magnitogorsk. It kept 80 engineers there on location for one year and then cut back to "one unit" when, in March 1932, the Soviets fail to pay. The company threatens to pull out "all its personnel from Magnitogorsk within one month".

It is not implausible that in 1929 when the Fed central bank tightened credit sparking the investor frenzy and speculation that crashed the Wall Street stock market setting off the Great Depression the Rockefeller-Morgan-Rothschild banking clique removed Hoover who now proved less than cooperative to their plans. By 1933, the Consortium barons replaced Hoover with the more pliable Roosevelt. Hoover felt he had been forced out by a fascist takeover of the American government and economy. Under his "New Deal" advocacy of corporate socialism, FDR used radical legislation to use federal powers to centralize domestic economy under tighter political control of the government. After the market meltdown and depression, the Consortium capitalists make even greater fortunes. Baruch does very well for himself and friends as does Secretary Mellon with hands-on control of Federal Reserve Bank, the Consortium's very own cash machine. Need cash? Just ask.

Not all Americans had forgotten how a decade earlier during the postwar heyday Mellon emerged unscathed in the Teapot Dome scandal that brought down the Harding presidency and may have led to his elimination. With civil war raging in Soviet Russia, Whites fighting Trotsky's Red Army, and Deniken's forces with

British military advisers driven into the Black Sea, and Warsaw captured by the Bolsheviks, the League of Nations became a major issue during the Presidential election of 1920. Republican candidate Warren G. Harding was on record as opposing the League and further attempts to ratify the charter. Harding said, "It will avail nothing to discuss in detail the League covenant, which was conceived for world super-government In the existing League of Nations, world governing with its super-powers, this Republic will have no part." Harding was opposed in the Republican primaries by General Leonard Wood, the Republican "war hawk" backed by a powerful group of rich men who wish(ed) a military man in the White House." Voters once again voiced their disapproval of the League. Harding outpolled his opposition by a greater margin than Wilson who had "kept us out of the war" during the election of 1916 with only fifty-two percent of the vote, while Harding, a Taft Republican, as President opposed the bankers and their Federal Reserve. Harding won the Presidency with sixty-four percent. Harding, too, had his own secrets to kee In August 1920, Harding was a Freemason elevated to the Sublime Degree of a Master Mason in his homeland of Marion, Ohio. Ohio is Taft-Rockefeller country.

After his election victory President Harding names Harry M. Daugherty who had been President Taft's campaign manager now as his Attorney General. Other cabinet appointments were not as astute. Harding is surrounded by oil men. Republican bishop and a Standard Oil lawyer, Charles Evans Hughes occupies the State Department top seat; Mellon, owner of Gulf Oil takes Treasury, Sinclair Oil lawyer, a subsidiary of Standard Oil of Indiana fills the Postmaster General slot; the Secretary of the Interior is Albert Fall who will go down for the Sinclair bribe taken for a lease of the Navy's oil reserves in Wyoming. Harding had long been an outspoken opponent of the League of Nations, and there was still a chance that its League supporters could get the US backing despite the Senate's earlier refusal to ratify the treaty. Daugherty prosecuted the oil trusts under the Sherman anti-trust laws but during the fight Harding suddenly died on August 2, 1923.

This was the era of the huge steel combinations between Carnegie, Frick, Mellon and Morgan. In Morgan's expensive buyout of Carnegie, Charles Schwab, another Pilgrim and Carnegie partner, pockets some $40 million, Carnegie gets $300 million. Mullins writes, "It was boom one year, bust the next, around the turn of the century, but neither state of the economy affected Mellon. In boom times he counted stock dividends, interest payments, trust charges, expanded production in companies he had purchased earlier. When the economy went bust it was foreclose; buy up property at a fraction of its value; force weaker companies to sell or merge. The aluminum company, the golden black profits of oil, the real estate and industrial companies acquired by foreclosure, the soaring assets of the banks and insurance companies, all combined to make Andrew Mellon one of the richest men in the world." (E. Mullins, *World Money Order*; W. Hoffman, *Mellon*, 43-4)

Andrew Mellon serves twelve years at Treasury, first with Harding, then with Coolidge, Hoover and Roosevelt. "No man appointed to public office," writes biographer William Hoffman, ever had to resign from as many corporate boards as Andrew Mellon did. There were fifty-one in all, and their activities spanned the spectrum of industry and finance. Included were aluminum companies, oil companies, steel companies, companies involved in coke, coal, carbon, shipbuilding, electricity, automobiles, land development, railroads, construction, insurance and banking. The Harding and Coolidge administrations particularly might better have been called the Mellon administration. "For eight years," wrote Drew Pearson, the well-known Washington syndicated columnist, "he dominated the national capital. For eight years his word was law with every banker throughout the land.

"For eight years Presidents served under him. So powerful was his influence, so great his prestige that he told them what to do and his judgment was final. Andrew Mellon was active in other areas behind the scenes. In 1922 aluminum import duties were increased 250 percent by the Republican sponsored Fordney-McCumber Tariff. Andrew Mellon had a 100 percent monopoly on American aluminum. Here we turn again to William Hoffman for a closer look at Mellon: "Insiders knew that the battle between Andrew Mellon and Herbert Hoover was simply a struggle between Morgan money and Mellon money. With the help of *The New York Times*, which thought it ludicrous that such a wealthy man should *openly* run the country, (Mellon was actually running it from behind the scenes), Herbert Hoover, the Morgan man, captured the Republican presidential nomination. Such was Andrew Mellon's power, however, that after the election he remained on in Treasury. If blame could be placed on one man for the Great Depression, that man would be Andrew Mellon. Andrew Mellon's optimism convinced investors that stock prices could go up forever." (W. Hoffman, *Mellon*, 48-9)

Reader, we defer to Charles Savoie in *World Money Order III*: "The impeachment hearings proceeded without a hitch. Patman dredges up at least a dozen scandals. It turns out that Andrew Mellon's Standard Steel Car Company built a plush club during World War I which was used to entertain government bureaucrats responsible for keeping war costs down. At the club all expenses–food, lodging, entertainment – were paid by Standard Steel Car. The bureaucrats were, of course, receiving expenses from the government since they were supposed to be on state business. During the hearings Patman demonstrates that Andrew Mellon was hardly suffering because of the Depression – 'The Union Trust Company is a Mellon owned corporation in Pittsburgh. It commenced business during the panic of 1893, prospered during the panic of 1907 and the hard times of 1914, and has been paying 200 percent dividends and more during the depression years of 1930, 1931 and 1932'."

Patman put the Mellon money in perspective – "The fortune I have mentioned is twice as much money as the average amount of money that has been in circulation during the past three years. *It is equal to two-thirds of all the gold in the entire world. It is equal to one-half the value of all the property in the United States in the year 1860.*" Astounding! Volumes could be written on the Mellon deals. (C. Savoie, *The Silver Investor: World Money Order III*, 2005; W. Hoffman, *Mellon*, 54-5, E. Mullins, *Secrets of the Federal Reserve*)

In his work *World Money Order III*, Charles Savoie writes, "In *The Mirrors of Wall Street* (1933) by Anonymous, we read – 'There can be no question that Mr. Mellon is one of the canniest cash collectors that this or any other country has ever developed. Mr. Mellon alone can explain why he did not raise his voice to avert the greatest financial cataclysm that had ever befallen the nation. He was a member of the Federal Reserve Board.' Mellon had no intention in alerting anyone outside his circle of you-know-what-by-now-(or you haven't been paying attention) because the crash and depression were calculated to strip others of wealth. Mellon, as Treasury Secretary, conferred with Montagu Collet "Archie" Norman, governor of the Bank of England, in Washington on February 6, 1929. Norman, another member of The Pilgrims, admitted– 'I hold the hegemony of the world.' Hegemony = leadership, in case anyone needs a vocabulary exercise. This was the same Montagu Norman who refused to visit any nation not having a central bank! He disapproved of countries not having covert British control!" (C. Savoie, Money Order III, on the web, 27-9)

Savoie refers to *Tragedy and Hope* (1966) by Carroll Quigley of the Newcomer Society, as "a Pilgrims Society front organization". The *Wall Street Journal*, November 11, 1927, described Norman as the "currency dictator of Europe". Since he was actually head of the Bank of England, yet the *Journal* said he had power over European finances, take that as an indication of European central banks colluding with the grandmaster of all central banking, the Bank of England, for such is the case. Let it not be thought that Norman was such a substantial power in himself, but rather he had power delegated to him by such as the Windsors, the British Royal family, and the Rothschilds. Just after the closed conference of Mellon – who was a substantial power in himself, in fact, surely one of the two most powerful men in the United States at that time, the other being John D. Rockefeller Jr. of The Pilgrims Society – with Lord Norman, the Federal Reserve reversed its cheap money policies and began tightening. A boom had been engineered, now it was time to stage a bust, so that the big rich could recapture their payrolls from the middle class, and break down many non-allied rich. By late October, the Crash was under way." Plausible and probably mostly all true. Check it out. It fits.

Pilgrims Society member Floyd Odlum went short the market, then bought tons of shares at 90% off their highs! Many other Consortium insiders did the same. Mellon did too. William Hoffman in *Paul Mellon– Portrait of an Oil Baron* (1974) described the world around Mellon at the time. Hoffman writes, "The Depression came, the greatest depression this country has ever experienced. It bothered Andrew Mellon not at all." Hoffman added, "It merely presented him with another business opportunity, a chance to swallow up weaker corporations and, when it was over, to emerge stronger than ever. As Drew Pearson pointed out, Andrew Mellon spent his first eight years in office predicting federal deficits. This was so the government could claim it was broke and thereby deny World War I veterans their bonuses and dissuade the hard-pressed from seeking assistance. Andrew Mellon's last four years in office, however, brought predictions of surpluses, so that the Depression plagued American public would not demand an increase in income and inheritance taxes. When the Depression refused to fade away, Andrew Mellon was a man no longer in touch with reality. He urged people to work hard and spend money that, he said, was the solution to the Crash. Yet how could people spend money when Andrew Mellon's banks refused to loan them any? How could they work hard when his companies laid them off and said there was no work? In May 1931, the Secretary of the Treasury said there should be no pay cuts, but in October of the same year his Aluminum Company of America slashed wages ten percent. In June 1932, the Aluminum Company slashed wages ten per cent more."

Hoffman went on: "At the Alcoa mills in a Pittsburgh suburb, more than half the normal work force of four thousand was laid off. A welfare worker revealed that those still working had been forced by the company to donate a day's pay to those who were unemployed, despite the fact that a high weekly wage for those working full time was only twelve dollars. The aluminum company itself paid nothing to those it laid off. Panic spread. By that time Mellon was gone, having shipped April 1932 to London, a full year after the moratorium banking crisis at Lausanne, and sent safely abroad far from Congressman Patman's calls for impeachment in the American press and into the arms of the Pilgrims Society at the Court of St. James in London. (W. Hoffman, *Mellon*, 49-50)

"On March 30, 1930," Hersh writes, "Pullman took possession of the manufacturing assets of Standard Steel Car; the Mellons acquire Pullman stock, 400,000 shares altogether, and a little over eight million dollars in cash. Each brother got 40 percent...". The settlement is worth $38,700,000. In September 1929, the Mellons look towards a merger with the Pullman Inc. railroad car business. Morgan controls Pullman. Jack Morgan and George Whitney worked out a deal with Pullman, and board a ship in England for America when the market crashed. The deal still goes through. (W. Hoffman, *Mellon*, 54-5; "The fortune I have mentioned is twice ...."; "On March 30, 1930 Pullman took possession ..."., B. Hersh, *The Mellon Family*, 262)

So Mellon escapes relatively unscathed by the market crash. Again Hersh: "Like Hoover, Mellon despised 'certain varieties of New York Banking' which he deemed were too often devoted to tearing men down and picking their bones. When the boom broke, he said, 'they deserved it'." By midsummer 1932 US Steel plunges from 262 to 22. But in just over a decade at World War II, US Steel is producing more steel than Stalin. Hersh writes, "...many of the business leaders were now concerned privately with stocking getaway yachts or, like the ever-resourceful Albert Wiggin, chairman of the board of the Chase Manhattan Bank, coordinating bear raids against the holdings of their own banks stockholders.

Hersh quotes from Ferdinand Lundberg book of the era, *America's Sixty Families* (1937) "that Hoover's 'two principal advisers' were Dwight Morrow and Thomas Lamont, both key Morgan partners at precisely the time 'the Morgan banks, alone of the nation's banking institutions were almost one hundred percent liquid, i.e. had almost all their resources in cash or government securities'. Lundberg concludes from this that the Morgan managers remained, at their most innocent, cheerful bystanders around the securities slaughterhouse. They waited with money; they anticipated choice cuts. That certainly was likely enough after a collapse which saw General Motors end up at eight dollars a share the summer of 1932, down from convincingly from 73 three action-packed years earlier. General Motors did well; US Steel was off from 262 to 22'."

Since these barons of capital were willing to stand on top of the hill watching the slaughter of their shareholders as corporate stock plunged, would they blink an eye at millions of Ukrainians starving to death unable to pay for a loaf of bread or even give bread to a starving Mother or child? Don't even think about asking the shareholders in these hard times. (B. Hersh, *The Mellon Family*, 290-93 re. "Like Hoover, Mellon despised 'certain varieties of New York Banking' (and) many of the business leaders")

In September 1931, 305 banks closed their doors; in October 522 banks closed. Thirteen million Americans were unemployed. National wages fell 60 percent less than in 1929. US industrial production dropped to less than half its peak levels. Winter grips the whole of the Ukraine and southern Russia in hunger and famine. With Pennsylvanians starving and freezing in the streets in the winter of 1931, Governor Gifford Pinchot visited Andrew Mellon at his Washington office. Before being allowed to see the Treasury Secretary, the governor admired the $1.7 million worth of gems Mellon pinched from the Soviet Union worth countless multiples today.

During this meltdown Mellon buys some 30 paintings from the Soviet Union worth valued then around $8 million, probably billions today. In 1931 Mellon's collection of Russian Hermitage old masters with an estimated worth of $3.2 million was destined for Washington's National Gallery not far from the White House. Mellon left another $20 million to build it but died in 1937 four years before it opened. According to biographer Seymore Hersh, Andrew Mellon also jumped in the carnival grab of art treasures from the cash-strapped Soviet Union at ridiculous depressed market prices. The press followed the art exploits of the Treasury Secretary buying Soviet art for millions while American workers vanquished in the streets. Hersh observes, "... insurgent Russia needed tractors, and credits fsor machine parts were out of the question in the unfriendly West without frozen foreign exchange. The Soviets were ragged. Colouste Gulbenkian, who appeared in Moscow to direct the worldwide Soviet dumping of oil, brought to the attention of the leadership its dowry in canvases."

A Berlin dealer eyed the Hermitage collection for Mellon's raid on Leningrad's invaluable collection of Czarist treasures. Selling priceless Russian property was tempting but life-threatening if caught. "Russia still needed money. An unnamed Soviet Treasury official secretly authorized the sale of a single canvas, as an experiment, to see whether confidentiality was possible," Hersh observes, and he adds, "In March 1929 agents for Mellon picked up *Lord Philip Wharton* by Van Kyck, and stashed it away in a New York vault; a Hals, and two Rembrandts arrived in New York in April. Then shipments stopped. The seller was liquidated. After the crash, more art filled Mellon's vaults including *The Annunciation of Jan van Eyck*, for half a million dollars. Mellon's art agents ventured to Leningrad and searched the Hermitage themselves for paintings now on display in Washington's

National Gallery of Art. Mellon payed some 6.5 million for 21 masterpieces among them Raphael's *Alba Madonna, Saint George and the Dragon*, Botticelli's *Adoratio of the Magi*, Titian's *Venus with a Mirror*." Mellon also bags a beautiful Velasquez. (B. Hersh, *The Mellon Family*, 282)

When the two patricians sat down to talk, Governor Pinchot made a proposition: let wealthy Pennsylvanians loan $35 million to the state coffers for emergency relief programs at the 4 percent interest rate authorized by a constitutional amendment. Mellon was asked to donate $1 million; Mellon refused and the rich capitalists followed their leader but not all. (W. Hoffman, *Mellon*, 50-1)

"I cannot believe that a national government will stand by while its citizens freeze and starve, without lifting a hand to help," Gifford Pinchot declared in January 1932. And he should know. Gifford Pinchot (Bonesman, Yale 1889) served as Teddy Roosevelt's conservation Secretary and Pennsylvania's Governor in the early days. A disgruntled Republican prohibitionist, Pinchot added, "I do not see how it can refuse to grant that relief which it is in honor, in duty, and in its own interest bound to supply." President Herbert Hoover still wasn't listening, at least not until it was too late for him to do much about it. The administration's 'fundamental policy is not to be changed', he said dryly.

Congress had other ideas, and by February 1932, introduces the first of many federal relief bills. In spite of Hoover's intransigence, one bill was agreed upon and passed above the heads of Hoover's beleaguered surrogates. The president vetoes the bill on the grounds that its proposed $2.2 billion public works program was a pork-barrel band-aid that would only bankrupt the nation. Congress bustles and came up with another version, the Emergency Relief and Construction Act. Public works are cut to $322.2 million. Another $1.5 billion in RFC loans is passed with authorization up to $300 million in RFC relief loans to states of particularly hard-pressed. Hoover was obliged to bite the bullet. He signed the act into law on July 21. (T. H. Watkins, *The Hungry Years, A Narrative History of the Great Depression in America,* NY: Henry Holt, 1999, 102)

Author T. H. Watkins in *The Hungry Years*, (1999) comes upon some relevant findings on unemployment in America during the summer 1932: "Unemployment rates continued to climb, relief caseloads swelled by 200, 300, or even 400 percent, individual relief allotments grew smaller and smaller, while larger and larger portions of city budgets went to finance them (in 1932, $256 million – 67% of all non-federal public money- would go for relief), until there was little or nothing left or either resources or energy. Voluntary relief efforts, writes former *Chicago Tribune* investigative reporter George Seldes writes in 1932, 'were bucket brigades fighting a skyscraper fire...The reason is that they all tried to make individual kindness cope with a national calamity which had gone far beyond the point at which kindness, even of the noblest sort and highest degree, could function'." Soup kitchens, Hoovervilles, and flop houses. A city mayor writes "Our one great achievement in response to this national catastrophe has been to open soup kitchens and flophouses." The head of the Children's Bureau of Philadelphia told a Congressional Committee "If the modern state is to rest upon a firm foundation, its citizens must not be allowed to starve. Some of them do." A new appeal for civil leadership and self-reliance struck at the heart of community leaders. A Morgan partner and president of Philadelphia's enfeebled "Committee of One Hundred", and a true believer in non-governmental action Horatio Gates Lloyd switched, saying, "The present need is on a scale that calls not for more charity but for governmental action to save the health and indeed the lives of a large portion of the citizenry." (T.H. Watkins, *The Hungry Years*, 100-1)

American investigative reporter and foreign correspondent George Seldes lived over a century, and died in 1995. His was a fascinating life and he wrote constantly since his education at Harvard under the same teachers as Reed, Lippmann and Eliot. His interview with Lenin in 1922 is recounted in *Witness of a Century* (1997) as is his interview with the Bolshevik Peters about the thousands of victims under Bolshevik terror. More pertinent to our story is his amazement to find Lenin reading *Course of Empire* written by the former Republican US Senator Richard F. Pettigrew (South Dakota) nearly impossible to find in the US, although published by the same company Boni & Liveright as John Reed. The book exposes the concentration of power and wealth in the American plutocracy. Pettigrew made national headlines when in 1917, in a newspaper interview he denounced the European war as a capitalist scheme intended chiefly to enrich further the wealthy, and he urged young men to dodge the draft. It was the same political line that got Socialist presidential contender Eugene V. Debs a ten-year sentence in federal prison under Wilson's notorious wartime measure, the Espionage Act. Pettigrew fought back with a top legal defense team headed up by his close personal friend, the prominent attorney Clarence Darrow. All charges were dropped. Along with three other reporters is expelled by Chicherin and the Foreign Office, in 1923 for violating Soviet censor measures and smuggling out their dispatches disguised as personal letters in the diplomatic pouch.

When he returns to the US, Seldes briefs the President on Soviet affairs, and talked with Secretary of State Hughes on the phone, told that the US would not normalize diplomatic relations but continues to trade and do business with Lenin's regime. When pressed on recognition and the double-standard, Hughes tells Seldes the Soviet regime was too immoral a partner for the American electorate. George Seldes spends the next ten years as an international reporter for the McCormick's *Chicago Tribune* until his articles on suspicious exploitation of mineral rights in Mexico in 1927 offend the Consortium's corporate finance there. Soon after he returns to Europe Seldes has a falling out with publisher McCormick and devotes himself to freelance work publishing material he could not get into the national press: *You Can't Print That!* (1929) and *Can These Things Be!* (1931). His 1933 book *World Panorama* is a narrative history of the interbellum period. In 1934, Seldes publishes a history of the Roman Catholic Church, *The Vatican,* and finishes his exposé of the global arms industry, *Iron, Blood and Profits* (1934) and on Benito Mussolini, *Sawdust Caesar* (1935). Seldes had covered Mussolini and the rise of Italian fascism for the *Chicago Tribune* but was expelled after he implicated the dictator in the murder of leading opposition politician Giacomo Matteotti. *Harper's Magazine* an carries his account of Italian censorship and intimidation of American reporters. More books follow that include two books on the news business and firmly position Seldes as a harsh critic of the America's national press racket: *Freedom of the Press* (1935) and *Lords of the Press* (1938), the latter titled from a speech by Roosevelt's Secretary of the Interior Ickes: "Our ancestors did not fight for the right of a few Lords of the Press to have almost exclusive control of and censorship over the dissemination of news and ideas."

Seldes did his best to convince Americans "that advertisers were a far greater threat to journalistic freedom than government censorship. "The press and news", he wrote, "are coming more and more under the domination of a handful of corporate publishers who may print such news as they wish to print and omit such news as they do not wish to print"

For his defense of professional integrity *Time* labels Seldes a "muckraker". For three years he reports on the Spanish Civil War critical of colleagues in bed with Franco and their Consortium-minded owners. During the Second World War he publishes *Facts and Fascism* (1943) and *One Thousand Americans* (1947) about Consortium power and informs Americans of the near dictatorial takeover of Washington in the early 1930s. *Time* is quick to denounce it "a collection of truths, half-truths and untruths about the US press and industry." Seldes introduces a wide audience to the conspiracy theory known as "the Business Plot", a supposed plan of America's corporate elite to overthrow the US government in the early 1930s.

In comparison to the Russian scene Depression in America may have been a rude and horrendous experience that put the spotlight on the weaknesses of the capitalist nations to control their economy and provide for their people. With fascism showing its evil white fangs writers in America often show little restraint in metaphor to describe it. "Poverty and hunger gripped the nation by its throat," wrote author William Hoffman. Riots were commonplace. A group of World War I veterans marched on Washington and demanded the cashing of soldiers bonus certificates. The Government drove them out of Washington with armed troops under the command of Douglas MacArthur. There was talk of revolution as desperate people called for desperate measures. Texas Representative Wright Patman was seething mad over Andrew Mellon's policies and by his lack of concern for widespread suffering. After the next war MacArthur

On January 6, 1932 Patman brings impeachment proceedings against the Treasury Secretary. Whenever Andrew Mellon's name is mentioned in print, it is as a "philanthropist" or "businessman" or "public servant." Very seldom is the word "impeachment" is brought up, though that drastic course of action is precisely what was taken." "Representative Patman went on to make the remarkable statement that "Mr. Mellon has violated more laws, caused more human suffering and illegally acquired more property to satisfy his personal greed than any other person on earth without fear of punishment and with the sanction and approval of three chief executives of a civilized nation." Soon, four "chief executives". (W. Hoffman, *Mellon*, 51-2)

The three executives must have been the President; Speaker of the House and Chief Justice of the Supreme Court, or the Vice President. So powerful are the Mellon interests that Gulf Oil is the only major oil company in the United States to hold its own against the group formerly known as Standard

Oil (Rockefellers, Harknesses, Whitneys and Pratts the biggest shareholders). Much later the Mellons would sell Gulf Oil to Chevron, after being enriched by gushers from Kuwait to Venezuela, where it extracted some 200,000 barrels of oil daily at its peak of operations. "Gulf Oil's assets were greater than the gross national product of most countries." Hoffman added, "Representative Patman also revealed that Andrew Mellon, while in office, had voting stock in more than three hundred corporations engaged in "mining properties, bauxite, magnesium, carbon electrodes, aluminum, sales, railroads, Pullman cars, gas, electric light, steel railways, copper, glass, brass, steel, tar, banking, locomotives, water power, steamships, shipbuilding, oil, coke, coal, and many other different industries." There were other questionable deals. All US banks (Andrew Mellon was chairman of the Federal Reserve Board) refused credit to the Columbian Government until it signed the Barco oil concession giving 1.5 million acres of oil land worth as much as $2 billion to Gulf Oil and a company owned largely by the Morgans. When finally the giveaway was signed, credit was miraculously available." (W. Hoffman, *Mellon*, 53, 97, 134)

Not all fortunes were lost in the Great Depression. Some of the sixty big United States fortunes had survived. The three greatest – Rockefeller, Morgan, and Mellon – came through nearly intact. ... The reporter Horan writes that both Percy Rockefeller, William's nephew and "the John D.s" all lost long-term paper holdings, "but they were largely offset by his hedge and other market operations". By 1932 Percy Rockefeller's holdings are doing well making him one of the richest men in the world with a fortune estimated near a billion dollars, reportedly greater than the old dime-pincher JDR himself. Horan wrote, "the John Ds in 1920 had had an annual income of between fifty and sixty million dollars; by 1932 they were down to between thirty and thirty five million." Rockefeller lost big in real estate, but Standard Oil prospered buying Jersey common during the crash at $50 and selling with a profit, and doing it again in the summer 1932 buying Jersey at $21, with the stock at $30 in October. Mellon's Aluminium Company (Alcoa) suffered too; its profitability drops from $10,868,000 showing a deficit in 1932 of $6,763,000.

"There was still capital, enough to cover the preferred. But how much longer?" observes Hersh in *The Mellon Family*. The Consortium capitalists were worried. By 1934 at the same time FDR prepares anti-trust proceedings Germany outstrips Mellon's corporation in ingot tonnage. Hersh writes, "The depression settled in. On Pittsburgh street corners too, entrepreneurs in spattered cravats were interrupting holiday shoppers with offers of disease-looking apples. Whoever couldn't look, bought. Movies seemed cheap; in Kansas in newsreels the cattlemen were lining up their livestock along gullies shallow enough for bulldozing. The soup in soup kitchens looked lifeless as water. In industrial Kensington, unemployed from the aluminium mills marched noisily upon borough hall to insist on gestures of relief." Around Prince's Gate, between strolls with the royalty Andrew Mellon sends his son Paul another gift of 75,000 shares of Aluminium company stock saying its "not paying any dividends at present...but this course is better for the stockholder."

The Mellons keep their banks open, the Mellon National and the Union Trust defy the trend when others close and readily displays cash if only to raise confidence for anyone wishing to withdraw their holdings. Pullman falls from 99 to 10. Alcoa collapsed from 539 to 22. Pittsburgh Plate Glass and US Steel bottom out. Insiders of Mellon empire fear the worst, saying, "If this thing goes any further we are going to be broke." Mellon's Gulf Oil had reported a deficit for 1931 near $24 million and pipelines ran at under-capacity; by 1935 Gulf is back up again operating at a profit paying off its Union Gulf loan. That year the corporation nets $10,500,000. (B. Hersh, *The Mellon Family*)

The Mellons are unique and all the same stand out as a paradigm example of Consortium success at the pinnacle of corporate power in FDR's America. In 1933, and again in 1935, the President signed legislation that prohibited commercial banking houses from underwriting securities. That would all soon change. In 1933 after he leaves the Treasury Andrew Mellon created Mellon Securities Company. By the end of the decade it had made a ton of money for the family and the company emerged as "one of the three or four biggest in the country". By 1938 Alcoa shares were performing at $160 a share. Sources "close to the family" said Andrew Mellon left a half billion dollars to his children. A year after the war Koppers called by *Fortune* "the dog of the Mellon industrial family", soared in profitability in 1951 helped by increasing sales climbing from $113 to $285 million while shares nearly double from $26 to $50.

The Mellons repeated their wartime windfalls of the First World War with the next one. Alcoa's government contracts with Washington were worth at least a half billion dollars. Oil discovered in Kuwait in 1938 offered enormous reserves of pure and light crude that hardly needed any cracking. Gulf owned half the Kuwaiti concession with production surpassing Arabia in 1953. The Mellons were also beneficiaries in the Iran coup where Kermit Roosevelt and the CIA in Teheran return the Shah to the throne. Kermit Roosevelt had been hired as a Gulf Oil executive in charge of government relations and seeking concessions more favorable to the Consortium forcing out the popular Iranian nationalist Prime Minister Mohammed Mossedegh, in August 1953, as the oil Consortium interests are split between the Anglo-Iranian (40%), Shell (14%), "and five American oil companies including Gulf, each of which might buy up to 8 percent of the production of the National Iranian Oil Company."

"Between 1950 and 1953 Gulf's sales nearly doubled," Hersh writes, "to close to two billion dollars annually." When the Consortium kings rule the land they can afford to give some pennies back to the people, for example, the art that they buy cheap and used to write off millions in taxes owed the government as endowments or philanthropy.

Andrew Mellon's towering legacy shadows and perpetuated political power. His son-in-law David Kirkpatrick Estes Bruce having married Mellon's daughter Alisa in London will direct the European branch of Donovan's OSS during the war as the uncontested number 2 in command with a bunch of Mellons under his command while serving as ambassador in Paris. Bruce also assumes seats on dozens boards of corporations "from Westinghouse Electric, and Tripps' airlines with William Rockefeller, Sonny and John Hay ("Jock") Whitney, "to the racetrack in Rockingham, New Hampshire". As a younger Consortium generation man, Bruce was a favorite of Ave Harriman, invested in the W. A. Harriman Company and sits on the board of Harriman's Union Pacific. When asked what he did for a living, R. K. Mellon (1899-70) quipped, "I hire company Presidents".

Jock Whitney (1904-82, Yale, Oxford) is the son of Payne Whitney, and grandson of William C. Whitney and John Hay, both Presidential cabinet members. When his father dies in 1926, he inherits a $20 million trust fund ($210 million), a quarter of what he later inherits from his mother. He also inherits his family's passion for thoroughbred racing, takes an active hand with his sister running his mother's Greentree Stables and becomes the youngest member in 1928 elected to the Jockey Club and still owns a few ships with his great J-Boat when big yacht racing is still the regal sport of millionaires, kings, emperors and commodores. He pursues his passion for polo but his four entries each fail to win the Kentucky Derby. During the height of the Holodomor in March 1933 Jock Whitney makes the cover of *Time*. By this time he increases his stakes in motion pictures, invests heavily in RKO Radio Pictures and Technicolor with his cousin Cornelius Vanderbilt Whitney. It was Jock Whitney who put up most of the money in David O. Selznick's production of Margaret Michell's Civil War love story, *Gone With the Wind* which also picks up the 1937 Pulitzer for non-fiction as the national bestseller. (B. Hersh, *The Mellon Family*, 270- 388)

Remember that both Harrimans, the Whitneys and Paul Mellon are all Yale men. Not many forgot it. Few could even dream of turning down Skull & Bones. Paul Mellon, Class of 1929 did. A Mellon could do that sort of thing. Why not? Tapped by Bones as preeminent among the fifteen radiant stars of his Class young Paul had so much money and status that he needn't bother. Mellon snubbed Bones. Afterall, that was now Harrimans' turf. So he joins Scoll & Key instead alongside Jock Whitney. Never keen on physical exertion either as a teen at Choate, unlike Averell Harriman who excelled at rowing at both Groton and Yale, Mellon helped out his mates by selling advertising for the *Yale Daily News* to local shop keepers in New Haven. Once when dragged to a hockey game he got smacked by a puck. He never went back. He turned a shoulder on the clubs and fraternities calling them "a bad system". A true liberal Democrat! This was a time when football frenzy and "The Game" against Harvard was still more socially correct than academics or pursuing a serious career. During the decade of Prohibition Mellon liked to take his friends to New York's speakeasies once shared a bar with gangster Legs Diamond.

In 2007 Yale's Sterling Memorial Library, a towering grandiose display of gothic architecture, cornered by gargoyles and encased in stained masterpieces, its walls adorned with secretly inscribed legends, housed a special tribute to Paul Mellon arranged by its top archivist. The Paul Mellon Gallery of Art houses part of their private collection with a value that rivals Yale's entire private endowment. One of Mellon's closest classmates was A. Whitney Griswold, Yale President (1950-63); during his tenure, Griswold and Mellon endowed professorships including the 1948 Bollingen Prize for poetry. (The Foundation's name was Mary

Mellon's way of honoring C. G. Jung, who owned a country house near Bollingen on Lake Zurich in Switzerland.) The Library of Congress jury decision naming Ezra Pound the recipient of the $1,000 award for his *The Pisan Cantos* while he remains institutionalized at St. Elizabeth's psychiatric hospital in Washington, DC for over 12 years sparked a national scandal. Was this the price he had to pay for having exposed secrets of the Federal Reserve? Pound had a statement delivered for Press: "No comment from the Bug House", but it was leaked by Walter Winchell that he really had said, "Democracy is more stupid than ever I said it was." Hemingway wrote, "The best of Pound's writing – and it is in the *Cantos* – will last as long as there is any literature." Princeton eventually took over the Bollingen Prize but then, in 1973, the Andrew W Mellon Foundation made an outright endowment of $100,000 to empower Yale's Beinecke Library to continue awarding the honors. The next year the prize went to Wallace Stevens ; other recipients include W. H. Auden, Archibald MacLeish, William Carlos Williams, Marianne Moore, Robert Frost, Conrad Aiken, E. E. Cummings... (William McGuire, *Poetry's Catbird Seat*, Library of Congress, Washington DC, 1988)

Always the Navy man weeks before his inauguration in February 1933 FDR can't resist getaway ten-day cruise to Miami on Astor's magnificent *Nourmahal* leading the fleet of sumptuous yachts owned by key Consortium skippers. Astor and FDR are very good friends and it was then to the *Nourmahal* in Miami that FDR rested after a failed assassination attempt killing the Chicago mayor. In fact, they are cousin many times over, a fact largely ignored by the press and forgotten at the time. His maternal grandfather Franklin Hughes Delano made a fortune in "the China Trade" trafficking opium; in 1844 he married Laura Astor (1824-02), the daughter of William Backhouse Astor. FDR's half-brother James Roosevelt Jr. was married to his aunt Helen Schermerhorn Astor, the oldest daughter of William Astor, in 1878, making them cousins. In a column on the wedding in Grace Chapel, *The New York Times* underplayed it calling it "a notable social event". (T. Morgan, *FDR*, 18; "A Notable Social Event", *The NYT,* Nov. 19, 1878)

After FDR was elected President, Vincent Astor put the *Nourmahal* at his disposal. FDR's son James and top adviser Harry Hopkins were often aboard. By 1935 FDR passed his "soak the rich" tax laws essentially killing the era of the great J-Boats and sleek yachts of the super-rich during these post-Depression years in an effort to distance himself from the infamous "The public be damned!" hardline adage of the rich memorialized by William H. Vanderbilt when asked in 1882 why he was shutting down a Chicago Limited extra-fare mail train; Vanderbilt tossed off any public responsibility, saying "I am working for my shareholders. If the public want the train, why don't they pay for it?"

DELANO, ROOSEVELT, RUSSELL & THE AMERICAN OPIUM CHINA TRADERS

After Roosevelt's victory, the president-elect sat down with Secretary Stimson in January for a one-on-one conversation. Stimson made a note in diary how FDR told him of "a personal hereditary interest in the Far East. He told me that one of his ancestors, I think a grandfather, had held a position there and that his grandmother had gone out to the Far East on a sailing vessel and had very nearly been captured by the (Confederate raider) *Alabama.* He took a very lively interest in the history (of our Far Eastern policy) as I told it." His advisers Rexford Tugwell and Raymond Moley suspect Stimson of pushing his foreign policy in that part of the world. Stimson agrees to confering with Roosevelt later in the month. Tugwell and Moley try to convince FDR that he is making "a tragic mistake." Months later Roosevelt tells Moley about the Delano china trade, saying "I have always had the deepest sympathy for the Chinese. How could you expect me not to go along with Stimson on Japan?." (Raymond Moley, *After Seven Years*, 1939, 93-5; Sumner Welles, *Seven Decisions That Shaped History*, 1951, 68; Stimson Diary, Jan. 9, 1933, Henry L. Stimson Papers, box 170, folder 20, Yale Univ. Library)

Roosevelt was in a dream of a long forgotten tale not finished yet, retreating to his roots lost in regression. Nearly a century has past since Warren Delano Jr, in a letter dated April 11, 1839, in Canton wrote his brothers defending smuggling profits gained by the opium trade by foreigners exploiting the Chinese though it had been banned by imperial decree. Delano justified the business since it would never have been possible "without the fostering care of those in authority" in China. "I do not pretend," he added, "to justify the prosecution of the opium trade in a moral and philanthropic point of view, but as a merchant I insist that it has been a fair, honorable and legitimate trade; and to say the worst of it, liable to no further or weightier objections than is the importation of wines, Brandies & spirits into the US, England &c." In other words, in the era when men are still active in the ancient trade of slaves, and in this time of extermination, war and Genocide at once when everything in civilization is at once darkly brilliant, Roosevelt' recalls his ancestor proudly defending his rightful role as a drug trafficker.

FDR's grandfather Delano admitted that the traffic was "doubtless a most injurious one to the Chinese." All in all he blamed the emperor and his mandarins, writing that if they "determine honestly to stop the trade, the Foreigners *cannot by any* possibility sell or smuggle the drug into the country." (See Frederic D. Grant, Jr., "Edward Delano and Warren Delano II: Case Studies in American China Trader Attitudes toward the Chinese, 1834, 1844", honors thesis, Bates College, 1976, 183-5, 260-1)

The Roosevelt-Astor family connection is easily traceable back to the evanescent adventures of Captain Warren Delano and his brother, Franklin Hughes Delano, born July 27, 1813, who became a partner in the New York shipping firm of Grinnell, Minturn and Co. in January 1839. He had done so well that by September 1844 he is able to marry Laura Astor, the daughter of William Backhouse Astor and granddaughter of John Jacob Astor, the richest man in America. The could be no mistaking the fact that Laura Astor Is one of the most sought after women in America when she joins with the Delano family with its fortune rooted in Chinese opium which gives rise to the huge fortunes of the British Empire and on which are built their magnificent country estates on hundreds and thousands of acres. As a wedding present the couple received a portion of William Backhouse Astor's "Rokeby" estate near Barrytown, New York; their house called "Steen Valetje" is constructed there around 1850. When Laura looks back into the Delano family line she'll see that many of the Delano family are descendents of Philippe de la Noye who landed in Plymouth, Massachusetts in 1621. A family of seafarers in the New England trade, FDR's great-grandfather Captain Warren Delano (1779 -66), of Fairhaven, Massachusetts, achieved success and prominence as a captain and shipowner. Warren Delano II, (1809-98) succeeded his father, sailing to China in 1833 on board the *Commerce* for the Canton Company; six years later he made partner in the Skull & Bones firm of Samuel Russell & Co. founded in Middletown, Connecticut.

Stimson may have found it more than slightly amusing this Delano-Roosevelt-Russell association to his Skull & Bones secret society which most certainly would not have escaped FDR's arcane sense of humor. It was after all fantastic commerce even while transforming the Chinese into a country of dope addicts ruined by opium. But commerce follows the flag and there is always collateral damage. It must have been justified as the cost of doing business. Except in the case of the Chinese trade, it was the business and trafficking drugs is not the same as consuming them. The traders took pride in the distinction and their profits to the bank.

But we have not finished yet; we can go deeper as I learned when I happened upon a most rare document in an antique book seller in Mystic, Connecticut, a New England harbor famous for pirates and whaling ships. According to a rare pamphlet, *Old Shipping Days in Boston* (1918), Samuel Russell first sailed to China in 1818. "In five years he and Philip Amidon, who represented Brown & Ives also of Providence, formed the partnership of Russell & Co.". The firm rapidly became "the most powerful house in the East, having connections in London with Baring Bros. & Co. and the Rothschilds in France; in India with Jamsetjee, Jejeebhoy & Sons; and in Boston at different times with J. and T. H. Perkins, Bryant and Sturgis, W. Appleton & Co., and Robert G. Shaw."

A small and most unassuming 1913 pamphlet titled "Some Ships of the Clipper Ship Era" (State Street Trust Co., Boston) states, "In China, acting as US Consul in Canton and Macao during the Opium War with ships loaded with tea sailing from Hong Kong ; Capt. Delano sailed home with his fortune to seek marriage and return to China with his bride, in 1846. Captain Delano lived in New York, invested in real estate and mining, and moves his family to "Algonac" near Newburgh, New York. In 1952 he was a founding member of the American Navigation Club with other clipper ship owners from Boston and New York including Daniel C. Bacon, Thomas H. Perkins, William H. Boardman, John M. Forbes, and Edward King. A club bet of 10,000 pounds is on to challenge their English competitors. But when he loses his fortune in the market crash of 1857 Warren Delano returns to China for another easy killing in the opium traffic. His mother follows him to Hong Kong in 1862, returning after the end of the Civil War.

"Franklin H. Delano combined his affairs as partner in Grinnell, Minturn and Co. with business of his brothers Warren, Frederick, and Edward and benefited from New York City property inherited from the Astors. They even sailed to Chile and handled government relations as the American Consul in Chile (1840-1851). The Delanos lived well, sailed frequently to Europe preferring the cosmopolitan life in Italy and Monte Carlo. Warren Delano III (1852-20) went to Harvard (1874) then joined Union Mining Company where he eventually made director, at Mt. Savage, Maryland. W.D. III invested in mines, banking and railroads while breeding race horses at "Steen Valetje" which he inherited. He missed the "Roaring Twenties" when unexpectedly he lost control of his horse, on September 9, 1920 when his horse ran into the path of an oncoming train at Barrytown, the Astor town. At the time of his death, Delano was a director of the Union Mining Company, President of the Delano Coal Company, and Chairman of the Board of the Vinton Colliery Company. FDR's mother, Sara Delano, born in 1854, was one of eleven children; she married Roosevelt's father James Roosevelt, in 1880, and young FDR was born two years later, January 29, 1882. She proved to be an overbearing, loving but excessively possessive and dominant mother. Once, when he was five, she persisted in asking him what was troubling him, and he exclaimed, with his hands clasped in prayer, "Oh, for freedom!" (Doris Kearns Goodwin, *No Ordinary Time*, Simon & Schuster, 76)

SOVIET GRAIN SHIPMENTS AND FARM COLLECTIVIZATION

In his book *Let History Judge, The Origins and Consequences of Stalinism* (1989) Soviet historian Roy A. Medvedev refers to what he called the "dramatic events, distortions and illegalities of collectivization from 1929 to 1933". Medvedev wrote, "The consequences of those events continued to be felt for many years. In 1937, although it was announced that the grain harvest had reached 7.3 billion poods, in fact the gross yield was only 5.9 billion and the average yearly harvest during the second Five-Year plan was only 4.45 billion, lower than in 1913 (1 pood/ 36.113 lbs.). 1938 and 1939 agricultural output dropped below 1937 level. 1940 level surpassed that by only 5-6 %. Instead of 8 poods, the 1938-40 average was under 5 poods (4.756). An enormous gap had developed by the end of the thirties between the rapid development of industry and the slow development of agriculture. This prevented the establishment of normal relations between the city and the countryside, between the working class and the peasantry. The heart of the problem was the forced transfer, or 'pumping' of funds from agriculture to industry."

In the Ukraine revenue from agriculture far exceeded that from industry. At a Central Committee plenum in 1929 Stalin acknowledged the "supertax", a sort of "tribute" on the backs of the peasants. Medvedev writes, "In the late thirties the prices paid to collective and state farms remained very low, while those farms continued to be overcharged for manufactured goods and for the services of the Machine Tractor Stations. Thus the forced transfer of funds from the countryside to the city continued. The war threw Soviet agriculture even further back. Agriculture suffered greater losses than any other branch of the national economy. In 1945 agricultural output was only a little more than 80 percent of the

1913 level. The number of farm machines had decreased several fold, and labor was in short supply (millions killed…). Many collective farms were staffed only by women, old men, and boys. In other words, the effort to improve agriculture had to start all over again. In 1946 the fourth five-year plan began, with ambitious goals for agriculture. Not one of them was reached. It was only with difficulty, in fact, that the 1940 level was reached. Though the number of horned cattle rose to 59.1 million, this was still lower than in 1916 and 1928. As for hogs, the number remained below the prewar level.

After the Holodomor it was next the war that devastated Soviet agriculture as well as industry.

"In 1953 gross agriculture output had increased by only 5 percent. The average yearly grain harvest in 1949-1953 was around 81 million tons. Per capita grain production in 1953 was 19 percent lower than in 1913." Collective farming staggers, machines and factories destroyed, tens of millions of young men and civilians killed. Roy Medvedev in *Let History Judge, The Origins and Consequences of Stalinism* (1989) observes, "It is hardly surprising that virtually no grain was available for fodder or export. The average yield of most crops was lower in 1949-53 than in 1913. The targets of a widely publicized three year plan from 1949 to 1952 for increased livestock raised by the state farms and collective farms was also not met. The main reason for the postwar stagnation in agriculture was the Soviet government's violation of the principle that farmers need personal material incentives. Continued pumping of funds to the cities … buying at prewar price levels, for grain, but industrial goods prices now inflated several fold." (Roy A. Medvedev, *Let History Judge, The Origins and Consequences of Stalinism*, Columbia Univ. Press, 1989, 97)

The depletion in livestock persists until the early 1950s, though without the war this might have occurred sooner. There are far too few agricultural machines to go around, so when, in 1932, "Motor Tractor Stations" (MTS) were established, each had to serve several collective farms. This meant collective farms had to compete with each other in bribing the local MTS and some always failed to attain arbitrarily set quotas. Also, there was shortage of trained farm managers; so at first, they were party workers sent down to run the farm and coerce the peasants. Peasants were unwilling to work hard because they were paid very little, if at all. As a result, in 1936, Stalin was inclined to allow them small private plots on which they could raise vegetables, fruit, and even some livestock, and sell on the open market.

Andrew Wilson's book *The Ukrainians* is a curious read indeed. Wilson describes the grim reality known to Americans and foreign workers in Kharkiv who dared not tell the horrid truth fearing the fatal consequences of offending their host. "The original capital of the Ukrainian SSR was Kharkiv (Kharkov). It was moved to Kiev in 1934, not so much to control a Ukrainianisation campaign that was already defeated as because the authorities were confident they could create a model proletarian Soviet city in the heart of Ukraine and proselytize its Soviet Ukrainian identity westwards."

Of the grisly famine Wilson writes, "Whole villages were wiped out, people ate domestic pets, grass, even next year's corn (notoriously defined as 'the theft of Socialist property' and made punishable by death), and cannibalism was widespread. Internal passports were introduced to prevent the starving leaving their villages in search of food. Russian abstract constructivist painter Kazimir Malevich's haunting *The Running Man* (1933-34) is eloquent testimony to the disaster showing a peasant fleeing across a deserted landscape." In fact, Malevich (1879-35), whose paintings by the end of the century sell for tens of millions of dollars, and is considered a world artist of the first rank, was born in Kiev of immigrant Polish parents; his father worked in the agriculture business and young Malevich grew to intimately know peasant life and celebrated their traditional way of life even while he becomes a master at Russian Suprematism and Cubist formality during its heyday with Picasso, Braque and Wilfredo Lam in Paris before the war when he was identified in the West as part of the Russian avant-garde. Malevich with Kandinsky and Tatlin are given posts by the regime to head commissions to sponsor the development of culture and counter criticism by traditionalists. Referring to "the Famine as an act of genocide", Andrew Wilson draws principally on the paper by Mace, *Famine in the Soviet Ukraine 1931-33* (1987), Conquest's *Harvest of Sorrow* (1986), and Ivan Drach, who concluded "in essence the Famine of 1932-3 was not an accidental or unique episode in the fate of the Ukrainian people ... just one stage in the planned eradication of the Ukrainian nation." Drach adds "almost a third of our peasants died 60 years ago just because they were and wanted to remain Ukrainians."

Andrew Wilson quotes Mace, citing "'enemy number one for Stalin and his circle was not the Ukrainian peasant nor the Ukrainian intelligentsia. The enemy was Ukraine itself." But in a stroke to reverse the tone of deliberate ethnic-cleansing, with the same breath Wilson brushes off the national thrust of the Terror-Famine. Furthermore, Wilson he chooses not to cite it as 'man-made' instead comparing mass murder on a scale never before witnessed in history to the status of the potato farming in Ireland's famine a century earlier during the apogee of the British Empire. Wilson's articulate treatment shows an equally adeptly absurd twist in disinformation the object of which is always to pervert and confuse the public record and mask the truth rendering the villains impervious to scrutiny. Andrew Wilson writes, "Many ethnic Ukrainians participated in the grain-requisition bands that descended on the villages, just as many Irish exploited their fellow-countrymen in the 1840s." How is the reader to believe that it is normal to take politics out of politics, or to pass off the Terror-Famine with the back of his hand saying that the cause of deaths was the result of Ukrainians killing Ukrainians just as Duranty did for Stalin and *The New York Times*. Later a parallel logic of comparison is applied later to insurgent nationalist Ukrainians killing Jews under their Nazi masters.

Alas, blame it on the poor Kulaks again! Wilson concludes the key cause of the famine in 1932 was Stalin's forty-four per cent increase in Ukraine's grain procurement quota. Guards were posted on the Ukrainian-Russian border." Fudging on Wilson writes, "It would be fair to say that the small holding 'rich peasant' (*kulak*, or *kurku* in Ukrainian) culture that Stalin sought to destroy was disproportionately vulnerable." Wilson suddenly veers into a maze of diversion with an academic flare for ambiguity, writing, "If Gennadii Ziuganov is right to claim that there is a natural affinity between (specifically) Russian peasant culture and Socialism via the tradition of the land commune (and if Stalin thought the same way), the implications for Ukraine are clear." Get that? Intellectual confusion is the best dope for oblivion. (A. Wilson, *The Ukrainians*, 147; J. Mace, *Famine in the Soviet Ukraine 1931-33*, Harvard Ukrainian Institute, Cambridge Mass, 1986; R. Conquest, *Harvest of Sorrow*, Oxford Univ. Press, 1986 quoting Ivan Drach, "'Chy pokaiet'sia Rosssiia? Vystup an mizhnarodnii naukovii konferentsii Holod 1932-33 rr. V Ukraini"', 1997, 354-8)

In his telling of the tale Wilson shifts to the Purges and now concedes that then and there Stalin deliberately steps up liquidation to target the Ukrainian intelligentsia. "These hit Ukraine particularly hard and were longer and more thorough-going than elsewhere. Up to 80% of the Ukrainian intelligentsia were killed or disappeared or sent to the camps; the party was completely purged twice, in 1932-34 and 1937-8." Wilson takes another swipe at the Ukrainians themselves, writing, "It was also true that many Ukrainians *benefited* from the purges, namely the so – called 'newly promoted' (*vydvizhentsy*) – hundreds of thousands of upwardly mobile proletarians and former peasants in the mold of Dovzhenko's Ivan, who filled the dead men's boots of the old intelligentsia." (italics added)

What else on God's Earth could they do? This is Stalin's godless turf! Forsaken and doomed to slavery and death by the Consortium investment – Ford trucks, Caterpillar machine reapers, General Electric turbines, Curtis-Wright aeroplanes, hundreds and thousands of American expert technicians, mechanics, planners and workers marching in step with communist propaganda bellowing about new markets for industry and the promise of consumer goods. There is no aid, no one to help them! Instead so many are starved, shot, exterminated. Filling "dead men's boots"? Virtually everyone had to work for food ration cards. No meal without a card! No card without work, Time pushes on in one giant rushing stream! Dizzy with success in a crash ten-year race for economic and military survival.

Years after Bullitt's embassy team discreetly monitors in monthly reports the Holodomor progress and its consequences, a few years later upon the outbreak of world war on the eastern front Chip Bohlen returns, this time with Ave Harriman for the Molotov-Roosevelt meeting. "The fact that Russians were carrying so heavy a load led to a guilt complex in our relations," Bohlen observes. Molotov cites the latest numbers on losses, the scale of destruction, Russian defeats at Kharkov and Kerch, the imminent loss of the Sevastopol port, and the *Werhmarcht* only 80 miles from Moscow. FDR asks General Marshall if he can tell Stalin that the Americans are preparing a second front. Marshall agrees, in Molotov's presence. No free meals here!

Finally the plan FDR sets in motion is essential and pays off in the Consortium bid to save England, save American lives FDR instructs Molotov to tell Stalin that "we expect the formation of a second front this year". D. K. Goodwin in *No*

Ordinary Time, writes "Molotov was jubilant. The ice was broken. The president felt that he was actually getting chummy with his Russian visitor. Molotov was put up in the family quarters, in the room Churchill had occupied across the hall from Hopkin's room." Molotov and the President's wife, First Lady Eleanor chat past midnight. "Eleanor later remarked that she liked him immediately." She considers Molotov "an open, warm sort of person". No diplomat ever thinks this of the icy diabolical communist. What utter fools the Americans can appear to be, so charming and naïve, so easily outmaneuvered without their luxuries and comforts. Passionately anticommunist, Churchill is furious to be outplayed by the Russians. Informed of Molotov's visit, he adamantly opposes a landing on the European continent, unwilling to risk another Somme when 60,000 British lives were lost in a single day of the Great War. A true warrior down to the lower depths of his soul he ought to know the human price of a military debacle; after his Gallipoli disaster in the Great War Winston Churchill served in the trenches commanding the 6th Battalion, the Royal Scots Fusiliers, 1916. He grimly tells Harriman present at the meeting that "he could not help but think of all the faces that were not there". Churchill leaves Washington, arriving June 19 at Hyde Park driving around the estate on the bluffs overlooking the Hudson and the home of his cousin Laura Delano. Yes! Churchill is related to the Roosevelts. Churchill also knows there is another deadly race underway and records in his diary the alarming German advance on heavy water experiments and atomic bomb research. Josef Goebbels had declared, "German science is at its peak in this matter."

"DEFEAT IS ONE THING, DISGRACE IS ANOTHER"

FDR had met Alexander Sachs, the Russian born American financier 11 October 1939 to know more about the progress of atomic research by the German refugee Albert Einstein of Princeton on fission of uranium atoms and the chain reaction to be harassed into a bomb. Sachs had Einstein's letter to the President but they talked about Napoleon instead and how he had spurned Fulton's steamship FDR ordered a bottle of Napoleon brandy, and poured two glasses while Sachs read an 800 word summary of atomic fission.

FDR listened and remarked, "Alex, what you are after is to see that the Nazis don't blow us up."

Roosevelt entrusts the bomb's top secret development to Stimson. Two months after Churchill's visit, FDR launches the Manhattan project which by 1945 under General Leslie Groves would involve over 120,000 people and cost $2 billion. FDR installed Churchill in the Rose Suite of the White House where they constantly strolled in and out of each others rooms like youthful lads. The next day at breakfast Churchill gets news that after 35 weeks of siege the British forces had fallen at Tobruk in Libya losing at least 25,000 to a German force half the strength. Churchill wrote, "Defeat is one thing, disgrace is another." (D. K. Goodwin, *No Ordinary Time*; J. E. Persico, *Roosevelt's Secret War*, 176-80)

William Shirer is excellent reading on Nazi Germany, and in particular, Hitler's invasion plan of Russia. In his book *The Rise and Fall of the Third*

Reich, he weaves his way through the debacle after the Holodomor. In the chapter "Barbarossa, The Turn of Russia", the American correspondent in Berlin reanimates events leading to how Hitler in 1940 prepared his betrayal of Stalin. The world suddenly awoke to the horrible truth of his ideas all there to know in advance and rooted in *Mein Kampf,* a book that Warburg dismissed as the mad ravings of a lunatic idiot.

James "Jimmy" Warburg, Bullitt's friend, son of the brains behind the Fed and heir to the wealthy Consortium Jewish banking family made several trips to Europe and Germany in the 1920s and knew who to fear. In 1929 Shirer listens with awe when Hitler transfixed a crowd at Bremen with his fascist tirade. Shirer writes, "Just watching the effect he had on people while talking what to me seemed like sheer nonsense, I had a goose-pimply feeling that this was a phenomenon that wasn't as unimportant as it might seem." Fritz and Max Warburg are slow to heed the danger. But how stupid could the Consortium be not to take him seriously at his word. Only they *did* take him seriously. He was *their* creation with a published blueprint for Nazi world supremacy.

For Stalin even then, ten years before the outbreak of WWII, it was too late to stop events from marching to war. Unlike the Brest-Litovsk deal negotiated with the Germans in the spring of 1918 pulling Russia out of the war so that Trotsky and Lenin could consolidate their Bolshevik regime in the midst of civil war, this time the Kremlin had no time to lose. As early as 1924 Hitler publicly declares his intention to invade and destroy Russia writing in *Mein Kampf*: "we National Socialists take up where we broke off six hundred years ago. We stop the endless German movement toward the South and West of Europe and turn our gaze towards the lands of the East. ... When we speak of new soil and territory in Europe today, we must think principally of Russia and her vassal border states. Destiny itself seems to wish to point out the way to us here...This colossal empire in the East is ripe for dissolution, and the end of the Jewish domination in Russia will also be the end of Russia as a state." (John G. Stoessinger, "Barbarossa: Hitler and Russia", *Why Nations Go to War*, NY: St. Martin's Press, 3rd ed., 1982)

BARBAROSSA: HITLER'S DOOM IN THE EAST

Hitler's worst nightmare of a two-front war East and West would not deter him from his plan nor shake him out of his madness. As early as the fall of 1940 Hitler outlines his plan for attacking Stalin, by July 1940, before launching *Sea Lion,* "if Britain were not invaded", writes Shirer. But his plan for the invasion of England fails to materialize and is doomed by aggressive RAF victories in August through October. The date is set for spring 1941. Hitler is told by his Army Commander-in-Chief Field Marshal von Brauchitsch that the Russian campaign will be settled in "four or six weeks", easily time enough to crush the Red Army and occupy territory "so that Soviet bombers could not reach Berlin or the Silesiana industrial area, while, on the other hand, Luftwaffe bombers could reach all important objectives in the Soviet Union".

Hitler's Chief of Staff Gen. Franz Halder – "probably the most brainy man in the army" –, Shirer tells us, "but is allowed no credit by Hitler". Late June 1940 Halder passed on Hitler's words during a conference at the *Berghof* above *Berchtesgaden*, Hitler's favorite sanctuary overlooking the Alpine mountains. Shirer recalls Hitler's dilemma when he retreated from his earlier plan to invade Britain, and announced instead plans to invade Russia. Shirer: "Britain's hope lies in Russia and America. If that hope in Russia is destroyed then it will be destroyed for America too because elimination of Russia will enormously increase Japan's power in the Far East.

"'Something strange has happened in Britain! The British were already completely down," Hitler exclaimed. "Now they are back on their feet ... if Russia is smashed, Britain's last hope will be shattered. Then Germany will be master of Europe and the Balkans ... Russia must be eliminated." By spring 1941 Hitler is impatient to get on with his Eastern Front. Shirer writes, "The sooner Russia is smashed the better. When it failed, Hitler railed against the General Staff. Chief Halder urged Field Marshal Brauchitsch to protest or resign their posts. Brauchitsch refused. Hitler was determined to advance to Moscow immediately." (W. Shirer, *The Rise and Fall of the Third Reich*, 793; Ron Chernow, *The Warburgs*, Vintage, 1993, 321)

In his history of the war *A World at Arms* (1994) Gerhard L. Weinberg writes that "until the end of the war in Europe in May 1945, the majority of fighting of the whole war took place on the Eastern Front: more people fought and died there than on all the other fronts of the war around the globe put together." Germans used 60 percent of its total strength, 2,700 war planes destroyed the Red Air Force, the largest in Europe, though mostly obsolete planes caught on the ground. In the first week of the campaign, over 4,000 Soviet planes are destroyed giving the Nazis near total control of the air. Three million Germans, half a million men from pro-German countries, 600,000 horses, two large encirclement battles, 300,000 Russians captured, but in both in the north and south more Soviet troops pushed back, evading capture. (Gerhard L. Weinberg, *A World at Arms, A Global History of World War II*, NY: Cambridge Univ. Press, 1994, 264)

Alexander Bevin in *How Hitler Could Have Won World War II* (2000) explores the military might of Hitler's carefully planned Barbarossa invasion launched across the Ukrainian border. Bevin writes, "For immediate use in the attack, Hitler assembled 107 infantry divisions, 19 panzer divisions, 18 motorized divisions, and one cavalry division, a total of three million men, with supporting troops, This represented the bulk of the total German strength of 205 divisions. The Barbarossa forces included 3,350 tanks, 7,200 artillery pieces, and 2770 aircraft." Panzer tanks, however, are not "fully tracked," and with the first rains "panzer mobility would end with the first mud". (Alexander Bevin, Chapter "Barbarossa", *How Hitler Could Have Won World War II, The Fatal Errors that Led to Nazi Defeat,* NY: Crown, 2000)

The West anticipates a crushing defeat of Soviet Russia. According to FDR biographer Ted Morgan the White House expects a quick German victory. "The question was, how long could the Russians hold out," Ted Morgan writes.

"Stimson conferred with the chief of staff and the men in the War Plans Division, who estimated it would take Germany one to three months to beat Russia." Once again the Russians proved themselves a force not to be underestimated and Stalin had millions of men and women eager to defend Mother Russia. Ted Morgan observes, "the Russians had kept their industrial capacity a secret. Their steel production was 70 percent that of America. In June 1940, Stalin had 24,000 tanks, 4000 of which had been built since the pact with Hitler. The Soviets had been making tanks since 1928, according to the Bolshevik dogma that war is normal and peace is abnormal. They had a new model tank each year, just as in America there was a new model car, and some of their tanks were better than the German tanks. So the Russians hung on." (T. Morgan, *FDR*, 592)

And although Hitler decided on the Russian invasion before he launched the air war against Britain, according to Bevin he switches his focus and his army away from Great Britain turning instead towards Moscow to take all of Russia by several spear-headed sweeps behind the Red Army."

Germany aimed to trap the Red Army and block a Russian retreat. "The tactic was different than used successfully in the Blitzkreig westward in 1940," observes Bevin, and he adds, "As early as July 31, 1940, "in a conference with his senior military chiefs Hitler announced his 'resolve to bring about the destruction of the vitality of Russia in the spring of 1941." Later, in private, many of his generals shook their heads in despair. This was another of Hitler's fatal blunders that cost him everything he had to lose. (A. Bevin, *How Hitler Could Have Won World War II*, 45)

Ukraine was to be Germany's greatest conquest. And the feudal city of Koenisberg situated halfway on the Baltic Sea coast between Danzig and Lithuania was to be the showpiece for a museum of Russian spoils. Both were destroyed, literally obliterated. The Nazi plan was that Ukraine would remain an "independent state in alliance with Germany" and feed the German population. White Russia would be annexed to the Reich. On December 18, 1940, Hitler's signed his attack plan in Directive No. 21: "The German Armed Forces must be prepared to 'crush Soviet Russia in a quick campaign' before the end of the war against England." The codename was clear: "Barbarossa", a war of annihilation based on racial extermination in honor of the Crusade commander of the 12th century drowned while crossing the River Calycadnus of modern Turkey. Mark Mazower in *Hitler's Empire* (2008) that the primary objective was "to erect a barrier against Asiatic Russia on the general line Volga-Archangel' which would definitely eliminate the USSR as an industrial and European power." Hysterical at not breaking England's back, Hitler clashed with his generals and pressed on to smash Russia as he had crumbled France. (Mark Mazower, *Hitler's Empire: How the Nazis Ruled Europe*, Chapter "War of Annihilation: Into the Soviet Union", NY: Penguin, 2008; C. Bellamy, *Absolute War*)

In the chapter "The Planning of the Terror" in *The Rise and Fall of the Third Reich,* William Shirer recalls how Gen. Halder records for posterity Hitler's vow in his own words to seize Russia in spring 1941: "The war against Russia will be such that it cannot be conducted in a knightly fashion. This struggle is one of ideologies and racial differences and will have to be conducted with unprecedented, unmerciful and unrelenting harshness. All officers will have to rid themselves of obsolete ideologies. ... I insist absolutely that my orders be executed without contradiction. The commissars are the bearers of ideologies directly opposed to National Socialism. Therefore the commissars will be liquidated. German soldiers guilty of breaking international law... excused. Russia has not participated in the Hague Convention and therefore has no rights under it."

In fact, from the beginning Hitler made clear how to conduct total war in the East. To all combat commanders in Ukraine on December 22, 1941 the German Army Group South issued a "Top Secret" Memorandum: "The following concept of the Fuehrer (Hitler) is to be made known ... to all commanders .... Each area that has to be abandoned to the enemy must be made completely unfit for his use. Regardless of its inhabitants every locality must be burned down and destroyed to deprive the enemy of accommodation facilities ... the localities left intact have to be subsequently ruined by the air force." With his Russian forces crushed and defeated in retreat Himmler on September 7, 1943 orders *SS-Obergruppenfuehrer* Prutzmann "to leave behind in Ukraine not a single person, no cattle, not a ton of grain, not a railroad track... The enemy must find a country totally burned and destroyed."

The German assault on Moscow follows "along the old road which Napoleon had taken to Moscow", Shirer observed. Soviet armies are quickly encircled between Vyazma and Bryansk, and some 650,000 prisoners are captured along with 1,200 tanks. By October 20, German forces advance to forty miles from Moscow. Even Gen. Halder calculates taking Moscow before the Russian winter, the rains of *Rasputitza*, and the thick impassable lush mud all of which had defeated the French over a century past. By November, total losses German of Eastern armies (not counting the sick) 743,112 officers and men, 23% of the entire German force of 3.2 million. By December 6, German troops had been beaten back from Moscow's suburb. Hitler's prophecies weeks late August that Russia was crushed "without any reservation" and had been "struck down and would never rise again" become haunting echoes of doom.

By July 9, FDR authorizes American forces to occupy Iceland, relieving the British there. Hitler, in *Wolfsschanze*, his wolf's lair headquarters (or entrenchment) in East Prussia from where he directs his generals, considered it "an aggression against Germany and Europe." Hitler resists declaring war on America. The Fuhrer is duped into believing that Nazi success in Russia will rally the Americans to join the German side. Events take another course as the once again the Consortium shows him the fool so well parodied by Charlie Chaplin. (W. Shirer, *The Rise and Fall of the Third Reich,* 859)

Ordered to leave behind complete destruction German soldiers destroyed 18,414 miles of railroad track, station, freight cars and locomotives. They flooded mines, dynamited factories, poisoned wells and reservoirs, and destroyed over two million homes and buildings. Gen. Eric Koch orders during the 1943 retreat that "the homes of recalcitrant natives ... are to be burned down; relatives are to be arrested as hostages." What the Soviets missed in 1941 the Germans destroy in 1943-44. (Lev A. Bezymenski research cited in Rolf Dieter Müller and Gerd R. Ueberschär, *Hitler's War in the East*, Berghahn Books, 3rd ed. 2009: Messeurs Müller and Ueberschär observe "over twenty-five million Soviet citizens lost their lives" on the Eastern Front; D. Dallin, 364. Both citations can be found in A. Gregorovich; Kondufor, *History Teaches a Lesson*, Kiev, 1986, Document no. 119, 172)

Nazi war files of Alfred Rosenberg, Reich minister for occupied eastern territories were "captured intact". American journalist Shirer gets it right when he notes that Rosenberg is Hitler's mentor back as far as the early formative Munich days when fascism first becomes fashionable not only in Berlin, but in London, Rome and throughout Europe as well as in Washington. Shirer covers Berlin and the rise of Nazi terror from the early thirties until 1940 and returns at war's end to see the rubble of Berlin and Nuremberg. In 1934 he is there in Nuremberg at the Adlon Hotel on November 15, along with the "disillusioned" American ambassador Bill Dodd who "looked most unhappy" attending the first of the *Bierabend* between beer and sausage and lectures by Rosenberg then head of the Nazi party's Foreign Affairs Office.

Hitler and the Nazi Party have grown into an alarming menace to the free world. *The NYT* on its front page August 19 in an eye-witness account by Fred Birchall reports a public poll gave Hitler ninety per cent popularity with the German people: "The endorsement assures Chancellor Hitler, who four years ago was not even a German citizen, dictatorial powers unequaled in any other country, and probably unequaled in history since the days of Genghis Khan. He has more power than Joseph Stalin in Russia, who has a party machine to reckon with; more power than Premier Mussolini of Italy who shares his prerogative with the titular ruler; more than any American President ever dreamed of." That year Birchall picks up his Pulitzer for "unbiased" reporting for *The NYT* in Germany, two years after Duranty.

Dodd and Shirer share a mutual contempt for the Nazis and remain throughout these turbulent days friendly and close observers. Shirer calls Rosenberg "a crack-brained, doughy-faced dolt...The official Nazi 'philosopher' was the most muddled of men: tedious, verbose and just plain stupid." Of events long passed but not forgotten, Shirer brings us back in *The Nightmare Years, 1930 to 1940*, writing in 1984, "His theory of race, which insisted on the superiority of the 'Aryan' Germans and the inferiority and sickness of the Jews – and also of the Slavs, Asians, Americans – were idiotic, and his ignorance of history was almost total." Even Hitler finds his best-seller book, *The Myth of the Twentieth Century,* impossible to read and few do. A leader of the Hitler Youth League with nearly 8 million members tells Shirer, "Rosenberg was a man who sold more copies of a book no one had ever read than any other author in German history." After the war the Nuremberg judges of the major war criminals sentence Rosenberg to death and he is executed.

Hitler detests this academic worm with a diploma from the University of Moscow just the same. Brown University's Norman Rich reasoned that without the support of the peasants it would be impossible for the Nazi's to secure the grain harvests. By spring 1941 Rosenberg moved his administrative servants into the former trade mission offices of the USSR in Berlin. However, Heinrich Himmler is the all-important *Reichsfuher SS* of the Germanization programs in Russia and personally liked by Hitler. The East, Himmler feels, is his special domaine and he spends more time dedicated to ruthless SS political persecution of non-Germans and wants nothing of Rosenberg's plans for collaboration with anti-Communist Ukrainian Slavic nationalists. (William L. Shirer, *The Nightmare Years, 1930 to 1940*, NY: Little, Brown, 1984, 180-2)

AMERICA'S SECRET AGENT IN BERLIN

It is in fact the Wehrmarcht's Chief-of-Staff, General Halder, involved in the 1938 anti-Hitler plot aborted by the Munich appeasement deal that seals the fate of the Czechs; Halder is a source for a US secret agent in Berlin giving advance warning of the invasion. Agent Sam Woods, ostensibly a US commercial attaché in US Berlin embassy, informed Washington that spring 1941 that Hitler's "Barbarossa" invasion plans to attack Russia had been known as early as January 1941 and transmitted in a confidential report to the US State Department. The FBI confirms the report as authentic. An economics professor and one of America's most valuable intelligence assets in Berlin Edwin Respondek passes information to Woods. But he's not his only source on the invasion plan. Respondek also gives Woods a tip on the Japanese Pacific war plans, and later provides essential information on German atomic experiments. Yhe West has sundry other sources; Consortium ace-in-the-hole Schacht in Berlin and other high ranking civil servants keep in regular touch with US Foreign Service men including Leland Harrison (1883-51), the American minister in Bern dealing ostensibly a trade and commerce official. Harrison and Woods, with diplomatic cover as head of the US Consulate in Zurich keep in touch with Allen Dulles living in Bern. Schacht, too, has been involved in the July 20 anti-Hitler resistance movement when troops march on Munich. Throughout this period Harrison occupies a slew of other sensitive posts including Sweden, Uruguay, and Romania. (Pratt-Hull, *The Memoirs of Cordell Hull*; W. Shirer, *The Rise and Fall of the Third Reich*, 830)

"I left Berlin in December 1940", Shirer writes. "George Kennan, the most brilliant Foreign Service officer at the embassy, who remained there, informs me that the embassy learned from several sources of the coming attack on Russia." Kennan knew that Clark Kuykendall (US Army 1917-19, wounded at Compiègne, Croix de Guerre, Columbia 1920), formerly Vice Consul Amsterdam 1920, Oslo 1928, Bergen 1930, Cherbourg 1933), before becoming US Consul at the doomed center of Germanic *kultur*, Koenigsberg, formerly the capital of Prussia founded by the Teutonic Knights in 1255, had relayed a report of the imminent attack "two or three weeks" prior to the invasion. Koenigsberg would be captured, its population decimated, killed, deported or starved, and the city renamed "Kaliningrad". Welles has information passed on to Stalin of German plans to invade the USSR "as late as May 19". But Welles dismissed the odds of a German Soviet invasion "only one in a hundred". As early as March 20, Sumner Welles passes the tip over to Soviet ambassador Constantine Oumansky in Washington. But war historian Alexander Bevin credits "the American commercial attaché in Berlin" Sam Woods as the primary source.

More messages are sent to Ambassador Steinhardt in Moscow who informs Moscow, a few weeks prior to invasion. Even Churchill warns his nemesis in the Kremlin in a personal note delivered April 19, 1941 with information garnered from a British agent "based on Ultra intelligence intercepts which he didn't reveal to Stalin ; Churchill informs Sir Stafford Cripps, British ambassador in Moscow but Cripps astoundingly delays delivering the news to Stalin. As early as late April British intelligence decoded an intercept from the Germans and know the exact day of the invasion as June 22. (W. Shirer, *The Rise and Fall of the Third Reich*; I. Gellman 229; conversations with S. Welles, L. Fischer papers, C. Hull, *Memoirs*; Frank Graff, *Strategy of Involvement, Diplomatic Biography of Sumner Welles*, Gardner, 1988; A. Bevin, *How Hitler Could Have Won World War II*)

"In April," Barton Biggs writes in *Wealth, War and Wisdom,* "Churchill instructed the British ambassador, to deliver a personal message to Stalin warning him that an attack was imminent. Cripps, thin, tweedy, stubborn with a touch of stoic self-importance, believed he had already warned the Russians and much to Churchill's irritation never does directly or in a timely fashion deliver the message to Stalin. Churchill later mused that perhaps if Cripps had given the warning, at the very least the Russian air force would not have been caught lined up in orderly rows on the ground on the first day of Barbarossa." Sir Stafford Cripps had replaced Lord Beaverbrook in the war cabinet with the title Lord Privy Seal, and before the outbreak of war is expelled from the Labour Party "for advocating a popular front with both Liberals and Communists". Cripps returns to London "trailing the glory of the Red Army". (B. Biggs, 98)

Stalin lives a morbid distrust of the English and demonstrates even less faith in his own intelligence sources. "The Soviet capacity to understand the political and diplomatic intelligence it collected, however, never approached its ability to collect that intelligence in the first place," writes Christopher Andrew and Vasili Mitrokhin in *The Sword and the Shield* (1999). "Its natural tendency," they underscore, "to substitute conspiracy theory for pragmatic analysis when assessing the intentions of the encircling imperialist powers was made worse when during the 1930s by Stalin's increasing tendency to act as his own intelligence analyst. Stalin, indeed, actively discouraged intelligence analysis by others, which he condemned as 'dangerous guesswork'. 'Don't tell me what you think', he is reported to have said, 'Give me the facts and the source!' As a result INO (foreign intelligence department Cheka, GPU, OGPU, GUGB sic) had no analytical department. Intelligence reports throughout and even beyond the Stalin era characteristically consisted of compilations of relevant information on particular topics with little argument or analysis. Those who compiled them increasingly feared their life expectancy if they failed to tell Stalin what he expected to hear. ... The main function of Soviet foreign intelligence was thus to reinforce rather than to challenge Stalin's misunderstanding of the West." (C. Andrew and V. Mitrokhin, *The Sword and the Shield,* 54)

FDR still has the Japanese biting at his feet. His economic pressures which include restricting oil supplies fail to coerce the capitulation of Admiral Tojo and the militarist clans. Roosevelt is directly challenged by the Commander of the American Pacific Fleet Admiral James O. Richardson extremely worried by the order from the Chief of Naval Operations Admiral Harold R. Starck that he was too keep his ships in Hawaiian waters after the completion of naval exercises in April 1940 in order to maintain "the deterrent effect which it is thought your presence may have on the Japs going into the East Indies".

War historian James Costello calls Richardson (1878-74) "the epitome of a seafaring admiral whose devotion to the Navy was matched by an unshakable temperament". Admiral Richardson flies to Washington July 1940 hoping to put his case forward to Roosevelt for moving the fleet to California where it would be less vulnerable to a surprise Japanese attack. Once in the capitol he immediately suspects the fleet had become "hostage to American diplomacy" in a game to bluff the Japanese. Roosevelt is facing reelection for an unprecedented third term on a campaign for peace while preparing for war. Richardson is not in the loop and the Consortium politics are complicated. FDR is surprised that Richardson would speak out and question the wisdom of his Commander-in-Chief. "I know that the presence of the fleet in the Hawaiian area has had and is now having a restraining influence on the actions of Japan", Roosevelt said. Richardson doesn't buy it and argues that the fleet remains at great risk "disadvantageously disposed for preparing for, or initiating war operations". Their encounter, the Admiral recalls, turns into a "hot and heavy" confrontation. Roosevelt is caught off-guard and offended that his logic or foreign policy should be challenged. He ends the meeting abruptly, saying "Joe, you just don't understand." Months later Richardson is replaced by Admiral Husband E. Kimmel. His career ended and he retires the next year a Rear Admiral. (George C. Dyer, *On the Treadmill to Pearl Harbor: The Memoirs of Admiral James O. Richardson,* Washington, DC, Naval History Div., Dept. of the Navy, 1973, 435)

The top brass at Pearl Harbor are rattled. The problem of American vulnerability is taken up by Secretary of the Navy William Franklin Knox (1874-44), a tough former US Army Rough Rider in Roosevelt's 1898 Cuban adventure during the Spanish-American War and part owner of the *Chicago Daily News.* Roosevelt appoints Knox in 1940 in a bid to gain support from the Republicans. A Hoover Consortium nominee for Vice-President Knox ran on the 1936 Republican ticket with Alf Landon. "I'm no New Dealer", he would say assuring Republicans Roosevelt was "a great man". Knox drafts a letter by Rear Admiral Richmond Kelly Turner and sends it to Stimson, declaring, "If war eventuates with Japan, it is believed easily possible that hostilities would be initiated by *a surprise attack upon the Fleet or Naval Base at Pearl Harbor.*" (Knox calls for an immediate correction by "taking every step, as rapidly as can be done, that will increase the readiness of the Army and Navy to withstand a raid of the character mentioned ...." (Sec. W. F. Knox communication January 24, 1941 concern for the "security of the US Pacific Fleet while in Pearl Harbor, and of the Pearl Harbor naval base itself". (James Costello, *Days of Infamy*, re. "Hearings Before the Joint Committee on the Investigation of the Pearl Harbor Attack, 79th Congress, Washington, DC, US Govt. Printing Office, 1946 - PHH 24:1363, Chapter 2, "A Strategic Error of the First Magnitude", 44-63, Simon & Schuster, 1994; italics added)

That May 1941 is a fatal month for the Ukrainians and the USSR. FDR is stricken down with a painful intestinal infection. Interior Secretary Harold I. Ickes considers the situation in the White House critical, and FDR's condition "inactive and uninspiring". He calls a special meeting for May 12 with Stimson, Knox, and Supreme Court Justice Bob Jackson to prepare a document for taking over executive authority. Stimson recalled the urgency, writing in his diary, "We all felt that the country was sadly in need of leadership and that only the President himself could supply the want. We know the defense program is not anywhere near what it ought to be ... We felt that the State Department was a bottleneck ... What we wanted is something dramatic, something that will arrest the attention of the world." (T. Morgan, *FDR*, 590)

Reader let us look again at Bevin's account here: "Ambassador Laurence Steinhardt informs Molotov of reports to US legations pinpointing the attack almost to the day. High-altitude Luftwaffe reconnaissance aircraft made more than 300 overflights of Soviet territory in the weeks leading up to the invasion. On June 16, the German embassy evacuated all but essential personnel. There were many more warnings. Up to the last day, the Soviet Union continues to supply Germany with raw materials, including 4000 tons of rubber, plus manganese and other minerals shipped from the Far East over the Trans-Siberian Railway." When in the morning June 22 the German ambassador Count Schulenburg – later shot in an assassination plot against Hitler in 1944 – presents Molotov with a declaration of war, the Commissar squeaked, "Do you believe that we deserved that?" (A. Bevin, 90; T. Morgan, *FDR*, 590)

Churchill waned. Cripps' popularity rose. At the time Singapore falls, Mandalay is evacuated and lost along with Rangoon. Europe's empire in Asia is in shatters collapsing like dominoes under the Japanese as Roosevelt expected they would. As the Nipponese war lords had dreamed soon one day all of the great resources of China will belong to Japan. Peter Clark in *The Last Thousand Days of the British Empire* (2008) observes, "The collapse of supercilious white imperialists before little yellow men whom they had systematically slighted and disparaged was an object – lesson at home, the British had salved their pride with the noble myth of 1940: a nation courageously pulling together with a unity that spanned all classes, in a fitting image of a democracy at war with Nazism. Churchill's timeless rhetoric captured this. Yet faced with the threat of the invader in their Asian empire, the British showed the ugly face of imperialism, leaving a shameful myth of 1942: an army and navy unable to protect the bastions of power, white officials ready to cut and run, saving themselves and their possessions while showing a racist disregard for others, even their own faithful servants. Here Churchill's imperialist rhetoric exposed him as the captive of his own decrepit assumptions."

The man who would be king (remember reader he was born in Blenheim Palace) gets a harsh rebuke from his libertarian friend and savior in the White House. The ground is shifting, rapidly, under the thundering fire of Nazi and

Soviet guns. Roosevelt in 1942, in a message to Churchill, criticized Great Britain's unwillingness "to concede to the Indians the right of self-government' and that American public opinion would not forgive the consequences should India be invaded as a result". Alright for the Indians, in time of war when England is on its knees about to be invaded by Berlin's Nazis and losing its empire to the little yellow Asians". Why hadn't Roosevelt given the Ukrainians a message about "the right of self-determination"? Of course this would have been out of the cards. FDR was not risking an incident with the Russians or meddle in their internal affairs. But these are ordinary facts arranged within time strung like beads along the length of one string. We are not living in two parallel worlds. Its a world war and there is only one world. But its too late for that now, no use telling the Ukrainians now caught up in Stalin's defense of the Motherland. Their heads are spinning if they still have one at all. More doom. Why are the gods punishing them? Any Christian would think Ukraine cursed for their sins. (Peter Clark, *The Last Thousand Days of the British Empire*, London: Bloomsbury, 2008, 21-2)

Biggs looked at how markets reacted to the war after news of Hitler's attack on the Russians. Western stock markets surged. "In the midst of the barrage of bad news and heavy bombing of London," Barton Biggs observes, "the stock market perversely but intuitively rallied. Was it anticipating Operation Barbarossa, the German attack on Russia? Even though the *Werhmacht* bit off great chunks of the Soviet Union, once Russia was involved, Britain no longer stood alone. The chances of a German landing in Britain had to be much diminished. After the late winter sinking spell, London stocks staged a resolute rally for most of the rest of the year. From the low in April the Index rallied 24% to its mid-December high ... Unquestionably it was buoyed by the growing alliance between the United States and Britain, and it must have sensed the rising odds of the United States being drawn into the war. Another example of the wisdom of markets." The war business is taking off and orders pour in pushing market confidence and shares higher. (B. Biggs, 100)

The Germans also predict a quick victory. On June 22, 1941 in the early morning hours the invasion of Russia was launched. "England has lost this war," Hitler wrote Mussolini, and he added, "Like a drowning person, she grasps at every straw. The destruction of France…has directed the glances off the British warmongers continually to the place from which they tried to start the war: to Soviet Russia. Both countries, Soviet Russia and England, are equally interested in Europe … rendered prostrate by a long war. Behind these two countries stands the North American Union goading them on ... Whether or not America enters the war is a matter of indifference, inasmuch as she supports our enemy with all the power she is able to mobilize. The situation in England itself is bad; the provision of food and raw materials is growing steadily more difficult. The martial spirit to make war, after all, lives only on hopes. These hopes are based solely on two assumptions: Russia and America. We have no chance of eliminating America. But it does lie in our power to exclude Russia. The elimination of Russia means, at the same time, a tremendous relief for Japan in East Asia, and thereby the possibility of a much stronger threat to American activities through Japanese intervention. I have decided under these circumstances to put an end to the hypocritical performance in the Kremlin." (W. Shirer, *The Rise and Fall of the Third Reich,* 850)

Just two weeks into the war General Halder wrote in his diary July 3, 1941: "the Russian campaign has been won in the space of two weeks". Hitler and his close adviser and double agent felt the same. "I will keep this day as precious in my memory". It would haunt him until he died with the Red Army assault on Berlin and his bunker German General Staff bunkers.

"BEST TANK IN THE WORLD" – THE SOVIET T-34

But the Soviet Russians were better prepared than German commanders ever imagined. "I realized soon after the attack was begun that everything that had been written about Russia was nonsense", Field Marshal Gerd von Rundstedt told Allied officers after the war. At first a large portion of the Red Army tanks "from the BT to the T-26 and 28, were obsolescent: more of the total of 23,000 tanks deployed by the Red Army in 1941 were lost through breakdowns than to enemy action", Evans observes in *The Third Reich at War.* The superior armor of the Soviet T-34 tank of catch the Germans unaware. Anti-tank shells bounce off harmlessly. And they keep coming, more and more of them. Russian fighter airplanes are easily shot down by the well trained *Luftwaffe* kept filling the sky with more and younger pilots with less training in the air. On the ground divisions replaced one after another even during the retreat. The Germans are quickly overwhelmed by numbers. Further, Hitler and his political advisers hope for a political upheaval and a mass revolt of Russians against Stalin and communism. But the Russians in contrast to the collapse in 1917 prove themselves more patriotic and determine with each day of combat. (R. J. Evans, 178-90)

British war historian Max Hastings offers a description shared by countless historians as well as the Nazi tank commanders themselves, of the fierce, unrelenting "stoicism of the Russian soldier", and the "spectacle of the Red Army in attack", and he writes of the experience from 1942 on of a Tiger troop commander of the *Grossdeutschland Panzergrenadier* Divison: "His unit often fought opposite the Soviet 'Red Flag' Guards Division. Each side collected the other's cap badges. But (Lieutenant) Saurma qualified his respect by saying: 'The Russians didn't think much. They were usually being driven by their officers.' The Germans feared the Soviet Stalin tank, but thought little of Soviet tank gunnery. In battle, Saurma sought to keep moving constantly. 'It's much harder to hit a running hare,' he told his own tank commanders ... T-34s would approach six, twelve abreast. The Germans would knock out four or five, but there were always more. 'You couldn't believe the way they kept coming – their infantry simply charging our tanks, running and shouting, even when the bodies were piled up in front of our positions. Sometimes our infantry seemed paralysed by the spectacle. One thought: 'How can we ever stop such people?'" (M. Hastings, *Armageddon,* 112-3)

In the 1930s Ukraine is the center of heavy industry in the USSR. Stalingrad to the east will assume later occupy a more conspicuous place in history in the production of armaments before the German invasion. Hitler's fascist army had to run up against the T-34 tank designed and built in the Kharkiv Tractor Factory. General von Runstedt finds it to be the "best tank in the world", and General von Kleist regretfully says it is the "finest in the world." The first Ukrainian T-34 tank, no. 1, was tested by successfully driving it 1,000 miles from Kharkiv to and from Moscow. A more powerful cannon, superior speed – 32 mph compared to 25 mph for the Panzers –, armour plating virtually impervious to German shells which bounced off. Its superior welded construction was the creation of the brilliant engineer and master builder Y. O. Paton (1870-53), and a Vice-President of the Academy of Sciences of Ukrainian SSR (1945-52). He was also the father of Borys Paton, long-term president of the National Academy of Sciences of the Ukraine, expert in electrometallurgy, recipient of dozens of most prestigious awards, and opponent of the ill-fated Chornobyl nuclear power plant.

The T-34 also ran on a wider track so it did not get stuck in the mud like the Panzers and the entire Wehrmacht invasion force, at least those who didn't freeze to death. The Germans decision to copy the Russian model failed but lacked the engineering technology to do it nor did they possess the necessary special alloys used in its construction. Even after the fall of the Soviet Union, the Ukrainian T-84 Tank built in the 1990s in Kharkiv was considered superior to rivals. (Andrew Kershaw, *Weapons & War Machines*, NY: Phoebus, 1976, 192; A. Gregorovich, "The Best Tank in the World", World War II in Ukraine, on the web)

Only a few years after Stalin's severe crushing of the peasants, as major events are not without minor consequences, the war situation described in an account with figures by Richard Evans helps to understand the backdrop of what happens next in the Ukraine. Overnight came the Germans: "On the first day alone, German air strikes against 66 Soviet airfields destroyed more than 1,200 Soviet aircraft, almost all of them before they had a chance to take off. Within the first week the German air force had damaged over 4,000 Soviet planes beyond repair.... It had already taken 600,000 prisoners by the end of the second week in July. By this time, more than 3,000 Soviet artillery pieces and 6,000 tanks had been captured or destroyed, or simply abandoned by the troops... Over 300,000 Red Army prisoners had died by the end of 1941 ... Over the whole course of the war, German forces took some 5.7 million Soviet prisoners. Official German records showed that 3,330,000 of them had perished by the time the war was over, or some 58 per cent of the total.... By comparison, 356,387 out of about 2 million German prisoners taken by the Red Army, mostly in the later stages of the war, did not survive, a death rate of almost 18 per cent. This was far in excess of the mortality rates of British, French and other servicemen in German captivity, which were below 2 per cent until the last chaotic months of war, not to mention those of German servicemen taken prisoner by the Western Allies." In his book on Japanese atrocities of Chinese in Manchuria in the 1930s, *Nanking, Anatomy of an Atrocity* (2000) Mashiro Yamamoto writes, "Only one in twenty five American POWs died under Nazi captivity, in contrast to one in three under the Japanese, and this in the war when "only about 90,000 American POWs – in the hands of the Nazis." (R. J. Evans, 179-84; M. Yamamoto, *Nanking, Anatomy of an Atrocity,* 2000, 286)

FDR'S $ LEND-LEASE GIVE-A-WAY TO STALIN: A DREAM BETWEEN HEAVEN AND HELL

Once FDR releases $40 million in funds for Soviet Russia late July 1941 prior to public acceptance of Lend-Lease shipments, the President sends his adviser Harry Hopkins on a special mission to the Kremlin. By August Hopkins is back with Roosevelt during FDR's secret meeting with Winston Churchill. In their first conference that takes place out at sea in Newfoundland's Placentia Bay Hopkins reported the mighty dictator appeared solid, small, only 190 pounds and built "like a football coach's dream of a tackle", and wore baggy pants, – not the *sharashka* of the Gulag!, – boots shining like mirrors, and talked direct and to the point in a low raspy voice. "It was like talking," Hopkins remarked, "to a perfectly coordinated machine, an intelligent machine." Stalin is obsessed with mistrust and suspicion of the West, in particular of Churchill and his fantastic anti-Soviet plots embellished by NKVD scenarios. Of course Stalin had his Cambridge agents and indispensable documents from their ace agent Kim Philby. Roosevelt himself does not figure in the same light. Hopkins and Stalin get along. Stalin convinces Hopkins that the old wolf knows Russia and military strategy that will overwhelm the German Army now 400 kilometers deep in hostile territory running low in supplies. "Even the German tanks run out of petrol," he said. The German tanks he said would find "moving mechanized forces through Russia was very different from moving them over the boulevards of Belgium and France".

Stalin asked the Consortium's emissary for "20,000 antiaircraft guns, thousands of heavy machine guns, a million rifles, high-octane gas, aluminum, 3,000 pursuit planes and 3,000 bombers." It would cost $2 billion. Hopkins asks General Yakovlev how much weighed the Russian tank. "It is a good tank," the Russian tersely replied.

Hopkins cabled FDR, "I feel ever so confident about this front. ... There is unbounded determination to win." In fact, the T-34 medium tank, superior to the German Mark IIIs and IVs, weighed 26.5 tons and could race at 31 mph (the Mark IVs moved at 25 mph with 25 tons). Stalin had some 1800 of these new tanks when Hitler attacked. Its guns were high-velocity 76-millimeters while the Mark IV carried a low-velocity 75-millimeter gun. The Soviet KV-1 (Klementi Voroshilov) heavy tank first developed in 1939 and at one time considered the most powerful tank in the world, was also superior in speed, guns and virtually impenetrable armour forcing German infantry to tackle the tanks head-on. Both tanks easily resisted German firepower except its 88-millimeter high-velocity antiaircraft gun. But the Germans had superior radio communications and logical support. (Alexander Bevin, Notes, 311)

In 1995, Gregorovich writes, "Today all over independent Ukraine there are discoveries of mass murder graves in the suburbs of cities (such as Bykivna in Kiev), and near all the KGB (NKVD) secret police stations throughout Ukraine.

The Ukrainian victims of Stalin's Soviet Russia number in the millions. Many Ukrainians are also buried in the mass graves of Siberia. It is unknown how many of these Ukrainian victims of the Soviet system perished during the war years. The retreating Soviet officials, for example, shipped 6 million cattle from Ukraine east to Russia, 550 large factories, thousands of small factories and 300,000 tractors. The USSR also evacuated 3.5 million skilled workers from Ukraine to the Russian Republic. In the Battle for Ukraine Soviet sources say the partisans blew up nearly 5,000 enemy trains, blasted 607 railway bridges, 915 warehouses, and damaged over 1,500 tanks and armoured carriers.

As the Soviet authorities and army retreated from Ukraine in 1941, Stalin's scorched earth policy left a trail of destruction including the Dniprohes Dam on the Dnieper River, which was the largest hydro electric power dam in Europe, countless mines and major industrial factories, and Khreschchatik Street in the capitol city of Kiev." (see <www.militaryfactory.com> for tank details)

Gregorvich tells of the terrible destruction: "On November 3, 1941 the famous architectural monument, the Dormition Cathedral in the Pecherska Lavra built 1073 in Kiev, was destroyed. Moscow tried to blame the Germans for destroying this superb example of medieval Ukrainian architecture but it was proven to be the work of a Soviet bomb squad which had mined it before their retreat and later set it off killing Germans. Moscow also ordered the evacuation to the east of the Government of the Ukrainian SSR, the Ukrainian Academy of Sciences, all Kiev, Kharkiv and other university personnel, scientists, skilled technicians, Soviet bureaucrats, and most NKVD (KGB) secret police to be evacuated east to Russia. The Ukrainian Government and the Academy of Sciences were relocated in Ufa, Siberia."

Roosevelt rattles his cabinet to get Stalin all he needs double-quick. He berates Stimson like no other. "The Russians have been given the run-around," he tells the old man. "I am sick and tired of hearing that they are going to get this and they are going to get that. Whatever we are going to give them, it has to be over there by the first of October, and the only answer I want to hear is that it is under way." FDR exploded when he learns 40 P-40 pursuit planes had been sent to England instead of Russia. "Get the planes right off with a bang next week!" he yells. (T. Morgan, *FDR,* 593)

That fall 1941 while Hitler and his press chief Otto Dietrich were clicking heels and glasses proclaiming victory in Russia Göering tells Mussolini's fascist foreign minister Constanzo Ciano, "This year between twenty and thirty million persons will die of hunger in Russia. Perhaps it is well that it should be so, for certain nations must be decimated. But even if it were not, nothing can be done about it. It is obvious that if Humanity is condemned to die of hunger, the last to die will be our two peoples. ... In the camps for Russian prisoners they have begun to eat each other." Interesting this analysis of hunger whether it be inflicted by an external invader, or an internal tyrant, the reaction of the outsider is the same, "Better the other than me."

"The Jews and the Slavic peoples," Shirer wrote, "were the *Untermenschen* ("subhumans"). Slavs like Jews had to be stamped out, used only to toil as slaves of the State in mines, factories and fields. Stalin's orders were clear. Zhdanov proclaimed Stalin's will to the Special Departments and Red Army. 'When moving forward don't try to capture one or other point but...burn to ashes these populated areas. So the German staffs and units will be buried...Toss away any sentiment and destroy all populated areas you meet on your way'." Even the American General Staff in July "confidentially informed American editors and Washington correspondents that the collapse of the Soviet Union was only a matter of a few weeks." The fascist Galeazzo Ciano, 2nd Count of Cortellazzo and Buccari (1903-1944), in 1931 marries the *Duce*'s eldest and favourite child, Edda, and becomes Mussolini's dauphin; his father Constanzo Ciano, born in 1876, had been a hero in the Italian navy in WWI, liked to be called "Admiral", turned fascist after the war becoming a MP in 1921, and acquired *Il Telegrafo* to promote his career in politics rising to serve Mussolini as foreign minister, and ambassador to Great Britain. In January 1944 he was executed by firing squad with five other prisoners; his son escaped a similar fate.(W. Shirer, *The Rise and Fall of the Third Reich,* 854, in Ciano's Diplomatic Papers, 464; R. J. B. Bosworth, *Mussolini's Italy, Life Under the Fascist Dictatorship, 1915-1945*, NY: Penguin, 2005, ed. 2007)

Hitler had given orders that Leningrad, formerly St Petersburg, was to be "wiped off the face of the earth". The elder Voroshilov is relieved swearing "we'll smash the Fascist scum!" Stalin in Moscow frets, "We might have to abandon 'Peter'." Under mortal threats from the Kremlin General Zhukov counter-attacked with hardened forces. Hitler was forced to call off the military assault and instead inflict a 900-day siege on the ancient city. But it is the German surrender at Stalingrad of Field Marshal Paulus and the Sixth Army February 2, 1943 that finally turns back the tide of war against Nazi conquest. It would never again mount its great Nazi blitzkriegs for a Nazi-ruled new order.

Financier-historian buff Barton Biggs calls Stalingrad "the greatest battle" of the "War of the Century". Nothing quite surpasses it. The population was to be annihilated. He himself called the invasion "the battle of annihilation" against "the Judeo Bolshevik conspiracy, commissars, and the Communist intelligentsia." Hitler added, "In this war for existence we have no interest in keeping even part of this great city's population." It would be Hitler's greatest defeat and spell the end of his "thousand-year Reich".

After Stalingrad all the horror fell upon Moscow. Hitler ordered his Panzers to spearhead Operation Typhoon. Some 2.2 million people were trapped and dying in Leningrad. In December 53,000 Soviet soldiers and civilians perish. Inhabitants are reduced to starvation. Once again cannibalism is not uncommon. By July 1942 it is thought since the start of the Nazi siege that the city lost a million more victims. Montefiore, who in the 1990s had access to unpublished Sovietfiles, reminds us "it was not rare to find a body lying in the hall of an apartment block with thighs and breasts carved off."

The ice of Lake Lagoda was the only way in for food and relief. Stalin raved at Zhdanov not to fall back but resort to extreme measures. "Don't waste time. Every moment's dear. The enemy concentrates power against Moscow. All other fronts have the chance to counter-attack. Seize the moment!" Stalin issues orders to shoot cowardly senior officers. Zhdanov replied, 'All will be done. … I've become as ferocious as a dog!'" If Moscow falls, Zhdanov and Stalin issue ultimate orders to blow up buildings, killing civilians but burying German officers and German staff entrenched in the city's cellars. Hitler's directive September 29 ordered Moscow totally destroyed: "The further existence of this large city is of no interest once Soviet Russia is overthrown." Bent to do to what they did to Stalingrad, Hitler issues orders to "raze it to the ground by artillery and by continuous air attack". (S. S. Montefiore, 388-90)

Somehow in all this chaos Stalin was able to host Harriman arrives in September to settle terms on belated American aid package in a last ditch effort to forestall the demise of Mother Russia. Along with Harriman is Lord Beaverbrook, member of the British War Cabinet and the Canadian press czar and some hundred guests seated in the regal 18th century Catherine Hall for a royal banquet hosted by Stalin in the Kremlin palace. Opposite him sat Molotov with Mikoyan who negotiated the western aid package. Stalin is observed "very restless, walking about and smoking continuously". He slams down an unopened letter from Churchill. "The paucity of your offers clearly shows you want to see the Soviet Union defeated!" Harriman, Beaverbrook and the guests feast on "hors d'oeuvres, caviar, soup, and fish, suckling pig, chicken and game, ice cream and cakes, washed down with champagne, vodka wine and Armenian brandy".

Stalin toasts victory. Molotov did what was expected. Thirty two toasts! Stalin clapped, drank (probably water) and talks uninterrupted. With his keen eye of a reporter on Stalin Lord Beaverbrook recorded the night activities, and queries the Great Executioner if President Kalinin still keeps a harem of Bolshoi ballerinas? Stalin jesters, "He's too old. Do you"? In the cinema, by the time Stalin suggests a third movie, the Germans have already smashed the Red Army on their advance to Moscow.

In June, when Churchill arrives on a mission which he considers no more practical than that of "carrying a lump of ice to the North Pole". Compelled to warn Stalin there would be no second front that year, Harriman gathers round British Ambassador Sir Archibald Clark Kerr and Commissars Molotov and Voroshilov to hear the bad news. Stalin answers, "You can't win wars without taking risks." He adds later, "You mustn't be so afraid of the Germans." During a sumptuous banquet held in Churchill's honor and Molotov – encouraged by Stalin – pumping toasts for three hours and nineteen courses, Stalin invites Churchill to retire to his quarters deep within the Kremlin for a private bottle, or two. "Have the stresses of this war been as bad to you personally as carrying through the policy of collective farms?" Churchill asks. 'Oh no', replied Stalin revealingly. That had been 'a terrible struggle'."

Montefiore reveals how the Big Three – Stalin, Churchill and FDR – all teased and jostled over inside jokes safe only for the ears of masters of the world while nations of the world and the human race are butchered at will. Brothers in war! Comrades! Drink to our Victory! Stalin asks for one of Churchill's cigars. On the last page of Montefiore's account the tone of this astounding tale is captured by Martha Peshkova, who as a child once played with Stalin but now she believes murdered her father and her grandfather, the famous writer and early Bolshevik Maxim Gorky: "Stalin was as clever as he was cruel. Politics in Stalin's time was like a closed jar with intriguers fighting one another to the death. What a frightening time!" (S. S. Montefiore, 422)

The death figures from the Second World War are atrocious as near the same as in the First. The masses hadn't yet learned their lesson but what could they do under the heel of the Consortium capitalists who controlled the industry and press in West while investing and financing the economies of totalitarian client states? What could they do, with bayonets at their back and flags waving them on. War is good business to the merchants of death proclaiming their holy mission with beautiful words of glory for the good and happiness of mankind. All it takes for a good world war is more fodder and fuel. Laurence Rees in his book *War of the Century, When Hitler Fought Stalin* (1999) figured the death toll of Soviet citizens at 25 million. These numbers, now widely accepted, are absolutely astounding to a westerner not familiar with Russian losses in the First World War or under Stalin's regime of purges and widespread terror and the Genocide of the Holodomor. Looking back with the vantage of perspective and hindsight is it any wonder that neither FDR nor other leaders in the West objected to Stalin's draconian Terror-Famine?

Reasserting Russia's economic and political prestige in the world beset by the plunge in the price of oil on which it staked its recent monetary visit to Poland in September, 2009, Vladimir V. Putin described the Second World War as the "bloodiest, most horrible war in the history of Humanity". In the same story, a recent Russian poll reported "two thirds of Russians think the Soviet Union could have defeated Nazi Germany alone". An alarming conclusion. Fortunately, a figure for how many more millions of patriotic Russians would have been lost fighting the full force of Nazi military fury to save Mother Russia, had there been no American Lend-Lease, or how many millions were saved because of it is inestimable. What is certain it shortened by years the war that still brings tears to their eyes. (Michael Shwirtz, "In a Visit, Putin Tries To Ease Rifts With Poland", *The NYT*, Sept. 2, 2009)

Corporate America's "Uncle Joe" had no problem eliminating his fellow citizens, friends and their wives, children and family alike all perished in his Soviet inferno. Stalin purged his own family killing at least two brothers in law, and imprisoning two sisters in law. A third brother-in-law Pavel Alliluyev was poisoned in the Kremlin. Alliluyev's daughter, and Stalin's niece, Kira said, "Of course, he knew he couldn't arrest my father. He wouldn't be able to prove to my mother that he was an enemy of the people. So he got rid of him." All the same, reader, Kira and her mother are imprisoned. She says her life after her father's murder "was like something out of a Shakespearean tragedy. … He was clearly above everyone else. He didn't see anything around him, he just wanted people to say 'Yes' to everything he did. … My life was really destroyed. But what should I do about it. I decided to be an optimist. So I go on living. You can't go back and change things." Her daughter Svetlana Alliluyev describes what it was like living in Stalin's world. "Did I know a single person whose life turned out well? It was as though my father were at the center of a black circle and anyone who ventured inside vanished or perished or was destroyed in one way or another."

Harrison Salisbury put the sentiment down another way, in his seminal work, *The 900 Days: The Siege of Leningrad* (1969, 1985), and he wrote, "Hardly a day passed in which someone in the Kremlin, some high official, was not threatened with execution or actually executed. This was the special quality of the epoch, the flavor of the Stalinist-Leninist system, the medieval concentration of power, the Florentine nature of Stalin's 'court', the paranoid aura of Kremlin life. Marshal Bulganin was not talking idly when he said once to Nikita Khrushchev, 'A man doesn't know when he is called to the Kremlin whether he will emerge alive or not'." (Laurence Rees, *War of the Century, When Hitler Fought Stalin*, NY Press, 1999, 27; Svetlana Alliluyev, *Twenty Letters to a Friend*, NY: Harper & Row, 1967; Harrison E. Salisbury, *The 900 Days: The Siege of Leningrad*, 1969, 1985 ed., Da Capo Press, 576)

We may include a brief note here on Nikolai Aleksandrovich Bulganin (1895-75) who survived Stalin, rising steadily in the ranks, a Bolshevik in 1919, in the Cheka; a Stalin loyalist in industry and electricity in Moscow by 1934 the Communist Party's XVII Party Congress elects him candidate member of the Central Committee and in the Great Patriotic War. Bulganin serves in the State Defense Committee as Stalin's link to the Red Army. As Chairman of the Soviet Council of Ministers, and officially head of the delegation, Khrushchev in his memoirs (1970) tells many anecdotes including their trip to London in April 1956 for a state visit when Eden is Prime Minister, and invited to stay at Eden's country home, and at Chequers. They also have a pleasant meeting with the Queen. "She met us as we came into the palace', Khrushchev recalls "She had her husband and two of her children with her... She was dressed in a plain, white dress. She looked like the sort of young woman you'd be likely to meet walking along Gorky Street on a balmy summer afternoon.... I was very impressed by the Queen. She had such a gentle, calm voice. She was completely unpretentious, completely without the haughtiness that you'd expect of royalty. She may be the Queen of England but in our eyes she was first and foremost the wife of her husband and the mother of her children." (N. Khrushchev. "Visit to London", *Khrushchev Remembers*, 401-14)

SS Chief Heinrich Himmler tells how it is for the Ukrainians and Belorussians who survived Stalinist persecution and now faced death under German occupation. On October 4, 1943 the Nazi SS butcher declares, "What happens to a Russian, to a Czech does not interest me in the slightest.... What the nations can offer in the way of good blood of our type we will take if necessary by kidnapping their children and raising them here with us. Whether nations live in prosperity or starve to death like cattle interests me only in so far as we need them as slaves to our Kultur; otherwise it is of no interest to me. Whether 10,000 Russian females fall down from exhaustion while digging an antitank ditch interests me only in so far as the antitank ditch for Germany is finished...". Kidnapping women, code-named "Hay Action", was carried out by Field Marshal Model's Army Group Ukraine-North. (W. Shirer, *The Rise and Fall of the Third Reich*, 937-8)

In violation of Hague and Geneva Conventions the Nazis impressed "hundreds of thousands" of POWs in addition to two million prisoners of war by the end of

September 1944 added to their foreign labor force half working armament and munition industries. Albert Speer admitted at the 1945-46 Nuremberg trial that forty percent of all POWs are employed in 1944 in weapons production, munitions and subsidiary war factories. The Nazis even used Russians to man their artillery; in 1943 Field Marshall Milch of the Air Force orders 50,000 Russian war prisoners in addition to the 30,000 already operating anti-aircraft artillery. "It is amusing that Russians must work the guns," Milch declares. (W. Shirer, *The Rise and Fall of the Third Reich,* 947-8)

The stocky pig-headed Gen. Koch was passionately contemptuous of Slavs. Hitler appointed this taskmaster of horrors and brutality to be his *Reichcommissar* of the Ukraine and Regional Leader of East Prussia. "We are the Master Race and must govern hard but just," declared Koch in his speech in Kiev March 5, 1943. "I will draw the very last out of this country. I did not come to spread bliss...The population must work, work, and work again. ...We definitely did not come here to give out manna. We have come here to create the basis for victory. We are a master race, which must remember that the lowliest German worker is racially and biologically a thousand times more valuable than the population here."

When German armies advanced on Russia's oil fields in the Caucasus, Martin Borman, Hitler's party Secretary wrote a long letter to Rosenberg resounding Hitler's racial dogma. Borman to Rosenberg: "The Slavs are to work for us. In so far as we don't need them, they may die. Therefore compulsory vaccination and German health services are superfluous. The fertility of the Slavs is undesirable. They may use contraceptives or practice abortion – the more the better. Education is dangerous. It is enough if they can count up to 100 ... Every educated person is a future enemy. Religion we leave to them as a means of diversion. As for food they won't get any more than is absolutely necessary. We are the masters. We come first." *Reichkommissar* Koch immediately closed local schools, declaring children needed to learn to obey instruction from their German masters. It was Koch who declared, His brutality is best exemplified by his remark, "If I meet a Ukrainian worthy of being seated at my table, I must have him shot." (W. Shirer, *The Rise and Fall of the Third Reich*, 939; R. J. Evans, 188; re. "If I meet a Ukrainian worthy ...", Norman Davies, *Europe at War*, Macmillan, 2006)

Ten years after Stalin's terror starvation repression devastates the Ukrainians, Shirer focused on the refined Genocidal techniques of Hitler's friend and the Nazi Reich's ideological philosopher and minister for the occupied eastern territories Alfred Rosenberg: "The job of feeding the German people stands at the top of the list of Germany's claims on the East. The southern (Russian) territories will have to serve ... for the feeding of the German people. We see absolutely no reason for any obligation on our part to feed also the Russian people with the products of that surplus territory. We know that his is a harsh necessity, bare of any feelings...The future will hold very hard years in store for the Russians."

Mass starvation and extermination have become morally acceptable justified by the superiority of a dominating dogma. Whereas the Holodomor might have served as a warning its methodology has become the practice, only worse as total war assumes the evil of limitless barbarism. We saw that in the Consortium support for Stalin. With Göering in charge of the economic exploitation of the USSR his long directive dated May 23, 1941 to his Economic Staff four weeks before the Nazi invasion of the Ukraine instructs that surplus food must go to Germans, and not to industrial areas in Ukraine targeted for destruction.

A week after the invasion Hitler appointed *Reichsmarschall* Göring responsible for running the economic affairs of Nazi occupied eastern territories, undercutting Rosenberg. It was Göring who had appointed Eric Koch as Reich commissioner of the Ukraine. By May 2, 1941 the Nazi high command agreed that Nazi victory in the West necessitated that the Wehrmacht "be fed at the expense of Russia" in spite of the eventuality that "tens of millions of men will undoubtedly starve to death". Famine and food were weapons of necessary destruction and key to victory. "Support of the war economy" had to be, as it was for Stalin and the Consortium support for the Socialist regime of state terror during the Holodomor, "the highest law" and the new conquered Slav territories would be "exploited economically with colonial methods."

These "methods" altogether understandable to Elihu Root and his protégé Henry Stimson and fellow lawyers, financiers and businessmen in the Consortium during America's occupation of the Philippines and his tenure there as Governor just prior to resuming the helm as chief of foreign policy for President Hoover. Göring had no trouble anticipating what he called "the biggest mass death in Europe since the Thirty Years War".

Neither the Holodomor nor the subsequent Holocaust would compare to the carnage Hitler's Wehrmacht vowed to inflict on the USSR. "The German Administration in these territories." Göering declares, "may well attempt to mitigate the consequences of the famine which undoubtedly will take place and to accelerate the return to primitive agricultural conditions. However, these measures will not avert famine. Any attempt to save the population there from death by starvation by importing surpluses from the black-soil zone would be at the expense of supplies to Europe. It would reduce Germany's staying power in the war, and would undermine Germany's and Europe's power to resist the blockade." (M. Mazower, *Hitler's Empire,* 146-7)

On May 2 a meeting of Nazi state secretaries estimated the death toll. "There is no doubt that as a result, many millions of persons will be starved to death if we take out of the country the things necessary for us." Göering and Rosenberg make it clear that the order must be "clearly and absolutely understood". Completely understood! No exceptions! On order of the Nazi state nationalism planning authorities from the great country of *Kultur* that had given the world Beethoven, Bach and Goethe, Shirer concluded that no German is on record for having protested these officially organized and systematically implemented measures "to put millions of human beings to death by starvation".

For Shirer the lack of protest seemed incredible, and he writes, "In all the memoranda concerning the German directives for the spoliation of Russia, there is no mention of anyone's objecting – as at least some of the generals did in regard to the Commissar Order. …For weeks and months, it is evident from the records, hundreds of German officials toiled away at their desks in the cheerful light of the warm spring days, adding up figures and composing memoranda which coldly calculated the massacre of millions. By starvation, in this case. Heinrich Himmler, the mild-faced ex-chicken farmer, also sat at his desk at SS headquarters in Berlin those days, gazing through his pince-nez at plans for the massacre of other millions in a quicker and more violent way."

But hadn't the Consortium partnership with Stalin showed Hitler the way and even given a clear green signal to what had become no longer unutterable but instead an officially sanctioned government policy of ethnic-cleansing here once again in the Ukraine by the fact of the recent historic precedence of the Holodomor of encouragement of, support for, and profit from their investment in the crime? Even worse, but inescapably true is the Consortium can not evade premeditated and complicit responsibility proven by their cover-up by all the means available including government collusion within the State Department and press organizations of complicity with Stalin's state socialist terror regime. Of course, the brilliant legal experts in the State Department and in the firms of Wall Street and around the country that serve the Consortium will argue against any guilt by association. Anything less would be moral suicide. Is that worse than patricide? (W. L. Shirer, *The Rise and Fall of the Third Reich*, 1960, 833)

Once the guns silenced in 1918 the victors escalated the war by economic means. "The Treaty of Versailles did not end hostilities between the participants in the First World War", wrote historian Benjamin Higgins who comments in *The Economic War since 1918*, "The scene of battle was merely shifted from military to economic fronts." This was no secret. Everyone at the table knew it to be so. Winner take all. The violence of lies, war and propaganda cut deep and tear the heart and soul out of all the words of rhetoric. Morality is the first casualty of war. In the usurpation of power and wealth the victor always holds the higher moral ground. Benjamin Higgins writes "for two decades the war was carried on with economic weapons. Slow, subtle, and unspectacular in their action as compared with military weapons, these economic weapons are none the less deadly in the destruction of national welfare; and, as is often the case with military instruments of war, the effective use of economic instruments exposes the user to grave danger and prompts retaliation in kind". Benjamin Higgins quotes Schacht on Germany's need for markets and need for capital and he observes how Germany fell into "severe financial straights" having invested in American stocks that crashed. These profound symptoms of economic woe mattered much less to FDR transfixed by America's surge as a global power and long unemployment lines. (re. on the effects of the First World War. (Benjamin Higgins, *The Economic War since 1918*, 135; Willard Waller, *War in the Twentieth Century*, Dryden Press/ Random House, 1940)

"THIS IS NO PEACE; THIS IS ONLY A TRUCE FOR TWENTY YEARS"

It was an outrageous treaty to formally end an outrageous war in order to create conditions for an outrageous New World Order set in an outrageous scene of the old world. And all the diplomats, lawyers and politicians, representatives of their countries arrived in Paris to sit at the conference table in the Hall of Mirrors which made them look even more ridiculous. Only the Bols stayed away and out of the muck. To blame for the Versailles fiasco must stand tall the US President Woodrow Wilson who betrayed the political mandate that got him re-elected in 1916, forced the resignation of his Secretary of State leaving the government at the mercy of Baruch's War Industries Board (WIB), Lansing's State Department dominated by Wall Street types and the Consortium stable of greedy corrupt bankers. No wonder the President went home mocked, humiliated and ridiculed for the pomposity of the spectacle he orchestrated with his bogus plan for a League of Nations that finally proves to be either too much a sham or too far ahead of its time and in a decade rejected by both Tokyo and Berlin.

Wilson expected to hold the laurels of victory before the whole world of true believers. With the British delegation in Paris is the British economist John Maynard Keynes; Keynes will return after World War II to lecture Bretton Woods. For the Americans, Paul Warburg, the Fed chairman represents the Consortium; his brother Max is there too representing the German Government as head of the banking firm of M. M. Warburg and Co. handling German finances and chief of German intelligence. British Foreign Secretary Lord Curzon, Consortium bigwig and a conference delegate dismisses the proceedings for its shadowy intent and declares: "This is no peace; this is only a truce for twenty years." The terms of the Versailles Treaty were setting the stage for a second world war. Lord Curzon is indeed prophetic: he picks the actual year that World War II will commence! Even John Maynard Keynes worries over the inherent flaws in the Treaty, writing, "The peace is outrageous and impossible and can bring nothing but misfortune behind it".

One of the planks of Versailles called for large amounts of war reparations to be paid by Germany to the victorious nations. This plank alone of the Treaty caused more grief back home than any other and precipitated at least three events: "hyperinflation" of the German mark (1920-23); the destruction of Germany's middle class actually rising before the war; Adolf Hitler, a dictator who promised to end inflation and restore pride to the German people and the country to its former high rank among the world powers. And who wrote the plank? The Consortium's prized Princeton lawyer in the firm Cromwell & Sullivan John Foster Dulles, one of the founders of the CFR, and later crowned as Eisenhower's Secretary of State.

In addition to writing the Treaty of Versailles, the nations who were victorious in the war also wrote the Charter of the League of Nations, which was ratified on January 10, 1920, and signed by President Wilson for the American government. Wilson brought the treaty back to the United States and asked the Senate to ratify it The Senate, remembering George Washington's advice to avoid foreign entanglements and reflecting the views of the American people who did not wish to enter the League, refused to ratify the treaty. Wilson was not pleased, possibly because he not only came to see himself as the nation sees him expressed by his arch nemesis Senator Henry Cabot Lodge as "a future President of the world." The

Treaty never is ratified by Congress. Wilson and Lenin, both frail and weak, cut off and isolated from their people, the spirit of life drained leaving them looking sick and ghostly are possessed by death in 1924.

Lord Riddell's *Intimate Diary of the Peace Conference and After, 1918-1923,* published a decade later, in 1934, recalls an interesting statement by British Labour PM David Lloyd George, March 30, 1919, on the subject of the Versailles Peace negotiations. Riddle and Lloyd George were both Pilgrims and very proud of it. "The truth is that we have got our way. We got most of the things we set out to get. The German navy has been handed over, the German mercantile shipping has been handed over, and the German colonies have been given up. One of our chief trade competitors has been most seriously crippled, and our Allies are about to become her biggest creditors. That is no small achievement." (Lord Riddell, *Intimate Diary of the Peace Conference and After, 1918-1923*, Reynal, 1934)

What was this arrangement of Anglo-American elite and how did it affect Soviet Russia and contribute to the Genocide of the Ukrainians of the Holodomor? How did this exclusive network intertwine with the Consortium capitalists of America's elite business establishment in pursuit of a new chapter of imperialist goals of empire in the 21st century?

These questions are essential to understanding the people who rule the world but shirk their role and responsibility in destroying it and without serious consideration of these questions issues of accountability, guilt and responsibility are mere hearsay. Consequently the culprits will all pretend their innocence and then always get away with mass murder and Humanity as we know it will fall deeper into a black hole of oblivion and lostness until it ceases to exist and no one knows the difference between what is Right and what is wrong because no one dares to ask the question. Charles Savoie researched the boney hand of the Pilgrims Society where only Might is Right is the cardinal creed.

STRANGE CONNECTIONS: SOVIET RUSSIA AND ENGLAND'S PILGRIMS SOCIETY

Much research needs to be done yet among many members already identified Charles Savoie finds plenty of interesting connections between Soviet Russia and England's Pilgrims Society to give the reader a good idea of how membership was tied to political influence and corporate power. To illustrate this Charles Savoie helps us to focus attention on some of the more important senior elite of the Pilgrims Society, and he writes, "So thoroughly were members of the Pilgrims involved with the Communist Revolution in 1916-1918, that certain of their young operatives present there, became members later. Included among these we note Norman Armour, of the fabulously rich Chicago meat-packing family, an embassy Secretary at Petrograd, Russia, 1916-1918 during the coup days (sic), and who later held ambassadorships to Canada, Chile, Argentina, Venezuela, Spain and Guatemala. He escapes with his wife, the White Russian Princess Myra Kondacheff, February 2, 1919 (*Who's Who* 1958); Walter Hampton Mallory, special assistant to the American ambassador in Petrograd and president of the China Institute in America, 1943-47, and a member of Pilgrims Society member in John D. Rockefeller Jr.'s China Medical Board beginning in 1947, Pilgrims Society member controlling their public kindergarten, the Council on Foreign Relations from 1927 into the 1960's and later an emeritus director. He was decorated the Order of Pure Gold by China; Post Wheeler (*Pilgrims United States, Who's Who*, 1927) was Secretary at the embassy in St. Petersburg, Russia, 1909-1911; Joshua Butler Wright, son-in-law of real admiral W. H. H. Southerland (*Who's Who* 1927) was counselor at the American embassy in Petrograd, Russia, in 1916, Secretary of the American delegation at the Opium Conference at The Hague, 1913, a whitewash of the Chinese opium traffic that brought fame and fortune to the founders of London's Pilgrims. Wright was US Commissioner at the Brazilian Centennial Exposition in Rio de Janeiro in 1922 and Secretary of the US delegation to the 5th International Conference of American States in Santiago, Chile, in 1923. Pilgrims Society member Isaac F. Marcosson (born 1877) wrote *The Rebirth of Russia* (1917), the same year he wrote *The Business of War*, very profitable for his Pilgrims Society cronies. Another Pilgrims Society member, Henry Cutler Wolfe (born 1898) wrote *The Imperial Soviets* (1940) and went long with the American Relief Administration in Russia in 1922, the Hoover front for assisting the Bolsheviks. Wolfe was a contributor to *Harper's* magazine, *Saturday Review, The New York Times, The Wall Street Journal.*"

Not many readers may be familiar with the name Walter Rathenau cited by Quincy Howe in his 1940 study *How the War of 1939 Began.* No matter, reader, so few are remembered or living today but their contribution is lasting. Look! It's clear for all to see. And to unravel the story it is not quite as dark and impenetrable as some may think. Howe, a leading establishment author in his time describes the dilemma of Walter Rathenau, the former head of Germany's public utilities company AEG, the GE subsidiary. A brilliant philosopher, engineer and industrialist after the war, in 1921, Rathenau becomes Germany's minister of reconstruction; the next year as foreign minister he negotiates the Treaty of Rapallo with the Soviets and Lenin's Russia still deep in chaos torn apart by revolution and civil war, famine and disease. (Quincy Howe, "How the War of 1939 Began", in *War in the Twentieth Century,* 1940)

Rathenau, a Jew of exceptional talent, "had done a superhuman job of conserving German resources during the First World War". Rathenau directs the wartime allocation of Germany's raw materials. Howe describes him as "a combination of Owen D. Young, Herbert Hoover, and Bernard Baruch", all Consortium collaborators. Howe observes that Rathenau signs a treaty with Moscow increasing trade, "exchanges of military secrets, and close political cooperation". Unfortunately, he maneuvers in sync with the Versailles reparations scheme and after the collapse of the German mark, in 1923, two right-wing army anti-Semites assassinate him. That triggers a spiral of violence that augers doom for the Weimar Republic and set events spinning through the Holodomor years towards WWII. This same year, in 1923, Schacht is appointed president of the Reichsbank, Germany's central bank. Still in his thirties Schacht takes over as head of the Dresdner Bank and the Bank of Issue in occupied Belgium. In fact Schacht is Germany's top banker who negotiates a huge loan to restore the worthless German currency with gold from the Bank of England.

During the Nazi era, however, the Rathenau men continued in his footsteps. "The Rathenau school was economic, not political", Howe writes. "It did not interest itself in what sort of government might exist in either Russia or Germany. It saw great possibilities for cooperation and exchange of goods between Germany, the most highly industrialized country in Europe, and Russia with its untapped store of raw materials and its enormous need for industrial goods." In fact, Rathenau is thought to be the role model for Arnheim, the German industrialist character in Robert Musil's well-known novel, *The Man Without Qualities.* Although he negotiates the Soviet's return to the bankers table and restores Germany-Russian trade, Rathenau in *Kritik der dreifachen Revolution* (*Critique of the Triple Revolution*) ultimately rejects the Soviet model as unworkable.

Rathenau observes: "We cannot use Russia's methods, as they only and at best prove that the economy of an agrarian nation can be leveled to the ground; Russia's thoughts are not our thoughts. They are, as it is in the spirit of the Russian city intelligence, unphilosophical and highly dialectic; they are passionate logic based on unverified suppositions. They assume that a single good, the destruction of the capitalist class, weighs more than all other goods, and that poverty, dictatorship, terror and the fall of civilization must be accepted to secure this one good. ... If ten million people must die to free ten million people from the bourgeoisie, then this is a harsh but necessary consequence. The Russian idea is compulsory happiness, in the same sense and with the same logic as the compulsory introduction of Christianity and the Inquisition." While that may seem incomprehensible and antithetical to moralists revolted by the trade-off in lives, unfortunately Rathenau was right. His assessment was accurate to the time. But his voice was silenced. It serves as a lesson to the present to wake up and take notice of life suspended in the balance of who lives and who is to die. Political leaders and tyrants, doctors and refugee relief workers are faced with making these decisions this very moment. (Quincy Howe, "How the War of 1939 Began", *War in the Twentieth Century*, 1940)

A history professor at Union College found that the total number of men killed in the First World War "was more than twice the number killed in *all* the wars participated in by European powers from 1790 through 1913". An incredible statistic! Civilian losses were even higher! Yet the Consortium still didn't finish the job. Serious estimates put the cost of the First World War at $337 billion. The Versailles Treaty or perhaps better known as the Carthaginian Peace stripped Germany of another $6 billion of foreign investments or one tenth of the Hohenzollern Empire's national wealth. It lost one eighth of her livestock, one tenth of factories, one sixth of its precious arable land. Its merchant marine, or those ships not picked up by Harriman, is cut to 500,000 tons, one eleventh its prewar size. The Weimar Republic's great navy was reduced to only a few aging vessels, no more than 15,000 personnel, and its army restricted to 100,000 or one sixth its prewar strength. Postwar Germany was forbidden to manufacture, purchase or own tanks, armored cars, military or naval airplanes, poison gases, or submarines. And it happened that the whole country is bankrupt, its currency worthless, its population near starving and burdened with Versailles debt and reparations.

Meanwhile, England is free to expand its empire of world resources to include 99.5% of world jute, 94% nickel, 58% rubber, 51% wool, 44.5 % lead, while its deficient in none of the basic raw materials of coal, iron, cotton, oil, rubber, and copper. In spite of all that, still not satisfied, the blood-sucking capitalist Consortium bankers ram through the Young Plan in 1929 and ratified the next year over the protests from both German nationalists and communists. It seems nothing will satisfy the Consortium except another war and they will do anything in their devious underhanded way to have it. (Walter Consuelo Langsam, Chapter "The Peace of Paris: Europe Between Two Wars", *The Quest of Empire*, Foreign Policy Association, 1939, 143-4)

The problem of raw materials weighs on the balance beam between the Holodomor and the Holocaust. On the other hand, with Rathenau out of the way, Germany's critical need for raw materials found another proponent in Hjalmar Schacht quoted January 1937 in the CFR's own flagship, *Foreign Affairs*. "Before the war," Schacht points out, "Germany's world investments were in round figures $12,000 millions, the profits of which could be used to buy raw materials all over the world. The markets where raw materials were procured were completely free." No monopoly of basic commodity supplies, smooth gold standard, immigration unrestricted. "All these elementary principles of international trade and intercourse have now disappeared", Schacht declared. German foreign investments were wiped out by Versailles. He lamented, "Germany remains the lone unsatisfied large Power." Schacht urges that Germany be allowed to "produce raw materials on territory under its own management. Second, this colonial territory must form part of her monetary system." (*Foreign Affairs*, January 1937)

So we know in the network of international finance as president of the Reichsbank Schacht holds a prominent role in reorganizing German finances under the Consortium's Dawes Plan (1924-29) as also does another German banker Carl Melchior. Charles G. Dawes is chairman of the Allied Committee of Experts in 1924. When that plan fails, Owen Young is appointed chairman of the Committee, in 1929, (another Five-Year Plan?) with alternates Morgan partner Thomas W. Lamont and T. N. Perkins, a banker close to the Morgan clan. The Consortium path to war through monetary reform is a bumpy road marked by trial and error. Throughout the government central bankers are beleaguered by the inexorable problem of reparation debts and Germany's inability to pay roughly 3 billion marks a year.

The capitalists are unrelenting inventing one scheme compounding interest upon interest. Quincy Howe described the Dawes Plan as "first of a series of agreements by which the Allies reduced Germany's reparations obligations and at the same time made loans to the German government and to German industry in order to increase her ability to pay". Consortium bankers and politicians finally fixed German reparations at an annual fee of 132 billion gold marks – about one quarter of Germany's total 1921 exports. By 1923 inflation was astronomical (1,261 *trillion* times the 1913 level).

The British are willing to cut the reparations bill in half. Germany is unable to meet its debt requirements to the bank and fails to pay. At the table the French balked. French and Belgium troops stormed into the Ruhr valley. In 1924 the Consortium appoints a committee of bankers led by American banker Charles G. Dawes to develop a new system of reparations payments. The new Dawes Plan is essentially a JP Morgan Co. scheme to arrange a series of foreign loans totaling $800 million with proceeds flowing to Germany raised for the most part in the US from dollar investors and used in the mid-1920s to create and consolidate the cartels of IG Farben and Vereinigte Stahlwerke. And reader it should be remembered that by 1924 Germany is struggling to pay its reparations war debt. Quincy Howe writes, "Germany met her obligations, paying altogether some 11,096 millions of marks" ($5.5 billion). That year Germany borrows another 18.2 billion from abroad destined to stimulate German industries and municipalities.

When the Dawes Plan fails to make the Germans pay the impossible reparation debts the bankers renegotiate, in 1929, and devise the Young Plan. But it doesn't fly; Schacht calls the latest reparations package inflationary and a deal with demands impossible to sustain. In protest Schacht resigns from the Reichsbank and in 1930 he is replaced by Hans Luther who tells his British confident John Wheeler-Bennett, "This is a historic day in German banking. For the first time in our history we have not enough gold to cover our paper." Schacht then quits the German Democratic Party in the Weimar regime.

By 1931 the impact of international financial crisis completely wacks Germany draining its gold reserves and foreign exchange from the Reichsbank forces Hoover's hand. Germany's creditors are now dangerous on the precipice too heavily in debt. In July Hoover announces his moratorium on German debt and Congress passes it into law. (Victoria Schofield, *Witness to History*, 66)

It should be obvious to the reader that the Morgan-Rockefeller-Harriman Anglo-American Consortium – add Mellon, Carnegie if you insist along with other billionaires too many to list – was playing a deadly game. But this is exactly the nature of their "Game". Sutton traces Hitler's rise to the failure of the Young Plan (1928). Accordingly we can trace the Holodomor to a parallel spiral of events by the key bankers of the Consortium, in particular the Soviet Five-Year Plans (1928). Both Schacht and Nazi industrialist Fritz Thyssen date the rise of Hitler in 1933 to the unrealistic goals set by greedy Morgan bankers. The German steel scion Thyssen is of the opinion "the financial debt thus created was bound to disrupt the entire economy of the Reich". Schacht is more specific, writing "Fritz Thyssen claims that, I turned to the National Socialist Party only after I became convinced that the fight against the Young Plan was unavoidable if complete collapse of Germany was to be prevented." He adds, "The difference between the Young Plan and the Dawes Plan was that, while the Young Plan required payments in goods produced in Germany financed by foreign loans, the Young Plan required monetary payments." (A. C. Sutton, "The Young Plan", *Wall Street and the Rise of Hitler*)

British historian A. J. Taylor summed up the folly of the bankers while excusing issues of responsibility or even accountability not wishing to point a finger this way or that. Taylor's explanation offers neither an excuse nor justification for the greed of the bankers and their grotesque ambition neither of which was short-sighted. Reader, Taylor reads well but his rhetoric is not very convincing at all. Those bloody stoic British principles! How well they served the colonization of Empire. "The British government feared to offend economic principle," Taylor writes, "even more than to offend Hitler. Pandora's secret box which Schacht had opened in Germany and which the American New Deal had also revealed was still unknown to them. Wedded to stable prices and a stable pound, they regarded increased public spending as a great evil, excusable only in the event of actual war, and even then lamentable... The British government still lived in the psychological atmosphere of 1931: more terrified of a flight from the pound than of defeat in war." (A. J. Taylor, 118-9)

Sutton writes, "Schacht's parallel charge that Owen Young was responsible for the rise of Hitler, while obviously self-serving, is recorded in a US Government Intelligence report relating the interrogation of Dr. Fritz Thyssen in September, 1945: 'The acceptance of the Young Plan and its financial principles increased unemployment more and more, until about one million were unemployed. People were desperate. Hitler said he would do away with unemployment. The government in power at that time was very bad, and the situation of the people was getting worse. That really was the reason of the enormous success Hitler had in the election. When the last election came, he got about 40%'."

Sutton added, "The Young Plan was assertedly a device to occupy Germany with American capital and pledge German real assets for a gigantic mortgage held in the United States. It is noteworthy that German firms with US affiliations evaded the Plan by the device of temporary foreign ownership. For instance, AEG (German General Electric), affiliated with General Electric in the US, was sold to a Franco-Belgian holding company and evaded the conditions of the Young Plan. It should be noted in passing that Owen Young was the major financial backer for Franklin D. Roosevelt in the United European venture when FDR, as a budding Wall Street financier, endeavours to take advantage of Germany's 1925 hyperinflation. The United European venture was a vehicle to speculate and to profit upon the imposition of the Dawes Plan, and is clear evidence of private financiers (including Franklin D. Roosevelt) using the power of the state to advance their own interests by manipulating foreign policy."

Reader, follow the path and see where it leads. The financial system in the hands of the Consortium politicians and public servants of Governments are directly aligned with the goals and objectives of the instruments they control and from which they derive benefits and rewards. The academic institutions, press organizations, think-tanks *et cetera* all partake of the same cultural norms. It is all one and the same world and they control it. Or at least they think they do. During the rise of Stalin and Hitler in the early thirties the "apex of the system" of financial and political control for the Consortium system is based in Basle, Switzerland – in the Bank for International Settlements (BIS).

Professor Quigley taught student Bill Clinton about BIS. Sutton observes how during WWII the BIS functions "as the medium through which the bankers–who apparently were not at war with each other– continued a mutually beneficial exchange of ideas, information, and planning for the postwar world...war made no difference to the international bankers." However, it is Schacht, not Young who hatches the idea which evolves into the Bank for International Settlements. A conference run by a leading NY banker Jackson Reynolds worked out the details assisted by Chicago's First National Bank director Melvin Traylor. Also present are Sir Charles Addis, formerly of the Hong Kong and Shanghai Banking Corporation, and various French and German bankers.

The Bank's international staff allow for a unique profile during the world war. Sutton explains it this way: "An American President was transacting the daily business of the Bank through a French General Manager, who had a German Assistant General Manager, while the Secretary-General was an Italian subject. Other nationals occupied other posts. These men were, of course, in daily personal contact with each other. Except for Mr. McKittrick they were of course situated permanently in Switzerland during this period and were not supposed to be subject to orders of their government at any time. However, the directors of the Bank remained, of course, in their respective countries and had no direct contact with the personnel of the Bank."

However, Schacht, president of the Reichsbank, has a personal representative in Basle ... The B.I.S. falls under Young's vision to promote international financial relations. Schacht himself later admits he gave Young the nexus that later became the postwar International Bank for Reconstruction and Development or World Bank. It is Schacht who declares, "A bank of this kind will demand financial co-operation between vanquished and victors that will lead to community of interests which in turn will give rise to mutual confidence and understanding and thus promote and ensure peace."

Here's Seymour Hersh's take on the unfolding financial crisis in May 1931: "Europe, those forever-whimpering Europeans. Those extensive European borrowings, privately solicited, discreetly granted, had already been flowing so long through the important American banking houses nobody really knew how much they represented. That train of private and governmental loans, reparations, interest payments coming due. … In May of 1931 it went." A dispatch reaches Washington; Vienna's largest bank, the Boden Kredit Anstalt is exposed, seriously in trouble. Depositors riot. Capital fled Germany in alarming sums and too quickly to stabilize markets. Hungarian banks totter on the brink of collapse. The NY Fed and Bank of England are called to intervene but are scuttled by the French.

Hoover sees the dikes busting. He calls for a moratorium. Treasurer Mellon declares it's Europe's mess, and leaves on vacation; he sends a five page telegram to President Hoover recommending the moratorium in order to keep a trade balance. Meanwhile Europe's central banks close, and western leaders demand gold to save deposited Eastern currencies. "Reserves were depleted overnight; smaller countries jumped off the gold standard like fleas off a drowning dog," Hersh writes.

Visibly shaken, Hoover demands the Comptroller of the Currency come up with accurate figures as to the extent of unsecured short-term borrowings from US banks about to sink; something about the relatively low estimates submitted by Federal officials doesn't feel plausible. Again Hersh on Hoover: "'Twenty-four hours later I received the appalling news that the total American bank holdings probably exceeded $1,700,000,000', much of it by banks for which large losses would critically 'affect their capital or surplus and create great public fears. Here is the consequence of the Reserve Board maintaining artificially low interest rates and expanded credit in the United States from mid-1927 to mid-1929 at the urging of European bankers. Some of our bankers have been yielding to sheer greed for the 6 or 7 per cent interest offered by banks in the European panic area'."

At the summer 1931 London banking conference with the British Foreign Office, Stimson and Mellon give Germany a year moratorium. Germany badly needs the money, about a half billion dollars. Hoover, however, now threatens to expose the banker's joint loan issued by the Bank for International Settlements at Berne. (re. "Europe, those forever-whimpering Europeans...", William Hersh, *The Mellon Family,* 292-5)

Banks are in crisis throughout the summer. Great institutions including Lazard Freres in Paris and London lean ominously when their "quaint" little foreign exchange house in Antwerp in Belgium goes bust. William D. Cohan in *Lazard Freres* (2007) tells of a secret meeting July 14, 1931 with Kindersley, Montagu Collet "Archie" Norman of the Bank of England, and David-Weill. "Kindersley told Norman about the huge loss Lazard Brothers had suffered and said the firm needed, immediately L5 million (pounds) (estimated today to be equivalent to 250 million (pounds), or $450 million) to 'put matters straight' or the firm would go under." German and Hungarian banks were now affected by the debt repayment moratorium. Norman intervened to rescued "one of its prized Accepting Houses" with the mediation of S. Pearson & Son Ltd. of London. In fact, events that year nearly result in "the total liquidation of Lazard". (William D. Cohan, *Lazard Freres,* 2007)

WHO WAS CHARLES G. DAWES? AND OWEN D. YOUNG?

Reader, let us return to the Consortium and see who is in control of the corporate banking system in a world overrun with mass murder and Genocide, totalitarian soviet socialism to creeping Nazi fascism in Germany. Who is this Charles G. Dawes who puts his name to the plan that helps seal the fate of Germany?

In 1892 Dawes authors *The Banking System of the United States.* Comptroller of the Currency (1897-01), Dawes organizes the Central Trust Company in Chicago in 1902 associated with the JP. Morgan. During WWI Dawes chairs the General Purchasing Board of the Allied Expeditionary Forces. By the time he turned 50 he is a ranking Pilgrim.

Not many Americans can tell you the Republican businessman Charles Dawes (1865-51) served as Vice-President under Coolidge during Stalin's iron-fist consolidation of power over the Kremlin (1925-29) before dashing off to London as Hoover's ambassador to Great Britain, 1929-32 preceding the Treasury Secretary Mellon. It is Charles Dawes who in 1932 chairs Hoover's $2 billion Reconstruction Finance Corporation. Owen D. Young, too, had worked at JP. Morgan Co. and is chairman of *both* GE and Radio Corporation of America (RCA) as well as a director of the NY Federal Reserve Bank (1923-40). In 1942 Young has a seat on the Pilgrims Society excomm.

Think about it, reader. During the Holodomor years the world order is stacked up in Washington and London with the pinnacle of financial power not only concerned but highly motivated, even ambitious to extend the power and control of business and armaments. For years everything had been set in motion against them; neither the Soviet Russians nor the nationalist Ukrainians ever had a chance to save themselves from their manipulations. As the Young Plan is launched in 1930 to replace the Dawes Plan both schemes have everything to do with the reparations debt and damages imbroglio to make the Germans pay for cost and devastation of property and human life caused by the First World War.

The Dawes and Young Plans gives the bankers means to float profitable loans for German cartels in the United States. Both plans are designed and managed by the same groups of central bankers who man the committees sponsored by the Government. Under these two plans from 1924 to 1931 Germany paid about 86 billion marks in reparations to the Allies including America. At the same time Germany borrows mainly from bankers in New York the sum of 138 billion marks making a net German payment of only three billion marks for reparations. The bankers work it out so actually the burden of German monetary reparations is paid for by Wall Street investment firms underwriting German bonds to foreign subscribers at a handsome profit for the banks. For them it was the best way to ensure that they can stay in business, hold Germany hostage, control Germany's economy and collect their exorbitant fees.

In January 1932, the Consortium bankers meet at Lausanne and reduce Germany's total reparations to 3 billion gold marks with bonds at 5% interest amortized with a 1 % sinking fund. The Lausanne Economic Crisis of 1932 had been a major stumbling block for Stimson and Hoover threatening global economic stability world. Germany's remaining war debt was nevertheless reduced to $714 million with Germany to pay it off through a bond issue. The June settlement at Lausanne 1932 meant an annulation of Germany's obligations.

Banks are falling like dominos, defaulting everywhere. Early 1932 Congress authorizes Hoover's creation of the RFC to shore up the nation's collapsing credit system. But the bankers make another of their "gentlemen's agreements" whereby the former Allies manage to add reduction of their war debts over Stimson's protests. The Bank of International Settlements (BIS) in Basel, Switzerland will not sell the bonds on the market until 1935 giving Germany in theory a little breathing time before having to resume payments. As it goes Germany is floundering with unemployment.

During the war the American Consortium bankers loaned $10.4 billion to the Allies by selling Liberty Bonds, and used the money to pay American producers for weapons, munitions and other war supplies then sold to the Allies. Germany still owes some $30 billion to the Allies. After 1932 Germany stopped paying; up till then it had paid $5.5 billion in reparations pulling it down into economic and political morass. (W. C. Langsam, *War in the Twentieth Century*, The Dryden Press, Random House, 1940, 109; W. Hersh, 292-5, re. "Europe, those forever-whimpering Europeans...")

Consortium loans include three billion dollars of contracts signed after the Armistice "to protect the profits of American investors". While America was pushed to the edge by the greed of bankers and consumer euphoria for prosperity, and dreams beyond dreams, so too did the Soviet people get taken to the cleaners by constant pressure on the Kremlin to meet their state socialist targets with nothing more to lose now than their lives now that their freedom was gone.

Author Cassella-Blackburn provides a readable account on German-Russian trade in the Soviet Union covering the Five-Year Plans from 1928 to 1933. Here too, reader, do not overlook the remark to "American businessmen", where Casella-Blackburn writes in *The Donkey, the Carrot, and the Club* (2004) though keeping Consortium investment very much in the shadows: "Although helpful, the Soviet Union had to use direct barter and short-term commercial loans, which did not meet the needs of the plan. Only Germany and Great Britain would grant long-term loans. Even while a substantial proportion of American businessmen took an active interest in Soviet economic development, many business leaders held back due to the American government's hostility toward the Soviet state."

Aided by Consortium investment streaming through Berlin Germany resumed its status as Russia's primary partner in trade. Again Cassella-Blackburn's sanitizing study of Bullitt does give some useful economic data while making a masked comment of overall Consortium investment: "By 1933 German imports reached 46 percent and exports from the Soviet Union to Germany reached 17 percent of the Soviet totals. The United States was for a short period (1930-31) the largest exporter to the Soviet Union, but Germany and Great Britain changed the trend by providing more credits, and were less concerned with charges of dumping, especially wood products and grain, against the Soviets." Cassella-Blackburn publisher Praeger in Westport, Connecticut reportedly a CIA publishing front ignores Sutton's classic three-volume study on US-Soviet trade. (Jonathan Haslam, *The Soviet Union, 1930-1933: The Impact of the Depression*, London 1983, 39-41, 53-5, 133n; B. Parrott, 19-75, *Politics and Technology in the Soviet Union*; A. C. Sutton, *US-Soviet Trade 1917-1965*, 346-8, 1246-9, 2295; A. J. Taylor; M. Cassella-Blackburn, *The Donkey, the Carrot, and the Club*: *William C. Bullitt and Soviet-American Relations*, 1917-1948, Westport, CT: Praeger, 2004, 81)

Meanwhile as France inserted trade protectionist barriers and quotas principally on agricultural goods and foodstuffs to protect its own domestic production, a gold and currency crisis threatened to sink the British Empire long before national liberation movements rose up and claimed independence. By 1934 when Schacht in Germany addressed the International Conference for Agrarian Science at Bad Eilsen Schacht he urged an end to the Consortium economic blockade with its excessive demands over tariffs, quotas and duties regulating global trade. France, for example, since 1913 to 1931 had imposed duties equivalent to 180% of prices on wheat, up from 39% to 160 % on the price of flour. Italy's duties had more than tripled on wheat, more than quadrupled on flour. Schacht calls the British and French tariff hikes "calculated materially to obstruct exportation from Germany".

A drain on England's bank reserves undermined the sacred Gold Standard. "Income from overseas investment fell off;" according to Benjamin Higgins in *The Economic War since 1918*, exports were cut in half by 1931; shipping receipts were less than half their 1929 level in 1931. ... Could the Bank of England hold out? Would England be forced off the Gold Standard again?" Prior to Ukraine's famine crisis and leading up to it the state of American banking was on already on critically dangerous course when the pound tumbled and threatened foreign exchange markets. A flight from the pound pushed up rates on foreign exchange leading to untenable drains on gold so that by December 1931 gold had fallen to \$3.37; the next year gold hit \$3.27 as the pressure on England lessened. (Benjamin Higgins, *The Economic War since 1918*, 158-170, re. currency devaluation)

Hoover faces the worst crisis in banking since the days of the earlier money crisis when bankers Morgan and Davison rescue New York from financial meltdown. Hoover now has to take the blame for the state of affairs he and the Consortium bankers had created when Reconstruction Finance Corporation (RFC) made public names of banks getting a financial bailout which started a series of runs on some but not all banks. Since the flow of money from the Fed is based on discount interest rates, as the money flowed and the rates drops when the sell-off hit people fear that the government would not be able to meet reserve requirements of the Fed necessary to meet demand thereby triggering a severe contraction where the banks and the Fed run out of money. The Panic continues until March 6, 1933. FDR declares a bank holiday. It's only a temporary break. Thousands of banks did run out of money and nearly all closed their doors.

Sunday March 5 1933. The nation prayed that their meager savings had not vanished with their paper fortunes bought on speculation and margin debt. Roosevelt extended the bank holiday four days. Further he prohibited gold hoarding, or the export, or foreign exchange deals. All gold bars, coins, certificates had to be exchanged. The reporter Horan observed that from 1930 to 1932 some 773 banks failed wiping out 7 million dollars of American savings and 3604 state banks with more than 2 billion dollars evaporating. The US Treasury reports \$1.212 million had been withdrawn precipitating the dollar to plunge.

The next day FDR's Treasury relents. Depositors find their banks opening doors to allow access to safety deposit boxes, loans for food, and to make change for small coins and bills, cash checks drawn on US Treasury. But gold payouts remain forbidden. In Chicago alone Americas returns \$2 million of gold in a day, \$1.2 million in Philadelphia within five hours. By midnight on the last day of the bank holidays, the Fed in Washington reported \$200 million in gold collected.

By May 12 FDR signs the Reconstruction Finance Corp. Act to \$500 million to bail out States in dire need. Ten days later on March 22 the administration passes the Beer Bill modifying the Volstead Act. Taps are reopened and it legalizes the sale of beer and wines. The nation deserves a good binge.

Especially if the authorities permit the people to see the horrors witnessed by people like Lev Kopelev, a young Jewish student in Kharkov lived under the specter of famine and death all around him. Kopelev's story figures to several accounts, in particular noted by invariably divergent writers such as Scott Palmer and Robert Conquest. He survives, and lives to be 85. His memories of the horror live with us today. "In the terrible spring of 1933 I saw people dying from hunger. I saw women and children with distended bellies, turning blue, still breathing but with vacant lifeless eyes. And corpses – corpses in ragged sheepskin coats and cheap felt boots; corpses in peasant hunts, in the melting snow of old Vologda, under the bridges of Kharkov…I saw all of this and did not go out of my mind or commit suicide. Nor did I curse those who had sent me out to take away the peasants' grain in the winter, and in the spring to persuade the barely walking, skeleton-thin or sickly-swollen people to go into the fields in order to 'fulfill the Bolshevik sowing plan in shock worker style. Nor did I lose my faith. As before, I believed because I wanted to believe."

Lev Kopelev was actually born in Kiev, in 1912, studied at Kharkov University, and published in *Komsomolskaya Pravda*. As a correspondent during the 1932 "liquidation" (the Bolshevik term for the peasants) Kopelev witnesses the NKVD's forced grain procurements. Fluent in German, Kopelev also survives Hitler's invasion serving as a propaganda officer in the Red Army in the East Prussian Offensive; after the "Great Victory" he survived one year in the gulag sharing the *sharashka* with Solzhenitsyn who immortalizes him as Rubin in his novel *The First Circle* (1968). Kopelev dies in 1997, in Cologne Germany; his memoirs were published in America in 1984. (*Education of a True Believer, Harper Collins,1976, 1988;* Scott W. Palmer, "Dictatorship of the Air: aviation culture and the fate of modern Russia," Part III, in *Soviet Aviation in the Age of Stalin, 1929-1945*, NY: Cambridge Univ. Press, 2006, 193)

A few years later, after the death winds had swept the Ukraine and with Stalin preparing his staged Purge of the Party, FDR thumped the 1936 campaign trail broadcasting government figures of factory employment rising from 4.9 million to 7.2 million "an increase of 45 %" with factory pay up 115 %. Of 168 leading corporations showing deficits in 1932 totaling 87 million dollars, they reported 580 million in profits for 1935. It was a substantial turnaround. Bank failures, Roosevelt told the nation, which numbered 1502 in 1932 were only 36 for the first six months in 1936. Business bankruptcies tapered off a third to 12,000 in 1935 with smaller liabilities "than in any year since 1920". To have a better picture just how serious became the economic crisis of the Depression, FDR reeled off figures declaring that during the three last years of Hoover's Republican administration from 1931-33, the national deficit soared to 5.8 billion while national income plummeted "from sixty-eight billion" in 1930 to 39 billion in 1932.

On May 17, 1933 FDR asks Congress to shorten the work week and special powers to create national employment program with $3.3 billion for public construction. That same day, in the USSR, at the height of the Holodomor

Terror-Famine Stalin assures his people. No famine! And no more waves of arrests! There are too many people already in the Gulag construction camps! How to feed them all? Only now will the nature of his totalitarian destruction of the Bolshevik Revolution become clear and legible to all victims and attentive observers. Solzhenitsyn recalls these dying dreadful days. "Now at last we can catch our breath! Now at last all the mass waves are coming to an end! Comrade Molotov said on May 17: 'We do not see our task as being mass repressions.' Whew! At last! Begone, nighttime fears! But what's that dog howling out there? Go get 'em. Go get 'em."

The previous month FDR had pushed through his Tennessee Valley Authority to develop power on the Tennessee River with massive employment in the region as well as creating the Civilian Conservation Corps (CCC) passed by the Democratic Congress in July 1933 with $350 million in appropriations helped take up the slack of 15 million unemployed men and women. Was that a concession to Hull in exchange he keeps quiet general operations in the State Department including the Ukraine? It's not unthinkable. Within four years more than 2.5 million youths find jobs in CCC programs. That rivaled anything that the Soviets could muster with its Komsomol youth communists. The CCC develops into a huge prewar government organization with more than $100 million of equipment for collective training, education and work programs this at a time with the World War II only a few years away. FDR also uses the federal program to combat illiteracy: 50,000 young boys and girls will graduate from grade schools and 400,000 teenagers will pass high school courses, and 40,000 college courses are offered to educate young adults. America is on the move again! (A. I. Solzhenitsyn, *The Gulag Archipelago*, 58)

Frustrated by the bankers whom he publicly damned for the financial market meltdown and Depression FDR drops the gold standard in June. That frees up the Fed to print more money and pump the economy to keep it moving again. FDR rejoiced at how he put bread back on the table of American homes. But across the Atlantic and Europe, while Ford tractors go unserviced, and factories short of workers for lack of food the doomed Ukrainians lose all hope of having any bread of their own. By January 1934 the dollar is fixed to 13.71 grains of fine gold at a gold standard devaluating dollars to 1926 American price index. Overseas the inflationary trend hit the British pound rising to over $5 dollars in 1934 and doubling the German mark, and the French franc to 6.21 cents.

George Creel, President Wilson's WWI propaganda czar returns to the government payroll and signs up as a publicist for the NRA. Creel has a national reach to all the newspapers and journalists of the country and he uses it to help push Roosevelt's New Deal government corporate socialism while doing nothing to expose Stalin's state terror communism and the Holodomor. Another feather in his hat and ribbon on his chest for the Consortium's bureaucratic hack! The NRA's New Deal public works projects created by the 73rd Congress on June 16, 1933 included the National Industrial Recovery Act giving FDR wage and price controls by extending mandatory powers to the government over industrial wages, hours, prices. It also allows for a $3.3 billion bond issue to finance construction of federal state local and public and private projects for employment.

FDR now has his hands firmly on the ship's wheel. He also now has authority to draft codes of fair competition for industry, and invested with power to compel compliance and subject fines for non-compliance. FDR also imposes a score of taxes including a 1 percent tax on corporation net worth, 5 percent on earnings above 12.5 percent, five percent tax on corporate dividends, a half-cent increase in the refiner's gas tax, and many taxes. In addition to the massive public works programs, it authorizes $100 million dollars for Farm Relief and $400 for highway construction projects to be disbursed in thirty days.

FDR pledges a million men back to work by the fall. And who does he appoint to manage the nation's between the wars of post-Depression recovery – Brig. General Hugh Samuel Johnson ("Old Iron Pants"), a graduate of West Point, adviser to Bernard Baruch in 1927, the author and administrator of the Selective Service Act during WWI, and *Time Magazine's* "Man of the Year" for 1933; his main duty in the Great War had been to coordinate Army purchases with Baruch's War Industries Board. One of their own.

In "*The Rise of Fascism*", Clifford Kirkpatrick observes the dangers left in the wake of Hitler's 1930 victory winning 6.4 million ballots of the popular vote. Hitler seizes 107 seats in the Reichstag. By 1932 the SA boasts having 600,000 men in the National Socialist party. Reich finance minister Otto Dietrich brought Hitler closer to the Rhineland's industrialists, Bavarian industrialists, White Russians, and money from France and "an American industrialist". "Schacht", Kirpatrick writes, "always with his nose in the air to catch the shifting political wind opened up new supplies of money; a united front was established with Hugenberg and Stahlhelm, a German veteran's organization led by Franz Seldte."

As it was for the Americans and Ukrainians 1932 is also a fateful year for the German people. Kirkpatrick describes it this way: "Bruning of the Catholic Center party was still Chancellor, but he was beset on every side with difficulties. Unemployment soars to 6 million. Agriculture was in a sorry plight. The small landowner was haunted by foreclosure. On the other hand the great Junker landholders of East Prussia were dipping into the public treasure to obtain *Osthilfe* (help from the East)."

In a dramatic shift in trade flows Russo-German trade "shrank from year to year until it had dwindled in 1938 to only one-tenth of the 1930 figure. Hitler raved and thundered against Communists and Jews in Moscow. At the Nuremberg Nazi Party Congress in 1936 he announced that Germany wanted the Russian Ukraine and the Ural Mountains." Two years after the Holodomor the Nazis set their sight on the Ukraine. Hitler's Nazis plan to finish the work begun by Stalin depopulating the people there. And we know who is backing them both. (Clifford Kirkpatrick, "The Rise of Fascism" cited in Willard Waller, *War in the Twentieth Century*, Dryden Press -Random House, 1940; Konrad Heiden, *Hitler*, Knopf, 1936, 221; Q. Howe, 340)

Norman Rich's book *Hitler's War Aims* (1973) has a chapter "The Instruments of Control: The Economy". History professor emeritus at Brown University Rich served on the State Department's board of editors reviewing seized Nazi Foreign Ministry documents. He explains how Nazi repudiation of Marxist theory did not deter them from recognizing in the economy the element they considered to be the basic source of their strength, and he writes that "by controlling the leadership of such enterprises they could control the enterprises themselves. This system had the added advantage of giving business leaders the temporary illusion that they were being left in charge of their own affairs. Not only were the great cartels left intact, but a compulsory cartelization law of July 1933 empowered the Reich minister of economics to integrate independent enterprises into the cartel system and thus bring them under cartel control."

The extraordinary Herr Schacht! The Consortium's own Nazi monopolist is empowered by the Nazi decree February 27, 1934 that leaves no illusion who controls these cartels. The law authorizes Schacht to form and control business associations "and eventually to ensure state control over all associations and their members". With the stench of death from the Holodomor's wheat fields blowing east over Germany, the economic Nazi czar now rules by decree within the newly formed Reich Economic Chamber within the Ministry of Economics; in May 1935 Hitler appoints Schacht the acting minister of economics and president of the Reichsbank and promotes him to a new post as general of the military economy (*Wehrwirtschaft*). This avails Schacht the broadest powers ever enjoyed by a Consortium man over Germany's national economy and war machine. Still not radical enough, in October 1936, Hitler delegates emergency powers to his friend Herman Göring as head of a new Four-Year Plan. It will all be too much for poor Schacht, and for Hitler who can no longer afford to have a Jew perceived at the summit of the Reich's glory. The next year he crosses the mighty Fuhrer and resigns, again.

Norman Rich, Ph.D (Berkeley 1949), and for a time Resident Fellow at St. Anthony's College, has an impressive academic pedigree that includes Oxford, Princeton, Guggenheim, Fulbright fellowships ... For five years immediately after the war Rich studied captured German Foreign Office documents, a project sponsored by State, FO, and the Quai d'Orsay. And reader, I can tell you the elderly Norman Rich resides in Lyme, Connecticut a few minutes from my home and dines regularly with close company. (Norman Rich, *Hitler's War Aims: Ideology, the Nazi State, and the Course of Expansion,* W. W. Norton, 1973)

Norman Rich examined source documents of Nazi intentions in Soviet Russia and Hitler's determination to "build a dike against the Russian flood" to protect Germany and Europe. Hitler declared, "we must meet it with a living wall'. For Hitler, might is right. 'It is success that justifies everything'." This is exactly the Consortium logic of war and destruction at work. Hitler told his staff after the invasion, "The real frontier is the one that separates the Germanic world from the Slav world. It is our duty to place it where we want it to be." Hitler's Aryan views remained loyal to the doctrines expounded in *Mein Kampf.*

Three weeks after the invasion of the Ukraine a conference is convened on July 16, 1941 with *Reichmarschall* Göring, General Wilhelm Keitel, a die-hard Hitler loyalist to the very end – Hitler refused his request for transfer and Jodl once intervened taking a gun away to prevent his suicide –, liaison between Hitler and his General Staff, Alfred Rosenberg, Reich minister for occupied eastern territories, Hans Lammers and Bormann. Hitler said the main thing was that the Germans must know what they want in the East. The task he said was first to "initiate a final settlement".

In the Ukraine, Hitler reverses his mistakes in Scandinavia and the Low countries, and urged his troops to enter as liberators, appearing as military instruments to impose only law and order. "This need not prevent us from taking all necessary measures – shooting, evacuations, etc. – and we shall take them." Nazi military objective to seize the Urals required that only Germans could bear arms. They would not use the subjugated peoples or the Ukrainians against Stalin. Instead, Hitler originally planned to send the Ukrainians to work in German war plants as forced labor.

Pacification of the vast region of the Ukraine had to be swift and immediate. "A permanent war on the eastern front," Hitler declared, "will help form a sound race of men, and will prevent us from relapsing into the softness of a Europe thrown back upon itself. It should be possible for us to control this region to the east with two hundred and fifty thousand men plus a cadre of good administrators. … The space in Russia must always be dominated by Germans." The Ukrainians didn't have a chance to resist. "Hitler said, "This could best be done by shooting everyone who looked in any way suspicious." Hitler now could blame Stalin and the Soviet government for mounting resistance, making it easier to exterminate them with police regiments in armored vehicles and using air power against the insurgents. Hitler planned to annex Ukraine's hinterland and the Crimea along the Black Sea as well as lands inhabited by Volga Germans, the Baku oil region, and the nickel mines of the Kola Peninsula all too irresistible for greed and glory not to take. (N. Rich, 326-7)

Hitler craved the Ukraine's vast open grain lands and those of the Upper Volga to become Europe's breadbasket while taking oil and iron from the East. Rich, in particular, quoted Hitler's fantasy of empire. "Where," Hitler said, "is there a region capable of supplying iron of the quality of Ukraine iron? Where can one find more nickel, more coal, more manganese, more molybdenum? And, on top of that, so many other possibilities! The vegetable oils, the rubber plantations to be organized. With 100,000 acres devoted to the growing of rubber, our needs are covered." In addition to rubber, the warmer climate of the Crimea would also yield citrus fruits and cotton. "The Pripet marshes will supply us with reeds… The Black Sea will be for us a sea whose wealth our fishermen will never exhaust. Thanks to the cultivation of the soya bean, we will increase our livestock. We will win from the soil several times as much as the Ukrainian peasant is winning at present."

This was his plan for the new Germany to reclaim its birthright! Rich confirms the Nazis Aryan conquerors intend to convert the southern ports of the entire seacoast into a German colony once rid of Slavs and Jews. "There will be no harm in pushing out the population that is there now. The German colonist will be the soldier-peasant. … These soldiering-peasants will be given arms, so that at the slightest danger they can be at their posts when we summon them."

The Nazis plan called for total domination of the Ukrainians who were reduced to sub-human level of existence with less rights than a German servant or stable-boy. The proud Cossack and the fearless Ukrainian warrior would be no more. "The Russian desert, we shall populate it. The immense spaces of the eastern front will have been the field of the greatest battles in history. We will give this country a past. We will take away its character of an Asiatic steppe, we will Europeanize it. With this object, we have undertaken the construction of roads that will lead to the southernmost point of the Crimea and to the Caucasus. These roads will be studded along their whole length with German towns, and around these towns our colonists will settle." (N. Rich, 329)

The Nazi German fascists had plans to use their concentration camps of Ukrainian slave labor to lay down four-track rails capable of transporting high speed trains at 200 miles per hour. "As for the two or three million men whom we need to accomplish this task, we will find them more quickly than we think. They will come from Germany, Scandinavia, the Western countries, *and America.* I shall no longer be here to see all that, but in twenty years the Ukraine will already be a home for twenty million inhabitants besides the natives. In three hundred years the country will be one of the loveliest gardens in the world." Germans would replant Reeds in the marshes to control the winds, reforest lands to control the rains… Hitler went on, saying "The German colonists ought to live on handsome, spacious farms. The German services will be lodged in marvelous buildings, the governors in palaces. Beneath the shelter of the administrative services, we shall gradually organize all that is indispensable to the maintenance of a certain standard of living. Around the city, to a depth of thirty to forty kilometers, we shall have a belt of handsome villages connected by the best roads. What exists beyond that will be another world, in which we man to let the Russians live as they like. It is merely necessary that we should rule them." Even after the invasion Hitler had reason to believe that the American Consortium would remain a loyal partner in the destruction and German plunder of the Soviet Union. (Italics added)

Germans would replace Slavs. Hitler compared his pacification of the Ukraine to the American extermination of North American Indians by the US government and cowboys. Rich wrote, "There's only one duty: to Germanize this country by the immigration of Germans, and to look upon the natives as Redskins." All potential leaders and Jews were to be eliminated. The Russian Ukrainians were to be expelled unless easily convertible from Soviet slave labor to Nazi slave labor. The order was clear. Ukrainians were in no way to benefit from German occupation. The Russian slave would be converted into a German slave state. "Our guiding principle must be that these people have but one justification for existence – to be of use to us economically. ... My long-term policy aims at having eventually a hundred million Germans settled in these territories. It is therefore essential to set up machinery which will ensure constant progression, and we will see to it that million by million German penetration expands." Hitler envisions within ten years 20 million Germans living there. "We will not succeed except by the application of the most severe measures." (N. Rich, 330)

Hitler's Pollyanna program of benevolent extermination of course would never work against the Ukrainians. In his role as deputy leader of the Political Department of Rosenberg's Ministry for the Occupied Eastern Territories, and a Reich diplomat, Dr. Otto Brautigam felt compelled to warn of some difficulties for the Reich's war effort inherent in Hitler's assault on Humanity. In a confidential report to his superiors written October 25, 1942 Brautigam admits "the prevailing limitless abuse of the Slavic Humanity" by the Nazi invasion forces that occupied the Ukrainian and other Soviet territories and united resistance against the fascist Nazi killing machine: "It is no longer a secret from friend or foe that hundreds of thousands of Russian prisoners of war have died of hunger or cold in our camps... We now experience the grotesque picture of having to recruit millions of laborers from the occupied Eastern territories after prisoners of war have died of hunger like flies. ... In the prevailing limitless abuse of the Slavic Humanity, 'recruiting' methods were used which probably have their origin only in the blackest periods of the slave traffic. A regular manhunt was inaugurated. Without consideration of health or age the people were shipped to Germany... Our policy has forced both Bolsheviks and Russian nationalists into a common front against us. The Russian fights today with exceptional bravery and self-sacrifice for nothing more or less than recognition of his human dignity.' Hitler was undaunted promising to meet resistance with greater Nazi brutality. Russian resistance provoked Hitler to urge harsher vengeance since "it enables us to eradicate everyone who opposes us". (W. Shirer, *The Rise and Fall of the Third Reich*, 940-2)

Throughout the years of German military defeats and Stalin's advances, Hitler repeated his Russian war aims. In his speech to army commanders in July 1, 1943. Hitler reaffirmed territorial ambitions for German expansion for "open space", or *Lebensraum* east and west. "The fight, gentlemen, is a fight for *Lebensraum*. Without this *Lebensraum* the German Reich and the German nation cannot endure. Germany must become the hegemonial power in Europe, but even if it does so, it cannot exist in such a ludicrous area as we inhabit today. In such an area one will not be able in the future to build up an army. ... Whoever has his industry squeezed into such a small space runs the risk of having it destroyed, I might say, overnight. In that event fine ideas are of no use whatever, for in the end man lives from the earth and the earth is the prize which Providence gives to those people who fight for it." (N. Rich, *Hitler's War Aims*, 1973, 331)

British establishment historian A. J. Taylor had a problem explaining Hitler's genocidal ambitions in the Ukraine and how they intertwined with the logic of mass murder. Taylor writes, "Hitler's claim to living space, *Lebensraum*, sounded more plausible – plausible enough to convince Hitler himself. But what did it amount to in practice? Germany was not short of markets. On the contrary, Schacht used bilateral agreements to give Germany practically a monopoly of trade with south-eastern Europe; and similar plans were being prepared for the economic conquest of South America when the outbreak of war interrupted them...*Libensraum,* in its crudest sense, meant a demand for empty space where Germans could settle,. Germany was not over-populated in comparison with most European countries; and there was no empty space anywhere in Europe. When

Hitler laments: 'If only we had a Ukraine …', he seemed to suppose that there were no Ukrainians. Did he propose to exploit, or to exterminate, them? Apparently he never considered the question one way or the other. When Germany actually conquered the Ukraine in 1941, Hitler and his henchmen tried both methods – neither to any economic advantage."

Hitler's mad push to the Black Sea is no less inspired by tales of actual ancient onslaughts when seas were once called *Oceanus Germanicus* and for thousands of years history did repeat itself, tribes conquering tribes, Romans defeating Celts, Celts burning Rome, and so forth on and on, time after time. Of course modern science and the Big Bomb finally put an end to all that barbarism replacing savage barbarity with more refined means of persuasion ... (A. J. Taylor, 105)

"Even the Fascist dictators would not have gone to war," Taylor would have us believe, rather euphemistically, "unless they had seen a chance of winning; and the cause of war was therefore as much the blunders of others as the wickedness of the dictators themselves. Hitler probably intended a great war of conquest against Soviet Russia so far as he had any conscious design; it is unlikely that he intended the actual war against Great Britain and France which broke out in 1939. He was as much dismayed on 3 September 1939 as Bethmann had been on 4 August 1914." Taylor got it wrong; evidently he had not read Rich on Hitler, and exaggerated England's ability to go it alone against Nazism which most definitely it could not do without its fate hinged on America to pull it out from most unfavourable circumstances. (A. J. Taylor, 118-9)

Ukrainians, in fact, frequently greeted the Nazis as liberators from communist tyranny as recorded by Nazi film crews. Their enthusiasm passed quickly. But Rich too gets it wrong when he wonders why the Nazi conquers fail to enlist Ukrainian support. "Among the most unfortunate of Hitler's policies from the point of view of the German administration in the east was his refusal on principle to enlist the aid of the Slavic peoples or to allow anyone but Germans to bear arms. This prohibition made it difficult – at first almost impossible – for the Germans to set up native nationalist or anti-Communist governments in the conquered areas against Bolshevik Russia, or to recruit manpower in the east for service in the German armed forces." Ethnic-cleansing doesn't take survivors! It exterminates them! Himmler, however, indifferent about their Slavic origins violated Hitler's Aryan principle by enlisting Ukrainians as police and members of the Waffen-SS and eventually persuaded his Chancellor to recruit General Andrei Vlassov and Russians to fight Stalin. (N. Rich, Vol. II, 331)

The fate of the Ukrainians was left hanging. Rich concludes, "The trouble was that, unlike Hitler, the Army High Command had no broadly conceived policies for dealing with Russia, nor was there any unanimity among German military leaders as to what Germany's ultimate aims in Russia should be. … All administrative plans were based on the premise that Russia would be conquered quickly and that there with the administration would be turned over to German civilian authorities." Even fascists get confused when Genocide turns on the killers and The Game goes haywire.

An essential part of the ideological thrust of Hitler's invasion plans was the extermination of all Bolshevik functionaries and Jews. His order dated July 22, 1943 to commanders instructed them not to demand more security forces but to overcome resistance "by applying suitable Draconian measures", Norman Rich observed. Against Moscow Hitler thundered. "'Everywhere the harshest measures' are to be used to crush the resistance movement in the shortest possible time...' Every case' of revolt against the German occupying power, no matter what the circumstances, must be ascribed to Communist origins". Hitler ordered one hundred communists for the death of a single German soldier. "The manner of execution must intensify the intimidating effect'. Goebbels recorded Hitler on Stalin, saying "Stalin is probably sick in the brain. Otherwise you can't explain his bloody regime." That didn't keep Hitler's Nazis from killing some three *million* Soviet POWs. For Josef Goebbels, Hitler was a moderate in comparison who pensioned army officers opposed to National Socialism while Stalin killed his "enemies of the people"; he quotes Beria, head of the NKVD soviet secret police for saying "an enemy of the people is not only one who makes sabotage, but one who doubts the rightness of the party line. And there are a lot of them among us, and we must liquidate them." (N. Rich, Vol. II, 332-3)

"Jewish-Bolshevism, you see, that was the big enemy," confirms Carlheinz Behnke, then a soldier in the SS-Panzer Division Wikiing. 'And these were the people to fight against because they meant a threat to Europe, according to the view at the time. ... And the Jews were simply regarded as the leadership class or as those who were firmly in control over there in the Soviet Union.' A soldier in the SS Calvary regiment fighting in the East told how it was to be out there. "Our task was absolutely clear to us...We knew that Bolshevism was the World-Enemy Number One. .... And we were told that their aim was to over-run Germany and France and the whole of Europe down to and including Spain. That's why we had to fight. ... We never really asked about the reasons for anything much. I mean they were just blokes who were supporting their system, just like it was with us. ... The commissars just had to be killed." (L. Rees, 51)

General Zhukov could not hold Kiev. When Kiev fell entire Russian army divisions were trapped, over 600,000 men captured in the greatest battle encirclement ever in modern warfare. Zhukov asks to be relieved. Stalin accepts, telling his commanders "Hold out as long as you can." But soviet soldiers are equipped with WWI vintage 60 mm guns, – one rifle for five men –, and told to take guns from the Germans. Russian officers fled in vehicles leaving their men behind; three out of four had been officers for less than a year, military and political. It was a rout.

Appointed Nazi *Reichskommissar* for the Ukraine Eric Koch is also Gauleiter of East Prussia. Koch joined the Party in 1922 and sported a Hitlerian mustache. Hitler had no interest in civilizing the Ukrainians, rather to make their life no better than a beast, leaving them ignorant like posting signs on the roads "just enough to understand our highway signs so they won't get themselves run over by our vehicles". Laurence Rees writes, "It's inconceivable he said that a higher people (the Germans) should painfully exist on a soil too narrow for it, whilst amorphous masses, which contribute nothing to civilization, occupy infinite tracts of a soil that is one of the richest in the world." (L. Rees, 51)

The Germans, especially the black uniformed SS troops in the East "took positive pride in starving the newly subject peoples", writes Niall Ferguson in *Civilization, The West and the Rest* (2011), and he adds, "it will pump every last thing out of this country', declared *Reichkommissar* Erich Koch, when put in charge of the Ukraine. 'I did not come here to spread bliss ...'. Göring bloated that he 'cold not care less' if non -Germans were 'collapsing from hunger'." Operation Barbarossa, in particular, was a campaign of organized extermination "all the way to industrialized genocide". Ferguson observes, "By February 1942 only 1.1 million were still alive of the 3.9 million originally captured. Herded together in barbed-wire stockades, they were simply left to the ravages of malnutrition a disease." (Niall Ferguson, *Civilization, The West and the Rest,* NY: Penguin, 2011, 192-3)

"'Hardly anything will be left standing in Kiev", Hitler tells General Koch. Notes recorded their conversation. "The Fuhrer's inclination to destroy the Russia's large cities as a prerequisite for the permanence of our power in Russia will be further consolidated by the *Reichskommissar* smashing up Ukrainian industry, in order to drive the proletariat back to the land." Koch closed the schools. "Ukrainian children need no schools. What they have to learn will be taught them by their German masters." Koch disputed constantly with Rosenberg and treated him with contempt and Rosenberg sheepishly obeyed, saying, "Ukrainians were destined to tend the cows, not study to be doctors or engineers."

Hitler in February 1942 declares, "No sooner do we land in a colony than we install children's crèches, hospitals for the natives. All this fills me with rage.... The Russians don't grow old. They scarcely get beyond 50 or 60. What a ridiculous idea to vaccinate them! ...No vaccination for the Russians and no soap to get the dirt off them. But let them have all the vodka they want." Upon his visit to Vinnitsa in western Ukraine, at his headquarters Werewolf, Hitler ordered contraceptives "not only be permitted but even encouraged, for one could have no interest in the excessive multiplication of the non-German population". Reminiscent of Stalin's racial marginalization of the Ukrainian Slavs, albeit for political reasons, the motive may differ but the methods and objective was the same – a reduction of the national population as a political and cultural threat. (L. Rees, 87-91)

Fast forward 1936-37. In Paris, with money gone, holding in hand a "bad offer from the *Paris Herald*, recovering from India, and Afghanistan, ill and hurting from and a skiing accident in the Alps and thinking he was going blind with only one good eye, any other journalist without Shirer's outstanding skill as a writer would have been an easy bet for suicide. Instead Shirer writes Bullitt, "What Roosevelt is doing at home seems to smack almost of social and economic revolution", Shirer declared to his friend now ambassador in Paris having left Moscow and the Soviet mess behind him.

In Paris reading Shirer passes time brushing up on Trotsky's *History of the Russian Revolution*, and Tolstoy's *War and Peace.* He plans Christmas 1937 in Vienna with the very talented and experienced foreign service diplomat John

Wiley and his wife, they too having been exiled a safe distance from the Kremlin. He tells Bullitt, "John, our chargé d'affaires here now. Walter Duranty there, as always ..." Shirer fills in Bullitt on all his insider friends, for example, Chip Bohlen, "on leave from the Moscow Embassy" living "next door to the Rothschild palace. The owners, being Jewish, have removed themselves to Czechoslovakia for greater safety…" As though Bullitt didn't know! Duranty, in fact, is living in Vienna "for a few months" and had long talks with Shirer who writes Bullitt on November 11, "Litvinov refuses to broadcast and seems worried by news from Moscow that his private Secretary has been arrested by the OGPU." Hitler has staged his purge of the SA, and Rohm's death Shirer calls a "suicide" in a Munich jail. In June Shirer aims for "a post in Berlin to cover the Nazi shakeup; there August 25 he writes in his diary Rohm "shot on orders from Hitler". Shirer meets Knickerbocker and Dorothy Thompson, author of *I Saw Hitler*. She too gets expelled from Naziland, and "Knick" figures "on Goebbels's bad list". (W. Shirer, *The Rise and Fall of the Third Reich,* 89-90)

Shirer and his friend Gillie formerly correspondent with the *Morning Post* takes him past "a building where a year ago for days on end, he said, you could hear the yells of the Jews being tortured". They call on Dodd at the embassy "a blunt, honest, liberal man with the kind of integrity an American ambassador needs here." Shirer covered the annual Nazi Party rally at Nuremberg September 4 and called it his "thorough introduction to Nazi Germany". Knickerbocker was reporting for INS and Shirer for Universal. "Like a roman emperor Hitler rode into this mediaeval town at sundown today past solid phalanxes of wildly cheering Nazi who packed the narrow streets…Tens of thousands of Swastika flags blot out the Gothic beauties of the place,…I got my first glimpse of Hitler as he drove by our hotel, the Wurtemberger Hof, to his headquarters down the street at the Deutscher. … He fumbled his cap with his left hand and as he stood in his car acknowledging the delirious welcome with somewhat feeble Nazi salutes from his right arm.,…for the life of me I could not quite comprehend what hidden springs he undoubtedly unloosed in the hysterical mob which was greeting him so wildly … there is something glassy in his eyes, the strongest thing in his face. He almost seemed to be affecting a modesty in his bearing. I doubt if its genuine." Shirer observes "a mob of ten thousand hysterics who jammed the moat in front of Hitler's hotel, shouting, 'We want our Fuhrer', ... and they looked up at him as if he were a Messiah, their faces transformed into something positively inhuman."

The next day William Shirer writes, "I'm beginning to comprehend, I think, some of the reasons for Hitler's astounding success. Borrowing a chapter from the Roman church, he is restoring pageantry and colour and mysticism to the drab lives of the twentieth-century Germans." Later that week at Nuremberg Shirer and other correspondents look on as Hitler harangued 50,000 SA storm troopers not long after the SA chief Ernst Rohm murder in the "Night of the Long Knives" killings by the SS and Gestapo late June and early July 1934. "We wondered if just one of those fifty-thousand brownshirts wouldn't pull a revolver, but not one did." Months later at the Nuremberg rally, Hitler announced a Four-Year plan "to make Germany self-sufficient in raw materials. Göring to be in charge. Obviously a war plan, but of course the Germans deny it. Party rally mostly concerned this year with attacking Bolshevism and the Soviets. There is talk of a break in diplomatic relations."

Not willing to miss the Nazi pageantry of the Olympic Games held in Berlin Shirer wrangles a pass with Holdomor journalist Ralph Barnes. In from London, on October 8, Shirer lunches with Bill Stoneman who has just replaced John Gunther as *Chicago Daily News* correspondent there. Stoneman is all excited about losing a sensational gossip scoop of Simpson divorcing her husband. Shirer notes in his diary "It's a tremendous scoop and should blow the story. Obviously the King intends to marry the woman now and maker her Queen."

Invited but not on the flight Shirer narrowly misses going down with his wife on the Hindenburg zeppelin at Lakehurst. Later that year he observes, on September 27, 1937, "Much of what is going on and will go on could be learned by the outside world from *Mein Kampf*, the Bible and Koran together of the Third Reich. But – amazingly – there is no decent translation of it in English or French, and Hitler will not allow one to be made, which is understandable, for it would shock many in the West." Hitler admits world domination by the Master Race "of the entire globe". Shirer makes it perfectly clear what Hitler writes in *Mein Kampf*. "France is to be annihilated, says Hitler, and then the great drive to the eastward is to begin."

This past summer 2013 discarded from a public library on Block Island I found a 1937 American edition of *Mein Kampf* (*My Battle*) first published by Houghton Mifflin in 1933. In his chapter "Eastern Policy" Hitler declares, "As a Nationalist, estimating humanity by the principle of race, I cannot admit that it is right to chain the fortunes of one's nation to the so-called 'oppressed nationalities', since I know how worthless they are racially... The menace which Russia suffered under is one which perpetually hangs over Germany. Germany is the next great objective of Bolshevism." (Adolf Hitler, *My Battle* / *Mein Kampf*, Boston: Houghton Mifflin, 1933, 285)

Shirer also notes that Lord Lothian had been once again called to Berlin for talks with Göering. By the time of his appointment to Washington, in 1939, Lord Lothian is a veteran of over two dozen crossings to the US; the minister knows his mission for Churchill is to secure Roosevelt's firm commitment to save England.

What is a silent night? What is a World War?

In just over two years once Barbarossa was underway the loss of life, – Ukrainian, Russian and German – is beyond the imagination of most people, including the typical American observer. On the siege and encirclement of Leningrad, for example, the most lethal siege in world history, Shirer writes, "The Red Army had lost nearly 3 million men – 44,000 a day – many of them in great encirclements at Kiev and Vyz'ma. Stalin started the war with almost 5 million soldiers under arms; now, this number was temporarily reduced to 2.3 million. By October 90 million people, 45 percent of Russia's prewar population, inhabited territory controlled by the Germans; two-thirds of the country's prewar manufacturing plant had been overrun...The Russians lost twenty casualties for every German, six tanks for every panzer; in October their losses were even worse than those of the summer, with sixty-four divisions written off. But other formations survived, and clung to their positions ... "The capture of Leningrad was one of the three strategic goals of Operation Barbarossa; for two and a half years that started on September 8, 1941 and endured until January 27. 1944. Up to one and a half million Russian soldiers and civilians died during the siege in Hitler's plan to raze the city and exterminate the population to burdensome to feed. At the Nuremberg war crimes trial in 1946 the courtroom was hushed to silence to hear the final cry from the diary of Tanya Savicheva, 11, her notes telling about starvation and deaths of her grandmother, then uncle, then mother, then brother, "Only Tanya is left." She died of progressive dystrophy after the siege. Between June 1941 and May 1944, each month Germany suffered an average of 60,000 men killed in the east; though the enemy's losses were far greater, this was a shocking statistic." (M. Hastings, *Inferno*, 155-63)

Richard J. Evans, Cambridge history professor and author of three large volumes on World War II is not bashful about describing genocidal atrocities but he pays no homage to the victims of the Holodomor in *The Third Reich at War*. His focus instead on the racial extermination agenda of Hitler's invasion plan are pertinent to the Holodomor history in view of how the Terror-Famine gave precedence to Hitler and reinforced his fundamental and well-known determination to eradicate the Slavs and Jews from Russian Ukraine and all other territories of the USSR. Inspired by legends of great Teutonic knights in a death-grip with a modern day Genghis Khan in the Kremlin, Hitler stated his intention to leave only behind and then they too would eventually disappear. Evans too refers to *Mein Kampf* where Hitler reveals in the early twenties his dream for the conquest of the Russian grain lands and the imperative historical right and urgency to acquire it for *Lebensraum* ("living space") of German expansion eastward.

As early as February 3, 1933, he emphatically reaffirms to his army chiefs his intentions to move quickly towards Eastern Europe in his land grab and depopulation scheme. Furthermore, the Americans and the British both had sophisticated code-breaking intelligence operations for decades, code-named "Magic", and "Ultra", respectively. Whatever they failed to gather from on the ground diplomatic and intelligence contacts government policy planners were privy to cable intercepts. By the end of July 1940 Hitler had informed his senior command to begin planning for an invasion. Evans writes of the Fuhrer's spirited optimism when he declares, "Eight to 100 divisions would be needed to crush the Red Army. It would be child's play in comparison to the invasion of France." (R. J. Evans, 160)

Reich architect and minister Albert Speer confides in his diary December 21, 1946 his consternation upon hearing the accusations and statements of his fellow Nuremberg prisoners of the Nazi plan of extermination and the slave labor concentration camps under his control as *Reichsminister* of the Todt and Armaments. It's an extraordinary admission of a self-demented war criminal forced to confront his own sick perversion once utterly defeated in war and incarcerated by the victor. He writes of Hitler's maniacal obsession extolling the eradication of Jews, Slavs and Bolsheviks. "And then this beastly way of talking! How was it I never really felt revolted by it, never flared up when Hitler- as he did almost all the time in the last few years – spoke of 'annihilation' or 'extermination'. Certainly those who would charge me with opportunism or cowardice are being too simplistic. The terrible thing, the thing that disturbs me much more, is that I did not really notice this vocabulary, that it never upset me. Only now, in retrospect, am I horrified ...'

"Afternoon. Of course all such talk was also connected with the ideological fever Hitler communicated to all events, but especially to the campaign against Bolshevism. He felt himself the protector of Europe against the Red hordes, as he used to phrase it. He believed I the most literal sense that it was a question of to be or not to be. Again and again he came back to that. The litany of the later years ran: 'We must win the war or the peoples of Europe will be mercilessly annihilated. Stalin will not stand still. He'll march on to the west; in France the Communists are already calling for him. Once the Russians have Europe, all our cultural monuments will be destroyed. Europe will become a dessert, cultureless, emptied of people, nothing but low scum left and chaos everywhere. Don't forget, Stalin is Genghis Khan come back from the abyss of history. Compared to what's going to happen if we should lose, the devastation of our cities is a joke. We with our two hundred divisions weren't able to stop the Russians; then how are a few Allied divisions going to do it? The Anglo-Saxons will abandon Europe without a struggle. I'm sure of that. They'll leave it to the cannibals. After the big encirclements we found human bones, you know. Imagine that, they ate each other up out of hunger. Just so they wouldn't have to surrender. They you have it, they're subhuman.' I heard him make this last remark repeatedly, and even then the contradiction struck me. For he charged the Russians with being *Untermenschen,* for conduct – at least as far as their unyielding determination to resist was concerned – that he again and again demanded of his own soldiers. But this contradiction which today strikes me as infuriating did not bother me at the time. How was that possible? Perhaps the contradiction was somehow resolved in the personality of Hitler and could appear obvious only after his death. It is generally admitted that Hitler admired what he hated; it is really more accurate to say that he hated what he admired. His hatred was admiration that he refused to acknowledge. This is true of the Jews, of Stalin, of communism in general." (Albert Speer, *Spandau, The Secret Diaries*, NY: Macmillan, 1976, 26-7)

With the spectre of victory of resurgent all-powerful Germany against Stalin armed with master weapons of atomic and rocket power, poison nerve gas, armed forces domination land, sea and air, slave labor and willing executioners of the master Aryan race at peace in the luxury of their comfortable homes, Hitler elaborated his "General Plan for the East" to his generals reaching across Poland, the Ukraine through Belarus and European Russia into the rich Caucasus oil fields of Baku. Evans writes, "In July 1941, Hitler amused himself by painting castles in the air for his guests on the subject of the future of Eastern Europe. Once conquest was complete, he said, the Germans would annex vast masses of territory for their own racial survival and expansion. 'The law of selection justifies this incessant struggle, by allowing the survival of the fittest.' 'It's inconceivable that a higher people should painfully exist on a soil too narrow for it, whilst amorphous masses, which contribute nothing to civilization, occupy infinite tracts of a soil that is one of the richest in the world."

The Crimea and the southern Ukraine would become 'an exclusively German colony', he said. The existing inhabitants would be 'pushed out'. As for the rest of the east, a handful of Englishmen had controlled millions of Indians, he said, so it would be with the Germans in Russia: The German colonist ought to live on handsome, spacious farms. The German services will be lodged in marvelous buildings, the governors in palaces... Around the city, to a depth of thirty or forty kilometers, we shall have a belt of handsome villages connected by the best roads. What exists beyond that will be another world, in which we mean to let the Russians live as they like. It is merely necessary that we should rule them. In the event of a revolution, we shall only have to drop a few bombs on their cities, and the affair will be liquidated." Great German roads, autobans, would connect the German towns of colonists, and German blood would be united from visitors returning to mix with their own kind "from all over Western Europe and even America". Hitler predicts only some 20 million Russians would remain by the sixties and Russian cities would "fall to pieces". (M. Hastings, *Inferno*, 152, cites the Nazi "plans for a transfer east of 30 million Germanic colonists" to resettle the Ukraine.)

Inspired by their Furher Nazi soldiers of the Wehrmacht dream of settling down in his "colonial existence" and ownership of their private farmland stolen from the Slavs, 50 million of them to be exiled to Siberia. Aly Goltz recalls in *Hitler's Beneficiaries* (2006) a typical reverie voiced in a letter to his parents, December 31, 1943, from Heinrich Boll, of the Wehrmacht in the east, and the Literature Nobel laureate in 1972. Writers of children's books animated the fantasy modeled after the American taming of the Wild West. "They concocted the following flights of fancy: 'Let us now borrow Tom Thumb's magic boots and take a walk through a foreign land. We'll need them if we hope to get there. ... Here we are in the fruitful terrain of black soil ... The corn rustles along the wheat and rye." (Aly Gotz, *Hitler's Beneficiaries: Plunder, Racial War and the Nazi Welfare State,* Henry Holt-Metropolitan, 2006, 31-40)

Max Hastings also provides a fair and relative description to help put the slaughter into perspective, and he observed, "Berlin was indifferent. Hitler sought to conquer as much land, and to inherit as few people, as his armies could contrive. He often cited the precedent of the nineteenth century American frontier, where the native inhabitants were almost extinguished to make way for settlers." Anyone who reads Teddy Roosevelt's writings of eradicating native American Indian tribes to clear lands for settlement may wonder of the genocidal connections of empire mentality in extermination behavior of the so-called civilized cultured elites of the world, and, in particular, men like McKinley, Roosevelt, Root, Taft and Stimson who celebrated the imperial thrust of Pax Americana of economic and military expansionism fostered by their leaders in Washington. (M. Hastings, *Inferno*, 146)

Hitler, again quoted in the excellent volume by Richard Evans, was mesmerized by his great extermination dream building Germany's Nazi empire with high-speed trains at 200 km per hour on special track for the Crimea "Reich Motorway" from Hamburg to the Black Sea. "'Larger carriages will be required – probably double-deckers, which will give the passengers on the upper deck an opportunity of admiring the landscape. This will presumably entail the construction of a very much broader-gauge permanent way than that at present in use, and the number of lines must be doubled in order to be able to cope with an intensification of traffic...This alone will enable us to realize our plans for the exploitation of the Eastern territories ... Of what importance will the thousand-kilometre stretch to the Crimea be,' he asked, 'when we can cover it at eighty kilometers an hour along the motorway and do the whole distance easily in two days!'" Extreme care was taken by construction engineer and armament-munitions *Reichsminister* Dr. Fritz Todt and his successor Speer to ensure that their detailed plans for an *Autobahnen* stretching across the plains to the Urals preserve a natural harmony guided by his "philosophy of the beauty of the highway" in sync with the contours of the landscape. (A. Speer, 400)

As Stalin had succeeded in liquidating Ukrainians and other non-Russian ethnic populations, Hitler launches his military campaign to efface Russian society and culture off the map "In comparison with Russia," Hitler raves, "even Poland looked like a civilized country." Germany, he said, offers "no remorse" in their mission of "annihilation" to eradicate the indigenous barbarians. "We're not going to play at children's nurses; we're absolutely without obligations as far as these people are concerned." The Reich would provide no health or educational facilities. A day before the Barbarossa invasion, SS chief Heinrich Himmler prepares a neat report of Hitler's ideas in the so-called "General Plan for the East"; months earlier in January he had told his SS officers during their meetings in their 17th century Wewelsburg Castle northeast of North Rhine-Westphalia. One week before Operation Barbarossa a special meeting is held at Wewelsburg assembling troops of the *Einsatzgruppen* SS paramilitary death squads that were responsible for mass killings, typically by shooting targeting Jews, gypsies and Soviet Communist Party commissars, in particular. Their main assignment is to kill civilians and to that end they review extermination procedures to systematically reduce the Slav population by 30 million starving them to death.

After Stalin's call for a partisan war, Hitler on July 16, 1941 responded in private, "The Russians have now issued an order for a partisan war behind our front. This partisan war has its advantage: it allows us to exterminate all who oppose us." Himmler meets with Hitler on December 18, 1941. When Himmer asks the Furher, "What to do with the Jews of Russia?" Hitler answers, "*als Partisanen auszurotten*" ("exterminate them as partisans"). A "second sweep" started in late December. *Einsatzgruppe A* had already murdered almost all Jews in its area, and had little else to do, so it shifted its operations into Belorussia to assist *Einsatzgruppe B*. In four days of slaughter, in February, *Einsatzgruppe D* reduced the Jewish population of Dnepropetrovsk from 30,000 to 702. (Yehuda

Bauer, *Rethinking the Holocaust,* Yale Univ. Press, 2000, 5; Raul Hilberg, *The Destruction of European Jews,* NY: Holmes & Meier, 1985, 368-72)

While Germany suffered its own bad harvests Nazi food specialists had studied Stalin's grain problem well. "Soviet cities," Richard Evans writes, "many of them created by Stalin's brutal forced industrialization in the 1930s were to be starved out of existence, while practically the entire food production of the conquered areas was to be used to feed the invading German armies and maintain nutritional standards at home, so that the malnourishment and starvation that (Hitler believed) had played such a baleful part in the collapse of the German home-front in the First World War would not be repeated in the Second. This 'hunger plan' was developed above all by Herbert Backe (1896-47), State Secretary, Food Supply in the Reich Agriculture Ministry." Yale history professor Timothy Snyder in his book *Bloodlands* (2010) Backe's extermination calculations resulted in "4.2 million Soviet citizens (largely Russians, Belarusians, and Ukrainians) starved by the German occupiers in 1941-1944". (Timothy Snyder, *Bloodlands*, London: Bodley Head, NY: Perseus, 2010)

The German masses and their military actually believed the Nazi fairytale of real-life utopia. They resented their economic misery imposed upon by them Versailles for having lost the war. Gotz writes, "Three memories were particularly traumatic: the food shortages caused by the British naval blockade, the devaluation of the currency, and the civil unrest that followed defeat. More than 400,000 people starve to death during the war – a number that does not include those who died prematurely by tuberculosis and other infectious diseases made worse by malnutrition." Gotz's book explores how the morally and financially corrupt, bankrupt and debt-burdened Nazi regime was unsustainable, and doomed economically. Gotz writes, "Hitler bridged what he and his leadership knew to be a precarious financial situation with military adventures that had terrible consequences for millions of people. Dispossession, deportation and mass murder became the major sources of state income." (A. Goltz, *Hitler's Beneficiaries*, 31-40)

Ukrainians who work ten hours a day must work eight for the Reich, declared Koch. "Everyone seems to think that their most basic task is to make their own lives as comfortable as possible by hoarding as much food as they can and sending it back home. In any case, superhuman feats have been achieved in this area. Illegal trading and black marketeering are in full bloom. What the Jews used to do is now being carried out in much more highly perfected form by 'Aryans'." Encouraged by Hitler and his commanders empowered with weapons and propaganda the Germans excelled in their greed and plunder. "The whole thing, writes one observer in Ukraine, is reminiscent of the 'trade' with Negro tribes and the 'exchange' of glass pearls for ivory." (A. Gotz, 113)

Before an assembly of educated and cultured members of a Gentleman's Club in Berlin, a Reich agricultural adviser Hans Deetjen explained the Nazi right of conquest and exploitation, and he declared "According to statements from the highest offices, Ukraine will be made to 'pay for the war'. Our policies toward the local population are designed with that goal in mind. Ukraine is to provide cheap labor both for the Reich and for the exploitation of agriculture and natural resources in that country itself... The standard of living there has to be kept low. Only then can the necessary surpluses be produced in Europe." (A. Gotz, 308)

Born May 1, 1896 in the Caucasus, Batumi, in 1914, Herbert Backe graduated from the Russian school in Tbilisi, Georgia. He survived the Great War interned in Czarist Russia, and later studied at the University of Gottingen; 1923 to 1924 he serves as assistant rector of the Technical School in Hanover; he joins the Nazi Party in 1925 becoming a member of the Nazi Party Congress convened by Hitler the next year, on February 14, in Bamberg, Bavaria, he helps develop a party program. A specialist in agricultural policy, Backe serves as minister of food supply from 1944 to 19 45. Backe kills himself in the Nuremberg prison, April 6, 1947.

Backe worked with Reich Agriculture Minister Richard Walther Darré (1895-53). In power since 1933 Darré is Hitler's leading Nazi ideologue extolling the rich Nordic blood of the peasantry, and for many years is on good personal terms with Reinhard Heydrich, SS head in Czechoslovakia. The transcript of a 1940 speech by Darré published December 9, 1940, in *Life* foretells their cosmogonic myth of regeneration and longevity: "by blitzkrieg ... before autumn ... we shall be the absolute masters of two continents ... a new aristocracy of German masters will be created (with) slaves assigned to it, these slaves to be their property and to consist of landless, non-German nationals ... we actually have in mind a modern form of medieval slavery which we must and will introduce because we urgently need it in order to fulfill our great tasks. These slaves will by no means be denied the blessings of illiteracy; higher education will, in future, be reserved only for the German population of Europe ...". Didn't America get the message clear yet? Darré was sentenced at Nuremberg to seven years imprisonment. He serves only three. Freed from prison in 1950, Darré soon drowns in alcohol. (Gesine Gerhard, "Food and Genocide. Nazi Agrarian Politics in the occupied territories of the Soviet Union", *Contemporary European History* v. 18, Issue 1, 2009, 57-62; T. Snyder, *Bloodlands*, 411)

Yale Professor Tom Snyder in *Bloodlands* (2010) avoids the issue Anglo-American investment in the fascist regimes. That the Ivy League university press as well as Oxbridge tend to publish writers who do so in alarming trend in this day and age. Likewise for the most part the issue of a Ukrainian Genocide is dismissed as too problematic for scholars. So they perpetuate the Holodomor taboo of Consortium investment, gulag totalitarian slave labor under Stalin, and the Anglo-American war strategy for a postwar New Order. It seems no less incongruous, nor odd, that Snyder ignores the significant contributions to Holodomor research in the sixties by the State Department agriculture specialist Dr. Dana Dalrymple, nor does he acknowledge the more recent published disclosures of fellow professor Dr. James Mace in Kiev.

For Snyder the subject of Genocide in the Ukraine comes not without some risk to his general thesis of Consortium neutrality of the blue-bloods and Roosevelt's war strategy for the postwar new world order of American dominance. Nor is it likely that the honorable Yale professor would venture to bite the hand that feeds him and risk his tenure. But Snyder's dismissal and denial of the Holodomor events is very odd, indeed. In fact, its more than odd, its absolutely outrageous. Perhaps, and reader we must hope it will come to pass that one day there will be, and it we should sit on our rear ends and wait for this but rather invite the professor to a conference for a proper hearing on this controversy. I assure you reader, the conference will be open and online.

In light of the fact that he introduces his book with a preface titled "Europe" with its first paragraph about the continuity of Genocide from the 1933 to 1945 era, and among its victims an eleven year old girl facing death when "Stalin was deliberately starving the Ukraine", and later after Hitler's invasion of the USSR, "a twelve-year-old Jewish girl in Belarus wrote a last letter to her father. … She was among the more than five million Jews gassed or shot by the Germans."

Albeit his exacting detail Snyder fails to consider that of the total number of Holodomor victims, Stalin exterminated "three million children in the Ukraine alone", *or one in three*, as recalled in the heart-rendering memoir published in 1989 by the young brave teenager Nina Markovna, with her red Pioneer kerchief and perfect junior communist salute, at home with her family in Feodosia on the Black Sea. Nina's poignant story tells how they suffered and sacrificed; then the Germans came in 1941, with more extermination while she secretly prays to her *Boshinka*. She pondered her dilemma: "That Pioneer kerchief and its pledge – to what, to whom? A strange, rebellious thought possessed my whole being. Can I serve two masters? Can anyone serve two masters?" She buried the kerchief, and sighed, "There, I thought, in great relief – now *Boshinka*-God will truly watch over my fat father." (Nina Markovna, *Nina's Journey*, Washington DC, Regnery Gateway, 1989, 153-9)

It seems most remarkable that a scholar with his talent and support from one of the finest universities in the world should use his skill to obscure the genuine issues of causality and continuity between these two events, the Holodomor that precedes the Holocaust. Instead, Synder groups all the victims together in so-called "killing zones" of Europe. In so doing, Synder writes, "The victims were chiefly Jews, Belorussians, Ukrainians, Poles, Russians, and Balts, the peoples native to these lands. The fourteen million were murdered over the course of only twelve years, between 1933 and 1945, while both Hitler and Stalin were in power." It's all too easy to get lost in the numbers while it remains academic not to.

Throughout Snyder appears to minimalize the Ukrainian Holodomor tragedy overshadowed as it was by the subsequent Nazi horrors of Wehrmacht extermination while America's "Uncle Joe" and the communist peoples of Soviet Russia were literally dying to win the war for the West. For example, he writes "The very worst of the killing began when Hitler betrayed Stalin and German forces crossed into the recently enlarged Soviet Union in June 1941. Although the Second World War began in September 1939 with the joint German-Soviet invasion of Poland, the tremendous majority of its killing followed that second eastern invasion. In Soviet Ukraine, Soviet Belarus, and the Leningrad district, lands where the Stalinist regime had starved and shot some four million people in the previous eight years, German forces managed to starve and shoot even more in half that time."

In the preface Synder writes, "Mass killing in Europe is usually associated with the Holocaust, and the Holocaust with rapid industrial killing. The image is too simple and clean. At the German and Soviet killing sites, the methods of murder were rather primitive. Of the fourteen million civilians and prisoners of war killed in the bloodlands between 1933 and 1945, more than half died because they were denied food. Europeans deliberately starved Europeans in horrific numbers in the middle of the twentieth century. The two largest mass killing actions after the Holocaust – Stalin's directed famines of the early 1930's and Hitler's starvation of Soviet prisoners of war in the early 1940s – involved this method of killing. Starvation was foremost not only in reality but in imagination. In a Hunger Plan, the Nazi regime projected the death by starvation of tens of millions of Slavs and Jews in the winter of 1941 and 1942."

Reader, you may well understand that other demonstrative examples are too numerous to cite but that is the Yale professor's general thrust. We know that Stalin "imagined" with nightmarish power of his capacity to dream sick in mind but not frightened of his full official powers, and he steadily plans the extermination by hunger of millions of the Russian Ukrainian peasants as early in 1929 if not sooner. Although he averts the moral issues of western engagement with the fascist regimes of Berlin and Moscow, while at the same time describing the "mass killing of the twentieth century is of the greatest moral significance for the twenty-first" century, in his attempt to write "the history of the bloodlands," – without any political engagement from the West which made it all possible, if not inevitable as it was well known in advance as most probable if not logically inevitable by agricultural experts, principally on the scene Bolsheviks, Germans and Americans, in both declared intention and deed – Prof. Snyder is correct when he writes, "Hitler was remaking the German political system in spring 1933 – at the same time that Stalin was asserting his own personal authority in the Soviet Union." In terms of the practical lessons to be gained by the utility of extermination demonstrated and duly noted mutual consolidation of power and means should not go down lightly. Meanwhile, London and Washington, too, waits comfortably from a distance, for the pieces and events to fall into place assuring their role as guardians of world power. (T. Snyder, *Bloodlands*, vii, xi)

But what are we to make of Snyder's calculations? Of course the numbers are mind-boggling but not totally beyond the reach of human comprehension. In writing his history of "the purposeful murder of fourteen million people by two regimes over a short time and in certain parts of Europe", he elaborates on what this means to him. "Fourteen million, after all, is a very large number. It exceeds by more than ten million the number of people who died in all of the Soviet and German concentration camps (as opposed to the death facilities) taken together over the entire history of both the Soviet Union and Nazi Germany. If current standard estimates of military losses are correct, it exceeds by more than two million the number of German and Soviet soldiers, taken together, killed on the battlefield in the Second World War (counting starved and executed prisoners of war as victims of a policy of mass murder rather than as military casualties). *It exceeds by more than thirteen million the number of American and British casualties, taken together, of the Second World War.* It also exceeds by more than thirteen million all of the American battlefield losses in all of the foreign wars that the United States has ever fought." What about twenty million Russian soldiers and civilians dead from all causes during the First World War alone? Those numbers just didn't mean very much to Churchill, Roosevelt and their friends in the Consortium just so long as British and American lives were spared. (T. Snyder, *Bloodlands*, 411; italics added)

THE YALE PROFESSOR WONDERS, "WAS IT GENOCIDE?"

Hitler's war quickly assumed the dimension of a post-medieval modern monstrosity of barbarism. Max Hastings writes in *Inferno*, "The ruthlessness of the invaders was swiftly revealed. In France in 1940, more than a million French prisoners were caged and fed; in Russia, by contrast, prisoners were caged only to perish. First in hundreds of thousands, soon in *millions*; they were starved to death in accordance with their captors' design, and inability to come with such numbers even had they wished to do so – the Reich's camps had capacity for only 790,000. Some prisoners resorted to cannibalism..." (M. Hastings, 146)

In fact, Snyder does not readily acknowledge the Terror-Genocide of the Holodomor. It's a problematic definition as he makes clear in his chapter "Numbers and Terms". "Was it genocide? he asks rhetorically?" Perhaps this investigation will bring him farther down the path lined with bodies and ghosts of the exterminated. Regarding the famine deaths Professor Snyder picked a low number of "3.3 million Soviet citizens in 1932-33 (mostly Ukrainians) deliberately starved by their own government in Soviet Ukraine". Snyder writes much about the Holocaust but he gets the clock backwards when he notes, "Stalin's crimes were enabled by Hitler's policies."

It was the other way around. Interestingly, Snyder does account for increasing postwar numbers of Ukrainian gulag prisoners, often transported in American Studebaker trucks. After some refinement in May, the Hitlerian "General Plan for the East" is adopted July 1942 as official Reich policy. The extermination plan proposes "to remove between 80 and 85 per cent of the Polish population, 64 per cent of the Ukrainian and 75 per cent of the Belorussian, expelling them further east or allowing them to perish from disease and malnutrition. Not counting the Jewish population of these areas", Evans observes, adding "the Plan thus envisaged the forcible uprooting of at least 31 million people from their homes, in what would no doubt be a murderously violent process of dispossession; some estimates, taking into account projected population increases, put the number at no fewer than 45 million. ... The space vacated by the Slavs would be occupied by 10 million Germans. The borders of Germany would in effect be extended a thousand kilometers to the east." Even after the precedent set by the horrors of the Holodomor it's no wonder why the overwhelming majority of Ukrainians and their fellow Russian Soviet citizens passionately defend their homeland with limitless fury. (T. Snyder, *Bloodlands*, 409-14; R. J. Evans, 173-4)

Without explicitly citing the Holodomor as a factor leading toward a total lack of moral will inured by years of mass killings Max Hastings comments on the executions *en masse* by German soldiers of the heavily indoctrinated Wehrmacht, and he writes, "Posterity is fascinated by the ease with which the Nazis found so many ordinary men – to borrow the title of Christopher Browning's study – *Ordinary Men* (1998) – willing to murder in cold blood vast numbers of innocents, of all ages and both sexes. Yet there is ample evidence in modern experience that many people are ready to kill others to order, once satisfied that this fulfills the wishes of those whose authority they accept. Hundreds of thousands of Russians were complicit in the deaths of millions of their countrymen at the behest of Stalin and Beria, before the Holocaust was thought of. Germany's generals themselves may not have killed civilians, but they were happy to acquiesce in and even enthuse about others doing so." Browning observes how the 500 soldiers of Nazi Battalion 101 in November 1943 summarily slaughtered some 38,000 Jews and hustled another 45,000 to certain death on trains bound for the Treblinka concentration camp. Hastings writes, "Browning found no evidence that any sanction was imposed upon those who refused to kill; in one of the most highly educated societies in Europe, it was easy to find men willing to murder those whom their rulers defined as state enemies, without employing duress." (M. Hastings, *Inferno*, 505)

From Berlin William Shirer on March 30, 1940 writes of the German Foreign Office press release of a "White Book containing what is purported to be sixteen documents discovered by the Germans in the Warsaw Foreign Office. Germany's Foreign Minister von Ribbentrop says they are secret reports of various Polish envoys. The most important are from the Polish ambassadors in London, Paris, and Washington. They 'implicate' American Ambassadors Kennedy, Bullitt, and Biddle (Anthony J. Drexel Biddle sic), and the point of them is that these diplomats, backed by Roosevelt, were leading conspirators in forcing this war on Germany!" Ribbentrop was convinced the "documents" would greatly strengthen the hand of the American isolationists by convincing the American people that Roosevelt and his personally appointed ambassadors had not only had a hand in starting the war but had done everything to get us in." Shirer dismisses the alleged reports as "probably only doctored" but possibly not "faked", and he later commented, "They gave an intimation of the machinations of that Jewish-plutocratic clique whose influence, through Morgan and Rockefeller, reached all the way up to Roosevelt." Who distorts the truth? When is the half truth also half lie? (W. Shirer, *The Rise and Fall of the Third Reich,* 688)

By December 1, 1940 seven months *before* Barbarossa Germany was producing 1500 to 1600 planes per month and looking for something superior to Spitfires and Cobras built in America. "Maximum German production capacity is 3,000 planes a month," Shirer writes in *Berlin Diary*, and he adds, "The German has two characters. As an individual he will give his rationed bread to feed the squirrels in the Tiergarten on a Sunday morning. He can be a kind and considerate person. But as a unit in the Germanic mass he can persecute Jews, torture and murder his fellow men in a concentration camp, massacre women and children by bombing and bombardment, overrun without the slightest justification the lands of other peoples, cut them down if they protest, and enslave them... It is the evil genius of Adolf Hitler that has aroused this basic feeling and given it tangible expression. It is due to this remarkable and terrifying man alone that the German dream now stands such a fair chance of coming true. First Germans and then the world grossly underestimated him. It was an appalling error, as first the Germans and now the world are finding out." (W. L. Shirer, *Berlin Diary*, 581)

Dodd and Schacht were together again, in Paris, on November 18, 1937, attending a dinner given by the French Embassy to celebrate Bullitt's arrival there. Bullitt promptly commits another of frequent and brandished blunders over Polish diplomatic documents supposedly captured by the Germans which allegedly revealed, as he now confides to Dodd arriving after three days in Warsaw, "that Foreign Minister Beck of Poland had assured him again and again that the Poles would do everything possible for peace, not ally themselves with any nation, except on commercial matters, and not intervene if Germany annexed Czechoslovakia or if Russia seized Finland." Bullitt insists to Dodd that the information confirms that the West would defend Poland if attacked. The next day, November 19, Dodd joins Schacht with Bullitt in Berlin for a luncheon with two dozen guests many of them intimate with Hitler's "Circle of Friends". Since 1933, SS General Himmler has been working closely with his favorite fascists in a nest of Morgan and Rockefeller bankers and industrialists in league with Schacht, with contact dating back even further. They were all high-ranked and well-informed with access to confidential diplomatic and military reports of the foreign ministry as well as the public press. To them the human tragedy of the starvation and unrest the Ukraine had been no secret. The Nazis as well as Stalin's commissars are preparing to exploit any surviving partisan Ukrainian nationalist on the outbreak of war.

Economics minister Dr. Schacht imploringly confides he'll take a job in the White House. "Yes," Schacht tells Dodd, "I would be delighted to see the President often." Dodd made a note in his diary, "I wonder what he was going to do with the Hitler statue in his parlor or with the painting of Goering which I saw in his house the last time I was there...Of course he will lose his property in the event that he is able to slip out some way..." (W. E. Dodd, *Ambassador Dodd's Diary*)

Within the "Circle of Friends" (which became known as *Freundeskreis Reichführer SS* or *Freundeskreis Himmler*) with Schacht is Dr. Karl Blessing (1900-71) chief economics expert in 1933 in Hitler's reorganized economic ministry with a seat on the inner council of the Deutsche Reichsbank "to finance, prepare and complete armament and war preparations".

In 1929 Blessing assists Schacht in Paris for the Young Plan talks. After the war to Blessing will emerge out of detention to direct Deutsche Bundesbank (1958-69), alongside other high-ranking Nazis including Dr. Guenther Frank-Fahle, former director of Farben and their liaison man with the Consortium's cartel of American chemical companies. Farben in a letter to a South African firm describes Blessing as "one of Schacht's closest collaborators". Blessing is never sentenced as a war criminal. Instead Blessing is appointed German governor in the International Monetary Fund headquartered in Washington and is a member of the governing council of the all-powerful BIS, in Basel. Hitler's senior economist becomes head of Germany's Federal Bank in 1957.

It is quite clear reader that this critical year 1933 is a very bad year for the Ukrainians caught in the Holodomor Terror-Famine Genocide. FDR is crowned in the White House, Hilter takes over in Germany and Stalin is firmly entrenched in the Kremlin. So, reader, why do people sing "Happy Days Are Here Again" in America? Just follow the bouncing ball…

Nor are these events we may fear as isolated or random events as news editors make them seem. Take another step, look down, and see the deep intertwining roots spread and grow and tighten and squeeze the world's patience sucking out the life until it order breaks down and all is torn apart. The Consortium men must have their war!

Blessing and Schacht in May jointly create the Metallurgische Forschungs GmbH (Mefo) to serve as a cover for Germany's secret rearmament with the firms Krupp, Siemens, Rheinmetall, and Deutsche Werkre... In 1941, Blessing is appointed chief of Kontinentale ÖL AG, the company in charge of Russia's Caucasian oil reserves vital to the Nazi war effort. Presently his grandson heads of the German Commerzbank.

The founding members of Schacht's "Circle of Friends" include Wilhem Keppler (1882-60), chairman of the IG Farben subsidiary Braunkohle-Benzin AG, exploiting oil from coal technology from Standard Oil of New Jersey. A trained chemical engineer he fought in the First World War, joined the Nazi Socialist Party (NSDAP) in 1927, was part owner of Odin Works, a small photographic gelatin factory. In December 1931 Hitler appoints Keppler Nazi Party economics adviser; two years later, on March 5, 1933 Keppler is elected to the Reichstag.

Condemned during the Nuremberg Ministries Trial to ten years in prison, on 14 April 1949, Keppler serves less than two years. Wilhem Keppler's nephew and *Wehrwirtschaftsführer* (Military Economy Leader) Fritz Kranefuss, a friend of Himmler and member of the board at Braunkohle-Benzin Aktiengesellschaft (Brabag), between 1938 and 1945, becomes the most important producer of synthetic fuel in the Reich and a leading user of concentration camp labor during the war; ITT Corp.'s executives include Kurt von Schröder and Emil Hinrich Meyer, a board member at the ITT's Germany-based subsidiaries Standard Elektrik Lorenz and Mix & Genest as well as AEG; August Rosterg, General Director of Wintershall; Otto Steinbrinck, Vice-President of Vereinigte Stahlwerke AG (a steel cartel founded in 1926 with Wall Street loans); Reichsbank President Schacht, Emil Helffrich of the German-American Petroleum Co. (94 per cent owned by Standard Oil of New Jersey); Friedrich Reinhardt, board chairman at Commerzbank; Ilseder Hütte chairman Ewald Hecker, and political figures Carl Vincent Krogmann and Gottfried Graf von Bismarck-Schönhausen.

Most of these senior industrialists are also members of the SS which attributes 18 per cent of its ranks grafted from the aristocratic class. Nazi Germany's success is dependent on maintaining a highly industrialized society. Germany's modernization of technology is stimulated by rearmament. Budget expenditures on arms increased from 5 per cent, in 1933 to 18 percent, in 1934, 25 per cent, in 1935 and more than doubles to 58 percent in 1938, or one-fifth of its gross national product requiring huge loans.

On the other side of the border, Stalin's extermination of the peasants and Nazi persecution of the Jews and preparations for the Holocaust are the backdrop of Hitler's economic plans for war and conquest in the Soviet Union. As late as December 1936 we find Dr. Schacht haggling over German-Soviet trade with a commercial rep sent by Stalin desperate for more time to prepare his defense and, on the verge of adding tens of thousands of senior military and Party officials to the lists of those millions of peasants killed and exiled in the Holodomor.

"Even at the XVII Party Congress in 1934, Stalin had hinted of the alternative policy of agreement with Germany," according to Robert Conquest in his book "The Great Terror", where he reviews Stalin's relations with Germany prior to the Nazi-Soviet Pact of 1939. "Of course we are far from enthusiastic about the Fascist regime in Germany", Litvinov declares. "But Fascism is beside the point, if only because Fascism in Italy, for example, has not kept the USSR from establishing the best relations with that country." Conquest omits to say, however, that also at that Party Congress of the AUCP(B) the all-powerful Stalin conveniently reports a population *increase* in 1933; from then on mention of the famine vanishes "even from secret documents", observed Holodomor researcher and writer Yuriy Shapoval of the National Academy of Sciences Ukraine in"Foreign Diplomats on the Holodomor in Ukraine" (2009).

Conquest went on, writing, "Litvinov was right. From 1936, and on the basis of the threat of his alternative anti-German policy, Stalin began to put out feelers to the Nazis, through his personal emissaries."

In 1933, Stalin's foreign trade commissar David Kandelaki under the guise of "commercial attaché" is dispatched to the soviet embassy in Berlin. By December 1936, he and Schacht negotiate a general framework for a Soviet-German trade agreement. Schacht insists first on a cessation of Communist agitation inside Germany. Back in Moscow Kandelaki obtains a written draft for a deal, secret or public. Kandelaki returns to Berlin to open direct negotiations, but Hitler tells Schacht to scrap it "unless Stalin committed "to develop further along the lines on an absolute despotism supported by the Army" since he refused to take Stalin at his word to cease forever promoting communism in Germany. Meanwhile Nazis and NKVD agents continue to meet secretly. Kandelaki returns to Moscow as deputy commissar in foreign trade. For his work negotiating trade and credit deals with the Germans Stalin awarded Kandelaki the Order of Lenin (1937), and the next year has him liquidated in the sweeping Purges. (R. Conquest, *The Great Terror, A Reassessment*, 196-7)

"THE HISTORY OF AN UNDERWORLD", SAYS LONDON'S RUSSIAN SCHOLAR

Men and women confront extreme difficulty in peculiar ways. A few rise to the challenge and resist the moral assault on their own Humanity. Most ignore the problem and do nothing which is not as damaging as those who pursue their own self interests and contribute to the problem. It is even worse when these people are experts, specialists with professional status and influence and shirk their responsibility as leaders in their particular domain of expertise escalating calamity into tragedy that overwhelms brave and strong individuals as well as defenseless. As founder and head of the London School of Slavonic Studies Bernard Pares falls in the latter category of Consortium experts who knowingly and willingly deceived the public about the Holodomor Terror-Famine. Even worse, the professor from a small country town in Surrey and an indefatigable Russian scholar and passionate lecturer, turned his back on his fellow Russians to please his paymasters.

Pares assiduously pushes Consortium and Soviet propaganda praising Bolshevik repression in the framework of socialist progress. Consequently he feels constrained and obliged to ignore the Holodomor, or risk a lifetime ban from the homeland of his professional interests. He compiles, in fact, a glowing account of the Soviet Union, published in 1936, a year after his trip there ending a sixteen year hiatus, – of the success of Stalin's state planning after a decade of foreign aid owing to the transfer of technology, technical training assistance and foreign credits.

For decades, Pares is able to stand out as England's imperial expert on all things Russian within the guidelines healthy to the Foreign Office dons. Before the October Revolution, he chronicled a sweeping narrative of his four years with the troops on the Russian Front during the First World War. Meanwhile Pares periodically visits Soviet Russia and remains attentive not to incur the suspicions of Soviet authorities. His affairs are more than just academic; the famous communist spies of the Oxbridge set, quite notably McLean, Burgess and Philby who are now burrowing holes deep within the British Establishment and which will wreak havoc during the war.

"State planning was set up by the Communists," Pares writes, "long before Stalin became the master, and the best minds were drawn into the work. It began with Lenin's attempt to achieve the quickest transition to the new State with the maximum of control by means of electrification (*Goelro*), which at the time was scoffed at by his critics as 'electrification'." The British Russian scholar fails to even hint of the existence of large corporate firms like Vickers, a Rothschild firm, and Westinghouse or GE responsible for Lenin's greatest gift to Russia's workers and peasants and symbol of the social transformation of the masses. The Red Star was illuminated by General Electric; Lenin pulled the switch. Let there be Light! Constant streams of Bolshevik propaganda proclaim Soviet success but no one ever sees the name of Owen Young's company blazing in neon signs. Never does the dictator of the Proletariat reveal the Consortium secrets many of which were well-known or otherwise walk the long trail of easily obtainable facts or introduce western capitalists as the saviors of the new Soviet economy. (B. Pares, 90-1)

Reader, read Professor Pares' masterly work, *A History of Russia*, – dedicated to key Consortium philanthropist and Jew-hater Charles R. Crane, – republished a half century after his 1944 edition where Pares bares his heart revealing a keen perception intrinsic to the outsider's understanding of the extraordinary predicament of the Russian and Ukrainian peasant class. "If the story," Pares writes, "of the people as a whole is the subject of study, it is almost throughout – I would not apply this so much to the glowing life of the Kiev period – *the history of an underworld.* Government and people are here more separate, even more foreign to each other, than elsewhere; in the main, it is the doings of the government that are chronicled, not the life of the people, so that of the latter we get ordinarily only glimpses. If these glimpses showed nothing more than a subject world of servants, we might not look further; but it is just in this underworld that we find those suggestions of shrewd wisdom, patient toil, a morale of suffering and endurance, and a broad humanity which have always encouraged even the most matter-of-fact of foreign observers to see in the Russian people the potentiality of a great future. This sense of potentiality was never entirely absent with their administrators, generals, or teachers; as for the educated class, from the first stages of its formation the instinct which gave shape to its thoughts and ideals was the powerful sense of solidarity which it felt for the peasant world below it and its sense of shame in presence of the standing contrast between the actual and the possible conditions of peasant life. This second peculiarity produced even more distinctive results. It was as if, among educated Russians, there were a kind of suppuration of the conscience; and it is only by taking account of this that we can get an understanding of the engaging but baffling mentality of the Russian intelligentsia." Apparent in Pares is that same "baffling mentality" of the uncanny British upper class, not without its supporters of Nazi fascism and many in the aristocracy harboring bitter contempt for the brazenly dialectic Marxist communist. (B. Pares, xvii; italics added)

Keep connecting the dots. See the big picture unfold in the details. Take a closer look at Westinghouse and General Electric. Czarist Russia. Charles R. Crane, Root, Stimson and the Republicans. Standard Oil. Rockefeller, Harriman and the Democrats. Its all one big show of the Consortium party. A decade before Stalin's vice-grip of the Communist Party line, President Wilson's Root's mission to Revolutionary Russia played out their roles in helping to stage the 1917 Bolshevik coup Crane, Root, and Wilson are all members of the select Pilgrims Society, backbone of the Consortium wing in the British Empire. Lenin and the Bols take all the credit for giving Russian peasants electricity and light which was used for years in propaganda as symbol of the progress and success in building the great socialist future. His son Richard Crane served as a confidential assistant to Wilson's Secretary of State Robert Lansing. In a strikingly curious meeting in Manhattan on the eve of his departure for Berlin, the newly designated US ambassador William Dodd observes Charles Crane as a man who "did much to bring on the Kerensky revolution which gave way to Communism ...." And while it was made to appear that Lenin "drove Crane out of the country', the Consortium had other irons in the fire, and after the war is dispatched for a year in China as Wilson's ambassador in 1920.

Soviet leaders feel an entire decade is required "to master the new processes, install all the equipment, train workers, bring the subsidiary plants into phase with the main plants (a major headache), and expand operations." Debunking the firebrand intellectual Trotsky first, then then his brilliant rival Bukharin, empowered with western support and within only the short span of a decade, Stalin initiates the ambitious and unprecedented two Five-Year Plans for state industrialization and collectivization, in 1928 and 1932, respectively. In one bold stroke Stalin put an end to Russia's peasants as a political threat and decimates insurgent Ukrainian nationalism with a barbarism on a scale not incompatible with the annihilation of the First World War, nor the worst crimes of Lenin or Ivan the Terrible who fought back the Mongols descendants of Genghis Khan. After the ravages and atrocities of both sides during the Russian Civil War, how much more could the Russians and peasant class endure? It should be remembered just how rapidly the world of the peasants had been turned upside down. Stalin's drive to transform industry and agriculture is announced as his empire celebrates the tenth anniversary of the Bolshevik October Revolution of 1917, which itself came to pass unexpectedly and suddenly as Russia's countryside, brutally devastated by the First World War had yet not recovered. (A. C. Sutton, *Western Technology and Soviet Economic Development, 1930-1945*, 344)

Never a true friend of the peasants Lenin was smart enough to know that nothing could be done in Russia without their support in the revolutionary councils of the soviets. With the peasants the vast majority Lenin Bolshevized the Petrograd Soviet. They fill the ranks of nearly the entire Czarist army. Alfred G. Mayer's exemplary study *The Impact of the War in the Countryside* (1915) gives us a vivid picture of how the world of the peasants, and Russia, radically changed in less than four years. Mayer is vice president of the American Association for the Advancement of Science. Mayer writes, "The Russian village was drained of its male work force more quickly and more thoroughly than was the Russian city. Of the more than fourteen million men mobilized by 1916, ten million were peasants. In the summer of 1914, 38 percent of all provinces in the empire had reported no labor shortage or only a negligible labor shortage during the harvest. By 1916 about half of the provinces registered an acute shortage of hands, and the other half reported a 'medium' shortage of labor during the harvest. With the men of military age gone, the people left to do the field work were women, children and the elderly. Women harvested the crops pulled plows and were obliged to do everything with severely reduced resources. For example, of 2,500 flour mills in 1916, 1,650 were useless for lack of grain or coal."

And the American publishes his account during the Great War (1914-18) just two years before Russia's autocratic Czar is secretly overthrown. Only then does America enter the bloody debacle. "The war drained Russia of its manpower, killing mostly peasants. By March 1917, between fourteen and fifteen million men are mobilize d in the armed forces – five million in the first five months of war. That represented 36 percent of the male population of working age, mostly wage earners and agricultural producers. Casualty figures vary between 7.3 million to 8.5 million, excluding civilian women, children and the elderly. While cities benefited from graft and corruption, and supplies still readily available, the countryside was lost its prime workforce. Industries closed or were drastically reduced.

"Fields were neglected, harvests limited, entire regions abandoned by war and more than ten million refugees are forced to flee advancing Germans and poured into the country or fled from near the front. After the civil war and a semblance of order restored under Lenin's NEP, the men, women and children who had survived the harshest times then faced with contempt and rage Stalin's coercive state industrialization and crackdown on individual peasant families with his new wave of terror and slave labor gulags." (Alfred G. Mayer, *The Impact of the War in the Countryside*, 1915, 216)

New York Times correspondent Harrison Salisbury, however, was more objective about Lenin and the peasants. Suffering from two near fatal attacks by assassins, Lenin briefly recovered and worked relentlessly leading his Bolshevik comrades throughout the critical civil war. He died in 1924 alarmed over divisions within the Party leadership and Stalin's crude ruthlessness. "In the struggle for survival Lenin never managed to work out any clear-cut Communist system," Salisbury wrote in his brief book *Russia*. "The Government expropriated the big industries, the banks, the insurance companies and other business and proceeded to run the enterprises itself. The peasants were permitted to seize and farm the landlords' land. Contrary to Marxian theory, the peasants had provided the main support for the revolution; if Lenin had tried to interfere with their land-grabbing, they would have quickly overturned him." (H. Salisbury, *Russia*, 20)

Ambassador Bill Dodd is an invaluable source of detail and sketches about Americans and Nazis in Berlin during the Hitler era. This modest professor turned FDR's ambassador called his Berlin days "confused and deteriorating … fraught with high tensions". We know before he leaves for Berlin he meets with two key pillars of American policy establishment – the inimitable and strange Col. House at his farm in Beverly, Massachusetts, and then in Manhattan with Charles Crane at his opulent Park Avenue apartment adorned with "a marvelous display of Russian and Asiatic works of art". It is Crane who sponsors the Rockefeller-endowed Samuel Harper now a Stalinist apologist who in turn promotes the Consortium line at the State Department, at universities, with contacts to journalists whenever and wherever it serves to endorse the spirit of repression of the Russian masses behind the communist Five-Year Plan. Their motto might just as well be placed atop a huge billboard on Broadway, "Build Till It Hurts".

Charles Crane is a useful tool in the Consortium who witnessed and covers up the Holodomor Terror-Famine. It is Crane who endows University of Chicago's first Russian chair – "Russian History and Institutions –, occupied by Sam Harper. Prof. Harper held it, Dodd notes, "for the last seven or eight years". We remember that JD Rockefeller endowed the University of Chicago with fifty million to eighty dollars – $40 million by 1930 – converting a small Baptist college directed by his father, William Rainey Harper, a Hebrew scholar, by 1900 into a world-class institution. JDR, Sr. later called it "the best investment I ever made." In return the plumbing scion becomes a university Trustee and uses his money to influence the younger Harper. It's an odd match; Crane is not timid to show his natural contempt toward Jews. (W. E. Dodd, *Ambassador Dodd's Diary*)

In 1900, Crane holds a chunk of stock in GE and is keen on the Russian business. When Sam is only eighteen Crane invites the Harpers to join him on a tour through Czarist Russia. Young Harper decides then to make Russia the focus of his academic career. Crane finances his language-training at Sorbonne's Oriental School for Languages, the same institution engaged by the US State Department. Harper returns to Russia in 1904, and is on the scene at the 1905 Father Gapon massacre of the failed revolution; Harper would also witness first-hand the devastation of famine during the Lenin-Trotsky era as member of Hoover's ARA. Dodd notes in his diary that Crane also gave "a million dollars to support the Institute off Current World Affairs" managed by Walter S. Rogers, director and fellow of the Institute. Dodd calls it "an organization which conducts surveys of conditions in all parts of the world and furnishes reports to the government." Crane, 75, visits Germany in July 1933 just after the failed assassination attempt on Hitler, Göering and Goebbels in the Roehm-Schleicher putsch after which Roehm is murdered.

Loyal and reliable Dodd transmits to FDR his interview with Hitler's foreign minister, Constantin von Neurath sending details on the failed coup. Overtly aristocratic von Neurath (1873-56) considers many Englishmen his friends having served as UK ambassador in London from 1930-32 during the doomed Weimar government. Von Neurath never cared to hide his distaste for Hitler's Nazi fanatical usurpation of Germanic *kultur* which his family had long served to maintain with pride. His grandfather having been foreign minister to King Charles I of Wurttemberg, and his father a Conservative politician in the Reichstag parliament, Von Neurath is replaced by the more compliant Joachim von Ribbentrop, in 1938, and exiled to serve as *Reichsprotektor* of Bohemia and Moravia (1939 -43). Von Neurath's his influence ends after he's sidelined for *SS-Obergruppenführer* Reinhard Heydrich.

US Consul in Berlin Raymond H. Geist knew more about Nazi self-enrichment methods than Dodd cared to tell in his memoirs. "I know that on many occasions," Geist told authorities in his 1945 testimony record in the US Embassy in Mexico, "where it was thought necessary to increase the pressure, the prospective purchaser or his agent would be accompanied by a uniformed S.A. or S.S. man. I know because I lived in the immediate neighborhood and know the individuals concerned, that Baron von Neurath, one time Foreign Minister of Germany, got his house from a Jew in this manner. Indeed, he was my next door neighbor in Dahlem. Von Neurath's house was worth approximately $250,000 ($4.2 million). I know too that Alfred Rosenburg, who lived in the same street with me, purloined a house from a Jew in similar fashion."

Dodd invites Gen. Hermann Göering to dine with Crane and his son Richard. Göering, Dodd learns "directed the killing of opponents for a week, more than seventy-five people" in the "Night of the Long Knives" episode. The German ambassador in Moscow, Rudolf Nodolny, a senior diplomat in Russia since he entered the Foreign Service, in 1902, and head of *Ostabteilung*, the Eastern

Section of the Foreign Ministry, had since been dismissed. Nodolny had also served as ambassador in Sweden, and Turkey until 1932.

With Germany withdrawn from the League, in November, 1933, Hitler sends Nodolny to Moscow to negotiate with Litvinov. Baron Von Neurath instructs Nodolny "to normalize the relations between Russia and Germany". Litvinov proposes they draw up an agreement "not to seize and annex the Baltic States". In June 1934 Nodolny meets with Hitler to draft some sort of agreement but Hitler refuses saying "he did not wish to have anything to do with those people"; soon after Hitler tells Nodolny he prefers to deal with the English. (W. E. Dodd, *Ambassador Dodd's Diary*)

Again Hitler and Von Neurath stall. Nodolny then resigned presenting his credentials through President Hindenburg. Nodolny recalls, "The agreement which I had envisaged was almost identical with the Friendship Agreement that Ribbentrop concluded in 1939". (Theodore Draper, "The Forlorn Dream of Rudolf Nodolny", *The Reporter*, July 7, 1953)

Crane's moral indignation over Hitler's fascist methods clashes with Dodd's self-righteous sense of compassion. Dodd is too discreet and alarmed to bring attention to his thoughts which remains private, and he writes. He is clearly disturbed by the fascist and anti-Semitism he encounters by these strange men of prominent influence from Washington and Wall Street. In his diary Bill Dodd writes, "The Cranes understood the absences, though they did not criticize all the ruthless terrorism of recent measures." And later in October when Crane travels to Germany to meet Hitler he praises the dictator as "simple, enthusiastic, bent on stirring the German people to passionate self-confidence and wanting in knowledge of foreign problems..." Dodd remarks, "This is the same story I have heard again and again." (W. E. Dodd, *Ambassador Dodd's Diary*)

In October Dodd learns from Ohio Senator Robert J. Bulkley (Harvard BA, Harvard Law) traveling in England that during a dinner German steel and arms industrialist Fritz Thyssen declares, "We compelled the German Government to withdraw from the League." Although Thyssen gave millions of Reichsmarks to the Nazi Party for the March 1933 Reichstag elections, he opposes Hitler's fanatical war program bankrupting Germany; after war broke out in 1939 he and his family flee to Switzerland but his escape to freedom is compromised; he and his wife spend the war in concentration camps until liberated by the Allies. (W. Dodd, *Ambassador Dodd's Diary,* 9-11)

There are religious people too passing through in Berlin that year. Oh yes, very religious people indeed having traveled across the great Atlantic Ocean to watch the spectacle of Nazi insurgence on the old continent. One of Dodd's visitors to the German embassy in Berlin is Dr. Charles S. MacFarland, a religious spokesman and general secretary of the Federal Council of Churches of Christ in America "traveling in the country a week or two". During an hour interview with Hitler, Dr. MacFarland vigorously tells the Chancellor that four thousand Protestant preachers reject his creed, two thousand and seven hundred have made formal protests after his election, "and that the Catholics were likewise in a similar revolt and the Pope was considering a remedy". Did the Federal Council of Churches ever take a position on the Terror-Famine? Not a sign of protest is uttered on behalf of the Ukrainians.

Dodd is joined by John White, a career Foreign Service man accompanied by Orme Wilson, brother-in-law to William Astor. White is the son of Henry White (1850-27), the senior ranking Republican in Wilson's Paris Peace Commission and one of the signers of the Versailles Treaty. Col. House hailed White as "the most accomplished diplomatist this country has ever produced." He was buried in Washington's National Cathedral near the former President. White is a leading figure in the capitol well-known for entertaining in grand style and his lavish evening parties always attract the elite to his palatial residence where his father at ease welcoming President Harding, Lord Cecil, or French Prime Minister Georges Clemenceau and other world statesmen and cultural dignitaries noted for their accomplishments. The next year John White, who is married to the sister of Jay Pierrepont Moffat, division head of Western European Affairs, and Dodd's immediate boss, sells his famous residence to Fed Bank chairman Eugene Meyer, proud of his latest acquisition and heightened status as publisher of the *Washington Post.* Meyer is the father of Katherine Graham, the paper's legendary owner and outstanding social hostess of the rich and powerful.

Dodd is not impressed by the false charms of pretentious wealth and its awkward intrusions on common civility more sympathetic to his southern country nature. He considers White's tastes "a little too English in veering and with a distinct Harvard-Oxford accent". White and Wilson are privileged insiders with access to power and information about events in Russia with a backdoor into Moscow and the Holodomor. They are not only there to check up on Dodd but also to touch base with the entire European continent which cannot afford to ignore events unfolding in Soviet Russia. However, Dodd leaves no instance to indicate that the subject of the Holodomor is raised. Dodd meets another of Teddy Roosevelt's vintage ambassadors, the notoriously famous and rich James Hazen Hyde, (1876–59), son of Henry Baldwin Hyde who founded Equitable Life Assurance. At twenty-three James inherited the majority shares in the billion-dollar Equitable Life Assurance Society incurring the wrath of Morgan and other partners who in 1905 publicly accuses him of embezzling $200,000 to pay for his Gilded Age ball. Hyde prefers the theater and actresses, and he's accompanied by a dazzling French beauty. Dodd privately notes the finds him "more agreeable and better informed than most millionaires I have met".

The mild and unassuming Dodd has come a long way in the last few months since having been catapaulted from academic obscurity into the world spotlight. That had been a very busy day for Dodd who met the charming First Lady Eleanor Roosevelt and FDR's son FDR Jr. She had personally bid farewell to Dodd sailing on the same ship to Europe, the *USS Washington*, with Rabbi Wise, and the wife of Senator Breckinridge Long, whom Dodd remarks in his diary is "descendant of the Blair family of Kentucky, Washington, and St. Louis, and very conscious of the fact". Roosevelt had appointed "Breck" Long ambassador to Mussolini in Rome. Sen. Long was a campaign contributor and an insider with "one of the most beautiful colonial houses in Maryland, Montpelier, near Laurel", according to Acheson. Spain went to Claude Bowers, a Mid-Western pressman. London goes to Robert Bingham, the newspaper publisher from Louisville, a Democrat lawyer and husband to the richest woman in America, the daughter of the founder of Standard Oil, Henry Morrison Flagler (1830-13). Although an original Standard Oil partner, Flagler is widely credited as the brain behind the booming oil refining business. According to a magazine story published in 1910, "When John D. Rockefeller was asked if the Standard Oil company was the result of his thinking, he answered, 'No, sir. I wish I had the brains to think of it. It was Henry M. Flagler.'" (Edwin Lefevre, "Flagler and Florida", *Everybody's Magazine*, Feb. 1910, 183, in Sidney W. Martin, *Florida's Flagler*, Univ. of Georgia Press, 2010, 56; W. E. Dodd, *Ambassador Dodd's Diary*)

Flagler is also known as the founder of Miami and Palm Beach, and the genius behind the Breakers Hotel, formerly called the Palm Beach Inn. Looking back at Flagler's life after his sudden death from a fall on May 20, 1913, Morgan banker George W. Perkins reflects, "But that any man could have the genius to see of what this wilderness of waterless sand and underbrush was capable and then have the nerve to build a railroad here, is more marvelous than similar development anywhere else in the world." It was so big that anyone in the Kremlin would feel like a Russian dwarf next to it. A peasant might think it came from the heavens on the wings of angels, destined for kings and lords but not for them. (Samuel Moffet, "Henry Morrison Flagler", *The Cosmopolitan,* 1902)

Once comfortably installed though feeling a bit odd and awkward at the sumptuousness of the old mansion with its ornate private gardens of the 630-acre Tiergarten once a royal hunting reserve, Dodd makes the rounds with Vienna Consul George S. Messersmith himself back in Europe after Antwerp and a stint in Curacao. In a few years after he's replaced by Phillips actually now in Italy when the Consortium's senior Senator Breck Long, in 1940, will first enjoy the splendors of the Renaissance before retiring under the sun in Havana replacing Messersmith there. Ah, such a wonderful life if you can stick it out and not step on too many toes.

Dodd meets regularly with Mowrer and the "young H. R. Knickerbocker". Before sailing to Europe, Dodd had also met with Edgar Ansel Mowrer (his brother Paul is an editor at the *Chicago Daily News*). His book, *Germany Puts the Clock Back* (1933) is banned and the German authorities demand his resignation as President of the Foreign Press Association in Berlin. Journalists have to walk a very fine line to keep their jobs. With every lie truth suffers another blow against Humanity and the free press is merely a myth of myths, ink on paper so convenient to sell newspapers for Consortium profits. A vicious circle for those caught in a trap. Mowrer know wars. He has covered battles during the Great War including the Italian front and lived in Rome for eight years before Berlin. He leaves for Paris where he continued reporting until the ignominious French defeat in 1940. During the war Mowrer joins the US government as Deputy Director in the Office of Facts and Figures (OFF) in the newly created Office of War Information, a spin-off of the predecessor to the OSS. After the war, in 1948, Knopf publishes Mowrer's book, *The Nightmare of American Foreign Policy*. (D. Acheson, 12)

A new face in Berlin, Dodd holds a press conference and invited the American community business leaders and their German friends and leaders. Afterward Dodd tells Mowrer how much he regrets Nazis repression of his book. The journalists likes the ambassador's relaxed style and natural candor. To them Dodd appears to have integrity, without airs, and most importantly, he's approachable. Sigrid Schultz of the *Chicago Tribune,* owned by "Colonel" Robert McCormick of the International Harvester family, Frederick Oechsner of UPI, and Louis Lochner, head of AP's Berlin desk (1919-46) all seek him out as does Hans Luther, Germany's envoy to Washington.

Dodd's arrival immediately turns into a scandal over Nazi persecution of Jews. He brazenly commits a public affront antagonizing Berlin's elite private community. In front of two-dozen shocked German journalists Dodd reads a statement *auf Deutsch* comparing FDR's Recovery Act to the proposed plan for German economic recovery by Nazi Minister of Economics Kurt Schmitt (1886-50), chairman of Allianz as since 1921. Schmitt had been a captain in the First World War, is wounded and received the Iron Cross.

Dodd awakes the next day and learns he has embroiled the embassy in the middle of hostilities between the Nazi Third Reich and the Jews. "Fifteen years ago the diplomatic bricklayers at Versailles raised many a high wall around Germany", *Time* writes in its June 11th edition. Neglecting to mention Nazi racist plans for enslavement and extermination of the population in southern Ukraine and the Crimea on the Black Sea, *Time* tells its readers, "Since last year Nazi persecution of Jews and Communists has raised several new ones. Last week Prussia's Premier Hermann Willhelm Göring shouted: 'The German nation needs room if it is not to suffocate. Germans, too, need air and sun'."

Meanwhile *Time* reports decreasing levels in trade between Russia and the Reich lacking cotton, wool, oil and metals. "Last week a mammoth trial of Communists on charges of 'preparing to commit high treason,' opened at Breslau. Soviet Russia's mounting resentment against Nazi abuse of Communists and Communism was reflected to a certain extent in the total of Russian imports from Germany in the first quarter of 1934: 21,000,000 marks as against 181,000,000 marks for the same period in 1932." The West continues to pressure Schacht to pay war debts now reduced to 40 per cent cash value. But Germany has no money to pay even under the latest arbitration. *Time* quotes the French paper *Le Soir* whose writer "badgered Nazi Foreign Minister Baron von Neurath into an equally damaging admission: 'That we have factories that can change to the manufacture of arms is a well-known fact in Europe. But in that respect we are still far from equality with other nations'." ("Germany: Air & Sun", *Time,* June 11, 1934)

Throughout July and August 1933 Dodd is concerned with daily Jewish persecutions. Through Schacht and other backdoor channels Dodd warns Hitler "that German exports would continue to fall if the ruthlessness were not abandoned; and that the belligerent tone of German conduct would almost certainly lead to an international boycott". By apparently Dodd is not aware that long before he arrived in Berlin, on December 18, 1932 Schacht and Kurt Schmitt had participated in a meeting to seal the loyalty of Hitler's "Circle of Friends of the

Economy" (*Freundeskreis der Wirtschaft*), or "Circle of Twelve" (*Zwölferkreis*) at the Berlin Kaiserhof. There the Nazi Party reaffirmed its support to Schacht's economic plans for the Reich. That led to the meeting February 20 when Schmitt joins Göering and other leading German industrialists to back Hitler. A member of the Nazi Party (membership no. 2 651 252) since early 1933 Schmitt makes a RM 10,000 election contribution to the Nazis. Schmitt also holds the posts of Vice President of the Berlin Chamber of Industry and of the Chamber of Commerce. In the shuffle, just three weeks after the Rohm massacre, Schacht, on July 30, 1934, becomes Schmitt's successor as *Reichsminister* of the Nazi economy, and receives the *Totenkopfring der SS* ("SS Death's Head Ring").

The Berlin embassy has an understanding with the foreign correspondents on what is deemed permissible if they want to get by the censor and cable their stories. No one knows this better than Lochner. The son of Maria Lochner born von Haugwitz and Johan Friedrich Karl Lochner, Louis Lochner (1887-75) liked to sign his name Louis. "Loch" is a Lutheran, and Phil Beta Kappa graduate of the University of Wisconsin. His peers see him as a pro who knows all the "ins and outs" of the journalist racket. Since 1909 before the war he'd been reporting for AP from Berlin. In 1915, Lochner sails to war-torn Europe on the Ford Peace Ship, press secretary to the industrialist Henry Ford himself, and earned the respect of the Germans of the doomed Weimar Republic. On his way he finagles an interview with its last president Gustav Stresemann, and former German foreign minister, just five days before he dies; in 1930 he sits down together with Hitler and Rudolf Hess and, then again does the same thing in the year of the 1933 Holodomor. Lochner also speaks fluent German so he is seamlessly at ease with the Nazi's who can use a friend in the world press. They used him too. Is it any wonder why so many journalists are agents, and double agents, and so on.

Don't kid yourself. It's a dangerous profession. Gareth Jones of the Holodomor stories found that the hard way and risked it all. Lochner plays a different game. Lochner blends in and is a familiar face at Nazi headquarters able to sway passed sentries so that he often sees Hitler in rare and confidential moments away from any propaganda staging; in 1939 the *Wehrmacht* invites him to witness Hitler's triumphant invasion of Poland. When its time to swallow the Lowland countries, Yugoslavia Greece and Lochner is there too embedded in the Nazi sweep through France and reported the ignominious French defeat at Compéigne. Lochner is not a threat; he doesn't cause them any problems. And they know how to make him helpful if they need to. For a journalist it is essential that he is able to move about with ease. It earns Lochner a Pulitzer that year.

Lochner has the tenacious skills of a a survivor who knows when to keep his mouth shut. The Consortium relied on Lochner, a good hound in the service of his masters. He could smell out a story anywhere. They own Associated Press and send him to Basel to cover the first annual meeting of the BIS. On his way back to Berlin he rolls into Munich to see why the Bavarians were making so much noise with their hero Adolf, leader of a tiny band in the National Socialist German Workers' Party. Lochner kept his eye riveted on Hitler whose "meteoric political career had often engaged my journalist attention. Ambassador Dodd writes, "It has often been remarked that Hitler's success is due in part to his ability to ingratiate himself with visitors whom he hopes to win over, by saying what he thinks they want to hear ... It should be easy to come to an understanding with the United States. The only thing that divides us is the problem of reparations which I insist are political debts. Investments, loans, and so forth, are good with us. But we shall see to it that political debts are cancelled." Lochner has no problem with access. He covers Hitler's rendezvous with Mussolini, in 1938, and accompanies Soviet troops when they attack Finland, earning him a Pulitzer. He died in Wiesbaden, West Germany 1975. (W. E. Dodd, *Ambassador Dodd's Diary,* 21)

Dodd has been well briefed on what to expect in Berlin. Consortium bankers and industrialists fill his diary book that note the steady stream of meetings. On August 11, 1933, Dodd writes in his diary, "Winthrop W. Aldrich, President of the Chase National Bank, New York, came at 11:30 to express satisfaction with the German financial plan under which the German bonds sold to Americans would not be announced." Nazi bonds quietly sold by American bankers to the Americans! Dodd laments, "How unfortunate for us these loans!" Before leaving to meet Riechsbank president Schacht over at Hitler's quarters eager to find ways to do business with the new totalitarian regime Aldrich tells Dodd his admiration for the new Chancellor. Why this should come as news to Dodd is not clear; Aldrich's mother is a Rockefeller and they are deep into Nazi business.

WHAT WHITING WILLIAMS TELLS AMBASSADOR DODD

During this same period a stranger walks into the Embassy with an eye-witness account with horrible information carried from the death fields of the Ukraine. Dodd is clearly unprepared for what he learns on August 29, 1933 in his meeting with Whiting Williams, correspondent of *The Saturday Evening Post*, a most reputable paper he can have no doubt. Dodd recorded the meeting in his diary. Williams "came to give me a strange tale of Russian woe, a ten-thousand word story, soon to appear in print, of starving millions of peasants. He asked for a letter to President Roosevelt *which I said I might give him, but I am not sure. I could hardly believe 20,000,000 were starving in Soviet Russia!"* Did he believe it? Does Dodd tell FDR? And why hadn't the circumspect Dodd taken more seriously American and foreign press reports or, for that matter, the sensational press conference by Gareth Jones in Berlin the previous March. Surely Dodd would have been informed. Berlin is a key hub for these correspondents. Or with the Nazis creating havoc is Dodd who is already deep up to his neck in the boiling pot simply overwhelmed? (Italics added)

Three weeks later Dodd sits down again with the venerable and super rich bankers Winthrop Aldrich and Henry Mann of National City on September 1 and learns of their chat seeking favor with Hitler. Dodd kept a record in his diary, writing, "Hitler is a fanatic on the Jewish problem. He has no conception of international relationships. He considers himself a German Messiah. Despite Hitler's attitude these bankers feel they can work with him."

The Consortium's top PR man is here too. It seems fairly incredible but so many of the most powerful and famous men are passing through Berlin and Moscow these days. Including Ivy Lee, who, according to ambassador Dodd, "showed himself at once a capitalist and an advocate of Fascism." The connections leading to inflammatory Nazi militarism, Soviet terror, and the Holodomor Genocide were all too obvious and enough to disturb the open mind of the ambassador feeling swamped by international fascism wearing different masks. Aldrich. Rockefeller. Ivy Lee ... Later this month, the ambassador dined with Schacht for a confidential evening with Senator McAdoo, President Wilson's son-in-law, and Consortium insider ever since he participated in the secret arrangements in the creation of the Federal Reserve Bank system exactly two decades before back in 1913. Dodd observes that McAdoo, looks astonishingly fit and young for his seventy-five years and very active life in the center of American power politics. The dinner is recorded as one of the Ambassador's most pleasurable evenings since his posting in Berlin.

Dodd feels he is now at the center of the storm overtaking Europe. The revelations of Whiting Williams are startling vivid and real. Williams is convinced that the reality of the Holodomor and its terrible scale of victims is also undeniably true. By God, man, he swore to the ambassador, he had seen the Holodomor with his own eyes! It was an undeniable reality to one of the most prestigious journalists in America and he intended to take the story to heart home. Dodd closed his diary but he could not close his mind. Surely he might have tried not to think about it and shake his head in disbelief. But what good would that do to clear his doubts or silence his conscience. This is not something easy to forget, ever! You live and die knowing it might in fact be true! Consortium men have no trouble here in a world without frontiers staging wars with no tears. But Dodd, this man of "candour" and apparent integrity, intent on publicly denouncing the Nazi persecution of Jews, why should he stay silent about the Ukrainians?

Dodd is already in way over his head. FDR had used him, and keeps him at bay. Now he dreads drowning in this volcanic hell. Dodd might have at least checked Williams' "facts" with embassy's own reports from Riga and with other friendly foreign legations in Germany. Certainly the French, British and Latvians know more about this Holodomor if it were true. Why doesn't the ambassador relay it immediately on to State in Washington or at least talk it over confidentially with his high-level friends like Schacht or through discreet channels to German foreign office linked to the *Wehrmacht*'s strategy for the occupation and pacification of the Ukraine. Or did he?

Dodd had been briefed to be particularly sensitive about the Jewish situation in Berlin even while many Consortium men and particularly the White Anglo-Saxon Protestants (WASPs) of America's north east coast from "Phili" to Boston show tolerance, even a stated preference toward favoring the Nazis. Lacking vision and powerless to overcome the magnitude and scale of events beyond his control of which he played now only an insignificant role as observer and intermediary, a messenger for the Consortium, the ambassador awaits the coming disaster incapable of changing the course already set. He speaks the language and plays his role, nothing more is expected of him. So Dodd too kept his place there in the Berlin embassy. Once peace is shattered the Germans would slaughter more than a million Jews in the Ukraine. What good are protestations now. But Whiting Williams has planted the seed he came to sow. Who else has Whiting been talking to in Berlin? (Dodd, *Dairy*, 21-30)

Nor have the American diplomats in Poland expected to see Whiting Williams when he drops in on the Warsaw Embassy on his way to Berlin having slipped out of Moscow unmolested by Stalin's secret police after two weeks in the Ukraine and undetected by GPU agents in the countryside. Through the doors of the embassy Williams carries his eye-witness account freshly imprinted in his memory like sticks of burning dynamite which he now planted inside the US Consulate.

Whiting is determined that US government insiders listen up to what was really going down in the Ukraine even while they slept in their beds not hearing what was going on. Whiting Williams took his story to the Warsaw embassy and there met US Consul Jerome Klahr Huddle – not a junior Vice Consul or Third Secretary. Consul Huddle promptly sends the Department a dispatch describing Williams "a qualified and capable observer" who sympathized "with the laboring classes" but was decidedly not "socialistic", and certainly not part of the contrived and false soviet "reality" of illusions catering to the "diktat" of a dominant totalitarian Communist Party hierarchy. Peasants and workers both had a right to bread for survival. How far had the world regressed to where children are shot for taking grain or seeds; what had the soviet socialist revolution accomplished since the days before the French Revolution when children were hung for stealing a loaf of bread?

In earnest Consul Huddle carefully notes Whiting's home address in the United States at 3030 Euclid Avenue, Cleveland, Ohio. That's home country for Huddle too, born there in 1891. Huddle and Whiting Williams have a lot to talk over about Middle America. America's farm belt studded with Rockefeller oil dregs. Just out of Russia and the Ukraine and beyond the tightening grasp of the evil hand of the GPU Williams explained how the Kremlin Bolshevik regime in Moscow was acting as "the most unscrupulous and the cruelest organization for the exploitation of the laboring man, whether industrial worker or farm peasant, that the world has ever seen". Huddle sends his dispatch No. 2812 on August 23, 1933 titled "Conditions in the Russian Ukraine–Observations of Mr. Whiting Williams". Bullitt put his customary stamp on the ten-page report on September 27th, – proof that he too read it already two weeks after Kelley's Far Eastern Division got it. The report is buried in the bustle of diplomatic recognition preparations. FDR wants no problem over the Holodomor. No meetings are scheduled to even discuss it, at least not for the record. The famine mass killings are not on the agenda. As long as they don't openly talk about it there is nothing to cover up and nothing to deny. The Consortium can pass over it in silence. It would be hard to prove a willing eagerness to be partners in the crimes committed even before there was a war.

The Williams memoranda may well have been the first documents with details of the Holodomor told by an American journalist touring the famine regions of the Ukraine. The American journalist for *The Saturday Evening Post* Whiting Williams spent two weeks "through the industrial and agricultural districts of the Ukraine". Williams tells US Consul Huddle of his visits to "Kiev, Kharkov, the Don basis and the Dnieprostroy" having skirted the Moscow ban restricting the international press corps "from leaving Moscow except under express authorization and in directions approved by the Soviet authorities". In Huddle's report to Washington, Williams is described for exactly who and what he is, "a well known American educator and economic investigator and adviser, who is possessed of degrees from a number of the better known American universities (*Who's Who*). He is engaged at the present time as lecturer and journalist as well as a technical adviser on economies. He has worked as a laborer in the coal fields of Pennsylvania, the Ruhr district of Germany and has also in the past observed labor conditions in Soviet Russia." Williams tells the government functionary and fellow American citizen that he's "familiar with the psychology and character of the laboring man through actual contact with him in his work". The Department notes that Whiting Williams speaks German but not Russian or Ukrainian.

"It is generally understood," the young Consul Huddle informed the Department referring to Stalin's ban on restricted territories, "that this prohibition has been instituted to prevent the Moscow press correspondents from visiting the Ukraine and observing and reporting on the alleged famine conditions existing there. It was in this very district covered by the present decree that Mr. Williams visited. *His report therefore would appear under the circumstances to be particularly significant.* It was apparent that Mr. Williams was much affected by what he saw during his fortnight in the Ukraine and he states he was greatly depressed at the plight of the inhabitants." If Huddle thought he would get any points here for a career advancement he was sadly mistaken. The memo report is shocking and makes no attempt to conceal the fact of State Department's knowledge of the Holodomor now in its most critical phase. (italics added)

"*Famine Conditions.* With respect to reports regarding conditions of famine which have been coming out of Russia for a number of months past, Mr. Williams confirms these in no uncertain terms. It is difficult to believe in fact that his statements with reference thereto are not exaggerated. Nevertheless Mr. Williams qualifications as an observer and his reputation are such as to make his statements authoritative. He says that he has seen during only the period of his two weeks' visit and has acquired personal knowledge of scores of deaths of laborers and peasants as a result of starvation. He has seen people dying in the streets from this cause. He cited a particular instance of a baby girl whose death from starvation he himself observed.

"He saw peasants falling from weakness occasioned by hunger, while they were working in the grain fields in the midst of food. From his conversations with Russian peasants and laborers and with foreigners of position in the districts he visited, he has gained the idea that during the past year not hundreds, not hundreds of thousands, but actually millions of Russians have died from starvation and the diseases occasioned by the lack of food. Mr. Williams actually believes that this is the case. He states that he saw villages completely depopulated and many others reduced to one-half their previous population from this cause. The shocking descriptions he gives of conditions as he saw them and heard of them first-hand are almost unbelievable.

Whiting Williams tells the Foreign Service bureaucrat "the mentality of both workers and peasants seems at the lowest possible ebb. They appear to be completely helpless and without hope. Their only interest is in a plea, not a struggle, for existence and it is difficult to converse with any individual among them for any length of time without his intrusion of a plaintive prayer for bread.

"It is a paradox that while the Soviet Government is admittedly working desperately to garner the season's harvest and while the peasant laborers are being forced to this end, they are at the same time perishing for lack of food. I am repeating Mr. William's comments."

"Condition of Food Available. Mr. Williams states that the only food available to the industrial laborer and peasant consists of the filthy substance called bread; on this with water he must live, supplemented only by occasional herbs and less nutrious vegetables. Potatoes he knows nothing of. Meats are entirely beyond his obtaining and even the meats sold by the Torgsin (*Torgovlya sinostrantsami* sic) for foreign valuta proved for the most part inedible. In response to my inquiry whether fowl was available, he said that occasionally a peasant might be found disposing of a chicken but that the scarcity of fowl was notable. He also stated that there is a lack of live stock for butchering purposes. If there is wild game, the laborer and the peasant have no means of shooting or trapping it. One of Mr. Williams' more illuminating statements is that in most of urban communities and the farming colonies, dogs and cats have completely disappeared. ... They have been eaten. So rarely is a laborer, a peasant, a small shop-keeper or an artisan able to have meat that meat is sometimes used by Americans and other foreigners in payment of debts to the small craftsmen."

The 1933 Harvest. "On the day which he left Russia, he saw vast areas of fields in which the wheat was still standing in shocks, contrasting this condition with the condition in Western European countries where it has all been taken in and threshed. He predicts that if the fall rains come with their usual regularity a very large percentage of the Russian wheat crop will be destroyed. He attributes the failure to complete the harvest first, to the sabotage on the part of the peasants which the Soviet authorities have admitted and second, to the decimation of the peasant population by starvation and disease." (A Warsaw commission agent told me this morning, – August 23rd – that he had approached the Soviet commercial attaché at Warsaw with a proposal that Russia buy a quantity of Bulgarian wheat. The Commercial attaché laughed at the offer and stated that Russia would soon have wheat to export to Bulgaria.)"

Williams confirms for Huddle's report "that the Soviet Government has rushed 'shock troops' of young communists and office workers from the cities into the agrarian regions to speed the harvest, but he says that these so called 'shock troops' have proved highly unsuccessful and that it is a fact that a considerable percentage of them, unable to withstand the rigors of labor in the harvest fields have succumbed. He cites a particular instance of this which came to his attention at Kiev where he was told that out of one group of a hundred Kiev inhabitants who were sent into the fields, seventy returned."

Non-workers were left without any resources to live. "It is considered a crime by the authorities for any person to give them alms." Workers have not enough money to pay for food. "According to Mr. Williams the only difference between the fate of the workers and the non-workers lies in the time factor. The non-workers are succumbing more quickly than the workers."

"Psychological Condition of the Workers and the Peasants. Mr. Williams is convinced that the question of creature comfort and the better things of life does not now enter into the calculations of the average Ukrainian worker or peasant. His mind further seems centered not especially on the question of existence but rather on how long it will be until he dies. In general they seem entirely without hope. The older and more experienced among them and those of higher grade of intelligence who realize the existence of an outside world are wondering whether help will come to them for that outside world but they have no hope. They merely wait. There is among them no spirit of active opposition to the Communistic regime. They are crushed." Williams did not see evidence of plague or typhus.

Huddle urges Whiting Williams to go talk with the Far Eastern Division in Washington so that Kelley could "learn from him first-hand the story of his experiences". If they hadn't hit it off so well as fellow Ohio boys there might be merit to consider that as perhaps a concealed attempt to send the correspondent to where he might be better advised to keep the Holodomor under the official radar to the public. But that doesn't seem likely.

On September 20, Bob Kelley sent copies of the Huddle-Williams report to Hull, Phillips and the newly appointed Undersecretary Harry F. Payer with a personal attached memo saying "The description of conditions in the Ukraine contained in the attached dispatch, as found by Mr. Whiting Williams during his visit there last month, is well worth noting." Payer, is a talented lawyer from Ohio, musician and linguist who spoke five languages in addition to commanding skills reading classical Greek and Latin. Of Czech origin he served on the Czech Relief Commission, and for a few months worked on FDR's RFC, resigning in April 1934. Kelley reaffirms that Williams is no casual witness but "a well-known lecturer and student of industrial and labor problems and is an adviser to large industrial concerns on personnel and economic matters." As he had "special training", Kelley underscores Williams' experience studying "labor conditions in Russia". For his part, Huddle eventually reaches ambassadorial rank, to Burma and is there for the dawn of Burmese independence under General Aung San, assassinated in July 1947, and the father of Daw Aung San Suu Kyi, Nobel Peace laureate and democratic leader under oppression of the military junta.

Although Kelley urged his superiors in the State Department to give it "special attention", it might seem odd to the reader that nowhere does Bob Kelley mention the word famine, starvation, or make reference to the food catastrophe and breakdown of Soviet economic infrastructure when he transmits this document.

In spite of the fact that Kelley refers to the 1933 travel ban on reporter Bill Chamberlin as further proof to validate the authenticity of the Williams report, and even with its mark for special consideration the document might have simply been buried in the blur of papers from around the world shuffled from desk to desk.

"From Mr. Williams' account of conditions in the Ukraine", Robert Kelley writes in his memoranda to his superiors, "it will be readily understood why the Soviet government recently established a rigid control of movements of foreign correspondents in Russia had refused permission to Mr. Chamberlin, who has been for eleven years correspondent in Russia for the *Christian Science Monitor*, to visit and observe the harvest in the principal agricultural regions of the North Caucasus and the Ukraine. Robert F. Kelley (signed)" That Whiting Williams also writes for the *Saturday Evening Post* famous for its promotion of the good American life with images of material progress, consumer consumption coloured with Norman Rockwell illustrations is not mentioned by Kelley in spite of the shocking revelations certain to turn the stomach of wholesome America. Next February 1934 Whiting Williams in London confirms the famine was common knowledge among Russians. (Whiting Williams, "My Journey Through Famine-Stricken Russia!", London: *Answers*, Feb. 24, 1934, 28; SDDF 861.5017 Living Conditions/706)

The day after processing William's report, the US consulate in Warsaw has another curious visitor with his Russian tale. Memo No. 331 contained the government's conversation with William Allen White (1868-44). Orsen N. Nielsen, from Wisconsin, served briefly as Vice Consul in Moscow in 1918, before his transfer to Sweden serving there until 1921 followed by Berlin where he stayed until 1924. Nielsen also served in Dublin and Teheran before returning to Berlin where now as Second Secretary he forwards the White memorandum to Kelley. Bullitt reads it November 17, the day after FDR's official recognition of Stalin's regime.

Bill White is traveling on a special Soviet tour with his wife Sallie. He's the famous publisher of the *Emporia Gazette* of Kansas. An icon of middle America opinion, Bill White is a former friend of Teddy Roosevelt, a Pulitzer poet and writer of biographies of presidents Wilson and Coolidge. Ten honorary degrees including Harvard where he stood on the commencement podium with Albert Einstein. White has friends all across America, in the press, in academia, and in Washington. Today the University of Kansas Journalism School today bears his name.

A newspaper publisher for nearly four decades, White is a staunch supporter *against* FDR in his presidential elections, but supports New Dealism and his drive towards a Second World War. Quixotic to a fault, Bill White publishes in 1933 the anti-war poem: "The boys who died just went out and died. To their own souls' glory of course – but what else? Yet the next war will see the same hurrah and the same bowwow of the big dogs to get the little dogs to go out and follow the blood scent and get their entrails tangled in the barbed wire." White asks a lot of questions but America, and Russian and Ukrainian workers and peasants need answers that speak the truth and not more capitalist and communist lies mouthed by self-censoring journalists.

In Warsaw, William White takes his seat across from Third Secretary Bernard Gufler, on August 24 and 25 who duly notes that White is a true American patriot in favor of US recognition of the Soviets and sailed from London on a Soviet steamer to see Soviet socialism at work with his own eyes. White stays only two days in Leningrad and Moscow before deciding to return taking the European route home passing first through western Ukraine into Warsaw. "His program in Russia," the Consul wrote, "consisted of the usual sight-seeing, visits with his acquaintances among the newspaper correspondents, and some entertainments, including a luncheon at the Foreign Office ... all he saw of the Soviet country-side was seen from the train."

His American embassy official notes that White is given the typical VIP welcome by the GPU-Intourist guide who "made a special effort to make Mr. White's stay in Leningrad pleasant"; he booked a room at the Savoy Hotel there finding the best cook's meat "lean and poor". From the American press corps White learns there "that it is true that the country is suffering from a great famine and from a widespread epidemic of typhoid." In his report Consul Nielsen mistakenly states that White is the "first correspondent who wrote a story about the famine". Or of this is what White leads him to believe, now could Nielsen be so ignorant of the other press famine stories.

The Soviets take special care not to make his visit unpleasant though all the time White, the American Consul noted, said he was "very much afraid that after the publication of his story in the American newspapers he would be expelled from Russia." White's version of the ban on the foreign press was a slightly different version of the secret agreement between the American journalists in Moscow nuanced to say it was a "gentlemen's agreement that all of them would write stories on the famine, so that if the Soviet Government expels correspondents for writing famine stories, it will have to expel the whole corps of American correspondents."

William Allen White was amused that the Russians would ever dare to make a "planned economy" calling it "a paradox ... since the Russians are, in his opinion, the most easy going, unpractical, and happy-go-lucky people in the world". A "paradox" indeed! But White, too, is a walking "paradox". Acting with the self-presumption as a keen observer of social conditions and human behavior, and decidedly not keen to play the fool, White said, that its exactly that quality of human nature "which makes the Communist regime possible", and that its "the easy-going character, combined with the extreme cheapness of human life in Russia, which makes it possible for the Government to sacrifice innumerable lives in the course of its experiment". The same argument is often used by colonial exploiters of native populations worldwide. To look at life that way is false and unjust but White doesn't seem to care to dispense with over-used stereotypes that can still be of value to the authorities and keep his name in print at home to sell newspapers. How many times do world travelers in exotic lands hear the refrain, "Just look at all these happy, cheerful smiling faces!" The Russians "looked very shabby and badly fed" White tells the experienced US consul. Yet, White, nonetheless, convinces himself to confess that these enduring and strong people suffering terrible hardships and the deprivation of their freedom and human rights "were not unhappy".

Apparently White knows little about Russian pride or the Russian "soul" but assumes he knows more than others including the Consul. His reasoning is simple enough. Anywhere else, William Allen White declares, "these conditions would lead to violent general revolution, but that in Russia seemingly the Government merely had to shoot a few thousand people on the quiet, finding itself able to keep the rest in order with band music and patriotic speeches."

White is confident that while the US government remains short-sighted to delay recognition of the Soviet Government to prolong the any longer would "look foolish, so it might as well recognize the Soviet Government now and be done with it." Russia he insists, "is a good credit risk", and needs big business and "large credits", and that only now "recognition will facilitate the granting of credit and control of credit".

White has Kansas on his mind; there are too many cheap pigs in Kansas and White hopes to ship hogs from his home state where "the oversupply of hogs is ruining the farmers of Kansas, since the hogs are too cheap to sell and too expensive to feed as long as the present relationship between meat and corn prices continues". White favors US government backed credits to buy and ship Soviet agricultural goods "upon the theory that such action would relieve the American farmer of his surplus, put cash into his hands, and thus assist American agriculture, even if Russia was 'slow pay' on the bill." (SDDF 861.5017 Living Conditions/704)

If Dodd now had any compassion for the suffering Ukrainians and famine-terror across his borders ravaging the snow-covered plains of the Ukraine this day he doesn't tell the Soviet ambassador or, FDR. Instead, Dodd opens his diary and writes, "November 23, 1933. Thursday. Since the United States Government has recognized Soviet Russia, I called today at the request of the State Department on the Soviet Ambassador. He said he had been a student here about 1880-90 and had taken his doctorate in Berlin. He spoke German a little more fluently than I do. He impressed me in no way as an extreme Communist. The talk turned almost exclusively to the Russo-Japanese conflict in Manchuria. Help in that area seemed one possible result of American recognition, with trade important only in a secondary degree."

Not a word of discomfort does he allow to intrude here in the peace of his private thoughts of terror and fear albeit Nazi or Soviet. It is curious though that Dodd admits to feeling ill at ease about meeting the Soviet ambassador to Berlin. Outside the embassy he brushes away an AP photographer waiting for a good picture of the occasion "telling him that certain reactionary papers in America would exaggerate the fact of my call and repeat their attacks upon Roosevelt for his recognition". Recognition of the Soviets with their communist propaganda remains for Dodd a bitter pill to swallow.

At the annual foreign press dinner ball hosted by Lochner of AP, "dean of American newspaper correspondents", Dodd again meets the Soviet Commissar. The sumptuous dinner scene of a ballroom feast in prewar Berlin as the two ambassadors and journalists banter pleasantries and tid-bits over champagne when they all know about the famine and suspect the foul hand of the Powers-That-Be behind these murderous Bols? Is it Stalin? Is it Roosevelt? Montagu Norman of the Bank of England? Sir John Simon, British Foreign Secretary? Baron de Rothschild? Berlin attracted the best of well-informed minds all of whom had good cause to wonder why Jewish professors were dismissed without pensions and Jews were beaten mercilessly in the streets only because they refused to salute the Brown and Black shirts.

Three days after his meeting the Soviet ambassador, Dodd wrote FDR "the Hitler regime is composed of three rather inexperienced and very dogmatic persons, all of whom have been more or less connected with murderous undertakings in the last eight or ten years ... Hitler's devices are the devices which men set up in ancient Rome, namely his flag and salute. He has definitely said on a number of occasions that a people survives by fighting and dies through peaceful policies. His influence has been wholly belligerent…In the back of his mind is the old German idea of dominating Europe through warfare…You have a unique triumvirate here. Hitler, the less educated, more romantic, with a semi-criminal record; Goebbels and Göering, both holding doctorates Doctors of Philosophy, both animated by intense class and foreign hatreds and both willing to resort to ruthless arbitrary methods." (T. Morgan, *FDR*, 395)

On December 4 Ambassador Dodd meets John Foster Dulles of the Sullivan & Cromwell law firm representing a group of "associated American banks" with a billion dollars in claims of US bondholders against German cities and corporations and reviews the bank's position for their meeting the next day with Reichsbank directors whom Dodd and Dulles meet regularly. The Dulles brothers are both participants in the 1932 Geneva disarmament talks; in the next war brother Allen Dulles heads the Swiss-based office of the OSS handling American intelligence in Germany, and his brother considered one of the finest legal minds in the country serves Eisenhower's White House as Secretary of State (1953-59). Dodd suspects but he doesn't admit to knowing that Dulles and his firm are financially helping Hitler in 1933 consolidate his industrial power base. (W. E. Dodd, *Ambassador Dodd's Diary,*)

Time for a breather, reader. We don't want to get too far ahead in our story just yet. Let's pause in our Holodomor story and grasp the importance of the Dulles brothers on the scene, a most intriguing pair of operators who ever mastered political power in the 21st American century. According to writer Charles Savoie, "The first Rockefeller agent to send money to the Institute of Pacific Relations as chairman of the Rockefeller Foundation was John Foster Dulles (Pilgrims Society). His brother, Allen Dulles, also from Princeton University, became the head of the CIA in 1953, and long before that had been a senior member the Pilgrims Society front, the Council on Foreign Relations (CFR). Both Dulles brothers are partners in Sullivan & Cromwell, located at 48 Wall Street, and one of the world's most influential law firms. Based in Geneva during the war Allen Dulles was instrumental in handling the surrender of the Germans in Italy and incurring the wrath of Stalin with his Red Army hammering the Nazi's defense of Berlin. Twenty years later, after his rude dismissal at the CIA, Dulles joined President Lyndon Johnson's Commission on the Assassination of President Kennedy (1963), the forerunner of the Warren Commission (1965), that looked more like a Pilgrims Society Round Table affair. Their sister Eleanor also served as a delegate to the 1944 Bretton Woods Conference that created the International Monetary Fund, considered by Savoie as "a leading instrumentality for wealth transfer to members of The Pilgrims Society. In 1932, Eleanor Dulles authors *The Bank for International Settlements at Work* adding to the family's awesome prestige; three decades later Dulles International Airport outside Washington DC and serving the capitol is dedicated by JFK, after he has fired Allen Dulles as veteran head of the CIA and only a year before his assassination. (Charles Savoie, *World Money Order III)*

Once again the world traveler man on a mission is at sea again *en route* to Moscow via Europe. This time Bullitt is accompanied by his nine-year old daughter, Anne, of his estranged wife Louise Bryant and little Pie-Pie, a West Highland terrier tagging after trunks of his finest wardrobe of Savoy Row suits, cutaways, tails and top hats. Bullitt had arranged for Holodomor's most capricious reporter Walter Duranty who books his cabin on the same ship. In Paris Bullitt is joined by his loyal aide George Kennan. There is a dramatic scene on the train platform at the Gare de l'Est; a woman tries to approach the ambassador. She is distraught, thin and frail, barely forty but her face is ghostly pale. It is Louise desperate to meet her daughter before she is gone forever out of her life. What a horrendously pathetic scene it must have been for the ambassador! Poor Louise. Her lover buried in the Kremlin, and now the other off to drink with the Stalin and his band of wretched Commissars! Bullitt. Bryant. Duranty. Kennan. There in the cold dark night on a Paris train platform they stand about to enter a new era of the Soviet tragedy that binds them all.

Later this week on Wednesday Dodd in Berlin receives a long message from Bullitt due to arrive and expecting to be joined by Litvinov on his way as he came a different route from Washington to Moscow via Rome. Annoyed but feeling compulsions of moral obligation if not outright indignation at the violation of his own traditional national values, Dodd conscientiously changes his itinerary and returns to Berlin to host Bullitt at his home in Berlin where he arrived six months before. He is stressed and worried by rising tensions and over twenty cases of US citizens assaulted by Nazis for refusing to salute Hitler and the Reich.

Saturday December 9, 1933. Dodd entertains FDR's Moscow emissary arriving in Berlin. Bullitt is radiant. "Litvinov has agreed to pay the debt of $100,000,000", Bullitt tells Dodd. Over the next three years the two ambassadors would scrupulously observe each other and compare notes about the consolidation of totalitarian power wielded by the dictators Hitler and Stalin. The Nazi's are only a few months from taking over power in Berlin. Dodd frets over how he can possibly accommodate his guests on his meager $17,500 State Department salary.

Just think about Andrew Mellon and those lavish dinners in London! So stretched and already to his limits living in impoverished Berlin even his German guests in their forced penury find it hardly credible. Dodd doesn't complain preferring to live modestly.

Bullitt misses Litvinov who instead proceeded directly to Moscow in advance of Bullitt's arrival. Bullitt is unable to restrain his ecstasy over their diplomatic victory. Dodd listens patiently while Bullitt envisions great advances in US-Soviet trade now that Stalin has agreed, he says, "to open Russian markets to American industrial goods and leave Germans in the lurch since they were indignant at Hitler's attacks upon all Communists." Odd, since Stalin kills more communists than the Germans ever did – and in a peacetime Genocide! Dodd adds, "One more thrust at the Third Reich." Dodd worries what will happen "if the United States monopolizes Russian markets and further isolates the Germans" closing off German markets when Germans owe Americans a billion dollars. The Consortium business weighs heavy on his mind. Dodd writes in his diary, "Collect one hundred millions from Moscow and lose one billion in Berlin. Bullitt never referred to this." Dodd wonders what on earth are those Morgan-Rockefeller-Harriman bankers really up to! Losing so much money invested in conspicuously fascist war machines behind leaders of mass destruction. How could it be anything but evil? The Devil's work, indeed. But these Consortium operators are determined to use all the power known to man to blow up the world and reshape it again once and for all and to do so as they see fit for generations to come. Dodd had even more to worry about. What would happen to the country if there was a Devil sitting in the White House? Behind whose face does he hide?

Dodd lunches with Bullitt joined by the Soviet chargé d'affaires, a German Nazi expert on Russia, John White, and John Cudahy, FDR's new ambassador to Poland, an adventurous soul, born in Wisconsin, son of a successful meat trader, since his days as a Harvard undergraduate when he once dove into an icy river to save an Indian Chief who returns the next day with 100 members of his tribe including his favorite daughter to show his gratitude, and a medicine man who leads a dance invoking Spirits. Cuduhy lives a raucous and charmed life shared in passions of the soldier, explorer and diplomat. After the First World War he serves in US Army Lieutenant (1918-19) and part of the Allied intervention forces of the Polar Bear Expedition sent to Archangel fighting communists in Russia's Civil War. On November 14, 1918, Lt. Cudahy led the counter-attack that routed 1,000 "Bolos" had encircled and attacked an Allied force of 600 American, Canadian and Royal Scots holding the village of Toulgas on the Northern Dvina River. Embittered and disillusioned, he writes his account of the doomed military campaign, *Archangel: The American War with Russia.*

After Warsaw, Cudahy will go Brussels where, in 1940, as FDR's ambassador to Belgium on one occasion he entertains Henry Luce prior to his meeting with King Leopold and the Queen of Holland when the war caught up to them and German bombs pulverize the city. What a group! What a world is turning towards the flames! And still no talk of Stalin's war on the peasants, the Terror-Famine or any of that unpleasant business surely inappropriate while they savor the delicacies of German cuisine far from the frozen faces of hunger in the Ukraine. Evil has a free pass; as Head of State, a Hitler or a Stalin can virtually kill anyone and get away with it. Kill or be killed: that's the motto of a good dictator. No wonder Hitler was always in mortal awe and fascinated by Stalin and remained supremely envious of his power til the end.

Nor dare they admit the folly of each one sitting across from the other, these wretched twisted creatures all playing out their hand destroying the lives of the beautiful, the natural and the good and pure. What little they know about it now, what little they care showed no trace in Dodd's diary that night. Dodd ruminates over cigars and cherry with British Ambassador Sir Eric Phipps, a quintessential Englishman descended from a distinguished family line that included officers at both Waterloo and Trafalgar. After King's College, Cambridge, Phipps has been in the diplomatic service since 1899, then Paris, Rome, St. Petersburg before the Great War, and Vienna in 1928, newly appointed to Berlin this year. Dodd is keen to share views with Sir Eric, who is also the brother-in-law of the Under-Secretary of State Sir Robert Vansittart (1930-38), succeeded by Sir Alexander Cadogan. In 1937 Phipps will head their embassy in Paris.

From the start Vansittart is suspicious of Hitler; anything Hitler says, he argues, is "for foreign consumption". He knows Hitler is an interminable liar and should never be taken for his word. Vansittart and his small group against appeasement are convinced that Hitler will launch the European war as soon as he "felt strong enough". Vansittart claims it was vital to revise the Versailles Treaty in Germany's favour but not with Hitler in power. As far as he's concerned Britain should be firm with Germany, and it was essential to bolster that firmness by a Franco-Soviet pact. Vansittart also urgently advocates rearmament. When he visits Germany in the summer of 1936 Vansittart claims he moved in an world that "the ghost of Barthou would hardly have recognized" and urged Britain negotiate at once with Germany. Hitler was exploiting fears of a "Bolshevist menace" merely as a cover for "expansion in Central and South-Eastern Europe". Satisfying Hitler's "land hunger" at Russia's expense was not only unacceptable but entirely immoral. It was, he believed, precisely because Germany had gained equality in Europe that Vansittart favours instead facilitating German expansion in Africa. Throughout this period of Stalinist repression and the Terror-Famine Vansittart remains a major figure in the loose group of officials and politicians opposed to appeasement of Germany. Lord Vansittart is also involved in intelligence work and Churchill's chief diplomatic adviser. (Maurice Cowling, *The Impact of Hitler. British Policy and British Politics 1933-1940*, Cambridge Univ. Press, 1975, 156-9)

Dodd and Sir Eric Phipps carefully weigh Hitler's plan for war in Europe. Hitler insists on a 300,000 standing army, guns and "defensive planes", saying that the "Germans wish a ten year pact against war", and agree to an international commission of arms inspectors "including supervision of the SA, and SS troops, 2.5 million strong". Dodd is hopeful, and literally believes it marks "a real move toward disarmament". Phipps is not convinced, and repeatedly warns the Foreign Office not to be duped by the character of the Nazi regime. After having only four meetings with Hitler this year, Sir Eric Phipps sums up his views to Foreign

Secretary Sir John Simon, in his dispatch on January 31, 1934, writing Hitler's "policy is simple and straightforward. If his neighbours allow him, he will become strong by the simplest and most direct methods. There mere fact that he is making himself unpopular abroad will not deter him, for, as he said in a recent speech, it is better to be respected and feared than to be weak and liked. If he finds that he arouses no real opposition, the *tempo* of his advance will increase. On the other hand, if he is vigorously opposed, he is unlikely at this stage to risk a break." On April 1, 1935 Phipps sends another warning, "Let us hope our pacifists at home may at length realise that the rapidly-growing monster of German militarism will not be placated by mere cooings, but will only be restrained from recourse to its *ultima ratio* by the knowledge that the Powers who desire peace are also strong enough to enforce it." (Correlli Barnett, *The Collapse of British Power*, Pan, 2002, 387-8)

The French government resists proposals for disarmament favoured by Britain's Labour government. The French, too, were less naïve. In August 1933 the French Conseil supérieur de guerre understood better stating that Nazi Germany was "preparing to impose its will with a policy of force... as soon as it has gained a clear military superiority". FDR's political backer and poor choice of an ambassador for Poland sees Hitler in quite a different light than Dodd.

More reports arrive for FDR declaring Hitler a fraud of the most treacherous calculations. John Cudahy sends Roosevelt a report dated December 27, 1933, "There is a unity in Germany, an intense feeling of national solidarity and patriotic buoyancy, which strikes one almost immediately, and the allegiance to Hitler borders on fanaticism. But the reports of training large bodies of troops for war, and assembling huge supplies of war materials are in my opinion entirely, baseless."

Ambassador Cudahy's aloofness, however, minimalizes Nazi brutality and denies the evil where it lurks. Too many times the witness needs a corpse to smell death. Here in Germany Hitler's Brownshirts and Blackshirts, SS Nazis and Hitler's Youth fascists are already marching down the long road of war but Cudahy doesn't see that. He sees instead, as he writes the President, "an outlet for the peculiar social need of a country which loves display and pageantry. Half of the Brownshirts are unemployed and the organization provides relief and cheap meals for needy members. These marching clubs are essentially social. The German feels important and distinguished in a uniform and what has been taken for a blatant display of militarism is merely an expression of the unique German gregarious instinct, accountable on the same grounds that our Elks.... are accountable." FDR rejects that sort of sophistry that masks Hitler's real objective and he replies underscoring that Germany was "heading consciously or subconsciously toward an idea of extension of boundaries". Anyone who thinks otherwise is a fool. (T. Morgan, *FDR*, 395-6)

Reader lets take another fix on the intrigue of nations. France improves its relations with Bolshevik Russia. The Soviet Union represents a vital eastern counter-weight against a resurgent Germany. Soviet Russia has been an important French ally until its breakdown from the strain of losses, corruption and disorganization in the First World War. Dodd cables his memorandum to inform Washington and British Foreign Secretary Sir John Simon of Fritwell Manor that predates the Roman conquest of Britain, and is a Liberal Minister in MacDonald's fragile coalition government. But it's all just another convoluted web of uncertainties and improbabilities and what-ifs with brutal Japanese aggression tearing into China and the Far East as the English, French, Americans and Russians had done before. So now it was their turn and the Japanese troops are given a free hand by London and FDR. Dodd wonders, "did he not think it would be far better for an English-German-French pact to be made on disarmament than to take the chance of an eventual Italian-German-Russian deal which might force France into a dictatorship?" Yes, there was a real threat that Paris fascists might seize power at any moment. Dodd laments writing in his diary that Sir Eric "wished American moral support but indicated, indirectly, that England had recognized Japanese claims in Manchuria. He seemed ready to acknowledge the danger to world peace if autocracies of Central Europe were allowed to compel French submission". For the sake of peace in Europe Dodd insists Communist Russia must come to the table and fix peace in the Far East.

Ambassador Dodd is slightly too naïve about the nefarious far-sighted designs of the Consortium which found no place in his classroom at Rockefeller's University of Chicago. Dodd writes in his diary again if only he could find the way. "I thought the English ought to compromise, then President Roosevelt might negotiate and Europe would be out of its impasse." Dodd writes December 20 after the British publicity press rave about scooping Bill Phillip's trip to London and Windsor Palace to meet the King and Prime Minister Ramsay MacDonald's Foreign Secretary John Simon before dashing off to Paris and Rome. A few days earlier Dodd had met with Von Neurath, and learns that the Germans are convinced Russia will soon spiral in chaos once the Japanese invade their borders. The Kremlin always suspicious of Anglo-American entente is all nerves over rumors circulating in London of a proposed British loan to the Japanese, the German says. (W E. Dodd, *Ambassador Dodd's Diary,* 63)

Had Dodd been more informed he might have easily known details of the Holodmor from John Cudahy in Warsaw and others not far from the border with the Ukraine. But there is sign of acknowledgment. And yet the Polish papers are full of it. And surely he should have known that all during this spring, summer and fall Europe's embassies and Washington received more detailed reports monitoring peasant resistance in the Ukraine to Soviet "russification of the administration of the Ukrainian SSR"; Premier Stalin and his underling commissar Postyshev intensify the confiscation of grain.

The US State Department is aware of Nazi plans for pacification of the Ukraine and their ambition to "colonize" it. "Pacification", "Russification", "Collectivization" –different words for the same thing, – extermination of millions of Ukrainians setting a new standard of immorality and the Consortium remains intimately locked on its course for mass destruction, more greedy and hunger for power than ever.

The World's Fair called "A Century of Progress" launched in 1928 by a non-profit corporation opens in Chicago on May 27, 1933. The Russians are not officially represented but have their commissars there eagerly examining closely the latest technological innovations. Rufus Dawes, organizer of the World's Fair, opened the event and said, "Here are gathered the evidences of man's achievements in the realm of physical sciences – proofs of his power to prevail over all the perils that beset him. Here in the presence of such victories men may gather courage to face their unsolved problems ..." Rufus Dawes, prominent Chicago businessman with a fortune in oil and banking, happens also to be the younger brother of Charles G. Dawes and great-great-grandson of the American Revolutionary War veteran William Dawes; in the 1920s he serves as an expert on the commissions to prepare the Dawes Plan and the Young Plan to manage German reparations to the Allies.

The fair's vision, described a noted observer, presented an image of modern society a scientific utopia of mass production that embraced the "hopes of the satisfaction without pain of almost limitless human wants." For the fair Detroit's top architect Albert Kahn built the Ford Rotunda. Hitler sent one of his show-piece airships, the 776-foot *Graf Zeppelin*, which circled Lake Michigan before landing at the nearby Curtis-Wright Airport. American manufacturers introduced their "dream cars": the Cadillac 16-V limousine, the Lincoln rear-engine concept car, Pierce-Arrow's Silver Arrow. Union Pacific Railroad sent its first stream-lined train, the M-10000, and the famous *Zephr* with a record run from Denver to Chicago in 13 hours. VIP Consortium men arrived in their impenetrable limousines smoking fat cigars gloated over the new industrial technology and scientific advancement and made more deals. Many brought their wives and children. This year alone 27 million visitors go to see it and marvel, and 21 million the next year until it closes in May. The Italian pavilion praised Mussolini's "heroic deeds of Fascism" mixing classic and modern architecture. International Harvester, Caterpillar and Deere all show off their mechanical wonders and tractors to improve farm productivity and profits for the farmer.

The same day, the May 27 story appearing in the Soviet state organ *Ivestiia* of grain and seed procurements is relayed to Washington along with a speech by the People's Commissar for Agriculture Mikhail Tshernov (1934-37) proclaiming the decision of the All-Union Corn Committee that "the farmers will be compelled to deliver the grain at set dates at the shipping points; the grain shipping and storing campaign must be conducted at a strong tempo from the beginning." He went on to say "The entire Communist press, without exception, is day after day shouting: 'The first load of grain from the present crop – to the State!' Or like this "The taxes in kind must be collected, the seed loans liquidated, the payments in kind from the collective farms for the use of Government tractors received, and the enemies must be treated with utmost cruelty.'"

This report to the US State Department continues: "Why all these unusual atrocious measures? As an answer we can use a speech by the red governor-general – one Posneeshev (Pavel Petrovich Postyshev sic) reported in *Economical Life,* June 23, 1933. He said that the farmers on collective farms are starving, even in the best districts, producing good crops. Thus the hungry villages are impatiently waiting for the new crop, in the hope to get a few good meals. In this very legitimate desire the peasants in the villages (sic) are supported by the Communists of lower ranks. These Communists are with the peasantry, they disagree with their superiors. Some sort of alliance between the peasantry and the Communists of the lower strata is a fact fully confirmed by Posneeshev himself. And so the policy of those on top drove a wedge in the ranks of the Communist party itself." He quotes,"*Evestia*" (22 VII, 1933) "informs that Commissar of Agriculture orders the collective farms to organize the guarding of the field crops by setting up a service of day and night watchmen and patrols". Then in a bold type 'GUNS GUARD HARVEST', the article quotes "Evestia" July 23, 1933 on collective fields under armed guards "Those guarding the socialistic grains are : First, the shift bosses, then there are the scale men, the wheat chiefs. Next are those in charge of means of transportation (teams, wagons, etc); and the patrol with a red band on his arm, and a rifle. Next the watchman sitting on an observation tower built for this purpose in the fields; and finally there are mounted patrols everywhere among the crops." The report continues to state "The open spaces of the countryside are now the battlefields ... The peasantry closed in with its deadly enemy – the Soviet power. On one side the authorities, armed to the teeth; on the other – the peasantry, robbed and beaten, animated with hatred, protecting its right to live, to enjoy the free labor and to own the land. The villages, which were forcibly collective, do not accept the slavery; they are freeing themselves from Soviet's fetters."

Commissar Postyshev's grain procurement and execution squads appear in more Department reports.

Half-way into the autumn harvest season, in October 10, US Ambassador John Cudahy, in Warsaw, transmits a number of highly significant documents with what he said were in "reference to the Embassy's confidential dispatch No. 215, May 27, 1933". These include translations on Russian living conditions in *Soviet Russia* from July and August "which have been received from an authoritative source". Cudany writes, "In general these reports treat of the efforts of the Soviet regime to insure a successful grain collection campaign and to prevent the withholding or diversion of grain." Among them, two documents "deal with conditions affecting the Central Government's control of the Ukraine with reference to the russification of the administration of the Ukrainian SSR" as well as "the control of the grain harvest by the political sections of the machine-tractor stations."

The thirty-one page Cudahy memorandum, however, includes another damaging article from *Rosja Sowiecka's* July issue No. 11 "Forecasts on the Autumn Struggle for Grain in the Ukraine": "Conditions in the Ukraine, autocratically ruled by Postyshev, Stalin's representative, are not satisfactory.

Copies of the long Cudahy memorandum are sent to Washington, to Riga and the military attaché in Warsaw. It includes an article from *Rosja Sowiecka's* July issue No. 11 "Forecasts on the Autumn Struggle for Grain in the Ukraine": "Conditions in the Ukraine, autocratically ruled by Postyshev, Stalin's representative, are not satisfactory. The feeling exists that the persons who were responsible for that memorandum (the Hugenberg memorandum "entrusting Germany with the right to colonize the Ukraine") must have been well-informed concerning the situation as regards loyalty in the Ukraine. Not so long ago the Moscow press did not disguise its indignation against the local authorities of the Soviet Ukraine who showed, it was alleged, great leniency toward anti-State elements. It was only in the beginning of June, as if in anticipation that the Ukrainian problem would suddenly arise in Europe, that this anti-Ukrainian campaign was abandoned."

Referring to Pavel Postyshev's June 10 speech ten days before its publication the Cudahy memorandum stressed the severity of Postyshev's crackdown "to show Europe that all hopes connected with the possibility of any separatistic movements in the Ukraine are under present conditions impossible of realization." Postyshev called particular attention to the previous January Central Committee's instruction to Ukraine about the harvest problem. Postyshev declared, "We have carried out sowings in a better manner than last year. However, we have extended sowings so that even now they are not yet concluded." But tractors are inadequate and livestock in poor condition. "Should things continue as at present, then we may have to go back to conditions of last year and make the same mistakes which were made in last year's campaign for the delivery of grain to the State. No, we Bolsheviks from the Ukraine will not permit this to happen as the proletariat of the USSR would never forgive us."

His warning is sharp and accusatory: "The weakening of the Bolshevik watchfulness over the class enemy – this was the gravest sin of the party organization in the Ukraine ... The lack of Bolshevik watchfulness has resulted in the gaining of a wide field of activity in the Ukraine by the sabotaging counter-revolutionaries ... Do not think that the enemy acts merely within our agricultural organizations. The sabotage and counter-revolutionary elements have succeeded in extending their activity to other fields of socialist construction. They have even succeeded in obtaining in such fields a number of important and commanding post." The Old Bolsheviks vanguard is on thin ice. (SDDF /11538)

These are busy days for the former University of Chicago professor from North Carolina obliged to sit long hours with Consortium bankers and Nazis. On January 22, 1934 Dodd meets John Foster Dulles over the problem of the National City and Chase National banks and their $100 million held in securities; Dulles represents creditors holding $1 billion of high interest loans in the doomed Dawes and Young Consortium plans. The American bankers then turned around selling them as safe $90 bonds to public investors. Dodd feared this was playing with fire. He writes that the bankers reaped "enormous profits for themselves".

Dodd deliberately stores notes in his private diary showing he's in no way unsympathetic to the bankers losses: "Money was put into city, state and corporation improvements, a vast building scheme like that of 1922-1929 in the United States. Now my job is to save as much of this as possible...." Last June Roosevelt had given Dodd the straight and narrow on the Consortium predicament when he said '...the bankers have gotten themselves into this. You must lend what personal, unofficial aid you can, but no more." Now the creditors, the New York bankers, have organized and pressed the government into fighting their battles. I shall do what I can..."

It's a busy day for Dodd. He dreads having to entertain Rockefeller's hatchet man Ivy Lee for lunch now traveling through Berlin with his son James. Dodd wrote, "Ivy Lee showed himself at once a capitalist and an advocate of Fascism. He told stories of his fight for Russian recognition and was disposed to claim credit for it. His sole aim was to increase American business profits." A few weeks earlier, on January 3, Dodd had lunches with Dulles and reporters including Junius B. Wood, a freelancer and former Far Eastern correspondent for the *Chicago Daily News*, based in Japan, in and out of Berlin for the next two years, and Joseph Flack, a career Foreign Service office. Much to talk is over the political problem arising from the German debt. Wood is a veteran foreign correspondent of virtually legendary status among his colleagues. From his earlier Moscow days he is certainly likely to be well informed the Holodomor deaths; four years before Wood told the US State Department's minister in Riga, Frederick Coleman, that Bolshevik "control of the food supply is an irresistible weapon" used to crush Ukrainian partisan resistance. Junius Wood has some stories to tell of Japanese invasion of Manchuria where passes two years observing the Japanese imperial army. He was with the American Expeditionary Force in Europe and Siberia, 1917-20. Later he is stationed in the Soviet Union, 1925-28, and generally "ridiculed" the communist regime. Wood returns to Moscow where he is based from 1925-1928, adding to his legendary adventures around the world in a 32-year career for *Chicago Daily New,* that also puts him at Vera Cruz, Mexico, for Wilson's army expedition to capture Pancho Villa and Zapata, in 1914 and a Cuban revolution in 1917. Junius Wood's assignments send him to the Balkans, Scandinavia, Central and South America, Japan, China, India, the Philippines, and Arabia. He reported more than a dozen national political party conventions, and flew across the country in the helium gas airship *Shenandoah*, in 1924.

Before the end of the month Dodd again is obliged to meet again with Ivy Lee. In the interim Lee had talks with Josef Goebbels and Nazi Economics minister Kurt Schmitt. Lee's reputation as the Rockefeller man precedes him as one of the best American PR men of Consortium Big Business. Acting like two advertising junkies with plans contrived in Hell, or, wherever they find themselves, Lee advises Goebbels how best to handle the Consortium-owned correspondents telling him to "see the foreign press people often and learn how to get along with them". It might seem odd that, or blatantly out of place, or maybe not that all. From Rothschild to Rockefeller, Morgan and Lee, now Goebbels gets primed on the urgencies and prompts of the propaganda tricks from America's spin doctor. Goebbels couldn't be more delighted and thinks he has the Americans deep in Nazi pockets.

An innate disdain for Lee's irreverent fascist lust for Nazi business leaves Dodd with a felling of moral indignation. Lee standing on the same side as the Nazis is morally repugnant and Dodd is conflicted between separating the man's moral fiber from his actions. He has seen a lot of strange characters since he took the embassy job and it makes him unwell and sick at heart as though the poisonous atmosphere is starting to take effect him personally. Not long ago Dodd sat in his hotel room with George Sylvester Viereck, the mysterious author and Nazi propagandist paid $100,000 by Goebbels "to push their cause". People can still recall when Viereck gained fame for his best-selling expose on President Wilson and Col. House in *The Strangest Friendship in History.* Dodd calls him "a curious sort of journalist with whom one would best not be too free".

Dodd admires a certain broad knowledge and efficiency shown by the educated elite in Berlin's diplomatic community that from time to time revives his waning enthusiasm for the place. The ambassador enjoys the opportunity to sharpen his German in conversation with his special friend and frequent dinner guest Dr. Schacht, Hitler's top banker. He savours Schacht's sagacity and sharp mind that challenge his own skills acquired at the Virginia Polytechnic Institute before he left his beloved South for Chicago's megaopolis. But for the most part, receptions given in his honor by wealthy American and German socialites leave the ambassador bored, and intellectually empty, and depressed. After a tea reception attended by German aristocrats at the Henry Wood mansion in Potsdam, Dodd remarks, "Everybody stood up in good Hohenzollern style" however sadly the grandeur descended to conversation of "the tone (that) was quite Hitlerite." (W. E. Dodd, *Ambassador Dodd's Diary*, 75)

Dodd will keep his post the full four years of his tour but by the end both he and the Nazis will have had enough of each other. Terror and persecution are not quite his cup of tea. In fact he abhors it all and the fascist relations of daily life have a perverted affect on his promiscuous daughter and wayward son. Dodd becomes a thorn in the Nazi's nest and unofficially *persona non grata* and recalled. Resigning from the service in November 1937, estranged and isolated from goose-stepping fascists with their ridiculous militaristic rigidity and salute which he finds utterly alarming, an no less obnoxious, ambassador Dodd could consider him lucky to get when the going is good before the apocalypse. In no small way he saved himself. Sincerely honest about his position Dodd tells reporters upon his return to America that he had found representing the United States in Hitler's Berlin nest a dim task.

"In a vast region where religious freedom is denied, where intellectual initiative and discovery are not allowed, and where race hatreds are cultivated", Dodd wonders, "what can a representative of the United States do?" In a curious way as we will see the same thing happens to Bullitt in Moscow. But Bullitt is a great conniver and already had been scheming against Dodd while seeking to gain more points with the President.

Bullitt writes FDR November 23, 1937 quoting General Göering that if America seeks good relations with the Germany then Dodd has to go. Göering tells him "he considered it simply disastrous that there should be no American Ambassador in Berlin." Bullitt shows his true colours; adamantly he is convinced by more than own loyalty to the President to betray and expose Dodd once and for all. Bullitt lands his *coup de grace* : "Neither he nor anyone else in the German Government could recognize Dodd as an American Ambassador. Dodd was too filled with venomous hatred of Germany."

His days there are numbered. In a few years Hitler appoints his friend Göering in charge of the economic exploitation of Soviet Ukraine and in all of Soviet Republics; on May 23, 1941 Göering officially orders Russia's food production to feed Germany and condemns the Ukraine to starve. The instruction announced, "Any attempt to save the population from death by starvation...would reduce Germany's staying power in the war. As a result, many millions of persons will be starved to death if we take out of the country the things necessary for us. This must be clearly and absolutely understood." The historian, professor and author of a dozen books on this period and issues, John Stoessinger (Harvard, MIT, Columbia, Princeton, NY City University...), who fled Nazi-occupied Austria first, then Czechoslovakia, to Siberia and Shanghai) observed, "Once again, there is no evidence that nay of Göering's subordinates who prepared the spoliation of Russia during that pleasant Germany spring of 1941 voiced any protest." (J. Stoessinger, *Why Nations Go To War,* 37)

Dodd dedicated to his father his diary memoirs *Teacher and Friend, Who Kept the Democratic Faith in an Age of Betrayal.* Of Hitler's rise to power in 1933, former Columbia professor and historian Charles Beard wrote in its preface that "the new Chancellor's fortunes were, at the moment, hidden from all vision, even his own...That he was a dangerous and ruthless personality was well known everywhere in the spring of 1933, but, as the veil could not be lifted on the future, several varieties of policy in relationship with his government were recognized as available in all diplomatic circles, including the Department of State in Washington". Constantly increasing his popularity among the masses, all of Hitler's generals have reason to suspect Hitler of erratic and emotionally volatile behavior and he outflanks them with his power. "You will never learn what I am thinking. And those who boast most loudly that they know my thought, to such people I lie even more." (John G. Stoessinger, *Why Nations Go to War,* 1982, 27)

Hitler's Germany is a ticking bomb. Everyone knows it. America was so radically isolationist that even with France on its knees, England fierce but trembling expecting invasion anytime, America, still proudly isolated and aloof as it had been in the First World War. Dodd's book appeared in 1941, the year to remember, a year when everything changed for the Americans: the German invasion of the Ukraine, in June; FDR's mission to Moscow in July, followed by Harriman to the Kremlin in September; the declaration of war after Pearl Harbor, in December. With history set in motion Dodd remained a very specious even casual reader of Consortium strategy of which he himself was not personally an advocate but suffered the consequences.

Among his peers Dodd is considered an expert on all that is noble and good in American history. His exhaustive volumes on the lives of Thomas Jefferson, Robert E. Lee, Jefferson Davis, Abraham Lincoln and Woodrow Wilson are already considered classics in American history. Now Dodd has a chance to serve a living American president and live history in the flesh in the making instead of writing about presidents long since dead. Yet Dodd stands deep in Consortium territory with his entire academic career indebted to endowments principally from Rockefeller. To say that Dodd was naïve is to risk understatement. To that extent he may be considered truly a public servant of the establishment's national interests. Coincidentally Dodd has already been selected President of the American Historical Association for 1934, the occasion of its 50 year anniversary, occupying the chair of his immediate successor, Charles Beard; Dodd's address to his distinguished colleagues in January 1935, is titled, "The Emergence of the First Social Order of the United States". Its an interesting commentary tracing back the birth of American freedoms built on the foundations of the British Empire derived from profits of "the East India Company and the new African slave trade corporation, in which the Duke of York and the king's 'devoted' sister, the Duchess of Orleans, were heavy stockholders." As Dodd well knew history is not lived by historians who make it.

This was a strategic choice by FDR breaking with precedents to pick a rich bagman of the Democratic machine. Charles Beard wrote "A selection from this class meant taking a financier, a rich lawyer, or a soldier of great fortune – a man little versed in the history of European politics and likely to use the Embassy as a debt collection or salvaging agency for American creditors, or in selling raw materials for German rearmament, while making lavish displays at dinners and entertainments". Nor was Dodd selected from the State Department's "second class of potential candidates…'career' men in the diplomatic and consular service … permanent civil servants more or less 'trained' in the conduct of foreign relations." Roosevelt was playing again. It was a cruel mean choice to pick Dodd as a harmless and inoffensive presidential servant and throw him into the Nazi fire inflamed with the Consortium fascists. It would break him completely, morally and physically.

Career men like Henderson, Kennan and Kelley, Bohlen, Messersmith, Coleman who to use Beard's characterization are reliably "'correct' in matters of protocol – precedence, propriety, formalities, and traditions". These true and faithful civil servants assure the continuity of the system. Still, they were not all mere pigeon-holed bureaucrats. In fact, many of these careerists most 'available' for the embassy in Berlin were either rich themselves or had married fortunes; they were ambitious, or had ambitious wives. Only innocence regarded them as purely objective agents of the national interest." Ellis Briggs, for example, recalls in his government memoirs *Proud Servant* how John Wiley impressed his peers as a "tough and articulate" career officer, in particular during the Spanish crisis with the King deposed and he stayed on in the tumult as chargé d'affaires even as the US ambassador fled. And Chip Bohlen, later with Harriman in Moscow during the last days of the German siege held out and witnessed the Wehrmacht assault repulsed by heroic Soviet citizens in last-ditch battles to save the soul of Russia and smash the Nazi will forcing a retreat. (W. E. Dodd, *Ambassador Dodd's Diary*, Charles Beard, preface, viii, 30; Ellis Briggs, *Proud Servant; Memoirs of a Career Ambassador*, Kent State Univ. Press, 2012)

So why does FDR pick Dodd for Berlin? What is FDR thinking? A concession to "Cord" Hull? Not likely. To know better we should look at the same logic in his choice of his Secretary of State. Poor Hull. Poor Dodd. The world is going to Hell all around them and there is really nothing they can do to stop it. Is FDR sending a message of southern respectability to Hitler and his Nazi gang of criminal thugs? The most sensitive diplomatic post at the time is held by a trustworthy University of Chicago man who could be counted on to send objective unbiased and unfiltered reports. Even with all his preparatory introductions from Crane to Root and Barach, Dodd remains out of the Consortium loop. FDR used Dodd like he uses everybody. Dodd will have to take the heat. When it was over for him Dodd returns to his farm in Round Hill, Virginia, a burnt-out case.

Fate had not been kind to Professor Dodd. He suffers pretty much a total crackup. Back in the United States his life spins out of control there too. First his beloved wife "Mattie" fell ill, and dies. Heart-struck and not completely sound mind he nearly runs down an Afro-American child and leaves the scene; in a highly publicized case he loses in court, fined court costs on top of the medical expenses he claims he'd already paid. Morally exhausted and alone, unable to reconcile his strict Baptist faith with the fascist and totalitarian clients of the Consortium's geopolitical intrigue he serviced in Berlin, and abandoned by his renegade communist-turned-soviet agent daughter, Dodd dies of pneumonia in 1940. Europe is already besieged by Hitler's advancing *Wehrmacht* army.

FDR and Stalin are the strangest of bed-fellows. They were inevitably united by economic forces controlling them in the guise of monopoly and only differed by the identity of the group and their methods of controlling power. The system of economic monopoly and international finance linked them together and made their union indispensable. It could have been no other way. If you believe that then it goes along that the evolution of the affairs of the world required it be so. Antony Sutton studied how the American and Soviet systems were very different but shared a common aspect of obedience to government under the control of a few individuals who held legal monopolies of financial and industrial control and thereby profited at the expense of everyone else.

Corporate socialism was the modern expression of the legitimate authority of America's government. "John D. Rockefeller and the turn-of-the century capitalists," Antony Sutton wrote, "were convinced of one absolute truth: that no great monetary wealth could be accumulated under the impartial rules of a competitive *laissez faire* society. Monopoly was the only sure road to the accumulation of massive wealth, and buying off politicians for state protection of your industry to ensure favorable government regulation. A legal monopoly was the most reliable path to wealth and power. The difference between communist or socialist state monopoly and a corporate state monopoly is essentially only the identity of the group and the means they use controlling the existing power structure." The essence of capitalism is monopoly. Rockefeller knew it. Morgan knew it. Harriman knew it. The law suits Brandeis fought so valiantly to advance told the story. All their friends and partners knew it as well as their public adversaries worked hard to inform the American people of the secret arrangements to create these monopolies. Likewise, or inversely, the essence of socialism is also monopoly. Lenin knew it. Trotsky knew it. Stalin knew it. And they perceived a certain dialectical amusement as they played with its intrinsic contradictions. So did FDR. Capitalism and socialism are politically run economies. Stripped of ideology and rhetoric they are very common in nature and more in common that met the eye. Combination of the two political run economies was necessary and inevitable.

Corporate socialism is the *modus operandi* of the Consortium. The state exerts its power of control using paid workers and obedient careerist academics. Soviet socialist workers received subsistence wages in roubles, and in most cases were provided with generous food and much sought after accommodations; both systems used writers, artists, hacks, Consuls and Commissars to reproduce ideas and propaganda and falsify history and the press. Its uncanny how dumb-witted most Americans appear to be when ignoring how the stupendous success of the Rockefeller banking and oil fortune primarily depended upon focusing public attention on distracting and superficial contrivances, such as the myth of a historical struggle between capitalists and communists, and the lobbying of political forces by large corporations or large centralized state entities of concentrated economic resources and power to exert control. They can thank Lee for that.

Rockefeller's public relations man is Ivy Lee shrewd at turning discretion into a pack of lies to conceal atrocities. Ivy Lee has a long tortuous history promoting trade with Soviet Russia. In 1930, England's former war Prime Minister, Lloyd George sends his personal assistant Gareth Jones to work with Lee. Linguistically gifted, Jones speaks fluent Russian and German, and brought back confidential information telling of the terrors of collectivization and the beginning of widespread famine breaking out inside the Ukraine. Lee and Lloyd George, however, are political animals, motivated by the tradition of their class and accorded measure to the way they experience it. Both lack idealism and compassion natural to youth, or, "preferred the faceless to faces", writes Russian writer Boris Pasternak, author of *Dr. Zhivago.* Pasternak is persecuted by Stalin and Khrushchev but spared. In 1958 Pasternak was awarded the Nobel Prize for Literature, but had to refuse under pressure; only fame kept him out of the Gulag. His pregnant mistress was not as fortunate, and lost their child in prison. After a trip to the Ukraine, Pasternak witnesses abhorring scenes of the Holdomor. He writes, "There was such inhuman, unimaginable misery, such a terrible disaster, that it began to seem almost abstract, it would not fit within the bounds of consciousness". (O. Mathews, *Stalin's Children*, 38)

Once there is some light shed on the privileged and honored servants of the Consortium willing to perform their duties, like Ivy Lee spinning propaganda to fuel the economies under Stalin and Hitler, we can understand how it was that men Lee and others like him were indifferent when personally told of the starvation in the Ukraine by eye-witness Gareth Jones, an aspiring personal assistant of former British Prime Minister Lloyd George. Lee probably used Lloyd George to pass on his offer to Winston Churchill to pen a glowing biography on J. D. Rockefeller, the world's richest man. Even at $200,000, a huge fortune in the thirties, the equivalent of $2 million today, Churchill declined. He couldn't be bothered as he was himself finishing up his classic five-volume history of the First World War (1928) and running his devoted staff ragged with his brilliant eccentricities and exhausting the ever-vigilant private secretary long after hours. (Churchill surpassed that extraordinary feat with six volumes on World War II.)

But this is tame stuff. Eustace Mullins reveals how Rockefeller in New York gave Trotsky $10,000 for his trip to revolutionary Russia in 1917 – he arrives late on the scene. And Britain's Prime Minister Lloyd George indignantly intervened when Trotsky was hauled off an ocean liner and arrested in Halifax by Canadian secret service unaware of the thickening deep plot to stage a Bolshevik "revolution" in Moscow and St. Petersburg. In the saga while Trotsky was interned by bewildered officials President Wilson and his advisors in Washington intervened and expedited a special passport along with their favorite socialist journalist Lincoln Steffens to escort Trotsky along his way to Russia. Steffens will return there with Bullitt on his House-Milner mission to seal a deal with Lenin in the midst of the chaotic Civil War.

Try to think out of the box. If you were to read, say, Frederic C. Howe's book (1906), *Confession of a Monopolist*, – actually a best seller in its day –, the monopolistic system based on an economy of corruption and privilege as it had evolved during the last half-century in America comes to light. Similarly, Presidential adviser Col. House wrote a cryptic book with a similar theme about a socialist hero in government. Howe and House are both Consortium types with particular interest in the takeover of Czarist Russia by a band of radical socialists. Howe's role in the 1917 Bolshevik Revolution surfaces in Sutton's book *Wall Street and the Bolshevik Revolution*. Meanwhile Howe is playing out a strategic role influencing Democratic administrations from Wilson to Roosevelt and reappears again aside Roosevelt's New Dealers as consumer counsel in the Agricultural Adjustment program in of all places the Department of Agriculture.

To understand the public philosophy of the international bankers and corporate socialists of the Consortium personified in Roosevelt and his pro-Soviet administration, Antony Sutton took a closer look at Frederick Howe to see what he was up to. Here we have Sutton to guide us through this maze of intersecting ideas, people and events, all bound by a common thread weaved through the Consortium's grab of wealth and power. "It is at the same time", Sutton writes, "also a system of disguised forced labor, called by Ludwig von Mises the '*Zwangswirtschaft* system', a system of compulsion. It is this element of compulsion that is common to all politically run economies: Hitler's New Order, Mussolini's corporate state, Kennedy's New Frontier, Johnson's Great Society, and Nixon's Creative Federalism. Compulsion was also an element in Herbert Hoover's reaction to the Depression and much more obviously in Franklin D. Roosevelt's New Deal and the National Recovery Administration. We call this phenomenon of corporate legal monopoly – market control acquired by using political influence – by the name of corporate socialism." It is also most obviously set in motion right through the Bush administrations and apparent in the Obama agenda as well.

FDR nationalizes the railroads, introduces Americans to the Social Security tax at the same time Stalin socializes the millions of rural peasants into factory workers of heavy industry and into tractor-centers, tractor plants and tractor "brigades" to harvest the wheat in the Ukraine once he had exterminated the best of the hardy and skilled peasants, wheat and food products Russia needs in order to survive.

A most curious place in the time of the Holodomor! As much as he dare Bullitt maintains personal relations with both Howe and House. Is it any wonder why these men just happen to always circulate in the same political circles where occasionally their orbits cross over. What is going on? It's not just because they belong there like some invisible or imperceptible destiny or chance or some odd or magical predetermined force. There is a selection process, appointments are made, nominations, instructions and directions are transmitted and the actors are there waiting to play a role, standing by, ready to take risks, serve the cause, gain a promotion, accelerate their career for the good and rich rewards of fame, status and mutual self-interests of their extended family. All is done to keep in step, stay in "the Game" and be a player. On January 9, 1934, for example, when he had barely had time to unpack his suitcases and get acquainted with the Moscow *apparatchiki* Bill Bullitt replies to a casual written request from Howe to help promote an art show in the United States. This not long after one of the plutocrats bought an entire museum for his collection, or Mellon donates some of his acquisitions to create America's National Gallery in Washington. Bullitt replied he was "very much excited over bringing the Rembrandt collection from Leningrad", smugly calling the Heritage Museum's Rembrandts "unofficial ambassadors of cultural relations".

Reader, keep your eyes open to see layer after layer in the hierarchy of relationships, here cultured by much more in play than Old Masters of the art world. Perhaps Bullitt would have himself better serve the country as a cultural envoy, but how ironic when Stalin is destroying one culture and Ukrainian nationalism to replace it with a latter day version of "Russianfication" more terrible than the Czar Ivan IV. Rembrandts! Bullitt is more comfortable admiring lifeless and priceless Rembrandts, Faberge eggs and other Czarist art treasures than he ever would be off touring the countryside to see dispossessed *kulaks* and the disenfranchised Russian masses. He really couldn't be bothered, and never was but such trifles. Not a word about famine to the new American government bureaucrat in the department of agriculture. Reader, don't you find this a bit too ironic? It's such a joke on the people, only the people aren't laughing. From Berlin to Moscow, New York to London and Paris, most of the people are living desperate lives, stressed and worried, hungry and living in fear.

Before the year is out Bullitt will realize how he'd been duped by his imposing duplicity of self-importance, and that what he suspected all along, and not unlike Dodd at sea in Berlin that he too was utterly superfluous in Moscow, that he too was merely serving his master, a timely useful tool in the hands of the President and the Consortium. Neither John Reed, the infamous communist and dead lover of his estranged wife, his nemesis, was unable to escape, to find peace and time to write novels, killed by typhus in 1920; delirious and dying in a Moscow hospital he uttered repeatedly to his wife Louise he'd been "caught in a trap". Four words Louise never forgotten. A bit more than a decade later, Louise Bryant, mother of

Bullet's daughter, once herself, too, an engaged and brave journalist in her own right, is dying in Paris, forsaken, alcoholic and addicted to heroin. Too many lives in America and in its prodigal proxy the Soviet Union destroyed by a mad carnage of corporate socialism. In keeping together their elite social network Howe tells Bullitt that he absolutely must contact their aging friend Lincoln Steffens "who has had a bad stroke" at his home in Carmel, California. "He seems so appreciative", Howe writes "of a letter which I wrote him some days ago." It has only been slightly over a decade since his secret diplomatic trade mission to Moscow with Steffens in 1919, when Reed had finished his epic, split the American socialist movement and gone underground soon to surface arrested in Finland and freed in a prison swap with Lenin. The socialist writer Steffens had been a mentor and loyal friend of John Reed ever since his days at Harvard when he shared essays with T.S. Eliot and Walter Lippmann. (A. C. Sutton, Chapter 5, *FDR*. Sutton notes "the sponsor of Howe's book was the same publisher who in 1973 put out a collectivist dirge by John D. Rockefeller III, *The Second American Revolution;* Frederic C. Howe, *Confessions of a Monopolist*, Chicago: Public Publishing, 1906)

That people all year are starving and crumbling in the streets of Kharkov, the capital of Soviet Ukraine, never does seem to perturb Washington or the State Department. Trade and the bogey-man of communist propaganda dwarf the food crisis. Even when gripped by "the Great Depression" Bolshevik methods of murder and extermination never take hold of the American psyche. At least not when America is confronted with the spectre of starvation at home. Mass starvation in America! Is it really possible? The Russian experience of Terror-Famine that held Russian villages spellbound with horror is antithetical to the isolationist American culture. Not with headlines of the tens of thousands of Hunger Marchers in Britain, or protest rallies of the unemployed and poorly fed millions across America. It didn't figure into the equation of daily life. Or did it? Well, not as they were told, – or not told.

Meanwhile American engineers sign contracts to launch Stalin's modern military industrial base under the First Five-Year Plan (1929-34). During the height of the famine in 1933, for example, the KHEMZ at Kharkov designed by General Electric is equipped with a fantastic turbine-manufacturing capacity two and one-half times superior to G.E.'s main Schenectady plant located under his nose just twenty miles north from Governor Roosevelt's office at Albany in upstate New York. The Urals-Emash combinat increased Soviet electrical equipment manufacturing capacity by sevenfold.

In the Zaporizhya Oblast in southern Ukraine the communists covert churches into social clubs, and as elsewhere priests are harassed constantly, arrested and some not infrequently killed after the most grim tortures. US State Department and British Foreign Office files bulge with reports of these murders since the fall of the Czar. By the end of 1932, all in all just over a thousand churches are estimated as having been closed in the Ukraine. The major offensive of 1933-34 is yet to come; in 1934-36 some 75-80% of the remaining churches in the Ukraine are destroyed. With its hundreds of church cupolas painting the skyline in Kiev only two small ones are still active in 1935.

This once proud homeland of Cossack legends and black earth rich in deposits of aluminum, iron and magnesium or became a show-case metallurgical complex built by American and Soviet engineers. Oilgear Co. of Milwaukee files reports from the giant Kharkov Tractor Plant servicing hydraulic presses and boring machines for cylinder blocks. In the Ukraine, on October 1st, 1931, the Kharkiv tractor plant produces its first tractor. That year the plant turns out 8 to 10 tanks a day with a top speed of thirty km per hour. Three years after a turbo generator (currently turbo engine) plant named after S. M. Kirov begins production. Machine tool plant, surveyor tools plant, crane equipment plant, sanitary engineering equipment plant, tractor spare parts plant, *Porshen* (piston) plant, *Hydroprivod* (hydraulic drive) plant, and various other plants are built in the 30's. By 1940, 1,200 enterprises operate in Kharkiv alone which by then houses three hundred thousand workers with twelve times more production than in 1913. Before the war Kharkiv plants account for 40% of the mechanical engineering production in Ukraine and 6% in the USSR.

From the Wheel Track Layer Corporation in 1932 the Soviets buy the chassis of the Christie M 1931 model medium tank (MB) designed by automotive and tank inventor Walter Christie. Not only it becomes the basic Soviet tank of World War II, the Soviet T-32 nicknamed the "the flying tank" for its maneuverability but it serves as the basis to develop other Soviet tanks including the 12 ton BT, followed by the BT-5 and the BT-28 produced at the Chelyabinsk Tractor School in 1938.

Founded in 1933 the plant manufactures a 60 hp tracked tractor C-60 (*Сталинец-60*, *Stalinets-60*) fueled by petroleum ether (Benzine). By 1937 the factory is producing its first diesel-powered vehicle C-65 (*Сталинец-65*, *Stalinets-65*), and by 1940 has turned out 100,000 tractors. For the war the massive plant produces 18,000 tanks, and 48,500 tank diesel engines as well as over 17 million units of ammunition. Production includes a huge part of the Soviet arsenal: the KV tank from 1941, T-34 tank from 1942, KV-85 tank and JS tanks from 1943, and T-34/85 tank and SU-85 self-propelled field gun from 1944.

Chelyabinsk becomes the Soviet's manufacturing center situated in the Urals far removed from the Front in the hinterland east of Moscow. The city swells to over one million workers and forever remembered as "Tank city" (Танкоград, *Tankograd*) for its T-34 tanks. That's long before its notoriety as the center of a region swamped by radioactive waste from a nearby nuclear-weapons facility. Other industrial entities include most of Leningrad's Kirov Plant; during the siege 15,000 workers are either wholly or partially relocated to boost production at Chelyabinsky; by 1944, the work force increases from 25,000 to 60,000.

At present it has become a major trans-shipment center for Afghan opium and heroin, which enters Russia from Central Asia. By 1945 workers proudly displayed their honors awarded by Stalin which include the Order of Kutuzov, 1st Class, the Order of Lenin, the Order of the Red Star.

Tanks and airplanes soon symbolize the Soviet recovery. Mass production accelerates everything. Manufacture of the world-beating T-34 medium tank, for instance, is adapted so that the turrets could be stamped, rather than cast. Troops still dub it the 'matchbox', partly because they expected it to catch fire as readily as its predecessors, nicknamed 'zazhigalki', 'lighters,' also because the T-34s poured off production lines in such prolific numbers after 1942. German Panzers are in shock at the numbers and resistance of the T-34s and suffer heavy losses of German tanks and found their tank superiority reversed after the battle northeast of Orel on October 11, 1941. Military historian Alexander Bevin observes, "German tankers found that the short-barreled 75-millimeter gun on the Mark IV could knock out a T-34 only if it could hit the grating above the engine in the rear, a shot rarely possible." (A. Bevin, Chapter "Barbarossa", *How Hitler Could Have Won World War II*)

Soviet manufacturing far exceeds in quantity the *Wehrmacht* which uses the best of German engineering but simply cannot match Soviet labor for quantity. Stalin had gambled that it was one way to beat the fascists. The price was costly. In only a few weeks in the summer of 1941 the Red Army lost nine-tenths of its total tank force as well as its main production factories in Kharkov and Leningrad. "In the entire war," Catherine Merridale tells how in *Ivan's War*, "German industry would produce only 1,354 Tiger I and 5,976 Panther machines. By 1943, the Soviets were turning out T-34s at a rate of over 1,200 a month." But the Soviets pay the price in manpower losing 70,000 dead in the heroic self-sacrifice against the latest German tanks on ravaged grain fields for their victory at Kursk in 1943 in one of the greatest epic battles ever in war history and liberates the region. Yes, it did figure into the equation of daily life in America. Tens of thousands of Soviet Russians sacrificed their lives destroying Hitler's Nazi machine which ultimately saves American soldiers facing a significantly less powerful resistance in the West true to the calculations of Churchill, Roosevelt and the Consortium. (C. Merridale, *Ivan's War*, 212; Werner Keller, *East Minus West Equals Zero*, 1961, 208-16; R. Conquest, "The Church and the People", *Harvest of Sorrow*, 199-213)

Detractors of Stalin's crimes might consider his zeal for tyranny against Soviet peasants and workers justified to build Soviet defense industries deep within the Russian hinterland far from aerial attack or massive assaults. Soviet planning, however, would be no match to counter the rapid speed of German military penetration deep into the heart of the Ukraine in 1941. If ever a strategy could be considered at the same time both brilliant and insane this was it. Where he lost in the blitz he gained when the Germans realized too late that they had fallen into the ancient trap once used by the ancient Scythians to evade marauding enemies lost in the hinterland. This would be Hitler's rude awakening. Six months later in the dead of winter outside Moscow and Leningrad and in only a few months of war the USSR lost nine-tenths of its tanks and nearly two-thirds of its prewar manufacturing including the main industrial production centers in Kharkov and Leningrad. Yet, all was not lost. What the Germans didn't capture or destroy could be quickly dismantled, packed and transferred east far beyond the Volga river to the Urals.

By 1941 Stalin still had only four large tractor plants - Putilovets, Kharkov, Chelyabinsk and Stalingrad. Much of the equipment evacuated from Kharkov was reassembled at the Altai Tractor Plant opened in 1944. Only three automobile-truck plants (Gorki, Moscow and Yaroslavl) and two giant-machine building plants both built for heavy industry (furnaces, kilns, compressors), Kramatorsk, the great heavy machinery plant Uralmash, and another giant plant slightly smaller than Kramatorsk opened in 1933 July; three years later plants was still working at only 60 % capacity and could prefabricate submarines. Nor did the Soviets expand more giant plants than those built in 1932-33; they remained subordinate to the large ones. During the later years 1936-40 contracts by American firms were less publicized and literally unknown to both the Soviet and American populace entailed cooperation for new plants.

Again we have Sutton's researched findings gleamed from State Department files to confirm these contracts: "Petroleum-cracking ... was one such sector; all oil refineries in the Second Baku and elsewhere were built by Universal Oil Products, Badger Corp., Lummus Company, Petroleum Engineering Corp., Alco Products, McKee Corp., and Kellogg Co.. Advanced steel-rolling mills were supplied under the United Engineering agreement, and in 1928-29 the Tube Reducing Co. installed a modern tube mill at Nilopol and supplied equipment for another. Outside Moscow Vultee Corp. built an aircraft plant outside Moscow." Sutton wrote, "These and similar agreements in half a dozen sectors ran from about 1936-1940 with few public news releases." Stalinist Terror did not keep American businessmen away. (A. C. Sutton, *The Best Enemy Money Can Buy*, 2000)

Stalin's brilliant strategy to tuck away war production plants far away in the Urals and Siberia, and the dismantling of some 3,000 plants and factories while destroying what they left behind from invading Nazis, prove to be the winning card as the Red Army retreats and survives to counter attack with adequate armament instead of material left behind to be used against them. Evans writes, "By the end of the year, the overwhelming mass of civilians in the occupied areas had come round to supporting the Soviet regime, encourage by Stalin's emphasis on patriotic defense against a ruthless foreign invader. Escalating partisan resistance went along with a dramatic recovery of the fighting effectiveness of the Red Army. The cumbersome structure of the Red Army was simplified, creating flexible units that would be able to respond more rapidly to German tactical advances. Soviet commanders were ordered to concentrate their artillery in anti-tank defenses where it seemed likely the German panzers would attack. Soviet rethinking continued into 1942 and 1943, but already before the end of 1941 the groundwork had been laid for a more effective response to the continuing German invasion.... war production facilities were undergoing a relocation of huge proportions, as factories in the industrial regions of the Ukraine were dismantled and transported to safety east of the Ural mountains.

The accounts of fellow historians Bevins, Evans and Hastings describe the arrangements: "A special relocation council was set up on 24 June and the operation was under way by early July. German reconnaissance aircraft reported what to them were inexplicable massings of railway wagons in the region – no fewer than 8,000 freight cars were employed on the removal of metallurgical facilities from one town in the Donbas to the recently created industrial centre of

Magnitogorsk in the Urals, for example. Altogether, 1,360 arms and munitions factories were transferred eastward between July and November 1941, using one and a half million railway wagons. The man in charge of the complex task of removal, Alexii N. Kosygin, won a justified reputation as a tirelessly efficient administrator that was to bring him to high office in the Soviet Union after the war. What could not be taken, such as coalmines, power stations, railway locomotive repair shops, and even a hydro-electric dam on the Dnieper river, was sabotaged or destroyed."

The Dnieper River Power Station by the famous American dam engineer Hugh L. Cooper, completed in October 1932 with an annual output capacity reaching 2.7 billion kilowatt-hours and an ultimate capacity estimated at 650,000 kilowatts. The first five giant power generators were manufactured by GE; four more generators of similar power produced by Elektrosila in Leningrad were installed during the second 5-year plan. The Dneprostroi Dam was the largest in Europe at the time of its construction; Yale's Russian professor emeritus George Vernadsky (1887-73) calls it "the pride of Soviet industry and a memorial to Russian-American cooperation". Soon after the Barbarossa invasion in 1941 the huge new dam is competently blown up by the Red Army demolition experts in the Soviet massive dismantling and shipment campaign of factories and equipment sent north to the Urals and east toward Siberia. Evans concludes, "The scorched-earth policy deprived the invading Germans of resources on which they had been counting." Kosygin rose to the Politburo under Stalin, and Soviet Premier under General Secretary Brezhnev. Two months out of office he died in 1980. (R. J. Evans, 196-7; George Vernadsky, *A History of Russia*, Yale Univ. Press, eds. 1929 to 1962, 355)

Immediately after the war, GE proudly replaced the destroyed generators announced in a 1945 press report from GE headquarters in Schenectady: "Declared to be the largest in physical size ever built, the armature frame and core for the first of the huge hydro-electric generators, being built by General Electric for Russia's famous Dnieprostroi Dam, have been completed in the company's Generator Division here. Shipment of the first complete generating unit, weighing more than 2,250,000 pounds, will be made next April, International General Electric officials said today. The new generators, which will replace those destroyed during the war, will have a 15 per cent greater output than the waterwheel-driven generators built by GE in 1931 for the same Soviet plant. Each of the new units will be rated 90,000 kilo-volt-amperes, as compared with the 77,500 kv-a of the original generators, which were the largest ever built for this type of service before the completion of Boulder Dam. ... With a frame diameter of 42 feet, 5 inches, the new generators will be the largest in physical size ever built, according to G-E engineers, and if set on their side they would be taller than a three-story building. Shipment of two succeeding units are scheduled for May and August, 1946."

On the evacuation of Soviet plants and factories M. Hastings observes in *Inferno:* "Russia's industrial migration eventually embraced 1,523 undertakings, including those 1,360 major plants. Fifteen percent were transferred to the Volga, 44 percent to the Urals, 21 percent to Siberia and 20 percent to Soviet Central

Asia, in 1.5 million railway wagons... The 1941 industrial evacuation proved one of the crucial achievements of Russia's war... Though astonishing industrial output was achieved amid chronic hunger, it would be mistaken to idealize this: production of a Soviet aero engine required five times as many man hours as in its US counterpart. Yet the evacuation represented part of what a British intelligence officer once called "the Russian genius for piecemeal improvisation." In the twenties Soviet engineers marveled at Ford's American machinery. When things broke or parts went missing, since they couldn't reproduce it, they improvised with natural peasant ingenuity and resourcefulness. (M. Hastings, *Inferno*, 150-2)

By late 1942, war materials from Russia's industrial plants recovered to the Urals strengthened the Soviet defenses. The Red Army began to reverse the Nazi advance but no one was prepared that autumn and winter for the carnage of Stalingrad. On one day, Sunday August 23, 600 planes of the Luftwaffe darkened the skies; on the ground everything appeared to perish in flames more than killing 40,000 civilians in 14 hours, half of them in London, and "almost as many as perished in the entire 1940-41 blitz on Britain", observed Hastings. That winter relentless bombardment fell on Leningrad and the city would suffer until January 1944 when the Red Army launched its assault pushing back Nazi artillery. Over a million Leningraders died in the siege. Soviet censors banned news of the horror of hunger and starvation. Stalin's orders permitted no surrender. In *Inferno*, Hastings makes clear how the Russians stopped Hitler when no one else could. "A people who could endure such things displayed qualities the Western Allies lacked, which were indispensable to the destruction of Nazism. In the auction of cruelty and sacrifice, the Soviet dictator proved the highest bidder." (M. Hastings, *Inferno*, 302-8)

By the summer of 1942, Soviet production of weapons, shells and tanks had recovered. In *Ivan's War* of the experience of the Red Army soldier in the countryside and the cities, Catherine Merridale observes the tremendous effort to overcome the Aryan Nazi fascists who systematically raped their country. "The revival of manufacturing seemed like a miracle, "Merridale observes.

Meanwhile, Lend-Lease military aid, principally from the United States, began to make a crucial difference in the supply of weapons, airplanes, and food. Studebaker trucks, 200,000 of which were to be shipped to the Red Army by 1945, became popular at the front, and soldiers learned to recognize the taste of Spam". (C. Merridale, *Ivan's War,* 161; R. J. Overy's *Russia's War*, London, 1997; A. Bevin, 105)

"WHY HAS THE HISTORY BEEN BLACKED OUT?"

However one's views of the moral or political aspects of the capitalist-socialist economic collaboration, it should strike you as particularly curious that the history of the US construction of the Soviet Union had for so long been kept out of the public eye. Referring to US-Soviet trade and technical collaboration, Antony Sutton asked, "Why has the history been blacked out?"

The closing of the curtain first began with trade, and then was virtually pulled tight over the Holodomor. Political expedience and economic gains are of keen advantage to Consortium's global strategy and interests. Walter Duranty of *The New York Times* received the 1932 Pulitzer Prize for excellence in journalism, – established by Joseph Pulitzer in his will in 1904, and first awarded in 1917, – for his falsification of Soviet Russia in order to please Stalin and his paymasters in the Consortium. That award still stands with the obfuscation of the Holodomor and US complicity with Stalin that all still remains a very a gray area today if not completely in the shadows. Hardly an American knows the tiniest truth of it all. The State Department documents of famine Soviet Union in the twenties and thirties remained classified until the 1960s and even as late as 1980. Unfortunately, there remain too many gaps most probably arising from missing or misplaced documents either accidentally lost or deliberately destroyed. Enough documents and records, however, do exist which leave more than a trace of history before the cultural conditioning of collusion by the press and governments could completely obstruct the truth.

For decades much of the key information remained under lock and key until historian-engineer Antony Sutton published his findings in the seventies. Sutton devoted ten years investigating the reasons for the black-out as he saw it. "Because 50 years of dealings with the Soviets has been an economic success for the USSR and a political failure for the United States," Sutton declared. "It has not stopped war, it has not given us peace." Peace was never an option. The 20th century proved America to be a war machine. The national economy of America, and the livelihood and comforts of a great many Americans depend on a war-based military and industrial economy of private companies of various size closely linked to a culture of government subsidized by hardworking American taxpayers.

FORD AND HIS FORDSON: "INDUSTRY MIRACLE MAKER" SAYS JOHN REED

It was the First World War that consolidated the players of the Game and firmly entrenched them on the center stage of national power. Most were dollar-a-year patriots in the war trade of Wilson's presidency. Henry Ford was one of those patriots. The Soviets loved Henry Ford without knowing him or the Ford Peace Ship that sailed to Europe in 1915 in a ploy to divert anti-war pacifism to re-elect Wilson. *The New York Herald* called it "one of the cruelest jokes of the century." Bullitt was on that ship too. Incredible? The more incredible it seems the more it makes sense once you figure the Consortium logic of "The Game".

In the twenties Soviet engineers marveled at Ford's American machinery. When things broke or parts went missing, since they couldn't reproduce it, they improvised with natural peasant ingenuity and resourcefulness.

Two British authors Overy and Wheatcroft in *The Road to War* (1987) raised the specter of Soviet dependence on western technology and trade. Published in 1987 during the era of *Glasnost* and the implosion of the Soviet Union Overy and Wheatcroft wrote, "Lenin himself was greatly attracted to the new ideas of Fordism, of industrial rationalization as a key instrument in the Soviet fight against the ways of old Russia. Lenin had a film of the Ford factory at work in his private collection; Ford engineers helped set up the Soviet Union's first tractor and motor-car factories. Between 1920 and 1926 over 25,000 Fordson tractors were acquired to revolutionize Soviet agriculture; Soviet apprentices were trained in the United States at the Henry Ford Trade School; and Soviet technical schools and factories hung banners on the walls proclaiming 'Do it the Ford Way because it is the best way'."

The Fordson, named after his son since both of them built it. The tractor, built at the Rouge River plant. Henry Ford is particularly proud of this model. He was proud to say it had been built with "no stockholders, no directors, no absentee owners, no parasites". The Fordson becomes the wonder of Soviet collectivization as well as his plants and vehicles easily convertible for military use. He probably would marvel at the ingenuity of the Russian peasant wit, having been a farmer himself and feeling comfortable behind a team of horses and a plow on his farm.

In 1919 the Ford Motor Co. "had received the largest return on risk capital in recorded business history" Ford estimates the value of the company then at $250 million; a few years later he's offered $1 billion for the shares he held with Edsel, or 97% or the company. JD Rockefeller, Sr. held only "two-sevenths of Standard Oil at the height of his power", Lacey writes. (R. Lacey, *Ford*, 176-7)

The family of Henry Ford did not live in Boston, Philadelphia or New York. He never went to the fancy New England prep schools or experienced the white-glove pampering of an Ivy League experience. He was happy to come from a simple farm country in the Midwest. The Ford family arrived from Ireland to escape the potato famine, in 1832, the same year Russell founded his secret society Skull and Bones at Yale and set off to join the British sea captains and patrons of the China opium trade. When they settled it only a year has passed since the French author of *Democracy in America*, Alexis de Tocqueville stepped on shores of Lake Erie at Buffalo, New York and bought a ticket on a steamer taking him into the thick Michigan forests of the New World finding where he finds "a restless, challenging, adventurous race which sets coldly about deeds that can only be explained by the fire of passion, and which trades in everything. ... Here he found the spirit of the American frontier and brazen or modest urge for innovation that would ensure America's future prosperity personified in "a nation of conquerors... who only cherish those parts of civilization and enlightenment which are useful ... a people who, like all great peoples, has but one thought, and presses forward to the acquisition of riches, the single end of its labours, with a perseverance and a scorn for life which one could call heroic, if that word were properly used of anything but the strivings of virtue." (R. Lacey, *Ford,* 4)

The Michigan lands were settled by Ford's parents and other peasant families like them, Poles, Scandinavians, Germans and East Europeans, Slavic types from the Ukraine and Russia a generation before the Romanov Czar proclaimed the end of serfdom. Ford's parents built a small successful farm when a acre of land could be bought for a day's work. If Ford had been a Russian he would have been called a *kulak.* There he grew up to learn and appreciate the simple good things of life, as he recalled when he turned fifty and long after his company had become the model of success in America, Russia and the entire world.

"The first thing that I remember in my life is my Father taking my brother John and myself to see a bird's nest under a large oak log twenty rods East of our home. I remember the nest with 4 eggs and also the bird and hearing it sing. I have always remembered the song, and in later years found that it was a song sparrow. I remember the log layed in the field for a good many years." There in those woods Henry Ford was born, in 1863, when the American Civil War raged in the Eastern coast to give birth to the Union and Lincoln was President. (R. Lacey, *Ford*, 5)

Reed and Lenin shared a mutual fondness; Lenin who personally liked Reed must have enjoyed many informative talks about the American industrialist and the American factory worker with the radical labor leader. Impressed by his first-rate book of the October Revolution, *Ten Days That Shook The World* (1919) Lenin was fascinated with Reed and gives him with Politburo status alongside his prominent Bols. In 1916, before America enters the war Reed met with the capitalist iconoclast Henry Ford at his Detroit factory. At the time the top writer for *The Masses* published by Max and Crystal Eastman in Greenwich Village of downtown Manhattan under the shadows of Wall Street he portrays Ford in a laudatory essay full of color and homespun anecdotes and not at all akin to the "mushroom millionaires" of the plutocratic elite New England cliques living mysterious secret lives while grinding down the working class for the sake of heartless greed and profits. Reed observes, "He hasn't a villa at Grosse Pointe; he lives on a farm in the little village of Dearborn, ten miles from Detroit. He does not move in Detroit's select social circles; he prefers sitting on a neighbor's back porch of an evening and talking things over with the farmers. He belongs to none of the exclusive clubs frequented by his fellow-millionaires. And frankly, they hate him." (John Reed, "Industry's Miracle Maker")

Stalin, however, in the mid-thirties, now would be equally impressed by Ford's repression of unions, using Detroit thugs and corrupt police in his pay to keep order in his factories and meet production output quotas..

Henry Ford never went to the Soviet Union. It would have been a historic meeting indeed. In 1908 Ford rolled out his first Model T; by the time he turns fifty in 1913 Ford factories produce enough vehicles to fill several football fields on a single day, and reach 2.5 million in two years as auto ownership explodes reaching 9.2 million by 1920. (R. Chernow, *Titan*, 556)

From the beginning his resilient and lightweight Model T was a booming success, especially after Albert Kahn, who had built the Packard Car Co. factory in Detroit, in 1905, links up with Ford and built his "Crystal Palace" on the former racetrack of Highland Park for Model T production with the first cars rolling off the line in 1910. The factories were constantly pushed to the limit by soaring demand; output doubled to 78,440 vehicles in just two years. Ford was swamped with streams of new orders arriving daily.

When in 1911, Frederick "Speedy" Taylor who since the 1880s had been applying time and motion techniques to machine shops, published *The Principles of Scientific Management*, automation became the new religion of industrial production from Detroit to Moscow and every shop line in between. Certainly Lenin would have been impressed by Ford's 1915 antiwar Peace Ship initiative and would have been eager to debate the practical tenets with the captain of American industry. Ford was not likely to convert to communism. "The present Jewish government of Russia was transported almost as a unit from the lower East Side of New York ... the Bolshevik revolution was a carefully groomed investment on the part of international Jewish finance." Consequently Ford developed an uncanny contempt for Jews, an attitude exploited by some strange encounters during the trans-Atlantic crossing.

Ford biographer Robert Luce writes, "It was quite simple, said Henry. The world was controlled by gold, and the gold was controlled by the Jews." And that was all there was to it. Further, Ford distrusted the Consortium Crowd of Rockefeller-Morgan-Harriman bankers with mutual disdain, and he wonders, "The capitalist newspapers began a campaign against me. They misquoted me, distorted what I said, made up lies... The invisible hand got at its work." Ford blamed everything rotten happening to America on the Russian Jewish conspiracy, from short skirts, rolled up stockings, jazz, and "a marked deterioration in our literature, amusements, and social conduct ... a general letting down of standards." One can only wonder what Ford today would say about movie America and the Hollywood film culture. To challenge his critics Ford argued, "This concealed international control of the world flourishes because people do not believe that it exists. They don't see how it can exist. ... Someday a world-wide exposure will be made and many things explained which have always puzzled the plain people ... We shall see that much which we have charged up to the 'mystery of life' has really been the deliberate effect of a deep-wrought, unified international but private program".

An inevitable backlash to his rabid anti-Semitic propaganda published in his newspaper *Dearborn Independent* became a major liability threatening his car sales now topping a million or more a year. He had stirred up a major hornets nest. For example, William Fox, the Hollywood producer proposed releasing a rash of films showing Ford auto accidents. (R. Lacey, 206-8. Lacey is forgiving about Ford's eccentric grandstanding anti-Semitic behavior. Apparently during the war when showed film footage of Nazi concentration camp atrocities Ford suffered a serious stroke. Lacey writes, "Henry stayed on the best terms with the architect Albert Kahn .... There were never fewer than 3,000 Jews in the Ford work force through any of these years. Henry Ford seems to have got on well with every Jew he met in his life, in fact.", 219)

In 1953 a Soviet representative to the United Nations denounced Ford as the symbol of parasitic capitalism that oppressed the working class. Eisenhower had appointed Henry Ford II to join a UN delegation. The young man was given the opportunity to respond and he did, talking calmly for ten minutes. Then he left the building and ran into a friend on First Avenue in front of the new UN Secretariat Building. "I'm going to catch it from my Mother-in-Law. I'm an hour late for Thanksgiving Dinner," he told his friend before taking a cab across town. (R. Lacey, 463)

In 1930 the giant Ford Motor Company establishes the Soviet motor car industry. The Ford plant at Gorki on the outskirts of Moscow had a production capacity of 140,000 cars a year. That decade it became one of Ford's largest manufacturing plants in the world; Ford licensed patents, provided technical training to the Soviets in assembling automobiles and support and inventory of spare parts. It was a model plant of Soviet automation capable of rapid military conversion. (Overy and Wheatcroft, *The Road to War*, 1987, 189)

Invited to Moscow to take part in the celebration of the 10th anniversary of the October Revolution Mexican artist Diego Rivera (1886-1957) arrives in the autumn of 1927.

The following year while still in Russia he befriends Alfred H. Barr Jr., newly appointed director of the Museum of Modern Art (MoMA) in central Manhattan built on the site of Rockefeller's former homes. It opened in 1927, largely due to the inspiration of his wife and Junior's $5 million. Diego gets a whole show there dedicated to him. Rivera is commissioned to paint a mural for the Red Army Club in Moscow, but work is abruptly halted, in 1928 when he's kicked out of the country for earlier counterrevolutionary associations. Rivera returns to Mexico and the next year Rivera he's expelled from Mexico's Communist Party. But none of that kept him from painting the mural *In the Arsenal* (1928) considered as evidence of Rivera's knowledge of the murder of Julio Antonio Mella allegedly by a Soviet assassin Vittorio Vidalli. It was a good year the controversial artist. He divorces Guadalupe (Lupe) Marin and marries the fabulously enchanting and talented painter Frida Kahlo, in August 1929, and then in New York American journalist Ernestine Evans publishes *The Frescoes of Diego Rivera* introducing the artist to English readers though he doesn't speak English and prefers Italian, French and Spanish. From Moscow to New York Rivera is now a sensation among the Consortium art collectors. Before the year is out Rivera accepts a commission to paint murals in the Palace of Cortés in Cuernavaca from Ambassador Dwight Morrow as souvenir for his daughter's marriage.

In 1931, Diego arrives with his new young wife and a large entourage in New York for his one-man show at the Museum of Modern Art (MoMA). In a five-week run it sets new attendance records. Actually he arrives a month and a half before the opening and occupies an on-site studio where he produces five portable murals featuring bold colourful images drawn from Mexican themes of revolution and class inequality. During the show Rivera adds three more murals with monumental images of workers city life under the Depression.

Diego Rivera arrives in Detroit on April 21, 1932. It has been a hard spring for Ford in the city that he virtually owns. Three thousand Hunger Marchers provoke the police and the crackdown wasn't pretty. For years ever since Ford was threatened by thugs with kidnappings he feared for his grandchildren, so he hires gangsters for protection. Now the rave in America is driving cars at break-neck speeds while shooting up rivals in Prohibition gang wars. But when his grandchildren leave the house bodyguards ride shotgun. Ford doesn't have a problem with that kind of crime in the city, yet he decries gangsterism and prohibition to the evils of drinking. "Just don't kidnap my kids!" Diego's wife thinks the Rouge Plant looks more like a war zone or a ghetto instead of the industrial marvel its rumored to be but these are hard times even for Ford and much of the construction work in progress is suspended and incomplete.

Their meeting is a success. Ford and Rivera share a mutual impression and respect each other's talents. Rivera tours Ford's Detroit mechanical world, overwhelmed by the industrial colossus of railcars, factories, salt mines, chemical plants, and of course the massive Rouge plant, "the largest single manufacturing facility that man had ever set down upon the face of the earth". Rivera's visionary genius now wants to transform all of it together artistically, celebrating both the bold new industrialist and the American working man and woman. Rivera declares, "In all the constructions of man's past... there is nothing to equal these." Rivera tells the *New York Herald Tribune* that Americans no longer need to feel inferior to artistic movements abroad or go to Europe to learn the arts.

"Here it is – the might, the power, the energy, the sadness, the glory, the youthfulness, of our lands." Ford biographer Robert Lace observes Diego Rivera "felt he had discovered the modern pyramids, and he fell to scribbling furiously in his sketchbook." Edsel, too, is wild with excitement when he sees the sketches. Henry Ford himself studies in awe Rivera's brilliant fusion of man and machine transformed and liberated in the process of production in his various natural settings combined in one vast vision and felt his $10,000 fee well worth every cent. (Edsel Ford lost a bundle in the stock market crash and had some difficulty arranging payment and the original check payment was worthless when the bank on which it was drawn shut down.) Here industrialist and artist, Ford and Rivera shook hands feeling the joint satisfaction, as Rivera described, that this new collective hero had mastered a feat "higher than the old traditional heroes of art and legend". The fresco entitled *The Industry of Detroit or Man and Machine Five* is completed during this 1932-33 period and later donated to the Detroit Institute of Arts. Only fie years previously he is spurned by Stalin; now Diego Rivera is embraced by Ford. During a private dinner his wife Frieda asks the miracle industrialist, "Are you Jewish?" (Robert Lacey, *Ford: the Men and the Machine,* 318-20)

Diego and Frieda make the rounds from Stalin to Trotsky and from the Fords back to the Rockefellers. During this tumultuous episode in the History of the world captured in their personal and panoramic paintings full of symbolic meaning and energy his work speaks of the personalities and extreme turmoil of this modern period. The tempestuous couple arrives in New York in the fatal spring of the 1933 Holodomor. That January Diego had arranged to paint a fresco for the World's Fair in Chicago on the theme of "Industry and Machinery". JD Rockefeller, Jr. himself preoccupied with his megalithic real estate investment and aiming introduce a bold European modernism smack in the center of Manhattan in the architecture of Rockefeller Center. His RCA building in the complex is nearly complete. Captured by the excitement in the art world of Rivera's success in San Francisco where he painted in 1931 a fresco for the San Francisco Stock Exchange Club increasing his popularity across the country New York's wealthy patrons are keen on taking him on again, especially Abby Aldrich Rockefeller who convinces her husband, John D. Rockefeller, Jr. to commission Rivera to paint a mural for the lobby of the soon-to-be-completed Rockefeller Center in New York City. His wife Abby bought watercolours and enjoyed the success of his one-man exhibition at the MoMA. It had opened with Matisse; both he and Picasso had declined the Rockefeller offer to paint the RCA building lobby. Diego and Frieda are invited to the Rockefeller mansion at 10 West 54th Street. Brother Nelson Rockefeller steps in to settle the commission work to decorate the lobby of the RCA building with the theme of the art "Man at the Crossroads Looking with Hope and High Vision to the Choosing of a New and Better Future". Rivera proposes a 63-foot-long panorama of workers facing symbolic crossroads of socialism and capitalism with industry and science and there is a general consensus of shared approval. After all, it all seemed harmless enough.

But the Rockefellers have no idea how the artists will personify the Earthly Paradise envisioned by these American capitalists. Their view of the world is cracking everywhere. Their paradise is abominable, demonic, unjust. Diego paints scenes symbolic of the corrupt and diseased world of capitalist tycoon speculators and card-playing gangsters of the ruling class contrasting against the revolutionary world of the struggle of workers and peasants. Inserted among red flags flying is a saintly image of Lenin in a Soviet May Day parade. Wall Street and the country is still in the grip of the Depression and Rivera feels no reason to concede his autonomy and sell out to the richest man in the world.

The Rockefellers are shocked by the insult to the ruling class with mountains of cash to pay for art and beg Rivera to remove Lenin. (Bury Lenin twice?) Diego refuses, embarrassed by the scandal, and asserts his reputation as an *artiste.* It may be their money, and their being but he is the master of his art. It is his art, his painting. If Art has a sacred Voice uttering the Truth of the World it is Here and Now in the RCA Rockefeller building. The press turn wild over the mockery adding more injury to insult; their words risk even exposing the Consortium leaders secret dealing with Stalin and the Communists. One headline brashly exclaims, "Rivera Perpetuates Scenes of Communist Activity for R.C.A. Walls – and Rockefeller Foots the Bill".

A negative press campaign slanders Rivera's pro-communist bent and calls for its removal shake the city and Rockefeller's image. What will happen if the press get wind of his investments in the Soviet Union? Rivera refuses to stop work. No matter, he offers to throw in for free a portrait of Lincoln. Rockefeller managers give Rivera his full fee and bar him from the site. Armed guards order him down from the scaffolding and kick him out of the lobby. Junior tells his father the art work is "obscene and, in the judgment of the Rockefeller Center, an offense to good taste." Screens are quickly mounted to hide the art work and eventually "every square inch of the frescoes that he had painted was methodically chipped away". Some surviving murals, such as *The Detroit Industry Murals* currently installed in the Detroit Institute of Arts are considered 20th century treasures. (Lacey, 328; R. Chernow, *Titan*, 669-70)

The scandal causes an uproar shaking the art world and disturbs the equanimity of the Society Queens of Fifth Avenue. Ensuing negotiations, and demonstrators urge the Rockefellers not to trash the Rivera art, or, at least transfer it to the MoMA. Appeals fall on deaf ears. On February 10 1934, workmen swinging axes demolish the mural. When he returns to Mexico City Rivera recreates the Rockefeller frescoes in the Palacio de Bellas Artes (Palace of Fine Arts) entitled *Man Controls the Universe* or *Man in the Time Machine.* Not afraid to show his sense of humour about the scandal of having offended the world's most famous capitalist he adds a portrait of John D. Rockefeller, Jr. in a nightclub. Diego swears never to return to the US. (He keeps his promise.) Did Rockefeller put him on the State Department no-entry black-list? Nor does it matter that Abby Aldrich Rockefeller is a MoMA co-founder.

In the WWII conference photos of FDR and Stalin at Teheran (1943) and Yalta (1945) both leaders appear surprisingly comfortable sitting together on top of the world. Winston Churchill kept his usual circumspect distance. Tehran was the first of the two trips ever taken by Stalin outside the USSR and his only trip by airplane. (FDR on the other hand thought flying was great fun.) Churchill goes out of his way to be agreeable and befriend the Commander of the Red Army which has sacrificed so much bringing Hitler near total defeat and dooming his plan to invade England. The Soviet ruler understands the necessary "correlation of forces" with the Americans while he negotiates gains in the Baltics; it had served him well in the thirties as it did during the war as they carved up Europe and redrew borders with not a little disregard for ethnicity and historical precedents. Their complicity during these head-butting conferences in the suffering and murder compounding violence and corruption in a deliberate betrayal of the truth would again have terrible and lasting consequences for peace and freedom. In some respects it could be said that it never changed to be sure.

The Holodomor is a clear sign to the world of what to expect in the future. Reader, really when you think of it at all, or ponder the resounding convergences and ripple effects of commercial and diplomatic exchanges, it does not beg the question to truthfully face the reality head on (as too few do), otherwise one perpetually lives, and endures with moral blinders. In Stalin's day, moral considerations were tossed out the window along with the victims. Political opposition was countered many steps before it could become a threat. There were short-term and long-term effects. The Great Purge of his officer's ranks may have nearly cost him the war. Look at the mediocrity of political leadership everywhere in the world today. Events had lasting repercussions. Churchill shuttered to think England might lose again an entire generation of its finest men. In reference to the Russian backhanded dismissal of the Holodomor as a man-made Genocide by Stalin, Ukrainian journalist Oxana Pachlowska observed in *The Day*, "Apparently they do not understand that playing down humiliations is an invitation to more humiliation." This has got to be taken seriously if we are going to move closer to peace, tolerance and resolution of the conflict seeped in original deceit and treachery of those responsible for the Holodomor. (Oxana Pachlowska, *The Day*, March 28, 2006)

Reader, lets catch a breath. Soviet huge military industrial defense plants were built by American engineers. FDR's "New Dealocracy" was the flip side of his so-called "New Diplomacy". Only it wasn't new and it was a diplomacy towards a military alliance. Internal and external affairs are the bread and butter of New World Order government without borders. Stalin's Terror-Famine against Russia's peasants and their extermination by decree in the Ukraine, German Nazi rearmament and Hitler's fascists taking power in Berlin based on the extermination of non-Aryan races are inseparably linked by a merger of two diametrically opposed social and economic systems, capitalism in the West and Soviet-styled communism in the Kremlin.

The Ukrainian Holodomor 1932-1934 Genocide opens a Pandora Box of world provocation. Pertinent questions were obscured by censorship which protected the men enriched by finance and corporations who controlled the existing power from high or unseen positions in and out of government with whom lay the ultimate responsibility for this tragedy of epic proportions. These were the forces operating on FDR when he sets out immediately to recognize the USSR in 1933.

Once Hitler is installed as Chancellor in 1933 Hoover steps aside as FDR is sworn in as President and occupies the White House. The Japanese watch all of this very closely as they push deeper slashing, raping and shooting their way through Manchuria claiming the Chinese had provoked an attack on the Southern Manchuria Railway bond loan handled by Morgan. First the Japanese withdraw from the League of Nations, then it's Germany's turn to do the same while European diplomats dashed about talking their heads off saving the world or saving their necks first. Europe looks about to blow any moment. It will still be another brief six years before the 1939 Nazi-Soviet Pact of Non-Aggression authorizes the two dictators to dismember Poland and Eastern Europe. In the accord Hitler agrees to let the Slavs annex of Latvia, Estonia and western Belorussia all of which secured western Trans-Carpathian Ukraine including Lvov, the largest city in western Ukraine, and a buffer for Leningrad. Although he had replaced the Soviet Foreign Affairs Commissar Litvinov with Molotov, a non-Jew and more congenial to the Germans, Molotov likes to recall how in the Kremlin Stalin places Lazar Kaganovich, Jewish commissar of railroads sitting one chair next to the Reich's Foreign Minister Ribbentrop. "And Ribbentrop had to drink to me!" Kaganovich tells Molotov, smirking about his Jewishness. Only Molotov meets Hitler.

Stalin never meets Hitler. Why should he? This is what Hitler says about the Russian Bolsheviks in *Mein Kampf,* "The present-day rulers of Russia have no intention of entering into an alliance honourably or of sticking to one. We must not forget that they are low bloodstained criminals, that it means dealing with the scum of humanity, and that, favoured by circumstances in a tragic hour, they overran a great State and in a fury of massacre wiped out millions of their most intelligent fellow-countrymen, and now for ten years they have been conducting the most tyrannous regime of all time.... We must not forget, that those rulers belong to a nation which combines a rare mixture of bestial cruelty and vast skill in lies, and considers itself specially called now to gather the whole world under its bloody oppression. We must not forget that the international Jew, who continues to dominate Russia, does not regard Germany as an ally, but as a State destined to undergo a similar fate." (A. Hitler, "Eastern Policy", *Mein Kampf / My Battle,* Cambridge: Riverside Press-Houghton Mifflin, ed.*1937,* 284-5)

How odd that this same wounded and decorated veteran of the First World War, cynical and cursing the international Jew alongside Anglo-Americans who conspired to secure a Bolshevik victory and feed starving cities to stabilize Lenin's ruthless retention of power, will then in the mid-thirties sit down with Herbert Hoover who led the American food relief program to feed the German Army and in so doing prolong the First World War long enough for American troops to launch their 1918 offensive against the last desperate thrust of the Kaiser's army. And so Hitler put could put forward the question, "Who was more cynical, Lenin or Hoover continues to dominate over Russia, does not regard Germany as an ally, but as a State destined to undergo a similar fate?"

"Hitler", Molotov recalls, "... There was nothing remarkable in his appearance. But he was a very smug...vain person. He wasn't at all the same as he is portrayed in movies and books. They focus on his appearance, depict him as a madman, a maniac, but that's not true. He was very smart, though narrow-minded and obtuse at the same time because of his egotism and the absurdity of his primordial idea ... he spoke in a calm voice, he didn't curse. He just tried to persuade ... he was also in awe of Stalin's personality."

After the war Molotov flies to San Francisco to address the United Nations. His airplane is sent by Harriman.

THE ARA: "FOOD IS A WEAPON"

From the beginning Lenin declared "Food is a weapon". Harriman and Acheson adopt the same *politik* in postwar Eastern Europe. The Bolsheviks and Herbert Hoover used the first famine in the 1921-22 phase of the Russian Civil War to destroy the opposition of the Old Regime and its Wilson's undeclared war against the revolutionaries.

Even Russia's greatest writer after Leo Tolstoy who died in 1910, Gorky (a pseudonym for "bitter" he started using in Tiflis for the newspaper *Кавказ* (*The Caucasus*) at first shows little enthusiasm in heeding the anti-communist intellectual Ekaterina Kuskova to speak to his longtime friend in the Kremlin with whom his relations are always rocky. Maxim Gorky is the pride of "Mother Russia"; his most influential writings in these years were a series of political plays, most famously *The Lower Depths* (1902).

By 1899, Gorky is openly associating with the emerging Marxist social-democratic movement which helps to make him a popular standout with the intelligentsia and a growing numbers of "conscious" workers. At the heart of all his work is a belief in the innate worth and potential of the human person (*личность, lichnost*). Gorky was attentive in a carefully crafted prose that pits individuals, aware of their inherent dignity, and inspired by natural energy and creative will, with people who accept and succumb to the degrading conditions of life. His writings and letters evoke often the "restless man" in a search conflicted by contradictory feelings of skepticism and faith, hope, and an abundant love of life threatened by the vulgarity and the pettiness of others he rejects with contempt.

Gorky is dispatched to the US, in 1906, to raise funds. During this difficult and revolutionary period his relations with Lenin are tested, especially when his newspaper *Novaya Zhizn* (*Новая Жизнь*/ *New Life*) is censored under the Bolshevik knife driven by tensions of civil war. It was then in 1918 when Gorky published essays critical of the Bolsheviks called *Untimely Thoughts* (re-published in Russia only after the collapse of the Soviet Union.). The essays compared Lenin to the Czar and labeled him a conspiring anarchist and repressive tyrant responsible for arbitrary arrests. "Lenin and his associates," Gorky observes from within their closely guarded circle, "consider it possible to commit all kinds of crimes ... the abolition of free speech and senseless arrests ...". Gorky easily sees through the political opportunism of Lenin: "a cold-blooded trickster who spares neither the honor nor the life of the proletariat."

The plan was to establish a public relief committee. The Politburo agreed and appointed Kamenev to create the All-Russian Famine Relief Committee. Gorky sends a personal plea to Herbert Hoover, Director of the American Relief Administration (ARA) urging humanitarian assistance to the starving population of Russia.

As Russia 's greatest young and radical writer with many Bolshevik friends Gorky lived a tortuous and dangerous liaison defending Russian culture against Bolshevik excesses. Gorky had warned against the Lenin's coup and the Bolshevik seizure of power bringing down the Provisional government saying "the Russian people will pay for this with lakes of blood"; in 1918 Lenin shut down Gorky's paper *Novaya Zhizn* for comments describing his friend Lenin: "A talented man, he has all the qualities of a 'leader', and also the requisite lack of morals and a pure landowner's ruthless attitude toward the lives of the masses." Not infrequently they argued; on at least one occasion Lenin loses his temper and obliges Gorky in 1921 to leave Russia "to recuperate and rest". Lenin tells him "If you don't go, we'll exile you." In 1929, Stalin, near 50, and close to the summit of his ascendancy over the Party uses Gorky to fulfill his management over the new proletarian Soviet culture molded in his image.

A former Soviet citizen and author (*St. Petersburg, A Cultural History* and *Shastakovich and Stalin*) living in New York City, Solomon Volkov writes in *The Magical Chorus* (1999), "The well-informed émigré journal *Sotsialisticheskii Vestnik* reported as early as 1933 (and it is thought now that their source was Babel) that Gorky 'is considered the second-most important person in the Union, by weight following Stalin. It must be said that the friendship of the latter with Gorky has taken on planetary scale: Gorky is the only man whom Stalin not only takes into account but courts.' ... Stalin had 'inherited' Gorky from Lenin, who had rated the writer very highly as a 'European celebrity'. Gorky certainly was the most major cultural figure whom Lenin knew personally, and one with a marked Bolshevik orientation even before the revolution." Gorky, however, was a lousy politician and ended his life as a pathetic stooge of Stalinism that first killed his son Maxim Peshkov in May 1934 followed by his own life two years later. (Solomon Volkov, *The Magical Chorus, A History of Russian Culture from Tolstoy to Solzhenitisyn*, NY: Vintage-Random House, 1999, 87-103)

Hoover's "humanitarian" aid mission to save millions of starving Russians in 1921 was in reality a pro-Bolshevik American front to gain access and power for the Consortium interests to seize resources and insert a decisive wedge to control the regime. The advantage is most opportune for Lenin and the Bolsheviks who make the most of it. These educated and hardened revolutionaries knew that humanitarian relief came at a price.

FROM LENIN AND TROTSKY TO HOOVER AND HARRIMAN ...

Trotsky once said, "Of course, help to the starving is spontaneous philanthropy, but there are few real philanthropists – even among American Quakers. Philanthropy is tied to business, to enterprises, to interests – if not today, then tomorrow." The bankers and businessmen now come to the Russians with the zeal of missionaries in their hearts and followed them all the way to the bank. Controlling populations by grain restriction is an ancient *regle du jeu* in war. Stanford historian Lyman Van Slyke observes in his study of European and American incursion into China and Nanking, "In 1841-1842 an Anglo-French naval force had penetrated far enough to blockade the Grand Canal, thus demonstrating the capacity to strangle the capital by preventing vital grain shipment, and to take Nanking under its guns. There the first of the Unequal Treaties, the Treaty of Nanking, was concluded in 1842." (Harold H. Fisher, *The Famine in Soviet Russia*, 1919-1923, 57; D. Acheson, *Present At The Creation;* Lyman; Van Slyke, *Yangtze*, Addison-Wesley, 1988, 154)

Hoover's reputation preceded him. The Bolsheviks know that Commerce Secretary Hoover is a rich and powerful organizer, an American living in Europe, a capitalist millionaire many times over and very secretive powerbroker eager to swallow Russia's vast natural resources. As a mining engineer he amasses a fortune before he was forty. From 1902-08, Hoover works for the Anglo firm Bewick, Moreing and Co. building a mining empire in sixteen countries. In British Burma (it becomes a colony of the Empire in 1885) he invests in an abandoned mine that proved to be worth a king's ransom in silver, zinc and lead. He leaves that firm to set up operations in New York, London, San Francisco and St. Petersburg where he teams up with Leslie Urquhardt, the British promoter of similar temperament eager to plunder Czarist holdings in the Urals. Urquhardt is chairman of the prewar Russo-Asiatic Corporation with well over a million acres to exploit and in league with his royal cousin Baron Mellor Zakomelsky. Hoover supervises the deal at a $2 million a year commission; the Bols later nationalize the Russo-Asiatic holdings. Hoover's successful handling of the Czar's royal Cabinet Mines in Siberia in 1919 lead to his taking a stake in the Irtysh mines, the richest iron ore mine in the world. But of course none of this figures in Hoover's highly publicized humanitarian handling of the ARA to stave off famine in Russia's revolutionary civil war...

In *Hoover and Famine Relief,* (1974) there is a chapter titled "The Politics of Retreat" that refers to "the Urquhardt Concession". Benjamin Weissman writes, "Department of Commerce and ARA officials kept Hoover informed on the progress of the negotiations between the Soviet government and Hoover's former business associate, Leslie Urquhardt, for a far-reaching concession in Russia." Weissman tells a good tale that has a particular importance to the Consortium Holodomor story, and he writes, "The Urquhardt concession is seen in international financial and government circles as a test case advanced by the Brits to determine the usefulness of the Anglo-Russian Trade Agreement of 1921. According to a report transmitted to Hoover in December 1921, however, Urquhardt is a far from reliable instrument for testing Soviet sincerity. One of his associates in the Russo-Asiatic Corp. is quoted saying that 'Mr. Urquhardt had great hope but little expectation that he would be successful ...." Urquhardt is also a favorite target of the Cheka.

Hoover pursues his "year-long quest for a concession with keen interest", confirms Weissman. On June 2, 1922, James Goodrich, a Hoover confident and former Republican Governor of Indiana, reports he met with Urquhardt, in Paris, to weigh prospects of putting together a lucrative business with the Russians. Urquhardt follows closely the ARA director-general's trip to Moscow and he proposes a deal with Soviet commissar of foreign trade transmitted on August 30 by Christian Herter to the State Department. Herter, too, enjoys a long stellar career there ever since he mixed with Princeton's Dulles brothers, the prodigious Adolf Berle from Harvard and other blue-bloods on Wilson's American Commission to Paris to negotiate Versailles with Col. House and Secretary Lansing.

The Urquhardt concession covers a huge tract in Siberia "that Hoover had managed with huge success when he was a director of the Russo-Asiatic Consolidated Ltd. before the war." At stake, Weissman explains, is "a substantial reimbursement to the British firm for losses incurred during the period of confiscation, the grant of a 99-year lease on the firm's former property, immunity from Soviet labor laws, and exemption from all export duties. These benefits are granted to the corporation in return for a royalty of 7.5 percent in lieu of all local and national taxes. The 'member of the corporation' comments that 'this is less than we had to pay under the old regime at Kyshtim'." Then in a strange turn of events and with Lenin ill and withdrawn from official duties the Bolshevik leadership reject the concession denouncing Urquhardt in *Pravda* and identifying him as "the real 'master' of capitalist England and its ruling oligarchy." (C. Herter to D. C. Poole, Aug. 30, 1922; Dr. Frank Golder to C. Herter, Oct. 9, 1922; B. Weismann, Chapter "The Politics of Retreat", *Hoover and Famine Relief,* 138-40)

Things are not going well at all for Russia and turn tragically worse. After four years war and the Russian empire disorganized and exhausted by corruption and political chaos, revolution and demands for peace and land led to the abdication of Czar. Nicholas, his wife the Tsarina and their beautiful daughters and poor sick Alexii, the Crown Prince are all doomed.

The Bolshevik takeover and subsequent separate peace at Brest-Litovsk in the spring of 1918 taking an exhausted and revolutionary Russia out of the capitalist bourgeois conflict. Trotsky had been appointed Commissar of Foreign Affairs and he sent his friend Adolph Joffe to head the peace negotiations for the Bolsheviks. Joffe had come a long way with Trotsky and took an active part in the 1905 Revolution and helped Trotsky edit the Vienna *Pravda* in 1908 and provided family funds for it. During this time Joffe underwent psychoanalysis with Dr. Alfred Adler; the Trotskys and the Adlers became close friends turning their attention to the work of Freud. After Trotsky's expulsion from the Communist Party on November 12, 1927, Joffe commits suicide. A farewell letter addressed to Trotsky is intercepted by Soviet agents and used by Stalin to publicly discredit both Joffe and Trotsky. Trotsky's eulogy at Joffe's funeral is his last public speech in the USSR. Joffe's wife Maria Joffe is arrested by the NKVD, yet she survived and writes her memoirs *One Long Night - A Tale of Truth* (1978). Joffe's daughter, Nadezhda, born in 1906, became an active Trotskyist and is arrested in 1929. After her second arrest Nadezhda Joffe is sent to the harsh Siberian camp Kolyma in 1936 where her husband is murdered there two years later. She survives the camps and also publishes a precious memoir, *Back in Time: My Life, My Fate, My Epoch* (1994). In 1996 Nadezhda died in a Brooklyn hospital, surrounded by her four daughters, two who had seen her taken away by the NKVD, and one who was actually born in the Kolyma prison.

Within months of disorganization and civil war fields lay untilled, factories stood idle. Industrial production plummeted to one-seventh of what it had been before the war when Czarist monarchy ruled. By August 1922 with the country engulfed in disease, hunger and famine comrades Lenin, Bogdanov, Krassin and others admitted their communist revolutionary program had failed. The Soviet economy was at the point of collapse; that same year Stalin is voted General Secretary of the Communist Party.

The 1921-22 period is etched in the memory of the Russian people as the worst famine in Russian history up to that date. Sutton writes, "The famine that struck large areas, particularly on the Volga and in the Ukraine, in 1921-1922, was caused only to a small degree by drought and other natural phenomena. In the main it was the consequence of the political developments of the preceding few years.... It was a man-made famine. By the summer of 1921 the disaster had reached such proportions, and the prospects for the future appeared so bleak, that the government was forced to deviate from the accepted methods of propaganda and admit the facts." (A. C. Sutton, *Western Technology and Soviet Economic Development, 1917-1930*, 345; Werner Keller, *East Minus West Equals Zero*, 1961)

At the time Lenin and Bolsheviks split over the thorn of concessions in the controversial debate over how to handle the capitalists and the Bolshevik need for economic reconstruction within a credible Marxist-Leninist ideology of proletarian socialist dictatorship. Sutton explained what happened to the Urquhardt-Hoover plan 1922. "Urquhardt was president of the Russo-Asiatic Consolidated, Ltd. which had held very large concessions in tsarist Russia. Negotiations with Urquhardt for operation of his former properties, then lying idle, would have led the way for other entrepreneurs. Although Urquhardt was well aware of Bolshevik strategy, he made a concession agreement with Krassin in 1921; the latter then went to Moscow for ratification by Lenin and Trotsky. Before this could be obtained, word leaked out and the hue and cry within the Party forced Lenin to scuttle the agreement, using British activities in the Middle East as a pretext." (A. C. Sutton, 305 v. 1; see Allen Wardwell, Graham R Taylor, Allen T. Burns in "*Draft Report on the Russian Famine 1921-22, 1922-23*, 264-310)

James Goodrich, 57, is the scion of the Goodrich family of Indiana. He is sent to Russia on a mission to head a small investigation fact-finding team with Colonel William N. Haskell and to convince American public opinion and the US Congress that the Russian famine and disease conditions are sufficiently catastrophic to merit humanitarian aid and neutralize critics about possible clandestine motives to intervene that might be other than overtly Christian and report back to Secretary Hoover himself, to Congress, "and, ultimately, the American people in hopes of obtaining relief."

Why wasn't this done for the Ukraine in 1932?

As World War I ended on Armistice Day November 11, 1918, the United States helped many countries around the world recover from war through the American Relief Administration (ARA). Hoover's work with the ARA was part of a general postwar reconstruction program of the Consortium's logic of war and destruction ergo reconstruction, profits and control. The primary goal of the ARA was to provide food relief but it also provided medical aid, clothing, and relocation services with Russia still gripped by Civil War and American and Allied intervention. Earlier attempts to enter Russia in 1919 and 1920 had failed. As for France and Britain, in 1919, they gave up all ideas of fighting the Soviets. By the summer of 1921, Litvinov, assistant commissar of foreign affairs in London worked out a deal with ARA's director for Europe Walter Lyman Brown on conditions for ARA presence in Russia. In the US-Soviet Riga Treaty agreement Brown reassured Litvinov that the ARA mission was not political but aimed solely at saving as many lives as possible. Hoover consents and appoints Col. Haskell to run the show on the ground. His hard-nose approach to the Bolsheviks is quite different than the artful style of Goodrich diplomacy and better suited to obtaining results.

Woodrow Wilson's armed intervention in the Russian Civil War (1919-20) remains a haunting memory. There's no mistaking that Goodrich is an odd choice; he has no previous experience in Russia, cannot speak the language and knows little if much at all about its unique, strange and diverse culture. On top of that everything is in a state of chaos Russian-style and in a bloody civil war when the people are fighting for survival. Goodrich will spend his first four weeks there for the ARA concluding that communism had failed. On the luminous side Goodrich develops a deep appreciation for the Russian people. "I am very impressed," he wrote to Hoover from abroad, "by the ability of the people to adapt themselves to the very trying situation that confronts them." Not forgetting how Leo Tolstoy helped organize aid to the Caucasus in the 1890 famine under the Czar now the famous Maxim Gorky pleaded in a public appeal that the Soviets were only able to provide 20 percent of the food needed in central Russia including the worst hit provinces Samara and Saratov.

Chosen solely to be a Hoover tool to implement the next step in the Consortium plans Goodrich possessed a practical knowledge of "the roles of banking, railroads, commodities, infrastructure, utilities, and government, generally", and stood relatively clean of scandal as high ranking Republican in Ohio, no mean feat in Rockefeller-Taft territory. Yet with virtually no foreign policy experience to speak of and no contact whatsoever with Russia or the Soviet Union his selection was more as a political figurehead between Congress and the public than a hands-on trouble-shooter in the wild regions of Bolshevik chaos.

Assigned to cover Goodrich on the trip is Hoover's agent Col. Haskell, a first-rate army intelligence man backed by impressive military record: West Point graduate, field service in the Philippine pacification, US Army Expeditionary member in Wilson's war against the Mexican revolutionary "bandit" Pancho Villa, and line officer in the St. Mihiel offensive during the First World War before becoming Deputy Chief of Staff and Chief of Ops of the Second US Army Corps on the British Front.

In Washington, the Govenor meets Hoover and Haskell, already at the helm as head of the Russia ARA unit. On route from England having departed October 3, they leave behind in their wake alarming reports in the British press inflaming their worst fears that 35 million Russians were starving. In the Volga region. Goodrich learns from US State Department officials "…dogs had been butchered for sausage; the same was true of newborn calves and piglets. Peasants in the Samara region were eating grass, leaves, bark, and clay in an attempt to starve off starvation." Peasants explained how they lost their harvest. A refugee women tells Goodrich of terrible and desperate days: "Last year and the year before they (government workers) took our grain. They did not even leave our men enough to sow. If we tried to keep what we needed for our children or our next crop they threatened to kill our men if we did not give up all. So our people were discouraged and each year they planted less. This year when the sun burnt up everything, starvation and death came and we had to leave or die." (Diane Starbuck, *The Goodriches, An American Family*, Liberty Fund, Indianapolis, 2001, 134-7)

Goodrich went to Moscow. No one was at the station to greet him. He walked through the desolate Russian streets to ARA headquarters and entered a sumptuous mansion belonging to a former millionaire before the Soviets nationalized it as state property of the Proletariat. It was one of only three buildings in the entire city heated by steam. Goodrich found inside "a veritable museum of art". Goodrich was assigned a room filled with paintings he estimated were worth at least a half a million dollars; portraits and landscapes from the great European masters, – Rubens, Van Kyke, Raphael, Mignard, Bonheur. Trotsky's wife had intervened to save the mansion and its furnishings from destruction. The former owner was still around to protect the art from damage or theft. In the local shops Goodrich discovered the black market where he exchanged "90 good American Dollars for 8,920,000 worthless Russian Rubles"; he was no less amused when he paid a taxi driver 5,000 rubles for a ride around Moscow, and he observed, "To me it was only six cents but to him it seemed to mean almost a fortune". It might have seemed that little changed in a hundred years since Tolstoy had a similar encounter with a peasant. (D. Starbuck, *The Goodriches*, 137)

Goodrich meets his friend and fellow investigator Dr. Frank Golder, chairman of the history department of Stanford University and originally from Odessa in the Crimea; Golder holds a Ph.D from Harvard. Along the way after leaving Samara they meet up with "special investigator" for the ARA, Lincoln Hutchinson (1866–40). These are all first rung authorities in their field and well-connected with the powers-that-be. Dean of the College of Letters and Science at Berkeley and head of its economics department, Hutchinson had studied at Berkeley before heading east for a Masters degree from Harvard (1899); he's also a Consortium player serving in consulates from South America to Europe. On top of that Hutchison is a tough guy; in the twenties he forms the Sierra Ski Club in Nevada, along with his brother James, a lawyer and charter member and director of the Sierra Club, which he enjoyed all his life until he dies up there in the Sierra, 92, just ten years after he last climbed Whitney glacier at 14,500 feet the highest summit in the US.

Hutchinson will stay two and a half years in revolutionary Russia. During the war he joins Baruch in the War Trade Board and the War Industries Board (Inter-Allied Munitions Council in London and Paris with the Nonferrous Metals Committee of that Council, on the Inter-allied Tin Executive), then heads Hoover's ARA for Eastern Europe. Later, in Prague, Hutchinson helps Jan Masaryk write the Czech national constitution.

Now they wait at the train station for their their Russian translator. When he doesn't arrive they board leaving without him. Golder speaks Russian. Along the way the Goodrich party talks to countless Russians learning that the "Reds" openly admitted that the Soviet Government had made concessions to capitalists as the capitalist powers themselves too often do just the same making concessions to socialists. Goodrich particularly likes that and finds the logic as convincing as it's true. "This argument set me to reflecting on the slow processes of human evolution in government and it occurred to me that it would be indeed strange if this experiment in Russia, starting as it did with pure Marxian government with its rule of the workers through a dictatorship should evolve into the capitalistic form, as was the experience of our ancestors in progressing from barbarism to civilization, while our capitalistic form should after long ages slowly disintegrate into socialism as it now shows evidences of doing in America and in England."

The three men traveled to Penza province to investigate eastern and southern Russia. "Russians" wrote Goodrich, "are proverbially careless in everything, and this includes gathering facts" and the Russian peasant "with true oriental cunning" had concealed reserves from the Red grain patrols. They find conditions completely inadequate to fight typhus and cholera; no doctors, medicine or supplies doubling the mortality rate; two thermometers in a hospital for 800 beds. Starbuck learned that the administrator's first assistant found the situation hopeless and committed suicide. Everywhere he went Goodrich found impressive the collective organization and ingenious character of the Russian peasant with an underlying common sense not unlike the American farmer. Some 80 million peasants worked in communes of one form or another. Regardless how the communist intellectuals predicted the abolition of family life and Russian traditions Goodrich thought "the Russian Peasant will go his way marrying and giving in marriage and rearing his family pretty much as the American farmer rears his family". (D. Starbuck, *The Goodriches,* 145)

Goodrich was there in the midst of the unfolding tragedy. According to Diane Starbuck in *The Goodriches,* the governor from Ohio chronicled how life as he found it where "commune leaders knew that death was a certainty for many. In Norga, a commune of 8,561, Jim Goodrich finds the majority of peasants to be satisfactorily nourished. It puzzled him, then, when the local officials predicted that half of the population would be wiped out by the end of the winter if foreign relief was not forthcoming. 'Why is it,' Goodrich asked the farmers at Norga, 'that when so many of you have plenty of bread and meat for the present you permit others at your doors to starve to death?' They were silent for quite a bit and then one strong faced man said slowly and gravely: 'You Americans do not understand. It cannot be helped. It is necessary that some must die in order that others may live, otherwise, if help did not come we would all die. It was so in the great drought of 1891. America helped us then. We hope that she will be able to save many of us again'."

Goodrich explains how he would share his last piece of bread "and both of us live or died together. But that Volga peasant had expressed the sentiment that I heard everywhere. It is not easy for us who have not been imbued with that something called oriental fatalism, and which I found expressed in every phase of life in Russia, to understand that indifference with which they look upon death from cholera, typhus or starvation, or at the hands of the government. They seemed to place little value on human life. To them it was the case of 'Kismet, it is fate'."

Riding on the train through the Kazan, playing poker and sleeping in his pajamas, Goodrich marvels at Russia's vast natural resources, writing, "Unless I am much mistaken, there will develop in this Russian timberland within the next fifty years a great people and a great country." Kazan was the capital city of the Tatar Autonomous Soviet Socialist Republic. They learn that already 300,000 Tartars had fled the famine. A decade later when Stalin's Holodomor hit the Ukraine "oriental fatalism" would return with a vengeance. (D. Starbuck, *The Goodriches,* 147-8)

"It would be impossible, I found, with the limited means of the American Relief Administration to give anything like adequate relief to all of the children of this Tatar Republic in the Volga valley. The only thing to be done was to select the worst districts and do the best that could be done with the relatively small amount of food stuffs at the disposal of the administration. Unless Uncle Sam himself came to the relief of these distressed people I felt that hundreds of thousands of them, many helpless children, were doomed." On November 1, 1921, Goodrich sent a fourteen-page report to Hoover, and another report to Secretary of State Charles Hughes. "On every hand," Goodrich wrote, "I see the most conclusive evidence of the return of the Government to a capitalistic basis … and there is a feeling everywhere I have gone that the Government has turned the corner and that every step from this time on will be a return to the capitalistic form of government."

Famine, disease, civil war and general bedlam. Political chaos and economic disintegration implodes the center, so it appears, and severely strains the Bolsheviks hold on power. Russia's wartime bankrupt Czarist economy literally goes over the edge falling into total collapse. Lenin and the Bolsheviks are forced to make more concessions to the peasants taking the same tactic Trotsky implemented with Germans at Brest-Litovsk to end that war so they can start fighting the Whites soon aided by the Allied intervention troops.

This doesn't leave Lenin much time to implement a revolutionary Marxist socialist economic program. Slavic scholar Sheila Fitzpatrick writes in *Stalin's Peasants*, "the Bolsheviks announced a new policy of alliance (*smychka)* with the 'toiling peasantry' as a whole – that is, with all exploiters who were natural opponents of Soviet power." With the end of civil war and rich landowners in flight, including priests the monarchy's extensive aristocratic family's landholdings, the new regime enjoyed a real estate bonanza of some around fifty million hectares, or 140 million acres, with one to five acres of arable land destined to each peasant living in the western Russia and the Ukraine. (S. Fitzpatrick, *Stalin's Peasants*, 24-5)

Harding and Hoover to the rescue! Commerce Secretary Hoover is remembered in the annals of history for his wartime humanitarian food work in the so-called Belgium Relief as Baruch's Food Administrator. On November 20 the Goodrich and Haskell boarded the steamship *George Washington* for the trip home. Commerce Secretary Hoover needs no more time to relieve Russia's calamity.

On December 6 in his first State-of-the-Union address to Congress President Harding requested $10 million to purchase ten million bushels of corn and one million bushels of seed corn. Two days later Haskell privately informed Hoover that five to seven million people "must die unless relieved from outside Russia" and that tragedy was in one area alone! This was a famine of epic proportions far worse than in 1891. Goodrich pleaded for more aid writing Harding, "As a Christian nation we must make greater effort to prevent this tragedy. Can you not ask those who have already assisted this organization to carry over eight million children through famine in other parts of Europe to again respond to the utmost of their ability?" (D. Starbuck, *The Goodriches,* 153)

Interestingly, that during the Russian Relief Hearings Hoover makes a clear distinction to Congress December 13, 1921 between a man-made and a natural famine. "The problem that we are confronting," Hoover declares, "is not a problem of general relief to Russia, for which there can be some criticism, but it is a problem of relief to an area suffering from an acute drought. In other words, we are making a distinction here between the situation created by the hand of man as distinguished from the situation that might be called an act of God. This Volga area, as has been stated, is practically all throughout an agricultural region. It has not been the scene of any extended socialist organization, as that is a city phenomena. It comprises a population of farmers, of which apparently one-third are of German extraction." Hoover adds, "I think you will find in Nebraska alone many thousands of farmers who migrated from the Volga Valley. You will find many thousands of farmers in the Northwest of the same population." Americans still have family members back in the old country! A decade later this distinction is ignored by Hoover, as President, and Roosevelt during the Holodomor.

Since August the ARA is able to raise only a half million dollars from public contributions. Hoover appeals to the economics of relief. "We are today feeding milk to our hogs; burning corn under our boilers. From an economic point of view there is no loss to America in exporting those foodstuff for relief purposes. If it is undertaken by the Government it means, it is true, that we transfer the burden of loss from the farmers to the taxpayer, but there is no economic loss to us as a nation, and the farmer also bears part of the burden." (D. Starbuck, *The Goodriches*, 38; US Congress, Russian Relief Hearings, Dec. 13, 1921)

The second day of testimony passed in closed door sessions. Goodrich noted the capitalist concessions to the peasants that the Communist regime had sanctioned: "farmers were now able to keep and sell for personal profit surplus crops; retail shops and banks were beginning to reappear; serious discussions regarding the role of private property and contracts were under way. All of this was very important to the members of the committee because of the desire, on the part of many in Congress, to investigate whether recognition of Russia and the establishment of diplomatic relations could or should be pursued." The House votes 181 to 71 in favor of a relief bill.

Still, Senator Tom Watson from Georgia raves over $200 million owed to the United States and complained "the Russians do not even know how to mill corn; they don't like it, won't eat it." By late January Congress had spent $12 million on food relief purchases – 6,945,000 bushels of corn, 1,370, 652 bushels of seed wheat, 9,800 tons of corn grits, and 340,000 cases of condensed milk; thirteen steamships had already left bound for the Soviet Union packed with three million bushels of grain. More ships awaited loading at docks in New Orleans, Philadelphia, Baltimore and New York for cargo destined for the starving Russians, Volga Germans and the Ukrainians. It is perhaps the largest relief effort ever launched in the world. Lenin pays $10 to $12 million in gold for seed, – not food, – "as stipulated in the agreement of December 1921". (D. Starbuck, *The Goodriches,* 156)

"Did the United States benefit economically from its generosity towards the starving Russians?" Weismann wonders. In 1923, the Department of Commerce claims that it did. According to a Department pamphlet, purchases for the relief program helped to maintain the price of corn during a critical period. According to an ARA official, this added hundreds of millions of dollars to the value of corn sold by American farmers." It should not be overlooked that Hoover was an expert in commodity trading and price fluctuations. Weismann adds, "The average price of corn did indeed rise more than 57 percent during the two years of the relief effort. But the price of wheat, which was shipped to Russia in substantial amounts as flour, actually fell by a few percentage points. During the same period, the price of cotton, which was not part of the relief program, went up over 95 percent." (B.

Weismann, *Hoover and Famine Relief*, 182-7. Weismann sources Joseph Brands, *Herbert Hoover and Economic Policy*, 11; Frank M. Surface and Raymond L. Bland, *American Food in the World War and Reconstruction Period*, 114)

As American food relief ships steamed through the seas Goodrich on February 12, 1922 returned to Moscow arriving there three weeks later March 9. With the passing of winter and spring in the air he found the streets bustling with renewed vigor. Remarkably much of the gloom already lifted. Stores seemed to display more goods for sale. Twenty thousand peasants on sleds converged at food distribution centers. Within a week 135 trains were transporting 50,000 tons of American corn to the famine-stricken heartland.

Goodrich attends a dinner on April 1 with Scheineman*, President of the Russian banking system. He met Lenin briefly. Soviet and foreign bankers urged official diplomatic recognition between the two countries to boost commercial exchange. Russia needed everything imaginable produced by the western industrial nations; the Soviets needed to deal with the American businessmen directly. "When I told him that America was in Russia spending $50,000,000 solely because the people believed it a Christian duty to feed the starving millions in Russia, with no ulterior purpose, and no hope of receiving anything in return, the expression on Scheineman's face indicated that he wondered if I thought he was foolish enough to believe that sort of thing." Goodrich assures Scheineman that Americans must first have assurances that "private property and contract, freedom of trade, free speech, and free press were guaranteed, not only to the nationals of other countries but to the Russian people as well." But surely the Great Powers have their "special interests", concurs Scheineman. (* Leon Trotsky in his *History of the Russian Revolution* identifies Scheineman as "a Bolshevik, the future director of the Soviet State Bank – a man of cautious and bureaucratic mold, but who at that time was marching abreast with the other leaders.")

In Moscow Goodrich attends a meeting at the Imperial Theatre of the Communist Party where he listens to Trotsky's address, and sharp criticism by an anti-Bolshevik dissenter in the audience. After a brief stay in London Goodrich June 7 heads straight back to Moscow. Pushing for recognition, trade, and more uninterrupted relief, this time he was invited to view Russian treasures of Empire collected over centuries of wars and treaties. The riches are beyond the dreams of most mortals and the envy of the world, and the world's greatest prize after Versailles. Few had ever seen such extraordinary treasures accumulated over centuries. Not even JP Morgan has ever seen such wealth. The Harrimans, Mellons, and Rockefellers, and Roosevelt's ambassador during Stalin's Great Purge Joe Davies will soon all have their turn at the Czarist loot.

"ALL THE CZARIST EMPIRE'S TREASURES ARE STORED HERE ..."

The Czarist treasure! This is what wars are fought for! On his mission for Hoover Goodrich arrives at a Soviet government storehouse to witness large sealed chests brought out and locks smashed. He can barely contain his astonished excitement. It need not be told how the revelation shook him other than for you reader to imagine how the sight of all the treasure sent feverish shivers down his spine. What any Consortium man would do to get his hands on it! "The old Czar's crown," Goodrich recalls, "the crown of the Czarina, and the various members of the royal family were there, brilliant with diamonds, varying from one to two hundred carats, all of purest water, and of wonderful color. There were crowns of diamonds, and pearls of emeralds, rubies, and amethysts; collars, bracelets, and necklaces of the precious stones. The scene begged description." He estimates the treasure worth a half billion dollars, undeniable proof that the charges aimed at Lenin and his gang of Bolsheviks had sold off the royal jewels were wicked lies and rumors. Goodrich's eyes watered as he beholds the magnificent royal treasures crafted for Kings and Queens, a priceless fortune of over three hundred years of Romanov tyranny. Here in the Czarist vaults lay the security for a loan to buy western agricultural equipment and supplies, and for whatever they need to finance their future.

Goodrich meets Rakovsky, Bolshevik President of the Ukraine. At last! A man who makes sense, and he finds him to be "the clearest headed man I had met in Russia" – and thought by many to be a double-agent for the ubiquitous hand of the Consortium but who isn't suspected by the jealous peering eyes of whispering on-lookers and the curious desperate for a loaf of bread. Rakovsky, too, pushes hard for official US recognition of the Soviet government. Lenin is dying! Why are the Americans so slow to act!

No one is too certain how long "the Bols" will be able to retain power. Goodrich telegrams Secretary of State Charles E. Hughes, the lawyer and 1916 GOP nominee for President: "The most definite and authenticated report is that while he (Lenin) has had a very light stroke of apoplexy and some mental disturbance his affliction is really due to an acquired or inherited syphilitic infection ... The executive committee of five of the communist party whom Lenine consulted on all important matters, considering of Lenin, Trotsky, Zinovev (sic) president of the Petrograd commune and Stalin, a Georgian prince who is very much trusted by Lenin has just been increased by the addition of Tomsky and Rakov (sic), very close friends of Lenine.... My judgment is that the death of Lenine will not mean the downfall of the Bolshevik government or even its serious embarrassment but that it will stand and continue to function." (Telegram J. Goodrich to C. E. Hughes, June 12, 1922, Frank A. Golder Papers, box 31, in D. Starbuck, *The Goodriches,* 169)

By summer 1922 disputes within the ARA back home as well as ARA conflicts with Soviet officials cast a shadow over the ARA's future. Hoover and Haskell seriously disagree over the real role and purpose of America's mission in Russia. Hoover plans for a reduced aid program after the harvest. By August, the ARA clash over Soviet insistence to sell Russian grain on the international grain market. With millions of Russians starving, V.G. Mikhailovsky, director of the Soviet Statistical Department of the Moscow Soviet, on August 1, 1922, argues that there is no home market for Soviet grain! The Bolshevik government is bankrupt with no money or manufactured goods with which to pay for the peasants. (Where are the Tsarist gold reserves?) Better to confiscate and sell the grain abroad and let them die, Mikhailovsky argues.

Meanwhile, American farmers enjoyed a grain surplus from abundant harvests. Hoover readily accepts for payment and persuasion Soviet treasures, crown jewels, and precious religious icons to pay for the American grain shipments. Haskell scores big with an inventory of $1 million worth of confiscated church treasures. Confiscated platinum, silver, rare metals, crown jewels, ikons, plate-ware etc. were all catalogued by another "expert" H. J. Larsons, Deputy Chief of Currency of Harding's Treasury. The list is never made public and remains a highly guarded secret far exceeding the low value estimates.

While the ARA was feeding one million children a day Commissar Kamenev pushes for Soviet grain exports on the international grain market to raise the money he informs Haskell on November 6 of preparations for Soviet grain shipments worth $50 million. Kamenev confides the Soviet government expects to gain "only $10 to $15 million urgently needed to buy mining equipment. Kamenev pledged the crown jewels and confiscated church property in exchange for an American loan in exchange the Soviets would suspend grain exports that year. Outraged over the Soviet grain exports, Hoover instructs Haskell, writing for the record, "The A.R.A. must protest against the Humanity of a government policy of exporting food from starving people in order that through such exports it may secure machinery and raw material for the economic improvement of the survivors. Any such action imposes the direct responsibility for the death of millions of people upon the government authorities." The Soviets went ahead anyway with the exports.

Eustace Mullins in *World Order* (1984) came across a fantastical reference to Maxim Litvinov, – (his real name is Meyer Wallach, born *Meir Henoch Mojszewicz Wallach-Finkelstein*, shortened to *Max Wallach* –, the second son of a wealthy Jewish banking family in the Podlasie Region of the former Polish-Lithuanian Commonwealth, then part of the Russian Empire), from an earlier biography by Arthur Upham Pope where Litvinov notes, and Mullins observes, "that in March, 1921, a trade agreement was signed with Great Britain providing that gold sent in payment for machines bought by Russia would not be confiscated towards old debts or claims. This insured that Czarist gold sent to England would not be seized by his cousins, the British Royal Family. On July 7, 1922, Litvinov reveals that the Russian delegation at the Hague Conference was negotiating with an important group of financiers which includes Otto H. Kahn of Kuhn, Loeb. 'The conference with the Russians,' Kahn declares a week later at the Hague in the Netherlands, 'will bring useful results and will lead to a closer approach to unity of views and policies on the part of England, France and the U.S.'." (E. Mullins, *World Order,* 1984)

When Otto Kahn's wife visits Russia in 1931 she is treated with the honors reserved for visiting royalty and world leaders. Her visit chronicled in a 1932 story on Otto Kahn is reported in the national French newspaper, *Figaro,* and cited in *The Rulers of Russia*, (1938), by the Irish catholic priest, Denis Fahey, of Dublin, and distributed in America by Rev. Chas. E. Coughlin. Fahey quoted the paper stating "She was officially received by the Soviet Government, which gave in her honour a grand diplomatic dinner and several brilliant receptions. The Red army lined the roads at the present arms...It was the least that the heads of the 'Proletarian Dictatorship' could do in order to honour the wife of one of their sovereigns."

Priest Fahey quotes from an article appearing April 2, 1934 in the *Daily Herald* from a man describing Kahn: "'I knew Otto Kahn, the multimillionaire, for many years. I knew him when he was a patriotic German. I knew him when he was a patriotic American. Naturally, when he wanted to enter the House of Commons, he joined the 'patriotic party'." Fahey adds, "We read, too, that an attempt was made to secure the nomination of Mr. Otto Kahn as president of the English-speaking Union, and the manoeuvre was defeated by the timely exposure of Kahn's Bolshevist activities. It was proved that Kahn's house was a meeting place for Soviet agents such as Nina Smorodin, Claire Sheridan, Louise Bryant and Margaret Harrison." Otto Kahn owns numerous spectacular mansions and country residences; the private school of the Convent of the Sacred Heart on Ninety-first Street and Fifth Avenue in uptown Manhattan occupies his former Italian-Renaissance-styled residence. (B. Weissman, 142-3; Betrand M. Patenaude, *The Big Show in Bololand, The American Relief Expedition to Soviet Russia in the Famine of 1921*, Stanford Univ. Press, 2002. Patenaude interprets the ARA within the framework of America's billion dollar postwar European reconstruction; Nora Levin, *The Jews in the Soviet Union Since 1917: Paradox of Survival*, NY Univ. Press, 1988, 330; Litvinov "was referred to by the German radio as 'Litvinov-Finkelstein'– was dropped in favor of Vyascheslav Molotov. 'The eminent Jew', as Churchill put it, 'the target of German antagonism was flung aside ... like a broken tool. ... The Jew Litvinov was gone and Hitler's dominant prejudice placated.'"; Rev. Denis Fahey, *The Rulers of Russia*, Dublin, 1938, US edition 1940, 31; E. Mullins, *World Order*)

Haskell quickly adapted to famine politics and gave the Soviets and Hoover a unique way of handling the crisis. At first Col. Haskell attacked the Bolsheviks for causing famine conditions and governing by terror without "the support or confidence of the people". Haskell denounced Soviet requisition of grain for export as the cause of the people's starvation. He called "ridiculous" Bolshevik claims that drought or foreign military intervention as the cause. Four months pass while Haskell aligned himself to an entente between the Bolsheviks and Hoover. One year later, after working closely with Cheka boss Dzerzhinsky (Felix Edmundovich) and the Soviet leadership, Col. Haskell sends a request to Christian Herter to immediately issue US visas for Radek, Litvinov and Krassin as they will "invariably come back with more reasonable ideas and always convinced that they have got to suppress the agitators in Russia and get on more friendly terms with America". Had Col. Haskell lost his head and gone Bolshevik? He wonders, what game are they playing with the Bols? And is this really a problem anyway? These are very confused times what with the US Attorney General Palmer's "Red Scare" anti-Bolshevik campaign blowing up bombs to get appropriation funds from Congress and FBI's J. Edgar Hoover chasing left-wing liberal-commie

"Reds" in capitols across America terrorizing the public. Many of those caught are sentenced to long prison terms.

Herter thinks different, flatly rejects the Goodrich plan and instructs Haskell who is also working in tandem with Kamenev's wife to exercise more caution and avoid falling into a Soviet intrigue that might prove too delicate for the diplomats this at a time when official relations have been severed since Francis closed the embassy in 1918. The Bolshevik Leonid Krassin, a former engineer for the rich Russian industrialist Morozov and an important conduit of funds to Lenin in the pre-1905 revolutionary organization, for example, Herter tells him is "completely untrustworthy and unreliable". By this time Haskell, not unlike Col. Raymond Robbins, formerly attached to the 1917 American Red Cross spy mission during the Russian Revolution, is confused by cross signals from State and has gone completely over to the Bolshevik side urging massive foreign economic assistance for the Soviet regime in the absence of which Robbins had said conditions would result in "misery and suffering by millions over a long period of years".

Christian A. Herter is another Consortium don at State and carries considerable influence. After Harvard he marries a granddaughter of Standard Oil scion Charles Pratt giving him access to the Rockefeller treasure chest. After the 1919 Paris Peace Conference where he helps draft the Covenant of the League of Nations he then works with Allen Wardwell and others to set up the Council of Foreign Relations (CFR). The Massachusetts Republican will then opt for career in politics serving twelve years in Congress during the Roosevelt years while considering himself a specialist in foreign affairs.

But this is not the first time the intelligence agent Haskell exceeded his ARA orders not to interfere with internal Soviet affairs and stay strictly focused on "humanitarian" relief work. Soviet editors at *Izvetiia* are quick to exploit the Haskell-Hoover rift. Then American press get wind of the split. *The Nation* headlines its editorial "Hoover Stabs Russia".

Haskell works closely in step with his friend Dzerzhinsky, a ruthlessly immoral Bolshevik commissar and Lenin's revolutionary head of the Chekha secret police to further the ARA's mission to back official recognition of the Soviets and open trade relations. Herter cabled back telling him to back off, that it was "inadvisable". Christian Herter also tersely disapproves of any reference to the Americans taking a million dollars in Soviet gold imported by the US Treasury for the "charity". Herter is another golden boy of the Consortium to go far at State. We will see more of Herter as his influence grows within the Consortium in the thirties. After World War II President Eisenhower appoints Herter to succeed Herbert Hoover Jr., as Undersecretary of State; Herter had been considered as a candidate over Richard Nixon for Vice President on the Republican ticket; instead Eisenhower appoints him Secretary of State when Dulles resigns. (B. Weissman, 152, Haskell to C. Herter, Feb. 12, 1923, HHL)

At the same time of ARA operations in Europe (1920-21) the Robert Dollar company, according to Sutton, "handled \$7 million of the total \$15 worth of United States exports to the USSR." That company's agent in Moscow is Jonas Lied (1881-69) who has, according to the State Department, an 'interesting dossier' in the Department of Justice (i.e., the FBI) and intelligence in the State Department." Lied is an explorer, Norwegian diplomat and adventurer who founded The Siberian Company, in 1912, opening Arctic sea routes through the Kara Sea. Success comes the next year when Fridtjof Nansen joins Lied's second expedition from Tromsa to Siberia. But by 1918 the Bolsheviks nationalized his company. Still he is manages to salvage a vast art collection safely expedited to his ancestral farm in Romsdal.

For his part Dollar shows no willingness to talk openly about his activities with the Soviets. Likewise, Sutton recalls, "Dollar was reluctant to say very much except to blast the 'radical element in this country (which sic) should not be allowed to block trade." What really was the use of that gold if not to facilitate trade and technology, grain imports, an end to civil war, and the stabilization of the Bolshevik regime? Anyway, that's peanuts compared to the extraordinary cachet of unaccounted Czarist gold secreted to Consortium's banks. (A. C. Sutton, v. I, 267-96; SDDF 316-109-1375, 316-107-451; *Jonas Lied, Prospector In Siberia*, Kessinger, 2010; Jonas Lied, *Siberian Arctic: The Story of the Siberian Company*, London: Methuen, 1960)

If the wake of the winter's death season Jim Goodrich investigates communities for survivors. He meets the president of the Tatar village Tahtalla commune and described wretched conditions there. "In last September we had 1177 souls in this commune', Goodrich observed. There are 522 people left. Nearly 300 starved and the rest emigrated or died of typhus. Only about 12 percent of our livestock is left. If it were not for America we would all be dead. We raised very little last year and are now getting 250 adult and 250 child rations for relief, so you see the Americans are practically feeding the whole commune." He found commune peasants as few as 5 % calling themselves "Reds". On his trip from Samara to Moscow Goodrich found ample reason to be encouraged and fields showing "evidence of good husbandry" helped by a mild spring weather. Goodrich expects a good harvest of wheat, rye and other grain. This leads him to believe "that in a few short weeks the work of American relief in Russia would be over".

Lenin's health suddenly deteriorates. He is wasting away, literally at times a skeleton of his former self. On June 18 the Governor and Dr. Golder meets with Soviet leaders Finance Commissar Sokolnikoff (1888-39) and commissars Kamenev, married to Trotsky's younger sister, Olga, whom he had met in Paris during one of his many trips there with Lenin; and they meet other professional Leninist revolutionary leaders – Litvinov, Krassin, Rykov, acting president of the Soviet Republic and president of the Soviet Council, and Sokolnikoff, who will eventually irritate Stalin over his call for freedom of discussion within the Party and economic reforms but more for exposing Zinoviev's "leftist" opposition. In 1929 he reappears in London as the Soviet ambassador, until 1932, he is replaced Maisky. Arrested in 1936 Sokolnikoff dies in the Gulag, likely shot. Born in 1884 Ivan Maisky (Jan Lachowiecki) is a Polish Jew ruled by the laws of the Imperial Czar. One day he finds luck at his door; he is one of a handful to survive Stalin and pops up at the Yalta and Potsdam conferences, dying in 1975. During the Holodomor years Maisky served as the Soviet envoy to London where he remains until 1943 meeting frequently with Churchill and Eden, and assuring the ever-suspicious Stalin of England's constant unwillingness to sign a separate peace with Nazi Germany. In 1953 Stalin has Maisky arrested. He thinks its his turn now, but much to his surprise the sentence is six years in the Gulag; two years later he is released by Khrushchev. He surfaces again, in 1966, his signature next to those of writers and cultural leaders on the "Letter of 25" addressed to Brezhnev in opposition to any rehabilitation of Stalin by the reactionaries.

The lives of Rykov and the others with Goodrich will be less fortunate. In a breathless hurry Aleksei Ivanovich Rykov (1881-38) tells Goodrich that Lenin's "stroke" on May 26 has left most of his body paralyzed. Trotsky is absent. Litvinov again is inclined to push forward the recognition card. Pressed by Sakaloff, "counsel for the commissariat of concessions", Goodrich writes Hoover June 22 telling of his invitation to talk "with the central executive committee including Trotsky and others ... I told him that I would give serious consideration to an invitation of that kind. I am rather expecting it. I have been standing rather stiff on this matter because I felt that if any discussion of America's attitude towards Russia was to be had at all it only should be with those men in authority."

Convinced America should help turn Russia around Goodrich has already written the Republican senior Sen. Hughes, on June 1: "It is only in the productivity of Russia that there is any hope for the Russian people and it is idle to expect resumptions of trade unless the economic basis of production are securely established." And, again, on September 29, Goodrich presses Hughes sending the same information to Evan E. Young, US Commissioner at Riga (1920-22).

During the war Evan Young had been Consul General in Halifax when Trotsky and other Bols emigrated from New York to revolutionary Russia and may have helped facilitate Trotsky's US passport in compliance with instructions from London and on direct orders from Wilson's White House; in 1920 Young is sent to another hot spot, Constantinople, and there hooks up with Col. Haskell entrenched in activities of the Bolshevik Civil War with tens of thousands of White Russians thrust back to the Crimea in southern Ukraine and eventually forced to escape or even suffer a fate worse than death. The Bols drowned them by shiploads rather than let them escape to freedom, yet another massacre in the suffering tragedy. The lucky or escaped include exiled novelist and poet Vladimir Nabokov, who a generation overnight sets the world on fire introducing an arousing style of literary erotica with the publication of his sensational novel, *Lolita* (1955); in the exodus he is a political refugee with a price on his neck who reluctantly flees with his family and are among the last White Russians of landowners and aristocrats to be evacuated in a flotilla of twenty-six vessels taking some 146,000 refugees to Constantinople. Only a true lover of freedom knows the terrible feeling of heartbreaking exile from their sacred Russian Motherland. (Andrew Field, *VN, The Life and Art of Vladimir Nabokov*, NY: Crown, 1986)

During three hours of debates ranging over securities and guarantees to individual and property under the Soviet system Rykov again returns to the debt problem imploring the prestigious American not to make it a thorn in harmonious relations between the vast former Russian Empire and the ascending American democracy. "You know that Russia cannot pay. It seems foolish to ask Russia to issue her obligations to pay when she knows that without financial help she cannot pay." Goodrich rebuts Rykov telling him to buck up. "The difficulty with you gentlemen is that you yourselves have no faith in Russia. … Russia can pay, once her industrial and economic system is restored. You ought to show your faith in Russia by frankly saying that you recognize your debts, that they are valid obligations, that you will give us your understanding to pay these debts, and will fix a definite time when interest and principal will be paid." (*The Goodrich Manuscript,* 4-7, in D. Starbuck, 169-170; Warren Harding Papers, roll 181)

On June 21 Goodrich returned to the Volga to examine relief operations. Once back in Moscow he tracked down American businessmen, managers of Westinghouse, International Harvester, and the head of the Soviet State Bank and Commission on Concessions. Goodrich found after his meetings that while the Soviets rejected private property they eagerly sought long lease contracts with foreign corporations. Americans preferred to manufacture in the United States then ship the new goods rather than get muddled in Soviet labor laws that drained 25 percent of a company's payroll, for example, allotting seven months paid maternity leave for women workers. (D. Starbuck, *The Goodriches*, 174)

TO SAVE RUSSIA : A MONOPOLY FOR THE COMMUNISTS AND THE CAPITALISTS

International Harvester has a long history in Russia. The US corporation is poised to be a major player in Stalin's Five-Year Plan of collectivization of State socialist terror against the peasants in the Ukraine and elsewhere. A Morgan-Rockefeller conglomerate absorbed the McCormick Harvesting Machine Company founded by Cyrus McCormick, the Mid-western pioneer inventor of the reaper. McCormick's great-great-granddaughter, Anne Blaine, married Gilbert A. Harrison; a year later Harrison dipped into the McCormick fortune to buy *The New Republic* magazine founded in 1914 by William Straight and his wife's Whitney money, one more example of how Consortium fortunes of the rich and powerful capitalists from the 19th century American industrial revolution era were used to shape the nation and control public opinion especially during these tumultuous war years. However Harrison is only 18 years old during the Holodomor; impoverished by the Depression he is compelled to travel cross-country selling jewelry from the family car. Harrison passed away during the writing of this book, mostly forgotten and scarcely a blip on the radar, in 2008.

The 1921-23 Russian famine was headline news in British and American newspapers. A nationwide network of Friends of Soviet Russia blossomed in every state, and nearly every city and factory across America. Famine Scout Clubs sprang up with children joining in the relief-for-Russia work. When the famine crisis passed, the FSR groups disbanded and did not arise as any significant force during the Holodomor 1932-33 famine for the reason that the Communist Party in America strictly forbids recognition of the famine or promotion of relief organizations to aid the Stalin's victims.

Think about it reader. Whereas in the beginning under Lenin's terror regime, Hoover, Mellon and the Consortium group pressed for recognition, and hold a conference at Riga, Latvia with Walter L. Brown their chief negotiator with Litvinov, the Bolshevik banker's son., to feed and strengthened the regime, then blacklisted recognition off the official agenda. The same group of insiders then invest economically and politically during Lenin's NEP reconstruction program and Stalins' Five-Year Plans for industrialization and modernization of the peasant system of agriculture. And as they remain silent about the Holodomor, all publicity and talk of the 1931-33 Holodomor famine is censored, while the White House recognizes Stalin's regime with negotiations. All this during the peak of the famine, terror and economic disaster. Faced with the prospect of a national banking crisis, domestic social unrest and economic upheaval in the first year of his radical New Deal administration, Roosevelt feared the public outcry over sensational headlines in black and white attacking America's Consortium power elite in the State Department. Of course that would never happen.

The Wasps and the Jews in the American-Anglo Consortium owned the news organizations. Public exposure of the bankers and war planners was not going to happen except in isolated cases such as Richard Whitney, president of the New York Stock Exchange, convicted for illegal trading, and his unpardonable betrayal of Consortium loyalties. Dick Whitney was arrested on grand larceny sent to Sing-Sing prison. John Kenneth Galbraith writes in his *The Great Crash, 1929* of how the 1932 Senate and Banking Committee investigation into the crash handled the syndicates and pools of millionaire investors who manipulated the markets and set up the market meltdown of the stock exchanges. "Under the later guidance of Ferdinand Pecora, this committee became the scourge of commercial, investment, and private bankers," Galbraith writes, and he added, "But this was not foreseen when it was organized. The original and more or less exclusive object of the inquiry was the market for securities. On the whole, this part of the investigation was unproductive ... the committee turned to the famous market operators. These, too, were disappointing. All that could be proved was what everyone knew, namely that Bernard E. ('Sell'em Ben') Smith, M. J. Meehan, Arthur W. Cutten, Harry F. Sinclair, Percy A. Rockefeller, and others had been engaged in large-scale efforts to rig the market. Harry F. Sinclair, for example, was shown to have engaged in especially extensive operations in Sinclair Consolidated Oil." (J. K. Galbraith, *The Great Crash, 1929*, 158)

No Lubyanka for Stalin! No calf butting the oak here! When the Consortium aided and abetted their man in the Kremlin Stalin consolidate his absolute demonic control over a totalitarian communist state of downtrodden enslaved populations. The prisons held only criminals, naturally, saboteurs and extortionists of the worst kind. The bottom might fall out from under FDR. Whether it be 1922 or 1932 it would never serve Consortium interests to demonize the demagogue nor appear aligned with the Commie Reds and having the American administration branded by Marxist-Leninist slogans of "capitalist enslavement" if the world knew too much of Soviet grain confiscated from the Ukraine as they did in 1922 and sold on the international market in exchange for gold used to buy American manufactured goods, or worse, American financed Nazi goods sold to the Soviet Union to modernize social terrorism. Remember reader, Hoover had even once censured Haskell for pursuing that very same Bolshevik policy of starving the victims in order to fill Soviet coiffures. That same quid pro quo was always the basis of the US-Soviet relations. How long could the center hold before all things fell apart? How long could the truth remain a lie? How long would Consortium power prevail over the free world.

Do you still wonder what might have happened to FDR had he listened with earnest to the appeals of the Ukrainians and defied the impossible and come to their aid? With soup kitchens and bread lines still feeding the poor, hungry and unemployed millions in America and with American trade in the balance, does anyone still even imagine that Roosevelt would have risked the stigma of communism in the White House? During the 1921 famine in Russia, America reeled with overproduction and an abundant wheat harvest while the price of wheat shipped to Russia as flour actually dropped. The price of corn increased 57 cents over two years benefiting American farmers. And while the British press publicized the "terrible facts" about the famine Chicherin and other Soviet authorities decry "a total misunderstanding about the situation in the starving provinces". But a steady stream of news from the British trade mission in Moscow feeds the papers of starving masses and people dropping like flies in the streets.

But we know famine is not new to Soviet Russia. In early 1921, Lenin tells Bolshevik delegates at the Tenth Congress of the Russian Communist Party "If there is a crop failure, it will be impossible to appropriate any surplus because there will be no surplus. Food would have to be taken out of the mouths of the peasants. If there is a harvest, then everybody will hunger a little, and the government will be saved; otherwise, since we cannot take anything from people who do not have the means of satisfying their own hunger, the government will perish." Fridtjof Nansen, the Norwegian explorer and head of the International Committee for Russian Relief estimates twelve of nineteen million people then starving would die without immediate aid. Estimates ran as high as 30 million people who faced death by hunger. Nansen tells Maxim Gorky to appeal to the Americans for aid. Fridtjof Nansen is awarded the Nobel Peace Prize in 1922 for his work to aid refugees and victims of the Great War. (B. Weissman, 2-5)

"Help is needed" declared Lenin in his appeal to the international proletariat against capitalist conspiracies that blocked urgent food relief from coming to the rescue of the Soviet state On August 2, 1921 Lenin appealed to war-torn Ukraine where he granted limited autonomy (he would soon reverse that call). Lenin said, "The well-protected Ukraine gathered an excellent harvest this year. Workers and peasants of the starving Volga region, who are presently suffering a catastrophe worse than the horrible disaster of 1891, expect help from the Ukrainian farmers."

Lenin was forced to slow down his radical socialization of Russia. Again Lenin readily accepted foreign aid and assistance from the powerful industrialists. Hoover responded by sending engineers, research scientists, and technologists. According to Werner Keller in *East Minus West Equals Zero* (1961) the arch opportunist Lenin found it advantageous to use them. Lenin knows not to be overly concerned, and he said, "They will furnish credits which will serve as a means to support the Communists parties, and by supplying us with materials and techniques which are not available to us, they will rebuild our war industry which is essential to our future attacks on our own suppliers. In other words, they will be laboring to prepare their own suicide." (Werner Keller, *East Minus West Equals Zero*, NY: G. Putnam's Sons, 1961,195-201; *Facts on Communism: The Soviet Union from Lenin to Khrushchev*, Committee on Un-American Activities, House of Representatives, 87th Congress, 1st Session, Dec. 1960, 130)

With the flux of change and events passing rapidly from war to peace, from revolution to civil war the confusion of chaos must have been overwhelming to live at the time, and later, but mark this reader, the Consortium was never spell-bound. It stays many steps ahead of the unfolding picture sailing through turbulent and murky seas. Its plans are carefully determined with calculated precision. The Consortium does not take kindly to miscalculations. Accidents of history are cumbersome and inconvenient. The reader should understand that this time in history was full of checks and balances, the give and take of war and peace. Lenin was a master player in The Game. Trotsky excelled. Stalin proves to be even more devious, cynical and ruthless revealing the basest of human instinct and even comic delight in murder and treachery. The Consortium plays its part shared with all of them, not to be left out or passed over, ready to help at every turn of fortune, changing tactics as the Russian scene unfolded until they could guarantee stability under the totalitarian dictatorship not of Lenin's Proletariat, but finally under the tyranny of state socialized terror of Comrade Stalin.

At the end of 1918, when the Bolsheviks seized power and opened peace negotiations with the Germans, the Allies retaliated extending their maritime blockade against Germany to also include Soviet Russia. The French further antagonized Moscow by intriguing with the Poles to seize Russian territory in April 1920; the French and British also meddled in the doomed Kronstadt uprising a year later in March. But postwar interference in Russia's internal affairs did not stop there. Lenin prevailed in the Kremlin as head of the Soviet government and sought an end to hostilities and a toning down of the propaganda war with the West linked to acceptance of his New Economic Policy (NEP) for international trade of Russia's vast resources essential to domestic growth at home. That too was turned down. Soviet commissars abroad asked for loans and trade credits from Europe and the United States, but most Consortium bankers and countries refused to advance money or even extend credits, except Germany's bankrupt Weimar Republic. After launching the NEP, Lenin's health deteriorated; he was forced to lighten his exhaustive work load and leave government duties to others in the Communist Party. By 1922 Stalin took over as General Secretary of the Communist Party.

Many of those who helped would later be killed, imprisoned or exiled by Stalin's goons. Even many of the provinces in the Ukraine had a poor or insufficient harvest, with fields spoiled, untilled, and abandoned by Revolution and civil war and little if anything to send; refugees from the Volga descended into the Ukraine to find relief. In the same speech Lenin was forced to retreat from the "the joyous but difficult task of overthrowing capitalism". Yet, reader, we know food aid was used in 1921 against insurgent nationalist Ukrainians in their abortive revolt for independence. At least five million Russians starved to death. Less than ten years later, Stalin used the same food weapon against the peasants. And in the same region of the Caucasus, the Rockefeller-Morgan interests were already making deals to extract oil in return for foreign exchange required to build Soviet communism.

Lenin and Stalin after him knew the strategic importance of winning over the peasants and not to lose the Ukraine. Soon after the Bolsheviks and their agents seized power the sting of the Soviet whip was sharply felt on the back of Mother Ukraine. The February 1917 Revolution inspired nationalists in the Ukrainian Central Rada parliament in Kharkov to break away from centuries of Russian domination. The Ukrainian National Republic was born. Russians, Poles, Germans, Ukrainians and Bolsheviks clashed over territory. From 1918-1920, the Ukraine, famous for its rich black soil making it the grain breadbasket of Russia and Europe it was the first country in Eastern Europe to fall after Trotsky and the Bolshevik Red Army repeatedly launched major offensives to ruthlessly prevent it from breaking away and annihilate its movement for national independence. Ukrainian nationalists were killed, imprisoned, exiled, and hid underground in groups like the Organization of Ukrainian Nationalists (OUN).

From the beginning the Consortium had supported the Bols against the nationalist Ukrainian independence fighters. As a truly international organization, the Consortium's military and political specialists supported the key players on different sides of Russia's civil war including the most famous White generals Kolchak and Deniken who received payments from the Morgan and National City banks. Whites fought Reds in dramatic cavalry charges. Freed from a Czarist prison after a general amnesty of the February Revolution in Russia in 1917, the young anarchist-communist leader and Ukrainian nationalist Nestor Makhno met with Lenin in the Kremlin along with Sverdlov, stalwart Bolshevik organizer of the Party who had been with Stalin in harsh barren arctic exile during the war. Their perceptions differ over Ukrainian independence and the peasants. With his wild band of Ukrainian Army of Insurgent Peasants Nestor Makhno fights the new government and the Whites, and soon controls vast tracts of Ukraine.

Much of the indigenous Ukrainian opposition to the Communists is fueled by traditional anti-Semitism. In contemporary and impoverished Ukraine where the national standard of living is very low hushed hostility towards Jews; anti-Semitism persists with ignorance and joblessness widespread. Salaries remain dismally low and working hours long. The Whites publish caricatured anti-Semitic posters showing a hideous Jewish Trotsky with Oriental Bolshevik soldiers. However, it is never proven that Makhno is anti-Semitic; he fought alongside Jewish officers in his army. Makhno is aided by Maria Nikiforova, the anarchist revolutionary whose terrorist activities over a decade against Czarist officials are repeated against the Bolsheviks. Born in Alexandrovsk, now Zaporizhia in southern Ukraine, in 1885, Maria's father was an officer and decorated hero in the Russo-Turkish War (1877-78). Widely known by her nickname "Marusya" her bravery and exploits earn her a command of a combat unit in the famous Black Guard regiment. Maria Nikoforova fights one regime after another, battling the Germans and the notorious General Denikin until she is executed in 1919 with her husband Witold Bzhostek, both captured while on a sabotage mission in Sevastopol in the Crimea.

On orders from Lenin Trotsky signs the Treaty of Brest-Litovsk buying time to consolidate the Bolshevik Revolution and fight the Whites in the ensuing civil war by making peace with the Central Powers but at a huge price of ceding large amounts of territory to Berlin including the Ukraine. The disenfranchised Ukrainians are unhappy to be ruled by the Central Powers after fighting a war against them. They rebel and all is chaos. Partisan units waged warfare against the Germans and Austrians. The rebellion turns into an anarchist revolution. Nestor Makhno is one of the main organizers of these partisan groups to take control fo the disorder united into the Revolutionary Insurrectionary Army of Ukraine (RIAU), also called the Black Army. (They fight under the Black Flag, the color of anarchism, Makhnovists or *Makhnovshchina* i.e.Makhnovism). The RIAU also battle against the Russians, Whites (counter-revolutionaries) and reactionary anti-semitic pogromists. In areas where the RIAU overcome opposing armies, villagers and workers struggle to abolish capitalism and the state through organizing themselves into village assemblies, communes and free councils. Land and factories are expropriated and operated under self-management.

By March 1918, the RIAU had successfully defeated Germans, Austrians, Ukrainian nationalists and various White armies. General Denikin defeats Trotsky's forces in the Ukraine. Makhno fought Deniken and won but soon betrayed by Trotsky. Makhno then loses half his army to the typhus epidemic. Makhno forces reach a new truce with Trotsky's Red Army in October 1920 when both armies come close to territories held by Wrangel's White Army. Makhnovshchina agrees to help the Reds. That all changes when Wrangle is decisively crushed in the Crimea.

As the Civil War drags on in order to neutralize Makhno and his followers Lenin agrees to recognize Ukraine as an autonomous anarchist region. A treaty is signed by three Jewish Commissars : Bela Kuhn, S. I. Gusev and M. V. Frunze. As soon as the other fronts are secure, the Red Army turn all its force against Makhno and the Ukrainian autonomous region. Again the communists betray Makhno. But Makhno intercepts three messages from Rakovsky, Bolshevik Commissar of the Ukraine, with orders to arrest Makhno and his men. He escapes again, in 1923, taking refuge first to Rumania, then to Poland and eventually settles in Paris. Bela Khun will perish in the Great Purge.

By the time Lenin and the Bolsheviks launch the 1917 October Revolution they are already deep in the pockets of the Morgan-Rockefeller-Harriman, all Consortium men of the same type, cast and style visibly scurrying about St. Petersburg and Moscow under the banner of the American Red Cross. The coalition of capitalists and Bolsheviks rise and falls with the tide swelling with a position of strength to stabilize a new Russian government in the chaos of war and revolution and save whatever success it can manage to score and push to the top and hold with popular support and guns.

Russia provides the capitalists with the largest untapped market in the world and cheap labor. Imagine taking over an entire empire the size of Russia with its vast inexhaustible wealth in mineral resources, including gold and oil. It dwarfs miniscule Europe and stands remotely too distant to the West to entirely comprehensible. With the highest accelerated rate of growth before the outbreak of the First World War, Czarist Russia had constituted the greatest competitive threat to the supremacy of the American-Anglo Consortium. For that reason it had to go. For a little more than twenty million dollars paid for in gold at today's value worth near a half billion dollars, the Consortium has their own team inside the Kremlin. They did what men could do in positions expecting them to use the power of their position to wage war for extraordinary profit to enrich and sustain their clans and corporations.

Who profits? Jacob Schiff, Otto Kahn, Kuhn Loeb... and, for example, the Guggenheim interests are represented by Daniel Guggenheim, son of Meyer and father to Robert, Harry, and Gladys. The scion of American Smelting and Refining (1901-19), he controls one of the largest mining conglomerates in the world owned with principals JP Morgan & Co., and Kuhn, Loeb. The Guggenheim mining and mineral fortune stretching from Chile and Bolivia to Mexico across the Northwest to Alaska where Guggenheim JP Morgan Sr., and their third partner Jacob Schiff together invest tens of millions taking up where the Russians left off when the Alaskan territory was sold by the Tsar to US Secretary of State William H Seward for $7.2 million in 1867 and called "Seward's Folly. During WWII nitrates essential in the production of munitions revived their business in Chile reap tens of millions more as even Hitler's synthetics cannot keep up with demand.

Daniel Guggenheim first impressed JP Morgan Sr. who invests tens of millions in his venture and becomes a director at Morgan's Guaranty Trust. Their Alaskan syndicate founded in 1906 became known the "Guggenheim Trust". But most of the Guggenheim empire (American Smelting & Refining, Anaconda, Kennecott Copper, Anglo, Pacific Tin, International Rubber, American Congo with King Leopold II of Belgium and Thomas Fortune Ryan, all exploiting natural resources, commodities, and cheap labor mostly in Latin American countries. In his Tacoma deal to refine Kennecott ore Baruch pockets a cool $1 million for arranging the purchase; Baruch is one of the pallbearers when Daniel dies in September 1930.

Three generations of Guggenheims, in particular, of those of Issac, Meyer and Daniel, each not satisified only "to gain control of all mining and smelting on the North American continent", and seek a monopoly and to take "a few steps further: gain control, also, of all mining and smelting on the rest of the planet". John H. Davis, *The Guggenheims, An American Epic*, NY: William Morrow, 1978, 110*)*

Guggenheim biography John H. Davis in his chapter "Lords of the Earth" 1905-23, in describes the family's concentration of wealth: "The Guggenheim epic is one of concerted family endeavor. Its only parallel in our time is the history of the Rothschilds of Europe". In *The Guggenheims, An American Epic* (1978), author John Davis writes, "The ultimate prize was too great. Dan Guggeheim's ambition had become nothing less than to control all the natural resources of Alaska. ... the 'Guggenheim Trust' bought Kennecott Mountain and several hundred thousands of acres of adjoining territory in the Wrangel chain, bought two hundred miles of railroad right-of-way to the sea, bought western Steamship Company, bought Northwestern Commercial, a service company, bought every Alaskan coal mine they could get their hands on, bought endless forests, and, perceiving that ships could transport fish as well as copper, bought, as a sideline, Northwestern Fisheries, the most important fishing and canning industry in the Western United States, Canada, and Alaska, for good measure." (J. H. Davis, *The Guggenheims*, 90, 95-136. No citing of Hitler or Stalin in the index)

Writer John Davis, a Bouvier cousin to Jackie Kennedy's clan, makes a relevant comment of Consortium power and influence of Guggenheim wealth and their friends. Herein lay one of the great American paradoxes. The American people, through their elected representatives, solemnly professed to the world in speech after speech that America sought no man's territory, that America had no imperialistic aims. Yet all the while, through the efforts of men like the Guggenheims, America was steadily building up the greatest commercial empire on the face of the earth; we are shown the ads with the thick paint oozing down over South America and Africa. America seeks no man's territory, but the Coca-Colonialization of the world must also extend to Easter Island, the Seychelles, Tasmania. It may not be the will of the American people, but it most certainly is the will of the officers and boards of directors of Sherwin Williams and Coca-Cola. Thus the American empire, the most extensive and powerful commercial and military empire in world history, was willed not by the American people, or their elected representatives – but by a handful of strong-minded, talented, industrious, acquisitive people like the Guggenheims." (J. H. Davis, *The Guggenheims*, 110)

The Guggenheims marry into the Loeb and Rothschild families. With Schiff, Morgan and their connections to the New York Fed they prove to be an essential element in the American-Russian syndicate formed in 1918 established to tap into the Russian Bolshevik concessions. It is a fantastic bargain between Jews and their partners in order to preserve their financial and industrial monopoly and abolish competition. With one bold stroke they converted Czarist Russia into a captive market and monopoly of Soviet-styled Marxist-Leninist socialism. It is their greatest coup, and the greatest fraud yet of the century.

A few of the Red Cross agents were denounced in the New York press as Wall Street Bolsheviks, in particular the Morgan and NY Fed banker William Boyce Thompson and his agent Col. Raymond Robins who secretly schemed to back the Bolsheviks as the only legitimate regime in Russia aided by the State Department, president Wilson and the British FO under prime minister Lloyd George. Just more nonsense in the press that covered their tracks. Their real motives were never about ideology. Their interest was not freedom or self-determination for the workers and peasants. They wanted a stable government and monopoly over Russia's coveted resources.

Thirteen years after the Russian spy mission Col. Robins wrote, rather enigmatically of his successor, "Major Wardwell" who he promoted and who remained active with the CFR.

Robbins writes, "Major Wardwell stayed in Russia all through the summer of 1918 and on into the fall. He saw the first great outburst of the Mass Terror. He lived in Russia in its days of greatest personal peril. But he differed from certain other representatives of foreign governments in Russia. He took no part in plots for the blowing up of railway bridges to interrupt the supplies of the Soviet government. He took no part in plots for the bribing of Soviet army officers to upset the military organization of the Soviet government. He remained neutral in the Russian civil war. Remaining neutral, he remained in perfect security. He stayed till October, seeing Russia at its reddest, attending to his own American Mission business, in full protection by the Soviet government; and then he came out in full liberty, unmolested and unhindered." A nice white-wash. It should be noted that the original book was published "with the income of Jacob H. Schiff Endowment for the Promotion of Studies in Human Civilization", a $100,000 endowment at Cornell University made by the German-born Schiff in 1912 originally for the study of "German "Kultur"; in June 1918 Cornell's trustees agreed to shift the Schiff Foundation theme to a study of "human civilization"; then there was the little problem of the war when Wilson followed London and the Consortium men invested in the government war business and declare the Kaiser a mortal enemy of the free world. (William Hard, *Raymond Robins' Own Story*, NY: Harper & Bros., 1930)

On Anglo-American support of Trotsky during the 1918-20 civil war historian Antony Sutton wrote "…it was Trotsky who appointed tsarist generals to consolidate the Red Army; that it was Trotsky who appealed for American officers to control revolutionary Russia and intervene in behalf of the Soviets; that it was Trotsky who squashed first the libertarian element in the Russian Revolution and then the workers and peasants; and that recorded history totally ignores the Green Army of 700,000 nationalists composed of ex-Bolsheviks, angered at betrayal of the revolution and who fought both the Whites and the Reds. In other words, we are suggesting that the Bolshevik Revolution was an alliance of statists: statist revolutionaries and statist financiers aligned against the genuine revolutionary libertarian elements in Russia." Stability of centralized dictatorship whose only legitimacy is tyranny by ruthless oppression was not in disfavor with the Consortium family of client states.

Linguistic and cultural differences dividing Russia and the Ukraine are profound, persisting after three centuries of Russian domination. They can be easily traced to the era when Kiev was the capital of Kiev Rus', a vast Slavic kingdom, seat of the grand prince, capitol from the 9th century upon the baptism of grand prince Vladimir in 988, and also the seat of the metropolitan o the Russian Orthodox Church, prior to the ancient Russian Empire that existed long before Peter the Great constructed St. Petersburg with French and European architects. Those cultural differences always irritated Stalin, Bolshevik Commissar of

Nationalities, a Georgian always inclined to smash Ukrainian separatism and its unique culture of social individualism.

Once the Red Army in 1920 takes Riga in the north and drives the Cossacks back down through the Ukraine and into the Black Sea, the new Bolshevik leaders consolidate their political authority under Lenin. The Central Committee Secretariat comes into existence formally after the Sixth Party Congress headed by Yakov Sverdlov until his sudden death, in 1919, succeeded by Stalin. It is at this time that the post of 'responsible Secretary' is created in the Secretariat; in 1921, Mikhailov and Yaroslavsky are appointed general secretaries. Molotov joins the Politburo, as a candidate member.

Events move feverishly knotting themselves wildly; nothing can be held back helplessly passing between seasons in the flood of revolution and breakneck zigzags under the weight and woe of Mother Russia. By 1922 Stalin becomes General Secretary replacing Molotov, and remains General Secretary in 1923-4 when the Secretariat expands to five members. With his seat in the Politburo Stalin dominates the "Orgburo" as well as sitting on the Central Executive Committee and, until 1923, oversees the Council of People's Commissars, the "Sovnarkom". Thus the lone Georgian wolf amasses what Lenin in his last Testament alerts the Bolsheviks to Stalin's "boundless power". They were warned. Russia is doomed.

Stalin gains support from Lazar Kaganovich, who becomes head of the Organizational Instruction Department of the Central Committee. Two other Bolsheviks, Syrtsov, head of Records and Assignments, and Bubnov in charge of Propaganda and Agitation, combine strength with Kaganovich and Voroshilov to form Stalin's first general staff helping him to mold his personal control over the Party apparat. They are not duped; these comrades know how the wolf bares his teeth.

Kliment Efremovich Voroshilov (1881-1969) also plays a major role under Trotsky's Red cavalry close to Stalin coordinating the defense of Tsaritsyn (later renamed Stalingrad, then again as Volgograd, "the Heroic City"). In Stalin's camp he emerges out of the party turmoil as People's Commissar of War in 1925 where he stays obediently loyal carrying out the absolute dictator's purge of the Red Army officer corps in 1937.

In 1923 Lenin sits incapacitated and dying under Stalin's control. His devote wife and firebrand revolutionary Nadezhda Krupskaya is censored and threatened not to cause any trouble. Stalin exploits the new "elections" to Party apparatus increasing his influence in a major reshuffle of provincial and regional committees in the Party's Central Committee.

Trotsky still possesses enormous power as the popular hero of the Civil War. But Trotsky is too vain to play the beguiling actor and instead too proudly tends to show his cards to comrade Stalin who deceptively changes circumstances to his own advantage. Trotsky keeps three posts: commander of the Red Army, chairman of the Revolutionary War Council, and People's Commissar for War. But when he's removed as chairman of the Revolutionary War Council, in January 1925 Trotsky is a doomed man and personally denounced by the Party leaders.

The previous year Mikhail Afanasyevich Bulgakov (1891-40), Russia's great satirist who despite official harassment is given time to live, – yes! Stalin the Great Defender of the Party, Hero of the Revolution, Master of the Sun, Moon and the Universe, – but of course only illiterate idiots believed it so) – gave him more life, twelve years writing his best work of which one is considered among the world's greatest novels, *The Master and Margarita,* and still perplexed, piquantly alive, he reads *Pravda* about Trotsky's "illness". Mikhail Bulgakov – (reader I must tell you how every day during those spirited years of the "Orange Revolution" thinking one day this book might see the light from the steps of Bulgakov's house on Andrievsky Spusk /"Witch Hill", a minute from the Historical Museum. Yes! reader go find his books, and read on the benches under the towering walls of the Historical Museum above the hill there as musicians play while lovers embrace ...) – notes the event in his diary confiscated by secret police: "On 8 January 1924 Trotsky was given the push. God alone knows what will happen to Russia. May He come to her aid!" Under constant watch by the secret police, his confiscated diaries and manuscripts are returned years later only after his protest reach Maxim Gorky. Poor but courageous he would not be disappointed and though he dies in 1940 it takes another generation before his work is published, – yes he hid it well! – and KGB chief Yuri Andropov denounces him in 1978 "a dangerous weapon in the hands of (Western) ideological centers engaged in ideological sabotage against the Soviet Union". So even if these monstrous idiots denounce it with such fattening vigor it must be something not to miss! During the years of chaos and Party disputes, Stalin is said to have absolutely nothing to do with all the troubles blamed on the dirty swine around him. Andropov becomes Premier in 1982 but dies within the year; yet Russia still must wait several years before Gorbachev makes his causal rounds unescorted in Moscow and Leningrad shaking the country out of its brutally dulled and schizophrenic paralysis. (C. Andrew and V. Mitrokhi, 11)

By September 1921, ARA kitchens in Petrograd and Moscow are feeding tens of thousands of children and moved operations into small towns and rural villages rural sometimes encountering opposition from local village leaders and Communist Party officials. Most rural local committees consisted of a teacher and two or three members who would serve the food to the children from the local schools. This fed the children, paid and fed the teacher, and continued some measure of education. In addition to feeding programs, the ARA employed thousands of starving and unemployed Russians to unload, transport, and distribute food to the most famine-stricken areas. ARA also furnished medical supplies for hospitals, provided treatments to tens of thousands of people, conducted health and sanitation inspections while providing eight million vaccinations between 1921 and 1923.

Lenin's doubts over American eagerness to help fight famine could scarcely conceal Hoover's race to seize Russia's riches for himself and his friends in the ARA, Washington, and elsewhere. On September 1, 1921 Lenin even sent Molotov to the Politburo for a vote on Hoover's request to act as the Soviet's purchasing agent of grain in the Balkans. Lenin was not going be outfoxed by an American capitalist there in Russia to do business. Hadn't the Americans helped install him in the Kremlin? Rockefeller was not yet a common name in the Soviet Union communist party hierarchy but soon that would change too. Does Hoover really care about saving Russian children from starvation? This is the man who had helped keep the Germans fed during the First World War and prolong the carnage until Wilson entered the foray and sacrificed more than a hundred thousand US soldiers. (Remember this was all part of the American war plan from the beginning of hostilities in 1914.) Why should Hoover care about Russian women and their children? In Politburo meetings, with Lenin absent, Stalin denounced the ARA remittance program officials who ship and transport the ARA food relief packages from ports to ARA warehouses for dispersal.

Lenin wrote the Politburo on October 18 that the ARA mission was a trade program, not charity, and liable for transport costs. The next day, Lenin argued, "If need is the goal – trade, then we ought to gain that experience, for they are giving us real assistance for the starving and the right of control, and the right of refusal in three months. Therefore, it does not follow that we should take payment for the food and clothing. Establish such control, with the approval of the Politburo, that will combine the hope and capability of supervision over everything."

Two days earlier Lenin writes Chicherin, "Hoover is really a 'plus'." A few days later Lenin will sent him another message: "Agreements and concessions with the Americans are super-important to us: with Hoover we have something worthwhile." Hoover's ARA mission strengthens Bolshevik authority enhancing its prestige with the confidence and gratitude of the masses. Lenin is convinced that US Congressional approval of the Hoover's mission will lead the capitalists to strengthen his seat of power and his plans for NEP for a partial free-enterprise system and marginal respect for private property rights to jump start the national economy.

Only four years after the Russian Revolution, on December 23 at the Ninth All-Russian Congress of Soviets, Lenin takes credit for the sudden increase in activity supporting famine relief. He tells Party delegates that with the ARA mission "we have achieved a very considerable success in our struggle against the famine". Unfortunately for the Ukraine of the thirties and with the communist regime tottering on the verge of bankruptcy Stalinist methods of law and order had evolved into the most systematic and ruthless modern dictatorship ever known to man and the extermination of a nationally resistant indigenous population in a region vital to the interests of the USSR. (B. Weissman, 122)

Reports from Soviet and foreign relief commissions during the fall and winter of 1921 report millions dead and starving; the official Soviet relief agency, the Central Commission for Aid to the Starving, (*Pomgol*) reported "seventeen provinces with an estimated population of over twenty-five million people, were closely affected by the famine in the fall of 1921." In his book *Herbert Hoover and Famine Relief to Soviet Russia: 1921-1923* (1974), Weissman observes that the actual number of starving victims "ranged from 55 percent of the population in Perm to 90 percent in Samara. In five provinces of the Ukrainian Republic, 12 percent of the entire population of ten million faced death by starvation in

December 1921. This figure rose to 48 percent by April 1922. Nevertheless by August 1922 over 1,100 carloads of food were shipped from the Ukraine to the eastern provinces of Russia; the contribution of the famine-stricken provinces was 74 carloads." (B. Weissman, *Hoover and Famine Relief to Soviet Russia: 1921-1923*)

Winter was rapidly approaching and despite worsening famine conditions and two million more children added to the relief rolls Soviet chairman of the All-Russian Famine Relief Committee Commissar Kamenev in September 1922 told the ARA to leave Russia. Famine is predicted for the next year. Dire reports on famine conditions in the Volga and the Ukraine reach the State Department; in December Hoover agreed to expand relief for three million children. American grain was shipped to Russia even as the Bolshevik authorities with their Cheka secret police deprived critical regions in the Ukraine and elsewhere of its own harvest. By late spring increased tonnage of ARA shipments are shadowed by larger exports of Russian grain. Commissar Kamenev's wife Olga heads a reorganized Soviet relief commission; by May 1923 she reports in the last five months four hundred thousand tons of Soviet farm products had already been shipped abroad in return for urgently needed foreign exchange. She calls it "absolutely unthinkable" to stop wheat exports and deprive the Bolsheviks from building Soviet Russia's Marxist-Leninist economy even though grain was confiscated from famine-stricken provinces. Stalin will use the same logic ten years later during the Holodomor. Meanwhile Kamenev argues that Hoover's ARA refuses to buy Soviet grain and attacks Hoover as politically motivated operating under special and non-humanitarian interests but is powerless to disclose them. (B. Weissman, 144)

At the time the Consortium staged a black-out on the pro-Soviet recognition lobby. By voting $100 million in relief aid the US Congress recognized the Soviets as the legitimate political authority in Russia. "The pro-recognition movement," Weissman writes, "gained few recruits among former members of the ARA. Of the veterans of the mission to Russia who were interviewed or polled forty-five years later (an admittedly small sample), none reported having been influenced by his experiences in Russia to change his mind about recognition; only one respondent stated that he had favored recognition in 1923. An impressive number of former ARA aides obtained executive positions in the organizations that favored recognition as little as Hoover did. The list includes the US State Department, the Department of Commerce, the US Chamber of Commerce, Standard Oil Company, Wilson and Company, the magazine *Foreign Affairs*, the Hoover War Library... Several former members of the ARA Division joined companies or groups that were directly interested in trade with Russia." Haskell asks to be discharged from the US Army to join the American-Russian Chamber of Commerce (ARCC). Its refused by Hoover who tells him to keep quiet and stay out of politics too far over his head.

William Haskell officially shuts down the ARA mission July 20, 1923 as its staff vacates their Moscow headquarters. ARA director for Europe Walter Lyman Brown snags a job as chief engineer of a Russian mining group in a botched grab for concessions. Meanwhile Republican President Harding keeps recognition of the Bols off his public agenda. Only a decade before Gorky's return to a Russia in the eye of death's grip of the Holodomor, Col. Haskell writes, on August 27, 1923, – and this in his final intelligence report of the ARA mission, – "Communism is dead and abandoned and Russia is on the road to recovery." It is an odd statement in absurd extreme conditions to further plunge the historical record into darkness.

By August 1923 Goodrich breaks with Hoover over the administrations non-recognition policy towards Russia. Unaware of the Rockefeller-Morgan-Harriman drive for monopoly control Goodrich insists on the need for "some sort of relations" between the US government and the Bols in the Kremlin. Goodrich is kept out of Hoover's closed circle of powerful friends in the Consortium. Radek ridicules Hoover's alleged "humanitarian" motives. Author Harold Fisher quotes Radek in his book *Famine in Russia*: "The Republican American administration has not yet decided to conclude a trade agreement with Russia, but one thing it knows; namely, 'if America wants at some time in the future to trade with Russia, she must now come to the aid of the starving'. (H. Fisher, *Famine in Russia,* 64; A. I. Solzhenitsyn, *The Gulag Archipelago, 1918-1956*, 241; B. Weissman, 181)

Hoover may be known to readers for his work directing Belgium Relief (CRB) during the First World War. Having earned a reputation as a methodical and tough businessman Senator Henry Cabot Lodge once objected to his unilateral manner in conducting negotiations with France and England, but then quietly acquiesced when told that Hoover's group included Robert Bacon, Morgan's man in Paris, and ambassador Page in London. CRB operations unilaterally seized ships and subsidies from the Allies worth some $300 million. The CRB fleet also manages to sail unmolested past U-boats of the German fleet. Hoover's CRB operations were managed by a small staff of sixty loyal subordinates without normal accounting records to indicate what happened to close to a billion dollars during four years of the war. Other directors included Lewis L. Strauss and Robert Alphonso Taft, Bones 1910, son of the former President, and keystone of Republican power politics. America did not know that Hoover was in fact feeding the hard-pressed German armed forces thereby prolonging the war long enough for the Americans to enter the fray once properly prepared and ready to join the table of victors at the Versailles peace talks for postwar reconstruction.

As the US Secretary of Commerce, and famous for ostensibly feeding the hapless Belgiums during his relief war work on a Dollar-a-Year salary, Herbert Hoover made a ton of cash for himself while actually feeding the Germans to keep them in the war long enough for the Americans to get into the Game. What a farce! And the flag-waving American patriots, proud purchasers of Liberty Bonds bought it hook, line and sinker within the carefully editorialized terms of reference. They had to. The war gang owned the press. Antiwar protesters are imprisoned under sedition acts. Ten years later President Hoover will occupy the White House surrounded by the same Wall Street banking gang during the early years of Stalin's Terror-Famine in the Ukraine.

The initiative came from the Consortium war planners and it was only due to their continuous relations with the American Relief Committee that the provisioning question was solved." In his book, *The Strange Career of Mr. Hoover* (1931) John Hamill declared, "That is what the Belgian Relief Committee was organized for–to keep Germany in food." Hoover was a businessman invested in Congo Copper and the Kaiping Coal Mines mixed up with Belgium royals and quite the contrary patriotic figure than popularized in establishment history textbooks. Wherever they could be found copies of John Hamill's book were systematically acquired and destroyed by government agents on the eve of President Hoover's re-election campaign. (John Hamill, *The Strange Career of Mr. Hoover*)

Hoover was a real psycho operator in business and government. Eight years as Secretary of Commerce, partners in crime with Mellon and the gang, Hoover literally stole the White House from the American people. And he wondered why he wasn't loved by the people who gladly kicked him out of the White House in 1932 not long after Mellon was forced by pressure to flee with his billions Mellon out the back gates before a public lynching in Congress. And that the Consortium might not withstand. Behind closed doors and in smoke-filled clubs for gentlemen there was serious talk about martial law and bringing out the troops to maintain law and order if the passive masses took to the streets in protest.

President Wilson's own Secretary of the Navy Joseph Daniels and FDR's boss (he needed a job, any job! in the Consortium's war effort so FDR served as Assistant Secretary of the Navy) observed the style how Hoover approached food distribution "as coldly as if he were giving statistics of production". Daniels adds, "From his words and manners he seemed to regard human beings as so many numbers." A few years after the Holodomor of the thirties, Hoover returned to his expertise in food distribution, saying "Famine fighting is a gigantic economic and governmental operation handled by experts and not 'welfare' work of benevolently handing out food hit or miss to bread lines… Some individual with great powers must direct and coordinate all this. Such an operation would be hopeless in the hands of international commissions or committees". This unmitigated self-serving American Czar of famine relief is President of the United States sitting majestically behind his great desk in the White House exactly when Stalin consolidates his power in 1928 and during the early thirties ruling over the Soviet Party writing notes and orders to exterminate the Ukrainians. To be sure these men together share a common fate imbued with a certain mutual cynicism and devious contempt for mankind. Thought little is known on the role Hoover played in 1900 directing food-relief for victims of the Boxer Rebellion in China we may expect that to change soon. (B. Weissman, 25)

When I began to study the Holodomor 1932-33 it seemed odd that the incumbent Hoover Presidency (1928-32) had not taken any steps to help the Soviet leaders address the grain problem. Only after a critical inquiry behind the back of history do we see the reasons. The First World War was a general debacle of terrific proportions. It befell Europe and all the world with the vengeance of a curse. Sickness and disease was even more extraordinary than four years of total war. The 1918 Spanish influenza is thought to have infected a *billion* people worldwide; estimates on those killed range from 20 to 100 million.

William Taubman, author of *Khrushchev* (2003) is an establishment American historian from Amherst College. Writing of the fatalities confronting Hoover in Bolshevik Russia, Taubman alludes to a few of Hoover's shadowy activities. "In the countryside as a whole," Taubman observes, "deaths from famine in 1921 and 1922 exceeded the combined total of casualties in the world war and civil war." Figure that! Wilson's Democrats have little to offer the Russian peasants. As head of the American Relief Administration (A.R.A.) Hoover sent 700,000 tons of food and supplies worth $60 million into Russia which Trotsky's Red Army in turn diverted to restore fronts against counter-revolution intensified by the famine. Much of the American food aid went to feed armies of the White Russians to persuade them to retreat. Women and children were abandoned unfed. Taubman's findings should be taken seriously although three generations removed. In time with good scholarship and research exponentially accelerated by the Internet more revealing details will paint a more accurate picture of what really happened. Yet we can be grateful for another good lesson in Yankee-Soviet pragmatism that shows how quickly they resolved the Russian situation, shortened the civil war, restored stability by violent and sustained repression and got the business of Lenin's NEP program for reconstruction on track in the interests of Consortium-communist collaboration. (W. Taubman, *Khrushchev*, 2003)

Was this communism or even socialism as espoused in the Marxist-Leninist tracts exalting the "dictatorship of the proletariat"? Many members of the Communist Party members thought not they saw NEP grounds for the betrayal of communist principles. Opening his office to Consortium emissaries seeking concessions Lenin himself saw NEP not as a departure from socialism, but as a temporary expedient; he called it "state capitalism" and claimed it was "the ante-chamber of socialism." Soviet Russia needed a breathing space to recover from the devastation and chaos of war and revolution. Lenin knew he needed the capitalists now more than ever.

The NEP policy was implemented in March 1921, primarily because massive peasant revolts all over Russia threatened Bolshevik power. The peasants were revolting against war communism, i.e. the forcible requisitioning of their produce to feed the army and the cities. War communism was carried out with particular ruthlessness in Tambov province; in the spring of 1918 Lenin had begun to implement it. The NEP policy directly aimed at fusing national cultures with communism, but it actually produced a vigorous development of these cultures, especially in Soviet Ukraine. In Moscow, this raised fears of Ukrainian nationalism and separatism; therefore, extensive purges of literary organizations took place in Ukraine in 1927. These purges were replicated in Belorussia and other non-Russian republics.

Without intending to do it writer Antony Sutton helps blow away the myth of altruism behind Hoover's critical Soviet food relief program. "The primary source of foreign exchange during the 1920s," Sutton wrote, "was export of raw materials – especially petroleum products, furs, minerals, and foodstuffs." He adds, "Export of food to regain prewar markets was implemented even while American relief was importing supplies into Russia for the famine areas." Sutton had very good reason to suggest we take another look at Hoover's ARA mission and examine the implications. He wrote, "In one case, the Soviets were loading a boat with Ukrainian wheat for export to Germany, while alongside was a boat from the United States unloading American wheat for the famine areas to the north of the Ukraine."

The American-Russian Chamber of Commerce (ARCC) was created during this time. American businessmen and manufacturers and financiers saw in the famine an opportunity to use it as "a major factor in the pressure for recognition of the Soviet Union and resumption of full trade with credits". ARCC sent a letter on February 27, 1922 to its friends at the US State Department pushing for a statement "announcing under what conditions you would be glad to cooperate with all nations in relation to the economic development of Russia". This during Hoover's ARA mission emphasizing the need to off-set German economic and political autonomy of the Kremlin. In fact, as German credits dried up in the mid-twenties the Department eased up on its ban against credits to the Kremlin. Reeve Schley, vice president of Rockefeller-Morgan's Chase National Bank was at the forefront of financing US-Soviet trade wanted a more favorable and aggressive policy than oozed out of the fortress-mentality of State of hands-off and long-arm distancing from formulating any clear policy towards the Soviets. A proponent of ARCC he became its president in 1929 during the implementation of the Consortium's Five-Year Plans with Stalin. That nebulous stance of the twenties of neither supporting nor intervening in business relations would later prove catastrophic by State's non-interposition in the Holodomor thirties. Sutton succinctly sums it up, writing, "The individual or firm was entirely on its own, and could expect no diplomatic or consular help in the event of trouble with the Soviet government." Yet we see how Henderson states that the consular services did what they could when they wanted to help American businessmen navigate the hazardous Soviet waters.

The ARCC, in fact, keeps very close tabs on its member activities in Russia. In late 1928, for instance, it polled its members to know if Russia means good business. Half the members responded favorably. The ARCC reports "that credits have been extended and that all obligations were carried out meticulously", at least for the majority of its responding members. The Bausch & Lomb company, for example, is satisfied with "prompt" payments from Amtorg; Black & Decker report the company remains "very optimistic about the possibilities of securing business" and declares its readiness to keep a permanent rep there. (K. Siegel, *Loans and Legitimacy*, 105)

Disillusioned and sickened by famine and terror, Russia's most famous living writer and Lenin's close friend Maxim Gorky suffers from tuberculosis and leaves his cherished homeland to live comfortably in exile seven years in an Italian villa in Sorrento. In 1932 Bertolt Brecht stages his epic play on Russia's first classic of social realism *The Mother* (*Мать* / *Mat'*). Without fame or money in fascist Italy each summer Maxim Gorky leaves his serene Mediterranean retreat to make triumphant visits to the USSR with no limit on the pomp and propaganda by Stalin and his surrogate communist slogan scribblers. The Kremlin treats its prize icon with state honors including the Order of Lenin, a house in Moscow formerly belonging to the millionaire Ryabushinsky, (now the Gorky Museum), a *dasha* in the suburbs, servants and cash from Yagoda, head of the GPU. Yagoda must persuade Gorky to remain permanently in the Soviet Union.

Gorky, growing weak, old and feeble, too, falls prey to seduction by the Soviet charade and his role in it that turned the "reeducation" of the peasants and workers into a country of slave labor. Its everything that Tolstoy abhorred.

When Gorky pays tribute to ten years of Soviet Party rule, many of his readers become his most fierce critics. "It is of course, fine to praise things that you have not yourself experienced," decries a Gorky reader from Moscow. "You live far away. In good time, you declined the pleasure of becoming a blind and mute object of an experiment that was conducted against your wish and that of almost all the population of your country… All are therefore amazed by your article – for 10 years he was silent and suddenly he begins to sing the praises… of something which even its creators are beginning to regard differently, and which has clearly led to a dead end. You chose a bad moment to speak out but, incidentally, writers always were bad politicians."

Another concerned Soviet citizen writes Gorky at the time of his impending return in March 1928 to receive official state honors for his 60th birthday presented by the Great Stalin himself and the entire Soviet Party nomenclature! "You will see for yourself what the USSR is like at the present moment. Don't go, like a VIP, for this purpose to the Volkhov hydro-electric dam or to the rebuilt factories and plants, as foreign delegations do. They only see the external, calm side of our culture, only observing what they are shown. … Do the opposite. Forget that you are a well-known writer. Do not travel anywhere with official guides, as if you were under arrest, but … go wherever your heart leads, as the nation's observer, as you did in your youth. … Without a doubt, you will soon see new divisions in the nation and among them new tendencies, new movements in thought. These new developments…penetrate everywhere under the tireless administrative influence of the authorities and as a consequence of a material dependence of the masses on the central authorities that is unheard-of and unprecedented in capitalist states. At the head of this movement are a small handful of people, Lenin's associates…"

In June 1929, Gorky visits Solovki and writes a favorable article about this most dreaded prison death camps, which had already gained ill fame in the West. During the worst times of the Holodomor in 1933, Gorky edits an infamous book about the White Sea Canal, presented as an example of "successful rehabilitation of the former enemies of proletariat". Gorky's return to the Soviet Union is motivated in part by material needs. In Sorrento, Gorky finds himself without money or fame. He visits the USSR several times after 1929; on October 11, 1931 Gorky read his fairy tale "A Girl and Death" to his fellow comrades in an audience including Joseph Stalin, Kliment Voroshilov and Vyacheslav Molotov and an event that was later depicted in a painting by Viktor Govorov. On that same day Stalin leaves his autograph on the last page of this work by Gorky: "Эта штука сильнее чем "Фауст" Гёте (любовь побеждает смерть" / "This piece is stronger than Goethe's *Faust* (love defeats death)".

And in the next year 1932 Stalin personally invites Gorky to return to the USSR for good. Gorky accepts.

It is not difficult to understand. You only have to open your eyes to see that there was no other living writer in Russia with his prestige and reputation. Even Stalin was envious as ever he could be jealous of anyone with all his power. Especially writers! This is the same man who frequently played chess with Lenin while living in exile before the Revolution, who was thrown out of a hotel during a tour in America because he dared to live with a woman who was not his wife. Gorky's articles in the Soviet press provoked a wave of bewilderment. Another letter attacked him for "an extraordinary degree of flippancy against the very same people, against those remaining representatives of the Russian intelligentsia who have not yet been finished off by the Soviet regime. In doing so you conceal behind your great name the outrageous falsehood of contemporary Russian life. From your fine distance, enjoying complete freedom and independence (if under the protection of the fascist government and blessed sky of Italy), inhabiting a superb villa with no limits on your living space, you repeat, after the official lying press of Soviet Russia, what those who have lived through the last 10 years of Soviet Russia, know to be falsehoods – untruths that cannot be justified by any, even the highest, goals and ideals ... Yes, you are a free writer and in your letters to the Soviet press, using that monopoly, you can say whatever you wish in defense of the Soviet authorities, you can harass us without any fear of reprisal. You cannot hear anything from us in reply; our hands our bound and the Soviet gag is forced into our mouths. But knowing this, do you suppose that you are acting as a champion of the free word?"

More letters arrived at his villa in Italy from people confused and angry by Gorky's betrayal of freedom in Russia. A peasant wrote, "We peasants, living far from the centre of Mother Russia...hope that your visit will correct our blunders and mistakes of our rulers, since there are great many of them somehow...We have so many rulers locally – our petty bosses, like the rural soviets – and they just behave like royalty, almost never carrying out the laws we have and, in particular, the Land Code...And if someone is a communist, ie, a Party member, then you cannot get anywhere near him and his word is law...They are not afraid of the law but of each other...". (Vitaly Shentalinsky, *Arrested Voices*, Martin Kessler Books, The Free Press, 1993, 247)

That Gorky returned in the critical year of the Holodomor 1933 to stay in his beloved Russia has to be a tell-tale of the utter pathos that had befallen the Soviet Union and its vassal state of the Ukraine under Stalin and the Consortium. It was an incredible coup by the communist dictator marking the success of his international propaganda campaign. Duped as Stalin stooge, Gorky walked hand in hand with the terror. Wherever he stepped in every shadow hid the NKVD agents. First they would kill his son, then Gorky himself will be poisoned in 1936. Poor Maxim! How pathetic when the revolution devoured its favorite son. In only twenty years he had fallen so low and lost the brilliance of his youth while Stalin evolved into robust and shimmering middle-age. Solzhenitsyn has no kind words for Gorky calling him Stalin's "slobbering prattler" and "apologist for executioners".

Four years after the Hoover ARA mission withdrew from Russia, Harold Fisher wrote the first ARA history titled *The Famine in Soviet Russia, 1919-1923*: "On ruined towns and desolate villages across the bleak, dreary steppes had fallen the heavy pall of black misery. Into this atmosphere of fatalistic hopelessness came the representatives of that distant and incredible land – America." But in 1931, the American aid would not come. After Wilson's armed intervention and hyped undeclared war on the Bolsheviks, the great publicity and controversy over the relief mission and America's role with the revolutionary leaders of the former Czarist regime did not lead to official recognition. The following year President Woodrow Wilson and Lenin died.

Americans were there supervising the construction of factories, dams and huge industrial projects and transferring invaluable state-of-the-art western technology to vital Soviet centers throughout the Ukraine, in Crimea along the Black Sea around Moscow, Leningrad and to the outer regions of the Urals. American companies sent engineers not food. Not this time. The world was different now. The disease and famine caused by the consequences of the First World War killed millions. It was said that Hoover was the Great Humanitarian who fed the world. Just over four years after the ARA officially ended Stalin is entrenched in power. By 1928 Lenin's NEP evolved into two Five-year economic plans promising a bright new future for the Russian people. Hoover is elected the 31st President of the United States but his administration is rocked by scandals involving the all-powerful Treasury Secretary Andrew Mellon, the plunge of stock market and an economy tumbling into the Great Depression.

Bertrand M. Petenaude lectured on international relations at Stanford and widely considered "an expert on modern Russia and European history" according to The Hoover Institution website which described Bolshevik and Soviet attitude towards the ARA and Hoover. When the US Congress was debating the Russian aid bill to grant a $20 million shipment of corn and grain, Stalin declares "It must not be forgotten that the trading and all other sorts of missions and associations that are now pouring into Russia, trading with her and aiding her, are at the same time most efficient spy agencies of the world bourgeoisie, and that, therefore, the world bourgeoisie now knows Soviet Russia, knows her weak and strong sides, better than at any time before, a circumstance fraught with grave danger in the event of new interventionist actions." Patenaude's book *The Big Show in Bololand* (2002) keeps within safe Consortium limits and within establishment parameters for the politically correct historical interpretation. Follow the money; readers should always be aware of the funding behind Patenaude's research and writing funded by the Hoover Institution, Title VIII grant, National Fellows Program. The Kennan Institute for Advanced Russian Studies supported research in Washington and he received a Herbert Hoover Presidential Library Travel grant. No problem risk there! (B. Patenaude, *The Big Show in Bololand*, 738; B. Weissman, 125-6)

Bertrand Petenaude pays respect to Conquest's findings while undermining the severity and cause of the Holodomor. "The devastating famine of 1921,"

Petenaude writes, "was indeed the largest in modern Russian history – that is, up to that time. Its significance has been obscured by the similarly deadly but politically more notorious famine of 1932-33, centered in Ukraine."

Eye-witness accounts filed in State Department dispatches indicated that the Holodomor was even more deadly than earlier famines. He writes, "Robert Conquest has called that calamity the 'Terror-Famine' because of its man-made character, though the extent of Stalin's culpability and whether the crime deserves to be called 'Genocide' are subjects of learned and emotional debate." This is quite an extraordinary statement in view of recent ground-breaking events in the Ukraine, in particular, that country's official recognition of the Holodomor placing it on a scale with the Jewish Holocaust. It would have been more clear perhaps if Petenaude had reviewed official Soviet commentary about the famine in the thirties from Stalin himself on record to the current Russian leadership under Putin which prefers ignorance over awareness, denial instead of transparency. Russian Soviet archives remain sealed.

The next statement by Petenaude is equally remarkable for what it reveals less than it omits. "The 1921 famine," he writes, "does not carry this political baggage, though it, too, was no simple act of nature." This is understatement on the edge of hyperbole. The American program of food and relief assistance transpired from 1920 to 1923. The ARA arrangement was officially signed August 20, 1921. The issue of Ukrainian sovereignty delayed sending food to famine-stricken regions in the Ukraine. At the time an American allied expeditionary force invaded the Ukraine and Russia; Germany continued to occupy regions torn by civil war, disease and chaos. Petenaude then inserts a statement hard to fathom when he writes, "Events would demonstrate the importance to hundreds of thousands of Ukrainians, among others, of the ARA's determination to keep its options open." Was Hoover's ARA campaign a sequel to Wilson's intervention? White Russians always claimed that the American forces actually helped Trotsky's Red Army and Lenin stay in power. (B. M. Petenaude, *The Big Show in Bololand,* 26-45. It is remarkable that Petenaude makes no reference to the published findings of Holodomor historian James Mace.)

Besieged and with bedlam reaping havoc everywhere Petenaude writes, "Only by early summer did the government at least seem to recognize the enormity of the problem and begin to act, though it took longer still to arrive at the decision to request outside assistance". He adds, "Having to seek food relief from abroad would have been embarrassing enough for any great power in eclipse, but for the pariah government in the Kremlin the prospect was supremely humiliating." Hello? Unlikely.

The Bolsheviks were arch strategists beyond the pangs of humiliation, expert dialecticians with mental reasoning that frayed the wits of Consortium diplomats and bankers making mincemeat of rival brains. Trotsky proved especially annoying during the fragile ARA negotiations. The *Manchester Guardian*, a paper with one of the better reputations, chides Trotsky for "looking a gift-horse in the mouth, complaining of the sharpness of its teeth and suggesting that it has an uncertain temper" when he exploited what Litvinov described as a "lack of confidence on one side and suspicion on the other". The Bols were ruthless. There could be no mistaking that and those who did paid dearly. (B. M. Petenaude, *The Big Show in Bololand,* 27-43)

Again, Petenaude indulged in the diversion so conspicuous of the establishment historic account declaring that the negotiations setting up the ARA in Bolshevik Russia nearly collapsed over Soviet calls for jurisdiction over the American aid workers, restricted territories and other complications arising between opposing sides of capitalists and communists. In what would seem like a *deja vue* a decade later when FDR replaced Hoover in the White House, the Soviets made a gesture of reconciliation when Lenin sent a message through Kalinin to President Harding and Congress to reconsider recognition of Lenin's government in Moscow. London and Moscow agreed on March 16 to open trade between the two countries, a traditional prerequisite to official diplomatic recognition. Germany, Austria, Norway and Italy did the same before the end of the year.

Hoover and his Secretary of State Charles Hughes resist having relations entangled over outstanding debts, Czarist claims stemming from nationalization of property, and the spreading of revolutionary Bolshevik propaganda to the workers of the world calling for the overthrow of imperial capitalist governments. This is the time in 1922 when journalist George Seldes and other Americans interview Lenin; on his return to America Seldes is told by Hughes that the US government would not obstruct investment in Lenin's regime while diplomatic recognition would be immoral and not in the cards. (B. M. Petenaude, *The Big Show in Bololand,* 43; George Seldes, *Witness to the Century,* NY: Random House, 1998)

Nous sommes perdus ("We are lost"), a driver in Odessa on March 1, 1922 tells Commanding Officer Webb Trammel of the destroyer *USS Fox* docked in Odessa and there to assist American supply ships arriving in the Black Sea. Hoover's ARA men were withdrawn in two waves, the last ships leaving in 1923. Americans bid farewells with "shower of rain and tears", Russian kisses and bear hugs under "a moonlit night". Love was in their hearts and food in their stomachs. They had survived when millions died. The food relief work throughout the Volga, the Ukraine and Russian territories had ended the years of death and destruction of the Great War, Revolution, Civil War and Famine. Tens of millions of Ukrainians and Russians were dead. Many of those who survived would soon be killed by the famine and extermination by Stalin and his communist cronies with Hoover and FDR on watch. At that time in 1922 and 1923, the popularity in Bolshevik Russia was at its summit, at least for the survivors, relief workers, families and friends. There were banquets and resolutions of the Council of People's Commissars, toasts to Col. Haskell and the departing Americans of the ARA. "Those three letters will not be forgotten", said a resident of Kiev. They pronounced it "A-RA", one word in two syllables. The *New York Evening World* wrote the "ARA" had been absorbed into the Russian lexicon and 'will survive for centuries". The Soviets as impatient as the many of the big American Consortium firms to enter into lucrative trade deals.

Lavish dinners and abundant praise for the ARA! "Due to the enormous and entirely disinterested efforts of the ARA, millions of people of all ages were saved from death and entire districts and even cities were saved from the horrible catastrophe which threatened them." It was said that the Soviets would never forget "the help given them by the American people, through the ARA, seeing in its pledge for the future friendship of the two nations". By this time Lenin is severely ill, sequestered in isolation by Stalin's agents, and in seven months dead.

Neither Stalin nor Trotsky show up at the farewell dinner June 23 at the Pink House for Haskell and his senior staff. Kamenev takes his place alongside Litvinov, Radek, Dzerzhinsky, Health Commissar Semashko and John Finley, *The New York Times* financial editor.. Haskell plays toastmaster, and carefully steered talk away normal relations. Away from Moscow Trotsky sent a message praising the "energetic and unselfish" contribution of the Americans. Foreign Affairs commissar Chicherin calls the ARA "the work of broad masses of the American people who at a most difficult moment have come to the assistance of the Russian people and have thus laid a firm foundation for the future unalterable relations of friendship and mutual understanding between them". A diplomat of the old school says America has at last come to Russia and to take "possession of a gigantic virgin continent and turned it into a miracle of most perfect technique of production and culture".

Grigorii Sokolnikov, Bolshevik finance commissar, praises ARA efficiency and American work methods calling it "a great lesson to all Russians who have come into contact with them". He says he hopes that "all Russians would take this lesson to heart and become as efficient as Americans after the true American fashion". Russia is not finished, he argues, far from it, perhaps indeed "poverty-stricken" but possesses "enormous wealth".

"The plan of the Soviet Government is to develop this wealth as efficiently as America has developed hers," Sokolnikov pleads, and in an extraordinary gesture he raises his glass high over the heads of his fellow Americans to his friend Dzerhinskii, with words of praise normally reserved for Lenin, Trotsky or Stalin, or Hoover. Haskell returns the jest with more laurels for the agent of Soviet Red terror citing his "worldwide reputation for efficiency, "one of the most practical and efficient men in the Government, who always accomplishes what he starts out to do and always keeps his promise." Dzerhinskii, sighting the soft spot in the American soldier, returns the compliment, portraying Haskell as "a soldier of peace as well as a "Knight of the Order of the Heart".

Next its the turn of the intellectual Polish Jew Radek, never short of words, who once taunted Westerners "only famine victims die of famine", and makes no secret that he had little in common with the Russian *muzhiki* and prefers to be in Germany agitating for communist revolution. Radek make jokes about Jews (he is one) and Russian Christians. He assures Haskell that Jews in Russia will not swindle the ARA. Radek tells his audience that he regrets never having been in America but remains an ardent reader of the American press "for a number of years" and considers "Europeans in general judged Americans very wrongly. In Europe the impression is that Americans are dry business materialists, but he was convinced, mainly through the work of the ARA, that Americans had been badly misjudged and have shown a rare combination of fine business efficiency and moral idealism of the highest order". Radek confesses he has read Hoover's book, *American Individualism*; he condescends to flatter and send the message that Hoover's own personal individualism had become "a model which every Russian desires to achieve".

Radek praises the 300 Americans of the ARA. "On the streets of Moscow," Radek declares, "one sees two kinds of Russian: the first type which slouches along in a dull, stupid manner, dressed in dirty boots, and wearing usually an oriental cap. The other type are men who walk smartly and energetically through the streets going straight about their business. The second type is now generally called 'the American type' and we look to these 'American Russians' for the future of Russia." During the Holodomor Radek towed the Stalinist line until he too perished in the purges. (B. M. Petenaude, *The Big Show in Bololand,* 707-26; See *ARA, Facts on Communism: The Soviet Union from Lenin to Khrushchev*, Committee on Un-American Activities, House of Representatives, 86th Congress, Second Session, 133-4)

Hoover is less keen about the Bols. In a conversation in Washington with Consortium State Department's Dewitt Clinton Poole, Hoover admits he "had never been so glad to finish a job as this Russian job; that he was completely disgusted with the Bolsheviks and did not believe that a practical government could ever be worked out under their leadership". It's a view diametrically opposed to the position of Secretary of State Hughes communicated on the telephone to journalist George Seldes recently returned from Russia and his meeting with Lenin.

But when Haskell meets with Lenin late 1922, Hoover has already described the Russian situation as "the most overshadowing tragedy of ten centuries in the heart-breaking life-and-death struggle with starvation by a nation with a hundred and fifty millions of people." And Hoover made it a point to slam the communist rulers, and he declares, "In Russia under the new tyranny a group, in pursuit of social theories, have destroyed the primary self-interest impulse of the individual to production." Still unwilling to establish normal relations, Hoover and ARA men agree that Lenin appears to have rejected his former radical economic program, the NEP. Russia remains an "economic vacuum" with a long way to before it regresses into the tone of moral depravity and economic collapse experienced under Stalin.

Once the Americans had completed their mission, the Bolsheviks quickly removed traces of that phase of Americanization of Russia. With the American mission gone, a wave of arrests followed as Cheka went to work tightening its grip. Once the ARA were gone the Bolsheviks pulled down signs at the Blandy Memorial Hospital in Ufa was pulled down and at the Blandy Children's Home. The Haskell Highway and the Hoover Hospital in Odessa dropped their American identities. ARA presence was replaced by more terror and a "considerable number" of arrests, according to reporter Walter Duranty.

By the spring of 1924, the Soviets used its attacks on Hoover's ARA to justify further repressions by the GPU; in May *Izvestia* reports the arrests of Ukrainians in Kiev on charges of espionage and improper payments of ARA food. The Soviets accuse Hoover with interfering in the Soviet Union's internal affairs. Duranty later writes the arrests were justified "ARA Spies in the Role of Philanthropists" but offered no proof. Skilled in their uncanny logic and empowered by their secret alliance with the Consortium heirs of empire the Bolshevik leaders know how and when to provoke and profit.

During the First World War Hoover is right in the epicenter of the violence in Europe. For example, the Rockefellers-Morgan banking interests linked to the Schroeder banking house of Baron Schroeder in Hamburg are an indispensable part of the Hoovers' Belgium Relief Commission that prevented peace with Germany in 1916, arranged American food relief to salvage their precious control over Lenin's Bolsheviks and their fragile monopoly during four years of civil war and famine, and bankrolled Hitler's national social fascism. Hoover was able to extend his extraordinary business and organizational skills across the world gripped by war, revolution and a decline in 19th century empires and with alacrity and acumen replace those anachronistic imperial vestiges with combinations of Consortium ingenuity and capital.

On closer examination an inquiry into the political leadership of the United States during the Holodomor of Stalin's man-made Terror-Famine unveils financial and corporate business connections within the American system of centralized banks under the Federal Reserve federal banking structure. Interlocking boards of dozens of strategic corporations reveal the extensive investment by the American political leadership and their friends in bed with Lenin and Stalin. From its inception in 1913, the system centralized Federal Reserve Banks through their shareholders and New York subsidiaries smoothly meshed with the institutions and members of Rothschild family and the Bank of England family of banks in London. A powerful group of American lawyers helped implement their business expansion, men like Charles Hughes, Elihu Root and Henry Stimson, all linked to the America's role in the First World War, the fall of the Great Russian Czarist Empire and Stalin's Holodomor of Soviet state terror and famine.

Its time to start to close the loop of the Consortium's key players within the inner circle with Commerce Secretary Herbert Hoover soon to be President Hoover. Henry Lewis Stimson (1867-50) returned to government as FDR's administration during WWII and with monitored the Manhattan Project's race to build and deploy nuclear weapons. In the early 1920s, the Federal Reserve System played the decisive role in the re-entry of Russia into the postwar finance system. His firm Winthrop and Stimson continued to be a link between Russian and American bankers. As Hoover's Secretary of State he oversaw the US-Soviet relations directly leading to Roosevelt's recognition of the Soviet Union. It was Stimson who first tipped off Litvinov in Geneva during the disarmament talks in 1932 that America was ready to deal openly with Stalin.

Nothing goes through the Consortium government program if it didn't pass by Stimson. That includes the Holodomor. If heads were to roll for crimes against

Humanity, Mr. Henry Lewis Stimson would be first in line. Stimson: Bones 1888. Just prior to the creation of the Fed and WWI, Henry Stimson was President Taft's Secretary of war (1911-13). His close friend William Howard Taft head Bonesman 1878. With his Yalemen Taft taps Stimson bringing the doctor's son into the secret society. We know Stimson serves US Attorney for the Southern District of New York (1906-09) and tried public publics but fails at the polls. During WWIthe former Secretary of War is "promoted" Colonel Stimson with the American Expeditionary Forces assigned to a field artillery unit on the Western Front. He is there during the German spring offensive of 1918 but its unclear if he saw action in the trenches. In 1927, he sails to Nicaragua where he enjoys imperial status under America's benign "Good Neighbor Policy" towards Latin America; later he is given the plumb post of Governor General of the Philippines (1927-29), stoically incarnating Anglo-British commitment to racial superiority over millions of island natives. Later, much to his initial regret, that idyllic paradise goes to FDR's son Theodore Roosevelt, Jr. (1887-44) who like his father leaves New York state politics to become Assistant secretary of the Navy (1921-24) before assuming the post of Governor of Puerto Rico (1922-32), and then Governor General of the Philippines (1932-33); in 1930 Nicolas Roosevelt is appointed Vice Governor of the Philippines; Secretary of State Stimson politely demurs, but strongly disapproves personally.

In 1929, the Consortium dons brought Stimson back into the White House to run Hoover's State Department (1929-33) in this critical period towards Soviet Russia leading up to and endorsing Stalin's consolidation of power. It is also the crucial year Ukrainian famine at the same time State secretly opens the door towards official recognition. During WWII Roosevelt will bring Stimson back into the cabinet as his Secretary of War with Harriman in London handling Lend-Lease war provisions in the Consortium's war with Hitler long before the President declares war on Japan, and subsequently German, much to the stupefaction of *Reichchancellor* Hitler.

But reader, lets check course again. While Hoover was working out the ARA famine relief program to prevent Lenin and Trotsky losing Petrograd and the Consortium from losing the Russian empire into breakaway factions and total chaos, Hoover keeps his hand in Consortium banking arrangements; in 1921 Hoover helps Morgan bankers establish the Soviet State Bank monopoly in Moscow. That same year Lenin announces his New Economic Policy, the NEP in a last ditch effort to save the Revolution with western capital and trade. Stalin will do the same before the end of the decade.

Remember during the Russian civil war Rockefeller's Standard Oil operatives were on the ground making deals with both Whites and Reds. While Armand Hammer is off hunting for his asbestos deal somewhere in the Urals writer Katherine Siegel turns our attention for a brief glance at Mason Day "and his associates at the Barnsdall Corporation…" in their ambitions for grabbing Soviet oil in Georgia in 1921: "The firm, newly christened International Barnsdall, dispatched three men to the Caucasus: Day, trade representative e Frederick G. Menard, and assistant Secretary Eugene F. Connors. In Tiflis, the Soviets presented them with two options: either start a 'mixed corporation' or form a concession.... Barnsdall wanted 'monopoly rights in the region and to export all kinds of raw materials from the Caucasus. The firm thus decided upon a concession that included raw materials ranging from tobacco to coal, but the primary interest of the firm was oil exploitation." (K. Siegel, *Loans and Legitimacy*, 120)

The International Barnsdall Corporation owned by Morgan Guaranty using advanced drilling technology reopens the rich Baku oil fields in the Caucasus, a vital source of foreign exchange without which will retard Lenin's New Economic Policy (NEP) for the reconstruction of Russia under the control of the Soviet Party. *The New York Times* reports in March 1922 that Henry Mason Day, president of Barnsdall is near to closing a deal with Commissar Krassin for the Baku oil since talks advanced in Genoa. While Barnsdall pushed for a deal in Moscow Commissar Krassin meanwhile is bogged down in negotiations in Genoa where he barters off Standard Oil against Royal Dutch Shell over oil rights. The British are furious having been left out of Standard's acquisition of Nobel's nationalized properties in the Caucasus indignant over rash treatment afforded them by Soviet trade rep F. Y. Rabinovitch, President of the Union of Georgia, Azerbaijan and Armenia.

By July it is a done deal. Emboldened by the helping hand of the Hoover-Rockefeller-Morgan capitalists, by late 1922 before the famine subsided Moscow recommenced grain exports the Bols again refine their macro-management style and nationalized privately operated businesses. But when the Bols travel to Genoa, Italy intercedes on an invitation to negotiate trade and loans with Consortium partners and banks,; the Soviet communists frustrate the negotiations, preferring to deal with the Germans and instead and sign the Treaty of Rapallo to renounce all claims of war debts and damages!

Antony Sutton writes, "Rapallo laid the groundwork for economic recovery." In fact, the military agreement of 1922 is the basis of long-denied protocols for German military, economic and technical assistance giving the Kremlin breathing space to consolidate the Revolution and open more doors to capital and technical assistance from the West. Rapallo helps bring the Soviet leaders back from the brink of complete disaster. And at the same time the USSR maintains good relations with Weimar Germany (1919-33). Ha! Whoever said the war was an honest mistake? (A. C. Sutton, *Western Technology and Soviet Economic Development, 1917-1930*, 317)

During the war years Lloyd George rose in rank privy to England's inner council most jealously guarded war secrets of corrupt backdoor armament deals since he took over Lord Kitchner's work in the munitions and armament sector. Throughout the next decade, both Lloyd George and Churchill have full access to intelligence reports of both internal and external affairs of the Soviets and Bolshevik atrocities as well as knowledge of the Consortium players behind the Soviet Five-Year Plans. That the turn-around in Soviet economic fortunes is linked to German technical assistance is also made clear after Rapallo yet foreseeable as early as 1917 when the German bankers played their cards to deal a final blow to the Czarist monarchy with funds to the Russian revolutionaries. During the

War General Ludendorff authorized Trotsky's return on a sealed train full of revolutionaries. Under the terms of the Rapallo agreement Germany and Soviet Russia renounce all reparation claims and all financial claims against each other; further, Germany, although in a state of economic and financial collapse, promises to aid Soviet Russia financially. Mutual trade relations are reestablished. It's a new beginning. Money and heavy industry promises to flow from the Consortium behind German's recovery. The American factories are already flooded with over-production from the war and the bankers have too much money and need to invest in reconstruction.

The Rapallo Treaty is signed on April 16, 1922. When Gareth Jones assists David Lloyd George in research for his official memoirs as British Prime Minister he most certainly has privileged access to details of the Soviet trade agreements with the Bolsheviks within the framework of Rapallo. There Lloyd George as Prime Minister tried to welcome back Soviet Russia into the "concert of powers" with a normal dialogue between partner nations instead of having to play off the venomous attacks of commissars spitting invectives with their sharp.-German relations since Rapallo's spirit, – "an era of wholehearted cooperation", – Soviet-Germ-tongue Bolsheviki denouncing imperialist secret treaties.

Lloyd George insists on Western credits and loans in a general stimulus package for the Soviet economy. Still entangled in a strange American military intervention during the Russian civil war the Bolsheviks are *persona non grata* having been denied seats at the Versailles Peace Treaty negotiations in Paris which they denounced as a banker's diplomatic farce of secret treaties dividing up countries, peoples and resources for the sole benefit of empire. Wilson, too, is too ill and preoccupied with France to deal with a Russian solution. Loy Henderson in the US Legation at Riga, Latvia, finds himself grading reports from superior ranking officers. Then, after weeks of negotiations in October 1925 in an effort to normalize relations since the Great War Germany, France and England sign their Locarno Pact, eventually repudiated by Hitler, in March 1936, when Nazi troops reoccupy the Rhineland. The Kremlin distrusts the French-Anglo detente with Germany and denounce Locarno

Back in New York Gumberg plays a key role as an expeditious agent promoting US-Soviet trade relations by guiding the American Russian Chamber of Commerce (ARCC). In correspondence January 1923 with Barnsdall, its vice-president Philip H. Chadbourne writes Gumberg: "Have closed contracts for all the machinery, ectcetera, and everything looks fine." A Tiflis agreement gives Barnsdall "exclusive rights to handle, sell, and market all or any of these goods: oil, tobacco, wool, skins, silk, timber, lumber, coal, licorice, root, cocoons, manganese". Siegel reveals "Barnsdall got the right to all of these products tax-free, and it would also have 'preference over any other shippers over all railway lines, steamship lines and pipelines at reasonable rates'." These guys also bagged deals on land. In return the Soviets and Georgians shared a thirty percent commission on exports of goods, not oil. Chadbourne also worked with Brown (Lyman) "vice president of Barnsdall New York". Engineers and equipment come from Lucey Manufacturing Corp. "Mr. Lucey" worked closely with Barnsdall president Henry Mason Day on the Baku and Grozni operations. Also with Day were Hunter Marston and Grant Forbes, reportedly Barnsdall "financial experts". ("American Obtains Baku Oil Concessions; H. M. Day of Barnsdall Corporation Reaches Preliminary Agreement with Krassin", *The NYT*, July 10, 1925. For a good account on Day, Barnsdall and Sinclair activities with the Soviets in Baku since Day's arrival on the shores there with his few engineers in 1923, see Steve Levine, *The Oil and the Glory: The Pursuit of Empire and Fortune on the Caspian Sea*, NY: Random House, 2008)

The Soviets, according to the Siegel account, exploit the Barnsdall deal for propaganda, and it works "'keeping the major oil companies off balance', particularly Standard Oil. ... It even drew in Harry Sinclair, who attempted to follow Barnsdall's success in the Caucasus...". However, Barnsdall "left Russia in 1924 having lost money." As Siegel tells it, "Its record was another in the annals of overambitious and unfulfilled Western concessions in Soviet Russia".

At State, Poole backs Barnsdall's exploitation of Soviet Russia's resources, writing Day "We will do anything possible to assist any legitimate American enterprise in securing these materials" of the Caucasus region. Poole even tendered the possibility of extending "official representation at Tiflis" with prior envoy of US Shipping Board transports to the area. The Commerce Department was already on the ground there. Where there are US ships, commerce follows, then diplomatic relations. The State Department authorized the US Shipping Board to send ships to Soviet ports. (K. Siegel, *Loans and Legitimacy*, 128)

For the period 1917 -30, American Consortium assistance in various forms was the primary factor of Soviet growth, first, in "the sheer survival of the Soviet regime and, secondly, in industrial progress to prerevolutionary levels". Sutton's research into US-Soviet trade during this period confirms it. The Allies are bankrupt, their crumbling empires sliding into rebellion, liberation struggles and national insolvency or bankruptcy, on the verge of the end of the colonial era.

After the First World War America floods Europe with dollars. Sutton's study shows that by 1929, American technology outstripped the German investment in rebuilding the Soviet Union. The Consortium bankers had seen to it already having stored away in Fed vaults gold on deposit sent from England, France and Russia. The influence of this industrial giveaway by US corporations and subsidiaries in Germany for US national security is never a seriously debated issue. Sutton writes, "Of the agreements in force in mid-1929, 27 were with German companies, 15 were with United States firms and the remaining ones were primarily with British and French firms. In the last six months of 1929, the number of technical agreements with US firms jumped to more than 40." (A. C. Sutton, *Western Technology and Soviet Economic Development, 1917-1930*, 346-7; A.C. Sutton, *1945-1965,* 412)

Therefore we know that from the beginning the Consortium of American bankers and British imperialists stepping in tune with the Fed and Bank of England, respectively, declared that trade with Lenin and Stalin was the primary stimulus towards regime stability and peace. Prohibited technology transfers use the same intentionally specious logic dating first back to Lenin in 1920 when the Bolsheviks were fighting famine, disease and civil war contesting their hold on Russia. "Hands Off Russia" declare the pro-trade CFR-ARCC lobbyists. Trade with the West saved Bolshevik tyranny and repeatedly squashed nationalist movements for independence and autonomy in the Ukraine. After the ravages of war Russia lacked supplies in every sector of the economy and desperately needed everything imaginable from manufactured goods, consumer items, foodstuffs and factories.

After the adoption of New Economic Policy (NEP) proclaimed by Lenin in March 1921 with the aim of restoring the economy and permitting private enterprise in agriculture, trade and small-scale industry Soviet Russia experienced "comparatively rapid economic development" during the 1924 to 1929 period. Economists generally agreed that the Soviet economy revived quickly from the devastation of the First World War, Revolution and Civil War. There was more food from the farmers; there were goods in the shops and outdoor markets.

According to research by historian Roy A. Medvedev in his book *On Stalin and Stalinism,* "It was in 1926 that industrial production reached roughly the prewar level, and production in agriculture approached that level as well. Towards the end of 1929 gross industrial output was one and a half times greater than in 1913, while production in heavy industry increased at an even more rapid rate. The output of coal reached 40 million tons (as against 29 million in 1913) and of steel, almost 5 million tons (4.3 million in 1913). The production of textiles, shoes, sugar, vegetable oil, and butter rose above the prewar level. Although collectivization had taken place only to a negligible extent (3.9 percent of peasant households), by 1927-9 agricultural production surpassed the prewar level, with the area of land under grain crops as well as the number of livestock restored to the level of 1913. For the first time since the civil war, the population rose above 150 million people, cities recovered, and the numbers of blue-and-white collar workers reached 95 per cent of the 1913 level. Thus in 1929, when the capitalist world faced the onset of its gravest, most protracted economic crisis, our country was experiencing an economic upsurge at an unprecedented rate." (R. A. Medvedev, *On Stalin and Stalinism,* 37-8)

Such progress was incredible! Unbelievable this, in Russia! How was it possible? In only a few short years prewar levels were surpassed! Huge advances in agriculture, heavy industrial production. Peasants now had shoes! Abundant sugar, vegetable oil and butter! And grain, too. Babushka had not one but two, perhaps three cows. And so many chickens to feed! These were days never to forget. "In this period", Medvedev writes, "also urgent measures were taken to overcome the cultural backwardness of the country. Illiteracy became a thing of the past. A broad network of primary and secondary schools came into being, while the expansion of higher education and scientific research led to the opening of many new institutes. Foreign trade increased as economic relations with a number of large capitalist countries returned to normal."

There was widespread agreement in 1928 that the success of technical transfer from the West prompted by Lenin's New Economic Policy (NEP) encouraged American entrepreneurs and companies to invest in the Soviet monopoly. From a production of almost zero in 1922 there was a recovery by 1928 to pre-World War I production figures.

By the late 1920s German predominance in technology was largely replaced by increased American technical assistance. The American and European capitalists quickly made progress with Lenin's New Economic Policy (NEP) though that fell apart in 1927 that "careless, well-fed year of the still untruncated NEP" remembers Solzhenitsyn in his *Gulag Archipelago* journals with mass arrests and the Lubyanka Cheka building shaking with terror when the Party suddenly declared peasants were too comfortable, that economic progress was proceeding too slow so they confiscated more livestock, raised grain procurements and inflated industrial targets. (A. I. Solzhenitsyn, *The Gulag Archipelago*, 41)

Meanwhile as Sen. Nye shows during FDR's first year as President, the munitions manufacturers of the Great War working hand-in-glove with Wilson's government make out handsomely. American bankers and industrialists make hundreds of billions of dollars in war profits and accumulated most of the world's gold. And it becomes clear how these money sharks concentrate their resources on European reconstruction, with investments in Germany and the Bolsheviks in Soviet Russia. The same international elite that financed the war that blew Europe to bits now took it upon themselves to rebuilt it. Destroy, make money, and rebuilt and destroy again. A simple policy of destruction and economic renewal and all very profitable if you can make it work. That's just what they did. With the First World War successfully concluded, profits rolled in and tens of millions of people died, lives and worlds destroyed, the international monetary elite settled down comfortably in tidy palatial surroundings from Versailles and the Quai d'Orsay to Blenheim and Wall Street, and planned phase two, reconstruction of Europe and Russia under the Soviet monopoly.

During the years preparing this book I came across yet another "play it safe" treatment of this era's persona titled, *Loans and Legitimacy: The Evolution of Soviet-American Relations, 1919-1933* leading up to and during this critical Holodomor period. It's a curious title of a "legitimate" work with research financed with funds – in this case by grants, not loans -, without which the very talented author Katherine Siegel declared in 1996, "this book would not have been possible". It has proven in the course of experience that indeed first "follow the money" to see what money is behind the work. In this case funds came principally from Princeton's Kennan Institute of Advanced Russian Studies. Other funds came from the Hoover Library Association; the Franklin and Eleanor Roosevelt Institute; the Hagley Museum and Library; the Institute on Global Conflict and Cooperation; the Society for Historians of American Foreign Relations, and departments at St. Joseph's University, the Interdisciplinary Humanities Center, and the University of California. That's quite a money bag. One wonders what they get for it. In this case, it turns out to be another pack of neatly twisted half-truths and misleading paths in the land that brought you *The Wizard of Oz* – in farmbelt USA. But reader, Dorothy Gale tells us in 1939: *"Toto, I've a feeling we're not in Kansas anymore."*

Few ever guessed that this film would become a great American classic with a musical score rated the best of all Hollywood films. Written by L. Frank Baum (1900), and directed by Victor Fleming. It is finally released in 1939 after years of gestation and stars Judy Garland, Frank Morgan, and Ray Bolger with superb casting. The darling innocent Dorothy Gale is swept away from the Kansas farm-belt to Oz. Written during the Great Depression by Oscar-winning lyricist E. Y. "Yip" Harburg, the film is considered an iconic fairytale and political allegory of the greatest financial collapse at the time with 30 per cent unemployment. Incidentally, just this month as I write August 2013 another of the Oz muchkins died, making national headlines, a news-worthy item of iconic significance not to be overlooked by American culture pundits, and now on the Internet are advertisements celebrating its 75th anniversary. All in the Land of Oz. You see, continuity is essential to keep all the lies in motion and the people dazed, confused and dumb.

Only in this case, its not Judy, its Stalin, who, incidentally, barely gets mentioned in Siegel's book. Like the omniscient all-powerful dictator isn't even there. Bloody hell! He ran the entire totalitarian show! (Or are you thinking, reader, "No way, it Rockefeller, Harriman and the Consortium gang all the time.) These establishment academics like a tidy house. But that's the way the State Department wanted to play its in the official record books for posterity historians as it very well knew there would be an official record-keeping, White Papers, Kennanesque treatments of critical historical events, processes and personalities. And of course, behind it all, the money trail. Be careful to cover the tracks, conceal clues, hide the trip-wires!

In this case a lot of Consortium Morgan-Rockefeller-Harriman money. Siegel makes extensive use of Sutton's research on Soviet dependence of American technology although seldom referring to him by name, apart from a token obligatory reference. Sadly she ignores the significance of the political and economic governmental role behind American investment in Soviet client state. To hell with the victims, right? Investors have to take risks! Nothing comes at a cheap price – except to the Consortium. More than a hundred million slave laborers! A bonanza for Big Business and everyone knew it would not last forever. Make hey when the sun shines! Sing and be merry. Look at all those happy smiling Ukrainian girls on the collective farms, hoes in hand, aloft mighty tractors made in America. Fords, Caterpillars, Deerings...From Kansas to Oz they got a whole lot of tractors and trucks.

Nearly ever writer will tell you that his or her accomplishment should never be prejudiced or compromised by its financial sources of support. Oh, yeah? God forbid, never that! Yet, forums do have their focus, platforms project agendas, so how on earth could there ever then be such a thing as the moral integrity of good scholarship without the dangling purse strings? In most case scenarios the agenda decides, and if you don't play by the rules you're out. That's exactly the problem. That is and will be for as far as the horizon is long a problem in democratic America where money rules a country that worships wealth. Well, until the Internet blew the old world away. Is it merely a coincidence that the

USSR collapsed just at the same time as the digital technology revolution and the dawning of the Internet for the world's information starved masses?

Fortunately, access to the Internet has changed the rules of the game, increasing the constant daily tension of conflict between government control, surveillance and secrecy, providing a wider scope for inquiry and cross-checking information with invaluable off-line sources. Julian Assange's breakthrough with Wikileaks followed a few years by NSA whistle-blower Edward Snowden contest government hegemony of the world information order and the limitations of citizen privacy. However, in the real world (it's really not so weird at all) – a certain independence may be compromised or denied in measure or degree one way or the other. For it is a fact that in the real nature of social intercourse, there is a sort of mutually implicit understanding and tacit acknowledge that the slant focus or orientation affecting the point of view of a grant recipient as well as the conclusions may be tainted by funding sources.

Let's not fool ourselves and play dumb. For example, in the taboo Genocide story of the holodomor cover-up and FDR's green light to Stalin's program of mass-murder launched and institutionalized on the foundations of massive western technology transfers and the assistance of thousands of highly skilled western engineers, the American academic Katherine Siegel who clearly has access to enough information to lift the curtain and see who and what is pulling the levers in Ozland instead kept silent about the truth of complicity and concealment. Not doing otherwise normally would seem to be a case of obvious poor scholarship. But there is nothing "normal" about mass-murder and the consolidation of a totalitarian war machine preparing for world war. Yet Ms. Sibling proved herself too capable to be that ignorant or careless of such an important oversight. Not that anyone can really blame her. Whoever might have the courage to stand up and expose the villains is scratched off the invitation list, or worse. Look what happened to Gareth Jones.

For Katherine Siegel pertinent facts of the Holodomor do not come into play in the financing of the Soviet socialist terror regime leading up to and responsible for Stalin's Genocide. She fit the mold set by Richard Pipes of Harvard and other Russian and Soviet scholars who top the agenda of academic protocol. Their institutions are built of granite and stone on top of billions of dollars of endowments and funding. If you try to shake that and intend to survive know your Shakespeare, forget the idyllic smooth career path, and prepare for a bumpy ride.

Clearly, the learned Katherine Siegel does not go near the question implicating the United States under Hoover or Roosevelt of guilt by association with Stalin's man-made Genocide. Yes, just the same, it is better to name funding sources rather than not, and even to do so is acknowledgment of a certain mutual appreciation. This author, nevertheless, too, is appreciative of her contribution for many details that do prove useful to provide some missing pieces of the puzzle that still remains too far from complete. Further, her oversight shines so blindly that the conspicuousness is all too obvious. Could this be intentional on her part to minimize and virtually dismiss the Holodomor as merely an incidental consequence of the Consortium-backed terror collectivization of Russian farmland. That loss is hers alone, the gain is ours, because as we know denial and deception are glaring signs of deceit and guilt by inference. This is how the Consortium perpetuates itself by exploiting academic research and scholastic skills that ought to be directed towards higher learning and not sacrificed to a pathetic agenda of crime when the innocent victims go punished, and are tortured to death. How utterly odd that this capable student of American Soviet history should mention only in passing in her extensive bibliography Conquest's *Harvest of Sorrow: Soviet Collectivization and the Terror-Famine.*

Evidently Siegel researched official Soviet records in the Russian archives. Yet, it's clear by her Consortium oriented promoters, university sponsors and foundation grant underwriters that Siegel sought and received the recognition of her taste-masters in and out of the academic foreign policy establishment, buying her line that the Soviets, – and not the Consortium, – "boldly sought American goods and money." In all fairness, – and I write this on the day *The New York Times* declares that finally that Russia thirty-six years after *The Gulag Archipelago* is published in the West mandates Solzhenitsyn's trilogy for Russian students –, so let's be clear that Katherine Siegel observes the dilemma posed to Americans educated so as to be able to detect distortions, albeit overt lies and misleading information about the US-USSR commercial relation. Reader, beware of treacherous waters where we encounter so often the "iceberg effect", - so little exposed that we can see concealing the real invisible danger underneath.

"Historians of early Soviet diplomacy," Katherine Siegel writes, "have given little attention to Russia's economic interests in the United States, emphasizing instead the Kremlin's successful establishment of official ties with the European powers during the first half of the 1920s. Yet over the course of the decade, Russian purchases of American goods served Soviet goals by promoting a significant change in US economic policy. Most notably, Soviet trade encouraged Washington officials, no longer as reluctant as they had been in 1919, to authorize private long-term credits. This cooperation of business and government to assist American economic relations with Soviet Russia is representative of New Era corporatism, that system of public-private collaboration to ensure 'order, progress, and stability' that is, often associated with Herbert Hoover." And that is how she opts to introduce the Consortium exploitation of the Soviet socialist monopoly and gulag slave state system, with the benevolent introduction of the ARA to save the Russians from famine. She is stumped, hitting the wall, unable to see why, as she readily admits, "the American government's flexibility on the Russian question before 1933 has gone unnoticed by historians". Oh my God! How could that possibly have ever happened? Oh, dear me, I do declare, how did they not see! And she adds, "Although Washington did not extend government financing to Moscow, its officials did entertain the subject of credits and responded positively to American firms' requests to offer long-term financing beginning in 1927." In view of Bullitt's tedious negotiations with Litvinov, shadowed with all the pretense of subterfuge, Siegel is obliged to confront the reality of Consortium investment. (K. Siegel, *Loans and Legitimacy,* 5)

Once Hoover's ARA mission withdrew the Soviets in 1923 resumed grain exports to earn foreign exchange. Four years later a fundamental shift is in the air. Coolidge's Secretary of State Kellogg in a reversal of the government's orientation towards Russia set by Hughes now made "significant adjustments in the policies that determined economic relations with Soviet Russia". Growing Soviet-American trade spurred him to shift so that by 1927, and this, for the first time, the State Department authorized long-term credit for an American sale to the Bolshevik regime. Stalin had made his move. The Consortium follows in step with events marching in Moscow. It was the American Locomotive Sales Co. which received a large contract from the Soviet government sugared with terms with a moratorium of five years before having to make a single payment, the kind of credit it was argued essential for a sizable heavy equipment order. This is a breakthrough that doesn't pass unnoticed at State. Bob Kelley who was advising the Department declares that the proposed financing "violated the carefully preserved distinction between the established and acceptable practice of offering short-term credit to Moscow" and as such represented the unprecedented and, in his view, unmerited practice of granting long-term credit. No matter. He is overruled by three men equally anticommunist in their outlook: President Coolidge, Treasury Secretary Andrew W. Mellon, and Commerce Secretary Hoover. Siegel observes that as long as securities sales were not in the deal the US government "would not look with disapproval upon banking arrangements incidental to the financing of contracts concluded...with the Soviet authorities".

The Consortium had breached the trade barrier flatly reversing Hoover's stance in 1921 that "trade with Russia on credit was out of the question" and that "trade with Russia on credit was out of the question", or more to the point then "communism and long term credits are incompatible". The Consortium now had other plans with Soviet Russia and their emerging dictator of stability and repression Comrade Stalin. (K. Siegel, *Loans and Legitimacy*, 98)

Evan Young's dismissal of trade with the Soviets in 1924 is cast aside by Secretary of State Frank Kellogg's February 1928 four-page memorandum authorizing routine long-term trade credits far exceeding the earlier short-term credits that had been extended to International Harvester years prior. Kellogg is determined not to lose ground to Great Britain and Germany both which have recognized the Soviet government. A bitter pill to swallow for Kelley who keeps up his anticommunist hardline resentment of Moscow and doing his best to push it across Kennan, Henderson and Chip Bohlen.

International Harvester had a long and important pre-revolutionary history which is not the subject of this book. However, by 1924, it was clear to both the Soviets and Harold McCormick that it was time to update with state of the art machinery and modernize its Lubertzy factory under NE Prior to the Plans, US-Soviet trade virtually staggers. In February 1924 the Department's Evan Young aptly lamented that "The experience of foreign business men has been that the practical working out of concessions has fallen far short of expectations with the result that many firms have withdrawn from their Russian enterprises." (K. Siegel, "International Harvester and the New Economic Policy", *Loans and Legitimacy*;

E. Young, Feb. 23, 1924, RG 59, 661.111/451; in a ftn. Siegel examines how Soviet fortunes changed under NE *Pravda*, "A Step Ahead", Aug. 9, 1924, IHP, BA2-01, box 2, 1384 cites 177 Siegel footnote 14; re. Harvester's profits see Carstensen, 205: "Its investment amounted to 60,450,000 gold rubles. Singer Sewing Machine, the next major investor, invested fifty million gold rubles in the USSR."; Lincoln Hutchinson, Aug. 8, 1922, "Confidential Supplement to Memorandum of July 24, 1922, on Foreign Capital in Russia Before the Revolution", A. Gumberg Papers, box 2)

Focusing on International Harvester as principal investor in Russia and the Ukraine Siegel writes, "This included $342,000 for the branch warehouses seized after the revolution; $36 million in cash, assets, and collections when the branch inventories were seized and the nation's currency inflated in 1918 (a 2000 percent inflation rate) ; $1.7 million in Lubertzy inventory, work in progress, machines, and more inflation between 1917 and 1924; and finally, $4.9 million from the Lubertzy plant and its equipment taken in 1924. The plant closed in 1922. Harvester stock diluted in value to virtually no value. Eventually *Vesenkha* takes control of the plant while Soviet officials sought Harvester managers to remain. Harvester essentially lost some $43 million from its Russian investment by 1924. The company was essentially taken over by the Soviet Trusts while on paper, the Russian company exists as a subsidiary of the American firm. In 1932 the company declares, "We have kept this company going now for 15 years since the Revolution. It is some expense and trouble to hold the annual stockholders' meetings and directors meetings and believe it would be safe to omit these." (K. Siegel, *Loans and Legitimacy*, see footnote 43, 179)

What about Russian gold? Here again items came to the surface in Katherine Siegel's book *Loans and Legitimacy* (1996) adding another long line of string on the cat's ball. Siegel: "Although Russian gold was not permitted entry, Western European nations routinely serviced their accounts in the United States using remolded Soviet bullion. The Moscow State Bank decided to test this prohibition in February 1928 and transported $5 million in gold bars directly to New York, consigning the shipment to the Chase National Bank and the Equitable Trust Company. Despite long acceptance of 'laundered' Soviet gold, this more straightforward use of the metal became an international issue. Within two weeks, the French ambassador told the State Department that his government would sue who ever took this gold, because he claimed it was owed to France. Chase National Bank and Equitable Trust refused to certify the Soviets' title to the gold shipments bearing the Bolshevik seal because they feared a French lawsuit. The Treasury Department ultimately rejected the gold bars on the attorney general's advice that 'acceptance might imply United States recognition of Soviet ownership'. Although Soviet officials had proof that the gold had been manufactured in the mid-twenties and not, as French representatives alleged, ten years earlier, they were wary of a court battle. The gold was recalled to Moscow." Published reports of gold shipments are more tentative than real.

The Consortium will get it later. A *Tass* correspondent furiously protests that the Americans had already processed through the American Treasury "hundreds of millions" worth of gold which "entered unprotected". (*Tass*, March 30, 1928, *Gosundarstvennyi Aarkhiv Rossiiskoi Federatsii* /GARF, fond 4459, op 2, del. 328, l. 523)

During NEP the race of American businessmen for Soviet concessions included Doheny hot for Russian oil, and Lenin's use of the clever Jew Armand Hammer, as "the first American concession operator", the "bellweather to induce other American capitalists to invest", according to Lenin who said, "I am sure *not a damn thing will be done* unless there is *exacting* pressure and supervision." By 1930, after making millions in concessions, Hammer and his brother, both from Princeton, sign off their Soviet deals taking away millions of dollars paid in rubles and Soviet bonds. He also crossed the border with his famous collection Russian art treasures including priceless Fabrege Easter eggs from the Czarist craftsmen. The Soviets are to promised ten percent at any auction. Subsequently, Hammer remains outside the USSR for over three decades and makes another fortune in Occidental Oil.

On the pre-Stalin period, the Consortium had no problem doing business without official diplomatic and commercial relations between their respective governments. For the State Department and Kremlin, it was business as usual between the capitalists and communists. Siegel sheds some light here important for our narrative: "Though Soviet Russia signed no treaties of political or economic cooperation with Washington, as it did with London, Berlin, and Paris, this diplomatic impasse seemed scarcely an obstacle to Soviet agents and their American brokers. These representatives set up NY offices and in other cities to buy cotton, agricultural implements, engines, and other goods, and found a welcome reception from business in the 1920s. In turn, despite their dislike for the Soviet system, most American businessmen could not help but notice the potential of Soviet Russia's 140 million people, who occupied one-sixth of the world's geography and the incredible natural resources that lay beneath the surface.

Between 1923 and 1930 American sales to the Soviets grow twenty-fold, as total trade with the Bolshevik state surpassed the half-billion dollar mark. American firms supply the Russians with over a quarter of their imports, including oil drilling, mining, metalworking, electrical, construction, and agricultural equipment.

By 1931 Moscow, in turn, purchases more than one-fourth of American industrial equipment exports. In certain fields, like power-driven metalworking equipment and agricultural implements, Moscow consumes fully two-thirds of manufacturers' foreign output that year. Vital to this growing trade are large credits, from firms such as GE and American Locomotive Sales Corporation, as well as smaller businesses, and from banks including Chase National, Guaranty Trust, and Equitable Trust." (K. Siegel, *Loans and Legitimacy*, 3)

In March 1929 Kirov's Leningrad Obkom voted into law Stalin's Five-Year economic plan. Leningrad's industry would increase gross output by 276 percent in five years producing sorely needed industrial products like generators, turbines and tractors, and. of course chemicals, all the while training new ranks of workers, engineers and technicians. Agriculture production failed to meet increasing demand; Leningrad suffered severe food shortages and insufficient quantities of grain; fuel supplies were only a third needed to run the factories that ran below capacity. As more factories were built by Consortium engineers but production failed to meet the new quotas. Soviet leaders screamed "Saboteurs", "Wreckers", "Counter-revolutionary scum"! Something had to be done!

In May 1928, 53 technicians and engineers in the Donbass region at the Shakty mines are been sentenced after a public trial and imprisoned for "sabotage" and "economic counter-revolution". Moscow's Central Supreme Economic Council (VSNKh) issued a torrent of draconian directives. One hundred new factories must be built, for example. The Putilovets plant was ordered to deliver ten thousand tractors in a year! Workers jeered at the quotas and mocked their supervisors. And ever since January when Stalin responded to the grain procurement crisis with his plan for a massive collectivization of agriculture, dekulakization and expropriation of property and grain, to May when he declared the aim of collectivization was "to transfer from small, backward and fragmented peasant farms to consolidated, big, public farms, provided with machines, equipped with the data of science and capable of producing the greatest quantity of grain for market", the Consortium committed to investment to sustain Stalin's dictatorship. (S. Fitzpatrick, *Stalin's Peasants*, 39)

By the summer of July and August the summer of 1929 proves to be a very important time for the American businessman in the Soviet Union. In this first year of the Soviet Plan ARCC sent a highly publicized "delegation of one hundred". This pro-Soviet lobby included businessmen and tourists, wives and celebrities all there to be feted and royally treated in the palaces and pavillons of the Czars now the fiefdom of the dictator and his band of murderous Bolsheviks. Chase National Bank organized the tour, in particular, Reeve Schley, Wardwell and Gumberg. This was the green light Stalin could not even have imagined. Waves and waves of American capitalists came one after another to marvel at the wonders of Moscow and America's new frontier. (K. Siegel, *Loans and Legitimacy*, *Loans and Legitimacy*, 105; See minutes of the board meeting of ARCC's directors Oct. 7, 1929; Report by Gumberg, Sept. 1929 "American-Russian Chamber of Commerce Delegation to the USSR, July-Aug. 1929 as well as correspondences A. Gumberg to Oswald L. Johnston, ARCC Secretary and treasurer, Dec. 17.1929; Schley to Smith, Oct. 24, 1929; Schley to ARCC directors, Dec. 5, 1929, all in ARCCP, box 21. ARCC members include Hugh Cooper, Wardwell, Simpson, Thacher and Bartlett, Equitable Trust, Chase National Bank, Chicago Pneumatic Tool, Remington Rand, Westinghouse Electric, Johnson and Higgins, Averell Harriman, Percival Farquhar, American Locomotive, Sullivan Machinery; A. Gumberg "Russian Trip of American Businessmen Brought Definite Results"; Leland Harrison and D. C. Poole followed the delegation closely, writing to Sec. HLS, Aug. 12, 1929, RG 59,661.111/11; Aug. 21, 1929, RG 59/ 661.1116/70; Reports in the foreign press include "America's Capitalists and Stalin's Russia", *Stokholms Tidningen* on Aug. 10, 1929. *New York Herald Tribune,* July 18, 1929; letters Gumberg to Schley 1929)

By 1930 Soviet industrialization and collectivization under the Plans is in full swing at breakneck speed with massive repression in the countryside and millions of exiles sent to forced labor camps and construction projects under technical supervision of western engineers. People who complained of unrealistic goals were either dismissed, shot or exiled as "enemies of the people".

Just prior to the big market bust on Wall Street jubilant Americans rush to Moscow aboard the ARCC's pro-Soviet trade delegation eager for concession made available owing to a liberalization announced by Moscow the previous September. Gumberg writes in his report of the mission trip, "Our delegation was the first large group of foreign travelers to make such an extensive trip in Russia under comfortable conditions." The group saw the sights in Leningrad, Moscow, at the new Ford construction grounds at Nizhni Novgorod (Gorki). Nothing like a trip in summer floating down the Volga to Stalingrad and along the Black Sea vacation spots past Rostov on the Don in the Caucasus where they also took in the obligatory speeches at the Donetz coal mines, Dniepropetrovsk steel factories, the General Electric-Cooper showpiece of the Dnieprostroi dam site, and of course a stay over at Kharkov and Kiev. This only four years before the Holodomor but now guests are paying the astronomical sum of $1000 a head ($13,000) for the six thousand mile tour by car, steamer and specially prepared luxury train. The American press followed it.

The Soviets make the most of its Five-Year Plan propaganda tour to boost the popularity of Stalin and the success over a decade of Soviet collective state communism of the socialist dictatorship. The Austin Company of Cleveland announces it will build a Ford-inspired model automotive plant at Nizhni Novgorod. In addition to sending technical experts sent abroad to train future soviet engineers and managers Ford also has an outstanding contract valued at $30 million to sell Ford parts. Austin Company designs six hundred plants in the USSR. That came in addition to Ford's $18 million factory with Ford investing forty percent with plans to assemble 30,000 automobiles and 20,000 trucks per year by 1933. When the first Ford rolled off the Nizhni Novgorod assembly line in 1932 the Soviet press went "dizzy with success" only that by this time the Holodomor special brigade OGPU clean-up rolls along on Ford tractors and trucks. Westinghouse reps now promise to power up the Stalingrad tractor factory. It seemed like everyone hurried to get first in line to sign new contracts: MacDonald Engineering from Chicago contracted to guild grain elevators and refrigerator plants; IBM made its deal as did Underwood Elliott Fisher, Remington Rand, Gillette Safety Razor, Bristol Patent Leather, Animal Trap Co. and some twenty odd other firms negotiating for soviet business. "By the end of 1925, ten thousand Fordson tractors had been shipped to Russia, and after Ford's new offer of a relatively meager ten-month, 25 percent credit, ten thousand more had arrived by April 1926. This compared with 2,400 total shipped by the more generous Harvester," Katherine Siegel writes in *Loans and Legitimacy*. (K. Siegel, *Loans and Legitimacy*, 174; C. A. White, *Ford in Russia*, 88-9; Soviet Foreign Trade, *Russian Review*, Feb. 15, 1926; re. Soviet view of Ford, Reuther, *The Brothers Reuther*, 91; White, *Ford in Russia*)

AND THE RUSSIANS COMES TO YALE

George Vernadsky (1887-73) taught for over a generation at Yale in New Haven, Connecticut from 1927 until he retires retirement during the Cold War period, in 1956, and just three years after the death of Stalin. He is evidently too far removed, physically as well as mentally, from the actuality of the Soviet regime and lacking sufficient documentation to ever fully comprehend the horrific magnitude of Stalin's Genocide of his fellow Russians and Ukrainians. That in itself is very odd for it is a fact that his career overlaps precisely the entire Stalinist era.

I wonder if this man standing on the shores of Connecticut looking out across the Atlantic Ocean eastward towards Europe and stretching his imagination further across the expanse of Russia and Ukraine had not lost touch completely with the land of his study which he left behind. Stalin's persecution of the Ukrainian nationalists and virtual wholesale suppression of Ukrainian national culture befell all surviving Ukrainians with devastating impact. And while there were millions of victims no Ukrainian or their descendants passed through the hell of the Holodomor unaffected by the trauma and its reverberations that flow as ripples on water through lives and society from generation to generation.

A child of Czarist St. Petersburg, George Vernadsky inspires students at Yale for thirty years with a wisdom and experience inherited from his homeland the culture of Moscow's University where he and his family of the Russian intelligentsia lived through the tumult of the tragic end of the Romanov monarchy and the debacle of the Great War ending 450 years of colonial oppression of the Ukraine (150 years under the Poles, and 300 years under Russians).

The Vernadsky family narrowly survives the Russian Revolution and Bolshevik coup that liberates or tears asunder the lives of the millions of workers, peasants and intellectuals and eradicated or exiled aristocrats and capitalists across the former empire engulfing cities, towns and villages in the countryside with civil war, famine and disease. Instead George Vernadsky assumes a politically correct Consortium position in the academic milieu of Yale.

Before emigrating to the West Vernadsky taught at Petrograd, Perm and Simferopol; in 1920 he escapes in the exodus of White Russia to Europe and, in 1927, joins Yale's faculty pursuing his work in the Slavic Studies Department nestled in within discreet courtyards of idyllic tranquility under Gothic towers of Ivy vines, gargoyles and ornately painted glass and darkly paneled reading rooms. It is a sublime environment far removed from the chaos and turmoil of Bolshevik politics and Chekha terror raging in his homeland. While millions of displaced Russians and Ukrainians toil in the gulag, Vernadsky publishes two years later the highly acclaimed *History of Russia* (Yale, 1929) frequently edited over the years, followed by *Bohdan, Hetman of Ukraine* (Yale, 1941), *Ancient Russia* (Yale, 1943), *Kievan Russia* (Yale, 1948), *The Mongols and Russia* (Yale, 1953), *The Origins of Russia* (Clarendon, 1959), *Russia at the Dawn of the Modern Age* (Yale, 1959).

The professor may have been a good historian but he was a lousy mystifier of the reality of life and death in the Soviet Union and while he enjoys a modicum of celebrity as Yale's distinguished authority on Russian history, but he is no expert on Stalin. In fact, Vernadsky appears to have known even less of Stalin's masterful manipulation of the Soviet Party machinery to inflict Communist terror as well as keeping the West in the dark. Prof. Vernadsky is a conservatively minded scholar of an old school mentality, not inclined to rock the boat and so a perfect tool of the Consortium academics of Yale.

In *A History of Russia* (Yale 1962) apart from vague and casual reference there is no mention of the Ukrainian Genocide, gulag of forced labor or the totalitarian communist state system of torture. Instead this exile of the Bolshevik takeover who became senior professor of the Yale's Slavic Department shows an unrestrained tolerance of the progressive improvements of living conditions and opportunities for the underprivileged and stoic sacrifice and endurance of his ancient homeland that in less than ten years rose from social, economic and political chaos to defeat the most powerful military offensive the world had ever known after Hitler launched his *Barbarossa* invasion June 22, 1941 with devastation that surpassed the guns of August 1914. Prof. Vernadsky nevertheless acknowledges the indispensable link of the transfer of western technology and engineers, in particular from the United States, to advance Stalin's Five-Year Plans. For the man who describes the Russians as essentially Slavs, and Kiev Rus' "the blossoming of Russo-Byzantium culture (972-1237), at first glance it might strike the reader as a most errant omission that the Holodomor, and in particular, that critical year 1933 is virtually overlooked.

Further, Vernadsky glosses over details of grain production, procurements as well as exports, consistently underplays as is Stalin's systematic policy of extermination of the nationalist Ukraine, and all this in spite of the professor's extensive and privileged interest in Ukraine in spite of his intellectual interest and passion for the Ukraine. Yet, upon closer inspection we find quite naturally that Vernadsky's unique academic position and work is very much the by-product of rare individual circumstances.

Vernadsky's route to Yale is circuitously destined with a fate that overcame the misfortune of the painful war years of penury and betrayal. Upon closer inspection we find that Vernadsky's unique academic qualifications are, in fact, no trivial affair and are influenced by personal circumstances. As a Russian Ukrainian scholar he follows a paternal tradition of the Ukrainian Intelligentsia. In fact, his father is Vladimir Vernadsky, the first President of the Ukrainian Academy of Sciences founded in 1918. Young Vernadsky enters the Moscow University (where his father is professor) in the years of the failed Russian Revolution of 1905. Obliged to leave Russia he then studies at the Albert Ludwigs University of Freiburg and the University of Berlin. Two years later George graduates from Moscow University; in 1910, and moves to Saint Petersburg where he teaches at the University for the next seven years, and even receives a Master's degree for his study on the influence of Freemasonry on the Russian Enlightenment.

Embroiled in the tumultuous progressive politics of university and urban life (his father is one of the leaders of the Kadet party enough to have both shot in the next decade) loyal to the Kerensky Provisional Government in 1917 in power briefly after the abdication of the Czar, Vernadsky remains in Russia during the Civil War in Perm on the banks of the Kama River (renamed Molotov for a time 1940-57) where he lectures for a year until Admiral Kolchak succumbs to the Reds.

Consequently, and without much choice, and with nowhere else to go in his calling, Vernadsky follows the route of the retreating Whites southwest to Kiev and the university of Simferopol in the ancient city of the Crimean Scythians where during the upheaval he teaches for another two years until the city was finally captured by the Bols in October 1921.

The Bolsheviks push the Whites and Tatar Cossacks into the Black Sea. Anti-Bolshevik resistance in the Crimea collapses. In 1920 between erratic spurts of Ukrainian independence George Vernadsky joins the exodus fleeing first to Constantinople, then to Athens and Prague, where he again returns to teaching at the Russian School of Law (1921-25) where evolves his Eurasian theory of Russian history and culture as the synthesis of Slavonic, Byzantine, and nomadic Mongolian Asiatic influences.

His work and profile are such to impress Yale.

In 1927 Vernadsky is offered a chair at the university through the auspices of another naturalized Ukrainian, Michael Rostovtzeff (1870-52), and who considered in his own right a renowned scholar on ancient Greek, Iranian, and Roman history. Rostovtzeff's life has also been thrown for a loop by the 1917 October Revolution. In Russia Rostovtzeff is recognized as the world's preeminent authority on ancient history of South Russia and the Ukraine. When he is obliged to take leave of Kiev and St. Petersburg, in 1918, Rostovtzeff emigrates to the US to teach at the University of Wisconsin in Madison. Appointed Sterling Professor of Ancient History and Classical Archeology at Yale in 1925 he heads their ten-year excavation of the imperial Roman city of Dura-Europos on the right bank of the Euphrates river in modern Syria. (A more up-to-date review of activities in 2012 at Yale's Gallery of Fine Arts includes a major exposition of an unearthed synagogue, a Christian building, Mithraeum and some 12,000 artifacts of daily life). Rostovtzeff's vast knowledge produced *Iranians and Greeks in South Russia* (1922) and *Skythien und der Bosporus* (1925). His most important archaeological findings at Yale are described in *Dura-Europos and Its Art* (1938), as well as in a book published by Yale field director Clark Hopkins (1932–35).

Vernadsky is helped by another Russian emigrant with an illustrious history relevant to our story of war, revolution and the American connection to Bolshevik Russia. Frank A. Golder (1877-29) born in Odessa, Ukraine of modest Jewish parents entered the United States with his family around 1881 probably to escape the Odessa Czarist pogrom that year. Golder manages to overcome a hard life of poverty in New Jersey, escaped the streets and eventually graduated from Bucknell Univeristy (1898). Perhaps enamored by the legend of Jack London's gold-digging Klondike adventures in upper regions of Alaska, Golder travels to Unga Island in the obscure territory of the Pacific northwest where he taught native Aleut Eskimoes until 1902 recalled in his *Tales from Kodiak Island.* Then he's off to Harvard where in a year he adds his second B.A. (1903) and a Ph.D., also from Harvard (1909). Golder teaches briefly at the University of Chicago; in 1914, during the first year of the Great War, Golder publishes *Russian Expansion on the Pacific, 1641-1850.*

Golder then travels to Paris, Berlin, and ends up in St. Petersburg, in 1914, just in time for the war. He remains there until 1917 when on behalf of the American Geographical Society he takes a job translating and editing the journals of the famous Danish explorer Vitus Bering. Swept up by war and peace, Golder mixes easily with adventuresome intelligence operatives and other American embassy officials, and various key groups including the Root diplomatic and Stevens railroad missions; there he catches the attention of Col. House's "Inquiry" Committee and joins his staff.

For two years Golder prepares government reports on Ukraine, Lithuania and Poland for the American delegation at the Paris Peace Conference before returning to teach at Washington State and Stanford. There he joins the Hoover team drafted as collector-curator in the gargantuan task of filing thousands of Russian war and revolution documents for the Hoover Library Archives with duplicates meticulously arranged for Harvard and the Library of Congress.

But Frank Golder yearns to return to Soviet Russia arriving August 1920, and soon one of Hoover's ARA famine relief workers. During the summer of 1922 Golder is with the Americans helping to feed "nearly 11 million people a day" and political observer of Lenin's government along with the ARA economist Lincoln Hutchinson, author of *On the Trail of the Russian Famine* (Stanford, 1927); there "Doc" Golder assiduously works as "the most traveled of all the ARA Americans, in tandem with Goodrich and Haskell and the Bolsheviks and journeying up and down the Volga and to the Ukraine, the Caucasus, and Dagestan".

As we see here with this note from Golder's diary: "*November 25, 1921.–* There is a cry for help from the Ukraine. The granary of Russia is empty and the inhabitants are suffering from hunger and the terrors of bandit raids. Hutchinson and I have been detailed to investigate, and after the usual delays we got away last night in a small second-class car at the tail end of a long train. The car has a flat wheel, and as we sit around the table to eat our schip we realize the truth of the saying, 'there's many a slip 'twixt the cup and the lip'. At three o'clock we reached Briansk, where a prison car was hooked on to the rear of our car to keep us company and steady. *November 27.–*We arrived at Kiev yesterday about one o'clock in the afternoon. This city, situated on wooded hills, is more beautiful than the other Russian cities we have visited until now.

Since the Bolshevik revolution Kiev has changed hands fourteen times, and that should give an idea of the extreme fighting and the destruction it has suffered; and yet its ruins are not flaunted in one's face as those of Samara, Astrakhan, and other Volga towns. Kiev, the cradle of Russian culture and Christianity, city of shrines and pilgrimages, the ancient seat of learning, has now become a provincial town. It is not even the capital of the Ukraine. That honor has been conferred on upstart Kharkov, and it is not quite clear whether this was done to punish Kiev for its resistance to Bolshevik rule, or to reward Kharkov for its loyalty. But neither the Whites nor the Reds can deprive "the mother of Russian cities" of her historic traditions, of her beautiful location overlooking the Dnieper, or of her marked individuality." During three years revisiting (1925-27), amassing a seminal collection of Slavic materials including posters, magazines, books, and government documents, much of it is gathered and assembled by Golder from journeys throughout Europe, and Russia, and before his premature death in 1929, shipped to California,. (Frank A. Golder and Lincoln Hutchinson, "The Ukraine November 25-December 6, 1921", *On the Trail of the Russian Famine*, Stanford Univ., 1927; Terence Emmons and Bertrand Patenaude, *War, Revolution, and Peace in Russia: The Passages of Frank Golder, 1914-1927*, 1992)

As a Russian exile emigrant professor Vernadsky, too, is not immune from the tumult or unaffected by the communist horror afflicting his family and friends and throughout the years tries to come to terms with Stalin's post-Bolshevik regime. He stops short of calling it a man-made famine and instead describes the government revamping of agriculture under soviet collectivization in the first Five-Year plan as a "necessary" step firstly "to raze the existing farm structure."

And while he calls kulakization as "an act of cruel madness" plunging the country into chaos and famine", the hard-pressed and cruel path of Soviet Russian path of modernization remains for him a scheme of "experiments which were carried out over a considerable time" and ranged from "a free cooperative association of farmers to a strict kolkhoz economy". When gradual taxation failed to produce desired results, Moscow resorted to more coercive methods. "as production slumped to new lows the threat of starvation hung over the whole country".

Nowhere does and educated and privileged Ukrainian Vernadsky characterize the extermination of his fellow countrymen and women, elders and children, as deliberate Stalinist inspired nationalist Genocide against his people. Again, he writes, collectivization instead was a scheme of "experiments which were carried out over a considerable time" and ranged from "a free cooperative association of farmers to a strict kolkhoz economy". When gradual taxation failed to produce desired results, Moscow resorted to more coercive methods described by Vernadsky with superb understatement: terror repression inflicted on the peasant population by the absolute dictatorship is characterized as "great hardships even when scores of years are allowed for the readjustment. In Russia, compressed as it was within the space of a few years, it resulted in a social convulsion."

Vernadsky writes, "The final decision to prepare for a rigorous and thoroughgoing collectivization of rural life in Russia came on January 6, 1930. The whole process was to be completed in the region of the lower and middle Volga and in the northern Caucasus by the autumn of 1930 or at least by the spring of 1931. In other regions it was to be put into effect by the autumn of 1931 or the spring of 1932. And how was Stalin to accomplish all this?

Vernadsky recalls how Soviet planning showed itself to be entirely impractical and inconsistent with rural conditions, caused principally by the lack of tractors and combines for the collectives. "Until 1930 there were not more than 25,000 tractors in the whole RSFSR, and because of the lack of repair shops and the scarcity of experienced operators nearly half of these were chronically in poor condition. The shortage of harvesting combines was even more acute. Although two immense factories capable of turning out 25,000 combines a year had been planned, in 1930 there were almost no such machines actually in operation anywhere in Russia. Few of the new farms could be furnished with the equipment which alone could justify their organization from the economic point of view. For most of them 'columns of tractors' remained only a slogan, and the majority had to be content to try to operate vast tracts of land with 'horse and columns,' the traditional equipment of the peasant farmer." (G. Vernadsky, "The five-year plan: collectivization of agriculture", *A History of Russia*, 358-9)

"The fall of 1929 was a bloody one in the villages, and before it was over hundreds of the richer peasants had been executed, Vernadsky writes. "In January 1930 the government decided to exterminate the whole class of richer peasants." Dekulakization went into "full swing, hundreds of thousands of these men with their families were deported to the north and the east where they were placed in concentration camps and set to work, under the supervision of the OGPU, at lumbering, canal digging, railroad building, and other heavy labor." Zealous repression of the expropriated peasants stripped of possessions and forbidden from joining the new collectives, impoverished without any means of support backfired. Demoralized peasant villages and communities with sons and friends in the Red Army threatened more resistance. Vernadsky observed, "The government made a few concessions; and deported kulaks who had children in the army, in civil service, or in the factories were returned to their villages – if they were still alive." (G. Vernadsky, 359)

The manner by which western scholars have treated the Holodomor, in particular, in the past few decades ought to raise serious and intriguing questions to the reader. Reader, let me tell you I have tried to pull many sources together to arrive at a fair and balanced understanding of the Holodomor as we can know it through the diligent work of historians and researchers and other writers with talent to illuminate and share their findings. Scholarship is a task of diligence and persistence and of course the art of writing falls under the influence of rhetoric and editorial discretion where the question of Consortium influence and academic integrity may influence a scholar's incentive to be published by the most prestigious and great universities, whether Oxbridge or Harvard, Princeton and Yale.

Reader, – and students of Genocide, – you have been warned. Culture has its rituals and myths laden in the historicity of false explanations. A return to "the Past" is always subject to political exigencies and persuasion of special interests. In the Holodomor there was much at stake to prompt Stalin's massive Terror and repression during the turbulent thirties between the two World Wars when some fifty million lives or more perished. As a professional publisher, editor, writer and journalist for over forty years I have earned my scars and walked miles countless around the world to remind you reader, beware of brilliantly written and neatly packaged books that shadow or distort the truth. Take heed from the wisdom of the philosopher Mircea Eliade writing in *Myth and Reality* (1963): "There is more than a destruction, there is reversion to Chaos, to a sort of primordial *massa confusa*." (M. Eliade, *Myth and Reality*)

In *A History of Russia*, written by Nicholas V. Riasanovsky (Oxford University Press) there is virtually nothing on the Holodomor or Gulag despite eight editions over the past half-century since it was first published in 1962 five years after taking degrees at Oxford and Harvard. Riasanovsky's treatment of Stalin's Five-Year Plans is introduced with a quote from Duranty still perpetuating Stalin's lies carried by *The NYT* and the Harvard-Yale Consortium academics, as does this Berkeley professor emeritus considered "one of the foremost historians of Russia" (Sidney Hellman Ehrman Professor of European History) teaching there since 1957. Riasanovsky also taught at Harvard where he took his graduate degree, and was rose in the ranks to become president of the American Association for the Advancement of Slavic Studies.

Nicholas Riasanovsky was born in Harbin, Russia in 1923. Before emigrating to the West, his father taught at Moscow University, and his mother was an accomplished novelist (*The Family*, 1940). He graduates from the Oregon University (1942) and after Harvard picks up his Ph.D. at Oxford (St. Johns College) on a Rhodes. With all that time and talent, Riasanovsky ignores the role of the western technology in the reconstruction of Soviet Russia suffice to write, "The famine and other horrors of the First Five-Year Plan (1928-32 sic) did not recur." Everyone was talking about it; all his friends knew.

Reader see here he does speak about the famine in the thirties: "... the great industrial spurt was accompanied by shortages of consumer goods, rationing, and various other privations and hardships which extended to all of the people, who at the same time were forced to work harder than ever before. The whole country underwent a quasi-military mobilization reminiscent of War Communism". In the next paragraph Riansanovksy continues with the same vogue of thought: "But the greatest transformation probably occurred in the countryside. As already mentioned, the collectivization of agriculture, planned originally as a gradual advance, became a flood. Tens of thousands of trusted Communists and proletarians – the celebrated "twenty-five thousand" in one instance, actually twenty – seven thousand – were sent from towns into villages to organize kolkhozes and establish socialism. Local authorities and Party organizations, with the police and troops were necessary, forced peasants into collectives. A tremendous resistance developed. About a million of the so-called kulaks, some *five million* people counting their families, disappear in the process, often sent to concentration camps in far-off Siberia and Central Asia. A frightful famine swees the Ukraine. Peasants slaughtered their cattle and horses rather than bring them into a kolkhoz. Thus from 1929 to 1933 in the Soviet Union the number of horses, in millions, declined from 34 to 16.6, of cattle from 68.1 to 38.6, of sheep and goats from 147.2 to 50.6, and of hogs from 20.9 to 12.2. Droughts in 1931 and 1932 added to the horors of the transition from private to collectivized farming." Even Riasanovsky admits he is quoting from "official – and doubtful figures". (italics added)

The professor writes of the Second Five-Year Plan (1933-38); by the time of the German invasion in June 1941 Riasanovsky is able to write, "In agriculture collectivization was virtually completed and, except for the wilderness, the Soviet countryside became a land of kolkhozes and sovkhozes. Slightly less than 250,000 kolkhozes replaced over 25 million individual farms. The famine and other horrors of the First Five-Year Plan did not recur. In fact, agricultural production increased somewhat, and food rationing was abolished in 1935. Still, the economic success of Soviet policy remained much more doubtful than the achievements of Soviet industrialization. Peasants regularly failed to meet their production quotas. They showed greater devotion to their small private plots than to the vast kolkhoz possessions. In other ways, too, they remained particularly unresponsive to the wishes of Communist authorities. A full evaluation of Soviet social engineering shold also take account of the costs. As one author summarized the salient human aspects of Soviet agricultual policies during the socialist offensive: 'As a result of collectivization the number of families on the land diminished from 26,000,000 to 21,000,000. This means that 5,000,000 families or approximately 24,000,000 individuals must have left the countryside. Of these the increase in the towns accounts for one half. *Twelve millions are not accounted for.* A part of them has undoubtedly perished, the other part has found new possibilities in the Far East, in the Arctic, or in Central Asia'." No word of Gulag here, nor do we find it figure in the index. This is more than outrageous oversight or a convenient forgetting. (Nicholas V. Riasanovsky, "The First Three Five-Year Plans, 1928-41", *A History of Russia*, Oxford Univ. Press, 1993, 497-501; first published 1962, the eighth edition (2010) with an excellent chapter on Kievan Russia; italics added)

If we examine more closely the unique historiography of the Holodomor by the prestigious academics, see, for example, the work by Geoffrey Hosking, *Russia and the Russians*, published by Harvard (2001). Hosking is professor of Russian History at the University of London. His other books include *The First Socialist Society: A History of the Soviet Union from Within*, (Harvard); and *Russia: People and Empire*. (Harvard). For some odd reason he completely ignores the findings of Dr. Mace and the US Congressional Commission on the Ukraine Famine held in Washington DC in April 1986. At that inquiry Mace tells the Commission members which includes the distinguished WWII aviator veteran Republican Congressman Ben Gilman from New York (1973-2003) that "Stalin had ample reason to know that a famine was going on in late 1932, early 1933. Through the Soviet press, we can trace his reaction to it, and this has passed largely unexplored. I found no publications on this in Western or Soviet scholarly literature." (US Congressional Commission on the Ukraine Famine, Washington DC, April 1986)

Hosking writes that the problem of Soviet communist repression of the peasants was not endemic to the communist system under Lenin. In his chapter "Collectivization of Agriculture" Hosking observes that Lenin when confronted with the problem of peasant cooperation with the Bolsheviks was less extreme in his approach to repression of the peasant class. "This confrontation threatened the whole basis of the NEP, which is why Bukharin and his 'rightist' followers objected to it so strongly. They quoted Lenin, and with some justification. Lenin had called the NEP a 'breathing space', but had increasingly inclined to the view that one should draw breath 'seriously for a long time'. He had not abandoned the ultimate aim of collectivizing agriculture, but toward the end of his life he was recommending that this be done gradually, through the creation of 'civilized cooperatives', whose advantages over family smallholdings would be so obvious that peasants would flock to join them voluntarily. Stalin's personal campaign of 1928-29 when he toured the Urals and Western Siberia signaled the abandonment of this long-term perspective, and the return to emergency wartime methods. Historian and a professor of Russian and European history for over thirty years Martin Malia, (*The Soviet Tragedy*) refers to this period of Stalin's program of emergency collection after "the famous shortfall in grain procurements of December 1927" as the equivalent of "an intra-Party coup d'état" with backing from the Politburo to mount his big thrust for grain collection (*prodrazverstka*) in a major campaign of War Communism in the countryside with orders to Molotov, Kaganovich, Zhdanov, Andreev ... (G. Hosking, *Russia and the Russians*, 449; M. Malia, *The Soviet Tragedy,* 191)

Hosking passes over the famine with only the slightest reference. Without deferential acknowledgment of the name Holodomor in the Ukrainian language as it is known around the world, or the existence of the man-made Genocidal terror campaign, Hosking writes that unlike the 1921-22 famine "remained unpublicized, in order not to disrupt the propaganda images of the success of the first five-year plan. Starving peasants who tried to make for nearby towns to find food were turned back at roadblocks, while foreign correspondents were kept out of the affected areas." Yet, Geoffrey Hosking asserts the death toll of famine victims "in the region of *four to five million.*" (G. Hosking, *Russia and the Russians*, 454; italics added)

Referring to the terrorist work brigades, *udarnik*, or shock workers – "one of the highest titles of honor among the working class", – sent in the summer of 1929 to repress recalcitrant peasants, Hosking writes, citing Lunn Viola's, *The Best Sons of the Fatherland: Workers in the Vanguard of Soviet Collectivization* (Oxford, 1987): "Beset by mounting chaos in the villages, the party decided that it needed to inject cadres from outside to make the new system work. In November 1929 an appeal was launched for 25,000 of the most class-conscious workers to be sent out to the villages to coordinate the collectivization campaign and to get the newly created farms working. The appeal emphasized the need to take the class war to the countryside, overcome the kulaks, modernize agriculture, and secure the food supply for the future. There was a lively response: more than 70,000 workers put forward their names in the next few weeks, and by early spring of 1930 some 27,000 had been selected, given brief training courses, and dispatched to the villages." And so by the end of that summer 1929 Stalin and his shock brigade grain procurers exerting massive pressure on the peasants in the Ukraine "by whatever means seemed appropriate" increased kolkhoz membership or collective farms from one to two million. (Geoffrey Hosking, *Russia and the Russians*, NY: Oxford Univ. Press, 2001, 452; M. Malia, 195)

In blatant disregard for the terror campaign Hosking quotes from Lev Kopelev's *The Education of a True Believer* (1981): "One of them, Lev Kopelev, later recalled the ideals which motivated him: 'Stalin had said 'The struggle for grain is the struggle for socialism'. I was convinced that we were warriors on an invisible front, waging war on kulak sabotage for the sake of grain that the country needed for the Five Year Plan. For grain above all, but also for the souls of peasants whose attitudes were bogged down in ignorance and low political consciousness, and who succumbed to enemy propaganda, not grasping the truth of communism.'" And that's it, apparently, and good enough for Geoffrey Hosking satisfied that he has fairly treated the subject well enough for his students, and to the satisfaction of higher authorities. Remember reader, these academics specializing in Russian and Slavic studies need a visa to enter Russia. Most recently author-journalist and Russian specialist David Satter failed to get his renewed as of December 2013.

On the drought and famine in 1931 Hosking called it "a dry summer" with "an exceptionally poor grain harvest". Again he stops there. And for the next year Hosking writes, "information came in from the regions about disappointing grain deliveries, Stalin resisted suggestions that the Soviet Union cease exporting grain 'in order not to undermine our credit abroad', and instead sent instruction that deliveries were to be *increased and policed more thoroughly*." Hosking is referring to the draconian August 7, 1932 "law" mandating execution and "emissaries" sent "to see that these instructions were obeyed" including death "for *any* theft of 'collective or cooperative property'. He dismisses the terror equating Stalinian repressions as not incompatible to "a revival of English eighteenth-century "hanging for sheep-stealing". Remember reader, Hosking is published by Oxford and Harvard. (italics added)

Another strange oddity in Hosking in his passing over the Holodomor Terror-Famine issues of Genocide against the Ukrainian people by an truncated reference to a warning of famine in a letter sent to Stalin by Roman Terekhov, a member of the Ukrainian Politburo, and the Regional First Secretary in Kharkiv until January 1933. Stalin replies, in writing accusing him of "concocting fairy tales" and sarcastically tells him he ought to join the Writers' Union. That's not what the US Congressmen are told. Somehow Terekhov survives both the famine and Stalin.

In an article published in 1964 by *Pravda*, Terekhov tells how he went directly to Stalin in late 1932 pleading for emergency bread deliveries to regional districts in the Ukraine. Stalin listened patiently then cut Terekhov off, telling him. "We have told you, comrade Terekhov, that you are a fine storyteller. You made up this story about a famine and thought you would frighten us, but it won't work! Maybe it would be better if you stopped being a secretary of a region and of the Central Committee of the Communist Party of Ukraine and went to work int he Union of Soviet Writers writing fairytales for idiots to read." Stalin's urged Terekhov and the Ukrainian Politburo "to collect even more grain from the countryside there". Professor Hosking also ignores to mention this US Government Investigation Report on the famine. (G. Hosking, *Russia and the Russians*, 453-4 citing Lev Kopelev's *The Education of a True Believer*, London: Wildwood House, 1981,

26; S. Fitzpatrick, "The Great Departure: Rural-Urban Migration in the Soviet Union, 1929-33" in William G. Rosenberg and Lewis H. Siegelbaum, eds., *Social Dimensions of Soviet Industrialization*, Bloomington, Indiana Univ. Press, 1993, 21-7; David L. Hoffmann, *Peasant Metropolis: Social Identities in Moscow*, 1929-1941, Ithaca: Cornell Univ. Press, 1994, 32-41, 73-4; "Investigation of the Ukrainian Famine 1932-33", *US Congressional Commission on the Ukraine Famine*, Second Interim Report, April 23, 1986, US Government Printing Office, Washington, DC, 1988; Dr. James Mace, re. Stalin's response)

According to the report, "On the Scope of Political Repression in the USSR under Stalin's Rule: 1921–1953" by N. G. Okhotin and A. B. Roginsky (2003), the number of arrests soared in 1929 and 1930, and the number of convictions nearly doubled and executions tripled in 1929, and 1930, respectively, with the biggest jump in 1930. In 1929, there were 219,280 arrests for trial, 147,210 convictions and 3020 executions; in 1930 the arrests for trial rose to 378,540, convictions 285,820 and executions 20,988. In 1931, arrests continue to soar until a lull in 1933; in 1931 there were 479,070 arrests for trial, 272,960 convictions, 11,290 executions, or 32,278 executions for the period 1930-31. Arrests for the Holodomor peak period in 1933 jump to 643,430, and 422,140 convictions with 5790 executions, or 670 more executions than the previous year. For the period 1929 to 1936, the total number of executions was 51,948, according to this same report. It appeared more practical to send the prisoners to the labor camps. The 1937-38 Great Terror of the Red Army Purge saw those figures leap to nearly 16 million arrests, 15 million convictions, and 764,590 executions. (N.G. Okhotin and A.B. Roginsky, "On the Scope of Political Repression in the USSR under Stalin's Rule: 1921-1953", Memorial Society, Moscow, 2003)

Reader let's try not to get too lost in the numbers. It's worth noting the contribution by Soviet Russian expert the author Christopher Andrew in an effort aimed at clarity on this problem. "Controversy over the level of incompleteness in the official records (which do not, of course, include deaths in the camps or the millions who died from famine) will doubtless continue." And he explains, "Among the growing number of studies of the Terror, the classic account remains that by Robert Conquest... There is however, vigorous controversy over the numbers of the Terror's victims. In 1995 Colonel Grasshoven, head of the Russian security ministry rehabilitation team, estimated that in the period 1935-45, 18 million were arrested and 7 million shot. Olga Shatunovskaya, a member of Khrushchev's rehabilitation commission, gave the figure of those 'repressed' (imprisoned or shot) from 1935 to 1941 as 19.8 million (a statistic also found in the papers of Anastas Mikoyan). Dimitri Volkogonov arrived at a total of 21.5 million (of whom a third were shot) for the period 1929-53. Conquest's own revised estimates are of a similar order of magnitude." (R. Conquest, 'Playing Down the Gulag', *The Times Literary Supplement*, Feb. 24, 1995, 8)

Recent studies based on incomplete official records suggest considerably lower, but still large figures. Stephen Wheatcroft, one of the leading analysts of the official figures, believes it "unlikely that there were more than a million executions between 1921 and 1953. The labor camps and colonies never accounted for more than 2.5 million prisoners." What is striking even in the official records is the enormous rise in executions during the Great Terror: 353,074 in 1937, and 328,618, as compared with a total of under 10,000 for the Five-Year period 1932-36. (S. Wheatcroft, The Scale and Nature of German and Soviet Repression and Mass Killings, 1930-45, *Europe-Asia Studies*, v. 48, no. 8, 1996)"; C. Andrew and V. Mitrokhin, "Terror", ft. 21, 585)

By 1930 "dekulakization" goes into "full swing"; over 800,000 arrests, over a half million arrests with over 32,000 executions in the USSR. After Stalin's "Dizziness from Success" letter published in *Pravda* March 30, peasants were no longer forced into collectives and those who joined were free to leave. The government responded with increased taxes on individual farmers and improved conditions inside the collectives, particularly machinery from the West.

Prof. George Vernadsky observes, "By 1933 the number of tractors actually in use reached the impressive total of 200,000 and 25,000 combines were in operation in the grain districts. For the first time service stations for the repair and maintenance of agricultural machinery became generally available, and in the south, in particular, great numbers of 'machine-tractor stations' were set up to serve the neighboring kolkhozes". Sounds wonderful, right? Although the conclusions of this distinguished Yale professor are contradicted by more graphic on the scene source reports of broken down equipment lacking parts and skilled mechanics to cope with the intense government procurement program.

While Vernadsky concedes "a Pyrrhic victory" by the exterminators "since in winning it the backbone of the Russian agricultural system seemed to have been destroyed", he concludes with only a single reference to the entire Genocidal year of 1933: "By 1932 the government had won the battle of the kolkhozes – in the sense that the peasants had at last reluctantly accepted the new regime... The first reports showed a catastrophic decrease in production, particularly in the raising of livestock. The famine of 1930-31 followed close on the heels of the chaos which existed everywhere in agriculture, *and in Ukraine in particular the suffering reached a scale which almost passes human comprehension.* Even this disaster did not permanently cripple the Soviet economy. Within a comparatively few years the tremendous innate vitality of the Russian people once more asserted itself in the reestablishment of a working agricultural and industrial system." No mention here by the Russian professor Vernadsky of the terror, gulag or mass extermination, or the military preparations for inevitable war with the capitalist states which ought to strike the reader as a striking omission in these years of the Cold War where everything evil and threatening is Red.

Vernadsky prefers a more innocent diluted interpretation of historical events without speaking out to denounce Stalinist dictatorial terror or Genocide. Yet further on he describes Hitler's alarming advance towards Poland with a non-aggression pact of 1934, and he writes, with exaggerated reference to former Polish claim to Western Ukraine: "It was clear to them that nothing good could be expected from a rapprochement between Hitler, who did not conceal his intention of eventually trying to seize Ukraine, and Pilsudski, who had already tried and might at any time be expected to repeat the attempt." Five years later Churchill feels the same in 1939 when the Nazi-Soviet pact doomed Poland. (G. Vernadsky, 360-73; italics added)

It is in the following chapter ("The Soviet Union in the thirties") George Vernadsky affords his students barely a glimpse of the horror, concluding that "results of the first five-year plan were in the main satisfactory, and in not a few fields even better than had been anticipated". Still, he does concede that "gaps existed", that "the whole industrial structure lacked stability and cohesion", the railways remained "entirely inadequate". And what of the 1933 famine? "The reorganized agricultural system," George Vernadsky observes, "was in such a chaotic state that even in 1933 the government could not be certain collectivization was a workable principle or would yield adequate returns within a reasonable length of time. The people as a whole were depressed by the severe and continuous privations by which they had to pay for the fulfillment of the plan, and in spite of the wholesale deportation of kulaks – or perhaps precisely because of it – the loyalty of the peasant masses was especially doubtful." In fact, reading Vernadsky one wouldn't know there ever was a Holodomor famine in these years. (G. Vernadsky, 371-3)

Regarding dependence on western engineers and technicians, Vernadsky writes, "The Soviet Government endeavored energetically to extend commercial relations with the United States. In connection with the launching of the first five-year plan and the program for industrializing Russia, a number of contracts had been assigned to American firms for constructing or equipping factories in the Soviet Union, and a sizable group of American engineers had been hired to work in Russia as experts and consultants. The volume of trade continued to rise during this period and in 1929 reached the round sum of $155,000,000. But although trade relations proceeded on a mutually satisfactory basis, diplomatic relations with the United States remained in a state of suspension." (G. Vernadsky, 366)

Yale Professor Vernadsky considers the Plans an evolution of ideas first forwarded by "a prominent engineer of pre-revolutionary training", Basil Grinevetsky, whose book published in 1919, *Postwar Prospects of Russian Industry,* is at the time "the most important and clearest blueprint for the reconstruction of Russian industry". Grinevetsky is credited, in particular, with the "mammoth relocation of Russian industry…of great military importance – the shift of productive centers far to the east out of reach of any foreign invader".

Whereas for the most part historians credit the far-reaching genius of Comrade Stalin for the vision to transplant Soviet industrial factories far beyond the reach of Hitler's *Wehrmacht*, incapacitated by attrition and inadequate supply lines, Vernadsky observes that "Grinevetsky suggested the rapid development of two areas of great potential wealth – the Ural region and the vast territory of western Siberia which had not hitherto been sufficiently exploited… On the basis of Grinevetsky's ideas *and others*, the members of the Gosplan prepared the outline for the first five-year plan, which was announced early in 1928 and went into operation that autumn." Convertible factories are a priority. His enthusiasm for the achievements realized in the plan revised to four years (October 1, 1928 to December 31, 1932) is seen as nothing short of "tremendous", as he explains, "In four years Russia's yearly national income rose from 27 billion rubles (1926-27 level) to 45 billion rubles in 1932. Capital invested in industry rose from 2 billion to over 9 billion rubles. On the basis of this enormous capital investment the Soviet Union was able to proceed with a vast industrial expansion." International financing and western capital prepares the Soviet communist war machine...

Without the educated skills, training and mentality required to implement modern progress, and possessing a "shortage of skilled labor, technicians and engineers due handicapped by a "reserve pool of skilled workers that has always been traditionally "low", Vernadsky explains, due chiefly to the emigration, not Bolshevik terror against the cultured, educated class, he nevertheless is obliged to concede Soviet dependence on western expertise. "Foreign engineers were invited to supervise the building of the more important industrial plans, but they were too few to take care of all the details of the work personally, and in addition, they could not be trusted by the government."

Vernadsky's historical accounting of Soviet progress paid tribute to the cooperation and development of the Russian people although he neglects to say the war mentality imposed on the population was at the price of freedom. Their lives depended on it unless they were to be arrested, displaced or killed as "enemies of the people", parasites, corrupt bourgeois "wreckers" and other vermin of the Bolsheviki vernacular. "The Russians believed that they were battling for survival, and under those circumstances they could and did bear extremes of privation." With the use of "shock brigades", fanatical youth indoctrinated in the Komsomol battalions, failures to achieve quotas in coal, pig iron, timber and even in Leningrad's factory goods production were met with increased quotas and unrelenting government incentive. Vernadsky writes, "the general rise of production at the end of the first five year plan was impressive enough. In the period 1928-1932 the yearly output of coal had increased from 35,000,000 to 64,000,000 tons; of oil from 11,000,000 tons to 22,000,000, of pig iron from 3,000,000 to 6,000,000. In 1928 less than 1,000 automobiles and only slightly more than 1,000 tractors had been produced, but in 1932, 24,000 automobiles and 50,000 tractors rolled from Soviet plants." (G. Vernadsky, 351-5; italics added)

January 1, 1933 will prove to be the most brutal year for the Ukrainians. Stalin launches his more ambitious second Five-Year Plan with unbridled ruthlessness. Any observer would have to be bent, or indifferent, to think it a mere coincidence that the increased demands on the population were independent and unrelated to the increased measures of repression imposed throughout the USSR at the same time as the Holodomor is killing its most victims? For the good of "God, Country and Yale", professor Vernadsky tallies its success, writing, "The annual gross output of Soviet industry, which by 1932 had reached 43 billion rubles (calculated on the 1926-7 price index), was to be expanded to 93 billion rubles by 1937, the last year of the second plan."

But Vernadsky omits to speak of factory conversion to war production; instead he extols Soviet concentration "on heavy industry in order to build up her military potential", citing "the Magnitogorsk plant, the Kramatorsk heavy machinery plant, and the Cheliabinsk tractor factory", with no references to western technology, technical onsite expertise of foreign workers. Improvements in railroads showed "a 10 % increase in car loadings for 1934 over 1933, several new lines such as that between Moscow and the Donetz basin", and, in 1933, the Baltic-White Sea Canal is completed. Bullitt and the embassy personnel have the opportunity to witness first-hand the building everywhere of the Moscow metro the first of its kind in Russia, launched in a publicity drive two years earlier and sufficiently deep in the ground to remain safe from bombardment. (G. Vernadsky, 374-5; *The Utopian Dream: Photography in Soviet Russia, 1918-1939.* NY: The Gallery, 1992)

Stalin's *volte-face* from Ukrainization of the 1927 period replaced by intensified repression of Ukrainian national elements is dismissed by the Yale professor who instead writes not unerringly that the "critical condition in agriculture was eased somewhat at the beginning of the second plan." Vernadsky spares his reader the meaning of "somewhat". For the fact all reports indicate that the Holodomor is nearing its peak. Vernadsky writes, "The critical condition in agriculture was eased somewhat at the beginning of the second plan. A vast amount of capital was poured into the collectives which were constantly being expanded and equipped for more efficient production. In 1933-34 alone agricultural investments totaled 5 billion rubles, most of which was spent on machinery and equipment. The extraordinary efforts previously put forth by the government to bolster the agrarian structure began to show results. The annual yield of grain crops in both 1933 and 1934 totaled more than 89,000,000 metric tons as compared to slightly more than 80,000,000 in 1913. The livestock situation continued to be troublesome. The number of horses continued to decline – though not at the previous rate – but the general food situation was improved somewhat by an increase in hog production." The peasants ate their horses and drank their reserves of vodka in a last feast celebrating centuries of tilling the land rather than surrender them to the State, and starve. Many flee to the cities to find employment and food, or to seek a new life in the wilderness while those who stayed behind faced the Soviet onslaught.

Pigs, however, reproduce in greater quantities, a fact that did not elude Orwell, author of the anti-Stalinian classic *Animal Farm,* – a must-read for all Russia watchers. Professor Vernadsky tells us, "With the mechanization and collectivization of farming, thousands of peasants were released for work in factories and the pool of skilled labor available to industry was rapidly augmented. On the whole, the morale of the Russian people was improving. Still, silk stockings and chocolates, cherished gifts from foreigners, will get you a long trip to the gulag for deviation from the Party line of the classless New Society. Better fed, stirred by sweeping industrial achievements, of great national significance, the people caught the spirit of growth and expansion which was being cultivated by the government." This is the same message from Stalin and FDR's ambassador Joe Davies: the Yale professor Vernadsky as well as the pro-communist wing in the Consortium prefers non-Russians to believe it so but the Russian-Ukrainians who survive were not fooled. (Vernadsky, 375)

And there is another book published in 1934, destroyed in 1937, reprinted in 1998, a book ordered by the OGPU to praise the success of "corrective labor" practices during the construction of the Canal. This is edited by Maxim Gorky and written by well-known soviet writers of the time and constitutes stories after multiple field trips when construction was under way. It is symbolic, that many of the heroes of the book and its authors alike did not survive the purges of 1937-38. According to a Soviet author, "Before they died, people often lost their senses and ceased to be human beings." Yet one of Stalin's lieutenants in Ukraine stated in 1933 that the famine was a great success. It showed the peasants "who is the master here. It cost millions of lives, but the collective farm system is here to stay."

> Addendum to the minutes of Politburo (meeting) No. 93. 6 December 1932
>
> RESOLUTION OF THE COUNCIL OF PEOPLE'S COMMISSARS OF THE UKRAINIAN SOVIET SOCIALIST REPUBLIC AND OF THE CENTRAL COMMITTEE OF THE COMMUNIST PARTY (BOLSHEVIK) OF UKRAINE ON BLACKLISTING VILLAGES THAT MALICIOUSLY SABOTAGE THE COLLECTION OF GRAIN.
>
> In view of the shameful collapse of grain collection in the more remote regions of Ukraine, the Council of People's Commissars and the Central Committee call upon the oblast executive committees and the oblast (party) committees as well as the raion executive committees and the raion (party) committees:
>
>> to break up the sabotage of grain collection, which has been organized by kulak and counterrevolutionary elements; to liquidate the resistance of some of the rural communists, who in fact have become the leaders of the sabotage; to eliminate the passivity and complacency toward the saboteurs, incompatible with being a party member; and to ensure, with maximum speed, full and absolute compliance with the plan for grain collection.
>
> The Council of People's Commissars and the Central Committee resolve:
>
>> To place the following villages on the black list for overt disruption of the grain collection plan and for malicious sabotage, organized by kulak and counterrevolutionary elements:

1. village of Verbka in Pavlograd raion, Dnepropetrovsk oblast.

5. village of Sviatotroitskoe in Troitsk raion, Odessa oblast.

6. village of Peski in Bashtan raion, Odessa oblast.

The following measures should be undertaken with respect to these villages :

1. Immediate cessation of delivery of goods, complete suspension of cooperative and state trade in the villages, and removal of all available goods from cooperative and state stores.

2. Full prohibition of collective farm trade for both collective farms and collective farmers, and for private farmers.

3. Cessation of any sort of credit and demand for early repayment of credit and other financial obligations.

4. Investigation and purge of all sorts of foreign and hostile elements from cooperative and state institutions, to be carried out by organs of the Workers and Peasants Inspectorate.

5. Investigation and purge of collective farms in these villages, with removal of counterrevolutionary elements and organizers of grain collection disruption.

The Council of People's Commissars and the Central Committee call upon all collective and private farmers who are honest and dedicated to Soviet rule to organize all their efforts for a merciless struggle against kulaks and their accomplices in order to: defeat in their villages the kulak sabotage of grain collection; fulfill honestly and conscientiously their grain collection obligations to the Soviet authorities; and strengthen collective farms.

CHAIRMAN OF THE COUNCIL OF PEOPLE'S COMMISSARS OF THE UKRAINIAN SOVIET SOCIALIST REPUBLIC - V. CHUBAR.

SECRETARY OF THE CENTRAL COMMITTEE OF THE COMMUNIST PARTY (BOLSHEVIK) OF UKRAINE - S. KOSIOR.

The 1934 negotiations between Stalin and Bullitt for improving the Russian railways fuel his intent on accelerating the geographical distribution of heavy industry to develop industrial bases in the Urals and western Siberia with an intent to exploit the rich natural resources and protect his centers of military production. Its during this second Plan with priority for the Ural-Kuznetsk *combinat* of mining and metallurgical plants already progressed since 1928, and reaffirmed at the 16th Congress in 1930 called for more iron from the Urals and coal from the Kuznetsk region. To move the materials in both directions through 1200 miles of wilderness Stalin needs track and freight cars.

By 1932, the Soviets had 83,000 kilometers of rail track, up from 58,000 in 1913, and top 100,000 by 1940. The Soviet regime was able to extract even greater results with a higher percentage in increased rail capacity expanding from 132 million tons (1931) to some 260 million tons (1932), and 553 million tons (1940). In just six years from 1932 to 1938, under the draconian gulag system of concentration camp and factory labor, industrial output rose considerably outpacing any production in the West; coal increased from 64 million tons to 132 million; oil from 22 million tons to 32 million; pig iron from 6 million to 14 million; steel from 6 million to 18 million; automobiles from 23,000 to 211,000; tractors from 50,000 to 176,000." Discoveries of coal deposits in northern Kazakhstan further impact a greater load on the Ural route. In cities along the Volga River more factories spring up producing locomotives, tractors and automobiles as well as turbogenerators from Moscow to Kharkov and Stalingrad as well as Gorky, Ufa and Sverdlovsk.

In 1938 while Bukharin, Rykov, Yagoda and others of the so-called Rightests and Trotskiites, are crucified industrial war production is intensified with the launching of the third five-year plan, bolstered by the announcement of oil deposits between the Urals and the Volga giving rise to a "the Second Baku. A second rail line is undertaken to the Far East along the north shore of Lake Baikal towards the Sea of Okhotsk but is incomplete before the German invasion.

Also constructed during the second Plan is an oil pipeline from Grozny in the north Caucasus to the Tuapse on the Black Sea. Here is Vernadsky writing on the second five-year Plan launched January 1, 1933: "The Soviet Union was forced again to concentrate on heavy industry in order to build up her military potential." He cites "the Magnitogorsk plant, the Kramatorsk heavy machinery plant, and the Cheliabinsk tractor factory", with no reference to western technology transfer, technical expertise of foreign or American workers, tank production etc. Improvements in railroads showed "a 10 % increase in car loadings for 1934 over 1933, several new lines such as that between Moscow and the Donetz basin", and, in 1933, the Baltic-White Sea Canal is completed. Bullitt and the embassy personnel had first-hand opportunity to witness the building everywhere of the Moscow subway, the first of its kind in Russia, sufficiently deep in the ground to remain safe from bombardment. (G. Vernadsky, *A History of Russia,* "Economic Progress, 1935-38, Yale, 1962, 355-88)

Vernadsky's figures confirm that the "spectacular" and "steady" progress of the Soviet increase in production in agriculture was due to the "increase in the production of tractors and agricultural machinery at home and in imports from abroad, chiefly from the United States". Even after the trials of Zinoviev, Kamenev, Rykov, other Bols, CP members and the Red Army officer ranks are decimated by the thousands, Stalin is still sending down orders through the NKVD to liquidate surviving Ukrainians. But Vernadsky musn't write about these killings of the Genocide.

By 1935, and once Stalin is mollified to some degree by the thoroughness of his sweeping repression of Ukraine's peasant and nationalist population, and food production stabilized, the regime ceased with the onerous ration books for bread and food products. Collectivization by 1939 results in 4,000 kolkhozes (state farms) on 12 million hectares, and 242,000 kolkhozes (collective farms) on 117 million hectares. Some 1.3 million individual farmers were still allowed to work on "privately used land" on a million hectares, which may seem odd. Vernadsky explained, "At first there had been considerable confusion about the internal organization of the kolkhozes; two different plans had been put into operation simultaneously, the one providing for strict collectivization and the other for a looser association.

"By the end of 1934 an intermediate form which included some elements from both of the original plans had become the prevailing type, and in 1935 a revised code for the *kolkhozes*, called the Stalin Code, was promulgated. Presumably this new system of organization was in part the result of the advice given b y Kirov. Each kolkhoz received a charter or deed for the land in its possession, and although the land still legally belonged to the state it was expressly provided that the farms should remain permanently in the control of each kolkho.... Each member was now permitted a small plot of land, varying from one quarter to one hectare in size, for his personal use, and the products of such plots could be disposed of by the holder for his own profit. Each member was also to share in the collective profit of the kolkhoz according to the amount of work he had contributed. All collectives were bound to sell a certain quota of grain and other products to the government at fixed prices, and to pay the machine-tractor stations, usually in grain, for their service. They were free to dispose of the balance on the open market." He added, "By the end of the second five-year plan more than 6,000 machine-tractor stations serving collectivized agriculture had been organized in the main farming districts of the Soviet Union – in Ukraine, the north Caucasus, and western Siberia. At the same time, the number of tractors operated by the stations increased from 7,000 in 1930 to 454,000 in 1941, and harvesting combines from 3,000 in 1932 to 125,000 in 1939." Training and domestic production gradually relieved Soviet dependence on imports and the necessity of the supervision of foreign technicians. (G. Vernadsky, 386-7)

In fact, while the Brits were importing more than the United States, the *Stokholms Tidningen* editors poked fun at Imperial England for having to cow down and more more: "accommodating" or be doubled by the American business man. Siegel quotes from a source that Stalin feared commercial rivalry in the West between the Americans, London and Berlin might make a mess of his Plans. "Germans constantly cry that the position of the Soviet Government is precarious and that it is not justified to open serious credits with Soviet economic organizations, but at the same time they try to monopolize trade relations with the USSR, and offer credit."

The dictator is confused how in the West anti-Soviet lobbies clash with cliques pushing for liberalizing credit terms with Moscow. Parliamentary democracy is a nuisance. "How to explain these two-faced German and English businesspeople? They want to monopolize to themselves the trade relations with Russia, abusing and driving away the United States from us". Meanwhile Stalin encouraged greater commercial ties with America. Poole now stationed as Consul in Berlin. Poole learns that IBM "did not business" with the Soviets at the time, and that their patents had been victims of industrial espionage complaining that some of their ideas had been "pirated" and patents "copied".

Other Americans have similar stories of grief. John L. Senior of Cowham Engineering told the embassy that he gave up all notions of working under the Soviets. For their part, Westinghouse favors increasing sales but without credit. Gumberg and his group for the most part know they were part of a propaganda tour, conspicuously playing out their roles in exceptionally staged "cleanliness of the entourage, the lack of beggars, the efficient supply of factories and mines and the satisfaction of the peasants …became obvious." All perfectly orchestrated. So who is fooling who? It takes two to dance. Gumberg has long been a National City agent. (K. Siegel, *Loans and Legitimacy*, 107-8)

We ought to take a closer work at how the Consortium did its business with the Soviets and how it particular strategic interests dominate US foreign policy with its tradition and generational impact still felt today. Of course it has become more subtle and sophisticated over time penetrating every corner of American life with its impact felt globally through the proliferation of its influence and institutions.

As is often the standard practice when reading establishment history you have to move on quickly from here to dig into the heart of darkness. David Allan Mayers treatment of the Terror-Famine in a chapter titled "In Stalin's Time" of his book *The Ambassadors and America's Soviet Policy* (Oxford 1995) merits a good read not for what it purports to reveal but rather how it conceals. Mayers throws in a curious quote about Harriman by Clark Kerr, Chancellor of the University of California, at Berkeley, who at this time takes his MA at Stanford, in 1933, in economics and industrial relations, and on the cover of *Time* in 1960 but unfortunately the description is more apt to sum up this establishment crony. Kerr apparently called the Yale billionaire a "champion bumsucker" with his unrestrained praise of the Consortium masters while straining backwards to do his best not to expose them. Clever but not convincing, though he does get his reward winning the "America Academy of Diplomacy for a Book of Distinction on American Diplomacy" (the Douglas Dillon Award); the following year Bush's Secretary of state picked one up. Other winners include Robert L. Beisner, 2007 (*Dean Acheson*, Oxford Univ. Press), James Chase, 1999 (*Acheson*, Simon & Schuster), Condoleeza Rice and Philip Zelikow, 1996 (*Germany Unified and Europe Transformed*, Harvard).

Firstly, Mayers will not recognize the Holodomor by name. While quoting Conquest he refrains from accepting descriptions minutely detailed in the Conquest book *The Great Terror*. Establishment history has an iceberg effect. It hides more below the surface. Mayers misses the whole story of American-Anglo investment in the Soviet Union. He follows that standard course naming mostly the same names in the same fashion with some added anecdotal stories here and there to spice the cake and dumb down the reader with filler that guarantees job placement in America's academic community. He's smart, deliberate and apparently fairly precise. In other words, his is exactly the dangerous kind of soap that stinks when you know what it really is all about. It exists in this great pluralistic world of fact and fiction. Just be careful and know what you that you are getting stuffed and mounted with this literary nonsense posing as fact.

Propagandists have to be very good at what they do which is why ad men, corporate lobbyists, TV newsmen get big bucks to spin, distract and daze viewers into states of idiocy. To be sure, university academics and political think tankers get their share in the twisted culture of modern Babylon. This is how Mayers introduces the initiation of the Consortium's Five-Year Plan: "The rapid industrialization, collectivization of agriculture, and decision to 'squeeze' the countryside's wealth to pay for machinery and foreign technology amounted to an attack by Stalin's government on the population. This massive but lopsided contest between coercive state power and its subjects resulted in countless more fatalities and led to the incarceration, exile and forced labor of millions of men and women. ... The setting of foundations for industrial complexes such as Magnitogorsk in the Urals, electrification of rural areas, and campaigns to raise popular awareness of everything from socialist precepts to personal hygiene impressed sympathetic observers as first evidence the sacrifices were not in vain. One US engineer explained in 1930 after living in the Soviet Union for three years: '(The worker) has been told – and he still believes – that the hardships which he undergoes now will end in a more glorious Russia, a Russia of plenty for him and his children'."

Of course, many did. Many knew better. Countless died knowing either way. In the end it didn't matter whatever you knew or thought. The *chef d'orchestre*, No. 1, the Great Dictator himself set the agenda. Party debates were conducted according to plan with pre-set outcomes. Mayers intentionally downplays and in so doing obscures the picture of US investment in the USSR. There is no reference to American fascist involvement behind the Bolshevik grab for power denying the Russians their freedom after millions died fighting for it in the First World War.

Mayers writes, "During the nonrecognition era, various US businessmen organized profitable trade and enterprises in the Soviet Union through the offices of Amtorg, that institutional expression of Moscow's eagerness for American capital and technology. Concessions were granted to Armand and Julius Hammer to mine asbestos and manufacture pencils. A manganese-mining operation was run by Averell Harriman in the Caucasus during the 1920s that began with the promise of development of a vital natural resource (though it ended in a confusion of red tape and inefficiency.) Oil companies, including Standard and Sinclair, won contracts to develop Soviet energy reserves. Substantial quantities of American-grown cotton were exported to Soviet textile industries, themselves partly financed with private US capital." Mayers implies that this was fair and competitive contract bidding instead of cartel price fixing under monopoly control of the giant Soviet industrial Trusts.

The "Great Turning Point" came by the time of Stalin's speech for the 1929 anniversary of the October Revolution, November 7. Bread was taken by force. Resistance to join the collectives meant that peasants who had farmed their own land since 1920 when it was taken from landlord estates now became slaves to their new masters. That meant mass deportations and more starvation and more purges.

By 1926 Ukraine's economy had recovered. Industrialization built 408 industrial enterprises; 421 were reconstructed in 1926-29. Stalin launched the construction of 371 industrial projects; by 1929 the Ukraine's machine-building output more than doubled. Persisting to look through a Czarist prism at all things wrong in Russia, Salisbury offers little praise for hapless Soviet Socialism, even after a few short years when the country faced near oblivion and total destruction in the First World War, Revolution and Civil War.

Harrison Salisbury writes, "When Stalin started to build 'Communism in one country' it quickly developed that his problems and methods were not unlike those of Russia's past rulers. In 1928 many projects for Stalin's first five year plan of the Czarist planning commission of 1915. His orders for 'collectivization' of peasants, forcing them into farm cooperatives, and the elimination of kulaks, or richer peasants, were carried out with the mass brutality of an Ivan the Terrible. His purges and paranoid use of terror rivaled those of his tyrant predecessors. His secret police followed Czarist patterns. Like his imperial precursors, Stalin turned Siberia into a vast labor camp. He used forced labor to run mines, fell timber, dig canals and build factories, and enslaved enormous segments of the population to provide an army of workers."

Salisbury omits to recall that Anglo-French imperial war planners in the First World War, joined by the financial power elite in Washington and New York, targeted the collapse of Czarism, engineered the destruction of its autocratic rule over the vast Russian resources and unskilled manpower, and once quickly defeated in the Civil War and immediately queued up with plans for concessions and profits certain to come from the inevitable peacetime postwar reconstruction with a socialist monopoly of dictatorship as their partner. (H. Salisbury, 21)

American-made locomotives, high on Stalin's shopping list, are sold in bulk. Easing of credit restrictions in 1928 permit the USSR to purchase more than $20 million worth of electrical equipment from the International GE, and "the Cooper Company" provides for a good price technical assistance useful in building the Dnieprostroy Dam. David Mayers (1995) assessed the figure of US-Soviet trade having reached a yearly value of about $100 million by 1930, at least twice the pre-1914 level when Czarist Russia had the fastest growing economy in the world and America was still a debtor nation. He observes, "Despite concern about Soviet dumping of cheap products in American markets, there was growing optimism among entrepreneurs that business with the USSR was lucrative and –after the 1929 stock market crash – could play a role in US recovery." (D. A. Mayers, *The Ambassadors and America's Soviet Policy*)

Soviet industry was for the most part paid for by peasant labor and the produce extracted from the countryside. And those locomotives are the pride of the USSR and dreaded by all the Gulag prisoners. Prices in the city were set at the highest level with the lowest return to the peasants leaving the most profit to the government to pay for the industrial program. The OGPU-NKVD police (The OGPU or United Main Political Administration was the title used by the secret police from 1923-34) cracked down on the Kulak richer peasants, then suppress after any sign of resistance by individual peasants who hesitate joining the collective farms or withholding any of their harvest.

Comparisons of the Salisbury type simply turn out to be ludicrous when the record of Czarism is contrast with the early years of Soviet Russia. Examine the contrary perspectives, for example, between the Consortium's own spy turned Cold War historian Conquest and Soviet dissident Solzhenitsyn. Consider the extent of slave labor, exile and imprisonment in labor death camps with numbers that skyrocket after the statute on Corrective Labor Camps adopted on April 7, 1930 soon after Stalin's decisive "Dizziness with Success" article is published in *Pravda*. It's an admonishment to the Party and triggers a wave of mass extermination of the peasants and sounds the final blow against his political opposition within the Party from both the Left and the Right.

Conquest describes Stalin's gulags in *The Great Terror, A Reassessment*, modified and republished in 1990. (President Bush honors Conquest a medal for his work; Solzhenitsyn got prison and exile.) Conquest: "The camps took their modern form at a time of vast expansion of the network. The most careful estimates of the camp population over the pre-Yezhov period run as follows: In 1928, 30,000. In 1930, 600,000. In 1931 and 1932, a total of nearly 2 million in 'places of detention' can be estimated from figures given for the allotment per prisoner of newspapers, and a Moscow scholar recently estimates that of 'over' 15 million dekulakized in the collectivization of 1930 to 1932, 1 million of the males of working age were sent directly to labor camps. In 1933 to 1935, Western estimates run mainly at the 5 million level (70 percent of them peasants), and in 1935, a little higher. But recent Soviet analysis suggests that (omitting deportees held in NKVD 'Special Settlements') the true figure may be lower, in the 2 to 4 million range. A Soviet textbook of the 1930s gives the maximum numbers at forced labor (*katorga*) in Czarist times, as 32,000, in 1912, and the maximum total of all prisoners as 183,949." Close examination is invaluable to understand the absurd bureaucratic rationale reserved for political prisoners and common criminals. Women were not allowed to keep their children born in captivity. They too belonged to the Security Organs. An estimate in a Soviet paper during the time gave the number of NKVD children of between 500,000 and one million. Amy Knight in *Who Killed Kirov* (1999) observes that collectivization in all of Soviet Russian peasant households increases from 6 percent in 1931 to 54 percent by January 1934. (R. Conquest, *The Great Terror*, 311; Amy Knight, *Who Killed Kirov*, 1999, 146; A. Knight, *Beria*, Princeton Univ. Press, 1995)

Soviet historian Roy Medvedev sheds more light in his treatment "The War Against the Peasants" in *On Stalin and Stalinism* (Oxford, 1979): "According to recently published data, 115,000 kulak families were deported to remote areas in 1930 and 265,800 in 1931 – a total of almost 381,000 during the two year period. Peasant families were large in those years, averaging not fewer than six or seven persons per family. Thus, even on the basis of official figures, something like 2.5 million persons were sent into exile. Official government sources also report that the deportation of kulaks and 'kulak-agents' continued during 1932, and that in addition to families sent to distant parts of the country, quite a number of families were resettled in other districts within their own region. There is every reason to believe, however, that all these statistics are considerably understated… A much larger number of peasants died during the appalling famine, more or less artificially created in the winter of 1932-33, which primarily affected the southern regions of the Ukraine, although the northern Caucasus, the Volga region, Central Asia and Kazakhstan suffered as well. In 'Population of the USSR once can find census data for the Ukrainian population according to which there were 31.2 million in 1926 and 28.1 million in 1939. The actual decrease in population over the thirteen-year people amounted to 3.1 million. Yet during the same years the number of Belorussians in the USSR grew to 1.3 million, an increase of almost 30 percent! ... For the period of 1926-39, the number of Kazakhs decreased by 860,000; there was also a decline in the number of Uighur, Altai, Yakuts, Tungus and other peoples of the north. There was virtually no change in the number of Kalmyks and Buryats."

The Marxist Medvedev quotes from a later document published with a French translation: "During the famine 1933-34 (writes a specialist on the demography of the USSR), an incredible number of children perished, particularly newborn infants. Of those living in the USSR at the time of the 1970 census, 12.4 million persons were born in 1929-31, but only 8.4 million in 1932-34. The difference between these figures cannot be attributed to any deliberate attempt to control the birthrate. Moreover, the collectivization campaign was at its height in 1929-31, but there was only a relatively slight decline in the birthrate compared to the preceding three-year period. Bearing in mind the fact that the famine of 1933 descended without warning and that birth-control methods were virtually unknown in the Russian countryside of that time, it is undoubtedly the case that no fewer than three million children born between 1932 and 1934 died of hunger."

(R. A. Medvedev quoting from *Cahiers du Monde russe et sovietique*, 1977 re. M. Maksudov, *Poteri naselenia SSSR v 1918-1958*, *On Stalin and Stalinism*, 74-6)

Note. In a blitz of propaganda in June 1936 Stalin outlaws abortion, long a target of criticism by western visitors and specialists who visited Soviet hospitals where it was the most frequent operation. Abortion was first legalized in Soviet Russia in November 1920, largely the work of Aleksandra Kollontai, a famous writer and close follower of Lenin who became the first woman elected to the Communist Party's Central Committee and appointed Commissar for Public Welfare. Heavy fines are levied on women who insist on having an abortion; a minimum sentence of two years in prison is imposed on those who performed the operations. Perhaps Stalin prefers the neo-conservative Czarist measure for family and Motherhood to compensate for the state's falling birthrate. Kollontai is attacked for "bourgeois feminist deviation" for advocating the ideal of the single woman and the emancipation of Soviet women from persisting patriarchalism. (Barbara E. Clements, Barbara A. Engel, Christine D. Worobec, "Women, Abortion and the State", *Russia's Women: Accommodation, Resistance, Transformation*, Univ. of California Press, 1991, 244)

Around 1970 an entire generation discovered Russia when the film *Doctor Zhivago*, written by Boris Pasternak. I saw it seventeen times as a kid working in the Darien movie theater and along with millions of Americans fell in love with his mistress Laura, played by Julie Christie. He died in 1960, and was buried at Peredelkino, in view from a window of his house in this writer's colony. His funeral with some two thousand people turned into "the first mass unofficial funeral ceremony in Soviet history". Pasternak is one of the few famous writers spared by Stalin. He witnessed those famine horrors during the Russian Civil War and ten years lived these Holodomor 1932 to 1934. Stalin and the Communist Party created the Writers' Union in 1932. It was the only professional organization for writers in the country. They are instructed to write for the people building communism in the factories and harvesting the grain for the great socialist future and to give the young wings to reach their dreams with a new culture of Soviet socialist ideas. (re. Pasternak funeral, S. Volkov, 197)

Stalin liked to call prominent writers on the phone to show that he too was human and real while the secret police confiscated their works and kept them under constant surveillance to make sure they didn't stray too far from the Party line. He liked their wit and their brains for describing life and writing the destinies of men. Stalin, too, is known for his wry Russian sense of humor.

A writer, Stalin said, is "the engineer of men's souls".

Once in the night when he called Pasternak, he asked the writer why he hadn't called him, and insisted that he must come to see him some time.

"What do you wish to talk about?" Stalin queried.

A long pause.

Pasternak replied, "Life and death".

Silence. Pasternak heard only the click of the phone as Stalin puts down the phone.

STALIN AND HIS FAVORITE WRITERS

Bulgakov was born in Kiev to Russian parents. The Great Dictator had a weakness for the writings of Mikhail Bulgakov, author of one of more famous works in modern literature *The Master and Margarita*, a realist magical satire about corruption and the Devil, which he began writing in 1928. Stalin liked his writings so much that they would occasionally talk on the telephone. But Stalin repeatedly refused to give Bulgakov permission to leave Russia and kept under constant surveillance by the Lubyanka.

Pasternak left notes in his unpublished memoirs: "In the early 1930s it became fashionable among writers to visit the collective farms and gather material about the new way of life in the villages. I wanted to be like everyone else and also set out on such a trip with the intention of writing a book. But there are no worlds to express what I saw. There was such inhuman unimaginable misery, such frightful poverty, that it began to take on an almost abstract quality, as if it were beyond what the conscious mind could absorb. I fell ill and could write nothing for an entire year." Pasternak could have been imprisoned and sent to the Solovetsky monastery in the White Sea to be shot or to any of the industrial labor camps. Instead Stalin chooses to intervene with a written order, "Leave that cloud-dweller in peace!"

Five years after Stalin's death, Pasternak wins the Nobel Prize for Literature in 1958, a year after an Italian publisher released *Dr. Zhivago*, but Pasternak is bullied – (Nabokov must be crunching his teeth!) –, by a wave of Soviet protest and Pasternak is forced to turn away from the accolades and rejects Stockholm. Not until 1988 does *Doctor Zhivago* see the light on bookshelves in Pasternak's Russia. (Vitaly Shentalinsky, *Arrested Voices*, Martin Kessler Books- Free Press, 1993, 149)

During these same years from 1928-35 American presidents in consecutive administrations once again allow US-Soviet trade and economic assistance to bolster Stalin's repressive regime. As a result, the Consortium kings Hoover and FDR strengthened Stalin's monolithic Soviet Party state socialism to spread terror over the Soviet Union and helped seal the fate of millions of people suffering extermination by starvation, torture and forced deportation to slave labor camps. Americans living safe and tranquil lives behind white picket fences would not even be able to imagine the horrors let alone believe such nightmares even if they found light in a stray newspaper beyond the purse-strings of the Consortium owned national press. Outraged Americans did, those who caught wind of it and kick up a storm, at least those few who saw under the veil of American and communist propaganda concealing the truth about the camps, and angered by the economic complicity and political silence in Washington.

Their protests were in vain. Mainstream America was kept in the dark about Stalin's agricultural campaign of extermination of the Ukrainian peasants and good Americans were deprived of even the slightest opportunity to exercise their democratic rights until it was too late. As far as the White House was concerned, it was not in the best interests of the nation, ergo, its strategic defense interests to irritate Stalin and derail FDR's plan for good relations with the dictator in exchange for the remote possibility of lessening the massive suffering that struck the Ukraine for half a decade.

Certainly, if an evil will prevailed in the Soviet Union it found a willing collaborator in the White House and its State Department. Roosevelt officially recognizes Stalin on November 16, 1933. In spite of the outcry of American Ukrainians and their friends in Washington and Berlin, plans for a second world war, more devastating than the first, were already drafted inside the Soviet military and industrial society constructed with American technology and engineers. (Oh yes, America had its own plans too, naturally.) Since food could be used as "a weapon", and Hoover knew this all too well, both he and FDR had good reason to fear exposure by the famine and other possible entanglements arising from Soviet internal affairs of perpetual state terror. Worse, it might have meant the abrupt end to their political careers and a different course of history than they secretly mandated for their country and the world. Thus it was also convenient for Washington to keep the taboo and not stir up the murky secrets of the foggy bottom. In another country, perhaps such an assault against Humanity might provoke revolt, even revolution. Not in America. The American people are not like that. Apparently they are sedate and comfortable in their isolated containment, secure and protected by a paternal government, and is content to live in a state of perpetual chronic fear and obey the dictates of the American Dream fantasy. Anyway, the Consortium would never permit such a revolt, and never did having amply invested for over a century to guarantee the perpetuity of their power over the country they control, through education, in the constant bombardment by the media's idiotic talking heads, orchestrating an inane dollar-endowed political process out of reach of the common man, with lawyers and bankers at the center of power, and most importantly, asserting its democratic dogma with the consent of the docile and loyal governed.

For over a decade the Americans were heavily invested in Lenin's regime of terror. As far as the war planners were concerned, famine was just another detail of soviet progress in their secret business of development and war. Hundreds of eager American consultants and technically-skilled engineers arrived to make a good buck on the Soviet monopoly which needed everything under the sun to match Germany's reconstruction and rearmament.

The lack of documentation on US companies building Stalin's Five-Year Plans speaks volumes of a black-out by government employees at the State Department and in the White House. Even if the Riga team and Washington's bureaucrats were woefully deficient in the area of technology and economic systems, the Soviet's technical dependency on American technology was incontestable and for long a well-kept secret. Did Riga and State Department's government officials have a particular bureaucratic aversion to "rocking the boat," or to forward research proposals to analyze Soviet industrial and technological capacity? This does not however explain why some of the outside consultants who are hired by all Western governments in such profusion, as Sutton observes, did not systematically explore the possibility. Western governments are not only aware but they also profited from Soviet dependency. Imagine the scandal! Here you have the Soviet Union dependent on American technology, building its colossal military industrial infrastructure dependent American engineers, American companies, and American innovation, while extolling the superiority of communist virtues and collective socialism, berating bourgeois contradictions and American capitalists for making imperialist wars. All the while Stalin's men are invoking more repressions, trials, seizures, executions, with freight cars packed with prisoners packed off to freeze to death in northern concentration camps and Siberia where life expectancy is two years. How could FDR dare speak about freedom when the Americans are deprived of the freedom to know the truth about Soviet terror or about their own government engaged in finance and trade deals with the Central Committee of the Communist Party (CCC). Some call it a travesty; others call it "the American way".

In a democratic society, the freedom to know is still not enough for freedom to flourish. Once the famine was exposed, the truth behind it was buried with the dead. Too much exposure can kill even a news story if left only partially told. There must be freedom to act, and accountability and transparency required of democratic leadership. However, the USSR government deprived Americans of both those essential freedom s while permitting and encouraging Stalin to stealthy plot his campaign of Terror-Famine and purges of Russians as well as Ukrainians. Both the Ukrainians and the American people then might have asked two Democratic Presidents, "Why are you killing the Ukraine?"

The contradictions of history are not so ironic as our inertia to understand the logic behind them. The technology of industrialized weapon systems developed in America during the First World War and subsequently refined in the 1920s is sold to the Soviets enabling them to transform the socialist economy into a formidable military and industrial power to withstand an assault by Hitler. On the eve of the Twentieth Anniversary of the October Revolution in 1937 Stalin could boast the success of his First Five-Year Plan of Industrialization that he had the largest iron and steel works that existed anywhere in the world. Between 1929-32 these industrial plants originating from the United States are built by American engineers employed by the McKee Company of Cleveland (Ohio) on the blueprints from Gary (Indiana), the perfectly planned industrial steel mill city.

With the Depression the promising future turns into one of the deadest towns in America. For the moment McKee signed a $2.5 million gold dollar contract with the Soviets in exchange for the technical plans and supervision needed to construct the Magnitogorsk plant where iron deposits were found to hold 228 million tons of iron ore making it one of the richest in the world and an important symbol of success for Stalin's socialist experiment. How long is the future? At present Gary, Indiana is a dump.

Workers dreamed how they were building a magnificent city with palaces, houses and a park. But the reality was different. The Party hierarchy cadre in the cities would rather commit suicide than be sent there, a real hell on earth for the unprepared in the distant wilderness hundreds of miles south east of Moscow. Workers even created a futurist park with metal trees because trees wouldn't grow on the steppe. With nearly all its thousands of workers living in tents or temporary barracks, freezing and weakened by "prolonged and severe food shortages", Magnitogorsk poured its first melting of pig iron February 1, 1932. Scott related, "Economic difficulties caused severe reductions of gold allocations for purchasing equipment abroad and often currency shortages and consequent salary delays in Magnitogorsk itself ... expensive imported equipment was not used with anything like the efficiency possible. Figures compiled by Soviet engineers in Magnitogorsk showed that their excavators did only thirty and forty percent as much work as machines of the same size and type did in the United States." And there was everything to be gained! No need to worry about the environment.

Forty years later, *Time* publishes an account of the costs to the land, rivers and lakes of this incredible industrial miracle of modern manufacturing. "The level of the Caspian Sea has dropped 81 ft. since 1929, mainly because dams and irrigation projects along the Volga and Ural rivers divert incoming water. As a result, Russia's caviar output has decreased; one-third of the sturgeons' spawning grounds are high and dry. Meanwhile, most municipalities lack adequate sewage treatment plants, carbon monoxide chokes the plateau towns of Armenia, and smog shrouds the metallurgical centers of Magnitogorsk, Alma-Ata and Chelyabinsk." (*Time*, November 30, 1970; John Scott, *Behind the Urals, An American worker in Russia's City of Steel,* NY: Houghton Mifflin, 1942, 73)

For nearly ten years in the thirties, John Scott lived and worked at the Magnitogorsk plant. His book *Behind the Urals, An American worker in Russia's City of Steel* is considered "the classic first-hand account of the daily life of Stalinism". It is an interesting detailed account of his life with Soviet laborers under the factory labor camp system and a very curious bit of authorship. It was not released until 1942 through an establishment house (Houghton Mifflin) by which time the German *Wehrmacht* forces had taken all of the Ukraine and Belorussia pushing their front line to the walls of Leningrad, to the Volga river and Stalingrad and into the Caucasus and over the east bank of the Don river and moved north to Moscow stopped only miles from the Soviet capital. Instead of denouncing Stalin and the Terror-Famine eradicating the peasant resistance Scott weighed his experience with Soviet Russia at war. American official diplomatic recognition sustained and even encouraged Stalin's determination to liquidate insurgent Ukrainian nationalism as an internal political threat. The Nazi Germans were too brutally racist against the Slavs to exploit them politically or militarily against Stalin so they killed them instead.

While Presidents Hoover and Roosevelt pursued their secret Consortium agenda in the Soviet Union John Scott (not his real name) labors at the giant plant for five years first as a skilled electrical welder. In fact he has been trained by General Electric in Schenectady, New York and, at age 22, picks up a Soviet visa in Berlin. After the harvest of 1932 which he would have had ample time to observe and is surely well-informed about the famine, the idealistic son of social radical professor Scott Nearing arrives September in the Urals. Scott quickly moves up the ladder to become an operator at a coke and chemical plant.

As an American with engineering skills, "John Scott" (1912-76) mixes with Russian workers as well as foreigners, even Germans. During a dinner in Chelyabinsk two hours by flight from Magnitogorsk, Scott observes how Germans and Russians openly spoke of Hitler's preparations for war. Scott writes, "Hitler was consolidating his position. The Soviet press in general was somewhat indifferent and most of the Russians had no particular antipathies for the Nazis, but the Germans in Russia, most of them Social Democrats and Communists, were profoundly disturbed." Hitler's war preparations are a badly kept secret only to idiots who believed pacifist lies published in the Consortium press. These German workers have good reason to be concerned. Most of them are either deported, or imprisoned, tortured and executed as spies by Stalin's secret police. Many are just "gulaged", and disappeared forever.

After the loss of their farms and independence, the Ukrainians had no special love for Stalin or his reign of terror. In 1939, Stalin seized the western Ukraine region including Lvov previously held by Poland that mounted little resistance to Hitler's invading army two years later. According to a former Czech communist trade official, "the Ukrainians, and for that matter the Baltic nations, welcomed the Nazi invaders, and the Ukrainians were particularly willing to join the German Nazis in their fight against the Soviets. Convinced that Germany was a superior nation Hitler did not accept the Ukrainians as allies and treated them as barbarians. For this blunder Hitler most probably lost the war against the Soviet Union; many military experts agree that he might have been able to enter Moscow and subdue the Soviets." (J. Scott, *Behind the Urals*; Eugen Loebl, *Mr. Solzhenitsyn And His Critics,* in *The Mortal Danger: How Misconceptions about Russia Imperil America, by Aleksandr I. Solzhenitsyn,* 2nd. Ed. Harper Colophon Books, 1981, originally published in *Foreign Affairs*, Council of Foreign Relations, Inc.)

Scott learns quickly that extreme conditions entailed extreme hardships are undeniably a part of the price paid to build the socialist future promised by Leninist-Marxism. School children worshiped Lenin as their savior. "Religious icons with the Mother of God still adorned the walls of peasant homes but all the socialist bureaucracy now had Marx and Lenin over their heads. While he suffers the 40 degree below freezing work conditions as well as the heat of the Purges, Scott justifies the "millions of expropriated kulaks, the political exiles in Siberia" dismissing them as "a lost tribe". He writes: "They had been sacrificed on the altar of Revolution and Progress. They would die off in twenty or thirty years, and by that time, perhaps, Soviet society would be able to function without scrapping blocks of its population every decade. "He called it "a cruel concept, but it was, one in a long list of expenditures ... for survival".

A supporter of Stalin's hardline socialism Scott learns the language, married a Russian and fathers two children before his return to America. "I survived black bread, rotten salt fish, the cold, and hard work, which was unusual. I did not survive the purge... I could not live with it ... Westerners have no place in Russia. It is the Russian's country, and it is their Revolution. Men and women from Western Europe and America may occasionally succeed in understanding it, but it is almost impossible for them to fit into it." Scott accepted the terror of collectivization with its mass deportations and fails to condemn Stalin for the famine. Like the stooge Walter Duranty and his embedded Consortium peers in the Moscow press pool, Scott blames the kulaks for the punishments they deserve and inflict upon themselves in defiance of the new collective socialist order. Like so many other observers there and abroad he is either unwilling or incapable of accepting the logical link of state terror and Genocide, of mass murder and mass repression by a faceless totalitarian state where nationalist Ukrainians as well as the Bolshevik political opposition or any dissident risks extermination by the absolute power of one cult of one man who incarnates the hope and pathos of the USSR and like his predecessor Lenin is always right.

On the surface carefree and idealist young John Scott emulated his father's unique blend of America's "rugged individualism" with all the characteristics of a strong-minded and physically fit American boy. His father Professor Scott Nearing is an accomplished writer and thinker, well-known anti-war civil libertarian and good friend of John Reed, who just also happened to be the founder of the American Communist Party. Had that been known, – and surely the secret police had files –, John Scott invariably stood on a pedestal in Soviet Russia even with no one around. Reed died in Moscow in 1920 on his return from a Congress meeting at the Baku oil port on the Caspian Sea coast where he rode against insurgents. His fatal mistake was to drink contaminated water.

Deep inside Russia, instead of riding official celebrity John Scott joins comrades in exile producing pig iron and iron ore with the latest American technology at the giant Magnitogorsk Metallurgical Combinat plant supervised by American engineers of McKee and the American firm of Koppers. Nor is the Consortium link mentioned by George Pettee, US military intelligence specialist who retired to Amherst University. In a 1950 discussion with General Sherman and students, Pettee refers to Scott as a prime resource on rare and reliable information of Soviet industry on the ground. It's a cover. He misleads the students. Pettee has no intention when he referrs to the WWII Strategic Bombing Survey on exposing American intelligence gathering or why Allied bombers chose not to destroy General Electric power plants inside Nazi Germany. Pettee, like so many college professors in universities around the country, are "spotters", responsible for selecting prime candidates to send up the ladder bound to Consortium careers in public service and private enterprise. Pettee knew better than to reveal Consortium secrets in open and unscreened university sessions. (J. Scott, *Behind the Urals*)

The Urals-Kazbas Combine huge Magnitogorsk metal plant is considered the greatest single project of heavy industry in Stalin's Five-Year Plan. It will prove invaluable for Soviet defense. Magnitogorsk iron is directly linked by rail with the new Kuznetsk coal basin on the Chinese frontier a thousand miles south. And it proves to be one of Stalin's bold successes in his crash program of forced industrialization and an indispensable alternative to the pre-revolutionary Krivoi Rog-Donbas coal-steel Combinat situated in the Ukraine and captured by the Germans early in the war.

Likewise the Kuznetsk metallurgical works in Kuznetsk figures in the Freyn Engineering Company operations of a 1930 technical-assistance contract (coke ovens, coal receiving, transport shops, trade school, blast furnace ore yard, foundry, rail shipping, rolling mills, merchant and bar mills, etc.) In 1932 an official *Izvestia* journalist and writer Ilya Ehrenburg (*Memoirs, 1921-1941*) visits Novosibirsk, Kuznetsk. His descriptions of the intensity of the summer and autumn work drives during this trip across the USSR confirm Scott's experience, and he writes, "These were extraordinary days; for the second time our country was shaken up by a tornado; but if the first one – during the Civil War years – had seemed elemental, bound up with the struggle between classes, with wrath, hatred and heartsickness, this time collectivization and the laying of the foundations of heavy industry, which churned up the lives of tens of millions, were determined by an exact plan, inseparable from columns of figures, subordinated not to explosions of popular passion but to the iron laws of necessity."

Ehrenburg observes, "Once I saw railway stations crammed with people and their belongings; a great transmigration was taking place. Peasants from Orel and Penza abandoned their villages and made their way eastwards where, they had been told, bread, smoked fish and even sugar were distributed. Konsomols, fired with enthusiasm, set off for Magnitogorsk or Kuznetsk; they believed that it was enough to build huge factories to create an earthly paradise. In freezing January metal scorched the hands. People seemed to be frozen to the marrow; there were no songs, no flags, no speeches. The word 'enthusiasm', like many others, has been devalued by inflation, yet there is no other word to fit the days of the First Five Year Plan; it was enthusiasm pure and simple that inspired the young people to daily and unspectacular feats..." (Ilya Ehrenburg, *Memoirs*, World Publishing, 1964)

Again Ehrenburg: "I saw parties of special deportees: they were former kulaks who were being taken to Siberia. They looked like the victims of a village fire. Others being taken the same way were traders in garden produce from the Moscow suburbs, petty speculators from Sukharevka, religious dissenters, embezzlers. In Tashkent and Ryazan, in Tambov and Semipalatinsk recruiting agents were taking on navies, bridge-builders, peasants who had fled from the villages after collectivization..." He tells of life in the giant steel city of Tomsk in Siberia ordered to built on the bare steppe."Life was hard; everybody talked about rations, about distribution centres. In Tomsk the bread was like clay; it reminded me of the year 1920. In the market they sold minute grubby lumps of sugar. Professors took their place in the queues between lectures. The Torgsin (*Torgovlya s inostrantsami* – 'for trade with foreigners') shops stocked tempting flour, sugar, shoes, but there you had to pay in gold – wedding rings or hoarded Czarist coins. In Kuznetsk new arrivals immediately asked: Do they issue meat? The typhus isolation building of the hospital was overcrowded: typhus was again taking a heavy toll. In Tomsk I saw a professor's wife boiling soap. It all reminded me of the rear in a war, but this rear was the front: the war was on everywhere." (I. Ehrenburg, *Memoirs,* 1963)

Ehrenburg wrote what he saw, painting pictures with words of the unfolding scenes around him of toiling masses, uprooted families, enthusiastic youth.

Ehrenburg: "This vast canvas was painted in two colours: rose and black; hope lived side by side with despair; enthusiasm with dark ignorance – some were given wings, others were destroyed by the experience." Ehrenberg encounters a few workers in a meeting "on the construction site of the Moscow-Donbas trunk-line" that was repeated thousands of times elsewhere in the Ukraine and Russia. "A navy in a lambskin cap with a weather-beaten face said 'We're a hundred times happier than the capitalists. They stuff themselves and die – they don't know what they're living for. When one of them makes a bad deal, he hangs himself with a hook. But we know what we're living for: we're building communism. The whole world's watching us'."

Ehrenburg's account is full of such vivid and human encounters with country folk from various Russian republics, like the young girl from Tomsk, a Russian city several hundred miles north of Kazahkstan in the far east of Russia. She could just as easily have been a Ukrainian, but she was "… a Shor, in the Tomsk museum; she was a medical student and had come to present to the museum a small carved wooden figure, a talisman against fever and evil spirits, which her parents had given her. She knew that the museum was collecting objects that belonged to the old way of life. She asked me a lot of questions about life in France, whether there were many hospitals, how they were combating alcoholism, whether the French liked going to concerts and Romain Rolland's age. She had trusting and eager eyes. Her parents had no doubt asked the shaman to exorcise the evil spirit that possessed their headstrong daughter."

Further on Ehrenburg observes foreign specialists amazed at the roughness and imprecision of Russian or Ukrainian building techniques…at first there were no roads or houses … "the workers were a floating population, and anyway they did not know how to treat the machines; the whole undertaking was doomed to failure. They formed their judgments on the basis of textbooks, of their own experience, of the mentality of people living in tranquil countries, and were totally unable to understand the spiritual climate and potentialities of this, to them, alien land." (I. Ehrenburg, *Memoirs*)

"Once again I realized how great was our people's fortitude in years of sore trail. Factories were built under conditions in which success was nothing less than a miracle, just as an older generation had seen the miraculous victory in the Civil War, when blockaded, hungry, barefooted Russia defeated the Interventionists. I do not know whether this is a universal human trait, but Soviet people have invariably shown themselves at their best in the worst of times..." (I. Ehrenburg, *Memoirs*)

"The young people never saw the earthly paradise which they had dreamt of, but ten years later the blast-furnaces of Kuznetsk enabled the Red Army to save their country and the world from the yoke of the racialist madmen … it was all unbearable and magnificent. … And what about the other steel, the human one? The builders of Kuznetsk, like all their contemporaries, did not have an easy life. Some died young – either in 1937 or the front. Others became prematurely bowed down and silent – there were too many sudden turns, there were too many things to adapt oneself to, to get used to. Now those heroes of The Second Day who had survived are on the wrong side of fifty. That generation had little time for reflection. Its morning was romantic and cruel: collectivization, the liquidation of the kulaks, the scaffolding of the construction. What followed, everybody remembers. The courage demanded of those who had been born on the eye of the First World War would have been more than enough for several generations: courage not only in work and in battle, but also in silence, in dismay, in anxiety. I saw these people given wings in 1932. Later, wings were no longer in fashion. The wings of the first Five Year Plan were inherited by the children, together with the gigantic factories paid for at so high a price." (I. Ehrenburg, *Memoirs*)

It was the same story at Magnitogorsk. Ehrenburg called conditions there "unheard-of severity". He added, "I think no one anywhere has built or ever will build like that again. Fascism had interfered with our life long before 1941. In the West feverish preparations were being made for a campaign against the Soviet Union; and the foundation trenches of the new construction works were the first battle trenches."

In 1933, Ehrenburg meets with American film director Lewis Milestone, director of *All Quiet on the Western Front*. He feels a special pride in his Russian roots, saying often, "I'm not Lewis Milestone, I'm Lenya Milstein." He was a Jewish immigrant from Bessarabia before the First World War, joined the US Army, made his fortune in Hollywood. "In Hollywood one can't do what one wants. And that goes for more places than Hollywood...", he said. Milestone urged Ehrenburg to write a scenario of Stalin's Five-Year Plan. "Let the Americans see what the Russians are capable of achieving." After the war, 1946, during Stalin's Zhdanovshchina anti-Semitic repression, Ehrenburg is introduced to a former Hungarian minister by Kaftanov, Soviet Minister of Education: "You know he's a Jew, but in spite of that he's a prominent Communist and a good Soviet patriot".(I. Ehrenburg, *Memoirs,* 222-3; I. Ehrenburg, *The Second Day*, 225-30; B. Levytsky, 194)

Winters are harsh in the extreme, accidents frequent. Even in the "free" zones ; safety was not a factor. At the spring peak of the famine in the Ukraine, with the Arctic winter broke without a thaw and everything frozen solid before turning to a sea of mud in May. Scott was badly burned in the mill. The Ural industrial district of mines, factories, and shops, fields and forests covered a five hundred mile square territory. Workers were encouraged to work overtime and usually forced to do it. Managers were party members; they drove the workers relentlessly, fearing the full measure of the risk of prison and deportation, or death for "sabotage" if they failed to meet arbitrarily set, and usually utterly absurd production targets. In 1928 the show trial of "wreckers" from the Skakhty industrial center in the Donbas region is one such propaganda fiasco and embarrassment for the Stalin's tightening regime that Stalin used it to ignite the beginning of a wave of terror against the intelligentsia while striking fear in the hearts of every soviet manager responsible to satisfy the demands of socialized state planning. Meet the production quotas or take a holiday hike to the timber camps in Siberia!

As John Scott tells the story the Magnitogorsk plant, "a child of the Five-Year Plan" originally planned in 1928 to open in January 1934, is completed years later.

From 1937 to 1942 it produces some ten million tons of steel destined for tanks and planes. Scott befriends Joseph F. Barnes of the *New York Herald Tribune* and takes him around for a tour of the coke and steel plant where he works during the purge years of the mid-thirties.

With his father famous in intellectual Bolshevik circles – Scott Nearing had written a preface for Senator Pettigrew's *Course of Empire*, a book much admired by Lenin, – young John Scott manages to visit many other plants of "the new Ural heavy-industry base" in Perm in the North Urals, Ufa located two hundred miles northwest of Magnitogorsk, at Sverdlovsk, the great tractor factory at Chelyabinsk known as ChTZ, and a factory for combine harvesters. He observes that as early as 1935 many were converted to military production building tanks, submarines, airplanes. Scott learns that they are building in Perm "an aviation motor factory which will make the largest plants in the United States look small". (J. Scott, *Behind the Urals*, 107; *Robert Conquest says this is B. Barnes in the only citation of Barnes in *Conquest of Sorrow*; O. Mathews, *Stalin's Children*, 31)

Ralph W. Barnes should not to be confused with Joseph Barnes (1907-70) with 18,000 items in 40 boxes of papers in his collection waiting for researchers at Columbia University. "Joe" Barnes became a top correspondent and later editor for the *New York Herald Tribune* setting up in Moscow fresh out of Harvard and London's School of Slavic Studies. His private papers included correspondences with prominent figures of the period including Bullitt, Kennan, Lippmann, and Muggeridge to name only a few. Apparently Joseph Barnes, too, was a talented and energetic writer with an instinct and intellect to excel as a first-rate foreign correspondent; why did he miss the Holodomor but instead ends up in Manhattan bank?

In 1934 for Doubleday Barnes edits *Empire in the East; China, Russia, US, & Japan*; then he passes a year in Manhattan at Time Inc., in 1935, attempting to launch a *Readers' Digest* competitor for Luce. In the war we find him deputy director in the Office of War Information at an overseas branch (1941-44). Still young and strong, at 43, he settled back from the daily rush of the newspaper world to be a book editor at Simon & Schuster where he remains until 1970. (Richard Kluger, *The Paper: The Life and Death of the New York Herald Tribune*, Knopf, 1986)

Born 1907, Joseph Barnes is the son of an itinerant lecturer, a self-taught, mildly famous British leftist political scientist and philosopher. Barnes is admitted to Harvard, only 14 years old; instead, he takes Latin at Oxford and adapts to British culture. Returning to Harvard (Class of 1927) and directed the *Crimson* living the good life with friends including Cornelius Vanderbilt Field, direct descendant of Cornelius Vanderbilt. Together, Barnes and Field enter London's School of Economics where Harold Laski is an instructor. There Barnes studies Russian, joins the School of Slavonic Studies and focuses on the communal agricultural changes overtaking Russia. Only 20 years old Barnes spends 7 months there on his own living in Moscow on meager resources. He managed to obtain a government pass to tour the Ukraine. Barnes then returns to Depression America and takes a banking job at Morgan's Equitable on Madison Avenue in Manhattan. His brother arranges newspaper accreditation for the *New York Tribune* and returns to Moscow, first in 1931 as a stringer, then again in 1934 assisting Ralph Barnes (no family relation) open up the *Tribune's* Moscow bureau. There he grabs a job as translator and guide for a visit by the Institute of Pacific Relations (IPR) crossing Russia on their way to Shanghai, and edits for the IPR, a Consortium front with funding from Rockefeller, Carnegie...

In 1937 Barnes and his wife Betty and young daughter Lila lived apart and somewhat aloof from the Moscow colony of foreign correspondents, preferring the family life in a district with "ordinary Russians" where he rents "a split-log house" with ample rooms, veranda and garden. He does very well on his $75 a week salary the advantage of the black market ruble exchange rate, drives an old Dodge with chauffeur and enjoys rare prestige with the Soviet authorities. He arrives at a critical time with the arrival of the new US ambassador, and the debut of the Great Purge. All cables and correspondence are censored, telephones closely monitored. Barnes is allowed access into the Ukraine and Ural industrial zone into Siberia "finding the sort of all-absorbing immersion in a new experience which some men would pay for". In a country where any news comes from sources other than the government Barnes might otherwise be considered an intelligence agent. He's given a free hand to do as he pleases, unrestrained by his publisher.

The excellent account by Richard Kluger in his book *The Paper, The Life and Death of the New York Herald Tribune* (1986) tracks his career there: "There were never any instructions from New York or Paris about what to cover, never a rebuke when the *Times'* veteran Moscow correspondent Walter Duranty scooped him, and only an occasional note of commendation from (managing editor sic) Wilcox or Sunday editor George Cornish. 'I got almost nothing,' he would write of his employers, 'but freedom and silence'. And from the Soviets, cold scrutiny and nightly struggles on the telephone with the censor." Brash and bold Barnes enjoyed taking risks. On one occasion he duped a censor during a call to Berlin and revealed "a list of 1,200 Soviet officials of every rank who had been victims of the purges." His wife recalls, "Joe was a very cocky guy, full of himself and ambition, and not fraught with anxiety or uncertainty." Kennan recalls Barnes was "much more pro-Soviet than the rest of us – naively so, it seemed to me. I saw him as a warm, generous, if naive, idealist, captivated, as so many had been in that early post-revolutionary period, by the excitement and the ostensibly progressive aims of the Soviet regime of that day."

Barnes knows Henry Shapiro, who started as a stringer in Moscow in 1933 for the *Herald Tribune* and remains a correspondent there for forty years. In the early days Shapiro became a Reuters bureau chief then took over from Lyons in 1937 as head of UPI. Shapiro finds Barnes more broad-minded and less arrogant than the other American correspondents there for the most part anti-Soviet. "The very fact that Joe knew the language," Shapiro recalls, "was enough to cast him under suspicion … Joe's problem was that he didn't suffer fools gladly – he was head and shoulders over the rest of the correspondents, and he'd let you know about it. He'd been used to dealing with academics and others with a background in the area.... He was very critical of the Soviet Union when dealing with people with whom he thought he might have an intelligent conversation."

Early 1938, Barnes ventures into the Urals on a two-week trip to the Magnitogorsk industrial zones representing, he told his editors, "probably the biggest single shift in economic and military geography since the opening of the American West or the industrialization of Japan." In March he covers the Moscow Purge trial of 21 leaders. The next month Barnes writes his editor Larry Hills, in Paris, to cover his expenses for a story to the Ukraine, where "this year's harvest is likely to have overwhelming importance for the whole Soviet situation." But the paper is having family problems over an internal dispute among its owners, the Reids, and a management shakeup affecting foreign news. Even Barnes is obliged to pay his own expenses while editors cut his copy arbitrarily. As incredible as it is they miss the Holodomor story and its aftermath leading to WWII.

The situation worsenes. By May Barnes is furious when his editors kill his May Day dispatch. Kluger recaps what happened: "Not only was the wire-service piece wrong on the facts, such as stating that US Ambassador Joseph E. Davies was present when he was actually in bed with indigestion, but it missed completely the point 'clear to nearly everyone except the A.'"

For his part, Duranty has returned on the scene and recaptures his zeal sending back stories daily for the *Times*. Barnes is obliged to sit it out with the "*Trib*" appearing to have given up the race for scoops and top-knotch reporting. "I never had the feeling that the *Herald Tribune* was more than remotely interested in my being there", Barnes laments, feeling used and abused with the owners disinterested on telling the Russian story. Paris editors are more eager to run a banner headline "Avenue de l'Opera to Be Lavishly Decorated / With Roses for Visit of British King and Queen" and worry about the current slump of American tourists in Paris and declining newsstands sales than they are in imminent war in Europe. At the end of 1938 Dorothy Thompson writes owner Helen Reid of the falling reputation of the paper, how" practically every American journalist in Paris was appalled". She adds, "I have many old friends there and they write me candid letters, and they tell me that the Paris *Herald Tribune* is playing the fascist game from start to finish. Inasmuch as this is certainly not the policy of the *Herald Tribune*, I feel that you ought to do something about it." And although the paper lost a half million dollars in operating expenses, it still only cost readers three cents a day to read the news from Moscow. (R. Kluger, *The Paper*, 297-305)

When his book appears in 2008 Owen Mathews is *Newsweek*'s bureau chief in Moscow. Of Russian-Ukrainian descent with a grandfather formerly an enthusiastic young communist Party worker in Kharkov raion, Owens recalls the intensity of Soviet construction of the first Five-Year Plan. Mathews writes, "Across the Ukraine new metal works were going up in Krivy Rog and Zaporozhiye, new anthracite mines were being sunk in the Donetsk basin. Each day of the first Five Year Plan one new factory was founded and 115 new collective farms opened." Pride and fear made success triumph and failure severely sanctioned by unforgiving proletarianism of collective single-minded consciousness against the bourgeois class-enemy of the Revolution.

With banks closing their doors all across America, and Japanese aggression unchecked deeper in Manchuria, Stalin addressed a workers conference in February 1931 passionately urging all Soviet citizens not to fail to reach their quotas and achieve the targets set by Party leaders. "To retard the tempo – this means to drop behind. And those who are backward are beaten. We do not want to be beaten! No, we do not want that! The history of old Russia was, among other things, that she was constantly beaten because of her backwardness. The Mongol khans beat her. The Turkish *beys* beat her. The Swedish feudal lords beat her. The Polish-Lithuanian nobles beat her. The Anglo-French beat her – for her backwardness, governmental backwardness, industrial backwardness, agricultural backwardness. They beat her because it was profitable and went unpunished. Remember the words of the pre-revolutionary poet: 'Thou art poor, Thou art abundant, Thou art powerful, Thou art powerless, Mother Russia ...'. We are fifty to a hundred years behind the advanced countries. We must make up this gap in ten years ... or they crush us!" And it was true. (*Horizon History of Russia*, American Heritage, 1970, 359)

Food is rationed. The unemployed are denied ration cards, nor a place to live. Housing is in very short supply. Workers often live in barracks without their families. The people who occupied existing housing had to share apartments, one family to a room, and the housing shortage is never overcome, though much would later be built under Khrushchev and Brezhnev. On top of all that, there is constant terror of the secret soviet police.

Scott is an astute observer and during his flight stopover at Sverdlovsk describes in vivid detail new soviet aviation facilities where he meets pilots and mechanics and learns how planes are built, tested, then dismantled and stored in crates to be shipped "near the places they may be needed... Particularly in the Far East, along the frontiers of Manchukuo, large numbers of crated planes were stored". Aware the planes will quickly become obsolete his informers tell him "their industry could not hope to keep up with the West in retooling for new models. They, therefore, count on the quantity rather than on the quality of their planes to overwhelm any possible enemy." (John Scott, *Behind the Urals*, 107)

BEHIND THE URALS: THE 'AMERIKANKA' AT MAGNITOGORSK

When he first arrives Scott is assigned housing with foreign engineers in the foreign settlements in Magnitogorsk. His is called *Amerikanka*. John Scott meets the American engineer consultant in charge Magnitostroi and until he completes it he's "paid good American dollars, being supplied with caviar in a country where there was little bread and no sugar". Scott observes, "A colony of several hundred foreign engineers and specialists, some of whom made as high as one hundred dollars a day and expenses, arrived to advise and direct the work. Money was spent by the millions – 170,000,000 roubles in 1931."

Scott's account of Magnitogorsk is much sought after by the Riga Legation who never miss a chance to get the first-hand information on life under the Soviets from American engineers and workers in constant need of a Soviet visa, or a new passport (the Soviets keep passports for blackmail). Scott writes, "Within several years, half a billion cubic feet of excavation work was done, forty-two million cubic feet of reinforced concrete poured, five million cubic feet of fire bricks laid, a quarter of a million tons of structural steel erected." The young Soviet industry lacks labor, supplies and materials. Aroused by Stalin's Bolshevik propaganda in the summer 1930 "Shock Brigades" pour in from all corners of the USSR. Production is tied to a wage and bonus system. It is not uncommon, for example, to find workers with increased wages and premiums while labor productivity increased and production costs drop.

Scott managed somehow to stay out of trouble. Not an easy thing to do at Magnitogorsk. Here life is cheap and anyone might be killed for a bottle of vodka or just for the mere fun of it. One still had to be very careful where bourgeois law and order is not the norm. Life could quickly turn rough living among these illiterate and ignorant brutes who will fight to the death just for the joy of it. Magnitogorsk is a steel town primarily housing single men. At times it is more like "one giant knife fight" typical of many towns and ports in the mid-thirties as depicted in the Soviet film *Moi Drug Ivan Lapshin* (*My Friend Ivan Lapshin*) directed by Aleksei German. (Steven Kotkin, *Magnetic Mountain*, Ph.D. dissertation, Univ. of California, Berkeley, 1988).

Caught in Stalin's paranoia web of purges, few foreign specialists or Americans choose to stay after 1937. Scott writes this is a time "when foreigners were dismissed, demoted, publicly discredited, sent home, sometimes arrested" for espionage, or because they had seen and knew too much. Scott's experience is unique. Many American workers seeking a job during the Great Depression, or life in the "New Society" become disillusioned or just want to get out but never did. The Soviets do not permit their departure. They have seen too much. "With the exception of slight letups in the middle twenties and again in the early thirties, few foreign specialists were allowed to come to the Soviet Union," Scott declares in clear contradiction of the reality.

Constantly suspected of espionage, Scott is lucky to get out when he does and he even manages to leave with his Russian wife Marsha and their two children. Indeed, that was highly unusual. Soviet secret police most likely have a thick file on Scott. But should Stalin risk an international scandal with his prestige soaring in the West. His father was thought to still be active at Columbia University, the Ivy League school in Manhattan. Nearing has a curious reputation and is more than just a symbol of the Greenwich Village's radical left-wing, something Trotsky would know more about. Nearing, too, has many good connections to the Consortium and any party comrade or commissar who knows that also knew that Scott was respected and virtually untouchable.

When Daniel Schorr becomes a CBS foreign correspondent in the Khrushchev era, in 1955 one of his encounters is with Robert Robinson, a former tool maker with Ford in Detroit first recruited in 1930. Schorr describes his plight as "a token black" elected to the Moscow Soviet where he met Stalin and Molotov. His repeated efforts to leave are thwarted; he was denied a passport. Robert Robinson finally manages to escape via Uganda, and survives to tell the story of his ordeal in *Black on Red* (1987). (J. Scott, *Behind the Urals*, 174; Daniel Schoor, *Staying Tuned*, Simon & Schuster, 2001, 60-1)

Remember reader as the Holodomor creeps across the Ukraine and in other stricken territories of the Soviet Union, Scott's account chronicles the construction progress on the ground and the mentality and attitude of his fellow workers of the Plans launched and manufactured with the financial and technical means of the Consortium. While "deployed on the iron and steel front", Scott lives Stalin's "war communism" and suffers hardships along with tens and hundreds of thousands of Russian workers building blast furnaces to make steel.

"Every since 1931 or thereabouts", Scott recounts, "the Soviet Union has been at war, and the people have been sweating, shedding blood and tears… All during the thirties the Russian people were at war. It did not take me long to realize that they ate black bread principally because there was no other to be had, wore rags because they could not be replaced." That brutal winter of 1933 in January is one of the coldest on record when the temperature drops 35 degrees below freezing. Accidents are frequent. Sometimes men froze to death working out-of-doors. Lips freeze. And when a worker spit it too would freeze in the air then hit the ground like a rock. Most of the workers have to learn their skills on the job in this intemperate conditions.

John Scott: "From 1928 till 1932 nearly a quarter of a million people came to Magnitogorsk. About three quarters of these new arrivals came of their own free will seeking work, bread cards, better conditions. The rest came under compulsion. In the summer of 1930, workers arrived to do the preliminary groundwork of rail and dam construction. Then herds of peasants came "because of bad conditions in the villages, due to collectivization. Many of these peasants were completely unfamiliar with industrial tools and processes. They had to start at the very beginning and learn how to work in groups. Nevertheless they learned so well that the first dam across the Ural River was finished the sixth of April 1931." Two years later they had a five-mile lake and ample water for the city and plant. (J. Scott, *Behind the Urals*, 70-1)

Scott minimizes Bolshevik force against the population. At first glance it may seem like a remarkable omission of oversight or zealous prejudice in favor of the awesome communist initiative, especially in when it is recalled that he is the son of the intellectual free-thinking stalwart and university professor Scott Nearing. But the omission is deliberate. In fact he never uses the word "terror" to build the USSR and "Stalin's Ural Stronghold".

By 1942, with the Ukraine devastated by Nazi occupation, Ural industries were "supplying the Red Army with the immense quantities of military materials of all kinds, spare parts, replacements, and other manufactured products necessary to keep Stalin's mechanized divisions in the field". FDR and his war planners were well aware that an American-Anglo invasion in France would have to wait at least two years while Soviet-Russia gradually pushed back the Germans. Even with Leningrad and Moscow under siege, Scott praised "the political sagacity of Joseph Stalin and his relentless perseverance in forcing through the realization of his construction program despite fantastic costs and fierce difficulties". Scott forgives Stalin for smashing the political opposition and the brutality and terror that accompanied the Five-Year Plans of industrialization and war against the Ukrainian peasants. "'Russia must overtake and surpass the most advanced countries in industry and military achievement within ten years or these capitalist countries will annihilate us,' said Stalin in February 1931.

With the vision of a true Consortium capitalist Scott asserts that new soviet industries must be concentrated in the Urals and Siberia thousands of miles away from the nearest frontiers, out of reach of any enemy bombers. Whole new industries must be created. This is the constant Soviet socialist line. Scott doesn't call it a Consortium plan. Scott asserts, "Russia had hitherto been dependent on other countries for almost its entire supply of rubber, chemicals, machine tools, tractors, and many other things. These commodities could and must be produced in the Soviet Union in order to ensure the technical and military independence of the country. Bukharin and many other old Bolsheviks, however, disagreed. … Step by step, one after another of these dissenting voices were silenced. Stalin won. Russia embarked on the most gigantic industrialization plan the world had ever seen. In 1932 fifty-six per cent of the Soviet Union's national income was invested in capital outlay. It is an extraordinary achievement. In the United States in 1860-1870, when we were building our railroads and blast furnaces, the maximum recapitalization for any one year was in the neighborhood of twelve per cent of the national income. Moreover, American industrialization was largely financed by European capital, while the man power for the industrial construction work poured in from China, Ireland, Poland and other European countries. Soviet industrialization was achieved almost without the aid of foreign capital. While a few thousand foreign technicians assisted in their work, the brunt of the immense task fell on the shoulders of the Soviet peoples. Russia was industrialized with the sweat and blood of the one hundred and sixty-odd million inhabitants of the vast country."

Scott marvels at the enormous natural wealth in the Soviet Union and Stalin's resourcefulness to capture it and remove any obstacle, political or indigenous, that opposed Soviet progress now defined by the urgency of military defense. It is curious that Scott ignored the Army purges that removed the Soviet's senior and experienced military personnel. In *Behind the Urals*, Scott described the immensity of the tractor plant that "covered a larger area than the entire old city of Chelyabinsk". From the air Scott could see "the 'Stankostroi' factory, originally planned as a light-machine building plant, but reprojected in the early thirties to make tanks". (J. Scott, *Behind the Urals*, 110)

"The Urals are rich in non-ferrous metals. Chelyabinsk is a zinc-producing as well as a tractor and tank manufacturing center. Some nickel is produced at Kalilovo and also at Ufalei. Bauxite is mined and aluminium produced at a large modern plant at Kaminsk, while copper is turned out in quantities at Kyshtym. A few miles from Magnitogorsk an immense deposit of manganese was found and in 1934 mining was begun on a large scale. Today this manganese is used in blast furnaces all over the Soviet Union and exported as well. Copper and sulphur are produced from pyrites in Blyava.... The Ural industrial district is not entirely dependent on the Caucasian wells for oil. The largest single known petroleum deposit in the world is situated in and around Ishembayevo. A pipe line connects these oil fields with Ufa, where large cracking and refining units have been erected and put into operation. Here, in 1939, nearly three million tons of oil was produced..." (J. Scott, *Behind the Urals*, 110)

In 1940, a high-octane gasoline plant was completed in Ufa for the manufacture of motor fuel for the Red air fleet. Its planned production was half a million tons annually and American engineers with whom I spoke, who had worked on the erection of the plant, told me that in their opinion it would produce nearly the planned amount of high-octane gasoline during the first year of production. Another high-octane gasoline plant was erected at Saratov on the Volga and is reported to have gone into operation early in 1941, though its capacity is not known. Beside its oil industry, Ufa boasts one of the largest internal combustion engine plants in the Soviet Union. Several times when passing through the town on the train, I saw the plant stretching for mile after mile along the railroad. Its equipment is new and it is thought to produce tank and airplane motors... However, during the last few months it has grown enormously. The industrial district created in the Urals during the thirties was formidable enough. No figures are available regarding the quantities of factories and plants evacuated from Western Russia to the Urals and Siberia. It is known, however, that even before the outbreak of war, large electrical equipment plants were removed from White Belorussia on the German frontier and also from the Leningrad district to the Urals and Western Siberia. One such plant is reported to have been removed to Sverdlovsk during 1940 and to have been producing normally in March 1941. Any plant except the largest smelting, steel-making, and chemical works can be moved by railroad fairly quickly and with little damage." Scott stayed a week in Sverdlovsk visiting the huge URALMASH plant and the Ural Heavy Machine Building Works outside the city, a child of the Soviet Five-Year Plan and "one of the best looking plants I have ever seen". (J. Scott, *Behind the Urals*, 260-62)

Scott was keen to compare American and Soviet technique essential to the success of the technology transfer. He wrote, "The first mechanical department was a beautiful piece of work. A building a quarter of a mile long was filled with the best American, British and German machines. It was better equipped than any single shop in the General Electric Works in Schenectady." Inside were lathes "as long as ferry boats" to make gun barrels. "The foundry was likewise a beautiful job, completely mechanized and laid out according to the latest American technique." It made turbines, rolling mills and heavy machinery. By 1936 the foundry built submarines "shipped in sections either to the Pacific Ocean or the Black or Baltic Seas, thousands of miles away." (J. Scott, *Behind the Urals*, 103)

Arriving in Soviet Russia in 1931, Scott observed first-hand instances of sabotage, corruption and "wrecking" by embittered kulaks as well as observe methods used by the NKVD secret police at the Magnitogorsk works. "During the late twenties and the early thirties the rich peasants, or kulaks, were liquidated.

Their property was confiscated and given to the collective farms. They were shipped out to some construction job for five years or so, to be re-educated. Some of the young ones, like my friends Shabkov, lent themselves to this re-education; but most of the old ones were bitter and hopeless. They were ready to do anything, in their blind hatred, to strike back at the Soviet power. But the Soviet power was not around to strike. There were only workers and engineers and other ex-kulaks building a steel mill. But the machines were symbolic of the new power, of the force which had confiscated their property and sent them out onto the steppe to pour concrete. And they struck at the machines." (J. Scott, *Behind the Urals*, 187)

The fact that Scott was raised by the American socialist and libertarian Scott Nearing makes his son's personal account even more ironic and tragic. With his invaluable first-hand experience inside the ranks of Stalin's slave laborers of "politicals" and common criminals John Scott fails to expose the systematic mass horrors, torture and executions lived by so many and described by only a few rare writers. Pasternak and Solzhenitsyn are two among millions who barely survive in conditions of brutality and inhumanity on a scale inconceivable in the mind of a "civilized" westerner accustomed to cherish bourgeois individual freedoms not having undergone the unrelenting struggle of class war in a depraved society of ruthless Bolsheviks intent on effacing all characteristics of defiant individualism. The magnitude of killing by two world wars of mechanized annihilation is roughly proportional to those killed by Stalin's extermination and Terror. In the "civilized" societies of the West, in America, England, and France, for example, the Consortium terror is more subtle and no less real, and even perhaps, more enduring and more threatening, and more painful in how it strips the soul of its Humanity. The Ukrainians are survivors. I know them. I lived with them and loved them. And I can tell you, they still have a soul. (Note. Robert Conquest's *The Great Terror, A Reassessment* provides an invaluable history of the horrible tortures common in the Soviet extermination labor camps inflicted on individuals and groups of victims.)

All the oil refineries in the Second Baku and elsewhere are built by Universal Oil Products, Badger Corporation, Lummus Company, Petroleum Engineering Corporation, Alco Products, McKee Corporation, and the Kellogg Company. Advanced steel-rolling mills are supplied under the United Engineering agreement. Later, the Tube Reducing Company installed a modern tube mill at Nikopol and supplied equipment for another. In 1937 the Vultee Corporation built an aircraft plant outside Moscow. The Americans also transfer invaluable tractor technology which becomes the model for Soviet tractor engineering. Tractors are a necessity to modernize Soviet agriculture in Stalin's great dream of collectivization. Illiterate and uneducated peasants many now landless whose families have tilled the black-earth land for generations and centuries in tune with the rhythms of nature and the heartbeat of animal and man must be transformed into a skilled mechanical worker.

An engineer from Detroit is engaged to design and construct the largest tractor factory in the world covering thirty acres in one giant building. To launch the Plan Stalin orders the construction in the heart of the wheat belt of south-central Russia of two huge tractor factories: in Kharkov in the Ukraine, and on the barren steppes of western Kazakhstan, in Chelyabinsk. A Party slogan compares the change from horse to machine parallel "to plough up the virgin soil of the peasant consciousness".

The tractors produced are copies of the American Caterpillar Company. The Ford Motor Company of Henry Ford and the British Austin Company build the Gorki plant – for over three decades the largest motor vehicle plant in the USSR. Gorki produces the Soviet jeep and half a dozen other military vehicles. In the 1960s Gorki produced many of the trucks American pilots in the Vietnam War observe streaming down the Ho Chi Minh trail. It also produces the chassis for the GAZ-69 rocket launcher used against Israel; in 1968 while Gorki is building vehicles to be used in Vietnam and Israel more equipment is ordered and shipped to Gorki from the US. The Stalingrad Tractor Plant begun by Ford in 1926 to produce 10,000 tractors a year, eventually produces a small three-ton armored car and a self-propelled gun at a rate of one per week; the T-37 tank, - modeled on the British A 4 EII, rolls off the Soviet assembly line every four days.

The success of the American tractor-tank in the First World War, as it evolved out of Peoria, Illinois Caterpillar Tractor Company factories "when Benjamin Holt, a combine maker in Stockton, California, first came up with the answer to one major drawback of the stream tractor for farming. Because steam engines were so heavy, the typical tractor was equipped with enormous wheels that distributed its weight and prevented it from sinking in the ground. Even so, tractors still sank in the spongy peat soil of the California delta, west of Stockton. Holt replaced the wheels with a pair of continuous tracks, gave his machines the evocative trademark 'Caterpillar', and outfitted them with gasoline engines instead of steam. Discovering that construction contractors liked them as well as delta farmers, he purchased a manufacturing plant in Peoria to help meet rising demand. By 1915, more than 2,000 Caterpillar tractors were operating in the field. During World War 1, the British adapted Holt's crawler – the 'Yankee machine that climbs like hell'- to develop the fighting contraption that became known as the tank. Holt converted his production for wartime demand, and the Caterpillar name became known throughout Europe, the Middle East, and East Africa." Nor did Caterpillar's success escape the attention of the Soviets." (Barbara Marsh, *A Corporate Tragedy, The Agony of International Harvester Company*, 73)

The Soviet War Mobilization Plan calls for a wartime output tripling the self-propelled gun rate and doubling that of armored cars, but maintaining the same tank production rate. But as with all the major construction projects in the Soviet Union it was held up waiting for plans and engineers from the United States. In fact, for the Stalingrad Tractor Plant, those plans didn't come until mid-1929. *Amtorg* declares, "While preliminary work on the site of the Stalingrad Tractor Plant had been conducted for some time, the actual work on the construction of the principal departments started only in June when the plans arrived from the United States." Sutton concludes that even the Five Year plan itself, although announced in 1928, the year Stalin grabbed supreme power, "contracts for construction were not let until 1929-30. Foreign engineers arrived on site a few months later." (*Amtorg No. 7*, April 1, 1930, 1340)

Early 1931 the State Department is surprised to learn seven Americans of the Stalingrad Factory Plant had been elected members to the soviets. *Pravda* on January 28, 1931 ran an article translated and sent by Felix Cole on February 3, 1931. J. Edgar Hoover gets a copy over at the Justice Department. The row is about an American assembly shop worker in the plant, Sharkino, who told *Pravda*, "There is no doubt that we will produce 150 tractors in two shifts in the forge and foundry ... In my capacity as delegate to the Soviet I shall struggle for the uprooting of everything that interferes with its work. I shall struggle for the execution of the program of the Tractor plant and for the shipment of a sufficient quantity of Stalin implements to the collective farms of the boundless Soviet Union."

Felix Cole asks the Department to inquire as to "these men's citizenship" as Americans and their "acceptance of an elective office in a foreign government". The USSR was pigeon-holing skilled American workers throughout Soviet industry to train hundreds and thousands of Soviet workers; many were slotted as members of politically elite party soviets, or councils. James Grafton Rogers replies that technically they remain American citizens "unless such acceptance should constitute naturalization or involve the taking of an oath or affirmation of allegiance to a foreign State". For that matter no one at State could defend their rights in the USSR "since at the present time there are no American diplomatic or consular officers in Russia". In other words, the Americans without an embassy to run to must fend for themselves. Rogers (1883-71) is the only Westerner ever on Stimson's staff and gets high praise from his boss. (SDDF 861.00/11456)

Numerous reports exist in the US government files confirming observations published by John Scott of the adaptability of Soviet plants for war use. An account by Scott, For example, states, "The heavy industry plants are fitted with special attachments and equipment held in reserve which in a few hours will convert the plants into munitions factories. ..." General design, construction management, and equipment for the gigantic plants built from 1929-33 are provided by Albert Kahn, Inc. of Detroit, the most famous industrial architectural firm in the United States equivalent to a Bechtel or a Cargill.

Data published on the Soviet "Plans" neglect to mention a fundamental feature of the Soviet industrial structure in this period: the giant units were built by foreign companies at the very beginning of the 1930s, and the remainder of the decade was devoted to bringing these giants into full production and building satellite assembly and input-supply plants. In sectors such as oil refining and aircraft, where further construction was undertaken at the end of the decade, we find a dozen top US companies (McKee, Lummus, Universal Oil Products, etc.) aiding in the oil-refining sector and other top US aircraft builders in the aircraft sector (Douglas, Vultee, Curtis-Wright ...).

Only relatively insignificant Soviet innovation occurred in this period: For example, SK-B synthetic rubber was dropped in favor of more useful foreign types after World War II; the Ramzin boiler, confined to small sizes; the turbodrill; and a few aircraft and machine gun designs. Stalin later received Douglas DC-3 Dakotas which the Russians called the "Duglas". They also had Cobras and Hurricanes. During the war women ("night witches"/ *nocha veydma*) barely twenty years old flew the Polikarpov U-2s, biplanes of the First World War; they'd cut their motors at night gliding in silence over their targets and bomb German lines at Stalingrad and Moscow or drop supplies to the Red Army. (C. Merridale, *Ivan's War*, 176; V. Grossman, *A Writer at War*, 80; J. Scott, *Behind the Urals*; A. C. Sutton)

Also part of the Five-Year Plan for industry, from 1927-32, the largest hydroelectric dam in the world was built on the Dnieper River at Dnieproges (Dnepropetrovsk, or Dneprostroi) by Col. Hugh Cooper famous for having built the dam at Muscle Shoals, Tennessee. The power plant increased Russia's hydroelectric system output by six times, and produced more power than Niagara Falls. The young writer from Wales, Gareth Jones visited several of these same industrial plants. Jones met briefly Cooper during his walking tour across the Ukraine in 1931. The electrical industry had the services of International General Electric (in two agreements), the Cooper Engineering Company and RCA for the construction of long range powerful radio stations, important for military communications and political propaganda.. Stuart, James and Cooke, Inc., – also visited by Jones –, contracts with various coal and mining trusts were supplemented by specialized assistance contracts, such as the Oglebay, Norton Company aid agreement for the iron ore mines and the Southwestern Engineering agreement in the non-ferrous industries.

In the late 1920s, long before the government officially endorses US-Soviet trade, the USSR is allowed to purchase unassembled US battleships, hence build the Soviet fleet in US shipyards, dismantle, ship and rebuild in the USSR. Or, using carbon copies, American battleships are subsequently assembled in the Soviet Union on plans drawn up by American naval architects. By 1938 the Soviets are placing orders to American firms for top-secret submarine specifications. The State Department approves shipments of ammunition as well as battleship(s). Roosevelt, for example, personally orders the State Department to "give all help" to the Soviets for a 45,000 ton battleship to be built in the US. America used to build battleships like the "Retvizan" for the Russia Czar launched in 1900, at a Philadelphia shipyard. After the French détente of 1933, Paris also agrees to provide military assistance to the Soviets; the Italians provide weapons and built the destroyer *Tashkent.* Vickers, in fact, supplied tank designs and tank models "which became the basis for the standard Soviet tanks of World War II". (1928 US Congressional Record. Re Soviet Shipping; A. C. Sutton, 238)

Historians generally agree that by 1932, Stalin's campaign of terror and collectivization is complete. That fatal summer the harvest was good. The peasants who had survived winter now faced more harsh measures of repression and deprivation. "Stalin won the drive to collectivize Soviet agriculture," Harrison Salisbury writes long after his employer *The New York Times* knowingly published the lies of its star Moscow reporter Walter Duranty. Here's Salisbury: "In a space of less than three years more than 95 percent of Russian farm lands were incorporated in farm collectives or state farms which were directly operated by the Government." That figure is miles from Taubman's 60% "of peasant households" in Russia collectivized by mid-1949. And even that figure is with far less peasants around after the Holodomor and the Second World War! (W. Taubman, 205; H. Salisbury, *Russia*)

Salisbury told a very different story in 1965 two decades after tens of millions of more victims sacrificed for Soviet victory over German fascism. "But the price was colossal." Salisbury wrote only a few years before Solzhenitsyn smuggled his Gulag manuscript to the West and while his books remained banned. In Salisbury's atoned version he writes, "Millions of kulaks, or rich peasants, were uprooted and shipped to Siberia. Civil war broke out in some regions. Peasants retaliated against the Kremlin by slaughtering their cattle, burning the harvests, concealing crops from the grain collectors. The toll in lives reached into the millions and many regions were struck by famine. The wounds to agricultural production were so severe that more than 30 years later they are still to be felt. Stalin confessed to Winston Churchill in a wartime conversation that had he to do it over again he never would have attempted the collectivization program."

And what about his precious Pulitzer? Is *The New York Times* now repudiating Duranty? Not really. Salisbury gets it right when he adds, "But two of Stalin's objectives were fulfilled. He did break the political power of the peasants and he did squeeze out of them the funds which he poured into the gigantic industrialized program." Perhaps the murder of Kirov would have been enough to trigger and maintain the years of purges, but Stalin nonetheless finds it more opportune in the spring of 1932 to blame his political rivals for the "excesses" committed by the Party against the Ukrainian peasants whom he was bent on destroying as they were too numerous to uproot and deport like numerous other nationalities he exterminated (Tartars…). And not only the peasants but the Ukrainian intelligentsia as well. Not only people were destroyed, but the intellect too was not spared. Conquest recalls, "Of the seven Principals of Kiev University (1921-38) six were arrested and one died a natural death." (R. Conquest, *The Great Terror*, 293)

Conquest recounts more ethnic cleansing by the Terror. "The Ukrainian creative intelligentsia, as we have seen, had been struck down on a vast scale every year since 1930. The Ukrainian poets perished in their majority for 'nationalist' reasons: sixteen, starting with Vlyzko in 1934, are named as executed or dying in camps between then and 1942 – almost all at Solovetsk, though a few were in Kolymar. A group of neo-classical poets, Mykola Zerov, Pavlo Fylpovych, and others, were tried in Kiev in January 1936 for nationalism, terrorism, and espionage. One temporary survivor, the poet Mykhalo Dray-Khamara, got a five-year Special Board sentence … but seems to have died in camp in 1938 or 1939 …", many others arrested, imprisoned, shot … "And so it was in all the non-Russian Republics. Their men of literature were almost automatically regarded as bourgeois nationalists, since, of course, they had been working in the national traditions of their own languages." With typical Soviet efficiency Stalin's purges proceed in all directions detecting "wrecking" from agriculture to industry and the sciences. "The Meteorological Office was violently purged as early as 1933, for failing to predict weather harmful to the crops. In part on similar grounds, astronomers connected with sunspot research fared badly. The Solar Service had in fact been set up in 1931 to help predict long-range weather patterns, with the usual imperfect results, though there were also charges of un-Marxist theories of sunspot development." (R. Conquest, *The Great Terror*)

Recognition of Stalin's dictatorship late November 1933 meant more than a gesture of legitimization of the Kremlin's terror and FDR's complicity of silence and policy of non-condemnation of Genocide; a new meaning to extermination of the masses is given by the White House allowing the Consortium gang off the hook closing the circle and openly joining hands with the most powerful and deadly dictatorship on the planet. The United States and the Soviet Union stand together on equal footing and this in spite of the terrible gap in inequalities between the two nations that lead to the mission of Bullitt's successor and FDR campaign supporter, the millionaire ambassador Joseph E. Davies. To close the gap even tighter while he lives aboard his glimmering Czarist-size yacht on the Neva, Hollywood produces the ambassador's propaganda film *Mission to Moscow* which claims the Russians are mind, body and soul just like Americans. Nothing is further from the truth. But to the banker and businessman consumers are all the same or should be. They fail to see, however, that much more is at stake than can be staked on the bottom line or market assessments based on American standards. The war proves again that the Russians are a very different kettle of fish.

One of the State Department's regular analysts is Harvard professor Bruce Campbell Hopper. Hopper (1892-73) had toured the Ukraine during the Holodomor years. At the US Army War College in January 1940 to teach "The Role of Soviet Russia", the title of his annual G-2 military intelligence course Hopper introduced his lecture with the "Dizziness from Success" 1930 Party speech by Stalin during the collectivization terror. For Hopper Genocide in the Ukraine is neither the cause, focus or consequence of Stalin's terror campaign. Human Rights don't figure in Hopper's or Stalin's calculations. Genocide is no*t kosher*, yet. Not until the Jews get burned alive in the Nazi camps does Genocide get taken seriously as a crime against Humanity. Hopper skips over it as a discussion topic. Instead he and the State Department observes Stalin's steady takeover as Russia's Soviet Czar. "Only one man is allowed to have enormous failures in Russia – Stalin."

Hopper writes. He adds, "Stalin was neither named, nor chosen his successor. Stalin gained that position by tough politics, outplaying the intellect of Trotsky with the cunning of the peasant. I venture to believe that history will record of Stalin that he was both builder and destroyer. He set out to fulfill the program of Lenin, to build socialism. But, in contrast to Lenin who was without fear, Stalin had been haunted by fear all his life." Strange that Hopper would use that cliché – "the cunning of the peasant – under the title of his notorious speech. This speech alone is a masterpiece in double-speak and another step in the cover-up of official US government complicity behind Stalin's regime or knowledge of the famine. Hopper leaves it unclear who suffered worst in Stalin's liquidation, the GPU secret police, political commissars and the Komsomols, the survivors or the victims.

Hopper declares, "Having gained supreme power in 1927, he set out to prove that socialism could be built in one country alone. To do that he had to set an over-rapid pace of industrialization of a backward country, hence the series of Five Year Plans. He likewise forced through the collectivization of agriculture, at terrific cost in human life, and sacrifice of life stock. In 1930, when the pace had gone too fast, he recalled his cohorts, lectured them on dizziness from success, and liquidated the most obedient. That was building and destroying." In the same speech Hopper is correct when he made a direct link between Stalin's foreign policy during the late twenties and early thirties and the suppression of the peasants. "In foreign affairs," Hopper writes, "his dominant fear was a return of the *cordon sanitaire*, which he was to use as a whip over the Russian people."

Hopper knows very well that for over a decade the Americans had profitably built both the Stalin and Hitler war economies and financed their industrial factories for world war. But he Consortium's Harvard academic stops far short from calling Stalin a mass murderer guilty of mass murder against the Ukrainian population, bottling up his population, restricting travel abroad, imposing deportations and exile to forced labor and death camps, and satisfying the western Consortium not to export revolutionary communism in exchange for foreign investment and trade. In this way Hopper explains Stalin's system of repression to his army students, "In foreign affairs he announced, in 1927, a policy of peaceful co-existence with capitalist states, joined their collective security system in 1934, and even made a United Front with democracies in 1935 against 'Fascism and War'."

The previous year Bruce Hopper had lectured on the Hitler-Stalin rapprochement "which at the time seemed a wild guess". Hopper calls the costly Soviet invasion of Finland "blasts the reputation of the Bolsheviks for hard realism and common sense". Logic he says "has departed from the game". "Since they are committed in the direction of folly, it is utterly impossible to predict what measures the Bolsheviks may adopt to get out of the trap. They are Russians, ergo, extraordinary." Still calling them Bolsheviks? Stalin had killed most of them. What "trap" does Hopper have in his mind? From the look of things, it appears that both Hitler and Stalin had been set up from the beginning. After the Soviet attack on Finland American trade and assistance tapers off replaced by a boost of German imports (machine tools, advanced equipment) in exchange for Russian raw materials.

Hopper, too, is adept at playing the establishment historian of US-Soviet affairs. He never refers to Consortium power management or Consortium money that endows Harvard and pays the bill of his career salary at Harvard. Litvinov's disappearance, he declares, is a Stalinist blunder. Even the illiterate peasants are aware of that but Hopper adds a unique twist. He states, "For 12 years Litvinov guided Soviet foreign policy. He, alone of the Bolsheviks, knew how to sit down with Western statesmen, and out-talk them, and out-maneuver them. If they proposed reduction of armaments, he shouted for total disarmament. If they talked of mutual guarantees, he offered everyone a treaty of non-aggression." Litvinov, he said, was "committed to the Geneva method of collective security". Well, he must have been a good stooge. Stalin replaced Litvinov with Zhdanov who unlike his predecessor did not survive the purges. Andrei Aleksandrovic Zhdanov (1896-48) joined the Bolsheviks when he was nineteen in 1915, remained loyal to Stalin, replaced Kirov as governor of Leningrad, and policed the wartime *Sovinformburo* and the *Cominform* in 1947. In 1939 in order to divide Eastern Europe with Hitler, the Soviet army invades Finland, is repelled and instead seizes Latvia and Estonia. Hopper calls that more "building and destroying." But he misreads history daring to second-guess the Soviet mastermind. Actually Stalin is preparing for the Soviet defense against Hitler's certain assault while he watches the West divide the European chessboard before FDR gives it all away at the Yalta conference.

When peasants are strategically insignificant, they tend to be overlooked by analysts like Hopper looking for more sensational subjects. Of course, it is largely the indoctrinated and trained workingclass of peasants who fill Stalin's war factories, man his tanks, fly the planes, and fill the ranks of the Red Army. With their unsurpassed courage and fierce pride this nation of peasants stop Hitler's invasion at Stalingrad leading to his ultimate defeat at Moscow and retreat to Berlin which they sack on their way westward before finally greeted and contained by the Allied forces in Germany.

The Consortium excels in the falsification of history and spends lavish private sums to do it. Harvard's young Soviet studies don overlooked Stalin's extermination of millions of peasants who provided the food to feed Russia's millions. What did it matter when there are so many of them! Stalin then liquidated his friends and enemies, Hopper said, those "old Bolsheviks, companions of Lenin, most of whom had known the dungeon smell of Siberia. Lenin declares : "Let not blood flow among you.' But Stalin sent them all, or nearly all, to the basement of the Lubianka, or other prisons, where the muzzle of the pistol fits behind the ear. We needn't recite the names. They are in the record of the Russian revolution, even to Yenukidze, whom Stalin dearly loved, – the friend of his childhood, a fellow Georgian." But love for Stalin is an illusory emotion of weak fools not to be taken seriously and he has a crueler fate in store for his friend. "In the Bukharin Trial, Yenukidze was to be made the central villain of terrorist activity, held responsible for the organization of the murder of Kirov, and said to have instructed Yagoda to tell Zaporozhets not to hinder the act; he is also to be responsible for plotting the murder of Gorky, shot. Abel Yenukidze, too, is liquidated by Stalin along with the Caucasian Bolsheviks in Stalin's scheme to rewrite and falsify his role in Bolshevik history. Yenukidze is shot October 30, 1937 along with Sheboldayev and "with other leading figures, including thirteen other full members of the Central Committee …". (Bruce Hopper, Essay, "Psychological Profile of a Madman", *The Red Book*)

"At 60 Stalin is still responsible for his face", an astute literary phrase by the Russophile. "He is not an evil man," Hopper concludes. History records Stalin killed tens of millions in the USSR. Is there nothing evil inherent in that? "Rather", Hopper explains, "he is a peasant raised to absolute power. The curse upon him is his misunderstanding of Lenin's legacy of monolithic power. By a monolith of power Lenin meant that the party should have freedom of discussion, a democratic centralism of comrades with a unity of will, once a course of action had been decided upon. By monolith of power Stalin understands that no voice shall be raised against the will of Stalin. And what is the will of Stalin? Stalin's will is his own (the peasant's) conception of the mystic absolute revolutionary conscience, the dictate of that awful majesty, Socialist Society. Other, equally ardent revolutionaries, would take a different route to Socialist Society, – let them be destroyed. More nimble brains, who count the cost of the tempo in human lives, would slacken the pace to gain surcease (sic) from the deadly monotony, – let them also be destroyed. These become Stalin's enemies because they offered his understanding of the monolith of power and the revolutionary conscience. …it is revealed as a pathetic travesty on human kind. (Finland) The Russian people, instead of being transformed into a wonder folk, seem to become spiritless cattle, which they never were under the Tsars; they then, at least, had God."

Hopper elaborates further: "… in these years of work I have acquired an abiding sympathy for the Russian people, the little brothers of the steppe whose air seems destined to be unfree. I now see economic collectivization and planning as a failure, except to organize human and material resources for military power. I now consider the furious tempo of industrialization as a historical mistake. There was a natural course laid out for Russia by geography as an agrarian hinterland, and a normal pace dictated by immense distances and extreme climate. But in order to attain revolutionary goals by military means Stalin interfered with that dictate of geography and that limitation of the human material, and set out to overtake and outstrip capitalist countries with a soviet industrialism based on materials. To maintain that tempo he has sent millions of Russians to forced labor in the northern woods, on the canals and railroads. He slaughtered the companions of Lenin. He built and destroyed, always trying to win the loyalty of the mass to his conception of the Socialist Society. Thus his many spectacular stunts – shock brigades, Stakhanovism, the mass trials, the purges, etc. And now he is as near to Socialist Society as he will ever get, because all Russia is a proletarianized peasantry. The revolution in 1917 exiled the flower of the talent of old Russia; the rest has been largely liquidated in the name of Monolith of Power."

"The Nemesis of self-devourment has overtaken Stalin. Russianism has overtaken Bolshevism; eventually Russianism will consume the Bolsheviks themselves," Hopper writes. It's the same theme as we find later with journalist Harrison Salisbury. "Stalin, remote like the old northern star, broods alone in the Kremlin. His is the loneliness of the god of terror. He broods over his pipe and his Gerogian wine. He wanted peace; he still wants peace." But Stalin now lived "the reality of his old nightmare, a war in the West". "He is a sick man. The adulation on his 60th birthday was that generally reserved for a dying man." Hopper erred. He said Stalin had "a heart disease, and can last but a few years at most". Hopper predicts "four casualties to one" in the Red Army "against a modernized Western Army". In 1940, Hopper wrote, "it would be folly to assume … that Russia could be easily invaded". Only four to one? Napoleon, of course, never wrote *War and Peace*, nor would he ever read it.

For years now the terror in the countryside was already taking shape and building force as early as 1928 when Consortium syndicates are pushing Bolshevik bonds to American investors willingly duped by propaganda as were more pliable and illiterate Russian peasants. Collective state farms had already been proven a horrific failure of militant communism when Stalin announced the Collectivization Plan adopted by the Communist Party leadership. The peasants wanted none of it. In his *History of Russia*, Bernard Pares, London's Slavic Studies Russian expert wrote, "either they had collapsed or they had fallen exactly into the hands of those for whom they were not intended, namely the more prosperous peasants, and state authority in the villages had itself fallen under peasant influence. ... What the peasantry wanted was to go forward with its individual farming, while widely cooperating with each other in securing machinery and in marketing their goods." They resisted, forced into collective farms, however, often by the Communist Youth Organization, the Komsomols, the young generation of pea-brain fanatics of the Motherland fed communist propaganda later liquidated or killed in the war.

Again Pares: "Force was used on the largest scale, and in the spring of 1930 the young enthusiasts reported that two-thirds of all the farms in the country were already collectivized. This was only on paper; the peasants might have been driven into collectivization but the farm work was being ruined." It was then Stalin sent his famous rebuke to the Party chiefs, deriding them for their "dizziness with success", urging the Party ease off the peasants to allow them get on with their work in their own way. It was only a temporary retreat. Individual farmers were hit by heavy taxes, and restrictions imposed by the government monopolies. The richer peasants – *kulaks* – were again targeted. Stalin's lower deputies then sent thousands of zealous Communists, Red Army soldiers and Cheka police to crack down on the country villages. Soviet cameras filmed despairing scenes homes ransacked, arrests and executions by gunshots or hangings of *kulaks*. Pares observes, "... the local paupers pointed out the victims. The condemned man and his wife were deprived of everything they had – house, stock, implements and everything else – put into carts in what they stood up in, and carried away to concentration camps, to work there as slaves of the Government."

And there is the experience of the well-known writer Maurice Hindus (1891-69), born in Russia, emigrated to America in 1905, and returned to his native village in 1929-30 to personally experience numerous scenes of repression and famine recorded in *Red Bread, and Broken Earth: Collectivization in a Russian Village* (1931). Albeit, pro-Soviet, he described scenes of indignation and hopelessness that were repeated in every village. "'Barracks for life,' says one. 'Serfdom – that's what it is,' says another. 'You cannot put together a broken heart as you can a broken wagon,' says a woman ...'. When we live in one place and have a family, we are like an oak,' says the old man, 'we get rooted deep in the very soil on which we live, and when we are pulled up we just wilt and die'."

The Ukrainians died with God in their heart. But God did not create the 1932-34 Holodomor Terror-Famine. There was an important distinction overlooked. "It was the Communist Party that governed Russia – not the Soviet government", Prof. Pares wrote in his *History of Russia*. As General Secretary of the Party Stalin controlled Party affairs "kept the books", distributed important posts and appointments, assiduously disciplined in the business of administering power, avoided direct confrontations and carefully plotted his moves. In his last testament written before he died in 1924 after a series of strokes that partially paralyzed him Lenin feared the worst and warned of Stalin's roughness.

By 1926 and the Party meetings of April and July Stalin had ousted his opposition rejected as a "gang of European adventurers"; Dzerzhinsky, head of the Cheka-GPU made a speech on the stability of the party and suddenly died soon after; well-educated radical from a prosperous family, Dzerhinsky had spent nearly all his life in prisons – certainly not the norm for the Bolshevik leaders. Zinoviev was suspended from his functions as President of the Third International or Comintern, controlling communists in foreign countries.

Stalin managed to deceive his contemporaries. He and his supporters intrigued to isolate both the brilliant theoretician and much beloved Bolshevik figure of the Revolution, Bukharin on the Left as well as the Trotskyists with Zinoviev and Kamenev on the Right who might have succeeded Lenin upon his death as Premier albeit he was a Jew not a Russian. In July 1927, Trotsky violently denounces Stalin in the Central Committee of the Party; Trotsky's days in Soviet Russia are numbered.

Trotsky is kicked off the Politburo, the inner executive of Commissars of the Party; then, in 1927, he's expelled along with Zinoviev from the Party Central Committee. Trotsky argued against state capitalism; Stalin favored his "Socialism in one country" doctrine of 1924 before world revolution. Refusing to be silenced, and too conspicuous to be killed, Trotsky sent into internal exile, then expelled from the country 1929. Stalin eventually has him killed in Mexico City in 1940, an ice pick through the brain. After Trotsky's exile, first Bukharin, then Rykov, are shot after the 1938 show trial in the Great Purge.

On the Trials and the system that devoured its children who created it, British historian Michael Hughes in *Inside the Enigma: British officials in Russia, 1900-1939* (2003) perpetuates the myth that the Bolsheviks willingly played along with Stalin's liquidation of the old Bolshevik organization thus crushing any remnant of genuine oppositional politics within the Soviet socialist Party ranks. "Yet even Bukharin," Michael Hughes writes "whose intellect allowed him to run rings round the prosecution, remained a prisoner of his life-long commitment to Bolshevism. He could not find it in himself to renounce outright the system that he had helped to build, even at the moment it destroyed him ... The lingering myth of the Communist Party's infallibility provided its leader with a powerful tool to manipulate and crush anyone who had any shred of idealism or ideological belief left intact." Unfortunately Hughes too plays his establishment role in concealing the invisible hand of the Anglo-American Consortium leaving the reader to infer that Empire politics simply no longer pursued any commercial interest in post-Czarist Russia. (Michael Hughes, *Inside the Enigma: British officials in Russia, 1900-1939,* Hambledon & London, 2003, 263)

In 1928, 98% of land is small farms; by June 1928, the number of collective farms, or *kolkhozes*, increases to 33,258 but it represents only a fraction of the total population affected and is unpopular among most villages. The next year special brigades terrorize the countryside taking militant action against peasants who resist to protect their property and confront the reality the Bolshevik revolution that promised land only aims to destroy them completely. In retaliation many peasants kill off their livestock; in 1929, 18 million of 34 million horses are slaughtered in Russia; 60 percent of the sheep and goats, and 45 percent of the cattle are destroyed. (*Horizon History of Russia*, American History Publishing, 1970)

By 1929 Stalin's decision to industrialize Russia paid for by the national produce from collectivization would protect its frontier from encirclement and invasion by the imperialist powers. He justifies the Terror-Famine in the name of national security to protect the Party and the Revolution of the Proletariat. Stalin, in fact, had adopted Trotsky's economic goals. Instead of stability and growth Stalin's repressions trigger wholesale peasant resistance risking general rebellion adding political breakdown to economic bankruptcy of the Communist Party.

From 1929 the peasants hoarded wheat so Stalin confiscated it. From 1929 to 1933 Stalin faces open warfare in the countryside. The Kulaks are steadily "eliminated" - but this soon includes all opposition. Two stages from 1928: take away Kulak land and power and use poorer peasants against Kulaks to force all peasants onto the collective farms. There was massive opposition - especially from Kulaks. The killing of livestock continues to some 100 million animals.

By 1938 - 90% of the USSR is under collectivization, but it does not resolve problems of efficient food production. However peasants are not now starving in the cities. In 1928-29 the NEP ceases to work; the Kulaks keep their grain stock off the market pushing up prices.

Massive state repression is directed against them – who were systematically killed.

Collectivization was put into effect. This was the famine. Perhaps ten million people died in forced collectivization. Millions were sent to forced labor camps and farms. State took control of farm machinery - could be withdrawn from opponents. Even after collectivization there was planned famine directed against the peasants. Millions were deliberately starved to death in one of the bleakest chapters in history.

A worse fate descended on Politburo member and author of the Communist Party Constitution the theoretician Nikolai Ivanovich Bukharin. Although by late 1927 substantial progress had been achieved by the New Economic Policy (NEP) Comrade Stalin "introduced an abrupt change in the economic policy of the Party which not only called for a violent offensive against the *kulaks* but virtually meant the abandonment of the NEP and even a reversion to certain elements of 'war communism'.

The peasant suffered the most. Stalin had declared their plight "the very essence of the nationality problem." By 1928, however, Stalin is ready to launch his latest attack against the "nationalist deviation in the Ukraine", and linking it with collectivization to destroy the bedrock of Ukrainian nationalism – individual land-holdings, and the kulak farms. The kulak is blamed as the bearer of nationalist ideas. Likewise, the Ukrainian nationalist is branded the sponsor of kulak attitudes: both must be eradicated by "war communism". The kulaks and other "anti-Soviet" elements are attacked by a variety of terrors.

In April at the 1929 plenum of the Central Committee in a speech never published in the US Bukharin launches a virulent attack directly at Stalin for destroying the NEP and imposing a reactionary feudalistic military repression of the peasants and bureaucratic centralism that while he spoke was ransacking the countryside and bringing the country to a crisis so that "at the very threshold of socialism we apparently will either have to start a civil war or fall by the wayside and perish from hunger." Rather than openly fight Stalin, Bukharin withdraws from the April Party Conference and abandons his seat on the presidium. The Rightists lose more ground in the Central Committee. Bukharin is removed as editor of *Pravda* and chairman of the Comintern. When Tomsky loses his trade union leadership, Stalin's henchman Kaganovich berate the opposition: "The greater part of the leadership has been replaced… It could be said that this was a violation of proletarian democracy, but, comrades, it has long been known that for us Bolsheviks democracy is no fetish..." Throughout the decade Stalin consistently exploits the Bolshevik factional in-fighting until all of them perished as kulak-deviationists and kulak-bourgeois elements. (R. Medvedev, 64; R. Conquest, *The Great Terror*, 18)

The dictator of the Proletariat was getting impatient. So was the Consortium behind the two Five-Year Plans and wanted a high return on each dollar invested in the so-called "New Society" of state socialized communism. Stalin justified forced collectivization and industrialization by claiming that Russia was "threatened" on its borders by the Western Powers, i.e. Great Britain and France so it had to "catch up" and surpass the capitalists in industrial production and this at a time when the West is confronted with economic turmoil and depression on their home fronts.

Summer 1930 marked the beginning of a new era of Bolshevik terror. By March, more than half of farmlands and half of the total peasant population are collectivized. At the Sixteenth Party Congress that June and July Bukharin made his strongest appeal to gain the leadership of the Party. Here Bukharin claims "a victory of the right in the party would lead in the end to a rebirth of capitalism". Stalin clashes with Trotskyists over the failed compulsory agricultural program. Kirov backs Stalin in the attack on Bukharin, Rykov, Tomskii and Uglanov, – all will soon perish in Stalin's final crackdown. Rykov has already been replaced by Molotov, Stalin's nominee for Premier, backed by his trusted henchman Kaganovich. Then all hell breaks loose.

Rural regions face imminent civil war in the first great crisis of Stalin's regime. The peasants abandoned the *kolkhozes*. Stalin now berates his *apparatchiki*. "The peasant is adopting a new tactic," Stalin warns. "He refuses to reap the harvest. He wants the bread grain to die in order to choke the Soviet Government with the bony hand of famine. But the enemy miscalculates. We shall show him what famine is. Your task is to stop the sabotage of the harvest; you must bring it in to the last grain and send it off to the delivery point. The peasants are not working. They are counting the previous harvested grain they have hidden in pits. We must force them to open their pits." Stalin insists on harsher measures, more terror. By 1936, 91 percent of all Russian and Ukrainian peasants are displaced to work on collective farms.

Sergei Kirov, second to Zinoviev in the Leningrad Party organization, has been one of the key authorities in the OGPU crackdown and decimation of the academic hierarchy in the Academy of Sciences headquartered in Leningrad; nor is Kirov opposed to Stalin's Terror and the use of forced labor in the death camps.

The ambitious and popular younger Kirov has an active role in the "Stalin Baltic-White Sea Canal" constructed exclusively by prison labour. Its even praised by the writer Maxim Gorky duped by his paymaster and hailed in the West. At Stalin's instructions work has to be fast and costs kept low. In 20 months between 1931 and 1933 prisoners equipped with pick-axes, wheelbarrows and hatchets dig a 227-kilometer long canal linking the Baltic and the White Sea. Built at a cost of some 280,000 workers, mostly exiled peasants who died in extreme cold conditions with meager nourishment to finish.

During the height of the Holodomor in July 1933 Stalin makes one of his rare trips to Leningrad, this time for the official opening of the Canal. Sailing on the steamship *Anokhin* for the inauguration Stalin is joined by Kirov, Voroshilov, defense commissioner, Yagoda, OGPU deputy chief in charge of the Canal project, and M. D. Berman, head of the Gulag labor death camp system. The Soviet Party Commissars hail their achievement saying, "To build such a canal in such a short time, in such a place – it is truly heroic work and we must give justice to our Chekists (original name of the political police in 1917), who led this business and who literally achieved a miracle." Stalin concludes to his disappointment that the canal is too narrow and not deep enough for his liking. (Shoot the architect! Did he? Reader, we may assume...) He orders a bigger one to be built. The blueprints are ready by 1936 but the project is never implemented. (Were they *all* shot?) Ice-bound half the year and too small for maritime vessels, the White Sea Canal never serves any significant economic or strategic purpose. (A. Knight, 149)

The Five-Year Plan has to be completed in four years! It is the primary military industrial priority of Stalin's Soviet totalitarian regime and the Consortium's winning card in the race towards world war. Forced labor lays thousands of miles of rails and track, filled the lumber camps, working the coal mines of Vorkuta and mined the gold of Kolyma. During the first two Five-Year Plans of 1929-39, giant hydroelectric dams and factories are built and assembled with western technology. These had to be ready in record time using both prison and free labor. The two-mile long Magnitogorsk dam is completed in 1932 equipped with giant GE turbines.

Staggering sacrifices for extraordinary achievements. Eighty percent of all industrial investment is spent on heavy industry. At least fifteen hundred new factories are built in this period. In the wilderness of western Siberia and deep in the Urals, vast industrial complexes were built, a brilliant stroke of genius by Stalin to entrap Hitler's crack Wehrmacht divisions when after a few months his Nazi invasion is stopped in the deep muddy black earth of the Ukraine from rain and snow. Half of the machine tools produced in 1932 are engaged in production. Coal production increased twenty-five percent as did the number of oil wells in production. Electricity produced from power stations doubled. Stalin boasted that the Five-Year Plan (FYP) for Industry has nearly reached its goal at 97.3 percent.

With the American economy struggling from financial ruin, by 1937 Russia's industrial output increases to 13.7 percent from 2.6 percent in 1913, and 3.7 percent in 1929. (*Horizon History of Russia,* 359)

Forced labour forms the crucial backbone of all FYPs, particularly after 1934 with intensified ethnic-cleansing of the Ukraine. Millions of people died of cold and malnutrition in these camps. What the peasants had not realized, however, was that the Bolshevik terror descending upon them were the direct result of Moscow's relations with the Consortium. Stalin had good historical reasons to distrust England surpassed only by his fear of German rearmament. But how on earth are the illiterate peasants to know that from the beginning Lenin, Trotsky, Stalin and the whole gang of Bolshevik leaders, Rakovsky, Rykov, Zinoviev and the others are no better than actors of a deadly drama financed by Allied (and Russian!) gold held in American vaults, the bedrock of the great American capitalist free-enterprise market system. Live and learn; when you walk under the eternal stars what's the point of living in starry indifference when you can discover the truth behind the lie.

Of course they read Lenin's Marxist essays on imperialism and "the capitalist war" and remember how he held strong and committed during the early years of defensive war fever. First Lenin and Trotsky tricked them, then those left behind Stalin finished off, killing and exiling the and disobedient resisters. Like his predecessors Stalin tolerated no opposition; Trotsky wouldn't have been much less cruel. Soon all Soviet industries will be equipped with technology imported from the West. After all, Lenin's vision is first and foremost to transform the great farmlands of the Ukrainian plains with harvests using advanced American-modeled machines from International Harvester. Westinghouse, Standard Oil, and other giant companies of the Consortium standing in line beckoning for Soviet business for the entire USSR and all it shining bright under the light of General Electric. And the great American people never got the clear picture in their heads; instead they get Luce, Readers Digest and the mass media propaganda machine to do the brainwashing of ethnic cleansing.

No sooner than December 1, 1930 when Walter Duranty interviews Stalin for *The New York Times* the dictator accepts paying part of the debt some $345 million with the $86 million owed First National included but only if President Hoover agrees to grant credits or a loan to the Soviet Union in a package deal considering Soviet claims against the United States. (M. Cassella-Blackburn, 99)

Important to understand in this story but not the central focus of this book is the role playing between the partners of the United States and Bolshevik Russia from the first days of takeover of Czarist Russia. Americans carefully aimed their diplomatic hands towards rising territorial ambitions of both Nazi Germany in Europe and Imperialist Japan in the East. With the Black Sea as its entire southern frontier Ukraine borders Moldavia, Romania and Poland to the West. Otherwise the Ukraine is entirely enveloped by Russia to the north and east. What's most important to understand here is that the Ukrainians got caught in official but carefully concealed government and private Consortium strategy and Stalin's obsession for absolute power. When in 1933 the Holodomor envelopes with all its force civilian and religious organizations in America were only able to urge in vain and far too late that Roosevelt intervene on behalf of the Ukrainians. FDR and his advisers turned away. In their professional arrangements there was no place for inconvenient sentimentality, or amateurs. They were to be laughed at as fools and manipulated by paid hacks occupying key positions as editors, publishers and personalities in the press industry, many of them members of government committees, research institutes, and the Council of Foreign Relations. Meanwhile, the powerful men and organizations of the Consortium are simultaneously financing Hoover and FDR in America, Hitler in Germany, and Stalin in the Soviet Union.

Antony C. Sutton's exhaustive findings reveal alarming similarities between the Roosevelt "New Deal" and Hitler's Four-Year Plan. During the Hoover administration, the Americans were praising Stalin's promise to push through Soviet Five-Year Plans of the Communist Party. These plans were actually engineered by the Consortium and its network of firms and financiers. Stalin cleansed the Soviet Party hierarchy of any political opposition that challenged capital's stronghold on the state socialist monopoly of terror and famine. Sutton's findings may seem to the establishment-educated readers at first almost too incredible to be true. Brainwashing by propaganda slogans are profound as any consumer fed constant advertisements knows all too well. That is, if there is any free will left to the mind to distinguish more than one ad from another. Sutton's conclusions come together with a simple logic as deadly as Stalin's campaign of extermination. Of course, once consumers are pacified and their minds "cleansed" to receive the propaganda doped with intentions to act a certain way, the individual will is threatened with instructions to obey. And when already pacified consumers feel threatened and scared, they bow their heads and cow-down with their tail between their legs, unable to stir up the passion of revolt. The illiterate but wise Ukrainian kulaks were built tough and hard. They resisted the propaganda and they were smashed.

Antony Sutton: "Why did the Wall Street elite, the international bankers, want Roosevelt and Hitler in power? "Wall Street ...wanted war in Europe between France and Germany. We know even from Establishment history that both Hitler and Roosevelt acted out policies leading to war." It may be hard to accept at first glance. But when you look closely at the individuals and their groups, review their objectives and activities, then the picture becomes more clear and convincing. When a crime is committed who benefits from the crime? Better there were no crime and not ask the question, right? Wrong! Once again, why should an international Consortium of capitalists choose to support Marxist communist Bolsheviks? In fact, these so-called enemies of capitalism were publicly denounced. That was all part of the ploy. "There was widespread criticism of the Bolsheviks," Sutton observes, "but this was not allowed to interfere with trade. In sum, there was no argument made against technical transfers while several influential political and business forces were working actively to open up trade ... What was missing in the Soviet Union was freedom. Its people had technical skills, but they had little incentive to invent, develop, refine, manufacture, and make a profit from science and technology. The USSR was dependent on imported science and technology from 1917 until 1991." (A. C. Sutton, *US-Soviet Trade 1917-1965*, 1973, 167, 417; A.C.Sutton, "Myth of 'Sidney Warburg", *Wall Street and the Rise of Hitler*)

Sutton's many published books on secret and elitist Wall Street dealings inside Nazi Germany and the Soviet Union challenge establishment history. They have become, nevertheless, classic material to any serious reader of US-Russian history. Yet they remain far from mainstream reading lists. Remember, the Consortium is omnipresent and unforgiving. While off-limits to most educators fortunately his three volumes on US-Soviet trade has become standard reading in American universities from MIT to Stanford. Try your local government library. His book *Wall Street and the Rise of Hitler*" revealed that key American financiers provided capital and industrial means to Hitler to launch World War II. International financing of the Russian Revolution is documented in *Wall Street and the Bolshevik Revolution.* Clearly it should be self-evident to the digital society that it's unquestionably time, and long overdue to toss into the dump that conventional textbook reading of historical events with its three generations of delusion and deliberate obscurantism of the actual causes of events. That was not an easy thing to do when the Consortium owned virtually all of the publishing industry and seeks to control the Internet.

Sutton points out that the Soviet economy might just as well have been tagged "Made in the U.S.A." More to the matter here Sutton's *Western Technology and Soviet Economic Development 1917-1965* demonstrates US deliverance of the bulk of technology, savoir-faire, raw material and most of the financing required to build the monolithic industrial and military machine with which "the Evil Empire" as President Reagan punned the Soviet Union threatened the free world.

FDR 1933: "THE ONLY THING WE HAVE TO FEAR IS FEAR ITSELF"

Having been dosed with printed lies for generations it may seem hard to believe how the Consortium managed to build a menacing military machine conceived to terrorize the free world and render a population hostage to their own government fit to be mostly middle-class paranoid and frightened taxpayers. Strange but the fact is the majority of contemporary Americans live in a state of perpetual fear. Fear for their jobs, fear for their taxes, fear for their credit and debts. That is very strange if you reflect that it was President Roosevelt himself who said in his first inaugural address in 1933, "The only thing we have to fear is fear itself." Whoever believes that government is to be trusted is living a fantasy that has forsaken freedom and courting doom.

It does not take a great leap of understanding to comprehend that the opaque Federal Reserve Banking central banking system squeaked into legislation by a pontificating son of a minister as President from Princeton University in 1913 and that financed nearly forty billion dollars of war profits for an American elite in the First World War as well laying down the road as the conditions for the

Second World War was also a primary factor in consolidating the Soviet socialist monopoly with Russian-styled Stalinist despotism. Understand the Fed factor. The Ukrainian peasants never had a chance in hell. (A. C. Sutton, *Western Technology and Soviet Economic Development 1917-1965*, A. C. Sutton, *Wall Street and the Rise of Hitler*, Seal Beach, CA. Press, 1976; A. C. Sutton, *Wall Street and the Bolshevik Revolution*, Rochelle, NY: Arlington House, 1981)

When I first became interested in the Holodomor story while living in the Ukraine during the politically contrived "Orange Revolution" of 2004-5, it seemed odd the American famine connection had not been seriously explored. Why? To quote my dear friend Sasha, "there were special considerations". Substitute "national strategic interests". But who decided the peculiar nature of these interests? What were they? Where do they come from? Who decides what these "special considerations" are much less how to implement them?

To find the right answers the compass needle needed an adjustment. Sutton's research combined with the famine reporting of Gareth Jones and others including the hacks and propagandists pointed the way to asking the right questions. Follow the money. The conclusions are dangerously embarrassing but not as frightening as the crime.

Sutton writes, "Looking at the broad array of facts presented in the three volumes of the Wall Street series, we find persistent recurrence of the same names…the same international banks … and the same location in New York: usually 120 Broadway. This group of international bankers backed the Bolshevik Revolution and subsequently profited from the establishment of a Soviet Russia. This group backed Roosevelt and profited from New Deal socialism. This group also backed Hitler and certainly profited from German armament in the 1930s. When Big Business should have been running its business operations at Ford Motor, Standard Oil of New Jersey, and so on, we find it actively and deeply involved in political intrigue, revolutions and war. The version of history presented here is that the financial elite knowingly and with premeditation assisted the Bolshevik Revolution of 1917 in concert with German bankers."

From then until the final collapse of the Soviet Union in 1991, this Consortium elite and its extended networked members spread through the globe like tentacles of a giant octopus engaged in industrial and banking operations with a colossal socialist monopoly and implicitly shared in the process of destruction of untold millions of lives of the Soviet society. It was all done in relative secrecy and suppression. For generations citizens in the so-called "free world" and the US were not privy to the reality of US-Soviet affairs. National "representative" government leaders lied to protect the Consortium of shared power and special interests groups.

Prior to his appointment to Moscow Bullitt spends much of his time with European bankers and diplomats, in London and Paris, in particular, Consortium people and their cronies negotiating outstanding debts and claims from the First World War. His passion was words, not numbers. Bullitt preferred books to balance sheets. But he gloated in social contacts, enjoyed playing the gallant host at extravagant parties and liked to charm his superiors which made him a good man-servant to FDR who liked to put his "boys" in the right place. Stalin finds Bullitt weak and ridiculous and exploits his weakness to the Kremlin's advantage.

Again we are indebted to Sutton's research and findings, as well as Georgetown's professor Carroll Quigley who alerted students that the "apex of this international financial control system after the First World War was the Bank for International Settlements (BIS), with representatives from the international banking firms of Europe and the United States, in an arrangement that continued throughout World War II."

In you read Sutton and I strongly encourage you do it and see more clearly the role of the BIS emerging as the Consortium's brain child in a global plan conceived at a conference presided over by bankers Jackson Reynolds in New York, Melvin Traylor of Chicago's First National, Sir Charles Addis from the Hong Kong and Shanghai Banking Corp. sitting abreast to German and French bankers. In other words, a global banking cartel. Sutton traces how Hitler's financial wizard and Reichsbank president Hjalmar Schacht is also Germany's rep at the Bank for International Settlements. It is Schacht, – not Charles Dawes or Owen Young, – "who conceived the idea which later became the Bank for International Settlements."

Schacht works closely with Young and the Morgan interests in New York; in fact, he blames them and their banking measures straining Germany's economy for causing the crisis that eventually brings Hitler to power in 1933 on tsunami wave of overwhelming popular support across Germany's entire national political spectrum. But the powerful Morgan bank with its reputation for starched elegance and groomed impeccability is only one sparkling facet of a vast and ambitious system of cooperation and international alliance binding governments determined to take control of the resources and affairs of the world. And, of course, Morgan, Rockefeller and the Consortium gang follows Hitler's ascent eager to cash in and invests heavily in the fascist Nazi regime spelling doom for the Ukrainians and a world longing for peace instead of war.

Professor Quigley called this Consortium system a global arrangement established over generations with a single purpose, "... nothing less than to create a world system of financial control, in private hands, able to dominate the political system of each country and the economy of the world as a whole." This feudal system worked in the 1920s, as it works today adapted and modified through the channels of private central bankers in each country who control the national money supply of individual economies. In the 1920s and 1930s the New York Federal Reserve System, the Bank of England, the Reichsbank in Germany, and the Banque de France easily influenced the political heads of their respective countries by controlling the money supply of the monetary environment. More direct influence was realized by supplying political funds or withdrawing support from political parties and their politicians. In the United States, for example, President Herbert Hoover moaned about his 1932 defeat having been promoted by Wall Street putting its money instead on Roosevelt. Politicians amenable to the objectives of financial capitalism and academics prolific with rhetoric for world control are always useful to the international bankers and kept on hand by a system of rewards and penalties.

From Vladimir Lenin to Mikhail Gorbachev the USSR was dependent on imported science and technology from the West. In the Soviet Union no one was exempt from the Marxist dialectics adapted to Bolshevik communist ideology. Everyone was a potential counter-revolutionary living under the blade of an inefficient and cumbersome communist bureaucracy of informers, secret police and arbitrary arrests justified under the Socialist State's revolutionary criminal code. Under such harassment Soviet Russians had technical skills, but they had little incentive to invent, develop, refine, manufacture, and make a profit from science and technology. What was missing in the Union of Socialist Soviet Republics was freedom. Of course, that was considered a bourgeois deviation, a false concept and counter-revolutionary and even more absurd than communism itself.

Nor did the Soviets ever develop the necessary broad changes from the bottom upwards required to successfully absorb western technology to justify trade with the West as a sufficient substitute for internal reforms. The US-Soviet system of collaboration and Cold War inevitably mutated to present realities. After centuries of beggarly existence of the peoples colonized by the Russian Empire and depleted human and material resources from decades of communism, independent Ukraine is still struggling to pick up the pieces of its shattered and fragmented experience burdened by Soviet-styled economy where corruption and a "mafia-type post-communism", have poisoned the political life and the media. Citing exactly this problem the former President of the Czech Republic Vaclav Havel observed in an opinion article in the Kiev-based newspaper *The Day* March 28, 2006 that Russian president Vladimir Putin called "the disintegration of the Soviet Union a tragic mistake;" the next year Putin made "Man of the Year" in *Time Magazine*. (*The Day*, March 28, 2006)

What did the State Department know about the Kremlin's internal affairs during Stalin's liquidation of Bolshevik comrades for their opposition to the Consortium socialist agenda? Washington is obliged to rely on Riga, and its close diplomatic ties with London and Paris. Britain's Foreign Office sends Sir Esmond Ovey to head its reopened Moscow embassy. Only six days after the British Cabinet reject the Ottawa trade Agreement binding both Britain and the USSR to an anti-dumping clause, the ambassador meets Litvinov mid-October. It does not go well. Litvinov is clearly agitated. He feels deceived, and worse, Stalin betrays Sokolnikov. Sir Esmund writes Simon October 22, 1932. (A. J. Williams, 203, 215 footnote 62, Overy to Simon Oct. 22, 1932, FO317/16320; G. Vernadsky, *History of Russia*, Yale, ed.1929, 1962, 362-6 re. Soviet diplomatic relations with Great Britain)

Sokolnikov – whose real name is "Brilliant" – is also chairman of the Petroleum Trust "responsible for the conclusion of the agreement with English oil interests which had been signed in February 1929. On December 20, 1929, he presented his credentials, and also exchanged formal assurances with Henderson that both governments would in the future abstain from agitation against each other." Litvinov's approach towards FDR in 1933 for normalization of diplomatic relations with the Americans follows much same emphasis for peaceful relations and Soviet restraint of propaganda activities, but spurned by Stimson after Litvinov's "blunt rebuff" over US meddling in the Russia-China dispute.

Sir Edmond Ovey's assignment will be most unpleasant in a most miserable post. In his book *Inside the Enigma*, Michael Hughes sketches a curious portrait on Britain's diplomatic scene in Soviet Russia during the thirties: "From the moment Ovey and his staff traveled to Russia at the end of 1929, they were struck by the greyness of daily life in Moscow and Leningrad. After the Ambassador settles in, he tells the Foreign Office, 'One becomes used, after a few months, to the general aspect of dinginess which strikes one so strongly on arrival. The average appearance of the crowds becomes gradually less remarkable, and one begins to notice the outstanding figures – those who are, literally, in rags, and those whom, by a stretch of the imagination or forgetfulness, one can actually describe as well-dressed." Hughes also notes that Ovey observes "the lack of food in the shops and the absence of almost any other goods available for purchased. The problems were particularly acute for 'the class of unfortunates … priests, ex-businessmen, ex-employees of the police force and the secret police, former military and naval officers', who received no ration cards and could not afford the high price of food sold on the open market." When Sir Ovey intervenes on behalf of some down-and-out soviet citizens, he's told in the standard rude Russian that 'their welfare was none of his business'." (M. Hughes, *Inside the Enigma*, 224)

By the early thirties conditions little improves and remain poor. Hughes writes, "Moscow was a desperately unpopular post throughout the 1930s. Only one individual volunteered for service there during the whole of the 1930s, while many others made little secret of their distaste for the country. … William Strang of the British Embassy writes in 1931 that no British representative should be posted to Soviet Russia for more than six months without a break. He suggests that any tour of duty there should be strictly limited, since a lengthy posting might create a level of stress that would damage the physical and psychological health of the individual official."

Sir William Strang knows his terrain well; in the summer of 1939 shortly after Hitler's troops complete their occupation of Czechoslovakia and target the Danzig on the Baltic and the Polish Corridor given to Poland in the Versailles Treaty, Lord Strang, head of the Foreign Office sits with Molotov "in a last ditch effort to secure an Anglo-Soviet agreement". However, the Nazi-Soviet Pact, announced in August leaves the door open for the German and Soviet occupation of Poland.

The British Embassy finds the situation in the cities in general utterly depressing. Writer Michael Hughes recalls how Douglas Keane observes in the summer of 1930 how conditions had deteriorated significantly since the Revolution, and Keane wrote, "All necessaries of life have become scarcer even during the short period I have been here. … Queues are now formed for almost every commodity, are of increasing length and begin to show less good temper than formerly." Special stores reserved for foreigners offered foodstuffs at significantly higher prices. The poor British Consul spent two weeks "scouring the city to find a broom-handle".

Keane and those who followed after him report frequently on the rise of disease, typhus, and the mounting death toll in Leningrad. Reader Bullard tells how the worsening housing crisis due to the influx of the country population into the cities created impossible health situation such as when a "room contains five beds nearly touching, and each bed contains a family of two or more persons". Strang is speaking for himself as much as his colleagues when he declares, "I must confess that after a year in the country I find more that makes for depression and less than makes for cheerfulness than I did a year ago. People seem less well-favoured (and many more positively ugly), less well-disposed, less buoyant."

By the end of 1931 William Strang is able to convey to London that signs of prosperity enjoyed by a certain tier of the Soviet Party ranks "one of the noteworthy developments in Moscow life during the past year or so is the emergence, perhaps temporarily, of a new urban *bourgeois* class. They are distinguished from the mass of the population by being obviously better fed, and by being well and even, by local standards, smartly dressed…They frequent the more expensive, if still modest, native restaurants, from which the poor and hungry are turned away. They live, by our standards, plainly, but in this country it is luxury to have enough." (M. Hughes, *Inside the Enigma*, 224-50, citing Lord Strang to Reading, Nov. 3, 1931; Keith Jeffrey, *The Secret History of MI6*, NY: Penguin, 2010, 312)

As in America a half century before when Rockefeller's oil boom brought misery and back-breaking exhaustion to the American workers while keeping just enough food in their bellies for another days hard labor Standard Oil now in Baku does little to improve the lives of Soviet workers there. Hughes writes that British observers on a trip in 1935 in the Caucasus report "material conditions faced by the population were still dismal. Workers in Baku lived 'in the most appalling plank hovels' while in Yerevan they had to make to with 'mud huts'." Such conditions were utterly offensive to the cultivated foreigner living in protected and relative sanitary bourgeois hotel in the Leningrad or Moscow. "A few days exposure to a diet of 'almost inedible food' quickly served to depress the spirits of even the most resilient official, encouraging them to scamper back to the comparative comfort of Moscow at the first opportunity." (M. Hughes, *Inside the Enigma*, 250, citing FO 37121105, "Vincent, 'Notes on a Car Journey from Moscow to Odessa'")

That picture of Baku contrasts with the memory of American Pulitzer journalist for *The NYT*, Hubert Knickerbocker for his book *The Soviet Five-Year Plan and its Effect on World Trade* published the year following his visit; that same year in 1931 "Knick" publishes another but highly critical anti-Soviet book, *The Red Trade Menace*: "I drove over the twenty miles of perfect asphalt pavement through mile after mile of new settlements, snowy white, the architecture neo-oriental' reported Hubert Knickerbocker, a correspondent for the *New York Evening Post*. 'The street car system that replaced horse cars four years ago is the best in Russia. The new electric inter-urban line connecting with the 'Black City' of oil, where wells are thickest, has the most artistic station and almost the only new big city railroad station in the country.' Walking through Baku, Knickerbocker heard a shot ring out. He traced it to a shooting gallery with a comic political overtone. 'Hit a capitalist and up rises a Social-Democrat; hit a hog and his head changes to that of a fat-jowled banker ... Baku, rich, is still red."(S. Levine, *The Oil and the Glory;* Hubert Knickerbocker, *The Soviet Five-Year Plan and its Effect on World Trade*, J. Lane, 1931; H. Knickerbocker, *The Red Trade Menace*, Dodd, Mead, 1931, 132-4)

Freelancer Steve Levine (*The Wall Street Journal, The New York Times, Newsweek...)* confirms the Consortium interest in backing Stalin's Plans. His book *The Oil and the Glory* recounts how Consortium investment from 1928 under Stalin "unabashedly employed American and European expertise to help carry it out. American engineers and equipment working at his command built the world's largest steel plant, its largest hydroelectric dam, its largest automobile factory, and more. Baku's oil fields, the country's greatest resource of foreign exchange, received special attention. Relying on American and German experts, but as hired help rather than as profit-earning co-owners, Stalin injected money and labor into Baku in 'savage determination to get out every barrel with the utmost speed and convert it as quickly as possible into the dollars so desperately needed by the five year plan'. In 1930, production rose to nearly 100 million barrels, just one-tenth of US production but still the third-highest in the world."

Levine concludes, "As Lenin had hoped a decade earlier, western know-how and equipment was instrumental in making the Bolshevik experiment work. The Great Depression motivated American professionals to seek jobs in the Soviet Union, and Washington not to bar their way. Since the economic plunge also reduced demand for their raw materials, the Soviets tapped national treasures for cash to pay the foreigners." (Steve Levine, *The Oil and the Glory,* NY: Random House, 2007)

How does Stalin rule with opposition in the wings able to "attempt to use Party committees and congresses to impose limits on his power"? Hughes explains how "Stalin instead exercised power through a complex ad hoc network of individuals and organizations that posed no corporate challenge to his position". Hughes would rather believe that the terrible conditions of mass terror, purges, gulag death camps deportations and executions were something to come much later, in 1937 and 1938.

Even Solzhenitsyn in *The Oak and the Calf* refers how the terror and famine came in perpetual waves with frequency stayed by a short pause here and there. "Until 1933, wherever there was a breath of Russia in the air ('White Guard' Russia, as they put it, or 'stick-in-the-mud Russia', as they called it when they were abusing muzhiks), people were executed, persecuted, exiled.... However viciously hostile the dogs, don't look to the Marxist wolf for help. Beat them with an honest stick, but don't call in the wolf. Because the wolf will end by gobbling up *your* liver." (A. I. Solzhenitsyn, *The Oak and the Calf*, 248)

No, Hughes and diplomats in the British Embassy would have us think that Stalin turned the socialist state into collective base of mass terror much later, writing "It was only as the decade wore on that terror began to be used systematically against leading figures in the Communist Party itself, however, as well as against those who occupied prominent positions in the economy, the military and the arts. Before the Great Terror, the Soviet political elite used violence primarily as a means of securing its position and advancing its chosen policies. Yet, at the very point when it had seemingly established its power absolutely, it began to destroy itself from within." Hughes cites Embassy files on "the Kondratiev trial of September 1930 and the arrest of three hundred GPU officers in June the following year", in 1931. (M. Hughes, *Inside the Enigma,* 253)

Lord Strang writes in the fall of 1930 "dissatisfaction is widely and openly expressed, it would not be wise to attach very great significance to this". Occasional satirical plays mocking Bolshevik party discipline. Sir Ovey reports Stalin secure as absolute dictator writing although he's not "regarded with affection by his followers, yet all the world knows and respects the terrific force of will which is his very being and which has raised him to the position of Dictator". (M. Hughes, *Inside the Enigma,* Ft note 115)

Peer inside into the offices of the Washington's Eastern European Affairs Division at the State Department and you will find Russian experts from Riga, Latvia under Henry Stimson, Bill Phillips and Bob Kelley. From Riga the US monitors intelligence and processed to Washington public information relating to famine crisis in the Ukraine. After the 1917 Bolshevik Revolution, America withdraws its ambassador withholding recognition of the new Soviet government. American Russian observers in the State Department maintained a listening post since 1922 in Riga, Latvia. Riga, founded in 1200 A. D. had formerly been the chief German foothold on the eastern Baltic when the Mongols ruled all of Asia, Russia and the Ukraine.

Stalin is talking to Duranty who talked to anyone who would listen in the State Department. A unique document on the problem of recognition, actually an intelligence report on political and economic conditions of the USSR, arrives at the State Department. It was written in December 1929 by Ivan I. Chernikioff, stamped "MCS". It is read by Kelley and others in the Eastern European Affairs Division. Written after the launch of the Five-Year Plans for collectivization and industrialization, Chernikioff's summary provides a blueprint for the framework of the recognition debate between Moscow and Washington and is remarkably similar to the issues raised by Kelly and the Russian experts at State which suggests the proposals for talks still unresolved have been on the table for some time.

"On the twelfth anniversary of the Soviet Republic the following dilemmas confront the Communist Party for the lst decade has governed all Russia:

"I. How to obtain long term credits and loans abroad without recognizing the old commercial and governmental debts and without compensating foreigners for property confiscated by the Communists (Soviet Government);

"II. How to establish friendly relations with foreign Governments and at the same time continue revolutionary propaganda in their respective countries against the existing order;

"III. How to obtain from the United States of America long time credits, loans and Government recognition, which would prolong the Communist rule in Russia and give the Soviet Government a 'breathing spell' until the world revolution against 'the oppression by the capitalists; starts, for as Lenin said, 'the capitalistic world and the Soviet State cannot exist side by side and either one or the other must be destroyed';

"IV. How they make the American business man believe the Five Year Industrialization plan is a 'good credit risk' and 'ideal outlet' for American manufacturers and could be used immediately, if the Americans would be willing to wait five years (until 1934) before the Soviet 'Accounts Receivable'."

Ivan Chernikioff wonders how the USSR can continue to spend heavily for defense; from 1927 to 1928 the US diverted $393,400,000 on military expenditures compared to around $552 million by the UK (1928-9) and $523 million by France (1929). He asks, "How to purchase grain from the Russian peasant for export and for feeding the army and city population by offering the peasants grain prices which are barely 25 to 30 per cent above the prewar levels, when they must buy manufactured goods from the sole supplier, the Government, at prices ranging from 300 to 400 per cent above the prewar level of prices? This discrepancy between the agricultural and manufactured price of goods may be regarded as an additional tax in disguise upon the peasant who thus have to pay for the inefficiencies of the Government, operated industries, and the Government distribution system. To surmount this difficulty the Soviet Government this year is again resorting to 'extraordinary measures', which last year saved the grain program from a complete failure."

It continues, "A partial description of the 'extraordinary measures' may be found in a following dispatch from Russia by Comrade Kretov: (*The NYT,* September 22, 1929) : 'Under the new government decrees here, all persons refusing to give up surplus wheat supplies to the government or hindering others from so doing may be fined five times the value of the grain affected. Kulaks, or rich peasants ... will also suffer loss of their property." "What the 'extraordinary measures' were supposed to be last year is explained by Mr. Rykoff in his speech entitled 'The Economic Conditions of the Soviet Union; (*Izvestia* No. 61, March 11, 1929)", these included an agricultural tax due on a date "advanced in order to 'pump out' surplus funds from the villages", the passing of a law of "self-taxation", measures against brewing vodka from grain, "Communist organizations started to pursue a more aggressive policy toward the villages and purged the grain purchasing organizations of all hostile elements". Soviet measures are described by Comrade Kretov in *Izvestia* July 27, 1929 "- a rule of thumb by the Soviet administration in the grain purchasing areas; infringement of the revolutionary lawfulness; illegal searches of private homes; the closing of market places', etc."

Kretov adds "these measures with logical inevitability affected not only the 'kulaks' but also part of the middle and poorer peasants… the latter were aghast and finally started to develop signs of discontent. These measures put the villages on guard and into the peasant heads entered doubts about the stability of their economic rights and the confidence of past wavered. At the same time the 'kulaks' and the counter revolutionary organizations did not sleep. They developed wild rumors and tried to create panic, thus trying to assume leadership among the peasants. As result we had examples of active protests in some sections of the country (minor Soviet officials and communists were murdered in the villages; government and collective farms were burned.)"

Chernikioff quotes the figure of *18 million* the total loss from Russian Civil War, famine during the Hoover ARA relief missions. (italics added)

Further reduction of food supplies described in the Chernikioff report is evident in the decrease in soviet export of cereals: "9,549,000 tons as compared to 10,115,000 for the year 1927-28". As regards Moscow's shortage of food, he writes, "Shortage of food, especially in the larger cities". We read in Sunday's *New York Times* for October 13, 1929 (Section 3, Page 1E) a dispatch from Moscow dated October 10: "... there has grown also a food shortage in Moscow, and one commodity after another is added to the rationing list. The most recent is milk, which can only be sold on 'children's cards', while cream and cheese have practically disappeared, and butter is lamentably scarce. At present almost every edible of popular consumption is rationed, with the exception of salt. Fruit, vegetables and even potatoes are lacking at most of the cooperatives despite the fact that Moscow, and the Northwestern provinces generally, have the best potato crop in years. The authorities defend the ration system on the ground that 'it prevents speculation' and 'insures food for workers at reasonable prices', but when the workers' wives must stand four in line to get food against their coupons, and often find the commodity they want is not obtainable, it seems that 'there's something rotten in the 'State of Denmark'."

The Chernikioff document also contains a detailed analysis of costs, production and supply. Chernikioff describes the Consortium's own Col. Cooper, "the great American engineer and dam builder" who attended a Bond Club luncheon in Manhattan on February 27. His talk "on the superpower project on the Dnieper River in the Ukraine" is featured in *The NY Times* article reporting, "Communism as it is practiced today in Russia must give way for something else because it is only for two classes, the peasant and the worker.... and that the Soviet system was doomed because it was founded on an idea that the State could do everything by edict, and that everybody must live on exactly the same plane of income." The writer notes that Cooper's opinion "seems to be well founded for it is the writer's belief that it will be most improbable that the Communist Party which is seventh-tenths of one percent of the entire population will be able to maintain its control over Russia indefinitely in the face of the growing opposition of the Russian peasantry, which comprises about 85 % of the population of the Soviet state, coupled with the increasing stability of the capitalistic world."

In the last year of the NEP, 1929, recruitment drives and Party propaganda raised membership to some 1,090,000. These were carefully profiled chosen and indoctrinated Marxist-Leninist comrades most of whom who had read Stalin's *Questions of Leninism.* "With a million such new men," observes Martin Mallia, "Stalin by 1929 had a political army more solid than any Lenin ever possessed, one ready to do battle, without discussion or haggling, at the call of the new

Leader." This was the year of "the Great Break" of 1929. (M. Malia, "The Road Not Taken: NEP, 1921-1928", 168-9)

Overlooked by both the Soviet writers and *The NYT* nor could they know that Stalin will swell the ranks of Party members in 1933 expelling some 400,000 of the "incompetent, the unmotivated, and the 'class-alien'; and weeding out another 200,000 in 1935, and again in 1936; then in 1937, Stalin liquidates rather than expels another 500,000 members from the Party's member lists, either shot or sent to the Gulag.

"Stalin knew very well he could get away with this coup," Martin Malia writes in *The Soviet Tragedy*, "as one cynic put it, he had 500,000 new jobs to give away each year. This is the number he purged in 1937, and by the end of 1938, 450,000 new men had taken their place in the first increase of Party membership since 1932. And in each of the next two years before the war, some 500,000 more were added, for a total of 1,500,000 new members since the great divide of the blood purge, 1937. In short, given the fact that some of the new men were also purged, more than half of the Party membership at the outbreak of the war had been recruited after the Purge." This is a significantly larger than the 120,000 vanguard Bolsheviks in 1917. (RG 59 T-1249, Reel 1, SDDF 861.00/11410; M. Malia, 248)

After meeting with Duranty for yet another briefing on the Five-Year Plan, the prescient and nimble John C. Wiley in Berlin sends Stimson and Phillips a 17-page memorandum No. 5262 marked "STRICTLY CONFIDENTIAL" and signed "Your obedient servant John C. Wiley" on January 29, 1930. Kelley stamps it February 17, 1930. Copies of the 17-page transcript of the Duranty interview with Wiley are sent to Riga, and the EIC in Paris. Wiley from Indiana is a career Foreign Service officer living with his wife Irena in both Riga and Tallinn; eventually in July 1938 he is appointed minister for two years to Estonia and Latvia. For the record Wiley says Duranty passed through Berlin "on a short vacation". Duranty has much to tell and here gives Wiley and Washington "an extensive account of the course of events, as he sees it, in Russia".

Duranty interpreted Stalin's consolidation of his dictatorial powers over the Communist Central Committee. Duranty was a two-track man inside halls of power and out on the street with the prestige of the most powerful newspaper in the world as well as middle and corporate America lay right outside Stalin's door. Duranty was Stalin's messenger to the White House, a paper boy. Stalin used him as the Kremlin's mouthpiece to corporate and mainstream America. Duranty told Wiley "a sweeping revision" from the Kremlin had rolled back the "features of the NEP (1921 to 1929) as permitted or actually encouraged private enterprise (business and retail trade, small banking and small industry in the cities, private building, etc., and individual farming, *kulakism,* (original emphasis) private dairies, mills, handcraft and village trading) have now been definitely eliminated."

The pace quickened. Duranty takes another step into the abyss of the Holodomor. He warns the Department of Stalin's intention to mercilessly hold his course regardless of the cost. Wiley, however, is none too alarmed. Duranty confirms Stalin's sudden shift to the Right of the CP "smashing the "'Leftward swing' that has been in progress since April". This in spite of the fact, Duranty tells Wiley, that Soviet production of raw materials for the first part of the year 1929 had declined "like oil, coal, timber, and ore", of some "five to fifteen per cent".

Why would *The NY Times*' foreign correspondent in Moscow on his "vacation" drop in to feed the diplomat information he knew that he expected would be relayed to Washington through the usual channels unless he was on a mission from the Kremlin with a message for Hoover and Stimson. Duranty is playing a dangerous double game serving many heads of the same monster. He must be careful not to lose it. Duranty might not have known but he certainly expected that his information about Stalin and Moscow reached the top of the Consortium. Duranty's intelligence work has to figure in *The New York Times* not withdrawing the Pulitzer. How could he know for sure who is doing intelligence for the Consortium. But he can't be certain who works for the Consortium, or for that matter, who is the Consortium. That's why it's secret. It's not really a conspiracy. It's just that not everybody knows who is doing what. The Consortium works on a need to know basis. The Consortium prefers secrecy and discretion. Or, it's not a secret anymore. Quiet channels. Their success depends keeping secret the secrets of their business. That's essential to their continuity, to their survival, and business as usual.

Duranty said this was due to "mismanagement and lack of coordination", "financial complications", he called it, and "impaired labor morale". Wiley struggled to get it right. "Why the amplification of the second year's schedule was imperative," Wiley writes in his memo, "is clear from the statistics of the collective movement. Instead of ten per cent of the harvested area being collectivized as was the case last spring, the autumn figures show a collective proportion of from 25 to 35 percent and it is expected that the proportion in the spring planting will average around 40 and in some important regions (Lower and Middle Volga North Caucasus and parts of the Ukraine) will be as high as 60 to 75 per cent.

"It is highly erroneous to suppose that the success of the collective movement and the rapid conclusion of the state grain collections campaign were due only to strong arm methods and direct compulsion. ...it stands to reason that so large a mass of the population, however ill organized politically, must have been moved by immediate advantages and hopes for the future." Either Wiley or Duranty or both doesn't wish to say or doesn't know exactly what he means by this, while they know with certainty Stalin is using terror to force the will of the peasants at the point of the bayonet to produce grain needed to feed the whole USSR. It's an incredible statement of political spin motivated by Duranty's hard-line Stalinism and contempt for the peasants.

Wiley then includes Duranty's standard argument which he will use throughout the Holodomor tragedy. In the memorandum sent to Washington, he wrote, "While it is true that recalcitrant peasants were blacklisted, boycotted and expropriated it is equally true that their more amenable brethren were given goods at low prices through their local cooperatives and were encouraged to join the collectives by the prospect of machines, tools, and implements, fertilizers, tested seeds, etc., on liberal credit terms., It is to provide these promised benefits that the industrial production has been speed up to over tax capacity. Similarly, the flow of goods to the villages is one of the principal causes of scarcity by all observers in urban centers. The spring sowings will show how far the countryside has been won over. But, the final test will, of course, be the quality and quantity of the harvest itself." And the credibility of Soviet state statistics!

Again Wiley a la Duranty: "It may be argued that the swing from Germany to America is fathered by the hope of eventual financial assistance. Some color is given to this view by the fact that American firms supplying agricultural implements, tractors, etc., are now being asked to give six months full credit with orders. On the other hand, this may be due to the Russian belief that, as the consequence of the Wall Street break, the United States now needs markets for money and manufactured goods so greatly as to incline America to accept business terms that she would previously have rejected."

Both Duranty and Louis Fischer acted as government intermediaries for the Consortium and repeatedly tried to broker a deal between Washington and Kremlin over debts and credits. All in vain. It was a subject not without a little interest to both Hoover and Stimson appreciated their effort and backdoor access to Stalin. Top Soviet watcher John C. Wiley now tells them that there "seems, however, little inclination to try to reopen the debt question which, if settled to America's satisfaction, would facilitate credits. Hints on the subject from Mr. Duranty met with but little response although he was assured that the theory advanced by Stalin eighteen months ago that payment of debts (without their acknowledgment in principle) might be admitted as a form of 'supplementary interest' on credit or loans (viz. General Electric agreement) still held good." Duranty fills in Wiley on the Schley-Smith affair inside the Russian-American Chamber of Commerce. Charles Smith, its Moscow re was "resigned" by the ARCC board and left for the US. In a joint cable the American correspondents sent a letter of regret to Reeve Schley of Chase National. Col. Raymond Robbins, formerly with Morgan's American Red Cross spy mission sent to Petrograd to unseat Kerensky was even listed as a possible successor but "rejected" by the Soviets. Still there was good reason to celebrate. "The Gillette contract has been the source of considerable Soviet satisfaction as the first real American concession since Harriman. Only an initial investment of some 200 to 250 thousand dollars is involved." Following the 2004 "Orange Revolution" Gillette razors were once again suddenly everywhere available in Kiev. The conglomerates came in force buying up Ukrainian brands and shelf space. (SDDF 861.00/11414, RG 59 T-1249 reel 1)

Wiley examined the data provided by Duranty with great interest to accurately describe the current situation of food production and distribution, both in the city and in the countryside, and the impact on the general population. He writes, "It may be taken for granted that commodity production has genuinely increased to about the same extent as claimed by Soviet statisticians. Why then should this scarcity occur? The answer is simple. First, a growing percentage of commodities, including foodstuffs, is being exported (to balance imports). Secondly, instead, as heretofore, of 20 per cent of the population (the urban centers) getting, say 60 per cent of commodities and manufactured articles in general demand, with the remaining 80 per cent of the population only getting 40 per cent of these commodities; at present the countryside is getting a more appropriate share."

It was clear to the American diplomat that the outcome of Stalin's political fight inside the Party was tied to the food issue. He wrote, "The effect is greatly to diminish the supplies in the towns without being able to satisfy the enormous rural demand. Many observers think that the 'lower moral' of urban labor is not disassociated from this development." Wiley concludes, "Stalin at present is more firmly in the saddle than ever and is carrying on a vigorous campaign in the Party against the Right Opposition – the Troika and their followers—and the remnants of the Left or Trotsky Opposition. Stalin's health is undoubtedly improved but he is suffering from cardiac trouble, and, in view of his arduous work, would not be considered a good risk by an insurance company. As long as he keeps going, no breach in party solidarity or change of policy is likely, unless there is a bad crop failure. But should anything happen to him confusion might ensue..."

Wiley then makes the following conclusion. How much is pure Wiley and pure Duranty is not exactly clear. Duranty is America's top foreign correspondent in Moscow with access to Stalin and feeding diplomats information from the Kremlin. "Generally speaking," Wiley tells his superiors "no one in Moscow attempts to deny that the present is a period of mounting tension. The issue depends largely on the strength of the Kremlin's, rather Stalin's nerves. This will be true for a year or two at least unless the harvest is exceptionally bad or good or extraneous circumstances intervene. Taking it by and large, with an average crop, the chances of success are fair but the possibility of a loss of nerve is not precluded."

The *World* on January 28, 1930 publishes news that both Ford and GE are building up the USSR. Eureka! Its source is a Standard Electric rep in Tallinn, Estonia, – M. M. Klemmer who had supplied a copy of his observations to the American Consul detailing in 57 pages (with an appendix) the industrial, political and economic development of the modern Soviet state.

On the peasants and agriculture, Klemmer is prophetic and pessimistic. "The agricultural population of Russia with its individual psychology and small housekeeping, has been always the concealed enemy of the communist ideas. During all the twelve years of the existence of the Soviet State, it has been always a problem how to get the food out of the country necessary for the army, workmen and other population of the towns.. This problem often stood so astute that it was necessary to use force against peasants in order to take away the grain and always there was a probability of a famine because peasants purposely did not produce enough food. "Besides the ideological reasons, the peasants are showing resistance as much as they can because the State is not able to supply them with enough necessary industrial products, textiles, etc., in exchange for the food."

More excerpts revealed Stalin's "proletarisation' of peasant and individual farmers": "The hostility between the communist State and peasants has lasted all the time, getting more and more severe. At one time it looked like though, the State would be forced to retire, or work out some kind of compromise policy to satisfy, in the minimum, the demands if only of the so-called 'poorest peasants'."; "In order to break down the resistance of the peasants, and at the same time, to provide the supply of food for towns, Stalin has cardinally changed the policy of the State also in regard to the country peasants."; State and cooperative collectives. "all individual farms in the country should disappear more or less soon." Replaced by large state farms, or *sovhoz*, sometimes called State Grain factories, as large as 50-100,000 hectares; and the rural commune *Kolhoz* organized by peasants themselves, but in reality controlled 100 precedent by the State.; "The present agricultural policy of the Soviet Government is the 'proletarisation' of peasant and individual farmers, by putting them into such conditions, so that they will be ruined and be forced to liquidate their individual enterprises and go into the State farms or agricultural commune as laborers."

The Klemmer report makes it clear to the Department where the Collectivization Plan is going. 'It can be easily imagined," Klemmer concludes, "what this policy really means. It means that the so called 'Social revolution' actually is now being made and that all what was done before, was only an introduction or child's play perhaps, compared with that what is going to be in future if the experiment is continued to its end. Before, the revolution touched directly only, may be, a million of more or less rich people and owners of the property in towns, now it is beginning to take hold of over a hundred of million peasants and the smallest land owners, who are about to be converted to the position of slaves or cerfs of the State." Of that, neither Hoover, Stimson nor the CFR-Consortium gang can now claim to harbor any doubt. (SDDF 871.00/11415)

The Americans are neither haphazardly blind nor stupidly ignorant in their interpretation of the information of famine and terror filling their cabinets. So many of the dispatched reports from US listening posts and embassies in Warsaw, Riga, Constantinople and other around places around the Ukraine were so hot with reports they could have stoked fires and smoked out the gang in London and Washington if they had been released to the press or leaked. One of the outside specialists known to the upper echelon in the State Department is A. D. Margolin, an expert on Ukraine and Russia. A lawyer living in Boston and a naturalized American citizen of Ukrainian origin Margolin corresponds often with Kelley.

On January 29, 1930 Margolin sends Kelley a confidential report prepared for the Executive Committee of the American Jewish Committee after his European trip to meet Jewish leaders in the Baltic States. In Poland, that fall, he explores "the question of Polish-Ukrainian relations". America had an opportunity to significantly alter the course of events in that part of the world, thought Margolin, and he concludes, "It is evident that Pilsudski and all his adherents continue to support the Ukrainian movement for the separation from Russia of the territories composing at the present time the Soviet Ukraine."

Margolin's recent trip to Eastern Europe left him with the conclusion that the road to Ukrainian autonomy and national independence was complex and full of peril but not hopeless. He advises Kelley accordingly, writing, "This policy aiming at the dismemberment of the present Russia has also strong supporters in Roumania, influential French circles, and among the members of the British conservative party. The present Polish government, however, does not intend to run the risk of any war with Soviet Russia for this purpose, as one of the spokesmen of Pulsudski recently explained in an informal talk, and prefers to see the Soviet government controlling Russia as long as possible, as such further existence of the Soviet mind can only result in a still greater weakening of Russia and in a still stronger development of separatist aspirations among the population of Ukraine, Crimea, and White Russia. Parallel with this sympathy toward liberation of Ukrainians who live in the Soviet Ukraine, Poland is in a constant bitter fight with its own Ukrainian population in eastern Galicia, Volhynia and Cholm region, in the endeavor entirely to subjugate them and to Polonize the territories in which they live."

Margolin visits Prague "the real center of both Russian and Ukrainian intellectual refugees". Here the government created "a Russian university, a Ukrainian university and other pedagogic and cultural institutions... it also finances the Podebrady (near Prague) the Ukrainian Agricultural Academy. Although it gives such a large support to the Ukrainian culture and Ukrainian language, the Czecho-Slovak government does not show much sympathy with the movement for an independent Ukraine. Unlike those of Poland and Roumania, Czecho-Slovak political leaders are opposed to the program of dismemberment of Russia." In Paris, Berlin, Warsaw, and Prague Margolin had interviews "with the leaders of all Ukrainian parties and also with many Russian political leaders." He informs Kelley that Ukraine was near a breaking point with Stalin and the Russians from the north. "These talks and also the information I had from Soviet Ukraine," Margolin concluded, "indicated that the abyss between Russians and Ukrainians becomes deeper and deeper and that the aspirations of the Ukrainian population in Soviet Ukraine and also in the Ukrainian territories under Polish domination for political independent existence are stronger than they ever were. The new generation in Soviet Ukraine and in Soviet Transcaucasia receives instruction in the schools in their respective mother languages (Ukrainian, Georgian, Tartara, Armenia). While supporting the local languages and culture in Ukraine and Caucasus (partly in Crimea and White Russia) as concessions for the purpose of pacifying the population, the Soviet government unwillingly increases the power of separatism prevailing in these constituent parts of the former Russian Empire." Margolin also underscores the lingering Ukrainian hostility towards the Jews, writing, "The attitude of the Ukrainians toward the new Jewish colonies in Ukraine continues to be negative."

On February 28, 1930 Louis Sussdorff Jr. from New York City, a junior official and chargé d'affaires, Riga Legation sends a memo to Stimson and Kelley. It states "...local authorities in the RSFSR have been given discretionary powers to recall village soviets and hold replacement elections by March 15th. The object sought is the activation of the soviets as agents of the Government and the Communist Party, particularly in the matters of collectivization of agriculture and extermination of refractory peasants." It refers to the decree of the Presidium of the All-Russian Central Executive Committee published in *Izvestia*, NO 36, Feb 6. signed by M. Kalinin, President, and A. Kiselev, Secretary.

Two weeks earlier, February 15, Sussdorff sends a memorandum on a report garnered from Mr. Olins, the Counselor of the Latvian Legation at Moscow and formerly in Washington. The memo tells of the peculiar role played by American journalists in Moscow. Sussdorff writes, "correspondents of foreign newspapers are the most useful informants of his Legation … however, Mr. Olins stated that foreign journalists in Soviet Russia, including American journalists, are not able, even through diplomatic or secret channels, to furnish their newspapers with plain, unvarnished accounts of conditions in the Soviet Union, since the publication of the real facts by any paper, no matter from what source it purported to come, would make its Moscow correspondent persona non grata to the Soviets. He said that, in general, foreign newspaper correspondents in Russia, receive large salaries and enjoy a social position which they do not have elsewhere, since, in view of the limited society in Moscow, they are treated virtually as members of the diplomatic corps. Hence, they do not want to do anything to jeopardize their positions. In this connection, it might be stated parenthetically that the Legation's own study of the American press confirms Mr. Olins' statement regarding the extreme caution of American correspondents in Moscow in sending in material that criticizes Soviet institutions. Two American correspondents in Moscow who passed through Riga some time ago admitted that they did not feel free to depict the worst phases of Soviet life."

The US embassy official made the point even more clear that articles published in the West sent by journalists based in Moscow were superfluous and unreliable. Riga Mission first secretary and chargé d'affairs Sussdorff adds, "With regard to information obtained through Soviet officials and the Soviet press, Mr. Olins regards this as of very little value. He considers that in general Soviet statistics are extremely unreliable and are only written to prove a thesis. No one who is employed in a Soviet bureau dares to speak of any Soviet undertaking save in terms of warm praise, since the slightest criticism would undoubtedly cost him his position." In other words, cross Moscow and no more easy gorgeous Russian women, no more ballerinas, no bargains at the food and drink commissariat, and forget the plush Moscow flat. Visa denied.

On February 25 the US chargé d'affaires in Warsaw cabled "Strictly Confidential" his telegram referring to his "strictly confidential dispatch No. 2985 of February 8, 1930, concerning conditions in Soviet Russia"; he now sends a "translation of a dispatch from the Polish Consulate General at Kharkov, the capital of Soviet Ukraine, written during the first part of 1930 concerning the a most alarming tendency of revolutionary economic method practiced by the Soviet authorities to liquidate" in their entirety local administrations of production in the provinces "and to replace these organizations under the direct control of some Moscow grouping." They include "a number of organizations, agricultural as well as industrial, which were operating in Soviet Ukraine under local administrations" now taken over by Moscow. Also included in the liquidation are the Donugal and Piwdenstal coal plants "and the Ukrpowitroszlah air way". The latter targeted "the works of the well-known engineer Kalinin in Kharkof". The Polish Consul General reports, "Different versions and comments among the local population can be added in this respect to the effect that beginning with the spring of 1930 a far-reaching liquidation of the local organizations of Soviet Ukraine will take place – with the possible maintaining of appearances of official Ukrainization, language and cultural." It warned, "It seems that the current year may bring serious changes with serious consequences for the Ukraine."

Mace observes that Lenin's NEP launched in 1921 and phased out by collectivization under the Plan before the end of 1929 had been essentially "a series of concessions to the peasant". It is familiar since 1923 to non-Russians as a policy of concessions known as "indigenization". Mace writes, "Since in 1926 about three-eighths of the Soviet Union's non-Russians were Ukrainians and the latter outnumbered the next largest non-Russian group by about 6.5 to 1, the nationality problem was to a great extent a Ukrainian problem. It is thus hardly surprising that the Ukrainian version of indigenization, Ukrainization, went much farther than its counterparts elsewhere in the USSR." (James E. Mace, "Collaboration in the Suppression of the Ukrainian Famine", Nov. 13, 1987)

Again here we can refer to Mace's findings which describe the cleansing process as it evolves according to plan under Stalin's central authority. "In 1932 and 1933 an artificially created famine made the Ukrainian SSR, the contiguous and largely Ukrainian North Caucasus Territory to its east, and the largely German and Tatar regions of the Volga Basin, in the words of Robert Conquest, 'like one vast Belsen'. A quarter of the rural population, men, women and children, lay dead or dying, the rest in various stages of debilitation with no strength to bury their families or neighbors. At the same time (as at Belsen), well-fed squads of police or party officials supervised the victims. 'In the Soviet case, the enemy was defined in terms of social class rather than-nationality, race or religion. However, the Communist Party held itself up as the embodiment of the class consciousness of the proletariat: anything it sanctioned was by definition proletarian, and anything it found convenient was by definition infected with hostile class content. Its ideology classified 'nationalism', as distinct from the party-sanctioned Russocentric 'Soviet patriotism', as 'bourgeois nationalism', that is, a form of bourgeois ideology. This allowed Stalinism to imbue class categories with national content. For Stalin the social basis of nationalism was the peasantry. Soviet ideology also posited the division of the peasantry into bourgeois and proletarian strata, which were never precisely defined, and thus, at Stalin's discretion, any segment of the peasantry could at any given moment be declared either proletarian and worthy of survival or bourgeois and worthy of 'liquidation'. Those whose relative wealth did not qualify them as class enemies could easily be classified as 'agents' of the class enemies." (Dr. James E. Mace, "Collaboration in the Suppression of the Ukrainian Famine," *The Ukrainian Weekly,* 1987)

This time Stalin intensifies his program for "Russification" or, at the least "denationalization" of the leadership of the non-Russian organizations and annihilates any threat from Ukrainization. Millions are killed; the Party ranks purged. The Ukraine and the Northern Caucasus are now besieged by a pilgrimage of young doctrinaire Russian communists brutally correct, dogmatic to Party logic and rigidly obedient to No. 1 with nothing else in their heads and little in common with the Ukrainians and entirely ignorant of their language or history. The impact of that cultural assault is still felt in the Ukraine of the 21st century. The political showdown in Kiev mounted by anti-government nationalist protesters against the pro-Russian regime of Viktor Yanukovch is ample proof of deep festering wounds.

On March 18, 1930, Frederick Coleman in Riga sends his memorandum "Counter-revolutionary activity – Russia". Coleman is a career Foreign Service man from Minnesota winding up his long stature as mission chief in Estonia since 1922 and was there during the famine under Lenin and Hoover's ARA intervention. In 1925 the Estonian Government honors their American friend with the Cross of Liberty 3rd Class in gratitude for his civilian services.

Coleman meets with veteran American correspondent Junius B. Wood. Coleman tells State, writing, "Junius Wood believes Govt. control of food supply is an irresistible weapon in handling the domestic situation in Russia and there is little chance that any internal trouble might develop into serious.." Wood is a regular in Russia, there in 1926 sleeping in Harper's room across from the Kremlin when asked to check on a cable report that Trotsky forces had attacked the Kremlin. He'd thought he overslept and missed it. False report, another of the countless rumours.... Writing for the *Chicago Daily News* he's stuck in Moscow waiting for Soviet permission to travel through the northern forest for a "first hand impression of conditions" there "particularly with regard to labor conditions" and incessant rumours of forced labor and the expanding gulag. (Samuel N. Harper, *The Russia I Believe In: The Memoirs of Samuel N. Harper 1902 to 1941*, 234. Harper's dateline for this period has no mention of famine or the Holodomor.)

The meeting between Woods and Coleman is no slight happenstance encounter. They are both highly trained in their professions and seasoned pros. Coleman takes Wood's story seriously enough to comment on it personally that it merits attention higher up. Coleman is an experienced senior Russian hand and in no way unfamiliar with the Soviet gulag system of forced labor and terror, a common subject shared among the foreign correspondents.

Before serving as a US Army captain in the First World War Frederic W. B. Coleman (1874-47) was trained as a lawyer, and worked legal counsel for a coal company in Norway and Czarist Russia. Born in Detroit, he moved to Minneapolis in 1910; in 1922 Coleman working for State and appointed to Riga, Latvia as the American minister there as well as accredited to Estonia and Lithuania. A steady, dedicated, hard-working civil servant there is no stain or hint of scandal in his career. About problems obstructing Woods doing his story, Coleman writes, "He anticipates, however, trouble in getting away from the controlled centers of production back into the woods where, he is confident, actual evidence of compulsory or convict labor can be obtained."

Woods tells Coleman that "he feels the trip would be useless if his investigations are limited to 'Potemkin villages'." Coleman adds that Wood spoke about "one occasion when he discovered that the entire labor gang which he was visiting had been brought in two days before his arrival. He fears that such replacement tactics could effectively conceal the utilization of compulsory labor at a limited number of investigation centers." Although contrary to assertions by the Soviet authorities neither Woods nor Coleman are able to confirm that practically all the lumbering in the north is the product of prison labor and likewise the canal connecting the White with the Baltic Seas.

Coleman tells State how food is used as a "weapon", writing, "Wood scouts the idea that any internal trouble might develop into serious counter-revolutionary activity. He believes that the government control of the food supply is an irresistible weapon in handling the domestic situation. While the entire population is at present on short rations, there is plenty of foodstuffs in the country and the prospects for the 1931 cereal crops are excellent, as the winter crops have been adequately protected by a snow blanket and sufficient spring moisture is in sight. As a result, Mr. Woods feels that the authorities can on short notice improve the standard of living by appreciably increasing the food ration..."

Woods relates to the American minister that terror and repression is "definitely" increasing "the domestic strength of the Soviet regime ... by its latent ability to raise the standard of living of the masses since the supply of food and other articles of consumption is increasing and is potentially available for domestic consumption. In this Mr. Wood differs from many who believe that the Soviet authorities can most effectively use their control of the food supply to starve recalcitrants into surrender rather than to bribe them into acquiescence at the risk of increasing their capacity for resistance."

After serving nine years Coleman leaves Riga on October 20, 1931, replaced by senior Foreign Service officer Robert Skinner, from Ohio, another careerist who served in London during the First World War and will stay on with his wife Helen but only until April 29, 1933. Coleman is sent out of the way where he can do no harm, first as ambassador to Denmark. But then two years later he abruptly resigns from the foreign service and is replaced the former army intelligence officer John Van Antwerp MacMurray. Fifty-two years old, a former ambassador to China and a seasoned Riga hand ever since his mission days with Haskell during the ARA Hoover famine intervention in the Bolshevik civil war MacMurray assumes his duties in August and stays a resident of Riga until February 1936 when Roosevelt and Welles do a general house-cleaning of the Russian observers. John MacMurray, always highly valued by Stimson, is eventually posted ambassador in Turkey across from the Crimea and Ukraine, in 1937, and serves there as the last US envoy resident in Istanbul before moving definitively to Ankar where he stays until 1941. For his part our dear with the Balkans on fire Wiley finally pulls out of Riga in July 1940. Whatever happened to the Haskell-MacMurray Mission documents? It's worth looking into, reader. (SDDF 861.00/11469)

"Things here are exciting", Duranty writes a friend staffer at *The New York Times.* "Stalin switched the whole works two or three days after I arrived and startled everyone – especially the younger *tovarishes* – a good deal". In a private letter Duranty tells of fellow Stalinist Paul Scheffer whose recent articles appeared in the *Berliner Tageblatt* and which are also relayed to Washington by ambassador Frederic M. Sackett in Berlin. "I do not think it's a real change of policy," Duranty adds, "but there is no doubt but that the younger element had succeeded in making the peasant almost fighting mad. But not quite, to the best of my knowledge, though there were 'demonstrations' in some places. Any way things have loosened up in consequence and it looks as if the Spring sowing might go all right. I at least remain optimistic, though, as I said before, it depends on the weather."

In his article "Moscow in Retrospect Progresses", Scheffer forecasts serious trouble and massive deaths by starvation in the months ahead, writing, "In the rural districts the effects of the prevailing disorganization will be felt at the time of the next harvest. There are still five months up to that time during which period famine can only grow worse." Again, the journalists take the Stalinist line that the problem is recalcitrant peasants who refuse to cooperate with Moscow and the Soviet Party dictated communist road to progress.

More alarm bells. By spring 1930 Moscow and Washington know that the risk of famine is real. The State Department receives a transmitted translation of the article "Moscow is Nervous" appearing in the pro-Soviet *Berliner Boersen Zeitung* on April 1, 1930. It states, "Anxiety about the spring sowing is beginning to hold sway in Moscow. On this sowing and the weather will depend a good or bad harvest, and if it is a bad harvest it may mean failure of the regime. Thousands of agricultural experts and workmen are being sent to the farms – mobilization for the sowing campaign. However, there is little hope of success. Although the country is still three months removed from harvest time, the spectre of famine is already haunting it. By this time in spring Washington's Russian experts know Stalin is now firmly entrenched in the Kremlin. His power is incontestable. "Stalin's position is stronger than ever before as there is no organized political opposition. Right and left oppositions have been vanquished and Stalin is in control. Due to strong position of present Soviet Government there is no talk about its overthrow." There is no doubt whatsoever now that to criticize Stalin in the Soviet Union is life-threatening; even in the White House and State Department negative talk about Stalin is taboo and a *faux pas* career end. (SDDF 861.00/11428)

On April 15, 1930 memorandum No. 6907 from Riga chargé d'affaires and first secretary of the mission Louis Sussdorff Jr. is sent to Kelley telling of "the views of Zinoviev, published in the *Moscow Bolshevik*, March 15 on the connection between domestic and foreign policy of American position against the USSR." Zinoviev's days too are numbered. "The United States," Zinoviev tells his comrades, "is being driven by economic factors into growing hostility to the Soviet Union, 'whose revolutionary role bars the road to many plans of American imperialism', in Germany, in China, in Latin America, and elsewhere. Moreover, American imperialists, knowing themselves to be the vanguard of the bourgeoisie in general, are made uneasy by the progress of socialism in the Soviet Union. All this, taken together, is spurring American imperialism, and is impelling it to assume the direction of the anti-Soviet campaign."

Frederick Coleman relay's Zinoviev's outburst over a recent agreement between Germany and Poland with the US, having "... immense importance for the preparation of a new war upon the USSR ..." This will remain a constant theme for Soviet preparation against an invasion from Europe and the West. The

State Department is informed that Zinoviev warned that "... if the imperialists should now decide to declare a new war upon us, tens of millions, both in our country and in the whole world will defend the Soviet Union. Industrial extension, collectivization of agriculture, raising the efficiency of the Red Army, belong equally to the Soviet external and internal policy'."

Coleman highlights more of the article for State, in particular where "Zinoviev called the Owen Young Plan a ploy to make the German economy dependent on America as the dominant world power. 'Poland is equally dependent, economically and politically'." The experienced old-guard Bolshevik denounces the German-Polish agreement "under the weight of the heavy hand of the American billionaires" which "increases the war danger to ourselves, for all the world proletariat". And he is not far off the mark, eh, reader?

For the next decade all Europe will repeat the question "What will happen to the Polish Corridor?" Eastern Poland and Western Ukraine are hotly contested territories with too many Ukrainians and too many Poles, respectively in each other's country yearning for a return to the homeland's former borders. With his world crumbling around him Zinoviev is fighting for political survival and had nothing to lose speaking out about the "the heavy hand of the American billionaires" inside the Consortium and pushing its agenda in Europe and in the USSR. It is there for anyone in the circle of power with access to see and know. The Americans are sure to have another mass famine on their hands only this time they know well in advance that it might blow up in their face along with public exposure of the Consortium's role in supporting the fascist dictator surely to let hell break loose. How would the old hands of the Consortium deal with this humanitarian crisis resulting from their own greedy and most wicked clandestine political designs? How many more world disasters of this magnitude are they prepared to micromanage. Another world war? No, they could not call up the troops again as they had done with Wilson's armed intervention followed by Hoover's ARA relief brigades. Stalin would have to go it alone. In his long career with food, famine and politics, President Hoover is an old hand at pondering these problems, calculating numbers and human beings rendered into abstractions for practical action or none at all. How far are they willing to go? How many will have to die this time? How could the people forget so quickly the horror of the Great War and the debacle of Versailles? Is there anyone in control of the world gone mad?

IN 1931 WHISTLE-BLOWER GARETH JONES SETS HIS EYE ON POLAND

One of Stalin's greatest fears was that trouble in the Ukraine might provoke Poland's expansion to the East. Two years before he breaks with the established FO policy on Russia to become the Holodomor whistle-blower, the young and bright personal Secretary of David Lloyd George publishes "Poland's Foreign Relations" in *The Contemporary Review*, July 1931. Territory, positioning, access and natural resources are the stuff of wars and competition between nations.

In a brilliant article and showing his skill at handling complex subjects with unabashed simplicity and directness Gareth Jones writes, "Poland's policy has been determined by permanent factors which never allow a Foreign Minister to stray far from a certain definite path. These factors are her geographical position, her history and her economic structure. Geography teaches Poland to be wary. Her straddling frontiers run for thousands of miles through the flat European plain. Not a single mountain bars the way to foreign troops; there is hardly a hillock between Warsaw and the Urals. To the east and to the west the frontier line winds through villages and farms and towns. The lesson of history is still more impressive. The Partition throws a shadow over modern Polish life. Although it was rectified in 1919, its psychological effect will not be wiped out for many a long day and there remains a lurking fear of a new partition. Finally, Poland's economic structure necessitates an outlet to the sea, which raises formidable barriers against friendship with Germany."

In the article Jones observes further, "Recent events have increased the anxiety for security which Poland's geographical position and her past inspire in her citizens. The rush of extreme nationalism in Germany, the Nazi cry for a strong conscript Army and the revolt of the German youth against Versailles, have made the Poles guard their security more tenaciously than ever. No Pole, with the threats of Herr Treviranus still ringing in his ears, can regard the Kellogg Pact as the guardian angel of his peace. The trade war which began in 1925 has also embittered Poland's relations with Germany. On her western frontier, therefore, Poland feels no security. Neither have her relations with Soviet Russia inspired her with great faith in her eastern neighbour, in spite of the signing of the Litvinov Protocol (1929) for the Renunciation of War. Poland has a propaganda value to the Communist Party. Soviet organs and theaters never cease vilifying the Poles in caricatures and plays, in order to provide an outlet for popular dissatisfaction and to unite the peoples of the Union in the face of the so-called menace of intervention from Poland. It is the belief in Moscow that war between the capitalist states and Communist Russia is inevitable and that Poland is destined to be the cats paw of France, America and Britain. In the Soviet Union propaganda banners blare out the slogans 'The Imperialists of the West are preparing war on Soviet Russia.' Great stress is laid on the war industry and everything is done to inculcate a military spirit into the masses. The Soviet child is taught that Bessarabia is Soviet territory temporarily in the possession of Rumania and that it was snatched away from the socialist fatherland by the capitalists. Poland cannot remain unperturbed by these developments in Russia, especially since most Poles remember that ten years ago the Soviet troops came within sight of Warsaw. Nevertheless, there is more fear of Germany than of Russia in Poland."

The fears of late winter turn into chaos by spring. Reports of uprisings and revolt in Ukraine cabled to Washington tell of worsening conditions for the kulaks and their families. On April 25, 1930 from the US Consulate in Teheran, Persia (Iran) comes a memorandum for Stimson with the header "Reported Disorders in Russian Caucasia". It lands on Kelley's desk over three weeks later on May 16. It reports more uprisings along the southern Soviet borders in the Ukraine met by harsh Soviet countermeasures, religious persecutions, and widespread unrest "especially marked among members of the so-called wealthier class, who are reported to be destroying their produce and livestock rather than subject them to communal distribution." Escalating food prices provoke a storm of outrage. Eggs costing forty cents!

"The great poverty of the populace makes starvation inevitable" is the message from Vice Consul Henry S. Villard. Thousands of refugees cross the Aras river into the Persian province of Azerbaijan. Villard adds, "Soviet patrols, however, are endeavoring to prevent such escapes, and it is a common rumor that all fleeing refugees *are shot on sight* ... individuals are picked off by rifle fire at will... Reports place the number of Soviet troops sent into the Caucasus at 400,000, with Tiflis as the concentration center." (SDDF 861.00/ 11430, italics added)

Reader, you see what is happening now, as early as 1930, – and you know now more than anyone in American then or, even now, would tell you. And yet the Americans consider themselves the most informed on the planet. Luce, Howard, McCormick and the press barons in America then, – and little has changed since except the names on the office doors, – consider themselves well-informed from their own men in the field and other multiple sources: journalists, foreign embassies, travelers, military agents, spies and informers...

Henry Villard is no small cheese either. He's a career diplomat with a full 28 years in the service in four continents and head of many US embassies. By the end of the decade he is well-established as one of State's top African experts and will play an important logistics role for the Allied invasion of North Africa. Now, after two years in his first posting and keen on Soviet aggressions, he sounds the alarm.

Or does he? Who is Henry Villard of Harvard?

His career at State takes off after FDR is elected President, though of course, that has little to do with it. Nonetheless, FDR was also a fellow editor, for two years of the Harvard *Crimson.* A true and dedicated Harvard man, is Villard, too, one of the thousands of alumni that fine day in June sitting in the Harvard Yard for the Solzhenitsyn commencement speech in the late seventies? That was not one to miss!

And how extraordinary that he be the nephew of Oswald Garrison Villard (1872–49), Harvard '93, a committed writer and journalist for human rights and civil liberties who denounces Empire and colonialism during his tutelage at *The Nation*, the country's leading national magazine on the Left dedicated to fostering liberal public opinion which he inherits from his father and a literary tradition of outspoken defiance dating back to his grandfather, William Lloyd Garrison (1805-79), a self-taught journalist and social reformer best known as the editor of the abolitionist newspaper *The Liberator*, which also happens be the title borrowed by Max and Crystal Eastman for the successor to *The Masses*, after it runs into trouble with the government in 1919.

Family traditions are not written in stone. After Yale (1938) where majored in English literature and won prizes for literary composition (he invested his winnings in technical engineering books), Oswald Garrison ("Mike") Villard Jr.

(1916-04) chose a different path, enters Stanford as a grad student in electrical engineering, joins the lab of Professor Frederick Terman ("the father of Silicon Valley") then at Harvard's Radio Research Lab (with William Hewlett and others) designing radio, radar and sonar for military applications vital to the war effort. Later at Stanford, Villard applies radar to study electrical disturbances in the upper atmosphere caused by meteor trails, nuclear explosions, and rocket launches; the results of his 1959 efforts in over-the-horizon radar, which worked by reflecting high-frequency radar from the ionosphere are highly praised. Later at Stanford Villard develops stealth technologies to counteract radar and sonar and even invented a small antenna so that dissidents in foreign countries could receive the Voice of America radio program, including the Chinese after the 1989 Tiananmen Square protests. A member of the National Academy of Sciences and the National Academy of Engineering, among his numerous awards include the highest civilian award given by the US Air Force and the Secretary of Defense Medal for Outstanding Public Service. So, in the end the Consortium gets their man. When questioned about the illustrious family heritage of pacifists and anti-war advocates, Mike Villard said he understood their arguments, but he prefers "to keep the powder dry", or, prepared superior deterrence is the best defense. Not long ago, in 2004 Mike Villard past on, at 87, to the end a dedicated patriot of the American global superpower.

On May 15, 1930, Coleman in Latvia dispatches memorandum No, 6969. "Trial of 45 persons for counter-revolutionary and separatist activity or leanings in Ukraine, Russia". Coleman transmits a summary of Soviet newspaper reports which was a sequel to dissolution of Ukrainian Autocephalous (Orthodox) Church. Trial was held at Kharkov, March 11 to April 19. Indictment and proceedings linked the Brotherhood of Political Independence of the Ukraine and the Association for the Liberation of the Ukraine." (SDDF 861.404/318; 861.00/11431)

On July 21, 1930, Frederick Coleman sends the translation of an article (memorandum No. 6998) on the "convergence concerning American Soviet relations" of a pro-Soviet business conference in New York, May 12, 1930 "organized by the board of industry" assembling some 150 business leaders and kept off-limits to the press. It was submitted from the Eastern European section June 9, 1930 and reported in the *Leningrad Krassnaya Gazeta*, No. 111, May 13, 1930. Soviet *Tass* correspondents, however, are there and reported among the conferencees is "the well-known grain dealer" Campbell as well as George Counts "the well-known worker in the sphere of education". Coleman observes that Campbell gave a speech praising Soviet collectivization of agriculture "sure to be a success". In January 1929 Stalin, in fact, had met with Campbell. The dictator is reported to have praised Russia's "peasants and workers delivered from their former landlords and capitalists ... and their demand is huge, both for personal and for industrial use." (K. Siegel, footnote, also Stalin, discussion with Campbell, Jan. 28, 1929, RTsKhIDNI, fond 558, o 1, del. 2884)

For his part, "Counts eulogized the way in which education is organized in the USSR." The State Department report adds that speeches by officials "were of a less friendly character". Coleman notes that Counts explained that "the five-year plan is rather a political than an economic program", quoting a Ministry of Trade official. Coleman observed that "Dewey, representative of the General Electric Company, and the engineer Hughes Fryne, who is keeping up business relations with the USSR, also took part in discussions with "very favorable views concerning the development of Soviet-American commercial relations." It's curious why the State Department would have to translate a story published in a Leningrad paper of a business conference with the Soviets in Manhattan during the rush-hour of investment by American Big Business in the Soviet Five-Year Plans. A New York black-out on US-Russian business news? What was wrong with US investment in the Soviet Union? Was it evil to invest in the godless Russians? Was it some dirty little secret? Little did Americans know that the Ukrainians are devout followers of a unique fusion of Christian and pagan religious traditions.

Note. The Cyrillic alphabet is named after St. Cyril, a Macedonian missionary of the 9th century, who, together with St. Methodius, was sent out of Constantinople to convert the Balkan peoples to the Greek Orthodox faith of the Byzantium Christians. They created a Slavic language written in a new alphabet based on Greek. From that time on, old Slavonic, or "Church Slavonic," has been used in the Russian and Balkan Orthodox Churches, whose missionaries traveled to Russia. When the ruler of Kiev Rus', Vladimir, accepted Christianity from Constantinople in 988 A.D., he accepted Church Slavonic with its Cyrillic alphabet along with the faith. Consequently all Russian as well as Serbian and Bulgarian writing uses the Cyrillic alphabet.

In 1988, the millennium of Russian conversion to Christianity was celebrated in the USSR. Gorbachev allowed the return of hundreds of churches to the faithful. He also visited Pope John Paul II, the head of the Roman Catholic Church, in Rome in December 1989. However, although the Ukrainian or Uniate Church was legalized in December 1990, there seems no end in sight for the bitter dispute over church property in western Ukraine between the Ukrainian (Uniate) church, the Ukrainian Autocephalous Orthodox Church and the Russian Orthodox Church. Underlying and enveloping this conflict is the fact that the Ukrainian Church lies at the core of Ukrainian national identity in western Ukraine, and that the Orthodox Church was used by the Czars as an instrument of Russification. Orthodox resentment of the Uniate and Roman Catholic churches is so strong that the Patriarch of the Russian Orthodox Church has twice put off meetings with Pope John Paul II, the last time in spring-summer 1997.

As the Five-Year Plans pressed forward the word was getting out of the technology transfer and presence of American engineers in the Soviet Union. From the US Embassy in Warsaw on the Ukraine border John C. Wiley, US chargé d'affaires and soon one of Bullitt's top staff advisers sends Kelley dated July 25, 1930 memorandum no. 136 translated from an opposition journal published July 17, 1930 the *Gazeta Warszawska.* Titled "Uncle Jonathan and Ivan the Terrible", the article covers US-Soviet commercial relations was written by Nowaczynski, a "well known journalist … a National Democrat and a prominent adversary of the Sanacja and Marshal Pilsudski." Wiley writes, "As a result of articles attacking certain army officers he was recently beaten and spent considerable time in a local hospital. The culprits have not been detected by the military authorities." Wiley highlighted that the article alluded to "the growing affinity between the two 'giants', the United States and Soviet Russia, as well as the aid being given by the United States for the fulfillment of the Five Year Plan. He forecasts dire consequences for other countries if Soviet Russia is vitalized into large-scale and efficient economic life after the American pattern'."

Frederick Coleman enclosed quotes the Polish paper *Robtnik*, and an article by Alexander Laczyslaw "an enthusiast of all which is American" which draws public attention to "a mysterious economic alliance". Coleman reports that both *Robotnik* "and even the *Gazeta Polska* are alarmed by the form and extension of the American-Soviet economic collaboration." In particular, Coleman highlights this excerpt from *Robotnik*: "A new center of factories and mines is being constructed a few kilometers from Sverdlovsk. A combination of granite and cement will give rise to splendid buildings where the productiveness of machinery will be concentrated. Also the living quarters for workmen are being built from cement and granite. Work is being supervised by the Americans; all equipment of plants will be furnished by the United States as long as proper workshops for the production of the best type of machinery are not yet constructed in Russia. This industrial center bears the name of *URALMACHINESTROJ*.

"Another set of American engineers are busy building a large tractor plant near Tscheljabinsk, 300 km south of Sverdlovsk. The annual output of the plant will be 50.000 60 H. tractors. 40.000 workmen will be busy therein. At Sormov, in the vicinity of Nishii-Novgorod, large docks and establishments for the construction of bridges are being reconstructed and 'rationalized' by Americans. It is planned to build at Sormov a Ford motor plant at the expense of 50.000.000 Dollars, with an annual output of 10.000 cars. A hydro-electric station on the Dnieper will be completed in 1932 at the cost of 100.000.000 Dollars. The management of the work is in American hands."

The Coleman memorandum encloses the following report form *Gazeta Polska*: "The American economic press informs us that the United States industry has been given, through the intervention of the AMTORG, orders a sum exceeding 200.000.000 Dollars. The following firms are interested therein; General Electric Company; Austin Co. of Cleveland; Ford; General Motors; DuPont de Nemours; International Harvester; Radio Corporation; Caterpillar Tractor and the United States Shipping Board which has already sold the Soviets 20 commercial ships. Standard Oil purchases in the Soviets quantities of Caucasion naphtha; besides, a series of other larger and smaller firms have been given concessions in the USSR."

"Yes, this is all true," Polish journalist Adolf Nowaczynski declares, and he adds, "Groups of engineers, instructors, technicians, scientific managers, experts in mechanization, standardization, motorization, etc. are proceeding to the Soviets not every month or week, but *every day*. Last week only 24 professors from all sorts of Universities; Campbell, the wheat king, Ralph Budd, Chairman of the Northern Railway, all went to Russia. Americans help Bolsheviks in establishing new railway lines, in electrifying old lines, in extending and modernizing old industrial works, in laying out enormous cotton plantations, in boring new oil shafts, and in the discovery of new mines and mineral riches (marble, granite, manganese). Red Moscow is full, is crowded with American businessmen." (Italics added)

The article is surprisingly accurate and detailed. It also makes references to Saul Bron, "the former chief of the London ARCOS, as head of all the business operations as chairman of AMTORG, the Soviet commercial mission in NY ... author of a pamphlet 'Soviet Economic Development' expounding "all advantages and profits of a close contact with the Soviets". Coleman extracts more salient revelations for Stimson and Kelley. "Evidently," states the Polish article sent to State, "it is under his influence and due to his suggestion that the large Jewish firm Albert Kalm (Albert Kahn sic) of Detroit is boldly exporting to the Soviets 40.000 tractors against a long-termed 10-years' credit whereas the International Harvester Co. is also sending tractors en masse to the USSR." He adds, "This must be really a splendid business if Ford himself gives a hand therein. There appeared recently in the American press an address by Ford to the American businessmen encouraging them to forsake all fears and help in the gigantic work of the industrialization of Russia. It has been calculated that 800 American engineers area employed at present in Russia in helping with the carrying out of the Stalin's Five Year Economic Plan, whereas a few hundreds of Soviet technicians have been delegated to America to study in the plants, works and laboratories of the United States all the wonders and trophies of the modern 'American civilization'. And he cites Soviet the highly controversial problem of Soviet 'dumping", disrupting European markets by flooding them "with their cheap timber, cotton, tissues from the Ivanovo-Vozniesienski plants, rubber boots, fish, linoleum and matches. At present the Soviet naphtha is known to the cheapest throughout Europe...".

Remember reader, this is political dynamite. The reference of financing through Amtorg several billions of dollars in current dollar exchange value of American-Soviet contracts and hundreds and thousands of engineers arriving and stationed in Russia to implement technology transfers from the West is of a scale of staggering proportions. Coleman is head of the Riga mission of Russian observers for the US government in the Baltics. The Polish journalist gets to the point about the scarcity of public news about US investment in the USSR and contrary statements and denials by the Soviet authorities and their friends. He writes, "In general, there is a quantity of common features thanks to which these two antipodes: the bloated capitalism of the Yankees and the consequent and starving collectivism and socialism of the Moscovites have been made to approach each other so closely within the present ear, or speaking with greater precision, within the last two years. A workman, in America, had been robbed of his soul, intellect and individuality in order to make of him an automaton or part of machinery; in Russia he has also been deprived of his individuality and turned into a cipher, a slave, a coolie."

The diplomats read the journalist's reporting of Stalin's veiled warning in his 1929 address to the American Communist Party when he declared, "a very definite task has been assigned by history to the United States Communist

Party. A revolutionary crisis in the United States is approaching... The American Communist Party should be ready to meet it with arms in hands, so as to be able to take upon itself the leadership in the next war." The Polish anti-Soviet journalist concludes, writing. "The really grotesque in this performance is the fact that the United States though so closely bound economically with the Soviets, refuse still to recognize them officially. But Mr. Bron, the Chief of the AMTORG, does not mind it at all. And he is right in not minding it."

Kelley's Eastern European Affairs Division also may have benefited from the Coleman memorandum and its extract of a comment appearing in *Kurjer Polski* the pro-government Warsaw daily dated August 8, 1930 stating, "The relations between the United States of America and the Soviets is *the greatest paradox of modern policy...* The annual meeting of the Political Institute at Williamstown was entirely consecrated to the problem of relations with the Soviets and this was initiated by ... which desire the *de jure* recognition of the Soviets by America. ... The Soviet representative declared that commercial relations between these two countries are developing very rapidly and that America is first on the import list of the Soviets." (Italics added)

Hoover's point-man in Berlin is a personal friend both of the President and Stimson, a wealthy and astute businessman, liked to the Federal Reserve banking system, and carries influence in the Senate and government, and an expert in food markets and distribution. From the embassy ambassador Frederic M. Sackett sends a translation of American correspondent Paul Scheffer's story in *Berliner Tageblatt,* titled *'Normal' Relations? America and the Soviet Union*, published three days earlier on August 24, 1930.

Taking a closer look at Sackett he turns out to be a trusted friend of Stimson. He leaves his elected office representing Kentucky when Roosevelt appoints him ambassador in Berlin (1930-33). Frederic Mosley Sackett (1868-41) has been a Republican US Senator since 1924. Son of a wealthy wool manufacturer in Rhodes Island. Private school, Brown (1890), Harvard Law (1893). Soon after making his reputation practicing law in Ohio he settles in Kentucky where he marries the daughter of James Breckenridge Speed, scion of a wealthy and prominent Kentucky family. Sackett joins their coal and cement business, learns the ropes and is soon president of the Louisville Gas Co. as well as the Louisville Lighting Co., and a director of the Louisville Branch of the Federal Reserve (1917-24).

During the First World War Sackett works with Washington's Republican hierarchy dominated by Root, Hughes and Lodge; during the war years he works under Hoover as a federal food administrator for Kentucky. Once stationed in Berlin Sackett monitors Hitler's rise to power and the flow of American technology and engineers to Berlin and into the Soviet Russian gulag regime just in time to get a good glimpse of the economic thrust of Stalin's Five-Year Plans and the Holodomor. A very wealthy Hoover Consortium Republican businessman from Kentucky, – just what the poor Ukrainians don't need peering over the borders from Nazi Berlin.

WHAT THE US AMBASSADOR IN BERLIN FINDS OUT – "THE EXPERIMENT"

In the Sackett dispatch, Paul Scheffer, Washington correspondent of the *Berliner Tageblatt*, and by 1935 editor (Goebbels promises he won't be forced to turn pro-Nazi...), resigning the next year while continuing to send it columns from abroad before the paper closes in 1939; in 1936 Scheffer, who meets frequently with Dodd a full carnet of notables, leaves for New York where he lobbies against Hitler's brand of German national socialism. Formerly correspondent in Soviet Russia and the author of *Sieben Jahre Sowjet Union.* Scheffer had been expelled by Stalin for writing about unsympathetic stories of collectivization. Now Scheffer leads Sackett on with a hard right this time.

"During the last two years business relations between the United States and Russia have multiplied considerably. It is probable that Germany will this year lose her place as leader among the countries which carry on business with Russia. But while Germany buys more from that country than she sells to it, the American trade balance with Russia is highly active. That is to say, what has already been known for a long time, that Germany pays for a considerable part of Soviet purchases in America." So, money from the Consortium is funneled through Germany to pay for Soviet purchases to bolster Stalin's failed state economy. Not that this is all news to Ambassador Sackett, an experienced Consortium insider and business leader back in his home state. Scheffer, however, goes about explaining how he believes the Consortium process plays out.

And Sackett further conveys it all to State, writing, "From the very beginning Russia brought great quantities of raw materials in America, chiefly cotton. But the purchase of industrial finished goods had gradually risen, particularly with regard to what is required for agriculture. Great numbers of tractors have been bought and only recently a new order has been place for 13 million dollars. The Soviet industry has imported spare parts (automobiles!), mining equipment, motors, and much else, and more than a thousand engineers followed, which is synonymous with large exports of foreign currency from the Soviet Union. The Bolshevists (sic) have been exporting lumber and cellulose more extensively and have tried their luck very successfully with a high grade of coal; they also export articles like caviar, images and peasant art."

And what about the banks? As a former head of a Federal Reserve bank Sackett would be well informed over Consortium credits linked to the success or failure of the Soviet grain harvest in the Ukraine affecting prices on the world grain market and take steps necessary to aid Soviet Russia avoid unstable grain-credit fluctuations impacting foreign and domestic markets.

In conversation with US ambassador the correspondent Paul Scheffer, as he discloses in his German news story, Rockefeller and other bankers are pushing for official recognition of Stalin's communist regime euphemistically called "the experiment". "The most interesting feature of Russian import and export operations", Scheffer writes, "is of course the financial conditions. While trade relations with America (sic) have gone up to considerably more than 100 million dollars in the last two years, the conditions on which the Soviets have been able to purchase have grown worse. This has been the case especially during the last six months. Some weeks ago the press published a statement, which originated in the Department of Commerce, to the fact that American industry now demanded 75 per cent in advance, whereas in the past 25 per cent was considered adequate security. The bank which usually grants the largest direct credits considerably curtained the volume of such credits a full year and a half ago.

"In spite of these difficulties Moscow continues its purchases. The main factor that played a part in such curtailment in America was the risk involved through the communist agrarian policy and the ever growing tension in the credit situation and the matter of foreign currency available to the Soviet Government. In the spring it was thought that the difficulties of the Soviet Government in the event of a poor harvest would be overwhelming. The fact that there appears to be a very satisfactory yield is not taken as a proof that collectivization is in a way a definite success. The yield of the soil in Russia has fluctuated between 50 and 70 per cent according to weather conditions during the ripening season. But, as it is pointed out here, the abundance of this year's crops, owing to unusual unfavorable conditions, cannot be taken as a proof that the shortage of grain and other foodstuffs, which as existed for years, will now come to an end. *Under such conditions as these a movement has recently sprung up in favor of recognition of Soviet Russia by America!* (Italics added)

"Rockefeller", the American Ambassador is told, "is supporting it as well as certain banking circles already in business dealings with Russia *but who do not come to the fore themselves;* also certain importers, as, for instance, importers of coal with whom the Russians furnish at the same prices as those obtained by Pennsylvania anthracite – and Russian anthracite is better. Big lumber dealers are selling Soviet wood products as a great profit, without however, contracting for definite consignments and without payments in advance. Much good propaganda has been carried on here for the Five Year Plan and this did not fail to make an effect, as for instance, in the case of the big steel manufacturers. One very large locomotive factory, however, has dropped off, and other firms are already in arbitration with the Soviets. The largest industrial association in the country issued a warning in May. But interest always awakens anew, roused by the general depression. It is supported by all sorts of visitors to Russia who, under the guidance of Moscow, make four or six week tours to inspect the 'experiment', and many others do their share, for instance, those who think 'bitter injustice' is done the Soviet regime by some of the attacks made on it – often by quite ignorant persons." Had Scheffer actually let the cat out of the hat?

Ambassador Sackett's boss still reigns in the Republican White House. Neither he nor Stimson hint at any inclination to officially renew diplomatic relations with the Kremlin. For Hoover secret backdoor diplomacy with the Soviet Bolsheviks is the best and only foreign policy. But now, just three years before FDR's recognition "gentleman's agreement", an open and highly publicized deal with Stalin is in the pipeline. "The big interests which have begun to advocate recognition of the Soviet Union," Scheffer writes, "are attracted by enormous possibilities contained within such a gigantic country of about 160 million inhabitants. The Standard Oil Company is drawing its circle closer and closer about Baku, and it may be assumed that it hopes to take a firm foothold there in exchange for a big loan. But big loans interest Wall Street too. Those are not plans for the moment but for a more distant future. The sooner recognition will be brought about, the sooner these circles hope to be able to materialize this promising future. The followers of these big interests believe their current business can be enlarged and that it may be possible to grant more favorable credit conditions as soon as the American Government stands back of them."

Scheffer gives a partial rendering of how Washington appears stalled in the recognition stand-off with Hoover and Stimson in the cockpit. "At present the Government declines," Scheffer writes. "But Coolidge directly urged business with Russia within dimensions consonant with the official position of the Government, which demanded the payment of Russia's debts and the guarantee that Moscow would leave off propaganda of every kind; this, however, could not be attained by other governments in spite of all promises given by the Soviets. The Hoover Government takes the same stand today. But in spite of all, the powerful forces mentioned above are on the offensive. They evince great optimism as to the ultimate success. They have even designated their candidate for the preparatory negotiations – Dwight Morrow – the hope of many in the United States who are seeking a strong personality to get control of the lethargy and growing confusion in internal political conditions. Morrow, as Ambassador, carried out the difficult adjustment with Mexico; he was a partner of Morgan's."

Scheffer's article reveals the on-going think-tank negotiations held at Massachusetts Institute of Politics in Williamstown "carried on under the leadership of an eminent 'publicity man'" (probably Rockefeller's own Ivy Lee, or another Morgan man). "Morrow's name was mentioned and that was a proof that the group in favor of recognition is determined to lead its forces into action now." Was this a Consortium plant to steer the mainstream press?

On August 1, 1930 chief engineer of industrial development and investment in the Soviet Union the Consortium's own Hugh Cooper of Cooper Engineering Co. gives an address on Soviet Russia at the Institute founded in 1921 by Williams College president Harry A. Garfield, son of the slain American president. During the First World War Garfield (Williams, Columbia Law, Oxford) also served the US Food Administration before becoming fuel administrator of the US Fuel Administration regulating price, production and distribution of coal. Another insider of the Baruch's WIB during the Great War on the side of the Republicans and a Hoover Consortium man. In fact, the history of Williams College dates back to the late 18th century when it was founded by its first president Ebenezer Fitch, valedictorian of his Yale 1777; Fitch gave Sunday sermons when not fathering his eleven children. At present Williams ranks first among America's liberal colleges and universities, ahead of Harvard, Yale or Princeton and is also a proud beneficiary of generous Rockefeller endowments and bequests.

Yet, nowhere in the entire Scheffer news story and Sackett memorandum can be found the slightest hint of Soviet gulags, state terror or forced labor in the death camps of the huge industrial projects of the Plans.

But Scheffer isn't finished with the story, not by a long shot.

Sackett finds more alarming details to send back to Kelley's desk that will surely raise an eyebrow or two on Stimson's stern profile. "In spite of everything," Scheffer observes, "all sorts of unpleasantness have just occurred. A commission headed by Hamilton Fish, by instruction of the House of Representatives, carried on an investigation of communist activities in America with special attention to their probably sources in Moscow. This commission invited Mr. Bogdanov, the head of the Soviet Trade Delegation in New York (Amtorg), to appear before it and put some very awkward questions to him.' In 1930 Bogdanov replaced Bron at Amtorg, 'a man of much higher standing in Russia'. Mr. Bogdanov and Moscow threatened to curtail economic relations, but they preferred to accompany this threat with immediate large orders. The members of the commission visited camps of young communists, similar to those we witnessed in Berlin under the name of the Soviet Minister of War, Voroshilov, and were received with warlike demonstrations directed against the 'capitalistic murderers' and in favor of Soviet Russia. The commission, greatly surprised, is now moving on farther and farther west, in spite of the greatest heat ever known in America. At the same time the Treasury put an embargo on cellulose shipments (lumber) from Murmansk which, according to the reports of a subaltern of the shipper in question, were loaded by compulsory labor of a very drastic nature. The law prohibits, rather indefinitely, the importation of goods produced by forced labor. The shipments were released, apparently because the loss to the Americans too would have been considerable. Friends of 'Recognition' voice the hope that these 'misunderstandings' will be instrumental in bringing the two parties closer through the 'explanations' which will follow."

MORGAN'S AMAZING DWIGHT WHITNEY MORROW

His father James was the principal of Marshall College. Born in West Virginia and raised in Pennsylvania, Dwight Whitney Morrow, 20, graduates from Amherst, in 1895, and studies law at Columbia before joining the firm of Stimson, Thacher & Bartlett in Manhattan. Anne Morrow, one of his four children, will one day marry world famous American aviator Charles Lindbergh. In 1913, Dwight Morrow partners at Morgan and sits numerous corporate and financial boards; Morrow with Davison and Lamont handle Allied war loans lending dollars in exchange for gold from the British and French central banks and passing it through the American Federal Reserve network, but mostly through the NY Fed. Morgan is then able to act as agent in Allied purchases of war materials from American manufacturers, always collecting its fees for the war business. When the US finally formally joins the War, Morrow takes over as director of the National War Savings Committee for New Jersey and is an adviser to the Allied Maritime Transport Council while also a member of the Military Board of Allied

Supply earning himself a Distinguished Service Medal, one Morgan partners to receive the nation's honor. As a civilian aide, he was moved to France and is part of General John J. Pershing's staff.

Morrow lives a full and charmed life. As a student at Amherst fellow classmate Calvin Coolidge picked Dwight Morrow as "most likely to succeed"; thirty years later as US President Coolidge appoints Dwight ambassador to Mexico (1927-30). Just prior to that during the controversial military court marshal of Billy Mitchell, Coolidge taps Morrow to head a study the Army's aviation policy with aviation experts (the Morrow Board) eventually to the establishment of the US Army Air Corps in July 1926.

It also leads to his daughter's marriage to Charles A, Lindbergh, when, the next year, Morrow, now ambassador in Mexico appointed by Coolidge in 1927 invites Lindberg for a goodwill tour when he's not too busy brokering oil deals with Mexican President Plutarco Ellias Calles. Lindbergh is a superstar on the world stage and everyone wants to meet this famous young and brave pioneer aviator in the modern craze of those powerful and revolutionary flying machines making the world smaller, time faster, and people closer together. Lindbergh falls in love with his beautiful daughter Anne in Cuernavaca where Morrow keeps a weekend villa. They marry soon after and to show the town his appreciation Morrow commissions Diego Rivera to paint a mural inside the Palace of Cortez.

As US Ambassador to Mexico Morrow negotiates arms and aircraft deals to assist the anti-Church government of Mexican President Plutarco Calles who in 1924 succeeds Gen. Álvaro Obregón Salido which helped end the Cristero War (1926-29). He successfully brings to the table an accord between the Calles government and the Standard Oil barons who had branded Calles a Bolshevik communist for his fierce dictatorial suppression of Catholics. Some 90,000 people on both sides have died in the conflict. The truce settled over a series of breakfast meetings with President Calles earns Morrow the nickname "ham and eggs diplomat". After the assassination of the new President Alvaro Obregon, Congress names Emilio Portes, who had been more open to the Church than Calles, as Mexico's interim president in September 1928 gives Morrow the wiggle space he needs to restore their peace initiative. By1929 Stimson's ambassador and friend manage to smooth over another peace agreement reached June 21 granting several concessions to the Catholics allowing worship to resume in Mexico.

It comes to pass the next year that by late that the nation's capitol settles back into the slumbering doldrums of summer formerly built on a swamp, and with Wall Street and Manhattan baking in the heat of August. The lawyers and bankers are away at their summer retreats in their cozy yacht clubs and country clubs and on vacation taking their families to their summer homes in New England or, on Desert Island, Maine, where Rockefeller bought a huge spread for a family summer home with hundreds of servants, and not far from the Skull & Bones retreat there; or somewhere on Long Island Sound, or Hobe Sound, or Jupiter Island or Palm Beach depending on the season, where the billionaires join Vanderbilt and his friends from their great Newport stone and marble mansions to cozy New England capes, or watching the giant sailing yachts for the annual races from their garden-party summits in Gatsby fashion of deluxe automobiles in parade. William K. Vanderbilt's palace mansion on Long Island "boasted a garage for one hundred motorcars. His brother George used more men on his North Carolina estate than the Department of Agriculture had for the entire country," quips Walter Lord. (W. Lord, *The Good Years*, 108)

Far from the coastal fog of remote tranquility elsewhere in Russia the food crisis takes another hostile turns towards a fatal mark on a tragic course heading towards a major national crisis. The Soviet collectivization plan is a disaster. It's not working. The Soviet Union is on the brink of another catastrophic famine. Revolt is reported "in all parts of Russia". Dispatches flood the State Departments Russian desk. There have been many warnings by now. State Department Dispatch No. 7164 dated August 8, 1930 is sent from Latvia by Riga's Russian watcher David MacGowan declares, "Famine in Russia."

THE SUMMER OF 1930: MORE FAMINE REPORTS INFORM THE WEST

It sounds the alarm. This is serious. It reports, "Shortage of food and other necessities is becoming more acute with each succeeding month. ...Strikes are occurring in all parts of Russia, in spite of the ruthless manner in which such protests are put down by the Government", announces dispatch No. 173 sent by M. Werlich in Poland August 11: "Dissatisfaction of the population in Russia due to the critical food supply. Beyond bread and sugar there are no other food articles in cooperatives". Dispatch No. 434, on August 12, by Lt. A. W. Kliefoth in Germany, a military intelligence officer, from Wisconsin. Klieforth reports, "Food and goods shortage in Russia. Harper* says that the tempo of the Five-Year Plan is responsible." (*Dr. Samuel Harper, Chicago University)

Immediately the next day there is another dispatch from Kliefoth, and dated August 13: "Exhaustion of the working class in Russia due to the inadequate and irregular supply of food ... the collectivization measures are having a particularly bad effect on the foodstuffs market; on August 14, 1930 from Thomas in Harbin in the center of Manchuria (renamed Manchukuo), an enclave of old Russia with a great portion of the population both Red and White.

And this from dispatch No. 5109: "Starvation in Southern Russia (Ukraine), especially in Krivorog, Maripul, and Herson. There is no divisions of crops until end of the year, and farmers will receive no subsistence until then. Food rations no longer given out in Amu region, and *starvation is much in evidence there also.* In Kiev where most of the peasants plant sugar beets collectively, they receive 200 grams of sugar per family each month." (SDDF 861.48/ Famine 1929-30/4;/ Famine 1929-30/42 to / Famine 1929-30/45; italics added)

The Riga team, too, has up to date harvest info streaming across the border into the little Baltic countries. David MacGowan heads the observer outpost; middle-age, born and bred in Tennessee, no fancy pedigree here. Born in Memphis in 1870 MacGowan went to Lee and Washington University, learns German at Halle and Berlin. His early career is spent as a desk editor, seven and a half years as a newspaper man in Memphis at the Knoxville *Sentinel* before taking on work in the field work, first as a correspondent for five years of American papers (*Chicago Tribune*) and AP (Berlin and Petrograd) before posting at Petrograd for a London newspaper. With Russia in the war, MacGowan passes the Foreign Service exams and joins State Department, in 1915, serving as Vice Consul in Moscow (1915), Vladivostok (1918-20), then assigned as First Secretary of the American Legation to Riga in August 1922. The former journalist turned diplomat quickly became fluent in Russian. He is assisted there by Russian-born John Lehrs, also fluent in Russian and German with family business in Russia confiscated by the Bols. Lehrs served as Vice Consul in the Petrograd embassy under Francis, Poole and Sumners during the Bolshevik Revolution, ARC spy mission and Lenin's coup; later he serves with the Hoover's ARA in Latvia.

Consortium ace Maddin Sumners finds MacGowan useful and brings him into the Embassy as Vice Consul in revolutionary Petrograd. John Lehrs had also assisted Poole and Ambassador David Francis (1850-20) in the embassy during the 1917 chaos and uprising. Remember, reader we know that Francis is an associate of Bert ("Bertie") Walker; a successful businessman, political crony, his positions included Democratic Mayor of Saint Louis, Governor of Missouri, Undersecretary of the Interior. Later, after some years in Eastern Europe as chief of the Liaison Division of the Russian Unit of ARA. Lehrs, 37, is posted to Riga where he stays until the Nazis makes it too hot and he too pulls out from that sector in 1940 with Kennan, Wiley and others. Neither Lehrs nor MacGowan, essentially field agents, are in the Consortium loop; their reports go mostly unnoticed except by Kelley. Two years later Lehrs and MacGowan are joined by Henderson to help with the paper filing. Married to a fiercely anticommunist Latvian, Henderson is assigned to the East European Affairs division in 1924 as Bob Kelley's assistant, and there keeps his head low, assuring himself a long successful career at State serving his senior Consortium masters.

In Moscow and Leningrad the Red Army out in force keeps order in the cities guarding breadshops and food shops. Foreign government observers suspect Soviet grain and sugar exports the cause for the scarcity. And this is only September in the harvest season. In the villages of the Ukraine religious agrarian festivals women appeal to their sister saints to protect them during the onslaught of winter. Many will not live to see spring. Enfants and older women will be first to succumb, along with the frail and sick.

On September 10, 1930, US ambassador Brodie in Helsignfors (Helsingborg) on the Baltic coast across from Poland sends extracts of a detailed report by Prof. Malbone W. Graham titled "New Governments of Eastern Europe". Brodie makes a point to identify Graham as "a keen observer and a close and persistent student of affairs of Eastern Europe". Prof. Graham had arrived in Warsaw late August and reports that "… the general level of well-being has definitely slumped during the last five years, particularly during the last two, and that the level of creature comforts is steadily sinking. There are soldiers guarding the long lines in front of bread shops all over Moscow and in certain instances in Leningrad, though there the food shortage, *produced by excess exports of grain*, was not quite as acute. Not more than a kilo of bread was given to a single family in Moscow, to judge by the size of loaf-fragments borne away by the people, and many got only the equivalent of a thick slice of distinctly inferior bread. Sugar, we learned, was virtually unattainable; butter was beyond the reach of the average citizen. The milk supply is of very dubious quality." (Italics added)

Graham states further that while in Riga "we were told on reasonably reliable authority that 85% of the milk supply in Leningrad was contaminated and the rest quite unfit for human consumption. I should incline to think that this represents a condition obtaining in most of the cities. *All estimates seemed to agree that the grain crop this year was the greatest in the history of Russia, as also the sugar crop, and that both were being largely marketed abroad. Thus it would seem obvious that the export policy of the government, rather than actual shortages in agricultural production, is to blame for the present crisis."*

Of the political repression of *kulaks*, Prof. Graham writes, "... there is a decided sharpening of the class struggle, a distinct endeavor to eliminate the last traces of the bourgeois groups which flourished under the capitalist system, and to individualize the incidence of the class conflict. We saw, just before leaving Moscow, the text of anew decree definite what the Soviet Government considers a kulak. If it s a series of categories descriptive of types; anyone employing the labor of another is a kulak; anyone who possesses more than 2 horses, 2 cows, etc. is a kulak; anyone maintaining any appreciable domestic industry is a kulak, etc. By exhaustiveness the definition embraces the principal economic opponents of the soviet regime. ... It is impossible to make extensive predictions ... at present there seems to be a neck and neck race between hunger and propaganda. The army is now well fed and it remains loyal; the GPU is omnipresent..." (Italics added)

We are now in autumn 1930 and headed straight into another perfect storm of famine monitored by diplomats and intelligence personnel. Winter is in the air. Doubt and fear are truly fatal. This tragedy won't be the last. The peasants are very worried. Far away in Washington what will Hoover and Stimson do to protect the Consortium investment in Russia when hell freezes over the Ukraine this winter? The people can hear the bells of the church but they are not ringing. Their suffering these terrible months has never before been told except to the famished survivors who look on helplessly when death came to their homes and villages in those terrible nights after day. Six months will pass before Stimson sends two of his top intelligence agents; Col. Haskell and "Ambassador" MacMurray, both with solid military and diplomatic experience are dispatched on two separate missions to investigate.

A few years earlier former US Secretary of State Frank Kellogg had sent MacMurray as minister to China when President Coolidge deployed the Marines 4th Regiment to occupied Shanghai in order to protect American citizens and property. It's all part of the unfolding series of events set in motion by nineteenth century imperialism bent on dismembering China ever since the British Opium Wars in 1842 led to a military defeat by Japan in 1895 and the quaint affair of the so-called Boxer Rebellion in 1900 when President McKinley deployed US Marines joining the British, French, German and Russian imperial troops ransacking the Imperial Palace – all of which led to a deep resentment of imperialist intervention and a profound nationalist insurgency. (The Japanese waited til night to go through the back door of the Forbidden City to do their ransacking.) The Holodomor Consortium men are for the most part born in that generation of the McKinley presidential campaign directed by Marcus Alonzo Hanna, political boss of the Republican Party, patron saint of Standard Oil, and the man who made McKinley President of the United States elected with an unprecedented $16,000,000 campaign fund from wealthy industrialists (the equivalent sum unmatched until the 1960s). It rang a bells for big business that echoes still to the current day with the slogan "what's good for business is good for the country." McKinley didn't live to see just how good; he is assassinated in 1901. (Richard Hofstadter, *American Political Tradition*, 109, reprinted in *The Irony of Democracy*, Dye and Zeigler, 82)

Bill Phillips and Morgan banker Willard Straight were not indifferent to the subsequent overthrow of the Manchu Dynasty in 1911 by Dr. Sun Yat-Sen and his revolutionary party many who are later killed by Japanese invaders in Manchuria. Dr. Sun Yat-Sen dies in the spring of 1925 and with him perished his vision of a unified China free of the yoke of foreign domination. China plunges into political chaos. After the First World War, Chinese and Soviet Communists lent their support to Dr. Sun's cause, as did the notorious military warlord General Chiang Kai-shek. In the turmoil Chiang undertook military operations in July, 1926 in an effort to wield Nationalist power throughout China and takes command of the National Revolutionary Army quickly Chiang's forces control the Yangtze Valley and moved northward toward Shanghai and betray their allies killing 5,000 labor organizers and Communists in Shanghai. Chiang unleashes the White Terror, a massive scale of atrocities to exterminate the agrarian population in the poor illiterate villagers of Jiangxi, including burning naked women at the stake. (Dean King, *Unbound, A True Story of Love, War and Survival*, NY: Little Brown, 2010, 8)

Tensions rise at the Shanghai's International Settlement where the enclave of foreigners tremble on the verge of panic fearing that their worst fate imaginable. During that time when Nationalist troops finally storm British settlement at Hankow on January 1927, MacMurray urgently requests Washington to immediately send 20,000 troops. Secretary of State Frank B. Kellogg stressed the US Marines were sent solely "for the purpose of protecting American life and property at Shanghai."

Dean King describes the scene in his book *Unbound* (2010): "On August 1, 1927, Communist soldiers in Nanchang, the capital of Jiangxi province, rose up against their former Nationalist allies and held the city for five days in what is considered the first battle of the Chinese Civil War. The Communists, under Zhou Enlai, He Long, Liu Bochen, Lin Biao, and Zhu De, captured thousands of small arms and a vast quantity of ammunition before being driven out. A month later, Mao Zedong leads the Autumn Harvest Uprising in Hunan. The rebellion, like other Communist outbreaks, is viciously suppressed; the Communists flee from the cities where they were subject to immediate execution." Mao reorganizes a hard core army of several thousand fighters in his mountain fortress refuge on

Jinggangshan, a mountain plateau on the Hunan-Jiangxi border in southeast China. (Dean King, 8-9)

That same day in September 1930 when Ambassador Brodie transmits the Graham report he urges State to take special note of the mounting urgency. From Finland he sends dispatch No. 100 headed "Famine in Soviet Russia" confirming the Graham report: "soldiers now guard the long lines in front of breadshops in Moscow and Leningrad. Not more than a kilo of bread is given to a single family in Moscow. Sugar is virtually unattainable; butter beyond the reach of the average citizen, milk supply of dubious quality. Grain and sugar crops are good, but being exported."

Meanwhile in Russia's cities in the north, in Petrograd and Moscow food products become more scarce. The Red Army patrols the streets. Three days after Brodie's report from Warsaw Coleman in Riga on September 13, 1930 memos State : "the Bolshevik rulers at Moscow are resorting to terrorism for the purpose of sustaining the currency, correcting abuses in connection with the food supply, and intimidating and disarming the opposition within the Communist Party itself."

In summer of 1930 Stalin steps up the pace of executions of pre-revolutionary intellectuals and professors of agrarian science; others are hauled off to "concentration camps". The government crackdown on educated professionals passes virtually unnoticed to the casual reader. Coleman remarks how the "news items" in *Izvestia*, the Soviet Government newspaper "were printed in small type, probably less for concealment than to impress the public with a sense of the usualness and inevitability of ruthless sanctions whenever deemed expedient, and of the unimportance of any person that gets in the way of socialistic progress. Some of the persons named in the third enclosure are economic writers and workers who have been in the service of the Bolsheviks." (*Izvestia* August 28) Ergo, propagandists for the state who also have to eat and put food on the table for their families. The list of new victims includes includes five professors on charges of "active spreading of counter-revolutionary rumors"; "noxious pilferers in the system of the Moscow lower consumer-cooperatives" guilty of "pilferage of acutely deficit foodstuffs, withdrawn from the cooperative by means of tens of thousands of counterfeit ration booklets"; those not shot were sentenced to "concentration camps" (*Izvestia* September 8); among the sentenced (*Izvestia* September 3) Professor Nikolai Dmitrievich Kondratiev, Director of the Cabinet of Agriculture Conjuncture of the Agricultural Instittue of Scientific Research, connected to the Timiriazev Agricultural Academy; in 1929 *Pravda* reported he had already been "attacked for his views by the agrarian-Marxists at the Conference of Agrarian Marxists in Moscow." Prof. Nicolai Pavlovich Makarov, formerly Chief of the Section of Organization of Agriculture at Timiriazev Academy and lecturer on grain husbandry at Plekhanov Institute suffer a similar fate. The Party needs a scapegoat. Somebody has to pay for the blundering mistakes. (SDDF 861.00/11440, Reel 1 RG 59 T-1249; *Izvestia*, No. 237, Aug. 28, 1930, No. 248, Sept. 8, 1930).

The famine situation in Soviet Russia comes as a rude surprise for Ed Brodie, arriving on his doorstep like unwelcomed and unexpected visitor. It has now unmistakably gone out of control and beyond the point of the extremely critical. He's not accustomed to turning an eye away from "just another famine". Ambassador Brodie is not a Consortium insider of the first rank but he is a Mason with connections. On September 15, 1930 Brodie sends dispatch No. 106, "Report that USSR has agreed to assist in relieving the famine situation in Russia." The American diplomat is inclined to call a famine for what it is and not what it's not. Nor does Brodie swallow the Soviet's propaganda line about abundant grain reserves and a plentiful crop available to feed the people. A resident of Oregon Brodie remains minister throughout the worst of the Holodomor until September 21, 1933, removed from the scene ironically only two months before the FDR's official recognition ceremony with Stalin's emissary in the White House. When he leaves Brodie is replaced by Edward Albright from Tennessee, another non-career political appointee in a sensitive post.

The info Brodie now sends about the famine with details of Soviet grain imports is gleamed from a translation of an editorial published in *Uusi Suomi* citing the Soviet delegation at Helsingfors as the source "denying that Russia has negotiated for assistance from America". Meanwhile the report in the press claims abundant news from American that a "Colonel Bell has been engaged by Russia to direct famine relief work in Russia." Brodie dismisses it all as pure bunk, and he writes "official confirmation has been lacking". In the same stride he transmits the Soviet Legation's statement insuring "that 'the Soviet Union's grain crop for the present year is large enough to suffice for the needs of the country, and in addition to which it will be possible to export considerable quantities of grain." Brodie, nevertheless, counters official Soviet denial of famine in Russia; instead Brodie is one of the few diplomats bold enough to step forward and emphasize the very serious and imminent danger to the population. While the Soviet Legation in Finland denies the reports of importation of grain into the Soviet Union, Brodie writes State, "Notwithstanding such assurance, there are persistent rumors *that famine conditions are already* noted in some sections of the Soviet Union." In the prevailing Soviet culture of suspicion, terror, fear and deceit and where "official" information albeit compounded by statements, reports, and "rumours", nonetheless, it is considered highly dubious it appears the diplomat finds it extremely difficult to know the truth of what is really going on under the spinning umbrella of the Consortium and Stalin's Bolshevik fairytale. (SDDF 861.00 B/591; italics added)

With the famine closing in on the village huts of stricken families in Ukraine and throughout Russia, and the State Department keeping it out of view of the Americans, a ghost from the recent American-Bolshevik past suddenly appears in the guise of a Yale Divinity student before Robert Kelley and growing more anxious about the notorious Sisson documents. Sufficiently haunting to annoy Kelley the demonstrative way he handles the inquiry is indicative of the same skill he later deploys in dismissing mounting alarm that risks exposing the Holodomor.

Jerome Davis of the Yale Divinity School at Yale University in New Haven is also a "lecturer on Russia". He writes Kelley, on October 30, 1930, asking for clarification if the Sisson documents from the Bolshevik revolutionary period are real or rather in fact forgeries "charging Lenin and Bolsheviks as German agents". John Reed had already denounced the documents as forgeries and slammed Edgar Sisson in a highly publicized and controversial rivalry. It's a touchy subject and Kelley doesn't want to take a stand. Anyway, this kind of scandal is way above his head, a minefield of dirty tricks, disinformation and espionage. Kelley, known in the Department as firmly anti-Bolshevik, backs off taking a stand and instead advises Davis that since the documents were "published during the World War by the Committee on Public Information", – the US government propaganda front run by George Creel –, he'd be better advised to pursue his inquiry elsewhere, and he writes Davis, "... I may say that I do not find that the Department of State has ever expressed an opinion as to the authenticity of the documents in question". He added, "There would appear to be no occasion, at the present time, for the Department to express an opinion with respect thereto." Just a lot of diplomatic double-talk, mumble-jumble. To appear sympathetic and obliging to his fellow Ivy Leaguer Kelley advises that he rely only on established government sources and consult the War Information Series document No. 20 October 1918 by CPI,"The German-Bolshevik Conspiracy".

Jerome Davis of Yale smells a rat. He persists, writing Kelley for government clarification which then prompts Undersecretary Colby sitting high on the Consortium rungs to instruct Kelley on December 17 how best to be rid of this ghost and this wayward Yale man with God at his side. Colby writes, "This is an almost impossible letter to answer, but I think that answer you have written, although perhaps I should not be able much to improve on it, would make us look a little bit ridiculous if it were published. After all the scoffer might well say that the Government must be carrying on a pretty funny business if it is not able to decide whether the documents were authentic or not." Colby suggests to Kelley that he tell "the scoffer" to dig up someone from the CPI to deal with it and get it away from Russian affairs. Kelley writes Davis, "The originals of the documents, are not in the files of the Department, and it is not even known where they may be at the present time, or even whether they are still in existence." Davis persists yet finds no trace of any investigation by State into the authenticity of the Sisson so-called "forgeries". (SDDF 861.00/11441)

Meanwhile, honorary board reps of the American Defense Society infuriated that "undersecretaries" Bob Kelley and Undersecretary Francis White are rumored to have dined with Soviet trade reps Bogdanoff and Skvirsky, write Secretary Stimson on November 13 requesting an explanation. The anti-Bolshevik group wants to know what kind of legal services for the Soviets and their trade organization Amtorg were performed by Hoover's Solicitor General Thatcher. As American citizens they also want to know why these government functionaries are doing hobnobbing with the Stalin's Red Commies when the US Government has no official diplomatic relations with the Kremlin. The American Defense Soviet group implores upon the Secretary to explain "the administration's attitude on

Soviet Russia". They are particularly disturbed by reports that Joseph Cotton, – Stimson's closest undersecretary and personal friend –, and his alleged cousin Thomas Cotton were both "working for the recognition of Soviet Russia..." Stimson replies, quite peeved, that Cotton is neither his cousin, nor had either Francis White nor Bob Kelley dined with Skvirsky as alleged. And that's all they get from the honorable Secretary who takes special offense at their intrusion into State's official affairs that are none of their business anyway. Francis White has a long successful career at State, appointed minister to Czechoslovakia (1933), and ambassador to Mexico (1953), and to Sweden (1957).

This time the reliable source is Poland's Consul General at Tiflis (Tbilisi) in the heart of Stalin's birthplace Georgia in the Caucasus across the Black Sea and the Crimea. An outbreak of clashes between insurgents and Soviet forces threatens "an armed uprising against the Soviet rule." On November 4, 1930 Felix Wiley transmits a document of the worsening food shortage and widespread "deplorable" economic situation. That's the euphemism generally used in diplomatic jargon for covering up the severity of an actual famine. If you don't admit a problem, then there is no problem, right? Not exactly, not now. The only practical thing for Stimson to do now is to ignore it completely and concentrate on the Japanese threat in Manchuria. But this is becoming harder each day as crisis reports steadily barrage the Department. There is already too much information circulating from embassy to embassy, from consuls to ambassadors, from junior officers to senior Foreign Service career officials.

From Berlin Wiley drafts his alarming memo for State, writing, "The Soviet authorities are greatly troubled by the turn of events in the Caucasus and feel that the situation there is very uncertain" to the extent that the Soviets supplied an armed train to protect delegates of the Communist Party of the Trans-Caucasuian provinces *en route* to the Moscow Assembly. They were forced to take automobiles to Wladikawkas before catching their train to Poti, then sailing to Noworossiisk and hitching a train to Moscow. "The Soviet press keeps silence on the true state of things... The economic situation is quite deplorable, although it is said that matters are still worse in other places of the USSR. There is a shortage of the simplest articles of food. The purchases of edible meat, flour and sugar, etc. is only effected with great difficulty and these commodities are inaccessible to many. There is no caviar at all. Even cigarettes are hard to obtain. ... All articles which seem fit for export (sometimes they are not) are shipped away, for money is much needed by the Government." No caviar! Officials in the Department scratch their heads in wonder. How bad can it get? It's not like this in the day of Czar Nicholas' Russian Empire.

Two weeks after Wiley's transmission come more reports of widespread Soviet terror.

On November 17, 1930 Coleman in Riga writes of the latest order of repression by Commissar Krylenko, Procurator of the RSFSR the decree is "designed to intimidate the remnants of the Russian intellectual classes and lay the ground for a bloody reckoning with these unfortunates, and based on testimony elicited through moral and physical torture." Coleman ventures inquisitively, "I suppose that the indictment pursued other aims also, as may be inferred from the Soviet editorial comment, which amounts to an appeal for the support of the masses of the population of other countries and to the workers of the Union to continue to strive for the accomplishment of the Union's industrial, agrarian and military program. Restoration and the enslavement of the industrial workers and the peasants are represented as the alternative to this program. In short, it is not only the intellectual classes whose intimidation is attempted, but the masses of the people. Possibly, the indictment also reflects the grave domestic conditions which the Soviet press would not willingly disclose directly." It is a reasonable assessment by the American diplomat. Why must he cast it in doubt, when the all too obvious is self-evident, or rather, as he does, write, "Quite possibly..." Yes, there is a dark hand of auto-censure in the Department reaching far and wide in the field affecting the reliability to process information of the most simple nature on the famine. Quite definitely, it is feared for Mr. Ambassador Brodie too.

News of a plot to overthrow Stalin arrives from Tallinn, the capital of Estonia on the Gulf of Finland west of Leningrad. The US Consulate sends a translation from an Estonian newspaper translation "Putsch in Moscow"! Estonia is one of the Baltic States in the orbit of Moscow. Published on November 29, 1930 it told of a botched assassination attempt on Stalin planned for the November 7 anniversary celebrations. But it's only a rumour. The plot is headed by Red General Blucher of the Moscow garrison; the garrison was to be shipped out of Moscow and replaced but lacked transport. It had been uncovered by a traitor. Observers of the Red Square celebration said the Red Guard in parade "looked worse and was not so well trained as in the previous years."

The Consul also keeps Washington up-to-date on the recent arrest of German engineers shortly after their arrival in Moscow. Are the English and Americans next? And there are more details of deteriorating conditions in Moscow: "The discontent is greater than ever before. The people in the streets are bitter faced and poorly clad. Leather shoes are seldom to be seen. A person with leather shoes is looked on as an exception. … shoes are made of cloth and felt are worn. … There are no queues, because in shops for food products one cannot get anything. The only queues before the cooperatives in the center of the city are for tennis shoes … and these are now sold in early winter... For two months no salaries have been paid. The government intends to improve the value of money by restricting the money in circulation. In some Government enterprises the employees instead of salaries receive 5 pounds of sugar." Tennis shoes in the Russian winter? In other words a very dysfunctional economy in extreme crisis.

The atmosphere is filled with "moody depression"; the population was losing its strength, and he added, "live as if in a daze. The number of suicides is increasing. The statistics relative to suicides are not published." Russian roubles are virtually worthless. "Nobody wishes to keep money; it is immediately changed into commodities. A Consul told me that he gets milk for a collection of old shoes. The milk woman does not want money, she wishes to have used things, particularly old boots." Try getting a cab in Moscow! There are none. "The Five

Year Plan provided for the construction of 25 million automobiles. Half of the time is over, but the automobiles do not appear."

"... In Moscow a messenger in a Consulate, who was a Soviet citizen, received a proposal to become an agent of the GPU. This man did not agree to the proposal and was arrested a short time afterward and shot... The new building of the GPU is ready now, it is on the Lubianka behind the old GPU building. It is a huge and modern building. Under the house there are vast tunnels through which automobiles enter from a distance of a kilometer away. In front of the house carriages or automobiles are never seen. The driving to Lubianka is performed secretly. ... For the foreigners there are two shops for food products, so called 'closed distributors' where they can get food, caviar, papiroses, fruits and other commodities against cards. The windows and glass doors of these shops are painted so that no one may look inside. The sight of food products would excite the people. Nevertheless people stop at the doors and abuse foreigners and members of foreign representations, and higher employees, coming out of shops. These last two classes in the USSR, also have the right to buy there."

Stalin survived. But few evidently understand the iron grip he holds on the Party, writing instead, "Stalin has succeeded in getting his way this time, too. Voroshilov's support has been of considerable importance in this effect... several high military persons have been arrested... The transfer of the Central Committee of the Party to the Kremlin (sic) is a further proof of this institution being in need of protection. Things have been similar with regard to the so-called sequestration for the troops of the GPU of all of the buildings near the Red Place, in front of the Kremlin"

While Coleman and the Riga Legation kept an eye on the grain problem, the State Department continues to keep its finger on the pulse of the Soviet economy. It closely monitors the banking and business activities of the Consortium effecting trade levels between Europe and the Kremlin whenever they might surface as in this memo citing "Harriman interests" in Poland accepting Soviet credit.

On November 12, 1930 a memorandum from US ambassador in Poland John N. Wiley recorded details about the business of Mr. George S. Brooks "President of the Executive Committee of Giesche Spolka Akeyjna", headquarters in Katowice, there on a visit to Warsaw. Wiley sends dispatch No. 389 writing, "Brooks informed me in private conversation that he has insisted in principle on doing business with the Soviets on a cash basis only. In practice he has accepted 50 per cent down and has discounted notes for the balance through the Polish Government...while previously first-class banks (Paris, London and Berlin sic) were ready to discount Soviet paper for his company for 18 per cent, at present only 5 or 6 banks were willing to accommodate him on such a basis. Mr. Brooks added that Harriman interests in Polish iron and steel industry have been accepting Soviet orders on a basis of 18 months credit. The Soviets have now demanded an additional six months, namely credit term of 24 months. This development was interpreted as eloquent in respect of Soviet lack of foreign exchange." Brooks talked about "the possibility of American recognition of Soviet

Russia in the near future … forecast to him in authoritative German business circles." (SDDF 861.51/2383)

State Department records show that before mid-July Kelley's Far Eastern Affairs division received detailed and confidential information of the approaching storm. Another shot is fired across the bow. This time it's a warning of mass famine issued from the Archbishop of the Black Sea Provinces and the City of Novorossijsk just east of the Crimean seacoast and southeast of Krasnodar north of the Caucasus Mountains. For some unexplained reason this particular report is not sent immediately to Washington and in fact may not have been sent until as late as mid-summer 1932 in the first year of the official Holodomor although Washington knew famine was the tragic state of daily life under both Five Year Plans. The most terrible famine in Russia it declared is now devastating the country in conditions *"much worse than that of nine years ago"*. And that was the worst in Russian history! How much more of this do the Russians have to take? Don't wait for the Americans to come again this time. Too much ease and prosperity has gone to their head, their will is weakened and their banks are closed. (Italics added)

The report is titled "Famine in Russia 1929-1930 in White Russia". Why "White Russia"? There is only one USSR! Or does the Department now consider a division, two separate Russias, "Red" and "White"? Does "White Russia", referring of course to the southern plains of the Ukraine and Crimea, constitute a breakaway state, or, at least the idea of a separatist nationalist Ukrainian independent state? Dispatch No. 3095 tells of failures of collectivization, 35% of White Russia collectivized, of some 2.5 million hectares, landowners "liquidating their movable property as far as they possibly can despite threats of punishment by the authorities. Horses and cows are being sold for $2.00 and $3.00 a head". This document gets the customary stamp as having been read by Kelley July 10, 1932; the document is curtly acknowledged by Stimson's office. Sergius, the Archbishop of the Black Sea Provinces and of the City of Novorossijsk (address in Yugoslavia at the Monastery of Prnika Glava) had warned of "the terrible calamity which threatens to strike within a short time the unfortunate people of Russia. I mean the famine which will carry away the lives of millions of men, women and children. *The famine will be much worse than that of nine years ago from which the Volga districts suffered and from which eight million perished.* This year's famine will spread throughout almost the entire country." (SDDF microfilm Reel 31, 861.48/ Famine 1929-30/46; italics added)

Figures about Soviet grain harvest and confiscation is always a central focus of George Kennan at the center of the tight group US Russian observers in Riga under Coleman, and later in 1930 just across the gulf to the north at Tallinn, in Estonia bordering Russia. A much read report dispatch No. 1106 from Riga prepared by George Kennan is sent to the Department January 27, 1933. Kennan writes, "While adequate statistical information is not available, there are indications that the harvest of the fall of 1932 was little better, if at all, than the poor harvest of 1931. If the total grain crop was larger, as Stalin claims, than the 1931 crop, the difference cannot have been very great, and the government procurements have quite evidently been less than in the 1931 season."

Kennan's figures on procurement put Soviet confiscations at 12,700,000 tons of grain "compared with 15,900,000 tons on the same date in 1930. Riga figures sent to the Department showed 1933 Soviet grain exports "on the same low level to which they declined in 1932". For July to September 1933, grain exports totaled 417,498 metric tons, against 348,735 tons for the same 1932 period, and 1,858,296 tons for July to September 1931. Wheat exports were 221,429 tons in 1933 for the same period, 164,950 (1932) and 1,156,591 (1931). It compares figures sent by the Riga Legation (Cole, Lehrs, Kennan) to State during the Holodomor 1933. Wheat exports are nearly five times the tonnage of wheat exports in 1933 for the same period (July-September); grain exports for the same period were quadruple in 1931. Accordingly, 15.9 million tons of grain in 1930 are confiscated compared to 12.7 tons confiscated in 1931 for the same period. Compare that to 15.9 million tons on the same date in 1930. The declining tonnage of wheat exports from 1931 to 1933 indicates a significant decrease in production.

"Owing to the depression in the West," Conquest observes, "the world price of agricultural products in proportion to that of agricultural goods was low in 1932. It is clear that Soviet agricultural exports were nevertheless of use in obtaining foreign currency. But the average grain exports over the Five Year Plan were 2.7 million tons a year; they had been 2.6 million in 1926-7; and meanwhile export of other farm products had declined by nearly 65%." (R. Conquest, *Harvest of Sorrow*, 171, cited in Jerzy Karcz, *The Economics of Communist Agriculture*, Bloomington, 1979, 457)

When the full fury of the Holodomor had finally quelled figures examined by Naum Jasny published by Stanford University in 1949 calculates government's grain procurements for the 1933-34 period higher than those for 1931-32 and 24 percent above 1932-33. Contrary to Department complacency toward the famine the Holodmor continues to rage throughout the summer of 1934. Naum Jasny estimates deaths in the Holodomor at 5.5 million *or more*. The Consortium plan of collectivization carried under the absolute dictatorship was an absolute failure as was the State Departments performance in not reporting it. (Naum Jasny, 621-2; figures from Moscow's *ZA INDUSTRIALIZATSIYU*, No. 246, Oct. 23, 1933; SDDF 861.50/828; italics added)

Particularly disturbing about the American government's silence during Stalin's man-made Holodomor is the fact that so many of the American diplomats in charge of information and conducting diplomacy on matters concerning the Soviet Union had extensive experience with Hoover then President Wilson's "Food Tsar" in the terrible famine 1919-1921 in revolutionary Russia under Lenin. That the silence is apparently a policy of deliberate intention suggesting an administrative agenda of deception makes it even more suspect. Further, that Roosevelt continued the policy and exploited it to his advantage transcends the border between Democratic and Republican partisanship operating upon the civil service bureaucrats of the foreign policy elite. At work here is a national agenda arbitrarily imposed on the apparatus of the executive authority of the US Government. From where? By whom? The operatives in the field, in the embassies and consulates process information to the White House. Consortium personalities in government and private firms file pass through the rotating doors walking up and down the corridors of power coming and going all the way to the bank.

DeWitt Poole, Bullitt, Kelley, Kennan, Haskell, MacMurray and many others were there in the twenties and thirties loyally processing their reports, never questioning Stalin's communist stranglehold over 160 million people and tightening grip choking the Ukrainians by famine and terror resulting in the Genocide of the Holodomor. Loy Henderson who like Kennan writes official State Department histories also gets his initiation as a good soldier serving under the same man, – like so many others like him, who fed millions of starving Russians immediately after the First World War.

America's great administrator Herbert Hoover nourished the occupied Belgiums as well as the German nation conveniently prolonging the First World War to the benefit of Wilson's war aims composed in part by the Consortium's own Walter Lippmann (Harvard 1910) and the race to a seat at victor's table with the "Big Four" at the Versailles Palace with its Hall of Mirrors. The American Expeditionary Force (AEF) was actually on the battlefields of France for less than ten months suffering 100,000 casualties; the Russians fought for three years and lost seven to ten million people including civilians. In 1919 Hoover donates $50,000 to Stanford University in California to entomb invaluable archives on the First World War and Russian Revolution along with his immortal name for posterity and historical perspective of future generations.

Son of a minister – seems to be a trend taking God into the Consortium's nefarious web; Ivy Lee and Woodrow Wilson both were sons of ministers. JD Rockefeller, Sr. is a True-Believer and a man of few words who declares his wealth came from God ...

Loy Henderson was born in 1892 and spent his youth living on the western frontier, studied law at Denver, and joins the American Red Cross during the war before his assignment to relief work in the Baltic. There Henderson experienced first-hand the misery brought on by civil war. Henderson worked in tandem with the military in prisoner repatriation handling trainloads of Russians from Lithuania and dealing with victims of influenza and typhus in Estonia. The Spanish Flu epidemic cut short the war as nations panicked to contain the disease ravaging the entire world. Perhaps one hundred million were killed. For his diplomatic memoirs Henderson recalls a scene with the Russians April 1919 a few months after the war: "The German and American officers in charge of the camp escorted us through it. The thousands of Russian prisoners, hearing that we were working on their early repatriation, became quite excited. They gave us cheer after cheer and in the afternoon a choir of the prisoners entertained us with Eastern anthems." Touching, isn't it?

That summer young Loy Henderson is sent from Berlin to Riga in Latvia to prepare American Red Cross (ARC) commission operations there "and ascertain the most critical needs of the Latvian people" and assess needs for sending personnel, medical and hospital supplies. He soon joins the ARC Commission to Western Russia and the Baltic States under Col. Edward Ryan in Riga. Their mission is to contain spotted typhus in Estonia "brought there by General

Yudenich's White Russian army, which, after having been defeated at the gates of Leningrad, had fallen back in Estonia." Henderson's "humanitarian" force was inserted into field operations of the Allied intervention into Russia's civil war. For the record Henderson wrote, "The bulk of the defeated Yudenich White army, twenty-five or thirty thousand men, had been interned either in or around Narva and of these at leaste eight or ten thousand were ill…many had spotted typhus. The disease was spreading among the armed forces and civilians in Estonia, particularly in Narva and Tallinn…" The great fear was that all of Europe might be invaded by the typhus epidemic raging through Russia, infecting White armies that would collapse with all of Europe in their wake. Henderson was part of the West's cordon sanitaire combined Wilson's armed intervention and Hoover's ARA mission to contain the spread of disease and stabilize the Bolshevik government and Lenin in the Kremlin. Henderson is a long way from home in Colorado, and standing out there in Riga in the mud and muck of disease and war he is even further from the white linen and champagne glasses of Versailles and the Hotel Crillon and the Ritz at Place Vendome where his Consortium masters draw borders and instill governments with the stroke of a pen and a good cigar. (G. W. Baer - L. Henderson, 25-71)

Around this time early 1920 Henderson met Bob Kelley in Riga with the Red Army attacking Warsaw. Henderson had already met the Far Eastern Division chief William Castle, in Paris, and soon met Earl L. Packer, third Secretary. Henderson liked Kelley and Young and was persuaded to sign on. After passing the Foreign Service exams in January 1922 he occupies his first post as Vice Consul to Dublin. Two years later while on leave in Washington he comes across Young again who took him into his new Russian section. Since clearing out after the Bolshevik coup in 1917, and still without an embassy in Moscow or diplomatic relations with Lenin's Bolsheviks, the Consortium people housed their Russian observers inside the Riga Legation in nearby Latvia. Henderson took the Berlin train to Riga as he had done in August 1919 "when I had traveled by German troop train as far as Mitau and thence had proceeded to Riga by riverboat." Kelley stayed in Washington to head Young's organized Division of Eastern European Affairs assisted by Packer. All these men were had every reason to be well aware of the Holodomor in the Ukraine.

The Dominican Republic might perhaps seem a strange place to send the Chief of the Bureau of Eastern European Affairs who lists his home residence as Sioux City, South Dakota. Evan Erastus Young (1878-46) was born in Kenton in Hardin County, Ohio, trained as a soldier serving with the US Army in the Spanish-American War before becoming a lawyer. He then joined the Foreign Service and is posted to Harput (1905-08), then Salonika (1908-09), in a few years the scene of a terrible British loss during WWI, and ends up America's ambassador to Ecuador in 1911. A meteoric rise from soldier to lawyer and diplomat and just over thirty.

How does Young becomes something of a Department Russian "expert"? Fate finds another victim.

The Consortium's own magazine *Time* gives Evan Young prominent mention after his appointment to the sunny Caribbean island as one of the "group of seven" in the Department of "bright young men". Phi Delta Phi, Sigma Alpha Epislon. With Kelley in place and his career unblemished by any unpleasantness over the Holodomor (he kept his mouth shut) Young later opts for an assignment in Bolivia where he can make use his fluent Spanish. And having had a brief stint at Commerce as a transportation expert Young has no problem with the shake-up of the Russian section. He ditched government work for a more lucrative post with Juan Trippe's Pan-American Airways using his smooth contact network to open up air routes in Latin America.

By early 1928 Pan American Airways founded by Trippe (Bones 1920) with partners Cornelius Vanderbilt "Sonny" Whitney and William A. Rockefeller, was easily able to exploit interdepartmental agents and the US Postmaster General's office in its penetration of Latin America. "The company was the beneficiary of the past as well as the "chosen instrument" of current governmental policy," notes Postmaster Wesley Phillips Newton, in "The Role of the Army Air Arm in Latin America, 1922-1931".

In the booming race for air routes Pan Am ruled the air. Routes were already charted out "in the Caribbean, Central America, and South America (and) had already been largely charted or tested by the Marine Corps, the Central American Flight, and the Pan American Flight." Newton adds, "In the Foreign Air Mail Acts of 1928 and 1929, PAA was given an indirect subsidy and by virtue of a provision in these acts that the Post Office Department could award a contract to a low bidder best suited to advance the interests of the United States, PAA could be and was favored in the awarding of contracts. The Department of State gave PAA extraordinary support. PAA also hired key personnel with experience in various branches of the government, including the military." Elizabeth "Betty" Stettinius, of Locust Valley, Long Island, and daughter of Edward R. Stettinius, a Morgan partner until his death in 1925, marries Juan Trippe, president of the Pan-American Airways, the Atlantic Gulf Caribbean Airways and the Southwestern Air Lines. That month, another Yalie, Armitage Watkins, graduates that year and promptly marries Mary White Merrill, granddaughter of Charles E. Merrill, founder of Merrill Lynch. Watkins' family owns a New York literary agency (Sinclair Lewis, William Saroyan...). During World War II Watkins does intelligence work and serves as the State Department's foreign press officer at the founding conference of the UN in San Francisco. In 1933 fellow Bonesman Henry Luce puts Trippe's face on the cover of his *Time* magazine. (Wesley Phillips Newton, "The Role of the Army Air Arm in Latin America, 1922-1931", *Air University Review*, Sept. - Oct. 1967; *Time*, June 1928).

Kelley and Henderson work well together. Fellow war vets they are and like buddies in the trenches they bear like brothers their exclusion from the snobs of the upper-class that fill the smug diplomatic corps which satisfies the Consortium backers of Stalin's bold expansion into a full-fledged totalitarian enterprise to the detriment of the enslaved peasant masses of Ukrainians and other nationalist elements striving for their cultural integrity and self-determination denied indigenous peoples of ethnic traditions. But none of that matters to these civilized barbarians with the luxury of government to raise status conscious among the millionaire-billionaire set which stocks the embassies around the world. In his memoirs Henderson gives his former boss Kelley a glowing review having overcome his lowly social status as a kid from public high school and "not, as were so many members of the department in those days, the product of an exclusive Eastern private preparatory school". Bob Kelley seems always was very keen "in matters relating to Russia".

Kelley's path to Harvard came on a scholarship. There he found out just what its like to be a poor boy in a rich man's world. The sons of Harvard were the elite of the elite in America, born to wealth, born to be Harvard's sons. To prove his worth and Harvard's confidence in him Kelley earns his degree *magna cum laude* specializing in Russian studies. He manages to win a year's fellowship at Paris, the customary stopover after graduation if can afford it and want to write, paint, chase women or just loaf. The sobriety and sacrifice of the war years however stole away much of the prewar joviality when academics rated a poor second to jock sports and Harvard football ranked as the top athletic team in the nation. Kelley always dreamed of becoming an instructor at Harvard.

When Wilson finally entered the European war as an official belligerent, Bob Kelley, without social connections and with only a commission in the regular army, stays behind to train other officers for combat leadership. By 1920, he gets his chance in the field and is sent abroad to the Balkans as an Army intelligence captain and military observer. There he crosses paths with Young who suggested he join the Foreign Service. Kelley passed the consular exams and is posted to Calcutta under the British Imperial Empire. Kelley might have floundered there with the Brits had Young not rescued him as his personal assistant. Earl Packer too, in early 1920, fluent in the language and knowledgeable about things Russian, was sent back to Washington to the Division of Eastern European Affairs. Packer returns to Riga in 1922 as Vice Consul and supervises Henderson building up the station's eternal links and organization of information. Three years later Packer joins Kelley as his assistant in Washington, not to return to Riga until 1936 as first Secretary during FDR's reorganization of the Russian section. Packer too, would be sent packing, first as Consul to Dresden, in 1940, then to Ankara as first Secretary, and later Consul General in Rangoon then to Tunis. Packer survives, and retired from the Department in 1950 after an unblemished career serving his country,

Kelley. Henderson. Kennan. Packer. Young. And others cut from the same cloth wearing the same shoes knew as concerned criticism of Soviet Russia that in keeping silent about the widespread use of terror and famine during the Holodomor years was a way to defend their collective opinion worked out under pressure of losing their jobs. To speak out meant to diverge from the President's foreign policy agenda. No one wanted to lose face. And so it was with their record of denial once it starts spinning, continues without stopping. So they kept their mouth shut about Stalin and the truth of the Consortium's role in building up

Soviet state socialism. These were not the men to lift the veil and say what truth lay in what the future would bring even when living in Hell.

In Washington Henderson found himself working alongside Preston ("Pete") Kumler "a quiet, reserved man in his late forties". Yale Law, editor of the *Yale Law Journal*. Kumler quits a lucrative practice in Chicago to join the army and Hoover's ARA. Deciding to stay on with Russian affairs, he takes a desk job under Young and Kelley. Kumler's career is cut short in the late twenties when he's killed in a car wreck.

Observing Stimson in the dingy old fortress building coined "Foggy Bottom" Henderson learns quickly "that the seat of authority in the State Department is the second floor. On it are not only the offices of the Secretary and the undersecretary but also those of the four assistant secretaries, the solicitor (later the legal adviser) of the department, and the chief clerk. This floor also houses the Division of Current Information and the Office of Coordination and Review. On the third floor were the so-called political divisions, which in the years to come developed into what became known as the Geographical Bureaus ... The Division of Eastern European Affairs occupied six rooms along the east corridor between the Division of Western European Affairs*, which was at the end of the corridor adjacent to the library, and that of Far Eastern Affairs. Three of these rooms were on the outside overlooking the executive offices of the White House, and the other four faced a noisy inner court. ... Members of the division whose windows overlooked the White House grounds sometimes find it difficult not to notice the activities of the presidents....". (G. W. Baer-L. Henderson, 123-7; * Austria, Belgium, Canada, Czechoslovakia, Denmark, France, Germany, Britain including Northern Ireland, British Dominions beyond the Seas, India, Irish Free State, Italy, Liberia, Morocco, the Netherlands, Norway, Portugal, Sweden, Switzerland, Union of South Africa, and international organizations in Europe.)

Although Henderson works two years under Stimson "grading and supervising the distribution of dispatches and reports" from posts in Eastern Europe, he seldom has contact with the venerable and elderly patrician of power. In his memoirs Henderson admits regularly debriefing visitors and businessmen about Russia. And, occasionally, when the door was ajar, Henderson stole a glimpse of the all-important Consortium strategist, but he is quick to point out, only "in conferences". (G. W. Baer - L. Henderson, 203)

Henderson's descriptions reveal how little he said or cared to show of what he knew about the rich and powerful who at this time formulate US foreign policy and control world affairs. "Secretary Stimson was a member of a rather closely knit fraternity of socially prominent Eastern business and professional leaders who, after graduating from exclusive preparatory schools and well-known universities and becoming affiliated with business or professional firms composed of people with similar backgrounds, tended to enter politics as liberals or progressives." Typical dribble. Skull & Bones, Yale, inside Root's most prestigious law firm, DA in NY when young, worked in TR's so-called anti-Trust-busting progressive campaign, Taft's Secretary of War. Appointed by Coolidge special commissioner during an uprising in Nicaragua for which he was granted governorship of the

Philippines. Henderson knows Stimson's team under Hoover for what they were, "a group of bright young men from Harvard, Yale, and Princeton – men with the proper background and the urge to enter public service at a high level". Henderson dares to say that the Secretary's "relations" engendered "extremely close" discretion with "prominent business and professional men of the cities of the East", as opposed to the Western coast of America. In other words, Stimson's private sanctum is what is known for generations as "The Eastern Establishment", – that iconic world of blue- bloodlines, old money, landed estates, pre-revolutionary ancestors, et cetera. All that still persists at present day (though much less hawked). It is no less in evidence inside the Obama administration packed with alumni from the prestigious Eastern training grounds. Of that *The NY Times* carried David Brooks' comment, "If a foreign enemy attacks the United States during the Harvard-Yale game any time over the next four years, we're screwed." (David Brooks, "The Insider's Crusade", *The NYT*, Op.-Ed., Nov. 21, 2008; G.W. Baer - L. Henderson, 187)

If there was a time when gentlemen didn't read other gentlemen's mail, there was good reason. They didn't have too. Henry L. Stimson was that kind of man, until his friends remade the world of radar, encryptology and code-breaking technology used in the First and Second World Wars. From Yale to the White House, Henry L. Stimson (Bones 1888) is friends with President Taft's Secretary of War (1911-13) and returns to steward Hoover's helm on foreign policy (1929-33), in particular, gold, war debts and Japanese expansion in China. Given the paucity of citations in Stimson's personal diary it becomes strikingly apparent that the puppet master is not too keen on keeping Russia in the record of official government business. Stimson also serves as FDR's intimate Secretary of War from 1940-45.

It is Stimson who will press President Truman to drop the atomic bomb on the Japanese. This decision involves much more than merely "pragmatic" military considerations. These Anglophiles, up through George Bush, have opposed the American republic's tradition of alliance with national aspirations in Asia. And they worried that the invention of nuclear energy would too powerfully unsettle the world's toleration for poverty and misery. Both the United States and the atom had better be dreaded, they thought. The present century owes much of its record of horrors to certain Anglophile American families which have employed Skull and Bones as a political recruiting agency, particularly the Harrimans, Whitneys, Vanderbilts, Rockefellers and their lawyers, – Root, Cromwell, Cravath, Stimson, Wardwell and many others interwoven with the Lords, Tafts and Bundys. The politically aggressive Morgan Guaranty Trust Company, run almost entirely by Skull and Bones initiates is another financial vehicle of these families in the early 1900s. Guaranty Trust's support for the Bolshevik and Nazi revolutions overlaps the more intense endeavors in these fields implemented by the Harriman brothers, George Walker, and Prescott Bush from their offices located a few blocks away with fronts as far away as Berlin and Moscow.

Stimson sees him rarely in his office or away at conferences. "I had few contacts with Secretary Stimson during the two years that I served under him.

... Henderson thought he was uninterested in the Eastern European Division or the Soviet Union. "I had the feeling that he had no strong views with respect to the advantages or disadvantages of recognition of the USSR by the United States. The fact that he was a close friend and admirer of Felix Frankfurter and frequently turned to the latter for advice tended to confirm my belief that he personally was not strongly opposed to the establishment of diplomatic relations ... Frankfurter had been for many years a strong advocate of recognition." Stimson was also close friend of Senator William Borah of Idaho "who had never abandoned advocacy of recognition". Stimson occasionally spoke with Kelley and briefed enough with Kelley's anti-Soviet viewpoint to know the general situation in the USSR from that point of view. Stimson also had his own private Consortium sources of information. He told him to speak with Senator Borah and have "a long talk" about it. In other words, it might be good for his career...

MORE REPORTS FROM US OBSERVERS IN RIGA

From his observer post at Riga in Latvia during 1929-30, Henderson prepares reports on "internal developments in the Soviet Union". That includes the Kremlin's deluge of propaganda celebrating Stalin's birthday December 21, 1929. "It seemed to me", he writes later for posterity, "that Stalin was carrying on a determined struggle to eliminate, or at least to silence, his opponents and to gain absolute control of the country." By Jove, safe assessment Mr. Henderson! By 1928, Stalin had already done that and Henderson knows it. He cites the November 1929 meeting of the Central Committee's endorsement of collectivization where "Stalin wins a victory that crushed his opponents temporarily and had a permanent effect on the internal and foreign policies of the Soviet Union". Soviet Russia celebrates Stalin's birthday across "the whole country" marked by "adoration" with language "of the kind customarily reserved for a deity". "It is doubtful if Lenin in the height of his power and popularity was ever given so much acclaim and praise", remarked Henderson's dispatch January 3, 1930 "as that accorded to the present leader of the Party". Soviet newspapers are "entirely devoted to Stalin". Portraits, photographs, congratulatory messages are reprinted from senders worldwide. Henderson adds, "little effort was made to disguise the fact that as chief of the all-Union Communist Party Stalin is also in fact the dictator of Soviet Russia and the controlling dictator of such international organizations as the Communist International and the Red International of Labor Unions." But there is something very important, and obvious about Henderson's dispatches. He doesn't ask the question about Stalin's total and ruthless domination of the Party or the real power behind the myth.

Of all people Henderson quotes Sergo Ordzhonikidze, and it appears he knew very little about his tested liquidator who Stalin had once dispatched, in February 1921, as head of a Red Army detachment to smash an anti-Bolshevik rebellion in Georgia. Since, he remains Stalin's trusted henchman in the entire Caucasus region until 1925. It was a time there of bloody civil war; Beria, a deputy police chief in the Azerbaidjan Cheka and later in the Trans-Caucasian GPU before he became head of the OGPU in the whole USSR is then ordered to assist in the horror of suppression. A former comrade of Beria in the Cheka who escapes from Russia in 1930, E. Dumbadze recalled how th Georgian Cheka perfected their "technical equipment" in the Georgian torture chambers: "Most people image that the torture chambers of the Cheka were gloomy cellars fitted out with instruments of torture. I cannot say that they were the same all over Russia, but as far aqs concerns the Georgian Cheka which I am describing the reality was much simpler and much more horrifying than those fanciful descriptions. Simpler because it is difficult to imagine anything more terrifying and revolting than the secret cellars of the Georgian Cheka.'" Boris Levytsky adds, "Dumbadze attended the executions of 118 persons in a single night. The condemned were taken into the inner courtyard of the Chekha building, the Chekists tore off their clothes and tied their hands. They were then thrown on to trucks and at the place of execution compelled to jump down. The victims were drawn up on the edge of open mass-graves. Two of Beria's men, Shulman and Nagatyepov of the 'death squad', walked along the rows and shot each man in the head. Dumbadze describes the ghastly scene in detail: some tried to run away, others wept, screamed or begged for mercy. Those who did not die at once were given a *coup de grace* by the escort. Beria waited in his office for the report on the executions. Some accounts allege that he sometimes took a personal part in the massacres." In 1931 Beria is promoted to First Secretary of the Central Committee of the Georgian Communist Party and Secretary of the Trans-Caucasian Regional Committee of the CP of the USSR. (B. Levytsky, 132-3)

Here Henderson quotes from Ordzhonikidze's story appearing in *Izvestia.* "The whole world is thinking of Stalin, his enemies with hatred, his friends with love," Ordzhonikidze declares. Henderson rightly contends, "This concept of unified leadership does not tend to confirm Soviet contentions that the Party, the State, and the Communist International, are separate and independent organizations." What he implies but doesn't say is Stalin *is* the State. The fellow Georgian and member of the Bolshevik Central Committee before the First World War, Ordzhonikidze had once been censured by Lenin who called for his expulsion from the Party over his brutality against Georgian communists in 1922. After he personally quarrels with his former friend and master over the ruthless repression of the peasants, Ordzhonikidze disappears from the political scene, never formally executed but dies during the Great Purges under "mysterious circumstances". Khrushchev thinks the rumors suggested "suicide". (N. Khrushchev, *Khrushchev Remembers*, 83)

At last the State Department finally decided to get serious about keeping a dossier on Stalin devoted to him. This was its first enclosure! What on earth had the Riga section been doing up til then? It cannot be oversight. It must be a ruse. There were documents somewhere on Stalin. File cabinets full of Riga files from these Russian observers. Here we find what appears to be the first mention, indirect, to Stalin's plans for economic reconstruction. It is in Henderson's recollection of the official record in early 1930 when Stalin marginalized the oppositional elements in the Party. The word "terror" doesn't yet figure into his analysis of repression during the Five-Year Plan, rather the fatuous rhetoric describes it as "the reduction of his opponents to a state of impotency". Henderson cites a crucial meeting in November 1930 of the Central Committee of the Party. Stalin's initiative that "the solution of the vexatious problems in the field of Soviet agriculture should have primary attention."

During the first half of 1930, therefore, while not neglecting other problems on the home front or those connected with foreign affairs, Henderson concentrates on agriculture, clearly the weakest sector of the Soviet economy." Henderson acknowledged that the success of Stalin's internal development of Soviet Russia was unavoidably "connected with foreign affairs". Brilliant, right? Henderson and the US Foreign Service staff communicate to the Department that Stalin's crash industrialization is hampered "by the inability of the responsible Soviet organs to supply technicians, skilled and unskilled laborers, food, raw materials, and transport."

Information gleamed from embassy documents and interviews with American workers confirm Henderson's concern that it is the Soviet government and not pressure from American industry that's needed to make the change of rapid conversion to a modern industrial state. He obviously didn't understand the nature of the monster. After the failure of collectivization and increased violent repressions contributing to increasing food deprivation and economic breakdown, empty factories and poor industrial output Stalin will blame his senior planners, engineers, managers and liquidate thousands of them all as "wreckers" and "enemies of the people" and "counter-revolutionaries" resisting Moscow's policies of central planning. In 1935 Beria will be awarded the Order of Lenin for his success in agriculture and industry for the Georgian and Azerbaidjan Republic, an essential distinction for the promotion of his career as Stalin's most trusted executants while the honorable and distinguished diplomats stand by and applaud in perfunctory ceremonial accord.

Stalin is doing exactly what is convenient and necessary according to plan. "The Soviet government", Henderson went on, "had taken and was continuing to take energetic measures for solving the problem of the shortage of technicians and of skilled and unskilled laborers. While Soviet technicians were in training, thousands of foreign technicians were being brought in from Europe and the United States. With the aid of special organizations created for the purpose, both skilled and unskilled labor had been organized into great flexible corps. Soviet workers were no longer allowed to decide for themselves the kind of work in which to engage or the places where they were to work. By judicious exercise of its control over food, other articles of consumption, travel and housing, the soviet government had gradually been able to reduce labor to a state of relative tractability." Incredible phrasing that, –"judicious exercise of its control over food, other articles of consumption, travel and housing" have the effect to render "labor to a state of relative tractability".

Henderson's charming euphemisms for slave or forced labor of the gulag concentration camps and factory divisions of tens of thousands of workers living on sweat and rations. Stalin's own press office couldn't' have come up with better rhetoric to keep the clean sheets of paper free of blotches of the truth. Stalin had enslaved the state using methods of torture and murder and exile by thug squads of secret police, but Henderson with his genteel education and safe in his remote post in the Gulf of Riga five hundred miles from Kiev, admittedly portrays the undisputed absolute dictatorship of Stalin as "judicious" while overtly dismisses forced labor and usurpation of all rights and dignities of ever enjoyed by a free man with one clean sweep of "relative tractability" by Stalin with western technology and technical assistance "from Europe and the United States". And this long after the Czar emancipated the peasants from serfdom! (SDDF 8611, 44, JV).

We stay with Henderson partly because he was so typically illustrates the both the delusion he projects and the pathos he inculcates as the seemingly innocent obliging diligent, the kind of civil servant that when duplicated by countless others like him create the inferno of dictatorship at home. Only it's more subtle, under the surface, beneath appearances, but its there all the same. And the evil comes back home with a vengeance sooner or later. Only Henderson doesn't see it that way. Some people never do. Those are the people the Consortium loves dearly. They got promotions when their victims got the bullet, the ax, and or just the grave.

Henderson writes, "The soviet labor union system had been developed in such a manner that it, as well as the Soviet police system, was a helpful adjunct in meeting the Soviet labor problem." No less incredible! "A helpful adjunct in meeting the Soviet labor problem." What in the world is this gobbledygook? A Jewish trick? More Bolsheviki nonsense? This is diplomatic non-speak and cover-up of the terror and methods so consistently well detailed under his nose in Riga, fascist rhetoric buried under the foggy bottom of State Department quicksand.

If the mind is rational to wonder what these pencil-pushing stamp-thumping bureaucrats are doing other than feigning the show of educated moral purveyors of democracy safe-guarding the world, and from what may I ask you reader, then it begs the question. From what? The tax-paying public never saw this dribble from their government servants? Henderson follows that up while still sticking his neck out claiming a seat in posterity's post-Holodomor heaven, writing in next sentence, "Considerable progress had also been achieved by the end of 1929 in increasing the output of the extractive industries and in improving the transport facilities. Similar successes however, had not been achieved in agriculture." Industry is a mess, the Five Year Plan is failing into shatters, and agrarian famine is climbing its ugly specter of death village after village. "Similar successes", is ambiguity dosed with baffled confusion. Well, the Consortium would reward Henderson right as he lost his grip. Had the Ukrainian sirens and ghosts from the Holodomor been circulating round his decrepit body when he outlasted almost the whole lot of them in his last year on earth? These men take an oath not to tell.

Unlike their communist rivals, both Kennan and Henderson enjoy a very long privileged and secure professional life passing away after nearly a century, 101, and 93 respectively. Henderson shifts the blame to the Communist Party for the inability of its leaders to agree on a general policy that resulted in Soviet failures in agriculture ("the sluggishness of agriculture"), the favorite Durantyesque line bought and sold by the Department. Not that Stalin had failed! Never. What had ever failed? Freedom? No matter. Freedom is just another concept like love with its illusions. Where were empires and massive wealth ever built upon freedom? Survival is more reliable. The Russians know better than to believe in such dreamy notions of the progressive, fat and weak-knee West. Words mean little. Everything is in the act. But what to do? How to think? Work for your rations before the sun goes down and the Consortium machine grinds you to a pulp! Yes! It will sell that too.

Here the State Department is taking Stalin, the Consortium's most important client – bulwark to a rapidly defiant Germany, and guardian of some of the greatest monopolies in natural resources in the world – at his word! The wolf has spoken and the sheepish diplomats dutifully type, file and send off their reports to Washington. "The agricultural policies of the party had been shifting to meet the urgent needs of the moment", Henderson concludes. Oh, really? And what would these "urgent needs of the moment" actually be? Hunger? Extermination? Genocide? Exile? Depopulation? Torture? Loy Henderson leads us closer to Stalin and the Consortium's magic word. He writes, "He was convinced that the time had come to meet the problems of agriculture head on and bring the Soviet farmer into the socialized sector of Soviet economy." And this is what they thought. The solution for economic success intrinsic to the Five Year Plans is socialized state terror imposed by Stalin and his cronies straight out of the horses mouth to reports by Henderson, to Kelley, then passed on to Phillips and Stimson who handed it over to the President who probably tossed his copy into the dust bin of history. (G. W. Baer - L. Henderson, 189)

Mixed with Henderson's myopic recall of the past are traces of truth but its all done with the play of rhetoric carefully construed to deceive and pacify suspicions. If you give a little truth no need to tell the big lie and get away with it. Henderson writes in his memoirs that "it had become apparent in 1930 that the year was to be an eventful one for Soviet agriculture". His superior David MacGowan asks Henderson to keep Washington "informed about what was taking place in the field". Curious choice of words that too – "in the field" but he's not referring to the farms.

So pressed to write reports that would be "comprehensible", Henderson undertakes it upon himself to prepare "a basic historical and analytical study of Soviet agriculture "from 1917 to the spring of 1930 to which I could refer from time to time". Henderson is so proud of that initiative, in fact, that he proposes it to MacGowan who assigns "a bunch of experienced translators and typists to assist him. Henderson is thrilled feeling like the Department's wonder boy. Bureaucracy rewards the master organizer.

After over two months his report is complete and ready in the first week of May 1930 just in time for the May Day fun. Five dispatches, the first number "6941-6945" is filled with "more than 200 decrees, resolutions, and statements" from Soviet publications – a huge reference book that would make any Soviet Party commissar drool with envy for a promotion or free cheap vodka. Henderson can hardly contain his joy, writing "These dispatches with their enclosures were put into neat volumes by an expert Riga bookbinder – a member of a guild that went back to Hanseatic days!" Only the best for the Department!

The impeccable orderly he has become Loy Henderson is ecstatic buried under the mass that he has been destined to shape, a heap of dusty files into a form easy to digest for his superiors in Washington. He recalls his predicament in his memoirs: "Each volume consisted of more than 600 typewritten pages. Several of these volumes were sent to the State Department for distribution among its various divisions and among other interested governmental agencies. One of them, which was placed in the central archives of the department, now rests in peace among thousands of other rarely read reports in the National Archives." Henderson doubted if anyone but himself used or even read the reports. "I am sure that I was the chief beneficiary of the study", he lamented during his last years. Undaunted and ambitious, committed to duty and convinced in the urgency of his mission, Henderson continued filing reports on "Soviet internal and external policies and developments" including many on "the outcome of the sowing and harvesting campaign of 1930". Only that it's no small matter that the statistics and numbers he uses are mainly falsified soviet figures, essentially worthless and of no use to anyone interested in accuracy. In the Soviet Union people learn quickly that truth is a falsehood capped with Stalin's shining star of CP socialism. Truth is valid only with the authorization of the authorities.

From a tiny apartment to a larger flat facing the chancery Henderson shares quarters with Lee Morse, commercial officer, the third secretary Landreth Harrison, and Norris Chipman, a vice consul and Dartmouth grad whose father is a Washington stockbroker. Harrison lives the raucous life of an American boy's' dream. First World War aviator he barely survives, shot down with a bullet lodged in his spine. Hospitalized for nearly two years, he recovered and studied at the University of Minnesota. Then two years in Paris before hooking up with the Department assigned to Riga in the Far Eastern Division during all the Holodomor years; in 1936 during the FDR-Welles shakeup Harrison is kept on in eastern Europe, at Warsaw where in 1939 he watched the Germans storm into Poland. After a brief tour in the USSR Harrison enjoys the benefits of a long career in the foreign office serving with promotions in Berlin, Berne, London and Paris. Chipman, too, based in Moscow remains in the Far Eastern Division. *Norris* B. *Chipman* is appointed Vice Consul in Tallinn in September 1929. When Chipman leaves for the special language school at the Sorbonne in Paris to learn Russian, Bernard Gufler from Kansas (Harvard, Princeton) replaces him with stints in Berlin during the war. Gufler has his share of promotions and perks, too, enjoying an ambassadorship to Ceylon before trading the tropics for ice in Finland across the Russian border. Henderson gets more than a just a career in Riga; he takes a Latvian woman for a wife, honeymoons on the French Mediterranean coast; and transfers to Washington in January 1931 to join his pal Bob Kelley in Eastern European Affairs. (G. W. Baer- L. Henderson, 190-91)

While the Consortium pursues its own agenda of killing millions by starvation State Department civil servants have to appear to be doing something useful if only diversionary from exposing the true agenda. Remember, supporting dictatorship and Genocide is not pretty business. It looks bad. It requires damage control rhetoric. It attracts unpleasant questions. It may even cause a sandal, heaven-forbid that greater catastrophe of upsetting the apple-cart! Henderson did his job. And it is exactly that kind of face-saving solipsism of a Stalinist apologist and Consortium hack who profited handsomely with a long career in the Foreign Service enjoying all the perks for having sacrificed and patriotically served his country with honor and distinction while others suffered and died *en masse* that makes it all the more grossly pathetic. The victims of genocide may forgive but they can never forget the crimes against Humanity by such cowardly self-serving officials as served on the Russian desks of the Eastern European Affairs Division. We can only hope others do not follow his path. But remember, diplomats are never supposed to tell the truth. They lie. That's what they are good at, all done with candor and a smile. Never forget it. It's what keepers of the secrets get paid to do. Smile! All is well that can be. (G. W. Baer- L. Henderson, Chapter 16, "Apprenticeship in the Department of State", 160-1)

We know from many declassified Department documents that Washington had steady and reliable information of events transpiring throughout Soviet Russia during this period of the twenties and early thirties leading up to and pertaining to the Holodomor Terror-Famine Genocide as well as to how the Department handled its aftermath. Henderson had to admit it, but he preferred not to speak of the technology transfer, the bank loans and credits, the colossal engineering projects supervised by American engineers. Instead the record he chose to leave behind tells of "communist activities" and "developments in the Soviet Union" without any specification whatsoever on his part. Embassies of friendly nations share and exchange informative. There is no way the Ukrainian Terror-Famine can be kept off the radar. Henderson, Kennan and the others make it a habit to keep famines and the Holodomor low profile and off the record books. The Holodomor is not recognized on the policy agenda and these bureaucrats in the American Foreign Service are paid to see that it's kept that way. (G. W. Baer - L. Henderson, 161)

The Riga base grows into the America's "most important source of information" on Lenin and the Bolsheviks in the Kremlin, the center of power in Russia and its Republics traversing twelve time zones. Long "before our recognition of the Baltic States," Henderson writes, "the department had established in its Riga office of the US commissioner to the Baltic states a section charged with collecting information on Soviet Russia". Most of the Riga team had experience in Russia and were fluent in Russian. Henderson said they were even well equipped in research and translation work" by "a number of local employees". Henderson is particularly proud of the commissioner's library, "a mass of Soviet books, pamphlets, newspapers, and other periodicals that was almost without parallel outside the Soviet Union". The two libraries "had complete sets of Soviet laws and decrees as well as numerous legal treaties, most issues of *Izvestia* and *Pravda* dating back to the early days of the Bolshevik revolution, and files of other newspapers published in Moscow, Leningrad, and the capitals of many of the constitutent republics." (G. W. Baer - L. Henderson)

After George Kennan leaves Princeton, in 1925, he passes his Foreign Service exams and is posted as a consul in Geneva; though during a visit to US minister Harry Carlson in Estonia he got along so badly its amazing he managed to leave with a high recommendation, and joins the Riga Legation early 1929, but not yet in the Russian Section then still under Coleman. Kennan then studies Russian history and language at the University of Berlin, and by 1931 speaks Russian fluently. In Washington the Department starts to take notice of Kennan in the fall 1932 when Castle praises his report on soviet gold reserves; that report was followed by another on soviet commercial treaties April 1933 "with the possibility of recognition in mind", and forwarded to FDR. During the recognition talks FDR choses opposite language than used by Kennan "relating to the treatment of foreign nationals in the USSR". (J. L. Gaddis, *Kennan*, 72)

To augment their information gathering the Riga station in the mid-twenties "subscribed to more than 50 different newspapers and other periodicals". Shelves were stacked with "books, brochures, and sets of periodicals relating to the programs, decisions, and proceedings of the organs of the Communist International and its affiliated organizations". Henderson finds "special interest" in "detailed instructions from the headquarters in Moscow of these international organizations to the communist parties and communist-manipulated organizations in other countries." Papers and periodicals arrive in Riga by train roughly a day and a half after they appear in Moscow except for occasions of "unexplained delays". Riga then telegraphs summaries considered urgent direct to State in Washington. Otherwise there is the diplomatic pouch. There is another problem; in the mid-20s the legation grossly lacks analysts to monitor developments having to suffice "from time to time" with "memoranda, some of which were quite exhaustive". The small staff is overwhelmed and has to cope lacking resources and personnel for its mission. Much to his regret his colleagues are unable to process and exploit to its "maximum advantage" the huge amount of intelligence collected on the Bols and "Russian conditions". Their failure to adequately secure and transmit data for the official record of the Holodomor is certainly adequate proof of that.

But FDR and Welles will change that basically throwing the Riga Legation's work to the winds. And to some measure Riga's deficiencies and mishandling by Kelley's Eastern European Affairs division has much to do in casting official silence of the Department over the Holodomor crisis. But that is not the only reason why not long after the Holodomor FDR decides to scatter the Department men from the Russian division. Perhaps even in their tireless effort not to fail they had to wonder if they had not already done too much of the wrong thing. Whatever they did it seems that the Consortium was not yet satisfied and makes a major shift in another direction to smooth over relations with Stalin during the height of the Great Purge as he too gets his house in order. (G. W. Baer - L. Henderson, 163)

Before normalizing relations in 1933 combing through Soviet publications for information is the daily routine at Riga. The occasional unexpected drop-in provides steady entertainment and breaks the office boredom between regular evening functions of the diplomatic set. Riga particularly prefers eye-witness accounts, observations by fellow travelers "of friendly countries", as well as "newspaper reporters, businessmen, and technicians". They eagerly bring true stories, the real stuff of life, passions and horrors vicariously shared with a variety to lighten up the day. Even horrid tales of famine finds the Riga team suddenly animated in their slumbering retreat far across the border from the action.

Henderson recalls "visitors usually had no hesitation in discussing privately with members of the legation their experiences in the Soviet Union and in giving their views on the developments and trends". Balkan officials were "particularly well informed … and their officials, while at times critical of Soviet practices, were inclined to lean backward in their endeavors to understand and rationalize Soviet actions that seemed shocking to many observers from Western Europe."

What is he saying?

Stupified by the horrendous nature of the crimes inflicted on the citizens of Russia the Americans were perplexed and nonplussed at Europeans who might try to find something worthwhile to do to lessen the utterly miserable existence of the Russian people. At the same time the Americans might even be expected to resonate their fate with the unbearable problem on their shoulders. Or, was there no word that need be said about the usual Soviet procedure in cases no less ordinary than their own. Each have their master to serve. The horror is real. When the time comes in many years they will not be allowed to forget. It is not so easy now to seek safety in the West so far beyond the sea. Work comrade, work! For the glory of the Soviet socialist Revolution and the glorious future! (G. W. Baer - L. Henderson, 163)

Since the US lacks intelligence agents in Russia except for a handful of sporadic military operatives Riga "arranged to obtain information from the secret services of several friendly countries" namely Britain, France and Italy. Diplomats in Moscow are closely watched by the Cheka (later called OGPU, NKVD, KGB) and other secret police. Diplomats in Moscow, Henderson writes, "found it almost impossible to prepare reports of the kind the department was receiving from Riga". Riga felt the pressure coming down hard on them from somewhere at the top; the Commerce Department constantly criticized State for not doing enough through the consulates to promote US exports. Centralized in the Consular Commercial Office where each report was "credited", "the author with the report and its grade" compelling the consular section to be more exacting in commercial work.

As a result the small staff at Riga is soon editing a "mass of information", political, economic and commercial reports. The information overload is so extensive that Henderson had to admit that "in spite of our lack of representation in that country, we were as well informed regarding developments and trends there as the foreign offices of any other country with the possible exception of Germany and the Baltic states". Get the picture? So what happened to result in the info black-out of the Holodomor years? A change in policy once the Stalin consolidates dictatorship and control over the Communist Party?

Stalin rams through the Consortium's Five Year Plans with consequent terror and famine from intensified collectivization and bankrupt inefficient industrialization all misguided in method and unrealizable? That is, unless an absolute dictator is firmly in place with a program of terror and forced labor... Is can hardly be any wonder why the experienced Minnesotan Frederick Coleman is transferred as ambassador to Denmark then quits the Foreign Service. (G. W. Baer- L. Henderson, 163)

In spring 1927 Kelley drafts a memo for Stimson's senior Undersecretary Wilbur J. Carr requesting that Henderson be sent back to Riga and promoted third Secretary. In Berlin Henderson meets John C. Wiley, first secretary, and the inimitable Dewitt C. Poole, senior head of the Russian section. Poole is another key Consortium player with knowledge and experience of the Morgan-Bolshevik American Red Cross spy mission. In those revolutionary days of 1917 their machinations assisting Lenin-Trotsky stage the Soviet coup allowed Ambassador Francis and the Americans in the embassy to make a clean sweep out of town taking the moderate provisional government interim President Kerensky with them. A decade has passed since Dewitt Poole left his post as Consul in Moscow during the Russian Revolution and return to Washington to organize the Division of Eastern European Affairs.

The precocious somewhat jaded but humorous Wiley impresses Henderson as already "a veteran diplomat". Henderson will work closely with both Poole and Wiley to smooth the rails of his long and successful career. Riga is a quaint city with a photo-perfect European flavor that beguiles Henderson daunted by its "picturesque buildings in the ancient squares that dated back to the era of the Hanseatic League, with the Opera House, with the steepled Gothic churches, and with the magnificent views across the broad Dvina River, I could understand why the Baltic Germans loved Riga and why they had been so determined to remain masters of it." Henderson assists David MacGowan in preparing Soviet reports on the Comintern and communist propaganda for world revolution.

The year 1930 proves to be pivotal in the history of Soviet espionage overseas. In the 1930s the Soviets reaped an espionage harvest that goes unmatched by the foreign powers. According to author Andrew Meier in his book *The Lost Spy* (2008) in the beginning "no more than a dozen men and women" formed what was called "The Center", agents using aliases, false passports, living in safe houses while appearing normal and above suspicion. Their small tight underground organization "stretched from Europe to America to Asia. How many hundreds of agents, informers, and couriers they recruited will never be known, but the Great Illegals help steal a generation of secrets. "And who were they? Clandestine Soviet communist sympathizers like Sidney Hook, then a philosophy student at Columbia University and close friend of the educator John Dewey form a nascent Soviet underground of spies, double-agents and idealistic cohorts. (Andrew Meier, *The Lost Spy*, 2008, 147)

Meanwhile Henderson devotes half his time "keeping the department informed on Soviet foreign economic developments, including the structure and activities of the Soviet trade monopoly and the institutions through which this monopoly was being exercised, Soviet concessions to foreigners, and the manner in which the foreign concessions fared." Henderson falls ill with fever and takes six months leave on "the Magic Mountain" in Davos, Switzerland for recovery.

He returns to Riga late 1930, joining David MacGowan and John Lehrs there. Then came George Kennan. State's crowning achievement in disinformation, "passionate and romantic" arriving from Tallinn, Estonia fresh from two years of Russian lessons at Berlin's Oriental Seminary in Berlin, Kennan is stationed in Riga (1931-33). He, too, finds the city romantic, vibrant with gypsies, vodka and *drozhkis*, and he recalls, "... Riga was still alive. ... To live in Riga was in many respects to live in Tsarist Russia." Also there is John A. Lehrs, an attaché who later serves as special assistant to Coleman. (D. A. Mayers, "In Stalin's Time", *The Ambassadors and America's Soviet Policy*)

Henderson takes charge of the reports in the Washington office while Kennan handles the Riga office, two like-minded instruments of the Consortium who had nothing to fear and nothing to lose while they kept their nose clear of any leaks or discrepancies that might open Pandora's Box and backfire the Plans and lose the monopolies to German competition. Who would fight Hitler then? Surely the Russians will never be able to organize themselves in time to crush an invading German Army. Stalin was running out of time. Better to submit the masses to unbreachable rules under an absolute dictator and keep up the propaganda that Russians and Americans are same-same, kin spirits and common foes of Nazi fascism. FDR's ambassador Davies and his Hollywood film would see to that! A generation later "Tricky Dick" Nixon would play for Khrushchev on his visit to the US the same propaganda game show of modeling the perfect American home tailor-made for every Natasha and her *Babushka*!

Once in Washington Henderson is bought up to speed by the staunch anti-Bolshevik Kelley and Evan Young. Throughout his Foreign Service career Loy Henderson carries out his administrative duties convinced that the Soviet Communists are determined to be masters of a world communist revolution instigating chaos everywhere from its Kremlin headquarters. He correctly swallows the official Washington-Moscow propaganda line of the Consortium regardless of what he may have thought contrary to what he was taught to believe. And he frequently handles matters calling into question "action that might be construed as recognition of the Soviet government" such as multilateral treaties that invoke recognition, *de jure* or *de facto*. "When it was clearly in the interest of the United States that we and the Soviet Union sign the same multilateral document" Henderson attaches a "caveat" to emphasize that signing was not an act of recognition, particularly in commercial transactions.

For the record and only when it is relatively safe to admit Henderson later inscribes an odd commentary of a prevailing mentality in the Russian section during this critical period of the late twenties. He does it through the Hoover years leading to FDR's unprecedented decision to recognize Stalin's regime. The Department has its own internal agenda collecting political and economic data on Soviet society with a particular focus on commercial relations beneficial to the expanding American industrial economy, ergo, the Consortium.

"Most of the time and energy of the Eastern European Affairs Division," Henderson admits, "was devoted to matters relating to Russia. Trade between Russia and the United States was slowly increasing. Information poured into the State Department about developments within Russia and about other events involving Russia. There were numerous communications in relation to Russia from other executive agencies of the government, from members of Congress, and from private US citizens or firms. One of the divisions most time-consuming activities was to observe developments in Soviet Russia's internal and foreign policies and practices what might justify a reconsideration of our policy of nonrecognition. If changes might be prepared to meet the conditions that our government had laid down as a prerequisite for recognition, it was important that the Department should be the first to note them in order to move in the direction of recognition without having to be pushed in that direction by critics in Congress." That can imply only one thing. They have said it before and say it again. The public be damned. The President, elected the 35th President of the United States by and for the People, had his own agenda. It is non-partisan and it is ultra-secret.

"HUGHESOVKA !!" – WELSHMAN GARETH JONES RETURNS TO UKRAINE 1930

For the West the story of the Holodomor begins with the newspaper reports of a young Welshman (the Welsh pride themselves as distinguished from the English). Gareth Richard Vaughan Jones, is the son of Major Edgar Jones, a loving family man of the British Empire. Born in Barry, Wales, in 1905, Gareth Jones is nine years old when the First World War began in August 1914. The Great War will cost Great Britain an entire generation of its best educated, an entire upper class of talent blown to bits, no less than a mortal death-blow to the Empire.

Gareth was always a cheerful lad, smart with God in his heart and prayers at the supper table. The young boy never forgot the tales of his mother and that place where she stayed in eastern Ukraine in Hughesovka, later named Stalino, and today known as Donetz. There as a young girl Mother Jones tutored the grandchildren of a steel industrialist from Wales. Ever since she impassioned his childhood with delightful stories recalling her happy days living peacefully there in 1889 to 1892.

As a boy Gareth yearns to visit that dreamy distant Russian land animated with mysterious tales and customs. In school he showed an ease for foreign languages, studied at Aberystwyth and graduated from Cambridge University in 1929 with First Class Honors in French, Russian and German. Alistair Cooke the elegantly distinguished American TV host who described Stalin as "The Maddest and Most Criminal of Tyrants" was also at Cambridge at that time. Gareth is a precocious seventeen-year old, in 1922 with a knack for languages when he first travels alone to Vilna (Vilnus), "the city of bones", north west of Minsk and only 120 miles from the Russian frontier. This is also the year when in Rapallo, Italy the trade Agreement is signed to reset relations between Russia's former enemy and essential commercial partner is signed by German and Bolshevik Soviet representatives in top hats and long tails, on April 16, 1922.

On New Years Day 1930, Gareth Jones officially begins his work as a personal assistant and foreign affairs adviser to Lloyd George. The ex-war minister caught wind that Jones might do well under his instruction. Gareth assists the famous statesman helping to prepare material for memoirs which should have been a most interesting first-hand view on the Consortium's powerful reach around the world. Jones has a full year to work intimately with Lloyd George, known as "the Cameleon" for his political longevity. Using his political connections Jones is introduced to the most powerful inner circle of men of the British Empire including key personages in the House of Lords and House of Commons.

Long before the First World War, in 1909, David Lloyd George had announced what became known as the People's Budget, increased taxes including a super tax for those earning £5000 or more a year, an increase in death duties on the estates of the rich and heavy taxes on profits gained from the ownership and sale of property. Staunchly opposed by the Conservatives, who had a large majority in the House of Lords, and who had objected to this attempt to redistribute wealth Lloyd George smashed their intentions to block his proposals touring the country making speeches in depressed working-class areas and stoking the fire of revolt. Learned noble men of the upper class were exposed for using their privileged position to deprive the poor of old age pensions. His radical actions cause a sensation forcing the Liberal government to curtail its powers. The 1911 Parliament Act drastically undercuts the authority of the Lords. When Prime Minister Henry Asquith appealed to King George V to intervene, and confronting a permanent Liberal majority in a reformed House of Lords, the Conservatives have no choice but to accept the Act.

During the Great War Lloyd George reaches his summit of power and the fame deserving of his infamous role in the four bloody years of Total War when he serves in government with a complicity as easily dismissed as his support for Stalin's extermination of the Ukrainians and practice of Genocide in the Holodomor. During the war years Lloyd George rises in rank privy to the British Government's inner council most jealously guarded war secrets of corrupt backdoor armament deals since he takes over Lord Kitchner's work in the munitions and armament sector. Throughout the next decade, both Lloyd George and Churchill have full access to intelligence reports of both internal and external affairs of the Soviets and Bolshevik atrocities as well as knowledge of the Consortium players behind the Soviet Five-Year Plans.

Time is too short for Gareth Jones to write his own account of the pacifist commitment of the labor minister if he truly had any. There is an interesting read, however when Lloyd George single-handily saves peace for the Bolsheviks. It's another twist on the Consortium secret takeover of the Czar's rich possessions. The Entente nations Great Britain and France, in fact, are largely credited for having stopped the initial Polish invasion of Russia by supplying money and arms in an armistice with Trotsky's Red Army.

According to Mikhail Heller and Aleksandr Nikrich in their book *Utopia in Power: The History of the Soviet Union from 1917 to the Present* (1985) if statesmen are to be credited for maintaining Lenin, Trotsky and the small bank of Bolsheviks in power, that infamous honor was earned by Lloyd George and his cabinet. Writers Mikhail Heller and Aleksandr Nikrich recall events in those turbulent days: "After January 1920 the Entente's policy in regard to Russia was based mainly on Lloyd George's views. While rejecting the Soviet system, as all other Allied leaders did, Lloyd George strongly opposed intervention in Russia's affairs, considering it a waste of time and money. On April 16, 1919, he declared he would rather see a Bolshevik Russia than a bankrupt Great Britain. Lloyd George formulated the principles of a policy that was to become standard for the West vis-a-vis the Soviet Union: to smother bolshevism with generosity. He declared that trade with the Soviet Republic would allow Russia's economy to revive, put an end to its chaotic state, and help surmount the difficulties that had given rise to bolshevism." (Mikhail Heller and Aleksandr Nikrich, *Utopia in Power: The History of the Soviet Union from 1917 to the Present*, London: Hutchinson, 1985, 97)

A little historical perspective casts light on Lloyd George and the significant role he played during the chaos of the Russian civil war and famine in the early twenties. With Riga still under siege Comrade Kamenev arrives in London on August 4, 1920 for talks on ending the Civil War, and keeping the Bols out of Eastern Europe. British troop withdrawals, famine and trade, the proletarian revolution are on the table. Kamenev is received as a royal guest in the great style fitting of the Great Britain's imperial tradition. In London he is treated with the respect reserved for ministers, royalty and the most opulent of the wealthy money men and women. Lloyd George negotiates a peace accord as mandated by Versailles conference on the basis of the Curzon line for the western frontier with Poland. Moscow puts pressure on Warsaw as Trotsky's Red Army advances there. An Anglo-French delegation to Poland reports peace with Poland might save her along with rebuilding Germany but Lloyd George calls the French bluff telling the Marshal Foch that England would send troops to Poland if France would do so as well. In a response that became classic French, Foch answers: "There aren't any troops."

General Maxime Weygand, dismissed the fable that he was the "father of the victory" on the Vistule. In his memoirs Weygand writes, "The victory was Polish, the plan was Polish, the army was Polish." The Riga peace treaty is signed the following year on March 18, 1921. Both sides consider it their victory of sorts; the Poles move their border further east, Lenin besieged by famine and terror finds a bit of respite from the general chaos; and Hoover's ARA agrees, and Lloyd George claim he had stopped Bolshevism from sweeping all of Europe into caviar tins. (M. Heller and A. Nikrich, 98).

That the turn-around in Soviet economic fortunes is linked to German technical assistance is also made clear after Rapallo foreseeable as early as 1917 when the German bankers played their cards to deal a final blow to the Czarist monarchy with funds to the Russian revolutionaries. General Ludendorff authorizes Trotsky's return on a sealed train full of revolutionaries. Once entrenched with the soviet councils the Bols are maintained in power by all major Western governments. Now with the backing by the international cartel of centralized banking of Consortium partners the Germans are the best placed to resume their status as Russia's first trading partner and the country most responsible for initially rebuilding the Russian industry. Plants emptied by the rallying calls of the communist leaders to the peasants and workers once again began to function. German management and workers assumed leadership abandoned by the propertied class in the majority of Russia's large industrial and mining enterprises.

When Gareth Jones is invited by former British Prime Minister David Lloyd George to assist him in research for his official War memoirs he most certainly will have access to details of the Soviet trade agreements with the Bolsheviks within the framework of Rapallo. That's part of his elite education and training in foreign affairs. There Lloyd George as Prime Minister tries to welcome back Soviet Russia into the "concert of powers" with a normal dialogue between partner nations instead of having to play off the venomous attacks by the sharp-tongued Soviet commissars talking "Bolsheviki" propaganda against the blood-thirsty imperialist parasites. Lloyd George insists on Western credits and loans in a general stimulus package for the Soviet economy. Still entangled in the strange American military intervention during the Russian civil war the Bolsheviks are persona non grata having been denied seats at the Versailles Peace Treaty negotiations in Paris which they denounced as a banker's diplomatic farce of secret treaties dividing up countries, peoples and resources for the sole benefit of empire. Wilson is too preoccupied with France to deal with a Russian solution.

It was an auspicious beginning. Rapallo imposes economic, military, and trade protocols meant to nudge Germany and Soviet Russia to put the First World War behind them. That means they must renounce all reparation claims and all financial claims against each other; further, Germany, although in a state of ruin, agrees to aid Soviet Russia financially, which of course leaves the door open to the Consortium. Germany is bankrupt, its currency worthless, its economy stripped and devastated by ruinous inflation. Mutual trade relations are established. Money and heavy industry will come from the Consortium. American factories are flooded with over-production from the war. Banks have too much money and needed to invest in reconstruction.

Rapallo was a long-time in coming and a windfall for the Soviets as well as Germany. The years 1923-33 see significant Soviet-German military cooperation. Sutton observes, "As late as 1928, Soviet industry was run by a partnership of German and prerevolutionary engineers independent of nominal Party control." German assistance was tremendous and saved Lenin and the Communist system. Terms of the Versailles Treaty stripped Germany of its air force. WWI flying legend Baron Richtoffen, Göering and other pilots immediately set about rebuilding the famous Luftwaffe in a secret exchange arrangement with the Soviets. German pilots are trained in Russia. Other sectors of collaboration include joint maneuvers in tank and gas warfare, the training of paratroops, technological transfer for the naval construction of submarines and aircraft prototypes. In this way the Germans circumvent the Versailles Treaty provisions banning German development and use of offensive weapons.

"The first modern aircraft factory in Russia was built by the German Junkers concern," Sutton writes. "Thus, Soviet air power was born. Large numbers of Soviet engineers and workers were trained; many hundreds of Russian pilots were thoroughly instructed by German pilots; and the first Russian airline network was created." For their part, the Soviets benefit from access to German military technology. By the mid-1930s both Germany and the Americans were arming the Soviets until 1939 under protests from Göering. Less than two years later, Hitler's troops invaded the Soviet Union violating his non-aggression pact signed in Moscow with Stalin. (A. C. Sutton, *Western Technology and Soviet Economic Development, 1917-1930,* 346; W. Keller, *East Minus West Equals Zero, 1961,* 202).

Diplomatic relations with Russia having been restored with Great Britain in 1924 suffered a breach three years later over Soviet espionage, – the Argos affair, but have since been normalized. leaving Jones more or less free to venture about on his first "pilgrimage" in August 1930. Then he visits Hughesovka, and on August 17 he writes a few carefully chosen words home to his mother in Wales commencing his letter exclaiming "Hughesovka !!"

Then two months later in the fall of 1930 his story "The Two Russias" is published by *The Times*, in London, with sequel parts appearing on several days through the week from October 13 to 16. It's a breakthrough for Jones and the Ukraine story. Written in the summer during the harvest season, but with winter now only weeks away and already awaited with dread in every village; the peasants are hungry, goods are scarce, many are already starving and many workers are too weak to perform their jobs in the factories. The Five-Year Plans are in full swing.

Before leaving the country Jones travels by car to State Farm, Giant No.2. Communists have transformed these desert steppes here into a huge farm extending a hundred thousand acres and maintained with modern agricultural machinery of the most sophisticated type found anywhere. Everywhere new buildings abound and various stages of construction. Everything he sees indicates that Soviet Russia is advancing rapidly under Stalin's Five-Year Plan of Industrialization. On a State farm he is is provided with excellent meals. Jones listens to "some rank-and-file opinion on the regime and its policies" and is shocked by the hardship of starving peasants he encounter. On his trip he finds was very little food, "only one roll of bread", and promptly leaves towards Kislovodsk in the Caucasian mountains.

Back in late summer upon his arrival in Berlin August 26, Jones had written a four page letter to his parents foretelling "many deaths", as a result of the Five-Year Plan" and "great suffering" from "starvation".

After only a few short weeks in southern Russia and on his way back to England Jones passes through Germany with his first hand account of the Terror-Famine imposed by Stalin's state system. Although Jones will return to the Ukraine taking more accounts back to the West of Stalin's campaign of grain and wheat confiscations escalated for each successive harvest culminating in the Holodomor apparently nothing is done whatsoever by the Consortium leaders in government or commerce to attempt to come to the aid of the Ukrainians or to lessen their suffering and save lives and prevent a wholescale slaughter of millions. The values of freedom and Humanity that were fairly much demolished in the Great War have meant little since to the men still in power.

For Stalin and for the Consortium this is not a morality play. "They cannot strike or they are shot or sent to Siberia," Jones writes home from Berlin. Jones' letter shows how sickened and morally shaken he was after the trip. He wrote, "Hurray! It is wonderful to be in Germany again, absolutely wonderful... ."Germany is a fine place."…. Thank goodness I am not a Consul in Russia – not even in Taganrog!

"Russia is in a very bad state; rotten, no food, only bread; oppression, injustice, misery among the workers and 90% discontented. I saw some very bad things, which made me mad to think that people like Bernard Shaw go there and come back, after having been led round by the nose and had enough to eat, and say that Russia is a paradise." The Soviet Union gloated over visits from England's left-wing intellectuals too spineless to call the Soviet bluff; George Bernard Shaw toured Russia with Lady Astor, wined and dined with aristocratic upper-class passion and delighted in how comfortable they were made to feel by the Soviet Intourist police agents. Here we see Jones' frustration finding it incredible that the learned and rich could be duped by communist propaganda theater. Shaw is one thing, a playwright, a champion of drama with moral responsibility before the public! But in a short time he will question his friend and mentor Lloyd George himself for supporting Stalin!

COLLECTIVIZATION: "THE MOST BRUTAL IN THE WORLD"

Jones feels nothing in common with these Consortium buffons all too eager play the fool and be duped by lowly uncivilized rotten scum. Jones is clearly worried about the future for the fine people he befriended and feels the pain of not knowing what he can do to help. "The winter is going to be one of great suffering there and there is starvation," he writes. Without mentioning Stalin or his band of murderous thugs by name he calls the communist government "the most brutal in the world".

Jones tells about the gulag system and executions. "The peasants hate the Communist," Jones writes, "This year thousands and thousands of the best men in Russia have been sent to Siberia and the prison island of Solovki. In the Donetz Basin conditions are unbearable. Thousands are leaving. One reason why I left Hughesovska so quickly was that all I could get to eat was a roll of bread – and that is all I had up to 7 o'clock. Many Russians are too weak to work. I am terribly sorry for them. They cannot strike or they are shot or sent to Siberia. There are heaps of enemies of the Communist within the country." But his moral outrage does not incline Jones to refuse a free air passage "from Rostov to Moscow as their guest". He is in a hurry to leave and get the truth out about the horror of state communism in Soviet Russia.

August 1930. Collectivization becomes "dekulakization" as repression in the countryside goes is in "full swing". Over 800,000 arrests, over a half million arrests with over 32,000 executions in the USSR. The communists ravaged the villages with their confiscations of grain and persecution of the peasants causing alarm in Moscow and prompting Stalin to relent from forcing peasants into collectives.

Jones withholds his doubts and credited Stalin with pushing the ravished USSR forward at the tremendous sacrifice of human lives. He cautiously tells his readers in *The Times* of London not to despair completely, and he writes, "Never-the-less great strides have been made in many industries and there is a good chance that when the Five-Years Plan is over Russia may become prosperous. But before that there will be great suffering, many riots and many deaths."

"The Communists", Jones declares, "are doing excellent work in education, hygiene and against alcohol. Butter is 16/- a pound in Moscow; prices are terrific and boots etc. cannot be had. There is nothing in the shops. The Communists were remarkably kind to me and gave me an excellent time." Jones keeps a communist propaganda postcard of smiling healthy peasant girls all "Members of the Collective Farms".

It is always the case and never a simple task that in the course of events leading to a world disaster of epic proportions that an individual has to see with his own eyes and hear with his own ears the naked unadulterated truth away from the rumors of the public press and the secrets kept in government files. Truth comes to the truth-seeker.

He's already on the trail which in three years leads him into the eye of the Terror-Famine of the Holodomor claiming its most victims in 1933. His extraordinary journey takes him across the propaganda barriers of the Consortium powers ruling the governments of the West, from America through Europe to the Kremlin and beyond into Manchuria and across the Tibetan planes of eastern China. As far as a man can see Jones had nothing to lose but his talented career and his life which he risks with the gift of his own good cheerful nature. Jones is carefree and confident, in fact, a little too careless when perhaps he ought to have been more wary when he was about to enter the lion's mouth.

As a precocious linguist Jones advanced in his brief academic career earning him the privilege to access power within the very exclusive ranks of the Foreign Office (FO) of the British Empire to become private secretary in matters of foreign relations to Lloyd George who just happens to be the former British Prime Minister (1916-22), a top-tier Pilgrim and key Consortium man who leans dangerously close to Hitler by 1935. Lloyd George had vowed to preserve the secrets privy only to the select few. Such men do not give secrets away lightly; rather they prefer to take their secrets of power to the grave making it ever so much more difficult for young men and women of a new generation to find the Truth if it is not granted to them naturally.

Serving His Majesty the King as the head of the England's government and chief of its war cabinet during the First World War Prime Minister Lloyd George was responsible as well for decisions of its government regarding foreign policy and its commercial relations of the Empire and its vast dwindling colonies and territories during the first five years of Bolshevik power. Lloyd George is one of the architects in the postwar Versailles planning commission for European reconstruction and very much aware of the British role in Bolshevik Russia. An astounding responsibility indeed, at a most exciting time of imperial statesmanship. That Jones was not able to "break the mold" in which he was cast as a promising candidate for a stellar career in the Foreign Office does not fault him for any slight of character from lack of will or impaired vision. On the contrary his eye is keen to grasp and understand what he saw. Jones has that uncanny skill that comes to the few, able to adapt with speed and acumen, deft at getting on collecting facts on wandering tours to Berlin, Moscow and the Ukraine, or taking a flight with Hitler. That he breaks the chains that bind him to the Consortium is to his credit and serves him in his journey. Later in 1935 his return to the scene of the world at war in Manchuria in the Far East will be his last great adventure. Not long after his 1933 press conference in Berlin shakes the world with the truth about starvation in the Ukraine Jones commits political suicide.

Disturbed and confused by the complexity of the tidal wave of changing cultures Jones returns the following summer to gather more eye-witness reports for a story no one wants to tell except the victims. During the years leading up to the Holodomor if Jones knew he was walking on a minefield any sign of alarm on his part might have doused the outsider's suspicion but not for long and certainly not in a land crawling with Cheka and OGPU secret police tailing virtually every foreigner or foreign correspondent. His boyish exuberance and sharp wit makes friends in dangerous places. The Ukrainian people could not have wished for much more than he is able to give in stories of the Humanity and suffering he witnessed and the lives they shared telling of their struggle to build the New Society of Soviet state socialism. We see in his writing a rare sensitivity to know and feel their joys are also his joys. When he describes their tragedy it also becomes his tragedy rarified in words but no less real and certainly no less tragic; rather, once the eye-witness makes his story known to the world it becomes all that much more real, and tragic, and never less. Which is why the taboo is so dangerous and effective to silence completely the resonances of the real and tragic reinforced and strengthened and made more clear with each utterance and sacred prayer.

PARES AND JONES: HIS MENTOR KNEW HIM WELL BUT HOW WELL DID HE?

Jones is a natural linguist. Fluent in Russian, German, French and English he took his degrees at Trinity College at Cambridge University and at the Sorbonne in Paris. It was when he was enrolled at the University of London under Sir Bernard Pares (Harrow School, Trinity College, Cambridge) that Jones falls into the orbit of fellow Welshman David Lloyd George (1916-22) assisting the wily politician as his personal Secretary to write his crusty memoirs before casting off into the world where he can easily apply his savvy skills for the Foreign Office, that elite tier of civil servants of the Empire. But Jones is neither economist, businessman or banker. Had he lived longer he most likely would have remained in the FO, most certainly in intelligence attached to an embassy. His untimely death ending a brief but brilliant adult life kept the seal of silence of Stalin's plan for collectivization and extermination of the peasants, a tragedy shadowed by another tragedy, the

Stalin Purges of the mid-thirties with more millions killed and imprisoned in the Siberian gulags recounted by Solzhenitsyn. Death silenced his voice and truth lost an ally devoted to telling the unknown horrors and missing links of the Holodomor with all its diplomatic traps and political snares of statesmanship leading to wars and groundless peace.

Pares is a romantic royalist with a 19th century liberal bent of the worst kind. Bernard Pares conceals his knowledge gained from many sources of the Terror-Famine. Bernard Pares (1867-49) is England's most prestigious Russian scholar who director of the great institution he founded, England's School of Russian Studies at Liverpool University, and at London University, where he is editor of the *Slavonic Review.* He lectures at Sarah Lawrence College and Cornell also bring him to the bosom of the Ivy League. Visiting Czarist Russia in 1898 during the reign of Nicholas II Pares makes four trips to Russia after the Revolution walking the battlefields of the Napoleonic Wars immortalized by Tolstoy's *War and Peace.*

During the First World War Pares serves as official observer to the Russian Army, with links to the staff of the British Embassy in Petrograd. During the Revolution he stays safely on the side of the Whites, riding with Kolchak's forces in the Siberia intervention, and for his services is knighted in 1919 by King George V with the KBE. After the Second World War, Pares chose to live in New York, where he finishes his autobiography, and dies, in 1949. During the writing of this book his Slavonic School in London honors Pares with a chair in Russian History in 2008.

Prof. Pares made several references to the Ukrainian famine but not by its proper name in his *History of Russia.* In two chapters, "Industrial Planning, and Agriculture Collectivized 1928-33", Pares observes peasants throwing kulaks out of their houses, writing "The kulak is the bourgeois in the village and he has to go." Pares is without remorse. He estimates the number of displaced kulaks, their families dispersed, homes and property confiscated, their lives and tradition destroyed with "as much as five millions" killed by Bolshevik henchmen. By the time of Stalin's Terror-Famine takes firm hold grinding its course on the rails of time this aging Russian scholar is set in his ways and unlikely to aid the Ukrainians or save his friend and protégé Jones. (A. Solzhenitsyn, *The Gulag Archipelago 1918-1956*, Harper & Row, 1973, transl. by Thomas Whitney; B. Pares, 101-2)

The discovery in 1994 of the Gareth Jones diaries came as a rare surprise on the occasion of the 70th memorial anniversary of the Holodomor Genocide Terror-Famine, at that moment only a few years after the US Congressional resolution on the famine in 1988 spurred on by the initiative of Dr. James Mace. Once again the light of truth exposed the terrible saga with details of history emerging as pieces of a broken mirror and now more accessible to reveal the deceitful practices of the administration of FDR's partnership with Stalin and American business and banking investment of the Nazi fascist and communist regimes when millions were sacrificed so that a few plotters could reap billions of dollars killing more millions while they restructured the world's geopolitical orientation in a monopolistic New World Order.

For years I had witnessed how America's elite Ivy League strata in the United States, families and friends of the super-rich Harvard-Princeton-Yale banking and Wall Street establishment enjoy fine liquors, expensive Cuban cigars, golf, trapping and backgammon, tucked away in their remote hideaway residences, protected behind iron-wrought gates and stone walls, as they maintain and extend their social and business networks. Many among them tend marry their own kind. That's logical given the proximity of their steady social relationships. Families and businesses thus thrive in an arrangement of interconnected of marriages. This new elite cemented in extraordinary wealth accumulated over the last 150 years might otherwise be called a conspiracy owing to the silence, deception and denial of any wrong-doing and the unavailability of details that remain inaccessible that permit it to thrive. Whether it's white Anglo-Saxon protestant (WASP) or Jewish or both, whatever you wish to call it, reader it's a matter of fact that members of the elite care very little about human life other than that in their own small world. They care more about their pet animals, for example, than they do for poor and starving populations unless they can be easily transformed into an obedient mass market for a good return on the dollar. The elite crave money more than anything to protect their status. Money likes money. Ergo, the cultural incest. These people are determined to keep power and wealth in the family and preserve it there for lasting continuity of succeeding generations.

PROPAGANDA PUNDITS: LEE, BERNAYS, PAGE, GOEBBELS & CO.

Jones walked the bridge of Anglo-American power establishment when months later he recalled his eye-witness account of the beginning of the years of terrible famine to the Wall Street insider, the corporate publicist and personal representative of JD Rockefeller, Ivy Lee. David Lloyd George sends Jones as a sort of foreign affairs specialist on personal loan. In that odd way Jones could prove to be useful to both Lee and the former PM and learn at the same time how the world really works from Wall Street to London. Perhaps then Jones would understand better what the Anglo-American Consortium is doing in Berlin and Moscow.

When the guns of August finally smash the fragile peace and launched the First World War in 1914 America's political elite is already deeply immersed in many of the customs of the British aristocracy. Consortium types such as Secretary of State Robert Lansing and the Rockefeller's agent Ivy Lee had already adopted the Victorian manners and customs of the British ruling class mimicked and suffered by the younger generation, sons of the British elite schooled at Cambridge University. Gareth Jones, nevertheless, was not inclined to be captive to style. His temperament and wit wouldn't grant that sort of concession to the upper class. Gareth comes from a modest, happy and loving home. It's not apparent that Jones with his simple Welsh family background had much of a welcome in New York's Social Register society of the rich and super rich. Nor is he a social climber and not the least bit interested in fake or superficial flamboyance or opportunistic self-aggrandisement. But Jones is clever enough to comprehend that Lee is engaged in pushing pro-Bolshevik PR for Rockefeller. Lee actually has a hand floating Bolshevik bonds for the Consortium syndicates, and he openly calls for recognition of the Soviet Union (on behalf of Rockefeller and his other clients) and investment into Nazi Germany. But Jones didn't leave much of a record to indicate what he might have known about these secret affairs of Ivy Lee inside the Pilgrim society with the Rockefeller Associates and advisors. When he arrives in the United States in 1931 he stays only briefly during the next three consecutive years, long enough to travel cross country, to meet Randolph Hearst in California, write, and move on.

From the beginning the Rockefellers and oil defined the 20th century. Wars for oil mark American foreign policy and lead to the First World War. No industrial power can survive without it. Lenin and Stalin depend on it for their industrialization to bulwark their communist experiment. It financed American politics and built the Great White Fleet under Whitney and Teddy Roosevelt at a cost of $100 million for all the sixteen warships, a hefty price when the annual budget for the Navy in 1900 is only $55 million. (A generation later one battleship will cost $250 million.)

Rockefeller oil ruled the world and with it America surpassed the British and French empires and quickly seize both German and Russian oil deposits. The Rockefellers use that oil and money to manufacture educational propaganda and finance medical institutions all of which were intended to extend their controlling interests. Their objective was not to save Humanity but to create and develop social institutions and resources closely affiliated with government to construct a homogenous American society while extending and maintaining their control over political leaders, governments and international nations.

David Lloyd George is not immune. Nor is he oblivious to the enormous power of the Rockefeller oil monopoly. He sends Gareth Jones to Rockefeller but not to save the Ukrainians. Not at all. It would have been, however, a most interesting meeting had Jones sat down with the Rockefellers to discuss the Soviet -Ukrainian problem. Men make history. This famine is man-made. Rockefeller has the potential to move the world for industry and Humanity. Jones never made that rendezvous.

Rockerfeller has a different agenda for Russia and the Ukraine. Rockefeller Soviet oil wells drill the earth in Baku and the Caucasus. The vast rich grain fields south of Kiev traversed by machines from Caterpillar, Deering and Ford became wastelands of death. And the once robust and healthy Ukrainian peasants bound to their soil over centuries starve looking like ghosts. In a few years these same fields bleed red as Soviet tanks fight desperately to stop the Nazi advance to Stalingrad and Moscow. Rockefeller money is everywhere. Is Lloyd-George on the take too? Reader you know now it would be inane and naive not to think so, now wouldn't it? And one can play the fool just so long…

Gareth Jones arrives at Wall Street on January 1st, 1931. A curious place for the foreign affairs specialist to celebrate the New Year after a year with the former British prime minister. He walks straight into Ivy Lee's inner sanctum. Thinking that he was on top of the world would make it even darker than hell. If he had a secret agenda no one had revealed it. Jones was no fool. Neither were his friends and adversaries. He had access to the entire US-Soviet economic club of investors right there. There wasn't anyone he couldn't get to if he had to. In easy reach are the Amtorg Trading Company 1927-32 files on US-Soviet trade as well as sensitive files on Otto Kahn and many more invaluable sources to explain the Bolshevik undercover political and financial operations in America. Remember, Jones was picked by Lloyd George because of his sharp mind and skills invaluable for the Foreign Service. Apparently he needs some practical experience on the field out in the real world. At least this how he is perceived by his peers. Is Jones a spy? Who is to know? How much does Jones really learn inside Lee & Associates? He is a very clever and privileged young man to be granted this kind of access, indeed.

The Consortium works inside and outside government. It has their channels everywhere like tentacles on a giant octopus. Their players changed hats and roles as often as the signs on the door. Lawyers and bankers leave their companies for jobs in government passing through the revolving door and *vice versa.* They talked the talk, they walked the walk. Once you're in, you're set for life, career, women, children, clubs, schools ... It's all so wonderful, every morning a blissful serenity of happiness and security and knowing that you and your kind control the world. At least that is, until the center cannot hold and hell breaks loose. Was Lee & Associates an intelligence front for the Consortium? The Game is the same the world over. One world, one Consortium, one Game.

Gareth visits Russia and Ukraine on at least three occasions. Each time he wrote articles for a number of newspapers regarding conditions in that country and the Five-Year Plans. As early as 1930, Gareth Jones grasped that the innocent and decent hard-working poor Ukrainian farm population were the tragic victims of "trade and politics" linked to the business of international bankers. But he doesn't write about American companies financing Stalin. Instead, Jones wings it on his own. Again, he will seek adventure and see for himself. How far would he go before he came back from the cold? Even if he were a mysterious intelligence agent of some sort there are times when no one can protect and he never lived to tell.

The year before Jones arrives in New York as a sort of political emissary – (what is this, really, friend to friend, favor for favor, or what?) –, Lee actually does publicity work for Lloyd George on Anglo-American relations. Ah, the smell of Rockefeller money... There could be no doubting that Jones realized he had been sent straight towards the center of the nervous system of America's brash capitalism, the subject of many of his articles that began with JDR himself when a dime is a dime and don't you ever forget that!, kid.

Unfortunately, as smart as he is, Jones is not the conceited sort or extrovert in a way to display the bravado of daring to appear to know the exact nature of the place. His intentions would be just approximations. The Consortium restricts access to the epicenter. Had Lloyd George told Jones of the Rockefeller-Stalin connection? Might he have acted any differently?

If Jones were to find out more about the secret dealings between the Consortium and the Soviet regime through Armtorg and other channels London and New York are the two places to search. Gareth Jones now has very powerful connections to the New York and London centers of the world power. Lloyd George most certainly tells Gareth Jones very little of what he knew about the secrets of Anglo-Soviet trade. Lee carefully maintains his London connections in the City, London's elite financial district, and a world of imperial intrigue more sophisticated and discreet than New York. Was Jones duped or playing a double game of concealment? Certainly Jones knew or at least had good reason and experience to suspect the pernicious and pervasive influence of the international banker cartel. He will soon learn for himself. Lee is the master spinner of corporate evils but Jones didn't put it all together. He is a man on a mission, linked directly to the Rockefeller labyrinth of Wall Street power. Jones had one foot firmly placed in the middle of Consortium and the other in the inner circle of London's post war empire.

Jones lived long enough to be influential even in these dark times, shining like a flash but he burned out too quickly flaming across the night sky. He was a good writer and journalist with a flair for capturing the heart and soul of the peasants besieged by Stalin's the Five Year Plans How useful could he be to the Consortium was yet to be proven. So far he had shown promise but had accomplished little to prove his worth. Would he ever more than a tool of the billionaires?

Now that Lloyd George sent Jones to New York he possessed a unique inside track within the publicity firm Ivy Lee Associates. How does he use this stepping stone to enormous corporate power symbolized by the towering office buildings of glass and concrete with shaking fortunes and tumbling stocks? By the end of the year Mellon has left Treasury for London and the Court of St. James and a swelling government deficit soon to pass $2 billion making the former President Calvin Coolidge cringe with fiscal pain, especially after he takes a five-figure loss selling his Standard Brands "depression-food" stock recommended by his close friend Dwight Morrow. GM Motors founder W. C. Durant denounces Mellon for pushing up the Fed's interest rates causing the crash. *The Wall Street Journal* declares, "the board's fault was in leaning backwards in its desire not to penalize business by high commercial money rates." (Amity Shlaes, NY: Harpers, 2013, 440)

Lee is considered in America as the founder of the concept of public relations. If anyone could do a whitewash on Stalin's crimes, it would be Ivy Lee. Lee was still the Rockefeller family's personal agent and J. D. Rockefeller, Jr.'s personal PR man for his image in the press and damage control. Besides Rockefeller, Lee's clients comprised a veritable *Who's Who* of the New York, Boston and Philadelphia Social Register, those cardinal anthologies as precious as Bibles of the Consortium society that Lee served since he created Ivy Lee Associates to broaden his reputation into the Rockefeller business and banking universe. With his own company Lee could further Rockefeller's interests while serving his own on a client basis and keep the billionaire and his family out of the spotlight. Lee's clients, mostly Pilgrims and CFR clans weaved their business and family lines together like a Gordian knot. Odd that Jones did not harbor a deep suspicion of the wealthy capitalist. It was not his nature. Jones was not the type to be intimidated. His instincts fathomed more humor than fear.

Because of his work promoting the Soviet Union's socialist economy, whether to build railroads or sell Bolshevik bonds on the Street, Lee could afford to be tagged a "Wall Street Bolshevik" along with fellow Consortium bigwig William B. Thompson of the New York Federal Reserve, while all the time promoting the interests of the Consortium first and foremost. Jones ignores Lee's Soviet investments instead of making them the object of a literary investigation. They don't appear to figure into his calculations concerning the Holodomor. Jones is careful not to attack the Consortium, at least not directly. But he came dangerously close. By exposing the Terror-Famine and his appeal to Humanity sickened the greedy warmongers bent on setting the world on fire again with another world war. In New York, Gareth Jones has the rare opportunity to observe Lee going about his business investing in dictators.

Ivy Lee seldom needs an introduction. He can sit down with any president or dictator in the world and readily present his business card. Stalin, Hitler, Mussolini. No problem there. Lee knows the top bankers of the Bolsheviks and their most powerful business partners on Wall Street. The White House is at his finger tips. So is every alumni benefactor of Princeton, his alma mata. Government officials at the highest level at State, Commerce and the Treasury always return a call from Ivy Lee. At the same time Jones steps into Lee's office, Prescott Bush celebrated his first days as a partner in Brown Brothers Harriman and Company and promptly bought an eight bedroom mansion. Lee too has too many secrets and a great deal of moral anguish.

Stalin tries to throw a blanket of silence over his terror of collectivization against the Ukrainian rural population but the truth invariably leaks out. Was it accident or fate how the public in the West first learned of the famine from the eyes and voice of a young Brit college boy who by able skill and sound wit managed to become special assistant to the British Prime Minister and who, was sent as his special representative to America where he would surely be able to give all the sordid details of the famine to Ivy Lee, head of the Rockefeller press network. Quite an extraordinary sequence of connections indeed for a young man with socialist ideals to lessen the burden of the oppressed!. But the man who whitewashed Rockefeller's massacre of immigrant miners in Colorado in 1914 including women and children, Lee, now nearly twenty years later is not interested in starving or dead Ukrainians. After examining certain records of Lee we don't need to second-guess why.

Who was Lee? The son of a southern minister like his mentor Woodrow Wilson, Ivy Ledbetter Lee was born in Cedartown, Georgia on July 16, 1877. A Rockefeller man all his life he dies in 1934 defending his work for Hitler's Nazis fascism and dictatorship. His mother was Emma Eufaula Ledbetter Lee and his father the Reverend Dr. James Wideman Lee was a well-known southern Methodist respected in those parts. Lee marries Cornelia Bartlett Bigelow in 1901. The couple have three children: Alice Lee (Cudlipp) in 1902, James Wideman Lee II in 1906, and Ivy Lee, Jr. in 1909. He passed his childhood in Atlanta, burned to the ground by General Sherman's Yankee army from the North during the American Civil War a decade before he was born. Lee attends Emory College before transferring north to Princeton when Woodrow Wilson, another southerner and minister's son, is the university President. Lee graduates in1898, a momentous year for Americans in Guilded Age millionaires swept up in the patriotic nationalist frenzy of the Spanish-American War. America seizes Cuba, the Philippines and Puerto Rico and claimed the rights of Empire now cast in sacred words of Democracy. At Yale this same year graduating contemporaries of his generation included Bonesmen Clifford Dudley Cheney, Payne Whitney, both members of that very rich and secretive in-crowd with Alfred Gwynne Vanderbilt and William Fitzhugh Whitehouse of the Class of 1899 (a family tradition honored by Edwin Sheldon Whitehouse 1905, Charles Sheldon Whitehouse, 1947, Sheldon Whitehouse, 1977, the former Attorney General of Rhodes Island and at present US Senator. Harry Payne Whitney (Bones 1894) marries Gertrude Vanderbilt; in 1912, Vanderbilt and Whitney figure among the largest of American fortunes listed in the Money Trust.

Lacking intimate connections, family background, or property or capital, Ivy Lee was not born to find himself privy to the elite world of Princeton clubs and estates nor figure among the prominent names of guest lists to their parties. Instead, Lee became their willing servant, a sharp-edged tool eager and ready to adjust the capitalist machine seamlessly and always in the spirit of serving "the public good" as they define it, and carrying the "White Man's Burden" farther down the road of progress and development.

Rising high above his humble beginnings, Lee learns quickly how to be a fixer, quite agile at wearing a confident smile and dash away the negative with a tricky phrase and distracting jest. Public relations work is a very serious instrument in corporate America where the public jumps like trained animals in a circus over the latest trifle or sensation. Clients paid big money then, thousands of dollars for his skill to spin a web of lies to beguile the public. At Princeton Lee is active on the college newspaper, won the Lynde debate prize, and participates in heated discussions over the controversy of private dining clubs and whether Princeton's President Wilson should abolish elitism on campus, not an easy thing for Wilson negotiating endowments from the fabulously rich Pynes of National City Bank money who when they weren't at Princeton might be found in the plush county of Somerset Hills with Senator Rivington Pyne at the Essex Hunt Club, all very much a perfect upper class English setting of stone and ivy Tudor estates adorned with blood hounds and thoroughbreds.

Throughout his life Lee remains a dedicated Princeton man, serving Princeton's President in the White House, handled PR for Morgan banker H. P. Davison's Red Cross work and the Kuhn Loeb-Harriman-Rockefeller brief nationalization of railroads during America's entry into WWI. It really didn't matter who he served. Democrats are virtually the same as Republicans to Ivy Lee as long as they're rich and powerful. Lee excels as a key fund-raiser, and that too, served him well with his corporate client contact list. After all, Lee learned fast how the world really worked. And he is well rewarded for doing his bit. Everyone who was anyone knew Ivy Lee. He was, after all, their kind of man. Lee made it his job to know them, too. I know something about the Princeton culture with close family there, like the Townend brothers; Uncle Frank was a four star US Army general, a lawyer with General Patton's commanding staff during WWII; his younger brother Hank was on a famous Princeton football team in the late thirties. Lawyer Frank Townend never missed a Princeton football game and jotted down every play in his tiny breast-pocket notebook.

The young Ivy Lee does post-graduate work at Harvard and Columbia but leaves to try newspaper work as a journalist learning the ropes at *The New York American*, *The New York Times*, and *The New York World*. Lee prefers to write about business and financial affairs. In 1903 J. P. Morgan and James J. Hill charted a new company to combine the Northern and Northern Pacific railroads with combined assets of over $400 million. The case of Northern Securities against the US government went to the Supreme Court. In 1904, the company lost a narrow 5-4 decision. Only two years on the Supreme Court Oliver Wendell Holmes writes the dissenting opinion. Holmes' appointment originally had been suggested to TR by Senator Lodge as a replacement of Horace Gray who resigned. Holmes stays on until 1932, and dies three years later, age 94.

Chief Justice Holmes was Harvard trained, College and Law, had served 20 years on the Massachusetts Supreme Court and eventually became Chief Justice. A veteran of the Civil War with three years in the 20th Massachusetts Volunteer Infantry called the "Harvard volunteers", he fought at Antietam, scene of the bloodiest battle ever in American history with 25,000 men killed in a single day, and at Fredericksburg. That day in 1931 on a jaunt with Stimson during one of their many delightful walks he tells the story how he had shouted to save Lincoln from taking a bullet. Holmes shares almost a mythical connection with America's roots even if it were true. Many families still have living grandparents born before the Civil War, sons and daughters of the American Revolution. The American nation was the youngest of the super powers, built with slave labor. Even the White House opened in 1880 was built by slaves from Africa. It's an ignominious history. On Inauguration Day 1933, the newly elected President breaks with official protocol and visits Holmes at his home and tells the new President a story about his father and Aaron Burr, Vice President of the US and author of the Federalist Papers. Holmes is a legend in his day, a living icon of shared American history, and shadowed lesser men such as the Consortium operators behind Roosevelt, he, too, a giant among men yet confined to a wheelchair. From the Lees of the world to the Rockefellers, Rothschilds and Roosevelts who now promote the Soviet communist collectivization and industrialization of slave labor and terror to sustain it their global interests, these reflections of America's past may have seemed to Stimson, himself no stranger to total war, signs of distant memories from another world far away.

Lee's first work in public relations came in 1903 as publicity manager for the Citizens' Union. He authored the textbook *The Best Administration New York*

City Ever Had used in Seth Low's unsuccessful campaign for mayor in New York. Before opening his first public relations firm in 1905, Lee took a job as a press agent for the Democratic National Committee. His partner George Parker provides the connections and Lee the brains. In this era of muckraking journalism, Lee sees the immediate benefit public relations work for Big Business believing if people are presented with all the facts on both sides of an issue they would not come down so harshly on business interests. Lee reinvents his role to interpret the public good to industrialists and the humanize the industrialist for the people. To achieve that end Lee believes in supplying the newspapers with as much information as possible. He's a newspaper man and his clients own the newspapers.

His "Declaration of Principles" drafted during the anthracite coal strike in the spring of 1906 explain the guiding precepts of his public relations theory that become hallmark in capitalist America. Lee sets out to find the facts that please his employers no different in kind than a proprietary company product and manage their distribution. It works and his employers rejoice.

Another opportunity to practice these principles came with work for the Pennsylvania Railroad, in 1906, said to be one of the most notoriously corrupt corporations in the country. The railroad's policy of refusing reporters access to all accident sites or granting interviews leaves owners and directors closing their doors to snooping journalists. Lee turns round the table to spin off the enmity and mistrust shared by reporters spurned for doing their work on behalf of the general public. Lee sees his role as a perfect job opportunity for the right man who knows how to give the press a good story.

Lee studies the company during a 40-day cross-country railroad trip in 1907 and records his observations in "A Trip Over the Harriman Railroads" (Union Pacific, Southern Pacific, Oregon Railroad, Oregon Shortline). Lee immediately smoothes over his reporting with frequent updates and arranges for reporters to travel to accident sites. Lee is so good at selling PR and whitewashing dirty companies with poor labor relations that the owners at Pennsylvania Railroad hire him full-time to direct their publicity business. Until the end of his life Lee remains a dedicated railroad man and his devotion seals his career in good graces of the ruling class of the all-powerful Morgans, Rockefellers, and Harrimans. Ambitious, smart and a good word twister not unlike his God-fearing father, Lee rapidly fulfills his upwardly mobile ambitions; by 1913, a year before WWI, Lee becomes the Pennsylvania Railroad's president executive assistant. Much of Lee's time is spent countering bad news over high freight rates and allegations of price-fixing between the railroad barons.

The dominant position in oil in America had been gained by a gangsterism that would make today's boardroom battles look like harmless fairy tales. Special railroad rates and rebates extracted by the railroad cartel also plays an important role in wiping out competition. In the process the railroads were notorious for practicing unsavory business methods ranging from theft to slaughter, not uncustomary in business for that era of pioneer industrial expansion. The immense fortune of the Rockefellers originally came from the Standard Oil Company. With tremendous skill Rockefeller built it into the powerful oil monopoly.

By 1915, the Standard Oil is producing nearly a third of the oil yield of the United States. Rockefeller wants a complete monopoly of the domestic American oil business. Lee targets Rockefeller. He adopts and defends their scheme of things as his own, and defines capitalism that preserves and extends their domination over American industry, the workingman, and the federal government. The writer Kris Milligan researched Rockefeller's wealth and studied his practices to accumulate it. He writes, "Rivals who were less successful in the application of the identical methods used by the Standard Oil Company, organized the 'liberals' and the 'socially minded', the social service cliques of that era, together with the demagogues, politicians, and crooked newspapers, for another type of battle on their successful competitor – commercial blackmail." (see Kris Milligan on the Internet)

Long before Lee came around to fix things Rockefeller is no stranger to bad publicity. For decades Rockefeller and Standard Oil are the target of reform-minded muckrakers. After President McKinley's assassination, public opinion forces Teddy Roosevelt who replaced McKinley – a Rockefeller puppet– to move against the trusts. President Teddy balks, weary of risking his political future. TR likened legislation drafted to stop the cartels would be "as effective as a papal bull against a comet." As resentment against the Oil Trust grew, politicians stood waiting for Standard Oil money, tying up the oil interests through "strike bills" but are harassed by investigations and court actions. The socialist muckrakers, church organizations and social service groups make their own investigations of Rockefeller monopoly control of workers' lives and communities in "company towns" obliged to live in ramshackled huts where "the Company" owned everything from the food they are forced to buy to the clothes on their backs. President Theodore Roosevelt, plays up to the public gallery attacking Standard Oil with one hand and with the other taking Standard's political campaign money.

Nevertheless, by 1907, six states went after Standard Oil, most notably Standard Oil of Indiana, indicted under the Elkins Act (1903) for taking bribes from the Chicago and Alton Railroad. In August 1907, Judge Landis of Chicago fines Standard Oil $29.24 million but the decision is overturned easily after the bankers and oil men hit back provoking the financial panic of 1907. HP Davison and JP Morgan personally intervene to save New York City from bankruptcy as well as saving Standard Oil. Four years later, in 1911 during the Taft presidency, the Supreme Court orders the dissolution of Standard Oil, an ironic windfall for Rockefeller and his partners. To calm public anger, the US Department of Justice also files seven suits of its own. In May 1911, Supreme Court Chief Justice White breaks up the Standard Oil Trust into 39 separate companies. The public outcry over Rockefeller's oil monopoly makes him a favorite item in the press. Robert Minor's famous cartoons in the *St. Louis-Dispatch* soon after are appearing in downtown Manhattan in *The Masses* with articles by Max Eastman and John Reed. One cartoon titled "A Hazardous Business" from the *New York World* depicts Rockefeller tiptoeing across a tightrope that says "Anti-Trust Law", and pushing a wheelbarrow with a money bag holding $400 million, and carrying a golf bag on his back. Another shows the billionaire hitting a golf ball out of a deep $29 million sand trap, suggesting Rockefeller could have anyone bribed and always evades prosecution. Ivy Lee counters the bad press setting a trend of Rockefeller style, for instance, staging films of the frail old man JDR, Sr. giving dimes to children when a movie cost a nickle.

Before he linked up with the Rockefeller crowd Lee takes his young family to Europe in the summer of 1910 where he arranges to open European offices for the investment firm of Harris, Winthrop, and Company. From then on Lee followed his client's interests and kept close ties with England. He emulates British traditions and customs, modifies his speech to mimic Elizabethan English, that distinct British art of elocution and all things Gothic, including cathedrals. Returning there late 1911 Lee delivers a series of business lectures at the London School of Economics on railroad investments and moves easily among his deep-pocketed listeners. As a member and host speaker of the Royal Institute of International Relations in London until his premature death in the thirties he keeps close ties with his London friends during the Holodomor years. Lee also joins the Royal Economic Society as does his son James.

Lee has considerable knowledge of financial matters from his days as a Wall Street reporter and his work for Harris, Winthrop & Co. takes him down the yellow brick road only that his is paved with gold of choice clients in the financial world readily opening their doors. Otto Kahn of Loeb & Co. (1916-31), for example, is an early client enlisting Lee Associates to handle to publicity, and speech writing.

Lee's approach to greater transparency and friendliness to the press, cultivating journalists and showing special favor also results in publishing publicity and investor information for his client's investors. It was not uncommon for Lee Associates, be it only a part of his activities, to produce a bulletin on European and foreign commercial affairs for Bankers Trust (1920-27). Other key clients include H. Davison's Liberty National Bank (1920-21), the forerunner of the NY Trust (1921-46), Speyer & Co., Dillon Read, Frazier Jelke, Kuhn Loeb .... The Ivy Lee Collection in the Mudd Library at Princeton is a goldmine awaiting the conscientious historian.

From New York to London Lee is a welcome face among the Consortium crowd. Lee's connection to Kuhn, Loeb & Co. is not at all incidental but, in fact, central to the Holodomor story though the actors are on the fringe. Kuhn, Loeb is a financial firm pivotal in the interconnected network at the center of power in America. Lee is their hired gun. He's positioned to make their corporate activities palatable to the working class and so an essential part of the main stream running through the new mythic culture transformed and enriched in the course of decades through the creative genius of demonstratively gifted individuals. These men are responsible for determining both private corporate and financial strategies as well as formulating national and international policies affecting government decisions at the highest level. They work inside and outside government channels and often pass through the revolving doors connecting them. In a world where money arbitrates decision-making, policy planning and social issues become especially complicated for public understanding of a democracy in practice. It is all an integrated network. Lee's mission is to keep the story simple and clearly in their favor to assure the corporations and their leaders look good with the appearance that the interests of American working men and women are always close to their hearts.

Lee is the privileged insider. He is paid to know how the real world of the Consortium seizes new opportunities, preserves its interests, prospers and ensures its continuity. Lee knows what to tell and not tell the public.

From the start everything known about Ivy Lee, properly speaking, ought to make it clear reader that he knows perfectly well before the Great War ends how the postwar New World Order would be set up. Lee works daily with the very same people who financed Trotsky and Lenin's Bolsheviks. Wall Street was his life. He understood how Wall Street financed Hoover and FDR as well as bankrolled Stalin's industrialization and collectivization Five Year Plans. The men behind FDR are foremost high on Ivy Lee's client list. They had the same friends, moved in the same orbit, were often seen together at the same clubs, trading visiting cards, clients, sharing drinks and cigars, and sometimes wives. The same men who for many years back Roosevelt's career lead him to spark his presidential ambitions and New Deal socialism. It is same the bridge across which all men of power walk in doing business with Stalin.

The kind of work Lee fashioned for Rockefeller reflects what he did for the Consortium during the Holodomor years which precipitated and directly contributed to the humanitarian catastrophe. Lee grooms the Consortium how to appear on the side of justice and law, their side, the stronger side, the side with all the money and power that thrives in war and destruction and deceit stripping Humanity of its common shared values for decency and cultural traditions that preserve rather than destroy the integrity of the human spirit and Mother Earth, that force of creation that is antithetical to the evil will and mental dementia of the most cruel, selfish and immoral architects of the world.

There is no need to dwell further on the earlier history before the Holodomor years. The desire to know the origin of Lee's beginnings is also characteristic of understanding his ends. Lee's reputation catches the attention of the Rockefellers, father *and* son. He is asked to remake the image of John D. Rockefeller, Jr. (1874-60) stained in the press outraged over dozens of murdered strikers, killed and burned along with women and children at the Rockefeller-owned Colorado Fuel & Oil Company mines and the infamous Ludlow Massacre of 1914. The United Mine Workers had asked for higher wages and better living conditions for the miners. Mostly illiterate and ethnic immigrants from Europe' s poorest countries, they lived in shacks provided by the company at exorbitant rent. Their low wages ($1.68 a day) were paid in "script" redeemable only at company stores charging high prices. The churches were the pastorates of company-hired ministers; their children were taught in company-controlled schools; company libraries excluded books that the Rockefellers deemed "subversive", such as *Darwin's Origin of the Species* which might give them the wrong ideas of how the rich and powerful survive and dominate the weak and feeble-minded lower forms of life unable to adapt in violent, predatory and aggressively hostile environments.

The Colorado Fuel & Oil company maintains a force of detectives, mine guards, and spies to quarantine the camp from unions and socialists. When the miners struck, JDR, Jr., then officially in command of the company, and the Baptist Reverend Frederick T. Gates, a director of the Rockefeller Foundation, refuse to negotiate. They order the strikers evicted from the company-owned shacks, and called in a thousand strike-breakers from the Baldwin-Felts detective agency. The mine-owners instruct Governor Ammons to call out the National Guard to help break the strike. Violence erupted. Guardsmen, miners, their women and children, who since their eviction camp in tents, are ruthlessly killed, in the conflict that rages out of control until the frightened Governor wires President Wilson for Federal Troops which crush the strike. *The New York Times*, report on April 21, 1914: "A 14-hour battle between striking coal miners and members of the Colorado National Guard in the Ludlow district today culminated in the killing of Louis Tikas, leader of the Greek strikers, and the destruction of the Ludlow tent colony by fire."

The following day *The NYT* reports: "Forty five dead (32 of them women and children), a score missing and more than a score wounded is the known result of the 14 hour battle which raged between state troops and coal miners in the Ludlow district, on the property of the Colorado Fuel and Iron Company, the Rockefeller holding. The Ludlow is a mass of charred debris, and buried beneath it is a story of horror unparalleled in the history of industrial warfare. In the holes that had been dug for their protection against rifle fire, the women and children died like trapped rats as the flames swept over them. One pit uncovered this afternoon disclosed the bodies of ten children and two women."

During the Ludlow strike, Rockefeller called in the local National Guard to bust it, mostly company thugs with guns, killing fifty-three people, including 13 of the miners wives and children. Muckrakers screamed for blood, calling Rockefeller a murderer. The public protested outside his home. Massive strikes and boycotts organized against all of Rockefeller's companies. The young journalist John Reed visits the camps and writes a series about Ludlow and Rockefeller's assault on the miners and their destitute families. It was a war of the richest capitalist against the oppressed in America; the drama will play out again in the USSR with Rockefeller's Consortium hidden in the shadow of Stalin but this time in the thirties millions perish.

The Ludlow massacre is not a spurious incident in Consortium affairs. National headlines shake the country. John Reed's story with interviews of survivors provoke a seething reaction hostile to Rockefeller personally and his violent exploitation of oppressed American workers by the ruling capitalist of money barons and the politicians they can easily buy for dollars. Reed makes it clear that from Ludlow and elsewhere across America that the denial of justice by violent repression of working immigrants and other citizens forced to live in intolerable conditions with their basic legal rights denied is odious and anathema to the American democratic experience.

Two decades later Democrat Senator Harry S. Truman wins votes echoing the violent repression of worker rights during the Depression years recalling the Ludlow massacre.

It is of interest to note that Truman denounces not the Consortium or an organized mafia of unseen power, but "wild greed", and he declares, "We worship money instead of honor. A billionaire, in our estimation, is much greater in these days in the eyes of the people than the public servant who works for public interest. It makes no difference if the billionaire rode to wealth on the sweat of little children and the blood of underpaid labor. No one ever considered Carnegie libraries stepped in the blood of the Homestead steelworkers, but they are. We do not remember that the Rockefeller Foundation is founded on the dead miners of the Colorado Fuel & Iron Company and a dozen other similar performers. We worship Mammon; and until we go back to ancient fundamentals and return to the Giver of the Tables of Law and His teachings, these conditions are going to remain with us. It is a pity that Wall Street, with its ability to control all the wealth of the nation and to hire the best law brains in the country, has not produced some statement, some men who could see the dangers of big business and of the concentration of the control of wealth. Instead of working to meet the situation, they are employing the best law brains to serve greed and self interest. People can stand only so much, and one of these days there will be a settlement.... Wild greed along the lines I have been describing brought on the Depression. When investment bankers, so-called, continually load great transportation companies with debt in order to sell securities to savings banks and insurance companies so they can make a commission, the well finally runs dry.... There is no magic solution to the condition of the railroads, but one thing is certain, – no formula, however scientific, will work without men of proper character, responsible for physical and financial operations of the roads and for the administration of the laws provided by Congress." (D. McCullough, *Truman*, citing *The New York Times*, Dec. 21 1937,1)

The master of spin helps the Rockefeller family out of this nightmarish debacle. Ivy Lee came to the rescue of Rockefeller's image transforming the dark horse into a white knight as he turns annihilation and destruction into a new beginning. Lee popularizes techniques that are quickly adapted as theorems for consumer marketing to humanize the capitalist avarice whether it be turn-of-the-century robber barons or contemporary corporate raiders and market speculators pirating mind-boggling sums. Soon everyone dreamed of the prophetic promise of prosperity and the potential to become a Rockefeller. By the twenties the frenzy of unlimited speculation and wanton greed bloated the financial and investment markets until the paper bubble burst in the big crash of '29.

Lee is hired as the Rockefellers publicist and paid $12,000. He carefully stages photo ops using only positive images of the old man Rockefeller mixing with his miners in another town and dancing with their wives, and kissing their kids. All filmed with authorized press releases ready to print. In fact, it is Lee who comes up with the ploy of handing out dimes to the kids making sure only positive pictures appear in press. Since JDR likes to play nine holes of golf every day, Lee gets the pictures released to the public. The billionaire looks human after all. Lee also produces pictures of JDR reading the Bible to young girls, apparently one of his favorite pastimes. He fed the propaganda into the news and the people bought it! Lee saved the day. It was a brilliant coup that turns the Rockefeller family into an American icon of world prestige. Then the Great War of 1914 burst on the front page, a capitalist war of clashing empires killing millions of workers inflamed with patriotic propaganda. The spin-masters were kept busy at their typewriters manufacturing the news selling the papers and making fortunes for the owners with God on their side and the son of a minister as their President fighting "to save democracy".

What concerns us here too is that JDR, Sr. credits the Lord Almighty for his good fortune. So much grace must be a God-given thing. "I believe that the power to make money is a gift from God." And he concludes that his earnings should be used for "the good of my fellow man … according to my conscience." Rockefeller truly believes he is blessed, but he never is quite able to clarify the connection between wealth and grace. Lee throws in a few dimes and some good press, and God does the rest. Reader, are we to believe in these new rites? Lee must be blessed too? Then, it logically follows with the same result of Lee's sacred press later for Hitler and Stalin? Were they all blessed and part of some new sacred ritual of mythic proportions in which the villains acquire a new mode of being with all the accompaniment of culture worship? In other words, it is possible to think and feel it so. This was his error and spells his doom.

Lee observes human behavior, and exploits the weak and defenseless. With his cunning and educated intelligence, he lies and manipulates the ignorant and illiterate converting the angry mob into adoring worshipers of wealth and greed. Since everyone is human, why not exploit it with the most base and primitive emotions and let them all swim in their own soup?

It works. From Princeton College to New York City gutter politics his experience had taught him well. Lee is successful and he profits handsomely. This is the man to whom the equally cunning wartime British prime minister, and most probably a London acquaintance, David Lloyd George, sends the young and talented foreign office specialist and linguist Gareth Jones. When Lee finished with his spins and lies, he lied some more. In fact, he never stops lying until he dies with a Nazi swastika burning on his forehead (it was a medal from Goebbels and Hitler). And the Ukrainians die starving with their hands raised to the sky asking for God's Holy Grace and maybe an answer why the Americans are not coming to help them in 1932, or 1933, or 1934, not when they came in 1919.

We should add that when Lee learns that the newly organized Rockefeller Foundation has $100 million lying around for promotional (re-generational) purposes without knowing what to do with it he goes to them with a plan to donate large sums - none less than a million- to well known colleges, hospitals, churches and benevolent organizations spreading the wealth in Rockefeller's name. The Rockefeller men and Society women love it! The plan is accepted. So are the millions. Together, the men with the millions make headlines all over the world, powerful rich and humane philanthropists helping the oppressed poor.

An end to oppression and the irksome struggle of the classes against capitalism! Remember reader, in these days of the gold standard and the five cent cigar there is a maxim in known to every newspaperman that a million dollars is always news. (Morris A. Bealle, *The Drug Story*; Emanuel M. Josephson, *The Strange Death of Franklin D. Roosevelt: A History of the Roosevelt-Delano Dynasty America's Royal Family*, Chedney Press, 1948)

For years Rockefeller knows how to handle the welfare liberal crowd, buying them off into complicit obedience, funding their church activities, taking them over one by one, or in one great sweep, including the radical church element, the Federation of Churches. Enter Reverend Gates and the Rockefeller "philanthropies". In 1937, Rockefeller Center, branded the "Eighth Wonder of the World", a commercial "Square" in the center of Manhattan nears completion. With the family fortune insulated from inheritance taxes and preserved for eternity John D. Rockefeller Sr. had become not only the richest man in the world but succeeded in adding to his fame as the greatest philanthropist ever in America giving away some $530 in addition to $537 million already given away by his son added to some $540 million passed through other Rockefeller philanthropies; over the weekend May 22 JDR, Sr. motors 40 miles, sits in his garden "comfortably for four hours", and that night asleep in his bed dies just before dawn on Sunday May 23, 1937. His daughter Abby writes her sister the next day, "really, it was a beautiful ending ... a remarkable record". (Peter Collier and David Horowitz, *The Rockefellers, An American Dynasty*, NY: Holt, Rinehart and Winston, 1976, 177; Ron Chernow, *Titan, The Life of John D. Rockefeller, Sr.*, NY: Random House, 566)

In fact the entire Rockefeller Empire constitutes an impregnable fortress of ultimate protection from government prying or unfriendly public will. The Rockefeller gifts are conceived for the dual purpose of taking the curse of the Rockefeller name and enabling the Rockefeller-Standard Oil interests to carry on without interference from a hostile public or the government. Historian Ferdinand Lundberg writes "The family today. is no slighter degree than two or three centuries ago in imperial Rome, is supreme in the governance of wealth – amassing it, standing watch over it, and keeping it intact from generation to generation. Because it is (unlike that relatively new device, the corporation) a private entity which in the strictest legality may resist public scrutiny, the family lends itself admirably to alliances of a formal character and serves as an instrument for confidential financial transaction. By definition, the family is a sacrosanct institution, and no agency of government may pry into it without offending inculcated prejudice.... The family alone provides a safe retreat from democratic processes, not outside the law, but above the law." (P. Collier and D. Horowitz, 179)

One can hardly expect a man of Rockefeller's efficiency and financial ability to fail to expect to profit royally from the disarming advantages of a "philanthropic" front. That Rockefeller realized the profitable business possibilities of a "philanthropic" set-up is indicated by an interesting and revealing story told of the inception of the plan to buy public opinion and confound his most defiant detractors.

The plan is initiated by Rev. Frederick Taylor Gates who has won John's D.'s respect by his sharpness clothed with piety. Rockefeller profits nicely from deals engineered by Gates through religious activities as an executive officer of the American Baptist Education Society. Especially appreciated is his aid in gaining control for a pittance of the Mesabi Mines, one of the richest iron deposits in the country. It nets many millions of dollars when later incorporated into U. S. Steel. In *John D. Rockefeller, A Portrait In Oil* author John K. Winkler quoting JDR, Sr. tells us: "Fred Gates was a wonderful business man,' says John D. with satisfaction. 'His work for the American Baptist Education Society required him to travel extensively. Once, as he was going south, I asked him to look into an iron mill in which I had an interest. His report was a model of clarity! Then I asked him to make some investigation of other property in the west. I had been told this particular company was rolling in wealth. Mr. Gates' report showed that I had been deceived. Now I realize that I had met a commercial genius. I persuaded Mr. Gates to become a man of business." (E. M. Josephson, *The Strange Death of Franklin D. Roosevelt*; John K. Winkler, *John D. Rockefeller, A Portrait In Oil,* Kessinger, 2005)

If religion helped net Gates inordinately large profits in his dealings with his fellow men, the manipulation of millions do not fail either. The winsome "philanthropies" established by this "wonderful business man" are expected to be hugely profitable. They have been more profitable than investments of identical sums in even the Standard Oil Company. The objective that lay at the back of the minds of Gates and Rockefeller at the inception of these "philanthropies" is long but clearly stated by Gates in the first publication of the General Education Fund, the, "Occasional Paper No. I," as it reads follows: "In our dreams we have limitless resources and the people yield themselves with perfect docility to our molding hands. The present educational conventions fade from our minds, and unhampered by tradition, we work our own good will upon a grateful and responsive rural folk. We shall not try to make these people or any of their children into philosophers or men of learning, or of science. We have not to raise up from among them authors, editors, poets or men of letters. We shall not search for embryo great artists, painters, musicians, nor lawyers, doctors, preachers, politicians, statesmen of whom we have ample supply. The task we set before ourselves is very simple as well as a very beautiful one, to train these people as we find them to a perfectly ideal life just where they are. So we will organize our children into a little community and teach them to do in a perfect way the things their fathers and mothers are doing in an imperfect way, in the homes, in the shop and on the farm."

One might have thought that the powerful Rockefeller interests behind Soviet economic development and FDR's New Deal would have been consequently persuasive in some sort of humanitarian intervention in the Ukraine and other famine-stricken regions. There are a number of factors why that didn't happen. Stalin was an absolute dictator. He used all the resources at his disposition to consolidate his power within the Communist Party and throughout the USSR state monopoly. That more than satisfied the Rockefeller interests busy at consolidating its global oil empire. Rockefeller's Standard Oil interests have long fueled dictatorships and used on the diplomatic chess board of gamesmanship. Ever since taking control of the oil reserves of the Americas the Rockefellers sought oil in the lands of the East and the Near East, Caucasus, and schemed with the British for rights in the Arab and Persian world Iran, Iraq and Saudi Arabia to supply the European and Mediterranean region. French and British government officials have always worked closely with their respective companies for the oil and the taxes it generates which is why nations compete fiercely in blocking rival interests and jealously guarding their spheres of influence.

The 20th century was the century of oil and war. For the first half of that century, the Rockefellers wanted nothing less than to see the British empire eclipse over the horizon releasing its territories to Standard Oil. It was for that reason alone, as far as the Rockefeller fortune was concerned, that America fought two world wars. Before the guns mobilized on the German-Russian frontier let loose all their fury, the strategic importance of Kaiser Wilhelm's Berlin to Bagdad Railroad plan had not escaped the attention of London's Foreign Office or the Rockefellers. In fact, it was one of the principal precipitating causes of World War One if not the overriding factor, that to grab Near Eastern oil from the control of the British. This goal existed long before the pontificating American President thought it better not to talk oil and thought better to talk about God Saving Democracy for America and the free world. The bony hand of Standard Oil can be seen in that move eastward that precipitated war. It was only after the British faced moral and economic bankruptcy in the long drawn out war of attrition, with the French expertly deceiving the Russian Czar to sacrifice everything to save Paris, did the British leaders agree to let Standard Oil and Wilson pushed their way into the "War to Save Democracy".

Following the First World War, Standard Oil obtains lucrative concessions in Romania, Bulgaria, Ethiopia, Sumatra, Persia, Kamchatka, Turkey and Saudi Arabia. It also seizes oil monopolies with the French Government, in Czechoslovakia and in China. The victorious British grab possessions in the Baku oil fields divesting the Turks and Germans. In 1920 Standard Oil of New Jersey purchases the Baku oil holdings of Nobel Oil Co. along with the Caucasian concessions.

For eight years the Rockefeller Standard Oil group battled Royal Dutch and Shell for Baku oil on the diplomatic front. Sutton maintains that the Rockefeller interests tendered official diplomatic recognition of the Soviet Government by the United States in return for oil but the deal collapses during the Harding oil scandal. After the big money secures the White House for Roosevelt, the Rockefellers get their man and recognition, and Stalin gets what he needs. A little more than year later, in 1935, the Socony-Vacuum Co. (a Lee client) announce that it has been buying oil from Russia since 1927 which pays for Stalin's Russian reconstruction along with Terror-Famine and the Gulag, all part of the package.

In the meantime the Rockefeller-Standard Oil interests are busy developing another source of oil in the Mediterranean. A subsidiary, the Anglo-American Oil Company had obtained, also in that fatal year 1933, an exclusive concession in the northern half of the Harrar Province in Ethiopia which remained largely unexploited. In 1933 the African Exploration and Development Co. affiliates with Socony Vacuum for the exploration of Ethiopian oil. And when Sir Francis Rickett, Rockefeller-Standard Oil negotiator made no headway with Haile Selassie he turns to Mussolini in Rome (another Lee client and favorite of the DuPonts) pushing for a deal on Abyssinian oil. In return for invading Abyssinia Rickett offers assurances of the Rockefeller empire that no sanctions would be exercised by the Rockefeller-controlled League of Nations of where Fosdick, the Rockefeller agent holds sway. Consequently Standard Oil undertakes to supply Mussolini with Roumanian oil (which explains H. P. Davison's Red Cross Mission there during the Bolshevik revolution) in return for a thirty year monopoly of the Italian oil market. Once the war starts Socony Vacuum builds two refineries in Naples. Although a signatory in June 1925 to the Geneva Convention whereby Mussolini joined Italy to twenty-four nations swearing against the use of chemical or bacteriological weapons in war – a provision he mocked – the *Duce* used gas in his 1928 campaign in Libya, and continued to deploy gas in battle with Ethiopia, prompting France, Britain and Stalin to stockpile chemical weapons if only for intended as a defensive deterrent as was the case when Hitler took the signal from London not to use them in his invasion plans. Bosworth writes in *Mussolini's Italy* (2007), "In 1935-6, during the invasion of Ethiopia, Italy unleashed an estimated 317 tons of chemicals on its hapless and defenseless black enemy, with its propagandists having the effrontery to claim that the real poison gas was being let of by the 'preachers' of Geneva." (R. J. B. Bosworth, *Mussolini's Italy*, NY: Penguin, ed. 2007, 297)

By December 1935 after two months of war, Haile Selassie is offered a peace deal whereby Mussolini gets the oil-rich Fafan Valley and the lands west of it. After the war and collapse of the farcical Italian fascists, in 1947 the Rockefeller interests take complete control of Ethiopian reserves with a concession granted Sinclair Oil.

Princeton's collection of Ivy Lee Papers stored at Mudd Library has boxes packed full of material on Rockefeller and the Rockefeller Institutes. Researcher will find press releases for the General Education Board (1914-41), International House (1932-38), Laura Spelman Rockefeller Memorial (1922-23), Rockefeller Center (1935-38) (see also Metropolitan Square material), the Rockefeller Foundation (1915-20), Rockefeller Institute for Medical Research (1915-39), and the Bureau of Social Hygiene (1917). There is also extensive collection of the family (weddings, birthdays, social events…) Printed material on philanthropies include annual reports, organization works. Also here are Lee's books and material on his Colorado Industrial Plan adopted by JDR, Jr..

Reader, perhaps it is not remarkable that the man who accumulated so quickly so vast a fortune convinced it was an act of God should also consecrate $26 million to build a monument of faith. On October 5, 1930 Lee and others gather together some six thousand believers on Morningside Heights for the opening of the massive Gothic creation of Christian unity with over thirty members of different denominations spirit embodied in the Riverside Church located a block away from Columbia University, that too another Rockefeller beneficiary. It is the pride and joy of JDR, Jr., who since Ludlow stands firm behind his conviction all his life "between labor and capital, trying to sympathize with and understand the point of view of each, and seeking to modify the extreme attitude of each and bring them into cooperation... The middle ground of sympathy with both", he emphasizes repeatedly, "recognizing the shortcomings of each, encouraging their improvement and helping to bring them together, has been the position which I have sought to occupy." (P. Collier and D. Horowitz, 153-4)

And of the Holodomor? Why do the Rockefellers not intervene to stop a world humanitarian crisis? Reader, it's not a brainteaser. They just didn't want to. Stalin is their special client. Oil and money are more profitable than humanitarian missions. Saving starving peasants of the Ukraine simply is not a political option. In America, social welfare is a means, after all, to domesticate and control the workers while supplying their needs. It's good for business. Give them jobs, sell them life insurance, dazzle their minds with entertainment. Make them active willing participants in the American Dream. That should be enough to make them passive and docile taxpayers funding government favorable expenditures fattened by tax credits and other incentives for Rockefeller corporations to walk their profits and Consortium politicians straight to the bank. "Follow the yellow brick road..."

Rockefeller researcher Kris Milligan writes, "Tremendous medico-political pressure has been brought to bear to protect the reputations of these supposed discoverers and of the Institute. It has created vested interests and rackets in medical research. Institutional and personal jealousies, intensified by tremendous power acquired by small cliques with the funds of the Foundation, have resulted in the suppression of needed researches by really capable, independent workers. It has barred many of them from the opportunity to engage in research. It has served to enable its employees to reestablish medieval dogmatism in medicine in order to protect their reputations and interests. Their efforts to protect their jobs have served to retard medical advance and to injure the interests of the public." (see Kris Milligan on the Internet)

Milligan adds, "The Rockefeller Institute was founded for the a. vowed purpose of directing medical practise in channels desired for various reasons by Gates and Rockefeller. It was designed for the purpose of control of medicine. Gates was convinced that the medical tradition built up through the ages was unsound and must be replaced by an arrogant "Medical Science" which insists that what it does not know is untrue. This ignorant dogmatism coupled with research politics has resulted in the Institute retarding the advance of medical knowledge, prostituting it to commercial interests, and has cost many lives. The Institute denies that it receives any royalties on its patents. It does not state whether it, or its sponsor, owns any stocks in the companies involved. It also refuses to make public its stock holdings. This refusal is surprising in view of the full and detailed publication made by the Foundation of all its holdings."

That's not all. Milligan again tells us, "Directly following the Supreme Court decision in 1911, ordering the dissolution of the Standard Oil Company,

Rockefeller sought of Congress a charter for the Rockefeller Foundation "to promote the well-being of mankind". Congress twice refused a charter to hold one hundred million dollars, on the grounds that it was a device for evasion of payment of taxes, that it was primarily intended for propaganda for seduction of public opinion and influencing politics, and that it would be a menace to the nation. The Foundation succeeded in securing from New York State in 1913 a charter to hold five hundred million dollars. The bill chartering the Rockefeller Foundation was introduced into New York State Legislature by a man who has discreetly served the Rockefeller interests though he has never permitted himself to be too closely identified with them in the public eye Senator Robert F. Wagner.

"The Foundation has supplemented the activities of the Institute and the General Education Board and has extended them into as many quarters of the world as go the ramifications of the Standard Oil Company subsidiaries and successors. It combines the functions of a tax-exempt business relations agency and super-diplomatic corps. Through its well-advertised and publicized subsidies it has gained entry into many governmental circles from which the interests which it represents would be excluded. Through a Director of its International Health Division, Dr. Thomas Parran, Surgeon General of the U. S. Public Health Service, for instance, the Foundation is directly represented in a division of our government that is important for its sponsors. He also interlocks the directorship of the Milbank Memorial Fund and a host of other agencies. Significant names on the directorate of the Foundation are: Arthur Hays Sulzberger, publisher of *The New York Times*, John Foster Dulles and John J. McCloy – two of America's future first examples of Cold Warriors.

"The creation of the Foundation followed closely on John D. Rockefeller Jr.'s shift in religious attitude toward the "new" or "liberal" theology which pragmatically decried fundamentalism and sectarianism In Protestantism. It is interesting to note that the fundamentalist ministers such as John Roach Stratton accused him of seeking to standardize education and religion through German rationalization. The Foundation supplanted the activities which had formerly occupied Baptist missions. It is the diplomatic corps that prepares the way for commercial conquests. By elimination of inter-denominational antagonisms attached to missionary work it no doubt proved more efficient. In China the medical missions prepared the way for the conquest by Standard Oil of the kerosene and oil market. They also lent impetus to the creation of modem China. The Bible-selling oil merchant, Soong, was the father of the commercial dynasty which now leads China. Oil is also an important factor in the background of the Chinese-Japanese wars.

"It is reasonable to suppose that an institution operated with the efficiency and in the spirit of the Rockefeller "philanthropies" would not be so unbusiness-like as to cast to the winds the large profits which have devolved from some of the Institute's products. Gates undoubtedly was a "business genius" of the rarest foresight and perspicacity. Then a munificently endowed research led the Government and the U. S. Public Health Service to withdraw its prohibition of this type of gasoline. As a result, the entire nation is now exposed to the danger of chronic lead poisoning by lead-filled, automobile-exhaust gases. In due time the mental and physical health of the people is certain to suffer.

"Initiated as a Baptist Church endeavoring to promote education among the Negroes, the General Education Fund was granted a charter by Congress through a bill introduced by Rockefeller's agent in the Senate, Senator Nelson Wilmarth Aldrich. The charter was virtually unlimited in its scope in the field of any activity that might be construed as remotely resembling education.

Kris Milligan writes, "The General Education Board was the chief agency employed in the drive for the destruction of democracy and the establishment of a dictatorship in the United States. For this purpose it fosters, as did Bismarck, Communism as the shortest route to dictatorship in a Democracy, and has converted the U. S. educational system into Communist propaganda agencies." (E. M. Josephson, *The Strange Death of Franklin D. Roosevelt*)

"The progress made by the Board was disclosed in an article in the *New York Globe* on March 28, 1919, by Dr. W. S. Spillman, formerly Federal Farm Management Chief, as follows: "I was approached by an agent of Mr. Rockefeller with the statement that his object in establishing the General Education Board was to gain control of the educational institutions of the country so that all men employed in them might be 'right.' I was then informed that the Board has been successful with smaller institutions but that the larger institutions had refused to accept the Rockefeller money with strings tied to it. My informant said that Rockefeller was going to add $100,000,000 to the Foundation for the express purpose of forcing his money on the big institutions." Was this propaganda, education, or both?

"The Board eventually succeeded in gaining control of almost every school, college and university in the country. They found it hard to resist the lure of the jingle of ready cash. They were forced to turn over to the Board power of dictation of their personnel and curriculum. Senator Kenyon, of Iowa, reported this to the U. S. Senate in January 1917.

"The Board has saddled on our educational system, in the guise of teachers and professors of the "social sciences," the high priests of class war and revolution, professional agitators and the chanters of the abracadabra of the "social philosophies" a la Bismarck and Marx. It has made them the haven of Socialists, Communists, distributors of wealth and other crack-pot New Dealers. It has helped make the foundation source of prostituted "professors" and "authorities" for the agents provocateurs (also known as "leaders") of labor. These professorial propagandists make most of their incomes as front-men, partners, cats paws and agents of labor union racketeers and as "neutral arbitrators" of labor disputes under the Wagner Act.

"To-day there are few professors in the larger American Colleges who are not thoroughly Marxist or openly Communist. Particularly the professors of social sciences, who are so often appointed by Presidents and other public officials to commissions as representatives of the public, can be depended upon to support the Communist or radical labor elements. The Commissions thus appointed under the New Deal, are "loaded" and biased. They can be depended upon to betray the public. They are on the payroll of the unions.

"In this respect, the General Education Board has been most damaging and dangerous. It has used its power over the schools, colleges and universities throughout the country to place on their teaching staffs hosts of advocates of radicalisms and outright propagandists of alien doctrines. It has placed its resources at the disposal of enemies of our country and its government.

"Senator Chamberlain of Oregon, in 1917 foresaw and sounded a warning of this danger in the US Senate. He stated: "The Carnegie-Rockefeller influence is bad. In two generations they can change the minds of the people to make them conform to the cult of Rockefeller or to the cult of Carnegie, rather than to the fundamental principles of American democracy.

"His prophecy is already fulfilled. The direct dividends derived from the activities of the General Education Board were many, including: Favorable publicity for the founders and advertising of their interests that was worth millions; The power to influence public opinion and the policies of the Government by propaganda distributed through the schools, colleges and universities; Control of researches and discoveries, and their application and profits; The power of voting the stock holdings of the institutions which they control and of dictating the expenditure of their funds; The power of appointment of personnel of the institutions which can be converted to the uses of nepotism and favoritism.

"The Rockefeller interests are well represented on the directorate of most of the more important social service agencies. Absurd and dangerous doctrines have been promulgated and incorporated into the law for the deliberate purpose of creating chaos for sinister ulterior motives. This explains why the resources of the General Education Board and of the Foundation have not been used to promulgate and to influence the adoption of a more rational concept of economic and social structure." (E. M. Josephson, *The Strange Death of Franklin D. Roosevelt*)

"With the aid of the machinery of the Foundation it would not take much effort to teach the nation that the menace to its security does not lie in accumulations of wealth, however large they may be; that on the contrary such accumulations constitute a factor of safety for the nation as well as for the individual. The real menace lies in the stupidly conceived and irrational monetary system which so limits the amount of money in circulation that accumulation of reserves by the nation and by individuals results in paralysis of exchange; and bars the setting up of reserves of essential commodities, the raw materials of the necessities of life.

POPULATION AND STARVATION: THE MALTUS EQUATION

"Little more than a century ago the distinguished economist Malthus enunciated, on the basis of a tremendous amount of statistical research, what was named the 'Law of Malthus.' The 'Law' states that population increases by geometric progression and must outstrip the production of food, which it says increases only by arithmetic progression. From this economic 'Law,' Malthus deduced the idea that the world would become over-populated and consequently reduced to starvation. Instead we are now ploughing under crops in order to prevent destruction of their value by supposed over-production. Man's ingenuity in improving production and in creating machinery of production was disregarded by Malthus. And they proved his 'Law' an absurd fallacy. An equally fallacious economic 'law', that of 'supply and demand' and 'marginal utility' (a euphemism for speculation, which is the real determining factor) bars us from remedying the reverse condition of that predicted by Malthus – an apparent over-production of food for our present-day populace. If one were to resort to the practice of framing fallacious thinking into 'laws,' the modern version would read as follows; 'The population and commodity production of the world grow to exceed the dimensions of its monetary system. For survival of that monetary system population and commodities must be destroyed. And that is being done by means of wars.'

"In final analysis the economy of the world requires one of two choices: Either the population and material wealth of the world must be destroyed to the point of bringing it within the scope of our present monetary system by a process of war and starvation, in conformity with the above-stated modernization of the 'law of Malthus;' or the currency and medium of exchange must be rationally based and soundly expanded to match expansion of population and real wealth.

"It is the first plan that rules throughout the world at the present time—identically in Russia as in the United States. It is taught dogmatically and without question in all our schools and universities, whether conservative or radical. Karl Marx in his 'Socialism' has justified its application to fixing the value of human beings and their labor. It is the mainspring of the so-called 'New Deal' and is the fundamental premise of all social service 'philosophy' and thought.

"It is apparent that there has been a deliberate fostering of these fallacious views in the classroom, in the land and in the rest of the world, for the insane purpose of precipitating a smashup of the world's economy that will result in absolute concentration of all the wealth and power of the world in a single hand.

"The insanity of such an objective is obvious to anyone who stops to think or to consider history. Stability or security, which, in final analysis, all men seek in the brief span of life, can never exist in the presence of a system that breeds starvation and violence. In such a system the master is as likely to succumb to the forces which he has set loose as are the mastered.

"There was far greater wisdom in John D. Jr.'s Sunday School homilies which taught that wealth is not essentially evil but a blessing. They did not point out that it is the stupid economic organization to which society clings that converts that blessing into the semblance of a curse.

"The General Education Fund has suppressed such views as those of the son of its founder. It has done much to crush the originality of thought that might have enunciated and popularized such rational views. Instead the Rockefeller 'philanthropies' have dogmatized the teachings of institutions of learning, and they have fostered destructive Bismarxian propaganda.

"It is significant that the Foundation was conceived at the time of the dissolution of the Standard Oil Company. Undoubtedly it had become apparent to the Rockefellers that in order to avoid interference with their enterprises by governments they must take them over more directly and completely than they had thus far done. Taking over governments would not insure absolute submissiveness. This required that the form of the governments of the world must be changed to absolute dictatorships and thatall concepts of democracy must be wiped out. That purpose is the obvious explanation of the objective of the Rockefeller interests in giving unlimited support to Communism, Nazism, Fascism, New Dealism and any other type of dictatorship."

"The international activities of the Foundation were invaluable in paving the way for the formation of a world-wide oil monopoly. Rockefeller personally directed these maneuvers. This is clear from the report made by Chairman Walsh of the United State Commission on Industrial Relations, who reported: '... Mr. Rockefeller is the Foundation. The testimony shows that the trustees exercised no authority that does not come from him'." (E. M. Josephson, *The Strange Death of Franklin D. Roosevelt*; Kris Milligen)

There is another factor: money. The Insiders have spent a lot of money to buy off the academic guild. They have paid well-respected social scientists and historians to write footnoted academic studies that self-consciously refuse to follow the money and family connections. This buy-off began when the Rockefeller foundation decide to fund a biography of John D. Rockefeller, Sr., to counter Ida Tarbell's famous muckraking book, *History of the Standard Oil Company* (1902) serialized in McClure's.

Ivy Lee is hired by the Rockefeller Foundation to locate a suitable author. He wants Winston Churchill, but Churchill's price is too high – $250,000 in advance in the middle of the depression ($3.5 million today). (In fact, Churchill is far too busy with his own literary work.) With Lee dead his successor persuades Allan Nevins, respected in the Establishment culture as a safe academic historian to write a two-volume book on "Senior". (Ray Eldon Herbert, *Courtier to the Crowd*, 1966. American universities used the Nevins-Rockefeller book as "the standard" biography of JDR, Sr. while Ida Tarbell's becomes a Main Street taboo with poor sales.)

At the time Stalin's Terror-Famine, Rockefeller had extensive investments in Nazi Germany and Communist Russia. Rockefeller's billions made and toppled governments determining the future of populations throughout the world literally holding their lifeline. Lee was part of the group that inspired Rockefeller giving millions away to create research centers, to fund medical laboratories and economic think-tanks, to cure diseases and social ills, many of them caused by industry and nervous disorders resulting from the world he financed and perpetuated, from the oil that gushed from the earth, to the ink of newspapers he owned, the blood and soul of propaganda and transfixing the national mind-set for public consumption or debate. That he owned their lives, more or less, wouldn't enter the minds of later generations, habituated to the culture that bred their lives as they struggled to survive and hold jobs that were connected to the Rockefeller empire like branches on a tree.

In fact, the Rockefeller business and banking Consortium with its friends in "high places" naturally prefer to dispense with the bad publicity of doing nothing to stop the loss of life or alleviate the human suffering of the Russians and Ukrainians by their Kremlin client. So, it must have come as a rude shock to Gareth Jones that the great philanthropic Rockefeller Foundation with all its medical and health services remain aloof unwilling to aid the Ukrainian peasant families.

Oh, the woes of Empire! What a world the Americans in the Consortium took over after the debacle of the First World War and Versailles! More than fighting for it, though some 108,000 Americans gave their lives to what the Consortium gang staged, bought and paid for with dollars and Allied gold, this inheritance of Empire was the great new adventure was the most ambitious Father & Son enterprise yet ever dared. While his servants prepared diner for the evening guests for a long time, certainly since taking the Philippines in 1896 and messing about in China Stimson is obliged to think about two hemispheres to manage including America's own backyard in Central America. So, that year with Stalin dealing with his Russian problems, on April 20, 1931 Henry Stimson recorded in his diary a particular entry upon learning that "John D. Rockefeller was so much interested in building unnecessary roads on Mount Desert Island to the detriment of the place, which everybody else objected to; and I had said that I wished to Heavens that he would build a few roads down in Nicaragua for me" for chasing "bandits" … thought of building "a trans-Atlantic road… A gift for that road, which would not be more than two or three million dollars probably would simply solve the Nicaraguan question, particularly if we also built another road up to the bandit provinces." Naturally Stimson didn't record in his diary the tiny detail that Skull & Bones owns the island.

The next day in for a talk with Hoover the President cautions against it preferring instead a loan "which otherwise could not be placed upon the market". The Nicaraguan ambassador Mr. Sacasa had approached Lee. Stimson writes April 30 in his diary, "of an attempt he had made to get John D. Rockefeller Jr. interested in Nicaragua… He had been to Ivy Lee and to Raymond Fosdick..." Raymond Fosdick (1883-72) a Standard Oil man has been on Rockefeller's payroll since 1913, about the same time Lee engages damage control to cover-up Ludlow. Raymond, brother of Reverend Harry Emerson Fosdick, Rockefeller's pastor installed in the Riverside Church on Park Avenue in Manhattan in the late twenties. House sends Fosdick to the Paris Peace Conference in 1919 with his "Inquiry" team of the Consortium gang which stack the American delegation at Paris. Later as Undersecretary General of the League of Nations, Fosdick works hand in hand with Jean Monnet, France's Undersecretary General; on July 31, 1919 Fosdick writes his wife that he, Monnet, and the British Undersecretary General are laying out "the framework of international government…". Even more interesting is Fosdick acting with Rockefeller money is a founding member of the CFR in 1921 along with many other men of the House "Inquiry" plan. Further, for five decades Monnet remains the driving force behind the creation of the European Common Market and the postwar European order. After the failure of the League, rejected by the US Senate vote, Fosdick devotes his life for the next thirty years as the sworn lawyer and protector of the great Rockefeller Foundation empire of funds, fortune and flourishing philanthropy. He graciously accepts, and not Winston Churchill who turns down the billionaire to write Rockefeller authorized biography (1956). (Raymond Fosdick, ed., *Letters on the League of Nations,* Princeton Univ. Press, 1966, 18. Fosdick, like Lee, Wilson, Kennan and many other Consortium players donated his private papers to Princeton.)

Lee's business is to keep secrets, not reveal them. It is awfully splendid, indeed, of Lloyd George to send Jones on to Lee's office and learn the ropes of how the Americans go about getting things done. But who knew who was spying on who? Lee is American and decidedly pro-British. Did Lee suspect foul play from the Brits and Lloyd George? Is Jones a spy? What game might the young lad with the boyish smile be playing?

Lee kept a long correspondence with all three generations of J. D. Rockefeller, eventually donating a part to Princeton University. He made a study of men and business turning his interest into an expertise on social psychology and political fortune-making that before his eyes made America the richest country in the world. Their battles became his battles, their problems, his problems and persuasion his method of marketing over the heads of the masses. Both Hitler and Stalin were Consortium clients and Lee would get into troubled waters defending them with less success than he enjoyed defending Rockefeller Even that was not always fair game, for example, when he seeks out the masterly writing skills of Churchill to pen the Rockefeller biography Rockefeller. And while he knew the rich and famous, most Americans today haven't the slightest clue who was Ivy Lee, and less of what he did. Perhaps more are familiar with the writings of the drug-inspired eccentric William S. Burroughs who lived on a Trust Fund and once shot his wife in the head; Ivy Lee was his not-so-favorite uncle.

A glance at the Ivy Lee Papers collection housed at Princeton University's Mudd Library will readily convince the reader of his list of Consortium of contacts, clients and activities; notably missing are the Nazi-Berlin Hitler files: Otto Kahn 1917-29, Guggenheim Fund, Bankers Trust, Bethlehem Steel Corp., Armour & Co., American Red Cross, 1917-29, Allied Chemical and Dye Corporation 1933, Roosevelt, Franklin D. (Interview with) memorandum 1933 Europe concerning summer trip memoranda 1934; Amtorg Trading Corporation 1928; Amtorg Trading Company 1927-32; Writings include "Public Opinion and International Relations" 1927; "The Problem of International Propaganda" 1934; Writings- "USSR A World Enigma" 1927; Speeches 1926-34: "Russia" 1930; "Problems of Propaganda: A Challenge to Democracy; "Meaning of Publicity," Harvard lectures 1924; "An Intelligent Citizen's Guide to Propaganda" mid-1920s; writings- Russia, miscellaneous (no date) Russian Revolution Notes (no date); Union of Soviet Socialist Republics 1928-1933; Radek, Karl, interview with by Gareth Jones 1931; Germany, Miscellaneous Material on 1931-34; Royal Institute of International Affairs 1934; John D. Rockefeller, Jr. and concerning Rockefeller interests 1914-35; Prime Minister of Great Britain Speaks on Anglo-American Relations Memorandum 1929; Thomas W. Lamont, 1930-31; Dwight Morrow, 1923, 1927, 1930; Otto Kahn, 1918, 1931, 1933 (1916-31); Mortimer L. Schiff, 1923, 1930; JP Morgan and Co. (French Bonds) 1920; James H. R. Cromwell,

1928; Dillon Read & Company 1927-29; Chrysler Corp. 1929-36; Chase National Bank 1923,1926; Chemical National Bank 1921-24; Frederic Ewing, (Standard Oil) 1932; Henry P. Davison, American Red Cross 1918…

Lee also has a correspondence in 1932 and 1933 with Winthrop W. Aldrich (1886-74), head of Rockefeller's Chase National Bank 1930-53, and one of eleven children of Senator Nelson W. Aldrich described by authors Collier and Horowitz as "the voice of the financial bloc in Congress, and a major force behind legislation creating the Federal Reserve System in 1913 and establishing a partnership between the bankers and the government in managing the nation's money", and the Rockefeller money as well. One of his three sisters, Abby marries John D Rockefeller Jr., grandson of William Avery Rockefeller, brother to JDR, Sr.. (P. Collier and D. Horowitz, 158)

Winthop Aldrich becomes an uncle to David and Nelson Aldrich Rockefeller, in the very big and tight clan. In 1929 Aldrich is president of Equitable Trust and is there to oversee the merger with Chase National. He too was rewarded with the Court of St. James as US Ambassador to Great Britain (1953-57) and received the Order of the British Empire most fit for an active member of Pilgrims Society and Royal Institute of International Affairs created in May 30, 1919 and stacked with prominent British and American personalities from the Versailles Treaty ordeal; its counterpart in the United States is the Institute of International Affairs arranged by Col. House in a meeting attended by various Fabian socialists, including economist John Maynard Keynes, a socialist in the British Versailles delegation.

Two years later Col. House renamed it the Council on Foreign Relations (CFR). Lee's Consortium corporate boards included director seats at Westinghouse Electric, AT&T, International Paper, ectera. In 1925, he spared with Charles Solomon in a debate the top of which was "The Interests of Humanity can Best be Served Under Capitalism". Jones would have to have some good answers to why this Capitalism's best spin doctor chose to do business with Hitler's Nazi fascists and Stalin's totalitarian dictatorship?

From the start Lee is interested Soviet economic development. That Lee is called a "Wall Street Bolshevik" along with the New York Fed's William Boyce Thompson seems to have escaped Jone's attention. In 1927 and 1928 Lee lectures almost exclusively on Russia coinciding with the publication of his book *USSR: A World Enigma*. In 1930 he prepares another manuscript on the Soviet Union; Lee hopes the bright young foreign policy ace Gareth Jones would have furnished him with primary material for a second book only it didn't work out that way. Jones harbored strong socialist leanings antithetical to Lee's high-pitched fascist twisted capitalism. Lee's Russia lectures are a series on communism and other aspects of social and political life ranging from women to the Comintern. A file in the Lee Papers at Princeton titled "The Russian Controversy" refers to accusations targeted at Lee in 1929 accusing him of working as a paid lobbyist for the Soviet Communist Party. The 1931 speeches document Lee's interest in Russian railroads. (Ivy Lee Papers, Princeton Mudd Library, Boxes 119-139:

Material includes the US Chamber of Commerce and recognition of the Soviet Union)

From his early days as a newspaperman and press agent for the Democratic Party in 1906, the bread and butter of Lee's work came from his skill at spinning a lie, transformed and carefully reinvented to appear as the truthful expression of a good idea. In 1906, he published his "Declaration of Principles" guiding his spin providing a favorable news twist, instead of advertising. By the mid-twenties after his war work for Morgan banker Davison in the American Red Cross and marshaling America's war spirit throwing the masses into Europe's trenches so the bankers could get their Versailles reconstruction deals, Lee wrote manuscripts on publicity such as "Publicity: Some of the Things It Is and Is Not" in 1924 careful to distinguish the difference between news from advertising. He followed that with *The Public Eye* recast as *An Intelligent Citizen's Guide to Propaganda*. In 1928 Lee's staff edited *Mr. Lee's Publicity Book* "an exposition of the methods and objects of publicity" describing how essential the spinning of information by adept public relations agents is to the image and process of democratic society. He called it *Constructive Publicity*, which also served as title of his collection on public relations and advertising. His last manuscript prepared in 1930 was entitled "Problems of Propaganda: A Challenge to Democracy. In the year of the Holodomor 1933 Lee's lecture titles include "Use of Publicity in Sales Promotion" and "The Virtues and Defects of Capitalism".

By 1934 Stalin had toned down the Kremlin's anti-western and anti-capitalist "Bolsheviki" rhetoric and adopted a softer line on economic cooperation with the Consortium. That year Lee gave a series of talks under the banner "The Contracts of Nations and A New Technique of Helpful International Propaganda". Stalin's shift proves how shrewd Stalin managed the propaganda beaming out of Moscow. The master who observed everyone was also the man everyone watched and feared. Stalin calculated each gesture; every move was aimed at cultivating the myth that he was a loving and wise leader. Clearly, diplomatic relations with the US is a prerequisite for the USSR before joining the League of Nations in September 1934. Lee responded with another essay on the theme in "The Problem of International Propaganda".

As the Consortium's most expensive mouthpiece Lee had an obligation to be well-informed on economic issues. He frequently wrote on the international monetary crisis, particularly war reparations and their effect on the world economy. His "Gold Standard Memorandum" dictated September 28, 1930, was not unlike the views of certain English leaders on the effects of the world-wide depression and the supply of gold on the world market. His 1933 essay "Gold Resumption in Great Britain," examined Great Britain's economic history from World War I with FDR's resumption of the Gold Standard. As a Pilgrim insider, with access to presidents and could call anyone on the phone. He interviews President Calvin Coolidge on war debts and reparations, argued intricacies of the Mellon-Beranger agreement (1927) on the elimination of Inter-Allied war debts believing that compelling full European payment of debts would hurt trade and undermine both the US and European economies. He interviews Dr. Gibbons.

Lee keeps a confidential memorandum written by Keynes to the British Prime Minister offering information and insight on the United States economic situation in 1931 and sends copies to many of his friends and business connections; Keynes is a former member of the British delegation to the Versailles Peace negotiations. And throughout 1932 Lee lectures on war debts and reparations, newspapers and news makers, publicity and advertising but seldom spoke about the 1929 stock market debacle.

The Consortium Wall Street gang made a fortune on the German hyper-inflationary crisis of 1923, and planned to package the cost of reconstruction and the debt burden of German reparations on American investors. Those loose ends came together in the 1929 market crash. Keynes too was playing the markets. Writer Barton Biggs notes how John Maynard Keynes also got caught with his buddy O. T. 'Foxy' Falk running a diversified hedge fund; Falk is massacred in the bust losing 63% in 1929; Keynes is down only 15 % while becoming rich speculating in commodities until his luck too, finally hits the wall, betting long on cotton, tin, rubber and corn. But he gets stuck holding near worthless Austin Motors. By then Keynes has lost 75% of his wealth. Game over.

By 1930, London's economy is also tittering on the brink with trade hit by protective barriers, rising unemployment and declining production. England and Scotland too had their share of breadlines. Not until 1932 when the British economy and stock market bottomed out were there signs of recovery, and by 1936 the *Financial Times* Index doubled to a record high. Keynes, not unlike so many others, then did very well for themselves. But the bubble burst again when stocks plunged in 1937 and London followed New York into recession.

Observing the shifting fortunes in the stock market upheaval Barton Biggs observes, "the Dow Jones Industrial Average by early 1937 had almost quadrupled from the 1932 low but was still down about 60 % from its 1929 high. Equities in the United States and Europe sold at five to eight times depressed earnings, at discounts to book value, and had yields considerably higher than bonds. The one exception was the German economy, which was booming by the standards of the 1930s, and the Berlin stock market, which was exhibiting sustained strength." Wealth creation and greed make uneasy bedfellows; Keynes took a beating, lost big, and suffered depression like his economy.

Rockefeller's man also keeps extensive files on Germany during Hitler's rise in the early 1930s. Lee was publicly attacked for working closely with the Nazi government. In 1923 Lee's fascist streak came out in his interview with Mussolini; he subsequently lobbies Mussolini's views to Americans. Ten years later his son James W. Lee II moved to Nazi Berlin and wrote letters home and kept a diary of daily activities and Nazi rallies. As we will see reader this will be the same time when Gareth Jones arrives in Berlin at the end of March 1933 and held his famous press conference on the Holodomor. An August 27, 1933 his diary entry has a long description of a Nazi rally in East Prussia. The Rockefeller-Nazi Standard Oil connections and Lee's enthusiasm for Hitler's Nazism erupted in a notorious public controversy parallel to the Holodomor. Unfortunately, Stalin's extermination of the Ukrainians made far less copy in the Consortium-owned press. From 1933 to 1934 Lee's son writes his father sending detailed information about the German situation which Lee needs for his father's work promoting IG Farben Industries. Lee responds in a letter dated November 15, 1933. (McCormack Committee folder, Ivy Lee Papers, Mudd Library, Princeton Univ.)

The Consortium's war business in Europe before and after 1933 is due in great part to Wall Street financial assistance in the 1920s to create the German cartel system, and to technical assistance from well-known American firms to build the German *Wehrmacht,* many of which we remember here and others will be identified later. This investment certainly is crucial to the German Nazi military war effort. In 1934, for instance, Germany produces domestically only 300,000 tons of natural petroleum products and less than 800,000 tons of synthetic gasoline; the balance imported. Yet, ten years later in World War II, after transfer of the Standard Oil of New Jersey hydrogenation patents and technology to IG Farben (used to produce synthetic gasoline from coal) Germany produces about six and a half million tons of oil, of which 85 percent (5 1/2 million tons) is synthetic oil using the Standard Oil hydrogenation process.

Moreover, the control of synthetic oil output in Germany is held by the IG Farben subsidiary, Braunkohle-Benzin A.G.; this Farben cartel itself was created in 1926 with Wall Street investors. The Nazi-Rockefeller business raises the bar setting a record high standard of moral irresponsibility and a precedent to follow for the Consortium.

Göering tells Eric Warburg, "Without fuel, nobody can conduct a war". In Ron Chernow's biographical account on the Warburg family interests, we learn of Eric Warburg's interviews with Nazis accused of war crimes at the Nuremberg War Trial. His encounter with Göering is in particular interesting since "Göering's economic bureaucracy had spearheaded the Aryanization of M. M. Warburg, and now fate, with a commendably poetic sense of style, created a fine opportunity for revenge. Eric would call it 'the grand finale' of his wartime work." It is of interest to note that *Reichsmarschall* Göering who has sworn no enemy bomber would ever menace Germany is then astonished at the range capability of the thousands upon thousands of Allied bombers that destroy city after city. Göering confesses that the strategic bombing raids at industrial targets including raw materials and synthetic fuels "inflicted the most damage". (R. Chernow, *The Warburgs*, 529)

The Rockefellers hold huge stakes in the chemical and pharmaceutical industries. They also have very large holdings in the German Dye Trust, IG Farbenindustrie, and are represented on the directorate by the late Walter Teagle, president of Standard Oil of New Jersey. Rockefeller's Chase National floats Dye Trust securities on the American market. The Rockefeller law firm Milbank, Tweed, Hope and Webb, headed by A. G. Milbank, chairman of the board of the Borden Co. and the Milbank Memorial Fund manages some of their interests. (E. M. Josephson, *The Strange Death of Franklin D. Roosevelt;* P. Collier and D. Horowitz, *The Rockefellers*)

We have seen how in order to build the Nazi regime Schacht harnesses powerful friends in high places and set their clever schemes and Jewish banking fortunes into play guiding the Nazi's Reich through the aristocratic channels of international investment banking in exchange for protection for himself and his friends and how he courts Hitler's favor who knows virtually nothing about finance. Schacht manages to block transfers of Jewish accounts diverted into the Nazi war machine. Imagine the sick irony here; Jewish fortunes controlled by Hitler aided by Rockefeller and the Consortium gang are nationalized with funds distributed to build the Holocaust concentration camps.

Schacht matched wits with Keynes with no less skill than when he discussed clever schemes with his close friend the British central banker Montagu Norman and senior Morgan partners. "He never joined the Nazi Party, but was given free rein from Hitler to run the Reichsbank. 'He (Hitler) understood nothing whatever about economics.' Schacht later writes, 'So long as I maintained th balance of trade and kept him supplied with foreign exchange he didn't bother about how I managed it.' He seems to have completely bamboozled Norman who told Tom Lamont of JP Morgan that the Nazis are 'fighting the war of our system of society against Communism. If they fail, Communism will follow in Germany, and anything may happen in Europe'." To save his own neck Schacht constantly underplays the Nazi menace to his inner circle persuading the Warburg family banks to hang on. (B. Biggs, *Wealth, War and Wisdom*)

Jones' published account denouncing Stalin and the Five-Year Plans for causing famine and repression in the Ukraine and elsewhere should have made Ivy Lee's silver hair stand on end. The man who first had a chance to help Gareth Jones save lives and possibly, if not prevent the Holodomor's full fury, lessen its impact and change the course of events leading to war and destruction was utterly void of moral will. Hence his surname "Poison" Ivy Lee. But Lee had the devil in him churning out fascist propaganda forcing him to forcing him to consecrate his days on earth defending his business with Hitler and Stalin.

If Lee and his capitalist friends doing business with the Soviets had the power to possibly influence events, it would seem irresponsible not to seek their cooperation in the interest of saving lives. But there was the problem. Who was interested in saving lives anyway? There is no apparent record that Jones ever received any cooperation whatsoever on the famine problem from Ivy Lee. What is one to do when confronted by evidence of an impending human catastrophe of epic proportions? Cry into the wind? Hadn't the horror of First World War taught everyone a lesson of the utter brutality and uselessness of Wilson's pedagogic imperative "to end all wars" and the folly of the Versailles treaty? Apparently not.

By the late twenties, with Europe well on its way to recover, publishers suddenly discovered that the public was interested to learn about the evil and unspeakable horrors of that war. Issues of war, debts, reparations and disarmament made daily headlines. Is the world either tragic or ironic, or is it just the way it is, with Humanity fatally flawed and justice miscarried? In fact, despite the inclination to think otherwise, neither Hoover, FDR nor Lee would lift a finger to ameliorate the conditions of millions of starving Ukrainians, and in so doing alter the course of American foreign policy speeding the world to an even more terrible holocaust. Lee will never see it. He dies in November 1934 defending his corporate work serving he thought the global interests of Humanity while working to advance the fascist regimes of Hitler and Stalin. Does that make the good-natured Lee a fascist? Or, he is just another harmless American businessman out to make an easy war-buck like most of his fellow club members. Is there any difference between them and whoring? (No slight intended towards prostitutes who earn their livelihood selling their bodies but not their souls.) Or was he just a creep anyway, from the Ludlow on through standing in the center of the stage visible to everybody, white tie and tails and top hat in hand "showing its empty white bottom". If only we could ask Bruno Schulz about this crocodile but the Nazis shot him dead.

Nothing knows innovation like war. Man's instinct for survival transforms into a dynamic of unparallel creative genius. Potential and necessity strike a natural balance when the stakes are unmistakably high and in order overcome defeat. The Harriman-Rockefeller-Morgan Consortium profits thrive on the logic of war destruction and aim to consolidate its centralized power in a tightly controlled and managed New World Order essential to the stability and future endowment of their activities. There is no greater unified enterprise than the war bureaucracy with its million dollar volunteer corporate managers to mobilize industrial production and the masses. Hitler and Stalin with their mass killing machines were essential to the plan to achieve it. And with assiduous planning to carefully put the necessary structures and operatives in place the Consortium and FDR were in position to win it with Bretton Woods and the United Nations to ensure its posterity. Nothing just happens, not when the stakes are this big.

If there were reports on the Ukraine filed for the President's, FDR turned a blind eye and ignored them. Roosevelt has his own key advisers, Consortium men like Walter Teagle (1878-62) Standard Oil president and the man responsible for making it a giant empire of the 21st century; Teagle serves on FDR's National Labor Board and is a director of the Fed. Teagle is also a principal in the Farben Nazi business; John J. ("Everybody Ought to be Rich") Raskob (1879-50), chief financial officer at both DuPont and GM (he resigns in 1928 in a split with GM chairman Alfred Sloan), is chairman of the Democratic National Committee from 1928-32; and Edward Filene (1860-37) of Boston who works with Pierre Jay to popularize banking for the people. Pierre Jay is the first chairman of the Federal Reserve Bank of New York (Bones 1892); in 1908 as banking commissioner for Massachusetts he and Filene help organize public hearings on creating credit union legislation leading to the passage of the Massachusetts Credit Union Act. Raskob's appeal to mainstream Americans to invest their weekly earnings in stocks (*Ladies Home Journal*) comes at the peak of the market's "gargantuan insanity" just two months before the 1929 Crash. When Raskob quits GM he cashed out his stock and builds the Empire State Building with funds reserved for his presidential nomination bid backing Al Smith.

Lammot DuPont of the E. I. DuPont de Nemours and Co. rebuff Soviet advances for concessions in 1927. But when the Soviets persist under the Plans DuPont agrees to sell its ammonia oxidation techniques to the giant Soviet chemical Trust *Chemstroi* to process Soviet fertilizer to boost grain production. Henry Francis DuPont (1880-69) studied horticulture, at Harvard (1902), and is the only son of Henry A. DuPont. With his interest in agriculture and animal husbandry he becomes the premier breeder of Holstein-Freisien cattle in America. He keeps a herd of cattle at *Winterthur*, his museum estate in Wilmington, Delaware. He might have made a gift of one to Stalin, or shown interest in the Ukrainians, but there is no evidence for it by this multimillionaire agriculture expert.

DuPont's entry into a pact with Stalin is broached on by professor Katherine Siegel but the treatment shows it in the most specious and superfluous style and kept within the bounds of her general treatment of US-Soviet affairs. And even more peculiar is Colby's extensive account into the DuPont family corporate fortune detailed in a 1000 page investigation that for its part fails to evoke a single instance of DuPont business with the Soviets as the powerful company imposes itself throughout the world.

That said Siegel does manage somewhat to put the bullish engineer Cooper together with the conservative DuPont in describing the leading Consortium man in the field as "the chief construction engineer for the $75 million Denieprostroi hydroelectric power station in the Ukraine" – a fact for the most part forgotten. Cooper praises fellow Consortium boss Lammot DuPont as among the "big men of the world". As one of the few directors with Harriman on ARCC, in March 1929 Cooper forwards to DuPont a report to promote business with Moscow. Unconvinced, he gets a negative reply.

Cooper, DuPont and H. H. Dewey of International GE carry on a correspondence weighing the Soviet propaganda factor with business. GE holds a five-year $25 million contract. Dewey tells DuPont's director of development Dr. Fin Sparre to be patient, and not to worry about the Soviet commissars who are "much less radical than they sound… But as yet (they) do not feel strong enough to admit openly that communism, as advocated by Lenin, is impossible." Dewey takes the line that commercial development will lead to prosperity among the Russian masses who will then "modify their radical ideas and … accept a more rational program" (K. Siegel, *Loans and Legitimacy*, 128; Correspondence Cooper-DuPont-Dewey cited in Siegel p 183, and in DPP files for March 1929; on Hugh Cooper also see Fithian, *Soviet-American Economic Relations*, 267; Fin Sparre to Lammot DuPont, April 20, 1929; H. H. Dewey to F. Sparre, April 19, 1929, accession 1662, DPP, box 35. H. Cooper continued correspondence with DuPont in July 15, 1929 letter; R. Fastenburg to Secretary July 23, 1929, DPP box 35, accession 1662; correspondence H. Cooper and L. DuPont 1931-32 in F. W. Pickard to L. DuPont, May 26, 1932, DPP; G. Colby, *DuPont Dynasty*, 1974,1984 ed.)

Hugh Cooper argues that the communists were "perfectly safe" as business partners. He tells DuPont to send his firm's top "pessimist" to see the USSR first-hand and if not convinced after three months then give it up. Lammot DuPont agrees to meet Bron of Amtorg at his office headquarters in Wilmington, Delaware and consider the Soviet proposal. DuPont men and the Soviet team hash out a draft agreement, "For Construction of Chemical Plants and Apparatus in the USSR", whereby Chemstroi technicians are to be trained in the US; DuPont agrees to sell chemical processes for creating lithopone necessary for the production of paper, inks and paints, or essentially revamping the printing processes fundamental for the production of Soviet propaganda. Ultimately, Lammot DuPont declares himself favorable to working with Stalin's dictatorial regime, saying "We do not regret at all the steps we have taken so far, and will be very glad in the future to discuss with you the sale of plans or processes … but each of these negotiations must contemplate an agreement independent of any other". DuPont insists on signing a general agreement and refrained from investing funds in the USSR while insisting that the Soviets be required to make prompt and full payments in dollars. And DuPont makes it clear that business with the company in no way could be used to claim any "establishment of industry in Russia under DuPont guidance". (K. Siegel, *Loans and Legitimacy*, 128)

Soviet engineers, – but only in groups of three –, are granted permission to enter DuPont's American plants. The USSR agrees to pay DuPont an advance of $70,000 on a $85,000 contract for the DuPont-owned Grasselli Chemical Company based in Cleveland to design the Soviet lithopone plant. Then upon closer examination of the deal Grasselli insists on $350,000. DuPont has millions already invested to produce ammonia oxidation technology but settles for $150,000 and the Soviets pay engineering expenses.

DuPont also invests in Soviet production of lacquer, in particular the essential ingredient nitrocellulose. For the record, the DuPont firm makes it perfectly clear that its operations with the Soviet communist regime are to remain secret nor are they to be considered part of any long-term engagement. In fact, shortly after the deal Lammot DuPont begins to regret ever contacting the Bolsheviks. "As time goes on, I am coming more and more to the conclusion that business relations with Soviet Russia by American corporations are undesirable, but have not yet come to the point where we should refuse to sell them goods", DuPont writes Hugh Cooper on January 19, 1931. (K. Siegel, *Loans and Legitimacy*, 128; DPP files, box 35)

Nor did the damage to the natural environment by DuPont's contribution to Soviet Russia's industrial progress in Soviet Russia ever figure into any cost assessment by the American company or its host. Generations would have to pay the price long after final battles are fought. Nature is still reeling from the blow. Over a generation later *Time* magazine writes, "In Russia, a huge chemical plant was built right beside a beloved tourist attraction: Yasnaya Polyana, Leo Tolstoy's gracious country estate. Unmonitored fumes are poisoning Tolstoy's forests of oak and pine, and powerless conservationists can only wince. With equal indifference, the Soviet pulp and paper industry has settled on the shores of Lake Baikal. No matter how fully the effluents are treated, they still defile the world's purest waters." (*Time*, Nov. 30, 1970)

Hugh Cooper uses the DuPont entry into Soviet affairs to draft GM into the Consortium Russian deals. Until recently General Motors has been virtually a DuPont-owned company. GM's James D. Mooney, a vice president in overseas operations, persuades GM chairman Alfred Sloan not to stay out listing "other American companies with a reputation for conservatism and foresight … (that) have already gone into this tremendously interesting and potential market". He calls pessimistic caution "bunk". And we know that at the Williams College's

Institute of Politics on August 1, 1930 Cooper gives an upbeat speech promoting Consortium investment in the Soviet dictatorship. (K. Siegel, *Loans and Legitimacy*, 131, D. Mooney to A. Sloan, Oct. 20, 1930; D. Mooney to DuPont, Nov. 21, 1930, accession 1662, DPP, box 35; Siegel ftn; D. Mooney to A. Sloan, Oct. 20, 1930 1-2, accession 1662, DPP, box 35; Mooney and Sloan continue correspondence on Russia throughout the year, see D. Mooney to A. Sloan Oct. 20, 1930, see Mooney speech at the American Automotive Club, Paris, Oct. 7, 1930, DPP, box 35)

Mooney is an aggressive capitalist, unwilling to give up market share to rivals. Mooney travels twelve days in 1930 to meet soviet planners and industrial plants. He is completely indifferent to Soviet politics or labor conditions of its citizens even so much as to say it was of no concern to him "whether that Government is autocratic or democratic or Bolshevik". He would suck up the life blood of the people if it meant selling more cars and reaping profits for shareholders. Convinced Stalin's government is "stable" Mooney says GM is ready to do business. But first GM needs to build an assembly plant for imports of Chevies, Buicks, and Bedford trucks; they could build Bedford trucks but Mooney refuses to let Soviet manufacturers take over building the famed Buicks. Mooney is satisfied that Soviet authority "provides the coordination and driving power, and keeps the unions in line; the leaders have vision; their ability as a nation to *pay* is self-evident."

DuPont is not of the same mindset as GM's Mooney. "These people seem to have no realization whatever of the virtues of truthfulness, integrity, and property rights." In 1936, DuPont maintained his dim view of Soviet "virtues" declaring, "the Russian government was looked somewhat askance at, if not trusted, by American business people generally." Siegel then writes, with obvious enthusiastic support for DuPont's business engagement with Stalin "Fortunately for both the Soviets and DuPont stockholders, the president's ambivalence about this trade relationship did not prevent his firm's continued involvement in what was a beneficial association. Once the company had launched trade with Moscow, its profit margins took precedence over the president's predilections. Vice President F. W. Pickard predicts in the early thirties that 'Russia will be a fairly important market for the United States'"; Pickard is determined to get what he says is "our share" of Russian spoils.

In 1933 this triumvirate runs the National Recovery Administration. When Sutton first looked at the rise of Hitler and Nazism he found GE and Vacuum Oil well represented. Standard Oil of New Jersey not only aids Hitler's war machine, but had detailed knowledge of this assistance. Emil Helfferich, board chairman of a Standard of New Jersey subsidiary, is a member of the Keppler "Circle of Friends" before Hitler seized power; Standard's man in Berlin continues to give financial contributions to Himmler's Circle as late as 1944. In 1935, John D. Rockefeller, Jr. owns stock valued at $245 million in Standard Oil of New Jersey, Standard Oil of California, and Socony-Vacuun. In 1936, Mellon traded their interest in the Barco concession to Socony for $12.5 million; Mellon's Gulf Oil Corp. enriched in 1952 by a Kuwaiti concession pumping 273 million barrels outstrips Iran and Arabia, and subcontracts to Socony and Atlantic what it doesn't sell to Shell. (*The NYT*, January 10, 1935; A. C. Sutton, *Wall Street and the Nazi Connection*; John Raskob, "Everybody Ought to be Rich", published two months before the 1929 market crash.)

For the next ten years the firm Lee and Associates performs public relations work for Socony-Vacuum Oil, the Standard Oil, also the producer of Mobil gasoline with interests in the German Nazi Reich and the USSR. Worn out with a suffering conscience, his son James Lee turns his back on the Nazis and takes refuge with God and the ministry. Many Nazis do the same after the war to escape one way or another and find grace and forgiveness for their sins in the Holy. In Ukraine the people don't get that option; most of their churches are destroyed by Stalin and the Nazis but their faith never dies.

Rich as they were and still are today the Rockefeller power is invincible, omnipotent and yet somehow assumes the most uncanny if not ironic dimension of ubiquity yet, at the same time it remains for the sheepish masses unwilling or unable to accept its dominance in everyday life, more or less invisible. That's real power. Nothing could hurt you, neither Stalin nor a famine even if it is *your* famine. Rockefeller money is virtually everywhere. In America, Rockefeller financial interests are extensively represented on the directorate of most of the more important social service agencies. Kris Milligan, well-known on the web for taking Skull & Bones out of "the Tomb", declares, "It has been related that German-born Senator Robert F. Wagner, whose name is synonymous with all the specious doctrines and the most destructive measures of the 'New Deal' has been identified with the Rockefeller interests and originally secured the New York State charter for the Foundation." Harry L. Hopkins, FDR's close advisor and director of Lend-Lease with Harriman and Stalin, readily acknowledges his debt to the Rockefellers, when he is appointed Secretary of Commerce; Hopkins offers the post of Assistant Secretary to Nelson Rockefeller. The Rockefeller's publicity people vetoed it. Nelson later becomes Governor of New York but his bid for the White House is again vetoed. Although charitable intervention might have been expected forthcoming from the colossal Rockefeller conglomerate of social institutions and foundations originally established to protect his fortune and circumvent taxes while securing loyal obedience of the faithful and well-paid Rockefeller servants, he never gets to call the Oval Office "Home Sweet Home". (Kris Milligan on the Internet)

Missing reports about the economic support for Stalin's Five-Year Plans and the Holodomor terror in the Ukraine they inflicted might in part explain the many remarkably inaccurate statements made to Congress by State Department officials and consultants in the Cold War period of the 1950s and 1960s. Still, if you believe in Alice in Wonderland, then perhaps there had been no real and pervasive knowledge of these technical transfers - even at the most "informed" levels of Western governments. Unfortunately for Jones he died before they surfaced. The irony of history is never without its riddle. Historian Antony Sutton's research led to findings which frustrated even the most articulate of pundits. A year before Solzhenitsyn revelations, in 1972, PBS *Firing Line* TV commentator and publisher of National Review magazine, William F. Buckley Jr. (Bones 1948) tried to marginalize Sutton, a former Hoover Institute Fellow by calling him "a jerk". (Ever listen to an inebriated Bill Buckley sing while playing his antique harpsichord. I did, in his home in Stamford, Connecticut.) Hoover Institute director Glen Campbell called Sutton "a problem", and justified his remark declaring, "The Russian Communist Party is not mellowing." Superfluous rhetoric of diversion.

In a curious turn of events the following year Solzhenitsyn breaks through the Cold War silence barrier with his secret publication in the West of *The Gulag Archipelago* to world acclaim shaking the Kremlin while in Washington the newly re-elected Nixon White House faces impeachment proceedings overshadowed by the Watergate presidential corruption scandal and losing the Consortium's doomed proxy war in Vietnam. Soviet concentrations camps still accommodated cells of doctors and engineers. The Soviet system of mental hospitals continue to take the overload. Religious persecutions did not end with Stalin's death in 1953. Harassment of Jews withstood the passing of time, practiced as it did under the Czars. Sutton reminded Americans who were not entirely doped and still had some free mental reflexes to assimilate the meaning of what he said that the only mellowing seemed to occur when a Harriman or a Rockefeller gets together with the bosses in the Kremlin. Don't be fooled. It's true.

See the photo history of Averell Harriman and David Rockefeller in Moscow or in the comfortable Crimean dachas. "That's good for business but not much help if you are a GI at the other end of a Soviet rocket in Vietnam," Sutton warns the House and Senate after a rising body count reported every night on the televised nightly news before Watergate evolved from a second-rate burglary at the Democratic Washington headquarters into an impeachment inquisition kicking "Tricky Dick" Nixon out of the White House. But Nixon, the Pepsi lawyer, friend of Prescott Bush and patron of his son George Bush's political career, had been just one of their tools, of course. The Americans lost the Vietnam War, withdrawing "with honor" but not before Nixon sent in thousands of giant bombers to obliterate Hanoi "to shorten the war". Who can forget the panic of the military helicopters on top of the US Embassy in South Vietnam while spies and collaborators dropped off the chopper's landing skids. "I've learned something about our military assistance to the Soviets", Sutton told a lecture audience. "It's just not enough to have the facts - these are ignored by the policy makers. It's just not enough to make a common sense case - the answers you get defy reason." Sutton is heard by those who are fortunate and smart to know the meaning of his message. (Russ Baker, *Family of Secrets: The Bush Dynasty, the Powerful Forces That Put It in the White House, and What Their Influence Means for America,* Bloomsbury USA, 2008)

THE HOLODOMOR HEINZE COMPANY CONNECTION

His journey leads him back to distant lands and more uneasy questions about the complexity of Consortium investment that will plague his fact-finding trip to the Ukraine in the summer in 1931. This is a critical time. By the end of the year Stalin will have plunged Ukraine into famine.

For his first visit to Russia still employed as Lloyd George's personal assistant Gareth Jones had arrived in Ukraine traveling alone. For this trip he returns accompanied by Jack Heinz who he had met in New York. Jones is twenty-five, H. J. Heinz II, his junior by two years is the heir of the H. J. Heinz Company, the Ketch-Up company and American brand trademark founded by his grandfather in 1869 in Sharpsburg, Pennsylvania. Jack Heinz II will eventually transform the family company after WWII into a multi-billion dollar empire.

Heinz likes to write and privately published an account of their trip to Moscow, Petrograd to Kiev, Kharkiv and numerous other Ukrainian farm villages. The book *Experiences in Russia, 1931* is based mostly on material written and translated by Jones. H. J. "Jack" Heinz II (1909-87) retreated from politics and controversy of the Holodomor to learn the family business. In 1930, a new company auditorium and service building at the Heinz factory in Pittsburgh had been dedicated to the Heinz employees by President Hoover himself in a broadcast from the White House. Now this year, in 1931, with his son abroad with Jones, his father Howard Heinz fights off bankruptcy in the aftermath of the Great Depression by innovating production with top-selling ready-to-serve quality soups and baby-foods in model factories with excellent working conditions.

Howard Heinze and Hoover have been good friends for good long while. In the days of war, famine and food relief their friendship is both a personal and governmental affair. The First World War is abruptly halted by the November Armistice. Massive famine and the deadly influenza, or as it was euphemistically called, "Spanish flu", and cholera and typhus, rages throughout Eastern Europe with the force of a black plague hitting the Near East and Russia. Literally no place on earth is immune to the wretched disease.

The world of power whether in Washington, London, Paris or Moscow is very small, tight, and confidential. Only bits and pieces of the truth are revealed in the press. Fortunately in the United States at present there is the Freedom of Information Act to serve and protect the vital interests of a free press and democracy in government. A simple reading of some Congressional documents that surface before the Senate Foreign Relations Committee Hearings, for example, on the Armenian Massacres during and after the First World War reveal that many of the same influential men informed and active in the proceedings then are still firmly in place in their seats of power in Washington during the Ukrainian Holodomor.

These men resisted for the most part any use of the phrase "crimes against humanity" during the first world war when, on May 24, 1915, the Allies of World War I, Britain, France, and Russia, jointly issued a statement explicitly announcing, for the first time, the commission of a "crime against humanity" in response to the Armenian Genocide and warned of personal responsibility for members of the Ottomon Government and their agents. An international war crimes commission after the war recommended the creation of a tribunal to try "violations of the laws of humanity". When the United States representative objects strongly to references to "law of humanity" as being imprecise and insufficiently developed the concept is not openly encouraged or seriously pursued as a proper conduct of foreign policy fitting of civilized powers.

Stimson and his fellow lawyers in the State Department are confident that no detailed public record is made on events in the Soviet Union *before* Roosevelt extends US formal diplomatic recognition of the USSR. Nor none after. It take another world war and the Nuremberg condemnation of the Nazi racist ideology and its enactment in the Final Solution of the Holocaust before the lawyers would define and protect "the laws of humanity" making Genocide irrevocably a crime of capital importance. (Robert Cryer; Hakan Friman, Darryl Robinson, Elizabeth Wilmshurst, *An Introduction to International Criminal Law and Procedure*, Cambridge Univ. Press, 2007, 188)

One of those strange coincidences in life is the chance encounter and trip to the Ukraine by Jones with his new friend Heinz, the son of Howard Heinze, one of the four children of Henry John Heinz, founder of the famous ketchup and pickle empire. Howard Heinze was chosen by Hoover to head the US Food Administration's relief efforts in Armenia (NER). By November 1918, famine and disease were killing more combatants and civilians then were mashed to bits by the slaughtering guns of war. Eastern Europe is on fire with typhus, starvation with no end in sight. The Allies need to immediately fix a *cordon sanitaire* on the Eastern European borders, along the Near East and Russia.

Near East Relief faced a devastating famine in the Caucasus. In January 1919 Howard Heinze arrives in Constantinople and sets up headquarters in the US Embassy. His task is to intervene in the Caucasus region of the Black Sea to the Caspian and effecting Georgia and Azerbaijan. This is Baku Standard territory with civil war disrupting the oil flow. Meanwhile the Bolshevik Red Army has pushed Wrangle's White Russian forces into the Black Sea having. Merrill D. Peterson in his book *"Starving Armenians": America and the Armenian Genocide, 1915-1930* cites both Heinze and Haskell in charge of military arrangements to secure food transport and rail facilities: "It was frigid, violent, and starving. The winter, following upon a season of drought, was one of the worst in memory; 20 percent of the people perished. A *National Geographic* author filed a story, 'The Land of Stalking Death', based on a journey aboard an American relief train from Batum to the capital, Erivan. At Tiflis 20,000 Armenian refugees are being fed by NER. At Alexandropol, a city left in ruins by the retreating Turks, the count of refugees had soared to 58,000 and 200 to 250 die daily. Conditions were no better in Erivan. A doctor who had ridden the relief train waved good-bye to the American journalist: 'God Bless America! For America, with God's help, will do it." "If anyone wants material for a treatise on human woe, intrigue, war, massacre, and governmental incompetence," Hoover wrote, "he can find ample sources in the mass of reports from relief officials in Armenia in 1918-1919."

Howard Heinze is Hoover's "trusted aide", an insider sent to take charge on the ground of Hoover's ARA's relief administration there. His main task was to assure that the Armenian Government "when and if they were recognized" would repay all the money expended by the United States Government for relief, and that the provisions could be transported and distributed." Who are these distinguished Americans now seeking full information on the humanitarian and political crisis south on Russia's borders? It is interesting to note on the Senate Foreign Relations Committee sat Ohio Senator Warren G. Harding, the next US President, senior senators William Borah of Idaho, Philander Knox from Pennsylvania, Williams, Hiram Johnson, of California... Harding presides. A document here cites at least 800,000 Armenians were already dead killed by Turks "either by massacre or by famine" and a half-million fled into the Caucasus mountains. This intelligence information is in numerous documents known to US ambassador Henry Morgenthau, Sr., father of FDR's closest adviser at Treasury.

Bill Phillips, State Department's point man during the 1932-33 Holodomor over a decade prior is a senior undersecretary and testifies to the Senate Committee on the Armenia question. He tells the Senators how best to handle the two key questions of what to do to prevent further "massacres" and how to counter "the famine conditions". Phillips declared that even with American aide "the dangers of an invasion of Russian Armenia and consequent massacres remains". Phillips also tells the Committee that Hoover's envoy agent Col. Haskell was "on the spot" having been sent a few months prior arriving mid-summer. Haskell's instructions to the Department make it clear that even one regiment would suffice to push back the Tartars from massacring Armenians.

Phillips tells the American legislators the urgent message agent Haskell had sent to State: "Unless troops are rushed the Armenians may at any time be exterminated." The situation for the Armenians was extremely desperate. A cable sent to Washington from the US Ambassador Gerard in Paris, having been received from an Armenian representative dated September 26, 1919 and which declared, "British already left Armenia. Haskell arrived without soldiers. Absolute lack ammunition... Have absolutely no money, population exhausted, people starving everywhere, from 30 to 50 persons found dead in streets daily. Population naked, no drugs, no more possibility resistance; will soon be completely annihilated. Within month absolute extermination is feared, thus solving Armenian question. Turks consider us responsible for overthrow their empire. Words lacking describe horror situation. You may come too late to save us." Why couldn't they have learned from their mistakes....("Maintenance of Peace in Armenia, Subcommittee Hearings of the Committee of Foreign Relations of the United States", Sixty-Sixth Congress, SRJ 106 A Joint Resolution for the Maintenance of Peace in Armenia, Washington Government Printing Office, 1919)

In "Britain and the Armenian question, 1915-1923" author Akaby Nassibian tells us of the plight of the Armenians, writing, "From nowhere in the Allied camp did she receive even diplomatic help. Neither could Armenian relations with Soviet Russia improve. Very soon after the Tiflis agreement... As to Kemalist Turkey, the summer of 1920 was for her a period of watching the victorious powers and balancing their unity of purpose and determination to implement the Peace Treaty against, on the other hand, securing any possible support from Soviet Russia. When, however, the American Senate decisively rejected Armenian mandate and the Allied powers showed no intention whatsoever of backing up the

Armenian clauses of the Treaty of Sevres which they had themselves drafted, and when Armenia herself was somehow unable to come to an agreement either with her Caucasian neighbors or with Soviet Russia, Kemalist Turkey felt herself in a position to act in complete freedom …" Haskell cables, "The country is a desert and the people nothing but professional beggars… There is no administrative or political capacity in the country, no money, and no resources to develop. Foreign Armenians who have amassed fortunes … will neither contribute nor return to the national home." Haskell returns to the United States from Turkey in 1920. Akaby Nassibian, *Britain and the Armenian Question, 1915-1923*, 212)

Ten years later tens of thousands of people in the USSR are dying each day killed by Stalin's "man-made famine" of socialist state terror. *Experiences in Russia, 1931*, a Jones-Heinz collaboration published anonymously in a small edition passed largely unnoticed despite the various reports of famine and the continuing polemic of US-Soviet trade and rumors of softening State Department policy of nonrecognition of the Kremlin. The irony of ordinary facts arranged within time is too irresistible to overlook.

Gareth Jones revisits the Ukraine, in 1933, and publicly exposes Stalin's crime of the Holodomor; his friend and fellow traveler Jack Heinz returns to his American family business and makes millions of dollars feeding consumer markets with over 200 Heinz products. No one apparently thought to ask why his father Howard Heinz and the Americans do absolutely nothing to lessen the Genocide. Nor does Jones mention the Armenian history or the Heinz family connection to Hoover and the ARA. Reader, can we risk to wonder why that would be so in spite of appearances and with hearts heavy with fear and facts? Perhaps a clue lay in the experience that his father too had known Genocide and seen it with his own eyes.

Instead of promoting a national sensation as Gareth Jones had wished with the release of a privately printed book *Experiences in Russia, 1931* – and this in spite of his broadminded connections to the publishing world so that he should have had no trouble securing a fine publishing house – Jones did little if anything to help relieve the suffering and still even to this day he is posthumously honored first among others. Nevertheless, with its vividly descriptive portrayals of the people suddenly compelled by revolution in the social experiment of Soviet communism, his book remains a gem of anecdotes and portraits of Soviet and Ukrainian life after centuries of repression caught in a modern transition under the pressure of western investment and political terror.

So why the Black Hole on US-Soviet economic collaboration? For his part, the two-month travel log with Heinz on their journey inside Russia and the Ukraine underplays the obvious controversy. On the contrary, Jones notes the conspicuous presence of American companies and engineers contributing to the technical and military conversion of the socialist Soviet economy. Yet it fails to strike Jones at all odd, albeit a curious adaptation after centuries of Czarist backwardness. The peasant population, he admits, proves instead to be a very clever and thrifty population and not averse to improving their lot.

Neither Jones nor Solzhenitsyn are able to move the world to stop Stalin or save the Ukrainians just as they could not stop Stalin's rise to absolute dictatorship of the Soviet Party. No one stopped him adding to the mythic cult of his invincible personality and bedeviling power. They did not die in vain, however. Their deaths and suffering was not to be neglected for all eternity. Now with the Internet, more people are realizing the lies and deception that have not been told in the mainstream corporately controlled press and media, which has contributed to the wars and corrupt democracies of the twentieth century. The information embedded in the American Ukrainian Holodomor story of US-Soviet relations is almost as unbelievable as the crimes committed against the people, and the terror inflicted on their unimaginable suffering by a regime dependent on western technology.

Any close look back at the period makes it perfectly clear that there were many powerful people who preferred Americans not know the vast differences that separated them from Russians. In fact, *Fortnightly,* the same journal that publishes the American foreign correspondents Ralph Barnes and Bill Chamberlin had remarked in 1929 that: "Since 1921, the daily life of the Soviet citizen is no different from that of the American citizen, and the Soviet system of government is more economical." Nothing could be farther from the truth but this is what the corporate socialists want people to believe. Did the editor wish to include American lynchings of 'niggers', too? Why would they spread such nonsense and lies about the Ukraine and Russia unless they wanted the readers to think it was true. This is what they did throughout the twenties and thirties. (See W. H. Chamberlin, "Impending Change in Russia," *Fortnightly Review*, n.s. 139 Jan. 1, 1933, 187-205. Soviet impressions of the talk seem optimistic in comparison; Bill Chamberlin's lecture at The Royal Institute of International Affairs, in "What Is Happening in Russia?" *International Affairs,* London, March 12, 1933)

Heinz may have been a client of Ivy Lee's publicity firm. (It was Lee who introduces Gareth Jones to Jack Heinze.) The company is a national brand name for slogans by the founder (or Lee): "It's not so much what you say, but how, when and where." Fast forward a few years. As a billion dollar publicly traded company the Heinz legacy is still strong today. His son, Jack Heinz III later marries the daughter of a Portuguese doctor, Maria Teresa Thierstein Simoes-Ferreira, who then marries Democratic Presidential contender Senator John Forbes Kerry, (Yale Bones 1966), and Secretary of State in the Obama administration. The billionaire Maria grew up in Mozambique making the rounds with her father to treat the poor. She often recalls, "How this little girl from Africa got here, I don't know...." For heaven's sake, reader. Sure she does. She met Jack Heinz in Geneva. She was a student. Heinz said his family make world famous canned soup. Heinz is the sole heir to a food empire, and later becomes a Republican senator from Pennsylvania. When he was killed in a 1991 plane crash Maria Heinz inherited a $500 million personal fortune with control over billions held in Heinz family trusts. Sometimes it really pays off to go to the right schools...

After the main thrust of the Holodomor had passed Jones made his way to Manchuria to look into Japanese expansion on the Russian frontier and see for himself what was happening on the ground there. Did he know that the Japanese Air Force after 1934 depends on US technology? How many people knew, or did it raise eyebrows to learn of Washington's curt dismissal of a precise report of US Consortium investment in the Japanese Imperial defense industry from the US Embassy in Tokyo in 1933 describing it as "not of great interest"? To whom? Likewise, while the Soviet's first Five-Year Plan is under construction by Western companies, there is apparently at some level within the State Department a clearly deliberate effort not to collect and store information to record this key aspect of joint US-Soviet industrial development. That raises suspicions. Is there a blind track onto which to shunt frightening events? What was the rationale prompting the US State Department to dismiss official accounting of US business cooperation and sales vital to sustain Bolshevik activities under Stalin now considered gross human atrocities? Nor, given the incestuous mingling and exchange between business leaders and government's public servants is it simply too incredulous and preposterous not to think that the information of such sensitive importance went undetected by the diplomatic community and their Commander-in-Chief in the White House. Does the government keep two sets of books, and two branch lines of time creating parallel realities, somewhat suspect and illegal?

The Riga team in Latvia fails to take note of what is openly observed by Gareth Jones and Jack Heinz of the Heinz family food fortune in the summer of 1931 when they walked freely through the Ukraine countryside villages and towns meeting notable persons including Consortium engineers in charge of huge Soviet industrial plants using forced labor along with workers and peasants and writing down what they saw as they went unhampered by the Soviet censor. Did Riga think the information irrelevant, redundant, just another famine in the countryside of dumb peasants? Not likely. Nor did Ambassador Dodd in Berlin who is no friend of the Morgan-Rockefeller crowd well-known to his commercial staff. The US Riga section decidedly chooses not to circulate the kind of information about Soviet industrial development potentially political dynamite in the wrong hands. They act by the criteria of "special considerations".

In 1935, on the eve of his 30th birthday, the man who first revealed to the world press and political leaders the truth of the famine is killed in Manchuko – Manchuria – in Inner Mongolia, a region known to be unstable a few years prior to the outbreak of fierce border fighting with the Japanese and Soviet forces. Soviet forces were better prepared than in the Czarist debacle of the fatal 1904-05 Russo-Nippon War when President Teddy Roosevelt negotiated the famous peace treaty at Portsmouth, New Hampshire. In one bold thrust TR, hero of America's Great White Fleet that sailed around the world in 1908 in a bold symbolic display of greatness after taking the Philippines in the Spanish-American War of 1898 projected American power among the declining powers of the world conquest and the pride of having arrived to pick up the pieces of crumbling old empires. When the ships representing America's first line of defense embarked on their voyage men of war along with their chaplains were driver to prayer. One witness declared, "I could see it it America's assertion of her right to control the Pacific in the interest of civilization and humanity." (W. Lord, 208)

Gareth Jones ventured deep there into forbidden territory taking with him his story of the Ukrainian Holodomor and what he had learned of a world set in motion by the Consortium's march of events. Fate would be cruel to the young man. When the Second World War erupted Jones was dead, allegedly murdered in a plot involving Soviet NKVD double agents, as well as Japanese and Chinese bandits.

But civilian policy makers seem to have no qualms about what they were doing, perhaps except for Secretary of War Henry Stimson. Ten years later, in August 1945, ninety divisions of the Red Army stationed in Manchuria in less than two weeks of fighting seized the Kurile Islands and Sakhalin. Stimson is hosting a refreshing dinner at their 740 Park Avenue residence in Manhattan with "LKT", Mabel and Helen Thorne, he casually tells his friends that the next day they and the whole world will know that the United States will to do something so big that is likely will end the war and dramatically alter the course of the world. At that same moment American airmen are flying toward Japan on a top secret mission.

On August 6 the Americans drop its first A-bomb on Hiroshima. It is a warning to the Soviets not to invade Japan or take any more Japanese islands. The day the Soviets launch their offensive against Japan. The Americans drop bomb number two on Nagasaki with equally devastating and horrible results. After forty years of imperial bloody conquests the Japanese Empire had come to its end. Within a week Emperor Hirohito agreed to the American conditions for surrender.

How many people remember that on the night of March 9-10, 1945 General. Curtis LeMay firebombed Tokyo with over 300 newly designed B-29 Super Fortresses each loaded with 2,000 tons of napalm and jellied gasoline blackened the skies over Tokyo. The Japanese old wood buildings burned like match sticks in a hell-fire indiscriminately killing at least 100,000 civilians in residential districts. The air raids continue for five months. Sixty-six urban centers are hit. All of Japan is considered "a military target".

The massive incendiary bombing did not come with warning except for leaflets with a message dropped to avert the doomed Japanese civilians: "Unfortunately, bombs have no eyes. So, in accordance with America's humanitarian policies, the American Air Force, which does not wish to injure innocent people, now gives you warning to evacuate the cities named and save your lives."

This is total war. "I suppose if I had lost the war," Gen. LeMay later comments, "I would have been tried as a war criminal. Fortunately we were on the winning side." In a confidential memo in June Brig. General Bonner Fellers, a key MacArthur aide, called the incendiary raids "one of the most ruthless and barbaric killings of non-combatants in all history." Stimson told Truman he was concerned about area bombing for two reasons: "First, because I did not want to have the United States get the reputation for outdoing Hitler in atrocities; and second, I was a little fearful that before we could get ready, the Air Force might have Japan so thoroughly bombed out that the new weapon (that is, the atom bomb) would not have a fair background to show its strength" – suggesting a rather subtle moral sensitivity."

In 1938, the State Department had declared aerial bombardment of civilians "in violation of the most elementary principles of those standards of humane conduct which have been developed as an essential part of modern civilization." Secretary Hull, in fact, condemned air attacks using incendiaries which "inevitably and ruthlessly jeopardize non-military persons and property". (Stephen R. Shalom, "Dollar Diplomacy, V-J Day: Remembering the Pacific War", *Z Magazine,* July-Aug. 1995, 71-82)

Oh my God! Its heart-wrenching how these stalwarts of Consortium mischief must suffer their intrigues! There is an eye-stopping account of Stimson's existential crisis in Richard Rhodes' book *The Making of the Atomic Bomb* and if true it behooves the reader to know it. Rhodes tells us, "Stimson abhorred bombing cities. As he wrote in his third-person memoir after the war, 'for thirty years Stimson had been a champion of international law and morality. As soldier and Cabinet officer he had repeatedly argued that war itself must be restrained within the bounds of humanity... Perhaps, as he later said, he was misled by the constant talk of 'precision bombing', but he had believed that even air power could be limited in its use by the old concept of 'legitimate military targets'", and firebombing was 'a kind of total war he had always hated'."

The US Secretary of War now in a position of confirmed victor leading the heroic warriors "seems to have conceived", Rhodes writes, "that even the atomic bomb could be somehow humanely applied, as he discussed with Truman on May 16: I am anxious to hold our Air Force, so far as possible, to the 'precision' bombing which it has done so well in Europe. I am told that it is possible and adequate. The reputation of the United States for fair play and humanitarianism is the world's biggest asset for peace in the coming decades. I believe the same rule of sparing the civilian population should be applied, as far as possible, to the use of any new weapons'." Had Stimson forgotten already Hamburg, Cologne, Dresden and so many other cities and the Allied "bombing which it has done so well in Europe", missing targets by miles, flying at night with Window barrages of aluminium strips jamming radar, wiping away 50, 000 civilians in minutes with incendiary and explosive bombs? Nine days after Stimson's rumination for historians Le May leads 464 B-29s, "nearly twice as many as flew the first low-level March 9 incendiary raid – once again successfully burned out nearly sixteen square miles of Tokyo, although the Strategic Bombing Survey asserts that only a few thousand Japanese were killed compared to the 86,000 totals for the earlier conflagration. The newspapers made much of the late-May raid; Stimson was appalled." Stimson is embroiled in debate and discussion with White House adviser and Director of War Mobilization with offices in the White House James ("Jimmy") F. Byrnes, Manhattan Project physicist Robert Oppenheimer and others on the use of the A-bomb. Rhodes writes of Stimson's "outrage at the mass murder of civilians and his complicity; Oppenheimer remembered such a statement at some time during the day ... (Stimson emphasized) the appalling lack of conscience and compassion that the war had brought about ... the complacency, the indifference, and the silence with which we greeted the mass bombings in Europe, and above all, Japan. He was not exultant about the bombings of Hamburg, of Dresden, of

Tokyo ... Colonel Stimson felt that, as far as degradation went, we had had it; that it would take a new life and a new breath to heal the harm'." (R. Rhodes, 639-47)

Did Stimson really have of decision at this time over the Air Force and US Army generals? According to the Rhodes account he did as becomes clear in a heated exchange between Manhattan Project chief General Leslie R. Groves and the Secretary May 30 in Stimson's office. Groves wants Kyoto nuked and wants General Marshall to approve a report on selected targets. Stimson cut Groves down to size, and Groves recalls, "I thought it was something that General Marshall should pass on first, Mr. Stimson said: 'This is one time I'm going to be the final deciding authority. Nobody's going to tell me what to do on this. On this matter I am the kingpin and you might just as well get that report over here.' ... I informed him that Kyoto was the preferred target. It was the first one because it was of such size that we would have no question about the effects of the bomb... He immediately said: 'I don't want Kyoto bombed'.... his mind was made up. There's no question about that." (R. Rhodes, 640)

In 1949, LeMay is first to propose that a nuclear war be conducted by delivering the nuclear arsenal in a single overwhelming blow, going as far as "killing a nation". Soon America will have thousands nuclear warheads. After the Russians successful blast in 1949, Stalin understood the wisdom of keeping Marxist-Leninist dialectics out of the way of Soviet physicists and the discipline of natural laws surprising the Americans with ability to keep up in nuclear arms race of the Cold War.

LeMay heads SAC until 1957, overseeing its transformation into a modern, efficient, all-jet force. LeMay actually advocates justified preemptive nuclear war. "He thought the term 'limited war' was an oxymoron," Louis Menand writes in *The New Yorker* (2013). "His theory of war was that if you kill enough people on the other side they will stop fighting." On LeMay's departure, SAC was composed of 224,000 airmen, close to 2,000 heavy bombers, and nearly 800 tanker aircraft. After bringing the world one step away from nuclear Armageddon during the Kennedy-Khrushchev missile crisis after numerous clashes with Secretary of Defense McNamara who had been his subordinate during World War Two Gen. Curtis LeMay is forced into retirement in February 1965; three years later McNamara resigns as Secretary of Defense no longer an advocate of the doomed war. (Louis Menand, "Nukes of Hazard", *The New Yorker*, Sept. 30, 2013)

Unfortunately, LeMay's influence makes Secretary of State Henry Kissinger incapable of using his intelligence to honorably end the Vietnam War. In 1972, in January, American fighter jets make a third as many strikes on North Vietnam as in all of 1971 and in February huge B-52s with eight engines thrusting their massive wings flew a record 19 missions in a single day. The war hawks and Nixon still hadn't had enough; the White House celebrates a beautiful spring Easter ordering Operations Linebacker. Four four days in April fighter jets flew 225 sorties; on April 10 B-52s took off and bombed North Vietnam for the first time since 1967 striking Hanoi and Haiphong. The Consortium media's pollsters hailed the bombing claiming popular support for the very unpopular war. Americans love to see their men in uniform blowing up the enemy. But the North Vietnamese refused to surrender to Uncle Sam.

So, Nixon, in a year facing impeachment for criminal activities, and soon to become the only US President to ever forced to resign, in disgrace, (claiming "I am not a crook!") only weeks after his reelection victory, launched Operation Linebacker II, in December 1972, a high-intensity Air Force, Navy, and Marine Corps aerial bombing campaign, which included hundreds of B-52 bombers that struck previously untouched North Vietnamese strategic targets, and more heavy bombing in populated areas in Hanoi and Haiphong. It was his way of saying "Merry Christmas, God Bless, Tricky Dick". LeMay's proud US Air Force drops some 40,000 tons of bombs on densely populated areas, and lost 26 planes, including 15 B-52s. It was meant to teach the Ho Chi Minh (Nguyen Ai Quoc) and his Vietcong leaders a lesson for having killed over 56,000 US troops, and wounding another 300,000 at a cost to US taxpayers of $139 billion. By the end of 1972 there were only 24,000 American servicemen left in Vietnam. In a few weeks in Paris Henry Cabot Lodge signs a peace agreement to end the war. An estimated 1.5 million North and South Vietnamese died in the war. The diplomats smiled, cameras flashed. Everyone went home knowing that the dream of Ho Chi Minh who once attended the French Socialist Party Congress more than fifty years ago in December 1920 and Vietnam's inevitable future would soon pass into reality. And America was kept in the dark over Nixon's disposition to use nukes against North Vietnam. You are encouraged reader to pick up Eric Schlosser's *Command and Control (*2013), reviewed by Louis Menand (*The New Yorker*) in which Schlosser confronts the alarming spectre of a nuclear accident and the need for greater safeguards and controls re-telling "hundreds of incidents of after 1945 when accident miscommunication, human error, mechanical malfunction, or some combination of glitches nearly resulted in the detonation of nuclear weapons." (Eric Schlosser, *Command and Control*, NY: Penguin, 2013; Louis Mesnand, "Nukes of Hazard", *The New Yorker,* Sept. 30, 2013)

Why kill Jones? Nobody really knows. Why not? Double-agents are everywhere. In the thirties Cambridge University is a nest of leftists and communist informers. Jones prefers to go it alone making his own way in strange and foreign territory. He likes to take risks. He excels at taking risks. And if Stalin feels even the slightest suspicion of betrayal even long before it ever happens and wants someone to disappear... Who is going to protect Jones now? In this world of Stalinist terror human life means nothing. People disappear every day never to be seen again.

When he came upon the famine Jones was on a trail leading very quickly and directly to world war, a trail of epic secrets and monstrous ambition. After he had been tipped off by an anonymous letter in 1935 the chameleon politician Lloyd George conceded with reserve, "Gareth Jones knew too much". If anyone had the authority to say that, truly it was this former employer, and ex-British MP and head of the Great Britain's war government. Jones had an uncanny ability, self-confidence and an insatiable curiosity to get to the heart of the matter not afraid to ask embarrassing questions to uncover the naked dirty truth. He persisted, proceeding into cul-de-sac. For some reason, and it often happens this way, Jones didn't fear too much for his own life. That didn't deter him from thinking that perhaps many people might want him out of the way. To men like FDR, Stalin, and even Lloyd George, Gareth Jones was in over his head. Jones was expendable even when serving "honorable" and "good" men. In a world of invisible government, every leader has his assassins and executioners. Honor has nothing to do with it. For modern Ukraine the memory of Gareth Jones has been resurrected with each new anniversary of the Holodomor. Were these secrets that kill worth dying for? What more did he know that he never lived to tell?

The year 1932 is a momentous year in America. Franklin Delano Roosevelt was about to take over the American government where he would conduct affairs as a virtual dictator for sixteen years, with a carefully controlled press, a New Deal economic plan to restructure the domestic economy to preserve the wealth of the richest fortunes in America, and launch a foreign policy known only to a few insiders to change the map of the world by gradual economic and military assistance to fascist Nazi Germany and communist Soviet Russia, culminating in the most destructive and violent war known that ever happened in the world. Although FDR would die before the end of the war, in 1945, he remained at the helm of the ship he steered for the federation of a New World Order, all consolidated a family of the new institutions that would dominate the world and preserve America as the dominant power for future generations: the Central Intelligence Agency, the Marshall Plan with its Cold War hawks, the Rockefeller supported United Nations, World Bank, International Monetary Fund, NATO…

Within that structure FDR carefully envisioned a unique role for himself and Stalin's totalitarian dictatorship. Before the end of his first year in office, FDR would welcome Stalin as the legitimate head of the USSR, thereby assisting in the liquidation of the Ukrainian insurgency and justifying in part their extermination by one of the most ruthless dictators that the world had yet ever known. Dictators make good business partners, and Stalin's monopoly in the Soviet Union was ideal business arrangement for Rockefeller, and his man, FDR. After all, dictators are the business of men who make politics. For big territory, and big resources. Never forget it.

In 1932, writing to his mentor and employer the former British Labour Prime Minister David Lloyd George the young Welshman Gareth Jones delineated details of the impending Holomodor in Soviet Ukraine. In London rumors were circulating throughout the city of the crisis. To informed circles it was no secret to the Anglo-American members of the Consortium. But by this time Lloyd George had passed the Russian Ukrainian famine problem on to the Americans. This was an American problem. Let the American Harrimans and the Rockefellers and the Morgan bankers deal with it. England had its own vast empire of problems with national liberation insurgencies popping up all over the world map. In fact, when the Nazi's first attack England that too becomes an American problem. Without American Lend-Lease aid England would have been unable to defend or feed itself to survive the Nazi onslaught from across the Channel.

Few people knew at the time, or today, just how extensive and controlling have been the Rockefeller banking and business interests in building and maintaining the communist monopolistic structure of the Soviet economy.

Rockefeller interests have been so dominant and extensive, as we shall see, that has been reported that David Rockefeller, chairman of the Council on Foreign Relations and president of the Chase Manhattan Bank, in October, 1964, made a special trip, to Moscow, specifically to recall Khrushchev from his resting health vacation at a sanatorium on the Black Sea the Ukrainian Crimea coast, once the resting place of Greek and Roman princes, and angered over millions of dollars of losses from weak Soviet fertilizer deals, fired the Soviet premier. "Out," is all he had to say. Is it so hard to believe, even if it's true? Writer Gary Allen writes, "Did David Rockefeller journey to the Soviet Union to fire an employee? Obviously the position of premier in the Soviet Union is a figurehead with the real power elsewhere. Perhaps in New York." A single man cannot wield so much power alone. He works in a network of organizations where the employees are "Associates", or members. Like the elitist CFR, or Pilgrims Society, for example. David Rockefeller once referred to $50,000 as "a few cents". For their power and money exudes almost aphrodisiac proportions. Even the illusion of its proximity makes them dizzy with excitement. (Gary Allen, *None Dare Call It Conspiracy*, 1972, 121; William Hoffman, *David: Report on a Rockefeller*, 1971, 141)

Jones' last visit to Ukraine inside the USSR was the most critical. In March 1933, he internationally exposed the famine and pointed to the failure of Stalin's Five-Year Plan of Collectivization and Industrialization. Obviously, this was an embarrassment to American investors and manufacturers of the Ivy Lee set. Genocide is not the best advertising when you want to sell the country to investors. Instead of the world press getting hot on the trail for more famine revelations, Jones now found himself having to fend off personal libel and misinformation by *The New York Times*' Soviet tool William Duranty as Stalin's main apologist for mass terror in the western press. Note. This author has since many times entered annual shareholder meetings on oil and gas investments under the Burmese military dictatorship responsible for ethnic cleansing of the Karen population. The overwhelming majority of shareholders, especially in the energy companies, are interested only in higher profits.

More famine stories by Jones are spiked by western editors and his own reputation discredited over the mock trial of six British company engineers accused of being spies. Stalin was determined to keep the collectivization repression out of the press – that was the message to the foreign press and, particularly Washington. The Moscow press corps knew very well that Stalin's instruction was "No famine stories."

But if neither Lee, Rockefeller, FDR nor *The New York Times* will help Jones and the Ukrainians take on Stalin, who would? Why would they? Should they?

Trade with the Soviet state monopoly augers good business. Stalin is a ready and able business partner. Businessmen generally are not interested in internal affairs they cannot easily understand or do much about. As we see later, Jones was ostracized from his Cambridge-Oxford foreign affairs crowd at Whitehall.

Nor was any relief forthcoming from the American establishment of the Council of Foreign Relations. On the contrary, the CFR, with its ranks filled with Pilgrims and Bonesmen included, at the State Department were strategically placed there to approve the sensitive transfer of western military technology to the Soviets as harmless manufactured goods. In fact, unknown to the American public, all the technology, the savoir-faire, much of the raw material and most of the funds to build the industrial and military machine with which the USSR used during the mythical Cold War to threaten the free world came from the US. That includes the tractors built in soviet plants, on models of imported western technology, that also depopulated the vast Ukrainian farmland. Gareth Jones writes of Ukraine's farmers adapting their lives under mechanized farm labor, replacing peasants and horses, and sending them away from their traditional villages to factories as part of the Soviet socialist plan for building the new proletarian society of the future. One tractor replaced ten or twenty peasants and if Stalin's logic of liquidating the Kulaks and Ukrainian peasant population *en masse* requires sending them away to increase productivity in factories –which it did not – or to Siberian gulags and timber camps of slave labor and where death and poor food and miserable living conditions are the only certainty, – then surely American capitalists ought not get in the way of modern progress! But at what cost in human lives?

As a result of the economic collaboration during the 1920s sustained well into the era of the Holodomor American companies and international banks of the Consortium created and maintained regimes of fascist and totalitarian terror in Berlin and Moscow while secretly developing a formidable threat to western civilization with the Soviet communist state completely dependent on western technology and innovation. The strategy of the Consortium towards Eastern Europe and the Soviet Union was horrifically simple, "Let it burn."

The two Five-Year Plans for agriculture and industry are built by American companies. Sutton's extensive research concludes that the Soviet communist regime "employed more than 350 foreign concessions during the 1920s". That's not a low number; more exhaustive research may find the number even greater. Russian concessions are greedily sought after once Lenin announced his New Economic Policy (NEP) enabling Hoover, Harriman and Rockefeller and other foreign businessmen and entrepreneurs to establish or expand operations in the Soviet republics. The Soviets do not give the foreign capitalists rights to property. There is no "private property" in the Soviet Union. Everything belongs to the State. Desperately in need of foreign capital, modern technical skills and state-of-the-art manufacturing and technology as well as products the Russian communists use their common sense to dissemble and rebuild in order to copy but too often with crude results as they lack the necessary skills and tools and spare parts to optimize precise requirements to make things work.

With concessions stimulating economic growth and employment in all sectors of the economy the Soviets are compelled by necessity and anticipate that in this way they could jump-start a national economy in ruins from a decade of war, revolution, famine and general chaos. For his part the foreign entrepreneur, naturally, expects a handsome business profit. Yet, the Russians have a peculiar historical experience and have emerged with a mentality compounded with Bolshevik impracticality and a logic that never intended to let the entrepreneurs have their way.

Sutton found that the Soviets offered three basic types of concessions: "Type I, pure concessions; Type II, mixed concessions; Type III, technical-assistance agreements." While Soviet methods might have been brilliant in theory, they were found poorly lacking in practice. In theory, this is how it worked, and again, we have Sutton to thank for illuminating the process. He writes, "Information was acquired on about 70 percent of those actually placed in operation. It was found that concessions were employed within all sectors of the economy except one (furniture and fittings), although the largest single group of concessions was in raw materials development. After information had been acquired on as many such concessions and technical-assistance agreements as possible, the economy was divided into 44 sectors and the impact of concessions and foreign technical assistance in each sector was analyzed. Nearly two-thirds of the sectors received Type I and Type 11 concessions, while over four-fifths received technical-assistance agreements with foreign companies. A summary statement of this assistance, irrespective of the types of concession, revealed that all sectors except one, i.e., 43 sectors of a total of 44, had received some form of concession agreement. In other words, in only one sector was there no evidence of Western technological assistance received at some point during the 1920s. The agreements were made either with dominant trusts or with larger individual plants, but as each sector at the outset comprised only a few large units bequeathed by the Tsarist industrial structure, it was found that the skills transferred were easily diffused within a sector and then supplemented by imported equipment. Examination of reports by Western engineers concerning individual plants confirmed that restarting after the Revolution and technical progress during the decade were dependent on Western assistance." (A. C. Sutton, *Western Technology and Soviet Economic Development 1945-65*, 411; W. Keller, *East Minus West Equals Zero*, 198-9)

Ukraine's iron and manganese ore deposits were thought to be the richest in the world. The Kryvyi Rih Basin and the Donetsk Coal Basin (Donbas) in eastern Ukraine had been Czarist Russia's leading industrial venues. They are still producing today. In 1890, Ukraine extracted 70% of the Czar's pit coal and produced 52 % of the Empire's cast iron. With pressure from the bankers and industrialists of the Consortium on Trotsky and the Red Army to rapidly resolve the problem of stability from eight years of war, revolution and civil war, Lenin didn't have much choice other than the NEP to turn the economy around. Between 1921 and 1925, Sutton calculated, "$37 million of machinery and equipment were pumped into the Soviet economy by American industry".

Without diplomatic relations, the industrialists went straight in to make trade agreements with the Soviet government in the grab for strategic minerals and oil. US firms make deals to prospect gold. The Consortium geologists went after the mines. Hitler would do the same in 1941 but his savage methods of fascist extermination followed a different political agenda. The Ukraine has enormous precious mineral reserves: titanium, nickel, chrome, mercury and other raw metal;

non-ore deposits include sulfur, phosphorites, potash salts, refractories, flux, granite, marble porcelain clay ... Harriman money built mines to dig up the manganese ore deposits, primarily in the Nikopol Basin and the Kryvyi Rih Basin with over 60 % pure iron. In the early 20th century, all of Russia's grain export came from the Ukraine reported to have one quarter of the globe's black topsoil ideal for harvesting grain. Hitler would ship trainloads back to Germany.

Rockefeller's Standard Oil Co. of New Jersey was first in line. Rockefeller was after Russian oil got his oil export concession. In return for the concession to the world's arch capitalist Lenin and the Soviets got stability for their regime and foreign exchange to pay for it. The Caucasus oil fields was key to Russian economic recovery. The Morgan men were in on the deal with the Guaranty Trust Company and its International Barnsdall Corp., introducing state-of-the-art rotary drilling techniques and pumping technology designed by the American oil men. No rotary drilling had ever been done in Czarist Russia.

It was in 1921 at the time of Hoover's ARA winding down and Lenin ramping up the NEP when Barnsdall Corp. went in and reopened the Caucasian oil fields; by the end of twenties the Soviets used Barnsdall for eighty percent of its drilling. Barnsdall also introduced a technical revolution in oil pumping and electrification of oil fields. (Antony C. Sutton, *Western Technology and Soviet Economic Development, 1917 to 1930*, Stanford University, Hoover Institution, 1968, v. 1; note from A. C. Sutton, Chapter 11, *FDR*)

In fact all Soviet refineries were built not by Soviet companies but by foreign companies; a Standard Oil lease at Batumi in southern Georgia near the Turkish border was the only one under a concessionary deal; all the others were built under contract. Again lets refer to Sutton on this. He wrote, "Numerous Type I and Type III technical-assistance concessions were granted in the coal, anthracite, and mining industries, including the largest concession, that of Lena Goldfields, Ltd. in Siberia, scene of a Tsarist massacre of miners in 1912. The Lena Goldfields operated some 13 distinct and widely separated industrial complexes by the late 1920s. The most sophisticated gold mining equipment in the world was installed in the USSR by the English. Once the goldfields began to produce, the English were pushed out. Money from the Lena Field Gold Mine provided much of the capital to pay the Great Capitalists for building the industrial capacity of the USSR. (In May 1934 Mellon faced indictment in the United States over his Lena business. The jury handpicked by the prosecution and the indictment was dropped; according to a personal letter to Bullitt from his friend, the lawyer Charles B. Wallace of Wilkes Barre, Pennsylvania. (W. C. Bullitt Papers, Yale Sterling Memorial Library Archives)

General Electric sold Moscow $20 million of electric equipment and other American firms set about re-equipping Russian industry in sectors such as iron and steel, for example, and particularly in the machinery and electrical equipment manufacturing sectors, agreements were made between Soviet Trusts and larger individual Czarist-era companies of the Consortium to reequip and start up the factories using modern technology developed in the West. AEG (German General Electric) and Metropolitan-Vickers (Westinghouse) were the major operators in the machinery sectors. "Only in the agricultural sector was the concession a failure," Antony Sutton writes, and in his chapter on Swope, he notes, "In the late 1920s G.E. and Westinghouse produced about three quarters of the basic equipment for distributing and generating electric power in the USSR General Electric, however was the dominant firm in the electrical equipment industry." (Harry W. Laidler, *Concentration of Control in American Industry*, Chapter XV, New York: Crowell, 1931; On 8 Sept. 1919 the British Westinghouse Electrical and Manufacturing Co. changed its name to Metropolitan Vickers Electrical Co..)

Vickers is a most interesting company of Rothschild activities. Mullins describes it as "one of the great Rothschild hoaxes" of the so-called ""disarmament movement" of the early 1930s". "The idea was not to disarm," Mullins explained, "but to persuade the nations to junk what arms they had so they could later be sold new ones. 'The merchants of death', as they were popularly known in those days, were never more than errand boys for their true masters, 'the bankers of death', or, as they were also known, 'the Brotherhood of Death. In 1897, Vickers, in which Rothschilds had the largest holding, bought Naval Construction and Armament Co., and Maxim Nordenfeldt Guns & Ammunition Co. 'The new Vickers-Maxim Co. was able to test its products in the Spanish-American War, which was set off by J. & W. Seligman Co. to obtain the white gold, (sugar), of Cuba; the Boer War of 1899-1901, to seize the gold and diamond fields of the Witwatersrand, and the Russo-Japanese War of 1905, designed to weaken the Czar and make the Communist Revolution inevitable. These three wars provided the excuse for tooling up for the mass production of World Wars I & II. In 1897, an international power trust was formed, consisting of DuPont, Nobel, Koln, and Kottweiler, which divided the world into four distinct sales territories. The chairman (sic) of Vickers, Sir Herbert Lawrence, was director of Sun Assurance Office Ltd; Sun Life Assurance, and chairman (sic) the London committee of the Ottoman Bank; directors included Sir Otto Niemeyer, director of the Bank of England, and the Anglo International Bank; S. Loewe, the German arms magnate, Loewe & Co.; Sir Vincent Caillard, President of the Ottoman Debt Council, financial expert on the Near East; and Sir Basil Zaharoff, the "mystery man of Europe".

One might have expected the Nye Senate investigation to have set off a storm of social protest in America, especially in the wake of a rash of antiwar novels about the horrors of the Great War that appeared with more frequency in the late twenties, but the masses had already been too dumbed down with belly aches hungry for consumer riches so that no matter how often the Committee "frequently came back to Zaharoff's activities, referring to him as 'a kind of super spy in high social and influential circles', nothing came of it. Even Gareth Jones, now embroiled in the Holodomor Genocide and political scandal was unable, or unwilling, to pursue the Zaharoff dealings with the mysterious scoundrel Lloyd George himself.

Mullins writes in *The History Project*, "For many years he exercised great influence on Prime Minister Lloyd George of England. Zaharoff, who began his career as a brothel tout and underworld tough, arranged for Lloyd George to have an affair with Zaharoff's wife. Arthur Maundy Gregory, an associate of Lloyd

George, was also a Zaharoff agent. Maundy Gregory for many years regularly peddled peerages in London clubs; knighthoods, not hereditary, were 10,000-12,000 lbs.; baronetcies went for as high as 40,000 lb., of which he paid Lloyd George a standard 5000 lb. each. Maundy Gregory was also closely associated with Sir Basil Thompson in British counter-espionage." Mullins adds, "Zaharoff, who was born in 1851 in Constantinople, married one Emily Ann Burrows of Knightsbridge. Maundy Gregory then introduced Emily Ann to the insatiable Lloyd George. From that time on, he was at Zaharoff's mercy. Although Zaharoff was closely associated with Lloyd George throughout World War I until 1922, when their association effectively ended Lloyd George's political career, the name Zaharoff appears nowhere in Lloyd George's extensive *Memoirs*. Lloyd George's political career came to an end after Zaharoff persuaded him to help the Greeks against Turkey in 1920, a disastrous adventure which brought about Lloyd George's downfall from political power. George."

Donald McCormick, in *The Mask of Merlin*, the definitive work on Lloyd George, states, "Zaharoff kept him (Lloyd George) closely informed on the Balkans. During the war, Zaharoff was sent on various secret missions by Lloyd George. The Big Three, Wilson, Lloyd George and Clemenceau, met in Zaharoff's home in Paris. On one occasion, Zaharoff went to Germany (in 1917) on Lloyd George's personal instructions, disguised in the uniform of a Bulgarian Army doctor. Clemenceau later said, 'The information which Zaharoff secured in Germany for Lloyd George was the most important piece of intelligence of the whole war.'" Zaharoff was awarded the Order of British Empire in 1918 for this mission. McCormick also notes, "Zaharoff had interests in Briey furnaces of the *Comite des Forges*. Throughout the war no action was taken against Briey or nearby Thionville, a German area vital to the German army. Orders to bombard Briey were canceled on orders of Zaharoff." M. Barthe protested this event in a speech to the French Parliament January 24, 1919. McCormick ascertains that Zaharoff made some interesting confessions to close associates. He boasted, for example, to Rosita Forbes, "I made wars so that I could sell arms to both sides." He offered astute political advice to Sir Robert Lord Boothby, "Begin on the left in politics, and then, if necessary, work over to the right. Remember it is sometimes necessary to kick off the ladder those who have helped you to climb it.'"

The McCormick account goes on: "In addition to his Vickers and Electric Boat stock, Zaharoff had large holdings in other armaments manufacturers, Krupp and Skoda. The Skoda Works of Czechoslovakia were controlled by the powerful Schneider family of Schneider-Creusot, headed by Eugene Schneider, whose grand-daughter married the present Duke of Bedford. The Nye Committee found that Vickers interlocked with Brown Boveri of Switzerland, Fokker, Banque Ottomane, Mitsui, Schneider, and ten other armaments firms around the world. Vickers set up a torpedo manufacturing firm, Sociétè Francasies des Torpilles Whitehead, with the former Whitehead Co., whose owner, James B. Whitehead, then became English Ambassador to France. Frau Margareta von Bismarck was a director of Sociétè Francasies, as was Count Edgar Hoyos of Fiume."

"At its peak in the 1930s, the Vickers network included Harvey Steel, Chas. Cammell & Co. shipbuilding, John Brown & Co., Krupp and Dillinger of Germany, Terni Co. of Italy, Bethlehem Steel and Electric Boat in the US, Schneider, Chatillon Steel, Nobel Dynamite Trust, and Chilworth Gunpowder Co." It just so happens that the trustee for the debentures of the arms manufacturers is the Royal Exchange Assurance Company of London with E. Roland Harriman of Brown Bros. who is one of the directors. (E. Mullins, *The World Order*)

Sutton concludes that there is no question that western technology and industry in the thirties provided the sole means to rapidly develop the Soviet economy, both militarily and commercially. He writes, "the US State Department pressed for the outright transfer of military technology to the USSR over the protests of the War Department (in the thirties) and the Department of Defense (in the sixties). When in the 1930s the War Department pointed out that the proposed DuPont nitric acid plant had military potential, it was the State Department that allowed the DuPont contract to go ahead. A Hercules Powder proposal to build a nitrocellulose plant was approved when the State Department accepted the argument that the explosives produced were intended for peacetime use. The new program was announced, however, only "after a sequence of construction and technical-assistance contracts with Western companies had been let. The Freyn-Gipromez technical agreement for design and construction of giant metallurgical plants is economically and technically the most important." Western observers like Jones and Pares were dumbstruck by Soviet advances during the early thirties particularly Gorki Ford Motor company and General Electric plant at Kharkov." (A. C. Sutton, *Western Technology and Soviet Economic Development, 1917 to 1930*, 347)

H. J. Freyn, director of Freyn Engineering Co. engaged as a technical consultant to the Soviet metal Trusts confirms American readiness to exploit to the max soviet industrial potential, and he declares "the aim of the Soviet Government is Americanization on as broad a scale as possible." If the State Department didn't recognize "the Soviet Government", its citizens and engineers certainly did.

Hoover prefers not to make a domestic issue out of the international Soviet trade. This and his failure to check the Japanese must go down in the historical record as two of his greatest failures. For it is reasonable to propose that had Hoover used the economic card in a gesture to favor Humanity instead of concealing the horrible denigration of Soviet workers under the monopolist gulag system, then perhaps Hoover might have been able to endorse moral persuasion to trump commercial advantages. However to take that proposal seriously, in view of Hoover and Stimson's imperialist persuasion and contempt for the oppressed masses, it is most unlikely that these two world leaders would have turned away from the incentive or reaping gross profits with the French, British and Germans ready to grab a greater share of the pie.

Further, the engineering director Freyn warns, "If American bankers, engineers, industrialists and merchants are unwilling to furnish the aid for which Soviet Russia stretches out its hand, other nations will have to do it, and will do it." Freyn's positioning is confirmed by others with similar experience, for example, the American contractor with the All-Russian Textile Syndicate, Samuel Newberger who praised his Soviet Party communist counterpart "most punctilious and correct in its manner of handling both actual cotton transactions and contracts of all forms." And Freyn himself concludes, "For the most part, these Soviet commercial agents were intelligent Jews in the Bolshevik party *nomenklatura* who knew how to do business and keep the client within arms reach."

Russians on the scene in the twenties and thirties, in general. corroborate Sutton's findings. The early Bolshevik civil war and revolution had crushed the Russian economy and infrastructure. That was obvious to anyone who visited Russia then. British Slavic scholar and Russian historian Bernard Pares wrote, "the Plan had almost to start from scratch, if it was to turn Russia into a great industrial country, and that, too, so soon after the smashing up of nearly everything that had been achieved so far."

And Pares observes further, "In 1928, when, after a year's preliminary study, the first Five-Year Plan was put into operation, Russia's supply of motors was equivalent to 2 percent of ours, or only equal to those of Greece, Egypt or China. The average income of the citizen was one-quarter of ours. To start from the beginning, the country had to be provided with the basic plant, which could not repay the State and its inhabitants until it could itself create those light industries which would be concerned in providing goods for consumers. This meant an enormous initial capital investment – as much as 30 per cent of the State budget, of which three-quarters was assigned to heavy industry. It was a colossal effort of 'collective saving', for which every individual citizen would have to tighten his belt, and, as the issue was clear, this was precisely the chief appeal in the Plan." Economy of savings, and the peasants had all their foodstuffs, grain and animals, and seeds, confiscated under Stalin's central planning. (B. Pares, "Industrial Planning", *Russia,* 89)

Pares stood by and saw how the Consortium seized the new Soviet market although unlike his student Jones he refused to protest against the injustice of Soviet brutality or the forced labor and "concentration camps" to achieve ambitious Soviet goals. For people such as Pares and Duranty who had been on the battlefronts of the First World War and witnessed, and experienced "Total War", Russia was merely going through another bad time and had to hang on and slog it through. That was all they could do, so thought the Consortium mind.

Aid follows repression and contributes to it. The foreign assistance continues to flow despite worsening economic and political conditions. England's foremost academic authority on Russia observes first-hand, "This effort had to be nation-wide, for all industrial production, which was the chief side of it, depended on food supplies for the greatly increased number of workers and on a surplus of grain for export, to provide the means of purchasing the necessary heavy machinery from abroad. This had to be done under the most disadvantageous conditions. The Soviet Union, after its wholesale confiscations, which included all foreign industrial capital in Russia, had the poorest credit possible, so that only short term loans were obtainable, whereas little can be done with short loans in Russia at any time, and least of all for such a gigantic enterprise as this. Just in the most critical year of the Plan came the European slump, which brought the prices of her goods so low abroad, that Russia had to pay dearly for everything that she bought there – an excess of 30 per cent, as has been calculated. And lastly the Plan involved a revolution in the supply and training of specialists, technician, and mechanics, which at first was bound to emphasize Russia's long-standing dependence on foreign help," Pares observed. (B. Pares, *Russia*, 90)

Pares explained the rationale of communist dictatorship: "Stalin's main part in the matter was the setting of various objectives with time-limits and providing the big drive both with compulsion and with stimulation exercised in turn; but that was, of course, the biggest contribution of all, and the Plan, in its essence, belongs to him. Just as foreign relations were eased by the new motto of 'Socialism in one country', so foreign capitalists sat up and took note of the opportunities opened to them by the Five-Year Plan. Anything to do with the Communist Russia was front-page news. The war, in alliance with the Western democracies, had brought all sorts of Allied missions to Russia. The Intervention had done much more to give numbers of intelligent foreigners of all nations a first-hand contact with the enormous possibilities of the country and particularly with its vastest and richest domain, Siberia. What a fascinating proposition – the utilization at long last of all this natural wealth! It was something which might capture the imagination of any man with capital and enterprise." (B. Pares, *Russia*, 90)

How different the enthusiasm provoked in an outsider of Pares' persuasion, duped as he was by the Potemkin masquerade to the extent he mimics Soviet propaganda when read in contrast with the personal experience of Soviet collectivity. Writing of the same period of Stalin's Five-Year Plans, Solzhenitsyn tells of a remarkably different reality below the surface of illusions that dazzled Pares, Shaw and others, both working class and aristocrat. Solzhenitsyn wrote, "The years go by, and everything that has not been freshly recalled to us is wiped from our memory. In the dim distance, we see the year 1927 as a careless, well-fed year of the still untruncated NE But in fact it was tense; it shuttered as newspaper headlines exploded; and it was considered at the time, and portrayed to us then, as the threshold of a war for world revolution. The assassination of the Soviet ambassador in Warsaw which filled whole columns of the papers that June, aroused Mayakovsky to dedicate four thunderous verses to the subject… Who was to be repressed? Whose neck should be wrung? … And in Moscow they began a systematic search, block by block. Someone has to be arrested everywhere. The slogan was: 'We are going to bank our fist on the table so hard that the world will shake with terror!'"

"It was to the Lubyanka, to the Butyrki, that the Black Marias, the passenger cars, the enclosed trucks, the open hansom cabs kept moving, even by day. There was a jam at the gates, a jam in the courtyard. They didn't have time to unload and register those they'd arrested. (And the same existed in other cities. In Rostov-on-the-Don during those days the floor was so crowded in the cellar of House 33 that the newly arrived Boiko could hardly find a place to sit down.)… But the Gulag Archipelago had already begun its malignant life and would shortly metastasize throughout the whole body of the nation." (A. I. Solzhenitsyn, *Gulag Archipelago*, 42-3)

While the Pares club of elite protagonists support Stalin's reconstruction repression, Solzhenitsyn attacks and ridicules it, for example, here when describing the situation of the foreign and Russian technician during the Bolshevik days: "It was the same for the foreign technician," Pares wrote, "with whose services Russia was less than ever in a position to dispense. In a country so poor in skilled knowledge as Russia, the immense casualties of the war, with the Civil War and the famine, in which it was especially the educated class that had been depleted,"– such a fine word, that! "Depleted". They were massacred by the thousands!) – "had to be reckoned not only in terms of officers or soldiers but also of technicians of all kinds, without whom even the existing rickety public services could not be carried on. The foreign technician saw a picture not only of a most novel and interesting experience but of scope for his vision and energy such as he could not hope to get in his own over-crowded country, and that in a land of the young, where seniority did not count." Solzhenitsyn's description of the Cheka-GPU reality of the NEP is more accurate: "If any pre-revolutionary engineer was not yet exposed as a traitor, then he could certainly be suspected of being one." (B. Pares, *Russia*, 90-1; A. Solzhenitsyn, *Gulag Archipelago*, 44)

Stalin can truthfully boast that he had the largest iron and steel works that existed anywhere in the world. Historian and Soviet watcher Antony Sutton wrote, "When the Soviet claim these units are the `largest in the world' they do not exaggerate; it would of course be impolitic of them to emphasize their Western origins." All Soviet iron and steel technology likewise came from the United States and its Consortium partners abroad. The Soviets use open hearth, American electric furnaces, American wide strip mills, Sendzimir mills and so on all developed in the West and shipped in as peaceful trade. It would take almost a half-century before US Congressman John Rarick summarized what he considered then to be the damage done to US national security, and he said, "The factories and steel mills that US aid built in Russia during the 1930s were used later to create the munitions that killed American GIs in Korea and Vietnam." (A. C. Sutton, *Western Technology and Soviet Economic Development, 1930-1945*, Stanford, CA.: Hoover Institute Press-Stanford Univ., 209-10, 343; US Congressional Record, June 27, 1973, E 4409)

These industrial plants built by the United States between 1929-32 were in fact "far larger than units designed and built by the same construction firms in the rest of the world and, in addition, combining separate shops or plants for the manufacture of inputs and spare parts". Sutton calculated at least one half of the equipment inside the plant was German, much of it "*manufactured in German to American design on Soviet account*". The Magnitogorsk steel plant, for example, where the American John Scott worked was good propaganda for the dictatorship of the proletariat, though it was built by American engineers from McKee Corporation of Cleveland, Ohio, on blueprints from Gary, Indiana, all courtesy of US Steel. It was truly the largest steel and iron plant in the world, and a symbol of national pride for young brainwashed kiddies of the Pioneers and teenagers of the Komsomols communist youth organizations who had no clue that it was a replica of the US Steel plant made in America by Albert Kahn." Remember reader, Cleveland, Ohio is oil country, Rockefeller territory ...

"Some of the Russian intelligentsia called it the *revolutsiya v soznanii*, the revolution in consciousness," Owen Mathews observes: "It wasn't really a revolution in consciousness. But that didn't begin to describe it. It wasn't really a revolution, because only a small minority chose or had the imagination to seize the day, to reinvent themselves and adapt to the brave new world. For the rest, it was more like a quiet implosion, like a puffball mushroom collapsing, a sudden telescoping of life's possibilities, not a revolution but a slow sagging into poverty and confusion." A young Soviet comrade would be more apt to describe the impact felt by the constant *blitzkreig* of Bolshevik Marxist-Leninist propaganda as "something of Russia inside ourselves, infecting out blood like a fever." (O. Mathews, *Stalin's Children*, 5)

Before 1932, Soviet factories rarely produced Soviet-manufactured equipment. They didn't have the capacity to do it until well into the Five Year Plan. It was the massive transfer of foreign technology that provided the impetus for Stalin's breakneck pace of industrialization for two years after the Great Depression. By mid-1932 with the Holodomor reeking more and more havoc in the Ukraine and across the Caucasus oil fields most of the foreign engineers fled. But they left behind everything western – equipment, standards, and manufacturing capacity. Not that everything worked too well at first; the Soviets didn't have the mentality to master at once the strange new modern techniques, properly install equipment or make it run efficiently for war production or do the necessary maintenance.

All the great powers prepared for war. Ever since the violent birth of the Soviet Union, military contingencies remained a priority with any industrial installation. German intelligence reports (OKW files) reveal that not a single Russian plant failed to produced war material or have military conversion capacity. Arms talks may prolong peace but not forever.

The major impetus behind his economic plans is first and foremost military. When Stalin looks across his borders he sees war on the horizon and admonishes his Party never to relent in their preparations for the inevitable. Military production always took priority over civilian needs. Plants were designed with specific requirements specifically conforming to military production. Neither Secretary Hull nor his underlings of Russian observers and their sources on the ground see fit to release that information to the public but they know it. So does the President. Otherwise the Americans would not have managed to prevail in a postwar Europe had not the Red Army "meat grinder" first destroyed Hitler's *Wehrmacht* stormtroopers outside Leningrad and Moscow using massively produced quantities of war materials, tanks, Katusha rockets, and airplanes from the Ural hinterland north and east of Moscow all the while Hull and FDR received reports safely installed in their isolated nests in Washington. (A. C. Sutton, *Western Technology and Soviet Economic Development, 1930-1945*, 344)

The thirties was a time of adjustment to this massive infusion of Western industrial might. Becoming accustomed to this tremendous windfall was not an easy task for the bulky, awkward economic programs of the communists. "The challenge", observes Sutton, "was to become familiar with this industrial overload and quickly convert it as quickly as possible to military strength. Unashlicht, Vice President of the Revolutionary Military Soviet, stated: 'We must try to ensure that industry can as quickly as possible be adapted to serving military needs...; (therefore) it is necessary to carefully structure the Five-Year Plan for maximum co-operation and interrelationship between military and civilian industry. It is necessary to plan for duplications of technological processes and absorb foreign assistance ...; such are the fundamental objectives'." (*Pravda*, no. 98, April 28, 1929, in A. C. Sutton, *Western Technology and Soviet Economic Development, 1930-1945*, 344)

In April 1928 opposition in the Communist Party to the first draft plan on collectivization leads to a new proposal in May by the Supreme Economic Council for industrial expansion of 130 percent over 5 years, or 26 percent per year! Trotsky's proposition is less radical calling for only 10% per year. It is rejected by Stalin. The collectivization Plan aims at providing the capital investment needed for industrialization with conversion to military production. For both the Consortium and the Kremlin collectivization is first and foremost a strategy of military defense vital to the survival of the Soviet Union. When collectivization began, there were protests and peasant riots in the North Caucasus. Bukharin openly criticizes the policy. Stalin answers that a "temporary peasant tribute was needed".

Three years before the Holodomor Stalin has played his card for the eventual extermination of the Ukrainian peasants although he doesn't say it as such but the seed is already planted. Bukharin teams up with Zinoviev and Kamenev against Stalin. In January 1929 Bukharin came out openly against him and sent a statement to the Central Committee that Stalin's policies were synonymous with a military-feudal exploitation of the peasantry, the disintegration of the Comintern, and the bureaucratization of the party. Stalin played the sly wolf and pretends to forgive Bukharin while he plots to rid the Party of all opposition. He will have to wait, however; Bukharin is too popular in the Party.

In March 1929 two versions of the Five-Year Plan are presented: a maximum and a minimum version. At the 16th Party Congress packed by Stalin supporters the Party adopts Stalin's maximum version. Bukharin is ridiculed by Stalin's sycophants. Stalin's plan now calls for the collectivization by 1933 of only 13% of the total farm population. By summer 1929 after Stalin has successfully fractured all opposition in the Party collectivization is pushed forward at breakneck speed and implemented by force. Peasants in the Ukraine and elsewhere throughout the Soviet Union resisted fiercely forcing Stalin to call for an all-out collectivization. Administration Security troops of the OGPU (later called NKVD) in massive force descend on the countryside to compel obedience to Moscow. They burn entire villages and shoot anyone who dares to resist. In retaliation the peasants killed off their livestock and burned the grain. Resistance is so strong that Stalin is forced to retreat and reconsider how he might best take the upper hand. For the Great Dictator of the Proletariat mass famine is no longer an unthinkable option.

He will let the peasants destroy themselves and steal the grain away. This is the world Gareth Jones would enter in 1930 before he entered the lions mouth on Wall Street in New York.

"There was nothing to be compared with it in all Russian history," writes Solzhenitsyn of the famine. "It was the forced settlement of a whole people, an ethnic catastrophe. But yet so cleverly were the channels of the GPU-Gulag organized that the cities would have noticed nothing had they not been stricken by a strange three-year famine – a famine that came about without drought and without war." Fortunately the WWII veteran and former gulag prisoner Aleksandr Solzhenitsyn survived to see his *Gulag Archipelago* memoirs published in his lifetime appearing under the co-title *Experiment in Literary Investigation.* His stories are *vignettes,* tales of outrageously absurd stupidity inherent in the Bolshevik- Soviet-Communist logic that seem so farfetched to the westerner that one might think he invented pure fiction instead of preserving a true memoir of the horrors that swept over the population in "waves" of terror. His was the Soviet State financed and engineered with western technology and forced into near total oblivion by the secret police and "the Organs", when every honest man was sure to be sent to prison or shot. In order to instill a culture of fear and corruption, no trick was overlooked, no one spared. During the late twenties while Ivy Lee visits the USSR and returns to use his vast resources to lobby for recognition of Stalin and the Bolsheviks, socialist state terror is already the order of the day throughout the land to an extent inconceivable to the West, and for most people entirely incomprehensible, unless perhaps you had been a victim of Jewish pograms and Tsarist repression; the Jews suffered unpardonable abuses, villages burned and people murdered under the Czarist regime. (A. I. Solzhenitsyn, *Gulag Archipelago 1918-1956*, 55)

"And so the waves foamed and rolled," Solzhenitsyn wrote. "But over them all, in 1929-1930, billowed and gushed the multimillion wave of dispossessed 'kulaks'. It was immeasurably large and it could certainly not have been housed in even the highly developed network of Soviet interrogation prisons (which in any case were packed full by the 'gold' wave). Instead, it bypassed the prisons, gong directly to the transit prisons and camps, onto prisoner transports, into the Gulag country. In sheer size this nonrecurring tidal wave (it was an ocean) swelled beyond the bounds of anything the penal system of even an immense state can permit itself." Three years of indiscriminate destruction and desecration, unchecked and ignored by western observers who had motives not to reveal it.

"This wave," continues Solzhenitsyn's chronicle "was also distinct from all those which preceded it because no one fussed about with taking the head of the family first and then working out what to do with the rest of the family,. On the contrary, in this wave they burned out whole nests, whole families, from the start; and they watched jealously to be sure that none of the children – fourteen, ten, even six years old – got away: to the last scrapings, all had to go down the same road, to the same common destruction. (This was the 'first' such experiment – at least in modern history. It was subsequently repeated by Hitler with the Jews, and again by Stalin with nationalities which were disloyal to him or suspected by him.")

We referred to Nikolai Tolstoy's recollection of Stalin's "secret war' subjecting the entire Russian population to the socialist imperative of military necessity and jamming the rail system with transports of prisoners from Latvia, Lithuania and Estonia at the cost of rolling stock need on the western front. At L'vov, where the Soviet 4th Army was fighting desperately to prevent its surrender, Stalin's major concern was that the NKVD finish liquidating potential Ukrainian opponents of the regime rather than order the local security forces to join in the battle against advancing Axis units. While Stalin pleaded with the British to rush more aid and take further action, the NKVD labor camp guards were doubled in number from 500,000 to one million heavily armed men. "Standard treatments of this period always claim that the Soviet Union lost over 20 million people during the Second World War. Tolstoy makes a convincing case that the actual total is probably closer to 30 million, maybe even more - with about a third of these deaths attributable to Axis actions. The blame for as many as 23 million deaths is placed with Stalin and his NKVD henchmen...". The Soviets are estimated to have shipped one million Poles to death camps in Siberia. Similar fates greeted the formerly hopeful residents of the Balkan states. (Nikolai Tolstoy, *Stalin's Secret War*, 1981)

The Kresy-Siberia website list brings into contact people from countries around the world with a special interest in the tragedy of the 1.7 million Polish citizens of various faiths and ethnicities (Polish, Ukrainian, Belorussian, Catholic, Orthodox, Jewish, etc.) deported from eastern Poland (Kresy) in 1940-42 to special labour camps in Siberia, Kazakhstan and Soviet Asia. Some 115,000 of these were evacuated through Persia in 1942 as soldiers of Anders Army and their families.

"From 1944 to the late 1950's, the Berianist Soviet government repressed the Ukrainians. A total of three million Ukrainians (out of a 1950 population of 53 million) were eventually deported to Siberian labour camps, while another million Ukrainians died as a direct result of political terror." In Moscow, on March 5, 2003 the academician Aleksandr Yakovlev: 'Recalling Stalin's oppression, Yakovlev said that after the Great Patriotic War (World War II) 1.8 million prisoners of fascist concentration camps, upon their return to Russia, were thrown into GULAG camps on charges of high treason. Many of them died'." Actual figures are not known, as documentation is scarce, per Stalin's instructions.

On February 26, 1930, six months before Gareth personally feels the pain of famine on his trip to the Ukraine, the CC AUCP(b) receives an alarming telegraph from Kharkiv, founded in the early 1650s, and eight hours east from Kiev on a slow train. A mass peasant uprising had shaken the Pluzhniansk border district. Other regions sent similar reports. At this time Stalin takes special notice of the grain-growing regions on the Ukrainian-Polish frontier. Minutes of the March 5 Politburo meeting show that on February 28 the Politburo approved amendments of a newly worded charter later published in newspapers, March 2, with an explanation by Stalin explaining the replacement of the peasants' commune by a peasants' *artel*, a form of collective farm oriented to the market economy (with collective cultivation, marketing, and ownership) but officially fall under the central administrative authority.

Thus, peasants for a short while are allowed to sell their production according to a free market of supply and demand. But it's all a trick. The Soviet government's apparent repudiation of the commune under the guise of the *artel* was addressed by Stalin in late March 1930, in his speech saying the party was "dizzy with success". Stalin publishes an article under the same title. He blames local party members for excesses, claiming to head off a mass revolt of the peasants, and promises collective farmers they had the right to keep a cow, small farm animals and a garden plot. Stalin knows how dangerous it was to take away the garden plot! The next month Stalin's government passed a law on grain procurements calling upon collective farms to supply the government a third to a quarter of their harvest, calculated according to the number of their work days.

All this is happening when the following year on his trip with his new friend the American Heinz traveling through the Ukrainian countryside on the 21st day of their outing his companion English journalist Gareth Jones records firsthand his account of the plight of peasants *in Russian Experience*. "'It is terrible," he said, as he shook his head. 'We can't speak or we'll be sent away. They took away our cows, and now we have only a crust of bread. It's worse, much, much worse than before the Revolution. But in 1926-27 - those were the fine years!'... Of course, I did not immediately understand what he had said, but his amazing change of face made it apparent that he was now telling a different story. It was an amazing reversion, but I think it significant that this is typical in many cases of enthusiastic supporters; they have many grave doubts and secret miseries.

Gareth writes on: "This fellow took us around to the Soviet offices again. A number of *muzhiks* were standing about. They stared at us and one old man with a cap on the back of his head came up and greeted us. 'And how is it with you, *tovarishch*?' we inquired. 'It is terrible in the Kolkhoz,' he whispered. 'They took my cows and my horse. We are starving. Look what they give us - nothing! nothing! How can we live with nothing in our *dvor*? And we can't say anything or they'll send us away as they did the others. All are weeping in the villages today, little brother.' We turned to leave and he followed us out into the dark corridor. Suddenly he seized us both by the arms and whispered hoarsely: 'For God's sake, don't say anything.'... 'Oh, do something for me!" she cried. 'They have taken away my cow. How can I live? Oh my! Oh my! They won't give me anything at all, and I am starving. Please, I beg, I beg of you. They say I can't get anything because I don't work, but I am ill. How can I work? And I have my little girl to feed! My *dvor* is empty and the land has been taken away. We are dying!' She wept - the tears streaming down her face. The young Konsomolka laughed, and shouted: 'Shut up, old woman! You ought to go to work.' 'But how can I work? I am ill!' she implored with outstretched arms, and then burst into tears again."

Collectivization does not increase Soviet agricultural output, but instead reduces it considerably. In 1930, the new status of the collective artel farm is reaffirmed at the 16th Congress.

Stalin kept the peasants wired in with a Catch-22 clause that underscored their dependence on the collective commune, as explained more recently by Kiev journalist and professor, Stanislav Kulchytsky who writes that "in line with the rising level of technical facilities, increasing collective farm membership, and the rising cultural level of collective farmers…It signaled to the managers of the planned economy when and where they should adopt measures to avoid difficulties with the sale of products, conversion of wages into goods, etc. Alongside free choice of employment, which the working class received without any efforts on its part, in 1930 peasants secured for themselves a garden plot with a cow and small farm animals. These two elements, which are alien to the communist economy, enabled it to function for a long time. It was ineffective, but it enabled the Kremlin to exploit the colossal mobilization resource that his economy possessed by virtue of its nature." (S. Kulchytsky, *The Day,* Kiev No. 39)

By July 1930, only 23% of the farms had been collectivized; by late 1931, that figure reached 52.7% as the pace of collectivization quickened. Still, the government record shows that even as late as May 1932, peasants on collective farms are permitted to sell at market prices. Under Stalin the problem of collectivization becomes endemic to the perpetuity of the Ukraine, and the survival of the Ukrainians themselves, and thus virtually an insurmountable proposition. Their very existence is at stake. The host of obstacles combined and spirals downward into the abyss of the Holodomor: the general demoralized state of agriculture, a breakdown from forced collectivization, forced procurements, seizures, liquidation of the skilled kulaks, deprivation of farm expertise, the terrorized and weakened population, the absence of work animals, tractors absent or in poor working condition, depletion of stocks, mass starvation… Fields went unattended, crops are neglected, fields unsowed, the rich soil infested and choked by weeds, harvests went to ruin, ungathered. For many it is a miracle that the crop of 1932 was not less than it was.

More recently Stanislav Kulchytsky revisited the ever present national controversy of the Holodomor in his article published in the Kiev daily *The Day,* on November 22, 2005, and titled "Why did Stalin exterminate Ukrainians? Comprehending the Holodomor. The Position of Soviet Historians". Here professor Kulchytsky refers specifically to a 1997 seminar held after the brief opening of the archives of the Stalinist period,"The Years of Hunger: Soviet Agriculture 1931-1933". The deputy director of the Institute of Ukrainian History at the National Academy of Sciences, Kulchytsky challenged statements by a colleague Stephen Wheatcroft (strange coincidence of name!) who rejects the "organized famine" thesis that Stalin deliberately forced starvation of the Ukrainians, and claims to the contrary that "the Kremlin did not know *anything,* and when information about the famine started to come in, (that) 'the Politburo of the Central Committee of the All-Union Communist Party (Bolshevik) was addressing the increasingly pressing problem of dispensing additional grain (to the peasants).' Between February and July 1933 the CC AUCP(b) and the Council of People's Commissars of the USSR issued 35 resolutions and decrees to dispense food grain." Russian visa approved! (Do you hear the stamp slam down on the passport as he smiles?)

Kulchytsky continues: "Interestingly enough, the cited facts were true. The only thing that is not known is why millions of people died of hunger… Of course, Stalin did not use terror by famine for the indiscriminate extermination of all peasants for whatever reason. Those lucky enough to survive were sent to perform agricultural labor and received food in the fields while they worked. They received food dispensed according to special resolutions from supreme government bodies. This was meant to show how much the government cared about keeping its citizens alive. In this way the peasants learned to work as part of state-owned collective farms." Kulchytsky refers to the research of Roberta Manning (Harvard) who found that "that before the 1933 harvest government stockpiles contained between 1.4 and 2 million tons of grain." That is enough to prevent the mass hunger. "What forced the Soviet government to seize and export such a large percentage of a very low harvest and stockpile more grain than it did during the previous grain crises?" Kulchytsky asks.

Kulchystsky is demonstratively clear about the logic of the pivotal terms for the debate: Famine-Starvation-Extermination-Genocide. He reminds us, writing, "The 1932-1933 famine in Ukraine should be analyzed within the context of the political and legal substance of the term 'genocide'. During a relatively short period Stalin purposefully exterminated the village population in two Soviet political-administrative divisions in which Ukrainians were the dominant population (the Ukrainian SSR and the Kuban province of the Northern Caucasus Territory of the Russian Soviet Federated Socialist Republic) … Stalin exterminated Ukrainians … the Ukrainian famine was a result not only repressive grain procurements, but also a perfectly organized campaign to seize all food stocks from peasants." (S. Kulchystsky, *The Day*, No. 37, 8)

"The reality, however, was different," professor Kulchytsky declares, and he reminds us writing,"In grain-growing regions, the government in fact reinstated food requisitions from Civil War times. For three years running almost entire harvests were confiscated from collective farms, condemning farmers to starvation. In grain-consuming regions the government restricted bread supplies and confiscated ration cards from entire categories of the population, which also resulted in starvation."

LORD MILNER'S "ROUND TABLE" MEN & LORD ROTHSCHILD

On his return from Russia and Europe, Gareth Jones briefed David Lloyd George at his country estate in Churt, Surrey. The former PM promptly sends the young man to meet his friend Lord Lothian, 11th Marquess Philip Kerr. Jones is well on his way to a stunning career, guided and controlled by the leading princes of the Anglo side of the Consortium clan assembled around Lord Milner's "Round Table" set that fills the ranks of Britain's Royal Institute of International Affairs. This Institute occupies a very special place in the Empire and Gareth Jones knows it. Predecessor to the American Council on Foreign Relations it was set up to exercise dominion over global monetary policy. Lord

Lothian happens to be a prodigy of none other than the Rothschild agent, Lord Alfred Milner who groomed a tight select nest of young men known as his "Kindergarten". They include, as Mullins recalls for our benefit, "John Buchan, the future Governor General of Canada; Geoffrey Dawson, editor of the *Times* and prominent supporter of (German) "appeasement" with the "Cliveden Set" (led by Lord Astor, who owned the *Times*)." Philip Kerr is only a few years from becoming Britain's ambassador to the United States (1935-1940). Lord Lothian is the youngest of the "Kindergarten" lot and shared a close relationship with Lloyd George in his cabinet from 1916-20 serving as his wartime private Secretary, his adviser, rather. Mullins writes that it was Lord Lothian who "was given credit as largely responsible for the German provisions of the Treaty of Versailles." Jones is now in step with the top of the top and not far removed from the King and Queen. Lothian was one of the royal ministers in the former days and is also on intimate terms with Waldorf and Lady Astor.

Let's take a closer look at the insidious unseen secret world of power now opening sealed doors to escort young Jones, a little too fast, and not fast enough to save the doomed Ukrainians. Others of Lord Milner's elite "Kindergarten" set Mullins writes in *The History Project: The World Order,* are George Jeachim Goschen, a Liberal who was hailed as the greatest Chancellor of the Exchequer, head of the Cunliffe Goschen banking house with Lord Cunliffe, Governor of the Bank of England. Goschen is also Chancellor of Oxford and the University of Edinburgh; his brother, Baron Sir Edward Goschen happened to be Ambassador to Berlin when Bethmann-Hollweg told him that the Belgian Treaty was a mere "scrap of paper"; Leopold S. Amery, who had two sons, Leopold, who will be executed as a traitor in 1945, and Julian, who marries Prime Minister Harold MacMillan's daughter, and serves as left-wing correspondent on the Spanish Front 1938-9, and later acted as Churchill's personal rep to Chiang Kai-shek, in 1945. After the war he also serves on the Round Table Conference on Malta, 1955, and on the Council of Europe (1950-56).

The senior Leopold Amery is described as "a passionate advocate of British imperialism"; he's on the staff of the *Times*, and compiles their seven volume history of the South African War, in addition to serving in the Cabinet from 1916-22, an MP 1911-45, First Lord of Admiralty, 1922-24, Secretary of State for India, 1940-45, and did his part to arrange independence for India. Amery is also a trustee of the Rhodes Trust.

The Milner-Rothschild relationship was described in Terence O'Brien's biographical work, *Milner*. O'Brien writes, "Milner went to Paris on some business with Alphonse de Rothschild. ... Business calls in the City included a formal visit to Rothschild.... weekend with Lord Rothschild at Tring, and visit with Edward Cecil, Lord Salisbury at Hatfield ... while spending a weekend with Lord Rothschild at Tring a Press Lord gave him a sleepless night (no further explanation given) ... talks with Rothschild.' Milner attended a Zionist dinner given by Lord Rothschild, sitting next to Lawrence of Arabia, who interpreted for him in a talk with King Feisal". O'Brien notes, "Milner lost no time in recreating his links with the City. He went first to Rio Tinto which reelected him to its Board and before long Rothschild asked him to be its chairman. Rio Tinto was one of the key firms in the Rothschild empire. Herbert Hoover was also appointed a director of Rio Tinto; he would soon be asked to head the 'Belgian Relief Commission' which prolonged World War I from 1916 to 1918." (E. Mullins, *The World Order*; Terence O'Brien, *Milner*, UK: Constable, 1979, 97)

Milner was principal in launching the South African War as described in *British Supremacy in South Africa* headed "Sir Alfred Milner's War". Mullins wrote, "The Rothschilds had decided upon the formula of a 'managed conflict" for the First World War because of the difficulty they had encountered in defeating the Boers [in South Africa] from 1899 to 1901. After illegally annexing the Transvaal in 1881, the British had been turned back with a resounding defeat at Majuba by Paul Kruger. In 1889, because of the discovery of vast wealth in gold and diamonds in South Africa, the Rothschilds came back to loot the nation with 400,000 British soldiers pitted against 30,000 'irregulars' – that is, farmers with rifles – whom the Boers could put into the field. The Boer War was started by Rothschild's agent, Lord Alfred Milner, against the wishes of a majority of the British people. His plans were aided by another Rothschild agent, Cecil Rhodes, who later left his entire fortune to the furtherance of the Rothschild program, through the Rhodes Trust – a by no means infrequent denouement among Rothschild agents – and the basis of the entire 'foundation' empire today. The British fought a 'no prisoners' scorched earth war, destroying farms and mercilessly shooting down Boers who tried to surrender. It was in this war that the institution of 'concentration camps' was brought to the world, as the British rounded up and imprisoned in unsanitary, fever-ridden camps anyone thought to be sympathetic to the Boers, including many women and children, who died by the thousands. This genocidal policy would next be used by the Rothschild-financed Bolsheviks in Russia, who adopted the Boer War concept to murder 66 million Russians between 1917 and 1967. There was never any popular reaction to either of these atrocities, because of the control of media which makes discussion of these calamities a taboo subject." (E. Mullins, "British Supremacy in South Africa", *The World Order*, 22)

How much Jones actually understood about this world of power and influence is unknown. Of that he doesn't say, but we can follow Jones as its torrential sweep takes him quickly into the future however uncertain and full of peril. For now Gareth Jones is recognized for his talents and the secrets that he is prepared to keep of the British ruling class.

"The career of Lord Alfred Milner (1854-1925)", Mullins wrote, "began when he was a protégé of Sir Evelyn Baring, the first Earl of Cromer, partner of Baring Bros. bankers, who had been appointed Director General of Accounts in Egypt. Baring was then the financial adviser of the Khedive of Egypt. Since 1864, Milner had been active in the Colonial Society, founded in London in that year. In 1868, it was renamed the Royal Colonial Institute, and was heavily financed by Barclays Bank, and by the Barings, Sassoons and Jardine Matheson, all of whom were active in founding the Hong Kong Shanghai Bank, and who were heavily interested in the Asiatic drug traffic. The staff economist of the Royal Colonial Society was Alfred Marshall, founder of the monetarist theory which

Milton Friedman now peddles under the aegis of the Hoover Institution and other supposedly 'right wing' think-tanks. Marshall, through the Oxford Group, became the patron of Wesley Clair Mitchell, who then taught (Arthur) Burns and Friedman. In 1884, Alfred Milner augmented the work of the Royal Colonial Society with an inner group, the Imperial Federation League; both groups now function as the Royal Empire Society. Vladimir Halperin, in *Lord Milner and the Empire*, writes: 'It was through Milner and some of his friends that the Round Table Group came into being. The Round Table, it should be said, is an authority to this day on all Commonwealth interests."

Mullins goes on to state how Milner raised a considerable sum for the work of the Round Table, including 30,000 pounds from Lord Astor, 10,000 pounds from Lord Rothschild, 10,000 pounds from the Duke of Bedford, and 10,000 pounds from Lord Iveagh. Milner launched a magazine called the *Empire Review*, later called the *Round Table* quarterly. Halperin also notes another contribution of Milner: "He played an important part in the drafting of the famous Balfour Declaration in December of 1917. It is a fact, that, with (Arthur) Balfour, he was its co-author. As far back, as 1915, Milner had realized the need for a Jewish National Home, and had never ceased to be warmly in favor of its creation. Milner, like Lloyd George, Amery, and many others, saw that the Jewish National Home could also contribute to the security of the Empire in the Near East'." (E. Mullins, *The World Order*; for more on the Earl of Cromer, see Pilgrim files; Vladimir Halperin, *Lord Milner and the Empire,* UK: Odhams Press, 1952)

Jones publishes his first story in *News Chronicle* of London appearing October 3, 1930, "The Snobbery of Soviet Russia". The editors keep secret his identity describing the journalist merely as "an Englishman recently returned from Moscow". Jones attacked the Soviet Party leadership for murdering peasants. Editors kept his identity a secret. It was Lord Lothian who helped Jones get his stories into *The Times.* The timing of the stories matches recent reports of "execution' of 'specialists' on a charge of sabotaging the food supply of Soviet Russia". Jones writes, "The story of 1931 is the story of how, creeping unawares upon an unsuspecting world, this new crisis, the world-banking crisis, came to add its burden to the already heavy load which trade and politics had placed on mankind."

In October 1930, Gareth Jones sent a series of articles published in *The Times* of London as well as reports to David Lloyd George; the next year he would tell Ivy Lee. The *Times* was careful to publish the articles unsigned with a byline "From a Correspondent". Jones writes, "Food difficulties arising from the slaughter of animals which followed the violent collectivization campaign in January and February, and from the Soviet policy of exporting foodstuffs to obtain credit at all costs, are already putting a brake on the progress of industrialization, as is proved by the decision to postpone the beginning of the Third Year of the Plan from October to January. This winter the difficulties confronting the Five-Years Plan will be greater than ever for thousands of workers are already returning from the towns to the villages and many will be too weak to work." (G. Jones, "The Two Russias, The Rulers and Ruled. Below the Surface", *The Times,* Oct. 13, 1930)

Jones' account is borne out by "K" writing about the grain expropriations. "Where did all the grain go?", and his source, the anonymous "K" asks. Writing of events of the market crash and economic meltdown in the West, Jones applied his first-rate mind to the problem of its impact Soviet Union. He writes, "In 1929 an unprecedented economic crisis engulfed the world, which came to be known as the Great Depression. In these conditions prices for industrial equipment dropped. Soviet foreign trade organizations happily bought everything at low prices and on preferential payment terms, paying in foreign currency. It turned out, however, that prices for agricultural products dropped even further. Nobody was issuing long-term loans, and to earn foreign currency the Soviet government had to sell more grain. Delayed exports of grain spelled big trouble. In order to find currency for yet another payment on its bonds, the Soviet government auctioned of museum treasures."

Particularly interesting is Jones alertness at the time to the Ukraine situation that summer and fall 1930. That he publishes his articles in *The Times* of London October 13-16 when he is still considered a protégé of Lloyd George might have had an inverse effect now that he was telling the truth as he saw it stamped out under Stalin's repression of the peasants. It's not at all unlikely that as he persisted to inform the readers of the reality of famine and terror in the countryside under the Consortium Five Year Plans Jones is burning bridges, distancing himself from his peers in the Foreign Service, and his protectors. Lloyd George may have already decided to cut him off, sending him to New York at a safe arm's length away from the inner circle of Empire aristocrats and their friends who never took too much to heart the suffering of illiterate workers of the lower class except at the polls..

The Consortium-Soviet relationship is a double-edged blade. In the same article Jones described advances in technology and industry. Gareth Jones writes, "In some branches of industries the boast of the Communists are fully justified. The power development of the electrified industry are tremendous and the quality of the materials used and of the products is far better than in other industries. The telephone system, for example, works well. The increased sales of Russian oil testify to the development of the Baku district. Aviation is progressing rapidly and a Trans-Siberian air route is being planned which will bring London, within a few days of Japan and thus revolutionize the postal services. New factories, mines and furnaces are being constructed everywhere. The State Publishing Company has created a network of bookshops throughout the country with vast sales of books at low prices." But the famine problem persists. In the same series of articles published October 1930 three years before the Holodomor, and still engaged with his work with Lloyd-George, Jones did his best to understand the justification for increasingly depressed economic conditions of the workers and peasants under the communist collective system mixed with the opportunity for progress under global capitalism.

Here in his second story in the series for *The Times* titled "The Two Russias: Fanaticism and Disillusion. Open discontent", Jones spoke with the miners at Donetz. He finds little if anything good in a way that could justify their hardship now. Jones observes of their "lost faith" in the communist program, "The views of the majority of the workers on living conditions under the Five-Year Plan can be gathered from the following conversations with workers. An employee of an agricultural implement factory said: 'Everything is bad now and we cannot get anything at all."

This is not what the Consortium or Stalin wants the world to hear and if it gets out the press will have a party with it bashing the communists and the failure of all that finance and industry from the west will be exposed. Washington and London already are dealing with a world economic slowdown from the Wall Street Crash and Great Depression in the US. The Soviet miner tells Jones, and he writes, "We cannot get boots and we cannot get clothes. Workers in my factory get 80 to 100 roubles (nominally £8 to £10) a month, and 120 roubles (£12) is the lowest figure on which one can live. We cannot obtain enough food and many are too weak to work. Eight hours is my day, but many seasonal workers do ten and twelve hours.' One of many thousands of miners, whose flight from the hunger and the housing shortage of the Donetz Basin the writer witnessed, expressed his opinion of what the Five-Years Plan was doing for Russia in the following words: 'Everybody is going away from the Donetz Basin, because there is no food here. There is nothing in Russia. The situation is terrible."

And the writer told Jones, "All that the Communists do for us is to promise us that when the Five-Years Plan is over we shall all be prosperous. My life is like a flower; it will soon wither away. I want to eat and live now. What does it matter to me what will happen in a hundred years?'"

"Another miner who was traveling hundred the same compartment nodded approval and said: 'A year or two ago we could got enough to eat, but now nothing at all. Now they are sending all our grain abroad and building factories. Why cannot they give us food and boots and clothing? I get 80 roubles a month. How can I live? The Five-Years Plan will not succeed. The Communists will not last very long, for we cannot stick it any longer. You see if there will not be a revolution.' Nor was this miner the only Russian who was so angry with present conditions as to speak of an uprising, for other citizens, especially in the south, spoke of revolution."

"Women are equally discontented with living conditions. A woman worker said: 'Times are bad. From 1922 until last year everything was satisfactory, but now things have become unbearable. With the money I receive for my eight-hour day's work I can only buy a small plateful of potatoes and tomatoes or a tiny portion of fish. I earn 52 roubles (nominally about £5 a month). How can I live?' Lack of faith in the future of the Plan and disillusionment characterized the conversation of most non-active workers."

In the same article Jones told how he learned from the peasants themselves that collectivization had quickly destroyed the free market resulting in the absence of food products. He called that 'the most vital problem of all', writing, 'The present food shortage was attributed by most Russians to two causes – the agricultural revolution begun last year and the absence of a free market. A caretaker and his wife explained: 'It is all the fault of this collectivization, which the peasants hate. There is no meat, nothing at all. What we want is a free market'."

Here again he let the Ukrainians, Cossacks and peasants of collectives speak out and tell his readers, and to be sure some who are actors in the drama, just how their Five Year Plan is destroying their life on earth. "While there is no reason to believe that the poor peasants support their Communist benefactors the point of view of the average peasant was well expressed in the following conversations, one with two members of a collective farm and the other with a Cossack individual farmer. 'It's a dog's life,' agreed the two collective members. 'It would be better to live under the earth than to live now. They force us to join collective farms. The very best people, those who worked day and night, were sent to the Urals and Siberia, and their houses were taken from them. What is the use of living?'"

Jones discovers that the people in the countryside have sparsely enough to live for once they were deprived of their livelihood and dignity gained from honest work spurred on by depossession of their homes, small farm plots, livestock and their community? The communists promised more coercion and forced labor and exile to death camps. Such as this embittered Cossack farmer who told his story of life under communism. Jones writes, "'It is hard to live. Just because we have our own holdings they make life a burden for us. I come here to the big town and I go to a shop to buy something. They say: 'Show us your collective farm card'. I reply: 'But I have no collective farm card'. They say: 'Then we cannot sell you anything. So in time I shall have to give up my land. Otherwise I shall not be able to buy a single thing and perhaps they will just take my house away and send me to Siberia. In my Cossack station in February they took 40 of the best and most hardworking peasants away with their women and children and sent them in freezing trains to Urals'."

The Soviets had divided Russia into two classes, the haves and the have-nots. Revolution did not bring prosperity but resentment and hatred of the privileged minority. Such was the so-called "Dictatorship of the Proletariat" of the Bolshevik Revolution. Jones describes a conversation with rail passengers. He wrote, "Bitter hatred of Communists and of the privileges they enjoy was often expressed. During a journey in the South a train passed ours and in were two cleanly dressed men traveling first-class. A workingwoman (a cook) who was in our compartment shouted: 'There's a party man and there's another. They are both traveling soft (first-class). They get everything and we have to starve.' With this there was general agreement among the people in the compartment. 'The Communists get the best rooms and we get none at all. They just send somebody off to the prisons of Solovki and take their room,' said a miner on another journey."

For the Consortium's dictator Jones spared no words of praise. With his fluency in Russian and friendly manner Jones found Russians and Ukrainians everywhere yearning to pour out their hearts even at the risk of death by informers or the OGPU. Everywhere he went he found Stalin the target of their derision and irrepressible Russian humor.

Stories are whispered about Stalin in corners of trains. Here is a typical story told me in the Donetz Basin:- Stalin had a dream in which Lenin appeared to him.

"Hello, Stalin! How are you?" asks Lenin.

"Oh, I'm fine," replies Stalin.

"How is Russia?"

"Oh, splendid," says Stalin. "You know, we have our Five-Year Plan now and our achievements are amazing."

"Really." says Lenin. "And what are you going to do when the Five-Year Plan is over?"

"Oh, we'll have another Five-Year Plan."

Then Lenin crushes Stalin by saying:

"By that time every man, woman, and child in Russia will have died and joined me, and you'll be the only man left to carry out your second Five-Year Plan."

Jones writes from his notes caring to quote the people in their original voice: "Stalin shares the unpopularity of his Party and most Russians evaded a reply to any question about him saying: 'If Lenin had only lived, then all would have been well.' An anecdote told with a warning that to repeat it would render anyone guilty of a counter-revolutionary act, illustrates the general attitude towards the dictator."

"Stalin has a dream in which Lenin appears and says to him: 'Good-day Stalin. How is Russia?' Stalin replies, 'We are getting on splendidly. Our achievements under the Five-Years Plan are wonderful.' Lenin asks 'But what are you going to do when the Five-Years Plan is over?' Stalin answers: 'Oh, then we shall have another Five-Years Plan.' Finally Lenin crushes Stalin by saying: By that time everyone in Russia will have died and have joined me and you will be the only man left to carry out your second Five-Years Plan'."

The *Times* editor introduced Jones and the series of articles as "impressions recently gathered by an unshepared visitor to Russia who was able to collect at first hand some rank-and-file opinion on the regime and its policies". Jones, in fact, mocked the Soviet propagandists acting as though they wished only to lead the dumb and blind. He slammed "the Socialist experiment". It's clear by the tone and focus of his stories that Jones found it difficult to resort to English reserve, seal his upper lip and restrain his disgust at the farce played out by the communists for the benefit of their masters with the only purpose to deceive and conceal the shortcomings of their repression now causing food shortages and famine. The tourists and businessmen duped by the charade are likewise objects of rebuke for their complacent ignorance, or worse, complicity in the spectacle.

Jones wrote, "Visitors to Tsarist Russia often returned to England impressed with the apparent loyalty of the whole population to the Emperor and entirely unaware of the rapidly growing discontent which was seething beneath the surface. Today history is repeating itself. Groups of tourists, biased from the very beginning in favour of the "workers' paradise," are being shown by competent and charming guides the facade of Soviet Russia and leave the country enthusiastic over the success of the Socialistic experiment. Not possessing the slightest knowledge of the language, and meeting few people other than active Communists, they leap to the conclusion that the majority of that they meet are ardent supporters of the present régime. The politeness of Communist Officials, and their willingness to spare no trouble in impressing their guests, disarm criticism and leave the foreign delegations blissfully ignorant of the hunger, discontent, opposition, and hatred which in the last few months have been steadily growing in intensity and are spreading through all parts of the Soviet Union and through all sections of the community. Few observers of the Soviet Russia are worthy of credence unless they can understand and speak Russian, unless they have carefully studied the Bolshevist Press, and have had contacts not only with that numerically insignificant section the Communist Party, but also with peasants, miners, nobles, restaurant workers, private traders, priests, Civil servants, and engineers."

Jones compares "the two views" essential to understand the causes and conditions of the antagonism between them. Jones was willing to concede that "a miner escaping from the Donetz Basin, where there has been a serious breakdown in food supplies is far more likely to exaggerate the gravity of the situation than a well-paid specialist working in the electrical industry, which is making great progress." He wrote, "In a vast country under the 'dictatorship of the proletariat' where the ballot box plays little part, it is difficult to draw a conclusion as to the exact amount of support which the régime has from the population, especially when that support varies according to such consideration as the quantity of meat or grain received in a certain town or the price of butter in a certain market. The population seems, however, to be divided into two sections, the "active", that is "the rulers" composed of less than 10 percent., and the "non-active," that is "the ruled" composed of more than 90 percent. of the total. Whereas most of the 'active', the 10% section, consisting of the members of the Party and of youth organizations, are filled with an enthusiasm, unknown in any other group of people save perhaps the National Socialists of Germany, the Fascist and the Salvation Army, the 'non-active' 90 percent are thoroughly disillusioned, have lost faith in the Five-Years Plan and dread the return in the coming winter of the conditions which reigned in 1918 and 1919. Most of the active minority are young in age and young in spirit. Many of them who are now 20 were only seven years old when the October Revolution broke out, and have no conception of life in a capitalist country. Having passed through the Communist training grounds of the Pioneers (the Communist Boy Scouts) and the Komsomol (the League of Communist Youth), they have had Leninism stamped upon them and have been educated to believe in the inevitability of the world revolution and of the forthcoming war which they are taught, the capitalists will wage war on Soviet Russia."

Of the terror, executions and depopulation of kulaks, Jones wrote, "Many are impatient with what they consider the slow progress of socialization in Russia. As a working woman said: 'The old people think that the Five-Years Plan is going too quickly, but for the young people it is not going quickly enough.' The millennium must come at once and every remnant of capitâlism must disappear. The Party, in their view, must not be guilty of any leniency either towards the class enemies at home or towards the Imperialist abroad. A conversation with among Red Army commander will best illustrate the attitude of the rulers of Russia: 'We must be strong and show no mercy. We are not a tender-hearted set of people. We must not hesitate, for example, to crush the kulaks and send them to cut wood in the forests of the north.' These were people who shot writers and painters as spies for the bourgeois because they created art that was too 'tender-hearted'." (sic)

Since the main purpose of the trip was to evaluate the progress of the Five-Year Plans, Jones reported his findings, writing, "The active minority firmly believes that ultimately Communism will be victorious. To attain this victory in Russia their method is the Five-Years Plan (October 1, 1928 to September 30, 1933), which has a threefold object – rapid industrialization, complete collectivization of agriculture, and the elimination of all capitalist elements in the country. The State Planning Commission, in collaboration with the whole country, prepares a vast plan for the whole country, for each district and for each factory. Thus the economic system is highly centralized and the means of production in industry are already almost entirely in the hands of the State. The whole energies of the ruling body are concentrated upon the execution of the Five-Years Plan, and all national activities, from education to art, are subordinated to one object, the rapid and complete socialization of the Soviet Union."

Jones describes the shock brigades enlisted to push forward the Five Year Plan calling them "groups of energetic and enthusiastic Communists who offer their services free of charge to the State and who rally the other workers to carry out or to exceed the plan of the factory or mine. Many thousands have been sent out to the villages, where they arouse the enmity of the peasants by their vigour and ruthlessness in forcing the households too rapidly into collective farms." Were they successful? Without referring to the transfer of technology and expertise from the West, Jones writes, "In some branches of industries the boast of the Communists are fully justified. The power development of the electrified industry are tremendous and the quality of the materials used and of the products is far better than in other industries. The telephone system, for example, works well. The increased sales of Russian oil testify to the development of the Baku district. Aviation is progressing rapidly and a Trans-Siberian air route is being planned which will bring London, within a few days of Japan and thus revolutionize the postal services. New factories, mines and furnaces are being constructed everywhere. The State Publishing Company has created a network of bookshops throughout the country with vast sales of books at low prices."

Soviet figures only tell part of the story. Jones looks for what's missing. He informs his readers of *The Times,* "Statistics conceal the poor materials used in many of the factories, such as the Putilov tractor factory, the bad quality of the boots and clothes and other goods produced, the correct way in which some of the figures are compiled and the failure to provide some factories with raw materials, with transport facilities or with engineers. Much expensive imported machinery is ruined by being treated with recklessness. Moreover, there is a great wastage of brainpower, since a man's political keenness is often more important than his business ability and an expert may lose his post because of his bourgeois parents. To counter balance many of these drawbacks are unbounded faith, energy, vigor, and ruthlessness of the Communists.

Taking into account "success" in "some branches of Soviet Industry" progress was slow, even breaking down and winter promised to be very difficult for the Soviet workers and peasants "as is proved by the decision to postpone the beginning of the Third Year of the Plan from October to January. This winter the difficulties confronting the Five-Years Plan will be greater than ever for thousand of workers are already returning from the towns to the villages and many will be too weak to work." Russia was far from meeting its goal of prosperity "in one or two years time". He adds, "Far nearer to the truth are the views of the rank and file, of the non-active workers and peasants."

Jones' conclusions painted a bleak picture of life under Stalin's system of state socialized terror. "Russia remains a poor and discontented country, "he writes. "In the last few months, the Five-Years Plan has met with a check and in many districts, especially the Donetz Basin, there have been many breakdowns. Food difficulties arising from the slaughter of animals which followed he violent collectivization campaign in January and February, and from the Soviet policy of exporting foodstuffs to obtain credit at all costs, are already putting a brake on the progress of industrialization…"

In the second story for *The Times* Jones tells of conversations with the Russians showing "the growing gulf between the 'rulers' and the 'ruled' and the profound discontent of the 'non-active' inhabitants" who had "lost faith" in the communist revolution and its economic program. "There is," the young Welsh journalist writes, "however, a section of the population, which belongs partly to the 'active' and partly to the 'non-active' sections. These are the highly-skilled artisans, the engineers and the mechanics, who are well paid, who are eagerly sought after, and among whom there is no unemployment. They are so indispensable to the execution of the Five-Years Plan that they receive wages varying from 150 roubles (nominally about £15) a month to 250 or 300 roubles (£25 or £35) and more. They are able, therefore, to obtain food beyond their rations from the private traders, who sell at a higher price than the cooperative shops. Thus unless they have a bourgeois past – they are happy compared with the unskilled worker, who may receive 80 to 100 roubles (nominally £8 to £10) a month, but often less. To this intermediate section of the population belong also those who enjoy the advantages of the Rest Houses and Sanatoria provided by the State.

Regime change seems unlikely, in not "impossible". Jones writes, "Chaos appears to be the only alternative to the present Government for there is no other group outside the Party to take control. It is probable, however that within the Party itself there will be changes. The Right Wing 'Opportunists' will make themselves felt this winter… Rykov and Tomsky are despised for their weakness in the 16th Congress of the Communist Party, when they showed abject humility before Stalin. One often hears praise, however of the right wing moderate Bukharin. The remark is frequently made: 'Bukharin is not done for yet.' In his last article the following day he may have touched a nerve in Stalin when he wrote, "Bukharin, is a power to be reckoned with."

On Stalin, Jones wrote, "It would be unwise, however, to underestimate the skill in intrigue of a man like Stalin, who was too strong for Trotsky." Jones hints at a possible "revolt" calling it "improbable, but there always is the possibility, so my informant seemed to think, of a Red military leader such as the adventurer Blücher loved by the troops and popular in Russia, obtaining control of the Army and throwing out the unpopular Stalin."

That previous fatal summer of 1930 Comrade Aleksei Rykov, Soviet Premier from 1924 to 1930, and one of Bukharin's allies in the Politburo, is sent south "to rest" replaced by the arch-villian Molotov (Skryabin), a steadfast Stalinist at the center of Central Committee of the Party of the seventy-one members and always seen close to Stalin mimicking his master. During the Holodomor Motolov is a ruthless executioner of the Ukraine. Ironically he out-lives Stalin. Comrade Rykov is not so lucky, executed in 1938.

Jones rejects Soviet marketing techniques by dumbing down the population to start up the ruined economy. Clever peasants were not smiling fools of monotonous communist propaganda shown in the postcards sold on the street to foreigners. He writes, "Nor do the methods used by the Party meet with the approval of the masses. The Communists have committed a tactical blunder in over-indulging in propaganda. "We do not read the notices because we know already what is written on them," was the remark of a teacher. A miner expressed himself in more vigorous terms: "I do not believe a word they say in the papers or on the placards. They are all lies, lies, lies. Nobody reads the posters, we are so tired of them."

In the second article, Jones writes, "One of the main weapons in the hands of the active section of the population is, of course, propaganda, from which one cannot escape wherever one may go. In the train one reads in large letters: 'Let us reply to the furious arming of the capitalists by carrying out the Five-Years Plan in four years.' Across the streets large red and white banners are stretched upon which are inscribed: 'The capitalist of the West are preparing war on the Soviet Union," or "Let us destroy illiteracy.' Sitting in any co-operative restaurant one sees on all sides pictures of Lenin, Stalin and Kalinin, and such appeals as: 'On May 1st remember the oppressed workers of the capitalist countries.' In a factory, besides excellent posters on health and accidents, there are such notices as: 'God and the drunkard are the enemies of the Five-Years Plan,' or 'All, all, all, come to a meeting on August 1 to hear a report of a comrade of the Third International who has come from Germany and other countries.' Outside the Tretyakovskaya Art Gallery in Moscow the following slogan strikes the visitor: 'Art is a weapon of class warfare.' Upon the House of Soviets the following words are written upon a banner: 'To Capitalism, the international revolutionary movement brings not peace but the sword.' Finally, upon the china in the Hotel Metropole, mainly frequented by foreigners, are the words, 'Workers of the World, unite.' Besides posters, there are other more effective propaganda methods. The theatre is an implement for the socialization of the country. The film industry, of whose success the USSR is justly proud, has as its aim the spreading of Communism. The museums, which are artistically arranged and admirably kept, all teach one lesson, the evil of Capitalism and the glories of the revolution. Even such a minor institution as a shooting range must have its political use; thus the targets are the Czar, a priest, a kulak (a peasant owning more than three cows), a Chinaman, and a drunkard."

"YOU MAY BE A SPY"...

Of OGPU terrorizing the countryside and tearing open the heart and soul of the Russian peasant Jones spoke their language and recorded their suffering and brought their story back telling his readers, "The action of the State Political Police in exiling peasants, members of the intelligentsia, the priests and bourgeois, to Solovki, to the Urals and to Siberia, is condemned by the majority of the non-active inhabitants, for the sympathy of the average Russian is still, as in Czarist days, with the under-dog, with the sufferer. Fear of the secret police closed the mouths of some fellow travelers. On being asked several questions, one skilled worker became silent and said: 'I am afraid of talking to you. A lot of foreigners, Latvians and others, belong to the OGPU (the State Political Police). There are spies – most of the Komsomoltsi (Young Communists), for example – who report you. You may be a spy'."

Jones wrote what he heard, and stressed that point to his readers in an earnest effort at objectivity. He wrote down the conversations practically by verbatim and emphasized they "are not chosen on account of the opposition they express to the Soviet regime, but because they are typical of views heard in many parts of Russia." He stressed the importance they "prove that the Communist Government has to face ever-growing opposition and hatred within the country. The openness with which many Russians expressed their dissatisfaction is another striking testimony to the extent to which public opinion has been roused."

In the third and last article on October 16 for *The Times*, "The Two Russias: Strength of the Communists. War Propaganda", Jones attacked head-on the Stalin's heavy-handed dictatorship. He wrote, In spite of widespread discontent, the government seems relatively stable for there is no organized opposition. Any attempt at forming a policy opposed to the general line of the party is immediately nipped in the bud. The O.G.U. (the State Political Police) is a strong body, with powers of life and death, which can ruthlessly and immediately suppress any counter-revolutionary movement. Never the less, peasant risings are possible, but these are not likely to affect seriously the position of the Government because they can be instantly crushed. Nor will the riots, which will probably take place this winter, bring about the downfall of the Soviet power, for they will be suppressed with equal thoroughness."

The regime stays in power with the support of the Red Army which Jones calls "a class army, strongly impregnated with Communist doctrines", and he argues, nonetheless, is not impregnable from dissent within and cites Stalin's "panicky letter, and retreat" during the first two months of the year. Jones writes, "There have, however, been signs of disaffection among the peasant soldiers who form the majority of the troops. When in the first few months of this year the country was being collectivized by force, rifles were smuggled by soldiers to their friends in the villages. It was the attitude of the Army that made Stalin change his tactics very suddenly in the beginning of March and condemn the excesses of local Communist authorities towards the peasants.

Once again Jones returns to the food crisis. Soviet authorities were constructing "grain factories" as the "solution" to feed the Red Army by converting "vast State farms in Siberia, the Volga district, the uncultivated steppes of North Caucasia and elsewhere." These "Sovkhozi" are managed "by the most modern machinery" and used as "schools for the training of agricultural mechanics". They spanned "a total area of over 2,400,000 acres, and are stations for agricultural experiments as well as for production". According to Soviet estimates 123 vast farms in 1931 would produce 4,000,000 tons of grain; 8,000,000 tons in 1932. Farm workers are "paid labourers", not enslaved kulaks. There would be no famine by Soviet guarantee of "a stable supply of grain, and, if the Soviet plans for building "pig and cattle factories" succeed, there will be a regular source of meat for the army and for the important factories." Jones chooses not to identify the western firms supplying "the most modern machinery" imported from the West nor does he mention estimates for future Soviet exports of wheat and grain on the international grain market except to say "concerted action against Russian cheap imports would certainly hinder the execution of the Five-Years Plan". Of course his readers know these household names and who they are.

If Jones were a Consortium player, – and spy, – he didn't let it show in these articles for *The Times.* With famine descending on the peasants and the majority of Ukrainians certain to undergo extreme suffering this coming winter, with a appeal towards moderation and tolerance instead of intensified collectivization, shock brigades and executions, writing, "the hardships of the next months might even make the Kremlin realize that a more moderate policy must be adopted, that trade must be more free, that the peasants must not be forced into collective farms, and that goods must not be exported at the price of hunger at home." What was suspected before the trip now seemed more certain that "there is no prospect of any slow evolution towards Capitalism, such as was expected when the New Economic Policy was inaugurated."

On Kremlin preparations for another war Jones quoted a Red Army commander that makes an declaration no less extraordinary because it is true: "War is bound to come. It is inevitable. The British may not make war against us, but they will certainly get other peoples like the Poles or the Chinese to do it." And to be sure the Consortium will make it so. We can hardly think that Jones, a sharp foreign policy specialist underestimated Consortium war strategy in Russia.

"At present Soviet foreign policy is emphatically one of peace," Jones tells us. "There is no desire for war and a fervent wish for time to carry out the Five-Years Plan. Whereas a peaceful Soviet foreign policy can be predicted for the next two, three, or even four years after, it is hard to be confident about the years after." But this misses the point. Soviet State Socialism was fundamentally pragmatic with an economic and political strategy deliberately set to meet the requirements of war. It defined it and was the ultimate force spearheading the Plans with Stalinist insistence not to waver in obtaining the targets and quotas established by the Central Committee of the Communist Party.

Jones was a child born in a lost generation fed on the passion, fear and loss of war. Great Britain had been devastated by the First World War. An entire generation sacrificed their lives, most of the Empire's most able men were blown to bits, many vanished in unmarked graves buried in the mud of sodden trenches in the sickly war waged by sickened minds unable or unwilling to stop the slaughter. Jones' own father is a retired Major. War is still on everyone's minds haunted by ghosts of loved ones. So it's only natural that Jones takes war as a serious element in Soviet Government policy.

Jones writes, "First, one hears on all sides, and the Communists do not conceal it, that the war industry is developing rapidly. The Soviet demand for nickel, which is presumably for the making of bullet envelopes and armour plating is greater than Britain's. Secondly, Communism has for the Red Army and for the party the force of a religion, and when one has always been taught that the millennium is close at hand one tends to be impatient at the slowness with which history moves. Nor is the feeling engendered among the young towards the Imperialists likely to increase the friendliness towards Great Britain. 'You wait; the world revolution will come although men like Cook have proved traitors to the working class," exclaimed a Communist in a private talk. "One day the unemployed of Manchester and of London will not think of sport, but of revolution, and at the same time the British will have trouble in their colonies'."

Jones finds the Soviet Communists in the Party in a frenzied state of delirium about the inevitable war in which "Communism will ultimately triumph". It's no secret here. The coming war is argued in terms of rival ideologies and "conflicting systems". In their logic the West would ultimately fail owing to "the disorganization of capitalism". Neither Jones nor his comrades account for the full weight of the master hand of the Consortium driving these Five-Year Plans. But they do feel the oppressive weight of Soviet war propaganda, and Jones, fluent in Russian has no trouble feeling it too, and he writes, "Soviet war propaganda in the form of placards and publications is intense and is having an effect upon the youth of the country. Among the magazines which have a wide circulation are the Red Army Soldier, Aviation and Chemistry and The Aeroplane. The *Osoaviakhim*, the Society for Air Membership and Chemical Warfare has an extensive membership, and its activities range lectures on poison gas to training in the use of rifles and machine guns for women and girls as well as for men and boys."

Jones captures the essential fighting spirit and endurance of the Russian warrior who in less than a decade will be urgently called to battle to defend his homeland against the Nazi traitors no matter the ideology or leader in the Kremlin. Jones cites this when he writes, "The fear entertained by some Communists that a war will lead to an immediate rising against the régime appears unfounded. A bitter opponent of Communism declares: 'I hate the Bolshevists, but if Russia were at war, whether the Bolshevists were in power or not, I should fight at once and so would every good Russian.' Indeed, war rumours are often a means of rallying the nationalism of the Russians to the support of the government and turning away the attention of the masses from the deficiencies in home policy, for this is the Achilles' heel of the Communist regime."

Jones doesn't quite get it yet. Or, at least he doesn't let on that he knows that all too well. To the extent that he dealt with propaganda of the Soviet kind for consumption at home, or abroad, was correct. But he misses the point and it may have cost him his life. It was this fighting spirit of the Russians that the Consortium feared most of all, that essential Russian spirit which threatened the West in the First World War and the very reason why they needed to strike Kerensky down during the Russian Revolution by supporting the Bolsheviks in order for the Consortium capitalists to take proxy control of the vast Russian monopolies and Trusts, seizing dominion over the vast resources of the former Russian Empire, imprisoning the population in gulags and death camps, for which they too ultimately take responsibility in knowingly permitting Stalin to "liquidate", exterminate, inflict Genocide upon the Ukrainians through man-made famine. Many of the Americans in the Consortium are experienced professionals at fighting famine in Russia. In the twenties and thirties they proved deft in managing it, so deft that through damage control in the State Department and censorship in the press which they own and control, the Holodomor proves to be just another step towards a common system of world government once the problem of Stalin and Hitler will have been resolved.

Jones returns to the "agrarian policy" as "the final test of communism". While the communists boasted of "an excellent harvest". The Five-Year Plan, he writes, "is now tottering, and although a series of bad harvests might change the whole situation, there still remains a chance that, provided collective farms succeed, there will after two, three, or four years be some improvement in the workers lot. But weaknesses of Communism – bitter class hatred, the persecution of individual thought and of freedom, the crushing of the bourgeoisie and of the intelligentsia and the subordination of art, drama, literature and even music (is compromised sic) to political aims."

Again, Jones misses the essential point indispensable to the entire spectacle of Soviet Russia under Stalin. The Rothschild-Morgan-Rockefeller-led Consortium is the ultimate master behind the power in the Kremlin, not Stalin.

Ivy Lee is more than willing to welcome David Lloyd George's personal Secretary and keen Russian observer into the 'Ivy Lee and Associates' propaganda agency in the heart of Wall Street, New York. In fact, Lee wrote papers and lectures on the nature of propaganda and information, or news, however you wish to spin it. Lee was a very experienced master spinner. Ivy Lee was the public relations agent and confidential an extensive network of the most powerful corporate leaders and companies in America: Harriman, Rockefeller, Chrysler, Standard Oil, Pennsylvania Railroad top the list. Ivy Lee also fancied himself as something of an expert on Soviet or Bolshevik after his trip there May 1927, as Rockefeller's rep and agent.

Lee is among the first of a steady stream of emissaries who in the following decade travel to Russia as Stalin's guests, even during the height of the famine when Stalin officially denys any existence of a famine. Gareth Jones, himself, had wanted to visit the Soviet Union that same year, 1927, but diplomatic relations between Britain and the USSR had soured over the Argos spy affair, and are suspended that summer. Instead, he roughs it as a stoker on a coal ship bound for Riga and spent the summer improving his Russian while boarding with poor Russian émigrés on the eastern frontier.

After his return from Russia 1927 during the 10th anniversary of the October Revolution celebrations Lee writes and publishes his masterpiece of propaganda pushing for American diplomatic recognition of Russia. It's his crowning work intended to mold American minds towards a more favorable perception of Stalin's terror and repression. He keeps silent about Stalin's policy of complete annihilation of the anti-Russian resistance of the peoples enslaved by Moscow, mostly Ukrainians. For Lee ought to have known better, for that reason, on the occasion of the 15th Congress of the All-Russian Communist Party, Stalin approves the general collectivization of agriculture; two years later collectivization is imposed on Ukraine.

Unfortunately at the time in the early thirties when millions of Ukrainians are wiped out by systematic extermination, the diplomats and Consortium people of the Morgan-Rockefeller-Harriman clans along with the Rothschild set in London could interpret the scale of the slaughter as a prelude for even greater and more violent destruction in a second world war. It is an extremely sophisticated affair. Preparations are already in place. Lee will repeat the act in 1932 on his return from Moscow to promote the Plans and official diplomatic relations with Stalin firmly entrenched inside the Kremlin palace.

THE RISE OF FASCISM IN EUROPE: "DOCTRINE OF THE 20TH CENTURY"

Early 1933 Hitler is installed as Chancellor of Germany. He is already well-funded. "The Nazi movement received millions," The *Brown Book* tells us, "from the banks and trusts to finance their election campaigns and to suppress the working class movement and all democratic forces by fascist terrorist gangs. As repayment, the tycoons expected profitable armament contracts from Hitler." For example, Emil Kordorf, founder and head of the Rhineland-Westphalia Coal Syndicate, first met Hitler in 1927 and gives the Nazi party money on every ton of coal sold amounting to more than six million Reichsmarks a year, already before 1933. On January 27, 1932, Hitler speaks to a privately assembled audience of German industrialists; Fritz Thyssen wrote about the meeting in his book *I Paid Hitler* (*Ich bezahlte Hitler*, 1941): "... practically, I established the connection between Hitler and the important industrialists of Rhineland-Westphalia. It is generally known that on 27 January 1932 – a year before he came to power – Adolf Hitler made a 2-1/2 hour speech in the Industrialists' Club in Dusseldorf. This speech made a deep impression on the assembled industrialists, and as a result, a number of substantial donations began to flow from the heavy industries into the funds of the NSDAP... In the last years before the seizure of power the large industrial associations provided funds continuously." But when war breaks out after Hitler invaded Poland on September 1, 1939 Thyssen writes to Gen. Göering that he will not support it and flees with his family. (*Brown Book of Nazi and War Criminals,* 1965; 2nd ed. 1968)

Before the dead were buried German fascists, bankers, industrialists, and the upper eschelon in the military and government are rehabilitated almost overnight. The *Brown Book* blames "conquest-mad German imperialism" for the evil of Hitler's Nazism, "armament monopolies and the big banks – IG Farben, Flick, Thyssen, AEF, Siemens, Krupp, Haniel, the Deutsche Bank, the Dresdner Bank, the Commerze-Bank and others". Anti-fascists in West Germany in the 1960s were alarmed by the resurgence "the same Nazi spirit" and neo-Nazis in the police force up to chancellor Kurt-Georg Kiesinger, and the Finance Minister, Franze Joseph Strauss.

The rise of fascism in Europe, in particular in Italy helps to put into the spirit of the time and place of events our Holodomor story with a view in mind of how many leaders in the State Department and within the Consortium suffer this perverse psychological bent toward extremism in every facet of normal life, something that FDR was acutely aware of and with characteristic nonchalance dismissed. Writing under the scholarly archways of All Souls College at Oxford to complete his book *Mussolini's Italy*, RJB Bosworth, reflects on the "number of immediate ramifications in Hitler's rise" for fascism in Italy while having enormous impact on democratic governments struggling and the dangers that threaten the freedom of the individual everywhere during this period.

"The morality of war and peace," Bosworth concludes," in other words, was simply that there was no morality. Fascism, with its habitual language of aggression – not for nothing did Mussolini regularly rejoice in his own savagery, seeing himself as a cat who walked by itself at night ready to scratch, claw and kill – deliberately tinctured such thoughts and assumptions. Yet Fascism did not by itself create its bleakly Darwinian view of the functioning of the international system. Perhaps the relatively weak are automatically inclined to doubt the moral preaching of the powerful and to seek any way to gain ground, whether metaphorically or literally. The conclusion that we live in a wicked world, is after all, one that frequently does seem to fit the state of humankind." That certainly applies to Stalin and his fundamental understanding of human nature which arouses his passion for cruelty and violence.

"In any case," Bosworth elaborates, "from 1930 onwards, in the day-to-day world of diplomatic dealing, developments outside Italy, although to a degree influenced by the Fascist story, began to play a searchlight on the regime's position in Europe and so require that the fudging and contradiction possible until then be abandoned or adapted to changing circumstances and opportunities. In September 1930 the National Socialist German Workers Party, under the Austrian-born demagogue Adolf Hitler, suddenly won more than 100 seats in the German Reichstag. In the two elections of 1932 it more than doubled that total and, on 30 January 1933, the Nazi *Fuhrer* was invited to become Chancellor of Germany. From then on every aspect of European politics was rendered unstable because of the menace of Nazism.... As the 1920s came to a close, the debate about the universal merit or potential of the Fascist revolution grew... The Nazi advance was one encouragement to think universally. The numerous retreats from the Wilsonian mixture of parliamentarianism, liberal capitalism and benign nationalism (self-determination), which by October 1938, left not a single liberal democracy surviving in all Europe outside its western fringe, were similarly influential in stimulating Italians to think that generic fascism might be 'the doctrine of the twentieth century', as the *Duce* took ambitiously to calling it.... From 1933 onwards it was no longer possible to be a 'fascist' in the same way as before." (R. J. B. Bosworth, 299-302)

These are not people who made a mistake and regretted it. They were "proven murderers of anti-fascists and resistance fighters, who are again at work in West Germany" along with 20 ministers and state secretaries, 189 generals and admirals of the Bundeswehr in leading NATO and Defense Ministry posts, 1,118 high judicial officials, 244 Foreign Office and embassy posts, 300 top posts in law enforcement and the Office for the Protection of the Constitution. They polled over two million votes, or 7.7% in seven provinces. "At the Reichstag elections in 1928, the 'handful of right-wing extremists' received 2.6% of the votes. That was exactly five years before 1933..." From 1945 to 1967 in East Germany (GDR) and the Soviet occudied zone a total of 16,583 persons are charged for war crimes and crimes against peace and Humanity; of the 12,818 found guilty, 119 were sentenced to death, 239 to life imprisonment, and 5,090 to imprisonment of more than three years. In West Germany which had three times the population of the GDR by 1964 only 12, 457 persons actually faced a tribunal with only 5,234 convictions; 9 are sentenced to death, and 71 persons are sentenced to life in prison. (*Brown Book of Nazi and War Criminals,* 1965; 2nd ed.1968, 12-3)

Ivy Lee is devilishly clever and knows how to manipulate the poor and uneducated masses. He picks up skills early working the political campaign route in New York City and grabs his big break when he shows the Rockefellers how best to manage their ugly public image in the city's newspapers with a little text and carefully staged family photos to show the simple nature of the everyman, the kind, generous, unpretentious and God-fearing true American. Lee quickly becomes the personal rep and chief public relations agent of JD Rockefeller, Sr., the world's richest man. Hired to clean up the scandal the Ludlow massacre at their Colorado Fuel and Iron Company mines in 1914, when hired Rockefeller death-squad thugs who gunned down and burned workers and their wives, women and children in the mining camps, Lee earned himself permanent employment to protect the Rockefeller image and transform the family name into a pillar of respectability and success and the shining icon of the American Dream. This he did for the next three decades until his death. Lee was already experienced with a career as image maker for America's richest capitalists. In 1908, he took over the publicity bureau of the Pennsylvania Railroad and became known as a trusted and clever Harriman man before moving over to the Rockefellers and Standard Oil Co.. Rockefeller had built up the powerful oil monopoly with shrewdness, luck and political skill helped by politically connected lawyers. The goal of the Rockefeller oil empire had always been the complete monopoly of the oil business in the United States and throughout the world. By 1915 during the war years, Standard produced almost one third of the entire oil yield of the United States. Lee lived briefly in London from 1911-2 and lectured at the London School of Economics

– "the paper money mob" – and became a member of the Royal Economic Society like his son James. When America entered the war in 1917 he handled publicity work for Morgan banker H. Davison, a director of the war cabinet and chairman of the American Red Cross. Lee worked as his personal assistant and served as ARC's head of public relations in the great mobilization drive to get young American men in the trenches overseas in Europe.

A 1952 book *Rockefeller Internationalist* by Emanuel Josephson describes the Rockefeller stake in the Soviet Union and Lee as a Pilgrims Society member directly linked to the center of Consortium power ever since he was hired by John D. Rockefeller Jr. to protect his father's fortune and his grandsons David, Nelson and Lawrence, and their grandchildren, and so on. Read the chapter titled "The Rockefeller-Soviet Axis", Josephson writes, "New fronts, hundreds of them, were created and sponsored, fostered and financed by the Rockefellers, their associates and allies, in order to build up sentiment in favor of Soviet Russia and recognition of the Bolshevik regime." Lee managed Rockefeller's pro-Nazi and pro-Bolshevik propaganda in the United States and taught the Bolsheviks another lesson in the discipline of advertising, propaganda and public relations.

First the Soviets under the rising star of Stalin, later Hitler's Nazis benefit from the wily Ivy Lee. A trip to Moscow that May 1927 to represent the Rockefeller banks and businesses is timed with Stalin's aggressive rejection of Lenin's NEP that had eased restrictions on private property affording the peasants a minimum of ownership and initiative in the countryside to eke out a living and manage their small produce. Stalin's policy was a plan within a plan having as its aim the complete annihilation of the anti-Russian resistance of the peoples enslaved by Moscow. For this reason alone Stalin on the occasion of the 15th Congress of the All-Russian Communist Party in 1927 approves the general collectivization of agriculture; in 1929 collectivization was imposed on Ukraine.

Lee was only one of the first of a steady stream of its Consortium emissaries who in the following decade traveled to Russia as royal guests of the Soviets. Lee was an ice-breaker and fixer. That same year Standard Oil of New York built a refinery in Russia. Lee then wrote and published his book pushing for normalization. In 1928, as part of Stalin's Five-Year economic plans, Chase National Bank, headed by the Pilgrims' Society member Albert H. Wiggin, a Lee client, and Morgan's Equitable Trust where another Pilgrim member Alvin W. Krech sells Bolshevik bonds in the US, with Lee's assistance inside the extensive Pilgrims Society – Consortium network. Morgan's favorite German banker Schacht heads the Berlin office and the critical link for the Americans needing information on Nazi and Soviet strategic industrial plans and programs.

From 1930 the aging Albert Wiggin runs the newly merged Chase National Bank with his successor Winthrop Aldrich there as president representing the Rockefeller money; Aldrich's father is Senator Nelson Aldrich from Rhodes Island, the power-broker setting up the centralized Federal Reserve Banking system. Winthrop married JD Rockefeller's sister. A Nazi family affair now. Aldrich also had important interests with the communists in Moscow.

With the famine killing millions of Ukrainians, elsewhere in Washington DC during June 1933, Congressman McFadden urges Americans during hearings to make an inquiry into Rockefeller's Chase bank deals with the Soviet State Bank. But who will listen? McFadden tells Americans they should think for themselves if they don't wish to be deceived by politicians and newspapers owned by the Consortium. He declares, "Open up the books of Amtorg, the trading organization of the Soviet government in New York, and of Gostorg, the general office of the Soviet Trade Organization, and the State Bank of the USSR and you will be staggered to see how much American money has been taken from the US Treasury for the benefit of Russia." The remarks of the experienced Congressman have to be taken into account as serious revelations of American engagement with Stalin and revealed to Americans at a critical time in the famine and public newspaper controversy when it was still possible for the American government to pressure Stalin or at least send a signal to end the bloodshed and forced death by starvation. McFadden is giving it to the Americans straight. And for the record he declares for the whole country to see, "The Soviet government has been given US Treasury funds by the Federal Reserve Banks acting through the Chase Bank and Morgan Guaranty Trust Co. and other banks in New York City." Congressman McFadden later died under "mysterious circumstances". But does anybody listen? Does anybody care? (E. Mullins, *Secrets of the Federal Reserve*)

To have an idea of the power of the Rockefeller fortune in the USSR, read Gary Allen's *None Dare Call It Conspiracy* (1972). It appeared in the era of Solzhenitsyn's visit to the United States during the thaw of détente and the winding down of the Vietnam War failure of US foreign policy. Allen writes: "A strange event occurred in October 1964. David Rockefeller, president of the Chase Manhattan Bank (they merged in 1956) and chairman of the Council on Foreign Relations, took a vacation in the Soviet Union. This is a peculiar place for the world's greatest "imperialist" to vacation since much of Communist propaganda deals with taking all of David's wealth away from his and distributing it to "the people". A few days after Rockefeller ended his vacation in the Kremlin, Nikita Khrushchev was recalled from a vacation at a Black Sea resort to learn that he had been fired! As far as the world knew, Khrushchev was absolute dictator of the Soviet government and, more important, head of the Communist Party which runs the USSR. Did David Rockefeller journey to the Soviet Union to fire an errant employee?

Obviously the position of premier in the Soviet Union is a figurehead with the real power elsewhere, perhaps New York. In *The Rockefellers, An American Dynasty* (1976) by Peter Collier, we find – "Ever after, David would have a special cachet in Moscow. After the 1968 elections, the Russians let it be known through diplomatic channels that chances for rapprochement would be dramatically increased if David were ambassador. George Guilder says– 'David goes through Russia and is treated royally. Ironically, nobody knows how to revere, blandish and exalt a Rockefeller half so well as the Marxists.' Chou En-Lai who as Premier of the People's Republic of China met with David Rockefeller in 1973 to work out financing and trade deals. America was led to believe that it was President Nixon who "opened up China." (C. Savoie, *World Money Order III,* 2005)

Is it possible for one man to command such international power? Yes, provided he has the support of many other powerful men– members of the Consortium Pilgrims on both sides of the Atlantic. Note the jubilant Pilgrims Society member David Rockefeller, who called $50,000 "a few cents" reveling in the knowledge of the plans shared with powerful associates– The financiers were interested not only in exploitation of America in the 19th century, which they did on a grand scale. They were the first "globalists". When *David: Report on a Rockefeller* by William Hoffman is published (1971) publicity on the back of the book states, "One President after another has done his bidding."

It was true. Hoffman writes, "The Governor of the richest state in the union is his brother. His life style would make Alexander the Great weep with envy. The power he wields crosses all borders, can make or destroy governments, start or stop wars, profoundly influence everyone's life – including yours! Yet by his own careful design, few people have known anything about David Rockefeller." The front cover caption reads– "For David Rockefeller The Presidency of the United States Would Be a Demotion! The Whole Story of the Single Most Powerful Man in the World." Of course, it was an unauthorized biography and it might be very hard to find a copy the Rockefellers didn't buy up. Yet Hoffman missed the Pilgrims Society connections, however, in anticipation of the tremendous influence he engaged Hoffman did mention David Rockefeller's founding of Bilderberg, in 1954, and that his "enormous" influence in the Council on Foreign Relations (CFR), grouping together diplomats, national politicians, military and intelligence officials, with people from finance, corporations, academia and the press. All together, they pretty much control the actors who implement the domestic and foreign policy setting the mindset and extending their power over the culture of the United States. (W. Hoffman, *David: Report on a Rockefeller*)

In a short but salient essay titled *World Money Order III* (2005), Charles Savoie zeroes in on the century old Rockefeller fortress of finance and corporate financing American society, a powerhouse unlike no other driving its capitalist economy at home and around the world. Savoie writes, "The Associated Press, October 20, 1969, announced that International Basic Economy Corporation (IBEC), a Rockefeller brothers holding, acquired as partners in Soviet trade, industrialization and development, and a firm of N. M. Rothschild & Sons of London. Once again we see reader how the two most important names in The Pilgrims Society took a fundamental position in building the monolithic totalitarian system of state Communism. On July 17, 1973, Pilgrims Society member David Rockefeller went before Congress urging it grant the Soviet Union most favored nation trading status. "In one country after another" Savoie observes, "Communism has been imposed on the population from the top down. The most prominent forces for the imposition of that tyranny came from the United States and Great Britain." (C. Savoie, *World Money Order III*, 2005)

Ivy Lee spends the last decade of his tragic life in denial and was very well paid for it. It set a standard for his day. Goebbels emulated him. Stalin imitated his methods. All these men admire Rockefeller capitalism and crave for his money. In the end Lee is doomed, his brain rotten with cancer. Rockefeller's Farben business is a dark cloud hanging over the choir-boy innocence the Rockefellers prefer for their family image. Their New Jersey company sends Lee to Germany in 1934 to clean things up and paint Farben and the Nazi business in a better picture for the news instead of thousands of SS *Brandenburgrs*, special forces, boot-stomping and saluting pursuing *Lebensraum,* living space, marching in file with arms extended in salute to their Fuhrer to seize an Empire in the lands of "savages".

Upon his return to the US a weary and exhausted Lee is immediately summoned to appear before the public and answer questions raised in Congress before a Special House Committee on Un-American Activities. A week after Hitler's SA blood purge by the Gestapo in the "Night of the Long Knives" late June and July the Committee testimony and a bold headline hits the press: Lee Exposed as Hitler Press Agent". Lee advises the Reich's foreign minister von Ribbentrop to tone down the militarist propaganda or rearmament, and Lee writes, "The National Socialist government has repeatedly proclaimed its sincere desire for international peace .... It should be clearly understood that the German people are not asking for arms but for equality of rights. Lee wants to carry to the world the message that the 2.5 million soldiers "between the ages of 18 and 60, physically well trained and disciplined, but not armed, not prepared for war, and organized only for the purpose of preventing for all time the return of the Communist peril". (P. Collier and D. Horowitz, *The Rockefellers*, 681-2, ft. 225, re. P. C. Hiebert, 290-1; US Senate SubCommittee on War Mobilization, Report on IG Farben, Washington, DC, 1946)

Time can be overcome. Lee dies denying he was a paid agent for Hitler. Lee succumbed to a brain tumor in 1934 while defending his publicity work for IG Farben. Dodd tersely notes his exit from the stage, and writes in his diary, "It is only another of the thousands of cases where love of money ruins men's lives ... I cannot say a commendatory word about him to the State Department." Nor does JD Rockefeller, Sr. whose reputation he salvaged during the 1914 Ludlow murders leave a trace of prayer for his salvation; reporters gathering outside his gates were told "Mr. Rockefeller could not under any circumstances be disturbed after six". There is no need to dwell on Lee. His grandson Nelson Rockefeller, the future governor of New York sends a polite telegram to Lee's widow calling Ivy Lee "a great leader"; nine months pass before JDR, Jr. sends kind condolences, writing, "What he did for us ... was of the greatest value", and sends a copy of his letter to each of his five sons, for the record. (W. E. Dodd, *Ambassador Dodd's Diary*, 155; P. Collier and D. Horowitz, *The Rockefellers*, 226 re. telegram to Mrs. Ivy Lee, Rockefeller Family Archives)

His hard-working paymaster JD Rockefeller, Jr. astounds his associates and sons with his constant dedication to preserving his father's extraordinary wealth that he inherited along with the wishes and intentions of its creator God Almighty and transformed by an unswerving faith in both. Collier and Horowitz's flattering book on the Rockefeller family describes the rapid expansion and dominance of the Rockefeller Chase banking empire and corporate investments and the religious convictions of JDR, Sr. and "Junior" but there is no reference whatsoever in the seven hundred page family history to Rockefeller war profiteering during the First World War (the Rockefeller Foundation led the money barons contributing millions to the war mobilization campaigns for the YMCA, American Red Cross, Salvation Army, Jewish Welfare Board....) when oil was essential to the Allied and American war effort, nor to financial and commercial dealings with Soviet Russia and, in particular, oil or grain deals. Reader, our best consideration cannot dismiss this as oversight or negligence. This omission is deliberate. But we do learn from Collier and Horowitz that JDR, Jr., or "Junior" by the early twenties and in the future exercises "control of a constellation of cultural and economic institutions whose reach was international and whose power was unrivaled in American life. He breakfasted with Presidents and was accepted in circles where his father's name had been anathema." To avoid new legislation in 1916 raising the estate tax from 10 to 25 Rockefeller, Senior steadily passed down over four years his entire fortune to his son amounting to nearly $500 million, or at present value, $12.5 billion. The oil tycoon still has a cool billion to play with and reads the stock prices devoutly every day after uttering his morning prayers, "God Bless the Rockefellers, God Bless Standard Oil ...". (P. Collier and D. Horowitz, *The Rockefellers*, 135)

THE DULLES BROTHERS & THE CONSORTIUM NAZI CONNECTIONS

Had Jones looked closer into Lee's circle of "associates" he might have learned of the importance of Rockefeller and the J. Henry Schroeder Corporation's plans for a second world war. As Stalin organized his national agricultural production with increased repression, intensified grain confiscations and deportations, Schroeder and the Rockefeller Consortium were financing Adolf Hitler's fascist usurpation of power in Germany. In his chapter "The Hitler Connection" in *Secrets of the Federal Reserve* Eustace Mullins writes: "Although any number of magnates have been given credit for the financing of Hitler, including Fritz Thyssen, Henry Ford, and J. P. Morgan, they, as well as others, did provide millions of dollars for his political campaigns during the 1920s, just as they did for others who also had a chance of winning, but who disappeared and were never heard from again."

Mullins tells us more: "In December of 1932, it seemed inevitable to many observers of the German scene that Hitler was also ready for a toboggan slide into oblivion. Despite the fact that he had done well in national campaigns, he had spent all the money from his usual sources and now faced heavy debts. In his book *Aggression* (London, 1934), Otto Lehmann-Russbeldt tells us that 'Hitler was invited to a meeting at the Schroeder Bank in Berlin on January 4, 1933. The leading industrialists and bankers of Germany tided Hitler over his financial difficulties and enabled him to meet the enormous debt he had incurred in connection with the maintenance of his private army. In return, he promised to break the power of the trade unions. On May 2, 1933, he fulfilled his promise'.

Present at the January 4, 1933 meeting are the Dulles brothers, John Foster Dulles and Allen W. Dulles of the New York law firm, Sullivan and Cromwell, which represented the Schroeder Bank." Allen Dulles holds a director seat in J. Henry Schroeder Company." Allen Dulles already heads the Near East Division of the State Department under Stimson. (Otto Lehmann-Russbeldt, *Aggression*, London: Hutchinson, 1934, 44; E. Briggs, *Proud Servant;* E. Mullins, *Secrets of the Federal Reserve*)

For at least four decades since the First World War the Dulles brothers invariably kept popping up in strategic places everywhere. Eustace Mullins, in *Secrets of the Federal Reserve* wrote: "The Dulles brothers often turned up at important meetings. They had represented the United States and the Paris Peace Conference (1919); John Foster Dulles would die in harness as Eisenhower's Secretary of State, while Allen Dulles headed the Central Intelligence Agency for many years. Their apologists have seldom attempted to defend the Dulles brothers appearance at the meeting which installed Hitler as the Chancellor of Germany, preferring to pretend that it never happened. Obliquely, biographer Leonard Mosley by-passes it in *Dulles* when he states, 'Both brothers had spent large amounts of time in Germany, where Sullivan and Cromwell had considerable interest during the early 1930's, having represented several provincial governments, some large industrial combines, a number of big American companies with interests in the Reich, and some rich individuals.' Neither Dulles nor J. Henry Schroeder were to be suspected of being pro-Nazi or pro-Hitler; the inescapable fact was that if Hitler did not become Chancellor of Germany, there was little likelihood of getting a Second World War going, the war which would double their profits." (Leonard Mosley, *Dulles*, NY: Dial, 1978, 88)

Again Mullins breaks new ground, writing here some startling revelations not easily found elsewhere in the plethora of dense darkness that oppresses memory and classified documents as tightly sealed and oppressed as the earth and more so. Mullins writes, "*The Great Soviet Encyclopedia* states, 'The banking house Schroeder Bros. (Hitler's banker) was established in 1846; its partners today are the barons von Schroeder, related to branches in the United States and England ...'." He adds, observing that "*The New York Times* noted on October 11, 1944 : 'Senator Claude Pepper criticized John Foster Dulles, Gov. Dewey's foreign relations adviser for his connection with the law firm of Sullivan and Cromwell and having aided Hitler financially in 1933. Pepper described the January 4, 1933 meeting of Franz von Papen and Hitler in Baron Schroeder's home in Cologne, and from that time on the Nazis were able to continue their march to power.' The financial editor of *The Daily Herald* of London wrote on Sept. 30, 1933 of 'Mr. Norman's decision to give the Nazis the backing of the Bank (of England.)' John Hargrave, in his biography of Montagu Norman says, 'It is quite certain that Norman did all he could to assist Hitlerism to gain and maintain political power, operating on the financial plane from his stronghold in Threadneedle Street. (Bank of England) Baron Wilhelm de Ropp, a journalist whose closest friend was Major F. W. Winterbotham, chief of Air Intelligence of the British Secret Service, brought the Nazi philosopher, Alfred Rosenberg, to London and introduced him to Lord Hailsham, Secretary for War, Geoffrey Dawson, editor of *The Times*, and Norman, Governor of the Bank of England. After talking with Norman, Rosenberg met with the representative of the Schroeder Bank of London. Managing director of the Schroeder Bank F. C. Tiarks is also a director of the Bank of England. After the Nazis gain power in 1933 Schroeder is appointed the German representative at the Bank of International Settlements in Basel, there in proximity to Allen Dulles. Hargrave says 'Early in 1934 a select group of City financiers gathered in Norman's room behind the windowless walls, Sir Robert Kindersley, partner of Lazard Brothers, Charles Hambro, F.C. Tiarks, Sir Josiah Stamp, (also a director of the Bank of England). Governor Norman spoke of the political situation in Europe. A new power had established itself, a great 'stabilizing force', namely, Nazi Germany. Norman advised his co-workers to include Hitler in their plans for financing Europe. There was no opposition'." (*The Great Soviet Encyclopedia*, London: Macmillan, 1973, v.2, 620; J. Hargrave, *Montagu Norman*, 217; E. Mullins, *Secrets of the Federal Reserve*)

Business abhors uncertainty. Well, that's the argument anyway that capitalist business enterprise require precise numbers and market targets that respect the bottom line. It requires stability and order. Stalin promised that, and in so far as America was concerned by the time of the late twenties and the Soviet Plans it was time to demystify the Bolshevik mythology and conceal communism within a mystery better adapted to accommodating good business with the West. Lee understood that it was better not to perceive the USSR as "an enigma wrapped in mystery" to paraphrase the famous Churchill axiom of the civil war interventionist days a few years before in the 1919-21 era. Lee doesn't need an official inquiry to know times had changed. All this is clearly apparent to the leaders. The ritual remains the same, however, by virtue of his new words and sacred powers. By the mid thirties after the tumult of the Holodomor had passed these leaders know that the USSR has progressed under Stalin and American business partnership as the exemplary model for a new beginning of the great Proletarian Revolution of "the New Man" and in New Soviet Society of the CP?

Unless endowed with the gift of hindsight one might otherwise have thought that Gareth Jones could not have found a more powerful and experienced publicity man to rally the cause of the Ukrainians. In another world, in another time, that might be near generations in the future. Here he was in New York City in the heart of Wall Street with the experienced and respected Ivy Lee who for nearly twenty years had been the personal representative of the great JD Rockefeller himself. He is after all reputed to be the richest man in the world, without equal, except for the Rothschilds. But Gareth Jones is no fool. And we know reader that Ivy Lee is the father American PR, a big man in Manhattan, the apex of corporate America.. No better expert could spin a lie and make evil look that benign. He had done it for Rockefeller, and was doing it now for both Hitler and Stalin. These kind men are poseurs, fakes. They appear harmless yet they are the most dangerous to be feared, controlled, or killed. In fact, killing is one of their most endearing professional traits. No stains, traces, smoking guns, Theirs is a dirty business but their hands are clean and they look spotless in their official suits and hats chauffeured in their private cars. And still the empires are speeding ahead madly insane with militarist fever and unbridled passions to conquer more territories with more powerful weapons when everything will be as it has been for centuries, with more Genocide and exterminations as it was before history began. Why Hitler ... why Stalin ... why Lee and all his corporate partners the Consortium? How much longer will the entire human race be held hostage to the exterminators?

Before Lee came to the attention of the richest and most powerful man in the world, he had to have a plan to get on the inside and bring attention to himself and show just how smart he could be and what he had learned at Princeton, how to debate the public and win at any cost. He didn't have family connections like Dulles. So he made it with the railroads and by serving the interests of the super rich. Their methods were the same. He never had to revise his 'principles'. "Those methods did not differ materially from those of the respected Morgans, Vanderbilts, Goulds and others in their class. According to conspiracy theorist of his day, Emanuel Josephson writes, in spite of his publicity efforts to create a favorable image, "Rockefeller's chief offense was his inordinate success and his taciturnity and independence." (E. M. Josephson, *The Strange Death of Franklin D. Roosevelt*)

The game of public relations, Lee knows perfectly well is the business of spinning lies around truths in the pay of corporations and putting a good face on wrong doing with the intention to create goodwill for a person or institution. Is it the other face of market capitalism, the falsehood of the negated truth, the deceit of despair yet made to seem as delectable as paradise or a false diamond? That's how he made his money. Edward Bernays (1891-95), fourteen years younger, is a blood nephew of Dr. Sigmund Freud, the father of psychoanalysis. It takes only one small step to apply his methods to the psychology of corporations to manipulate public opinion and control the masses. Bernays steps into adulthood just as the Anglo-American propaganda machine of WWI won the war at home and blurs the distinction between patriotism and treason in a climate intolerant of free speech or political dissent.

If Stalin engineered the soul, Lee and Bernays "engineered consent". Born in Vienna, Austria, Bernays pioneered the PR industry's use of psychology and other social sciences to design marketing campaigns using innovative techniques of public persuasion. Bernays declared, "If we understand the mechanism and motives of the group mind, it is now possible to control and regiment the masses according to our will without their knowing it."

Bernays actually calls this scientific technique of molding public opinion in the machine age the "engineering of consent", and he advocated "third party authorities" in much the same fashion, though now with modern techniques of psychology, to fashion society as did the Gillman of Yale in the 19th century. A year after the end of war, in 1919, Bernays opened his Manhattan office guided in part by the US publication of Freud's *General Introduction to Psychoanalysis*. "If you can influence the leaders, either with or without their conscious cooperation, you automatically influence the group which they sway," he said with a smile. One of his clients, was President Calvin Coolidge who became President in 1923 after Harding's mysterious death. So was Procter & Gamble, General Electric, American Tobacco, CBS and other firms of the Consortium. Bernays brought PR to AT&T and there worked with Arthur Page, son of Wilson's ambassador to the UK during WWI. Together they shaped the almost superhuman identity of the global communications giant. Bernays stayed there for twenty years.

By 1933 the Bernays book titled simply *Propaganda* has become a most important model textbook Hitler's Nazi propaganda minister Joseph Goebbels. Not that he ever intended it that way, or maybe he did. In the chaos and conflict of the postwar era, Bernays replaces the priesthood of indoctrination with scientific manipulation of public opinion which he describes is necessary for the survival of "democratic society". He has a lot in common there with Harvard's national syndicated columnist and Washington insider Walter Lippmann, another willing publicist for the Consortium myth-makers, or illusionists. Anything to distract public attention and preoccupy the masses, diversions from the real skullduggery going on. Better to get them all lost and stuck in comprehensible gibberish, rhetoric and other literary nonsense. Anything but the true facts to see the real picture of what's going on behind the news that seldom gets into print. Fill the news with nonsense and they will have no sense at all. Just good obedient faithful consumers and taxpayers believing that their government loves and protects them. "Smile for the camera, Mr. President...".

In fact, Bernays advocates a continuation of the same logic of war and destruction for capitalist profits of the Wall Street elite, now shielded and enriched by their corporations as defenders of buzz-words of individual freedom and democracy now defined by the market place. He wrote, "The conscious and intelligent manipulation of the organized habits and opinions of the masses is an important element in democratic society. Those who manipulate this unseen mechanism of society constitute an invisible government which is the true ruling power of our country... We are governed, our minds are molded, our tastes formed, our ideas suggested, largely by men we have never heard of. This is a logical result of the way in which our democratic society is organized. Vast numbers of human beings must cooperate in this manner if they are to live together as a smoothly functioning society. ... In almost every act of our daily lives, whether in the sphere of politics or business, in our social conduct or our ethical thinking, we are dominated by the relatively small number of persons ... who understand the mental processes and social patterns of the masses. It is they who pull the wires which control the public mind."

In his autobiography, titled *Biography of an Idea*, Bernays recalls entertaining Karl von Weigand, foreign correspondent of the Hearst newspapers, during a dinner at his home, and he writes, "Goebbels had shown Weigand his propaganda library, the best Weigand had ever seen. Goebbels, said Weigand, was using my book *Crystallizing Public Opinion* as a basis for his destructive campaign against the Jews of Germany. This shocked me... Obviously the attack on the Jews of Germany was no emotional outburst of the Nazis, but a deliberate, planned campaign." Nothing new here. All you had to do is read fellow Austrian Hitler's own *Mein Kampf* to know that, and it is freely available to any pro-fascist publicist, like Hitler-admirer Ivy Lee, whose private papers are now carefully tended by archivists of Princeton University Mudd Library.

All of Ivy Lee's connections to Rockefeller-funded medical institutes, universities, and foundations, including the vastly rich Rockefeller Foundation, were now at Jones' disposal. Had the great wealth of America heard the prayers of the folded hands of the Ukrainian Babushkas and the sweet healthy young Christian and pagan girls, a land forever rich in folk songs and spiritual forces. Well, not exactly. As fate would have it, Lee turned out to be most ineffective in helping the Gareth Jones publicize the tragedy of the Ukrainian people. Another cruel trick of fate, or is this destiny? Where lay the chance of it? It seems too cheap, too cute to call this merely "highly coincidental". But here Jones finds himself directly responsible to an agent acutely responsible for promoting western financial and technological support for Stalin's radical totalitarian agenda. Will he continue to play puppet to the Consortium masters holding the strings? Or will he become the whistle-blower of the first order to blow the Holodomor Genocide sky high?

Lee was not disposed to offend either his clients in industry and finance with unfavorable news about Stalin or Hitler. On the contrary, he would do his professional best to suppress any unfavorable news that would hamper recognition of the Soviet regime. Even with the allegations from Jones while still employed in his office and directly reporting to him about Soviet atrocities. Questions remain. Is Jones in his pay?

Is Jones not also Lee's rep? In politics life is short and usefulness is a virtue for the employer, not the employed. In gross violations of human rights, Lee fails Jones utterly. Was Lee communicating secretly through his own back channels to David Lloyd George about what to do with this "Mr. Jones"? Apparently Lee doesn't tell Jones the Consortium angle of modernization of the Soviet State. (We certainly don't have a record of it from Jones or Lee that he ever did.) Nor would he be obliged. Jones is smart enough to know and see for himself all that first hand. Furthermore, Gareth Jones may have read some if not all of Lee's published works, or certainly should have simply as a professional state of the obvious in their special circumstances. In fact, Jones does not just perform only one but two fact-finding trips for Ivy Lee Associates; the first trip during the winter 1930-31; and again when he takes off on his journey in 1932. It is during this time that Jones demonstrates a special interest in the financial consequences of the Consortium's onerous reparations deal bankrupting Germany since it was imposed by the 1919 Treaty of Versailles at the war's end.

Ivy Lee made national headlines in 1926 after he wrote a letter to the President of the United States Chamber of Commerce arguing for recognition of the Soviet Union. It was a curious tactic in a orchestrated calculation to gain Soviet favor and press forward the time-table. Throughout the twenties he had good insider reasons to lobby hard for recognition of the USSR. Many critics call him a Wall Street Bolshevik for doing it and charge that he was employed by Stalin for propaganda. Lee is a Rockefeller's publicist. The rush and blur of the daily news obscures the long view. People do not see that certain US business firms are doing a booming trade with the Soviet state monopoly. Ford is already a sensation and expected to sell where there. Americans only had to look back at their own recent past where the growth of the motorcar was exponential since the first American motorcar was bought on April 1, 1898; in less than two years eight thousand cars are crossing the country in all directions and a hundred taxis service Manhattan.

Lee is the first of a steady stream of emissaries who for the next ten years traveled to Russia as privileged guests of the Soviets. After his return from Moscow, Ivy Lee writes and publishes his masterpiece of propaganda in favor of Russian recognition titled *The USSR, An Enigma*; six months later his publisher Macmillan changes the title to *Present Day Russia* for a revised edition. In the book Lee sketches out the highlights of his two-week trip proclaiming that Bolshevism was "a dead dog and just needed to be buried". There was nothing to fear from the Communists. They had renounced world revolution he argued. It is a clear signal for Stalin that he get on with his business of consolidating his totalitarian dictatorship with the American Consortium business gang standing in the wings off-stage ready to do business; US recognition of the USSR in 1933 must be the first step of normalization.

By then, knee deep in the Ukrainian Holodomor, Lee and the Consortium capitalists will be up to their necks with the Nazi business. Equitable Trust Company, was headed by another Pilgrim Alvin W. Krech who helped Lee arrange the Morgan-Rockefeller banking syndicate to sell Bolshevik bonds in the US mostly using the Pilgrims Society's network to keep the Bolsheviks in power and stabilize the cash-poor Soviet regime from bankruptcy and collapse. Stalin consolidated his power in the Party. By 1927, with the bankers collaboration, Stalin is ready to launch his plan for collectivization of agriculture announced at the 15th All Soviet Congress. In reality this cover for the wholesale extermination of Ukrainian nationalism brings Stalin one step closer to the internal liquidation of the CP and most everyone in the Bolshevik commerce and banking apparatus who know anything about the US deals. Thousands of sincere genuine Party men and women perish.

In 1928 Chase National, headed by Wiggin is a star at the bank ever since he became the youngest vice president ever in 1904. From 1917 on Wiggin runs Chase National as chairman and is credited for making it a Rockefeller bank. By 1930 Wiggin, born 1868, the son a Massachusetts Unitarian minister, is now director of the New York Fed. He holds directorships in more than *fifty* American corporations.

The unidentified author of *The Mirrors of Wall Street* describes Albert Wiggin as "an uncanny genius", and a master at manipulating markets through a network of investment pools and security dealers and cashing out before the call money is withdrawn. "There was a blue-ribbon stable of seventy-two financial sharks as board members," he wrote. Although his name is inseparable from the bank Wiggen steps down in 1932 leaving him more time to admire his art collections of thousands of masterpiece paintings soon sprinkled about in sparkling donations to public museums and libraries in Boston, New York and Baltimore. Consortium bankers have indeed a sharp eye when it comes to the practicality of investing in things like paint on canvas immortalizing their names attached to iconic representations of culture instead of the basic fundamentals to improve the conditions of human life especially for families struggling to survive. We remember reader that again it rings of Marie Antoinette's rebuff of the oppressed masses in need of bread, saying, "Let them eat cake." And some day even charge the public the price of a ticket of admission! (*The Mirrors of Wall Street,* published anonymously)

William Dodd, US Ambassador to Germany in 1933 witnessed with amazement a steady stream of Wall Street bankers and industrialists that filed through the his Berlin embassy expressing their admiration for Adolf Hitler – and anxious for the ambassador to find ways to ease business with the Reich. On September 1, 1933, for example, Dodd records that Henry Mann of the National City and Winthrop W. Aldrich of the Chase both meet with Hitler, and Dodd notes, "these bankers feel they can work with him." Aldrich is the uncle of David and Nelson Rockefeller, the latter recently graduated from Dartmouth and married with all the banner press due a young prince coming into his own. Dodd also records that Ivy Lee, "showed himself at once a capitalist and an advocate of Fascism". Let's defer a moment reader. Who is this patriarch Aldrich?

Besides Harvard and U.K. Pilgrims Society member, Aldrich is high-end Consortium blood born to the inner circle. He will later become uncle to David Rockefeller, head of Chase, and Nelson, New York Governor, respectively, both ("PUS" or, Pilgrims United States). Three years before his meeting with Hitler Aldrich oversaw the greatest banking merger in American history carried through in the spring of 1930 when John D. Rockefeller Jr. withdraws from Bankers Trust and merges Chase National Bank with Equitable Trust. In the deal Winthrop W. Aldrich, – a Rockefeller –, moves from Equitable to join the brilliant taciturn Wiggin.

The sums at Chase National involved are awesome, the equivalent of nearly a third of the world's known gold supply. The Morgan-Rockefeller interests works jointly, choosing together their common target as partners, not competitors. In this particular situation they worked to a common purpose. They exerted some of their great power to strengthen the banking structure and the commercial system, and to benefit themselves and their seemingly limitless power and expanding reach in the world economy. Gary Allen writes, in *The Rockefeller File*, "Rockefeller thereby concentrated his holdings under one roof and became the dominant force in the greatest bank in the world. The entire New York banking situation was stabilized by Rockefeller gold and the magic name of the Oil King." (Gary Allen, *The Rockefeller File*, Chapter 9, "Building the Red Machine"; see A. C. Sutton.)

So it is Winthrop W. Aldrich (1885-74), President of the Chase National in 1933 during the years of Holodomor. Winthop is son of Senator Nelson Aldrich (1841-15) and the uncle to Nelson Rockefeller, the future governor of New York and the man who wanted to move into the Oval Office of the White House but it was never to be. It was largely due to Winthrop's father's work on centralized banking that laid the foundation for the Federal Reserve Act years before he joined the other bankers on Jekyl Island. Wealth and the privilege that comes with it was all Winthrop. It was the air he breathed and he was accustomed to the atmosphere of both ever since he was in diapers. His father-in-law is JD Rockefeller; JDR, Jr. is his brother-in-law married to his sister. In his prime his father Nelson led Congress with Senator Henry Cabot Lodge and spent thirty years there including the boom year prior to the Great War presiding with Brahmin character America's emergence to the top rank of world empires.

Nelson Aldrich was considered the best informed man in America on currency and fiscal questions. For at least two decades his home easily compared to the White House as a cornerstone of American financial and political force. Since American colonial days the Aldrich family lived in New England, true keepers of "the "Yankee sense of acquisition". For a quarter of a century some of the most successful, best educated, influential and political minds in America were entertained in the Aldrich home in Providence, Rhodes Island and their house in Washington DC. Senator Nelson W. Aldrich died in New York City, April 16, 1915. It is a most curious and obvious omission by the *Dictionary of American Biography* that there is no mention of the fact that he was a founder the US Federal Reserve Bank. Though Wiggin retires in 1932, Aldrich, however, remains head of Chase National from 1930 during the Hoover-Roosevelt bank negotiations with the Soviets and stays there during WWII until 1953, leaving the bank to take one final step up closer to heaven at the Court of St. James with the gait of a diplomat straight to the gateway of the King and Queen of England. There as US Ambassador Aldrich like his Consortium predecessors enjoyed the rights of knights with the honors due America's richest money men including the Order of the British Empire. His speech at The Pilgrims Society dinner on March 19, 1953 is a very royal affair and hallmark occasion for the Consortium celebrating the passing of Stalin. ("Nelson W. Aldrich, A Leader In American Politics", *Dictionary of American Biography*, 1930)

STIMSON AND HIS BOYS AT STATE

January 1, 1931. For the first few days of the New Year, Stimson is occupied with another revolution in Panama. This time the President was captured in the presidential palace he noted in his diary "and the revolutionists were in control of the city. This makes this the seventh Latin American revolution, six of them successful since this administration took office…" Stimson is relieved, however, that there was "no real danger to US troops there." Meanwhile, Stimson expressed outrage "in the case of torture in Honduras" by agents of United Fruit. Strange that he would not protest the mass brutality by Stalin who enjoyed the backing of some of the most powerful American industrial corporations in the world.

A Stimson memo of February 27, 1931 states "At Cabinet meeting this morning, we had quite a tentative discussion with regard to Russia, but it was agreed that I might bring up the whole matter after March 4th. HLS". No mention who is in attendance. He sends it to Kelley the next day.

A few days later, on March 4, 1931, Bob Kelley in Washington sends Undersecretary Castle a report from Norman Armour in the embassy in Paris, a member of the Chicago meatpacking family that made a fortune in the war, – a Pilgrims Society man, on Soviet "outstanding indebtedness" estimated by the French at 400 billion francs or, "approximately $400,000,000". Kelley omits to state that this is, in fact, the exact amount of Czarist wealth deposited "in the Chase Bank, National City Bank, Guaranty Trust Bank, the Hanover Trust Bank, and Manufacturers Trust Bank."

Kelley writes that figure "strikes me as a little high. I feel that it is closer to $300,000,000... Their chief indebtedness would seem to be to Germany in the amount of $120,000,000; to England, $50,000,000; and to the United States about $50,000,000." That is significant in light of future negotiations orchestrated by Kelley and Bullitt with Litvinov, Stalin and FDR over the debt and credit issue; fifty million dollars is the very same figure that Litvinov later proposes in a deal to end the squabbling that Bullitt uses to drag US-Soviet relations in an undertow bordering on comic farce and tragedy during the eclipse of the Holodomor and his brief stay in Moscow while the Kremlin resumes wheat exports to cover mounting debt obligations. The matters are never linked.

Kelley went on, writing, "I doubt whether their commitments in other countries are sufficient to bring the total much above $300,000,000." And he added,"I understand this is a matter in which the President himself is particularly interested..." Hoover, Castle and Stimson met to weigh the issue of bonds and credits to the Soviet Union as a means to finance trade including a large shipment of steel to Germany. (SDDF 861.51/2407-9)

Lawyers of the firm Milbank, Tweed, Hope and Webb at 15 Broad Street in Manhattan representing Rockefeller's bank Chase National inquire at the State Department and the Treasury for clarification of the government's position on importation of Russian gold into the US. Kelley is still head of Eastern European Affairs and replies on March 11 enclosing press statement from Treasury dating March 6 that the US Government had placed "...no restrictions" on either bullion or gold coin shipped "from Russia". He states, however, in his unsigned memo dated April 10, 1931 that Treasury still refuses "to have United States mints and assay offices accept Soviet gold, which affects in practice only gold that has already been imported". Kelley had talked with Cunningham over at Treasury where it everyone is in the dark and confused if the US has a policy of restriction. No one seemed to know, not even Kelley. The Customs Office confirms it's "aware of no restrictions affecting the importation of gold coin or bullion from Russia, but that certain restrictions do exist which affect the importation of jewelry from all countries." American banks", Kelley's man states, acted only as "agents in this case for the Soviet Government". And he adds, "I said that while the American banks were acting for the Soviet State Bank, it would seem that anyone was entitled to know whether restrictions against the importation of gold from Russia exist and could secure a statement from Treasury...".

The men at the Riga station continue to monitor millions of dollars of gold shipped from Moscow to Berlin. He adds, "Mellon's press statement March 6, 1928 of Treasury policy on Russian gold shipments imported into the US was said now to remain unchanged." Then, he states, "Some days ago there arrived in New

York from the National Bank of Soviet Russia some $5,000,000 ($50 million sic) of gold, half of which was consigned to the Chase National Bank and the other half to the Equitable Trust Company as agents. Since 1920, the Treasury Department has refused to accept at the United States mints and assay offices gold coming from Russia, the State Department having declined to give assurances that the title to Soviet gold will not be subject to attack internationally or otherwise." American banks, he went on to say which are "unwilling to present the gold as owners" could not deposit the gold in the NY assay office. So where does the gold actually go? Kelley is not able to provide an answer. It is a Consortium problem. He passes the memo to Stimson's office. In addition to shipping out hundreds of millions of gold rubles authorized by the Kremlin to pay for industrialization, the Soviets are shipping out millions of gold rubles worth of iridium, platinum, palladium and other precious metals and for the most part all mined with gulag slave labor. (SDDF 861.51/2419-22)

Stimson remains throughout 1931 and 1932 preoccupied with problems relating to the Manchurian crisis in the Far East and Japanese incursions there, war debts and reparations, Germany's fragile economy and disarmament issues threatening to upset the balance of power in Europe. If these concerns weren't enough to distract him from problems of the Consortium's Plans in Soviet Russia that might expose an industrial military strategy embarking the nation into a world war, Stimson also had to contend with various crises in the western hemisphere would have exposed the Consortium. That left Stalin virtually unstrapped and with his hands free to increase his repressive measures in the Ukraine. So while American banks and industry invested heavily to develop the socialized economic system of terror Stimson would take no initiative that might be perceived as interference in the internal affairs of the Soviet Union. To do so would have certainly raised questions in the press about the exact nature and role of American corporate investment in a prison economy of concentration camps, forced labor and gulags and derail the Consortium which had already invested billions of dollars from reaching its goals. (L. Henderson, *A Question of Truth*, 204; M. Casella-Blackburn cites two sources on Far East-Manchuria problem; Ulam, *Expansion and Coexistence*, 167-78; G. Kennan, in Cassella-Blackburn, 266. Both standard establishment academic sources; adjusted dollar value re. R. Chernow, *Titan*)

That spring the increase in Soviet terror and obstruction caused by the secret police prompts the Near East Foundation in the Caucasus to shut down operations in Tiflis, Georgia. Robert Skinner, in Athens sends dispatch No. 1668 on March 20, 1931 titled "Conversation with Laird Archer of the Near East Foundation concerning decision of the Near East Relief to withdraw from Armenia and Georgia." Archer was a former director of the foundation headquartered in downtown New York City on 151 Fifth Avenue. Archer met Skinner that day arriving in Athens from the Caucasus "where he had been to inspect the philanthropic activities of his organization…". Archer decides "to close them immediately and to terminate the Near East operations in that section on March 31, 1931". It had been running a trade school at Tiflis in Georgia, "a school of agriculture at Leninikan, Armenia, and a nurses' training school at Erivan." Some 3,800 persons had graduated "of whom 500 are constructed in agriculture, 270 in nursing, and 250 as teachers". He gave as his reasons for closing that "the work in Russia could no longer be called emergency work, and that the institutions were merely being used by the Soviet Government as a means of procuring competent directors for the carrying out of the Five Year Plan." Fear and terror of Soviet repression was the real reason for the closing. Skinner's memorandum to the Department reads, "During the last 18 months, 30 Russians of the Near East foundation staff have been 'removed', of whom it is quite certain that 6 were executed. The others are supposed to be in prison or in exile somewhere. No reasons were ever given for the arrests and punishment of these victims..." Archer is also upset that he was forced on arrival in Russia to exchange his dollars for roubles at the official rate, five times less the rate he could have got on the black market! (SDDF 861.48/2415)

March 26, 1931 is a "red hot busy day" but not because of the Reds in Russia. Stimson makes other notes in his diary that day that begins with a meeting at Woodley with his friend George Harrison of the New York Federal Reserve Bank, and Undersecretary Allen T. Klots, son of a Yale classmate who excelled at Winthrop & Stimson and becomes a key aide for thirty years. Stimson needs to appoint a man to the Bank of International Settlements in Switzerland. Harrison has been Joe Cotton's "informant" at the Fed. Cotton is Stimson's closest friend and unabashed confident always inclined towards outspoken honesty and sharing his basic attitudes with Stimson as they were the same. Harrison proposes Allen Foster Dulles; Stimson preferred Lansing Reed or the dapper lawyer Irving Olds, chairman of the board of US Steel (1940-52), a Yale Corp. Trustee, and also chairman of the New York Public Library. Olds once opened a speech by declaring, "Directors are like the parsley on fish – decorative but useless." (It must be a very exotic fish delicacy.) His good friend Lansing Reed (Bones 1904) is the lawyer at Davis Polk Wardwell Gardiner & Reed, and counsel for Guaranty Trust with a seat on the board of directors (1924-33). We know already reader, that Davis, Polk & Wardwell have always been the legal reps of Morgan and the Rockefellers.

George Harrison tells Stimson he is opposed having a Fed member on the Bank of International Settlements (BIS). Stimson notes in his diary, "On the other hand, he thinks it is important that we should have a more ready access to information as to what it is doing than we have now". Stimson then adds an important point that Harrison also discreetly tells him "of a proposition to form what is virtually an invested trust company under the control of international men to lend money in the rehabilitation of Europe which would not be owned by individual countries themselves, and he told me how he had tried to stop this".

The next day, Friday, March 27, 1931, Stimson meets with undercover agent William N. Haskell. Haskell had written Stimson "that he was going to Russia to take a look around and check upon what was going on there and I had invited him to come and see me". It would be a decade before the United States used military appropriations to build its global intelligence network at the outset of

World War II under William Donovan better known as "Wild Bill" and key men in the Consortium. In 1931 Stimson needed good intelligence men he could rely on. Stimson knows little about actual events in the Soviet Union and relied on information from Bill Haskell and John MacMurray, attached to the War Department. Bob Kelley had his own jealously guarded sources, Hopper, Harper, and other academics, preferably Harvard-Yale-Princeton men. Cornell, Amherst and Williams College will also do. "He had been all over Russia", Stimson notes in his diary about Haskell "probably more than any other American and almost any Russian, having first been at Tiflis, when he was High Commissioner General of Armenia (1915) and then afterward in Moscow and Russia Proper for two years while he was engaged in feeding the Russians during the great famine." So here, in the spring of 1931 the Secretary of State Henry Stimson has a private talk with Haskell about Soviet Russia and famine intervention under Hoover long before he became President.

Stimson was mesmerized, and fascinated to listen while Haskell recounted tales of the President Wilson's armed intervention adventure with the Bolsheviks. Haskell held his attention riveted on every word. Haskell had lived famines and knew their horror of suffering, disease and death. Haskell had been appointed by Wilson in 1919 as Allied High Commissioner to investigate conditions for the breakup of the pro-German Ottomon Empire and escaped capture by the Bolsheviks when he had to withdraw his mission under the Red Army advance as the Bols recaptured Armenia. Stimson notes in his diary, "Haskell says one of the requests of one of the First National Banks of Boston is to look over the situation and see what the five-year plan is doing, and how the Russians are likely to come out with it. He will be able to give us probably a more intelligent view than almost any one I can get."

The old Colonel admired Haskell, stirred out of the doldrums of debts and dollars by Haskell's details personally relayed of his "great experience" in military intelligence from the field. Stimson wrote Haskell is "a very intelligent man; and he has no motive in doing it, except to go there and find out." In other words, not a Consortium opportunist out or get a concession or turn a dollar.

Stimson brings Haskell into the loop now telling him that he is working with John MacMurrary at "the Page School at Johns Hopkins" are preparing their own "Russian investigation" and his mission already approved by the Secretary as "a good thing to do". Now Stimson briefs Hoover about the two missions but he keeps the details off the diary record.

"Hoover agreed", Stimson writes in the diary. Hoover tells his Secretary "the only thing is to look out that they don't put the investigation in the hands of the pinks." Hoover has in mind the American Russian Chamber of Commerce (ARCC) and its pro-Soviet business lobby of the Consortium. This is another example of how Stimson builds links between State and the White House to conduct separate intelligence-gathering missions for the President by personally dispatching highly qualified and experienced officers with military experience. Secretary Dean Acheson belittles this fact in his memoirs published over a generation later. (D. Acheson, *Present at the Creation*)

Two days after the Stimson-Haskell meeting the *Chicago Tribune* in its Sunday edition publishes Henry Wales' story, "Russia Seizes Rich Peasants as Colonists Uses Kulaks to Open Vast Lands in North". It features a photo of sleds hauling timber with the caption, "A redwood 'train' entering the city of Vologda in Soviet Russia." Wales toured lumber camps to investigate tales of "forced" labor. The Wales article is another example of the travesty of disinformation passed off to pacify the readers living in the Chicago community of Ukrainian descent with family relatives back home. "Ten thousand kulaks (rich peasant) families transplanted in north Russia, are not exiles; they are colonists brought here to develop new territory and take over settlements", explains a member of the Archangel Soviet to the *Tribune* reporter. Wales sees kulaks living in stench "ravenously" devouring raw fish while hired Norwegian lumberjacks lived in heated bunk houses. "But I saw well-fed mill workers and volunteer timber cutters 'wolf' down frozen herring just as voraciously." The article discounted forced labor or a Soviet gulag of concentration death camps. No attempt was made to explain why rich peasants would willfully abandon their traditional homesteads and farm work to cut and haul timber in the freezing north, or died by the hundreds and thousands on the way with inadequate food or clothing. The diplomats, however, acted as though they knew better and had countless officially-filed reports of escaped prisoners and other witnesses that proved beyond a doubt the use of forced labor in the Soviet labor concentration camps. "The Soviet press", Wales tells Chicago readers "frequently published reports of millions of starving Americans ranging in number from five to ten million followed usually by the statement that in the Soviet Russia there are today no unemployed."

With Kaganovich and Khrushchev at the top of city government, Moscow undergoes a major transformation. Foreign contractors proposed new construction projects in and around the city. "New industries were building flagship factories in the capital while older enterprises retooled and expanded. A vast military-scientific-industrial complex was forming in and around the city. Inundated with new construction projects (one hundred new factories came on line in 1931 while three hundred were rebuilt during the first five-year plan), Moscow was further swamped by migration from the countryside; 411,000 new residents (an increase of 15 percent) in 1931; 528,000, or nearly 1,500 a day, in 1932; and a total of 1.5 million, or a 70 percent rise, between 1928 and 1933." In William Taubman's account the exodus was for better jobs and wages in building up the new socialist state, however many of the workers no doubt come from the villages where life had become brutally difficult, if not impossible. (W. Taubman, 89)

WHAT KHRUSHCHEV KNEW

In 1963 Soviet Premier Nikita Khrushchev's comments in 1963 about the famine were confined to the period of 1947 during postwar food shortages and starvation. "Their method was like this", Khrushchev declares, "they sold grain abroad, while in some regions people were swollen with hunger and even dying for lack of bread." It was an unusual and candid revelation. But Khrushchev is actually describing conditions of the Holodomor of 1932-34 of which he had detailed knowledge and experience. The Gulag system and the Holodomor tactics of terror and famine are part of the Plans from 1930. During the Great Purge in 1937 Khrushchev joined Molotov and Yezhov (Nikolai Ivanovich Ezhov) and "a trainload of NKVD troops to Kiev to prune the local apparat, but the Ukrainian leadership refused to cooperate," observes Martin Malia in *The Soviet Tragedy* . "Moscow therefore decided on a clean sweep of all Ukrainian structures. By 1938 the Party and state apparats of Ukraine at all levels, as well as the cultural elite, had been replaced not once but twice or thrice." That year Khrushchev is given more powers as First Secretary of the "Ukrainian" Party and orders to entirely rebuild. Postyshev clashes openly with Stalin, and is executed; Khrushchev is elected in Postyshev's place as candidate to the Politburo, now in the same group with Zhdanov and Beria. And one day, in 1956, he would lead the violent crushing of Hungary's popular revolt for independence when young mothers crossed minefields to escape Soviet repression. (M. Malia, 258)

With peace restored and workers returning to the fields, harvests in 1947 to 1948 improved beyond state targets; by 1949, collectivization under Khrushchev absorbs 60 percent of Ukrainian peasant families. Soviet propaganda proclaimed bold progress in reducing the differences between the city and the rural villages; Cherkassy, for example, on the Dniepr is transformed into a model agro-city under his direction from Kiev, a present to Stalin for his 70th birthday anniversary.

Khrushchev's ties with Ukraine were ancestral and political. He is a good example of Stalin's new Party man who went from Kiev to Moscow on the coat-tails of Kagonovich. In 1934 he becomes Moscow Party chairman and Stalin's administrative deputy there. In 1908, Khrushchev, then a fourteen-year-old son of poor Russian peasants, moved to the eastern Donbas mining region of Ukraine where his family settles in Kuzovka (or Yuzovka, later renamed Stalino, in 1924, and Donetsk, in 1961). It had been developed after 1869 during the time of the Czar by Scottish industrialist John Hughes.

Khrushchev liked to say that Stalin knew Marxist-Leninist theory, but wasn't practical with his own hands; Stalin couldn't fix things. By fifteen Khrushchev distanced himself from the peasants' life, apprenticed to the boiler workers section and "dreamed of being a fitter"; he is soon in the shops assembling parts and machines and living in Yuzovka before the First World War, in the Ukrainian Donbas mining region. Khrushchev has a good job as a skilled metal worker earning 30 gold rubles a month. A reader of radical papers when in April 1912 news of the Czarist massacre of striking miners at the Lena gold fields in Siberia radicalizes his opposition to the regime with the result that he's fired from the German-owned Bosse and Genefeld Engineering Works and Iron Foundry when Czarist police found he had gathered donations for the families of strike victims. Khrushchev finds a job in a machine repair shop in the adjacent town Rutchenkovo where he organizes political study groups and distributes Social Democratic literature. His friendly manner amuses and assures his fellow workers when he indulges his loquacious frank and folksy humor. One woman finds Nikita especially irresitable, and in 1914, he marries Yefrosinia Pisareva, soon is the mother of two children, Yulia Nikitichna Kruschevna, and Leonid. He is exempted from military service in WWI with his good job and pay as a skilled metalworker with a large apartment. But Yefrosinia Pisareva dies of typhus during the terrible civil war period.

Khrushchev's third wife is Nina Petrovna, born in the Ukrainian part of the Vasiliev village in Kholm (Chelm) province of the former Polish kingdom then under Russian dominion. "Ethnically Ukrainian, she spoke the language far better than her husband, the future Communist party boss of Kiev," writes Taubman and his account of Nina Petrovna is an interesting profile of the emerging new Party communist of a militant woman with a decidedly strong Ukrainian background joining the CP in 1920. That summer Trotsky's Red Army is fighting a bitter civil war to around Warsaw to capture Poland. (W. Taubman, 59-60)

Nina Petrovna is sent near the front into Ukrainian villages to help win over the peasants with Bolshevik party propaganda. When the Communist party of western Ukraine was formed Nina Petrovna heads the women's section. When the Red Army retreats from Poland Nina Petrovna is sent to Moscow for six months study at the recently formed Sverdlov Communist University. Her next assignment in the Donbas is to help carry out purges (still nonviolent in the twenties) screening out careerists and other scoundrels who attached themselves to the Party during the Civil War. Next in her reeducation she is listed to go in the field to teach 'the history of the revolutionary movement and political economy' at a province party school, but she falls gravely ill with typhus. She is one of the lucky ones, and recovers to resume her duties at Taganrog in a teacher-training program. In autumn 1922 Nina Petrovna arrives in Yuzovka teaching the Marxist-Leninist dogma of political economy to the district party school.

Years later Khrushchev recalled, "it was painful for me to remember that as a worker under capitalism I'd had much better living conditions than my fellow workers now living under Soviet power." In New York, in 1959 with Governor Nelson Rockefeller, the Soviet Premier dismisses the American's bluff that a half million Czarist Russians emigrated to New York in search of freedom and "opportunity". "Don't give me that stuff," he counters. "They only came to get higher wages. I was almost one of them. I gave very serious consideration to coming." Whereas he became a Party *apparatchnik*, both his son Sergei and grandson Yuri became engineers. Khrushchev participated in strikes by the Rutchenkovo miners and organized demonstrations against the war. When the Czar abdicated in February 1917, he leaves the Donbas region for Moscow, and returns to Yuzovka in the December winter as a union leader chairing the Council of Mining and Metalworkers Union. There he first learns of Lazar Kaganovich, his future mentor and Stalin's right-hand man of the Ukraine famine terror. In the civil war conflict Kaganovich had led Bolshevik comrades into battle against Whites and reactionaries. By then, civil war had already broken out. In December 1917, White Czarist army of General Kaledin leads fierce Cossack cavalry charges against Red workers but is eventualy defeated in February 1918. A third of the miners in Donbas are lost in the war. Khrushchev joins up with Ivan Danilov leading a battalion of Rutchenkovo Red Guards in bloody fighting. (W. Taubman, 40)

By this time the anti-Bolshevik nationalist Ukrainian Central Rada in Kiev had declared itself an independent government. It fell in April as the Germans backed Hetman Pavlo Skoropadsky and the Whites near Yuzovka. Maurading bandits and armies ravaged through towns and the countryside. Lenin sought an immediate armistice to gain time to organize the Red Army against the imperialist forces soon to be unleashed against it by both the Germans and the Allies, including President Wilson's ill-prepared American armed intervention; People's Commissar of Foreign Affairs and Defense Commissar Trotsky signed the Brest-Litovsk Treaty with the Germans declaring a policy of "neither war nor peace".

In the ebb and flow of chaos, Khrushchev flees with the Bols and joined the Red Army. By spring the Red Army began confiscating grain stocks from the peasants to feed Petrograd and Moscow. Those who resist are shot and their grain seized. This is the period during the summer Lenin hangs a hundred Kulaks to set an example for the others still think they can resist the Bolshevik program. With revolutionary fervor, armed Bolsheviks bands impose collectivization, distributing the land from rich landlords as well as from rich peasants. Khrushchev joins the Red's Ninth Army fighting against General S. V. Denisov in Yuzovka who orderes one of every ten workers arrested to be hung without trial leaving hundreds of bodies suspended in the streets for days. The Reds shoot engineers and technicians of the educated classes in retaliation.

This was the era of chaos and bedlam as Makhno's anarchist forces cross with Bolsheviks, Whites and Skoropadsky agents massacring peasants and Jews in open warfare of class struggle taking their hatred and violence from village to village across the plains throughout the countryside. The historian William Taubman recalls the violence that overwhelmed tragic Ukraine: "Farther south, where Khrushchev was now stationed with the Red's Ninth Army, the fighting was even more barbaric. Although Commissar of War Leon Trotsky had barred executing prisoners, 'wounded or captured (White) officers were not only finished off and shot but tortured in every possible way. Officers had nails driven into their shoulders according to the number of stars on their epaulets; medals were carved on their chests and stripes on their legs. Genitals were cut off and stuffed in their mouths'."

The Whites captured Kharkov, Yekaterinoslav (the Cossack region of Dnepropetrovsk) and Tsaritsyn (Stalingrad) on the Volga river. But the Red Army reversed its losses in southern Russia and General Wrangle's Whites by November 1920 were pushed into the Black Sea and out of the Crimea, along with their imperialist backers. Wrangle was the last commander of the White Army in the south; in 1924 he created the Russian Armed Services Union (RASU) for a united front against the Bolsheviks. Wrangle eventually settles in Belgium until poisoned by the Bols; his deputy Kutepov is abducted in 1933 along with his assistant.

Khrushchev emerges from the chaos and war as a junior political commissar in a Red Army battalion promoted to instructor in the Political Department of the Ninth Army. By 1922, Khrushchev personally experienced the poverty and famine caused by the revolution and civil war. The Yuzovka territory was devastated. Coal production had stopped. The Donbas mines lacked owners or workers; most had fled or been killed. Food and supplies were scarce, crops failed, and bare fields left unplowed without seeds to sow. A thirty-pound sack of flour cost two million rubles, a pound of meat nearly forty thousand rubles, and its origin uncertain. Unsanitary health conditions resulted in breakouts of cholera and typhus epidemics. And there was cannibalism.

William Taubman in *Khrushchev*: "In the countryside as a whole, deaths from famine in 1921 and 1922 exceeded the combined total of casualties in the world war and civil war. In the spring of 1922 approximately 38 percent of the Yuzovka district population was going hungry, and some four hundred thousand children were starving in the Donbas as a whole. Father Neveu, an Assumptionist priest who lived through the famine in Makeyevka, saw scenes 'reminiscent of Flavius Josephus' description of the siege of Jerusalem. Mothers kill their children and then commit suicide to put an end to their suffering. Everywhere we see people with haggard complexions and swollent bodies, people who can hardly drag themselves around, and who are driven to eating dogs, cats, and horses. And their own children, one at a time... In Shakhty, a man bought and ate cooked meat from an old woman whose house was subsequently searched; in it were found 'two barrels containing parts of children's bodies, sorted and salted, and scalped heads." To think that Khrushchev is not familiar with this kind of barbarism then rampant throughout the stricken areas of the Russian republics is absurd; that starvation and famine would reoccur in the late 1920s culminating in the 1932-34 famine renders the subsequent tragedies even more grotesque and morally inhuman. (W. Taubman, 49-53)

For the peasants in the countryside 1925-26 would turn out to be their best years, a respite of reasonable calm and productivity unlike the turmoil and disorder of the Civil War. William Taubman writes "life was relatively good ... Coal production had been largely restored, and the NEP had stabilized the countryside. The brilliant Bolshevik Nikolai Bukharin was urging the peasants to 'enrich themselves' as a way of getting agriculture back on its feet. But that clashed with the Bolshevik antipathy to kulaks (well-off peasants), who did particularly well on Ukraine's rich soil." Peasants were producing again, fields were sowed, and harvests increased the food supply to the towns and cities. Kulaks and Party officials competed peacefully in the markets.

"'We were supposed to (beat) them at their own game'," recalls Khrushchev who has educated himself enough by Party work that by 1925 he is a full alternate delegate to the 14th Party Congress. "'We tried hard to underprice the NEPmen in state cooperatives and also to offer higher quality and better service. But we didn't have much success. Merchants who were in business for themselves could put up better displays of their products and give their customers more personal attention. Private stores catered to housewives, who like to have choice when they shop; they like to browse around and examine everything carefully'." Taubman observes, "But dealing with ornery peasants brought to the surface one of his own vices, his irritation at people and incidents that reminded him of his own peasant past."

That was the year, in 1925, when Stalin clashed with Zinoviev and Kamenev while they joined Trotsky in a united opposition dividing the Party against him. The Bolshevik "Right" had won the industrialization debate

But 1927-28 brought the "scissors crisis"; prices of agricultural products plummeted on world markets leaving peasants in Russia too poor to buy what they needed. The peasants reduced their harvest, producing food especially grain causing shortages in the cities and forcing a drop in exports. In 1927-28 the crisis of the countryside spurred an internal debate on the first Five-Year Plan. In December 1927, Khrushchev is a voting delegate at the 15th Party Congress that confirms the Central Committee Resolutions of October to contain the power of *kulaks* (rich peasants) in the villages. Collectivization was also part of the Resolutions but the Party remains divided on tactics how to achieve the support of peasants, either by incentives, or repression. Heavy taxes imposed by Stalin are collected by force. (W. Taubman, *Khrushchev*)

In 1928, for the first year of the Plan, Kaganovich sends Khrushchev back to the Ukraine, first to Kharkov, then Ukraine's capital, to reorganize the Ukrainian Central Committee with instructions "to proletarianize the apparat", and soon after to Kiev. There he settled with his wife and two children in a comfortable large party-owned house on Olginskaya Street off Kreshchatik in the city's center all of which was destroyed in the war and rebuilt after by German prisoners of war. Had he not become a Party functionary, Khrushchev would have been happiest as an industrial factory manager, a job that perhaps he was mentally better prepared to manage than a political career. (W. Taubman, 62-9)

Stimson might have been a little confused about the frequency of famines in the Soviet Union under the Plan, but not Haskell nor Khrushchev and his Party thugs and of course the NKVD dreads. As Solzhenitsyn recalls in *Gulag Archipelago* there were many famines. Solzhenitsyn writes, "Shakhty* came in Moscow in 1928…in September, 1930 the 'famine' organizers were tried with a great hue and cry. They were the ones! There they are!. There were forty-eight wreckers in the food industry. At the end of 1930, the trial of the Promparty was put on with even greater fanfare. It had been faultlessly rehearsed. In this case every single defendant took upon himself the blame for every kind of filthy rubbish … In 1931, following the trial of the Promparty, a grandiose trial of the Working Peasants Party was being prepared – on the grounds that they existed (never, in actual fact!) as an enormous organized underground force among the rural intelligentsia, including leaders of consumer and agricultural cooperatives and the more advance upper layer of the peasantry, and supposedly were preparing to overthrow the dictatorship of the proletariat…. Then all of a sudden, one lovely night, Stalin 'reconsidered'. Why? Maybe we will never know. Did he perhaps wish to save his soul? Too soon for that, it would seem…Stalin simply figured out that the whole countryside, not just 200,000 people, would soon die of famine anyway, so why go to all the trouble." (re. Shakhty Case, Trial of "wreckers", May 18-July 15, 1928, A. I. Solzhenitsyn, *The Gulag Archipelago 1918-1956, An Experiment in Literary Investigation I-II,* NY: Harper & Row, 1973, ed. 1975, 47-50, 373-6)

On April 1 Stimson is back to relax at Highhold now under "a northeast blowing with very heavy rain". He could find peace and calm there and clear his mind on this 123-acre Long Island estate in the West Hills of the Huntington Township two hundred and forty miles from Washington. There Stimson sought tranquil refuge in baronial seclusion from his packed daily routine in Washington. That day he ventured into Manhattan and drops in at Bonrights to see two of his closest friends Alfred Loomis and Landon Thorne. Both are very talented, rich and shrewd investors. "Alfred was full of Russia; and gave me a talk on it before I could stop it. He said that it was the last word and was the best thing on the subject printed here" referring to a book *The Fall of Russia* (1928) written by Father Edmund Walsh, a well-known Catholic Jesuit. Stimson remarked that he already knew Walsh "and had talked to him about Russia". The Catholic Church is vehemently against recognition of the heathen Bolsheviks. Stimson then went over to the Federal Reserve Bank of New York for a meeting with his close friend George Harrison and Montague Norman, head of the Bank of England (1916-44). Norman is all in a fuss over "the price of labor"; – he aims to lower it, – "at the same time as often as commodities and that unless that was done, he said, that he felt sure that we would come down to the dole next winter."

With another international financial doomsday on the distant horizon Stimson notes it all in his diary then visits his law firm Winthrop and Stimson for lunch with Winthrop and George Roberts. "They insisted on talking over Russia for a while", the Secretary noted, and he adds, "I told them that I was going to study that during my absence, but that I was more interested in studying the economic conditions which underlay the question of Russia than to jump to Russia itself first; that if there was no economic depression nobody would be thinking of Russia. This seemed to strike them as sound." Stimson did not elude further why he thought "nobody would be thinking of Russia" now that two incomparably massive economic plans linking the Washington and Moscow had been launched during his watch, and he knows so little about it, and seems to care even less, now that the American economy is still unraveling sliding stocks hitting new lows, mounting inflationary pressures and a constrained money supply.

Although Stimson won't know about it for days, even weeks, Department Agent Warrington Dawson on that same day April 1, 1931 in Paris sends to Washington a special report 885 which includes an article which appeared in the French press citing the "great majority of the 10,000 foreign engineers and technicians employed in the various branches of Soviet industry are German. To their numbers must be added 5,000 German engineers and technicians who have been sent to Russia by German firms, such as Siemens and Schukert, Krupp, Junkers, and AEG, for supervising the execution of their contracts in Russia". That includes "Junkers Aeroplane works near Moscow, Krupp's works in Maikop, and Grozny and the machine gun factory in Penza". In all, nearly 80 percent of the workers are German. The French also mentioned that it had "sufficient evidence to show that the German reactionaries not only help the Bolsheviks in procuring armaments, but also act as military experts and advisers to the Red Army General

Staff." "German reactionaries"? Oh, my God! Tell Stimson and Hoover that can't be true? Call Harriman now! Thyssen, where are you! Is this really true?

The Dawson report doesn't name names. It didn't have to. To the people who mattered and needed to know who did what with the Soviets. It was the business of the Consortium to know. And everyone knew in Paris that the Rothschilds never need wait long to get answers. Neither Dawson nor the French refer to Consortium financial and industrial investment driving the German economy towards rapid recovery. What is this about "German reactionaries"? Mr. Hoover knows literally everyone there is to know in Germany. He traded with them when America was at war with their Kaiser and fed his people when his own Prussian generals had failed and he arranged for food shipments to take care of Lenin and Trotsky's Red Army. So what's he up to now? (761.00/200, T1247 roll 1, SDDF 761)

In this period of acute monetary tension with banks and the economy severely strained in America, and London, Paris, and Berlin threatening to stop reparation debt payments, Stimson soothes over the anxiety of the day with regular meetings with NY Fed legal counsel and fellow Bonesman George Harrison (Harvard Law then secretary to his longtime friend Chief Justice Oliver Wendell Holmes) to ruminate about how to rearrange the world from inside the paneled luncheon room at the New York Fed. Harrison is also president of the New York Life Insurance Company. Wall Street is rocked daily with more reports of suicides over the stock market fiasco by greedy and ruined investors buying on margin. Most of the Consortium players held firm and recovered losses and picked up cheap stocks to make new fortunes on ther rebound. Old money can afford to wait out the crash while the new suckers get wiped out. Harrison is a frequent and most welcomed visitor at Highhold and keeps a farm only fifty miles from the capital within easy distance for cabinet meetings in Washington with his friend, Treasure secretary Andrew Mellon or President Hoover.

On April 8, 1931 Stimson again meets Harrison and Montague "Archie" Norman. Stimson notes, "I had a most interesting talk with him. He is very gloomy about the general situation in Europe…." The flight of capital from both Germany and England was alarming. Stimson gets another briefing on the Soviet Union. "Russia was the very greatest of all the dangers," Montague Norman told him. "Russia was in the background," Stimson noted in his diary. "I asked him whether he did not find that Germany had a good many secret affiliations with Russia, and he said that yes there was; that she necessarily tended that way with a good deal of her commerce, although she wanted to keep out. But he said that all of the other little countries around Russia, referring particularly to Hungary, were in the terrible position that they were not getting help from the capitalist system to stand the expenses of remaining capitalistic; that they were being kept out by tariffs and other things from the natural development which they should have, and all the time while they wobbled and wavered Russia was welcoming them to come over to her system." In other words, the USSR was eating up the Balkans.

In his expose *Secrets of the Federal Reserve* Eustace Mullins was particularly struck by the "collaboration" between Lord Montague Norman and Benjamin Strong and describes it "one of the greatest secrets of the twentieth century".

Strong married the daughter of the president of Bankers Trust in New York becomes her father's successor. According to Carroll Quigley (*Tragedy and Hope)* "Strong became Governor of the Federal Reserve Bank of New York as the joint nominee of Morgan and of Kuhn, Loeb Company in 1914."

On the internet the *Financial Times* (London) in 2012 showed a quaint photo of Montague Norman accompanied by Schacht, the Consortium's key banker in Germany who becomes Hitler's chief finance adviser and President of the bank of the Third Reich. Mullins provides some eye-popping background on Lord Montague Norman (1871-50) "the only man in history who had both his maternal grandfather and his paternal grandfather serve as Governors of the Bank of England." His father happened to be with Brown, Shipley Company, the London Branch of Brown Brothers, later Brown Brothers Harriman. Yes, the very enigmatic and ubiquitous top man at State and the Consortium's key link to Moscow, linking Stalin to Churchill in London and FDR in Washington. Lord Norman remains Governor of the Bank of England from 1916 to 1944.

In 1894, only 23, Montague Norman arrives for work at Brown Brothers in Manhattan. Here he befriends James Markoe of Brown Brothers, and in close circles with the Delano family and friends. He stays in America for thirteen years returning to London in 1907 to be named to the Court of the Bank of England. His work there is interrupted in 1912, when he leaves for Switzerland for treatment under the psychoanalyst Carl Jung. During his reign as Governor of the Bank of England at the apogee and transition of the British Empire, and, as Mullins observes, "he participated in the central bank conferences which set up the Crash of 1929 and a worldwide depression". Mullins draws from Brian Johnson's *The Politics of Money*: "Strong and Norman, intimate friends, spent their holidays together at Bar Harbour and in the South of France ... Norman therefore became Strong's alter ego… ". Strong's easy money policies on the New York money market from 1925-28 were the fulfillment of his agreement with Norman to keep New York interest rates below those of London. For the sake of international cooperation, Strong withheld the steadying hand of high interest rates from New York until it was too late. Easy money in New York had encouraged the surging American boom of the late 1920s, with its fantastic heights of speculation." (Brian Johnson, *The Politics of Money*, 88, see E. Mullins)

Benjamin Strong dies suddenly in 1928. *The New York Times* obituary, Oct. 17, 1928, opted then to recall the conference between the directors of the three great central banks in Europe in July, 1927, "Mr. Norman, Bank of England, Strong of the New York Federal Reserve Bank, and Dr. Hjalmar Schacht of the Reichsbank, their meeting referred to at the time as a meeting of 'the world's most exclusive club'. No public reports were ever made of the foreign conferences, which were wholly informal, but which covered many important questions of gold movements, the stability of world trade, and world economy." The meetings at which the future of the world's economy are decided are always reported as being "wholly informal", off the record, no reports made to the public, and on the rare occasions when outraged Congressmen summon these mystery figures to testify about their activities they merely trace the outline of steps taken, and develop no information about what was really said or decided."

Stimson's close friend George Harrison succeeds Strong at the NY Fed. At the 1931 Senate Hearings investigating the Federal Reserve System, H. Parker Willis, one of the authors and First Secretary of the Federal Reserve Board (1914-20), for the public record queries Harrison:

"What is the relationship between the Federal Reserve Bank of New York and the money committee of the Stock Exchange?" "There is no relationship," Governor Harrison replied.

"There is no assistance or cooperation in fixing the rate in any way?" asks Willis.

"No," said Governor Harrison, "although on various occasions they advise us of the state of the money situation, and what they think the rate ought to be."

Evidently this was sufficient to satisfy public curiosity during these very insecure Depression days with the nation's financial industry tittering on bankruptcy and real estate crash belittling their assets. But not for Mullins who rejects that insipid betrayal of the public trust.

"This was an absolute contradiction of his statement." Mullins writes, the New York Fed "which set the discount rate for the other Reserve Banks, actually maintained a close liaison with the money committee of the Stock Exchange."

Testimony before Congressional committees by Federal Reserve officials and investment-pool operatives as well as speeches by public officials and communiqués between the Federal Reserve Board and the New York Federal Reserve Bank reveal a tightly linked fiscal coordination between London, New York and Washington. Apparently Adolph Miller of the Fed Board favors selective credit controls to restrain speculators. George Harrison, for his part, urged a general tightening of credit to get the funny money under control. In the wake of increasing uncertainty and inaction by the Fed Harrison finds no mechanism to implement fiscal restraint. Adding to the confusion, Roy Young, another Board member unattuned to implementation problems, announces publicly, "It seems to me that it would be the (better) part of prudence for all who are lenders to see first that business gets credit at reasonable rates and let the others get what is left".

Two weeks later, on Tuesday, April 22, 1931 Stimson sits with Hoover for another cabinet meeting with Mellon. Stimson noted in his diary that the Soviets are causing a problem again "on the cargo of lumber and how it had been accepted because the Russians had brought out a case which the Treasury could not combat." Mellon explains how it opened a can of worms over "the whole question of doing business with Russia". Stimson and others do make "propositions" for the US response. However Stimson disagrees, as he notes in his diary: "I, therefore, brought forward the question of the application of the Russian Government to have students sent to different universities for instruction in engineering and pointed out that the only thing that I was immediately interested in was to protect the Administration from being charged with nullification of the policy set down in the Immigration Law." His strict legal interpretation wasn't adequate to the reality of the present problem of future relations with the Soviet government.

Further Stimson is not prepared to officially recognize Stalin's regime as either a legitimate or legally constituted government; its a rude predicament and awkward in view of the extensive investment of Mellon but his concern for the entire American-Anglo Consortium in the communist dictatorship.

Ever since he was groomed as a arch-deacon of the Skull & Bones secret society gang at Yale, the civilized Stimson prefers a more subtle approach to business with the Great Butcher. Evidently, and this we are led to believe Stimson really doesn't grasp the radical political dynamic set in play since Lenin and exploited by Stalin's usurpation of absolute power and control of the Party hierarchy. By 1929, the year of the Great Break Stalin is the unchallenged master of the Communist Party having narrowed the field and eliminated Bukharin, and his allies Rykov and Tomskii. But in most every State Department document and private papers this fact of Russian reality is absent from the record. Were the Americans so badly informed that they couldn't see straight or get it right? It would be incredulous to think they could have been that wrong in their assessment especially when the Consortium is investing millions in backing Stalin's Plans for the rapid economic development of his regime. and the survival of totalitarian dictatorship of the Gulag which is now the way of life in the Soviet Union.

"But the discussion went into the broader field," Stimson notes further, "and it became rather clear that the President was getting more vigorous against Russia, although he still adhered to the policy of doing business with her." Poor Hoover. He knew that he was that Stalin could hold on in one of the strongest empires of the world while Hoover's economy was in a tailspin and his reelection far from certain with a new Consortium gang in the White House while the entire Soviet Union assisted by American engineers worked feverishly to complete its Five-Year Plans. It was now only a question of time when again the world would burst in flames.

In order to appease Mellon and his investors in Bolshevik Russia, Hoover, on old hand in the Consortium game with Russia, told them how they should do it, saying, – and we can read Stimson's diary notes of the meeting, – "that when the students applied for admission to our consuls, they should be required to make statements in line with the statutes that they were not affiliated with any organization which was seeking to overturn the Government of the United States, etc., etc., and that they should promise not to engage in communistic activities while in the United States. This should be followed up by the Department of Labor watching them while they were here and deporting them if they did go into these activities." Then there was "the difficulty of transporting them after they got here, the practical difficulties, shipowners would not take them without a passport and that we could not give them passports … he could only do it under a guarantee to bring them back in case Russia refused to allow them to land, and that Russia would probably not allow them to land." Stimson is at a loss. He wants to avoid publicity over any incident with Russia. Stimson feels uncomfortable with a situation that he might be able to control, for example, stuck with Reds in America calling for world revolution. He had never been, unlike his deceased friend President Taft, inside Russia. Stimson was never very comfortable talking about Russia, or the Bolsheviks, or the Soviets, or whatever they wanted to call themselves now. In the cabinet meeting, nobody tells Stimson who these "students" really are. Industrial spies, subversive agents, engineers? But what does Stimson know about contemporary Russian life under Stalin anyway? Or for that matter, how can Stimson empathize with Americans living humble quiet and desperate lives isolated in their solitary homes and communities under the capitalist system not knowing if they would have dinner that night, or the communists living in terror not certain if they would even be there for dinner or taken away deported or shot under Russia's new communist culture dictated by Party dogma of "socialist realism".

As he often did Stimson sent the problem to Undersecretary Klots "to get busy with the Labor Department and try to work out a plan...". There is no record of any mention about reparations, debts, credits or loans, or pressuring the Russians for an opportune *quid pro quo.* The Soviet foreign ministry needs US government cooperation at a time when no formal diplomatic relations could manage their problem, so it is left to Mellon and the Consortium to oblige the Soviet placement of Russian "students sent to different universities for instruction in engineering" in the United States. A sort of quiet foreign exchange student program only nothing is said about the Americans who traveled to the USSR with no guarantee they would ever see America again. Stimson was not happy about the whole show but in the end he had to chuckle just a bit under his perfectly trimmed mustache about a Russian Jewish communist well known in the New York Yiddish community.

GARETH JONES AND JACK HEINZE ENCOUNTER THE FAMINE

Lets return reader to the oncoming storm of the Holodomor 1931 with Gareth Jones and Jack Heinze travelling in the Ukraine. As we know Ivy Lee plays a part in encouraging Gareth Jones to return to Russia and collect material on contemporary Russia to enable Lee to write a book promoting the Plans and Russia's future. Curiously, Lee proposes to Gareth that he take along as a traveling companion Jack Heinz II, the young millionaire heir to the "Pittsburgh food corporation" of the same name. Eureka! Was this a flash of genius or a strange paradox would be anyone's guess without an answer to explain the madness of the frightening world they will soon enter. Gareth stocks up with condensed food from the Heinz company. A great idea, and making the cover-up by FDR, the State Department and their friends in the press even more ironic. Imagine Heinz "Ketchup" to the rescue! To save the doomed Ukrainians, starved and murdered in cold-blooded will take a lot more than ketchup.

In fact, I observed how Heinz had returned to the shelves of Ukraine's big food markets ever since the 2004 victory of the people's Orange Revolution against the Russian-backed Kuchma-Yanukovitch regime, symbol of the country's new status of global big name-brand capitalism heralded as the new market economy alongside MacDonalds, Coca-Cola, Proctor & Gamble, Kraft Foods, Chrysler *et cetera.* In 2006, inflation is up to 40 % on food products, wages remain unacceptably low, the Verakova Rada parliament is stacked with over 300 oligarchic millionaires (where did they get all that money?) and Ukrainian television is saturated with inexpensive consumer advertising of products beyond the reach of 95% of the Ukrainians. Meanwhile, the best Ukrainian products cannot hold out against the massive resources of the giant foreign corporations.

Jones took the opportunity for future summer stories by first priming his readers back home in Wales with anecdotes of the Red Kremlin last fall. Jones placed five signed articles on deteriorating economic conditions of the Soviet Union for Cardiff's *The Western Mail* published in the spring April 7-11, 1931. "Communists' Five-Year Plan. How It Is Working In Russia. Its Origin and Purpose. 'No More Compromising With Capitalism'". Both articles show Jones' exasperation trying to understand the origins of the Five-Year Plans. He doesn't see the Consortium capitalists behind the plans. It's a rambling satirical essay on lampooning the "efforts of the Bolshevik revolution to build a new industrialized Russian where the machine will take the place of God.

"With the plan already two and a half years old, Jones writes, "This Revolution of the Five-Year Plan is now stirring every village, every street, every factory to its depths and affecting the life of every man, woman, and child in the Soviet Union." In the second article titled "Russia's Future. Stupendous Plan of Communists. Coal, Iron & Steel. A Vast Scheme for Agriculture" published April 8, Jones wrestles with how the Plan was launched. He wrote, "The Communists are aiming a converting 50 per cent of the peasants of Russia into members of collective farm by the end of this year. If that succeeds it will be a striking revolution in the lives of the 130,000,000 of Russian peasants. Besides these "collectives," vast State farms, covering hundreds of thousands of acres, are to be set up. These are to produce millions of tons of grain for export. How could the American farmer compete with that? Would it be wiser for the Americans to slow down the rate of progress in the USSR?

"In the realm of agriculture the Plan is no less ambitious. It is attempting to revolutionize the Russian village. Large collective farms are being set up. The "Kulak" class (the peasants owning three or more cows and employing labour) is to be crushed out of existence. The policy of collectivization aims at doing away with the millions of individually owned patches and strips and at establishing large farms run by machinery and owned in common. The peasants are allowed to keep their cottage, one cow chickens, perhaps a pig or two, but the tractors and the land are common property.

"This year 1931 is to see the production of Russia increase by 45 per cent! Wages are to be doubled. New factories of all kinds arc to be built. Electrification is to go ahead rapidly. A network of railways is to be constructed at breakneck speed, opening new regions to industry and trade. Waterways and roads are to be developed to carry the ever-growing amount of goods produced. The Plan - as a Plan - is, indeed, stupendous.

"...The hopes of the Communists were high. Although they only numbered 1 1/2 millions out of a population of over 150 millions, they were determined to make Russia into an industrialised Communist State. Wherever one went one saw huge banners stretched from one lamp-post to another across the street with the words, "Let us reply to the furious arming of the capitalists by carrying out the Five-Year Plan," or "God and the drunkard are the enemies of the Five-Year Plan...

"At street corners, in factories, in villages, Communists would harangue the crowds and tell them of the three main aims of the Plan and how its fulfillment would bring them health and happiness and save them from being attacked and murdered by the foreigner who was waiting to pounce on Mother Russia. This is what the factory workers, the peasants, the teachers, and the miners learned as they listened, open-mouthed, to the Bolshevik orators. They learned that the Five-Year Plan had three great aims. It would first of all convert the Russia of the peasant into the Russia of the mechanic; it would industrialise Russia and set up factories and mines everywhere. It would, secondly, turn the millions of strips the private property of the small peasants into big Socialist farms, where the land would be owned in common and where the tractor and the latest machinery would double or treble the amount of grain produced. It would, thirdly, exterminate all capitalist elements." An odd choice of words. But Jones repeats it again with a twist, here referring to the disappearance of the peasant by the "extermination" of the capitalist under the program of state socialized terror. He wrote, That meant that by 1933 every hawker, shopkeeper, barber, tailor who worked or sold for his own profit and not for a State shop or co-operative shop would disappear. That meant also that the individual peasant who had his own land would be no more. With its three aims, the industrialisation of Russia, the socialization of agriculture, and the extermination of the private trader, the Five-Year Plan is the most thorough revolution which has ever been attempted in the history of the world.

"What it seeks to achieve in the industrial field is stupendous. The exact figures of what production must be in each year up to 1933 are worked out. Did not the whole daring of the scheme take one's breath away, one might almost be compelled to laugh at some of its stipulations. For example, it was laid down that the average number of eggs eaten per head by the people in the towns between October 1, 1932, and September 30, 1933, was to be 155. The allowance of boots was to increase from .40 of a pair in 1927-8 to .74 of a pair in 1932-3!

"In other branches of industry the progress planned is enormous. Take coal. In 1913 Russia produced 29 million tons of coal. By the year preceding the Five-Year Plan this had increased to 35 million tons. By the end of the Five-Year Plan it is planned to produce 125,000,000 tons of coal! That is almost five times as much as in 1913! This year the figure is to leap up to 83 million tons. The Donetz Basin takes the first place In the Soviet coal plans. Its output is to increase from 27 million tons in 1927-28 to 70 million tons in 1933. The Donetz Basin has thus undertaken the task of more than doubling its coal production within live years. An immense construction programme is being carried out; seventeen new large shafts have recently been sunk. By the end of the Plan 50 large new mines will be in process of construction. The very face of the Donetz Basin is to be changed. Mechanisation is to go ahead full-speed, and a great housing programme is to be carried out.

"Then comes what is known as the sleeping giant of Russia, the Kuznetz Basin in Siberia. Its coal reserve is estimated at the incredible figure of 300 billion tons. Eight new large (plants sic) are to be constructed in the Kuznetz Basin. Its output will be small at the end of the Plan, viz., Six million tons, but the Soviet authorities intend to push ahead its development after the Five-Year Plan is over. The Ural coal region is to increase its production from two million tons in 1927-28 to six million tons in 1932-33. The Moscow district, where there are large reserves of low-grade coal, comes next. Its output is to increase from one million to four or five million tons between the first and the last year of the Plan. Even in the far-off Soviet lands of Central Asia and Transcaucasia coal development plans are to be pushed ahead.

"There is going to be a great drive in increasing the production of iron and steel. The iron and steel mills in the two important metallurgical regions of the country (the Donetz Basin and the Urals) are to be rebuilt. Many new blast furnaces are to be constructed. The output of oil is to reach 42,000,000 tons by 1933. This is a tremendous rate of increase compared with the 11,000,000 tons of 1927-28. The production of agricultural machinery, of copper, zinc, lead, aluminium, boilers, textiles-indeed, of all goods, is to be doubled or trebled. The timber and the fur plans are also exceedingly high."

Is Jones overwhelmed by inflated heady Soviet estimates, or is he pushing the pedal of public relations selling the Consortium's package to bring in more investors? Has he changed his tune? His editors at *The Western Mail* where has become something of a mysterious celebrity certainly are not unimpressed with his credentials; from the office of the former War Prime Minister Lloyd-George the paper announces Jones new appointment foreign affairs Secretary to Mr. Ivy Lee, who is "public relations counsel" to a number of important manufacturing companies. No mention of Rockefeller or Lee's promotion of the Five-Year Plan.

Now for his third article in a series of five: "Communist's Five-Year Plan. Forces Behind Stalin's Dictatorship. Peasant's Submissiveness. Method's Which Britons Would Not Tolerate". It's published in *The Western Mail* on April 9. Jones asks difficult if not rhetorically impossible questions "tormenting the men and women in all countries" about the Soviet program. He writes, "If the Five-Year Plan were carried out in full, then it would revolutionise the life and the trade of the whole world. Will it be carried out?

"We are in a state of war," said a Bolshevik Commissar as takes his Welsh visitor around the latest machinery in his factory. "Russia is fighting a war at construction, the war to build up the Socialist State and to change the whole face of the earth. We are fighting a battle royal for the Five-Year Plan. There are forces in Russia which will help the Communist to win the war of the Five-Year Plan." Could Ivy Lee himself say it any better?

"The first factor which will help the Bolsheviks to win the battle is the vast resources of Russia. Think of the amount of coal untouched stored beneath the soil of the Soviet Union. Her forests cover an area of about 2,000 million acres, by far the largest lumber supplies in the world. Riches untold lie within her boundaries.

"Oil? More than one-third of the whole worlds oil reserves are believed to by within her borders. Corn? The south of Russia deserves the name of the granary of the world. Cotton and flax? Gold? Platinum? Iron ore? All these are abundant.

"The Five-Year Plan will be helped the stability of the regime. The Bolsheviks seem to have come to stay. A revolution against the Communists seems impossible. Any attempt at by rising is at once nipped in the bud by the O.G.U. (the State political police). This feared body has power of life and death and it members have the right to shoot a counter revolutionary without trial. In any case Soviet justice is on the side of the regime and the law courts are used to suppress any enemies of the Five-Year Plan. 'Law courts', says Krylenko, the Public Prosecutor of the Soviet Government, 'are organs for disposing of the enemies of the Revolution.' Not only the O.G.U., which has a well-trained army of about 130,000 men, with the best weapons and aero-planes, but also the Red Army will probably support the regime."

"It is well fed and it is taught Communist doctrine. Recently a decree was issued to the effect that 60 per cent of the Army must be composed of workers. This will make the Army more Communist and make less likely the repetition of the troubles which arose among the peasants in the Red Army last year. With the O.G.U. and the Red Army on their side the Soviet Government can concentrate on the carrying out of the Five-Year Plan.

"Modern inventions make the grip over Russia firmer and help the Government to force on the Plan. The wireless, the theatre, the cinema, spread Communist ideals throughout Russia, while the machine-gun, poison-gas, and the aeroplane are invaluable in crushing any opposition which may arise."

Here in 1931 Jones introduces his readers to Stalin "brutal", "the dictator" who "has no mercy". He calls him "the son of a Caucasian shoemaker and of a washerwoman". Yet, he survives in power "a brilliant organizer".

Jones writes, "The next factor which will help the Five-Year Plan is the character of Stalin, the dictator. This ruthless, honest man is just the man to drive a nation. He is brutal and has no mercy. He allows nothing to stand in his way when his mind s made up. This son of a Caucasian shoemaker and of a washerwoman is a brilliant organizer. Without material he has one aim in life - to make the Five-Year Plan a success."

"The enthusiasm of youth is going to be the force which will help the Plan. For many young people Communism has the power of religion. They would sacrifice their lives willingly for the sake of the Plan. They would obey the command of the Communist party to leave their homes and to work in a mine in the depths of Siberia, just as a missionary would plunge for the sake of Christianity into the savage forests of Africa. They would work nine, ten, eleven, twelve hours, they would give up all their leisure for the success of the Five-Year Plan."

Jones visits a Moscow circus where he befriends "a fair-haired Russian boy aged thirteen". "'Would you like to go to Britain?' he asked the boy. The boy was shocked. 'No, never,' he said; 'it must be terrible there in a capitalist country where all the workers are oppressed. I am sorry for them. But they will be Communist one day, because we young people are going to make the Five-Year

Plan a success. Won't it be fine when we've turned Russia into a country of factories? I'd do anything to make the Five-Year Plan a success and so would a lot of my schoolfellows.' That is the spirit which is going to push the plan ahead rapidly. The youth of Russia is being trained to devote itself to the Five-Year Plan by the excellent work done for education in Russia. The State is sparing no efforts to set up schools and to teach reading and writing to young and old. 'We must give the workers books, but we do not give them boots,' said a communist to me.

"The command which is the State has over the lives of the worker is also a factor which will weigh in favour of the Plan. If there is a shortage of labour in the forests of the North, then many thousands of workers or peasants can be drafted to fill the gap In January when the transport was failing, the Commissar of labour issued an order by which all employees who had at any time been engaged in railway work of any kind had to report within five days and take any job offered in whatever part of the country where the Labour Exchange might send them."

"The State deprives the population of most commodities in order to get money to invest in industry and to buy machinery from abroad. Foreign trade is a Government monopoly. Thus no luxuries are imported, and butter, eggs, grain, and bacon, badly needed at home, are exported to get currency wherewith to buy tractors, textile-making machinery, and engines necessary to carry out the Plan."

Jones doesn't describe the Russian as lazy, apathetic or docile. "Submissive" only because "he has never tasted liberty", Jones explains further: "The character of the peoples who form the Soviet Union is another force which enables the Communists to press forward in industrializing. The average Russian is long-suffering, and having been a serf up to 1861 he has never tasted liberty. A British worker would never allow himself to be commandeered and deprived of his food and of his liberty as the Russian does. Bill Smith or John Jones would very soon stand up for his rights! But the Russian is submissive and lets the rulers go on ruling."

Initially Jones' reporting is upbeat and enthusiastic about the bold success of the Plans. His editors highlight the "excellent harvest" of 1930 calling it "a great stroke of good fortune for their policy of collectivization". Jones is right on the money when he writes about Soviet Russia. He is precise and unambiguous with a flair for humor and metaphor to explain, not beguiled with dialectical postering that marks the American foreign press correspondents in Moscow.

Jones writes, "In agriculture there are very many forces which will help the Communists to carry out their Plan. Last year's wonderful harvest was a great stroke of good fortune for their policy of collectivisation. The use of machines which the Communists advocate is bound to increase the production of grain in the flat stretches of fertile land in South Russia. A great deal, however, will depend upon the number and the quality of the tractors which can be produced under the Five-Year Plan, modern methods and excellent research Russian scientists will campaign for turning the into modern farms run by machinery."

"Tremendous State farms (covering hundreds of thousands of acres), where the workers are wage-earners, have been set up in the virgin steppes. These will be able to provide grain for the Red Army and for export. Large State pig and cattle farms are to be to make up for the terrible shortage of meat which was caused by the peasants massacring their cattle a year ago, when being forced to join the Communist collective farms."

Jones tells his story as he sees it with increasing anxiety, looking into the soul of the villagers gagged under their garments. His fluency in languages provides a blueprint of the anguish, people he yearns to understand so completely that all their gestures and appeals are in character and set before the reader with the economy known to the great writers like Anton Tchekov (1860-04) without moralizing and in a way that we accept under intolerable conditions as inevitable. The story signed and titled "Russian Workers Disillusioned. Forces Against the Five-Year Plan. Scarcity of Food and Clothing. Hundreds Shot for Failing at their Job" runs in *The Western Mail*, April 10, 1931.

"THE FIVE-YEAR PLAN? IT'S ALL LIES, LIES, LIES!"

Jones writes, "'Why can't they give us workers enough to eat?' suddenly burst out the Red-faced Russian miner in the corner of the carriage 'Their Five-Year Plan indeed! All they do is to promise us sausages and boots in a few years time! Let them give them to us now. We can't stick it, any longer. A revolution is sure to come.'."

Jones: "There was no meat to be had in the Co-operative Restaurant in Rostoff. The sausages had been sold out since nine o'clock in the morning. There were a few bars of chocolate (about a 6d. size) at 12s. per bar. There was no butter to be had except in the private market at 10s. per lb. There was a long queue of nervy people in the restaurant."

Jones: "'Anybody got any silver – there's no small change?' each other asked. There were grumblings and cursings. A young worker, slightly drunk, sidled up to me and said: 'That's what they are doing to us in Soviet Russia. The Communists are killing us workers and peasants. Everything's bad, bad, bad. We can't get boots and we can't get clothes. We can't get food, except bread. How can we work all day with our bellies empty. There's nothing in Russia. The Five-Year Plan? It's all lies, lies, lies!'."

Jones: "Two peasants, in their rough sheepskin coats, were furious. The train rattled along across the North Caucasian steppes. We were talking about the Soviet policy of making the peasants give up their land and join collective farms. 'It's a dog's life,' they said. 'It would be better to be under the earth than to live now. They force us to join collective farms. The very best, those who worked day and night, were sent to Siberia and the Urals and their houses were taken from them. They won't let us keep more than one cow. What's the use of working? It's terrible'." (What happened to the cow and the garden plot? sic)

Jones: "These glimpses of life in Soviet Russia show that the Communists are not having all their own way with the Five-Year Plan. The difficulties are formidable and they are putting a serious brake on the progress of the Plan. There are industrial difficulties, there are agricultural difficulties and there are human difficulties."

Jones: "What are the industrial difficulties? The first is the weakness of workers from lack of nearly all foods except bread. Meat is exceedingly scarce. All fats are almost impossible to obtain unless one is a manual worker or a member of the Communist party. Even a manual worker is rarely able to get enough. The bad quality of the goods produced under the Five-Year Plan is another drawback. The Soviet press publishes frank letters stating that clothes often fall to pieces in not much more than a month after purchase. Tractors often break within a few hours of use. This is easily understood. A factory is told to produce 1,000 tractors by a certain date under the Five-Year Plan. The manager may be arrested, perhaps shot or his bread-card may be taken away from him if the order is not carried out. Hence those 1,000 tractors are turned out regardless of quality."

Jones: "The ever-growing lack of engineers and of skilled labour is going to be a serious barrier to the success of the Plan. It is impossible to train engineers and mechanics in a year. Often a generation ion or more is needed to provide a trained body of workers. A South Wales collier cannot be made in six months. He is the skilled result of generations of experience. The Soviet Government is setting up industrial and engineering schools everywhere but they will find out that they can not run an industrialised State on unskilled and untrained engineers mechanics, and workers." (Jones here doesn't say that trained and skilled engineers from Czarist era died in the wars, fled, arrested, shot or imprisoned by the Revolution)

Jones: "The railways of the USSR are now in a state of confusion. Terrible mistakes have been made. Men have been shot for muddling the transport organisation. A millions tons of coal was left standing idle in the Donetz Basin this year because there were not enough wagons and locomotives to carry it away. Unless transport is improved and unless the railways planned a are built in time, and, what is more, in built well, then Five-Year Plan will be in grave danger of failing."

Jones is aware how dangerous it is to be an engineer in the new socialist society. By late 1930 Stalin had arrested 2,000 engineers, eight at the top and all convicted in an Industrial Party show trial. Engineering schools are set up to train loyal party members but with only limited engineering knowledge, all very life-threatening but nothing now threatens Stalin's political powers.

Jones: "It has been difficult for the Soviet authorities recently to keep the workers in the factories. They have been leaving one district for another or returning hungry from the towns to their villages where they have parents or brothers or cousins. The flight of workers was most marked in the Donetz Basin, the coal, iron and steel district where 93,000 workers fled last summer. The Soviet Government has had to make regulations which amount to the tying of workers to their factories or mines and to the tightening of the grip of the State over the life of each citizen."

Jones: "Failure in supplying factories with raw material such as cotton or flax, &c., the famine in fuel which caused so much suffering this winter, the disappointing results of the co-operative movement all these have put a brake on the fulfillment of the Plan. In agriculture the Government have had to face the opposition of masses of the peasants. There are probably at this moment many Communists being murdered in the villages by peasants want to at stick to their land. The wholesale massacre of cattle and pigs which followed upon the violent campaign of collectivization a year ago has caused a shortage of live-stock which will affect Russia for several years. By the class-warfare in the villages and extermination of the richer peasants (the Kulaks) by exile, confiscation, or sometimes by shooting, the Communists are depriving Russian agriculture of its hardest workers."

Jones: "There are, finally, serious human drawbacks which will prevent the Five-Year Plan making Russia into a happy prosperous country. There is, first, the clinging of average human being to property. Secondly, managers of factories and directors of trusts and many people in good positions are afraid of taking responsibility. It has been dangerous. During the last winter hundreds of men have been shot for failures in the branches of industry in which they had leading posts. When your actions are dictated according to a set plan and when failure may bring about death, your feeling of initiative is sure to suffer. Another human drawback is the stress which is laid upon political keenness and on orthodoxy rather than on practical ability. If you are a Communist then you have a far better chance of becoming the director of a factory than a non-Communist. A good street-corner orator is not necessarily a good organiser. There is thus waste of brain-power."

Jones: "The building up of an ideal State is going to be handicapped by the lack of freedom of expression which is an obstacle to the thinker, the artist, the writer, the politician, and to the man in the street. Finally the disillusionment which is spreading through the ranks of workers and peasants and which contrasts so violently with the optimism of the Communists and of youth has shattered the first fine careless rapture of the Plan."

On April 11, *The Western Mail* publishes Jones' third of the series, "Communists Five-Year Plan. Mixture of Successes and Failures. Progress at Expense of Happiness". He repeats the 'How is Russia' joke about Stalin's planned economy –'Stalin had a dream in which Lenin appeared to him....'"

Jones: "The Soviet Five-Year Plan has been working for two and a half years. What have been the achievements? There is no doubt that; great progress has been made in some branches of industry. The electrical power developments have been tremendous and the output is five times that of 1913."

Jones: "Air-lines now penetrate into the distant solitudes of Siberia. A Trans-Siberian air-line will soon revolutionise the postal and passenger services between Europe and Japan. A Welshman who flew from the South of Russia to Moscow last summer was struck by the excellent arrangements of the Soviet Aviation Company. Under the Five-Year Plan the book trade is to develop quickly, and masses of books are now offered to the peoples of Russia at low prices. The export of grain last year astonished the world although it was only one-half of the average prewar exports (1930 sic). The export of oil is jumping up, and the output in 1930 was almost double that of 1913. Education is provided for under the Five-Year Plan and is progressing favourably as is the excellent propaganda for health and temperance. New technical colleges are being established, and this part of the

Plan is also succeeding. Stalin's Five-Year plans resulted in Ukraine's industrial potential seven times the 1913 indices."

It's a very interesting economic report. In 1913, Czarist Russia had the fastest growing economy. The First World War, financed by the Americans, put an end to the Czarist economic threat. After the war, the Americans dominated the world market. Would Stalin's Russia change that under the Five-Year Plans. If Stalin is exterminating farm workers in the Ukraine, and letting fertile fields go unplowed and seedless, wouldn't that boost American grain profits on the international market? It would appear that the Russians would even have to import grain if Stalin continued to destroy Europe's breadbasket. That would be a boom for the American grain producers. That much should have been perfectly clear to Jones. And the Soviet Republic's cotton production would be a deathblow to the British Empire's hold on production in their East Indian Empire and throughout their colonies. Had the Americans put a strangle-hold on Stalin's economic development with their credits, loans and machinery that they could squeeze Stalin whenever necessary to balance world trade and control the equilibrium of world markets.

Did the Consortium's international bankers exercise that much control over the postwar world? Had House, Warburg, Rockefeller, Harriman and the Morgan men planned it differently? Certainly Ivy Lee and the Pilgrim set in the CFR knew better the answers to those questions. Stalin was a reliable liquidator; Hitler, on the other hand, was a real firecracker, a true fire-breathing dragon.

Reader we see where Gareth Jones is taking us. His is a very intriguing trail of facts, figures, with the compass needle pointing towards an ominous future. It would seem that if the Anglo-American wasn't in bed with Stalin, they most certainly, simply for the economic realities of political stewardship, ought not to have missed this megalithic opportunity at monopoly. Surely, Stalin needed America industry and innovation. It was only a question of years before the vast cloak of imperial possessions began to unravel, torn asunder by violent and non-violent national liberation movements seeking independence from the England. For now the sun still rises and sets always on the great British Empire.

Jones saw the pitfalls of the Five Year Plan just as easily as the British "Tommies" saw their death in the mud trenches of the First World War. And where is all this taking us now? Stalin's success is plunging almost as fast as his ratings in the West. Jones writes, "In spite of these achievements there have been very serious breakdowns in the Plan. Coal production dropped rapidly last summer, and while the output in March was 4,700,000 tons, it was only 2,900,000 tons in August. There has been a severe shortage of fuel this winter. The coal position is gradually improving, but it will be impossible at the present rate to reach anywhere near the 83 million - tons aimed at this year." But Jones has to admit some progress, and he adds, "Nevertheless, the output will develop, and the figure for 1930 (47,000,000 tons) was a two-thirds increase over the 1913 figure." All from the benefits of forced labor and the gulag system.

"The Moscow Trial showed that the Five-Year Plan was doing badly in many branches. While the first year of the Plan was a success, the second was disappointing to the Communists. Production did increase, but it was at the expense of quality and at the expense of the standard of living of the workers. Transport was disorganised throughout the country. The lack of skilled labour was felt keenly. These difficulties are going to increase with the extra burdens which the Plan places on the country."

"The rapid speed at which Stalin is trying to industrialise Russia has led to great hunger and suffering. Food is scarce. The health of the nation may be affected by the present privations. The discontent of the masses has been tremendous, and there has been talk of revolution against the Communists … and "a wave of hatred against Stalin". He adds, "As I walked past the Kremlin, the citadel where Stalin lives, I saw sentries everywhere, and in one place where the rampart was broken a Red soldier walked up and down with his painted bayonet ready.

Stalin is at present supreme, but if there is much more hunger and suffering his position will be weakened. This would not mean, however, the breakdown of the Communist regime, but the victory of the moderates in the party.

"What of the future? … The figures at which the Bolsheviks aim are fantastic and can never be carried out by 1933."

Of course the Russians have made "progress". Jones writes. "Russian progress was inevitable. But as far as one is able to judge Soviet Russia will in time be able to increase her exports of coal, grain, oil, and timber. Her shipments of coal abroad are at present small, but she is trying to get a foothold in several British markets and such as Italy. Her exports of grain will depend on the harvest, but if her crop is as good this year as it was last year, then Canada is going to suffer still further and the grain market will be seriously disturbed. Russia's oil supplies are vast and she will continue to increase her oil exports. Her timber will also continue to hit Canada, the Scandinavian States and the Baltic States, and France."

Of the Consortium billionaires in America interested in Russia's vast resources and the Soviet Russian market, Jones wrote, "Harriman, Rockefeller, Weyerhauser, International Harvester. They all took notice of Russian economic statistics. But they had a decade at least not to worry of America being left behind in the wake of Soviet progress. Soviet Russia will probably, therefore, be a competitor in such natural products as coal, grain, oil, timber, and furs. Where manufactured goods are concerned, however, it will be a. long time before she will gain the experience and the skill and the organization of the Western countries. Moreover, Russia herself will be a market absorbing vast quantities of manufactured goods and her need for machinery from abroad to make the goods will be great for a long time yet."

To be sure, Jones hits the nail on the head. American businessmen love monopoly as long as they can capture supply and control prices. Winsome greed and monopoly made Rockefeller the world's richest man, Mellon and Harriman too. Stalin came from a Russian egg. When Stalin died, they found unspent cash in his room small quarters. He never needed it. He owned the Soviet Union and held the whole country in his pocket. Everyone knows that the very rich don't need money. Unfortunately, two thirds of his vast library of some 15,000 volumes disappeared soon after his death. Stalin was no idiot, a voracious reader, and he did make a lot of private notes….

Jones: "Soviet Russia's trade system, by which export and import are a State monopoly, enables her to sell at any price. If she makes a large profit on oil, then she can afford to sell grain or coal far below cost price. The Soviet Union has become one vast centralised business concern controlling 158,000,000 people with a miserable standard of living. So far the Five-Year Plan has been a mixture of successes and failures. It is increasing the production of Russia, but at the expense of quality and human happiness. Difficulties galore lie in its path, but if these difficulties are overcome, then Soviet Russia will be a powerful competitor. The success of the Plan would strengthen the hands of the Communists throughout the world. It might make the twentieth century a very different kind of society than envisioned by the CFR."

A shrewdly bold understatement!

Jones is actually warning the Consortium when he says that. The CFR is a creature of the Consortium pushing forward its world economic agenda of international finance and big business within the political fratricide of state socialized terror and famine. Jones is thrashing his sword in the apocalyptic sky overhead before it comes crashing down on their heads.

1931: THE STATE DEPARTMENT RUSSIA WATCHERS

Felix Cole in Riga is sensitive to Stalin's raising the tone and pushing the throttle on industrialization and his war against the peasants. Cole will have a long career at State, a gem of iconoclast perfection and satirical wit who enjoys the friendship of Joseph Grew who after the war comes to his defense before ambassador Cole is declared *personna non grata*, in 1947, in Ethiopia for having confiscated German archives from Adis Ababa, as entitled under the Potsdam agreements, and for refusing to wear proper attire at a government ceremony, an insult taken personally by Emperor Haile Selassie. Cole is hustled out of the country and compensated with the salubrious charms of the East and the Sri Lanka embassy instead.

Cole reads with interest a transcript of Stalin's speech dated February 9, 1931 given "at a recent conference of industrial heads … in which he demanded the speeding up of the program of industrial expansion on the ground that this is required by obligations not only to the country but also toward the labor class of the whole world, to the world proletariat." Cole doesn't let tactical changes in Stalin's grip on power go unnoticed. In his memorandum to Washington he remarked Stalin as saying, "These later obligations, he adds, "are more serious and important than those to the workers and peasants of the Soviet Union ...", printed in *Izvestia*, No. 35, February 5. "Stalin's position is consistent," Cole declares, "with his position in the past" referring to his earlier September 1927 interview with American representatives of trade unions "reported in the Legation's dispatch No. 4749, of September 26, 1927". Stalin now exhorts his countrymen with a new brand of feverish Bolshevism: "It is said that our country represents the shock-brigade of the proletariat of all countries. This is well said… We were the first to commence the building of socialism. By the fact that we are doing something which in case of success will turn the whole world upside down and liberate the whole working class... We have doubled the output of industry as compared with the prewar output. We have created the largest agricultural production in the world. But we might have done still more if we had really tried during this time properly to get hold of production, of its technique, of its financial and economic aspect. At the most within ten years we must rush through that distance which we are now lagging behind the advanced countries of capitalism." Stalin lay extra stress on technique. In his bid to surpass the West, he berated the communist workman who failed to emulate the American passion for management organization and innovation while gloating over American technology and success. "The Bolsheviks must acquire technique. It is time for the Bolsheviks themselves to become specialists ... technique decides everything ... a managerial worker who does not wish to study technique and does not want to acquire technique is a joke and not a manager." (SDDF 861.00/ 11461)

By late 1931 the record shows Stalin keeps Moscow transfixed in a state of terror with a thousand people shot *each day* by the OGPU in the Lubyanka prison. On February 24, 1931, an internal memorandum sent to the Department's Western European Affairs division recounts another Kremlin tale of ethnic cleansing, falling wheat prices and famine. Paul Culbertson and his chief in Western European Affairs at State Ted Marriner initialize it. William R. Castle, undersecretary and head of the Western Europe Division also gives it his "WRC" ink stamp. Present too and on board is Moffat along with the very wealthy Hugh D. Auchincloss (whose son after Yale joins a Schiff brokerage house on Wall Street and in the future takes as his third wife the mother of Jackie Bouvier and holds her hand down to the aisle to marry JFK). Castle meets the *Nation's* man in Moscow Louis Fischer back from Russia and takes him to lunch riding a crest of laurels for his latest book, *The Soviets in World Affairs* (1930). (A good read on the Auchincloss family in John H. Davis, *The Bouviers, From Waterloo to the Kennedys and Beyond,* Maryland: National Press, 1993)

Two days later the same memorandum reaches Bob Kelley and his desk telling alerting him to be on his guard with Fischer in Washington looking for material and a scoop on US-Russian "relations", and declares that "the Comintern was tending to become the laughing stock of the responsible Russian officials, that Stalin had cleared them out of the Kremlin and that Soviet diplomats both in Moscow and in Kiel (Kiev sic) were constantly complaining of the deleterious effect on Russian foreign relations with this body pledged to world revolution. The observer notes that the shortage of Russian funds, occasioned by the Depression and by the necessity for financing the Five-Year-Plan, had led the Russian Government to discontinue a subsidy to the Comintern... In this connection he stated that the Soviets had been impelled to engage in 'dumping' by absence of credit in Europe and that they were heartily sick of selling their exports at a low price in order to raise ready cash." Very rarely at this time does Stalin ever get referred to in name. (Louis Fischer, *The Soviets in World Affairs*, Cape & Smith, 1930)

Stimson, and Roosevelt's State Department men are a breed apart from the mainstream America and all are keenly aware of the fact. Some fit the Consortium mold and the sweetness of domination over peoples and lands, others aspire but never get the chance to find their way into that customary boredom with only a single thought in their heads and possess everything they can to fulfill it. Brigg's account on the diplomats depicts Ted Marriner with a habit of displaying a decorum considered acceptable, even preferred of the quintessential Foreign Service officer of the Stimson elite, by not getting too mixed up in internal affairs of a host country, or, as he dubbed it, "hang your clothes on a hickory limb but don't go near the water".

J. Theodore Marriner is a strange choice to head division of Western European Affairs, a post he doesn't keep long. Born in Portland, Maine he studied at Dartmouth, took degrees at Harvard and during the early war years teaching English at Harvard College and Radcliffe. Then with America formally in the war he passes his Foreign Service exams that summer and enlists in the army but is discharged with a heart condition. In October he's sent sent to Stockholm as 2nd Secretary, three years later to Bucharest where he attends the indulges his passion for royalty at the coronation of the King and Queen of Romania. Then back to Washington at State for the summer 1923, assigned to, of all things, the Publications Committee from 1925-26, then back to Europe, this time to Berne, 1st Secretary and Chargé d'Affaires, then once again back in Washington on February 1927 to take over the Division of Western European Affairs. He also serves as on several delegations: Preparatory Commission for Disarmament Conference (Geneva, 1926-27); Special Commission for the Preparation of a Draft Convention on the Manufacture of Arms (Geneva, 1927); Pact for Renunciation of War (Paris, 1928); London Naval Conference (1930).

After four years as secretary to the US legation in Berne, Moffat returns to Washington to replace Marriner, who April 1, 1931, is sent to Paris to run the new embassy as Counselor and Chargé d'Affaires adjacent the Hotel Crillon just down from the Louvre museum on Rue de Rivoli with its fine view of the Eiffel Tower overlooking the Seine. Marriner leaves for London and the Conference of Ministers for a Moratorium on International Debts (London, 1931). He later attends the General Disarmament Conference (Geneva, 1932); Eighth General Conference on Weights and Measures (Paris, 1933). He leaves Jay Pierrepont Moffat to head the Western Europe Division. Moffat is a seasoned State Department career man with a gold-plated background. Born 1896, New York law, he's posted around the world: personal secretary to the US ambassador to the Netherlands (1917-19), secretary to US legation in Warsaw during the Russian Civil War (1919-21), Tokyo (1921-23), then chief of protocol in the Coolidge White House. Ellis Briggs in *Proud Servant* describes Moffat as "an equally competent and considerate chief, though two men could scarcely have differed more widely in character and work habits. Ted was amusing, cynical, intellectually and socially a snob; he was a bachelor without independent means, a man from Maine who entered diplomacy via Dartmouth College ... not Yale or Princeton but still Ivy." Ellis recalls, Jay

Pierrepont Moffat "was steady, intelligent, and literal-minded, with no great sense of humor". (E. Briggs, *Proud Servant*)

Moffat carried a lot more personal cultural history in his baggage. He marries Lilla Cabot Grew, eldest of Ambassador Joseph Grew's three daughters, and so, he too now is related to the wealthy Rothschild August Belmont and America's most illustrious naval family, the Perrys. And we know reader that Ambassador Joe Grew married Alice Perry, a granddaughter of famed American naval commodores Oliver Hazard Perry, hero of the War of 1812 who later dies of yellow fever in the Caribbean days chasing fortune and pirates, and brother of Mathew Perry who arrived with a small fleet in 1853 to compel the polite and formal Japanese to engage in open its ports to unrestricted free trade with America and its government where Daniel Webster is an avid expansionist and proponent "in all measures which extend and increase our means of intercourse with foreign countries, and strengthen and enlarge our foreign commerce", he declares to his friends in Congress.

Not to overlook are the Grews, cousins to the JP Morgans; Jane Norton Grew marries Jack Morgan, son of JP Morgan himself. It's all a very tight, comfortable, happy and very rich family of cousins and powerful influence from the State Department to Wall Street and around the world. The Grews are also related to the Belmonts; Commodore Mathew Perry's daughter Caroline, 21, marries August Belmont, the highly successful German Jewish banker who emigrated to New York as an agent fronting the Jewish Rothschild funds from Europe during President Jackson's Panic of 1837 banking crisis and ends up financing two loans to the US government and soothing the Mexican government over its recent war reparations when the navy bombarded Vera Cruz and blockaded the Mexican coast. For the wedding Belmont gave his new bride over two city blocks of valuable New York real estate. In help with Perry's payments to maintain his Hudson Valley family farm near Tarrytown, Belmont extends generous loans and tips other prime city properties including a piece of Central Park. During the 1850s Belmont loans Perry another $20,000 to buy new house in Manhattan on 38 West Thirty-second. To suppliment his various investments Perry, 62 years old with advancing arthritis, and his merchant-adventurer friends arranged that the US Congress provide $400,000 (relatively the same cost of a large sailing or steamship) for 34,000 copies of his three volume South China Seas and Japan narrative completed in 1857 advancing his expansion vision for American expansion, ports and old colonial territory. His books sit on the same shelves with those of his friends James Fenimore Cooper, Herman Melville, and Richard Henry Dana.

Moffat proves well to a dependable administrative instrument – a rare and priceless virtue in any division head. It was said you could set your watch when Moffat emerged from his doorway on 19th Street, furled umbrella in hand, or by the time, just before nine, when he paused at the Metropolitan Club to scan the *Wall Street Journal*, or by the moment, just after ten, when from his office he spoke to his broker in New York, on which occasions he was not to be interrupted by anything short of a summons from the Secretary of State himself. You always knew where Pierrepont Moffat could be found – he was meticulous about leaving word of engagements – and, wherever he was, he was accessible to his colleagues and ready to transact business, which was the diplomacy of the United States.

Moffat has the reputation among his peers of being a first-rate Foreign Service officer performing the nitty-gritty often tedious work necessary to an orderly bureaucracy. He's a career man rewarded with permanent tenure in Washington with skills much appreciated to get through the dense jungle of red tape ensnaring the Foreign Service. Ellis Briggs writes, at the time conditions were "by no means perfect, but with an organization so small that it did not take a newcomer long to find out who did what, the arrangement functioned with surprising efficiency. It broke down after the war, with the invasion of hundreds of enthusiastic amateurs – too many to assimilate, and too many of them suffering from an illusion of mission and a palpitating eagerness to remake foreign societies." Nevertheless, Moffat leaves little if any impact on the Department. That memorandum and dispatches on the Holodomor pass through his hands, Moffat, who was formerly in charge of protocol in Coolidge's White House is for the most part out of the picture of events that make the world turn. When the Japanese declare war, and with his father-in-law in Tokyo, Moffat finds himself out of the loop sent on mission in Canada; there in 1943 Moffat succumbs to a fatal blood clot. (E. Briggs, *Proud Servant,* 57-61)

In fact Ted Marriner impressed his younger colleague Briggs who recalls how although Ted "looked and sometimes acted like a dilettante, he was in fact hardworking and conscientious and an astute and skillful negotiator" specialized in "problems stemming from World War I", a neat euphemism for disarmament. "Privately, he was interested in royalty and was impressed by dynastic rank and ramifications; his knowledge of the *Almanach de Gotha* and Burke's *Peerage* would have impressed a chamberlain. The lower classes did not interest him, and he was dubious about the ability of colonial peoples to master the tools of self-government. He would have deplored the post-World War II eagerness to establish irresponsible, unviable new countries as contrary to common sense, statesmanship, and the best interest of the inhabitants." In fact, he too had little experience in Europe, with assignments only in Stockholm, Bucharest, Berne and Geneva. While serving two years as Consul General in Beirut, then part of Syria, on October 12, 1937, Ted Marriner, 45, is killed in the doorway of his office, apparently shot by an outraged Armenia-born naturalized US citizen ten years later. He won't be the first American diplomat killed there. And that year his colleague Moffat finishes up Consul General in Australia and before long is back in Washington, once again head of Western Affairs. We have good reason reader never underestimate Moffat. He has intelligence, wealth and access, and he speaks German, Russian, and French. And not unlike Grew, his superior and father-in-law, he's a man of the world who knows how to get around and get things done, a Consortium man, a real man among men. (E. Briggs, *Proud Servant,*50; J. Theodore Marriner Papers, Columbia; Jay Pierrepont Moffat Papers, Harvard; Jay Pierrepont Moffat, Jr. follows his father's footsteps: Harvard '53, US Army intelligence, State Department, ambassadorial rank to Japan, Europe, Africa, Caribbean, Chad.)

Known to have privileged access to Stalin, Fischer tells Carter at State that "the Russians were willing to enter into an international wheat pool – including United States, Canada, the Argentine and Australia – for the purpose of stabilizing the price of wheat and dividing the world markets." Fischer is clearly on an errand for Stalin badly in need of cash for the grain and tells the State Department the Soviets will lighten up on anti-capitalist Comintern propaganda but doesn't want press reports of grain exports at falling prices to backfire feeding more sensational reports about famine and miserable starving peasant farmers and their dying children.

The Soviet agent Fischer delivers this quid pro quo from the Kremlin. "He stated that the Soviet authorities were afraid to advertise this fact because of the effect which it might have on mass opinion in such countries as England, where they would appear to be making food more expensive for the proletariat." This at a time of hostile reports by grain merchants in the British press angry cheap Russian grain. "He added that he understood that Mr. Meshaluck, who had recently been in Washington and who represents the Russian State Economic Council, had told the Federal Farm Board of Russia's willingness in this regard." This is the same Meshaluck who in a few short years becomes one of the favorite Bolsheviks of Ambassador Bullitt whom he considered genuinely "honest"; Bullitt actually believed he could trust a Bolshevik even this Soviet mouthpiece who lied about famine and the ruinous state of Russian agriculture! But few in the Kremlin and even less at the Department trusted Bullitt for saving more than his own ass.

When the execution's blade sliced through Wall Street's frenzy of greed and unrealistic stock prices during the summer of 1929 anxious Americans worried over inflation and the rising cost of bread. Soviet journalist Ilya Ehrenburg observes, "Americans were disturbed by a small newspaper item : in the USA the surplus of wheat exceeded 240 million bushels. It became apparent that in Canada, Australia, Argentina and Hungary there was also too much wheat. The price of wheat was falling rapidly. Farmers were ruined and reduced to beggary. Hoover didn't dare touch the gold standard and play inflationary voodoo politics with the dollar as his successor would do in order to raise farm prices. "The words about a world surplus of wheat should not be taken literally," Ilys Ehrenburg in Berlin writing for *Izvestia* recalls in his *Memoirs 1921-1941.*

Ehrenburg adds, "Whole continents were starving. There were forty million registered unemployed in the world. The import of wheat into West European countries decreased sevenfold. Representatives of forty-six countries assembled in Rome for a conference to discuss what was to be done with the wheat surplus. That was in the spring of 1931. People seemed to have gone mad. In Brazil they burnt coffee. In the USA they burnt cotton. It was suggested at the conference that wheat should be denatured by means of eosin: the red grain could be used as cattle-fodder. The propaganda began: 'Feed cattle on wheat, it is cheaper and more nourishing than maize'. Banks went on failing. Hungry peasants abandoned their fields and went to the ends of the earth in search of bread. Cows ate wheat of the best quality – from Manitoba or Barletta. But a few months later the newspapers carried the information that there was too much butter and meat in the world; and for precisely that reason men died of hunger." Might it be true, "Whole continents starving"?

Ilya Ehrenburg saves his neck as an apologist for Stalin and of course is gagged and unable to speak of millions of starving Russians and Ukrainians. That summer Ehrenburg is allowed to travel abroad; in Denmark he watches as pigs are ground up into "round flat cakes used as pig-food". Ehrenburg writes, "England was buying bacon, but it was already clear that there was too much fat in the world, and if the general situation did not improve pigs would have to be done away with soon…" Ehrenburg is able to comprehend the meaning in the distinction between men and their means, and how once they overcome their differences and transcend the systems that separate them and hold them apart there is a common ground for the good, intelligent and kind-hearted. He writes, "I realized that it was not the character of men that mattered: among the factory owners, the financiers, the kings of industry and the financial magnates there were both kind and cruel men, intelligent and stupid ones, pleasant and repellent ones. The matter lay not in some devilish quality of theirs but in the senselessness of the system itself." But it won't excuse the tyranny of the beast or deny the greed and corruption of the ignoble predator out to destroy for selfish profit. As a creature of Soviet communism where everything good and perfect emanates from Stalin the Leader of the Proletarian Revolution criticism out of step with Party dogma is life-threatening.

In 1932 and during these critical two years Ehrenburg finds temporary solace from the Soviet madness in bohemian obscurity in Paris. Between the wars the decadent life returns to "gay Paree" with expatriate artists, exiles and millionaires mingling in the cafes on the Left Bank, or in the *Quartiers* of Montparnasse and Montmartre watching the world go by, and catching a glimpse perhaps of Picasso in lust for his new love, a teenager he met on the streets and marries. He was 45, and she provides the muse to launch his erotic paintings immortalized as the tall and sinewy Marie-Therese Walter; in *The Dream*, one of the paintings in a Picasso's retrospective that much later will be bought for $139 million by hedge fund mogul Steven A. Cohen, in 2009, a few months before the international financial meltdown. (I. Ehrenburg, *Memoirs 1921-1941*)

Long after his pro-Stalinist complicity, Ilya Ehrenburg wrote about the famine he saw and knew to be true. "The *Torgsin* shops stocked tempting flour, sugar, shoes, but there you had to pay in gold – wedding rings or hoarded Tsarist coins. In Kuznetsk new arrivals immediately asked: 'Do they issue meat?' The typhus isolation building of the hospital was overcrowded: typhus was again taking a heavy toll. In Tomsk I saw a professor's wife boiling soap. It all reminded one of the rear of a war, but this rear was the front: the war was on everywhere." (I. Ehrenburg, *Memoirs 1921-1941*)

"There were, of course, different types of men among the construction workers. Cynics came and adventurers and drifters who moved form one site to another in search of what was called a 'long rouble'. Peasants looked mistrustfully at the machines; when a lever would not work they grew angry and treated it like a baulking horse, often damaging the machine. If some of the men were spurred on by noble feelings, others exerted themselves in order to get a pound of sugar or a length of material for a pair of trousers. I saw parties of special deportees: they were former kulaks who were being taken to Siberia. They looked like the victims of a village fire…" (I. Ehrenburg, *Memoirs 1921-1941*)

"A peasant in a village near Tomsk said to me: 'A fellow came and said: 'Anyone who wants to build Socialism, he's welcome to join the collective farm voluntarily; and anyone who doesn't want to, he's welcome, it's his own full right. But get this clear: to chaps of that sort all we have to say is to hell with his soul, and string his guts on the nearest telephone pole'." (I. Ehrenburg, *Memoirs 1921-1941*, 223-4)

"Two hundred and twenty thousand builders were working in Kuznetsk. … Foreign specialist who worked in Kuznetsk said it was impossible to build like this, that roads had to be made first and houses put up for the builders, the workers were a floating population, and anyway they did not know how to treat the machines; the whole undertaking was doomed to failure. They formed their judgments on the basis of textbooks, of their own experience, of the mentality of the people living in tranquil countries, and were totally unable to understand the spiritual climate and potentialities of this, to them alien land. … I do not know whether this is a universal human trait, but Soviet people have invariably shown themselves at their best in the worst times." (I. Ehrenburg, *Memoirs 1921-1941*, 225)

THE MANCHURIAN PROBLEM WORSENS

William Castle from a wealthy family settlement in Hawaii and formerly chief of the Far Eastern Affairs in the early twenties and staunch bearer of Stimson's confidence also sends his boss clarification of GE's latest corporate dealings with the Kremlin. Castle gets the info "direct" from Owen D. Young. In his memorandum Castle writes, "The General Electric Company was owed a certain amount of money by the Russian Government. It also decided, in spite of this, to make a loan, I think of $25,000,000 to the Soviet for the purpose of supplies. It was, however, not willing entirely to give up the principle involved in the non-payment of the earlier Russian indebtedness and it, therefore, went through the form of saying that 2 % of the interest to be paid by the Soviet on the new loan was to be considered as amortization of the old loan. Inasmuch as this 2% was taken out of the regular rate of interest, not added to it, the transaction (sic) struck me as a face-saving performance on the part of the General Electric, which was a little bit silly. The General Electric, furthermore, considered the whole thing a gamble." The writer of Castle's memorandum to Stimson declares, "I have no doubt that the Russian Government would promise not to engage in propaganda. Whether it would order the Third International not to do so is entirely another problem and, furthermore, Mr. Fisher puts the cart before the horse inasmuch as it is not the Soviet Government which gives orders to the Third International, but exactly the other way around." Well, "WRC" was dead wrong about that and didn't figure who ruled Moscow and the Russians. (The writer of the Castle memorandum is identified as "Carter".)

The Manchurian problem was critical to the Consortium power play. From one administration to the next, it cuddled FDR's war strategy for the Consortium's interests. How it would pan out through FDR's socialist New Deal and the New World Order for enthusiasts of the next postwar reconstruction and the Marshall Plan, World Bank, IMF and the creation of the United Nations was all part of the excitement of the era. Roosevelt would never see the end of it all. Now the Hoover-Stimson doctrine of non-recognition of seized territories was embroiled in it. non-recognition of Japanese aggression coupled with recognition of the Soviet Union.

The perfect balance for the perfect storm. Grew too plays his hand. They all did. What else can they do with the cards they dealt. The "Stimson Doctrine" remains a hollow assertion of non-recognition of territorial gains taken by force following Japanese aggression in Manchuria in 1931 and most deliberately played a part in not recognizing the Soviets until FDR decides to undermine Kelley the pull the rug from under him and his entire tiny operation at State. After Stimson "retired" after serving three decades in the cabinets of four Presidents, he leaves a hard act for Hull to follow. Hull would never be more than a front in a tensely divided State Department where Sumner Welles had Roosevelt's ear. Stimson was always there behind the scene. When war finally breaks out (much to the relief of FDR and Stimson), it's the elder Henry Stimson who becomes Roosevelt's War Secretary returning to the post he had with his friend Taft. And when the Japanese finally attack Pearl Harbor, FDR's first call from the White House is to Col. Stimson at Woodley during lunch; when Truman drops the A-Bomb, Stimson has his favorite man of spin write the note to tell his story to the Americans and the world.

Establishment historians prefer to consider Manchuria in the Far East when Presidents Hoover and Roosevelt are first forced to rethink America's non-recognition policy toward the USSR. In May 1929 the Chinese seized the Chinese Eastern Railway and expelled the Soviets. After frequent clashes on the border the Soviets finally accepted the 1929 status quo but not until December 1932. The Red Army remained on alert in area. Stimson relaunchs the recognition issue when he entangled US interests in the Russo-Sino Manchurian border dispute. He sent "an advisory note" to both the Soviets and Chinese. Soviet Foreign Commissar Litvinov who fires back Stalin's response on December 3, 1929, writing that the Kremlin was amazed "that the Government of the United States, which at its own wish, maintains no official relations with the Government of the Soviet Union, finds it possible to address advice and directions to the latter". Stimson considered to interfere, but is rebuffed by Litvinov since Stimson's note was addressed to Great Britain, France, Germany, Italy and Japan "proposing joint diplomatic intervention to maintain the Kellogg Pact and to prevent war" between Russia and China over the Manchuria invasion in the direction of Harbin. Litvinov further adds that in view of clashes between Chinese troops "loyal to Nanking and the armies of the generals who had refused allegiance to the central government… neither Nanking nor the military governor of Manchuria was willing to accept the demands of the Soviet Union".

Ultimately, on December 22, 1929, the Chinese negotiate and accept the return of the Chinese Eastern. Subsequently, the Japanese began their conquest of China calling it their right of "self-protection" of Japanese residents occupying Manchuria on a claim that the territory had been ceded to Japan in 1907 following their victory in the 1905 Russo-Japanese war.

Time races on.

China protests to the League of Nations; in September 1931. Japan occupies more territory in northern Manchuria including Harbin and installs a puppet government with the heir to the Manchu dynasty, Pu-yi (1906-67), under its protection. Stalin, unprepared for war, later agrees to sell Russia's share of the Chinese Eastern Railway to Manchukuo for a nominal price that went unpaid and giving Japan direct communication with Vladivostok and calling for a demilitarization of the Russian frontier pushed back northward as far as the Amur. The border remains tense with violent clashes not infrequent. Soviet troops seize territory in Outer Mongolia and control the Sinkiang province of Chinese Turkestan. (M. Cassella-Blackburn, 81-2, DVP v. 12, 605; G. Vernadsky, 369-70; Mashairo Yamamoto, *Nanking, Anatomy of an Atrocity*, Westport, CT: Praeger, 2000)

Soviet support of the nationalist Chinese cites Chiang Kai-shek as the primary cause. "As the invasion heated up, the Russian Communist Party tried to mobilize the Comintern to stop shipments of military supplies to Japan and to persuade the Chinese communists that Japan was more of a threat than the Kumingtang. Moreover, the Foreign Commissariat suggested a non-aggression pact to Japan as well as offering to sell the Chinese Eastern Railway to the new Manchurian state… "Such a pact in the strategic interest for US and the USSR should try to forestall Japanese aggression in the Far East". Non-recognition remains Hoover's cornerstone to doing business with the Soviets despite any military threat from the Japanese or Chiang Kai-shek. Kelley writes anti-communist Congressman Hamilton Fish (NY) on October 19, 1929 that the USSR "is not prepared to conform to the accepted practices in the field of international relations". The Bolshevik communists are "subversives", and always will be. "They would only cause us trouble", declares Kelley. "They would have to stop their terrorism and threats to overthrow capitalism if they wanted American recognition". And he adds, paradoxically, "The domestic aims and policies of the Soviet government (big s, small g!) have nothing to do with the question of recognition of the government of the Soviet Union." Kelley would repeat his standard phrase often, and four years during the 1933 summer recognition work, here declaring, in 1929, "friction and controversy have been the inevitable result of recognition".

As far as he, Henderson or MacGowan are concerned in spite of persistent optimism over prospects for trade from the Commerce Department and ARCC there is likely to be little if any change after recognition. "Stalin was convinced the capitalist nations hated the Soviet state and they would do whatever necessary to destroy it," confirms Bullitt scholar Cassella-Blackburn. And it was true to such a great extent that he repeatedly dismissed Churchill's warnings of the imminent German invasion in June 1941 as treacherous "disinformation".

Marxist-Leninist dogma and Marx himself always pronounced the inevitable collapse of capitalism. The same argument runs throughout Stalin's history of mistrust, fear and suspicion bordering on psychotic paranoia and one of the reasons put forward by historians for his not taking seriously tip-offs of the day month, week and day of the German invasion June 21, 1944, these coming in from Churchill and the Americans as well as his own agents whom he dismissed as *agents provocateurs*. He distrusted everyone, inside and outside the Soviet Union. The question is whom to trust. And Stalin trusts no one. However he lets a few live like Chicherin, Litvinov, Molotov, but not too many others… (M. Cassella-Blackburn, 82-4; D. Dallin, *Soviet Espionage*)

Nor does Bullitt in the Cassella-Blackburn account comment on great changes in Soviet society after the industrial leap of Stalin's Five Year Plan. Caseslla-Blackburn cites "considerable industrial expansion… However, even in 1930 the Soviet leadership recognized that the fire-year plan was quickly producing chaos from structural imbalances of development, *especially with priority given to military industries*". This is rarely mentioned. "Transportation and power plants were severely underdeveloped to handle the strain of maintaining the industrial pace. The peasants in the military had little willingness to suppress their own drive for collectivization, pushing loyalties to the breaking point." (M. Cassella-Blackburn, 109, citing Robert Lewis, *Foreign Economic Relations*, and *Technology and the Transformation of the Soviet Economy*, and R. W. Davies, "Industry," in R. W. Davies, Mark Harrison and S. G. Wheatcroft, eds. *The Economic Tranformation of the Soviet Union*, 1913-1945, Cambridge, 1944; J. Haslam, Chapter 3, Appendix 1; original emphasis)

The Secretary makes another note in his diary after a cabinet meeting a week later May 1: "I finally settled the form of the letter to the different universities about the Russian students who wish to come over to study engineering ... A delicate issue of granting a passport to the American Communist "of Russian descent".

All that about an insignificant Jewish Russian communist although there is, for the record, an Olginskaya Street off Kreshchatyk, the Champs Elysée of central Kiev. Nor is the Secretary referring to Trotsky, or a whole number of 1917 Jewish Bolshevik revolutionaries well known to Sands, Poole, Wiley and the Department but who went undetected by Stimson's "undersecretaries" such as Alexander Gumberg, a shady double-agent, the *Nation's* Moscow correspondent in bed with Stalin, Louis Fischer, Karl Radek, the ravenous intellectual, Litvinov, Rosengoltz, Yagoda, head of the OGPU, even Karzhentsev, Commissar of the Arts. Only the Jews could afford "the expensive and fashionable summer resort on the Black Sea", Bullitt exclaims with gutless envy revealing once again his schizophrenic denial of the fact that he himself is part Jewish. But Stimson is beyond all this now, lost in his own thoughts and feeling rather disconnected and out of touch with the momentary present of how things really are played out in the Soviet Union. Stimson will have a second chance, and he could take a special delight in that. Most old men never do. Of all the dons in the State Department he was the first. He had outlasted presidents, administrations, wars and revolutions.

Soon FDR will rely on Stimson as his Secretary of War when he calls him the day the Japanese bomb Pearl Harbor. Quite an honor from a Harvard man to a elder patriarch of Skull & Bones. It was not in his character to be impressed by an Jewish communist even if he was one of our own.

As it were the case of Moissaye J. Olgin (1878-39) went all the way up to Stimson's office. The "American Communist 'of Russian descent' was actually a Jewish Communist and writer, the very talented Moissaye J. Olgin who edited the Jewish communist newspaper, *Freiheit,* founded in 1922, the year he helped split the Jewish Federation of the Workers Party of America. Olgin is also editor of the Yiddish Communist paper and he has written extensively on Russia and its peasants. In 1932, once in New York and let loose and free to do his revolutionary thing, Olgin publishes a tract, "Capitalism defends itself through the Socialist Labor Party" (Workers Library Publishers). Not a bad title, Olgin, since capitalism had been given a pretty bad time once the Consortium wiped out the stock market. In 1934, Olgin is at it, again, this time publishing his work, "Why Communism? Plain talk on vital problems". He just won't take a break, or do a thing to help the Ukrainians and get at the real rub of the problem. Instead, he dallies around town again, this time, taking on the high and mighty, thinking he too deserves to share the podium. In 1935 his work *Trotskyism: Counter-Revolution in Disguise*, are dismissed as the ramblings of an obvious Soviet agent or someone who wished he was.

This is the individual who Stimson just four days after a high-level cabinet meeting invests his own time and authority to issue a US passport. Stimson hopes to silence Olgin ; his logic is curt and simple, and as he records in his diary, "I think that the harm which might be thus done among the ignorant and at present suffering members of our population is much greater than anything that Olgin could do by his propaganda or his present proposed trip to Europe." His fears are not aroused that Olgin will "confer with the Communist authorities in Moscow, with a view to further propaganda on their behalf in this country." Only Kelley would have been adamantly against it alarmed that the communists are relentless in their call for world revolution, more fiction than reality. (HLS Diary)

A more important and rewarding matter transpires that day. Stimson speaks on the telephone long distance with his friend Dwight Morrow just returned from Europe where he met with the Italian fascist leader Benito Mussolini and his Foreign Minister. "Mussolini seemed to trust him much more than before ..." Stimson notes it in his diary and looks forward to meeting Mussolini in July on one of his rare trips overseas. (M. Olgin, "New Peasants of New Russia", *Asia, the American Magazine of the Orient*, NY: Asia Publishing Co., v. 21 Dec. 1920 - Jan. 1921)

The evening of April 3rd Stimson is "waylaid" by Joe Baird of UPI. Stimson finds the journalist testy questioning the nature of his choosing advisers. UPI's Baird wants the scoop on filling the vacancy at the top left by the death of Joe Cotton, one of his two key undersecretaries. Hoover later will appoint William R. Castle to fill Cotton's slot much to Stimson's regret. To set him right Stimson tells him "my theory and my practice as to never appointing applicants but only taking so-called dollar-a-year men", the WWI euphemism for the elite Consortium independently wealthy types who don't live on wages or salaries and are considered more able to think independent of material distractions. It might also explain the low salaries of government employees even at that level. State Department salaries in 1930 are atrociously low stemming from the tradition that only the rich should apply. Stimson's salary is set at $15,000, undersecretaries Cotton, $10,000, Carr, $9,000, White, $9000. Division chiefs, Hornbeck, $8000 (Grade eight), Kelley $7,500, Wallace Murray $6,600 (Grade Seven), Packer $5,600 (Grade six). Senior professionals (appointed) were paid significantly less than career officers, Culbertson, for example picks up a paltry $4,600. And Kennan, the Department's future icon with his name enshrined at the Princeton Institute when he's still alive, in 1930, signs up as a Foreign Service linguist on a salary of $3,000.

Stimson considers three men to fill the opening: Allen Dulles, Harvey H. Bundy and Dr. Herbert Feis. It was Allen Klots who brings Harvey Bundy to the Stimson team. Bundy is a lawyer from Boston with experience in finance. Castle and Carr approve. Stimson notes in his diary, May 8, 1931, "He is a great friend of Klots, who had been too modest to suggest it before; but he was highly endorsed by George (Harrison sic) and I remembered linking him very much when I saw him." Stimson tells Hoover during a cabinet meeting. Hoover knew Bundy and concurs. Stimson wants Harvey Bundy in his office "as soon as possible." Two days later they meet. Stimson goes for his regular ride on his favorite horse and again meets with Bundy who proves to be one of his closest advisers in these last two decades of Stimson's life; Bundy's son "Mac" and future Dean of Harvard follows his father and becomes Stimson's official biographer – a power three-some.

To help with the European economic crisis the previous November Stimson brings in his law partner Allen Klots, son of a Yale classmate; for three decades Stimson and the elder Klots were tight partners at the firm of Winthrop & Stimson. Klots, too, carries an impressive war record. That spring May 14 Klots brings in another man to meet the Secretary as economics adviser. Earlier that year Herbert Feis had been convinced he's a shoe-in for the top economic research position at the CFR. A flaming talent he and his book *Europe: The World's Banker* are the talk of the town with a new analytical twist on the science of international political economy.

A year after its publication in 1931, *Foreign Affairs* offers Feis the prominence he knows he deserves. *The New York Times* had publishes his long treatment of The Bank for International Settlements (BIS). Feis had also scribed a long article on Mexican trade since 1881 for *The Survey of American Foreign Relations*. At 38, and already a CFR member, in February Feis is hired as a research assistant at $1000 a year by James Shotwell of the Social Science Research Council. Feis' spot inside the CFR, however, is suddenly compromised when Charles Howland of the CFR group resigns a senior position leaving Feis jobless. For the next twelve years Feis remains a senior economics adviser at State. After the war Klots returns to Winthrop, Stimson, Putnam & Roberts. This is the same firm that retained former Yale President Kingman Brewster as their resident partner in London when he stepped down from his ambassadorship at the Court of St. James, in London.

Pravda and *Time* played partners in crime over a story on Legge and surplus American wheat. The story bounces between New York and Moscow titled, "Russia: Hoover Plot" is a curious blog of diversion published April 20, 1931 of a botched plan of invasion of Soviet Russia by the French. Apparently *Time's* are drunk with disinformation. *Pravda,* the official organ of the Soviet Communist Party pushed a story titled, "How the United States Prepared Intervention".

So, not to be bettered, *Time* picks up the baton and writes, "President Hoover has not yet been burned in effigy at Moscow, differing in this respect from Aristide Briand, Sir Austen Chamberlain and the President of China, Marshal Chiang Kai-shek who crushed the communists and leads the Kumingtong. But last week both Mr. Hoover and ex-Chairman Alexander Legge of the US Federal Farm Board became in Moscow popular candidates for stuffing & burning. Reason: "The Hoover Plot against the Soviet Union." *Time* adds, "... Wilson discovered that Mr. Legge, while chairman of the Farm Board, had not only bought huge stocks of wheat and cotton but also that 'Legge stored these supplies in Atlantic ports, although this was more expensive than storage in interior depots'. From this Wilson concluded that President Hoover had assigned Mr. Legge to assemble edible supplies for a French Army that was to invade Russia. During the Great War, as Wilson found out, 'Legge was food and raw material director of the United States and chief of service of the armies of the anti-German coalition'."

Grain for gold converts to cash for increased manufacturing, boosting exports, consumerism and the consequent demand for increased trade and greater imports. If the export barons could sell American surplus grain, it just might help the American farmer out of the deep hole of Wall Street's Depression. Or, as it was put this way in a study by three experts who happen to refer to the Consortium and its link to grain, government and gold in a 2004 essay titled "Harvests and Business Cycles in Nineteenth-Century America", written in part by Joseph H. Davis of the Vanguard Group investment firm. They also refer to the observations made in 1935 in the study *Wheat and the AAA,* prepared by Dr. Joseph Stancliffe Davis, a Harvard and Stanford economics professor and member of the American Farm Economic Association.

The recent observers saw fit to quote Wilson's adviser and backdoor member of the banker's clique which created the Federal Reserve Bank in 1913: "In the words of A. Piatt Andrew (1906) in a country where agricultural products form an important factor in foreign commerce, the size of the crops will exert a considerable influence upon the balance of trade and the international movement of gold. The extent of the bank reserves in the great financial centres and the contraction or expansion of general credit may in consequence depend most importantly upon the output of the season's harvests... When the American crops are abundant, our exports very naturally tend to increase, and gold imports are apt to occur. That, in turn, means large cash holdings in the banks, with, under normal conditions, the accompaniments of expanding credit and buoyant trade. Joseph Stancliffe Davis (1935) noted that the coincidence of good wheat crops here with short crops in Europe in 1879, 1891, and 1897, 'led to large exports at attractive prices and gave a pronounced stimulus to business in this country, twice facilitating revival from depression, and once (1891-92) helping materially to reverse a recession under way'."

To crown his years of service Joseph Stancliffe Davis (1885-75) is appointed to President General Eisenhower's US Council of Economic advisers (1955-58). But what is the Harvard professor doing at Hoover's Stanford University, in 1922, when the Commerce Secretary Hoover is stashing away for future save-keeping his vast Russian Bolsheviki documents? What on earth is he up to?

As an expert economist Joe Davis might have had something valuable to reveal about the US-Soviet wheat deals during the Holodomor years, for that matter since the First World War when he collaborated with ARA head and Commerce Secretary Hoover. Unfortunately for the victims of the government-planned economy of Soviet collectivization and industrialization, Dr. Davis is, in fact, little more than a tool of the Consortium. Harvard-bred Class 1905 with a Ph.D (1913), professor Davis ends up teaching at Stanford in California where he helps set up the Hoover Institute of the carefully guarded Russian Revolutionary war documents. That in itself would not seem worthy of interest if it were not for the fact that in 1935 the Consortium CFR's Brookings Institute publishes his book *Wheat and the AAA*. His other works included *Food as an Implement of War* (1905, reprinted by the Food Research Institute, 1943); *On Agricultural Policy, 1926-1938,* (Food Research Institute, 1943); *The World Between the Wars, 1919-39, An Economist's Perspective* (Johns Hopkins Univ., 1975).

Legge's days too are numbered. Legge will come to the end of his road in the year of the Holodomor 1933. (Andrew, A. Piatt. "The Influence of the Crops Upon Business in America." *Quarterly Journal of Economics,* 20 (3), May 1906, 326, and Joseph Stancliffe Davis 1935, 2, both quoted by Messers. Joseph H. Davis, Vanguard Group, Christopher Hanes, NY State Univ., Paul W. Rhode, Univ. of North Carolina, "Harvests and Business Cycles in Nineteenth-Century America", June 2004).

Eustace Mullins looked into how Hoover took it upon himself to marshal together thousands of government officials to assemble documents pertaining to the First World War and Russian Revolution. At the time of the Armistice and the Versailles Treaty negotiations in Paris (1918-19) the war planners were still suffering from shock, not from trench warfare but their hangover of overwhelming profits compared with millions dead. Mullins writes, "Even then, no one was sure just how World War I had gotten started."

In *The World Order* (1985) Mullins observes, "It was to someone's interest to see to it that as many pertinent and secret documents from the warring powers should be gathered in one place, gone over, and, if necessary, secluded from prying eyes. Hoover was able to call upon Gen. Pershing to provide hundreds of Army officers to aid him in his quest. In the 'Foreword to The Special Collection of the Hoover Library', Hoover says that he recruited 1,500 officers from the American Army, and the Supreme Economic Council, and sent them to all parts of Europe. *The New York Times* February 5, 1921 says that Hoover had as many as 4,000 agents in Europe, going from country to country to gather these documents."

Eustace Mullins explores deeper into this extraordinary government documentation campaign culminating in Hoover's "collection of 375,000 volumes". One has to wonder what on earth for? Only the Consortium could pull off such a campaign without Congressional support or public information.

Mullins writes, "Even in those pre-inflationary times, the cost of maintaining 4,000 agents in Europe must have been prohibitive. *No one has ever found out who was paying them.* Also, many of the documents were purchased outright. The only expenditure Hoover ever made public was the original $50,000 he had given in 1919 to establish the library. Who spent millions of dollars to put this collection together? It is most unlikely that Hoover would have parted with such sums, but no one has ever admitted putting any money into this project. *The NY Times* notes in the Hotel Commodore story that Hoover, a member of the first graduating class at Stanford, had presented the school with a collection of 375,000 volumes. It included the most valuable collection of secret Bolshevik records in existence, among them, the lists of the original district Soviets, which had been bought from a doorkeeper for $200. The *Times* noted that the Soviet Government had no copies of these rare archives! The *Times*, June 30, 1941, noted that the Bolsheviks had allowed Hoover to remove 25 carloads of material, at a time when Russian refugees were permitted to leave only with the clothes on their backs. (Ten days after the Nazi invasion of the USSR. sic) The solicitude for Hoover's collection may have been influenced by the fact that he had saved the infant Bolshevik regime from extinction by rushing large quantities of food to them. Hoover's collection also includes the complete secret files of the German War Council during World War I, a gift from President Ebert; Mata Hari's diary, and sixty rare volumes from the Czar's personal library. Many of the collections are permanently sealed.

The Times notes that the Hoover Institution contained 300 sealed collections, which no one has ever been allowed to examine. The initial organization of the material was done by a Stanford professor of history, Ehpraim D. Adams (1865-30). Adams and his wife are installed in an office in Paris May 22, 1919, to receive the first shipments of documents. Other offices were opened in Berlin, London, and New York. Aiding Adams were Dr. Alonzo Engelbert Tyler, who had been educated at the University of Berlin, served on War Trade Board 1917-19, and staff member of Stanford Food Research Institute; Dr. Carl Baruch Alsberg, also educated at University of Berlin, worked for the Dept. of Agriculture; and Dr. Joseph Stancliffe Davis, a Harvard professor of economics. The advisory committee of the original Hoover Library consisted of Dr. James R. Angell, president of Yale, and president Carnegie Corp.; Dr. J.C. Merriam, educated at the University of Munich, chairman National Research Council, and Carnegie Institution; Herbert Hover; and Julius H. Barnes".

Who was Julius H. Barnes? *Time* featured Barnes May 5, 1930 on its cover. Another Consortium crony Julius Barnes, too, figures in the American-Soviet Holodomor cover-up. Barnes knows just how profitable natural resources can be. A tough grain dealer from Duluth, Minnesota deep in the heart of the Midwestern farm-belt Barnes held a seat inside Hoover's US Food Administration war business as President of the Grain Corporation (1917-18). Barnes happens to be the former Director of the US Wheat Corp. Since 1922 Barnes heads the American Chamber of Commerce. On March 1922 Barnes in Chicago declares in a speech promoting agriculture citing progress in the booming world economy where even "Russia that is recovering from its destructive debauchery of communism is plainly approaching saner relations with the world". Barnes also praises the War Finance Corporation for "its well distributed loans" but in the same breath he disparaged government regulation, saying "The easy and happy thought that Government operation could spell relief for all human distress has lost its seductive charm."

After his war business Barnes joins Wall Street partners at J. Henry Schroeder Banking Corporation where makes an even larger fortune in sugar and grain; Schroeder owned most of Cuba's sugar industry. Schroeder partners did very well during the war: G. A. Zabriskie ran the US Sugar Equalization Board and became president of several big American baking companies including Empire Biscuit, Southern Baking Corporation, Columbia Baking; M. E. Rionda, president of Cuba Cane Corporation, director of Manati Sugar Company, American British and Continental Corporation, and others; senior partner Baron Bruno von Schroeder was a director of North British and Mercantile Insurance Company. Baron Rudolph von Schroeder of Hamburg, his father, was a director of Sao Paulo Coffee Ltd., a huge Brazilian company. Schroeder partner in London, F. C. Tiarks a director of the Bank of England. ("Agriculture Entering New Era; Julius H. Barnes Declares Its Problems Are Assured of an Early Solution", *The NYT*, March 21, 1922; see Mullins and Sutton for more on Schroeder).

For all his paranoia and vigilant distrust Stalin has good reason not to trust the British. According to Antony Sutton, the London Schroeder Bank in 1938 became Germany's financial agent in Great Britain. Two years earlier, the New York branch of Schroeder had merged with the Rockefellers, as Schroeder, Rockefeller, Inc. located at 48 Wall Street. Carlton Fuller of Schroeder is president of this firm with Avery Rockefeller vice-president. For years, Avery Rockefeller has been a quiet partner of J. Henry Schroeder, and created Bechtel Corporation, the construction giant whose employees played a leading role in the Reagan's administration with Secretary of State George Pratt Schultz (Pratt-Rockefeller Standard Oil heir) and Reagan's Defense Caspar Weinberger.

From Sutton we learn that after the Nazis gained power in 1933, Schroeder is also the appointed German rep at the Bank of International Settlements (BIS). That would have put him closer in touch with Allen Dulles. According to Sutton, "The Kilgore Committee in 1940 stated that Schroeder's influence with the Hitler Administration was so great that he had Pierre Laval appointed head of the French Government during the Nazi Occupation. The Kilgore Committee listed more than a dozen important titles held by Kurt von Schroeder in the 1940's, including President of Deutsche Reichsbahn, Reich Board of Economic Affairs, SS Senior Group Leader, Council of Reich Post Office, Deutsche Reichsbank and other leading banks and industrial groups. Schroeder served on the board of all International Telephone and Telegraph subsidiaries in Germany." Baron Kurt von Schroeder (1889-66) Adolph Hitler's personal banker, advanced funds for Hitler's accession to power in Germany in 1933*; German representative of the London and New York branches of J. Henry Schroeder Banking Corporation; SS Senior Group Leader; director of all German subsidiaries of I.T.T; Himmler's Circle of Friends; adviser to board of directors, Deutsche Reichsbank (German central bank; * Kurt Freiherr von Schroeder, a member of Nazi Party (NSDAP), joined de Circle of Friends of de Economy / *Freundeskreis de Wirtschaft* and who hosted a notorious meeting between Franz von Papen and Hitler and facilitated Hitler's seizure of the Chancellorship.).

In *Wall Street and the Rise of Hitler*, Antony Sutton writes, "The Nazi Baron Kurt von Schroeder acted as the conduit for ITT money funneled to Heinrick Himmler's S.S. organization in 1944, while World War II was in progress, and the United States was at war with Germany." Kurt von Schroeder, born in 1889, was partner in the Cologne Bankhaus, J. H. Stein & Co., which had been founded in 1788. Victor Perlo writes, in *The Empire of High Finance*: "The Hitler government made the London Schroeder Bank their financial agent in Britain and America. Hitler's personal banking account was with J.M. Stein Bankhaus, the German subsidiary of the Schroeder Bank. F. C. Tiarks of the British J. Henry Schroeder Company was a member of the Anglo-German Fellowship with two other partners as members, and a corporate membership." (Victor Perlo, *The Empire of High Finance*, International Publishers, 1957, 177)

The success of the Schroeders in duping Hitler into this belief explains several of the most puzzling questions of World War II. Why did Hitler allow the British Army to decamp from Dunkirk and return home, when he could have wipe them out? Against the frantic advice of his generals, who wished to deliver the *coup de grace* to the English Army, Hitler held back because he did not wish to alienate his supposed vast following in England. For the same reason, he refused to invade England during a period when he had military superiority, believing that it would not be necessary, as the Anglo-German Fellowship group was ready to make peace with him. The Rudolf Hess flight to England was an attempt to confirm that the Schroeder group was ready to make peace and form a common bond against the Soviets. Rudolf Hess continues to languish in prison today, many years after the war, because he would, if released, testify that he had gone to England to contact the members of the Anglo-German Fellowship, that is, the Schroeder group, about ending the war. The Hess flight is another enigma. Was it really Hess in the British prison? Or a double? Tn his book *They Cast No Shadows* (2002) writer Brian Desborough provides some answers to that riddle, when he wrote that Rockefeller's imposed a *quid pro quo* with the British to get a deal on British controlled Saudi Arabian oil or otherwise the Rockefellers would ship oil to the Nazis from their holdings in Venezuelan oilfields "in the expectation that Germany would defeat Britain". According to Desborough, "Suffering defeat at Dunkirk, the British were forced to promise the Rockefellers access to their Arabian oil deposits at the conclusion of the war, provided that the Venezuelan oil shipments to the Nazis were terminated. After the conclusion of hostilities, American troops constructed the Rockefeller's Arabian oilfields at American taxpayer's expense." Desborough describes how Rockefeller put pressure on the Chinese to block shipments of oil to Japan in order to preempt a Japanese attack on the Soviet Union and the consequent loss of oil and timber reserves. As a result Japan was pressured to launch its attack on Pearl Harbor. The sky was blanketed with waves of Japanese planes passing over the Philippines. General MacArthur was ordered to keep all US bombers on the ground. All were destroyed. Desborough also has some very interesting material on UFOs, a subject that may have driven President Truman's first Secretary of Defense James Forrestal out of his normal mind. (Brian Desborough, *They Cast No Shadows, A Collection of Essays on the Illuminati, Revisionist History, and Suppressed Technologies*, Writers Club Press, 2002, 307)

On May 14 1931 Stimson lunches with Senator Borah at Woodley for a roundup, he records, on "current affairs" and the world situation. Stimson fears "that Russia would come to South America when the inevitable fall came". The next day Stimson talks over Russia with Governor Baxter of Maine "a fine upstanding brilliant man". Baxter, he notes, "came in to tell us about Russia". Hoover had warned Stimson that Governor Baxter "used to be a little 'pink', but his experience in Russia, where he had gone to look over the situation in view of its effect upon the Maine lumber industry, had quite converted him." Baxter, however, impressed Stimson as decidedly "anti-Soviet, to put it very mildly". The Governor stressed the Soviet's "war psychology". Stimson sends him to Klots and Kelley. That afternoon Stimson took his usual car on the Senator train, returned to New York City and on to Highhold. "The country is at its most beautiful; the dogwood blossoms are better than I have ever seen them," the Secretary wrote in his diary, ever the consummate gentleman riding around his estate marveling at the wonder and beauty of Nature. Grandfather, tell me, do they do that in Hell, too? If Hell is the Soviet Union then the answer is affirmative.

Nothing is noted between the Governor of Maine and Stimson of forced labor camps or the Soviet timber gulag industry where "workers are held like dogs to their masters will". That's odd, since this month in the Chamber of Commerce in London, and in the British press, a scandal over reports of a vast network of communist "slave-work" has erupted and threatens to disrupt the Consortium's international timber and grain market. We know however, that from A.C. Ratshesky in Prague came an alarming official document dated May 25, 1931 about "the horrors" of "slave-work" in the Soviet timber camps "by disinherited peasants and political prisoners". Worse for the diplomats, the subject rages in public discussion inside London's Chamber of Commerce. The memorandum is sent to Kelley and stamped by an assistant Secretary of State (White) on July 13, 1931 of a meeting with Senor Roberto Levillier, Argentine's ambassador in Prague, "on the present situation in Russia" – subject which the minister proposed for "to boycott Russia both economically and morally" over grain shipments. The Argentinian diplomat suggests "a Pan-American Conference be called" in order to do it but that the call for such a conference "come from the United States". Ratshesky urges the document be sent direct to Secretary Stimson himself as he "was very interested in the Russian situation". Ratshesky writes that at the current debate inside the Chamber of Commerce in London over timber shipments from Russia "a decision of the United States of America have abundantly proved that this product is to be obtained by slave-work". He adds, "Many sailors of all nationality have seen the timber camps and written down the horrors of what they saw. Refugees themselves have handed the proofs of the facts and these have been gathered by Commander Bellairs who leads in the House of Commons and in THE TIMES, the movement of protest against the acceptance of goods obtained by slave-work. … most of Russian exports consist of goods either stolen or produced by disinherited peasants and political prisoners".

Ambassador Levillier tells the US officer how the slave system worked under Stalin's socialized terror and Ratshevsky dutifully informed Washington writing, "Practically all industries are carried on in Russia against the principles of personal liberty and Humanity. By the card that gives them a right to eat and live, workers are held like dogs to their masters will, and do not earn enough to support their family. The former proprietors are little by little shot or sent to the mines and timber camps. By such unhuman proceedings, the Soviets manage to produce goods at a much lower cost-price than any civilized country, can furnish, and when they don't for any reason, they sell at a loss, cash, thus getting a quick return and destroying the industries of other nations. In agriculture, for instance, they are increasing their wheat-acres, and it has been calculated by an American expert who published his report in the *American Geographic Review*, that they will be able to place about 233,000,000 bushels of wheat on the market in 1933. If they are thus allowed to go on underselling, no other country possessing wheat surplus, and paying reasonable human wages to the workers will export. This is only one example of one industry. They are planning to do the same in cotton and sugar in a larger scope than they have already done, and are equally busy in undermining the commerce of timber, cement, coal, tobacco, etc., in other countries." It's unlikely that Governor Baxter ever saw this cable; yet we can infer that it should have been read by Stimson. Hoover, however, was overwhelmed by turmoil in the national economy to give it much attention if any for which we have no record. (SDDF 761.000/ 861.000/600.6112/610.000)

Ratshesky's cable is consistent with reports on the Russian situation we find in recent academic studies, for example, in Michael Ellman's "The Role of Leadership Perceptions and of Intent in the Soviet Famine of 1931-1934" (2005). "The USSR in the early 1930s," concludes Michael Ellman in a paper on the Holodomor published in 2005, "was not engaged in an international war but was engaged, in the perception of its leaders, in a fierce class war with a ruthless and determined enemy which used starvation, murder, beatings and arson as weapons. In 1930, just in the Urals region (oblast') in the period 1 January – 10 November, the state security organs recorded 866 cases of 'kulak terror'." (S.I. Golotik & V.V. Minaev, *Naseleni i vlast'*, Moscow, 2004, 119, quoting two studies by Plotnikov about dekulakisation in the Urals cited by Michael Ellman, "The Role of Leadership Perceptions and of Intent in the Soviet Famine of 1931-1934", 2005)

Stimson prefers sending agent John Van A. MacMurray (1881-60) to investigate Russian conditions. MacMurray is an expert on the Far East with a solid military and State career including counselor in 1917 in Tokyo. President

Coolidge appointed him Minister to China from 1925-29 where he worked closely on the Chinese Customs Tariff with Secretary of State Frank Kellogg, Chief Justice Charles Evans Hughes, chief of the Division of Far Eastern Affairs Stan Hornbeck, and Bill Phillips. Stimson makes notes of his meeting April 13, 1931 in his office with MacMurray "of the Walter Hines Page School at Johns Hopkins University in Maryland" as it was then called before it was changed to SAIS and moved to Pennsylvania Avenue in Washington DC. Page had been President Wilson's close friend and adviser whom he trusted to send to the Court of St. James as his ambassador to Great Britain. Klots and Kelley of the Eastern Europe Division are also present at the meeting with MacMurray.

Stimson reviews "the organization of the investigation into Russia which MacMurray is planning to organized and carry on, and which we have given our blessing to." Stimson left his office and "hired a horse, as Larry is still lame, and went out for an hour and a half horseback ride". The exercise always did him good and makes him strong for another day and eases his troubled mind. The note by Stimson on MacMurray in fact leaves much in the dark. He is one of the very few without equal having had extensive experience as a observer during the Bolshevik coup days when he was chief of the Riga Legation and America's top Russian expert. It can be said too that MacMurray had been Kennan's first mentor before the latter joins Kelley, Bullitt and Harriman. A full two years will pass before Bullitt and Kelley collaborate that fatal Holdomor summer 1933 to iron out the wrinkles of the Soviet recognition deal for FDR with Bullitt pushing hard for Moscow; MacMurray will end up again in Riga, appointed August 28. Among those who know there is little doubt inside State that Bullitt bamboozled FDR by the back door, something that MacMurray would never do. When Bullitt is away in Moscow for his first meeting with Stalin, MacMurray presents his credentials, in Riga, on January 4, 1934, and is joined there by Keith Merrill.

Secretary Stimson has another important meeting June 3, 1931 on the Russian situation this time with General Haskell recently returned from Moscow. Stimson never visited Russia nor did he express any interest to go there or meet with the Soviet dictator himself. "What for?" he might have queried. Now he brings all his Russian team into the circle – "Rogers, Kelley and Klots, and part of the time Castle ... to hear what Haskell has to say. Stimson is captivated by Haskell's report of Soviet progress under the Five-Year Plan. "It was very interesting because Haskell was in Russia so long at the time of the famine in charge of the American relief and knew Russia thoroughly," Stimson noted in his diary, recalling the postwar famine and Hoover's operations there. Stimson's diary records notes of the meeting: "In general he noted this time the tremendous improvements that had been made in the management of the railroads and also the very great activities of construction that were going on, the building of the new dormitories for the peasants and the laborers and the enormous dam that was being built on the Dnieper river." Stimson was particularly interested in Stalin's military build-up Haskell, Stimson writes, told of the May Day Soviet parade and "the tremendous improvement in the Army". Haskell "counted four hundred tanks, where five years before when he saw a similar review, there were only four old tanks". The Soviet "aviation service",

Haskell tells the Stimson team "was either the best or second best only to France in Europe". Stimson notes that "Mitchell confirmed this view … of great progress", a reference most likely to Billy Mitchell, the controversial General of the US Signal Corps during the First World War commanding 1,500 Allied planes in 1918.* Haskell tells Stimson the Soviet Union lagged behind the United States in every category "except raw products". Stimson notes in his diary Haskell's attention to Russia's grain production. "Russia's estimate," Stimson observes, "was that now they could produce wheat at 38 1/2 cents a bushel ultimately. This was, however, not making allowances for certain factors of exchange and it was in terms of their own currency and computation." For Stimson, the world as understood by American foreign policy of which he was responsible was best interpreted in the "cost figures" – the terms of doing business, rates, money, production. Known by his peers as distant, cold and unflappable, "the ice-cycle", Stimson was an Empire-builder imbued with a 19th century outlook of international law and agreements, the covenants and contracts between nations that defined relations and the power to enforce the status quo over the poor oppressed and unstable or undeveloped regions of the world. Not unlike his peers Teddy Roosevelt and Churchill, Stimson fervently believed in the superiority of his own race over the indigenous natives of smaller nations. (*Not to be confused with Charles E. Mitchell, chairman of National City Bank, director on IG Farben Henry Ford and Paul Warburg, and chairman of the NY Federal Reserve Bank.)

A few weeks earlier, on May 5, 1931, Soviet officials, lobbyists and American businessmen gathered for a business luncheon at the Mayflower Hotel in Manhattan in full view of the city and national press. Undersecretary James G. Rogers, a senior Russian expert is particularly favored by Stimson and it's he who compiles a summary of the conference. Rogers had been appointed late winter in February to fill the slot long since vacant. Rogers is the only Westerner on Stimson's staff and brought gusty "relief from the dismal burden of State Department duties". In his memoirs Stimson notes while no one was able to fill Cotton's shoes, Rogers rose to become Stimson's "constant adviser, at first largely on legal questions and later on matters of major policy".

Among those present he notes was the slippery American Bolshevik Alex Gumberg, Col. Hugh Cooper, Richard B. Scandrett, and Cooper's assistant Lapean. Cooper is the top engineer building Stalin's "New Society" for the Consortium with close contacts to DuPont, GM, GE and other principal constructors of the Soviet infrastructure. He has Stalin's ear and can walk into the Kremlin whenever he cares to talk to the Supreme Ruler. A member of the Russian-American Chamber of Commerce, Cooper is described by Rogers as having been introduced as "the builder of the great Government power plant in the Ukraine" and who "has for five years been, as consulting engineer, designing and overseeing the construction of this plant in which now about 18,000 men are excavating, pouring concrete, et cetera." Alex Gumberg observes, "The magnitude of the Five-Year Plan probably scares more people than it attracts. The thing is too stupendous and complex. Russian business is concentrated in too few firms." Harvester and other companies have repeatedly been favored with Soviet business and in some cases reached the 'saturation point' in extending credits," Siegel observes. Americans like one executive had extended a $700,000 credit and when asked for more, told the Soviets pay up and then let's see. (K. Siegel, *Loans and Legitimacy*, 133)

Cooper's work is of course well-known to the CFR Consortium gang but its worth noting updated details here now related to the conferencees and delivered directly to Stimson by a top adviser. Assistant Secretary Rogers informs Stimson that Cooper told his audience that he worked with "a staff of nine engineers on the ground", and he adds "Common reputation says that he is *the most active technical man dealing with Russia and closer to Stalin than any other foreigner.*" Rogers updates a profile on Gumberg as having originally been presented to State "by the Solicitor General as with many convincing and impressive connections and acquaintances in Washington and New York, has been a Bolshevik agent in the past, is now working for the Chase Bank as a go-between between Russia and the United States". Actually, the FBI and the State Department have lengthy files on Gumberg dating as far back as the Lenin-Trotsky revolutionary period; his feud with John Reed was common gossip among the Col. Robbins and Americans of the 1917 Red Cross spy mission. Rogers tells his boss he also ran into the New York lawyer Scandrett, a close relative of Stimson's friend and Hoover adviser to Morgan banker Dwight Morrow. Cooper privately passed on the latest news from Stalin to Rogers for Stimson and the President. Rogers finds Cooper "hard boiled, clear headed, a veteran engineer, strongly anti-communist but eager to make money and achieve professionally." Cooper conveys Stalin's message to Washington through Rogers confirming to the White House the Kremlin's readiness to conform to the requirements of the United States Government to meet the needs of the Consortium's economic plans for the Soviet Union, which he says, are "already in a stage of advance socialism only as distinguished from communism". So defines the Consortium view of fascist totalitarianism under Stalin at this time as perceived by the most high-ranking American engineer in the USSR building the Soviet military industrial complex. Not a hint of any of this surfaces in Stimson's memoirs published in 1946.

"Apparently his main purpose," Rogers adds, "was to persuade me that the Russian program afforded no real threat to the world, that it was in the hands of practical politicians who while devoted to the cause were modifying the situation so rapidly that they were already in a stage of advance socialism only as distinguished from communism". Cooper stressed the point to the State Department official that he had "at considerable length conversations with Stalin about America." As related by Rogers, the message to the White House is clear: "Stalin did not now desire recognition; that he considered, until the foundation of mutual trust and commercial relations were built, recognition was precarious, using the simile of not desiring to put the roof on the house until the walls were built. He said they were anxious for commercial relations with America, that he thought they had turned away from us temporarily because of the emotional arousal of America against them and their consequent Russian emotion, partly also because of the extraordinarily favorable terms given by the Central European nations, but they wanted American standards of living, American goods, and had more confidence in us than anybody else." Stalin deliberately instructed Cooper, according to Rogers, in terms intended for Hoover, that the program for the construction of the Soviet socialist state "would carry on as near as he could give us indefinitely for 10 or 20 years". Stalin, he added, "denied any desire for propaganda in America, that he thought troops but particularly supplies would be given to any European communist revolution which originated internally, but Stalin insists the Soviet government is not actively propagandizing in America or elsewhere. He thought the military machinery was considerable and well trained, but that unless the policy changed there was no danger of any idea of foreign conquest." In other words, all is well with Stalin and Consortium investment. Dictatorship in the USSR still portends to be a timely boom for American Big Business at a time when America needs it most. (James Rogers, Mayflower Hotel memo, 711.61/223)

The builder Hugh Cooper, who stands to personally benefit from giant construction contracts with Stalin, cautions Rogers not to be a sucker to bad press about the communists. "America", Cooper told Rogers, "was full of false views of Russia and the most desirable thing was to get rid of illusions and fear psychology. He said he would not work for Russia for an hour if he felt there was any real threat to American institutions." Cooper gives Rogers a detailed profile of Stalin's political nature and ignorance of world affairs describing him as a pragmatist "much deceived in regard to America, and would modify any theories to meet the situation".

Author-historian Antony Sutton is also a trained engineer. His findings reveal Stalin's dependence on the US cooperation confirmed by Cooper and other American engineering firms collaborating with the Soviets during the Holodomor repression of the Ukraine. Sutton writes, "by 1930 largest hydroelectric installation and dam in the world was built at Dnieproges in the Cossack region of Zaporigia by Col. Hugh Cooper who built the Tennessee dam at Muscle Shoals." According to Sutton, "Two agreements with Orgametal by other American companies completed assistance in the heavy engineering field. International General Electric worked with the Cooper Engineering Company and RCA building long-range radio stations. Stuart, James and Cooke, Inc. contracted with Soviet coal and mining trusts. Specialized contracts, with the Oglebay, Norton Company, for example, signed with the Southwestern Engineering agreement in the non-ferrous industries for the iron ore mines. DuPont and Nitrogen Engineering worked with the Soviet chemical industry as well as with Westvaco and H. Gibbs connected with IG Farben and the Aniline Dye Trust. This was supplemented by more specialized agreements from other countries; ball bearings from Sweden and Italy; plastics, artificial silk, and aircraft from France; and turbines and electrical industry technology from the United Kingdom. The penetration of this technology was complete. At least 95 percent of the industrial structure received this assistance." (A. C. Sutton, *Western Technology and Soviet Economic Development, 1917-1930*, 347-348; Ibid., 216-7)

To advise the Soviet Coal Trust the Kremlin relied on the services of Charles E. Stuart, head of Stuart, James and Cooke, Inc., and represents "the largest group of foreign engineers in Russia"; in a passing reference to famine author Katherine Siegel in her book *Loans and Legitimacy* dismisses it, writing, "Although Stuart had heard rumors of starvation and other difficulties, he could find little evidence of them." Siegel confirms Cooper's optimism for western investors. "The Soviets paid their bills," she wrote, and Siegel elaborated how they showed a "consistently positive approach on Soviet payments and potential … those who sold to the Soviet Union rarely found reason to complain about payments on current accounts. It was the old debts that were unmet." No complaints. Prompt payment for goods and services bought and sold with the latest technology transferred from the West. No need to bother about reports of famine and starvation when they paid their bills on time. (K. Siegel, *Loans and Legitimacy*)

Evidently Oswald Garrison Villard, the wealthy liberal patron of the *Nation,* noted non-interventionist and good friend of Stimson, is his sometimes guest at Woodley. A big advocate of US-Soviet trade Villard has recently returned with news of conditions in Germany. They walk and relax as they chat together and play "bowls with Rogers" in the fresh air and shade away from the stuffy offices of the Department. Here they talk foreign policy in the light summer air that cools as it whispers through the trees overhead. Stimson can breathe and think at ease with his friends and not feel so alone with the world in his hands.

The Secretary ends his week Friday, June 12, 1931 over lunch at Woodley after having welcomes promptly at ten that morning his close friends from the Fed banks including Governor Eugene Meyer (Federal Reserve Board), Governor Harrison (NY Federal Reserve Bank) and Ogden Mills, both top-level Consortium players. Stimson is covered by Klots and Boal. It's a power meeting the kind Stimson enjoys. He feels well and fit to meet the challenges that await his well-advised under-takings.

As Assistant Secretary at Treasury Ogden Mills works closely with Mellon. A prominent Consortium player Mills is a key inside player, and member of London's Pilgrims Society at home in the capital of the world. The oddest thing about the debt talks with the Soviets during the years of false negotiations is that at any time all documents of the Czarist debts could have been tossed out the window with worthless Tsarist roubles erasing the so-called "debt" with a mere scratch of the pen and millions transferred overnight from a few of these blue blood Consortium billionaires who represent America's extraordinary capitalist wealth earned from industry and abundant natural resources shrewdly invested on Wall Street and in London's City banks and firms. (Not should we overlook the untold riches and loot smuggled out of Russia during the Bolshevik coup and chaos of civil war.) Of course that is not to be since the debt negotiations present a neat and workable structure to conceal fraud and farce as they know it. Such good fun! It's so easy to hoodwink the masses!

We shall, reader, take a closer look at exactly who is Ogden Livingston Mills, Jr.. Son of Ogden and Ruth T. (Livingston) Mills and grandson of Darius O. Mills, who left his son over $40 million (close to $700 million) Ogden Mills Jr. was born in Newport, graduates Harvard (1904) and Harvard Law (1907) and practices law in New York (1908) where he dabbles in politics there (as does Stimson) delegate to the Republican National Conventions (1912, 1916, 1920), serving as NY State Senator (1914-17). It was his father, however, Darius Ogden Mills (1825-10) with a huge fortune in Nevada silver who became a very rich banker and opened the National Gold Bank in San Francisco in 1840, and the D.O. Mills & Company in Sacramento at the start of the Gold Rush and the great drive westward of the young rowdy-dowdy republic.

Originally from Westchester County and only an hour by train north of Manhattan, Mills, at 16, headed west after his father died when like so many others is transfixed with gold fever; by 23 Mills struck it rich; branching out from mines to railroads, and he bought up huge tracts of forests around Lake Tahoe, with more gold and quicksilver from mines in Nevada added to vast tracts of cattle country and other properties. A step ahead of the mighty Cape Horn clipper ships rounding Tierra del Fuego through the Drake Passage and beating up the South America coast, by 1848, Mills is by far the wealthiest man in the State of California.

With the Civil War raging back East, in 1864 he opens the Bank of California in San Francisco. Mills and his bank rapidly become a financial power in its own right offering high credit in the financial centers both of Europe and Asia. Just shy of fifty in 1873 Mills resigns the presidency, leaving the bank with a capital of $5,000.000 ($90 million) and unlimited credit. While abroad in Europe he is betrayed by an inside swindle, hurriedly returns home and seizes control of his bank. As the flag-bearer of a $7 million subscription drive Mills restores credit operations and his bank's solvency. After having put his affairs in order Mills then moves his private accounts east and builds the largest office-building in Manhattan. This is the era when Rockefeller and Standard Oil prepare to take over the oil industry.

Mills did not turn his back on California; he left behind the University of California with $75,000 for the Mills Professorship of Moral and Intellectual Philosophy. The marble statue by Larkin G. Meade, – "Columbus before Queen Isabella" –. prominently at the center of California's state-house rotunda is another testimony to Mills legacy. So is the San Francisco Airport along the San Francisco Bay formerly called Mills Field, a parcel of the original 150 acre Mills estate named "Milbrae" which gave its name to the town nourished on Mills' money.

When Darius Mills returns to New York and settled in with the New York Society Register Consortium billionaires are at the height of America's Gilded Age of tax free unrestrained capitalism. To save their fortunes as chartered philanthropists he joined the ranks of Fifth Avenue multimillionaires contributing to the Met, the Natural History Museum, and the American Geographical Society. One of his bequeaths is the Bellevue mental illness building costing $100,000 ($1.75 million). Tired of banking Darius Mills turns his ambition and fortune towards New York Manhattan real estate investing in schemes with the Astor-Vanderbilt-Harriman-Rockefeller clique and enjoys his prestige on the board of numerous charitable and cultural institutions of the rich.

On his climb up the government ranks the younger Ogden Mills entered city politics, oversees the NY State Tax Association, and takes his seat in New

York's 17th District (1921). Before long he's a frequent visitor to the capitol joining the Hoover cabinet men such as undersecretary at the Treasury (1927-32) where he picks up some shrewd points about capitalism in America from Andrew Mellon, ranked high among the country's most rich Americans. During the peak of the Holodomor its Ogden Mills who is selected to replace Mellon in 1932 auspiciously abroad to join his Empire "aristos" at the Court of St. James in London as ambassador to Great Britain where he can oversee the world money crisis with intermittent ship crossings to New York and Washington.

After Hoover's defeat in 1932 Mills remains on the scene an ardent critic of FDR's New Deal socialism publishing *What of Tomorrow* (1935) and *The Seventeen Million* (1937). He also keeps his board seats in Lackawanna Steel of Atchison, Topeka, the Sante Fe Railway, Mergenthaler Linotype, and Shredded Wheat, a General Mills company. Mills dies in 1937 and was buried at St. James Churchyard, in Hyde Park, near his estate and not far from the Roosevelts, the Delanos and the Rockefellers.

Understand reader we are dealing with the cream of the cream of our Consortium men in charge of the corporate, financial and political power of the nation. We merely needn't dwell on the top tier of Morgan, Rockefeller, and Harriman families to the exclusion of our fellow princes of finance and knights of Wall Street. Americans are fascinated with family genealogy in their quest to know who they are and from where they came yet ignore much of their country's rich history that structured society as they live it today. It is their inheritance so they'd better know it, or watch it vanish from sight. Better to see it for what it was, and in many cases still may at present be larger than ever.

The wife of Mill's father, Ruth Livingston Mills, descended from the Livingston family, seventeenth century landowners settling in the Hudson Valley. Their 1,600 acre estate at Staatsburg had been originally purchased in 1792 by her great-grandfather, Morgan Lewis married to Gertrude Livingston of Clermont. Lewis served under Washington as quartermaster general of the northern Continental Army during the American Revolution; by 1804, he became New York's third governor and in the War of 1812 served as quartermaster general of the United States Army. In 1895, they commissioned New York top architectural firm of McKim, Mead and White to remodel and enlarge "Staatsburg" transforming it into one of the most prominent monuments in America with a Beaux Arts façade of sixty-five rooms and fourteen bathrooms all furnished with elaborately carved and gilded furniture, oriental rugs, silk fabrics and art from Europe, ancient Greece and the Far East, mixed with portraits of Mrs. Mills's ancestors. The Millses indulged their American Renaissance splendor primarily in the fall, as a setting for numerous house parties, balls and dinners on the estate grounds over-looking the Hudson River, where guests enjoyed all the sports true to the heart of the idle rich golf, tennis, horseback riding, yachting, ice skating, and ice boating. For the other seasons from their homes in Manhattan, Paris, Newport and Millbrae, the Millses mixed with the families of the Whitneys, Vanderbilts, Morgans, Astors and all their best of friends in the same schools, and clubs and companies of "High Society".

In fact, a century after their heyday the Mills family is at present still prominent and frequently in the news. The Mills folk marry with the Phipps and Reid families (steel and publishing). Upon Ogden Mills Sr. death in 1929, Gladys Mills Phipps takes over Staatsburg, in 1937, and the next year gave the mansion and 192 acres to the State of New York as a memorial to her parents.

As yachts are to the Vanderbilts, thoroughbreds are to the Millses. They remain socially prominent, in particular, as leaders with winning breeds. The Phipps, Carnegie and Mills families are all represented by Mrs. Henry Carnegie (Gladys Mills). Mrs. Phipps and Ogden Phipps both held seats on the Board of Trustees of the New York Racing Association, patronize the very exclusive Jockey Club, and owned nine national or Eclipse Award champions, including great thoroughbreds for the Phipps Stable as *Buckpasser*, *Easy Goer* and *Personal Ensign.* Among his champion winners, the aptly named *Inside Information* was inducted into Racing's Hall of Fame in 2008; *Personal Ensign*, topped an undefeated, 13-race career is "pensioned" in 2006 and still a princely thoroughbred at age 22. Americans today are likely to be more familiar with the Mills' horses than they are with the people sometimes glimpsed around the track, sitting in their booths or standing with their prized breed in the winner's circle. Ogden and Gladys also own the Wheatley Stable which produced the indomitable *Seabiscuit*, and *Bold Ruler,* a leading sire with bloodlines to the legendary *Secretariat.* If thoroughbred racing were still the sport of Kings, the Phipps are the kings of the sport.

Writer Charles Savoie tells us more about the extension of power through family connections and influence that made America's Consortium power center so pivotal in corporate and global power. An essay titled "Pilgrim$" published on his website (May 2005) takes the reader on a whirling spin through the Anglo-American power structure held together in The Pilgrims Society where are found the elite of the elite, the puppeteers who hold the strings over democratic society and who determine how it is to function and continue for generations to come. It is the Pilgrim Consortium players who inherited and took over The Great Game of Empire and who played the Holodomor card in their war games.

Henry Phipps life spanned almost a century of America's rise to global power. He made his fortune in Carnegie steel netting at least $75 million by 1900 and joined the Pilgrim set in 1903. At 22, Phipps (1839-30) became a partner in Bidwell & Phipps, agents for the DuPont Powder Company which made a killing in the Civil War, literally. He was married to Ogden's sister, Gladys Livingston Mills. In his book *The Rich and the Super Rich*, (1968) Ferdinand Lundberg tracks the Bessemer Investment Co. (later Bessemer Securities Corp.), the Phipps family holding company heavily invested in New England Power, International Hydroelectric and International Paper. Charles Savoie notes that the Bessemer website claims the Bessemer Trust operations "has been defining wealth management" for at least "a century" and in 2005 held some $42.4 billion. (F. Lundberg, *The Rich and the Super Rich,* 1968, 199)

Another Consortium billionaire with his hands on the press was Ogden Mills Reid, son of Whitelaw Reid (1837-12), Mills' son-in-law bought the *New York Tribune* from Andrew Greely; after Yale his son Ogden Mills Reid (1882–47) assumes ownership and a job as editor of the *New York Herald Tribune*. The family eventually sold the paper in 1958. Today the spin-off *International Herald-Tribune* where this writer was briefly employed in the 1980s remains headquartered in Neuilly, Paris owned and operated in part by *The New York Times*. Young Ogden Reid lived in Paris at 35, avenue Hoche, his residence described as being more like a "palace" by *The New York Times* on December 16, 1912 while he's off sailing abroad on one of his grand yachts. His father Whitelaw Reid had the former mansion, belonging to the Countess de Gramont, whose father had been French Consul-General in Egypt, rebuilt when appointed ambassador by Teddy Roosevelt to London, then Paris when he died. At the height of the postwar boom in 1928, Ogden sells at a King's ransom his Paris residence subsequently converted into the posh Le Royal Monceau Hotel.

All very chic. That same year their thoroughbred, *Kantar* wins the Prix de l'Arc de Triomphe. It was a very good year and the last of an era. Mills is on the top of the world. Nazi fascism is the vogue. Stalin stages his Purge show trials. The Duke of Windsor abdicated the English throne, in 1937, and dodged the world spotlight with his American divorcee, mingles with Ambassador Bullitt in Paris and sought privacy secluded in an Ogden Reid estate in the heart of France.

THE GERMAN-AUSTRIAN BANKING CRISIS SHAKES WASHINGTON

In May and June 1931 Europe is trembling with another the bank crisis. This time it's Vienna and Berlin. Stimson is at home at Woodley preparing his trip to Europe and entertaining his friend, ambassador and Morgan banker Dwight Morrow when he gets a telephone call from George Harrison, Governor of the NY Federal Reserve Bank. Austria's banks are on verge of financial collapse. The Kredit Anstalt, Austria's largest commercial bank that finances 70 per cent of the national industry is unable to absorb the heavy losses incurred by the Boden Kredit Anstalt, a real estate financial firm that it bought in 1930. Germany is rumoured to soon declare a moratorium on their war reparation payments. The Consortium fears a panic in the banking industry further undermining currency and crippling an unstable government sorely weakened by the world recession.

Wealthy Germans, businesses and foreigners in 1930 have already withdrawn some 900 million gold marks ($180 million). Historian Geoffrey Hodgson writes "much of it had been invested by Americans in German stocks and bonds, and as they were sold American money began to leave Germany at the rate of several million dollars a day. Moreover German public finances depended on about a billion dollars of short-term credits, more than $700 million of which had come from the United States." A collapse in Vienna will take down Berlin if the bankers don't act quickly to avert the storm. "The Americans would call in their loans," Hodgson observes, "and Germany could face – as Stimson put it to the British ambassador, Sir Ronald Lindsay – real bankruptcy and default." (G. Hodgson, *The Colonel*, 1990, 199)

The financial meltdown continues. By mid June Harrison tells Stimson Germany and Austria's bank reserves decrease to dangerous levels. The Germans report $107 million gone in three or four days; between mid-May and the first week of June the Reichsbank reserves drop from $613 million to $445 million. On June 14 Hoover leaves on his trip across mid-western states and visits the grain states where good harvests push market prices down further. Wheat drops to 44 cents a bushel, cotton drops to five cents. Unable to stop the slide Wall Street and the farmers watch prices press downward. Further political instability will worsen market stability with buyers unable to pay for corn and wheat. Loans would go unpaid, triggering a rise in farm foreclosures. Next to go would be Wall Street and the investment houses and banks in New York. Stimson stays on course traveling with his wife Mabel to Europe. During these few weeks now few people know that he is "at the height of the crisis, the arbiter of Europe". (G. Hodgson, 201-3)

But on that day in June 1931 as the national banking crisis strains American banks and with unemployment figures over the brink, Stimson writes in his diary of their confidential talk that morning on what he calls cryptically "the situation". He writes, "To my surprise Meyer (Federal Reserve Bank chairman and owner of the newly acquired *Washington Post* sic) was more pessimistic… He said that he had been so ever since last summer as to the economic condition of Germany. He spoke very harshly of it. After a long discussion they agreed that there would be time probably, although it was risky, for Harrison to go abroad and to ascertain the facts at firsthand."

Fed central banker George Harrison sails the following evening on the *Bremen.* For lack of a better plan Mills and Harrison propose backing the Hoover plan "of postponing for one or two years all payments by all countries" of war debt payments. Meyer disagreed, preferring a suspension of half the payments for five years. Mills returned to his office and drafted "a consensus" of their opinions:

"1. We feel that there is the greatest danger that a situation is going to arise which will produce a very prompt financial crisis in Germany and ultimately a most serious economic crisis there. "2. The situation is such that inevitably within the course of a very few months the whole question of debts and reparations is going to be presented to our Government. This is borne out by all of the information which comes through diplomatic and financial channels."

From their meeting we know that Stimson and the country's top bankers who themselves control the country's financial future opted for postponement, and, for Stimson what he considers as the bleakest scenario: "the general suspension by Germany of all payments", and consequently dragged into a conference with an "infinitely greater and more difficult" problem when "it will be too late from the standpoint of the economic harm which will be done to this country."

That afternoon Stimson met President Hoover in the East End of the White House "so as not to attract attention". Hoover is fatally pessimistic. Stimson read a confidential cable from Governor Norman:

"1. As regards the Reichbank this has been a difficult day. Circulation satisfactory but looses of foreign exchange increasing and serious due mainly to foreign withdrawals.

"2. As regards politics, situation is more difficult owing to uncertainty about emergency decree and constant possible effect on Government finances.

"3. The above modifies to some extent the cable sent to you yesterday from Berlin and may force the Reichsbank to adopt measures of stringency without delay. Indeed it seems to me the moment has come." Norman sought "means for preventing further foreign withdrawals". These were the longest days spent with Young, Gilbert, Mills and Harrison. Harrison cancels his trip to Europe. (HLS Diary)

The next day, June 13, 1931, Stimson writes of the deepening economic crisis: "Governor Harrison's Summary of Financial situation, showing the withdrawal of gold. The financial and monetary positions of Austria, Hungary and German have very much worsened in the past two weeks. … As a result of foreign withdrawals, no doubt much accentuated by some flight from the reichmark on account of German nationals, the Reichsbank has exported to or released from earmark in England approximately $35,000,000; in France at least $40,000,000; in the United States $22,000,000; and in other countries probably at least as much as $10,000,000 or $15,000,000, making a total of at least $107,000,000, most of which has been paid out in the last three or four days. These losses of gold do *not* include losses of foreign exchange holdings of the Reichsbank, which have been very considerable. The Federal Reserve Bank has received orders to make payments on Monday from the account of the Reichsbank of an additional $30,000,000, which will be covered by gold transferred to it by the Bank of France for the account of the Reichsbank. Further similar transfers of gold amounting to over $17,000,000 will be made by the Belgium National Bank today or Monday of next week through the Federal Reserve Bank." Stimson ended his summary writing that the crisis is "a more serious problem in Central Europe than we have had in any recent years". He fears more bank failures and total collapse of the German economy and uncertain mayhem.

June 14 Hoover places several calls to Stimson away from his office. Hoover later tells him he had consulted with "two prominent Democrats, of which Baruch was one". In his diary for the record Stimson does not name the second man. Another diary entry reads surreptitiously that Hoover had said "he thought that these two men, Baruch and the other, thought that Germany should go through with the remedy provided in the Young Plan."

Hoover fears an onslaught from the Democrats. Stimson writes that President Hoover "had decided that any independent action would be fraught with instant disaster". Stimson may be disturbed but he is not shaken; he has lived in the center of power his entire professional life and seen the world turn and evolve around him in a universe of unnamed constellations and undiscovered galaxies. In all this he has seen men and civilization rise with incredible capital and wealth in the adventure of the Great Game. So it is with stoic calm again Stimson returns to the peace of Woodley and Highhold where he is lord of his own manor.

On June 5, 1931 Kelley had sent Stimson a personal memo on how he understood Soviet pressure in foreign markets by "dumping" as a ploy in their bid to pressure America towards official diplomatic recognition of the cruel dictatorship. Kelley is well-known for detesting the Bols and their regime and as incredible as it may seem apparently Kelley is completely incapable of grasping Consortium strategy nor is he ever privy to know where dwells the ultimate power. But he is aware of his place and the precarious role he is there to play as is the singular fate of all lower mortals. Bob Kelley turns Stimson's attention to the issue that "it was clear that Russia needed money very much at present and therefore was inclined to be more compromising in regard to dumping and other economic warfare."

That same day Frederic W. B. Coleman attaches for Kelley his dispatch No. 7769 with a report on the American Workers' May Day Delegation to Moscow and fraternizing of Americans and the Russians. The May Day activities had finally ended weeks before on May 20th and workers were only now returning to Leningrad after a four-week show tour of the Soviet Union accompanied by similar European delegations traveling "throughout central and Southern European Russia" which meant the Ukraine. Coleman adds, "Visits were made to industrial plants, including the Stalingrad Tractor Plant, to Red Army barracks, to welfare institutions, railroad shops, power plants, and collective state farms." Statements, propaganda and resolutions were published in the soviet and world press.

"They have been shown the accomplishment of the Five-Year plan and of collectivized agriculture," Coleman declares, and he adds, "The welfare work of the Soviet state which reaches but a small minority of the population, has been emphasized. Unemployment abroad has been unfairly contrasted with the alleged shortage of labor in Communist Russia. They have been greeted by Comrades Molotov and Stalin; every effort was made to convince them that, in the Soviet Russia, the Government is of, by, and for, the proletariat... The American delegation has promised to aid Comrade Stalin to 'obtain the trust of the working class of the United States'." Here Coleman stressed, "Competent American observers have reported to the Legation that the general mass of industrial workers and peasants in Russia now believe that their lot is far superior to that of the farmers and workers in the United States. Intelligent Russians of the professional classes put full credence in the reports of mass starvation in the United States... Capitalistic America, in a period of acute depression, is to be discredited abroad through Soviet manipulation of disaffected American workers." (USDF 911.61/213)

Stimson's office is well-briefed with these and more reports streaming into the State Department about Stalin's terror in the countryside and weakening resistance of the Ukraine peasants under the pressure of intensified repression and confiscations. Yet it is not overtly evident what US government officials were at this time prepared to do in terms of forming a response other than their typical bureaucratic "wait and see" do nothing approach outside the guidelines of Stimson's principles and covenants to meet the pending disaster. Apparently neither Stimson and his men in State Department nor the President and his cabinet could do the humanly impossible to avoid the total breakdown of the American financial system at home as they could forestall the human calamity of the Consortium's secret Big Business support of Stalin state of mass terror against the Russian population including the Ukraine. So these brilliant and affluent privileged political leaders and statesmen chose the more simple course of action, that is, – do nothing. Hold course, sail hard and fast, and go through the motion of conducting business as usual. That sends a clear signal to Stalin to do the same. And of course as a result more Ukrainians died as Stalin tightened his grip, increased confiscations and grain exports, exiled more kulaks and recalcitrant peasants, and targeted the intellectual and professional sectors of the Ukrainian population.

Apart from war breaking out in Eastern Europe or Manchuria and the Far East, the Russian observers in the State Department had other more immediate problems on their mind, namely, their career and pay. Life during the Depression there isn't so cheery for junior Foreign Service civil servants. The stuffy atmosphere is often thick with morose and stagnation.

These days too are hard times at State. An account by Loy Henderson gives a good description on the penury and hardship of a low-level career in the Foreign Service. "An atmosphere of old-world courtesy permeated the State Department" during those mid and late years of the twenties. The Division was housed in the old State, War and Navy Building widely seen as "an ugly, antiquated, eyesore that should be replaced by a more 'tasteful' modern structure'. "The Depression held down salaries everywhere. Federal employees took 15% cut in salary that year; the "elite" Foreign Service was no exception. Budget cutbacks starting July 1931 had meant promotions were suspended for three years; a hiring freeze meant no new jobs for a year starting from January 1932 to March 1933. That left only enough vacancies to be filled once the new President was elected. FDR in 1933 devalues the dollar and imposed NRA relief legislation. The impact from Roosevelt taking the US off the gold standard is devastating to employees in the Foreign Service. The devalued dollar sends living expenses soaring. Many see fifty percent of their salary vanish overnight. Bureaucrats in the State Department's Foreign Service earn only a fraction more than they had a decade earlier and if you were in a government job in Washington or some God-forsaken backwater outpost during the glamorous "Roaring Twenties" and stock boom, then life in the early thirties needed a special spark or two to keep an eye on the bright side. In his memoirs *A Question of Truth* (1986) Henderson writes, "It can be rough living in a strange and foreign place. If you were lucky your ambassador had private means. Entertainment allowances were canceled. There were sixty-five percent cut for rents." For the Foreign Service beginning July 1, 1930 the US Congress approves a $17.2 million budget considered a huge appropriations increase of 2.5 million dollars in a year mostly lost in cutbacks. (G. W. Baer-L. Henderson, *A Question of Truth*)

The Russian section has a particularly tough time. Wilbur Carr, the administration hatchet-man responsible for cost-cutting and budget reductions wants to level the Riga mission staff. Carr, under Stimson and Hoover, refused to increase the number of translators and office assistants which overburdened Kelley, Henderson and Kennan. What perks? Pratt sums up life under Hull's tenure writing, "The results were hardship, low morale, and in a few cases, loss of sanity and suicide."

Henderson confirms the grim mood at State and the forced departure in two years of most of the Hoover men after FDR take over the White House and his closest advisers Welles, Moley, and Henry Morgenthau Jr. and launch their own purge at State to get rid of nearly a decade of Hooverites. Henderson describes how FDR uprooted Hoover's influence and impact over the Foreign Service and Commerce personnel. "As Secretary of commerce," Henderson writes, "he had expanded its activities in the United States and had instituted its own Foreign Service. Some of the members of the Department of Commerce and its Foreign Service had served previously under Hoover in various capacities during the period of the First World War and immediately thereafter. The White House insists that these two institutions were riddled with Hoover appointees who had been given Civil Service or Commerce Foreign Service cover and that these appointees be terminated and dismissed. The cowed Civil Service Commission agreed and the Department of Commerce and its Foreign Service were fragmented. On short notice many members of the commerce Foreign Service who had entered it with the impression that they were embarking upon a lifetime career were brought back from their posts abroad, fired, and replaced by persons on the administration's list of applicants. The unanticipated loss of their positions represented stark tragedy for many of those who had been serving abroad. They had lost contact with their home communities. Some of them, unwilling to join the lines of the unemployed, committed suicide on the way home or shortly after their return." Henderson might have been thinking about the fate of the US Consul George Hanson in Harbin, Manchuria, by FDR and the shabby backhanded treatment by right wing of the pro-Soviet Consortium gang to remove one of their finest Foreign Service men in the field. (G. W. Baer- L. Henderson, 217-26)

Herbert Feis is no light weight. Serious and unpretentious Feis graduates from Harvard (1916) where anti-Semitism more akin to inferior minds permeates the snobbery of club life. Born and raised on New York's lower East Side, he takes his degree in economics. When *Europe: The World's Banker* appears Stimson, in particular, ushers Dr. Feis, in 1931, into his elite entourage as economic adviser and speech writer. When he joins FDR's team *Time* (May 21, 1934) runs a story titled "Jobs & Jews" singles out Feis as "Hull's leading Jew" in a wilderness of blue-bloods. Feis doesn't miss the chance to marry into the fold taking for his wife the granddaughter of former US President James Garfield; shortly before his assassination Garfield had declared that he who controls the supply of currency would also control the activities and business of the country and its people, a typical Rothschild maxim; a hundred years earlier Jefferson warned that a private central bank issuing the public currency was a more terrible threat to the freedom of the people than a standing army. In his prolific writing career after the war Feis earns a history Pulitzer for *Between War and Peace: The Potsdam Conference* (Princeton 1960) on the origins of the Cold War, another establishment work useful to the Consortium's expansive historiography of propaganda. Other Feis books include *Churchill, Roosevelt, Stalin* (1957) and *Japan Subdued* (1961) on the decision dropping the atomic bomb; his *Three International Episodes, Episode Number Two: The Government Gives Attention to the Oil of the Middle East* (1946) explores America's interests in Israel, oil and politics in the Middle East. As a White House adviser Feis is privileged to observe America's strategic interests exercised by the Consortium grab for oil at the end of the Second World War to secure sources, access and supply. (W. Brownell and R. N. Billings, 130; H. Feis, 104; No mention of Feis in J. P. Lash, *Eleanor and Franklin*, or in D. McCullough, *Truman*)

INSIDE THE HOOVER - STIMSON WHITE HOUSE

Hoover now decides to call a moratorium on the reparation war debt. Feis had told Stimson he feared the German crisis "much worse today that it was in 1924". Stimson makes a note of it in his diary dated June 16, 1931. Three days later and only three weeks before his ship leaves Stimson records Hoover's "plunge" on Europe's war debts. "This was a busy day on top of a night without any sleep," Stimson notes. "At Cabinet Meeting the President took his plunge and announced that he was going ahead with this plan for proposing a suspension of all debts, reparations, etc., for the aid of the situation in Germany, and I am bound to say that having done it, he went in like a man. He had been in touch all of the evening and most of the night trying to get hold of Congressmen. Baruch had worked until two o'clock, and the merry task went on all the morning." Hoover's proposal Stimson observes was "a proposal for the suspension for one year of all inter-governmental claims and obligations, including reparations, debts, relief debts, and everything except debts owed to private individuals or banks".

More reports of Russian slave labor break out in the news in London and arrive at the Department that spring from a confidential diplomatic conversation in Prague, but it takes nearly two months for the lethargic US officials to inform the Russian desk in Washington. A document sent to Bob Kelley from A. C. Ratshesky in Prague, Czechoslovakia May 25, 1931, stamped by Undersecretary White on July 13 1931 tells of the alarming conversation with Argentina's Minister in Prague Senor Roberto Levillier "on the present situation in Russia". Argentina is a cartel grain exporter. He fears the economic consequences when Russia dumps thousands of tons of wheat from slave labor forcing down the world market price with inevitable economic impact on other grain producers and repeated in all other commodity markets depressed by cheap Russian exports. Ambassador Roberto Levillier is morally outraged by living conditions there where "workers are held like dogs to their masters to do their masters will". He has a plan "to boycott Russia both economically and morally" over grain shipments and suggests the US Government call for "a Pan-American Conference in order to do it. Czechoslovakia to the east sits under Poland and wedged by the Carpathian Mountains. Prague is a stone's throw from Warsaw and only a few hundred miles from Ukraine's most western border. A vibrant community of well-informed Ukrainians escaped the chaos leaving their cherished homeland since the Revolution and settled in the capital. Ratshesky urges that the Levillier interview be sent with urgent haste to Secretary Stimson as he "was very interested in the Russian situation" and is surely a man of true faith with many friends in South America and this effort would be nothing to him with God on his side beyond all measures and calculations. Of particular interest now he said was the current debate in the Chamber of Commerce in London over timber shipments from Russia "and that a decision of the United States of America have abundantly proved that this product is to be obtained by slave-work". This was political dynamite on the home front which could disrupt markets everywhere. He states further, "Many sailors of all nationality have seen the timber camps and written down the horrors of what they saw. Refugees themselves have handed the proofs of the facts and these have been gathered by Commander Bellairs who leads in the House of Commons and in THE TIMES, the movement of protest against the acceptance of goods obtained by slave-work … most of Russian exports consist of goods either stolen or produced by disinherited peasants and political prisoners".

This summer 1931 when he returns to Europe after a very long hiatus Stimson will have the opportunity to renew friendships and meet foreign leaders to see head-on what progress really means. In London, Paris and Berlin. German debt, rising unemployment in Europe, inflationary pressures and protectionism mixed with whispers of the Soviet's gulag pool of mass labor and "dumping" of cheap Soviet goods produced under Stalin's communist repression of the Plans is whispered between politicians, statesmen and industrialists throughout Europe's diplomatic community and in the ornate rooms of state parliaments, council rooms and private clubs.

The minister from Argentina is not duped by the enormous parades of May celebrations with thousands of hands raised in eulogy and voices raised in praise for their leader Stalin. "Practically all industries are carried on in Russia against the principles of personal liberty and Humanity", the ambassador tells the US diplomat in Prague. He ventures on, saying "By the card that gives them a right to eat and live, workers are held like dogs to their masters will, and do not earn enough to support their family. The former proprietors are little by little shot or sent to the mines and timber camps. By such unhuman proceedings, the Soviets manage to produce goods at a much lower cost-price than any civilized country, can furnish, and when they don't for any reason, they sell at a loss, cash, thus getting a quick return and destroying the industries of other nations. In agriculture, for instance, they are increasing their wheat-acres, and it has been calculated by an American expert who published his report in the *American Geographic Review*, that they will be able to place about 233,000,000 bushels of wheat on the market in 1933. If they are thus allowed to go on underselling, no other country possessing wheat surplus, and paying reasonable human wages to the workers will export. This is only one example of one industry. They are planning to do the same in cotton and sugar in a larger scope than they have already done, and are equally busy in undermining the commerce of timber, cement, coal, tobacco, etc., in other countries." (SDDF 761.000/ 861.000/600.6112/610.000)

Another American politician drops in at the Berlin Embassy on his way home from Moscow and tells his story to ambassador Frederick Sackett who promptly sends a memorandum of the conversation to Stimson. On June 21, 1931 New York Congressman F. M. Davenport on a trip to Moscow fatuously admits "he was much impressed with the appearance of the people on the streets, – he found them better dressed and fed than he had expected." Davenport conveyed his most sincere and most absurdly false impressions to his Government's civil servants. "The Russians," the Congressman tells Sackett, "on the whole were extremely loyal to the Government because of their conviction that they were better off under the present regime than under any other form of government." Davenport is part of that group of American visitors voicing the same impressions based on superficial appearances. Davenport adds, "there was no organized opposition to the present regime and the officials were incorruptible."

The American ambassador feels the temerity to record it all. After his carefully arranged visit, the Congressman now takes the opportunity to urge "the removal of all 'trade' restrictions by the United States against Russia" and liberalizing visa requirements. An avid supporter of free trade and engagement with the communists of the pro-Soviet lobby Davenport tells of his encounter with Edward Deuss, an American correspondent for the International News Service and "very 'level-headed and able, but not as well informed as Mr. Chamberlin (sic) from whom he received the greater part of his information and impressions." This is the standard Consortium line pushing for normalization of relations and recognition of the Soviet regime. Yet, the Congressman is quick to inform Sackett of a quite different story than he passed around to the American correspondents in Moscow. Alarmed, he says, by the "growing Russian production in raw materials", the Congressman calls Soviet economic progress "a most serious danger to the peace and security of the world – including the United States – and that upon his return home he would do everything in his power to induce American businessmen to refrain from trading with Russia on a credit basis without security, as the American support in the form of manufactured goods and machines as well as technical aid merely strengthened Russian communism in its efforts to overthrow the United States." Such wicked devils these Consortium communists! And after that the Congressman tipped his hat, bid farewell and left secure in his notion that he is neither a fool nor an idiot but an honest politician.

Two years later the reporter Edward Deuss is expelled by the Nazis, in 1933, but not before several interviews and a plane trip with the Fuehrer leads him to expose Hitler as a carefully self-contrived eccentric "genius". Deuss writes, Hitler "sees the world as a clash of opposing forces, and genius in man as the power to synthesize these opposing forces for the purpose of evolving a third and more powerful force." American government authorities are interested in his psychological profile of the leader. In a brief memorandum titled simply "Recollections of Adolf Hitler", the result of many close encounters Deuss concludes how Hitler flew to speak on average five hours a day despite his fear of flying and masterfully works the crowds: "Hitler always seemed pleased at the plaudits of the crowd but never without smirking as if to say, 'the poor saps are being taken in.' He despised the masses as so many sheep. They have always in his mind been led for causes almost always profane, but whatever the cause the leader must never forget to impress upon the masses that God has thus commanded and molded him in His image, though the truth be the reverse. The secret of Hitler is found not in him, but in history."

STIMSON IN EUROPE JULY 1931

On July 9, 1931 Stimson meets with Mussolini in the famous baroque setting arranged by the little *Duce* to meet visitors. Stimson keeps a written record in his diary to record scene for history: "We were taken through a series of rooms until we reached a very large room with Mussolini sitting behind the desk at the other end. He came and greeted me as I entered the door and walked back with me to two chairs standing opposite each other to the nearer side of the desk. Vitetti (of the Italian Foreign Office sic) remained standing throughout the interview ready to act as interpreter. Whenever Mussolini was at fault for an English sentence he would turn to Vitetti and say something in Italian and Vitetti would say invariably the same formula, 'The Chief of the Government says so and so and so and so.' So the interview was decidedly formal; more or less like Alice in Wonderland in that pose. I felt a little as if he might say 'Off with his head' like the King of Hearts."

Mussolini asks Stimson if the Depression is "passing over". Stimson recalls his answer to Italy's Generalissimo: "I disliked to prophesy, but we felt there were indications that the bottom had been reached and that we were on the upgrade, but I said I thought it would be a long pull." Mussolini insists Italy is "for disarmament". Stimson tells the Italian dictator "even if America abolished its entire army and navy it would not alter the problems existing between France and Germany, and France and Italy, to which he agreed, and I said that therefore there must be preliminary work in Europe on their political questions." The American president he says wants Italy to agree to "a two year naval holiday in laying down ships". Stimson tells the fascist dictator that "in America we felt that the coming year was likely to be a very critical one in respect to disarmament; that the world must choose whether it is going to try the new methods which we hoped would lead towards peace or whether it would drift into the old cycle of competition and war." Mussolini agrees repeating that "Italy stood for disarmament and peace…" When asked about restricting the free movement of American citizens, particularly communists, Stimson tells the Italian foreign minister Grandi, and he says in speaking for "every American laborer ... that America's chief defense against Communism was the satisfaction of the American citizens with their own Government and that our American Federation of Labor was our chief barrier against Communism." And he assures his Italian audience, that at heart on the bottom line "*every American laborer wanted to be a capitalist.*" (Italics added.)

It is precisely at this time that Stimson is in Europe when the bankers are carving out their relationship with BIS. He notes "that $500,000,000 of new money would be required ... deposited with the B.I.S. and then by the B.I.S. advanced not to the German Government but to the Reichsbank under orders of this international committee ..." On July 15 a telephone memorandum from Ambassador Sackett in Berlin to Stimson in Paris and Hoover in the White House. There is fear of a national banking crisis any day in Germany straining Europe's central banks and the reserves of the Bank of England. Two bank holidays in Germany. Stimson writes, "one bank had failed and everybody was anxiously awaiting what would happen tomorrow morning when the banks opened again... The Government was very short of cash. The Reichsbank had not enough to rediscount the eligible paper in the hands of the other banks... Germany was still expecting to get bank credits..." Of all the loans issued only a handful of financial houses in New York handle the German reparations. In particular, three houses – National City, Dillon, Read, and Harris, Forbes, – issued at least three-quarters of the loans taking small profits to create Germany's Nazi cartels. National City holds 20 percent of the loans with $5 million profit on 173 million shares issued in the American market of a total $826,400,000 in loans sold at a mere $10.4 million profit. (Robert R. Kuczynski, *Bankers Profits from German Loans*, Washington, DC, Brookings Institution, 1932, 127)

In Berlin on July 25 Stimson dines at a state dinner with Chancellor Heinrich Bruening's ministers including finance minister Hermann Dietrich. Stimson assures the Germans that Hoover is "trying to stabilize $600,000,000 of credits in Germany, but that our success depended upon the banks and the bankers would not loan money to a man who said he was broke, and that Germany had better get off that key and turn to courage and self-help". Evidently Stimson doesn't see the Brown Shirts lurking in the shadows. This time the carrot and stick method is due for a rude treatment.

Later in London at eight in the morning on August 27 Stimson meets with Britain's Prime Minister Ramsay MacDonald at 10 Downing Street. He stays only 50 minutes then returns to his hotel for a haircut and shower before sitting down with his ambassador Sackett for the latest briefing on Berlin. Sackett speaks of Mellon's meeting with Bruening as having "been the most helpful thing that had happened on his trip to Paris and London". But Sackett has some bad news for his boss: the German Finance Minister informed him "in view of the long term credits granted by American industry to Soviet Russia, Germany would be forced to increase its terms for the present calendar year". Stimson asks about Schacht becoming a problem recalling that Schacht had last told the Secretary that Germany didn't need the money "and that it would be a harmful thing for her to get it". And Schacht strongly opposes any further debt repayments. Sackett confirms that Schacht "had thrown his political fortunes with the Nazis". And Schacht refuses to tell the American ambassador what he would do if he were to become Germany's finance dictator. Schacht, he says, "would always switch off to what he would do politically... Schacht talks about forming a dictatorial group of five, including Bruening and himself and to give them dictatorial powers."

Stimson notes, "Hindenburg backs Bruening on the question that Germany is facing a Russian menace. They believe that eventually Russia will be compelled by public opinion to take back Bessarabia and that this will reopen the whole question of the spread of Bolshevism throughout Europe. In this maelstrom Germany will be the buffer state and must be ready to defend itself and the rest of Europe against Bolshevism. For this purpose, purely defensively, it must be armed to meet the crisis." Who will strike first? Has Stimson told the capitalist American worker about Germany's rearmament program "to meet the crisis"? (K. Siegel, *Loans and Legitimacy*, 133)

Europe's financial debacle is worse than Stimson had feared. The bankers lead him to believe they were already going bust and overextended with "700 to 800 million dollars in short loans in Germany." JP Morgan says their exposure is "more like a billion". "If German industry crashes," Stimson records in his diary "these banks will lose all of this because it no longer exists in improvements; it has gone into current expenditure. It can only be paid back by the proceeds of new business." Sackett is less alarmed and cautions Stimson that no more than a $50 million loan put forward "as a voluntary suggestion of the part of our banks" would suffice to turn Germany's economic crisis around. The Morgan bank, he tells Stimson has no German loans. "They had kept out," the US ambassador insists. Secretary Stimson knows decidedly more about Morgan investments and disagrees. "I rather supposed they had," Stimson declares in his diary, "but his leadership in American banking was such that I wanted him to know the situation in case the situation came before him in any way. I told him of the experience of Mellon and myself in the London Conference and how he had been against giving Germany any more money at first, so that we did not approach the question from the standpoint of people who had been stampeded. This present proposition seemed to me to be the best banking proposition I had heard of for meeting the situation."

WASHINGTON FALL 1931

As two of the most important men in Hoover's cabinet they could not have been more different in their personal temperament. Its not always easy for the tall and straight Henry L. Stimson to do business with Mellon. Stimson cherished his own old-fashion values and he holds Treasury Secretary Mellon in low personal esteem and strongly disapproves that Mellon had divorced his wife half his age over her tryst with another man. His son, Paul Mellon, one of the world's richest men, will forever feel the absence of the paternal love he craves from the man whom he confides to have known less than the father knew his personal servants. Whereas Stimson prides himself as a pillar of moral rectitude and unswerving and dedicated loyalty and willingness to compromise Mellon for his part remains aloof and uncompromising showing far more restraint in his attitude of severity towards fiscal policy both at home and abroad than might serve him better there and in personal relations as well as he leaves both his wife and son emotionally estranged and distressed.

On September 16, Stimson is delighted to invite for lunch by his young friend Trubee Davison, the son of HPD, "Harry", the late banker who passed away in 1924 and who was the unflappable pillar of the House of Morgan taking over the bank when JP Morgan, Sr. was obliged to retire from the stress of affairs with only a few years to live. It was Davison who negotiated final details of the British gold shipments for war loans. A devoted husband and loving father and family man, Davison missed by a hair the Republican presidential nomination when he died lost the reins to the leadership of the Republican Party that instead fell into the hands of Harding and Hoover. The younger Bonesmen feels a special honor to introduce the Secretary of State to "Dr. Peabody", legendary headmaster of Groton and now his father-in-law. As a boy Stimson had prepped at Phillips Andover Academy, a rival school in the brotherhood of the private elite boys schools. Stimson keeps close ties to the Andover and is an important benefactor to the endowment of the institution, financially as well as, and perhaps even more important to him personally, protecting the high moral standards he feels are necessary for the preservation of leadership in the youth of future leaders of the country. As it were for them in their world of moral rectitude and public service the honor of respect was mutual. Other men would shake, or bow, at the sound of their names, Stimson, Peabody and Davison.

Reverend Peabody is an icon in establishment circles in Washington, patron saint of all sides of the Consortium's political, economic and social power establishment. His boys from Groton spread across the country seeds of continuity and perpetual power assembled in his church every year every day including Sunday where clouds hover and crown golden skies and church bells ring every song. At their dining table Davison, Stimson and Peabody elicit the expression of Gothic gargoyles serenading a Christian triumvirate of the nation's destiny each convinced their intentions are excellent, and their purpose noble and divine. They are the chosen elite, the Select. Stimson, an Andover boy and Yale blue-blood with a degree Harvard Law School (1889-90). Stimson penned in his diary: "We had a very pleasant luncheon and Dr. Peabody proved to be a very pleasant and intelligent gentleman as I had expected." It's hard to believe that this was their first meeting ever but Stimson was not a Groton man where the bonds of boyhood are sealed for life. It's interesting sometimes how life intermingles, meshes and connects people with events, crossing generations, tradition and power: A decade later Trubee Davison will embrace into his family the dynamic niece of Stimson's close friend, President Alphonso Taft; his other daughter-in-law is a White Russian princess who marries another member of London's Pilgrim Society, the very swank Morgan banker, head of the New York and London office and who delivers a stunning performance at US Trust a half century later.

Back at State Stimson sets J. Pierrepont Moffat working on disarmament issues for the upcoming Geneva conference. Moffat, too, has a gold-plated pedigree: Groton, Harvard, a New York Social Register family. He may have had many rivals but few can match his intelligence. In the Foreign Service since 1918, Moffat took a first in his exams, and is promptly dispatched to Antwerp in the

Netherlands as private Secretary to the ambassador. Not long after Moffat marries one of the daughters of Joseph Grew. Career and Consortium unity is assured.

While Hornbeck handles the "flood situation in China", on September 18 the Secretary attends a conference with Hoover, Mellon, Secretary Tom Lamont, and Harry Robinson of California to talk about "the whole situation". Stimson writes, "Everybody felt the seriousness of the situation, and the worst of it was that there was nothing we could do. We canvassed each possibility in turn. The Federal Reserve Bank was loaned out. No more money could be gotten through private means. No money could be loaned by the Government without the consent of Congress. Congress could not be called, or gotten into operation, or any such measure gotten through in time to do any good… To suggest loaning any more money abroad would only open the door to a flood of domestic relief legislation which would occupy such a time and delay the other so long that it was out of the question…" That fall the White House is living in an abyss. The government is broke. Neither Stimson nor Hoover know what to do to stop the financial crisis from taking America and the world over the brink with no relief in sight.

That night Hoover telephones Tom Lamont. Stimson writes, "The President told me the same message which I had received from the British Embassy had been telephoned to George Harrison of the Federal Reserve Bank, early in the afternoon and had come to the President. It had come through some unknown informant in England; evidently some friend of the Government had rushed to the telephone and talked with Harrison about it even before it had got to him, a rather curious performance." Such "friends" and mysterious "informants" have a way of getting their business done, and all very quietly. Stimson, Harrison and Lamont are at the top of the pyramid and even from their lofty view they too can be surprised when their closed circle tightens. But who are these "informants" of the Consortium with their secret keys that turn the locks of power that keep governments in business.

Thomas Lamont is one of Stimson's closes friends and sources, a prince among princes, rulers of men pulling the strings doing God's work for Morgan, Rockefeller and his Consortium's true believers, dedicated, faithful servants of the Order absolutely convinced their Cause is Right. Luce put him on the cover of *Time* in November 11, 1929, days after the Wall Street Crash and ten years to the day after Armistice Day 1919. Writer-researcher Lundberg writes, "An extraordinarily complex and resourceful personality like Thomas W. Lamont, who has been the brains of J. P. Morgan and Company throughout the postwar period and was a mentor of Woodrow Wilson in Wilson's second administration as well as of President Herbert Hoover throughout his fateful single term in the White House, has exercised more power for twenty years in the Western hemisphere, has put into effect more final decisions from which there has been no appeal, than any other person. Lamont has been the First Consul *de facto* in the invisible Directory of postwar high finance and politics, a man consulted by presidents, prime ministers, governors of central banks, the directing intelligence behind the Dawes and Young Plans. Lamont is Protean; he is a diplomat, a publisher, a politician, a statesman – an international presence as well as a financier... Before that, in 1919, he was the representative of the United States Treasury in Paris with the American Commission to Negotiate the Peace, which wasn't negotiations in any sense, but everything forced on Germany." (F. Lundberg, *America's 60 Families,* 33)

During the day September 21, 1931 Stimson confers with Feis on the British threat to go off the gold standard. Stimson is fast to grasp the details and gist of the monetary problem reviewed by "Dr. Feis" who, he said, gave him "a sort of lesson in exchange… I found that he pretty well agreed with my own views as I had worked them out yesterday", Stimson noted. Then in even somber tone, Stimson focuses on the big picture. "The situation in Manchuria, however", Stimson writes, "has grown worse, as the movement by the Japs seems to have been much more extended that we had expected, and it is not possible yet to tell how far the Government is committed in it. It does look, however, as if the Ministry of War must be in it pretty deep, and that makes a very serious situation."

Two days earlier, on Saturday, Stimson had instructed Hornbeck to meet the Japanese ambassador straight away and "tell him how troubled I was about the situation and how I wanted information". They meet Monday. Stimson is relieved feeling he got the assurances he needs, and he notes, "The one good feature is that the Government, the Foreign Minister and the Cabinet, are apparently sitting tight and are doing their best to prevent the Ministry of War from running amok. They had directed that the movement cease and that no reinforcements be sent." The Secretary of State believes that he can restrain the Japanese militarists, at least during these tense days when no great power wants an all-out for war. In just over a decade, when Stimson is again War Secretary for the White House under FDR he won't have this problem of not knowing Japanese intentions; by that time both Anglo-American intelligence services will have almost daily decoded electronic intercepts from German Ultra and Magic Enigma ciphers and long memoranda from the Japanese ambassador in Berlin Baron Oshima. Hitler was caught completely fooled by the Allied landing in Normandy, in June 1944; Eisenhower's chief of staff George Marshall considered the Oshima transcripts the "main basis of information regarding Hitler's intentions in Europe". "Oshima", writes Ben Macintyre in his spellbinding and explicit book, *Double Cross, The True Story of the D-Day Spies* (2012), "supplied the most interesting reading of all: some seventy-five of the ambassador's reports were picked up in 1941, a hundred in 1942, four hundred in 1943, and no less than 600 in 1944. His commentaries were like having a bug in Hitler's headquarters, only more efficient." (Ben Macintyre, *Double Cross, The True Story of the D-Day Spies,* NY: Crown, 2012, 307-8)

Stimson is also pleased with his press conference that day, declaring to himself, "I think the matter was well handled". But overnight his brief respite is shocked by very bad news and it hits Stimson head-on. The enormous problem of the Japanese advance in Manchuria that he worked hard to avoid and underpins his precious Stimson Doctrine for the Far East now lay in shambles splashed in headlines for all the world to see. Hoover's Secretary of State adds another personal note, writing, "At Cabinet this morning I brought up the Manchurian situation which has now reached a very threatening condition. The Japanese have seized Southern Manchuria with their army, and while the Foreign Ministry seems to be fighting to stop the movement, it is now in possession of the country and a clash with Chinese troops may occur at any moment." Hoover is overwhelmed with the bank crisis. Stimson further notes in his diary, "The President is pretty well occupied with other things now, and this was just an additional chore, but he saw that it represented a major emergency and agreed with my propositions. My problem is to let the Japanese know that we are watching them and at the same time to do it in a way which will help Shidehara*, who is on the right side, and not play into the hands of any Nationalist agitators on the other." But Stimson remains secret about Morgan's stake in the Imperial Japanse expansion. "By 1932, the United States invested $466 million in Japan, almost twice the amount invested in China," Suzie J. Pak in *Gentleman Bankers* observes tracking the Morgan syndicated loans for the most part "readily floated in the United States, especially those for public utility companies and municipalities". (Baron Kijuro Shidehara, formerly ambassador to the US, in 1929 is the Japanese foreign minister, and postwar Prime Minister from 1945 to 1946; S. J. Pak, ft. 331)

Poor Hoover isolated in the White House, fuddles about "the question of saving the banks of the country". While Stimson advances his foreign policy towards Stalin and the Japanese, the President's failure on the domestic front will prove the administration's downfall. Even Mellon with all his billions can do nothing to keep Humpty Dumpty from tumbling down. Mellon tells Stimson that he "had allowed the big bank of Pittsburgh to fail just because he was unwilling to subscribe his million dollars when three of the four million had already been made up by others". Stimson observes, "All through the country now banks are in a precarious position because of the runs made upon them by their depositors, and we are trying to find some way of restoring confidence." With the world economy falling apart and badly hemorrhaging stuffing the banks with stop-gap cash for a quick fix will have no more effect than a band-aid. The bankers created the problem in the first place and now they don't know what to do.

Hoover then surprises Stimson by appointing "Ted" Roosevelt Jr. to the Philippines Governorship. Stimson is not pleased when young Teddy drops in to personally give him the news on September 25. After all, it was his father, President TR, Sr. who in 1905 had plucked Stimson, only 38, from his prosperous law practice, to act as his trust-busting US Attorney for the southern District of New York (1906-09) thus launching his career into the apex of national politics and American global power. About the Roosevelt the Younger, Stimson notes, "This was rather a staggering news to me. I can't imagine why the President has done that..." Stimson knew so many other more promising and influential candidates for that idyllic post posting in the tropical eastern sun. Stimson bows to form and extends a hand of congratulations with a promise to help him "and we had a frank talk which cleared the air a little bit". Even crusty baronial Stimson could sometimes be left out of the loop when forces greater than his own prevail.

The Far East will preoccupy the State Department for the next two decades. People slaughtered, Chinese women and children raped and the "Ice-Man" calls it "the Manchurian trouble". Stimson feels totally lost and in the dark about Japan. This is one of the low points of his long distinguished career. So far from the scene and out of touch from events on the ground and admits in his diary, "I have been getting a little worried because we really don't know what is going on in Manchuria". (Are we really supposed to believe this contrived recorded version of events? Remember reader, Hoover is an expert on Japanese affairs, and will plunder Japan in 1945 when he brokers gold deals with the imperial clans and their war criminals.) Japan and the Chinese he thinks are sending "contradictory statements and probably both of them are more or less untrue". Ambassador Grew doesn't figure into his calculations this day when he regrets lacking good intelligence. Stimson wants the able Consul General George Hanson in Harbin "to look it over" along with Salisbury in Tokyo where the militarists defend the Kwantung Army's activity in Manchuria as "action taken solely for national survival." (S. and P. Seagrave, *The Yamato Dynasty*, 167)

Stimson's premonition is not without good cause. In a few years that industrial city to the north will undergo an urban transformation from a remote village into a cosmopolitan hub with over 100,000 Russian émigrés and a thousand factories manned with gulag laborers mostly displaced kulaks marched and railed in across the Siberian tundra. Many of them will suffer more hardship and poverty of an uncertain fate under Stalin when they return to Soviet Russia rather than remain utterly helpless under Japanese occupation after Moscow sells its stake in the China Eastern Railway to the Japanese in 1935.

On September 29, 1931 Stimson wakes up after an early night and "a long sleep". This morning he feels "bright and fresh" reinvigorated by the crisp autumn morning with his dogs who also "seem to feel a fresh influx of spirits". Stimson stops at the White House "for a short talk with the President" mulling over reparations and debts. Both men feel mutually "cautious"; Hoover is morose, and tells him "that he felt more and more that it would be impossible to get the American people to approve of any more sacrifices in Europe unless it was tied up with a plan to alleviate distress in this country; and so he was thinking over the present situation as his first problem". Hoover, the Consortium's organization man and senior Republican has penciled out his list of problems and men to handled them. Stimson asks to see it, he says, "so that I could be thinking of them myself."

Hoover's list is long and foreshadows FDR's New Deal recovery legislation. He gives the list to Stimson, who recalls, "They included a plan for the rescue of the Farm Loan System, the Farm Loan Banks being some of them in trouble. Incidentally at Cabinet we discussed this matter, and I found that there was on foot a plan to advance new capital to those banks on the terms on which the original capital had been advanced, namely, so that it would be eventually paid back to the Government. Then he had a plan for the relief of the banks which had stocked up with frozen mortgages; another plan for the release of the credits amounting to something over a billion dollars in certain banks which had suspended; another plan for the relief of insurance companies which he tells me will surely go down in case the building associations which are in such trouble should crash. Then there was his plan for organizing a general movement among banks for a center of relief for general troubles in banking."

Wall Street is still on the skids with people left holding bags full of virtually worthless shares. Hoover tells Stimson the real government's dilemma was "the financial trouble". The President is convinced he can fix things. He weathered the Depression hadn't he? Stimson swallows his doubts. Both Landon Thorne and Arthur Page warn Stimson that "artificial aid…. might only postpone or make worse the ultimate liquidation…" They all fear an unraveling of the national economy. Stimson pointed out to the President "the delicate line which lay between artificial help which would be successful and one which would only produce more evil".

But Hoover is all bully and out of touch. He's sitting on top of a world economic tsunami and feels he can masterly control all the elements to arrive safely on shore. Sitting in the White House dreaming about his reelection in a year, and all that's at stake, Hoover is determined to hold the helm steady to pass through each problem. Stimson doesn't know what to do. In his diary he writes, "He is so painstaking in his own studies and has such good head that it is very hard to discourage him, and I don't like to do it. But I do wish I could be sure that he had always the best economic advice at his elbow." No matter how good an organizer had been in the past, Stimson worried that Hoover was shunning good advice and keeping too much "prejudice on his part against some types of economic advisers. He is not always judicial in his judgments of men who differ from him …" Stimson knew what both men feared most. The worst is far from over and neither the President nor his close advisor can see light through the deadening matter of darkness.

In the shifting sands of the world power balance Stalin consolidates his grip tighter. The Five Year Plans of spawned in the genius of Consortium planners and organizers will soon spiral out of control. Bungling attempts to mechanize production find the Russian people too far out of step and the effort to modernize Soviet agriculture and industry without the proper training and education too reckless. Too much is done too quickly. When the government fails to reach its projected targets Stalin will eliminate countless numbers of the he top level managerial ranks. What took the generations in the West the Kremlin urgently needs a decade to transform the Russian mentality to adapt to American methods. Factories lack spare parts and proper precision tools leaving workers with only their ingenuity to improvise.

When the USSR reduces grain exports it will be unable to conceal the famine. In two weeks London will be rocked by several stories on Soviet Russia's economic problems provoked by forced labor, starvation conditions and widespread discontent. But Hoover seeking a second term in the White House is not at all focused on the impending Holodomor overseas. The domestic crisis reaches a feverish pitch. America is going to get hit from within shaking the nation to its foundations. On October 5, a note found in his diary reveals renewed preoccupations of the Secretary. "News from America is very bad. The banking situation is very tough, and we seem to be on the brink of a serious crash."

Stimson meets with banker Odgen Mills. The previous night Hoover met with New York's top bankers at Mellon's residence. There assembled in secrecy – Mitchell of City Bank, Potter of Guaranty Trust, Lamont of Morgan. "The Press has not yet got on to it", Stimson observes. "In my opinion it is a sound conservative proposition calling upon the help of the bankers individually but without legislation, but along lines which apparently would be very helpful and which are recommended by the best economist's advice as sound." The meeting, however, leaves Hoover feeling "discouraged particularly by Mitchell and Potter.

More dark clouds descend over the Secretary. Stimson is suddenly hit by yet another "staggering blow" no less than a rude cosmic catastrophe. The first victim of the banking crisis is Dwight Morrow, Stimson's key man for the Disarmament Conference. Morrow unexpectedly dies at his home in Englewood, New Jersey. Stimson is extremely shaken, even quietly, but deeply devastated, and suffers a great personal and professional loss. The vulgarity of the cruel joke of losing his close friend need not remind the reader that events in Russia are far from his mind and find no solace in his heart. In 1930 after Ambassador Morrow returns from Mexico he joins his friends in the US Senate taking Walter E. Edge's seat in 1930 vacated when Hoover sent Edge to Paris as ambassador. Still a senior partner at Morgan, Morrow's wealth makes him one of the richest men in the state when he dies in October 1931 of a brain hemorrhage leaving behind an $100 million estate in current value. His will provides significant bequests: $200,000 to Amherst College, $200,000 to Smith College, $100,000, the Smithsonian Museum in Washington DC, and a $1 million trust for his daughter Anne. An engaged life of dedicated work and strenuous commitment left Morrow no time to enjoy retirement with his wife Elizabeth Reeve Cutter who authors several books and for two years served as President of Smith College. (Dwight Whitney Morrow Personal Papers, Archives, Frost Library, Amherst College)

There is no room in our story other than to say at this time reader the Secretary feels utterly forsaken by the foul turn of events that seem to come from all directions combining the impact of their assault. Its a miracle he can still stand up! The tall and erect Secretary is no slacker in the storm. But Stimson had only just met with his close friend Morrow the previous Friday and now he has lost forever not only one of his most precious friends but a cool and persuasive architect of the Consortium. With Morrow he could have conquered the whole world, or at least, perhaps, found a way out of the abyss in Manchurian where Grew and the Morgans have their own plans as they prepare to deal a second blow to Russia and Germany. It is with profound pain that he notes in his diary, "I do not know whom to turn to. He was one of the most helpful men I ever met, always cheerful, always sympathetic, always hardworking, and with a most penetrating and keen intelligence." Dwight Morrow had worked with Stimson at the London Naval Conference and on many other sensitive government problems. Stimson recalls how the banker diplomat "filled in more gaps … that I can remember, always ready to help out when others could not do it." Besides Morrow had been "the one man" among his "contemporaries" with whom he could talk openly on foreign affairs after losing Joe Cotton. Dwight Morrow always had "a perfectly ready sympathetic response" for the Secretary.

Trubee Davison who heads the New York Museum of Natural History finds time between his safari and world junkets to have his chauffeur drive down to Washington and pick Stimson up to catch their flight to Peterboro Airport at Hasbrouck Heights, New Jersey, and proceed to Morrow's funeral and eulogies before sending him off to the Elysian Fields. Morrow had been a classmate of former President Calvin Coolidge at Amherst, took his law degree at Columbia, in 1913 and quickly made partner at Morgan during the boom war years. It was Morrow who had handled several big Consortium deals for DuPont with General Motors and 3M. During the First World War he supervises state finance in New Jersey and Allied maritime shipping before serving as chief civilian aid to General Pershing. However he may have permanently etched his name in the American memory as having pushed for the repeal of National Prohibition ban on alcohol consumption.

On October 9 Stimson is hit by more bad news from the Far East. The Japanese militarists are running "amok" in Manchuria. International treaties and the League of Nations now fail to hold the peace. Stimson feels his own frustration. "We have nothing but 'scraps of paper'," he writes, and he confronts, "with brutal candor the failure of his own "Stimson Doctrine". For a lesser man the blow might have been too much. Stimson is "Old School" and feels dazed and vulnerable as he watches the modern world racing by too fast. He wonders if he is not out of sync with this brave new world for which he carries a heavy burden. Even when mocked by the gods these men with their fixed views are not inclined to change their ways. Elections may rearrange the men but not their ways. Radical fundamental shifts in policy seldom occur without a popular revolution and Stimson abhors a revolution he cannot control. This is what the leadership in both the Republicans and Democrats Parties has to prevent from occurring.

Stimson traces out his thoughts in his personal diary. The Secretary writes, "This fight has come on in the worst part of the world for peace treaties. The peace treaties of Modern Europe made out by the Western nations of the world no more fit the three great races of Russia, Japan, and China, who are meeting in Manchuria, than, as I put it to the Cabinet, a stovepipe hat would fit an African savage. Nevertheless they are parties to these treaties and the whole world looks on to see whether the treaties are good for anything or not, and if we lie down and treat them like scraps of paper nothing will happen, and in the future the peace movement will receive a blow that it will not recover from for a long time. As I pointed out to the President in Cabinet, if Japan runs amok, Congress will never let him cut a single dollar off on navies."

Whereas Stimson envisioned an inevitable clash with Japan starting with the Manchurian invasion, the Japanese leap into Asia is viewed more sympathetically by Hoover and his friends in the Consortium. "There is something on the side of Japan," Hoover declares. "Ours has been a long and deep-seated friendship with her and we should in friendship consider her side." His team of Hornbeck, Klots, and Feis, joined by Cameron Forbes, gets busy rephrasing the policy on

Japanese inroads in Manchuria. Hoover keeps Japan in the backstage of things and throughout the Second World War, well aware of the resources and billions of dollars of gold and loot building up in the secret Nippon Treasury of the Emperor and the militarist clans which use the Imperial Palace as their front of shady operations. At the war's end General MacArthur oversteps Truman to carve out a winners-take-all postwar peace deal worth undisclosed hundreds of billions of dollars in gold and loot much of which was recovered from elaborate mines in the Philippines and stashed away in close to two hundred secret bank accounts in exchange for the heads of Japanese war criminals (G. Colby, 334-5; S. Seagrave and P. Seagrave, *The Yamato Dynasty*)

Stimson invites the press to a grand luncheon at Woodley on October 12. Fifteen heads of the Washington bureaus come to hear his brief on Manchuria. Stimson noted in his diary, "They had all come flying. … I took up the situation from the time I had last met them at dinner, and explained what we were trying to do; what my policy of cooperation with the League was; and the things that I had been doing privately through diplomatic channels. I told them also that I was going to have Seymour Parker Gilbert represent us at the meeting of the Council and explained just how far we would go and what our limitations were. They were all very much interested…this meeting had satisfied them very fully." Formerly with the law firm Cravath, Henderson & De Gersdorff, this his year Gilbert is made a partner at JP Morgan & Co. soon joined by Charles D. Dickey (Brown Brothers).

The next day, October 13, while at home Stimson reads "a second report" from Harbin by George Hanson and Salisbury now in Manchuria. Stimson notes in his diary, "It relates to the way in which the Japanese had seized Kirin…" He calls it "most powerful report" and "a very admirable report, giving the details of a very dirty movement and conspiracy by the Army and all the names of witnesses." He knows that if it leaked to the press "it would inflame public opinion here against Japan almost beyond redemption". Stimson decides "sending a resume of it privately to Geneva, and after we get all we can from Hanson and Salisbury, I think I shall eventually send the facts to Shidehara." In a few years Hanson would run afoul of the Consortium with influence at State and lose the protection of Stimson over his outspoken contempt for Stalin's destruction of Russia fatally ending his career.

On October 14 precisely at 3:35 a.m. Stimson meets with Bob Kelley just back from Eastern Europe (Warsaw, Berlin, Prague). They discuss the Polish Corridor "and the eastern boundaries of Germany". Neither Russia nor Stalin are mentioned but clearly inferred in Stimson's diary notes. On October 16, at half-past noon Stimson holds another "enormous Press conference". On the same day, in London, *The Times* publishes the first article by Gareth Jones still attached to the Foreign Office on Soviet Russia in an unsigned series titled "The Real Russia". It runs for three days as his editors had done exactly a year before under the heading "The Two Russia's."

Starvation in the Ukraine is the last thing Stimson would care to think about now. After months of barely any mention if at all of Russia, Undersecretary Harvey Bundy on October 21, hands his boss a telegram from Christian Herter "telling me that President Lowell of Harvard, is going to attack the Stimson doctrine of nonrecognition before the Foreign Policy Association in Boston." Lowell wants another war feeling cheated in the last one. Herter is outraged. Stimson notes, "Herter is a great friend of Hoover's and wants to prepare a proper defense." Stimson, Bundy and Feis decide on giving the unhappy task to Castle. But Hoover tells Stimson "to write to Lowell and tell him what an unpatriotic thing it was to make this attack at this time and to try to get him to stop". They intend to put the Harvard president shut tight in his ivory bell tower. If there was a clear line between Consortium interests, national security and domestic politics its not there in Cambridge across the Charles River from Boston. Recognition of the Soviet regime is not going to happen on Hoover's watch and definitely not before his reelection bid that would certainly expose the terror and gulag system of Consortium business inexorably linked behind Stalin's bold economic reconstruction of the Plans.

Sunday November 1, 1931 finds the Secretary in better spirits for a day of rest at home at Highhold away from Washington all the worrisome affairs of the darkening skies overhead the steel-cold seas of Long Island. At least here he is able to record in his diary, "Another beautiful, bright, sparkling day. I took a long horseback ride in the morning. *Andover* has been exercised by the new man Duncan, and went better than I have ever known him to go. So I had a perfectly delightful ride. On the way I stopped at the Livingstons, and saw Mr. and Mrs. Livingston and their two children. Then I went over and saw old John Leiper, who was running for Justice of the Peace. Had a very nice chat with him. He was very grateful for what Arthur Page and I are trying to do for him with Meadowbrook. He is a good example of a true old friend. In the afternoon we drove to Cold Spring Harbor and called on Walter Jennings and his wife and had a delightful afternoon with them at tea. Constance and her husband and some friends they had been entertaining came in. Walter and Jean told us that a religious revival had come up which these young people and a number of others were interested in, and which seems to be making big progress among young people. It has taken them very seriously and I was very much interested to hear it." Stimson and his wife Mabel then returned to Highhold "just in time to dress for dinner" and joined his closest friends and partners at Bronson Winthrop's grand home at Syosset. Assembled for dinner are George Roberts, Herbert Semler, Allen Klots, and Willie Chanler with their wives, and joined is Perry Williams. They all share "a delightful evening."

Who are these confidential companions of America's senior statesman and head hancho of Skull & Bones? Shall we reader have a closer look at this intimate gathering? The guests need no name cards to know their place at the table. William ("Willie") Astor Chanler and G. Herbert Semler, Jr. (Yale Law, 1914) Semler is a partner in the New York law firm of Winthrop, Stimson, Putnam & Roberts. Herbert G. Semler, is listed in a government archived document of a 1940 Senate investigation into the "Investigation of Concentration of Economic Power" made under the "auspices of the Securities and Exchange Commission for the 67th Congress, Third session "pursuant to resolution 113". The inquiry concerns investor holdings in the nation's largest "nonfinancial" 200 corporations, and prepared for the National Economic Committee chaired by Senator Joseph C. O'Mahoney (Wisconsin), with Sumner T. Pike, Commissioner for the Justice Department, and Garland S. Ferguson, Commissioner of the SEC. Both Semler and Candance C. Stimson are at Wellsley College (Class 1892); she is the sole sister to Henry C. Stimson. An extraordinary woman in her own right, in 1913 she led her university as chairman of Wellsley's 1913 million dollar campaign drive. Herbert Semler and Lady Stimson amass a considerable fortune as important shareholders in General Telephone, later AT&T. John Winthrop Chanler, Willie Chanler's grandfather, had been a very rich banker, lawyer and US Congressman, as well as a boss of the infamously corrupt gang of cockroach politicians infesting New York City's barren politics at Tammany Hall in the mid 19th century. An Astor on his mother's side, his grandfather had married Margaret Astor Ward, the daughter of Emily Astor and William B. Astor and the great-grand-daughter of John Jacob Astor.

William A. Chanler is one of America's grand and robust adverturers, explorer and author. But his high-living lifestyle so irritated the Astors that when his wife dies in childbirth, the elder Astors seized the Chanler children. Little William Astor Chanler Jr. is only ten when his father dies, in 1877, and raised at the Astor Rokeby estate in Barrytown-on- the-Hudson in Dutchess County. This Roosevelt Hyde Park country and not far from the Vanderbilt and Harriman estates. Billy Chanler was born in Newport, R.I., attended St. John's Military School Ossining, then sent to Phillips Academy, Exeter, in New Hampshire before two years at Harvard joining the freshman class of 1886. But he makes his mark elsewhere – as a Fellow of the Royal Geographic Society of London and takes off from Harvard to conquer the world and find himself.

The adventures of Chanler in Africa in a region in Zanzibar near Mount Kilimanjaro in 1889 became legendary recounted in the book *Quest for the Jade Sea: Colonial Competition Around an East African Lake* by James Imperato (1998). Hardened by his odyssey Chanler returns to New York politics 1896 an ardent Republican delegate to the State convention held at Saratoga and the next year joins the State Assembly. Here is where Chanler's story with the Consortium gang becomes interesting as, when in 1898 during the Spanish-American War the adventurer Chanler is appointed captain and assistant adjutant general of "Volunteers" and serves as an ordnance officer with the Cavalry Division, Fifth Army Corps, where he applies his expertise in munitions for three months (May to August), and takes part in the Battle of Santiago. Apparently, Chanler and his brothers smuggled arms to the Cuban insurrectionists and later tells Bill Bullitt the real story how America grabbed Cuba after he, now a distinguished US Congressman, William Astor Chanler Jr. himself, – wild "Willie" – in rousing piratical form had helped blow up the *Maine*. "Remember the Maine" became the battle slogan of American nationalists and other patriots and Willie's favorite ballad. One sunken ship loses Spain an empire. It was all so easy for the Americans. As they move their eyes eastward with their eyes of China, Japan and Manchuria there is still the little problem of Imperial Russia. In a few years another war will expose her fatal weakness.

Right under their nose America's lust for Cuban real estate is hardly a secret. Senator Henry Cabot Lodge of Massachusetts set the stage for it a few years before the *Maine* when he visits Cuba. The Boston Brahmin Lodge ought to be given more credit for his influence and vision in building up the ranks of the State Department on equal footing with America's global ambitions. From the summit Lodge declares, "England has studded the Atlantic seaboard with strong places which are a standing menace to our Atlantic seaboard. We should have among those islands at least one strong naval station, and when the Nicaragua canal is built the island of Cuba ... will become to us a necessity."

Convenient popular rebellions in Cuba and the Philippines against Spanish rule provide Washington with conventional wisdom and just cause for military intervention there and throughout the South Pacific and the Southern American hemisphere in line with President Teddy Roosevelt's emboldened doctrine of American expansionism under the racist creed of "Manifest Destiny", America's peculiar justification for Darwinian slaughter of the savages in order to save them from eternal perdition. Roosevelt and Lodge were brothers-in-arms and cut from the same Crimson cloth. American press barons such as William Randolph Hearst and Joseph Pulitzer embraced the war cry of American expansion exaggerating Spanish atrocities in much the same way and the Consortium press lambasted Germans as baby killers and rapists in Belgium during the First World War. Theodore Roosevelt, in October 1897, as assistant Secretary of the Navy under President William McKinley wires US Admiral George Dewey in the Far East to ready an attack on the Spanish fleet in the Philippines. On April 23 Congress adopts a resolution declaring that a state of war exists with Spain even though the Spanish authorities had already accepted defeat. But America needs a good war to satiate the public train its troops, and a new chapter to the glowing saga of the great American Expansion. The Spanish deny any role in sinking the *Maine,* offer polite apologies for the loss of their ship and condolences for 266 dead Americans but no one is listening. (Hugh Thomas, *Cuba: The Pursuit of Freedom,* 1971; "The press and US militarism– a lesson from history," Shannon Jones, *World Socialist Web Site*, Aug. 21, 1998, <www.wsws.org/news/1998/aug1998/main-a21.html>)

Stimson may have lost his right hand with Morrow's passing but he still has Winthrop. The Secretary always found time to step out of the topsy-turvy world to find hours of peace relaxing with his wife and tight circle of intimate friends and law partners. Four decades before, Bronson Winthrop founded the Winthrop, Stimson law firm. What deals they brokered! What secrets they would never tell! These are the days of the notoriously corrupt McKinley administration, labor riots, violent strikes, muckraking and trust-busting when railroads, steel and oil fortunes crowned America's industrial progress. In the era when family ancestry was literally required knowledge for any Harvard, Yale or Princeton freshman candidate, Winthrop is a true American blue-blood who could trace his ancestry directly back to exiles and refugee immigrants and in particular, John Winthrop, future governor of the Massachusetts Bay Colony at the forefront of the American pioneer civilization.

Stimson's chum Bronson Winthrop was born in Paris in 1863 to parents "sojourning abroad at the time." He received the proper English education at Eton living with the sons of Lords of the British Empire during its heyday and later took degrees at Trinity College, at Cambridge. In New York Winthrop earns a law degree at Columbia (1891), then clerks briefly at Carter, Ledyard, & Milburn. Nearly the same time Stimson leaves Harvard Law School (1890) and joins the country's top law firm Root and Clark. Elihu Root built his reputation as Whitney's attorney. Winthrop joins Stimson at the Root firm, becoming partners in two years.

The closed circuit of their not ordinary connections with Root's tight inner network of Consortium power did not elude Stimson nor escape the attention of Antony Sutton where they surface in his pioneer book, *America's Secret Establishment: An Introduction to the Order of Skull & Bones* (1986). "Whitney's attorney and close associate was Elihu Root," Sutton writes. "Although not a member of The Order, Root has been called 'Whitney's artful attorney'. Root, one of the sharpest legal minds in American history and a power in his own right, worked along with the purposes of The Order. In 1890 along comes young Henry Stimson, fresh out of Yale, The Order, and Harvard Law School. Stimson joins Root's law firm, then called Root & Clark. After a while, in 1897, it became known as Root, Howard, Winthrop & Stimson and by 1901 it became Winthrop and Stimson."

Sutton has the pedigree of a thoroughbred but for all his digging he just scratched the surface. Before he died Sutton did some fine early research that helps us understand the importance of the Yale Skull & Bones hierarchy in the Taft-Stimson duo in their mission to shape and mold with dubious manipulations and outrageous abuses the American cosmos as they perceive its rightful destiny. "In the meantime," he writes with a patience that if it were not absolutely essential might cease to be amusing, "Stimson married Mabel White daughter of Charles A. White, Yale, Bones 1854 and classmate of Edward Payton Whitney. Charles A. White had married Mabel Jewett, the daughter of Edgar Boardman Jewett (1843-23) who was born in Ann Arbor, Michigan. His father owned a company that manufactured refrigerators popular with consumers, the John C. Jewett Manufacturing Company. Charles White stays in New York's national guard rising to the rank of Brigadier General of the 8th Brigade in 1884. Ten years later he's elected Republican mayor of Buffalo. William C. White (Cornell AB) joins the law firm of his brother, Charles A. White at 1200 Morgan Building, in Buffalo, New York; Andrew Dickson White (Bones 1853) is the first president of Cornell which he founds in 1865 with a half-million dollar gift from Ezra Cornell. Here we have a vital link to the Daniel Coit Gilman connection (Bones 1852) which ought to interest more the a few enlightened scholars.

The Stimson-White Bones connection is particularly relevant to the Washington's imperialist mindset of foreign policy architects crafting policy approaches towards Stalin during the Holodomor. President Taft is Bones and a descendant of its co-founder. Stimson is chosen as Taft's Secretary of War. Andrew D. White (1832-18), graduates Yale in "the famous class of '53", serves the next year as attaché to the American Legation in Tsarist Russia in the reign of Alexander II, the Czar Emancipator; President Harrison appointed him Minister to Russia forty years later (1892). He stays there for two years and resigned to write a two tome opus titled *History of the Warfare of Science with Theology in Christendom*. President Cleveland engages White to handle border negotiations between Venezuela and British Guyana; President McKinley sends him off as his Ambassador to the Kaiser's Germany. White leads the US delegation to the world's disarmament conference in the Hague (1899) despite the call by the Russian Czar "to put an end to the constantly increasing development of armaments". After spending a week with Carnegie in September 1901 at his Skibo estate in Scotland, White prevails upon him to fund a foundation for international peace; the next year White creates the Carnegie Institution in Washington appointing as its first president the same Daniel Coit Gilman of Yale and Bones. White remains a Carnegie Trustee. (*Dictionary of American Biography*, Volume X, Troye-Zunser, Ed. Dumas Malone, NY: Charles Scribner's Sons, 1936, 88-93; *Autobiography of Andrew Dickson White*, 1905)

Antony Sutton describes the Stimson Yale-Bones connection in quite another and perhaps more pertinent revealing aspect. Connections of the Stimson-Root-Whitney triad are easy enough to follow but reader, be careful where they may lead you in their charming and magnetic strange personalities: "Stimson proved he was capable in the law and when Taft (The Order) was looking for a Secretary of War in 1911, he appointed Stimson (The Order). Then Stimson's career went like this: As Secretary of War Stimson completed a reorganization begun by his predecessor none other than Elihu Root." In 1904, Root leaves the firm to become Teddy Roosevelt's Secretary of State. Now with Stimson in charge, the firm is rechristianed "Winthrop, Stimson". In fact, Henry and Bronson were boyhood friends and remain close throughout their lives. During the First World War they exchange letters when "Colonel Stimson" takes a commission as commander with the 305th Field Artillery of the American Expeditionary Forces (AEF) in France on the Western Front during the great German offensive of March-April 1918.

After the war their law firm expands to Winthrop, Stimson, Putnam & Roberts. This is the same firm that represented Zapata Petroleum, the company founded by George H. W. Bush, and Clark Estates Inc., "a trust benefiting the descendants of a founder of what would become known as the Singer sewing machine company … setting up British factories in 1868, Singer earned the distinction of being perhaps the world's first multinational corporation," according to Sutton. In WWI, – so ironically called "the Great War" until the second closed the gap like two book ends of total horror binding the Civilization's parody of the tragic epic, – Stimson stays of five years in the US Army rising in rank to Brigadier General. President Coolidge appoints him in 1927 to get experience some abroad and carry on the White Man's Burden as Governor-General of America's Pacific archipelago of the Philippine Islands until he must leave Manila in 1929 to return to Washington as Hoover's Secretary of State. That in itself is interesting but without much meaning or definition, yet, and it all seems rather empty and dull at first like "a questioning empty shell for the admission of an unknown content", borrowing a phrase from the imaginative and highly gifted writer from southern Poland (now the Ukraine) Bruno Schulz, a Jew shot dead in the street in 1942 by a vengeful Gestapo officer. You see, reader, we must tread carefully as issues of Genocide and strategies for Terror, disarmament, violence, war and peace are juggled in the hands of civilized moralists in responsible positions of power, and the leadership in the family of nations raise the most delicate questions of a strange and paradoxical nature full of a sweet and terrible bitterness for the common uncivilized brute. (Bruno Schulz, *The Street of Crocodiles and Other Stories*, Penguin Books, 2008)

From 1926 up into the peak of the Holodomor 1932-33, Stimson's friend and law partner Bronson Winthrop is Treasurer of the New York Bar Association; Stimson serves as its president (1937-39), followed by Allen Wardwell (1943-45). Other presidents included William G. Choate, Elihu Root, Francis Lynde Stetson, Henry W. Taft, Allen T. Klots, Francis T. Plimpton, Cyrus R. Vance (Bones, a White House lawyer during the Kennedy-Johnson Vietnam years, and Carter's Secretary of State) and the former US Attorney General George W. Wickersham, whose grandson I knew at Yale and raced with aboard his father's yacht, a Morgan banker. (A. C. Sutton, *America's Secret Establishment; An Introduction to The Order of Skull & Bones, Liberty House Press, 1986*; R. Baker, *Family of Secrets: The Bush Dynasty*, 17; *National Encyclopedia of American Biography*, Volume 33, s.v. "Winthrop, Egerton Leigh, lawyer and financier"; NCAB, Volume 33, s.v. "Winthrop, Bronson, lawyer"; James A. Dunlap III, *A Rothbardian Power Elite Analysis Of Modern American History*)

Stimson spends the weekend at Highhold quietly thinking about disarmament issues and his note he must prepare to the Japanese foreign minister when he returns to the office on Tuesday. He's up early the next day, Monday, enjoys a delightful ride with *Andover* before breakfast, nostalgic for the peace of the "old foxhunting days, the bright clear sunshine, the autumn woods, and the heavy dew over field and meadow". Immediately after breakfast the Secretary takes his driver into Manhattan for "social visits" with his cousin Alfred Loomis and his brother-in-law and cousin Landon Thorne. (Stimson is also a cousin of Albert Thorne's wife.) Loomis and Stimson meet often to talk over his securities and investments which today would be considered insider trading. Stimson notes, "He still advises holding all my balances in cash and not making any investment... I was rather inclined to begin, but he said that I had better hold it in cash for a little while yet. They are still very conservative."

Stimson has strong paternal feelings for Alfred Loomis whose father had died when he was a boy. Loomis excels at Yale does undergraduate work in mathematics and science, and graduates *cum laude* from Harvard Law School in 1912. Landon Ketchum Thorne (1888-64) also graduates from Yale (1910) and shares his cousin's passion for science studying at Yale's Sheffield Engineering School. Of Sheffield Sutton sheds some light, in particular, on a few secret society details: "The Order now had funds for Sheffield and proceeded to consolidate its control. In February 1871 the School was incorporated and the following became trustees: Charles J. Sheffield Prof. G. J. Brush (Gilman's close friend) Daniel Coit Gilman (The Order, '52), W. T. Trowbridge, John S. Beach (The Order, '39)

William W. Phelps (The Order, '60). Out of six trustees, three were in The Order. In addition, George St. John Sheffield, son of the benefactor, was initiated in 1863, and the first Dean of Sheffield was J. A. Porter, also the first member of Scroll & Key like Whitney, (the supposedly competitive senior society at Yale)." For the record Henry Sage, the lumber scion (1844-24) graduated Yale (1865) and was also Scroll & Key. And we know reader that the White brothers are close friends to Gilman and fellow Bonesmen. (A. C. Sutton, *America's Secret Establishment*; Fabian Franklin, *The Life of Daniel Coit Gilman*, NY: Dodd, Mead, 1910)

No one is better positioned in the US government to witness and appreciate the advance of technology essential to winning the next war than Henry Stimson who is one step away from the President and the decision to drop the Atomic Bomb on Japan in July 1945. But it is during the First World War with family matters in hand when he helped evolve the technological edge of American and Allied efforts against the Germany. Immediately after Harvard, Loomis joins his uncle's law firm, Winthrop and Stimson. The First World War gives Loomis a break to leave the tedious world of corporate law and wear a military uniform in a science lab blowing up things. Straight away Loomis volunteers, commissioned a captain and quickly moves up the ranks innovating ballistics and modernizing tank warfare. As Taft's War Secretary Stimson is able topull some strings for his talented nephew who becomes head of R&D at the Aberdeen Proving Ground in Maryland. Capt. Loomis invents and patents the Aberdeen chronograph, the world's first portable instrument for measuring the speed of shells which allows the military to calculate time over distance and hit a target. In the lab he works physicist Robert W. Wood from Johns Hopkins who encourages his research in experimental and practical physics.

The war ends and Loomis puts his missiles and physics away and walks out of the lab for the last time. He has the brilliant idea to stick to inventing and is soon piling up patents and financing a fortune in electric companies that wire America's postwar boom. He joins his best friend Landon and they make a fortune together living the American Dream with their Wall Street Consortium chums.

Briefly, after Yale cousin Landon Thorne began his career selling bonds on Wall Street for the Central Trust Company, predecessor of Hanover Trust before Howard Bonbright hires him. Once he leaves the US Army and the war behind Landon returns to Wall Street selling more bonds because he's good at selling bonds.

Thorne, Stimson, Taft. All are Yalemen and in the circle of the Bones brotherhood. As reader we know Stimson gained national prominence when he is appointed by Taft to replace Jacob Dickinson in 1911 as Secretary of War serving until Taft's loss to Woodrow Wilson but not before he sends US troops to Mexico to protect Consortium interests and firm up the dictatorship against Zapata and Pancho Villa. Before America's entry into WWI, Stimson tried his hand in city politics as a Republican delegate at the 1915 New York State constitutional convention and again at the 1916 Republican National Convention backing Hughes against Wilson. Stimson knows some very powerful and important people in both parties with fortunes on Wall Street.

After the Great War 1914 to 1918 Thorne applies his genius to business. But by 1920 although he had made partner the firm teeters near bankruptcy. Bonbright asks Thorne to take over the company. With funds from uncle Samuel Brinkerhoff Thorne (Bones 1896), he retools the firm as the preeminent investment banking-house on Wall Street specializing in public utilities and overnight he is underwriting 15% of all US securities in the public utilities sector.

The next year Landon and Alfred pair together to form their investment company simply called Thorne Loomis; in 1923 they create American Superpower, a company dedicated to improve the market for utility securities while they sit on a rising ocean of dollars and join the boards of several banks and electric utilities. In fact, Stimson's closest friends Loomis and Thorne pioneer the concept of the holding company, consolidating electric companies along the Eastern seaboard. Insider trading is both legal and common helping Loomis multiply his fortune many times over. Too wise and practical to be duped by the illusion of greedy and unsustainable speculation when the Wall Street crash finally hit Loomis and Thorne had already cashed out.

No fool to the game Alfred Loomis then scoops up securities at rock bottom prices. Dillon, Baruch and other Consortium insiders do the same. When the market bounces back Loomis ranks among the America's richest of the elite, next to the Vanderbilts and Astors with whom he races the famous sleek giant J-Class yachts of the thirties. Alfred Loomis is editor of *Yachting* when he sails *Yankee* against the 1905 record-holder *Atlantic*, the 185 ft. three-master and "grandest schooner yacht of all", helmed by Commodore Gerard B. Lambert (Princeton 1908). Lambert Pharmical, one of the backers of Lindbergh's 1927 transatlantic solo flight – in 1931 takes over the Gillette Safety Razor company with his pay "in stock paid to earnings". The firm helps shape the structure of the US power industry. FDR's banking legislation eventually forces Thorne to retire from the firm to avoid conflict with other bank directorships under the 1933 Banking Act aimed at limiting the concentration of economic power in the United States and making Roosevelt the target of slander denounced as a "traitor to his class". By now some of the biggest Consortium clients include American Power & Light, Electric Power, American Power & Commonwealth Power. Thorne sits on the boards of countless companies including Commonwealth & Southern, Niagra Hudson Power, Commonwealth Power of New Jersey, United Corp., Bankers Trust, First National Bank of New York, Southern Pacific, Federal Insurance, Vigilant Insurance... (Joseph E. Garland, *The Eastern Yacht Club*, Marblehead, Mass., 1989)

Landon Thorne lives at "Thorneham, a baronial 230 acre estate on New York's Bayshore, groomed with palatial landscaped gardens designed by architect Ferruccio Vitale and dominated by a 30-room Tudor mansion. Loomis also owns the most prominent property on Hilton Head Island, the "Honey Horn Plantation"; when the Depression hit Thorne and Loomis buy the entire Hilton Head Island, all 17,000 acres for a cool $120,000 and use it as their private shooting plantation. Twenty years later they sell for an even cooler $11.2 million. At present it's worth untold billions. These men also help Stimson become a very rich country gentleman, the democratic prince he so longed to be. Unfortunately, when his war work takes its toll he will not live long to enjoy it.

Let's jump ahead with a small leap. The mild and quixotic genius Mr. Loomis had been to Great Britain and knew many of the England's top scientists busy on radar research. In the late thirties Loomis had the brilliant idea to convert part of his family mansion into a vast secret private laboratory. The Loomis Laboratory in Tuxedo Park started with simple experiments in radio detection. Helped by his son Henry, the Loomis team builds a crude microwave radar mounted in the back of a van and deployed over a golf course by the local highway. Excited by its success they then take their contraption to the local airport and tracked planes to lend a hand in repulsing *Luftwaffe* planes attacking England in night bombing raids over London to force England's surrender. Loomis is appointed by Vannevar Bush to the National Defense Research Committee as chairman of the Microwave Committee and vice-chairman of Division D (Detection, Controls, Instruments) in 1940.

It's Loomis who sets up research facilities at the Massachusetts Institute of Technology in the "MIT Radiation Lab". Over protests from the US Army, Loomis uses all his business acumen, backed by powerful and wealthy friends to optimize "the Rad Lab" until a government pipeline comes up with public money. The resulting 10cm radar is a technology vital in detecting German U-boats, and bombers headed for the British coast, and is also vital during the D-Day invasion of northern France. "Radar won the war; the atom bomb ended it," Lab director Lee DuBridge liked to declare. Loomis also is the father of Loran, once the most popular long-range navigation system replaced by GPS. All his inventions in which he took much pride were no less important than his development of air controller ground-controlled approach technology that deployed radar to "talk-down" pilots when poor visibility rendered visual landings nearly impossible. After WWII Henry Loomis went back to the radiation laboratory at MIT before joining President Truman's Psychological Strategy Board; later he works with President Eisenhower's Commission on International Information as head of the Office of Research and Intelligence at the US Information Agency, and director of Voice of America where he stressed English as the global language. But in the sixties Loomis is disgusted by President Johnson and the crassness of this fake man and his vulgarity; Johnson's endorsement of the secret bombing of Laos in the Vietnam War is the last straw. Johnson is no leader, just a weak broken down old man kept captive of the dangerous reactionaries of the armed forces. Loomis rejects the Commander-in-Chief and hands in his resignation. Henry Loomis, 89, dies in November 2008.

So, after socializing with Albert and Landon, Henry Stimson went back uptown and met his wife Mabel at Penn Station to catch their 16:30 train to Washington. When they arrived waiting for "HLS" at Union Station is his loyal servant and bodyguard Captain Eugene Regnier by his side since his days as US Commissioner in Manila.

November 3, 1931 Tuesday. Early morning Stimson meets with Hoover then that morning sits with Rogers, Castle, Hornbeck and Klots. He finds Hoover depressed, overwhelmed and "deep in a financial problem…the real estate situation of the building and loan companies." Stimson is satisfied with Castle's draft on Manchuria that "rather cleverly met the difficulties which faced us of putting our statements in an inoffensive form." It seems rhetorical but true that how one perceives a problem is nearly equivalent to resolving it. Words can even bury the dead but in the case of the Ukraine apparently there would never be any cabinet paper or diary notes. There are too many dead and its been out of control for too long and not in Consortium hands. Such is the convenience of ruling by proxy dictators. The Cold War method of war by proxy is an unending evolution using the same logic of political and military expediency of Anglo-American Consortium power extended without the inconvenience of moral platitudes. It's illogical and fallacious it grows and continues just the same all the while the people caught up in their pursuits and preoccupations no matter how grand or petty and they are easily convinced by the Consortium leaders morphed into larger than life celebrities tracked, worshipped and adore by the media which they own and control by any means one way or another always assured to sway the day and get their way.

Its half past four and Stimson is impatient to get out of the office none too late after "a pretty good, lively, stiff day"; by six he was back in the saddle for "a very good horseback ride in the cool frosty air". Then back for dinner with his aide Capt. Eugene A. Regnier and Betty Rogers for dinner and an evening "deciding various points about the Grandi entertainment", referring to the Mussolini political circus coming to the White House and all the party amusements once the Italians come to town.

HOW STIMSON & THE CONSORTIUM CONCEAL MORGAN INVESTMENT IN JAPAN

Sterling and Peggy Seagrave in *The Yamato Dynasty* (1999) confirm the role of the Consortium players in the State Department's play for Manchuria and the Japanese invaders. In *The Yamato Dynasty*, (a must read!) Sterling and Peggy Seagrave write, "There are many linkages between conservative US business and the Japan Crowd. Morgan Bank was now run by Russell Leffingwell (1948-50). The Japan Crowd influence Washington at the highest levels. Secretary of Commerce W. Averell Harriman is a principal in the investment firm of Brown Brothers, Harriman, and was part-owner of *Newsweek*.... Secretary of Defense James Forrestal was a key figure at the investment bank of Dillon Read.... Dillon, Read, headed by future Treasury Secretary C. Douglas Dillon, was one of a group of investment banks called the Club of Seventeen, which handled 70 percent of Wall Street underwriting.... Former Secretary of War Henry L. Stimson had ties to Morgan and Dillon, Read through his law firm. In their thinking about Japan, all were influenced by Lamont, Hoover and Grew." Joe Grew marries Alice Perry, grand-daughter of the famous naval hero Oliver Hazard Perry II; her mother is a well-known impressionist painter in her own right, Lilla Cabot Perry; we know reader that one of their daughters Lilla Cabot Grew married Jay Pierrepont Moffat.

Joe Grew, Hoover's ambassador to Turkey based in Constantinople (1927-32) is well-placed to be fully informed on events reporting to his boss Stimson and by his own discreet sources on the Soviet situation does not surface in the files sourced for this book. (It would be most interesting to know how Grew divided and allotted his five years as head of the embassy in Constantinople at the crossroads of East and West in the former Byzantium Empire and a veritable center of the world. However, no evidence surfaced that showed that Grew showed the slightest concern for the Ukrainians during the Holodomor years. No does he demonstrate significant contact with fellow ambassador Bullitt in Moscow there in place two years after Grew arrives with his wife well-connected to Japanese family clans and royal hierarchy in Tokyo. Grew is tied up tight up with the Morgan partners heavily invested in Japan; he is a cousin by marriage of Jane Norton Grew to Jack Morgan, son of JP Morgan the America's premier banker. Perry, Belmont (Rothschild), Morgan, Grew, – all together these players make quite a team for Hoover, Roosevelt and their global agenda. In public, Consortium financiers criticize Japan's monopolies, but privately hold them in high esteem for which they are generously rewarded. The Seagraves write, "As Eleanor Hadley put it in *Antitrust in Japan* : 'American political mores require everyone to denounce monopoly and cartels, which all conservative critics were careful to observe'." (S. Seagrave and P. Seagrave, *The Yamato Dynasty,* 349, note 230)

Grew has been a Hoover man from the beginning of his days at State serving under Baruch in the President Wilson's War Industries Board (WIB) where among his duties once he belatedly leaves his beloved Berlin when America entered the war in 1917 he sold Liberty Bonds and making propaganda speeches against his former friends now America's enemy. He is soon immersed with Hoover's "core group of wealthy American conservatives" and is active helping to supervise Hoover's food distribution organization in Europe and relief after the war in Germany.

Nor does his miss the victory festivities and talks at Versailles in Paris with status as an official observer were he and Hoover "cultivated influential Japanese delegates (and former Allies sic), including Prince Saionji and Count Makino, the senior advisers to the Japanese throne." When Grew is posted to London in the early twenties he also befriends Japanese ambassador Matsudaira, and renew the bond between their wives' childhood friends, Nobuko and Alice. As far as the Japanese are concerned Grew's family ties to Morgan make him "a member of the great Morgan *zaibatsu."* To the Japanese his bond is sealed in family blood. His loyalty to the Japanese cause is considered of great unquestionable honor to be cherished as no less important than life itself. There can be no suspicion of betrayal which would be mortally fatal. "In Tokyo as in Boston," the Seagraves observe, "multi-generational ties between families implied interlocking directorships that created solidarity at home and extended economic influence overseas. Thanks to their family ties, both Joe and Alice would be cultivated by the most elegant members of Japan's elite, the tycoons discreetly financing the growing power of the army." Ergo, Asian partners of the Consortium empire. (S. Seagrave and P. Seagrave, *The Yamato Dynasty,* 143)

Undeterred by their increasing aggressiveness in Manchuria the Japanese remain important partners in commerce with America. The Seagrave account tracks Grew after he returns to America and is financially useful backing Hoover's election in 1928, and they write, "Despite the Great Depression, Japan remained the most important Asian market for American goods." – an essential persuasive detail Stimson but one that he is not inclined to dwell upon and prefers to overlook. Nor can it be discounted that Hoover, Grew, Root principal among others in the Consortium establishment, as the Seagrave findings corroborate, consider "that the seizure of Manchuria was the only way Japan could recover from its social and financial crisis" since the 1923 earthquake and unprecedented investment there by the Morgan banking syndicates. The next year 1932 Hoover makes his next vital move key to American strategic interests in the Pacific: he sends Grew as US ambassador to Tokyo. Banco Banco.

"Preserving and expanding American commerce in the Pacific is part of Grew's new job in Tokyo. Hoover, Morgan, Lamont and other Republicans preached the doctrine that national economies linked together by private enterprise would stabilize the world. In Asia and the Pacific, trade privileges could be used as carrot and stick to ensure cooperation, peace and prosperity. In their view, Roosevelt's New Deal Democrats were nascent Bolsheviks. In this, their attitudes were surprisingly similar to those of Japan's elite, who regarded all liberals as Bolsheviks.... They argued," the Seagraves disclose, "that Manchuria was an ideal source of food and raw materials to fuel Japanese industry. Western financiers like Tom Lamont supported the takeover and neatly blamed China for provoking it. In public, President Hoover denounced the Japanese takeover, but he supported it in private. Manchuria became Japan's puppet, 'ruled' by Emperor Pu Yi." (S. Seagrave and P. Seagrave, *The Yamato Dynasty,* 143-5)

The main worry for the Japanese Emperor Hirohito is Stimson's threat of a retaliatory economic embargo by sanctions or boycott (the "big stick") or, perhaps even a direct armed confrontation with the United States or Great Britain. Manchuria, not Russia, stays top on Stimson's agenda.

On November 4, 1931 Stimson meets with the Japanese Ambassador in his office and hands him a copy of the memorandum which he had already dispatched to Japan. Stimson records in his diary that he is not pleased at all with Japanese aggression in Manchuria and is inclined to "line up" against Japan "all the nations of the world". Stimson then laughs about the problematic but not insurmountable impasse and assures the Japanese ambassador that in order to make it as conciliatory as possible I had Castle draw the language. He laughed and told me that there was no danger of his government thinking that we were unfriendly; that they had been angry at first, but they realized now that we had treated them fairly. I told him that it was a very serious thing to get all the public sentiment of the world aligned against a man, but he is so thoroughly against the action of his own country that it is hard to argue with him. He makes no defense." Stimson retires to clear his head and plays deck tennis with Feis, Keith Merrill, a Russian expert, and his "perfect aide" Capt. Regnier. Forbes in Tokyo delivers the memorandum to Baron Shidehara. Gentle talk. "This was a good deal of relief from the tension." Stimson prepares for his morning press conference next day.

"I found that the Press Conference had been getting a little out of hand on the Manchurian problem", he recalls. Stimson had to set the record straight, and straight meant seeing it his own way as to unfolding events. He resumed how it went down. "They had no news from us and there was a good deal of disquieting news form the Press, so they were beginning to speculate and beginning to distrust our position as being afraid that something really unfavorable was happening." Stimson decided to hold "another confidential one" assembling at 3:35 p.m., and talks about Japan using occupation to apply pressure in negotiations on "treaties out of China". The Seagraves write, "The emperor asked his advisers if the navy and army were prepared 'in case we are subjected to an economic embargo or if we open hostilities with the Great Powers.' Ten more years would pass before that happened. But his aide's notes reveal that as early as 1931 Hirohito believed that war with the West was likely if his army continued its aggressive moves on the mainland. Because he did not intervene forcefully, and let the perpetrators off with mild scolding, he sanctioned their conduct. He was not a passive bystander, and praised the army for 'cutting down like weeds large numbers of the enemy... I deeply appreciate their unswerving loyalty'." (HLS Diary, Seagrave and Seagrave, ibid.)

This afternoon Stimson learns of Czech President Masaryk's speech two years before calling "attention to the Polish corridor as the principal evil" of the German crisis. How had Stimson ever missed that?

November 6. "The news is gets darker", Stimson notes in his diary. "The Japanese troops have gotten into a fight with the Chinese way north of their zone, up in the neighborhood of Tsitsihar, and there are various exciting rumors from Russia which I do not credit. But the worst news concerns the attitude of the Japanese people at home. They are getting more and more excited and more and more militaristic." A cable from Ambassador Cameron Forbes in Tokyo leaves Stimson suspecting that the Shidehara government will fall "in the face of this excited populace".

Stimson holds another press conference feeling better "they have acted pretty well so far." Hoover calls, alarmed and not knowing what to do. Stimson tells him "that I had reserved our freedom (in the League's Council sic) and we could do what we wanted". He expects a showdown on the Far East soon to take place "in Paris". Hoover tells the Secretary "saying that he had heard that Mr. Root was much worked up over the situation in Manchuria and suggesting that it might be a good plan to get hold of him."

Stimson calls on his former employer and mentor Elihu Root on the 7th. But Root is too old, lacks essential information and facts "to have any real opinion", Stimson observed, and instead sends Klots. On November 14 Stimson is surprised to hear that "Root is more sympathetic with Japan than with China; and he is very fearful lest we do not recognize her real claims to Manchuria." The Consortium message is clear. Back down on Japan and let the Imperial militarists have their way. Yet, after a briefing by Klots, Stimson is satisfied that his mentor and friend

Root "backed us up a hundred per cent on what we had done to date." Stimson leaves the office to exercise and unwind and tees off for nine holes of golf with Hugh Wilson.

On November 16 Stimson adds this note in his diary: "The dispatches from Manchuria are not good. The Japanese apparently are going right ahead in trying to set up their own puppet government throughout the country. The Army is doing this, and the Government at Tokyo is afraid to stop them. I am worried and I don't know what can be done except to watch the thing go through to its conclusion."

Stimson is caught totally unprepared to meet the latest Japanese expansionist moves in Manchuria. Without US pressure to restrain the Japanese militarist leaders consider that a green light and clear go-ahead. The crisis in the Ukraine is even a much worse case scenario. There Stimson knows Big Business interests of the Consortium are up to their necks behind Stalin's economic reconstruction. Only this time there will not be progress updates in weekly press conferences and he's soon out of a job.

There is not the slightest reflection by the Stimson team about Russia and the famine in the Ukraine. Dead communists don't figure, and Ukrainians are communists. American corporations may do business with the dictatorship but that's the business of private corporations and humanitarian aid just doesn't add up to good business with the US government on standby and diplomatic recognition in the cards. During the Hoover era in Lenin's famine of 1919-21 and the Russian Civil War it was a different game altogether. Lenin and Trotsky agreed to the Red Cross humanitarian aid, the US Congress approved it and the Bolsheviks used it to consolidate power and feed their Red Army. And we know reader how the US government and did so easily suppress that side of the story and then use State Department cronies like George Kennan to write the history of American armed intervention there so well contrived that people actually still believe that it was true and happened the way he told it.

What a farce! (Kennan always said he wanted a writing career; well, the government took him for his word making good use of that!) Now when Stalin is intent on liquidation of Ukrainian culture appeals for foreign humanitarian aid clash with the inevitable political fallout of cursed evidence of a failed state with Stalin's penchant for increased repression as a bulwark to further domestic disintegration and economic mismanagement. Its inherent in the method of the proletarian revolution that the promised miracle of the Communist Party is never attainable. That alone is reason enough for Stalin and his Plans not to figure on the map of Stimson's daily agenda, nor in a question at a press conference nor a detail in his diary, nor even a ping on Washington's radar.

More Japanese saber-rattling needles Stimson's composure. While Hoover fidgets over the sputtering national economy Stimson remains firm backing the traditional line on "the history of our American policy and the Open Door Treaty, the Treaty of 1922, the Nine Power Treaty". In other words, the failed Versailles postwar configuration prevails. Annexation and a puppet government under Japan, Hoover and Hurley concur "would not be in itself a diplomatic defeat for us".

Major Patrick J. Hurley is a wealthy tall ambassador from Oklahoma appointed Secretary of War by Hoover; FDR uses him occasionally as a "personal representative" as Roosevelt likes to do quite often with his Consortium friends and operatives sending them on various free-wheeling secret missions here and there. (Remember reader, the CIA is created *after* OSS activities in the next world war.) During the Second World War, as ambassador to China he tries in vain sending food and ammunition to save doomed US troops in Bataan. Hurley is part of the ill-fated pro-Mao China lobby at State that opts for Chiang Kai-shek; Chiang referred to Hurley as "a damned fool". FDR recalled Gen. Stilwell in 1944, and muddled in Chinese politics between Chiang's KMT nationalists and Mao. (Sterling Seagrave, *The Soong Dynasty*, Harper & Row, 1985, 402; see Barbara Tuchman, *Stilwell*)

The Italian delegation arrives for their state visit to the White House. Hoover meets with Italian president Dino Grandi, November 18. Stimson learn that "the general situation in Germany is bad" on all counts "morally, socially and economically. There was everywhere grave apprehension, particularly against Communism." Grandi, born in 1895, lawyer, editor, and a brave young captain during the Great War became a confirmed black-shirt fascist by 1920, and gives Hoover and Stimson a good lesson in how Germany is now feverish with fear of Communism. Grandi tells Stimson "Signora Grandi had employed a German nursemaid for their children, taking her home with her. In the contract which they had made, the nursemaid had insisted that there be inserted a clause which would enable her to obtain relief in case Germany should go over to Communism, in order she might go back and take care of her old mother. This, Grandi said, was a typical example of how the fear of Communism had pervaded the German people. In Berlin there were 500,000 unemployed, which is the equivalent of the total number of unemployed in Italy." Germany is still bound by treaties "from having tanks, submarines, capital ships, and big guns." Talk turns to international finance. "France", Grandi declares," has no international financial policy such as Britain has. Britain from long experience was wise in regard to the requirements of international financial policy. France was not. French loans had been purely political, not economic. She had made loans purely for the sale of securing allies. He said that it was a common saying in Italy, "Let us wait, all of this will be wasted just like French loans to Russia before the war." In a few years under Hitler, fascist Italy will significantly link economic dependency on Nazi Berlin with lower import-export trade levels to both Britain and France. By 1943 with the Americans landing on the Italian coast Grandi will be plotting the downfall of his *Duce*.

Hoover sketches out his own view "of the attitude of the American man on the street." Long isolationist, America had emerged in his generation deeply invested in the global grab of "the Game". Hoover and Stimson talk between themselves how they would leave a secure record for posterity far from disclosing the truth of intrigue and secrecy of their group of Consortium players. "For a hundred and fifty years," Stimson notes in his diary for his historical record, quoting President Hoover, "we had kept out of Europe; then in 1917 we had been dragged in a great war. We had spent forty billions of dollars in the war, and we had added ten billions more in the shape of loans after the war. We were spending a billion dollars a year on our disabled men. And yet Europe was in a worse condition than she was before the war." Hoover tells Stimson that "the ordinary American citizen" is tired of the war problems of Europe "and now he just wanted to keep out of the whole business." Hoover says "the American public" will not allow the US government to "take the leadership in any direction" overseas. The Old Guard was showing its age. In other words, the president will not go to Congress to stop the Japanese in China.

The next day at Woodley Stimson dines with Arthur Page hoping to improve his mastery of public relations. Page is a master Consortium PR spin doctor. Arthur Page (1883-60), son of Walter Hines Page, one of Wilson's closest friends and US Ambassador to Great Britain – and Pilgrim Society member – during the First World War. Stimson knew his father well and works closely with the younger Page on the finer points of how what style is best for the art of deception when the aim is display convincing confidence and assurance for security, prosperity and order while getting away with a little coup of democratic change or non-interference in the internal affairs of a foreign country while complicit and accessory to conspiratorial murder on a grand scale. Page will later be credited with another little delicate drafting for Stimson: Truman's presidential declaration of America's nuking of Japan. Born in Aberdeen, North Carolina, a writer and journalist by profession, his peers describe Page "an outstanding public relations practitioner, churchman, educator and statesman". Others may call him a real shit and a born killer. From PR to corporate lobbying, the Lees, Bernays, and Pages mark a line straight to the Nazi Goebbels.

The "Arthur W. Page Society" on the Internet proclaims Page as "the first person in a public relations position to serve as an officer and member of the Board of Directors of a major public corporation"- organized PR for 21 Bell System companies – at the time when Bell became "the largest publicly held corporation in the world". His father founded the book publishers Doubleday Page. A pioneer in corporate PR, Arthur Page served as vice president of PR for American Telephone and Telegraph (1927-46) working for Bernays. According to AT&T vice president Edward Block, "Every one currently engaged in the practice of corporate public relations owes their careers, in large measure, to his pioneering work." Page went to Lawrenceville prep school, near Princeton, then Harvard (1905), and makes his mark editing *The World's Work* magazine. In 1927, AT&T chairman Walter Gifford choose Page to write a book on AT&T and when he refused hired him as the company's prince of PR. In 1931 during the Holodomor years, Page sits on AT&T's board with a handful of other directorships in his deep pockets, including companies invested in Germany and Soviet Russia among them Chase, Westinghouse, Kennecott Copper, Continental Oil .... A contemporary of Lee at the top of corporate PR it would be totally absurd to even consider the possibility that Page was unaware of events in the Ukraine during these days of Soviet terror and famine under the CP Five Year Plans.

Westinghouse, for example, has huge operations and a long history in Russia. As a mainstream publicist Page is also selected as a Trustee of the some of the nation's most prestigious cultural and academic institutions like Bennington College for women, Teachers College at Columbia University, Metropolitan Museum of Art, as well as Carnegie Corp., the Morgan Library, and the Southern Educational Foundation and Farmers Federal of Asheville, North Carolina. Harvard names Authur Page a member of its Board of Overseers, fit to his rank as son of a UK Pilgrim. Since Page has always been master spin doctor of the Consortium he applies his talents during the Cold War overseas as a founder of the Free Europe Committee precursor to Radio Free Europe. What better way to lobby for the all-embracing unity of freedom to the whole world above all walls and partitions with the staggering secrets of the reality of power remain taboo and far from public view. This is the way of the Establishment, the system of the Consortium for America's popular landscape cultivating prestige and tradition even when there is none. And as the young nation ages, time will tell it that it was so.

Looking closer at the role of Page-Bernays in charge of corporate PR at AT&T responsible for articulating how the liberal capitalist functions in a world of "communications" i.e. propaganda the AT&T executive explains: "Mr. Page was an adviser, a counselor", Block observes. "He most certainly acknowledged the importance of communications and communications techniques. He was himself a gifted writer as well as an innovative communicator. He refers to the communications functions as "necessary" and states, "... it seems a good idea to combine them in a single department or organization as a matter of administrative convenience." In fact Page sees his mission as laying down the foundation for the corporate *kultur* of the capitalist masses.

Ed Block further describes how Page and Bernays established at AT&T the basic "principles" of Consortium PR to set the textbook standard for students of American corporate communications in "Society" and it becomes the corporate behavior model to follow up through the sixties when you could always tell who was the AT&T corporate man, impeccably dressed, straight and narrow : "For example, here are a few of the "principles." "Tell the truth." This is not always easy to do. Even so, this first principle means what it says, no exceptions. Tell the truth all the time, every time to your customers, your employees and to all your stakeholders. It means get the truth when the truth, as so often happens, comes in different versions, differing perceptions, when management is thrashing about trying to find the right course of action, the right policy. To us, it means tell the truth to your boss and to the Chief Executive Officer and to your client. *Truth is a habit of the mind, a basic building block of character and integrity in a business no less than in an individual.* To my mind, that's a highly desirable working principle. 'Both in belief and practice,' the 'Society' declares, he held that 'all business in a democratic country begins with public permission and exists by public approval...'. He contributed his energy and inspiration to enterprises such as the Marshall Plan and Radio Free Europe." Think about it. "A habit of mind"?

STIMSON FACES JAPANESE ADVANCE: "I REACHED THE END OF MY TETHER..."

Habits are not necessarily good things, patterned responses in a world of constant change. "Truth"? Page talked utter nonsense but people nodded their heads happy to know someone was putting the pieces together in a nice array of "truths". The Consortium had its "truth", Stalin had his "truth", Hitler had his "truth". In a world of multiple truths, the power of money was ultimate persuader of what the people would be led to believe is true. Heaven help them to find out dialectically that truth is only a concept and doesn't exist at all... Meanwhile, the people are soon starving to death in the millions and they said it wasn't true...

Friday 13 November. The League of Nations pushes for sanctions against the Japanese. That morning Stimson calls a Cabinet meeting. War Secretary Hurley "gently turned on Manchuria and suggested that we were making a mistake to get into it at all". He says "the Japanese were going to seize Manchuria anyhow, and we were simply letting our country in for a rebuff and a loss of prestige." Hurley has information from "some of the generals", Stimson records in his diary. But Hoover gives full support to Stimson's diplomacy saying "how the only alternative when this thing came up was either to lie down and destroy all the peace treaties, or else to do the best we could with the force of public opinion and that alone". It seems Page has taught him well. "I pointed out the policy of imposing sanctions of force, which Hurley suggested as the only thing possible, had been rejected by America in its rejection of the League of Nations; and America had deliberately chosen to rest solely upon treaties with the sanction of public opinion alone; and this was not the choice of this Administration, but a deliberate choice of the country long before we came in; and that, therefore, we had the alternative only of letting down our country entirely on its determined policy, or else going on and doing what I had done." Stimson relied on what he called "the historical precedent of Shantung and the success of public opinion there". Stimson cautioned the Japanese population knew very well "how economically Japan was being forced out of her position..." Later that afternoon William Curtis Bok of the World Court meets with Stimson "in great discouragement about the World Court". It seems it has become a political football.

This year DuPont powder merchants went into business with the Japanese militarists. As long as they kill Chinese it was good business for DuPont. Author Gerard Colby wrote, "Shortly after Secretary of State Stimson condemned Japan's attack on Manchuria, Japanese executives from the Mitzui Chemical combine met with DuPont executives in Wilmington and handed over $900,000 in exchange for DuPont's ammonia explosive formula, a process of manufacturing cheap munitions. The State Department, despite Stimson's public oratory, privately gave the DuPont sale its full approval." (G. Colby, 335; R. L. Beisner, 17)

This mid-November weekend Stimson relaxes at Woodley with a dinner Saturday evening for Elizabeth Morrow "very attractive and bright, although she looked very frail and rather delicate" since the passing of Dwight. Then Stimson is in the saddle again out for a Sunday ride with Mabel. The pressure of work feels heavier now with the chill of the Atlantic off the Long Island shore. Stimson falls from his horse. "The crash which I have expected for some time came this morning," he writes, "and I came down with my old friend *Lumbago*. He feels that he has been "getting along remarkably well all the fall, sleeping better than I have for almost years". But the business of Manchuria and other pressures in the week have taken a toll on his strength, "I reached the end of my tether and have been sleeping badly every night …". (HLS Diary)

Stimson returns to the stalls and takes a ride this time with Justice Holmes having met with Felix Frankfurter a few days earlier at Fort Stevens near the Walter Reed Hospital. Holmes and Stimson both live the lives of legends. Holmes tells him of the day there he "saw President Lincoln in 1864, when General Early attacked Washington". It is a rare moment for Stimson eager to learn more of his father's world when the famous surgeon first served as a young man in the Civil War. For Justice Holmes this was the world he knew well having fought in that bloody carnage and witnessed the end of slavery after generations of American slave ships stacked four decks high with Africans chained tightly together shoulder to shoulder.

Stimson notes, "There is a tablet which commemorates President Lincoln's presence there, and the old Justice showed me where the President was standing and showed me where he was, and showed me where General Wright, his commander, was pacing along the top of the earthworks. He showed me where they could see the attack being made by the Federal skirmishers upon the Rebels… Holmes had been a staff officer on the Sixth Corps under General Wright, which had been hurried up from Petersburg, Virginia, where they were under Grant's army, to rescue Washington." Holmes recalls how Americans had never endured anything like it when thousands of corpses of Union and Confederate soldiers lay scattered across the countryside, alongside thousands of dead mules and horses, human and animal flesh swollen and blackening under a stinging stench. In four years two percent of the US population, North and South, 600,000 men die in uniform.

"The war's staggering human cost demanded a new sense of national destiny", the President of Harvard University once wrote, "one designed to ensure that lives had been sacrificed for appropriately lofty ends." Stimson records Harvard's call for noble principles bloodied by American lives all sounded "very nice and interesting". Had either the Czar's liberation of Russia's serfs in 1861 that left them without civil rights and at the mercy of the estate owning aristocrats and at the mercy of unscrupulous landlords or the emancipation of the Afro-American slaves by bloody fratricide accomplished much in the way of global liberation? He may have wondered about the Philippines? And Cuba? What is America going to do about stopping the bloodbath Manchuria? Masses of American workingmen and women as well as Russia serfs now face a growing gulag of enslaved Soviet "proletariat" albeit their nations remain worlds apart yet had more in common than they are given to understand united as they were by suffering bonds under the bridle of Consortium masters.

Stimson liked to think he runs the State Department bureaucracy. He holds the reins of America's foreign policy tight in hand, steady, firm and unflappable.

There is always some room for decisions within the framework of the consensus of the Consortium. But a government man obeys instructions.

Yet, the world is strained and the risks of a breaking point are great. The elder statesman and lawyer is distracted by much too much from the main crises in the Far East, Europe and Russia. For example, revolutions and coups in Cuba and Latin America preoccupy him. One day that fall Harry Guggenheim, Hoover's ambassador in Cuba since appointed in 1929 a few weeks after the market crash – his father Daniel had made a generous campaign – is stirring up more trouble with the dictator mixing in politics and attempting, Stimson notes, to "run the country", Guggenheim "is not quite like Dwight Morrow", and he notes with regret, "I have had to hold him in a good many times." Tall, handsome, fluent in Spanish from his days in Chile, Yale, (he leaves after an anti-Semitic incident). Cambridge in England is more to his liking; athletic, blue-eyes, and filthy rich Harry Guggenheim cuts a fine colonial silhouette in his tropical white suit.

What Stimson does not put in his diary are the facts that Guggenheim is there looking after the interests of foreign capital. The Cuban government is completely controlled by the banks and American control of the sugar industry; in the one crop economy America owns 70 percent, own Havana's street railway system. Cuba's insurance companies are owned by Canadians. "Presiding over this vast slave camp of foreign capital was a brutal, graft-ridden gangsterism headed by a cruel dictator who worked hand in glove with Wall Street and Chase National Bank," writes biographer John H. Davis (*The Guggenheims, The Bouviers*, *Venice*).

There the Machado gang is gaining strength daily; on the island his son-in-law is head of Chase. Just prior to Guggenheim's arrival Machado proved he could be a good dictator for Uncle Sam by massacring hundreds in a violent repression of an alleged anti-government rebellion organized by the Union Nacionalistas and imposing martial law. Stimson is gravely concerned, and writes a note to himself in his diary, "unless we do something or make our position clear that we are not supporting Machado, we will lose prestige." More than that, the market plunge kills sugar prices resulting in overproduction forcing thousands of Cubans to lose their jobs and fermenting revolution. Under the Platt Amendment approved after the Spanish-American War America reserved a unilateral right to intervene militarily to protect and preserve "life, property and individual liberty". Protected by US Marines in his residence at Vedado Guggenheim assisted by his friend and Root biographer, Phillip C. Jessup, (Harvard Law 1924), a specialist in international law, he now possessed the fate of Cuba in his hands.

The Secretary urges Hoover "to make a statement that we would not intervene. But coming at this time, I told him that that would probably give the impression that we were really thinking of intervening; that it would come like a bolt out of the blue." On May 26, 1932 Stimson writes that "Guggenheim's only attitude is not to get us too much entangled with Machado's fortunes when what seems to be the inevitable crash comes along". His brother, Col. Bob Guggenheim is also an undersecretary attached to the State Department. (Phillip C. Jessurp, *Elihu Root*)

In his book on the Wall Street 1929 crash Harvard economist and professor J. K. Galbraith recalls how more Rockefeller money is funneled stirring up

Cuban politics. "Chase extended President Machado of Cuba," Galbraith writes describing him as, "a dictator with a marked predisposition toward murder, a generous personal line of credit which at one time reached $200,000. Machado's son-in-law was employed by the Chase. The bank did a large business in Cuban bonds. In contemplating these loans, there was a tendency to pass quickly over anything that might appear to the disadvantage of the creditor." Elsewhere, for example in Peru,. National City made suspicious loans and bribes "losing some $85 millions default." A Chase employee wrote the ambassador "It is only due to our close contact and friendship with General Machado and the Secretary of the Treasury (Paul Mellon) that we are receiving interest payments at so early a date, as the payments mean a real sacrifice on the part of the government." Ambassador Guggenheim naturally defends Machado and ignores the political opposition denouncing its leaders "motivated by their own political gain, not the nation's welfare" and for "taking advantage of a bad economic situation". He even encourages the dictator to ban the free press or risk "very definite dangers". More violent unrest leads to increased repression and dead civilians. The ambassador is threatened and he doubles his bodyguard. Ambassador Guggenheim has become the ugly American in the white tropical suit. By the fall of 1932 the papers carry headlines of more bombings and murders. Terror on the streets leaves hundreds killed. Friends of the ambassador plea for American intervention but the State Department leaves Harry and his embassy on the hook and he sees more of his friends in Havana's business community die and disappear. Decades pass until in the late fifties Havana falls to Fidel Castro, Robert Guggenheim is appointed by Eisenhower ambassador to Portugal's military dictatorship. (J. K. Galbraith, *The Great Crash, 1929*, 1955 ed.; J. H. Davis, *The Guggenheims*, 304)

Stimson diverts much of his time to work with the ambassador from the U.K. to prepare for the 1932 Disarmament Conference on agreements limiting such requirements as the tonnage of battleships, submarines, cruisers, and so on. "Ham" Armstrong wants him to write something in *Foreign Affairs* for January just prior to the Disarmament Conference. For half a century Hamilton Armstrong (1893-73) is senior editor of *Foreign Affairs,* and all Princeton carrying with him a ton of Ivy League distinctions. Stimson is doubtful of an agreement and declines telling Armstrong that "for a year we had been doing all we could to get the nations who had the future of that conference in their hands to lay the foundations for a successful conference and they hadn't done it." A few days later on November 20 Stimson talks by telephone with Walter Lippmann, the columnist and a leading political philosopher of America's unique democratic liberalism. He assures Lippmann he'll have the information he needs for a story going into *Foreign Affairs*. When they meet November 27 for the CFR story Lippmann curries favor and praises Stimson on his Manchurian policy. On November 28, 1931 Lippmann (Harvard, 1910) is invited to the Secretary's residence for a Stimson dinner with the Bundys. "Walter Lippmann was very strong in feeling that it was an outrage for the Secretary of State to put up with what I have to put up with in those conferences. So I have made up my mind to reform these young men down in the Department and withhold myself from them and insist upon knowing their questions beforehand," the Secretary notes in his diary. Then he turns his mind Sunday morning November 29 to the quiet of nature and his calm retreat. Stimson goes riding with Mabel for two hours relishing the fresh wet "rainy sultry weather". Again Stimson opens his diary and writes: "We did not get very wet and it gave us a good freshening up, because the strain for the past two or three days over the Manchurian affair has been pretty tense." Stimson is Old School and he tries hard to get along with the younger set in Washington. It disturbs him that Hamilton Fish will be married three times; and it pricks his 19th century sense of civic propriety that when Lippmann married Fish's first wife the union breaks his friendship with Hamilton.

Harvey Bundy is assigned to keep up debt reparations talks as they drag on; James Rogers stays on disarmament issues as a delegate to the conference. On the afternoon of November 25 Stimson is obliged to brief John Willys, US ambassador in Warsaw. Willys is a political appointee "who by the way", Stimson observes, "is not a very good ambassador." Stimson tells Hoover he wants Willys out of the embassy "as soon as possible". John N. Willys (1873-35) is the Ohio businessmen who founder, in 1908; the Willys-Overland Motor Company is soon the second largest car manufacturer in the US; in 1940 Willys contracts 360,000 jeeps in government war orders. The Red Army loves the Willys jeep.

To clear his head that afternoon Stimson plays some deck tennis at Woodley before speaking at another press conference "and then to cap it all" he notes, "I had a trans-Atlantic telephone call from Dawes" on a matter of a higher order, sorting out the fray over his disarmament delegates. Stimson listed Frank Polk, Charles Dawes, Henry Fletcher and Gibson. Both Fletcher and Dawes want to be chairman of the US delegation. Fletcher tells Hoover that he won't go "if Dawes went". On Sunday, December 13, Stimson sits down with Hoover reviewing Republican candidates from the Senate Foreign Relations Committee. Hoover found Moses "quite impossible from the President's own standpoint"; Vandenburg "who ... had a number of failings", and Swanson, too far "on the Democratic side". Hoover prefers another Republican Senator. Stimson concedes "it is very hard to match him", and he personally declines, not wishing to be away in "particularly as there will not be anything which fits my talents going on at Geneva during the first part of the session". Stimson agrees when Hoover recommends sending a woman delegate "if he could get a sensible one and a good one and not a member of the Women's Party, a professional woman advocate". Stimson thinks it over and concurs "it would be a very good thing"; he proposes two college women, "Miss Woolley", president of Holyoke, and "Miss Pendleton" of Wellesley. Stimson prefers Pendleton noting her previous experience in international affairs "although not as a delegate". Hines and Fletcher bow out, replaced by Gen. Frank McCoy's back in the country after his "success in Nicaragua" transforming imperialist policy there "into a real truly great reform". In a diary note on December 22 Stimson decides "McCoy is a better man than either of those two."

Immediately following his 10:30 morning press conference on November 30 Stimson meets reps of the Eastern Gulf Oil Company "at the request of Mr. Mellon". They are joined by Paul Alling, Assistant Chief of the Division of Near

Eastern Affairs. Nothing in Stimson's diary reveals details of what transpired; at 12:30 Stimson meets with the Associated Press newsman Frank Noyes. Stimson is irked over "the new habit" of press freedom demonstrated by AP "in the way of bringing in interpretations and opinion". He considers their reporting "stuff" a problem with "foreign connections" and too "easily distorted into great trouble for our Government." Stimson is uneasy with AP's "featuring the stories of the anti-Fascist agitation" on the streets of Italy during Grandi's visit to Washington. He reprimands Noyes warning him to back off and tone it down. Mussolini is bombastic and hallow and in a palace of spineless henchmen of corporate fascists all of whom will crumble within months of the American landing in Naples and Mussolini hiding in a German coat will be caught by partisans and shot before the end of the war and the liberation of Rome on June 4, 1944 when Hitler is caught sleeping and his generals duped by Pas de Calais while the Americans land on the Normandy beaches but for now Mussolini is the Consortium's man in Rome and not unlikely on the Rockefeller payroll. Frank Noyes is no greenhorn. In 1900 Noyes was elected president of AP when he was at the *Washington Star*. Noyes, approaching 70, lords over a veritable news empire with the agency wires feeding 35 million readers with AP dispatches in 1400 newspapers making it one of the two greatest wire news services in the world. "Noyes for 38 years had carefully avoided expressing personal opinions on public questions", *Time* writes in May 1938 when he retires.

UKRAINE IN FAMINE LATE 1931

By the end of the year 1931 Soviet Russia is plunged into winter famine. The Ukraine descends into the massive Holodomor. How do we find Stimson and his Consortium insiders? He leaves a trace in his diary. Its tells us what was on his mind. "December 3. Cabinet dinner at the White House. "It was a very large affair. Mabel went out with the President, and I took our Mrs. Hoover, and after dinner I had a short talk with President Hopkins, of Dartmouth … also with President Farrand, of Cornell; George Vincent, of the Rockefeller Foundation... It was a brilliant dinner…" Stimson always keeps very tight with his blue-blood clique of Ivy Leaguers. Do they discuss their little problem in the Kremlin? Evidently its not even that. For over two years the State Department has been well informed of the severely worsening food conditions in the USSR and particularly in the Ukraine. People are now starving to death. And the dam is about to burst wide open into intense political fratricide as the merciless Stalin eliminates the remnants of the Bolshevik revolutionaries. Hoover and Stimson will have to step aside and give room to FDR and his Democrats. Japanese expansion into China and along the Far Eastern Russian Frontier remains their principal preoccupation. A week later on December 11 Stimson notes, "Called the Japanese ambassador over to talk over speeches by Cabot Lodge about a possible embargo of Japan." Stimson is irritated that Lodge is rattling the saber and "making those speeches" and inflaming public opinion to force his hand. Stimson consoles himself for the record for having maintained "a friendly attitude towards Japan". Stimson added another diary note for the record, and he wrote, "Out of that stuff has come these rumors which an irresponsible and malignant little devil like young Lodge is now turning into an assertion as if I had betrayed my government. It all goes to show how difficult it is to conduct diplomacy between governments with a free press." But it's a game he knows well how to play and he has his own people ready to help in damage control.

Dispatch No. 679 of September 4, 1931 prepared by the US Consul Ernest Harris in Vienna, contained a transcript of an interview with the banker William E. Herrlich of Lee Higginson & Co, one of Boston's oldest and most respectable investment houses that may have shared in the fortunes of Boston privateers in the China opium trade boom exploiting the Chinese.

The six-page Herrlich-Higgenson document, is marked "Confidential". Harris writes "MARRIAGE AND DIVORCE WERE SO FREQUENT in Russia that queues were now established to facilitate the transactions. Divorce queues in Moscow resembled those for bread, rubber shoes or vodka." He may have been jealous it was that easy to leave one woman or man and be free to find another. Didn't anyone tell the poor sot that sex in Russia since the Revolution is as normal as drinking a glass of water? How ironic that once again we find the hand of Duranty at work. Harris went on writing down the banker's cogitations, "Walter Duranty ... understands the Russian psychology and sympathizes with their system. Even if the plant managers are well paid, and other workers might get good wages, it is not necessary that a class system should be developed; it could be the same way, for instance in the American army where they have the different grades and nevertheless are on the same class. The chief of a touring agency explained that the ambitions of the young men in the United States and Russia are entirely different. In the United States it is sport and to make money; in Russia to make the Soviet system a complete success. Naturally somebody trained under Anglo Saxon conditions cannot understand their condition, for instance their lack of family life. But they are different." Had Higginson's Herrlich ever read Tolstoy, Doestoevsky, Turgenev, Pushkin, Tchekov, Gorky? Or Lesia Ukrainka (Laryssa Kosach-Kvitka), Volodymyr Vynnychenko, Taras Shevchenko, and, of course, one of the exemplary Ukrainian writers Ivan Franko put on trial in 1878 with fellow left-wing nationalist Mykhailo Pavlyk. All of these writers felt they were someway in the Russian and Ukrainian vanguard, lovers of the peasantry (*khlopomany*) working together towards a growth in national consciousness and for the personal development and benefit of the people (*narod*). (O. Subtelny, *Ukraine, A History,* 221-335; original emphasis)

It is difficult for Duranty to stray from the official Soviet line. Take a good look at his copy and you'll see the pro-Soviet propaganda of the Soviet censor. But in his case it was a willful and deliberate act to conceal. He would never falter. In 1931 on one of his many visits to Berlin Duranty stops to have a chat with Lt. A. Kliefoth in the US embassy who memos the gist of their conversation to State: "Duranty pointed out that, 'in agreement with *The New York Times* and the Soviet authorities, his official dispatches always reflect the official opinion of the Soviet regime and not his own." Some readers of the *Times* would have been surprised to know what they were never told about Stalin's American reporter in the Kremlin dishing out intelligence to junior embassy officials intended for the White House for which the *Times* rewarded him with a Pultizer! But Lt. A. W. Kliefoth from Wisconsin is no fool. A military intelligence officer Kliefoth speaks five European languages, and served three years in the US embassy in Petrograd during the Czarist rule; he was there for the Kerensky-Lenin-Trotsky regime change. (Before that he was stationed in Sweden and Finland)

The Higginson banker does make, however, some astute observations of the harvest and the Ukrainians.

"The Ukrainians are as well as the Russians of a hard type," he tells Consul Harris, "but they have more culture. Kiev has also a few church services." Further, Herrlich is annoyed by the tiresome constant propaganda about Russians to the detriment of the Ukraine. Herrlich declares, "There is very much written on Russia and Russian problems. Russia does not deserve all the publicity it is getting. Moscow is supplied and much supported by Ukraina. After a while the Ukrainians may tire of helping the other Soviet Republics. It is a question in my mind if the sale of manufactured goods (machinery) to the Soviet Union is important enough to counterbalance the destruction they render in such commodity markets as wheat, lumber, oil." Consul Harris is one of the few US officials to regularly hand incoming reports on the famine. (SDDF 861.48/327)

Meanwhile the Germans begin taking care of their own in Russia by starting a delivery service providing food and clothing relief. According to information sent from US Consul George A. Gordon in Berlin and cited in Dispatch No. 1106 dated August 28, 1931, "the German branch of the soviet freight and transportation department "Derutra" ("Deutsch-Russiche Lager und Transportgesellschaft") has granted an exclusive agency to Herman Tietz and Company and the Kaufhaus des Westerns, two of the large Berlin department stores, for a parcels delivery system to private persons in Russia. The parcels may include food, clothing and 'objects of the daily requirements'." The system Consul Gordon notes is "modeled on the food and clothing packages of the American Relief Administration", and immediately put into effect. "It is also planned to grant similar agencies to organizations in the United States, England and other countries." Russian experts in the German Foreign Office called it, Gordon observes, "another demonstration of Stalin's new policy to appease the Russians by rewarding them for the sacrifice made in behalf of the Five Year Plan, similar to the decree which restored certain rights of the intellectuals and increased the pay of deserving workers". (SDDF 861.48/2419)

In order to gain more foreign exchange from the flow of goods to foreigners living inside the country, the Soviets announce that they too are revamping Torgsin store procedures for shipping food and clothing. On September 11, 1931, Frederick Coleman sends Washington a six-page memo "to inform the Department that the soviet authorities are effecting a complete reorganization of the system by which friends and relatives abroad have been supplying residents of Soviet Russia with foodstuffs and clothing." Frequently the Soviets imposed "prohibitive customs charges" or the recipient was "afraid, for political reasons, to accept delivery".

The new system was organized by *Sovtorgflot* in major cities (Berlin, Paris, London, New York, Riga and elsewhere) and includes a food-draft system for money drafts at Torgsin stores. It's intended to draw out foreign currency hoarded by Soviet citizens and increase the valuta collected in the Torgsin stores. "The great advantage of the reorganization", Coleman writes, "lies in the fact that it will enable the soviet authorities to collect the high customs tariffs in foreign currency and thus add to their supply of valuta". Coleman points out that this new measure was not going to help the millions of starving peasants, and he added, "It is pertinent to point out that the unlimited and unrestricted remittance of commodities or funds with which to purchase commodities now permitted will be mostly to the advantage of the non-proletarian elements as it is mainly the 'former people' in Soviet Russia who have relatives and friends abroad able to make such remittances."

Stimson is not necessarily indifferent when addressed through the proper official channels, for example, by a Senator or Congressman, as in the case of a Mr. Uditsky who needed to send foodstuffs and clothing to his destitute relatives, former "millionaires" in Russia. On this occasion Stimson shows he's capable of a prompt and personal response providing useful information to individuals in distress. In his memoranda to the Secretary, Coleman, however, omits to explain why the recipients fear the Soviet authorities for which he cites only "political reasons". In fact the status quo of repression under the Soviet dictatorship life is endured in a state of constant terror, uncertainty and fear of arrest, or worse. The confiscation of their private goods by the impoverished and hungry petty customs officials is the least of their worries. (SDDF 861.48/2420; 861.48/2421)

The chief engineer from California Zara Witkin who speaks fluent Russian and travels with a pass marking his high status shared the Torgsin experienced to readers who still believe that the Soviet Russian ways are readily transferable to the lifestyle of the average American citizen. Witkin observes, "Waiting for our train afforded us another day in Rostov. A school for formerly illiterate women was shown us. The alertness of these girls and their eagerness to learn was remarkable. Afterwards we cut loose of our guide and took a long walk through the town. In the Torgsin store, which sold only for gold, silver or foreign currency, we purchased some dried prunes and dried apricots. Back again in our hotel, we opened our packages and found they contained all prunes! The Soviet sales "system" in stores is an interesting example of unshakable bureaucracy. To buy an article, one must first stand in line and indicate the article desired. Then one is obliged to get into another line to pay for the purchase. Finally a third line is entered to receive one's purchases, which are already wrapped. No inspection of the wrapped article is possible. In this amazing process, without sense or reason, the purchaser frequently gets what he did not buy. There is no recourse. In the USSR the customer is always wrong."

Lets resume and take a bearing where we are. With Ukraine already under ice and snow the harsh winter 1932 will yet be more brutal than in previous years. While the White House is burdened by the world monetary crisis, Japanese aggression in China and fascism spreading in Berlin and Rome, these years 1930 to 1932 find the Russians and Ukrainians suffering forced starvation, famine, forced displacements and destruction of the kulaks as "class enemies", with executions *en masse*. Anyone who resists Soviet collectivization is a likely target to be shot along with their friends and family. Stalin put the question of progress of Soviet justice in the New Society of communism this way: "Either *backward* to capitalism, or *forward* to socialism. There is no and can be no third path." (I. V. Stalin, *Sochineniia*, Vol. 12, Moscow, 1952, 146 cited in S. Vokov, *The Magical Chorus,* 79)

After the bad harvest of 1931, and three years of harassment, arrests and executions in the countryside, Stalin who has suspected plot after plot by the peasants to withhold grain from the cities now ruthlessly struck back at the Ukrainians allegedly to punish thrifty peasant bourgeoisie for resistance to Soviet measures to socialize agriculture thus depriving the an entire population of peasants of a free market. Stalin hopes to succeed where Lenin had failed. A quota of 7.7 million tons is demanded for 1932 and nearly 7 million is collected. Peasants are left to starve in their barren villages. Collectivization has failed to feed the peasants or bring prosperity to the villages and foreign exchange to the Kremlin coffers. But from standpoint of Soviet government Kremlin policy is a success. Grain procurements for the year 1931-32 despite a smaller harvest will surpass previous levels. That is counter to the conclusion of the State Department's own agricultural expert Dana Dalrymlpe published in 1964 after his thorough study of official Soviet procurements numbers. "The factor," Dalrymple writes, "which really turned the below-average crop years of 1931, 32 and 33 into famine years was the food procurement policy of the government. He examined tables of soviet grain procurements for 1931-32, and they showed, he wrote that "Even though production during the three famine years was *down* 12 percent from the previous four year average, procurements were *up* 44 percent. The result was that the amount of grain left in the peasants' hands was decreased substantially. During the 1931-32 crop year the old "Iron Broom" technique which had been used during the years of war communism was put into use again." Dalrymple tells us, 'Grain, needed by the Ukrainian peasants as provisions, was stripped from the land... by grain collectors desirous of making a good showing." Even Stalin's hack journalist at *The NYT* concedes that a particularly heavy procurement is made in March 1932. "The *muzhik* has hidden rye in his storeroom – kill him!" That was the slogan of the anti-peasant horror in Stalin's regime.

So while in Washington Stimson and Hoover are bumbling about the fallout from the Wall Street crash and the meltdown of the domestic national economy with rising unemployment at home and the rise of fascist militarism abroad, financed by Consortium investors watching daily the prices of their stocks portfolio rising and falling, eager to buy, obliged to hold, and afraid to sell, by the spring of 1932, the food situation worsens in the USSR and degrades until it is dangerously out of control. Stalin's response is typical. He blames the Old Bosheviks in the Party, Trotsky Rightists and insurgent Ukrainian nationalist deviations. State Department agriculture specialist Dana Dalrymple during research in the sixties concludes that in order to meet Stalin's quota for 7.7 million tons for 1932, authorities had to cope with the total yield a meager 14.7 million tons, compared to 23.9 million tons in 1930. As a result Stalin demanded more repressive procurements and punishments for the "traitors". Soviet state terror particularly severe in the Ukraine took another sinister turn when Stalin learns that the procurement agencies obtained *less* grain from the villages after the 1932 harvest than after the 1931 or 1930 harvests. Stalin and his cronies then assert that the 1932 harvest had actually been good!. But again it was the kulaks again who held back their grain despite the fact that rural workers and families were refused rations and dying in much greater numbers in addition to those thousands of peasants already exiled or dead.

"The same procedure was carried on in the months following the harvest of 1932", Dalrymlpe further noted. Two decades later, the book *The History of a Soviet Collective Farm* gave a rare glimpse into the dim reality of life in Ukrainian villages. Author Fedor Belov found that by "autumn the 'red broom' passed over the kolkhoz and the individual plots, sweeping the 'surplus' for the state out of the barns and corncribs. In the search for 'surpluses,' everything was collected. The farms were cleaned out even more thoroughly than the kulak had been." Even so, the grain deliveries began to lag, reserve stocks had been cleaned out the previous year, and the Ukrainian Communists who were supposed to carry out the collections apparently began to get too soft-hearted for the Soviet leaders leading to more repressions, dismissals executions, exile and all other "pacification" tortures that Stalin's man-made famine imposed on the population. (Clarence Manning on D. Dalrymple, 103-4; D. G. Dalrymple, "The American Tractor Comes to Soviet Russia: The Transfer of a Technology," *Technology and Culture*, Johns Hopkins Univ. Press, 1964; R W. Barnes, "Grain Shortage in the Ukraine Results From Admitted Failure of the Soviet Agricultural Plan," *New York Herald Tribune*, Jan. 15, 1933, pt. II, 5; W. Duranty, *US, The Story of Russia*, NY: J. B. Lippincott, 1944, 190-2; N. Jasny, 794; F. Belov, 12)

END BOOK I

Printed in the United States
By Bookmasters